# Derivatives: Principles and Practice

**Rangarajan K. Sundaram**
*Stern School of Business*
*New York University*
*New York, NY 10012*

**Sanjiv R. Das**
*Leavey School of Business*
*Santa Clara University*
*Santa Clara, CA 95053*

## McGraw Hill Education (India) Private Limited
NEW DELHI

*McGraw Hill Education Offices*
**New Delhi** New York  St Louis  San Francisco  Auckland  Bogotá  Caracas
Kuala Lumpur  Lisbon  London  Madrid  Mexico City  Milan  Montreal
San Juan  Santiago  Singapore  Sydney  Tokyo  Toronto

**McGraw Hill Education (India) Private Limited**

**DERIVATIVES: PRINCIPLES AND PRACTICE**

**McGraw Hill Education (India) Edition 2013**

Second reprint 2014
**RDABCRYULCAQB**

Reprinted in India by arrangement with The McGraw-Hill Companies, Inc., New York

Sales territories: India, Pakistan, Nepal, Bangladesh, Sri Lanka and Bhutan

**Library of Congress Cataloging-in-Publication Data**

Sundaram, Rangarajan K.
    Derivatives : principles and practice / Rangarajan K. Sundaram, Sanjiv R. Das.
        p. cm.
    Includes index.
    ISBN-13: 978-0-07-294931-5 (alk. paper)
    ISBN-10: 0-07-294931-7 (alk. paper)
    1. Derivative securities. I. Das, Sanjiv R. (Sanjiv Ranjan) II. Title.
HG6024.A3S873 2011
332.64'57—dc22

                                                    2009053836

ISBN-13: 978-1-25-909709-6
ISBN-10: 1-259-09709-9

Published by McGraw Hill Education (India) Private Limited,
P-24, Green Park Extension New Delhi 110 016, and printed at
Pashupati Printers Pvt. Ltd., GT Road Shahadara, New Delhi 110095

To Urmilla and Aditi

...RKS

To my parents
and
Priya and Shikhar

...SRD

# Brief Contents

## The following Web chapters are available at www.mhhe.com/sd1e:

# Contents

# Author Biographies

**Rangarajan K. ("Raghu") Sundaram** is Professor of Finance at New York University's Stern School of Business. He was previously a member of the economics faculty at the University of Rochester. Raghu has an undergraduate degree in economics from Loyola College, University of Madras; an MBA from the Indian Institute of Management, Ahmedabad; and a Master's and Ph.D. in economics from Cornell University. He was Co-Editor of the *Journal of Derivatives* from 2002–2008 and is or has been a member of several other editorial boards. His research in finance covers a range of areas including agency problems, executive compensation, derivatives pricing, credit risk and credit derivatives, and corporate finance. He has also published extensively in mathematical economics, decision theory, and game theory. His research has appeared in all leading academic journals in finance and economic theory. The recipient of the Jensen Award and a finalist for the Brattle Prize for his research in finance, Raghu has also won several teaching awards including, in 2007, the inaugural Distinguished Teaching Award from the Stern School of Business. This is Raghu's second book; his first, a Ph.D.-level text titled *A First Course in Optimization Theory*, was published by Cambridge University Press.

**Sanjiv Ranjan Das** is Professor of Finance and Chair of the Finance Department at Santa Clara University's Leavey School of Business. He was previously Associate Professor at the Harvard Business School and a visiting Associate Professor at the University of California, Berkeley. Sanjiv has postgraduate degrees in Finance (M.Phil and Ph.D. from New York University) and Computer Science (M.S. from UC Berkeley) in addition to an MBA from the Indian Institute of Management, Ahmedabad. The holder of an undergraduate degree in Accounting and Economics from the University of Bombay's Sydenham College, Sanjiv is also a qualified Cost and Works Accountant. He is the Co-Editor of the *Journal of Derivatives* and Senior Editor of the *Journal of Investment Management*, and is a member of the boards of other journals. Prior to moving to academia, Sanjiv worked in the derivatives business in the Asia-Pacific region as a Vice-President at Citibank. His current research interests include the modeling of default risk, algorithms for harvesting financial information from the web, derivative pricing models, portfolio theory, and venture capital. He has published over 70 articles in academic journals and has won numerous awards for research and teaching.

# Preface

The two of us have worked together academically for more than a quarter century, first as graduate students, and then as university faculty. Given our close collaboration, our common research and teaching interests in the field of derivatives, and the frequent pedagogical discussions we have had on the subject, this book was perhaps inevitable.

The final product grew out of many sources. About three-fourths of the book came from notes developed by Raghu for his derivatives course at New York University as well as for other academic courses and professional training programs at Credit Suisse, ICICI Bank, the International Monetary Fund (IMF), Invesco-Great Wall, J.P. Morgan, Merrill Lynch, the Indian School of Business (ISB), the Institute for Financial Management and Research (IFMR), and New York University, among other institutions. Other parts grew out of academic courses and professional training programs taught by Sanjiv at Harvard University, Santa Clara University, the University of California at Berkeley, the ISB, the IFMR, the IMF, and Citibank, among others. Some chapters were developed specifically for this book, as were most of the end-of-chapter exercises.

The discussion below provides an overview of the book, emphasizing some of its special features. We provide too our suggestions for various derivatives courses that may be carved out of the book.

## An Overview of the Contents

The main body of this book is divided into six parts. Parts 1–3 cover, respectively, futures and forwards; options; and swaps. Part 4 examines term-structure modeling and the pricing of interest-rate derivatives, while Part 5 is concerned with credit derivatives and the modeling of credit risk. Part 6 discusses computational issues. A detailed description of the book's contents is provided in Section 1.5; here, we confine ourselves to a brief overview of each part.

**Part 1** examines forward and futures contracts, The topics covered in this span include the structure and characteristics of futures markets; the pricing of forwards and futures; hedging with forwards and futures, in particular, the notion of *minimum-variance hedging* and its implementation; and interest-rate-dependent forwards and futures, such as forward-rate agreements or FRAs, eurodollar futures, and Treasury futures contracts.

**Part 2**, the lengthiest portion of the book, is concerned mainly with options. We begin with a discussion of option payoffs, the role of volatility, and the use of options in incorporating into a portfolio specific views on market direction and/or volatility. Then we turn our attention to the pricing of options contracts. The binomial and Black-Scholes models are developed in detail, and several generalizations of these models are examined. From pricing, we move to hedging and a discussion of the option "greeks," measures of option sensitivity to changes in the market environment. Rounding off the pricing and hedging material, two chapters discuss a wide range of "exotic" options and their behavior.

The remainder of Part 2 focuses on special topics: portfolio measures of risk such as Value-at-Risk and the notion of risk budgeting, the pricing and hedging of convertible bonds, and a study of "real" options, optionalities embedded within investment projects.

**Part 3** of the book looks at swaps. The uses and pricing of interest rate swaps are covered in detail, as are equity swaps, currency swaps, and commodity swaps. (Other instruments bearing the "swaps" moniker are covered elsewhere in the book. Variance and volatility swaps are presented in the chapter on Black-Scholes, and credit-default swaps and total-return swaps are examined in the chapter on credit-derivative products.) Also included in Part 3 is a presentation of caps, floors, and swaptions, and of the "market model" used to price these instruments.

**Part 4** deals with interest-rate modeling. We begin with different notions of the yield curve, the estimation of the yield curve from market data, and the challenges involved in modeling movements in the yield curve. We then work our way through factor models of the yield curve, including several well-known models such as Ho-Lee, Black-Derman-Toy, Vasicek, Cox-Ingersoll-Ross, and others. A final chapter presents the Heath-Jarrow-Morton framework, and also that of the Libor and Swap Market Models.

**Part 5** deals with credit risk and credit derivatives. An opening chapter provides a taxonomy of products and their characteristics. The remaining chapters are concerned with modeling credit risk. Structural models are covered in one chapter, reduced-form models in the next, and correlated-default modeling in the third.

**Part 6**, available online at http://www.mhhe.com/sd1e, looks at computational issues. Finite-differencing and Monte-Carlo methods are discussed here. A final chapter provides a tutorial on the use of Octave, a free software akin to Matlab, that we use for illustrative purposes throughout the book.

## Background Knowledge

It would be inaccurate to say that this book does not pre-suppose any knowledge on the part of the reader, but it is true that it does not pre-suppose much. A basic knowledge of financial markets, instruments, and variables (equities, bonds, interest rates, exchange rates, etc.) will obviously help—indeed, is almost essential. So too will a degree of analytical preparedness (for example, familiarity with logs and exponents, compounding, present value computations, basic statistics and probability, the normal distribution, and so on). But beyond this, not much is required. The book is largely self-contained. The use of advanced (from the standpoint of an MBA course) mathematical tools, such as stochastic calculus, is kept to a minimum, and where such concepts are introduced, they are often deviations from the main narrative that may be avoided if so desired.

## What Is Different about This Book?

It has been our experience that the overwhelming majority of students in derivatives courses go on to become traders, creators of structured products, or other users of derivatives, for whom a deep conceptual, rather than solely mathematical, understanding of products and models is required. Happily, the field of derivatives lends itself to such an end: while it is one of the most mathematically-sophisticated areas of finance, it is also possible, perhaps more so than in any other area of finance, to explain the fundamental principles underlying derivatives pricing and risk-management in simple-to-understand and relatively non-mathematical terms. Our book looks to create precisely such a blended approach, one that is formal and rigorous, yet intuitive and accessible.

To this purpose, a great deal of our effort throughout this book is spent on explaining what lies behind the formal mathematics of pricing and hedging. How are forward prices determined? Why does the Black-Scholes formula have the form it does? What is the option gamma and why is it of such importance to a trader? The option theta? Why do term-structure models take the approach they do? In particular, what are the subtleties and pitfalls in modeling term-structure movements? How may equity prices be used to extract default risk of companies? Debt prices? How does default correlation matter in the pricing of portfolio credit instruments? Why does it matter in this way? In all of these cases and others throughout the book, we use verbal and pictorial expositions, and sometimes simple mathematical models, to explain the underlying principles before proceeding to a formal analysis.

None of this should be taken to imply that our presentations are informal or mathematically incomplete. But it is true that we eschew the use of unnecessary mathematics. Where discrete-time settings can convey the behavior of a model better than continuous-time settings, we resort to such a framework. Where a picture can do the work of a thousand (or even a hundred) words, we use a picture. And we avoid the presentation of "black box" formulae to the maximum extent possible. In the few cases where deriving the prices of some derivatives would require the use of advanced mathematics, we spend effort explaining intuitively the form and behavior of the pricing formula.

To supplement the intuitive and formal presentations, we make extensive use of numerical examples for illustrative purposes. To enable comparability, the numerical examples are often built around a common parametrization. For example, in the chapter on option greeks, a baseline set of parameter values is chosen, and the behavior of each greek is illustrated using departures from these baselines.

In addition, the book presents several full-length case studies, including some of the most (in)famous derivatives disasters in history. These include Amaranth, Barings, Long-Term Capital Management (LTCM), Metallgesellschaft, Procter & Gamble, and others. These are supplemented by other case studies available on this book's website, including Ashanti, Sumitomo, the Son-of-Boss tax shelters, and American International Group (AIG).

Finally, since the best way to learn the theory of derivatives pricing and hedging is by working through exercises, the book offers a large number of end-of-chapter problems. These problems are of three types. Some are conceptual, mostly aimed at ensuring the basic definitions have been understood, but occasionally also involving algebraic manipulations. The second group comprise numerical exercises, problems that can be solved with a calculator or a spreadsheet. The last group are programming questions, questions that challenge the students to write code to implement specific models.

## Possible Course Outlines

Figure 1 describes the logical flow of chapters in the book. The book can be used at the undergraduate and MBA levels as the text for a first course in derivatives; for a second (or advanced) course in derivatives; for a "topics" course in derivatives (as a follow-up to a first course); and for a fixed-income and/or credit derivatives course; among others. We describe below our suggested selection of chapters for each of these.

A first course in derivatives typically covers forwards and futures, basic options material, and perhaps interest rate swaps. Such a course could be built around Chapters 1–4 on futures markets and forward and futures pricing; Chapters 7–14 on options payoffs and trading strategies, no-arbitrage restrictions and put-call parity, and the binomial and Black-Scholes models; Chapters 17–19 on option greeks and exotic options; and Chapter 23 on interest rate swaps and other floating-rate products.

A second course, focused primarily on interest-rate and credit-risk modeling, could begin with a review of basic option pricing (Chapters 11–14), move on to an examination of more complex pricing models (Chapter 16), then cover interest-rate modeling (Chapters 26–30) and finally credit derivatives and credit-risk modeling (Chapters 31–34).

A "topics" course following the first course could begin again with a review of basic option pricing (Chapters 11–14) followed by an examination of more complex pricing models

**FIGURE 1**
The Flow of the Book

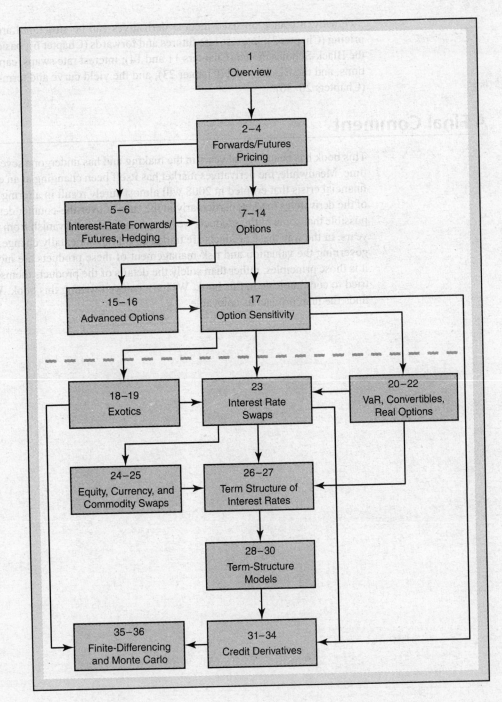

(Chapter 16). This could be followed by Value-at-Risk and risk-budgeting (Chapter 20); convertible bonds (Chapter 21); real options (Chapter 22); and interest-rate, equity, and currency swaps (Chapters 23–25), with the final part of the course covering either an introduction to term-structure modeling (Chapters 26–28) or an introduction to credit derivatives and structural models (Chapters 31 and 32).

Finally, a course on fixed-income derivatives can be structured around basic forward pricing (Chapter 3); interest-rate futures and forwards (Chapter 6); basic option pricing and the Black-Scholes model (Chapters 11 and 14); interest rate swaps, caps, floors, and swaptions, and the Black model (Chapter 23); and the yield curve and term-structure modeling (Chapters 26–30).

# A Final Comment

This book has been several years in the making and has undergone several revisions in that time. Meanwhile, the derivatives market has itself been changing at an explosive pace. The financial crisis that erupted in 2008 will almost surely result in altering major components of the derivatives market, particularly in the case of over-the-counter derivatives. Thus, it is possible that some of the products we have described could vanish from the market in a few years, or the way these products are traded could fundamentally change. But the *principles* governing the valuation and risk-management of these products are more permanent, and it is those principles, rather than solely the details of the products themselves, that we have tried to communicate in this book. We have enjoyed writing this book. We hope the reader finds the final product as enjoyable.

# Acknowledgments

We have benefited greatly from interactions with a number of our colleagues in academia and others in the broader finance profession. It is a pleasure to be able to thank them in print.

At New York University, where Raghu currently teaches and Sanjiv did his PhD (and has been a frequent visitor since), we have enjoyed many illuminating conversations over the years concerning derivatives research and teaching. For these, we thank Viral Acharya, Ed Altman, Yakov Amihud, Menachem Brenner, Aswath Damodaran, Steve Figlewski, Halina Frydman, Kose John, Tony Saunders, and Marti Subrahmanyam. We owe special thanks to Viral Acharya, long-time collaborator of both authors, for his feedback on earlier versions of this book; Ed Altman, from whom we—like the rest of the world—learned a great deal about credit risk and credit markets, and who was always generous with his time and support; Menachem Brenner, for many delightful exchanges concerning derivatives usage and structured products; Steve Figlewski, with whom we were privileged to serve as Co-Editors of the *Journal of Derivatives*, a wonderful learning experience; and, especially, Marti Subrahmanyam, who was Sanjiv's PhD advisor at NYU and with whom Raghu has co-taught Executive-MBA and PhD courses on derivatives and credit risk at NYU since the mid-90s. Marti's emphasis on an intuitive understanding of mathematical models has considerably influenced both authors' approach to the teaching of derivatives; its effect may be seen throughout this book.

At Santa Clara University, George Chacko, Atulya Sarin, Hersh Shefrin, and Meir Statman all provided much-appreciated advice, support, and encouragement. Valuable input also came from others in the academic profession, including Marco Avellaneda, Pierluigi Balduzzi, Jonathan Berk, Darrell Duffie, Anurag Gupta, Paul Hanouna, Nikunj Kapadia, Dan Ostrov, N.R. Prabhala, and Raman Uppal. In the broader finance community, we have benefited greatly from interactions with Santhosh Bandreddi, Jamil Baz, Richard Cantor, Gifford Fong, Silverio Foresi, Gary Geng, Grace Koo, Apoorva Koticha, Murali Krishna, Marco Naldi, Shankar Narayan, Raj Rajaratnam, Rahul Rathi, Jacob Sisk, Roger Stein, and Ram Sundaram. The first author would particularly like to thank Ram Sundaram and Murali Krishna for numerous stimulating and informative conversations concerning the markets; the second author thanks Robert Merton for his insights on derivatives and guidance in teaching continuous-time finance, and Gifford Fong for many years of generous mentorship.

Over the years that this book was being written, many of our colleagues in the profession provided (anonymous) reviews that greatly helped shape the final product. A very special thanks to those reviewers who took the time to review virtually every chapter in draft form: Bala Arshanapalli (Indiana University–Northwest), Dr. R. Brian Balyeat (Texas A&M University), James Bennett (University of Massachusetts–Boston), Jinliang (Jack) Li (Northeastern University), Spencer Martin (Arizona State University), Patricia Matthews (Mount Union College), Dennis Ozenbas (Montclair State University), Vivek Pandey (University of Texas–Tyler), Peter Ritchken (Case-Western Reserve University), Tie Su (University of Miami), Thomas Tallerico (Dowling College), Kudret Topyan (Manhattan College), Alan Tucker (Pace University), Jorge Urrutia (Loyola University–Watertower), Matt Will (University of Indianapolis), and Guofu Zhou (Washington University–St. Louis).

As we have noted in the Preface, this book grew out of notes developed by the authors for academic courses and professional training programs at a number of institutions including

Harvard University, Santa Clara University, University of California at Berkeley, Citibank, Credit-Suisse, Merrill Lynch, the IMF, and, most of all, New York University. Participants in all of these courses (and at London Business School, where an earlier version of Raghu's NYU notes were used by Viral Acharya) have provided detailed feedback that led to several revisions of the original material. We greatly appreciate the contribution they have made to the final product. We are also grateful to Ravi Kumar of Capital Metrics and Risk Solutions (P) Ltd. for his terrific assistance in creating the software that accompanies this book; and to Priyanka Singh of the same organization for proofreading the manuscript and its exercises.

Michele Janicek, our editor at McGraw-Hill, was a delight to work with, always tolerant of our procrastinations and always accommodating of our eccentricities. A special thanks to her and to the team at McGraw (especially Barb Hari, Meg Maloney, Dean Karampelas, and Christine Vaughan) for the splendid support we received. Thanks too to JaNoel Lowe for her meticulous copyediting job; Sue Gottfried for her careful proofreading; and Dheeraj Chahal for the patience and care with which he guided this book through the typesetting process.

Our greatest debts are to the members of our respective families. We are both extraordinarily fortunate in having large and supportive extended family networks. To all of them, and especially to Urmilla and Aditi, Priya and Shikhar, Ram and Preethi, Gaura and Shankar, Nithu and Raja, Romith and Angana: thank you. We owe you more than we can ever repay.

**Rangarajan K. Sundaram**
*New York, NY*

**Sanjiv Ranjan Das**
*Santa Clara, CA*

# Chapter 1

# Introduction

The world derivatives market is a *huge* one. The Bank for International Settlements estimates that by December 2008, the volume of derivatives outstanding worldwide, measured in terms of notional outstanding, was a staggering $592 *trillion*. The gross market value of these derivatives was a more modest, but still respectable, $33.9 trillion. By way of comparison, the gross domestic product in 2007 of the United States, the world's largest economy, was "only" about $13.8 trillion.

Not only is the market immense; it has also been growing at a furious pace. The notional amount outstanding in derivatives contracts worldwide increased more than *sevenfold* in the nine years ending December 2007, doubling in just the last two years of that span (Tables 1.1 and 1.2). The global financial crisis that erupted in 2008 took its toll on the market, but at the end of December 2008, the notional outstanding was roughly the same as at the end of December 2007, and the gross market value of these derivatives was more than 130% higher.

The growth has been truly widespread. There are now thriving derivatives exchanges not only in the traditional developed economies of North America, Europe, and Japan, but also in Brazil, China, India, Israel, Korea, Mexico, and Singapore, among many other countries. A survey by the International Swaps and Derivatives Association (ISDA) in 2003 found that 92% of the world's 500 largest companies use derivatives to manage risk of various forms, especially interest-rate risk (92%) and currency risk (85%), but, to a lesser extent, also commodity risk (25%) and equity risk (12%). Firms in over 90% of the countries represented in the sample used derivatives.

Matching—and fueling—the growth has been the pace of innovation in the market. Traditional derivatives were written on commodity prices, but beginning with foreign currency and other financial derivatives in the 1970s, new forms of derivatives have been introduced almost continuously. Today, derivatives contracts reference a wide range of underlying instruments including equity prices, commodity prices, exchange rates, interest rates, bond prices, index levels, and credit risk. Derivatives have also been introduced, with varying success rates, on more exotic underlying variables such as market volatility, electricity prices, temperature levels, broadband, newsprint, and natural catastrophes, among many others.

This is an impressive picture. Yet derivatives have also been the target of fierce criticism. In 2003, Warren Buffet, perhaps the world's most successful investor, labeled them "financial weapons of mass destruction." Derivatives—especially credit derivatives—have been widely blamed for enabling, or at least exacerbating, the global financial markets crisis that began in late 2007. Victims of derivatives' (mis-)use over the decades include such prominent names as the centuries-old British institution Barings Bank, the German industrial conglomerate Metallgesellschaft AG, the Japanese trading powerhouse Sumitomo, and the giant US insurance company, American International Group (AIG).

**TABLE 1.1**    BIS Estimates of World Derivatives Market Size: 2006–2008

| | Notional Amounts Outstanding | | | Gross Market Values | | |
|---|---|---|---|---|---|---|
| | End 2006 | End 2007 | End 2008 | End 2006 | End 2007 | End 2008 |
| **Total contracts** | **414.8** | **596.0** | **592.0** | **9.7** | **14.5** | **33.9** |
| **Foreign exchange contracts** | **40.3** | **56.2** | **49.8** | **1.3** | **1.8** | **3.9** |
| Forwards and forex swaps | 19.9 | 29.1 | 24.6 | 0.5 | 0.7 | 1.7 |
| Currency swaps | 10.8 | 14.3 | 14.7 | 0.6 | 0.8 | 1.6 |
| Options | 9.6 | 12.7 | 10.5 | 0.2 | 0.3 | 0.6 |
| **Interest rate contracts** | **291.6** | **393.1** | **418.7** | **4.8** | **7.2** | **18.4** |
| Forward-rate agreements | 18.7 | 26.6 | 39.3 | 0.0 | 0.0 | 0.2 |
| Interest rate swaps | 229.7 | 309.6 | 328.1 | 4.2 | 6.2 | 16.6 |
| Options | 43.2 | 57.0 | 51.3 | 0.6 | 1.0 | 1.7 |
| **Equity-linked contracts** | **7.5** | **8.5** | **6.5** | **0.9** | **1.1** | **1.1** |
| Forwards and swaps | 1.8 | 2.2 | 1.6 | 0.2 | 0.2 | 0.3 |
| Options | 5.7 | 6.3 | 4.9 | 0.7 | 0.9 | 0.8 |
| **Commodity contracts** | **7.1** | **9.0** | **4.4** | **0.7** | **0.8** | **1.0** |
| Gold | 0.6 | 0.6 | 0.4 | 0.1 | 0.1 | 0.0 |
| Other commodities | 6.5 | 8.4 | 4.0 | 0.6 | 1.8 | 0.9 |
| Forwards and swaps | 2.8 | 5.6 | 2.5 | | | |
| Options | 3.7 | 2.8 | 1.6 | | | |
| **Credit default swaps** | **28.7** | **57.9** | **41.9** | **0.2** | **0.9** | **5.7** |
| Single-name instruments | 17.9 | 32.2 | 25.4 | 1.6 | 1.6 | 3.7 |
| Multi-name instruments | 10.8 | 25.6 | 16.1 | 0.0 | 0.0 | 2.0 |
| Unallocated | 39.7 | 71.2 | 70.7 | 0.0 | 0.0 | 3.8 |

Source: Bank for International Settlements (BIS) website (http://www.bis.org).

What *is* a derivative? What are the different types of derivatives? What are the benefits of derivatives that have fueled their growth? The risks that have led to disasters? How is the value of a derivative determined? How are the risks in a derivative measured? How can these risks be managed (or *hedged*)? These and other questions are the focus of this book. We describe and analyze a wide range of derivative securities. By combining the analytical descriptions with numerical examples, exercises, and case studies, we present an introduction to the world of derivatives that is at once formal and rigorous yet accessible and intuitive. The rest of this chapter elaborates and lays the foundation for the book.

## What Are Derivatives?

A *derivative security* is a financial security whose payoff depends on (or *derives from*) other, more fundamental, variables such as a stock price, an exchange rate, a commodity price, an interest rate—or even the price of another derivative security. The underlying driving variable is commonly referred to as simply *the underlying*.

The simplest kind of derivative—and historically the oldest form, dating back thousands of years—is a *forward contract*. A forward contract is one in which two parties (commonly referred to as the *counterparties* in the transaction) agree to the terms of a trade to be consummated on a specified date in the future. For example, on December 3, a buyer and seller may enter into a forward contract to trade in 100 oz of gold in three months (i.e., on March 3) at a price of $900/oz. In this case, the seller is undertaking to sell 100 oz in three

**TABLE 1.2**  BIS Estimates of World Derivatives Market Size: 1998–2008

| | Notional Amounts Outstanding | | | | | |
|---|---|---|---|---|---|---|
| | Dec. 1998 | Dec. 2000 | Dec. 2002 | Dec. 2004 | Dec. 2007 | Dec. 2008 |
| **Total contracts** | **80.3** | **95.2** | **141.7** | **257.9** | **596.0** | **592.0** |
| **Foreign exchange contracts** | **18.0** | **15.7** | **18.4** | **29.3** | **56.2** | **49.8** |
| Forwards and forex swaps | 12.1 | 10.1 | 10.7 | 15.0 | 29.1 | 24.6 |
| Currency swaps | 2.3 | 3.2 | 4.5 | 8.2 | 14.3 | 14.7 |
| Options | 3.7 | 2.3 | 3.2 | 6.1 | 12.7 | 10.5 |
| **Interest rate contracts** | **50.0** | **64.7** | **101.7** | **190.5** | **393.1** | **418.7** |
| Forward-rate agreements | 5.8 | 6.4 | 8.8 | 12.8 | 26.6 | 39.3 |
| Interest-rate swaps | 36.3 | 48.8 | 79.1 | 150.6 | 309.6 | 328.1 |
| Options | 8.0 | 9.5 | 13.7 | 27.1 | 57.0 | 51.3 |
| **Equity-linked contracts** | **1.5** | **1.9** | **2.3** | **4.4** | **8.5** | **6.5** |
| Forwards and swaps | 0.1 | 0.3 | 0.4 | 0.8 | 2.2 | 1.6 |
| Options | 1.3 | 1.6 | 1.9 | 3.6 | 6.3 | 4.9 |
| **Commodity contracts** | **0.4** | **0.7** | **0.9** | **1.4** | **9.0** | **4.4** |
| Gold | 0.2 | 0.2 | 0.3 | 0.4 | 0.6 | 0.4 |
| Other commodities | 0.2 | 0.4 | 0.6 | 1.1 | 8.4 | 4.0 |
| Forwards and swaps | 0.1 | 0.2 | 0.4 | 0.6 | 5.6 | 2.5 |
| Options | 0.1 | 0.2 | 0.2 | 0.5 | 2.8 | 1.6 |
| **Credit default swaps** | | | | **6.4** | **57.9** | **41.9** |
| Single-name instruments | | | | 5.1 | 32.2 | 25.4 |
| Multi-name instruments | | | | 1.3 | 25.6 | 16.1 |
| Unallocated | 10.4 | 12.3 | 18.3 | 25.9 | 71.2 | 71.2 |

Source: Bank for International Settlements (BIS) website (http://www.bis.org).

months at a price of $900/oz while the buyer is undertaking to buy 100 oz of gold in three months at $900/oz.

One common motivation for entering into a forward contract is the elimination of cash-flow uncertainty from a future transaction. In our example, if the buyer anticipates a need for 100 oz of gold in three months and is worried about price fluctuations over that period, any uncertainty about the cash outlay required can be removed by entering into a forward contract. Similarly, if the seller expects to be offloading 100 oz of gold in three months and is concerned about prices that might prevail at the end of that horizon, entering into a forward contract locks in the price received for that future sale.

In short, forward contracts may be used to *hedge* cash-flow risk associated with future market commitments. Forward contracts are commonly used by importers and exporters worried about exchange-rate fluctuations, investors and borrowers worried about interest-rate fluctuations, commodity producers and buyers worried about commodity price fluctuations, and so on.

A slightly more complex example of a derivative is an *option*. As in a forward, an option contract too specifies the terms of a future trade, but while a forward commits both parties to the trade, in an option, one party to the contract retains the right to enforce or opt out of the contract. If it is the buyer who has this right, the option is called a *call option*; if the seller, a *put option*.

The key difference between a forward and an option is that while a forward contract is an instrument for *hedging*, an option provides a form of financial *insurance*. Consider, for example, a call option on gold in which the buyer has the right to buy gold from the seller at a price of (say) $900/oz in three months' time. If the price of gold in three months is greater than $900/oz (for example, it is $930/oz), then the buyer will exercise the right in the contract and buy the gold for the contract price of $900. However, if the price in three months is less than $900/oz (e.g., is $880/oz), the buyer can choose to opt out of the contract and, if necessary, buy the gold directly in the market at the cheaper price of $880/oz.

Thus, holding a call option effectively provides the buyer with protection (or "insurance") against an *increase* in the price above that specified in the contract even while allowing the buyer to take full advantage of price decreases. Since it is the seller who takes the other side of the contract whenever the buyer decides to enforce it, it is the seller who provides this insurance to the buyer. In exchange for providing this protection, the seller will charge the buyer an up-front fee called the *call option premium.*

Analogously, a *put* option provides the seller with insurance against a *decrease* in the price. For instance, consider a put option on gold in which the seller has the right to sell gold to the buyer at $900/oz. If the price of gold falls below $900/oz, the seller can exercise the right in the put and sell the gold for $900/oz, but if the price of gold rises to more than $900/oz, then the seller can elect to let the put lapse and sell the gold at the higher market price. Holding the put insures the seller against a fall in the price below $900/oz. The buyer provides this insurance and will charge an up-front fee, the *put premium*, for providing this service.

Options offer an alternative to forwards for investors concerned about future price fluctuations. Unlike forwards, there is an up-front cost of buying an option (viz., the option premium) but, compensating for this, there is no compulsion to exercise if doing so would result in a loss.

Forwards and options are two of the most common and important forms of derivatives. In many ways, they are the building blocks of the derivatives landscape. Many other forms of derivatives exist, some which are simple variants of these structures, others much more complex or "exotic" (a favorite term in the derivatives area for describing something that is not run-of-the-mill or "plain vanilla"). We elaborate on this later in this chapter and in the rest of the book. But first, we present a brief discussion on the different criteria that may be used to classify derivatives.

## Classifying Derivatives

A popular way to classify derivatives is to group them according to the underlying. For example, an *equity derivative* is one whose underlying is an equity price or stock index level; a *currency* or *FX* (short for foreign-exchange) *derivative* is one whose underlying is an exchange rate; and so on. Much of the world's derivatives trade on just a few common underlyings. Table 1.1 shows that *interest-rate derivatives* (derivatives defined on interest rates or on interest-rate-sensitive securities such as bonds) account for almost half the gross market value of the derivatives market, with smaller shares being taken by currency, equity, commodity, and credit derivatives.

While these are the most common underlyings, derivatives may, in principle, be defined on just about any underlying variable. Indeed, a substantial chunk of the growth in derivatives markets in the first years of the 2000s came from *credit derivatives* (derivatives dependent on the credit risk of specified underlying entities), a category of derivatives that did not even exist in 1990. As noted earlier in this chapter, derivatives have also been introduced on a number of exotic underlying variables including electricity prices, temperature levels, broadband, newsprint, and market volatility.

Derivatives can differ greatly in the manner in which they depend on the underlying, ranging from very simple dependencies to very complex ones. Nonetheless, most derivatives fall into one of two classes: those that involve a *commitment* to a given trade or exchange of cash flows in the future and those in which one party has the *option* to enforce or opt out of the trade or exchange. Included in the former class are derivative securities such as *forwards*, *futures*; and *swaps*; derivatives in the latter class are called *options*.

Forwards and options have already been defined above. Futures contracts are similar to forward contracts except that they are traded on organized exchanges; we discuss the differences more precisely below. Swaps are contracts in which the parties commit to *multiple* exchanges of cash flows in the future, with the cash flows to be exchanged calculated under rules specified in the contract; thus, swaps are like forwards except with multiple transactions to which the parties commit.

Tables 1.1 and 1.2 use both of these schemes of classification, first breaking down the world derivatives market by underlying and then into forwards, swaps, and options. The breakdown reveals some interesting variations. For example, while swaps account for the great bulk (roughly 80%) of interest-rate derivatives, options constitute over 75% of equity derivatives.

A third classification of derivatives of interest is into over-the-counter (OTC) or exchange-traded derivatives. Over-the-counter derivatives contracts are traded bilaterally between two counterparties who deal directly with each other. In such transactions, each party takes the credit risk of the other (i.e., the risk that the other counterparty may default on the contract). In exchange-traded contracts, the parties deal though an organized exchange, and the identity of the counterparty is usually not known. Forwards and swaps are OTC contracts, while futures are exchange traded. Options can be both OTC and exchange traded.

## 1.1   Forward and Futures Contracts

A *forward contract* is an agreement between two parties to trade in a specified quantity of a specified good at a specified price on a specified date in the future. The following basic terminology is used when discussing these contracts:

- The buyer in the forward contract is said to have a *long position* in the contract; the seller is said to have a *short position*.
- The good specified in the contract is called the *underlying asset* or, simply, the *underlying*.
- The date specified in the contract on which the trade will take place is called the *maturity date* of the contract.
- The price specified in the contract for the trade is called the *delivery price* in the contract. This is the price at which delivery will be made by the seller and accepted by the buyer.

We will define the important concept of a *forward price* shortly. For the moment, we note that the forward price is related to, but is not the same concept as, the delivery price.

The underlying in a forward contract may be any commodity or financial asset. Forward contracts may be written on foreign currencies, bonds, equities, or indices, or physical commodities such as oil, gold, or wheat. Forward contracts also exist on such underlyings as interest rates or volatility which cannot be delivered physically (see, for example, the *forward-rate agreements* or FRAs described in Chapter 6, or the forward contracts on market volatility known as *variance* and *volatility swaps,* described in Chaper 14); in such cases, the contracts are settled in cash with one side making a payment to the other based on rules specified in the contract. Cash settlement is also commonly used for those underlyings for which physical delivery is difficult, such as equity indices.

As has been discussed, a primary motive for entering into a forward contract is *hedging*: using a forward contract results in locking-in a price today for a future market transaction, and this eliminates cash-flow uncertainty from the transaction. Foreign currency forwards, for example, enable exporters to convert the payments received in foreign currency into home currency at a fixed rate. Interest-rate forwards such as FRAs enable firms to lock-in an interest rate today for a future borrowing or investment. Commodity forwards such as forwards on oil enable users of oil to lock-in prices at which future purchases are made and refiners of oil to lock-in a price at which future sales are made.

Forward contracts can also be used for *speculation*, that is, without an underlying exposure already existing. An investor who feels that the price of some underlying is likely to increase can speculate on this view by entering into a long forward contract on that underlying. If prices do go up as anticipated, the investor can buy the asset at the locked-in price on the forward contract and sell at the higher price, making a profit. Similarly, an investor wishing to speculate on falling prices can use a short forward contract for this purpose.

## Key Characteristics of Forward Contracts

Four characteristics of forward contracts deserve special emphasis because these are exactly the dimensions along which forwards and futures differ:

- First, a forward contract is a bilateral contract. That is, the terms of the contract are negotiated directly by the seller and the buyer.
- Second, as a consequence, a forward contract is customizable. That is, the terms of the contract (maturity date, quality or grade of the underlying asset, etc.) can be "tailored" to the needs of the buyer and seller.
- Third, there is possible default risk for both parties. Each party takes the risk that the other may fail to perform on the contract.
- Fourth, neither party can walk away unilaterally from the contract or transfer its rights and obligations in the contract unilaterally to a third party.

We return to these characteristics when discussing futures contracts.

## Payoffs from Forward Contracts

The payoff from a forward contract is the profit or loss made by the two parties to the contract. Consider an example. Suppose a buyer and seller enter into a forward contract on a stock with a delivery price of $F = 100$. Let $S_T$ denote the price of the stock on the maturity date $T$. Then, on date $T$,

- The long position is buying for $F = 100$ an asset worth $S_T$. So the payoff to the long position is $S_T - 100$. The long position makes a profit if $S_T > 100$, but loses if $S_T < 100$.
- The short position is selling for $F = 100$ an asset worth $S_T$. So the payoff to the short position is $100 - S_T$. The short position makes a profit if $S_T < 100$, but loses if $S_T > 100$.

For example:

- If $S_T = 110$, then the long is buying for 100 an asset worth 110, so gains 10, but the short is selling for 100 an asset worth 110, so loses 10.
- If $S_T = 90$, the long is buying for 100 an asset worth only 90, so loses 10, while the short is selling for 100 an asset worth only 90, so gains 10.

Table 1.3 describes the payoff to the two sides for some other values of $S_T$. Two points about these payoffs should be noted. First, forwards (like all derivatives) are *zero-sum* instruments: the profits made by the long come at the expense of the short, and vice versa. The sum of the payoffs of the long and short is always zero. This is unsurprising. Except when the delivery price $F$ exactly coincides with the time-$T$ price $S_T$ of the underlying, a forward contract involves an *off-market* trade (i.e., a trade at a different price from the

**TABLE 1.3** The Payoffs from a Forward Contract

This table describes the payoff to the long and short positions on the maturity date $T$ of a forward contract with a delivery price of 100. $S_T$ is the price of the underlying asset on date $T$.

| Time-$T$ Price $S_T$ | Payoff to Long | Payoff to Short |
|---|---|---|
| ⋮ | ⋮ | ⋮ |
| 70 | −30 | +30 |
| 80 | −20 | +20 |
| 90 | −10 | +10 |
| 100 | − | − |
| 110 | +10 | −10 |
| 120 | +20 | −20 |
| 130 | +30 | −30 |
| ⋮ | ⋮ | ⋮ |

prevailing market price). In any off-market trade, the benefit to one side is exactly equal to the loss taken by the other.

Second, as Figure 1.1 illustrates, forwards are "linear" derivatives. Every $1 increase in the price $S_T$ of the underlying at date $T$ increases the payoff of the long position by $1 and reduces the payoffs of the short position by $1. Linearity is a consequence of committing to the trade specified in the contract. In contrast, as we will see, options, which are characterized by their "optionality" concerning the trade, are fundamentally nonlinear instruments, and this makes their valuation and risk management much trickier.

## What Is the "Forward Price"?

By convention, neither party pays anything to enter into a forward contract. So the delivery price in the contract is set so that the contract has zero value to both parties. This "breakeven" delivery price is called the *forward price*.

**FIGURE 1.1** Forwards Are "Linear" Derivatives

The figure shows the payoffs to the long and short positions on the maturity date $T$ of a forward contract with delivery price $F$ as the time-$T$ price $S_T$ of the underlying asset varies.

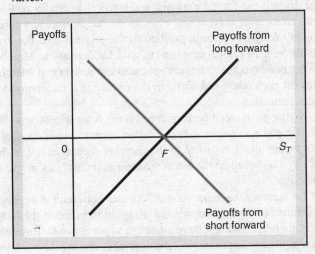

Is the forward price a well-defined concept? That is, is it obvious that there is only *one* breakeven delivery price? At first glance, it appears not. Certainly, it is true that if the delivery price is set very high, the short will expect to profit from the contract and the long to lose; that is, the contract will have positive value to the short and negative value to the long. Similarly, if the price is set too low, the contract will have positive value to the long (who will expect to profit from having access to the asset at an excessively low price) and negative value to the short. But it is not obvious that between these extremes, there is only one possible breakeven delivery price at which both parties will agree the contract has zero value. Intuitively, it appears that such idiosyncratic factors as risk-aversion and outlooks concerning the market ought to matter.

In Chapter 3, we examine this issue. We show that under fairly general conditions, the forward price *is*, in fact, a well-defined concept and that regardless of attitudes to risk and other factors, everyone *must* agree on the breakeven delivery price. Possible violations of these conditions and their consequences for the pricing theory are examined in Chapter 4. The principal assumption we make there, and throughout this book, is that markets do not permit *arbitrage*. The no-arbitrage assumption is just the minimal requirement that identical assets or baskets of assets must trade at identical prices.

## Futures Markets

A *futures contract* is, in essence, a forward contract that is traded on an organized exchange. But while futures and forwards are functionally similar (i.e., they serve the same economic purpose), the involvement of the exchange results in some important differences between them.

First, in a futures contract, buyers and sellers deal through the futures exchange, not directly. Buyers submit buy orders to the exchange, sellers submit sell orders, and these are matched via the exchange. The counterparties are unlikely to know each other's identities.

Second, because buyers and sellers do not meet, futures contracts must be *standardized*. Standardization covers the set of possible delivery dates and delivery locations, the size of one contract, and the quality or grade of the underlying that may be delivered under the contract, and is one of the most important functions performed by the exchange.

Third, counterparties are not exposed to each other's default risk. Rather, the exchange interposes itself between buyer and seller and guarantees performance on the contracts. (This is necessary because the counterparties have no way of gauging each other's credit risk.) Thus, each party to a futures transaction is exposed only to the default risk of the exchange. In well-run futures exchanges, this risk is generally very low.

Fourth, an investor may, at any time, close out or *reverse* a futures position. Closing out involves taking an opposite position to the original one. For example, if the investor was initially long 10 futures contracts in gold for delivery in March, closing out involves taking short positions in 10 futures contracts for delivery in March. These positions are netted against each other, and, as far as the exchange is concerned, the investor has no net obligations remaining.

Fifth, having guaranteed performance on the futures contracts, the exchange must put safeguards in place to ensure it is not called upon to honor its guarantee too often. That is, it must ensure that the parties to the contract do not default in the first place. For this purpose, a system based on the use of "margin accounts" (a.k.a. "performance bonds") are commonly used.

Table 1.4 summarizes these main differences between futures and forwards. The institutional features of futures markets are designed to enhance the integrity and liquidity of the market, thereby making it more attractive to participants. However, they also have economic consequences. For example, futures prices—the breakeven delivery prices for futures

**TABLE 1.4**
Differences between
Forwards and Futures

| Criterion | Futures | Forwards |
|---|---|---|
| Buyer-seller interaction | Via exchange | Direct |
| Contract terms | Standardized | Can be tailored |
| Unilateral reversal | Possible | Not possible |
| Default-risk borne by | Exchange | Individual parties |
| Default controlled by | Margin accounts | Collateral |

contracts—are typically close to, but do not quite coincide with, forward prices because of these differences, as Chapter 3 discusses.

# 1.2 Options

An *option* is a financial security that gives the buyer the right (but not the obligation) to buy or sell a specified asset at a specified price on or before a specified date. In dealing with options, we adopt the following terminology:

- Buyer = Holder = Long Position: The buyer of the option, also called the *holder* of the option, is said to have a *long position* in the option.
- Seller = Writer = Short Position: The seller of the option, also called the *writer* of the option, is said to have a *short position* in the option.
- The asset specified in the option contract is called the *underlying asset* or simply the *underlying*.
- The price specified in the contract is called the *strike price* or the *exercise price* of the option.
- The date specified in the contract is called the *maturity date* or the *expiration date* of the option.

We differentiate between options along two fundamental dimensions:

- **Calls vs. Puts** If the option provides the holder with the right to *buy* the underlying asset at the specified strike price, we call it a *call* option. If the option provides the holder with the right to *sell* the underlying at the specified strike price, it is a *put* option.
- **American vs. European** If the right in the option can be exercised at any time *on or before* the maturity date, it is called an *American-style* (or simply, *American*) option. If the right can be availed of only *on* the maturity date, it is called a *European-style* (or simply, *European*) option. American options are generally more valuable than otherwise identical European ones.

Traditional call and put options, whether European or American, are referred to as *plain vanilla* (or just *vanilla*) options. Options that differ from plain vanilla options in any way are called *exotic options*. Bermudan options are an example; in a Bermudan option, exercise is allowed on any one of a set of specified dates. Not quite as valuable as American options, which may be exercised at any time, they are more valuable than European options, which may be exercised only at maturity.

Options can be written on any asset, though financial options are the most common. Options on equities, equity indices, and foreign currencies are traded both in the over-the-counter market and on exchanges. Options on interest rates come in many forms. Exchange-traded interest-rate options include options on bond futures (i.e., the option is written on a futures contract that, in turn, is written on an underlying bond). In the over-the-counter market, popular interest-rate options include *caps* and *floors*, which are options written directly on London Interbank Offered Rates (or "Libor") rates, and *swaptions*, which are options on interest rate swaps.

In addition to options *qua* options, many financial securities are sold with embedded options. A common example is a *callable bond*. A callable bond is a bond issued by a corporation or other entity that may be purchased back by the issuing entity under specified conditions at a fixed price. Thus, a callable bond is a combination of a straight bond and a call option that gives the issuing entity the right to buy back (or "call") the bond under specified conditions at a fixed price. A more complex example is a *convertible bond*. A convertible bond is a bond issued by a company that may be converted, at the holder's option, into shares of equity of the issuing company. Convertible bonds in the United States are usually also callable, so both the issuer and the buyer of the bond hold options. Embedded options are also present in more mundane securities. In the United States, for example, mortgages may be prepaid at any time, usually without penalty, at the mortgage-holder's option.

As discussed earlier in this chapter, an option is a form of financial *insurance*. Since an option comes with a right but not an obligation, the holder of the option will exercise it only if it is in his interest to do so. Thus, the option protects the holder against downside risk, but provides full upside potential. In exchange for providing this insurance, the buyer of the option makes an up-front payment to the writer, called the *option price* or the *option premium*.

## 1.3 Swaps

A *swap* is a bilateral contract between two counterparties that calls for periodic exchanges of cash flows on specified dates and calculated using specified rules. The swap contract specifies (a) the dates (say, $T_1, T_2, \ldots, T_n$) on which cash flows will be exchanged and (b) the rules according to which the cash flows due from each counterparty on these dates are calculated. Importantly, the frequency of payments for the two counterparties need not be the same. For example, one counterparty could be required to make semiannual payments, while the other makes quarterly payments.

Swaps are differentiated by the underlying markets to which payments on one or both legs are linked. (The "leg" of a swap refers to the cash flows paid by a counterparty. Thus, each swap has two legs.) The largest chunk of the swaps market is occupied by *interest-rate swaps*, in which each leg of the swap is tied to a specific interest-rate index. For example, one leg may be tied to a floating interest rate such as Libor, while the other leg may specify a fixed interest rate (e.g., 8%). Other important categories of swaps include:

- *Currency swaps*, in which the two legs of the swaps are linked to payments in different currencies. For example, the swap may require the exchange of US dollar (USD) payments calculated on the basis of the USD-Libor rate for Euro payments calculated based on a fixed interest rate.
- *Equity swaps*, in which one leg (or both legs) of the swap is linked to an equity price or equity index. For example, the swap may call for the exchange of annual returns on the S&P 500 equity index for interest payments computed using a fixed interest rate.
- *Commodity swaps*, in which one leg of the swap is linked to a commodity price. For example, the swap may call for an exchange of the price of oil (observed on the payment dates) against a fixed dollar amount.
- Credit-risk linked swaps (especially *credit-default swaps*) in which one leg of the swap is linked to occurrence of a credit event (e.g., default) on a specified reference entity.

### Uses of Swaps

Swaps are among the most versatile of financial instruments with new uses being discovered (invented?) almost every day. A principal source of swap utility is that swaps enable converting the exposure to one market into exposure to another market. Consider, for example, a three-year equity swap in which

- One counterparty pays the returns on the S&P 500 on a given notional principal $P$.
- The other counterparty pays a fixed rate of interest $r$ on the same principal $P$.

In such a swap, the first counterparty in this swap is exchanging equity-market returns for interest-rate returns over this three-year horizon. An equity-fund manager who enters this swap is converting his equity returns into fixed-income returns through the swap. The second counterparty is doing the opposite exchange. A fixed-income manager who takes this side of the swap is converting his fixed-income exposure into equity exposure.

In similar vein, an interest rate swap that involves (say) the exchange of Libor for a fixed rate of interest enables converting floating-rate interest exposure to fixed rates and vice versa; a currency swap that requires the exchange of (say) USD payments based on USD-Libor for Japanese yen (JPY) payments based on JPY-Libor facilitates converting floating-rate USD exposure to floating-rate JPY exposure; and so on.

A second valuable contribution made by swaps is in providing pricing links between different financial markets. Consider the equity swap example again. By convention, swaps do not generally involve up-front payments, so at inception, the fixed rate $r$ in this swap is set such that the swap has zero value to both parties, i.e., such that the present value of all cash flows expected from the equity leg is equal to the present value of the cash flows from the interest-rate leg. This means the interest rate $r$ represents the market's "fair price" for converting equity returns into fixed-income returns. Thus, the equity swap not only enables transferring equity risk into interest-rate risk but also specifies the price at which this transfer can be done.

Similarly, interest rate swaps provide a link between different interest-rate markets, for example, between floating-rate markets and fixed-rate markets; currency swaps provide a link between interest-rate markets in different currencies, for example, between USD floating rates and euro fixed rates, or between euro floating rates and JPY fixed rates, and so on.

# 1.4 Using Derivatives: Some Comments

Derivatives can be used for both hedging and speculation. *Hedging* is where the cash flows from the derivative are used to offset or mitigate the cash flows from a prior market commitment. For example, an exporter who anticipates receiving foreign currency in a month can eliminate exchange-rate risk by using a short forward contract on the foreign currency, or by using a put option that gives the exporter the right to sell the foreign currency received at a fixed price. *Speculation* is where the derivative is used without an underlying prior exposure; the aim is to profit from anticipated market movements.

Derivatives usage in various contexts is discussed throughout this book. Here we present two examples to make some simple points about the advantages and disadvantages of using different derivatives to achieve a given end. Ultimately, the examples illustrate that there are pluses and minuses to all courses of actions–including not using derivatives at all. There is no one strategy that is dominant.

## Derivatives in Hedging

A US-based company learns on December 13 that it will receive 25 million euros (EUR) in the coming March for goods that it had exported to Europe. The company is exposed to exchange-rate risk because the USD it receives in March will depend on the USD/EUR exchange rate at that point. It identifies three possible courses of action:

1. Do nothing. It can wait until March and convert the money received then at the USD/EUR exchange rate prevailing at that point.

2. Use futures. It can enter into a short futures contract and commit to selling the euros at a fixed price.

3. Use options. It can buy a put option contract that gives it the right to sell the euros received at a specified strike price.

To keep things simple, we ignore "basis risk" issues, i.e., possible mismatches concerning the delivery dates of the futures and options contracts, and the date the company will receive the money.

If the company decides to go with futures, it will use the euro futures contracts available on the Chicago Mercantile Exchange (CME). Like all futures contracts, these are standardized contracts. One futures contract calls for the short position to deliver 125,000 euros. To hedge the entire exposure of 25 million euros, the company must therefore take a short position in 200 March futures contracts. Finally, suppose that on December 13, the futures price (USD/EUR) for March expiry is 1.0328; this is the fixed exchange rate the company can lock in if it decides to use the futures contract.

If the company decides to use options, it will use the euro options contract available on the Philadelphia Exchange (PHLX). One options contract on the PHLX calls for the delivery of 62,500 euros, so to cover the full amount of 25 million euros, a total of 400 contracts with March expiry must be used. A final decision the company must make concerns the choice of strike price. Suppose that the company has decided to use a strike price (USD/EUR) of 1.03 and that a put option with a strike of 1.03 and March expiry costs USD1,056.25 per contract. Then, if the company decides to use options, the total outlay required is

$$USD\,(400 \times 1{,}056.25) \; = \; USD\,422{,}500.00$$

To illustrate the impact of the different alternatives, we consider two possible exchange rates (USD/EUR)in March: (a) 0.9928 and (b) 1.0728. The following table summarizes the USD cash flow in March from each of the three alternatives. Note that the options cash flow does not include the initial cash outlay of USD 422,500. The payoffs are obtained in the obvious way. For example, under the do-nothing alternative, if the spot rate of $0.9928/euro were to prevail, the cash flow that results is 25 million × 0.9928 = $24.82 million.

| Alternative | $0.9928/euro | $1.0728/euro |
| --- | --- | --- |
| Do nothing | 24.82  million | 26.82  million |
| Futures contract | 25.82  million | 25.82  million |
| Put option | 25.75  million | 26.82  million |

There are three important criteria under which we may compare the alternatives:

1. *Cash-flow uncertainty*. This is maximal for the do-nothing alternative, intermediate for the option contract, and least for the futures contract.

2. *Up-front cost*. The do-nothing and futures contract alternatives cost nothing. However, there is an up-front cost of $422,500 for entering into the option contract.

3. *Exercise-time regret*. With an option contract, exercise-time outcomes are guaranteed to be favorable (if the USD/EUR exchange rate is greater than the strike rate, the option is allowed to lapse; otherwise it is exercised). With the other two alternatives, this is not the case:

   • In the do-nothing case, a "favorable" spot price movement (i.e., the high USD/EUR exchange rate of 1.0728) is beneficial, but an "unfavorable" spot price movement (the low USD/EUR exchange rate of 0.9928) hurts.

**TABLE 1.5**
Derivatives in
Hedging: Comparing
the Alternatives

| Alternative | USD/EUR Increases | USD/EUR Decreases | Cash-Flow Uncertainty | Cost |
|---|---|---|---|---|
| Do nothing | Gain | Lose | Maximal | 0 |
| Futures | Lose | Gain | Minimal | 0 |
| Options | Gain | Protected | Intermediate | +ve |

- In the futures contract, the high spot exchange rate hurts (we cannot take advantage of it because the delivery price is locked-in); however, the low spot exchange rate leaves us off for having locked in a higher rate.

Table 1.5 summarizes this comparison. The key point that emerges here is that there is no outcome that is dominant, i.e., that is better in all circumstances. Doing nothing is sometimes better than using futures or options but sometimes not. (In a sense, doing nothing is akin to betting on a favorable movement in prices, in this case, on the USD/EUR rate increasing. Like all speculation, this bet can go wrong.) Using futures provides cash-flow control, but the ex post outcome may not always look good. For instance, if the exchange rate moves to $1.0728/euro, the company is worse off for having hedged using futures—and it is useful to keep in mind here that regardless of our ex ante intentions, we are almost always judged in this world on ex post outcomes. Using options provides protection but involves a substantial up-front cost that may not be recouped by the gains from exercising the option—and that is fully lost if the option lapses unexercised.

## Derivatives in Speculation

The preceding example dealt with *hedging*: the reduction of cash-flow uncertainty from a prior market commitment. Derivative securities can also be used to *speculate* i.e., to make profits by taking views on market direction.

Suppose, for example, that an investor believes that the Japanese yen (JPY) will appreciate significantly with respect to the US dollar (USD) over the next three months. The investor can speculate on this belief using derivatives in at least two ways:

1. By taking a long position in JPY futures deliverable in three months.
2. By buying a call option on JPY with an expiry date in three months.

(There is also the third alternative of buying the JPY in the spot market today and holding it for three months, but this strategy does not involve the use of derivatives.) In both cases, the investor makes money if his belief is vindicated, and the yen appreciates as expected. With the futures contract, the investor has locked-in a price for the future purchase of yen; any increase in price of yen over this locked-in rate results in a profit. With the call option, the investor has the right to buy yen at a fixed price, viz., the strike price in the contract. Any increase in the price of yen above this strike results in exercise-time profits for the investor.

However, there are costs to both strategies. In the case of the futures, the cost is that the anticipated appreciation may fail to be realized; if the price of JPY instead falls, the futures contract leads to a loss, since it obligates the investor to buy yen at the higher locked-in price. In the case of options, the up-front premium paid is lost if the yen depreciates and the option lapses unexercised; but even if the option is exercised, the profits at exercise time may not be sufficient to make up the cost of the premium. Thus, once again, there is no one "best" way to use derivatives to exploit a market view.

# 1.5  The Structure of this Book

The main body of this book is divided into five (unequal) parts with a sixth technical part supplementing the material.

**Part 1** of the book (Chapters 2–6) deals with futures and forwards. Chapter 2 discusses futures markets and their institutional features. Chapters 3 and 4 deal with the pricing of futures and forward contracts. Chapter 3 develops the pricing theory, while Chapter 4 looks at the empirical performance of the theory and discusses extensions of the basic theory. Chapter 5 is concerned with hedging strategies in futures and forward markets, in particular the development and implementation of *minimum-variance* hedging strategies in situations in which a perfect hedge is impossible because of a mismatch between the risk being hedged and the available futures or forward contracts. Chapter 6 looks at a special class of futures and forward contracts—those defined on interest rates or bond prices, a category that includes some of the most successful contracts ever introduced, including eurodollar futures and Treasury futures.

**Part 2**, which deals mainly with options, is the longest segment of the book, comprising Chapters 7–22. Chapters 7 and 8 cover preliminary material, including the role of volatility and a discussion of commonly used "trading strategies." Chapters 9–16 are concerned with option pricing, beginning with no-arbitrage restrictions on these prices (Chapter 9) and put-call parity and related results (Chapter 10). Chapter 11 then provides a gentle introduction to option pricing and its key concepts (such as the option delta and risk-neutral pricing). Building on this foundation, Chapters 12 and 13 develop the binomial model of option pricing, while Chapters 14 and 15 present the Black-Scholes model. Chapter 16 discusses several generalizations of the basic binomial/Black-Scholes approach including jump-diffusions, stochastic volatility/GARCH-based models, and local volatility models.

Moving from pricing to the management of option risk, Chapter 17 looks at the "option greeks," measures of option sensitivity to changes in market conditions. Chapters 18 and 19 move this discussion beyond the realm of plain vanilla options. Chapter 18 examines a range of "path-independent" exotic options, while Chapter 19 studies "path-dependent" exotics.

The remainder of Part 2 looks at special topics. The measurement of portfolio risk and the concepts of *Value-at-Risk* (or *VaR*) and *risk-budgeting* are introduced in Chapter 20. Convertible bonds and their pricing and hedging are the subject of Chapter 21. Finally, Chapter 22 examines the field of "real options," optionalities embedded within investment projects.

**Part 3** of the book (Chapters 23–25) examines swaps. Chapter 23 looks at interest rate swaps, which constitute the great bulk of the swaps market. The workhorse of the interest rate swap market, the plain vanilla fixed-for-floating swap, is examined in detail, as are several others. This chapter also introduces caps, floors, and swaptions, and presents the so-called "market model" commonly used to value these instruments. Chapter 24 moves on to equity swaps, their uses, pricing, and hedging, while Chapter 25 completes the swap material with a discussion of currency and commodity swaps. As we noted in the Preface, other products that bear the "swaps" moniker are discussed elsewhere in the book: volatility and variance swaps are discussed in the chapter on the Black-Scholes model, and total return swaps and credit default swaps are discussed in the chapter on credit derivative products.

**Part 4** of the book (Chapters 26–30) deals with interest-rate modeling. Chapters 26 and 27 deal with the yield curve and its construction (i.e., estimation from the data). Chapter 28 provides a gentle introduction to term-structure modeling and its complications and discusses the different classes of term-structure models. Chapter 29 presents several well-known "factor models" of interest rates. It begins with a detailed presentation of two well-known members of the "no-arbitrage" class of term-structure models from the 1980s and early 1990s, namely, the models of Ho and Lee (1986) and Black, Derman, and Toy (1992). Then, it develops one-factor and multi-factor models of interest rates, including, as special cases, the models of Vasicek and Cox-Ingersoll-Ross, among others. Finally, it presents the important result of Duffie and Kan (1996) on "affine" term-structure models. Building on this background, Chapter 30 develops the two classes of models that have formed the backbone for much of the modeling of interest-rate risk in practice: the framework of Heath-Jarrow-Morton and that of the Libor and Swap Market models.

**Part 5** of the book (Chapters 31–34) deals with credit-risk modeling and credit derivatives. Chapter 31 introduces the many classes of credit derivatives and discusses their uses. Chapters 32 and 33 deal with credit risk measurement. Chapter 32 details the class of models that comprise the "structural" approach to credit-risk extraction, while Chapter 33 does likewise for the "reduced-form" approach. The structural and reduced-form approaches are concerned with extracting information about the default risk of an *individual* entity from the market prices of traded securities issued by that entity. Chapter 34 discusses the modeling of *correlated default*, i.e., of modeling default risk at the *portfolio* level rather than at the level of the individual entity.

**Part 6**, the final part of the book, deals with computational methods. Chapter 35 looks at the method of finite-differencing, and Chapter 36 describes Monte-Carlo methods. An introduction to the programming language `Octave`, a freeware version of Matlab that we use throughout the book for illustrative purposes, may be found in Chapter 37.

## Case Studies

The book provides a number of full-length case studies. These studies include the rise and fall of the GNMA-CDR futures contract, the first interest-rate futures contract to be introduced on a futures exchange; the Procter & Gamble–Bankers Trust scandal of the 1990s; and the sagas of Amaranth, Barings, LTCM, and Metallgesellschaft, major derivatives disasters all. Shorter case studies are also scattered throughout the book, especially to assist in highlighting specific points. In addition, the website of this book (www.mhhe.com/sd1e) contains a number of other case studies including the stories of the Ashanti Gold hedge that failed, Orange County's 1994 bankruptcy, Sumitomo Corporation's huge copper losses, the Son-of-Boss tax schemes, and the AIG debacle of 2008, among others.

## 1.6 Exercises

1. What is a derivative security?
2. Give an example of a security that is not a derivative.
3. Can a derivative security be the underlying for another derivative security? If so, give an example. If not, explain why not.
4. Derivatives may be used for both hedging and insurance. What is the difference in these two motives?
5. Define *forward contract*. Explain at what time cash flows are generated for this contract. How is settlement determined?
6. Explain who bears default risk in a forward contract.
7. What risk is being managed by trading derivatives on exchanges?
8. Explain the difference between a forward contract and an option.
9. What is the difference between value and payoff in the context of derivative securities?

10. What is a short position in a forward contract? Draw the payoff diagram for a short position at a forward price of $103 if the possible range of the underlying stock price is $50–150.

11. Forward prices may be derived using the notion of absence of arbitrage, and market efficiency is not necessary. What is the difference between these two concepts?

12. Suppose you are holding a stock position and wish to hedge it. What forward contract would you use, a long or a short? What option contract might you use? Compare the forward versus the option on the following three criteria: (a) uncertainty of hedged position cash flow, (b) up-front cash flow, and (c) maturity time regret.

13. What derivatives strategy might you implement if you expected a bullish trend in stock prices? Would your strategy be different if you also forecast that the volatility of stock prices will drop?

14. What are the underlyings in the following derivative contracts?
    (a) A life insurance contract.
    (b) A home mortgage.
    (c) Employee stock options.
    (d) A rate lock in a home loan.

15. Assume you have a portfolio that contains stocks that track the market index. You now want to change this portfolio to be 20% in commodities and only 80% in the market index. How would you use derivatives to implement your strategy?

16. In the previous question, how do you implement the same trading idea without using futures contracts?

17. You buy a futures contract on the S&P 500. Is the correlation with the S&P 500 index positive or negative? If the nominal value of the contract is $100,000 and you are required to post $10,000 as margin, how much leverage do you have?

# Part 1

# Futures and Forwards

# Chapter 2

# Futures Markets

## 2.1 Introduction

Futures markets offer an excellent platform for the study of several market phenomena including market design, contract design, market manipulation, and financial crises. The broad characteristics of futures markets and contracts were described in Chapter 1. This chapter looks in further detail at these markets. It describes their important common features, the economic rationale for these features, and their desirable and sometimes not-so-desirable consequences. Three case studies involving futures markets are used to highlight some of the chapter's main points.

While futures markets have been around for quite a while, they have undergone some dramatic changes in recent years. Hollywood afficionados may recall the image portrayed in the Eddie Murphy–Dan Ackroyd film *Trading Places*: frenzied traders in loud jackets using extraordinary hand signals to trade in commodities such as wheat, corn, or even—as in the case of Mr. Ackroyd's and Mr. Murphy's characters—orange juice. Colorful though this image is, it is no longer representative of futures markets both in terms of how trading is done and what is traded. To put the rest of the chapter in prespective, we begin with a description of the changing face of futures markets.

## 2.2 The Changing Face of Futures Markets

As economic mechanisms go, forward contracts are very old. The Futures Industry Association cites evidence of forward trading going back as many as 4,000 years. (Appendix 2A reviews the history of futures trading and its regulation.) Organized *futures* trading is more recent, but it too is several hundred years old. The world's first futures market was likely the Dojima Rice Market set up in Osaka, Japan, in 1730. Active futures trading in the US began with the establishment of the Chicago Board of Trade (CBoT) in 1848.

Three trends have marked the recent evolution of futures markets and have radically altered the face of these markets in terms of *where* trading occurs, *how* it occurs, and *what* is traded.

### Fewer and Larger Exchanges

The first trend is one of consolidation. Of the more than thousand commodity exchanges that existed in the US in the late 19th century, only a small handful survive today. Consolidation has been the watchword of especially the last two decades. The two largest New York exchanges, the New York Mercantile Exchange (NYMEX) and the Commodity Exchange (COMEX), merged in 1994, and the two largest Chicago exchanges, the Chicago Mercantile

Exchange (CME) and the CBoT, in 2007. In 2008, the CME acquired NYMEX too, making it the world's largest and most diversified derivatives exchange.

Europe's largest futures and options exchange, Eurex, was similarly a joint creation of German and Swiss exchanges. Its principal European rival, Euronext, was formed as a holding company through the merger of the Amsterdam, Brussels, and Paris exchanges in 2000; the Paris exchange had itself been formed in 1999 through the merger of four French entities. In 2002, Euronext acquired the London International Financial Futures and Options Exchange (LIFFE), and, in a cross-Atlantic expansion in 2007, merged with the New York Stock Exchange (NYSE) to create NYSE Euronext.

Nor has consolidation been limited to the developed economies. In 2008, the integration of the Brazilian Mercantile and Futures Exchange (BM&F) with the Sao Paolo Stock Exchange (Bovespa) resulted in the formation of BM&FBovespa, Latin America's leading exchange.

## Technology and the Trading Platform

The second trend is technological. Until recently, most exchanges worldwide used some version of a floor-based trading system with traders in the exchange's "pits" calling out buy and sell orders and determining futures prices through an open-outcry system. In the last decade, many trading floors have fallen silent as the use of electronic trading systems has spread. European exchanges, including Eurex and LIFFE, are now wholly electronic. While large US exchanges including the CME, CBoT, and NYMEX have maintained some of their trading pits, they have also introduced electronic trading—and with considerable success. The CME, for instance, estimated that 61% of its total trading volume in the third quarter of 2004 was electronic, up from 44% in the first quarter of 2003.

## The Rise of Financial Futures

The third, and perhaps the most significant, trend has been the changing product mix in futures exchanges. Through most of the 4,000 year history of forward and futures trading, the underlying asset in the contract was a *commodity* such as wheat or gold. The picture changed dramatically with the introduction of *financial futures*—futures contracts written on a financial security or variable—in the early 1970s.

The first financial futures contracts were currency futures introduced in 1972 by the CME. Futures contracts on mortgage-backed securities (the GNMA contract discussed in Section 2.7) were offered in 1975 by the CBoT and were the first interest-rate futures contracts. Treasury bill futures were introduced by the CME in 1976 and Treasury bond futures on the CBoT in 1977. Futures on stock indices and other products followed soon thereafter.

Although total trading volume has increased significantly since the 1970s, the increase in volume of financial futures has been far more spectacular. Table 2.1 describes the changing

**TABLE 2.1** The Changing Nature of Futures Trading

This table describes the spectacular growth in the trading of financial futures in the first two decades of their existence. The volume numbers in the table are in terms of the number of contracts traded at the CBoT and indicate the changing product mix at the exchange.

| | Volume | | |
|---|---|---|---|
| | **1976** | **1981** | **1990** |
| Financial futures | 0.13 million | 16.36 million | 114.39 million |
| All futures | 18.90 million | 49.08 million | 154.23 million |
| Financial futures % | 0.68% | 33% | 73% |

**TABLE 2.2**  The Top 15 Futures Contracts Worldwide

This table describes the most widely traded futures contracts in the world during the first half of 2008 measured by trading volume (in millions of contracts). The figures are from the Futures Industry Association. NSE is the National Stock Exchange of India. The remaining exchanges are mentioned in the main text.

| Contract | Underlying | Exchange | Volume |
|---|---|---|---|
| Eurodollar | Interest-rate | CME | 356,262,782 |
| E-mini S&P 500 | Equity | CME | 276,146,082 |
| DJ EuroStoxx 50 | Equity | Eurex | 194,904,054 |
| 10-year US Treasury Note | Interest-rate | CME | 154,732,086 |
| Euro-Bund | Interest-rate | Eurex | 150,263,897 |
| Euribor | Interest-rate | LIFFE | 132,965,091 |
| Euro-Schatz | Interest-rate | Eurex | 101,894,877 |
| 5-year US Treasury Note | Interest-rate | CME | 98,689,353 |
| 1-day Inter-Bank Deposit | Interest-rate | BM&F | 97,955,779 |
| Euro-Bobl | Interest-rate | Eurex | 87,222,810 |
| S&P CNX Nifty | Equity | NSE | 87,072,050 |
| White Sugar | Agricultural | ZCE | 70,853,581 |
| Light Sweet Crude Oil | Energy | NYMEX | 70,507,281 |
| Short Sterling | Interest-rate | LIFFE | 64,801,289 |
| E-mini Nasdaq 100 | Equity | CME | 53,295,145 |

product mix at the CBoT in the first two decades since the introduction of financial futures. In 1976, the volume of financial futures trading at CBoT was negligible, but by 1990, it accounted for almost three-fourths of the number of contracts traded.

Table 2.2 describes the top 15 futures contracts worldwide based on the volume of trading (measured in terms of number of contracts) during the first half of 2008. There are no non-financials in the top 10, and only two in the top 15: the White Sugar futures contract on China's Zhengzhou Commodity Exchange (ZCE) at No. 12 and the Light Sweet Crude Oil futures contract on NYMEX at No. 13. This dominance in terms of number of contracts is even more impressive when one considers that the typical financial futures contract is substantially larger in monetary terms than the typical commodity futures contract (see Table 2.4 further below).

# 2.3 The Functioning of Futures Exchanges

A futures exchange performs two essential functions. First, it provides a marketplace where buyers and sellers may interact and arrive at agreements. Second, it provides a mechanism to protect either party from a possible default by the other. The two organizations central to the functioning of every futures market, the exchange corporation and the clearinghouse corporation, perform these tasks.

The exchange corporation provides the marketplace. It determines such matters as the rules of trading (who may trade? when and how may they trade?); the standardization of contracts and provision of delivery options (what may be traded? how is settlement to be effected?); and margin requirements (how much collateral should be required of participants?). The details of futures trades—quantity, price, time of delivery—must be agreed to under the rules of the exchange.

After a trade has been agreed to, it must be recorded ("cleared") by the clearinghouse. Clearing is the matching of buy and sell records to ensure there are no discrepancies in the price and/or quantity. Once the trade is cleared, the clearinghouse corporation guarantees the trade by assuming ultimate responsibility for contract performance. Effectively, the clearinghouse becomes the buyer to all sellers and the seller to all buyers.

Of all the features that distinguish futures markets from forward markets, three are of particular importance:

- The standardization of contracts.
- The ease of reversing positions.
- The use of margin accounts to manage default risk.

Each of these is discussed in a separate section below (see Sections 2.4–2.6).

First, however, it is useful to review briefly several concepts of importance to the functioning of a futures exchange, such as types of orders, prices, how delivery is effected, etc. The remainder of this section takes us through this material. The presentation is in eight parts: (a) players in futures markets, (b) kinds of orders, (c) opening, closing, and settlement prices, (d) price ticks and price limits, (e) delivery and settlement procedures, (f) position limits, (g) the clearinghouse and contract performance, and (h) reading futures prices in the financial press.

## (A) Players in Futures Markets

Buyers and sellers in futures markets may be divided into three broad categories based on their motivation for trading: hedgers, speculators, and arbitrageurs.

### Hedgers

Hedgers are investors who have a pre-existing commitment to buy or sell and are using the futures market trade to offset the price risk from this commitment. For example, an exporter who anticipates receipt of foreign currency in the future might use short curency futures to lock-in an exchange rate at which the foreign curency can be converted to the home currency; a jewelry manufacturer who makes regular gold purchases might use long gold futures to eliminate the risk of fluctuations in the spot price of gold; and a mortgage banker might use interest-rate futures to offset the sensitivity of the value of her existing portfolio to changes in interest rates.

### Speculators

Speculators are those who take directional bets either on prices or on the difference of two prices (for instance, that this difference will narrow from existing levels). Unlike hedgers, speculators have no prior risk that is being offset by the futures trade. To bet on individual prices (e.g., that silver prices will rise), speculators can simply use the relevant individual futures contracts (in this example, long silver futures). To bet on the difference of two prices, strategies known as "spread orders," that involve the simultaneous use of two futures contracts, are used. Spread orders are described further below under "(B) Kinds of Orders." Exchanges generally treat speculators less generously than hedgers, for example, restricting their maximum position sizes more severely.

### Arbitrageurs

An *arbitrage* or riskless profit opportunity is one where two equivalent securities or baskets of securities sell for different prices. *Arbitrageurs* are those who exploit these profit opportunities. In the context of futures markets, this may simply involve trading the same futures contract on two different exchanges. For example, futures on the Nikkei 225 index are traded both in Osaka and in Singapore, and any difference in futures prices in the two markets creates an arbitrage opportunity that may be exploited by buying in one market and simultaneously selling in the other. Alternatively, as we describe in Chapters 3 and 4, futures arbitrage may involve simultaneous trading in futures markets and the underlying spot market if the futures contract becomes over- or under-valued relative to the spot price.

### Intermediaries

Of the intermediaries in futures markets, the most important are *futures commission merchants,* or FCMs. FCMs are the stockbrokers of the futures world, connecting customers to exchanges. They provide the facilities to execute customer orders on the exchange and maintain records of each customer's positions and margin deposits. FCMs may be independent institutions or have a parent institution such as a bank or be affiliated with a national brokerage.

Other intermediaries include *introducing brokers*, or IBs, who are individuals or organizations who solicit and accept orders to buy or sell futures contracts and direct the business to FCMs; *commodity pool operators*, or CPOs, who, akin to mutual funds, pool funds collected from investors and use them to trade commodity futures or options; and *commodity trading advisers*, or CTAs, who offer trading advice in futures in exchange for a fee. Finally, there are *associated persons*, or APs, individuals who solicit orders, customers, or customer funds on behalf of an FCM, IB, CTA, or CPO. APs are effectively salespersons for the other categories of intermediaries.

### Other Participants

Traders on the floor of an exchange are divided into two groups. *Floor brokers* are those who execute trades on behalf of others. *Locals* trade on their own accounts. Locals are of particular importance in futures markets since they add substantially to the market's liquidity. Locals who hold positions for very short periods of time are known as *scalpers*.

## (B) Kinds of Orders

A futures order must specify the particular futures contract (wheat? gold? eurodollars?), the delivery month for the contract (contracts expiring in June? July?), and whether the position is a long or short one. If a customer wishes, further contingencies may be specified in the order. The three most popular kinds of orders are *market orders*, *limit orders*, and *stop orders*.

### Market Orders

Market orders are the simplest kind of orders: they are just buy or sell orders with no restrictions. Market orders are matched as soon as possible at the best available price. (For a buyer, "best available price" means the lowest price currently being offered by sellers; for sellers, it is the highest price currently available from buyers.) In some cases, safeguards may be applied to the principle of immediate matching. For example, the price at which the order is executed may be required to lie within a maximum range around the last trade.

### Limit Orders

A limit order is one where the customer specifies a *limit price*. For a buyer, the limit price represents the maximum price he is willing to pay; for a seller, it is the minimum price she is willing to accept. For example:

- A limit order to *buy* 10 May wheat futures contracts with a limit price of $3.60 per bushel is an order to take long positions at a price of $3.60 per bushel *or lower*.
- A limit order to *sell* 10 May gold futures contracts with a limit price of $350 per ounce (oz) is an order to sell at a price of $350 per ounce *or higher*.

Limit prices are typically *below* the current futures price for buy orders and *above* it for sell orders.

Limit orders may be placed with restrictions regarding the time frame over which the order remains valid. The popular types are described below. Not all exchanges offer all of these variations, but virtually all exchanges offer most of them.

- A *fill-or-kill* (FOK) limit order (also called a *complete volume* or CV order) is one that must be filled immediately and completely or not at all.
- An *immediate-or-cancel* (IOC) limit order is one that must be filled immediately either partially or completely, or not at all.
- A *good-for-day* (GFD) limit order is one that is canceled at the end of the trading day if it has not been filled by then.
- A *good-till-canceled* (GTC) limit order is one that remains valid until the customer cancels or a maximum time limit (e.g., one year) is reached.

Limit orders have the advantage that they will never be executed at a price less favorable than the one the customer wants, but it is also possible that the order may never be executed. Consider, for example, a limit order to buy May wheat futures with a limit price of $3.60 a bushel. If the order is executed, the futures price will not exceed $3.60 per bushel. However, there may be no seller willing to sell at $3.60 or lower, or there may be buyers willing to pay more than $3.60 per bushel whose offers take precedence, so the order may never be filled.

### Stop Orders

A *stop order* is an order that becomes a market order once the market price for the contract reaches a specified price limit (the "stop price"). *Stop-buy* orders are orders to buy as soon as the stop price is reached; *stop-sell* orders are orders to sell as soon as this price is reached.

A stop order offers a way of limiting one's losses in the face of an unfavorable trend in prices. A prospective buyer who sees prices increasing can wait to see if they come down before buying. The danger with this is that prices may continue to increase and the price the buyer finally pays may be very high. A stop-buy order allows the buyer to wait until a specified point is reached and then have his order executed before prices get too high. The price limit is typically set *above* the current price for stop-buy orders.

For example, consider an investor who wishes to go long gold futures but is hesitant to do so at the current futures price of (say) $365 per oz. By using a stop-buy order with a price limit of $370 per oz, the investor ensures that if gold prices increase further, he will at worst be able to get a futures price of around $370 per oz.

Similarly, a prospective seller who sees the price declining can place a stop-sell order to limit her losses before prices get too low. The price limit in a stop-sell is typically set *below* the current price.

Besides market, limit, and stop orders, futures exchanges typically offer several other types of orders too (though not all exchanges offer all of these). Here is a description of some of them:

### Market-if-Touched Orders

A *market-if-touched* or MIT order is one that must be executed at the best possible price once a trade occurs at a price at least as *favorable* as a specified limit price. The limit price is typically *below* the market price for an MIT-buy order and *above* it for an MIT-sell order. An MIT order offers a way of locking-in one's gains in the face of favorable price moves. A buyer seeing declining prices or a seller seeing increasing prices can lock-in their gains beyond a point by using MIT-buy and MIT-sell orders, respectively. Thus, an MIT order serves the opposite function of a stop order.

### Stop-Limit Orders

A *stop-limit* order is a stop order that becomes a *limit* order once the stop price is reached. The stop price and the limit price may be the same, but they may also differ. For example, a stop-limit buy order for gold futures may have a stop price of $375/oz and a limit price of $380/oz. This effectively means that as soon as the futures price reaches $375/oz, the investor is willing to buy, but only at a price of $380/oz or below.

### Spread Orders

A *spread* order involves simultaneous long and short positions in two futures contracts. It is typically a bet on the behavior of the price differential (or "spread") between two commodities or securities, e.g., that the spread will widen from its present level. Spread orders can involve different months of the same commodity (e.g., buy May wheat futures, sell July wheat futures) or can involve futures on two different underlyings (e.g., buy 10-year US Treasury futures, sell 5-year US Treasury futures). A spread order can be entered at the current price (like a market order). Alternatively, the investor may specify a price difference between the commodities that triggers when the order is to be filled (e.g., if the spread exceeds a given amount).

### One-Cancels-the-Other

In a *one-cancels-the-other* or OCO order, the investor places two simultaneous orders on the same contract with the understanding that the execution of one cancels the other order. For example, an investor may submit the following orders on S&P 500 index futures: a limit-buy order with a limit price of 1,195 and a stop-buy order with a stop price of 1,215, OCO. In this case, the investor is interested in going long S&P 500 futures; ideally, the order will be executed at a price of 1,195 or below, but in the event of the market's sharply trending up without the limit price being reached, the stop order limits the investor's downside.

### Market-on-Close/Open

A *market-on-close* or MOC is an order that will be filled during the closing seconds of the market at whatever price prevails then. Its twin is the *market-on-open* or MOO order which is filled at the best available price in the opening range.

As these descriptions indicate, the flexibility offered to customers in placing orders in futures exchanges is quite substantial.

## (C) Opening, Closing, and Settlement Prices

As buy and sell orders are matched, futures prices are determined. This price will fluctuate over the day and over the life of the contract as the patterns of buy and sell orders vary. Three daily prices for each futures contract are commonly reported in the financial press: the *opening price*, the *closing price*, and the *settlement price*.

The *opening price* is the first price at which the contract is traded at the beginning of a trading session. The term *opening range* is used more generally to describe the first bids and offers that were made. The exchange recognizes an opening range only after the first trade is made.

The *closing price* is the last price at which a contract is traded at the close of a trading session. The *closing range* is that of the high and low prices or of bids and offers during the *official close*, which is usually the final 30 seconds of trading for most contracts and the final 60 seconds for currencies.

The *settlement price* is a representative price from the closing range chosen by the exchange, and is the official closing price of the exchange. The settlement price plays a major role in futures exchanges since margin accounts gains and losses are calculated with respect to this price (see Section 2.6). Deliveries are also invoiced at this price. The procedure guiding the selection of this price is of obvious importance. As one example, the Eurex website notes that in the Euro-Bund futures contract on Eurex,

> [The daily settlement price is] the closing price determined within the closing auction. If no price can be determined in the closing auction or if the price so determined does not reasonably reflect the prevailing market conditions, the daily settlement price will be the volume-weighted average price of the last five trades of the day, provided these are not older than 15 minutes; or, if more than five trades have occurred during the final minute of trading, the volume-weighted average price of all trades that occurred during that period. If such a price cannot be determined, or if the price so determined does not reasonably reflect the prevailing market conditions, Eurex will establish the official settlement price.

A related concept is that of the *final settlement price*, the settlement price on the last trading day of a contract. The rules for determining the final settlement price may differ from those for the daily settlement prices. For example, for the Euro-Bund futures contract on Eurex, the Eurex website states that

> The volume-weighted average price of the last ten trades, provided they are not older than 30 minutes—or, if more than ten trades have occurred during the final minute of trading, then the volume-weighted average price of all the trades during that period—is used to determine the final settlement price.

## (D) Price Ticks and Price Limits

Exchanges place limits on the *minimum* amount by which prices can move up or down. This amount is known as the *tick*. The tick varies from contract to contract. Specification of the tick is part of the standardization of the contract. Here are some examples, all corresponding to tick sizes in July 2009.

- On the corn futures contract on the CBoT, the tick is 0.25 cents per bushel. Since one corn futures contract on the CBoT has a standard size of 5,000 bushels, this means the minimum futures price move per contract is $\$(5,000 \times 0.0025) = \$12.50$.
- On the Light Sweet Crude Oil futures contract on NYMEX, the tick is $0.01 per barrel. Since one futures contract is for 1,000 barrels, this corresponds to a minimum futures price move of $10 per contract.
- On the S&P futures contract on the CME, the tick is 0.10. Since one contract is for 250 units of the index (i.e., of the basket of stocks that comprise the index), this implies a minimum futures price move of $25 per contract.
- On the Gilt futures contract on LIFFE, the minimum price move is £10 per contract.

Exchanges also establish *maximum* limits by which the futures prices can fluctuate in a day. These are called the *daily price limits*, and are stated in terms of movements measured from the previous day's closing price. The limits vary from contract to contract. For example, the daily price limit in August 2009 was $1,200 on the Live Cattle futures contract on the CME, and $10,000 on the Light Sweet Crude futures contract on NYMEX. For some contracts (e.g., the corn or wheat futures contracts on the CBoT), daily price limits are eliminated during the spot month (i.e., the month the contract expires).

The operation of the daily price limit varies from contract to contract. In many cases, once the daily price limits are hit, no trading outside the limits is possible until the next trading day. In others, the price limits act as "circuit breakers." For example, as of August 2009, trading in the Light Sweet Crude futures contract on NYMEX halts for five minutes each time the price limit is reached. When trading resumes, the price limit is expanded by $10,000 per contract in each direction from the previous limit. However, there is no maximum price fluctuation during any one trading session. A similar, but more complex, set of circuit-breaker rules holds for the equity futures contracts on the CME, though there is also a maximum amount by which prices may fall in a given trading day.

Daily price limits set by the exchanges are subject to change. They may, for instance, be increased once the market price has increased or decreased by the existing limit for a given number of successive days. The presence of such limits implies that it may not always be possible to close out futures contracts when desired.

## (E) Delivery and Settlement Procedures

Each futures contract is associated with a specific maturity month (e.g., the "May 2004 wheat futures contract"). For assets involving physical delivery (see below), delivery can often take place at any time during the delivery month.

There are three ways in which futures contracts are settled: physical delivery, cash settlement, and exchange-for-physicals. The normal method of settlement on most futures contracts is physical delivery. The contract specifies a set of locations where delivery may be made. If alternative locations are permitted, the contract may specify price adjustments to be made. Commodity futures contracts and many financial futures contracts including currency futures and Treasury futures are settled by physical delivery.

For some financial futures contracts, settlement by physical delivery is nontrivial. With stock index futures, for example, delivering an index requires delivering the basket of stocks in the index in the exact proportions in which they are present in the index. Given the complexities of physical settlement, such contracts are *cash settled*, i.e., one side pays the other cash equal to the change in contract value occurring on account of changes in the index level. Cash settlement takes place through the margin account described in Section 2.6.

An EFP or *exchange-for-physicals* is an alternative settlement mechanism for futures contracts in the US authorized under the Commodity Exchange Act. In an EFP, a long position and a short position with equal position sizes negotiate a price off-exchange and communicate their decision to settle their trades with physical delivery at the agreed-upon price. There are typically no restrictions on the prices at which EFPs may occur, but the EFPs must involve a trade with *physical* delivery at that price. EFPs are examples of ex-pit transactions, transactions done outside the trading framework of the exchange. EFPs are also known as "cash for futures" or "vs. cash" transactions; the word "cash" here refers to the cash market (i.e., spot) transaction accompanying the EFP. In the context of interest-rate futures, EFPs are also called *exchange basis facilities*, or EBFs.

## (F) Position Limits

Exchanges and regulators establish limits on the maximum number of speculative positions a single investor may hold at a time. These *position limits* vary over different underlying assets. Table 2.3 provides examples of position limits on several contracts on the CBoT and CME. The purpose of these limits is to prevent any one trader from exercising excessive influence over prices. Limiting any one trader's positions also acts as a soft curb on the benefits from market manipulation.

In the US, the Commodity Exchange Act (CEA) authorizes the Commodity Futures Trading Commission (CFTC) to set limits on the size of speculative positions. The CFTC may stipulate limits to be imposed by the exchanges, or it may provide guidance on the limits, which are then implemented by the individual exchanges. In addition, exchanges may also choose to set limits on nonspeculative positions.

In terms of magnitude, a rough average of the position limit tends to be around 10% of the open interest up to about 25,000 contracts of open interest with small increases thereafter. In the spot month (i.e., the delivery month of the contract), position limits may be set lower to offset the natural increase in price fluctuation from physical trading.

**TABLE 2.3** Position Limits in Futures Contracts

The table lists position limits for various futures contracts as of July 2009. The units in the table are in numbers of contracts. The "spot month" is the delivery month of the futures contract.

| Underlying | Exchange | Position Limits (No. of Contracts) in | | |
|---|---|---|---|---|
| | | Spot Month | Single Month | All Months |
| **Agri commodities** | | | | |
| Corn | CME Group | 600 | 13,500 | 22,000 |
| Soybean | CME Group | 600 | 6,500 | 10,000 |
| Wheat | CME Group | 600 | 5,000 | 6,500 |
| Oats | CME Group | 600 | 1,400 | 2,000 |
| **Livestock** | | | | |
| Live cattle | CME Group | 450 | 5,400 | None |
| Lean hogs | CME Group | 950 | 4,100 | None |
| **Forest** | | | | |
| Lumber | CME Group | 435 | 1,000 | None |
| **Interest rate** | | | | |
| 30-year US T-Bonds | CME Group | None | None | None |
| 10-year US T-Notes | CME Group | None | None | None |
| 5-year US T-Notes | CME Group | None | None | None |
| US T-Bill | CME Group | None | None | 5,000 |
| 3-month Eurodollar | CME Group | None | None | None |
| 1-month Libor | CME Group | None | None | None |
| **Currency** | | | | |
| Euro (EUR) | CME Group | None | None | None |
| British pound (GBP) | CME Group | None | None | None |
| Japanese yen (JPY) | CME Group | None | None | None |
| Swiss franc (CHF) | CME Group | None | None | None |
| Canadian dollar (CAD) | CME Group | None | None | None |
| Brazilian real (BRL) | CME Group | None | 24,000 | 40,000 |
| Israeli shekel (ILS) | CME Group | 2,000 | None | None |
| **Stock indices** | | | | |
| S&P 500 | CME Group | None | None | 20,000 |
| Big Dow | CME Group | None | None | 50,000 |
| Nasdaq 100 | CME Group | None | None | 10,000 |
| Nikkei 225 (yen) | CME Group | None | None | 5,000 |
| **Metals** | | | | |
| Gold | COMEX | 3,000 | 6,000 | 6,000 |
| Silver | COMEX | 1,500 | 6,000 | 6,000 |
| **Energy** | | | | |
| Light sweet crude | NYMEX | 3,000* | 10,000 | 20,000 |

* Last 3 days of spot month

An important aspect of the limits is that they be set relative to the likely physical supply of the commodity, decreasing when supply is likely to be short. Thus, there are no position limits on currency futures contracts at the CME or on Treasury futures contracts at the CBoT, since supply is not a constraint in these markets.

Accounts that are under common ownership, even though they are booked as separate positions, are subject to position limits in aggregate so that the spirit of the regulations is adhered to. Limits may also be aggregated across time, that is, across expiry months. The idea here is that since speculation across maturities may also result in unreasonable price fluctuations, control needs to be exercised for all contracts against a given underlying.

Once a market has been in place for at least 12 months, position limits may be replaced by *accountability rules*. This is usually done in liquid markets. Traders that reach a preset accountability level (and satisfy other stated criteria) are granted exemption from position limits.

Investors accepted by the exchange as bona fide "hedgers" do not normally face formal position limits. In practice, this means they may be given much higher limits than those allowed speculators so that there remains in place some limit that prompts future review if necessary.

## (G) The Clearinghouse and Contract Performance

At the end of the day, all positions must be recorded ("cleared") by the clearinghouse. In many futures markets, the clearinghouse corporation is a separate legal entity from the exchange corporation (though they may share common members). The same clearinghouse may serve several exchanges simultaneously. For example, in April 2003, some years prior to their merger, CBoT and CME announced an agreement for CME to provide clearing and related services for all CBoT products. In some cases, however, the clearinghouse is organized as an entity within the exchange itself. NYMEX is one such case.

Members of the clearinghouse are called *clearing members*. Non-members must clear their transactions through clearing members. Clearing members are responsible to the clearinghouse for contract performance. If an investor on an exchange defaults and his margin balance is inadequate to cover his losses, the clearing member who cleared that investor's contracts is first held responsible for the defaulted amount. If the clearing member also defaults, then the clearinghouse assumes ultimate responsibility for contract performance.

Duffie (1989) describes the incentives used by clearinghouses to provide clearing members with an incentive to fulfill their obligations. First, members are required to maintain a margin with the clearinghouse. Margin accounts are described in Section 2.6 below. Second, members pay a fee per contract cleared (and sometimes also a monthly fee) that is held in a *surplus fund*. Third, members are required to post a performance bond that is held in a *guarantee fund*.

Upon any default by a clearing member, the clearinghouse closes out all of that member's positions. Any deficit is then met by using in succession the member's margin account, the member's guarantee bond, the surplus fund, and the guarantee fund. If all of this still proves insufficient, the system collapses. No clearinghouse in US history has yet defaulted on its obligations.

## (H) Futures Prices in the Financial Press

Figure 2.1 describes the presentation of futures prices in *The Wall Street Journal* and is a typical example of how futures prices are reported in the financial press. The upper panel presents the prices as they once appeared in the print edition, the lower panel as they now appear online on the paper's website. There are some differences in the details (the online version does not provide the lifetime highs and lows, and the settlement price in the upper panel appears as the last price in the lower one), but these are minor and unimportant, so we focus our description on the upper panel. In this panel, the contract underlying ("Cattle-Live"), the exchange on which it is traded ("CME"), the size of each contract ("40,000 lbs."), and the units in which prices are quoted ("cents per lb.") are listed on the top.

## FIGURE 2.1

Futures Prices in *The Wall Street Journal*

| | | | | | | | Lifetime | Open |
|---|---|---|---|---|---|---|---|---|
| | Open | High | Low | Settle | Change | High | Low | Interest |

**Thursday, October 26, 1995**
**Open Interest Reflects Previous Trading Day**

**—LIVESTOCK & MEAT—**

CATTLE—LIVE (CME) 40,000 lbs.; cents per lb.

| | Open | High | Low | Settle | Change | High | Low | Interest |
|---|---|---|---|---|---|---|---|---|
| Dec | 67.85 | 68.25 | 67.85 | 68.17 | +.40 | 68.25 | 61.75 | 30,828 |
| Fb96 | 67.10 | 67.40 | 67.05 | 67.35 | +.27 | 68.30 | 62.80 | 15,490 |
| Apr | 67.20 | 67.42 | 67.20 | 67.37 | +.17 | 68.32 | 63.90 | 9,324 |
| June | 63.37 | 63.55 | 63.37 | 63.50 | +.17 | 63.55 | 60.95 | 4,161 |
| Aug | 62.00 | 62.12 | 61.92 | 62.05 | .... | 62.90 | 60.05 | 1,768 |
| Oct | 63.05 | 63.05 | 62.87 | 62.95 | +.10 | 63.05 | 61.30 | 531 |

Est vol 8.888; vol Wed 9.426; open int 62.110. +325

**FEEDER CATTLE**

Data retrieved at Nov 30 13:49:31 GMT • All quotes are in Greenwich Mean Time • Data provided by eSignal

| | Contract | Month | Last | Chg | Open | High | Low | Volume | Openint | Exchange | Date | Time |
|---|---|---|---|---|---|---|---|---|---|---|---|---|
| 📊🔲📺 | FEEDER CATTLE | Jan '10 | 92.500s | -0.800 | 92.900 | 92.950 | 91.900 | 436 | 16548 | CME | 11/27/09 | 18:11:13 |
| 📊🔲📺 | FEEDER CATTLE | Mar '10 | 93.150s | -1.125 | 93.600 | 93.925 | 93.000 | 381 | 6133 | CME | 11/27/09 | 18:11:13 |
| 📊🔲📺 | FEEDER CATTLE | Apr '10 | 94.550s | -1.150 | 94.750 | 95.050 | 94.350 | 8 | 979 | CME | 11/27/09 | 18:11:13 |
| 📊🔲📺 | FEEDER CATTLE | May '10 | 95.450s | -0.925 | 95.850 | 95.900 | 95.200 | 43 | 2078 | CME | 11/27/09 | 18:11:13 |
| 📊🔲📺 | FEEDER CATTLE | Aug '10 | 97.350s | -0.850 | 97.350 | 97.350 | 97.350 | 2 | 535 | CME | 11/27/09 | 18:11:13 |
| 📊🔲📺 | FEEDER CATTLE | Sep '10 | 97.950s | -0.100 | 97.950 | 97.950 | 97.950 | 0 | 5 | CME | 11/27/09 | 18:11:13 |
| 📊🔲📺 | FEEDER CATTLE | Oct '10 | 97.650s | -0.050 | 97.050 | 97.650 | 97.650 | 0 | 4 | CME | 11/27/09 | 18:11:13 |
| 📊🔲📺 | FEEDER CATTLE | Nov '10 | 97.800s | 0.000 | 97.800 | 97.800 | 97.800 | 0 | 0 | CME | 11/27/09 | 18:11:13 |

📊 - Chart 🔲 - Options 📺 - Quotes

Save Quote Board

Each horizontal line corresponds to a particular contract maturity month. All entries in each line barring the last pertain to price information. The first entry is the opening price of the contract in the last trading session. For example, the December futures contract in Figure 2.1 opened at a price of 67.85 cents per lb. The next two entries give the maximum and minimum prices on that contract observed in the last trading session. The difference between these two is one indicator of how volatile trading in the contract was during that session.

The fourth entry is the all-important settlement price while the fifth provides the change in settlement price from the previous day. A positive sign indicates the settlement price has increased, while a negative sign indicates it has decreased. The use of settlement prices in calculating gains and losses is described in Section 2.6 below.

The sixth and seventh entries describe the highest and lowest prices observed on this contract since it began trading. Observe that the December Live Cattle futures contract settled at close to its lifetime high.

Finally, the last entry indicates the number of contracts currently held by market participants. It is the sum of all the contracts held by long positions or, equivalently, the sum of all the contracts held by short positions. (As we discuss in Section 2.5, futures positions do not have to be held to maturity, but may be closed-out or "reversed" before then. The open interest measures only the number of futures positions that have not yet been reversed.) The size of the open interest is an important measure of the liquidity of that contract; a high open interest indicates a large number of participants and so a relatively liquid contract. As is typical in most futures markets, Figure 2.1 shows that open interest is high in short-dated futures contracts, but liquidity rapidly dries up as one looks at longer maturities.

# 2.4    The Standardization of Futures Contracts

The remainder of this chapter focusses on the three features that distinguish futures markets from forward markets:

• The standardization of contracts.

- The ease of reversing positions.
- The use of margin accounts to manage default risk.

This section deals with the standardization of futures contracts. The next two examine reversal and margining, respectively.

The standardization of futures contracts is perhaps the most important task performed by the exchange. It involves three decisions: specifying the *quantity* or *size* of one futures contract; specifying the minimum acceptable *quality* that may be delivered; and specifying the *delivery options* available to the short position. Successful standardization goes a long way in promoting contract liquidity; poor standardization, as in the case of GNMA futures discussed later in this chapter, can lead to the failure of the contract.

## The Size of a Futures Contract

Futures contracts are traded in standardized sizes. Table 2.4 summarizes the standard sizes of several futures contracts and the approximate value of the delivered quantity at spot market prices observed in July 2009.

As the table shows, commodity futures contracts in general have a value under $50,000. For example, one corn futures contract on the CBoT calls for the delivery of 5,000 bushels of corn, worth roughly $17,250 in July 2009 prices. The aluminium futures contract on the London Metals Exchange (LME) requires the delivery of 25 tonnes, which puts the worth of the delivered quantity at around $38,250 in July 2009. Of course, with fluctuations in commodity prices, the values of the assets in these contracts fluctuate too.

Financial futures contracts tend to be larger in size. One Treasury bond futures contract on the CBoT calls for the delivery of $100,000 in face value of US Treasury bonds; one S&P 500 Index futures contract on the CME was worth around $225,000 in July 2009, while the British pound futures contract on the PHLX was worth a little over $100,000 around the same time.

Many futures exchanges also offer what are called "mini" futures contracts in smaller standard sizes aimed at attracting smaller investors. Thus, while one wheat futures contract on the CBoT is for 5,000 bushels of wheat, the exchange also offers a mini-wheat futures contract of size 1,000 bushels. The Dow Jones Index futures contract on the CBoT is for 10 times the Dow Jones index, but there is also a mini-Dow Jones futures contract that is for 5 times the index. (There is also a "Big Dow" contract for 25 times the index.) Mini-futures contracts have now become popular and established presences in futures exchanges.

## The Standard Grade in a Futures Contract

Every futures contract also specifies the standard deliverable grade or grades of the underlying asset. For example, the LME's aluminium futures contract requires the delivered aluminium to have a purity of at least 99.7%; the COMEX gold contract requires the delivered gold to be of at least 0.995 fineness; and the oat futures contract on the CBoT calls for the delivery of either No. 2 Heavy or No. 1 grades.

For some financial futures contracts, quality is a non-issue (e.g., currency or index futures), but for others such as Treasury futures, it is of central importance. The "quality" of a bond depends on two features: the coupon paid by the bond and the bond's maturity. Every Treasury futures contract must spell out the acceptable quality on these two fronts. The standard coupon in the US Treasury bond and note futures contracts on the CBoT is 6%. The Treasury bond futures contract requires the delivered instruments to have at least 15 years to maturity or first call while the Treasury note futures contract calls for the delivery of Treasury notes with between $6\frac{1}{2}$ and 10 years left to maturity. US Treasury bills are discount instruments that pay no coupons; the Treasury bill futures contract on the CME requires the delivered instruments to have 13 weeks to maturity.

**TABLE 2.4**  Futures Contract Sizes

This table describes the standard sizes of several futures contracts and the approximate value of the asset in one contract measured using July 2009 prices. For the US Treasury futures contracts, the "contract size" and "market value" refer to the face value of the instruments that must be delivered, while for the Eurodollar futures contract, these terms refer to the principal amount on which interest is computed.

| Underlying | Exchange | Contract Size | Approximate USD Value (July 2009) |
|---|---|---|---|
| **Agri commodities** | | | |
| Corn | CME Group | 5,000 bushels | 17,250 |
| Wheat | CME Group | 5,000 bushels | 25,000 |
| Oats | CME Group | 5,000 bushels | 10,250 |
| Soybean | CME Group | 5,000 bushels | 56,000 |
| **Livestock** | | | |
| Live cattle | CME Group | 40,000 lbs | 34,000 |
| Lean hogs | CME Group | 40,000 lbs | 24,400 |
| **Forest** | | | |
| Lumber | CME Group | 110,000 board feet | 19,800 |
| **Interest rate** | | | |
| 30-year US T-Bonds | CME Group | USD 100,000 | 100,000 |
| 10-year US T-Notes | CME Group | USD 100,000 | 100,000 |
| 5-year US T-Notes | CME Group | USD 100,000 | 100,000 |
| US T-Bill | CME Group | USD 1,000,000 | 1,000,000 |
| 3-month Eurodollar | CME Group | USD 1,000,000 | 1,000,000 |
| 1-month Libor | CME Group | USD 1,000,000 | 3,000,000 |
| **Currency** | | | |
| Euro (EUR) | CME Group | EUR 125,000 | 173,750 |
| British pound (GBP) | CME Group | GBP 62,500 | 101,250 |
| Japanese yen (JPY) | CME Group | JPY 12,500,000 | 135,000 |
| Swiss franc (CHF) | CME Group | CHF 125,000 | 115,000 |
| Canadian dollar (CAD) | CME Group | CAD 100,000 | 86,000 |
| Brazilian real (BRL) | CME Group | BRL 100,000 | 49,000 |
| Israeli shekel (ILS) | CME Group | ILS 1,000,000 | 250,000 |
| **Stock indices** | | | |
| S&P 500 | CME Group | USD 250 times index | 225,000 |
| Big Dow | CME Group | USD 25 times index | 210,000 |
| Nasdaq 100 | CME Group | USD 100 times index | 142,500 |
| Nikkei 225 | CME Group | JPY 500 times index | 46,250 |
| **Metals** | | | |
| Aluminium | LME | 25 tonnes | 38,250 |
| Copper | LME | 25 tonnes | 121,000 |
| Gold | COMEX | 100 Troy oz | 91,000 |
| Silver | COMEX | 5,000 Troy oz | 63,000 |
| **Energy** | | | |
| Light sweet crude | NYMEX | 1,000 barrels | 60,000 |

## Delivery Options

Specifying the deliverable grade narrowly in a commodity futures contracts may limit overall supply and facilitate market *corners* or *squeezes*. Corners and squeezes are market manipulation attempts in which the manipulator takes on more long positions in a given futures contract than the short position has ability to make delivery. This is achieved by the long either controlling all of the available spot supply (a "corner") or at least a sufficient quantity so that the short position has difficulty finding adequate deliverable supply (a "squeeze"). In a successful attempt, the price of the commodity is driven up by the lack of supply. The short position must buy the required quantity for delivery at a high price and sell it back to the long position at the fixed price agreed to in the contract (or equivalently must compensate the long position for the difference in prices).

Partly to reduce the opportunity for such behavior, the short position in a futures contract is provided with *delivery options*. Delivery options allow the short position to substitute an alternative grade or quality for the standard quality at an adjustment in the delivery price. The specification of the contract lists the alternative deliverable grades to the standard grade and describes how the price will be adjusted for each grade.

| | |
|---|---|
| **Example 2.1** | The standard grade in the corn futures contract on the CBoT is No. 2 Yellow. However, at the time of writing, the contract also allows the short position to deliver No. 1 Yellow or No. 3 Yellow with the proviso that if No. 1 Yellow is delivered, the delivery price is increased by 1.5 cents a bushel, while if No. 3 Yellow is delivered, the delivery price is lowered by 1.5 cents a bushel. ∎ |

| | |
|---|---|
| **Example 2.2** | Several delivery options are also offered in US Treasury bond futures contracts on the CBoT. The most important is the "quality option" (other options are discussed in Chapter 6). The quality option allows the short position to deliver any coupon rate in place of the standard 6% as long as the delivered instruments meet the maturity requirements. The delivered cash flows are then discounted at the standard 6% rate to obtain a "conversion factor" for adjusting the delivery price. |

If the delivered bond has a 6% coupon, the conversion factor equals 1, since we are then discounting 6% coupons at a 6% rate. However, if the delivered bond has a coupon rate that is higher than the standard 6% (so is of "superior" quality to the standard), the conversion factor exceeds 1 because we are discounting higher-than-6% coupons at a 6% rate. Similarly, if the delivered bond is inferior to the standard grade (i.e., it has a coupon under 6%), the conversion factor is less than 1.

Section 6.5 and Appendix 6C describe the general formula used to calculate Treasury futures conversion factors, but here is a simple example. Suppose the short position in a Treasury bond futures contract delivers a 20-year, 8% coupon bond. Assume for simplicity that the last coupon was just paid. Then, on a face value of $1, the delivered bond will provide cash flows of $0.04 every six months for 20 years and a cash flow of $1 (the principal) after 20 years. To obtain the conversion factor, we have to discount these cash flows at a 6% rate. Since the Treasury market follows a semiannual compounding convention, a 6% discount rate means a semiannual discount rate of 3%. Thus, the conversion factor for this bond is

$$\frac{0.04}{1.03} + \frac{0.04}{(1.03)^2} + \cdots + \frac{0.04}{(1.03)^{39}} + \frac{1.04}{(1.03)^{40}}$$

which is approximately 1.23. This means that the long position must pay the short position 1.23 times the agreed-upon delivery price. Conversion factors for each deliverable bond are published and updated by the various exchanges. ∎

### The Impact of Delivery Options

As both the corn and US Treasury futures examples indicate, a mechanical rule is often used to determine the price adjustment in a futures contract for delivering a grade different from the standard. This means the price adjustment may not equal the actual difference in *market* prices between the delivered and standard grades.

This presents the short position with a profit opportunity. The price adjustment specifies what the short position *receives* for delivering a particular grade, while the market price is the *cost* of that grade. The short can search over the deliverable grades and select the one that is the most profitable to deliver. This is (somewhat confusingly) called the *cheapest-to-deliver* grade.

The profit opportunity presented by delivery options comes at the expense of the long position and has consequences for both pricing and hedging using futures contracts. From the standpoint of hedging, delivery options degrade the quality of the hedge for the long position. One particular case of interest is the GNMA CDR futures contract discussed in Section 2.7 in which the quality of the hedge was so degraded that the contract itself failed.

Delivery options also affect the pricing of futures contracts. Futures prices depend on not only the standard grade but also the cheapest-to-deliver grade (since that is, by definition, the grade that will be delivered). However, the cheapest-to-deliver grade will not be known with certainty until maturity of the contract, so the price really depends on the market's anticipation of the grade that will be the cheapest-to-deliver. This complicates the theoretical pricing problem substantially.

Nonetheless, one implication of the provision of delivery options is clear: other things being equal, the futures price will be *lower* than the forward price for a contract written on the standard grade. The reason is simple: the forward contract provides no delivery options to the short position, while the futures contract provides such options. The presence of such options makes the futures contract more attractive to the short (who cannot lose from having this extra option) but less attractive to the long. With fewer "buyers" (long positions) and more "sellers" (short positions), the futures price will be lower than the forward price.

## 2.5    Closing Out Positions

Unlike forward contracts, the holder of a futures contract can unilaterally reverse his position by *closing it out* or *offsetting it*. To close out a futures position, the investor must simply take the opposite position to the original. The investor then has no further obligations to the exchange. For example, suppose an investor has a *long* position in 10 COMEX gold contracts for delivery in May. To get out of this contract, the investor need only take a *short* position in 10 COMEX gold contracts for delivery in May. In contrast, if the holder of a long *forward* with one counterparty (say, Counterparty A) enters into an offsetting short forward position with a different counterparty (Counterparty B), she is not freed of her obligations to Counterparty A. To the contrary, her obligations now extend to both contracts and counterparties.

Of course, reversal of futures positions may not be costless. The investor can take positions only at the prevailing futures price at any point, so the initial price and the close-out price could differ, leading to a profit or loss for the investor. For example, suppose the long position in the 10 COMEX gold contracts was taken at a futures price of $340 per ounce. Suppose the price at the time of close-out is $332 per ounce. Then the investor has effectively agreed to buy at $340 per ounce and sell at $332 per ounce for a net loss of $8 per ounce. Since one COMEX gold contract is for 100 ounces of gold, this leads to a total loss on the 10 contracts of $10 \times 100 \times 8 = \$8,000$. This loss is settled through the margin account described in the next section.

Futures exchanges permit reversal of positions for a number of reasons. The most important is that investors may not desire to make or take delivery from the standard locations prescribed in the exchange contract (for example, because it would be inconvenient given their geographical location or because they would rather buy from their usual vendor). By entering into and closing out the futures contract, investors can obtain the relevant hedge without delivery.

| | |
|---|---|
| **Example 2.3** | Consider a bakery that estimates its requirement of wheat in May as 50,000 bushels. The bakery can hedge its price risk by going long 10 May wheat futures contracts on the CBoT at the currently prevailing futures price for May delivery (say, $3.25 a bushel) and then accepting delivery at this price in May. The cost to the bakery is then $\$(50,000 \times 3.25) = \$162,500$. |

As an alternative to taking delivery, the bakery can adopt the following strategy:

1. Take 10 long May wheat futures contracts at the prevailing futures price of $3.25/bushel.
2. Close out the futures position in May at the futures price $F_T$ that prevails then.
3. Buy 50,000 bushels of wheat in the spot market in May at the spot price $S_T$ prevailing then.

On the futures market, the bakery buys 50,000 bushels at a price of $3.25 per bushel and sells them at a price of $F_T$ per bushel for a total gain of $50,000 \times (F_T - 3.25)$. On the spot market, the bakery incurs a cost of $50,000 \times S_T$. Thus, the net cost to the company is

$$50,000\, S_T - 50,000\,(F_T - 3.25) = 162,500 + 50,000\,(S_T - F_T) \qquad (2.1)$$

However, the futures contract is already at maturity in May, so it is a contract for immediate delivery. This means the futures price $F_T$ must equal the spot price $S_T$ at this point. (This is called the "convergence of futures to spot.") The last term in (2.1) drops out, so the net cash outflow for the company is just $162,500. This is the same outcome as accepting delivery on the futures contract. ∎

## Closing Out Contracts Prior to Maturity

The ability to close out positions means that even in the presence of a delivery mismatch (i.e., when the investor's desired date and the delivery date of the futures contract do not coincide), the investor can still obtain an approximate hedge by opening a futures position and closing it out.

For instance, suppose that the bakery in Example 2.3 needs the wheat by April 20. Consider the same strategy as described in the example, except that both the closing out of the futures position and the spot market purchase take place on April 20. Since April 20 is "close" to the maturity date of the futures contract, the futures price $F_T$ and the spot price $S_T$ on that date will be "close" to each other. The last term in (2.1) will be small relative to the first one, resulting in a cash flow of approximately $162,500. Of course, the hedge is only approximate now, but a perfect hedge is impossible in the event of a mismatch. Chapter 6 explores "optimal" hedging in such circumstances.

Overwhelmingly, futures positions in the US are closed out prior to maturity. Only a very small number of contracts (probably under 5%) are actually held open for delivery. Of course, delivery is still important: it is the possibility of making delivery that forces the convergence of futures price to spot at maturity and so makes the hedge in (2.1) feasible.

# 2.6   Margin Requirements and Default Risk

Since futures exchanges guarantee performance on the contracts, they are exposed to risk of default by investors. To control this risk, exchanges require investors to post *margins*. Futures margins are collateral against default by the investor and should not be confused with stock margins, which are a form of down payment. Indeed, the CME calls its margins "performance bonds."

The level at which futures margins are set is crucial to providing market liquidity. If margins are set very high, they can virtually eliminate default risk, but market participation will be inhibited. If they are set too low, market participation is encouraged, but default risk increases. Thus, setting the level of margin requirements can be a delicate task.

In practice, margin requirements are set using sophisticated statistical techniques that take into account the volatility of the price of the underlying asset and other factors. A methodology known as SPAN (an acronym for *Standard Portfolio Analysis of Risk*) has become particularly popular in the industry with many exchanges now using it to determine their margin levels. An important input into the computations is the *volatility* of the price of the underlying: greater price volatility means greater price movements over the course of a trading day, and this in turn means that a larger "cushion" is needed as collateral to guard against default.

## The Margining Procedure

The margining procedure has three parts. First, an investor opening a futures account is required to deposit a specified amount of cash into an account called the *margin account*. The amount deposited initially is called the *initial margin*.

Second, at the end of each day, the balance in the margin account is adjusted to reflect the investor's gains and losses from futures price movements over the day. This process is called *marking-to-market*. The changes to the margin account are called *variation margin*.

Third, if the balance in the margin account falls below a critical minimum level (called the *maintenance margin*), the investor receives a *margin call* requiring the account to be topped up back to the level of the initial margin. The maintenance margin is typically set at around 75% of the level of initial margin. (More accurately, the initial margin is typically set at 135% of the maintenance margin.) If the account is topped up, the position continues until the investor decides to close out his contract or the contract is at maturity. If the investor does not meet the margin call, then the account is closed out immediately.

**Example 2.4**   Suppose that on March 1, a customer takes a long position in 10 May wheat futures contracts at a futures price of $3.60 per bushel. One futures contract calls for the delivery of 5,000 bushels. Thus, the initial futures price is $18,000 per contract.

Let the initial margin be $878 per contract, and let the maintenance margin be $650 per contract. Since the position involves 10 contracts, the total initial margin is $8,780, and the maintenance margin is $6,500. The initial price and margin balance and the remainder of the example are summarized in Table 2.5.

Suppose that the settlement price at the end of the first day is $3.58 per bushel (or $17,900 per contract). The customer's original position called for a delivery price of $18,000 per contract. Thus, she has made an effective loss of $100 per contract, or a total loss of $1,000. This $1,000 is immediately debited from her margin account, taking the margin balance to $7,780. Of course, the short position on these contracts has made a gain of $1,000, so the short's margin balance would increase by $1,000.

**TABLE 2.5** The Margining Procedure: Example

This table describes the evolution of the margin balance for Example 2.4. The prices are all in terms of prices per contract and the total gain or loss refers to the gain over loss over the example's holding of 10 long futures contracts.

|  | Initial/Settlement Price | Change in Price | Total Gain or Loss | Margin Account Balance | Margin Call? |
|---|---|---|---|---|---|
| Contract Opening | $18,000 |  |  | $8,780 |  |
| End of day 1 | 17,900 | −100 | −$1,000 | 7,780 | No |
| End of day 2 | 17,800 | −100 | −1,000 | 6,780 | No |
| End of day 3 | 17,650 | −150 | −1,500 | 5,280 | Yes |

Now suppose the settlement price on the second day is $3.56 per bushel (or $17,800 per contract). The customer has effectively lost an additional $(17,900 − 17,800) = $100 per contract. The total loss over 10 contracts is another $1,000. This amount is removed from the margin account, reducing the balance to $6,780. Since the balance is still above the maintenance margin level of $6,500 for 10 contracts, there is no margin call.

On the third day, say the settlement price fixes at $3.53 per bushel (or $17,650 per contract). This means a further loss to the customer of $(17,800 − 17,650) = $150 per contract, or a total loss over 10 contracts of $1,500. This amount is removed from the margin account, reducing the balance to $5,280.

Since the margin account balance is now below the maintenance margin amount of $6,500, the customer will receive a margin call requiring her to bring the balance back up to $8,780. If the extra funds are deposited, the situation continues. If not, the customer's position is closed out. Of course, the account can be closed out only when trading resumes by which time prices may have fallen further. Any further loss incurred as a consequence of the close-out is met by the $5,280 balance in the margin account. ∎

## Margins and Default

As the example shows, the marking-to-market procedure involves (a) rewriting the investor's futures contract at the *current* settlement price, and (b) settling immediately the gains or losses to the investor from the rewriting. The procedure breaks up the total gain or loss that occurs over the life of a futures contract into daily gains or losses, and requires the investors to pay as they go along. The economic motivation for daily margining is obvious: an investor who is unable to meet "small" losses (as occur from daily price movements) is unlikely to be able to meet larger losses that might result over a longer time span.

Historically, margining has worked very well in inhibiting default. Defaults have occurred, but these have been few and far between. One of the largest defaults that occurred was in the now-defunct Maine potato contract on NYMEX in May 1976. The default appears to have been caused by a classic market squeeze play in which the supply of Maine potatoes was simply not enough to cover the open long positions, leading to default on thousands of contracts.

Exchanges can typically alter margin requirements at any time. This right has been invoked in specific cases to defuse market-threatening situations. One was in the Silver Crisis in 1980 when COMEX margin requirements were increased dramatically, in some cases to $60,000 per contract (see Appendix 9B of Duffie, 1989). Another was during the Metallgesellschaft episode in 1994 when NYMEX doubled the firm's margin requirements; we discuss the Metallgesellschaft case in Section 2.7.

## Margin Sizes and Leverage

Table 2.6 summarizes initial and maintenance margin requirements for several futures contracts. As a comparison of Tables 2.4 and 2.6 shows, margins are typically small relative to the value of assets underlying futures contracts. In many contracts, margins are under 5% of the value of the contract, and in a comfortable majority of contracts, they are under 10%.

**TABLE 2.6** Futures Margin Levels

This table describes initial and maintenance margin levels for several futures contracts as of July 2009. The margin levels are for nonhedgers. For hedgers, the initial and maintenence margins are typically both equal to the maintenance margin level given here.

| Underlying | Exchange | Initial Margin (USD) | Maintenance Margin (USD) | Initial Margin as % of Contract Value |
|---|---|---|---|---|
| **Agri commodities** | | | | |
| Corn | CME Group | 1,620 | 1,200 | 9.4% |
| Wheat | CME Group | 2,700 | 2,000 | 10.8% |
| Oats | CME Group | 1,080 | 800 | 10.5% |
| Soybean | CME Group | 4,050 | 3,000 | 7.2% |
| **Livestock** | | | | |
| Live cattle | CME Group | 1,080 | 800 | 3.2% |
| Lean hogs | CME Group | 1,418 | 1,050 | 5.8% |
| **Forest** | | | | |
| Lumber | CME Group | 1,650 | 1,100 | 8.3% |
| **Interest rate** | | | | |
| 30-year US T-Bonds | CME Group | 4,320 | 3,200 | 3.6% |
| 10-year US T-Notes | CME Group | 2,430 | 1,800 | 2.1% |
| 5-year US T-Notes | CME Group | 1,350 | 1,000 | 1.2% |
| US T-Bill | CME Group | 405 | 300 | 0.04% |
| 3-month Eurodollar | CME Group | 1,148 | 850 | 0.11% |
| 1-month Libor | CME Group | 810 | 600 | 0.03% |
| **Currency** | | | | |
| Euro (EUR) | CME Group | 4,725 | 3,500 | 2.7% |
| British pound (GBP) | CME Group | 2,700 | 2,000 | 2.7% |
| Japanese yen (JPY) | CME Group | 4,050 | 3,000 | 3.0% |
| Swiss franc (CHF) | CME Group | 4,185 | 3,100 | 3.6% |
| Canadian dollar (CAD) | CME Group | 2,430 | 1,800 | 2.8% |
| Brazilian real (BRL) | CME Group | 4,900 | 3,500 | 10.0% |
| Israeli shekel (ILS) | CME Group | 8,100 | 6,000 | 3.2% |
| **Stock indices** | | | | |
| S&P 500 | CME Group | 28,125 | 22,500 | 12.5% |
| Big Dow | CME Group | 32,500 | 26,000 | 15.5% |
| Nasdaq 100 | CME Group | 17,500 | 14,000 | 12.3% |
| Nikkei 225 (in JPY) | CME Group | 625,000 | 500,000 | 13.5% |
| **Metals** | | | | |
| Gold | COMEX | 5,399 | 3,999 | 5.9% |
| Silver | COMEX | 8,100 | 6,000 | 12.9% |
| **Energy** | | | | |
| Light sweet crude | NYMEX | 7,763 | 5,750 | 12.9% |

The size of the margin requirement determines the extent of leverage provided by a futures contract. A margin requirement of 5% of contract value means that by putting 5% in cash up front, the customer gets full exposure to movements in futures prices, implying a leverage ratio of 20:1. Given the small size of margins in practice, it is clear that futures are highly levered instruments.

## Margining and Valuation

From the standpoint of valuation, margining complicates matters because it creates uncertain interim cash flows. Typically, the initial margin earns interest, but the variation margin does not. (Investors are, however, free to withdraw any balance in their margin accounts in excess of the initial margin, so this does not impose an economic cost.) The interest rate could itself change over the contract life. Thus, the holder of the contract receives uncertain cash flows that earn interest at possibly uncertain rates. It is not easy to see whether this implies futures prices will be higher or lower than the corresponding forward prices. We examine this issue later (see Section 3.8).

## Margining and Hedging

Daily marking-to-market also has a subtle effect on hedges using futures contracts. The purpose of hedging, by definition, is to reduce cash-flow uncertainty from market commitments. If a forward market commitment (say, a commitment to deliver wheat in four months) is hedged using a futures contract, there is a cash-flow mismatch. On the forward contract, any gains or losses are realized only at maturity, whereas in a futures, you settle as you go along. If these interim cash-flow requirements are large, they may complicate— or even ruin—an otherwise sound hedging strategy. The most spectacular case in which this occurred was the more than $1 billion in losses taken by Metallgesellschaft in 1994 (see Section 2.7).

## Clearinghouse Margins

Just as an investor is required to post margins with clearing members, the latter are required to post margins with clearinghouses. In this case, the initial and maintenance margins usually coincide. The clearing member must maintain the account at the original margin times the number of contracts outstanding.

# 2.7 Case Studies in Futures Markets

This section presents three case studies in futures markets, each of which provides important insights into and lessons concerning futures markets operations and trading.

The first concerns the GNMA CDR futures contract on the CBoT, the very first interest-rate-sensitive futures contract to be introduced on a US exchange. It offers an excellent look into the intricacies of futures contract design, particularly the specification of delivery options. A detailed analysis of the rise and fall of this contract is presented in Johnston and McConnell (1989); our presentation reports their research.

The second case study is that of the Metallgesellschaft episode of 1994, perhaps unique in the annals of derivatives-related debacles in that many analysts believe it involved not deliberately speculative positions (as, for example, in the case of Barings Bank) or attempted market manipulation (as in the case of Sumitomo) but rather what appeared to be a theoretically sound *hedging* strategy.

The third case study looks at the case of the hedge fund Amaranth whose $4-billion-plus losses from trading in natural gas futures and related derivatives made it the largest hedge fund failure of its time, and, indeed, among the largest losses suffered by a financial institution prior to the financial crisis of 2008. The Amaranth case highlights, in particular, the leverage and liquidity risks that can arise in futures market trading.

## Case Study 1

# The GNMA CDR Futures Contract

The Government National Mortgage Association (GNMA) Collateralized Depository Receipt (CDR) futures contract was introduced in 1975 on the CBoT. It was the first interest-rate futures contract traded on an exchange. The assets underlying the futures contract are GNMA mortgage-backed securities. Deliverable securities in the contract were backed by pools of single-family mortgages with initial maturities of 29–30 years. The mortgages were insured against default by either the Federal Housing Association (FHA) or the Veterans Administration (VA). Every mortgage in the pool could be prepaid ("called") at any time.

Figure 2.2 describes the rise and fall of the contract. The contract enjoyed spectacular success in its early years with trading volume growing rapidly from 1975 to 1980. It remained stable for about two years and then began declining rapidly, reaching near-zero trading volumes by 1987. The spectacular rise and fall of the contract can be traced directly to its design, notably the delivery options in the contract that made it a bad hedge vehicle.

An important—and intuitive—point in hedging with futures is that for a futures contract to provide a good hedge vehicle, the futures price must bear a close relationship to the spot price of the asset being hedged. (Hedging with futures is examined in detail in Chapters 5 and 6 where this point is formalized.) In the case of commodities, the underlying spot risk is usually well defined (the prices of lumber, corn, crude oil, etc.), but in dealing with interest-rate securities, one must be careful in identifying precisely *which* risk it is that investors are seeking to hedge.

GNMA CDR futures contracts are futures on mortgage-backed securities. The question is: *which* mortgage-backed securities are investors seeking to hedge? It turns out that

**FIGURE 2.2**
GNMA CDR Futures
Trading Volumes

This figure describes the growth and decline in trading volumes in the GNMA CDR futures contract between its introduction in 1975 and 1987.

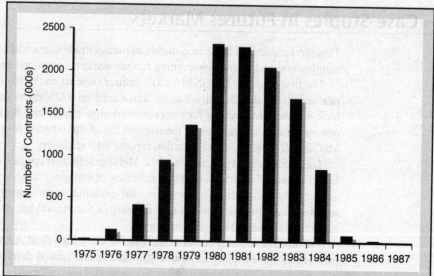

hedging demand in mortgage-backed securities is concentrated in *current-coupon* mortgages. Hedging demand comes primarily from mortgage bankers who originate mortgages and then package and sell them in the secondary market. Mortgage bankers are exposed to interest-rate risk on mortgages written at current coupon rates between the time the loans are made and the time they are sold on the secondary market.

Therefore, for the GNMA CDR futures contract to be useful as a hedge vehicle, it is necessary that the futures price of this contract bear a close relationship to current-coupon mortgages. In the presence of delivery options, the futures price is determined by the cheapest-to-deliver grade. Thus, it is the cheapest-to-deliver grade that must bear a close relationship to current coupon mortgages. Did the specification of the contract meet this requirement?

## Key Features of the GNMA CDR Futures Contract

The "standard" contract called for the delivery of GNMA securities with $100,000 in remaining principal and an 8% coupon. Several delivery options were also provided. Unusually, and perhaps uniquely among futures contracts, one of these was provided to the *long* position in the contract: at maturity, the long could elect to receive a Collateralized Depository Receipt (CDR) entitling him to receive $635 per month in interest payments as long as he held the CDR and to exchange the CDR for the actual GNMA securities at any time by giving 15 business days' notice.

The most important delivery option, however, was the "quality option" provided to the short. The quality option allowed the short to deliver any interest rate in place of the standard 8%. In the manner later used in the successful US Treasury bond futures contract, the contract provided for an adjustment in the price through a "conversion factor" which was calculated by discounting the cash flows from the delivered mortgage at the standard 8% rate. One problem here, however, lay in the length of time for which these cash flows could be assumed to last, since the mortgages could be prepaid at any time. The GNMA CDR futures contract assumed that cash flows from delivered mortgages would continue for exactly 12 years at the end of which the mortgage would be repaid in full. The conversion factor was calculated under this assumption, and the principal balance the short was required to deliver was stated as $100,000 divided by this conversion factor.

## The Problem

In practice, mortgage prepayments often occur because mortgage holders are able to refinance their mortgages at lower interest rates. Given this motivation, borrowers holding mortgages with high interest rates are more likely to find lower interest rates and prepay their existing mortgages than holders of low-coupon mortgages. The quality option in the GNMA CDR futures contract ignored this propensity for high-coupon mortgages to be prepaid earlier. By assuming that all mortgages last 12 years, the contract *undervalued* the prepayment option in high interest-rate mortgages relative to low interest-rate mortgages; equivalently, it *overstated* the maturity of high interest-rate mortgages relative to low interest-rate ones.

## The Consequence

The impact of this is not hard to see. By overstating the relative maturity of cash flows from high-coupon mortgages, the conversion factor of high-coupon mortgages is *overstated* relative to that of low-coupon securities. (Intuitively, the higher cash flows are assumed to last

**FIGURE 2.3**
US 30-Year Mortgage
Rates: 1975–1987

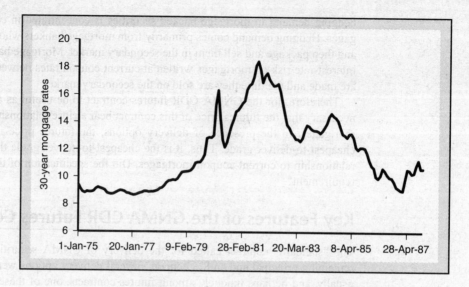

longer than they really do.) Ceteris paribus, therefore, the short will find it advantageous to deliver high-coupon mortgages; i.e., high-coupon mortgages will be the cheapest-to-deliver grade. Reflecting this, the futures price will bear a close relation to the high-coupon mortgages.

However, we have seen that for the GNMA CDR futures contract to be a good hedge vehicle, its price has to bear a close relationship to current-coupon mortgages. Thus, as long as high and current coupons are the same, there is no problem.

Between 1975 and 1982, this was in fact the case. In March 1975, the interest rate was 8.25%. It rose more or less steadily to a peak of 17% in September 1981 and remained at around 16%–17% through early 1982. (See Figure 2.3.) In late 1982, however, interest rates began a rapid decline. A low of 11% was reached by 1983, and until 1987, interest rates remained well below 16%. As a consequence, until 1982, it was the case that the GNMA CDR futures contract was an effective hedging vehicle for current-coupon mortgages, but by late 1983, this was no longer the case. Johnston and McConnell show that by this time, Treasury bond futures contracts had become better hedge vehicles for current-coupon mortgages than GNMA CDR futures contracts, and the contract died.

## Case Study 2
# Metallgesellschaft AG

The Metallgesellschaft episode was, as we have mentioned, unusual in the annals of derivatives-related debacles of the 1990s in that it involved a *hedging* strategy gone sour.[1] The protagonist in this episode was Metallgesellschaft Refining & Marketing (MGRM), a subsidiary of Metallgesellschaft AG of Germany. Metallgesellschaft was, at this time,

[1] Several postmortem analyses of the Metallgesellschaft episode are available, some siding with Metallgesellschaft's senior management in their terminating the hedge, and others faulting them. One vigorous presentation of the latter viewpoint is Culp and Miller (1995). Our summary here draws on their work among others.

a 112-year-old company mostly owned by institutional investors such as Deutsche Bank, Dresdner Bank, and Daimler Benz.

Begining in 1992, MGRM began selling contracts to supply gasoline, heating oil, and diesel fuel at fixed prices over 5- and 10-year periods. The details in the contracts varied to some extent. Many called for monthly delivery for the period specified in the contract, while others had lower delivery frequencies. The contracts were marketed aggresively and very successfully. By November 1993, MGRM had built up long-term supply commitments of 160 million barrels. This was eight times the commitment of October 1992, and more than twice the commitment of May 1993.

The fixed-price contracts left MGRM exposed to increases in spot prices. The company decided to hedge this exposure using gasoline, heating oil, and crude oil futures contracts on NYMEX. This allowed the company to focus on the storage and marketing of oil products where it possessed special expertise.

The hedge was complicated by the immensity of MGRM's total exposure. Position limits on NYMEX made it impossible to completely hedge MGRM's total commitments of 160 million barrels using only futures contracts. MGRM used long futures positions of 55 million barrels on NYMEX. It then entered into bilateral over-the-counter (OTC) swaps arrangements to hedge the remaining exposure. These large positions also made it impossible for the company to maintain anonymity in trading, a fact that compounded its problems when it ran into cash-flow difficulties.

# The "Stack-and-Roll" Strategy

The "ideal" hedging strategy would have been to match the maturity of the exposure with the maturity of the futures contract. For example, if there is a commitment to deliver 1 million barrels in three months, this particular exposure is hedged using a three-month futures contract. Although NYMEX offers oil futures contracts several years out, the contracts are relatively illiquid beyond the first few months. Culp and Miller (1995) note that liquidity was an important consideration in MGRM's approach because it lowered the cost of managing its positions to meet seasonal changes in the demand and supply of heating oil and gasoline.

As an alternative, MGRM decided to use a "stack-and-roll" hedging strategy using futures contracts. Such a strategy involves the following steps. The firm takes long positions in futures contracts to cover its entire exposure. All positions are in the nearby futures contract, i.e., for delivery at the end of the current month. (This is the "stack" part.) At the end of each month, the company closes out its position, and opens new long positions to cover its remaining exposure. (This is the "roll" part.)

As a simple example, suppose the commitment is to supply 1,000 barrels a month for the next 60 months. In a stack-and-roll hedging strategy, we take long positions in the entire commitment of 60,000 barrels in one-month futures. At the end of the month, we roll over the remaining part of the commitment (59,000 barrels) by closing out the existing futures positions and reopening long positions in 59,000 new one-month futures.

Theoretically, it can be shown that under some assumptions, a stack-and-roll strategy should provide a good hedge for the forward exposure. A proof is provided in Section 3.2. Intuitively, hedging using a stack-and-roll strategy is a matter of offsetting losses on the forward commitments with gains in futures and vice versa. If oil prices rise, there would be a loss on the forward contracts but a gain on the long futures positions. If oil prices fall, there would be losses on the long futures positions, but these would be offset by the increased economic value of the forward commitments.

# Potential Problems with the Hedge

In practice, a number of cash-flow-related problems may arise in implementing such a strategy. MGRM's strategy entailed two specific risks: (a) a steep fall in oil prices leading to margin calls on the long futures positions and (b) a change in the oil market from *backwardation* to *contango*. (The terms backwardation and contango are defined below.) In addition, MGRM faced *basis risk* from the futures/forward mismatch, viz., the problem that the values of short-term futures and long-term forwards react differently to changing market conditions. We examine each of these in turn.

## Problem 1: A Fall in Oil Prices

The first problem MGRM faced had to do with the interim cash-flow pressures potentially created by the use of futures contracts in general. MGRM had long positions in 55 million barrels of futures contracts. Thus, every $1 fall in oil prices would lead to a $55 million cash outflow on the futures margin accounts alone. A steep oil price fall would thus create an immediate and large cash requirement to meet margin calls and keep the hedge alive. Of course, the fall in prices would make the forward contracts with their locked-in prices more attractive, but the corresponding gains on the short forward positions would not translate into cash inflows until some date in the future. Thus, although the economic value of the position is unaffected (it remains hedged), a severe short-term cash-flow requirement is created.

Unfortunately for MGRM, this scenario came true: oil prices plummeted in late 1993. This led to an immediate cash requirement of around $900 million to meet margin calls (on the futures positions) and the demand for extra collateral (on the OTC positions).

## Problem 2: From Backwardation to Contango

A futures market is said to be in *backwardation* if futures prices are below spot. It is said to be in *contango* if futures prices are above spot. As we will see in Chapters 3 and 4, in a typical commodity market with a positive cost-of-carry, the theoretical futures is above the spot, i.e., the market should be in contango. However, in some commodity markets (especially oil) futures prices are often below spot. This phenomenon is commonly attributed to the presence of a large "convenience yield" from holding the spot commodity, an issue we discuss further in Chapter 4.

The "roll" part of MGRM's strategy meant it faced the risk of a possible shift in the oil market from backwardation to contango. Why? Rolling over futures positions at the end of each month involves closing out the existing long futures position by taking a short futures position in the expiring contract and taking a long futures position in the new nearby contract. The existing contract is at maturity, so it is being sold at the current spot price. Thus, rolling the contract over involves effectively *selling* at the current spot price and *buying* at the current one-month futures price. In backwardation, rollover creates cash *inflows*, but in contango, rollover creates cash *outflows*.

Through much of the mid- and late-1980s, the oil futures market was in backwardation. If this situation had continued, MGRM could have expected to receive cash inflows on the rollover. Unfortunately for MGRM, in late 1993, the oil market went into contango. As a consequence, by end-1993, MGRM was incurring a cash outflow of up to $30 million each month on rollover costs alone.

## Basis Risk: A Further Issue?

It has been suggested that a further issue that hurt MGRM is *basis risk*. MGRM was hedging *long-term forwards* with *short-term futures*. These two prices may not move in lockstep, that is, long-term forward prices may react to movements in the spot price of oil differently from short-term futures. Thus, perfect offsetting of cash flows is not generally possible, so there is what is known as *basis risk* in hedging. In the presence of such risk, a well-developed theory (see Chapter 5 for details) shows that it is not, in general, optimal to use a hedge ratio of unity (i.e., to hedge exposures one-for-one with futures). However, MGRM does appear to have used a hedge ratio of unity, which may have further degraded the quality of the hedge, adding to losses.

## The Denouement

When MGRM's cash requirements became public information, its problems were compounded. NYMEX first doubled MGRM's margin requirements. Later, NYMEX also removed MGRM's hedger's exception, effectively halving MGRM's position limits. Counterparties on their OTC contracts also demanded increased collateral for rolling over contracts.

In response, Metallgesellschaft AG's senior management decided to close out the positions and terminate the hedging strategy in place. A number of arguments were offered in favor of terminating the hedge. It was suggested that the strategy's cash requirements had become excessive; the rollover costs alone were around $30 million a month. It was also suggested that the long-term forward contracts were not "watertight," i.e., significant credit-risk existed. The possibility of basis risk from mismatch in assets underlying forward and futures contracts was also cited.

Led by Nobel Prize—winning economist Merton Miller and his student Christopher Culp, counter arguments appeared in the financial press and academic journals suggesting that the parent company's actions had been intemperate and unwise. For one, the termination of the hedge converted paper losses into real ones. Second, if the market went back into backwardation (which had, after all, been its "normal" state for several years), rollover profits would arise; removal of the hedge eliminated this possibility. Third, the removal of hedge left MGRM vulnerable to price increases.

As it happens, MGRM's positions were unwound near the bottom of the market: oil prices rebounded during 1994 (see Figure 2.4), though this could not have been foreseen at the time of closeout. But the eventual consequences were severe. The termination of the hedge resulted in losses of well over $1 billion, bankrupting the parent company.

**FIGURE 2.4**
Crude Oil Prices: November 1992–July 1994

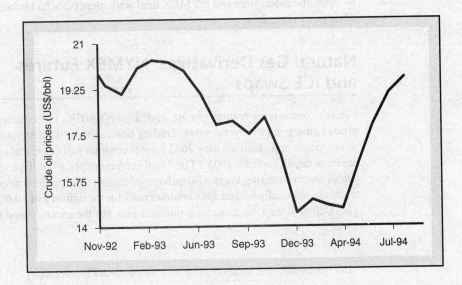

## Case Study 3

# Amaranth

Amaranth LLC started as a hedge fund specializing primarily in the trading of convertible bonds. As returns from its conventional areas of strength tapered off in 2004, the fund greatly expanded its energy-trading book, an area into which it had entered in 2002 following the collapse of Enron. This expansion coincided with the hiring of Brian Hunter, the principal author of Amaranth's spectacular success in 2005 and its even more spectacular implosion in 2006. What follows is a summary of the Amaranth saga.[2]

## The Natural Gas Market

Natural gas is one of the principal energy sources of the US economy, accounting for nearly a quarter of the country's energy consumption. Around half of US homes use natural gas heating in winter. Natural gas is also used to generate around a fifth of US electricity and is used in other commercial and industrial activities. Natural gas is commonly measured in terms of its energy content (British thermal units or Btu). Both cash and futures prices are usually quoted per million Btu, written MMBtu.

The natural gas market is an unusual one in many ways. Demand is highly seasonal with winter demand exceeding summer demand, especially if the winters are severe. (As one might expect, the seasonality is primarily caused by residential heating demand.) The relatively inelastic nature of winter heating demand means that winter prices tend systematically to be higher than summer prices and that winter price spikes are common if there is a cold snap.

There is a large and active spot (or "cash") market in natural gas. Traditionally, spot market pricing referenced spot price indices constructed by industry groups such as Platts; these indices are based on surveys of spot transactions at key delivery locations or "hubs," such as the Henry Hub in Louisiana. In the years preceding the Amaranth episode, the market moved increasingly towards referencing the near-month NYMEX futures contract in cash market trades, using the final settlement price for that contract. As a consequence, by 2006, the index price and NYMEX final settlement price had become virtually the same thing (see Figure 2.5).

## Natural Gas Derivatives: NYMEX Futures and ICE Swaps

Futures contracts on natural gas are traded on NYMEX. The contracts have monthly expiries running out to several years. Trading ceases on the third business day before the delivery month (e.g., the February 2005 futures contract will cease trading on the third-to-last business day of January 2005.) The "final settlement price" of the contract is based on the prices observed during the last 30 minutes of trading prior to the contract's expiry. The contracts are physically settled. One contract calls for the delivery of 10,000 MMBtu of natural gas. Delivery must be made at a uniform flow (to the extent possible) over the delivery month.

---

[2] Our presentation of the case draws mainly on the Senate Report (2007).

**FIGURE 2.5**
Index Prices and
NYMEX Final
Settlement Prices

This figure appears as Figure 14b in the Senate Report (2007). It shows the difference between the popular cash market Platt's index and NYMEX final settlement prices on the near-month contracts. The difference is very small except for the spike in September 2005 that followed Hurricane Katrina.

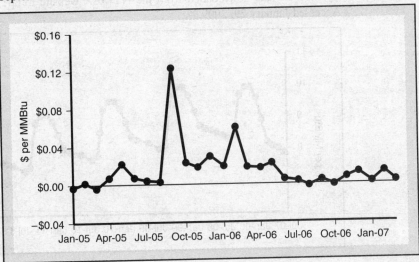

While NYMEX is a regulated US exchange, futures-like contracts on natural gas also trade on the InterContinental Exchange or ICE, an unregulated US electronic exchange. Called natural gas "swaps," these contracts trade in standardized sizes of 2,500 MMBtu and have monthly expiries out to several years. Unlike the NYMEX futures contracts, they are cash settled at maturity but are otherwise designed to mimic the behavior of the NYMEX futures contracts. Indeed, at the time of the Amaranth episode in 2006, the ICE swap contract even specified that its final settlement price would be set equal to the final settlement price of the corresponding NYMEX futures contract, so the two contracts were functionally identical.

There was, however, one important operational difference. As a regulated exchange, NYMEX specified position limits and/or "accountability levels" (position levels that triggered disclosure requirements and could lead to mandatory reductions at the exchange's discretion) for all its participants, although these limits could be (and, in practice, were) relaxed for specific participants by NYMEX. In contrast, as an unregulated exchange, ICE imposed no position limits at all, so participants coming up against trading or position limits at NYMEX could always shift into equivalent contracts on ICE. We will see the importance of this shortly in the context of Amaranth.

Finally, reflecting the seasonality of demand for natural gas, natural gas futures prices also reflect an oscillatory pattern as Figure 2.6 illustrates. Both panels of the figure show futures prices out to five years; the upper panel presents prices observed on June 1, 2007, while the lower panel shows prices observed on January 28, 2009.

## Amaranth's Trading Strategies

Amaranth's problems leading to its collapse in 2006 were largely caused by futures trading, but its energy-trading book also used a number of other strategies and instruments. One, for example, that proved a hugely successful bet in 2005 was the purchase of deep out-of-the-money call options on natural gas futures. These options gave Amaranth the right to

**FIGURE 2.6**
Natural Gas Futures
Prices

The upper panel of this figure shows natural gas futures prices as of June 1, 2007, for a range of maturities, while the lower panel shows the futures prices as of January 28, 2009. The upper panel appears as Figure 17 in the Senate Report (2007). The lower panel is based on data downloaded from the NYMEX website http://www.nymex.com. Accessed January 29, 2009.

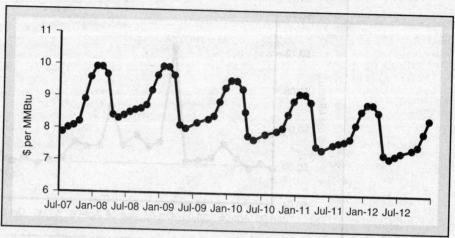

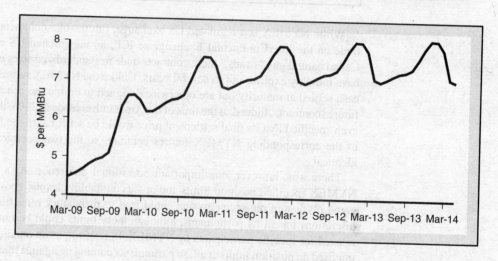

enter into long futures contracts at fixed futures prices. (Options on futures are described in Chapter 14.) When Hurricanes Katrina and Rita hit the US in 2005, natural gas prices soared and Amaranth recorded handsome returns.

The main strategy followed by Amaranth in 2006 is often described as one that was long winter–short summer, that is, as based on a view that the difference between futures prices for winter delivery and those for summer delivery would widen. Broadly speaking, this is correct, but the actual implementation, using NYMEX futures and ICE swaps, was more nuanced and involved several different substrategies. Some of the key substrategies are described below.

**Short Summer** At the beginning of 2006, based on the relatively warm 2005–06 winter and the presence of plentiful gas supplies, Amaranth took the view that gas prices would fall and so took a large short position of over 30,000 contracts in Mar-06 futures. In February, this was rolled over into short Apr-06 futures, and the rollover continued through the early summer as Amaranth continued to bet on falling gas prices through summer and early fall. The position sizes were also increased so that by end-July 2006, the short position in Sep-06 futures was over 60,000 contracts.

**The Jan-07/Nov-06 Spread** A second key component of Amaranth's strategy concerned the behavior of winter 2006–07 prices. Amaranth's view was that winter prices would rise and particularly that January prices would rise more sharply than November prices, that is, that the Jan-07/Nov-06 price differential would increase. So, in February 2006, Amaranth went long around 25,000 Jan-07 contracts and short around 25,000 Nov-06 contracts. These positions were gradually built up over the following months until, by June 2006, Amaranth was long around 60,000 Jan-07 futures contracts and short over 50,000 Nov-06 futures contracts. From mid-July-06 onward, the short Nov-06 position in this strategy was replaced with a short Oct-06 position.

**The Mar-07/Apr-07 Spread** Historically, with March signifying the end of the winter heating period, the March-April price differential has been very volatile. Amaranth bet on an increase in the Mar-07/Apr-07 differential, going long Mar-07 futures and short Apr-07 futures. In May 2006, Amaranth was long 20,000 Mar-07 and short 20,000 Apr-07 futures. By end-July, these positions had grown enormously; Amaranth was long around 59,000 Mar-07 futures and short around 80,000 Apr-07 futures.

Besides these, Amaranth had a vast range of other positions in other maturities including long or short positions in many other months in 2006. By late summer, Amaranth also had positions in the Mar-08/Apr-08 and Mar-10/Apr-10 spreads.

Unquestionably the most striking feature of Amaranth's trading book was the size of each position. These were immense measured in dollar terms and in relation to Amaranth's capital base. For example, assuming a price of $8 per MMBtu, each futures contract of size 10,000 MMBtu represents a notional value of $80,000. A futures position of 30,000 contracts then represents a notional value of $2.4 billion in this one contract alone. As we have seen, Amaranth held several positions of this size or bigger (much bigger in many cases).

But the sizes of Amaranth's positions are even more impressive when taken as fractions of the *entire market*. Amaranth's positions in many contracts often exceeded 50% of the total open positions in that contract on NYMEX. For example, in mid-June 2006, Amaranth held around 52% of the open interest in the Jan-07 futures on NYMEX and around 57% of the open interest in the Nov-06 contract. By end-July 2006, the size of Amaranth's long position in the Jan-07 futures was nearly equal to the entire actual nationwide consumption of natural gas by US residential customers during January 2007! These huge position sizes created severe liquidity issues for Amaranth, as we shall see shortly.

## Performance: Early 2006

Through most of early 2006, Amaranth's strategies did very well. The fund's year-to-date returns by end-April exceeded 30% with returns of over $1 billion in April alone. Much of this success came because prices behaved as Amaranth had bet. For example:

- In April 2006, the price of the Jun-06 futures fell by over $0.80 per MMBtu, or $8,000 per contract. Since Amaranth had a short position in approximately 30,000 of these contracts, this position alone would have resulted in a marked-to-market profit of around $240 million.

- The Jan-07/Nov-06 spread, which had been less than $1 in January 2006, increased steadily and in April 2006 widened sharply by $0.63, moving from $1.59 to $2.22. This meant a profit of around $6,300 on each long Jan-07/short Nov-06 position. Amaranth had, by April 2006, around 30,000 contracts in this spread, implying a marked-to-market gain of over $180 million on this position.

## The First Sign of Trouble: May 2006

In May came a sharp reversal, the "worst month since inception," as the firm later reported to its investors. Amaranth looked to lock-in the profits registered on some of its positions and exit the market but ran into a problem: in many contracts, it held a huge share of the total open positions, so it was hard for the firm to exit—or even reduce—its positions without triggering large price effects. In post-mortems of the Amaranth collapse, it has been suggested that Amaranth's marked-to-market profits in the year to date were, at least to some extent, illusory because they had been created by Amaranth's own trading. That is, for example, its continued large purchases of the Jan-07/Nov-06 spread themselves widened the spread, making Amaranth's previously obtained positions in the spread appear profitable. Given the huge shares of the open positions Amaranth held in many contracts, this appears plausible; it is not then surprising that Amaranth was unable to "capture" the marked-to-market profits by liquidating its holdings.

Compounding this liquidity problem, the market too turned sharply against Amaranth, particularly in the last week of May. There was widespread sentiment in the market that spreads had grown too large relative to fundamentals and to historical patterns (perhaps driven precisely by Amaranth's trading). The Jan-07/Nov-06 spread fell from $2.15 to $1.73, resulting in large losses on that position for Amaranth. Overall, the firm lost over $1.15 billion in May. But thanks to the strong performance in earlier months, it ended May still comfortably up for the year.

## Buildup: June-July 2006

After the liquidity problems it had encountered in May, Amaranth reportedly had internal discussions concerning reducing its portfolio and liquidating its positions even at a loss. Ultimately, however, the firm spent most of June and July *increasing* many of these positions:

- Amaranth continued rolling over its short position for the summer and early fall months. In June, the firm was short over 40,000 Aug-06 contracts. In July, it rolled these into Sep-06 positions, ending the month short around 63,000 Sep-06 contracts.
- Amaranth's long Jan-07 position reached 60,000 contracts in June and nearly 80,000 contracts in end-July. Against this, it had a short position of 51,000 Nov-06 contracts in June, which it changed to a short position of 42,000 Oct-06 contracts in July.
- The Mar-07/Apr-07 position increased by end-July to a long position in nearly 59,000 Mar-07 contracts and a short position in nearly 80,000 Apr-07 contracts.

The buildup of the Mar-07/Apr-07 spread was particularly sharp. On a few select days (May 26, June 15, July 31), Amaranth dominated futures trading in these contracts, accounting for between 40% and 60% of the trading volume with a noticeable effect on the spread on those days (see Figure 2.7). By end-July, Amaranth held around 40% of the total open interest in the 2006–07 winter months futures contracts on NYMEX.

**FIGURE 2.7**
The Mar-07/Apr-07
Natural Gas Futures
Price Spread

This figure shows the behavior of the difference between the futures prices for the Mar-07 and Apr-07 futures contracts on NYMEX. The figure is taken from the Senate Report (2007) and appears there as Figure 38.

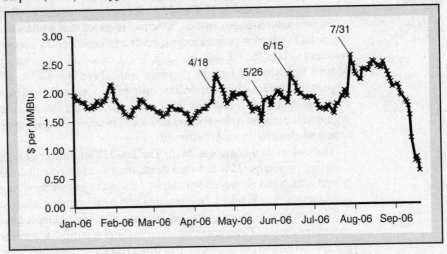

## More Volatility: August 2006

In early August 2006, concerned by the size of Amaranth's positions, NYMEX forced Amaranth to reduce the size of its positions. Amaranth complied but simultaneously opened or increased its positions on the unregulated ICE with the result that its overall exposure actually *increased*.

One particular position it adopted was to increase its short Sep-06 position while buying back some Oct-06 contracts. In the presence of plentiful supplies that pointed to a downward trend in prices, this was effectively a bet that September prices would fall faster than October prices. In the last week of August, the price of Sep-06 futures fell by over $1 (or over $10,000 per contract), possibly aided by Amaranth's own enormous increase in its short Sep-06 position during this week from under 60,000 contracts to over 100,000. Simultaneously, the Oct-06/Sep-06 spread widened dramatically to around 35 cents compared to its normal level of 7–8 cents.

The sharp departure from historical spread levels despite no obvious change in fundamentals led many traders to take the position opposite to Amaranth. The largest of these was another hedge fund, Centaurus. On the final day of trading in the September contract, Amaranth ceased its trading activities an hour before trading terminated, mainly at NYMEX's request. But Centaurus continued trading in enormous quantities, and as a consequence, the Oct-06/Sep-06 spread fell almost 40 cents in the last hour even as the price of the September contract rose by 60 cents, or $6,000 per contract. The resulting one-day loss to Amaranth was a staggering $600 million, over 6% of its total assets under management.

## The End: September 2006

Despite the huge loss on August 29, Amaranth still finished the month up over $630 million. But the size of the firm's positions and the volatility of its profit and loss (P&L) had started creating serious concerns in the market. Its margin requirements, which had exceeded

$2 billion by mid-August, crossed $3 billion in early September. Concomitant with the increased portfolio size, the firm's leverage had also increased. Chincarini (2006) reports that by end-August, the firm's leverage (the ratio of the value of its futures positions to its capital base) exceeded 5. This made it especially vulnerable to sharp moves in the market.

Subsequent testimony in the US Senate revealed that while a number of market participants had viewed winter/summer spreads as overpriced in summer 2006, they had been reluctant to take the opposite position, being mindful of the sharp price effect Hurricanes Katrina and Rita had had the previous year. There was also a general perception that a large market trader with considerable resources (Amaranth) had been buying these spreads propping up the price. But Amaranth no longer had the resources to increase its positions. As hurricane season ended with no major catastrophes and gas supplies heading into winter appeared plentiful, spreads collapsed.

The end when it came was swift. The Jan-07/Oct-06 spread registered a sharp decline, tumbling by almost 25% between September 1 and September 15. The Mar-07/Apr-07 spread, which had already fallen almost 25% in the last week of August, continued to slide precipitously (see Figure 2.7). Amaranth was hemorrhaging money.

In an attempt to shore up its cash position, the firm attempted to sell its Mar-07/Apr-07 spread position to Centaurus, but the offer was rebuffed. Centaurus' CEO, John Arnold, noted in his e-mail communication to Brian Hunter at Amaranth[3] that in his opinion, despite its tumble in recent days, the spread at $1 was still substantially overpriced. He suggested a fair price of 45–60 cents for the spread, which Amaranth refused.

Mr. Arnold's estimates proved prophetic. A week later on September 21, on what would turn out to be Amaranth's last trading day, the spread stood at 58 cents. Other spreads had similarly collapsed. Amaranth sold its energy book to JP Morgan Chase and liquidated the remainder of its portfolio to meet margin calls. In just three weeks in September, the fund had lost $4.35 billion, or 45% of its total assets under management of $9.67 billion.

## Leverage, Liquidity, and Volatility

A little reflection shows that three factors did Amaranth in, the first two related to Amaranth's strategy and the third to market characteristics:

**1. Leverage** All futures contracts are levered positions in that a small margin payment supports the entire position value. A margin payment of (for example) 20% implies a 5:1 leverage. Naked futures positions are, thus, very sensitive to changes in the levels of futures prices. With spread positions, the risk is somewhat different. It is not the *level* of futures prices that matters so much as its *term-structure,* that is, the way futures prices change with maturities. In particular, what matters is how the differences between futures prices at different maturities change. Speculative trades on seasonal effects are levered bets on the shape of this term structure.

In either case, it is leverage that creates the possibility of both large returns and large losses. Chincarini's (2006) estimate of a leverage of 5.29 for Amaranth by August 2006 means that the firm's total assets under management of $9.67 billion were supporting futures positions of over $50 billion! It is easy to see that a sharp change in futures prices (and/or the shape of the term-structure of futures prices) could cause catastrophic losses. Amaranth estimated that the probability of such price moves was small, but judging from the reactions of other participants, this view was not widely shared.

---

[3] See Senate Report (2007), p. 113.

**2. Liquidity**. The ill-effects of leverage are compounded by taking on too much of the same leveraged trade. It is even worse when that trade is a significant part of the entire market. Amaranth found that the size of its positions just did not allow it to unwind trades profitably, and in fact, even partial unwinding resulted in immediate adverse price moves, ensuring that the remaining positions would sell only at a loss. Marked-to-market "profits" in such situations can be largely illusory.

Leverage amplifies the impact of price moves. The absence of liquidity means that larger (adverse) price moves result when attempting to trade out of a position. Together, the two Ls can form a lethal combination as they did in Amaranth's case and as many financial institutions learned to their cost in the crisis of 2008–09.

**3. Volatility**. Commodities markets are characterized by high levels of volatility. Large price swings and swift changes in the term structure of futures prices are not uncommon. Around the time of the Amaranth debacle, natural gas options were trading at volatilities in the 80%–100% range. (By comparison, the volatilities on major equity indices were in the 15%–20% range.) High volatility means larger price swings, so combined with leverage, you can win big but you can lose just as big too. Certainly, when things began to go badly for Amaranth, the high volatility did not help.

Amaranth's case stands out because of its size, not because of the uniqueness of the factors that led to its collapse. Eight years earlier, another hedge fund had incurred catastrophic losses and had almost threatened the stability of the financial system. The 1998 failure of Long-Term Capital Management (see Chapter 23) had also been caused by the lethal leverage-liquidity combination. There really is not that much new under the sun, at least not in terms of the behavior of financial market participants.

## 2.8 Exercises

1. What are "delivery options" in a futures contract? Generally, why are delivery options provided to the short but not to the long position?

2. How do delivery options affect the relationship of futures prices to forward prices?

3. To what do the following terms refer: *initial margin*, *maintenance margin*, and *variation margin*?

4. What are price ticks?

5. Explain price limits and why they exist.

6. What are position limits in futures markets? Why do we need these? Are they effective for the objective you state, or can you think of better ways to achieve the objective?

7. What are the different ways in which futures contracts may be settled? Explain why these exist.

8. What is meant by *open interest*?

9. Discuss the liquidity and maturity of futures contracts.

10. Describe the standard bond in the Treasury Bond futures contract on the CBoT and the delivery option regarding coupons.

11. Suppose the delivered bond in the Treasury Bond futures contract has a remaining maturity of 20 years and a 7% coupon. Assume the last coupon was just paid. What is its conversion factor?

12. Suppose there are two deliverable Bonds in the Treasury Bond futures contract, a 15-year 8% coupon bond and a 22-year 8% coupon bond. Assume the last coupon on both bonds was just paid. Which bond has the higher conversion factor? (Guess the answer first, and then verify it by computation.)

13. What is meant by the "delivery grade" in a commodity futures contract? What is the problem with defining the delivery grade too narrowly?

14. Identify the main institutional differences between futures contracts and forward contracts.

15. Explain the term "delivery options." What is the rationale for providing delivery options to the short position in futures contracts? What disadvantages for hedging are created by the presence of delivery options? For valuation?

16. What is the "closing out" of a position in futures markets? Why is closing out of contracts permitted in futures markets? Why is unilateral transfer or sale of the contract typically not allowed in forward markets?

17. An investor enters into a long position in 10 silver futures contracts at a futures price of $4.52/oz and closes out the position at a price of $4.46/oz. If one silver futures contract is for 5,000 ounces, what are the investor's gains or losses?

18. What is the settlement price? The opening price? The closing price?

19. An investor enters into a short futures position in 10 contracts in gold at a futures price of $276.50 per oz. The size of one futures contract is 100 oz. The initial margin per contract is $1,500, and the maintenance margin is $1,100.

    (a) What is the initial size of the margin account?

    (b) Suppose the futures settlement price on the first day is $278.00 per oz. What is the new balance in the margin account? Does a margin call occur? If so, assume that the account is topped back to its original level.

    (c) The futures settlement price on the second day is $281.00 per oz. What is the new balance in the margin account? Does a margin call occur? If so, assume that the account is topped back to its original level.

    (d) On the third day, the investor closes out the short position at a futures price of $276.00. What is the final balance in his margin account?

    (e) Ignoring interest costs, what are his total gains or losses?

20. The current price of gold is $642 per troy ounce. Assume that you initiate a long position in 10 COMEX gold futures contracts at this price on 7-July-2006. The initial margin is 5% of the initial price of the futures, and the maintenance margin is 3% of the initial price. Assume the following evolution of gold futures prices over the next five days, and compute the margin account assuming that you meet all margin calls.

| Date | Price per Ounce |
|---|---|
| 7-Jul-06 | 642 |
| 8-Jul-06 | 640 |
| 9-Jul-06 | 635 |
| 10-Jul-06 | 632 |
| 11-Jul-06 | 620 |
| 12-Jul-06 | 625 |

21. When is a futures market in "backwardation"? When is it in "contango"?

22. Suppose there are three deliverable bonds in a Treasury Bond futures contract whose current cash prices (for a face value of $100,000) and conversion factors are as follows:

(a) Bond 1: Price $98,750. Conversion factor 0.9814.

(b) Bond 2: Price $102,575. Conversion factor 1.018.

(c) Bond 3: Price $101,150. Conversion factor 1.004.

The futures price is $100,625. Which bond is currently the cheapest-to-deliver?

23. You enter into a short crude oil futures contract at $43 per barrel. The initial margin is $3,375 and the maintenance margin is $2,500. One contract is for 1,000 barrels of oil. By how much do oil prices have to change before you receive a margin call?

24. You take a long futures contract on the S&P 500 when the futures price is 1,107.40, and close it out three days later at a futures price of 1,131.75. One futures contract is for 250 × the index. Ignoring interest, what are your losses/gains?

25. An investor enters into 10 short futures contracts on the Dow Jones Index at a futures price of 10,106. Each contract is for 10 × the index. The investor closes out five contracts when the futures price is 10,201, and the remaining five when it is 10,074. Ignoring interest on the margin account, what are the investor's net profits or losses?

26. A bakery enters into 50 long wheat futures contracts on the CBoT at a futures price of $3.52/bushel. It closes out the contracts at maturity. The spot price at this time is $3.59/bushel. Ignoring interest, what are the bakery's gains or losses from its futures position?

27. An oil refining company enters into 1,000 long one-month crude oil futures contracts on NYMEX at a futures price of $43 per barrel. At maturity of the contract, the company rolls half of its position forward into new one-month futures and closes the remaining half. At this point, the spot price of oil is $44 per barrel, and the new one-month futures price is $43.50 per barrel. At maturity of this second contract, the company closes out its remaining position. Assume the spot price at this point is $46 per barrel. Ignoring interest, what are the company's gains or losses from its futures positions?

28. Define the following terms in the context of futures markets: market orders, limit orders, spread orders, one-cancels-the-other orders.

29. Distinguish between market-if-touched orders and stop orders.

30. You have a commitment to supply 10,000 oz of gold to a customer in three months' time at some specified price and are considering hedging the price risk that you face. In each of the following scenarios, describe the kind of order (market, limit, etc.) that you would use.

    (a) You are certain you wish to hedge and want to take up a futures position regardless of the price.

    (b) Gold futures prices have been on an upward trend in recent days and you are not sure you want to enter the market right now. However, if the trend continues, you are afraid you will be locked into too high a price. Weighing the pros and cons, you decide you want to take a futures position if the price continues to trend up and crosses $370 per oz.

    (c) Consider the same scenario as in b, but now suppose also that you expect a news announcement that you think will drive gold prices sharply lower. If matters turn out as you anticipate, you want to enter into a futures position at a futures price of $350/oz or lower. However, you recognize there is a probability the news announcement may be adverse and gold prices may continue to trend up. In this case, you want to buy futures and exit if prices touch $370/oz.

    (d) You want to institute a hedge only if you can obtain a gold futures price of $365/oz or less.

    (e) Gold futures prices have been on a downward trend in the last few days. You are hoping this continues but don't anticipate prices will fall too much below $362/oz, so you are willing to take the best price you can get once prices are at $364/oz.

31. The spot price of oil is $75 a barrel. The volatility of oil prices is extremely high at present. You think you can take advantage of this by placing a limit order to buy futures at $70 and a limit order to sell futures at $80 per barrel. Explain when this strategy will work and when it will not.

32. The spread between May and September wheat futures is currently $0.06 per bushel. You expect this spread to widen to at least $0.10 per bushel. How would you use a spread order to bet on your view?

33. The spread between one-month and three-month crude oil futures is $3 per barrel. You expect this spread to narrow sharply. Explain how you would use a spread order given this outlook.

34. Suppose you anticipate a need for corn in three months' time and are using corn futures to hedge the price risk that you face. How is the value of your position affected by a strengthening of the basis at maturity?

35. A *short hedger* is one who is short futures in order to hedge a spot cash-flow risk. A *long hedger* is similarly one who goes long futures to hedge an existing risk. How does a weakening of the basis affect the positions of short and long hedgers?

36. Suppose you deliver a grade other than the cheapest-to-deliver grade on a futures contract. Would the amount you receive (the conversion factor times the futures price) exceed, equal, or fall short of the spot price of the grade you deliver?

# Futures Trading and US Regulation: A Brief History

As economic mechanisms go, forward trading is very old.[1] The Futures Industry Association traces the origin of forward trading to India around the year 2,000 BC. There is also evidence of forward markets in Greco-Roman Europe. More recently, there were organized forward markets in 17th-century Japan and Europe. The world's first futures exchange was likely the Dojima Rice Market set up in Osaka, Japan, in 1730.

Nonetheless, it is with 19th-century America, particularly the grain markets of Chicago, that modern futures markets are most closely associated. Their immediate predecessor in the US was a contract form called the "to arrive" contract by which buyers and sellers contracted for the delivery of grain in the future at a fixed price. By the time of the US Civil War, the "to arrive" contracts had themselves become traded instruments, bought and sold in anticipation of price movements and used for both speculation and hedging. These were replaced by standardized "futures contracts" on the Chicago Board of Trade (CBoT), the first organized futures exchange in the US.

The CBoT was established in 1848 and received a charter from the State of Illinois in 1859. It was swiftly followed by a number of other exchanges. The Milwaukee Chamber of Commerce was organized in 1858 to serve as a mechanism for trading grain. The New York Produce Exchange opened for commodity trading in 1861, and the New York Gold Exchange, New York Cotton Exchange, and New York Butter and Cheese Exchange (later the New York Mercantile Exchange) followed in 1864, 1870, and 1872, respectively. The Kansas City Board of Trade was incorporated in 1876, the same year the Merchant Association of St. Louis was organized. In all, over a thousand exchanges sprang up all over the US by the late 19th century.

The rapid growth was accompanied by rampant abuses and attempts at market manipulation. "Plungers," as market manipulators were called, made repeated attempts to corner or squeeze the market. Such attempts were commonplace. According to Markham (1987), "it was reported that [at the CBoT in 1868] there were three corners in wheat, two in corn, one in oats, one attempted corner in rye, and another threatened in pork."

Many corners were run successfully and made fortunes for the plungers. Others were spectacular failures leading to huge losses. One such failure was the attempted corner of the December 1897 wheat futures contract on the CBoT by Joe Leiter, a speculator. The corner was broken when the "meat king" P. D. Armour, who was the largest short, hired a fleet of boats to break through the ice and bring grain into Chicago. Another was "Black Friday" in New York's gold market in 1869. An attempted corner of the gold market by Jay Gould and Jim Fisk failed when President Ulysses Grant's decision to sell gold from the US Treasury led to a collapse in the price of gold and a suspension of gold dealings for a week.

Instances of market manipulation have come down dramatically in recent years but have not vanished. A huge default in 1976 on thousands of contracts on the now-defunct Maine potato contract on the NYMEX appears to have been caused by a classic squeeze play in which the size of the long positions far exceeded available supply. In 1980, the "Silver Crisis"

---

[1] An excellent reference, and the source of much of the historical material in this section, is Markham (1987).

occurred when the Hunt brothers of Texas attempted to corner the world silver market. It is estimated that at one time, between their long spot and long futures positions, they controlled about 200 million oz of silver, about 50% of the US annual consumption level. The price of silver rose from about $6/oz in December 1980 to around $50/oz six months later. The attempted corner was broken by a combination of intervention by regulators and tough action by the exchanges that forced the Hunt brothers to unwind their positions and take losses in the billions of dollars.

# Futures Regulation in the US

The earliest attempt at US federal regulation of futures markets came in 1861. In the early years of the US Civil War, the price of gold rose and fell with the fortunes of the Union army. Congress responded by prohibiting futures trading in gold in an attempt to stabilize its price. The legislation was repealed after a few weeks when it proved ineffective. By the late 19th century, however, speculative trading in futures markets was widely—and in the eyes of its supporters, unfairly—blamed for price swings in agricultural commodities. Congress and the states made numerous attempts to regulate or abolish futures trading.

Federal involvement began in 1914 with the Cotton Futures Act, which established the use of federal standards for grading cotton. Active regulation came in 1922 with the Grain Futures Act, which established a licensing system for futures exchanges or "contract markets" as they were called. The Grain Futures Act was replaced by the Commodity Exchange Act (CEA) of 1936. The CEA extended regulatory oversight to traders and brokerage firms and established the Commodity Exchange Administration, the principal regulator of futures trading in the US for almost four decades. In 1974, Congress enacted the Commodity Futures Trading Act, giving birth to the Commodity Futures Trading Commission (CFTC) as the regulatory agency in charge of futures markets.

The birth of the financial futures market in the 1970s (see Section 2.2) was the first challenge to the regulatory authority of the CFTC. The Securities and Exchange Commission (SEC) challenged the CFTC's approval of futures trading on GNMA mortgage-backed securities. The SEC argued that since the asset underlying the proposed futures contract was a security rather than a commodity, the SEC, not the CFTC, should have the power to approve trading in the contract.

The enactment of the Shad-Johnson Accords by Congress in 1982 delineated responsibility between the agencies. (John Shad was then the chairman of the SEC and Phil Johnson was his counterpart in the CFTC.) The SEC was given jurisdiction over options on securities and options on indices of securities (e.g., stock indices). The CFTC was given jurisdiction over all futures contracts including futures on securities, futures on indices of securities, and options on futures on such indices. But the 1982 legislation gave the SEC effective veto power over new stock index futures contracts to ensure they were not capable of easy manipulation.

In 2000, the Commodity Futures Modernization Act (CFMA) was signed into US law by President Bill Clinton, after very little debate on its provisions in either the House or the Senate. The CFMA provided for a major overhaul of the CEA as well as regulatory domains of the SEC and CFTC. It allowed the trading of futures contracts on single stocks and on "narrowly based" stock indices, futures contracts that had been prohibited under the Shad-Johnson Accord. The SEC and CFTC were given joint regulatory oversight of these instruments. The CFMA also explicitly excluded certain over-the-counter derivatives transactions (mainly swap agreements) from CFTC oversight. Perhaps the most controversial part of the CFMA was the "Enron loophole," which exempted most over-the-counter energy trades and trading on electronic energy commodity markets from government regulation.

Following the financial crisis of 2008–09 and the heavy losses incurred by AIG and others from dealing in credit default swaps among other instruments, the CFMA has come in for substantial criticism for de-emphasizing regulation of the derivatives industry. It seems very likely at the time of writing this chapter (early 2009) that the CFMA will be repealed or modified in important ways in the near future.

# 3

# Pricing Forwards and Futures I: The Basic Theory

## 3.1 Introduction

This chapter and the next mark the begining of our exploration into the pricing of derivative securities. This chapter is mainly theoretical: it presents and develops the basic ideas that drive the pricing of forwards and futures, first in the context of forward contracts, then futures. Building on this foundation, Chapter 4 then examines how well the theory does in practice and also a number of other issues of importance.

The pricing of forward contracts—actually, the pricing of *all* derivatives—is based on a simple but very powerful concept known as *replication*. Simply put, replication is the idea that the price of a derivative should be the cost of creating the same outcome synthetically (i.e., by using other securities). A maintained assumption in this process is that of *no arbitrage*, that is, that markets do not permit the creation of something out of nothing. We begin by making this assumption precise.

### The Main Assumption: No Arbitrage

Throughout the book, we assume that markets do not permit *arbitrage* opportunities. The word "arbitrage" has acquired a variety of meanings in the popular finance lexicon, ranging from its original connotation of a *riskless* profit opportunity to a more liberal interpretation as a portfolio that generates a superior risk-adjusted return. In this book, we use the word only in its narrow classical sense: *an arbitrage is a portfolio that guarantees net cash inflows without any net cash outflows*. Such a portfolio is a free lunch, the equivalent of the metaphorical $10 bill lying on the pavement. It represents an extreme form of market inefficiency in which two baskets of assets that are essentially identical trade at different prices.

The no-arbitrage assumption is not to be taken literally as implying that arbitrage opportunities can never arise in the market, but rather that they cannot *persist*. That is, while a misalignment of prices may create such opportunities, market participants take advantage of them as they arise, and prices adjust to eliminate the arbitrage. (Someone eventually trousers the $10—it does not continue lying there.) As such, the no-arbitrage condition is a statement of minimal market rationality.

## The Guiding Principle: Replication

The principle of replication that underlies the pricing and hedging of all derivative securities is based on a simple idea. The payoffs of a derivative are determined by changes in the price of the underlying asset. Therefore, it "should" be possible to re-create these payoffs by directly using the underlying asset and, perhaps, cash (borrowing or lending at the risk-free rate). If such a portfolio can be constructed, it is called a *replicating portfolio*; the derivative is then said to be "synthesized" by the replicating portfolio.

The derivative and its replicating portfolio lead, by definition, to identical outcomes, so, under the no-arbitrage condition, they must have the same cost. The cost of the replicating portfolio is readily computed since it consists of only the underlying spot asset and cash. Thus, the cost of the derivative, its so-called "fair price," is identified.

The key step in exploiting these ideas is identifying the composition of the replicating portfolio. For forward contracts, this is a simple task, as we now describe.

## 3.2 Pricing Forwards by Replication

Some notation first. Let date 0 denote the current date and date $T$ the maturity date of a given forward contract. The length of the contract is thus $T$ years. (We always measure time in years.) Let $S$ denote the current price of the asset underlying the forward contract and let $S_T$ denote its price at $T$.

Consider an investor with a long position in a forward contract with delivery price $F$. At maturity of the contract, the investor receives one unit of the underlying asset and pays the agreed-upon delivery price. To replicate this final holding, the investor can simply buy one unit of the underlying asset at date 0 and hold it to date $T$. Both strategies result in the investor's holding one unit of the asset at time $T$. Therefore, their costs in present value terms must also coincide.

What are these costs? The forward contract involves no cash flows up to date $T$ and a single cash outflow equal to the delivery price $F$ on date $T$. Viewed from date 0, the cost of this strategy is $PV(F)$, the present value of an amount $F$ payable at time $T$.

The replicating strategy results in a cash outflow of $S$ at date 0 for purchasing the spot asset. It may, in addition, involve other cash flows. These could be cash *inflows* such as dividends or coupons received as a result of holding the asset (e.g., if the asset is a financial security like a stock or bond); we call these "holding benefits." Alternatively, there may be further cash *outflows* such as storage or insurance costs ("holding costs"), especially if the asset is a physical commodity such as wheat or gold. Let $M$ denote the present value of the net holding costs:

$$M = PV(\text{Holding Costs}) - PV(\text{Holding Benefits}) \tag{3.1}$$

The net cost of the replicating strategy is then

$$S + M \tag{3.2}$$

Setting this equal to the cost of the forward contract, we have

$$PV(F) = S + M \tag{3.3}$$

Equation (3.3) is the fundamental theoretical pricing equation for forward contracts. If it does not hold, an arbitrage opportunity arises:

- If $PV(F) > S + M$, the forward is *overvalued* relative to the cost of replication. We can sell forward, buy spot, and make a riskless profit. This is called "cash-and-carry" arbitrage.

- If $PV(F) < S + M$, the forward is *undervalued* relative to the cost of replication. We can buy forward, sell spot, and make a riskless profit. This is "reverse cash-and-carry" arbitrage.

From (3.3), the unique delivery price $F$ at which arbitrage is not possible may be determined from knowledge of three things: (i) the current spot price $S$, (ii) the present value $M$ of the cost of holding the spot asset to date $T$, and (iii) the level of interest rates, which is needed to calculate present values. This is the central message of this chapter. The argument leading to (3.3) is called the "cost of carry" method of pricing forwards since it determines the forward price as a function of the cost of "carrying" the spot asset to maturity.

## Some Assumptions

To develop these ideas in a simple and concise manner, we will make use of three assumptions in addition to the main no-arbitrage condition:

**Assumption 1.** There are no transactions costs.

**Assumption 2.** There are no restrictions on short sales. In particular, the full proceeds of short sales are available immediately for investment to the short seller.

**Assumption 3.** The (default-)risk-free rate of interest is the same for borrowing and lending.

These assumptions are imposed in the interests of simplicity and to keep attention focused on the main ideas. They are not, of course, always realistic (particularly Assumption 2). In the next chapter (see Sections 4.2–4.4), we show that each assumption can be dropped at the cost of adding a bit of complication to the analysis. In particular, we obtain an arbitrage-free "band" of prices rather than a single price, with the size of the band depending on the extent of violation of the assumptions (e.g., the size of transactions costs).

## Interest-Rate Convention

Finally, to compute the present values in expression (3.3), we need the interest rates to be used for discounting cash flows occurring between dates 0 and $T$. In practice, the convention for quoting interest rates varies widely across markets and contracts. Appendix 3A describes different compounding conventions (annual, semiannual, continuous, etc.).

Different compounding and interest-rate conventions are, however, merely different measuring sticks for the same concept, analogous to measuring height in feet and inches instead of meters and centimeters. As illustrated in Appendix 3A, interest-rate quotes under one compounding convention may easily be converted to quotes under any other convention. The exact convention we choose to use to develop the theory is solely a matter of convenience.

We adopt the convention in this chapter that interest rates are quoted in continuously compounded terms on an annualized basis. Thus, a $T$-year interest rate of $r$ means that \$1 invested for $T$ years at the rate $r$ grows by maturity to $\$e^{rT}$. In the numerical examples, we further simplify matters by treating each month as 1/12 of a year. Thus, a three-month interest rate of 10% means that \$1 invested at this rate for three months grows to

$$e^{(0.10)(1/4)} = \$1.0253$$

## Forward Pricing Formulae with Continuous Compounding

Let $r$ be the rate of interest applicable to a $T$-year horizon. Under the continuous compounding convention,

$$PV(F) = e^{-rT} F$$

Using this in the formula (3.3), we obtain $e^{-rT}F = S + M$, or

$$F = e^{rT}(S+M) \qquad (3.4)$$

Equation (3.4) is the promised forward pricing formula under continuous compounding. For the special case where there are no holding costs or benefits ($M = 0$), it becomes

$$F = e^{rT}S \qquad (3.5)$$

## 3.3 Examples

We present two examples in this section to illustrate the mechanics of arbitrage when the forward pricing formula is violated. The first example keeps matters simple by assuming no holding costs or benefits, while the second example allows for such interim cash flows.

**Example 3.1**

Suppose the current spot price of gold is $S_0 = \$350$ per oz, the risk-free three-month rate of interest is 3%, and there are no costs of holding gold. What is the three-month forward price of gold?

From (3.5), the unique arbitrage-free forward price is

$$F = e^{(0.03)(1/4)} \times 350 = 352.635 \qquad (3.6)$$

Any other forward price will lead to an arbitrage opportunity as we now show.

### (A) Arbitrage from an Overvalued Forward

Suppose $F > 352.635$, say $F = 355$. Then, the forward is *overvalued* relative to spot by the amount $355 - 352.635 = 2.365$. To take advantage, we sell the relatively overvalued contract (the forward) and buy the relatively undervalued one (the spot asset). The specific strategy is:

1. Enter into a short forward position to deliver 1 oz of gold in three months at the delivery price of $355.
2. Buy 1 oz of gold in the spot market and hold it for three months.
3. Borrow $350 for three months at the interest rate of 3%.

Why is borrowing part of this strategy? The short forward position results in a cash inflow only in three months' time whereas purchasing the spot asset requires a cash outflow today. This cash outflow must be funded either explicitly (by borrowing) or implicitly (by utilizing surplus cash, in which case we are borrowing from ourselves, so the interest represents an opportunity cost). As a consequence of the borrowing, all net cash flows are moved to the maturity date of the forward contract.

The resulting set of cash flows is summarized in Table 3.1. There are no net cash flows at inception since the required cash outflow of $350 to buy the spot asset is matched by

**TABLE 3.1** Cash Flows in Example 3.1 from Arbitraging an Overvalued Forward

| Source of Cash Flow | Initial Cash Flow | Final Cash Flow |
|---|---|---|
| Short forward | – | +355.000 |
| Long spot | −350.000 | – |
| Borrowing | +350.000 | −352.635 |
| Net cash flows | – | +2.365 |

**TABLE 3.2** Cash Flows in Example 3.1 from Arbitraging an Undervalued Forward

| Source of Cash Flow | Initial Cash Flow | Final Cash Flow |
|---|---|---|
| Long forward | – | −351.000 |
| Short spot | +350.000 | – |
| Investment | −350.000 | +352.635 |
| Net cash flows | – | +1.635 |

the inflow of $350 from the borrowing, and, of course, there is no up-front cost to enter a forward contract. Nor are there any interim cash flows between inception and maturity since there are no costs of holding gold by assumption.

At maturity of the forward contract, the 1 oz of gold is delivered to the long forward position, resulting in a cash inflow of $355 from the forward. There is also a cash outflow of $e^{(0.03)(1/4)} \times 350 = \$352.635$ towards repaying the borrowing. Thus, there is a net cash inflow of $2.365 at this point, representing the arbitrage profits.

## (B) Arbitrage from an Undervalued Forward

Now suppose that $F < 352.635$, say $F = 351$. Now the forward is *undervalued* relative to spot by $1.635, so we buy forward and sell spot to take advantage of the mispricing. Specifically:

1. Enter into a long forward position to purchase 1 oz of gold in three months at the delivery price of $351.
2. Short 1 oz of gold in the spot market and hold the short position for three months.
3. Invest the proceeds of $350 from the short sale for three months at the interest rate of 3%.

The investment in this strategy plays the same role as the borrowing in the earlier strategy. The cash flows are summarized in Table 3.2. Once again, there are no net cash flows at inception since the cash inflow of $350 from the short sale is matched by the cash outflow of $350 for the investment. There are no net interim cash flows since gold has no holding costs.

At maturity, we pay $351 and receive 1 oz of gold from the forward contract that we use to cover our short position. We also receive a cash inflow of $e^{(0.03)(1/4)} \times 350 = \$352.635$ from the investment. Thus, there is a net cash inflow of $1.635, representing our arbitrage profits. ∎

The assumption that there are no holding costs or benefits is often not a reasonable one. Holding financial assets such as bonds or equities may result in holding benefits in the form of coupons or dividends. Holding commodities may involve substantial storage and insurance costs; the costs of storing oil, for instance, amount, on an annualized basis, to about 20% of the cost of the oil itself. Such interim costs or benefits affect the cost of the replication strategy and should be taken into account in calculating the forward price. The following example deals with such a situation.

**Example 3.2**

Consider a six-month forward contract on a bond. Suppose the current spot price $S$ of the bond is $95 and that the bond will pay a coupon of $5 in three months' time. Finally, suppose the rate of interest is 10% for all maturities. What is the arbitrage-free forward price of the bond?

In terms of our notation, we are given $S = 95$, $T = 6$ months $= 1/2$ year, and $r = 10\%$. Since holding the bond involves a cash *inflow*, $M$ is negative and is given by *minus* the present value of $5 receivable in 3 months:

$$M = -e^{-(0.10)(0.25)} \times 5 = -4.877$$

Therefore, from the forward-pricing formula (3.4), we have

$$F = e^{(0.10)(1/2)} \times (95 - 4.877) = e^{(0.10)(1/2)} \times (90.123) = 94.74$$

Any other delivery price leads to an arbitrage opportunity.

## (A) Arbitrage from an Overvalued Forward

Suppose $F > 94.74$, for example, $F = 95.25$. Then, the forward is *overvalued* relative to spot by $0.51, so we should buy spot, sell forward, and borrow. There are many ways to set up the precise strategy. One is to split the initial borrowing of $95 into two parts with one part repaid in three months with the $5 coupon and the other part repaid after six months with the delivery price received from the forward contract. More precisely:

1. Enter into a short forward position to sell the bond in six months' time for $95.25.
2. Buy 1 unit of the spot asset for $95 and hold it up to $T$.
3. Borrow $PV(5) = e^{-(0.10)(1/4)} \times 5 = \$4.877$ for repayment in three months and $90.123 for repayment in six months.

The cash flows from this strategy are summarized in Table 3.3. There are no net cash flows at inception since the cash outflow of $95 required to purchase the bond is matched by the total inflows from the borrowings ($4.877 + 90.123 = 95$). The only interim cash flows occur in three months. At that point, an amount of $5 is due to repay the three-month borrowing, but we receive $5 as coupon from the bond we hold. Thus, there are no net cash flows at this point either.

At maturity of the forward contract, there is a cash inflow of $95.25 from the forward position when the bond is delivered, and a cash outflow of

$$e^{(0.10)(0.50)} \times 90.123 = 94.74$$

towards repaying the six-month borrowing. Thus, there is a net cash inflow of $95.25 - 94.74 = 0.51$, representing the arbitrage profits.

## (B) Arbitrage from an Undervalued Forward

Now suppose $F < 94.74$, say $F = 94.25$. Then the forward is undervalued relative to spot by $0.49, so we buy forward, sell spot, and invest. In greater detail:

1. Enter into a long forward position to sell the bond in six months' time for $94.25.

**TABLE 3.3** Cash Flows in Example 3.2 from Arbitraging an Overvalued Forward

| Source of Cash Flow | Initial Cash Flow | Interim Cash Flow | Final Cash Flow |
|---|---|---|---|
| Short forward | – | – | +95.25 |
| Long spot | −95.000 | +5.000 | – |
| 3-month borrowing | +4.877 | −5.000 | – |
| 6-month borrowing | +90.123 | – | −94.74 |
| Net cash flows | – | – | +0.51 |

**TABLE 3.4** Cash Flows in Example 3.2 from Arbitraging an Undervalued Forward

| Source of Cash Flow | Initial Cash Flow | Interim Cash Flow | Final Cash Flow |
|---|---|---|---|
| Long forward | – | – | –94.25 |
| Short spot | +95.000 | –5.000 | – |
| 3-month investment | –4.877 | +5.000 | – |
| 6-month investment | –90.123 | – | +94.74 |
| Net cash flows | – | – | +0.49 |

2. Short 1 unit of the bond for $95 and hold the short position up to $T$.
3. Invest $PV(5) = e^{-(0.10)(1/4)} \times 5 = \$4.877$ for three months and $90.123 for six months.

Table 3.4 summarizes the resulting cash flows. There are no net initial cash flows. There is a cash inflow of $5 after three months from the three-month investment, but there is also a coupon of $5 due on the short bond. Thus, there is no net cash flow at this point either. After six months, the contract is at maturity. At this point, we receive

$$e^{(0.10)(0.50)} \times 90.123 = \$94.74$$

from the six-month investment. We pay $94.25 on the forward contract and receive the bond, which we use to close out the short position. This leaves us with a net cash inflow of $0.49 representing arbitrage profits. ∎

## 3.4  Forward Pricing on Currencies and Related Assets

An important difference between a currency and other underlyings such as wheat is that when we buy and store one bushel of wheat, it remains one bushel of wheat at maturity (assuming, of course, that the rats don't get at it!). In contrast, when we buy and store currency, the currency earns interest at the appropriate rate, so one unit of the currency grows to *more* than one unit over time. This means that the fundamental forward pricing formula (3.3) must be modified for such cases.

As a specific motivation, consider a currency forward contract (say, on British pound sterling denoted £) maturing in $T$ years. An investor taking a long position in this contract pays the delivery price $F$ at time $T$ and receives £1 at that point. To replicate this outcome using the spot asset, the investor cannot simply buy £1 today and hold it to $T$. Why not? The pound sterling the investor holds earns *interest* at the rate applicable to $T$-year sterling deposits, so the £1 would grow to *more* than £1 at $T$. For example, if $T = 3$ months and the three-month interest rate on sterling is 8%, then the initial £1 will grow to

$$e^{(0.08)(1/4)} = £1.02$$

in three months, so the investor will end up overreplicating the outcome of the forward contract.

To correct for this, we must take interest yield into account in constructing the replicating strategy. We do this by adjusting the number of units of the spot currency we buy at the outset so that we are left with exactly one unit at maturity. In this example, this may be accomplished by buying only £(1/1.02) = £0.98 initially. When this amount is invested at the 8% rate for three months, we will receive £1 at maturity.

We describe the forward pricing formula that results when the replicating strategy is modified in this way. Then we provide an example to illustrate the arguments.

## The General Pricing Formula for Currency Forwards

For simplicity, we continue referring to the foreign currency as pound sterling (GBP). Denote the spot price of this currency by $S$. As usual, $S$ denotes the current price in US dollars (USD) of one unit of the underlying spot asset. Here, the underlying is pound sterling, so $S$ refers to the exchange rate USD per GBP. Here, and elsewhere in the book where it helps to simplify exposition, we shall use the common symbols $ for USD and £ for GBP.

If we take a long forward position with a delivery price of $F$, then in $T$ years, we pay $\$F$ and receive £1. Viewed from today, the cost of this strategy in USD is $PV(\$F)$, or what is the same thing,

$$F \cdot PV(\$1) \qquad (3.7)$$

(We write the $ sign inside the parentheses to emphasize that present values are computed using the USD interest rate.)

To replicate the outcome of the forward, we must construct a strategy that leaves us with £1 in $T$ years. But this is a simple task: all we need do is buy the present value of £1 today and invest it so that it grows to £1 by time $T$. Of course, to calculate this present value, we must use the interest rate on pounds, not on dollars, since we can invest the purchased pounds only at the pound interest rate. To emphasize this point, we write $PV(£1)$ for the present value.

The cost of this replicating strategy in dollars is the number of pounds purchased today (which is $PV(£1)$) times the current dollar price per pound (which is $S$):

$$S \cdot PV(£1) \qquad (3.8)$$

Equating the costs of the two strategies, we obtain

$$F \cdot PV(\$1) = S \cdot PV(£1) \qquad (3.9)$$

so that

$$F = S \, \frac{PV(£1)}{PV(\$1)} \qquad (3.10)$$

Expression (3.10) is the fundamental pricing equation for foreign currency forwards. It is also referred to as *covered interest-rate parity*. It expresses the arbitrage-free forward price as a function of three variables: the spot exchange rate, domestic interest rates, and interest rates on the foreign currency.

## Currency Forward Prices under Continuous Compounding

Suppose we express interest rates on both currencies using a continuous compounding convention. Let $d$ denote the $T$-year interest rate on pound sterling, and, as usual, let $r$ be the $T$-year interest rate on the dollar. Then, from (3.10), we have

$$F = S \, \frac{e^{-dT}}{e^{-rT}}$$

Rearranging this expression, we obtain

$$F = e^{(r-d)T} S \qquad (3.11)$$

Expression (3.11) is the currency forward pricing formula when interest rates are expressed in continuously compounded terms. This formula has an intuitive interpretation. When we buy the spot asset, we give up dollars, which has an opportunity cost represented by the dollar interest rate $r$. However, we receive pound sterling in exchange, which carries a holding benefit represented by the sterling interest rate $d$. The difference $r - d$ represents the net cost of holding spot that is reflected in forward prices.

**Example 3.3**

Consider a forward contract on pound sterling. Suppose the spot exchange rate is \$1.60/£. Suppose also that the three-month interest rate on dollars is 6% while the three-month interest rate on pounds is 8%, both in continuously compounded terms. What is the arbitrage-free three-month forward price?

In terms of our notation, we are given: $S = 1.60$, $T = 3$ months $= 1/4$ year, $r = 0.06$, and $d = 0.08$. Therefore, from (3.11), the unique arbitrage-free forward price is

$$F = e^{(0.06-0.08)(1/4)}(1.60) = 1.592$$

## (A) Arbitrage from an Overvalued Forward

Suppose the delivery price in the forward contract differed from this quantity; for example, suppose we have $F = 1.615$. Then, the forward is *overvalued* relative to spot, so we sell forward and buy spot to create a riskless profit. The complete strategy is:

1. Enter into a short forward contract to deliver £1 for \$1.615 in three months.
2. Buy $£e^{-dT} = £0.98$ at the spot price of \$1.60/£.
3. Invest £0.98 for three months at the interest rate of 8%.
4. Finance the spot purchase by borrowing \$(0.98)(1.60) = \$1.568 for three months at 6%.

Note that we buy only $£e^{-dT}$ units at the outset because we want to have only £1 at maturity.

There are clearly no net initial cash flows in this strategy, nor, of course, are there interim cash flows. At maturity, we receive £1 from the investment, which we deliver on the forward contract and receive \$1.615. We must also repay the borrowing. This leads to a cash outflow of

$$\$1.568 \times e^{(0.06)(1/4)} = \$1.592$$

Thus, there is a net cash inflow of \$0.023 at maturity representing arbitrage profits from the mispricing.

## (B) Arbitrage from an Undervalued Forward

Similarly, suppose the delivery price in the forward contract is less than 1.592, say $F = 1.570$. Then, the forward is *undervalued* relative to spot, so we should buy forward and sell spot. The complete strategy is:

1. Enter into a long forward contract to buy £1 for \$1.57 in three months.
2. Sell $£e^{-dT} = £0.98$ at the rate of \$1.60 per pound and receive \$(1.60)(0.98) = \$1.568.
3. Borrow £0.98 for three months at the interest rate of 8%.
4. Invest \$1.568 for three months at the interest rate of 6%.

Note, once again, that we borrow and sell only $£e^{-dT}$ initially, since this will lead to a cash outflow of £1 at maturity, which we can meet from the £1 received on the forward contract.

Once again, there is no net initial cash flow and there are no interim cash flows. At maturity, we pay \$1.57 and receive £1 from the forward contract. We owe

$$£0.98 \times e^{(0.08)(1/4)} = £1$$

on the borrowing. Finally, we receive

$$\$1.568 \times e^{(0.06)(1/4)} = 1.592$$

from the dollar investment. Summing all this up, we have a net cash inflow at maturity of \$0.022 representing arbitrage profits from the mispricing. ∎

## Pricing Forwards on Stock Indices

In addition to currency forwards, the formula (3.11) has other uses also. One lies in the pricing of forwards on stock indices. A stock index is a basket of a number of stocks constructed according to specified rules. In the next chapter, we consider stock index forwards and show that one simple way to price these forwards is to use the formula (3.11) with $d$ denoting the dividend yield on the index. The details are in Section 4.6.

# 3.5 Forward-Rate Agreements

The idea of replication can also be used to price forward contracts such as forward-rate agreements or FRAs—and generalizations of FRAs such as interest rate swaps—that depend directly on the level of an interest rate rather than on the price of a traded asset or commodity. FRAs are treated in detail in Chapter 6, so we do not present the ideas here.

# 3.6 Concept Check

In recent years, several countries have pegged their currency to a foreign currency, thereby fixing the exchange rate. Argentina and Hong Kong, for example, have used pegs tying their currencies to the US dollar.

Consider a currency (call it the "tiger") that is pegged to the dollar. Suppose for specificity that it is pegged at 10 tigers per dollar. Suppose that the peg is widely considered credible in financial markets, i.e., market participants do not believe it is likely to break. What is the one-month forward price on the tiger? Think carefully before attempting an answer!

A little reflection shows that the forward price cannot be greater than 10 tigers per dollar. Suppose, for instance, that it is 11 tigers/dollar. Then an arbitrage can be created by buying tigers forward at 11 tigers/dollar (i.e., roughly at \$0.09/tiger), waiting until maturity of the forward contract, and selling the delivered tigers at the spot price of 10 tigers/dollar (i.e., at \$0.10/tiger).

Similarly, it cannot be less than 10 tigers per dollar. Suppose it were (say) 9 tigers per dollar. An arbitrage can be created by selling tigers forward at 9 tigers/dollar (i.e., roughly at \$0.11/tiger), waiting until maturity of the forward contract, and buying and delivering the required tigers at the spot price of 10 tigers/dollar (i.e., at \$0.10/tiger).

Thus, the forward price *must be* 10 tigers/dollar. We have identified this arbitrage-free forward price without knowledge of the interest rates as required by the formula (3.11) for currency forwards. Does this mean that (3.11) does not apply to this case?

On the contrary! We have shown that (3.11) *must* always hold or there is an arbitrage. So how are these two statements to be reconciled?

The key lies in noting that we derived the forward price of 10 tigers/dollar *assuming the peg was fully credible.* But if the peg is fully credible, the dollar interest rate $r$ *must be* the same as the tiger interest rate $d$. If the dollar interest rate is lower, we can create a simple arbitrage by borrowing in dollars at the dollar interest rate, converting to tigers, investing at the tiger interest rate, and converting back to dollars at maturity. The reverse strategy creates an arbitrage if the dollar interest rate is higher. Thus, we must have $r = d$, so using the formula (3.11) would have given us the same answer.

All these arguments rely on the peg being credible beyond doubt. If there is some suspicion that the peg might break, spot and forward prices will not coincide; neither will dollar and tiger interest rates. In all cases, however, forward and spot prices *must* be linked via (3.11), or an arbitrage opportunity arises.

# 3.7 The Marked-to-Market Value of a Forward Contract

In dealing with a portfolio of derivatives, we are often faced with the question: how much is a particular derivative contract, entered into a while ago but not yet at maturity, worth today? That is, what is its *marked-to-market* value? This value is used in practice to settle forward contracts prior to maturity. This section examines the answer for forward contracts.

## An Intuitive Answer

Consider a specific example. Suppose we hold a long position in a forward contract on copper with a delivery price $D = \$0.80$ per lb that was entered into earlier and now has one month left to maturity. Suppose that the *current* forward price for the same contract (i.e., copper of the same grade with one month to maturity) is $\$F$ per lb. What is the marked-to-market value (henceforth, simply "value") of the contract we hold? That is, how much better or worse off are we for having locked-in a delivery price of $D = \$0.80$ per lb compared to the prevailing forward price of $F$?

An intuitive answer to this question is easily given. Suppose $F > D$, say $F = \$0.82$. Then, we are better off by $\$0.02$ per lb for having locked-in the delivery price of $D = \$0.80$. This difference of $\$0.02$ in the delivery price is realized only in a month's time when the contract is at maturity, so has a present value of $PV(0.02)$. This is the value of the contract we hold.

Analogously, suppose $F < D$, say, $F = \$0.79$ per lb. Then, we are worse off by $\$0.01$ per lb for having locked-in a delivery price of $\$0.80$ per lb, so the contract now has a value of $PV(-0.01)$.

These arguments suggest that, in either case, the value of the contract to the long position is $PV(F - D)$. The value to the *short* position is just the negative of this value and is given by $PV(D - F)$. If $F > D$, the contract has positive value to the long position and negative value to the short. If $F < D$, the opposite is true.

## Valuation by Reversal

We can derive these expressions more formally by examining the question: how much value would be gained (or lost) if we were to unwind the contract right away and lock-in our profits or losses?

We cannot unwind a forward contract by selling it unilaterally. Nonetheless, we can achieve the functional equivalent of a sale by *reversal*. Reversal simply involves taking the opposite position to the original in another forward contract with the same maturity date as the original. Thus, for example, if our original contract was a long position in a forward contract to buy 100 barrels of oil in April, we enter into a short forward contract to sell 100 barrels of oil in April.

Note that reversal entails some credit risk unlike the closing-out of a futures position. If the counterparty with whom we signed our original forward agreement defaults, our obligations still remain on the contract used to reverse the original one.

Ignoring credit risk, reversal achieves the same outcome as a sale of the contract in that there is no net obligation in the underlying at maturity: the long and short positions are equal in size and cancel each other out. However, there *is* a net cash flow: the original long position had a delivery price of $D$ while the new contract used for reversal can be entered into only at the prevailing forward price $F$. This means we pay $D$ on the original long forward position but receive $F$ on the short forward contract used for reversal. The net cash flow is $F - D$. The present value of this net cash flow, $PV(F - D)$, is the value of the original contract to a long position. The negative of this quantity, $PV(D - F)$, is the value of the original contract to a short position.

---

**Example 3.4**

A US investor holds a one-month short forward position on pound sterling. The contract calls for the investor to sell £2 million in one month at a delivery price of $1.61 per pound. The current forward price for delivery in one month is $F = \$1.5850$ per pound. Suppose the one-month rate of interest is 6%. What is the value of the investor's position?

The investor has locked in a delivery price of $D = \$1.61$ per pound compared to the prevailing forward rate of $F = \$1.5850$ per pound. As the holder of a *short* forward, the investor is better off by $0.0250 per pound. This difference will be received in one month's time, so its present value is

$$PV(D - F) = e^{-(0.06)(1/12)} \times 0.0250 = 0.024875$$

Since the contract calls for the delivery of £2 million, the value of the investor's position is

$$2{,}000{,}000 \times 0.024875 = \$49{,}750$$

If the parties to the contract agree to unwind it today, the long position in the contract would have to pay the investor $49,750. ∎

---

**Example 3.5**

Suppose an investor holds a long forward position on 10,000 shares of Microsoft stock with a delivery price of $25 per share and maturity in two months. Assume no dividends are expected from Microsoft over the next two months. Suppose the two-month interest rate is 4% and Microsoft stock is currently trading at $24.50. What is the arbitrage-free forward price $\$F$ on the stock for delivery in two months? Given $\$F$, what is the marked-to-market value of the investor's position?

In our notation, we are given $D = 25$ (the delivery price already locked in) and $T = 2$ months $= 1/6$ year. We are not given $F$, but are asked to calculate it from the given information. Since no dividends are expected on the stock, the arbitrage-free forward price can be obtained using the zero holding costs formula (3.5). This results in

$$F = e^{(0.04)(1/6)} \times 24.50 = 24.664$$

Since the investor has a long forward position, the value per share of having a delivery price of $D = 25$ is

$$PV(F - D) = e^{-(0.04)(1/6)} \times [24.664 - 25] = -0.3339$$

Since the forward contract calls for the delivery of 10,000 shares, the total marked-to-market value of the investor's position is

$$10{,}000 \times -0.3339 = -3{,}339$$

Thus, if the two sides to the contract agree to unwind it today, the investor would have to pay the short position in the contract $3,339. ∎

# 3.8   Futures Prices

Valuing a futures contract analytically (i.e., identifying an exact relationship between futures and spot prices) is difficult for two reasons. The first is the presence of delivery options in futures contracts, which creates uncertainty about the grade that will actually be delivered at maturity. The second is the daily marking-to-market procedure in futures markets, which creates interim cash flows of uncertain size. Either factor raises the difficulty of the pricing problem considerably.

So rather than focus on the technical issue of valuation, we discuss the *qualitative* relationship between otherwise identical futures and forwards. "Otherwise identical" means (a) that the two contracts have the same maturity date and same delivery price, and (b) that the grade of the spot asset in the forward contract is the standard grade specified in the futures contract. The only differences in the contracts are that the futures contract has daily marking-to-market and perhaps also delivery options.

## The Impact of Delivery Options

As we have seen, delivery options are provided only to the short position in a futures contract. The presence of this option makes the futures contract more attractive to the short position than an otherwise identical forward, while the long position, who is effectively the writer of this option, finds the futures less attractive. Ceteris paribus, therefore, the price of a futures contract will be lower than that of a forward contract;[1] indeed, the difference in prices on this account will be precisely the value of the delivery option.

How much lower will the futures price be? That is, how valuable is the delivery option? In general, this depends on the range of alternative deliverable grades and the price adjustment mechanism specified in the futures contract. Economic intuition, however, suggests a plausible answer.

The delivery option in futures contracts is provided mainly to guard against squeezes by the long position. The presence of this option, however, degrades the hedge offered by the contract to the long position since it creates uncertainty about the quality that will be delivered. The more *economically* valuable this option to the short position, the more the hedge is degraded, and the less attractive the contract to the long position. In a successful contract, then, one would expect that while the range of delivery options is wide enough to ensure market integrity, the economic value of the option will be low so as to degrade the hedge minimally.

Empirical studies support this position. Hemler (1990) and Duffie (1989) examine the value of the delivery option on the Chicago Board of Trade's Treasury bond futures contract. They compute the loss to the short position from fixing the grade to be delivered a given length of time before maturity compared to choosing it at maturity. Duffie finds that if the bond to be delivered is chosen three months ahead of time, the average loss suffered by the short position is $270, or 0.27% of the contract's face value of $100,000. If the choice is made with six months to go, the average loss is $430, or 0.43%, of the contract's face value. (The higher values at longer maturities reflect the fact that interest rates can change more over longer periods.) Fixing the delivered bond one year ahead of time, Hemler finds the average loss to be around $660, or 0.66%, of the contract's face value.

One final point is important. As discussed in Chapter 2, delivery options have economic value only when the price adjustment mechanism specifies price differentials between

---

[1] Intuitively, short positions represent "sellers" and long positions "buyers" in these markets. If shorts find futures more attractive and longs have the opposite preference, the futures market has more sellers and fewer buyers, hence a lower price.

alternative deliverable grades that differ from the price differentials prevailing in the spot market at delivery time. The more the price adjustment mechanism reflects actual differences in spot prices of the different deliverable grades at delivery time, the lower is the value of the delivery option. The option ceases to have economic value when delivery price adjustments on the futures contract exactly equal the prevailing spot price differentials at that point.

## The Impact of Daily Marking-to-Market

The presence of margining and daily marking-to-market in futures markets creates uncertain interim cash flows that have no counterpart in forward markets. Two questions of interest arise as a consequence: (a) Given that the margin account earns interest, is there any reason to expect futures and forward prices to differ? (b) If so, in what direction is the difference?

The key to answering these questions turns out to lie in the joint behavior of interest rates and futures prices. It can be shown that:

- If futures price movements and interest rate movements are *positively* correlated, then futures prices will be *higher* than forward prices.
- If futures price movements and interest rate movements are *negatively* correlated, then futures prices will be *lower* than forward prices.
- If futures price movements and interest rate movements are uncorrelated, then futures and forward prices will coincide.

A formal derivation of these results may be found in Cox, Ingersoll, and Ross (1981) and Duffie and Stanton (1992).[2] The proofs are quite technical, so here we limit ourselves to discussing the intuition behind them. Appendix 3B considers the case of constant interest rates (a special case of zero correlation) and shows that futures and forward prices are indeed equal in this case.

Suppose futures price changes are *positively* correlated with changes in interest rates. When futures prices increase, the margin account balance of a *long* position also increases. The positive correlation implies that this larger balance earns interest at a higher rate. Positive correlation also means that when margin balances fall on account of falling futures prices, the losses are financed at lower interest rates. Thus, with positive correlation, long positions find the daily marking-to-market of futures more attractive than the one-time settlement at maturity offered by forwards.

For short positions, the opposite preference obtains. The short's margin balances move in the opposite direction to futures price movements. When futures prices rise and margin balances fall, the losses have to be financed at higher interest rates. When futures prices fall and margin balances rise, the increased balance earns interest at a lower rate.

Thus, with positive correlation, longs prefer futures to forwards while shorts prefer forwards to futures. This means futures prices will be *higher* than forward prices.

An analogous argument indicates that with negative correlation, short positions find futures more attractive and long positions find them less attractive, so futures prices will be *less* than forward prices. Combining these arguments suggests that with zero correlation, futures prices will be equal to forward prices.

Of course, even if futures and forward prices differ, the relevant question from a practical standpoint is how large these differences can be. Once again, the empirical answer

---

[2] Other relevant papers include Jarrow and Oldfield (1981) and Richard and Sundaresan (1981). Amerio (2005) provides a description of forward prices in terms of futures prices by means of a convexity drift adjustment that captures the instantaneous correlation between futures prices and interest rates.

appears to be: not very, at least not for short-dated futures contracts. Intuitively, margining exists to inhibit default. Subject to achieving this end, it is best, from a hedging standpoint, to minimize the interim cash-flow uncertainty this procedure creates. In practice, margin requirements are quite small as a percentage of the face value of the contract (see Chapter 2). The impact of interest-rate changes on the changes in margin account is even smaller relative to the face value of the contract. Typically, therefore, we would expect the difference between forward and futures prices caused by margining to be small on short-dated contracts.

Empirical investigations support this expectation. The "best" laboratory for testing the impact of marking-to-market is in currency markets where delivery options do not exist. A study of currency markets by Cornell and Reinganum (1981) reported that currency futures and forward prices typically differ by less than the bid–ask spread in the currency market; later studies by Chang and Chang (1990) and Dezhbaksh (1994) report similar findings. A more broad-based study by French (1983) compares futures and forward prices in several markets and finds the differences to typically be very small.

Over very long horizons, however, the factors that differentiate futures and forwards can drive a measurable wedge between the prices. For example, Gupta and Subrahmanyam (1999) compare rates derived from swap and Libor futures markets and find that, for the period 1987–1996, there were substantial differences that cannot be explained by default risk effects, term structure effects, or information or liquidity differences between swaps (forward) and futures markets. They attribute this to a "convexity effect" arising from the daily marking-to-market in futures markets that is absent in the forward market.

## In Summary . . .

. . . empirical studies show that neither delivery options nor daily marking-to-market appear to be very important from a pricing standpoint, especially for short-dated contracts. Economic intuition suggests too that this should be the case. In the sequel, therefore, we often treat futures and forward prices as if they are the same. This is an assumption of convenience that works well for short-dated contracts, but some caution should be employed in applying this to long-term contracts.

## 3.9 Exercises

1. Briefly explain the basic principle underlying the pricing of forward contracts.

2. True or false: The theoretical forward price decreases with maturity. That is, for example, the theoretical price of a three-month forward must be greater than the theoretical price of a six-month forward.

3. List the factors that could cause futures prices to deviate from forward prices. How important are these factors in general?

4. The forward price of wheat for delivery in three months is $3.90 per bushel, while the spot price is $3.60. The three-month interest rate in continuously compounded terms is 8% per annum. Is there an arbitrage opportunity in this market if wheat may be stored costlessly?

5. A security is currently trading at $97. It will pay a coupon of $5 in two months. No other payouts are expected in the next six months.
   (a) If the term structure is flat at 12%, what should be the forward price on the security for delivery in six months?
   (b) If the actual forward price is $92, explain how an arbitrage may be created.

6. Suppose that the current price of gold is $365 per oz and that gold may be stored costlessly. Suppose also that the term structure is flat with a continuously compounded rate of interest of 6% for all maturities.

   (a) Calculate the forward price of gold for delivery in three months.

   (b) Now suppose it costs $1 per oz per month to store gold (payable monthly in advance). What is the new forward price?

   (c) Assume storage costs are as in part (b). If the forward price is given to be $385 per oz, explain whether there is an arbitrage opportunity and how to exploit it.

7. A stock will pay a dividend of $1 in one month and $2 in four months. The risk-free rate of interest for all maturities is 12%. The current price of the stock is $90.

   (a) Calculate the arbitrage-free price of (i) a three-month forward contract on the stock and (ii) a six-month forward contract on the stock.

   (b) Suppose the six-month forward contract is quoted at 100. Identify the arbitrage opportunities, if any, that exist, and explain how to exploit them.

8. A bond will pay a coupon of $4 in two months' time. The bond's current price is $99.75. The two-month interest rate is 5% and the three-month interest rate is 6%, both in continuously compounded terms.

   (a) What is the arbitrage-free three-month forward price for the bond?

   (b) Suppose the forward price is given to be $97. Identify if there is an arbitrage opportunity and, if so, how to exploit it.

9. Suppose that the three-month interest rates in Norway and the US are, respectively, 8% and 4%. Suppose that the spot price of the Norwegian kroner is $0.155.

   (a) Calculate the forward price for delivery in three months.

   (b) If the actual forward price is given to be $0.156, examine if there is an arbitrage opportunity.

10. Consider a three-month forward contract on pound sterling. Suppose the spot exchange rate is $1.40/£, the three-month interest rate on the dollar is 5%, and the three-month interest rate on the pound is 5.5%. If the forward price is given to be $1.41/£, identify whether there are any arbitrage opportunities and how you would take advantage of them.

11. Three months ago, an investor entered into a six-month forward contract to sell a stock. The delivery price agreed to was $55. Today, the stock is trading at $45. Suppose the three-month interest rate is 4.80% in continuously compounded terms.

    (a) Assuming the stock is not expected to pay any dividends over the next three months, what is the current forward price of the stock?

    (b) What is the value of the contract held by the investor?

    (c) Suppose the stock is expected to pay a dividend of $2 in one month, and the one-month rate of interest is 4.70%. What are the current forward price and the value of the contract held by the investor?

12. An investor enters into a forward contract to sell a bond in three months' time at $100. After one month, the bond price is $101.50. Suppose the term-structure of interest rates is flat with interest rates equal to 3% for all maturities.

    (a) Assuming no coupons are due on the bond over the next two months, what is now the forward price on the bond?

    (b) What is the marked-to-market value of the investor's short position?

    (c) How would your answers change if the bond will pay a coupon of $3 in one month's time?

13. A stock is trading at 24.50. The market consensus expectation is that it will pay a dividend of $0.50 in two months' time. No other payouts are expected on the stock over the next three months. Assume interest rates are constant at 6% for all maturities. You enter into a long position to buy 10,000 shares of stock in three months' time.

    (a) What is the arbitrage-free price of the three-month forward contract?

    (b) After one month, the stock is trading at $23.50. What is the marked-to-market value of your contract?

    (c) Now suppose that at this point, the company unexpectedly announces that dividends will be $1.00 per share due to larger-than-expected earnings. Buoyed by the good news, the share price jumps up to $24.50. What is now the marked-to-market value of your position?

14. Suppose you are given the following information:

    - The current price of copper is $83.55 per 100 lbs.
    - The term-structure is flat at 5%, i.e., the risk-free interest rate for borrowing/investment is 5% per year for all maturities in continuously compounded and annualized terms.
    - You can take long and short positions in copper costlessly.
    - There are no costs of storing or holding copper.

    Consider a forward contract in which the short position has to make *two* deliveries: 10,000 lbs of copper in one month, and 10,000 lbs in two months. The common delivery price in the contract for both deliveries is $P$, that is, the short position receives $P$ upon making the one-month delivery and $P$ upon making the two-month delivery. What is the arbitrage-free value of $P$?

15. This question generalizes the previous one from two deliveries to many. Consider a contract that requires the short position to make deliveries of one unit of an underlying at time points $t_1, t_2, \ldots, t_N$. The common delivery price for all deliveries is $F$. Assume the interest rates for these horizons are, respectively, $r_1, r_2, \ldots, r_N$ in continuously compounded annualized terms. What is the arbitrage-free value of $F$ given a spot price of $S$?

16. In the absence of interest-rate uncertainty and delivery options, futures and forward prices must be the same. Does this mean the two contracts have identical cash-flow implications? (*Hint:* Suppose you expected a steady increase in prices. Would you prefer a futures contract with its daily mark-to-market or a forward with its single mark-to-market at maturity of the contract? What if you expected a steady decrease in prices?)

17. Consider a forward contract on a non-dividend-paying stock. If the term-structure of interest rates is flat (that is, interest rates for all maturities are the same), then the arbitrage-free forward price is obviously increasing in the maturity of the forward contract (i.e., a longer-dated forward contract will have a higher forward price than a shorter-dated one). Is this statement true even if the term-structure is not flat?

18. The spot price of copper is $1.47 per lb, and the forward price for delivery in three months is $1.51 per lb. Suppose you can borrow and lend for three months at an interest rate of 6% (in annualized and continuously compounded terms).

    (a) First, suppose there are no holding costs (i.e., no storage costs, no holding benefits). Is there an arbitrage opportunity for you given these prices? If so, provide details of the cash flows. If not, explain why not.

    (b) Suppose now that the cost of storing copper for three months is $0.03 per lb, payable in advance. How would your answer to (a) change? (Note that storage costs are *asymmetric*: you have to pay storage costs if you are long copper, but you do not receive the storage costs if you short copper.)

19. The SPX index is currently trading at a value of $1265, and the FESX index (the Dow Jones EuroSTOXX Index of 50 stocks, subsequently referred to as "STOXX") is trading at €3671. The dollar interest rate is 3% per year, and the Euro interest rate is 5% per year. The exchange rate is $1.28/euro. The six-month futures on the STOXX is quoted at €3782. All interest rates are continuously compounded. There are no borrowing costs for securities. For simplicity, assume there are no dividends on either index.

   (a) Compute the correct six-month futures prices of the SPX, STOXX, and the currency exchange rate between the dollar and the euro.

   (b) Is the futures on the STOXX correctly priced? If not, show how to undertake an arbitrage strategy assuming you are *not* allowed to undertake borrowing or lending transactions in either currency. (Assume that the futures on SPX is correctly priced.)

20. The current level of a stock index is 450. The dividend yield on the index is 4% per year (in continuously compounded terms), and the risk-free rate of interest is 8% for six-month investments. A six-month futures contract on the index is trading for 465. Identify the arbitrage opportunities in this setting, and explain how you would exploit them.

21. In the US, interest rates in the money market are quoted using an "Actual/360" convention. The word "Actual" refers to the actual number of days in the investment period. For example, if the interest rate for a three-month period is given to be 7% and the actual number of calendar days in the three-month period is 91, then the actual interest received on a principal of $1 is

$$0.07 \times \frac{91}{360}$$

Many other countries too (including the Euro zone) use the Actual/360 convention, but the British money-market convention uses Actual/365. This question and the next four pertain to calculating forward prices given interest rates in the money-market convention.

   Suppose the 90-day interest rate in the US is 3%, the 90-day interest rate in the UK is 5% (both quoted using the respective money-market conventions), and the spot exchange rate is £1 = $1.75.

   (a) What is the present value of $1 receivable in 90 days?

   (b) What is the present value of £1 receivable in 90 days?

   (c) What is the 90-day forward price of £1?

22. The 181-day interest rate in the US is 4.50% and that on euros is 5%, both quoted using the money-market convention. What is the 181-day forward price of the euro in terms of the spot exchange rate $S$?

23. The three-month interest rate in both the US and the UK is 12% in the respective money-market conventions. Suppose the three-month period has 92 days. The spot exchange rate is £1 = $1.80. What is the arbitrage-free three-month forward price of £1?

24. The spot exchange rate is $1.28/euro. The 270-day interest rate in the US is 3.50% and that on euros is 4%, both quoted using the money-market convention. What is the 270-day forward price of the euro?

25. The three-month interest rates in the US and the UK are 3% and 6% in the respective money-market conventions. Suppose the three-month period has 91 days. The spot exchange rate is £1 = $1.83. What is the arbitrage-free three-month forward price of £1?

26. Consider three exchange rates, dollar/euro, yen/euro, and yen/dollar. Provided below are their spot FX rates and one-year interest rates (assume a continuous-compounding convention):

    Spot exchange rates:
    dollar/euro = 1.2822
    yen/euro = 146.15
    yen/dollar = 113.98

    Interest rates:
    dollar = 3%
    euro = 5%
    yen = 1%

    (a) Check whether triangular arbitrage exists in the spot FX market.
    (b) Check whether triangular arbitrage exists in the one-year forward FX market.
    (c) Why does or why does not triangular arbitrage hold in forward markets?

# Compounding Frequency

Interest rates in practice are quoted with a *compounding frequency* that indicates how often interest is compounded on an underlying investment. For example, if interest is compounded annually, then interest is computed once a year. Thus, an interest rate of 12% means that an investment of $1 will grow in one year's time to

$$1 + 0.12 = 1.12 \tag{3.12}$$

If the compounding is *semiannual*, then interest is computed and compounded every six months. So an interest rate of 12% on a principal of $1 means that the principal grows to

$$1 + \frac{0.12}{2} = 1.06 \tag{3.13}$$

in six months' time. If the investment lasts a year, then this augmented principal earns interest for the next six months. Thus, at the end of one year, a principal of $1 grows to

$$1.06 \times \left(1 + \frac{0.12}{2}\right) = (1.06)^2 = 1.1236 \tag{3.14}$$

Similarly, if the compounding takes place three times a year, interest is computed and compounded every four months (= 1/3 of a year). An interest rate of 12% on a principal of $1 means that the principal grows to

$$1 + \frac{0.12}{3} = 1.04 \tag{3.15}$$

in four months' time. If the investment horizon is one year, interest on this augmented principal is computed for the next four months, and then the procedure is repeated for the last four months. So the initial investment of $1 grows at the end of one year to

$$1.04 \times \left(1 + \frac{0.12}{3}\right) \times \left(1 + \frac{0.12}{3}\right) = (1.04)^3 = 1.124864 \tag{3.16}$$

Similarly, we can define interest rates that are compounded four times a year, five times a year, and so on. By applying the above arguments, if interest is compounded $k$ times a year, then an interest rate of 12% means that a principal of $1 grows in one year to

$$\left(1 + \frac{0.12}{k}\right)^k \tag{3.17}$$

Of course, there is no reason the investment horizon has to be one year. If we take an investment horizon of $t$ years and are given an interest rate of $r$ that is compounded $k$ times a year, then an investment of $1 grows at the end of $t$ years to

$$\left(1 + \frac{r}{k}\right)^{kt} \tag{3.18}$$

A special case of (3.18) that comes in especially handy in modeling is the case of *continuous compounding* $k = \infty$. In this case, it can be shown, by letting $k \to \infty$ in (3.18), that an investment of $1 at a continuously compounded interest rate of $r$ grows in $t$ years to the sum

$$e^{rt} \tag{3.19}$$

where $e$ is the exponential constant (given by $2.71828\ldots$).

As these expressions and examples indicate, specifying the compounding frequency is very important. A principal of $1 invested for a year at an interest rate of 12% will return

- 1.12 if interest is compounded annually ($k = 1$).
- 1.1236 if interest is compounded semiannually ($k = 2$).
- 1.1255 if interest rate is compounded quarterly ($k = 4$).
- 1.1275 if interest is compounded continuously ($k = \infty$).

Thus, an interest rate of $r$ compounded twice a year is evidently not the same as an interest rate of $r$ compounded four times a year.

## Present Values under Different Compounding Frequencies

Suppose the interest-rate applicable to a $t$-year horizon is $r^{(k)}(t)$ expressed in terms of a compounding frequency of $k$ times a year. What is the present value of $1 receivable at time $t$?

With a compounding frequency of $k$ times a year, $1 invested for $t$ years at the rate $r^{(k)}(t)$ grows by time $t$ to

$$\left(1 + \frac{r^{(k)}}{k}\right)^{kt} \tag{3.20}$$

Thus, the present value of $1 receivable at time $t$ is

$$\frac{1}{\left(1 + \frac{r^{(k)}}{k}\right)^{kt}} \tag{3.21}$$

With continuous compounding, $1 invested for $t$ years at the rate $r$ grows to $e^{rt}$ by time $t$. Thus, the present value of $1 receivable at time $t$ is

$$e^{-rt} \tag{3.22}$$

## Converting from One Frequency to Another

What is important in carrying out an investment is the amount to which the investment will grow by maturity, not how interest rates are quoted. So, ideally, no matter what quotation conventions are used, we would like to convert them to a common convention. How do we accomplish this? That is, for example, suppose we want to express everything in terms of continuous compounding. Given an interest rate of $r^{(k)}$ that is compounded $k$ times a year, what continuously compounded rate $r$ is equivalent to this rate?

An investment of $1 at the rate $r^{(k)}$ for one year would grow to the amount

$$\left(1 + \frac{r^{(k)}}{k}\right)^{k}$$

in one year, while an investment of $1 at the continuously compounded rate of $r$ for one year would grow to

$$e^{r}$$

If the two rates are to be equivalent, these amounts have to be the same, so we must have

$$e^r = \left(1 + \frac{r^{(k)}}{k}\right)^k$$

or

$$r = \ln\left[\left(1 + \frac{r^{(k)}}{k}\right)^k\right] = k \times \ln\left(1 + \frac{r^{(k)}}{k}\right) \qquad (3.23)$$

Expression (3.23) describes how to convert rates under any compounding frequency to *equivalent* continuously compounded rates. For example, suppose we are given an interest rate of 12% compounded annually. From (3.23), this is equivalent to a continuously compounded interest rate of

$$\ln(1.12) = 11.334\%$$

In a similar way, we can convert rates under any frequency to equivalent rates under any other frequency. For example, suppose we are given an interest rate of $r^{(k)}$ compounded $k$ times a year. To what interest rate $r^{(\ell)}$ that is compounded $\ell$ times a year is this rate equivalent? Following the same lines of argument, we have to find the value of $r^{(\ell)}$ such that an investment of $1 leads to the same sum under either rate at the end of one year, that is, the value of $r^{(\ell)}$ such that

$$\left(1 + \frac{r^{(\ell)}}{\ell}\right)^{\ell} = \left(1 + \frac{r^{(k)}}{k}\right)^k \qquad (3.24)$$

This gives us

$$r^{(\ell)} = \ell \times \left\{\left(1 + \frac{r^{(k)}}{k}\right)^{k/\ell} - 1\right\} \qquad (3.25)$$

For example, suppose we are given an interest rate of 10% compounded semiannually ($k = 2$) and we wish to convert this to an equivalent rate $r^{(4)}$ that is compounded quarterly ($k = 4$). From (3.25), this equivalent rate is

$$r^{(4)} = 4 \times \left\{\left(1 + \frac{0.10}{2}\right)^{2/4} - 1\right\} = 9.878\% \text{ (approx)}$$

In summary, knowledge of the compounding frequency is important to be able to compute accurately the interest due on an investment or borrowing, but it has no significance beyond that. It does not matter whether we measure the distance from London to Glasgow in miles or kilometers as long as we know how to convert distances from miles to kilometers and vice versa. Analogously, what is important is knowing how to convert interest rates from one compounding convention to another, not the one with which we actually work.

## Appendix 3B

# Forward and Futures Prices with Constant Interest Rates

In this appendix, we show that forward and futures prices must coincide if interest rates are constant. This is a special case of a more general result that forward and futures prices are equal whenever futures price changes are uncorrelated with interest-rate changes.

Since futures contracts are marked-to-market on a daily basis, it helps to change notation and count time in days. So suppose we are looking at futures and forward contracts with $T$ days to maturity. Let day 0 denote the current day, and day $T$ the maturity day of the contracts. Let $\rho$ denote the constant *daily* interest rate expressed in simple terms and unannualized. That is, an investment of \$1 grows to \$$(1 + \rho)$ at the end of one day. For notational simplicity, let $R = (1 + \rho)$. Finally, let $\widehat{F}$ denote the forward price on date 0 and $F$ denote the futures price at this point. We wish to show that $\widehat{F} = F$; we show that if this equality does not hold, an arbitrage opportunity arises.

Consider first a strategy of taking a long position in $R^T$ forward contracts. Each forward contract has a payoff of $S_T - \widehat{F}$ on date $T$, where $S_T$ is the (currently unknown) spot price of the underlying on date $T$. Thus, the total payoff on date $T$ from $R^T$ forwards is

$$R^T (S_T - \widehat{F}) \qquad\qquad (3.26)$$

Now consider the following strategy with futures contracts:

- On day 0, open $R$ long futures contracts at the futures price $F$. Close them out on day 1 at whatever futures price $F_1$ is prevailing at that point. Carry the net cash flow $R(F_1 - F)$ to day $T$ by rolling it over at the rate $\rho$ up to day $T$.

- On day 1, open $R^2$ long futures contracts at the futures price $F_1$. Close them out on day 2 at whatever futures price $F_2$ is prevailing at that point. Carry the net cash flow $R^2(F_2 - F_1)$ to day $T$ by rolling it over at the rate $\rho$ up to day $T$.

$$\vdots$$

- On day $t$, open $R^{t+1}$ long futures contracts at the futures price $F_t$. Close them out on day $t + 1$ at whatever futures price $F_{t+1}$ is prevailing at that point. Carry the net cash flow $R^t(F_{t+1} - F_t)$ to day $T$ by rolling it over at the rate $\rho$ up to day $T$.

$$\vdots$$

- On day $T - 1$, open $R^T$ long futures contracts at the futures price $F_{T-1}$. Close them out on day $T$ at the futures price $F_T$ at that point. Receive the net cash flow $R^T(F_T - F_{T-1})$.

What are the time-$T$ cash flows from the futures strategy? The day 1 total net cash flow of $R(F_1 - F)$ is invested for $T - 1$ days. Thus, by day $T$, it grows to

$$R^{T-1} \times R(F_1 - F) = R^T(F_1 - F)$$

The day 2 net cash flow of $R^2(F_2 - F_1)$ is invested for $T - 2$ days. Thus, by day $T$ it has grown to

$$R^{T-2} \times R^2(F_2 - F_1) = R^T(F_2 - F_1)$$

In general, the day $t$ net cash flow of $R^t(F_t - F_{t-1})$ is invested for $T - t$ days. Thus, by day $T$ it has grown to

$$R^{T-t} \times R^t(F_t - F_{t-1}) = R^T(F_t - F_{t-1})$$

Summing up these cash flows, the total day-$T$ cash flow from the futures strategy is

$$R^T(F_1 - F) + R^T(F_2 - F_1) + \cdots + R^T(F_t - F_{t-1}) + \cdots + R^T(F_T - F_{T-1})$$

which after canceling common terms is just

$$R^T(F_T - F)$$

However, on the last day $T$, the spot and futures prices must coincide since the futures contract is now at maturity, so the total cash flow from the futures strategy is given by

$$R^T(S_T - F) \tag{3.27}$$

Compare (3.26) and (3.27). If the former is larger, we have an arbitrage opportunity in which we go long the forward strategy and short the futures strategy. If the latter is larger, there is an arbitrage opportunity in which we go short the forward strategy and long the futures strategy. There is no arbitrage opportunity only if the two are equal This occurs only if $\widehat{F} = F$, that is, if futures and forward prices coincide.

# Rolling Over Futures Contracts

We discussed the mechanics of rolling over futures contracts in Chapter 2. Based on the pricing formulae derived in this chapter, we demonstrate in this appendix that under constant interest rates, rolling over a futures contract has the same cash-flow implications as taking a single long-term contract. This result provides a theoretical justification for the common practice of hedging long-term exposures with short-term futures contracts and rolling them over.

For simplicity, we consider only a single rollover. With additional notation, the arguments easily extend to multiple rollovers. Consider time points 0 (the current time), $T_1$ (the time of the first rollover), and $T_2$ (the maturity date). It may help to think of $T_1$ and $T_2$ as one and two months, respectively.

We compare a futures contract with maturity $T_2$ to a futures contract with maturity $T_1$ that is rolled over at $T_1$ into another contract with maturity $T_2$. Throughout these arguments, we treat futures contracts as if they are forward contracts. This is justified by the constant interest rate assumption, but in any event, as pointed out in the text, the empirical differences between futures and forward prices tend not to be too significant. For simplicity, we also assume that the underlying asset has no payouts.

Let $S_0$, $S_1$, and $S_2$ denote the current spot price and the spot prices on dates $T_1$ and $T_2$, respectively, and let $F_1$ and $F_2$ denote the *current* futures prices for contracts of maturities $T_1$ and $T_2$, respectively. If $r$ denotes the interest rate, then we must have

$$F_1 = S_0 e^{rT_1} \quad \text{and} \quad F_2 = S_0 e^{rT_2}$$

The payoff at $T_2$ to a $T_2$-maturity long futures position taken today is

$$S_2 - F_2 = S_2 - S_0 e^{rT_2} \tag{3.28}$$

Consider a long futures position taken today in the $T_1$-maturity futures contract. At $T_1$, this contract has a payoff of

$$S_1 - F_1 = S_1 - S_0 e^{rT_1} \tag{3.29}$$

The rollover process involves closing out this contract at $T_1$ and opening a new futures position with maturity $T_2$. Note that the futures price for this contract (denoted $F_{12}$, say) is given by

$$F_{12} = S_1 e^{r(T_2 - T_1)} \tag{3.30}$$

The rolled-over contract has cash flows at $T_2$ from two sources. First, there is the settlement amount (3.29) on the original futures contract carried over to $T_2$ at the rate $r$. By date $T_2$, this amounts to

$$e^{r(T_2-T_1)}[S_1 - S_0 e^{rT_1}] = e^{rT_2 - rT_1}S_1 - e^{rT_2}S_0 \qquad (3.31)$$

Second, there are the resettlement profits from the rolled-over futures contract. These amount to

$$S_2 - F_{12} = S_2 - S_1 e^{r(T_2-T_1)} \qquad (3.32)$$

Combining (3.31) and (3.32) and canceling common terms, the total cash flow from the rolled-over contract at time $T_2$ is

$$S_2 - e^{rT_2}S_0 \qquad (3.33)$$

This cash flow is identical to the cash flow (3.28) from the single long-dated futures contract, completing the proof.

# Chapter 4

# Pricing Forwards and Futures II: Building on the Foundations

## 4.1 Introduction

In the last chapter, we examined the theoretical pricing of forward and futures contracts based on replication. We now build on this theoretical foundation in several important directions.

Section 4.2 looks at the empirical performance of the theory. Section 4.3 then develops the concept of the *implied repo rate*, the rate at which one can effect synthetic borrowing or investment using spot and forward (or futures) markets. Section 4.4 examines the impact of *transactions costs*, while Section 4.5 discusses the relationship between the forward/future prices and the expected price of the spot asset at maturity of the contract. Finally, Section 4.6 presents the notion of *index arbitrage*.

In the course of developing these ideas, this chapter achieves a second important objective. The theory developed in Chapter 3 utilized three assumptions: (a) short-selling is costless with the full proceeds of short sales available immediately to the investor, (b) borrowing and lending rates are the same, and (c) there are no transactions costs. In this chapter, we show that the violation of any of these assumptions results in a band of possible prices within which the forward price could lie without giving rise to arbitrage opportunities. Short-selling costs are discussed in Section 4.2, a wedge between borrowing and lending rates in Section 4.3, and transactions costs in Section 4.4.

## 4.2 From Theory to Reality

The pricing formulae derived in Chapter 3 were identified under ideal market conditions such as the ability to take long and short positions with equal facility. How well do they fare in the less-than-ideal real world?

In a few special cases, the answer is obvious. The replication argument depends on being able to buy and hold the spot asset. In some contracts (catastrophe futures, for example), the underlying is not a traded asset. In others—such as electricity forwards—the spot asset is traded but cannot be stored except at extraordinarily high cost. In either case, the derivative

**TABLE 4.1** Currency Futures Prices

This table describes futures prices on the British pound (dollars/pound) and the euro (dollars/euro) as of December 15, 2003. The data is from PHLX and is the set of settlement prices on that date for the different contracts. The December 2003 price is the spot price. The theoretical futures prices are computed as described in the text.

| Contract Month | British Pound Settlement Price | British Pound Theoretical Price | Euro Settlement Price | Euro Theoretical Price |
|---|---|---|---|---|
| Dec 2003 | 1.7470 | 1.7470 | 1.2294 | 1.2294 |
| Jan 2004 | 1.7423 | 1.7428 | 1.2282 | 1.2283 |
| Feb 2004 | 1.7385 | 1.7386 | 1.2273 | 1.2274 |
| Mar 2004 | 1.7342 | 1.7344 | 1.2263 | 1.2263 |
| June 2004 | 1.7210 | 1.7218 | — | — |
| Sep 2004 | 1.7083 | 1.7094 | — | — |

cannot be replicated and so is not a "redundant security" (one whose outcomes can be synthetically created from the spot asset). The theory simply does not apply. Forward and futures prices in such markets are determined by demand and supply factors including expectations of future spot prices and degrees of risk-aversion, and not just by no-arbitrage arguments.

Now for the good news. The vast majority of assets on which active futures or forward contracts exist are themselves traded assets that are storable. In such cases, the predictions of the theory are violated only to the extent that the assumptions fail to hold. The rest of this section elaborates.

## Financial Forwards and Futures

When the underlying asset is a financial asset (e.g., a stock or an interest rate or a currency), the assumptions we have made are very good approximations of reality. Transactions costs are quite low, especially for large players, and taking short positions in the spot asset does not typically pose a problem. Consequently, the theory does very well at predicting forward/futures prices in these markets.

As an example, Table 4.1 looks at futures settlement prices on the Philadelphia Exchange of British pounds and euros. The table compares these prices to the theoretical prices that obtain using the forward pricing formula (3.11) for currencies. In computing the latter, we use the simple assumption of a constant continuously compounded interest rate in each of the three currencies (1.2% for the dollar, 4.1% for the pound, and 2.2% for the euro). In reality, during the period in the table, the dollar Libor rate varied from about 1.15% for one month to 1.27% for six months. On the pound, the one- to six-month range was from about 3.90% to 4.20%, and on the euro from about 2.15% to 2.25%.

Despite the approximations, the table shows that the cost-of-carry model does remarkably well in approximating currency futures prices.

## Commodity Forwards and Futures

With commodity forwards and futures, the story can be a little different. An important difference between a commodity and a financial security is that the former is used in production and gets consumed in the process. Inventories of commodities are held by producers because this provides them with the flexibility to alter production schedules or with insurance against a stock-out that could cause business disruptions. The value of these options to consume the commodity out of storage is referred to as the commodity's *convenience yield*.

The convenience yield is not an observable quantity but it is nonetheless very real. It distinguishes commodities from financial securities. Its presence implies that those with inventories will not be willing to lend the commodity to an arbitrageur without charging a fee (for example, a lease rate) to compensate them for the loss of this yield. Thus, short-selling becomes more expensive, and this affects the pricing theory.

To put this in formal terms, let $c$ denote the annualized convenience yield on a commodity in continuously compounded terms. Suppose, for simplicity, that there are no storage or other costs. Then, ignoring the convenience yield, the thoretical forward price is $S_0 e^{rT}$. In Appendix 4A, we show that the convenience yield introduces a band in which arbitrage-free forward prices must lie: there is no arbitrage as long as $F$ satisfies

$$S_0 e^{(r-c)T} \leq F \leq S_0 e^{rT} \qquad \qquad \textbf{(4.1)}$$

The intuition leading to (4.1) is simple. $F$ cannot *exceed* the theoretical price $S_0 e^{rT}$ since an arbitrageur can always then buy spot and sell forward. However, if $F$ lies below the thoretical price $S_0 e^{rT}$, an arbitrageur looking to short sell the commodity has to compensate the holder for the loss of convenience yield $c$, so unless the forward price is below the theoretical level by more than the convenience yield, there is no arbitrage.[1]

A practical problem with (4.1) is that the convenience yield $c$ is unobservable. This makes (4.1) of limited use in pricing forwards, but it does enable us to understand observed deviations from theoretical prices. From (4.1), the range of permissible deviations depends on the size of $c$.

If the current supply of a commodity is "large" relative to its consumption demand, its convenience yield will be low since producers desiring to use the commodity can always access it via the market. For such commodities, short-selling costs will be low, meaning the lower and upper bounds in (4.1) are close together. So the observed and theoretical forward prices will not differ substantially.

The gold market is one such case. Gold's available supply has generally equaled several years' worth of consumption demand. The consequent low convenience yield from gold is reflected in the low lease rates for gold (about 1% per year) observed empirically. The theoretical model does well at pricing such futures/forwards.

Table 4.2 provides an example. The table considers gold futures settlement prices taken from NYMEX and compares them to the theoretical price computed using the simple zero cost-of-carry model. As in Table 4.1, interest rates are assumed constant at 1.2%. The theoretical prices are very close to the actual settlement prices.

However, if spot supplies are tight relative to consumption demand, the convenience yield is large, so theoretical and observed prices may differ considerably. The oil market is, perhaps, the pre-eminent example of this situation. In this case, forward prices may not just be substantially less than the theoretical level but (as in the case of oil) less than even the spot price of the commodity itself.

Table 4.3 illustrates this point. The table describes settlement prices on NYMEX for light sweet crude oil futures. The settlement prices are obviously inconsistent with the theoretical pricing formula (3.4) for assets with a positive holding cost. The theoretical formula predicts that the forward price should be above spot and should also increase with maturity (since holding costs increase with the horizon). Both conditions are violated in the table.

---

[1] The convenience yield accrues only to those such as producers who have a use for the commodity, and not to arbitrageurs who are long the spot asset. Hence, the convenience yield does not affect the upper bound in (4.1). Of course, if an active lease market existed for the commodity that reflected the convenience yield, and if any long investor were in a position to lease out the commodity at this rate, then the forward price would simply be equal to $S_0 e^{(r-l)T}$ where $l$ is the lease rate.

**TABLE 4.2** Gold
Futures Prices

This table describes gold futures prices ($/oz) as of December 15, 2003. The data is from the COMEX division of NYMEX and is the set of settlement prices on that date for the different contracts. The December 2003 price is the spot price. The theoretical futures prices are computed as described in the text.

| Month | Settlement Price | Theoretical Price |
|---|---|---|
| Dec 2003 | 409.4 | 409.4 |
| Jan 2004 | 409.7 | 409.8 |
| Feb 2004 | 410.1 | 410.2 |
| April 2004 | 411.0 | 411.0 |
| June 2004 | 411.9 | 411.9 |
| Aug 2004 | 412.8 | 412.7 |

**TABLE 4.3** Oil
Futures Prices

This table describes futures settlement prices ($/bbl) on light sweet crude oil as of December 15, 2003. The data is from NYMEX.

| Month | Settlement Price |
|---|---|
| Jan 2004 | 33.04 |
| Feb 2004 | 32.95 |
| Mar 2004 | 32.36 |
| April 2004 | 31.78 |
| May 2004 | 31.23 |
| June 2004 | 30.70 |

## Backwardation and Contango

*Contango* refers to a market situation where forward (or futures) prices exceed spot prices. If convenience yields are ignored, contango is the "normal" situation predicted for commodity forward prices by our pricing model: since holding commodities typically involves storage and other costs, theoretical forward prices exceed the spot price. Moreover, since carry costs are greater for longer horizons, the predicted forward price increases as $T$ increases, a situation referred to as a *normal market*.

For commodities with low convenience yields, the predicted structures match observations well. Gold futures prices, for example, exceed spot prices and increase with maturity of the futures contract (see Table 4.2). Normal markets are also the predicted and actual cases for those financials for which the yield $d$ on the underlying asset is less than the interest rate $r$.

However, for commodities with high convenience yields, we have seen that forward prices may be lower than the theoretical price (a situation called *weak backwardation*) and perhaps lower even than the spot price $S_0$ (a case referred to as *strong backwardation* or simply *backwardation*). The oil futures market is one example of a market that has frequently been in strong backwardation and for large periods of time. Oil futures prices, moreover, are often observed to decrease as maturity increases, which is called an *inverted market*. (Oil futures prices also exhibit other patterns such as a hump shape with futures prices first increasing and then decreasing with maturity.) Table 4.3 illustrates all of these points.

One plausible source of an inverted market in oil is the volatility of spot prices. The convenience yield measures the value of the option to consume the asset out of storage, and as we will see later in this book, the value of an option increases as the volatility of the price of the underlying asset increases. The greater volatility of spot oil prices over longer horizons gives rise to rapidly increasing convenience yields that likely cause futures prices to decline as maturity increases.

# 4.3  The Implied Repo Rate

In our development of the pricing theory, we have assumed that borrowing and lending costs are the same. We now examine how arbitrage opportunities from mispricing may be identified when this assumption is dropped. A central role in this process is played by the concept of the *implied repo rate*.

Intuitively, the implied repo rate is the interest rate embedded in futures or forward prices, i.e., it is the interest rate that would make observed forward or futures prices equal to the theoretical prices predicted under no-arbitrage given values for the spot price and other variables. Suppose, for example, that the forward contract is on an asset that involves no payouts. Then, the forward and spot prices are related by the expression

$$F = Se^{rT} \tag{4.2}$$

Therefore,

$$\frac{F}{S} = e^{rT}$$

so taking natural logs on both sides, we obtain

$$\ln\left(\frac{F}{S}\right) = rT$$

Rearranging this expression and using the fact that $\ln(F/S) = \ln F - \ln S$, the implied repo rate given $F$, $S$, and $T$ works out to:

$$r = \frac{1}{T}(\ln F - \ln S) \tag{4.3}$$

Similarly, if we consider an asset that has a continuous dividend yield of $d$, the forward and spot prices are linked via

$$F = Se^{(r-d)T} \tag{4.4}$$

Manipulation of (4.4) along similar lines as above shows that the implied repo rate in this case is given by

$$r = d + \frac{1}{T}(\ln F - \ln S) \tag{4.5}$$

## The Implied Repo Rate as a Synthetic Borrowing/Lending Rate

A numerical example will help illustrate how implied repo rates are interpreted. Let the underlying asset be a stock on which no dividends are expected over the next three months. Suppose the current spot price of the stock is $S_0 = \$25$ and the forward price for delivery in three months is $F = \$26$. Note that the implied repo rate in this case is

$$r = \frac{1}{1/4}[\ln 26 - \ln 25] = 15.69\%$$

Consider a strategy in which you simultaneously go short the stock and long the forward (as, for instance, you would in an arbitrage strategy where the forward was undervalued). Then, you have sold the spot asset today for $25 and have agreed to buy it back at $T$ for $26. From a cash-flow standpoint, this means a cash inflow at time 0 of $25 and a cash outflow at time $T$ of \$26. Effectively, it is as if you have borrowed \$25 at time 0 and agreed to repay \$26 at time $T$. Thus, this strategy represents just a synthetic borrowing using the spot and forward markets.

The implicit interest rate in this synthetic borrowing is the rate of interest that would make \$25 at time 0 grow to \$26 by time $T$. That is, it is the interest rate $r$ that solves

$$26 = 25e^{rT}$$

But this expression is just (4.2) with $F = 26$ and $S = 25$, so the required rate $r$ is just the implied repo rate (in this case, 15.69%)! Thus:

- *The implied repo rate represents the rate at which an investor can borrow synthetically by simultaneously going short spot and long forward.*

Consider the opposite situation now where you go long spot and short forward. Then you have bought the spot asset for \$25 today and agreed to sell it for \$26 at time $T$. From a cash-flow standpoint, this means a cash outflow of \$25 at time 0 and a cash inflow of \$26 at time $T$. This is effectively a synthetic investment using the spot and forward markets. The rate at which this investment occurs is, once again, the implied repo rate (here, 15.69%). Therefore:

- *The implied repo rate also represents the rate at which an investor can effect a synthetic investment by simultaneously going long spot and short forward.*

These interpretations of the implied repo rate do not depend on the no-dividends assumption. Consider, for example, a currency forward in which the current forward price is $F$, the spot exchange rate is $S_0$, and the foreign currency yield is $d$. Suppose we go long $e^{-dT}$ units of the spot foreign currency and short one forward contract (as we would in an arbitrage strategy where the forward was overvalued). Assume, as usual, that the spot holdings are invested at the rate $d$ and grow to one unit of the foreign currency by $T$.

From a cash-flow standpoint, this strategy implies a cash outflow at time 0 of $e^{-dT} S_0$ and a cash inflow at time $T$ of $F$, with no interim or other cash flows. This is just a synthetic investment of $e^{-dT} S_0$ at time 0, which grows to $F$ by time $T$. The implicit interest rate on this investment is the interest rate $r$ that solves

$$F = e^{rT} \times e^{-dT} S_0 = e^{(r-d)T} S_0 \qquad \textbf{(4.6)}$$

Thus, $r$ is just the implied repo rate given by (4.5). That is, the implied repo rate $r$ in (4.5) represents the rate at which investors can invest synthetically by simultaneously going long spot and short forward in the currency market. By reversing the strategy, it also represents the rate at which investors can borrow synthetically by going short spot and long forward in the currency market.

## The Implied Repo Rate and Arbitrage

The identification of the implied repo rate with a synthetic borrowing/lending rate makes it easy to see how the implied repo rate may be used to identify arbitrage opportunities:

- Suppose the implied repo rate in a given market is $r$, and you can borrow at a rate $r_b < r$. Then you can create an arbitrage by borrowing at the rate $r_b$ and investing synthetically at the rate $r$, i.e., by borrowing at the rate $r_b$, buying spot, and selling forward.
- Suppose the implied repo rate is $r$ and you can lend at a rate $r_l > r$. Then you can create an arbitrage by synthetically borrowing at the rate $r$ and lending at $r_l$, i.e., by buying forward, selling spot, and lending.

Arbitrage is precluded as long as the implied repo rate lies *above* the best interest rate available to lenders who can short the asset and *below* the best rate available to borrowers, i.e., we have $r_l < r < r_b$. This means that there is an interval of forward prices that is consistent with no-arbitrage when borrowing and lending rates differ. For example, on an asset with zero costs of carry, the forward price can vary from

$$F = S_0 e^{r_l T}$$

to

$$F = S_0 e^{r_b T}$$

without there being arbitrage opportunities. The closer $r_b$ and $r_l$ are to each other, the narrower is this permissible interval of forward prices, and, of course, when $r_l = r_b$, we obtain a unique forward price consistent with no-arbitrage.

---

**Example 4.1**

Suppose the current spot price of gold is $330 per oz, and the forward price for delivery in one month is $331.35. Suppose also that the one-month borrowing and lending rates you face are 5% and 4.85%, respectively. Finally, suppose that it costs nothing to store gold. Is there an arbitrage opportunity?

In our notation, we have $S_0 = 330$, $T = 1/12$, and $F = 331.35$. Since there are no costs of carry, the implied repo rate given these prices may be calculated using (4.3):

$$r = \frac{1}{1/12} [\ln 331.35 - \ln 330] = 4.9\%$$

Since the implied repo rate lies between the lending and borrowing rates, there is no arbitrage opportunity here.   ∎

---

**Example 4.2**

This second example is based on the formula for pricing stock index futures developed below in Section 4.6 on index arbitrage. It should be read subsequent to reading that section.

Consider a futures contract on a stock index. Suppose that the current index level is 1400, the three-month index futures level is 1425, the dividend yield on the index is 2%, and you can borrow for three months at 8%. Is there an arbitrage opportunity present here?

Since we are given only the borrowing rate, we use the implied repo rate to check if there is an arbitrage. Treating the index as an asset with a continuous dividend yield, the implied repo rate is given by expression (4.5):

$$r = d + \frac{1}{T} [\ln F - \ln S]$$

We are given $S = 1400$, $F = 1425$, $d = 0.02$, and $T = 1/4$. Thus:

$$r = 0.02 + \frac{1}{1/4} [\ln 1425 - \ln 1400] = 0.0908$$

or 9.08%. Since you can borrow cheaper than this rate, there is an arbitrage opportunity in which you borrow, buy spot, and sell forward. The complete strategy is:

1. Enter into a short forward position.
2. Buy $e^{-dT} = 0.995$ units of the index.
3. Borrow $Se^{-dT} = 1393.02$ for three months at 8%.
4. Invest all dividends into buying more of the index.

Note that we buy only $e^{-dT}$ units of the index initially since the reinvested dividends make our holding grow to one unit by date $T$.

At inception, there are no net cash inflows from this strategy: the cash outflow of $1393.02 towards the spot purchase is matched by the cash inflow of $1393.02 from the borrowing. There are no net interim cash flows either since all dividends are reinvested in purchasing more of the index. At maturity, there is a cash inflow of $1425 from the forward. There is also a cash outflow of

$$1393.02 \times e^{(0.08)(1/4)} = 1421.16$$

towards repaying the borrowing. This leaves a net cash inflow of $+3.84$, representing arbitrage profits. ∎

## 4.4 Transactions Costs

Transactions costs are costs that create a wedge between what one obtains for selling a commodity or a security and what one has to pay to buy it. Since brokers and market makers charge a fee for their services, the "ask" price (the price at which one can buy) is larger in practice than the "bid" price (the price at which one can sell). Suppose there is such a bid-ask spread. Let $S_0^a$ denote the ask price and $S_0^b$ denote the bid price on the spot asset; define $F^a$ and $F^b$ analogously. Note that we have $S_0^a > S_0^b$ and $F^a > F^b$.

How do these bid-ask spreads affect our pricing results? The answer is simple: exactly as the wedge between borrowing and lending rates did, this spread creates an interval of forward prices at which arbitrage is not possible. Outside this interval, there is an arbitrage opportunity.

To see this, note that arbitrage involves one of two strategies: either we buy spot and sell forward, or we sell spot and buy forward. Assuming for simplicity that there are no costs of carry, the former strategy involves a cash outflow of $S^a$ at time 0 and a cash inflow of $F^b$ at time $T$. In present value terms, the net cash inflow from this strategy is

$$PV(F^b) - S^a \qquad \text{(4.7)}$$

The latter strategy—selling spot and buying forward—involves a cash inflow of $S^b$ at time 0 and a cash outflow of $F^a$ at time $T$. Thus, the present value of the net cash inflow from this strategy is

$$S^b - PV(F^a) \qquad \text{(4.8)}$$

For there to be no arbitrage opportunities, each of these net cash inflows must be nonpositive. Any spot and forward prices outside this set leads to a riskless profit opportunity.

## 4.5 Forward Prices and Future Spot Prices

A commonly held belief regarding forward prices is that they reflect the market's expectations of future spot prices. This is called the *unbiased expectations hypothesis*. Yet the central point of the preceding sections is that for many assets, the price of a forward contract can be identified solely from knowledge of interest rates and the cost of buying and holding spot. To what extent are these statements mutually consistent?

For financial assets, the answer is easily seen. Consider, for example, a forward contract on a stock that is not expected to pay dividends over the life of the contract. If $S_0$ denotes the current price of the stock, then the arbitrage-free forward price of the stock is

$$F = e^{rT} S_0 \qquad \text{(4.9)}$$

Suppose the forward price is also the expected spot price at $T$:

$$F = E[S_T] \tag{4.10}$$

From (4.9) and (4.10), we then have

$$E[S_T] = e^{rT} S_0 \tag{4.11}$$

Equation (4.11) states that the expected rate of growth in the stock price between dates 0 and $T$ is the risk-free rate $r$. But the stock is a risky asset and—unless its risk is fully diversifiable—investors in a risk-averse world will demand a risk-premium to hold it. That is, the expected return $z$ on the stock will strictly exceed $r$. This means $F$ cannot be the expected time-$T$ stock price. Indeed, $F$ systematically *underpredicts* the expected future stock price since $z > r$ implies

$$E[S_T] = S_0 e^{zT} > S_0 e^{rT} = F$$

Thus, the unbiased expectations hypothesis fails to hold for financial assets. More generally, it fails for any underlying for which the smoothness conditions of Chapter 3 hold at least approximately. There is no more information in the forward price concerning the future spot price than is already available in the current spot price and interest rate information.

For commodities with large convenience yields, however, the cost-of-carry model predicts only a range (4.1) within which forward prices may lie. Where in this region forward prices actually lie may be influenced both by expectations of future spot prices and factors such as risk-aversion. In such markets, therefore, forward prices may contain some information concerning the market's expectations about the future. This is also evidently true of markets where the cost-of-carry model does poorly because of very large storage costs, such as electricity.

## 4.6   Index Arbitrage

A stock index is simply a basket of stocks weighted according to specific rules. The level of the index represents the price of this basket. As such, we can specify a forward or futures contract on a stock index in the same way we do for other financial assets.

There are many actively traded futures contracts on stock indices. As just a few examples: in the US, there are futures on the Dow Jones Industrial Average traded on the CBoT; on the S&P 500 index traded on the CME; and on the Nasdaq 100 also on the CME. In Asia, futures on Japan's Nikkei 225 index trade in Osaka as well as in Singapore on SGX (formerly SIMEX), and futures on the Korean KOSPI 200 trade on the Korean Stock Exchange. In Europe, futures on the British FTSE 100 index trade on NYSE Liffe, while futures on the Dow Jones STOXX 50, the Swiss SMI, the Finnish HEX 25, and the German DAX all trade on Eurex.

Index futures contract sizes are standardized in size, with the standard size specified as a multiple of the index (i.e., as multiples of the basket of stocks underlying the index). Thus, one Dow Jones Industrial Average futures contract on the CBoT is for 10 times the Dow Jones index, meaning that at maturity of the contract, the short position has to deliver 10 units of the basket of stocks that go into defining the Dow Jones index. Similarly, one S&P 500 futures contract is for 250 times the S&P 500 index, while one Nasdaq 100 futures contract is for 100 times the Nasdaq 100 index.

Unlike many other financial assets, however, the physical delivery of an index (i.e., the actual basket of stocks underlying the index in the correct proportions) is difficult, particularly so in the case of broad-based indices consisting of a large number of stocks. As a consequence, index futures are *cash settled*, not by physical delivery of the actual index.

Contracts are marked-to-market at the end of the last trading day, and positions are declared closed.

Index futures contracts have a wide variety of uses. Equity portfolio managers can use them to change the nature of risk in the managed portfolio in a relatively costless manner. Consider, for example, an equity fund manager whose portfolio tracks the S&P 500 index. Since S&P 500 index futures must move in lockstep with the spot level of the index, the manager can eliminate equity risk in the portfolio by shorting an appropriate amount of S&P 500 index futures. By going long Treasury bond futures in addition, the manager can change the exposure of the portfolio from equity risk to interest-rate risk. More generally, as we discuss in the next chapter, index futures can be used to change (increase or decrease) the beta of an equity portfolio.

## Pricing Forwards on Stock Indices

A stock index may be viewed as an asset that pays dividends, so forwards/futures on the index may be priced accordingly. Operationalizing this idea, however, involves some tricky issues. There are two ways of proceeding, each of which has its supporters.

One method is to use the known cash holding costs formula

$$F = e^{rT}(S + M) \qquad (4.12)$$

with $S$ denoting the current level of the index, and $M$ the dollar value of dividends that will be received over the $T$-year horizon of the contract. Computationally, one issue with this method is that with a large number of stocks, we have to predict the dollar value and timing of dividends from each of the stocks and sum up their present values to obtain $M$.

An alternative procedure is to use the dividend *yield* on the index. The dividend yield on a stock index is expressed in annualized terms and refers to the value of dividends received over a year from the stocks in the index expressed as a percentage of the cost of the index. Put differently, a dividend yield of 2% means that if we reinvest the dividends received in buying more units of the index, then the number of units in our holding of the index will grow at a 2% annualized rate.

This points to an analogy between holding a foreign currency and holding a stock index. If we hold one unit of a foreign currency and invest it at the applicable interest rate for that currency (say, $d$) for $T$ years, our holding of the foreign currency at maturity is $e^{dT}$ units. If we hold one unit of a stock index that has a dividend yield of $d$ (expressed in continuously compounded terms) and we reinvest all the dividends in buying more units of the index, then in $T$ years, we will have $e^{dT}$ units of the index.

This means we can use the formula (3.11) developed for currency forwards to also price forward contracts on a stock index. If $S_0$ denotes the initial level of the index and $d$ the dividend yield expressed in continuously compounded terms, the forward price is

$$F = e^{(r-d)T} S_0 \qquad (4.13)$$

Treating forward and futures prices as the same thing, (4.13) also represents the futures price on an index whose current level is $S_0$.

It should be recognized, however, that this is an approximation. There is no problem in using this formula to price currency forwards since we can lock in the interest rate earned on investing the foreign currency when making the investment. With stock indices, one cannot be certain of the dividends that will be received at the time of investing in the index. The dividend yield $d$ used in the formula represents an estimate, and the accuracy of the forward price depends on the accuracy of this estimate. Put differently, (4.13) should be interpreted as the correct forward price *given* the anticipated dividend level $d$.

Of course, analogous comments are also true if we use the formula (4.12). In that case, the computation of $M$ is based on forecast dividends over the life of the futures contract, so the formula is accurate only to the extent the forecast is.

## Index Arbitrage

*Index arbitrage* is the exploitation of differences between this theoretical price for the futures contract and the actual level of stock index futures. An example will help illustrate the concept. The example is based on the dividend yield formula (4.13).

| | |
|---|---|
| **Example 4.3** | Consider a three-month futures contract on the S&P 500 index. Suppose that the present level of the index is 1020, the dividend yield on the index is 1.4%, and the three-month rate of interest is 3%. To keep the exposition simple, we treat the futures contract as if it is a forward contract with a single marking-to-market once at the end of the contract. In our notation, we have: $S_0 = 1020$, $r = 0.03$, $d = 0.014$, and $T = 1/4$. Therefore, the index futures price should be: |

$$F = e^{(r-d)T} S_0 = e^{(0.03-0.014)(1/4)}(1020) = 1,024.80$$

Suppose the observed level of the index futures is 1,027.40. Then, the futures is *overvalued* relative to spot, so we should sell futures, buy spot, and borrow. The specific strategy is:

1. Enter into a short futures position to deliver the index at a futures price of 1,027.40.
2. Buy $e^{-dT} = 0.9965$ units of the index for $(1020)(0.9965) = \$1,016.43$.
3. Borrow $1,016.43 for three months at 3%.
4. Reinvest all dividends into buying more of the index.

Note that, analogous to the currency forwards situation, we buy only $e^{-dT}$ units of the index initially. When dividends from the index are reinvested in buying more of the index, our holding of the index grows at the rate $d$, so we are left with one unit of the index at maturity.

There are no net initial cash flows from this strategy, and since all dividends are reinvested in the index, there are no net interim cash flows either. At maturity, there is a cash inflow of 1,027.40 from the futures position. There is also a cash outflow of

$$e^{(0.03)(1/4)}(1,016.43) = 1,024.80$$

to repay the borrowing. The net result is a cash inflow of 2.90 representing arbitrage profits from the mispricing. ∎

## Comments and Caveats

Index-arbitrage strategies have grown considerably in popularity since their introduction. For example, Shalen (2002) reports that in July 2002, over 8% of trading volume at the NYSE was related to index-arbitrage programs.

Of course, in reality, implementing index-arbitrage strategies is not as simple as the example above suggests. Several problems may arise. One that we have already mentioned is that the dividend level used in the calculations represents only a forecast. If we use the cash dividend formula (4.12), we must estimate $M$, the present value of dividends expected over the life of the futures contract. This must be done by using estimates of cash dividends expected from each of the companies in the index and summing these up.

The alternative procedure of using a dividend yield is computationally simpler but conceptually requires a bit more care. Since dividends tend to be bunched, there are seasonal effects to be taken into account. That is, the average dividend yield over a year may be higher or lower than the yield over a specific shorter period. The dividend yield *d* used as an input into the formula must be the appropriate one given the maturity of the futures contract.

In either case, it is possible that the realized dividend rate will differ from the estimate. Thus, the profits from the strategy are uncertain and could even be negative. The use of the word "arbitrage" in this context is somewhat liberal.

A second problem is that index-arbitrage strategies require buying or selling the spot asset, which is the underlying index. Literally buying or selling the index (i.e., the basket of stocks comprising the index) will entail substantial transactions costs among other problems. In some cases, one can use traded instruments that track specific indices (for example, Standard and Poor Depository Receipts, or SPDRs, which track the S&P 500 index). If no such instruments are available, one can use a smaller basket of stocks that tracks the index closely. In many countries, the emergence of exhange-traded funds (ETFs), which track broad-market and sectoral indices, has also helped diminish the severity of this problem. Of course, a tracking error may still remain between the exact performance of the index and that of the tracking portfolio.

Other issues too may arise that are common to most derivatives arbitrage strategies. One is execution risk. In the ideal case, the two legs of the arbitrage strategy should be executed simultaneously at the observed respective prices. While electronic trading has facilitated simultaneity considerably, some room for slippage exists. For example, the uptick rule restricts when short-selling may be possible. Second, transactions costs (bid-offer spreads) and differences in borrowing and lending rates must be taken into account in calculating whether or not arbitrage opportunities exist.

Collectively, all of these factors suggest that while large deviations from the theoretical fair price cannot persist, small deviations may not represent genuine arbitrage opportunities. The data bears this out: index futures often deviate by small amounts from their theoretical levels but rarely by substantial levels (see, for example, Figure 4.1 on the percentage mispricing in the CBoT futures contract on the Dow Jones Industrial Average). Shalen (2002)

**FIGURE 4.1**

Mispricing in the Dow Jones Industial Average Futures Contract

This figure, taken from Shalen (2002), shows the percentage mispricing in the closing level of the CBoT futures contract on the Dow Jones Industrial Average. The mispricing is relative to the theoretically fair price.

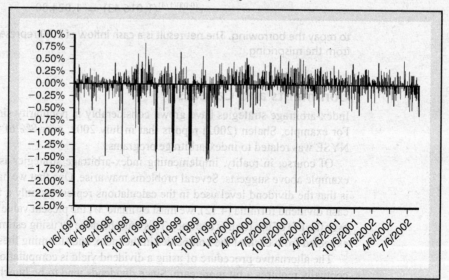

reports that, for example, the mean absolute mispricing in the DJIA futures contract on the CBoT has been less than 0.20% since 2000 and less than 0.15% since 2001. Mispricing tends to be highly correlated with volatility of the underlying index, perhaps because higher volatility levels increase execution and implementation risk in the arbitrage strategy.

## 4.7 Exercises

1. What is meant by the term "convenience yield"? How does it affect futures prices?

2. True or false: An arbitrage-free forward market can be in backwardation only if the benefits of carrying spot (dividends, convenience yields, etc.) exceed the costs (storage, insurance, etc.).

3. Suppose an active lease market exists for a commodity with a lease rate $\ell$ expressed in annualized continuously compounded terms. Short-sellers can borrow the asset at this rate and investors who are long the asset can lend it out at this rate. Assume the commodity has no other cost of carry. Modify the arguments in the appendix to the chapter to show that the theoretical futures price is $F = e^{(r-\ell)T} S$.

4. What is the "implied repo rate"? Explain why it may be interpreted as a synthetic borrowing or lending rate.

5. Does the presence of a convenience yield necessarily imply the forward market will be in backwardation? Why or why not?

6. How do transactions costs affect the arbitrage-free price of a forward contract?

7. Explain each of the following terms: (a) normal market, (b) inverted market, (c) weak backwardation, (d) backwardation, and (e) contango.

8. Suppose that oil is currently trading at $38 a barrel. Assume that the interest rate is 3% for all maturities and that oil has a convenience yield of $c$. If there are no other carry costs, for what values of $c$ can the oil market be in backwardation?

9. The spot price of silver is currently $7.125/oz, while the two- and five-month forward prices are $7.160/oz and $7.220/oz, respectively.
   (a) If silver has no convenience yield, what are the implied repo rates?
   (b) Suppose silver has an active lease market with lease rate $\ell = 0.5\%$ for all maturities expressed in annualized continuously compounded terms. Using the formula developed in Question 3, identify the implied repo rate for maturities of two months and five months.

10. Copper is currently trading at $1.28/lb. Suppose three-month interest rates are 4% and the convenience yield on copper is $c = 3\%$.
    (a) What is the range of arbitrage-free forward prices possible using

    $$S_0 e^{(r-c)T} \leq F \leq S_0 e^{rT} \qquad \qquad \text{(4.14)}$$

    (b) What is the lowest value of $c$ that will create the possibility of the market being in backwardation?

11. You are given the following information on forward prices (gold and silver prices are per oz, copper prices are per lb):

| Commodities | Spot | One Month | Two Month | Three Month | Six Month |
|---|---|---|---|---|---|
| Gold | 436.4 | 437.3 | 438.8 | 440.0 | 444.5 |
| Silver | 7.096 | 7.125 | 7.077 | 7.160 | 7.220 |
| Copper | 1.610 | 1.600 | 1.587 | 1.565 | 1.492 |

   (a) Which of these markets are normal? inverted? neither?

   (b) Which are in backwardation? in contango?

   (c) Which market appears prima facie to have the greatest convenience yield?

12. Suppose the convenience yield is close to zero for maturities up to six months, then spikes up for the forward period between six and nine months, and then drops back to zero thereafter. What does the oil market seem to be saying about political conditions in the oil-producing countries?

13. Suppose there is an active lease market for gold in which arbitrageurs can short or lend out gold at a lease rate of $\ell = 1\%$. Assume gold has no other costs/benefits of carry. Consider a three-month forward contract on gold.

   (a) If the spot price of gold is $360/oz and the three-month interest rate is 4%, what is the arbitrage-free forward price of gold?

   (b) Suppose the actual forward price is given to be $366/oz. Is there an arbitrage opportunity? If so, how can it be exploited?

14. A three-month forward contract on a non-dividend-paying asset is trading at 90, while the spot price is 84.

   (a) Calculate the implied repo rate.

   (b) Suppose it is possible for you to borrow at 8% for three months. Does this give rise to any arbitrage opportunities? Why or why not?

15. If the spot price of IBM today is $75 and the six-month forward price is $76.89, then what is the implied repo rate assuming there are no dividends? Suppose the six-month borrowing rate in the money market is 4% p.a on a semiannual basis. Is there a repo arbitrage, and how would you construct a strategy to exploit it?

16. The current value of an index is 585, while three-month futures on the index are quoted at 600. Suppose the (continuous) dividend yield on the index is 3% per year.

   (a) What is the implied repo rate?

   (b) Suppose it is possible for you to borrow at 6% for three months. Does this create any arbitrage openings for you? Why or why not?

17. A three-month forward contract on an index is trading at 756, while the index itself is at 750. The three-month interest rate is 6%.

   (a) What is the implied dividend yield on the index?

   (b) You estimate the dividend yield to be 1% over the next three months. Is there an arbitrage opportunity from your perspective?

18. The spot US dollar-euro exchange rate is $1.10/euro. The one-year forward exchange rate is $1.0782/euro. If the one-year dollar interest rate is 3%, then what must be the one-year rate on the euro?

19. You are given information that the spot price of an asset is trading at a bid-ask quote of 80 − 80.5, and the six-month interest rate is 6%. What is the bid-ask quote for the six-month forward on the asset if there are no dividends?

20. Redo the previous question if the interest rates for borrowing and lending are not equal, i.e. there is a bid-ask spread for the interest rates, which is 6 − 6.25%.

21. In the previous question, what is the maximum bid-ask spread in the interest rate market that is permissible to give acceptable forward prices?

22. Stock ABC is trading spot at a price of 40. The one-year forward quote for the stock is also 40. If the one-year interest rate is 4%. and the borrowing cost for the stock is 2%, show how to construct a riskless arbitrage in this stock.

23. You are given two stocks, A and B. Stock A has a beta of 1.5, and stock B has a beta of −0.25. The one-year risk-free rate is 2%. Both stocks currently trade at $10. Assume a CAPM model where the expected return on the stock market portfolio is 10% p.a. Stock A has an annual dividend yield of 1%, and stock B does not pay a dividend.

    (a)  What is the expected return on both stocks?

    (b)  What is the one-year forward price for the two stocks?

    (c)  Is there an arbitrage? Explain.

# Forward Prices with Convenience Yields

The presence of a convenience yield makes short-selling commodities more complex and costly than short-selling financial securities. To see the impact of this on our theory, consider, for simplicity, a commodity with zero storage costs. The theoretical forward price is $F = Se^{rT}$. Let $F^{obs}$ denote the observed forward price.

If $F^{obs} > F$ (i.e., the forward is seen as overpriced), a price correction can always be forced by arbitrageurs who buy spot and sell forward. Thus, forward prices cannot *exceed* the theoretical price we have identified and we must have

$$F^{obs} \leq Se^{rT} \tag{4.15}$$

If $F^{obs} < F$ (i.e., the forward is perceived as underpriced), a similar price correction requires that arbitrageurs who do not own the spot asset be able to short sell the commodity by borrowing it costlessly. Such borrowing has to be done from producers and others who hold inventories of the commodity and are in a position to lend it to the arbitrageur. In the presence of a convenience yield, however, those with inventories will not agree to lend the commodity out costlessly; rather, they will charge a fee as compensation for the loss of this yield.

Let $c$ denote the annualized convenience yield on the commodity expressed in continuously compounded terms. Then, an arbitrageur short-selling the asset will have to repay $S_0 e^{cT}$ units of the commodity for every unit borrowed today. Equivalently, for every unit to be repaid at maturity, the arbitrageur receives $e^{-cT}$ units today.

Now consider the position of an arbitrageur who finds the forward undervalued at $F^{obs}$. The arbitrageur

- enters into a long forward position,
- borrows and sells $e^{-cT}$ units of the commodity in exchange for returning one unit at maturity, and
- invests the proceeds of the short sales, $S_0 e^{-cT}$, for maturity at $T$.

At $T$, the arbitrageur pays $F^{obs}$ on the forward contract and receives one unit of the commodity, which is used to close out the short position. He also receives $e^{(r-c)T} S_0$ from the investment. Thus, the net time-$T$ cash flow is

$$S_0 e^{(r-c)T} - F^{obs}$$

This is positive (i.e., arbitrage profits exist) only if $S_0 e^{(r-c)T} > F^{obs}$. Therefore, there is no arbitrage possible from short-selling the spot commodity if

$$F^{obs} \geq S_0 e^{(r-c)T} \tag{4.16}$$

Combining (4.15) and (4.16), there is no arbitrage as long as

$$S_0 e^{(r-c)T} \leq F^{obs} \leq S_0 e^{rT} \tag{4.17}$$

Thus, the presence of a convenience yield on commodities results in a range of possible values for the forward price; in particular, forward prices may be less than not just the theoretical level, but even the spot price of the commodity itself.

# Chapter 5

# Hedging with Futures and Forwards

## 5.1 Introduction

The most important economic function played by a futures or forward contract is enabling investors to *hedge* exposures, i.e., to reduce the riskiness of cash flows associated with market commitments. In principle, hedging with a forward or futures contract is simple: if an investor has a commitment to buy or sell a quantity $Q$ of an asset $T$ years from now, cash-flow risk can be eliminated by locking in a price for this purchase or sale through a forward or futures contract. We begin with a simple example to illustrate this point, and then explain why matters are not quite as simple as the example suggests.

**Example 5.1**

Suppose a gold-wire manufacturer estimates its requirement of gold in three months' time to be 10,000 oz. The manufacturer can eliminate price uncertainty by entering into a long futures (or forward) contract to buy 10,000 oz of gold in three months. Ignoring interest on the margin account, the cost of gold to the company in three months is then $10,000\, F$, where $F$ is the current three-month futures price of gold.

Of course, the manufacturer can also obtain the required hedge without actually making or accepting delivery on the futures position by using the following strategy:

1. Take long positions of size 10,000 oz in three-month gold futures contracts at the current futures price $F$.
2. Close out the futures positions in three months' time at the futures price $F_T$ prevailing then.
3. Buy 10,000 oz in the spot market in three months' time at the spot price $S_T$ prevailing then.

Ignoring interest, the gain on the futures margin account is $10,000\,(F_T - F)$, while the cost of buying 10,000 oz spot is $10,000\, S_T$. Thus, the total cash outflow is

$$-10,000\,(F_T - F) + 10,000\, S_T = 10,000\, F - 10,000\,(F_T - S_T) \qquad (5.1)$$

At time $T$, however, the futures contract is at maturity, so we must have $F_T = S_T$. Thus, the last term in (5.1) drops out and the net cash flow is just the certainty amount $10,000\, F$. ∎

In practice, as mentioned in Chapter 2, the vast majority of hedges are implemented in this way, i.e., by closing out the futures position prior to delivery and covering the market commitment through spot market purchases or sales. Only a very small percentage of futures contracts are held open until delivery.

Nonetheless, implementing a hedge using futures contracts is not as simple an affair as this discussion suggests. The sections below explain.

## The Problem: Basis Risk

The *basis* in a futures contract refers to the difference $F - S$ between futures and spot prices. (Sometimes the basis is defined as $S - F$.) As (5.1) shows, for a hedge to be perfect, the basis $F_T - S_T$ must be *riskless* on date $T$ when the hedge is terminated—only this will ensure a certainty cash flow from the hedge.

Market practitioners often comment that the only perfect hedge is in a Japanese garden. This may be an overstatement, but there are at least two reasons why the basis $F_T - S_T$ may fail to be riskless on date $T$.

The first is a possible commodity mismatch. Futures contracts have standard grades (see Chapter 2), and the standard grade underlying the futures contract may not be the same as the grade of the asset being hedged. As a consequence, the futures price $F_T$ may not coincide with $S_T$, the time-$T$ spot price of the asset being hedged. The basis $F_T - S_T$ in (5.1) is nonzero and of uncertain size. This is *commodity basis risk*, basis risk caused by a commodity or grade mismatch.

The second is a possible delivery date mismatch. Futures contracts have standardized delivery periods, and the available maturity dates contracts may not coincide with the investor's date of market commitment. (The wheat futures contract on the CBoT, for example, has only five delivery months.) In this case, the futures position used for hedging must be closed out on the date $T$ of the hedger's market commitment, before the contract is at maturity. At this point, even if there is no commodity mismatch, the futures price $F_T$ will not typically equal the spot price $S_T$, so the basis $F_T - S_T$ in (5.1) will be nonzero and of uncertain size. This is *delivery basis risk*.

Basis risk may also arise in hedging with forward contracts. An instance is *cross-hedging*, that is, when exposure on one asset is hedged with a forward contract on another asset (e.g., when exposure to fluctuations in the Norwegian kroner/US dollar exchange rate is hedged with a euro/US dollar forward contract). Cross-hedging obviously implies commodity basis risk. It is typically used because there is no actively traded forward contract on the underlying asset (Norwegian kroner in this example), so a forward contract on a "closely related" asset (here, the euro) is used instead.

In this chapter, we develop a theory of optimal hedging in the presence of basis risk that is equally applicable to both forwards and futures. For expositional simplicity, we use the term "futures contracts" throughout in referring to the instruments used for hedging. The only material in this chapter specific to futures contracts is Section 5.8, which considers the impact of daily marking-to-market.

## Handling Basis Risk: The Questions

The presence of basis risk implies that cash flows cannot be made entirely riskless by hedging. What then is the best we can do in terms of reducing risk? This is the issue that concerns us in this chapter.

The first thing we need is a measure of risk. As is usual in finance, we measure the risk of a cash flow by its *variance*. To be sure, the variance does not completely capture all that is meant by the word "risk," but it is certainly a good first approximation. Thus, the task is to identify the hedge that leads to the least cash-flow variance among all possible hedges. We refer to this as the *minimum-variance hedge*. Identifying the minimum-variance hedge involves the answers to three questions:

1. What is the best choice of futures contract to be used for hedging?
2. What is the size of the futures position to be opened today?
3. Should this be a long position or a short position?

These questions form the focus of this chapter. Some comments outlining the intuition of the results to come will be helpful.

## 5.2 A Guide to the Main Results

Hedging is an offsetting of risks. In hedging a spot exposure with futures (or forwards), we are trying to offset the effects of spot price movements with futures price movements so that the resulting net cash flow has minimum risk. For such offsetting to work well, futures and spot prices must move "together" so that the effects of one can be canceled by the other. That is, futures and spot price changes must be *correlated*. The higher the degree of correlation, the greater the co-movement and the easier is the offsetting of risk. In the limit, when correlation is perfect, the offsetting is also perfect, and we obtain a riskless hedge.

These observations suggest that in selecting a futures contract for hedging purposes, we should choose one whose price changes are maximally correlated with changes in the spot price of the asset being hedged. We show that this intuition is on the mark; indeed, we show exactly how cash-flow uncertainty declines as a function of this correlation.

### The Hedge Ratio

A central role in this process is played by the *hedge ratio*, denoted $h$. The hedge ratio is the variable used to implement the optimal hedging strategy once the futures contract has been chosen. It measures the number of futures positions taken per unit of spot exposure. In notational terms, suppose the investor has a spot market commitment of $Q$ units on date $T$ and hedges this with a futures position of size $H$. The hedge ratio $h$ is then defined by

$$h = \frac{H}{Q} \tag{5.2}$$

For example, if the gold-wire manufacturer of Section 5.1 hedges his exposure of 10,000 oz using futures contracts for 8,000 oz, he is using a hedge ratio of $h = 8{,}000/10{,}000 = 0.80$.

### The Main Result

The most important lesson that will be derived in this chapter is the following:

*In the presence of basis risk, it is not generally optimal to hedge exposures one-for-one, i.e., to use a hedge ratio of unity. The variance-minimizing hedge ratio $h^*$ depends on the correlation between spot and futures price changes and increases as this correlation increases.*

Specifically, in the central result of this chapter, we show that the minimum-variance hedge ratio is given by

$$h^* = \rho \, \frac{\sigma(\Delta_S)}{\sigma(\Delta_F)} \tag{5.3}$$

where:

- $\sigma(\Delta_S)$ is the standard deviation of spot price changes over the hedging horizon.

- $\sigma(\Delta_F)$ is the standard deviation of futures price changes over the hedging horizon.
- $\rho$ is the correlation of spot and futures price changes.

That is, the minimum-variance hedge ratio is the correlation $\rho$ multiplied by a "scaling factor" $\sigma(\Delta_S)/\sigma(\Delta_F)$.

## The Intuition

To see the intuition behind (5.3), consider the correlation first. With zero correlation between spot and futures price changes, there is no offsetting of risks at all from hedging using futures. Any hedging activity only *increases* overall cash-flow risk by creating cash-flow uncertainty from a second source (the futures position). Thus, the optimal hedge ratio becomes zero. As correlation increases, however, greater offsetting of risks is facilitated, so we want to use a higher hedge ratio to take advantage.

Why scale the correlation by the ratio of standard deviations? The aim of hedging is to offset the effect of spot price changes with futures price changes. Suppose a "typical" move in futures prices is twice the size of a "typical" move in spot prices. Then, other things being equal, the size of the futures position used for hedging should be only half the size of the spot exposure. With the size of "typical" price moves measured by their respective standard deviations, it is this adjustment that the scaling factor provides.

## Layout of this Chapter

The next three sections of this chapter are devoted to deriving this optimal hedge ratio $h^*$ and identifying various properties of the optimally hedged position. Readers not interested in the derivation of $h^*$ can skip ahead to the numerical examples we present in Section 5.6. Sections 5.7 and 5.8 discuss implementation of the hedging strategy. The final sections of this chapter discuss extensions of the minimum-variance hedging idea to hedging equity portfolios and fixed-income portfolios, respectively.

## Some Mathematical Preliminaries

We recall some basic definitions and properties of random variables. Let $X$ and $Y$ be random variables with variances $\sigma_X^2$ and $\sigma_Y^2$, respectively. Let $E(\cdot)$ denote expectation. Then, the covariance of $X$ and $Y$ is defined as

$$\text{cov}(X, Y) = E(XY) - E(X)E(Y)$$

The correlation $\rho(X, Y)$ between $X$ and $Y$ and $\text{cov}(X, Y)$ are related via

$$\rho(X, Y) = \frac{\text{cov}(X, Y)}{\sigma_X \sigma_Y}$$

If $a$ is any constant, then

$$\text{Variance}(aX) = a^2 \text{Variance}(X) = a^2 \sigma_X^2$$

Finally, if $a$ and $b$ are any constants, then

$$\text{Variance}(aX - bY) = a^2 \text{Variance}(X) + b^2 \text{Variance}(Y) - 2ab\,\text{cov}(X, Y)$$

# 5.3   The Cash Flow from a Hedged Position

Suppose that a specific futures contract has been chosen for hedging purposes. (We formalize later the criterion that should guide this choice.) Let $F$ denote the current price of the contract and $S$ the current spot price of the asset being hedged. Let $F_T$ and $S_T$ denote, respectively, the time-$T$ values of these quantities.

We stress that one or both kinds of basis risk may be present: the asset underlying the futures contract may not be the same as the asset being hedged, and the date $T$ may not be the maturity date of the futures contract. Thus, we may not have $S_T = F_T$.

We treat the futures contract as if it is a forward contract that is marked-to-market once at termination. That is, the resettlement profits (or losses) from taking a long futures position at inception and closing it out at time $T$ are given by $F_T - F$. The impact of daily marking-to-market on the optimal hedge position is considered in Section 5.8 (see "Tailing the Hedge").

Consider first an investor with a commitment to buy $Q$ units of the asset on date $T$. To hedge this position, the investor

1. Takes a long futures position of size $H$ at inception at the futures price $F$.
2. Closes out the futures position at time $T$ by taking a short futures position of size $H$.
3. Buys the required quantity $Q$ on the spot market at time $T$.

To handle the possibility that the initial futures position may be a *short* one, we will allow $H$ to take on negative values also and interpret a long position of (say) $-10$ units as a short position of 10 units. Under this strategy, there is a cash outflow of $QS_T$ at time $T$ towards the spot purchase. There are also resettlement profits from the futures position at this time of $H(F_T - F)$. Thus, the net cash outflow is

$$QS_T - H(F_T - F) \tag{5.4}$$

The investor must choose $H$ to minimize the variance of the cash flow (5.4).

Now consider an investor with a commitment to sell $Q$ units of the asset on date $T$. To hedge this, the investor

1. Takes a short futures position of size $H$ at inception at the futures price $F$.
2. Closes out the futures position at time $T$ by taking a long futures position of size $H$.
3. Sells the quantity $Q$ on the spot market at time $T$.

Once again, we allow $H$ to be negative to allow for the possibility that the initial futures position is a long one. Under this strategy, there is a cash inflow of $QS_T$ at time $T$ from the spot market sale. There are also resettlement profits from the futures position of $H(F - F_T)$. Thus, the net cash inflow is

$$QS_T + H(F - F_T) \tag{5.5}$$

which is identical to (5.4). Thus, both a long and short investor want to choose $H$ to minimize the variance of the cash flow (5.4).

## 5.4 The Case of No Basis Risk

If there is no basis risk, identifying the minimum variance hedge ratio is a simple matter. In this case, we must have $S_T = F_T$, so (5.4) becomes

$$QS_T - H(F_T - F) = QS_T - H(S_T - F)$$
$$= (Q - H)S_T + HF \tag{5.6}$$

At the time the hedging strategy is initiated, $Q$ and $F$ are known quantities, so the only unknown here is $S_T$. If we set $H = Q$, the term involving $S_T$ drops out of (5.6) and the cash flow reduces to the *known* quantity $HF = QF$. The variance of this cash flow is zero. Since variance cannot be negative, we cannot improve upon this situation. Thus, if there is no basis risk, it is optimal to hedge completely, i.e., the minimum-variance hedge ratio is $h^* = 1$, and this eliminates all risk.

The important question is, of course, what if basis risk *is* present? The next section provides the answer.

## 5.5 The Minimum-Variance Hedge Ratio

To identify the minimum-variance hedge ratio, we first rewrite the cash flow (5.4) from a hedged futures position in terms of price *changes*. Let $\Delta_S = S_T - S$ and $\Delta_F = F_T - F$ denote the changes in spot and futures prices, respectively, over the hedging horizon. Add and subtract the quantity $QS$ to (5.4) to obtain

$$QS_T - QS + QS - H(F_T - F) = Q(S_T - S) - H(F_T - F) + QS$$
$$= Q\Delta_S - H\Delta_F + QS \qquad (5.7)$$

Now, let $h = H/Q$ denote the hedge ratio. The cash flow (5.7) can be expressed in terms of the hedge ratio as

$$Q[\Delta_S - h\Delta_F] + QS \qquad (5.8)$$

We want to pick $h$ to minimize the variance of this quantity. Note that the last term $QS$ is a known quantity at the time the hedge is put on, so contributes nothing to the variance. From (5.8), the variance of hedged cash flows comes from three sources:

- The variance of spot price changes $\Delta_S$. Denote this quantity by $\sigma^2(\Delta_S)$.
- The variance of futures price changes $\Delta_F$. Denote this quantity by $\sigma^2(\Delta_F)$.
- The covariance between these quantities, denoted $\text{cov}(\Delta_S, \Delta_F)$.

Using this notation, the variance of hedged cash flows (5.8) is

$$\text{Var}[Q(\Delta_S - h\Delta_F)] = Q^2 \text{Var}(\Delta_S - h\Delta_F)$$
$$= Q^2 \left[\sigma^2(\Delta_S) + h^2\sigma^2(\Delta_F) - 2h\,\text{cov}(\Delta_S, \Delta_F)\right] \qquad (5.9)$$

The presence of the $h^2$ term ensures that the last term is U-shaped as a function of $h$ (see Figure 5.1). To identify the point of minimum variance, we take the derivative of (5.9) with respect to $h$ and set it equal to zero. This yields

$$2h\,\sigma^2(\Delta_F) - 2\text{cov}(\Delta_S, \Delta_F) = 0$$

or $h\sigma^2(\Delta_F) = \text{cov}(\Delta_S, \Delta_F)$. Thus, the variance-minimizing value of $h$ is

$$h^* = \frac{\text{cov}(\Delta_S, \Delta_F)}{\sigma_F^2} \qquad (5.10)$$

To express $h^*$ in terms of the correlation $\rho$ between $\Delta_S$ and $\Delta_F$, note that by definition

$$\rho = \frac{\text{cov}(\Delta_S, \Delta_F)}{\sigma(\Delta_S)\,\sigma(\Delta_F)} \qquad (5.11)$$

Thus, $\text{cov}(\Delta_S, \Delta_F) = \rho\sigma(\Delta_S)\sigma(\Delta_F)$, so $h^*$ can also be written as

$$h^* = \rho\,\frac{\sigma(\Delta_S)}{\sigma(\Delta_F)} \qquad (5.12)$$

Expression (5.12) is the main result of this chapter. In words, as mentioned earlier, it says that the optimal hedge ratio is the correlation $\rho$ between price changes adjusted by a "scaling factor" $\sigma(\Delta_S)/\sigma(\Delta_F)$.

**FIGURE 5.1**

The Minimum-
Variance Hedge Ratio

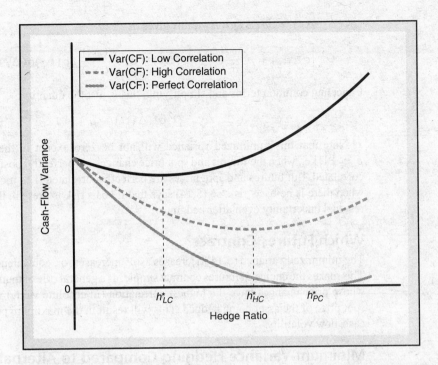

The minimum-variance hedge ratio is illustrated graphically in Figure 5.1. The figure considers a low level of correlation, a high level of correlation, and the limiting case of perfect correlation. It highlights two points. First, the minimum-variance hedge ratio increases as correlation increases. Second, the minimized cash-flow variance (i.e., the variance of cash flows under the minimum-variance hedge ratio) is lower as correlation is higher, which is intuitive: higher correlation implies a superior ability to offset cash-flow risk by hedging. In the limit, when correlation is perfect, the minimized cash-flow variance is also zero.

## Long or Short Futures Position?

The *sign* of the optimal hedge ratio is determined by the sign of the correlation $\rho$. If $\rho > 0$, the hedge ratio is positive, meaning that if the hedger has a long spot exposure (i.e., a commitment to buy on date $T$), he must take a long initial futures position, and if he has a short spot exposure (a commitment to sell on date $T$), he must take a short initial futures position. If $\rho < 0$, the hedge ratio is negative, meaning that a long spot exposure is hedged with a short initial futures position while a short spot exposure is hedged with a long futures position.

These sign implications are easily understood if one keeps in mind that hedging is basically an offsetting of risks. Suppose, for example, that the investor has a *long* spot exposure. Then, as a buyer, the investor "loses" on the spot position if spot prices increase. Under the hedge, these losses must be offset with gains on the futures position. With *positive* correlation, futures prices also increase when spot prices increase, so we must gain on the futures position when futures prices increase. This mandates a *long* futures position. With *negative* correlation, futures prices decrease when spot prices increase, so making a gain on futures requires a *short* futures position.

## The Minimized Cash-Flow Variance

What is the variance of cash flows from the hedged position under $h^*$? To identify the answer, we substitute the value of $h^*$ into the cash-flow variance (5.9). Using the identity

$\text{cov}\,(\Delta_S, \Delta_F) = \rho\sigma(\Delta_S)\sigma(\Delta_F)$, this gives us

$$Q^2 \left[ \sigma^2(\Delta_S) + \rho^2 \frac{\sigma^2(\Delta_S)}{\sigma^2(\Delta_F)} \sigma^2(\Delta_F) - 2\rho \frac{\sigma(\Delta_S)}{\sigma(\Delta_F)} \rho\sigma(\Delta_S)\sigma(\Delta_F) \right] \qquad \textbf{(5.13)}$$

Canceling common terms and simplifying, this is just the quantity

$$Q^2 \sigma^2(\Delta_S)(1 - \rho^2) \qquad \textbf{(5.14)}$$

Note that this minimized variance will not be zero except in the trivial case where $\rho = \pm 1$, i.e., when the futures and spot price changes are perfectly (positively or negatively) correlated. But futures and spot prices are perfectly correlated (i.e., move in lockstep) only when there is no basis risk, so (5.14) says that if basis risk is present, there is always some residual uncertainty even after hedging.

## Which Futures Contract?

The minimized variance (5.14) decreases as $\rho^2$ increases, or, equivalently, as $|\rho|$ increases. This makes the choice of futures contract simple: as a general rule of thumb, pick the contract whose price changes have the highest correlation (in absolute value) with changes in the spot price of the asset being hedged. This will result in the maximum possible reduction in cash-flow volatility.

## Minimum-Variance Hedging Compared to Alternatives

There are two questions about the minimum-variance hedge ratio that are of interest:

1. By how much does optimal hedging reduce uncertainty over the alternative of not hedging (i.e., using $h = 0$)?
2. How much larger is the variance of cash flows if we hedge one-for-one (i.e., set $h = 1$) rather than using $h^*$?

### (A) The Alternative of Not Hedging

If we do not put on a hedge, then $h = 0$. Substituting $h = 0$ in (5.9), the variance of the unhedged cash flow is

$$Q^2 \sigma^2(\Delta_S) \qquad \textbf{(5.15)}$$

Comparing (5.14) and (5.15), we see that optimal hedging reduces cash-flow variance by a factor of $\rho^2$. For instance, if $\rho = 0.90$, then $\rho^2 = 0.81$, so optimal hedging removes 81% of the unhedged cash-flow variance, i.e., the variance of the hedged position is only 19% of the variance of the unhedged position. On the other hand, if $\rho = 0.30$, then $\rho^2 = 0.09$, so even optimal hedging removes only 9% of the unhedged cash-flow variance.

### (B) The Alternative of Hedging One-for-One

If we use a hedge ratio of $h = 1$, the cash-flow variance in (5.9) becomes

$$Q^2 \left[ \sigma^2(\Delta_S) + \sigma^2(\Delta_F) - 2\text{cov}\,(\Delta_S, \Delta_F) \right] \qquad \textbf{(5.16)}$$

which can be rewritten as

$$Q^2 \left[ \sigma^2(\Delta_S)(1 - \rho^2) \right] + Q^2 \left[ \sigma(\Delta_F) - \rho\sigma(\Delta_S) \right]^2 \qquad \textbf{(5.17)}$$

Comparing this to the variance (5.14) under $h^*$, we see that using a hedge ratio of unity *increases* the variance by the amount $(\sigma(\Delta_F) - \rho\sigma(\Delta_S))^2$. The lower is $\rho$, the greater this quantity. This is intuitive: a lower correlation implies a lower minimum-variance hedge ratio $h^*$, so the greater is the error we are making by using a hedge ratio of unity.

Indeed, hedging one-for-one may even be worse than not hedging at all! Compare (5.17) and (5.15). The difference between these quantities is

$$Q^2 \left[ \sigma^2(\Delta_F) - 2\text{cov}(\Delta_S, \Delta_F) \right] = Q^2 \left[ \sigma^2(\Delta_F) - 2\rho\sigma(\Delta_S)\sigma(\Delta_F) \right] \quad \textbf{(5.18)}$$

If $\sigma_F > 2\rho\sigma_S$, this difference is positive, which means the variance of the cash flow with a hedge ratio of unity is *higher* than the variance of the unhedged cash flow.

# 5.6 Examples

In this section, we present two examples to illustrate minimum-variance hedging. Both examples involve basis risk arising from commodity mismatches. The first example looks at cross-hedging in currencies. The second example concerns hedging an equity portfolio using futures on another portfolio.

## Example 5.2  Cross-Hedging with Currencies

Suppose that a US exporter will receive 25 million Norwegian kroner (NOK) in three months and wishes to hedge against fluctuations in the US dollar (USD)-NOK exchange rate. Assume there is no active forward market in NOK, so the company decides to use a forward contract on the euro (EUR) instead. The company has gathered the following data:

1. The standard deviation of quarterly changes in the USD/NOK exchange rate is 0.005.
2. The standard deviation of quarterly changes in the USD/EUR forward rate is 0.025.
3. The correlation between these changes is 0.85.

What should be the company's minimum-variance hedging strategy?

The spot asset in this example is the NOK, so one "unit" of the spot asset is one NOK. The company will receive 25 million NOK in three months, which must be converted to USD. Thus, it is effectively as if the company has a commitment to sell $Q = 25$ million NOK in three months, i.e., it has a short spot exposure.

The forward contract used to hedge this exposure has the euro as its underlying asset, so one "unit" of the forward contract is a forward calling for delivery of one euro at maturity. There is commodity basis risk since the asset underlying the forward contract and the asset being hedged are not the same.

We are given $\sigma(\Delta_S) = 0.005$, $\sigma(\Delta_F) = 0.025$, and $\rho = 0.85$. From (5.12), the variance-minimizing hedge ratio is given by

$$h^* = \rho \frac{\sigma(\Delta_S)}{\sigma(\Delta_F)} = 0.85 \times \frac{0.005}{0.025} = 0.17$$

In words, the optimal hedge position is to take 0.17 units of forwards per unit of spot exposure. Why only 0.17, i.e., why is the hedge position so "small"? Loosely speaking, the euro trades roughly on par with the dollar (at the time of writing, around USD 1.45/EUR), while the Norwegian kroner costs only a fraction of that (at the time of writing in September 2009, around USD 0.17/NOK). Reflecting these price differentials, the quarterly standard deviation of the USD/EUR forward rate in the example is five times larger than the 0.005 quarterly standard deviation of the USD/NOK exchange rate.

In hedging NOK price risk with the euro, we are trying to compensate for losses from NOK price movements with gains from euro price movements and vice versa. Since the typical euro price move is five times as large as the typical NOK price move, we want to use far fewer euros in the hedge position than the number of NOK in the spot exposure.

Returning to the computations, since $Q$ is given to be 25 million and we have estimated $h^* = 0.17$, the optimal forward position calls for the delivery of

$$H^* = h^* Q = 4.25 \text{ million euros}$$

Finally, note that since the hedge ratio is positive and the company has a short spot exposure, this forward position must be a *short* one.

To summarize: the company's optimal hedge is to take a short forward position calling for the delivery of 4.25 million euros in three months. If the company's data is correct, this optimal hedge will remove $\rho^2 = (0.85)^2 = 0.7225$, or about 72% of the variance associated with the unhedged position. ∎

## Example 5.3   Cross-Hedging with Equities

Consider the problem of hedging a portfolio consisting of S&P 100 stocks using S&P 500 index futures.[1] Suppose that:

1. The value of the portfolio is $80,000,000.
2. The current level of the S&P 100 index is 800.
3. The current level of the S&P 500 index futures is 960.
4. One S&P 500 index futures contract is for 250 times the index.

The underlying asset in this problem is the S&P 100 index. That is, one "unit" of the underlying asset is the basket of stocks used to construct the S&P 100 index. The current price per unit $S$ of this asset is simply the current level of the index, so $S = 800$. Since the portfolio value is given to be $80 million, the number of "units" in the portfolio is $[80,000,000/800] = 100,000$. Therefore, $Q = 100,000$.

The asset underlying the futures contract is the S&P 500 index, i.e., one "unit" of the asset underlying the futures contract is the basket of securities used to construct the S&P 500 index. The current futures price per unit is simply the current level of the S&P 500 index futures, which gives us $F = 960$. Note that the futures contracts are standardized in size: one futures contract calls for delivery of 250 units of the S&P 500 index.

There is evidently basis risk in this problem since we are hedging one asset (the S&P 100 index) with futures written on another asset (the S&P 500 index). To determine the optimal hedging scheme, therefore, we need information on variances of spot and futures price changes over the hedging horizon, and the covariance of these price changes. Suppose we are given the following information:

1. $\sigma(\Delta_S) = 60$.
2. $\sigma(\Delta_F) = 75$.
3. $\rho = 0.90$.

Then, the optimal hedge ratio is

$$h^* = \rho \frac{\sigma_S}{\sigma_F} = 0.90 \times \frac{40}{50} = 0.72$$

i.e., to take 0.72 units of futures positions per unit of spot exposure. Since $Q = 100,000$, the size of the optimal futures position is

$$H^* = h^* \cdot Q = (0.72)(100,000) = 72,000$$

---

[1] This example is adapted from the class notes of Menachem Brenner at NYU.

That is, the optimal futures position calls for the delivery of 72,000 units of the S&P 500 index. One unit of the futures contract is for 250 units of the index. Therefore, we should take a futures position in $(72,000)/250 = 288$ contracts.

Should this be a long or short futures position? By hedging, we are trying to protect the value over the hedging horizon of the S&P 100 portfolio that we hold. Thus, it is as if we have a short spot exposure in three months and want to lock-in a value for this. Since the hedge ratio is positive, our futures position should also be a *short* one.  ■

# 5.7   Implementation

To implement a minimum-variance hedging scheme in practice we must identify $h^*$. There are two equivalent ways in which this may be accomplished, both using historical data on spot and futures price changes. The first is to estimate each of the three parameters ($\sigma(\Delta_S)$, $\sigma(\Delta_F)$, and $\rho$) that go into the computation of $h^*$. The second, and easier, method is to estimate $h^*$ directly from the data using regression analysis. We describe both approaches below.

In each case, we rely on the use of data on spot and futures prices at specified sampling intervals. For specificity, we take the sampling interval to be daily, though, of course, data of different frequency could also be used.

So, suppose that we have data on daily spot and futures price changes. Assume that price changes across different days are independent and identically distributed. Let $\delta_S$ denote the random daily spot price change and $\delta_F$ the random daily futures price change. Further, let

- $\sigma^2(\delta_S)$ denote the variance of daily spot price changes $\delta_S$.
- $\sigma^2(\delta_F)$ denote the variance of daily futures price changes $\delta_F$.
- $\mathrm{cov}(\delta_S, \delta_F)$ denote the covariance of $\delta_S$ and $\delta_F$.
- $\rho(\delta_S, \delta_F)$ denote the correlation of $\delta_S$ and $\delta_F$.

Each of these quantities may be estimated easily from historical time-series data on daily spot and futures prices.

## A First Method

Suppose there are $K$ days in the hedging horizon. Since price changes over successive days are independent, the total spot price change $\Delta_S$ over the hedging horizon is just the sum of $K$ independent daily changes, each with a variance of $\sigma^2(\delta_S)$. Thus,

$$\sigma^2(\Delta_S) = K\,\sigma^2(\delta_S) \tag{5.19}$$

Similarly, the total futures price change is just the sum of $K$ independent daily futures price changes, each with a variance of $\sigma^2(\delta_F)$. Thus,

$$\sigma^2(\Delta_F) = K\,\sigma^2(\delta_F) \tag{5.20}$$

Similarly, we also have

$$\mathrm{cov}(\Delta_S, \Delta_F) = K\,\mathrm{cov}(\delta_S, \delta_F) \tag{5.21}$$

From (5.19)–(5.21), the minimum-variance hedge ratio (5.10) can be written in terms of the *daily* price changes as

$$h^* = \frac{\mathrm{cov}(\delta_S, \delta_F)}{\sigma^2(\delta_F)} \tag{5.22}$$

Of course, we can also express this hedge ratio in terms of the correlation rather than the covariance. From (5.19)–(5.21), the covariance $\rho(\delta_S, \delta_F)$ of daily price changes is equal to the correlation $\rho$ between $\Delta_S$ and $\Delta_F$ since

$$\rho = \frac{\text{cov}(\Delta_S, \Delta_F)}{\sqrt{\sigma^2(\Delta_S)\,\sigma^2(\Delta_F)}} = \frac{K\,\text{cov}(\delta_S, \delta_F)}{\sqrt{K\sigma^2(\delta_S)\,K\sigma^2(\delta_F)}} = \rho(\delta_S, \delta_F) \qquad \textbf{(5.23)}$$

Thus, we can also write

$$h^* = \rho(\delta_S, \delta_F)\,\frac{\sigma(\delta_S)}{\sigma(\delta_F)} \qquad \textbf{(5.24)}$$

In either case, $h^*$ depends only on the properties of daily price changes and may be estimated from historical data.

### A Second Method

The second method estimates $h^*$ directly without first estimating daily variances and covariances. Suppose we have data on daily spot price changes (denoted $\delta_S$) and daily futures price changes (denoted $\delta_F$). Consider the regression

$$\delta_S = a + b\,\delta_F + \epsilon$$

Let $\widehat{a}$ and $\widehat{b}$ denote the estimates of $a$ and $b$. Then, the regression estimate $\widehat{b}$ is precisely the hedge ratio $h^*$!

Why is this the case? The regression estimates are, by definition, chosen to be unbiased (i.e., to satisfy $a + b\,\delta_F = \delta_S$ on average) and to minimize the variance of the error term $\epsilon$. Now, since $a$ is a constant, the variance of $\epsilon$ is

$$\text{Var}(\epsilon) = \text{Var}(\delta_S - a - b\,\delta_F) = \text{Var}(\delta_S - b\,\delta_F)$$

Thus, the estimate $b$ minimizes the variance of $(\delta_S - b\,\delta_F)$, the difference between daily spot price changes and $b$ times the daily futures price changes. The optimal hedge ratio $h^*$ was chosen to minimize the variance of $(\Delta_S - h\Delta_F)$, the difference between spot price change over the hedging horizon and $h$ times the futures price change over this horizon. Since total spot and future price changes over the hedging horizon are simply the sum of daily price changes, the problems are the same and must have the same solution.

This gives us a quicker and more direct way of obtaining an estimate of $h^*$ from the data, but, of course, the two methods are equivalent.

# 5.8   Further Issues in Implementation

In this section, we complete the discussion on implementation by focusing on three questions:

1. Thus far, the analysis has focused on using a single futures contract for hedging. Can we extend this to the use of *multiple futures contracts*?
2. What about hedging *multiple risks* simultaneously?
3. How do we account for the effect of daily resettlement and marking-to-market in futures contracts?

## Hedging with Multiple Futures Contracts

In the presence of basis risk, there is no a priori reason why only a single futures contract should be used in setting up the hedge. In hedging a single stock or a portfolio of stocks with index futures, for instance, it is plausible that using two different index futures contracts simultaneously may result in a better performance than using just one. Similarly, high-yield or "junk" bond returns tend to be highly correlated with equity returns. In hedging a portfolio of high-yield bonds, using a combination of equity index futures and interest-rate futures may be superior to using just one of the two.

When there are multiple futures contracts used for hedging, there are multiple hedge ratios (one for each futures contract) to be determined in the optimal hedging strategy. Determining these hedge ratios is simple. As earlier, let $\delta_S$ denote daily spot price changes. Let $\delta_{F_1}, \ldots, \delta_{F_n}$ denote the daily price changes in the $n$ futures contracts chosen for hedging. Consider the regression:

$$\delta_S = a + b_1\delta_{F_1} + \cdots + b_n\delta_{F_n} + \epsilon \qquad (5.25)$$

Then, the regression estimates $\widehat{b}_1, \ldots, \widehat{b}_n$ are precisely the hedge ratios of the $n$ contracts. The reasoning is the same as in the case of a single contract.

Should we use more than one contract? It is not possible to give an unambiguous answer to this question. Much depends on the specifics of the problem. Statistically, one can always improve the performance of a hedge by using more than one contract for exactly the same reason that one can reduce the standard error of a linear regression by adding more explanatory variables. However, one should proceed with caution here. It is well known that the improved standard error in a regression may be illusory if the added explanatory variables are unrelated ones. Analogously, there may be no real improvement in the hedge performance from using additional contracts; indeed, including a poorly related futures contract in the hedge may actually worsen the hedge.

There are statistical tests (such as the $F$ test) for comparing the fit of two regressions that we can use to gauge the improvement. At a minimum, we should check to see if the regression estimates are statistically significant and eliminate those futures that are not significant. Ultimately, common sense is the best guide here.

## Hedging Multiple Risks Simultaneously

So far we have considered hedging a single spot commitment (i.e., a single "risk") with futures. What if a firm faced several simultaneous risks, e.g., a firm that exports to many countries and faces simultaneous foreign exchange risk in all the currencies? What is the optimal hedging rule in such a situation?

The answer is a simple additive rule: identify the optimal size of the futures hedge for each risk *separately*, and then add them all up. The optimality of this rule is easily checked using the same approach as in deriving the optimal hedge ratio for a single risk. The details are left as an exercise.

## Tailing the Hedge

Thus far, we have treated the futures contract as if it is a forward contract that is marked-to-market once at the end of the contract. Now we examine the impact of *daily* marking-to-market on the size of the optimal hedge.

From (5.8), in determining the optimal hedge ratio, we are looking for the value of $h$ that minimizes

$$\mathrm{Var}\,(\Delta_S - h\Delta_F) \qquad (5.26)$$

The term $\Delta_S$, which represents spot price changes over the hedging horizon, is unaffected by daily marking-to-market, but the term $\Delta_F$, which measures resettlement profits from the futures position, depends on interest payments on the margin account. Suppose, as earlier, that there are $K$ days in the hedging horizon. Let $R$ denote one plus the daily interest rate paid on margin accounts, i.e., \$1 grows to \$$R$ at the end of one day. When daily marking-to-market is ignored, we showed that the optimal hedge ratio is

$$h^* = \frac{\text{cov}(\Delta_S, \Delta_F)}{\sigma^2(\Delta_F)} \qquad (5.27)$$

If we take daily marking-to-market into account, it can be shown that the optimal hedge ratio, denoted $h^{**}$, is simply $h^*$ multiplied by a "tail factor" $g(R, K)$:

$$h^{**} = g(R, K)\, h^* \qquad (5.28)$$

where the tail factor $g(R, K)$ is given by

$$g(R, K) = \frac{K}{1 + R + R^2 + \cdots + R^{K-1}} \qquad (5.29)$$

A proof of this result is given in Appendix 5A.

The tail factor $g$ measures the impact of daily marking-to-market. This factor is equal to 1 if $R = 1$ (i.e., net interest rates are zero) but is strictly less than 1 if $R > 1$ (i.e., interest rates are positive). However, it is very close to 1 if $R$ and $K$ are small. For example, if the interest rate on margin accounts is 5% (annualized), then the tail factor is

- 0.9994 if $K = 10$.
- 0.9967 if $K = 50$.
- 0.993 if $K = 100$.
- 0.93 if $K = 1000$.

Thus, daily marking-to-market does not make a big difference for relatively short horizons. However, over very long hedging horizons (such as the multiyear horizon of Metallgesellschaft in the case discussed in Chapter 2), tailing can make a substantial difference. Ignoring tailing in such situations will result in "overhedging," i.e., in the hedge ratio being larger than optimal, and this can increase cash-flow risk substantially.

## 5.9 Index Futures and Changing Equity Risk

In the second example in Section 5.6, we saw that futures on the S&P 500 index could be used to provide a hedge for an equity portfolio. We now examine a more general question: how we can change the nature of risk in an equity portfolio (more specifically, the beta of the portfolio) by using index futures. For this purpose, we assume that there is an index that represents the "market portfolio" and that there is a futures contract that trades on this index. In the US, the S&P 500 index futures contract plays this role; the S&P 500 index is widely viewed in practice as a proxy for the market portfolio and is used as the performance benchmark for managers of mutual funds and hedge funds.

Let $P$ denote the value of the equity portfolio and let $\beta^o$ denote its current beta. Suppose that the portfolio manager's objective is to alter this beta to a new value $\beta^n$. Let $F$ denote the current futures price per contract and suppose that the portfolio manager takes a futures position of size $H$ contracts. We allow $H$ to be positive or negative; $H > 0$ indicates a long futures position and $H < 0$ a short one.

Then, the question we are interested in is: what is the value of $H$ that will produce the required change in the portfolio beta? The required number of futures contracts is

$$H^* = -\frac{P}{F}(\beta^o - \beta^n) \qquad (5.30)$$

In particular, if the objective is to make the portfolio riskless (i.e., a zero-beta portfolio), the number of futures contracts required is

$$H^* = -\frac{P}{F}\beta^o \qquad (5.31)$$

## 5.10 Fixed-Income Futures and Duration-Based Hedging

All hedging strategies using futures contracts are based on the same idea: that by choosing the size of the futures position appropriately, it is possible to offest losses arising from spot price movements with gains on futures positions and vice versa. Hedging fixed-income instruments (e.g., a portfolio of bonds) with interest-rate futures is no different in this regard. However, fixed-income instruments have one feature that distinguishes them from other assets: both the spot price of such an instrument and the futures price of a contract written on a fixed-income instrument depend on a *common* underlying variable—the level of interest rates. This makes it possible to devise a special hedging strategy called *duration-based hedging*.

Duration-based hedging is explored in the next chapter. Intuitively, duration-based hedging looks at how much a change in interest rates would affect (a) the value of the portfolio we are looking to hedge and (b) the price of the interest-rate futures contract we are using for hedging. We then choose the number of futures contracts to be used in the hedge so that these value changes offset each other.

## 5.11 Exercises

1. What is meant by *basis risk*?

2. What is the minimum-variance hedge ratio? What are the variables that determine this?

3. How does one obtain the optimal hedge ratio from knowledge of daily price changes in spot and futures markets?

4. What is tailing the hedge in the context of minimum-variance hedging? Why does one tail the hedge?

5. In the presence of basis risk, is a one-for-one hedge, i.e., a hedge ratio of 1, always better than not hedging at all?

6. If the correlation between spot and futures price changes is $\rho = 0.8$, what fraction of cash-flow uncertainty is removed by minimum-variance hedging?

7. The correlation between changes in the price of the underlying and a futures contract is $+80\%$. The same underlying is correlated with another futures contract with a (negative) correlation of $-85\%$. Which of the two contracts would you prefer for the minimum-variance hedge?

8. Given the following information on the statistical properties of the spot and futures, compute the minimum-variance hedge ratio: $\sigma_S = 0.2$, $\sigma_F = 0.25$, $\rho = 0.96$.

9. Assume that the spot position comprises 1,000,000 units in the stock index. If the hedge ratio is 1.09, how many units of the futures contract are required to hedge this position?

10. You have a position in 200 shares of a technology stock with an annualized standard deviation of changes in the price of the stock being 30. Say that you want to hedge this position with the tech stock index that has an annual standard deviation of changes in value of 20. The correlation between the two is 0.8. How many units of the index should you hold to have the best hedge?

11. You are a portfolio manager looking to hedge a portfolio daily over a 30-day horizon. Here are the values of the spot portfolio and a hedging futures for 30 days.

| Day | Spot | Futures |
|-----|--------|---------|
| 0 | 80.000 | 81.000 |
| 1 | 79.635 | 80.869 |
| 2 | 77.880 | 79.092 |
| 3 | 76.400 | 77.716 |
| 4 | 75.567 | 77.074 |
| 5 | 77.287 | 78.841 |
| 6 | 77.599 | 79.315 |
| 7 | 78.147 | 80.067 |
| 8 | 77.041 | 79.216 |
| 9 | 76.853 | 79.204 |
| 10 | 77.034 | 79.638 |
| 11 | 75.960 | 78.659 |
| 12 | 75.599 | 78.549 |
| 13 | 77.225 | 80.512 |
| 14 | 77.119 | 80.405 |
| 15 | 77.762 | 81.224 |
| 16 | 77.082 | 80.654 |
| 17 | 76.497 | 80.233 |
| 18 | 75.691 | 79.605 |
| 19 | 75.264 | 79.278 |
| 20 | 76.504 | 80.767 |
| 21 | 76.835 | 81.280 |
| 22 | 78.031 | 82.580 |
| 23 | 79.185 | 84.030 |
| 24 | 77.524 | 82.337 |
| 25 | 76.982 | 82.045 |
| 26 | 76.216 | 81.252 |
| 27 | 76.764 | 81.882 |
| 28 | 79.293 | 84.623 |
| 29 | 78.861 | 84.205 |
| 30 | 76.192 | 81.429 |

Carry out the following analyses:

(a) Compute $\sigma(\Delta_S)$, $\sigma(\Delta_F)$, and $\rho$.

(b) Using the results from (a), compute the hedge ratio you would use.

(c) Using this hedge ratio, calculate the daily change in value of the hedged portfolio.

(d) What is the standard deviation of changes in value of the hedged portfolio? How does this compare to the standard deviation of changes in the unhedged spot position?

12. Use the same data as presented above to compute the hedge ratio using regression analysis. Explain why the values are different from what you obtained above.

13. A US-based corporation has decided to make an investment in Sweden, for which it will require a sum of 100 million Swedish kronor (SEK) in three-months' time. The company wishes to hedge changes in the US dollar (USD)-SEK exchange rate using forward contracts on either the euro (EUR) or the Swiss franc (CHF) and has made the following estimates:

    - If EUR forwards are used: The standard deviation of quarterly changes in the USD/SEK spot exchange rate is 0.007, the standard deviation of quarterly changes in the USD/EUR forward rate is 0.018, and the correlation between the changes is 0.90.
    - If CHF forwards are used: The standard deviation of quarterly changes in the USD/SEK spot exchange rate is 0.007, the standard deviation of quarterly changes in the USD/CHF forward rate is 0.023, and the correlation between the changes is 0.85.

    Finally, the current USD/SEK spot rate is 0.104, the current three-month USD/EUR forward rate is 0.471, and the current three-month USD/CHF forward rate is 0.602.

    (a) Which currency should the company use for hedging purposes?

    (b) What is the minimum-variance hedge position? Indicate if this is to be a long or short position.

14. You use silver wire in manufacturing, looking to buy 100,000 oz of silver in three months' time and need to hedge silver price changes in three months. One COMEX silver futures contract is for 5,000 oz. You run a regression of daily silver spot price changes on silver futures price changes and find that

    $$\delta_s = 0.03 + 0.89\delta_F + \epsilon$$

    What should be the size (number of contracts) of your optimal futures position. Should this be long or short?

15. Suppose you have the following information: $\rho = 0.95, \sigma_S = 24, \sigma_F = 26, K = 90, R = 1.00018$. What is the minimum-variance tailed hedge?

16. Using the equation for tailing the hedge, can you explain why the tailed hedge ratio is always less than the ratio for untailed (static) hedge?

17. You manage a portfolio of GM bonds and run a regression of your bond's price changes on the changes in the S&P 500 index futures and changes in the 10-year Treasury note futures. The regression result is as follows:

    $$\delta_P = 0.02 - 0.2\delta_{S\&P} + 0.5\delta_{TRY}, \quad R^2 = 0.7$$

    where the regression above is in changes in index values for all the right-hand side variables. What positions in the two index futures will you take? What proportion of the risk remains unhedged? What implicit assumption might you be making in this case?

18. You are asked to hedge the forward price of a security $S$ over a maturity $T$. The correlations of $S$, and futures contracts $F_1$, $F_2$ are given by the following correlation matrix:

    |       | S       | $F_1$   | $F_2$   |
    |-------|---------|---------|---------|
    | S     | 1.00000 | 0.98757 | 0.82923 |
    | $F_1$ | 0.98757 | 1.00000 | 0.84939 |
    | $F_2$ | 0.82923 | 0.84939 | 1.00000 |

    If the standard deviations of the returns on the three assets are given by

    $$\sigma(S) = 0.30$$
    $$\sigma(F_1) = 0.25$$
    $$\sigma(F_2) = 0.15$$

then, find the minimum-variance hedge for $S$ using both futures contracts $F_1$ and $F_2$. Express your solution in terms of the number of dollars you will place in positions in $F_1$ and $F_2$ to hedge a $1 position in $S$. What can you say about the solution(s) you have arrived at?

19. Our firm receives foreign exchange remittances in several different currencies. We are interested in hedging two remittances in six months time from Europe (200 in EUR) and from Japan (400,000 in JPY). If the sales were made today, we would receive the USD equivalent of these remittances at today's spot exchange rates. However, there may be a big change in spot FX rates by the end of the six-month period. In order to ensure that there are no surprises, we want to hedge the risk of changes in FX rates from now to six months ahead. The following tables give the correlations and covariances of changes in spot FX and forward FX rates. The notation below is such that $S(usd, eur)$ stands for dollars per euro.

| CORRMAT | $\Delta S(usd, eur)$ | $\Delta S(usd, jpy)$ | $\Delta F(usd, eur)$ | $\Delta F(usd, jpy)$ |
|---|---|---|---|---|
| $\Delta S(usd, eur)$ | 1 | | | |
| $\Delta S(usd, jpy)$ | 0.1480 | 1 | | |
| $\Delta F(usd, eur)$ | 0.7099 | 0.0914 | 1 | |
| $\Delta F(usd, jpy)$ | 0.1441 | 0.7419 | 0.1008 | 1 |

| COVMAT | $\Delta S(usd, eur)$ | $\Delta S(usd, jpy)$ | $\Delta F(usd, eur)$ | $\Delta F(usd, jpy)$ |
|---|---|---|---|---|
| $\Delta S(usd, eur)$ | 0.000107 | 0.000015 | 0.000106 | 0.000021 |
| $\Delta S(usd, jpy)$ | 0.000015 | 0.000096 | 0.000013 | 0.000103 |
| $\Delta F(usd, eur)$ | 0.000106 | 0.000013 | 0.000206 | 0.000020 |
| $\Delta F(usd, jpy)$ | 0.000021 | 0.000103 | 0.000020 | 0.000200 |

Note that the matrices of changes above reflect the change in USD amounts per unit of the foreign currency. This follows from the fact that the exchange rates are expressed as dollars per unit of foreign currency. If we want to hedge an inflow of EUR 200 and JPY 400,000, how many units of foreign currency must we hold in forward FX contracts to get the best hedge? Note that the best hedge is one that minimizes the variance of changes in the total remitted amount. Carry out your analysis in the following three steps:

(i) Compute what the variance of changes in remitted USD amount is if we do no hedging.

(ii) Compute what the variance of changes in remitted USD amount is if we do one-for-one hedging.

(iii) Compute what the variance of changes in remitted USD amount is if we do minimum-variance hedging.

20. HoleSale Inc. USA exports manhole covers to Japan and Germany. Over the next six months, the company anticipates sales of 1,000 units to Japan and 500 units to Germany. The price of manhole covers is set at JPY 10,000 and EUR 80 in Japan and Germany, respectively. The following information is given:

- The standard deviation of the JPY/USD exchange rate is 5.
- The standard deviation of the EUR/USD exchange rate is 0.05.
- The correlation of the JPY/USD and EUR/USD exchange rates is −0.4.
- The standard deviation of the EUR/USD six-month forward rate is 0.06.

HoleSale Inc. is going to use the EUR/USD forward FX market to hedge all currency risk across countries to which it sells its product by booking a single forward contract that minimizes the company's risk. How many units of this contract should the firm buy/sell?

21. You are attempting to cover a short forward position of $S$ with a long futures contract for the same maturity. Which do you prefer as a hedge: futures contract $F_1$ or $F_2$, where $\sigma(F_1) > \sigma(F_2)$, and given that the correlation of both futures contracts with $S$ is the same? Explain your reasoning.

22. You are planning to enter into a long forward hedge to offset a short forward position. If you choose a futures contract over a forward contract, which of the following circumstances do you want?

    (a) Do you want the term structure of interest rates (i.e., the plot of interest rates against maturities) to be sloped up or down?

    (b) Do you want the volatility of interest rates to be increasing or decreasing?

    (c) Do you want the volatility of the futures price change to be higher or lower than that of the forward price?

    (d) Do you want the correlation of the spot to futures to be higher or lower than that of the spot to forwards?

23. You are trying to hedge the sale of a forward contract on a security $A$. Suggest a framework you might use for making a choice between the following two hedging schemes:

    (a) Buy a futures contract $B$ that is highly correlated with security $A$ but trades very infrequently. Hence, the hedge may not be immediately available.

    (b) Buy a futures contract $C$ that is poorly correlated with $A$ but trades more frequently.

24. Download data from the web as instructed below and answer the questions below:

    (a) Extract one year's data on the S&P 500 index from `finance.yahoo.com`. Also download corresponding period data for the S&P 100 index.

    (b) Download, for the same period, data on the three-month Treasury bill rate (constant maturity) from the Federal Reserve's web page on historical data:
    `www.federalreserve.gov/releases/h15/data.htm`.

    (c) Create a data series of three-month forwards on the S&P 500 index using the index data and the interest rates you have already extracted. Call this synthetic forward data series $F$.

    (d) How would you use this synthetic forwards data to determine the tracking error of a hedge of three-month maturity positions in the S&P 100 index? You need to think (a) about how to set up the time lags of the data and (b) how to represent tracking error.

25. Explain the relationship between regression $R^2$ and tracking error of a hedge. Use the data collected in the previous question to obtain a best tracking error hedge using regression.

# Derivation of the Optimal Tailed Hedge Ratio $h^{**}$

Recall that to identify the minimum-variance hedge, we must find the value of $h$ that minimizes

$$\Delta_S - h\,\Delta_F \qquad \text{(5.32)}$$

where $\Delta_S$ is the change in spot prices over the hedging horizon and $\Delta_F$ represents the resettlement profits on the futures position. When we ignored interest payments on the margin account, we took the futures resettlement profits to be

$$\Delta_F = (F_1 - F_0) + (F_2 - F_1) + \cdots + (F_K - F_{K-1}) \qquad \text{(5.33)}$$

With an interest rate of $R$, the first day's profit or loss, $(F_1 - F_0)$, will accumulate interest at the rate $R$ for $K-1$ days and so will amount to $R^{K-1}(F_1 - F_0)$ by maturity. The second day's profit or loss, $(F_2 - F_1)$, will accumulate interest for $K-2$ days and so grow to $R^{K-2}(F_2 - F_1)$ by maturity. Doing the same thing for the profits or losses on each of the $K$ days shows that the total resettlement profits from the futures position amount to

$$\Delta_F = R^{K-1}(F_1 - F_0) + R^{K-2}(F_2 - F_1) + \cdots + (F_K - F_{K-1}) \qquad \text{(5.34)}$$

Assume daily price changes are independent and identically distributed (i.i.d.) Let $\delta_F$ denote the random daily futures price change with variance $\sigma^2(\delta_F)$. Then, viewed from time-0, the overall resettlement profits amount to

$$\Delta_F = \left[ R^{K-1} + R^{K-2} + \cdots + R + 1 \right] \delta_F \qquad \text{(5.35)}$$

For notational simplicity, let $f(R, K) = 1 + R + \cdots R^{K-1}$. Then,

$$\Delta_F = f(R, K)\,\delta_F \qquad \text{(5.36)}$$

The total spot price change $\Delta_S$ remains, as earlier, the sum of daily price changes

$$\Delta_S = (S_1 - S_0) + (S_2 - S_1) + \cdots + (S_K - S_{K-1}) \qquad \text{(5.37)}$$

If $\delta_S$ denotes the random daily spot price change (with variance $\sigma^2(\delta_S)$), then

$$\Delta_S = K\,\delta_S \qquad \text{(5.38)}$$

Therefore, with daily marking-to-market, the total cash flow (5.32) from the hedged position can be expressed in terms of daily price changes as

$$\Delta_S - h\,\Delta_F = K\,\delta_S - h\,f(R, K)\delta_F \qquad \text{(5.39)}$$

The variance of this total cash flow is

$$K^2\sigma^2(\delta_S) + h^2[f(R, K)]^2\sigma^2(\delta_F) - 2h\,Kf(R, K)\,\mathrm{cov}(\delta_S, \delta_F) \qquad \text{(5.40)}$$

The $h^2$ term once again ensures that this variance is U-shaped as a function of $h$. To find the point of minimum-variance, we take the derivative of (5.40) with respect to $h$ and set it equal to zero. After simplifying and eliminating common terms, this gives us

$$h\,f(R, K)\sigma^2(\delta_F) = K\,\mathrm{cov}(\delta_S, \delta_F) \qquad \text{(5.41)}$$

from which we finally obtain the optimal hedge ratio as

$$h^{**} = \frac{K}{f(R, K)} \frac{\text{cov}(\delta_S, \delta_F)}{\sigma^2(\delta_F)} \tag{5.42}$$

The last term on the right-hand side of (5.42) is exactly the optimal hedge ratio $h^*$ that obtains when daily marking-to-market is ignored. Thus, if we define

$$g(R, K) = \frac{K}{1 + R + R^2 + \cdots + R^{K-1}}$$

the optimal hedge ratio with daily marking-to-market is simply the old hedge ratio $h^*$ multiplied by the "tail" factor $g(R, K)$:

$$h^{**} = g(R, K) h^* \tag{5.43}$$

# Chapter 6

# Interest-Rate Forwards and Futures

## 6.1  Introduction

Interest-rate forwards and futures are contracts where the underlying is an interest rate or depends on the level of interest rates. Two of the most widely used contracts of this form are forward-rate agreements, which are over-the-counter (OTC) products, and eurodollar futures, which are exchange-traded. In both contracts, payoffs depend directly on specified interest rates. There are also other popular contracts, such as futures contracts on US treasuries, German government bonds or "bunds," UK gilts, and Japanese government bonds, in which the underlying asset is a bond. This chapter describes each of these products and their characteristics.

Following these descriptions, this chapter looks at the notion of hedging fixed-income risk. All strategies that aim to hedge spot price exposure with futures contracts are based on the same idea, that of offsetting the effects of spot price changes with futures price movements. Hedging fixed-income instruments (e.g., hedging a portfolio of bonds with bond futures) is no different in this regard. However, fixed-income instruments have one feature that distinguishes them from other assets: both the spot price of such an instrument and the futures price of a contract written on a fixed-income instrument depend on a *common* underlying variable—the level of interest rates. This makes it possible to devise a special hedging strategy called *duration-based hedging*. The final section of this chapter examines duration-based hedging.

Some of the most important products described in this chapter depend on the London Interbank Offered Rate or Libor. We begin this chapter with an introduction to Libor rates and the convention used to compute interest in this market.

## 6.2  Eurodollars and Libor Rates

US dollar deposits maintained in banks outside the US (including foreign branches of US banks) are called *eurodollar* deposits. The term *eurocurrency deposits* or *eurodeposits* is used more generally to refer to deposits in a currency maintained offshore relative to the country of origination. For the most part, the eurodeposit market operates outside the control of central banks. The euromarket operations of US banks are, for example, exempt from reserve requirements and no FDIC premia are imposed against their eurodollar deposits. Thus, every eurodollar received can be invested.

The interest rate on eurodollar deposits in interbank transactions is called the London Interbank Offered Rate or Libor. The spot Libor market is huge with especially great depth in the three- and six-month segments. Libor is now the benchmark rate for several other markets; swaps, commercial paper, and floating-rate eurodollar loans are, for example, all indexed to Libor.

Libor rates are quoted using the money market day-count convention. In the US, a "year" in this convention is treated as 360 days. The interest payable per dollar of principal is then computed as

$$\text{Libor} \times \frac{d}{360} \tag{6.1}$$

where $d$ is the actual number of days in the investment horizon. This is the "Actual/360 convention." The euro money market similarly uses an Actual/360 day-count convention, but the money market convention for pound sterling is Actual/365.

For example, suppose the Libor rate for the three-month period begining March 16 and ending June 15 is 4%. Consider the interest payable at maturity on an investment of $1 million. The number of days in this investment horizon is 15 in March, 30 in April, 31 in May, and 15 in June for a total of 91 days. The interest due at maturity is

$$0.04 \times \frac{91}{360} \times 1{,}000{,}000 = 10{,}111.11 \tag{6.2}$$

We denote by $B(T)$ the present value of $1 receivable in $T$ months' time computed using Libor rates for discounting. If $\ell_T$ denotes the $T$-month Libor rate and $d$ the number of days in this horizon, a dollar invested at Libor for $T$ months grows to

$$1 + \ell_T \frac{d}{360} \tag{6.3}$$

Thus, the present value of a dollar due in $T$ months is

$$B(T) = \frac{1}{1 + \ell_T \frac{d}{360}} \tag{6.4}$$

For example, suppose the current three-month Libor rate is 9%. Suppose there are 91 days in these three months. Then, $1 invested today will grow to

$$1 + (0.09) \frac{91}{360} = 1.02275 \tag{6.5}$$

in three months. Thus, the present value of $1 receivable after three months is

$$B(3) = \frac{1}{1.02275} = 0.9778 \tag{6.6}$$

## 6.3 Forward-Rate Agreements

*Forward-rate agreements* or FRAs are forward contracts written on interest rates rather than on the price of a traded security or commodity. Hugely popular in their own right, they are also the bulding blocks of other popular interest-rate derivatives such as swaps.

FRAs enable investors to lock in an interest rate $k$ for borrowing or lending a specified principal amount $P$ over a specified investment period $[T_1, T_2]$ in the future, i.e., a period beginning in $T_1$ years and ending in $T_2$ years. Such an FRA is referred to as a $T_1 \times T_2$ FRA. By market convention, the investment period is stated in terms of months; for example, a

$4 \times 7$ FRA refers to the three-month investment period beginning in four months and ending in seven months. We adopt this convention in this chapter.

## Payoffs from an FRA

An FRA is very similar to a commitment in which the long position agrees to borrow from the short position the amount $P$ at the fixed interest rate $k$ for the period $[T_1, T_2]$. However, there are some important differences. In an actual borrowing/lending of this form, the long position would receive the principal amount $P$ from the short position on date $T_1$ and would return the principal plus interest at the fixed rate $k$ on date $T_2$. The FRA modifies these cash flows in two directions.

First, no actual exchange of the principal $P$ takes place in an FRA. Rather, the long position in the FRA receives from the short position the *difference* between a reference interest rate $\ell$ and the agreed-upon fixed rate $k$ applied to the principal $P$ for the period $[T_1, T_2]$. Of course, if the difference $\ell - k$ is negative, then this is interpreted as a payment from the long position to the short position.

Second, in an actual borrowing or lending, the interest payment is due only at the maturity date $T_2$. Rather than wait until $T_2$, however, the difference $\ell - k$ in an FRA is settled on date $T_1$ itself by discounting the cash flows due on date $T_2$ back to $T_1$.

The reference interest rate in an FRA is commonly the Libor rate applicable to a period of length $[T_1, T_2]$. For example, if the period $[T_1, T_2]$ is three months long, then $\ell$ is taken to be three-month Libor. Throughout this section, we take the reference rate to be the appropriate Libor rate.

The following example illustrates FRA payoffs. FRAs are money market instruments, so the money market day-count convention is used to compute interest payments. In the US, this is the Actual/360 convention described in the previous section.

| Example 6.1 | **FRA Payoffs** |

Suppose today is March 15 and an investor enters into a long $4 \times 7$ FRA where the floating rate is three-month Libor, the principal amount is $P = \$5,000,000$, and the fixed rate is $k = 5.00\%$. The investment period in this FRA begins on July 15 (four months from today) and ends on October 15 (seven months from today), which is 92 days.

Suppose the actual three-month Libor rate that prevails on July 15 is $\ell = 5.40\%$. The difference $\ell - k$ is $+0.40\%$. Applying this difference to the principal amount of $\$5,000,000$ for 92 days results in

$$0.004 \times \frac{92}{360} \times 5,000,000 = 5,111.11 \qquad (6.7)$$

This amount must be brought back to July 15. To do so, we discount it at the three-month Libor rate prevailing on July 15. This gives us:

$$\frac{5,111.11}{1 + (0.054)\frac{92}{360}} = 5,041.54 \qquad (6.8)$$

This is the amount the investor receives from the short position on July 15.

Alternatively, suppose the three-month Libor rate on July 15 is $\ell = 4.70\%$. The difference $\ell - k$ in interest rates is now $4.70 - 5.00 = -0.30\%$. Applying this to the principal amount of $\$5,000,000$, the difference in interest rates amounts to

$$-0.003 \times \frac{92}{360} \times 5,000,000 = -3,833.33 \qquad (6.9)$$

**FIGURE 6.1**

FRA Payoffs

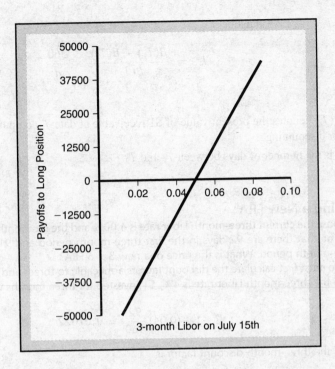

Discounting this payoff back to July 15 at the three-month Libor rate $\ell$, we obtain

$$-\left(\frac{3,833.33}{1+(0.047)\frac{92}{360}}\right) = -3,787.83 \qquad \textbf{(6.10)}$$

The investor must now make this payment to the short position on July 15. ∎

Figure 6.1 plots the payoffs that result to the long FRA position in Example 6.1 for various possible values of the Libor rate $\ell$ on July 15. The formula used to compute these payoffs is

$$\text{Payoff to long position} = \frac{(\ell - 0.05) \times \frac{92}{360}}{1 + \ell \frac{92}{360}} \times 5,000,000 \qquad \textbf{(6.11)}$$

Note that although the payoffs in Figure 6.1 appear to be linear in $\ell$, there is actually a very slight curvature present since the quantity $\ell$ appears in both the numerator and denominator of (6.11).

More generally, in an FRA with an investment period of $d$ days, a principal amount of $P$, and a fixed rate of $k$, we have

$$\text{Payoff to long position} = \frac{(\ell - k) \times \frac{d}{360}}{1 + \ell \frac{d}{360}} \times P \qquad \textbf{(6.12)}$$

where $\ell$ is the realized floating rate on the settlement date.

## Pricing a New FRA

At the inception of an FRA, the fixed rate $k$ is chosen so that the contract has zero value to both parties. This rate is referred to as the "price" of a new FRA. In Appendix 6A, we describe how this rate may be determined by replication, i.e., by constructing a portfolio that mimics the cash-flow structure of the FRA. We show that the arbitrage-free price of a new $T_1 \times T_2$ FRA must be

$$k^* = \frac{B(T_1) - B(T_2)}{B(T_2)} \times \frac{360}{d} \qquad \textbf{(6.13)}$$

where

- $B(T)$ denotes the present value of \$1 receivable at date $T$ computed using Libor rates for discounting.
- $d$ is the number of days between $T_1$ and $T_2$.

## Example 6.2 Pricing a New FRA

Suppose the current three-month Libor rate is 4.00% and the six-month Libor rate is 4.50%. Assume that there are 92 days in the first three-month period and 91 days in the second three-month period. What is the price of a new $3 \times 6$ FRA?

We must first calculate the discount factors applicable to three- and six-month horizons. Since the three-month Libor rate is 4%, \$1 invested for three months will grow to

$$1 + (0.04)\frac{92}{360} = 1.01022$$

Thus, the three-month discount factor is

$$B(3) = \frac{1}{1.01022} = 0.98988 \qquad \textbf{(6.14)}$$

Similarly, \$1 invested for six months grows to

$$1 + (0.045)\frac{183}{360} = 1.02288$$

so the six-month discount factor is

$$B(6) = \frac{1}{1.02288} = 0.97763 \qquad \textbf{(6.15)}$$

Now, using these discount factors in (6.13), the arbitrage-free price of a $3 \times 6$ FRA is seen to be

$$k^* = \frac{0.98988 - 0.97763}{0.97763} \times \frac{360}{91} = 4.96\% \qquad \textbf{(6.16)}$$

∎

## Valuing an Existing FRA

Consider an FRA with notional principal amount $P$ entered into some time ago with a fixed rate of $k$. Let date 0 denote the current time and suppose that the FRA period is $[T_1, T_2]$, i.e., the FRA begins in $T_1$ months and ends in $T_2$ months. How much is the FRA worth today?

Let $d$ denote the number of days between $T_1$ and $T_2$. With $B(T)$ defined as above, we show in Appendix 6A (see expression (6.66)) that the value of the FRA is then given by

$$P \times \left\{ B(T_1) - B(T_2)\left(1 + k\frac{d}{360}\right) \right\} \qquad \textbf{(6.17)}$$

Indeed, the price (6.13) of a new FRA is obtained just by setting this value to zero and solving for $k$.

---

**Example 6.3**

### Valuing an Existing FRA

Consider the 3 × 6 FRA from Example 6.2 above. The FRA is entered into at the fixed rate of 4.96%. Suppose the principal amount is $25,000,000. After one month, the FRA has become a 2 × 5 FRA. Suppose that at this time, the two- and five-month Libor rates are 5.50% and 6%, respectively. How much is the FRA worth today? Assume that there are 61 days in the first two-month period from today, and, as in the original example, that there are 91 days in the three-month period of the FRA.

An investment of $1 for two months at the Libor rate of 5.50% grows to

$$1 + (0.055)\frac{61}{360} = 1.00932$$

by maturity. Thus, the two-month discount factor is

$$B(2) = \frac{1}{1.00932} = 0.99077 \tag{6.18}$$

Similarly, the five-month discount factor is

$$B(5) = 0.97529 \tag{6.19}$$

Substituting these values in (6.17), the current value of the FRA is seen to be

$$25,000,000 \times \left\{ 0.99077 - (0.97529)\left(1 + (0.0496)\frac{91}{360}\right) \right\} = +81,150.40 \tag{6.20}$$

The positive value of the original FRA reflects the fact that interest rates have gone up since the FRA was entered into. ∎

## Hedging with FRAs

If an FRA involves only an exchange of the difference in interest rates, how does it allow borrowers and lenders to hedge interest-rate risk, i.e., to lock-in rates for borrowing/lending in the future?

Consider a corporation that can borrow at Libor and that anticipates a borrowing need for the period $[T_1, T_2]$. Suppose the corporation (a) enters into a long FRA today with a fixed rate $k$, and then (b) borrows the required amount at time $T_1$ at the then-prevailing Libor rate $\ell$. Under this strategy, the corporation pays the interest rate $\ell$ on the borrowed amount but receives the difference $\ell - k$ from the FRA. The *net* rate paid is $\ell - (\ell - k) = k$, which is the fixed rate in the FRA.

Similarly, consider an investor who wishes to lock in an interest rate for lending over the period $[T_1, T_2]$ in the future. The investor can enter into a short FRA today and then lend at $T_1$ at the then-prevailing Libor rate $\ell$. The investor receives $\ell$ from the lending but pays $\ell - k$ on the FRA, so receives a net rate of $k$, the fixed rate in the FRA.

Thus, by combining a position in an FRA with borrowing or lending at the Libor rate $\ell$ at time $T_1$, borrowers and investors effectively lock in the fixed rate in the FRA. The following example provides an illustration.

---

**Example 6.4**

### Hedging with FRAs

We build on Example 6.1 above. On March 15, a corporation anticipates a need to borrow $5,000,000 for the three-month period from July 15 to October 15. The corporation enters into a long $4 \times 7$ FRA on March 15 and borrows the \$5 million at Libor on July 15. The fixed rate in the FRA is $k = 5.00\%$.

We consider two possibilities for the Libor rate on July 15, $\ell = 5.40\%$ and $\ell = 4.70\%$, and show that the corporation's net cash flows are the same in either case. Of course, these two Libor rates are only illustrative; as the reader may check, the net cash flows are the same whatever the Libor rate on July 15. For the calculations, note that there are 92 days in the three-month period between July 15 and October 15.

### Case 1: Libor on July 15 Is 5.40%

In this case, as we saw in Example 6.1, the long position (here, the corporation) receives \$5,041.54 on July 15 in settlement from the FRA. Investing these receipts at the prevailing Libor rate of 5.40% for three months, the corporation receives the following cash inflow on October 15:

$$5,041.54 \times \left( 1 + (0.054)\frac{92}{360} \right) = 5,111.11 \qquad (6.21)$$

The corporation must also pay interest on the \$5,000,000 loan taken on July 15 at Libor. This interest amounts to

$$5,000,000 \times (0.054)\frac{92}{360} = 69,000.00 \qquad (6.22)$$

Thus, the net cash outflow facing the corporation is

$$69,000 - 5,111.11 = 63,888.89 \qquad (6.23)$$

### Case 2: Libor on July 15 Is 4.70%

As we saw in Example 6.1, the long position must now *pay* the short position an amount of 3,787.83 on July 15. Suppose the corporation borrows this amount on July 15 for three months at the Libor rate of 4.70%. The resulting cash outflow in three months is

$$3,787.83 \times \left( 1 + (0.047)\frac{92}{360} \right) = 3,833.33 \qquad (6.24)$$

In addition, the corporation also owes interest on the \$5,000,000 loan taken at Libor on July 15. This interest is

$$5,000,000 \times (0.047)\frac{92}{360} = 60,055.56 \qquad (6.25)$$

Thus, the net interest cost the corporation incurs is

$$60,055.56 + 3,833.33 = 63,888.89 \qquad (6.26)$$

which is identical to (6.23).

### Remark

In practice, such perfect hedges are infeasible since companies may not be able to borrow or invest at Libor flat for odd cash flows. The actual hedge will be very good but involve some slippage. This raises an interesting question: why are FRAs settled in discounted form rather than at maturity, when the latter would allow companies to obtain better hedges? One reason, suggested by Flavell (2002), is that discounted settlement is preferred by banks because it reduces the bank's credit exposure to the holder of the FRA. ∎

# 6.4  Eurodollar Futures

Eurodollar futures are the exchange-traded counterparts of FRAs in that they too are instruments designed to enable investors to lock-in Libor rates for future investment or borrowing. But while they are similar to FRAs in many ways, there are also important differences that stem from their standardization.

For practical purposes, a eurodollar futures contract may be thought of as an instrument that enables investors to lock in a Libor rate for a *three-month* period beginning *on the expiry date of the contract.* (Precise definitions of the contract and its payoffs are offered further below.) So, for example, for a futures contract expiring in September, the locked-in Libor rate applies to the three-month period from September to December. At any point in time, the CME and SGX (the two dominant exchanges in eurodollar futures trading) offer 44 expiry dates on eurodollar futures contracts: contracts expiring in March, June, September, and December for each of the next 10 years plus contracts in the four nearest serial expiry months outside the quarterly cycle. This means investors can lock in three-month rates as much as 10 years out in the future.

Note the contrast with FRAs here. In an FRA, the investment/borrowing period can be specified as the counterparties wish; for example, a $4 \times 10$ FRA locks in an investment/borrowing rate for a six-month period beginning in four months. In the eurodollar futures contract, this period is standardized both in terms of length (three months) and in terms of its starting date (one of the 44 standard expiry dates of the futures contract). Other differences with FRAs will be pointed out as we go along.

A more detailed description of the contract and its use in hedging interest-rate risk follows. But first, some remarks to put the contract into perspective.

## A Historical Note

Eurodollar futures were not the first interest-rate futures contracts. The Treasury bill and Treasury bond futures contracts launched in 1976 and 1977, respectively, had come earlier, and the short-lived GNMA CDR futures contract discussed in Chapter 2 preceded both of these.[1] But while Treasury futures were useful in managing interest-rate risk on US Treasury obligations, the volatile nature of the spread between Treasury borrowing rates and rates on private money market instruments meant that they did not do nearly as well in hedging private short-term liabilities.

In the late 1970s, the Chicago exchanges introduced futures contracts on private debt instruments such as commercial paper (CP) and certificates of deposit (CDs). These efforts ultimately floundered because there was a lack of homogeneity in the instruments deliverable at the contract's maturity. The troubles of such large banks as Continental Illinois and Chase Manhattan during this period showed that CDs issued by even large banks could have dissimilar credit risk, while Chrysler's near-bankruptcy experience in 1980 highlighted the same problem for issuers of CP.

The eurodollar futures contract was introduced against this backdrop in December 1981. In a short period of five years, the contract overhauled CD futures and other competitors to become easily the money-market futures contract of choice, indeed to become one of the largest traded futures contracts in the world. So how did it handle the settlement obstacle that earlier contracts had tripped over? The answer is simplicity itself. Unlike its predecessors that

---

[1] Burghardt (2003) presents a detailed analysis of eurodollar futures including a discussion of their evolution. The historical description here is based on his work.

had required physical settlement of the contract (so homogeneity of the delivered instrument became a matter of concern), eurodollar futures contracts proposed *cash* settlement of the contract. The acceptance of this then-novel proposal by the CFTC had far-reaching consequences. Among other things, it paved the way for other cash-settled futures contracts such as stock-index futures that have subsequently enjoyed great popularity.

## Trading Volume and Liquidity

Eurodollar futures contracts are consistently among the largest traded futures contracts in the world. Open interest in all contract months combined exceeded 3 million contracts in June 2000 and 4.5 million contracts in June 2002. Since each contract has a face value of $1,000,000, these figures represent a total notional outstanding of several trillions of dollars.

A noteworthy feature of eurodollar futures contracts, and one that distinguishes them from virtually all other futures contracts, is the high trading volume and liquidity along the entire maturity spectrum. In particular, there is substantial volume and open interest even in back-month contracts. In contrast, for example, almost all the open interest in Treasury futures contracts is concentrated in the first two expiry months.

## Contract Specification

As we have seen, the payoffs of an FRA are specified directly in terms of the difference between a fixed interest rate and the actual realized Libor rate at maturity. Eurodollar futures payoffs are specified somewhat differently, but the net effect works out to be roughly the same. This segment describes the formal specification of the eurodollar futures contract. The following segments then discuss how eurodollar futures may be used to lock in interest rates and so to hedge borrowing or investment exposure.

The underlying unit in the eurodollar futures contract is a $1,000,000 three-month (or, more precisely, 90-day) eurodollar time deposit (TD). Time deposits, unlike CDs, cannot be transferred or traded, so cash settlement is the only option in the eurodollar futures contract.

The price of a eurodollar futures contract is not quoted in terms of the interest rate directly but rather as 100 minus a three-month Libor rate expressed as a percentage. For example, a price of 95.50 corresponds to a Libor rate of $100 - 95.50 = 4.50\%$. It is this interest rate that gets locked-in via the futures contract as we explain below. Note that an increase of 1 basis point (one-hundredth of a percentage point) in the interest rate corresponds to a decrease of 0.01 in the price and vice versa.

As in any futures contract, long positions lose and short positions gain from a price decrease. In the case of eurodollar futures, the contract specifies that every 0.01 decrease in the price leads to a loss of $25 for the long position in the contract and a corresponding gain of $25 for the short position. Why $25? Because that is the impact of a 1 basis point change in interest rates on a 90-day $1,000,000 time deposit. That is, from (6.1), an increase of 1 basis point in the interest rate increases the interest payable on a 90-day $1,000,000 deposit by

$$1,000,000 \times \left[ 0.0001 \times \frac{90}{360} \right] = \$25$$

The price tick in the eurodollar futures contract is 1 basis point (i.e., a price move of 0.01), which has a dollar value of $25. The *minimum* price move on the expiring eurodollar futures contract (the one currently nearest to maturity) is 1/4 tick or a dollar value of $6.25. On all other eurodollar futures contracts, it is 1/2 tick (or $12.50).

Trading on a eurodollar futures contract halts at 11:00 am London time on the second London bank business day immediately preceding the third Wednesday of the contract month. When trading in the contract ceases, the exchange sets the final settlement price of the contract to 100 minus the spot three-month Libor rate, or, more precisely, to 100 minus the British Bankers Association Interest Settlement Rate (BBAISR) for three-month interbank eurodollar TDs rounded to the nearest 1/10,000th of a percentage point. Thus, for example, if the spot three-month rate is 4.60%, the final settlement price is just $100 - 4.60 = 95.40$. To compute the BBAISR, the BBA polls a given number of major banks in London (at least 8; for the eurodollar at the time of writing, 16 banks are polled) and asks them for rates at which they could borrow in the interbank market. After rank-ordering the results, the arithmetic average of the middle two quartiles forms the BBAISR. This fixing is done at 11:00 am London time.

## Hedging Interest-Rate Risk Using Eurodollar Futures

Suppose it is currently December and you anticipate a three-month borrowing need for $1,000,000 begining in June. Suppose also that you can borrow at Libor flat, and you wish to hedge the risk of interest-rate changes between now and June. One option is to take a long position in a $6 \times 9$ FRA with a principal of $1,000,000 and use this to lock in a Libor rate for that period.

An alternative is to use eurodollar futures. You can then adopt the following strategy:

- Take a short eurodollar futures position today that expires in June.
- Borrow the required amount at whatever Libor rate prevails in June at expiry of the futures contract.

To see the cash flows that result from this strategy, let $P$ be the current contract price and $k = (100 - P)/100$ the Libor rate (expressed, as usual, as a decimal) implied by the current price. Let $\ell$ denote the Libor rate prevailing in June at contract maturity. Then, the change in interest rates in basis points is $10,000(k - \ell)$. So the cash outflow on the futures contract is

$$25 \times 10,000(k - \ell) = 250,000(k - \ell) \tag{6.27}$$

If $d$ denotes the number of days in the three-month borrowing horizon, then the cash outflow on account of the interest costs of borrowing is

$$1,000,000 \times \left[\ell \times \frac{d}{360}\right] \tag{6.28}$$

Adding (6.27) and (6.28), the total outflow is

$$250,000(k - \ell) + \left[1,000,000\,\ell \times \frac{d}{360}\right] \tag{6.29}$$

rearranging which, we get

$$250,000\,k + \left(1,000,000\,\ell \times \left[\frac{d}{360} - \frac{1}{4}\right]\right) \tag{6.30}$$

In particular, when $d = 90$, the net cash flow from the hedging strategy is just

$$250,000\,k \tag{6.31}$$

This depends on only the fixed rate $k$ locked in through the eurodollar contract and not on the Libor rate that happens to prevail in June. Thus, we have a perfect hedge.

## Matters Are Not Quite That Simple . . .

There are two reasons why the hedge from this strategy will not be as perfect as expression (6.31) suggests. One is that in practice, the three-month hedging horizon will typically have 91 or 92 days in it, not 90. In this case, the second term of (6.30) will be small (since $d/360 \approx 1/4$), but it will not be zero, so the hedge will be only approximate. We ignore this problem to keep notation simple; that is, we treat the borrowing as a 90-day borrowing from now on.

The second reason has to do with cash-flow timing. The cash flow (6.27) occurs at expiry of the futures contract, which is the *beginning* of the loan period. The cash flow (6.28) is interest on the borrowed amount, which occurs at the *end* of the loan period. Clearly, we cannot ignore this and just add up these cash flows. Rather, we must evaluate both cash flows at the same point in time.

So suppose we move the former cash flow also to the end of the loan period by reinvesting the quantity (6.27) for 90 days at the rate $\ell$. The cash outflow from futures resettlement (6.27) then becomes

$$250,000\,(k - \ell) \times \left(1 + \ell\,\frac{90}{360}\right) \tag{6.32}$$

With $d = 90$, the total interest cost on the borrowing (6.28) becomes $250,000\,\ell$. Summing these up, we see that the net cash flow at the end of the 90-day borrowing horizon is now

$$250,000\,k + \left[250,000\,(k - \ell) \times \ell\,\frac{90}{360}\right] \tag{6.33}$$

This cash flow has a term dependent on $\ell$, so the hedge is no longer perfect.

## . . . but "Tailing" the Hedge Helps

In principle, there is a way to restore the perfect hedge: rather than use one full futures contract in the hedging strategy, we use only $\alpha$ futures contracts, where $\alpha$ is given by

$$\alpha = \frac{1}{1 + \ell\,\frac{90}{360}} \tag{6.34}$$

This is called "tailing" the hedge. If we tail the hedge in this way, then the cash outflow from futures resettlement is given by $\alpha$ times the quantity (6.32), which is simply $250,000\,(k - \ell)$. This restores a perfect hedge, since, from (6.28), the cost of a 90-day borrowing at the rate $\ell$ is $250,000\,\ell$.

Unfortunately, we cannot do this in practice because the rate $\ell$ is known only in June at expiry of the futures contract and not in December when we are setting up the hedge.[2] In practice, therefore, we must rely on approximations. One way to proceed is to use $\hat{\alpha}$ futures contracts where

$$\hat{\alpha} = \frac{1}{1 + k\,\frac{90}{360}} \tag{6.35}$$

Here, $k$ is the eurodollar futures rate at the time we enter into the contract. Loosely speaking, (6.35) treats the observed eurodollar futures rate as a good predictor of the eurodollar futures rate that will prevail at maturity of the contract. Of course, $\hat{\alpha}$ cannot ensure a perfect hedge, but it usually provides a good approximation. The example below illustrates.

---

[2] Note that the payoffs from FRAs *are* tailed using the factor (6.34)—this is the discount factor used to bring FRA payoffs back to the maturity date of the FRA contracts. See expression (6.12).

**Example 6.5**   Suppose it is currently December and you anticipate a three-month borrowing need for $100,000,000 begining in June. Suppose also that you can borrow at Libor flat, and you wish to hedge the risk of interest-rate changes between now and June using eurodollar futures. Finally, suppose that the eurodollar price of the June contract is currently 92, so the implied eurodollar rate is $k = 8\% = 0.08$. We continue assuming that the three-month borrowing horizon has 90 days.

From (6.35), the hedge ratio should be

$$\hat{\alpha} = \frac{1}{1 + (0.08)\frac{90}{360}} = 0.9804$$

so the hedging strategy you will follow is:

- Take a short eurodollar futures position in 98.04 contracts today that expire in June.
- Borrow the required amount at whatever Libor rate $\ell$ prevails in June at expiry of the futures contract.

(For purposes of illustration, we assume that one can take positions in fractional contracts.) To see how well this hedge works, consider two possible values for the three-month Libor rate $\ell$ in June.

**Case 1: $\ell = 8.25\%$**
From (6.28), the cash outflow in September on the three-month borrowing made in June is $250,000\,\ell$ per $1,000,000 of borrowing. (Recall that we are assuming $d = 90$.) Thus, the total cash outflow in September on account of the borrowing is

$$100 \times 250,000\,\ell = 2,062,500 \qquad\qquad (6.36)$$

In addition, there are the cash flows from the eurodollar futures positions. From (6.27), there is a cash *inflow* in June per contract of $250,000\,(\ell - k) = 250,000 \times 0.0025 = 625$. Moving this amount to September by investing it at the Libor rate of 8.25% results in a cash inflow in September per futures contract of

$$625 \times \left(1 + (0.0825)\frac{90}{360}\right) = 637.8906$$

Since we have a position in 98.04 futures contracts in all, the net cash inflow in September on account of the futures contracts is

$$637.891 \times 98.04 = 62,538.30 \qquad\qquad (6.37)$$

Subtracting (6.37) from (6.36), the net cash outflow in September is 1,999,961.70.

**Case 2: $\ell = 7.75\%$**
In this case, the cash outflow in September on account of the June borrowing is

$$100 \times 250,000\,\ell = 1,937,500 \qquad\qquad (6.38)$$

However, there is now a cash *outflow* on the futures position: per futures contract, this outflow in June is $250,000\,(k - \ell) = 625$. Moving this amount to September at the Libor rate of 7.75%, there is a cash outflow in September per futures contract of

$$625 \times \left(1 + (0.0775)\frac{90}{360}\right) = 637.11$$

Since there is a position of 98.04 futures contracts in all, the total cash outflow on account of the futures positions is

$$637.11 \times 98.04 \,=\, 62{,}461.70 \tag{6.39}$$

Summing (6.38) and (6.39), the total cash outflow in September is 1,999,961.70, the same as the cash flow in Case 1. ∎

## Remark: Daily Marking-to-Market and PVBP Analysis

In the analysis above, we have implicitly assumed that the gains/losses on the futures positions are realized only at the maturity of the contracts (in the example, for instance, these cash flows occur in June). In reality, gains and losses in futures markets are realized on a daily basis. In Appendix 6B, we examine how to design a hedging strategy that takes this into account. The analysis is based on looking at the present value of the effect of a one-basis-point change in interest rates on (a) the eurodollar futures position used for hedging and (b) the borrowing that is being hedged. The objective is to choose the number of futures contracts so that these effects cancel out, leaving the value of the position unchanged. This is called PVBP analysis, short for the present value of a basis point.

## FRAs vs. Eurodollar Futures: The "Convexity Bias"

While FRAs and eurodollar futures are very similar instruments, there are some important differences between them. One is the so-called "convexity bias," which we describe in this segment.

Consider the following setting. Suppose we anticipate today that in six months, we will need to borrow $100 million for a three-month period. Suppose too that we can borrow at Libor flat. We consider the cash flows from two situations: (i) we hedge the borrowing with a position in a long $(6 \times 9)$ FRA with a principal value of $100 million, and (ii) we hedge the borrowing with a short position in $100\,\hat{\alpha}$ six-month eurodollar futures contracts, where $\hat{\alpha}$ is given by (6.35). Suppose that in both cases, the locked-in rate is $k$.

Consider the FRA first. If the actual three-month interest rate in six-months' time is $\ell$ and $d$ is the actual number of days in the three-month borrowing horizon, then expression (6.12) shows that the FRA leads to a cash inflow in six months of

$$100{,}000{,}000 \times \left( \frac{(\ell - k) \times \frac{d}{360}}{1 + \ell \times \frac{d}{360}} \right) \tag{6.40}$$

If we take $d = 90$ as the eurodollar futures contract implicitly assumes, this becomes

$$100{,}000{,}000 \times \left( \frac{(\ell - k) \times \frac{90}{360}}{1 + \ell \times \frac{90}{360}} \right) \tag{6.41}$$

Now consider the eurodollar futures contract. If the actual three-month rate in six-months' time is $\ell$, the difference between the locked-in rate $k$ and the actual rate $\ell$ expressed in basis points is

$$(\ell - k) \times 10{,}000$$

Per basis point change, each short futures contract provides a cash inflow of $25. Therefore, the total cash inflow received from the short eurodollar positions is

$$100\,\hat{\alpha} \times [(\ell - k) \times 10{,}000 \times 25] \tag{6.42}$$

Substituting for $\hat{\alpha}$ from (6.35) and rearranging and rewriting the resulting expression, this is exactly the same thing as

$$100,000,000 \times \left( \frac{(\ell - k) \times \frac{90}{360}}{1 + k \frac{90}{360}} \right) \qquad (6.43)$$

*For any value of $\ell$, the amount (6.43) under eurodollar futures exceeds the amount (6.41) under the FRA, i.e., either the eurodollar futures leads to a greater cash inflow or it leads to a smaller cash outflow. This is the so-called "convexity bias."*

Before we show that the difference between (6.43) and (6.41) is positive in general, we illustrate it with numbers for two cases. In both cases, we take the locked-in rate to be $k = 0.08$.

### Case 1: $\ell = 11\%$

In this case, the cash flow from the FRA is given by

$$100,000,000 \times \left( \frac{(0.11 - 0.08) \times \frac{90}{360}}{1 + (0.11) \times \frac{90}{360}} \right) = +729,927.01$$

The cash flow from the eurodollar futures position is

$$100,000,000 \times \left( \frac{(0.11 - 0.08) \times \frac{90}{360}}{1 + (0.08) \times \frac{90}{360}} \right) = +735,294.12$$

The difference between the two is $5,367.11 in favor of the eurodollar futures.

### Case 2: $\ell = 5\%$

Now, the cash flow from the FRA is given by

$$100,000,000 \times \left( \frac{(0.05 - 0.08) \times \frac{90}{360}}{1 + (0.05) \times \frac{90}{360}} \right) = -740,740.74$$

while the cash flow from the eurodollar futures position is

$$100,000,000 \times \left( \frac{(0.05 - 0.08) \times \frac{90}{360}}{1 + (0.08) \times \frac{90}{360}} \right) = -735,294.12$$

The difference between the two is $5,446.62, again in favor of the eurodollar futures.

It is not hard to show directly from (6.41)–(6.43) that the cash flows are always biased in favor of eurodollar futures. Subtracting (6.41) from (6.43), we obtain

$$100,000,000 \times \left( \frac{(\ell - k) \times \frac{90}{360}}{1 + k \frac{90}{360}} - \frac{(\ell - k) \times \frac{90}{360}}{1 + \ell \frac{90}{360}} \right)$$

Taking a common denominator for the terms inside the parentheses, some algebra shows that this difference is

$$100,000,000 \times \left( \frac{(\ell - k)^2 \times \frac{1}{16}}{(1 + \ell \frac{90}{360})(1 + k \frac{90}{360})} \right)$$

which is, of course, always positive regardless of $\ell$.

### Remark

The convexity bias has a simple mathematical source. The payoff (6.42) from eurodollar futures is a linear function of the actual Libor rate $\ell$ that prevails at maturity of the contract.

On the other hand, the term $\ell$ appears in both the numerator and denominator of the FRA payoff (6.40), so the FRA payoff is not linear in $\ell$. In fact, this FRA payoff is concave in $\ell$, so the difference between eurodollar and FRA payoffs is convex in $\ell$.[3]

The convexity bias shows that eurodollar futures rates *cannot* be the same as the FRA rates for the corresponding period. This convexity bias is typically small at short maturities (in the example above, it is of the order of about $5,000 on a $100 million borrowing), but it can be substantial at longer maturities. For a more detailed treatment of this topic, see Burghardt and Hoskins (1995a), Burghardt and Hoskins (1995b), Pozdnyakov and Steele (2001), or Burghardt (2003).

## 6.5 Treasury Bond Futures

The US Treasury is charged with the responsibility of borrowing money from capital markets to meet government expenditures. Acting on behalf of the Treasury, the Federal Reserve Board regularly auctions fixed-income securities of various maturities. Treasury securities with less than a year to maturity are known as Treasury bills; those with maturities between 2 and 10 years are called Treasury notes. The term Treasury bonds refers to the longest-dated of Treasury securities, those with a maturity of 30 years.

Begining in 1976, futures contracts have been introduced in US exchanges on many of these instruments. In this section, we look at one of the most popular of these contracts—the Treasury bond futures contract. The two sections following look at Treasury note futures and Treasury bill futures, respectively.

Treasury bond futures were introduced by the CBoT in 1977 and enjoyed great success almost immediately. For most of the period since then, they have been the instrument of choice for hedging long-term interest-rate risk. However, the decision of the US Treasury to de-emphasize issuance of 30-year bonds has led to a fall-off in the importance of this contract (although this may change if and when the Treasury reintroduces the 30-year bond).

US Treasury bonds are 30-year fixed-income obligations of the US government that bear a semiannual coupon. Treasury bond prices are quoted for a face value of $100 and are measured in dollars and 32nds of a dollar rather than dollars and cents. That is, a quote of 99-05 means the quoted price is $99\frac{5}{32}$ for a bond with a face value of $100. The actual cash price paid for the bond is the quoted price plus the accrued interest on the bond. The accrued interest is calculated using an Actual/Actual day-count convention.

To illustrate, suppose, for example, that the quoted price for a 7% coupon US Treasury bond on October 13 is 100-05. Suppose that the last coupon was paid on June 5 and the next coupon is due on December 5. There are 130 days between June 5 and October 13, and 183 days between June 5 and December 5. Since each coupon is of size $3.50 (per face value of $100), the accrued interest is

$$\frac{130}{183} \times 3.50 = 2.48$$

Thus, the cash price of the bond is $100\frac{5}{32} + 2.48 = 102.64$. For a bond of face value $100,000, this translates to a cash price of $102,640.

---

[3] A function $f(x)$ is *concave* in $x$ if the second derivative of $f$ with respect to $x$ is negative for all $x$; it is *convex* in $x$ if this second derivative is positive for all $x$. If $f$ is a concave function of $x$, then the negative of $f$ is a convex function of $x$. (For example, the function $f(x) = -x^2$ is a concave function of $x$, and the function $g(x) = x^2$ is a convex function of $x$.) Visually speaking, convex functions are bowl-shaped (they can "hold water"), while concave functions are like inverted bowls.

**TABLE 6.1** Futures Contract Specifications

This table compares the specifications of five futures contracts: the US Treasury bond futures contract, the US Treasury note futures contract, the bund futures contract, the long gilt futures contract, and the Japanese government bond (JGB) futures contract. The numbers 3, 6, 9, and 12 in the Expiry months row stand for March, June, September, and December, respectively.

|  | Treasury Bond | Treasury Note | Long Gilt | Bund | JGB |
|---|---|---|---|---|---|
| Face value | $100,000 | $100,000 | £100,000 | €100,000 | ¥100 million |
| Standard coupon | 6% | 6% | 7% | 6% | 6% |
| Minimum maturity | 15 years | $6\frac{1}{2}$ years | $8\frac{3}{4}$ years | $8\frac{1}{2}$ years | 7 years |
| Maximum maturity | 30 years | 10 years | 13 years | $10\frac{1}{2}$ years | 11 years |
| Expiry months | 3,6,9,12 | 3,6,9,12 | 3,6,9,12 | 3,6,9,12 | 3,6,9,12 |

## Specification of the Futures Contract

The success of the Treasury bond futures contract is often attributed to its specification. The contract has been copied widely. The Treasury note futures contract on the CBoT, the UK gilt futures contract on Euronext.liffe, the German government bond or "bund" futures contract on Eurex and Euronext.liffe and the Japanese government bond futures contract on the Tokyo Stock Exchange and Euronext.liffe all have designs based on the Treasury bond futures contract. In particular, each defines a standard coupon and conversion factors in a similar manner to the Treasury bond futures contract. Table 6.1 lists some other features of these contracts.

The "standard" bond in the Treasury bond futures contract is one with a face value of $100,000, at least 15 years to maturity or first call, and a coupon of 6%. (Prior to March 2000, the standard coupon was 8%.) The quoted price for the futures contract uses the same convention as the cash market: prices are quoted in dollars and 32nds of a dollar per face value of $100. Since the contract provides for a number of delivery options, the actual price the long position has to pay depends on the delivered bond as well as the quoted price.

### The Quality Option

The most important of the delivery options in the contract is the "quality option" that allows the short position to substitute any coupon for the standard 6%. The price that the long position has to pay is the quoted futures price times a conversion factor that depends on the bond that is actually delivered. The conversion factor is calculated by discounting the cash flows from the delivered bond at the standard 6% rate. The discounting process uses semiannual compounding (i.e., we discount at 3% per six months) since coupons on Treasury bonds are paid semiannually.

For example, suppose the bond that is delivered is an 8% 20-year bond. On a face value of $100, this bond will result in cash flows of $4 every six months for 20 years and a repayment of the principal amount of $100 after 20 years. For simplicity, suppose the last coupon was just paid. Then, the conversion factor is

$$\frac{1}{100}\left[\frac{4}{1.03} + \frac{4}{1.03^2} + \cdots + \frac{4}{1.03^{40}} + \frac{100}{1.03^{40}}\right] = 1.2311 \qquad \textbf{(6.44)}$$

Thus, the long position has to pay the short position 1.2311 times the quoted price.

It is easy to see that if the delivered bond:

- has a coupon equal to the standard 6%, the conversion factor will be equal to 1 since we are then discounting 6% cash flows at a 6% rate.

- has a coupon higher than the standard 6% (so is of "superior" quality to the standard), the conversion factor will be greater than 1.
- has a coupon less than the standard 6% (so is of "inferior" quality to the standard), the conversion factor will be less than 1.

In practice, delivered bonds may have a wide range of maturities. The CBoT uses a method of calculating the conversion factor that involves rounding off the maturity of the bonds to the nearest quarter (i.e., three months). If after the rounding off the bond has a maturity that is an integer multiple of six months, then the bond is treated as if the last coupon was just paid and the next coupon is due in six-months' time. The calculations then proceed as in the above example. If after the rounding off the bond's maturity leaves a three-month remainder when divided by six months, then the next coupon is assumed to be paid in three-months' time, so accrued interest for the first three months must be subtracted from the price. The details and a general formula for calculating the conversion factor are provided in Appendix 6C.

### Other Options

Besides the quality option, the Treasury bond futures contract also provides the short position with other delivery options. One of these is the "wild card" option. Treasury bond futures trading on the CBoT halts at 2 pm, and the settlement price is determined at this point. However, the clearinghouse accepts delivery from the short position until 8 pm. So the short position has time from 2 pm to 8 pm to decide whether to deliver that day at the fixed settlement price, and if so, which of the deliverable bonds to deliver. This is the wild card option. If the cash prices of the deliverable bonds experience a significant decline after 2 pm and before 8 pm, the option becomes valuable to the short position.

If the wild card option is not exercised on a particular day, the short position again has a wild card option the next day based on the next day's settlement price. Delivery in the Treasury bond futures contract can take place on any day during the delivery month. There are roughly 15 trading days during this month, so the contract provides the short with about 15 of these options in all.

A third option, and one similar to the wild card option, is the end-of-month option. Trading in the Treasury bond futures contract closes seven business days prior to the last business day of the delivery month, and the final settlement price is fixed at this point. However, the clearinghouse accepts delivery until the end of the month, so any decline in bond prices during this period accrues to the short's advantage. Of course, the price of the futures contract will reflect the short's holding of these options and will be lower than if these options were not present.

### Implications for Delivery

The presence of these options gives the short position a powerful incentive to delay delivery until the end of the contract period. Broadie and Sundaresan (1992) look at the empirical patterns of delivery on this contract. In accordance with intuition, they find that when the yield curve is normal (long-term rates are higher than short-term rates), 90% of deliveries take place in the last five days of the delivery month. However, with inverted yield curves, there is negative carry and this militates against late delivery. In this case, deliveries tend to take place earlier in the delivery month.

## Pricing Futures on Treasury Bonds

It is mathematically very complex to take the delivery options into account in pricing a Treasury bond futures contract. If we ignore the delivery options and assume there is only one deliverable bond (or we know which bond it is that will be delivered), then matters are simplified considerably. Treasury bond futures may then be priced using the known cash cost of carry formula $F = e^{rT}(S + M)$ where $S$ denotes the current price of the underlying bond and $-M$ is the present value of the coupons that will be received from the bond during the life of the futures contract.

## 6.6 Treasury Note Futures

US Treasury notes are fixed-income obligations of the US government with maturities between 2 and 10 years and with a semiannual coupon. Futures on 10-year US Treasury notes were introduced by the CBoT in 1982. More recently, futures on 5-year US Treasury notes were also introduced by the CBoT. Both contracts have been received well (see Table 2.2 on their trading volumes). The former, in particular, has overtaken the Treasury bond futures contract as the Treasury futures contract of choice on long-maturity Treasury instruments (although this may change if and when the Treasury reintroduces the 30-year bond).

Treasury note futures are similar in their design and specification to Treasury bond futures, so the analysis above applies to Treasury notes futures too. The main difference between the bond futures contract and the notes futures contracts is in the admissible maturities of the deliverable instruments. In the case of the 10-year Treasury notes futures contracts, deliverable instruments are US Treasury notes with remaining maturities between $6\frac{1}{2}$ and 10 years. In the case of the 5-year Treasury notes futures contract, US Treasury notes with remaining maturities between 4 years 2 months and 5 years 3 months may be delivered.

## 6.7 Treasury Bill Futures

Treasury bill futures were introduced by the CME in 1976 and were the first futures contract on Treasury securities. Popular at one time, their importance has waned since the introduction of eurodollar futures.

Treasury bills are obligations of the US government and are issued with maturities of 91, 182, or 364 days (13, 26, or 52 weeks). Treasury bills bear no coupon; rather, they are issued at a discount to their face value and accrete to par at maturity.

Prices on Treasury bills are quoted on a face value of $100. The quoted price is not the cash price (i.e., how much it costs to buy the Treasury bill) but rather what is called the *discount rate* on the Treasury bill. To motivate this convention, suppose the cash price of a Treasury bill with maturity in $d$ days and a face value of $100 is $P$. Then, the cash return from investing in this Treasury bill is $\$(100 - P)$. This cash return is "annualized" in the money market day-count convention by multiplying it by $360/d$. This annualized return is the quoted price $Q$:

$$Q = (100 - P)\frac{360}{d} \tag{6.45}$$

$Q$ is referred to as the *discount rate* on the Treasury bill. From (6.45), given a quoted price of $Q$, the cash price $P$ of a Treasury bill is

$$P = 100 - Q\frac{d}{360} \tag{6.46}$$

For example, suppose a 91-day Treasury bill has a quoted price of 4.00. Then the cash price of the Treasury bill is

$$P = 100 - (4.00) \frac{91}{360} = 98.989$$

## Specification of the Futures Contract

The Treasury bill futures contract on the CME requires the short position to deliver bills with a face value of $1,000,000 and 90 days to maturity. The delivery options in the contract allow for the delivery of bills with 90, 91, or 92 days to maturity.

The Treasury bill futures price quote convention is similar to the cash market convention in its use of a discount rate. However, the quoted price here is 100 minus the discount rate, not the discount rate itself. Given a quoted price of (say) $100 - Q$, the invoice price on the futures (the amount the short position will receive) is determined by expression (6.46) with $d$ being the days left to maturity on the delivered instrument.

For example, suppose the quoted price is 94.60. Then, the discount rate is $100 - 94.60 = 5.40$. If a 90-day Treasury bill is delivered, the short receives

$$100 - (5.40) \frac{90}{360} = 98.65 \qquad \textbf{(6.47)}$$

per $100 of face value delivered. Since the delivered face value must be $1,000,000, the short position receives $986,500.

## Pricing Futures on Treasury Bills

Since Treasury bills are zero-coupon instruments, we can price futures/forward contracts on them using the zero cost-of-carry formula. Let $T$ denote the maturity of the futures contract and $T^*$ denote the maturity of the underlying Treasury bill. (We must obviously have $T^* \geq T$.) Let $r$ and $r^*$ denote the interest rates applicable to horizons of length $T$ and $T^*$, respectively, expressed in continuously-compounded terms. Finally, let $P$ be the current price of the $T^*$-maturity Treasury bill. Assume the bill has a face value of $100.

The futures price $F$ is given by

$$F = e^{rT} P \qquad \textbf{(6.48)}$$

We can make (6.48) sharper. Since $P$ is itself a zero-coupon instrument with a face value of $100, we must have $P = 100\, e^{-r^*T^*}$. Therefore, the futures price can be expressed as

$$F = e^{rT} \times 100\, e^{-r^*T^*} = 100\, e^{rT - r^*T^*} \qquad \textbf{(6.49)}$$

# 6.8 Duration-Based Hedging

The purpose of this section is to describe a special hedging strategy called *duration-based hedging* used to hedge portfolios of fixed-income instruments (e.g., bonds) with fixed-income futures. Duration-based hedging exploits the observation that both spot and futures prices in this case depend on a common underlying variable—the level of interest rates. Intuitively, duration-based hedging looks at how much a change in interest rates would affect (a) the value of the portfolio we are looking to hedge, and (b) the price of the interest-rate futures contract we are using for hedging. We then choose the number of futures contracts to be used in the hedge so that these value changes offset each other.

To implement a scheme of this sort, we need to be able to measure the sensitivity of portfolio values and futures prices to changes in interest rates. We address these issues first. Duration is most naturally presented in the context of a continuous-compounding convention for interest rates, so we adopt that convention in the remainder of this chapter.

## The Notion of Duration

Let a portfolio of bonds be given. Suppose that the portfolio will result in a cash flow of $c_i$ in $t_i$ years, $i = 1, \ldots n$. Suppose also that the interest rate applicable to a period of length $t_i$ years is $r_i$ in continuously-compounded terms. Then, the present value of the $i$-th cash flow is $e^{-r_i t_i} c_i$, so the current value $P$ of the portfolio is

$$P = c_1 e^{-r_1 t_1} + \cdots + c_n e^{-r_n t_n} \qquad (6.50)$$

The weight $w_i$ contributed by the $i$-th cash flow to the overall portfolio value is

$$w_i = \frac{c_i e^{-r_i t_i}}{P} \qquad (6.51)$$

The *duration* of the portfolio, denoted $D_P$, is defined to be its weighted maturity:

$$D_P = w_1 t_1 + \cdots + w_n t_n \qquad (6.52)$$

The duration is a measure of the portfolio's sensitivity to interest-rate changes. Namely, a small parallel shift $dr$ in the yield curve results in a change of approximately $\Delta_P$ in the portfolio value given by

$$\Delta_P = -D_P P \, dr \qquad (6.53)$$

Appendix 6D explains why this is the case.

Thus, for example, suppose the portfolio consists solely of a zero-coupon bond. Then, the duration of the portfolio is just the maturity $t$ of the zero-coupon bond. In other words, every basis point *increase* in interest rates will *decrease* the value of the portfolio by $-tP \, (0.01)$.

Two points should be stressed here. First, the accuracy of duration as a measure of sensitivity is only approximate. It is very accurate for small changes in the interest rate (say, a few basis points) but becomes progressively less accurate as the size of the interest-rate change increases. Second, it is an important part of the definition that all interest rates shift by the same amount $dr$, i.e., that the yield curve experiences a parallel shift.

## The Duration of a Futures Contract

Consider a futures contract written on a specific underlying bond. Let $F$ be the current futures price. How does $F$ change when interest rates change by a small amount $dr$?

If we could define a duration measure for the bond futures price (denoted, say, $D_F$), then, analogous to (6.53), the change $\Delta_F$ in futures price would be

$$\Delta_F = -D_F F \, dr \qquad (6.54)$$

Can we, in fact, define such a measure $D_F$? The answer, it turns out, is yes! It can be shown that the duration of a bond futures contract is simply the duration of the bond underlying the futures contract but *measured from the date of maturity of the futures contract*. A proof of this result may be found in Appendix 6E.

For example, consider the Treasury bill futures contract on the CME. At maturity of the contract, the short position is required to deliver to the long position US Treasury bills with a face value of $1 million and with 90 days left to maturity. Thus, the underlying in this contract is a zero-coupon bond maturing three months after the futures contract. When measured from the maturity date of the futures contract, the duration of this underlying asset is simply the duration of a three-month zero-coupon bond, which, from (6.52), is 1/4. Thus, the duration $D_F$ of the Treasury bill futures contract is 1/4.

## Duration-Based Hedging

Suppose we have a portfolio of bonds worth $P$ with duration $D_P$. Suppose that we wish to protect ourselves from changes in the value of this portfolio over some given horizon. Finally, suppose that we have chosen for hedging an interest-rate futures contract whose current price is $F$. For specificity, assume this is a futures contract written on a bond.

How many futures contracts should we use? Consider a position of $H$ contracts where $H > 0$ denotes a long position in the futures and $H < 0$ a short position. Suppose that interest rates shift by a small amount $dr$, and that, as a consequence, (a) the futures price changes by an amount $\Delta_F$, while (b) the portfolio value changes by an amount $\Delta_P$. The *net* change in the value of our position is then

$$\Delta_p + H \Delta_F \qquad (6.55)$$

Thus, for $H$ to be a good hedge, we would like it to satisfy

$$\Delta_p + H \Delta_F = 0 \qquad (6.56)$$

or, what is the same thing,

$$H = -\frac{\Delta_P}{\Delta_F} \qquad (6.57)$$

Equation (6.57) states that to identify the optimal size of the futures position, we need to know the changes $\Delta_P$ and $\Delta_F$ in portfolio value and futures prices, respectively, that are caused by the interest-rate change $dr$. But these quantities are easily calculated. If $D_P$ and $D_F$ denote the respective durations of the portfolio and the futures, then we have

$$\Delta_P = -D_P P \, dr \qquad (6.58)$$

$$\Delta_F = -D_F F \, dr \qquad (6.59)$$

Combining equations (6.57)–(6.59), we have

$$H^* = -\frac{\Delta_P}{\Delta_F} = -\frac{D_P P \, dr}{D_F F \, dr} = -\frac{D_P P}{D_F F} \qquad (6.60)$$

The hedging strategy given by expression (6.60) is called a *duration-based hedging strategy*. In words, the strategy states that the optimal size of the futures position can be determined from four variables:

1. The current value of the portfolio $P$.
2. The duration of the portfolio $D_P$.
3. The current futures price $F$.
4. The duration of the futures contract $D_F$.

---

**Example 6.6**

Suppose we are managing a portfolio of bonds whose current value is $P = \$5,000,000$ and whose duration is $\Delta_P = 1$. Suppose also that we wish to hedge this portfolio using Treasury bill futures. Finally, suppose that the current futures price is $F = \$990,000$. How many futures contracts should we use?

From what we have seen in Section 6.8, the duration of the Treasury bill futures contract is $1/4$. Therefore, from (6.60), the optimal hedge size is

$$H^* = -\frac{(1)(5,000,000)}{(0.25)(990,000)} = -20.20 \qquad (6.61)$$

which is, approximately, a short position in 20 contracts. ∎

## Potential Problems in Duration-Based Hedging

There are some problems that could result in duration-based hedging not working well in practice. We review some of these potential pitfalls here.

First, duration as a sensitivity measure has two shortcomings. It works well only for *small* interest-rate changes and it presumes parallel shifts in the yield curve. Duration-based hedging implicitly involves the same assumptions. To the extent that these assumptions are violated, duration-based hedging schemes will not perform well.

Careful choice of the futures contract can mitigate some of these problems. For instance, suppose the portfolio being hedged consists of bonds with roughly the same maturity. If we use a futures contract whose duration is "close" to the duration of these bonds, this will ensure that the portfolio value and the futures price depend on similar interest rates. If the portfolio consists of a large number of disparate bonds, we can separate it into blocks of roughly similar maturity and hedge each block separately with a futures contract matching it in duration.

Another problem in implementing a duration-based hedging scheme with a bond futures contract is that the duration $D_F$ of the futures contract may be hard to identify on account of delivery options in the futures contract. For instance, in the Treasury bond futures contract on the CBoT, the short position may deliver any bond with at least 15 years to maturity (or first call) and any coupon. Using the duration of the standard bond in the contract is also problematic since the standard bond specifies only a coupon rate; its set of possible maturities remains large. One alternative in such a situation is to estimate the likely cheapest-to-deliver bond and use its duration.

## 6.9 Exercises

1. Explain the difference between the following terms:
   (a) Payoff to an FRA.
   (b) Price of an FRA.
   (c) Value of an FRA.

2. What characteristic of the eurodollar futures contract enabled it to overcome the settlement obstacles with its predecessors?

3. How are eurodollar futures quoted?

4. It is currently May. What is the relation between the observed eurodollar futures price of 96.32 for the November maturity and the rate of interest that is locked-in using the contract? Over what period does this rate apply?

5. What is the price tick in the eurodollar futures contract? To what price move does this correspond?

6. What are the gains or losses to a short position in a eurodollar futures contract from a 0.01 increase in the futures price?

7. You enter into a long eurodollar futures contract at a price of 94.59 and exit the contract a week later at a price of 94.23. What is your dollar gain or loss on this position?

8. What is the cheapest to deliver in a Treasury bond futures contract? Are there other delivery options in this contract?

9. Describe the standard bond in each of the following contracts: (a) Treasury bond futures, (b) 10-year Treasury note futures, (c) 5-year Treasury note futures, and (d) Treasury bill futures.

10. Describe the conversion factor that applies if the delivered bond in a Treasury bond futures contract is different from the standard bond.

11. Explain the notion of duration of a bond. Under what conditions is this measure reasonably accurate?

12. How does one measure the duration of a futures contract? That is, how is the duration of a futures contract related to the duration of the underlying bond?

13. Explain the principles involved in duration-based hedging. How does the computation of the hedge ratio here differ from that of the minimum-variance hedge computation?

14. On a $1,000,000 principal, 91-day investment, what is the interest payable if we use an Actual/365 basis? What is the interest if the basis is Actual/360?

15. If the six-month interest rate is 6% and the one-year interest rate is 8%, what is the rate for an FRA over the period from six months to one year? Assume that the number of days up to six months is 182 and from six months to one year is 183.

16. If the three-month (91 days) Libor rate is 4% and the six-month (183 days) rate is 5%, what should be the 3 × 6 FRA rate? If, at the end of the contract, the three-month Libor rate turns out to be 5%, what should the settlement amount be?

17. In Japan, if the three-month (91 days) interbank rate is 1% and the six-month (183 days) interbank rate is 0.25%, what is the 3 × 6 FRA rate? Is this an acceptable rate? Why or why not?

18. If you expect interest rates to rise over the next three months and then fall over the three months succeeding that, what positions in FRAs would be appropriate to take? Would your answer change depending on the current shape of the forward curve?

19. A firm plans to borrow money over the next two half-year periods and is able to obtain a fixed-rate loan at 6% per annum. It can also borrow money at the floating rate of Libor + 0.5%. Libor is currently at 4%. If the 6 × 12 FRA is at a rate of 6%, find the cheapest financing cost for the firm.

20. You enter into an FRA of notional 6 million to borrow on the three-month underlying Libor rate six months from now and lock in the rate of 6%. At the end of six months, if the underlying three-month rate is 6.6% over an actual period of 91 days, what is your payoff given that the payment is made right away? Recall that the ACT/360 convention applies.

21. You have entered into the 6 × 9 FRA above at the rate of 6%. After three months, the FRA is now a 3 × 6 FRA. If the three-month Libor rate is 5%, and the nine-month Libor rate is 7%, what is the current value of the FRA? Assume that the number of days from three to six months is 92.

22. Given a 3 × 6 FRA with a rate of 10% and a time interval between three and six months of 92 days, plot the settlement amount if the three-month rate after three months ends up anywhere from 1% to 20%. Is your plot linear, convex, or concave? Why? If you are using FRAs to hedge your borrowing risk, does the shape of the payoff function cause you concern and why?

23. You anticipate a need to borrow USD 10 million in six-months' time for a period of three months. You decide to hedge the risk of interest-rate changes using eurodollar futures contracts (=90 days). Describe the hedging strategy you would follow. What if you decided to use an FRA instead?

24. In the question above, suppose that the underlying Libor rate for three months after six months (as implied by the eurodollar futures contract price) is currently at 4%. Say

the underlying period is 91 days. Using the same numbers from the previous question and adjusting for tailing the hedge, how many futures contracts are needed? Assume fractional contracts are permitted.

25. Using the same numbers as in the previous two questions, compute the payoff after six months (i.e., at maturity) under (a) an FRA and (b) a eurodollar futures contract if the Libor rate at maturity is 5%. Also compute the payoffs if the Libor rate ends up at 3%. Comment on the difference in payoffs of the FRA versus the eurodollar futures.

26. The "standard bond" in the Treasury bond futures contract has a coupon of 6%. If, instead, delivery is made of a 5% bond of maturity 18 years, what is the conversion factor for settlement of the contract?

27. Suppose we have a flat yield curve of 3%. What is the price of a Treasury bond of remaining maturity seven years that pays a coupon of 4%? (Coupons are paid semiannually.) What is the price of a six-month Treasury bond futures contract?

28. What is the price of a Treasury bill with a discount rate of 6% and maturity of 182 days? What is the price of a 91-day futures contract on the 91-day Treasury bill if the 91-day Treasury bill is trading at 95?

29. In the previous question, write down an expression for the payoff of the futures contract if after 91 days the discount rate of the remaining 91-day Treasury bill varies from 1% to 8%. Is the payoff function linear, convex, or concave? Why?

30. Suppose you own a zero-coupon bond with face value $3 million that matures in one year. The bond is priced off the continuously compounded zero-coupon rate that is currently at $r = 7\%$. Suppose you want to hedge the price of the bond six months from now using the three-month eurodollar futures contract that expires in six-months' time, assuming that the rate at that time remains unchanged for the shorter maturity. How many contracts will you need to trade to construct this hedge? Can you explain intuitively why this number is in the ballpark expected?

31. If we wish to hedge a bond that pays a cash flow of 2 million after six months and another cash flow of 102 million after twelve months, suggest a hedging scheme using eurodollar futures contracts. Assume that the bond is priced on a semiannual compounding basis and has a current yield to maturity of 4% per annum.

32. Qualitatively discuss how you would hedge a portfolio of bonds using eurodollar futures contracts.

33. (Difficult) Assume that the yield curve is flat at 6%. All bonds pay semiannually. Bond A has a coupon of 5.5% and a maturity of seven years. Bond B has a coupon of 6.2% and a maturity of five years. We wish to short bond B to offset the risk (duration-based hedging) of a long position in bond A. How many units of bond B do we need to short for every unit of bond A to achieve this?

34. Refer to the previous question. A futures contract on bond B trades as well. What is the price of the one-year bond futures contract on bond B? How many units of this contract do we need to short to offset a one-unit long position in bond A over the next year?

35. We are given a portfolio of bonds with value $P = 100$ and duration $D_P = 1$. The six-month Treasury bill future trades at price $F_1 = 95$ and duration $DF_1 = 0.4$. Also, the twelve-month Treasury bill future trades at price $F_2 = 92$ and duration $DF_2 = 0.9$. Suggest a duration-based hedging strategy for portfolio $P$. State clearly the assumptions for your choice.

36. The following market-based FRA rates are provided.

| Period (months) | Forward Rates (%) |
|---|---|
| 0–6 | 3.00 |
| 6–12 | 4.00 |
| 12–18 | 5.00 |
| 18–24 | 6.00 |

Answer the following questions:

(a) Find the price of a two-year maturity security with a coupon of 4.5%.

(b) Find the price of a six-month bond future on this bond.

(c) What is the price of a twelve-month bond future on this bond?

(d) Find the durations of all the three instruments above.

(e) If we invest $100 in the two-year bond, then how many units of the two futures contracts should we buy such that we have equal numbers of units in each contract, and we optimize our duration-based hedge?

(f) After setting up the hedge, the next instant, the entire forward curve shifts up by 1% at all maturities. What is the change in the value of the hedged portfolio? Is it zero? If not, explain the sign of the change.

# Deriving the Arbitrage-Free FRA Rate

Let the current time be date 0. Consider a $T_1 \times T_2$ FRA entered into today. We are to identify the value of the fixed rate $k$ in the FRA that will make the contract have zero value to both parties.

From expression (6.12), the payoff to the long position in an FRA at time $T_1$ is

$$\text{Payoff to long position} = \frac{(\ell - k) \times \frac{d}{360}}{1 + \ell \frac{d}{360}} \times P \qquad (6.62)$$

where $\ell$ is the realized floating rate on date $T_1$ for the period $[T_1, T_2]$. For any given $k$, we identify the present value at time 0 of these payoffs to the long position, and then choose $k$ so that the present value is zero.

To this end, for any $T$, let $B(T)$ denote the present value at date $T$ of \$1 receivable at time $T$. As the first step, add and subtract the principal amount $P$ to the numerator of (6.62) to obtain

$$\text{Payoff to long position} = \frac{P + P\ell\frac{d}{360} - P - Pk\frac{d}{360}}{1 + \ell\frac{d}{360}} \qquad (6.63)$$

Expression (6.63) can be separated into two parts:

$$\frac{P + P\ell\frac{d}{360}}{1 + \ell\frac{d}{360}} - \frac{P + Pk\frac{d}{360}}{1 + \ell\frac{d}{360}} = P - P\frac{1 + k\frac{d}{360}}{1 + \ell\frac{d}{360}} \qquad (6.64)$$

The first part of this cash flow, $P$, represents a certainty cash inflow at time $T_1$. The second part is an outflow of uncertain amount viewed from time 0 since the floating rate $\ell$ is not known until $T_1$. However, regardless of the realized value of $\ell$, if this amount is invested at rate $\ell$ at time $T_1$, it grows to the certainty amount

$$P\frac{1 + k\frac{d}{360}}{1 + \ell\frac{d}{360}} \times \left(1 + \ell\frac{d}{360}\right) = P\left(1 + k\frac{d}{360}\right) \qquad (6.65)$$

Thus, the uncertain cash outflow at time $T_1$ in (6.64) is *equivalent* to the certainty outflow at time $T_2$ of the amount on the right-hand side of (6.65). This means that, viewed from time 0, the cash flow (6.62) from the FRA is equivalent to the sum of the following two quantities:

1.  A certainty inflow of $P$ at time $T_1$.
2.  A certainty outflow of $P(1 + k(d/360))$ at time $T_2$.

The time-0 present value of these outflows is just

$$B(T_1)\, P - B(T_2)\, P\left(1 + k\frac{d}{360}\right) \qquad (6.66)$$

Expression (6.66) is the value of a general FRA with fixed rate $k$ and an investment period beginning in $T_1$ months and ending in $T_2$ months. At inception of a $T_1 \times T_2$ FRA, this value is zero. Setting it equal to zero and solving for $k$ gives us the arbitrage-free FRA price as

$$k^* = \frac{B(T_1) - B(T_2)}{B(T_2)} \times \frac{360}{d} \qquad (6.67)$$

# PVBP-Based Hedging Using Eurodollar Futures

The analysis of hedging using eurodollar futures in Section 6.4—in particular, the analysis leading to expression (6.35) and the example following—assumed implicitly that the gains/losses on the futures positions are realized only at the maturity of the contracts (in the example, for instance, that these cash flows occur in June). In reality, gains and losses in futures markets are realized on a daily basis. We examine here how to design a hedging strategy that takes this into account.

For specificity, continue assuming as in the hedging example from Section 6.4 that it is currently December and we are looking to lock-in a borrowing rate for a three-month borrowing of $100,000,000 to be made next June, i.e., in six-months' time. Our hedging strategy is to take a short position in $\hat{\alpha}$ futures contracts today, close it out next June, and borrow then for three months at whatever Libor rate happens to prevail at that point. What should $\hat{\alpha}$ be if we wish to take daily marking-to-market into account?

To motivate the answer, consider the impact of a 1-basis-point increase in interest rates. This has two effects. On the one hand, it leads to a cash inflow on the futures position. On the other, it leads to a larger cash outflow on our borrowing. However, the cash inflow on the futures position takes place immediately, while the cash outflow on the borrowing takes place only at maturity of the borrowing, that is, in nine-months' time. Our challenge in designing a hedge is to choose $\hat{\alpha}$ so that the *present value* of these effects cancel out, leaving the value of our position unchanged. This is called PVBP analysis since we are using the present value of a basis point to identify the optimal hedge.

Applying PVBP analysis to the current example, an increase of 1 basis point in interest rates results in an immediate cash inflow of $25 per contract, so over $\hat{\alpha}$ contracts, there is an inflow of $25\,\hat{\alpha}$. On the borrowing, suppose the three-month borrowing period consists of $d$ days. Then the increase in borrowing costs occasioned by a one-basis-point increase in interest rates is

$$I = 1,000,000 \times \left( \frac{0.01}{100} \times \frac{d}{360} \right)$$

For example, if $d = 90$, then the increase in borrowing cost is $I = 25$. However, this extra outflow takes place only at maturity of the borrowing, i.e., in nine-months' time. If $\ell_T$ denotes the current one-year Libor rate and $D$ the number of days in the nine-month period, the *present value* of this outflow is

$$PV(I) = \frac{I}{1 + (\ell_T \times \frac{D}{360})} \tag{6.68}$$

Thus, we want to choose $\hat{\alpha}$ so that $25\,\hat{\alpha} = PV(I)$, or

$$\hat{\alpha} = \frac{PV(I)}{25} \tag{6.69}$$

Expression (6.69) idenitifies the hedge ratio to be used if we take daily marking-to-market into account. Of course, hedging using this ratio must be dynamic since the ratio itself changes as time progresses. For a discussion of this and other practical aspects of hedging using eurodollar futures, see Chapter 5 of Burghardt (2003).

# Calculating the Conversion Factor

To calculate the conversion factor on a given bond in the Treasury bond futures contract, the CBoT rounds off the maturity of the bonds to the nearest quarter (i.e., three months). If after the rounding off the bond has a maturity that is an integer multiple of six months, then the bond is treated as if the last coupon was just paid and the next coupon is due in six-months' time. If after the rounding off the bond's maturity leaves a three-month remainder when divided by six months, then the next coupon is assumed to be paid in three-months' time, so accrued interest for the first three months must be subtracted from the price.

For example, suppose the delivered bond is an 8% bond with a maturity of 20 years and one month. Rounding off this maturity to the nearest three months, we obtain a maturity of 20 years. Since 20 years is an integer multiple of six months (it contains exactly 40 six-month periods), the bond is treated as if its last coupon was just paid and its next coupon will be in six-months' time. Thus, its conversion factor is precisely as obtained in expression (6.44) in the text, i.e., it is 1.2311.

Now suppose that the delivered bond instead has a maturity of 20 years and four months. Rounding off this maturity to the nearest three months, we obtain a maturity of 20 years and three months. This maturity is no longer an exact multiple of six months, so we treat the bond as if the next coupon will be in three-months' time. In three-months' time, we receive a coupon of 0.04 per $1 face value. The remaining portion of the bond is a 20-year 8% coupon bond on which the last coupon was just paid. We have just seen that the conversion factor for this remaining portion of the bond is 1.2311. Adding this to the coupon of 0.04 that will be received in three months, we see that the delivered bond has an overall conversion factor of 1.2711 in three months. We first discount this to bring it back to the present. Since the discount factor for six months is 3%, the present value of 1.2711 receivable in three months is

$$\frac{1.2711}{\sqrt{1.03}} = 1.2525$$

Next, we deduct accrued interest. Of the coupon of 0.04 receivable in three months, the accrued interest component is 0.02. Subtracting this from the discounted conversion factor, we obtain the final conversion factor $1.2525 - 0.02 = 1.2325$.

## A General Formula

In general, the conversion factor may be computed using the following formula. Let $N$ be the number of whole years left to the bond's maturity or first call (whichever is earlier), let $c$ denote the coupon on the delivered bond, and let $x$ denote the number of months by which the maturity of the delivered bond exceeds $N$ years rounded down to the nearest three months. Note that we must have $x = 0, 3, 6,$ or $9$ months. The conversion factor is then given by the formula

$$(1.03)^{-x/6} \left\{ \frac{c}{2} + \left( \frac{c}{0.06} \left[ 1 - (1.03)^{-2N} \right] + (1.03)^{-2N} \right) \right\} - \frac{c}{2} \left( \frac{6-x}{6} \right) \quad \textbf{(6.70)}$$

# Duration as a Sensitivity Measure

In this appendix, we derive (6.53); that is, we explain why the weighted maturity of a portfolio (i.e., its duration) measures the sensitivity of the portfolio value to changes in interest rates.

Consider first a zero-coupon bond with a maturity of $t$ years and a face value of $B$. The duration of this bond is simply $t$. If the $t$-year interest rate is $r$, the current price of the bond is

$$P = e^{-rt}B \tag{6.71}$$

If interest rates change by a small amount $dr$, then the price of the bond becomes

$$P' = e^{-(r+dr)t}B = e^{-rt}e^{-dr\,t}B \tag{6.72}$$

Thus, the *change* $\Delta_P$ in the bond value is

$$\Delta_P = e^{-rt}e^{-dr\,t}B - e^{-rt}B = e^{-rt}B\left[e^{-dr\,t} - 1\right] \tag{6.73}$$

Now, for small values of $x$, the exponential function $e^x$ is approximately[4] equal to $1 + x$. Since $e^{-rt}B = P$, we can rewrite (6.73) as

$$\Delta_P = P\left[(1 - dr\,t) - 1\right] = -tP\,dr \tag{6.74}$$

which is precisely (6.53).

An analogous, if notationally more complex, argument establishes that (6.53) holds for coupon bonds and, more generally, for portfolios of bonds. Consider a bond (or a portfolio of bonds) with cash flows $c_i$ at times $t_i$, $i = 1, \ldots, n$. If the interest rate for a period of length $t_i$ years is $r_i$, the current price of this bond is

$$P = e^{-r_1 t_1}c_1 + \cdots + e^{-r_n t_n}c_n \tag{6.75}$$

Suppose all interest rates change by an amount $dr$. Then, the change in the present value of the first cash flow is

$$\Delta_1 = e^{-(r_1+dr)t_1}c_1 - e^{-r_1 t_1}c_1 \tag{6.76}$$

The same arguments as used above show that this quantity is approximately

$$\Delta_1 = e^{-r_1 t_1}c_1((1 - dr\,t_1) - 1) = -e^{-r_1 t_1}c_1 t_1\,dr \tag{6.77}$$

Similarly, the change in the present value of the $k$-th cash flow is

$$\Delta_k = -e^{-r_k t_k}c_k t_k\,dr \tag{6.78}$$

The total change in the value of the bond $\Delta_P$ is the sum of all these changes and so is given by

$$\Delta_P = -\left[e^{-r_1 t_1}c_1 t_1 + \cdots + e^{-r_n t_n}c_n t_n\right]dr \tag{6.79}$$

Now define $w_k$ to be the contribution of the $k$-th cash flow to portfolio value:

$$w_k = \frac{e^{-r_k t_k}c_k}{P} \tag{6.80}$$

Note that the duration of the portfolio (its weighted maturity) is given by

$$D_P = w_1 t_1 + \cdots + w_n t_n \tag{6.81}$$

---

[4] More precisely, $e^x$ is defined as the infinite sum $1 + x + x^2/2! + x^3/3! + \cdots$. For small $x$, terms of the order of $x^2$ and higher become tiny and can be ignored as a first approximation.

Moreover, $w_k P = e^{-r_k t_k} c_k$ for each $k$. Substituting this into (6.79), we obtain

$$\Delta_P = -[w_1 t_1 P + \cdots + w_n t_n P] \, dr$$
$$= -P[w_1 t_1 + \cdots + w_n t_n] \, dr$$
$$= -P D_P \, dr \tag{6.82}$$

Expression (6.82) is exactly the relationship (6.53) that we wanted to prove.

---

**Appendix 6E**

# The Duration of a Futures Contract

We show here that the duration of a bond futures contract is just the duration of the underlying bond measured from the expiry of the futures contract. We consider only the case where the underlying in the futures contract is a zero-coupon bond (such as the CME's Treasury bill futures contract). The arguments may be easily extended to coupon bonds, but, as in the previous section, this gets notationally messy.

Let $T$ and $T^*$ denote, respectively, the maturity dates of the futures contract and the underlying zero-coupon bond. Let $r$ and $r^*$ denote, respectively, the interest rates applicable to these maturities. Finally, let $B$ denote the face value of the zero and $P$ its current price.

By treating the futures contract as a forward contract, the current price of the futures contract may be determined from the zero cost-of-carry formula developed in Chapter 3. This futures price is:

$$F = e^{rT} P \tag{6.83}$$

But $P$ itself is simply the price of a $t^*$-maturity zero, so its current price is simply

$$P = e^{-r^* t^*} B \tag{6.84}$$

Combining (6.83) and (6.84), we have

$$F = e^{rT - r^* T^*} B \tag{6.85}$$

Now suppose interest rates change by an amount $dr$. The change in the futures price $\Delta_F$ is then

$$\Delta_F = e^{(r+dr)T - (r^*+dr)T^*} B - e^{rT - r^* T^*} B \tag{6.86}$$

Pulling out the common terms, this is

$$\Delta_F = e^{rT - r^* T^*} B \left( e^{dr\,T - dr\,T^*} - 1 \right) \tag{6.87}$$

Using the approximation $e^x = 1 + x$ (which, as mentioned above, is a very good approximation for small $x$), we have

$$\Delta_F = e^{rT - r^* T^*} B (1 - [1 + (T - T^*) dr]) = e^{rT - r^* T^*} B [-(T - T^*) dr] \tag{6.88}$$

Now, $e^{rT - r^* T^*} B$ is just the initial futures price $F$. Moreover, $T - T^*$ is the maturity of the underlying zero measured from the expiry date of the futures contract, which is $D_F$ as defined in Section 6.8. Thus,

$$\Delta_F = -D_F F \, dr \tag{6.89}$$

which is exactly the result we are to prove.

Part

# 2

# Options

# Chapter 7

# Options Markets

## 7.1 Introduction

Options are often perceived as "new" financial instruments compared to, say, forwards or futures, but they too have been around for a very long time. Luenberger (1997) cites an early story involving successful speculation with options by the Greek scientist and philosopher Thales of Miletus (624–547 BCE). It is likely that, like forwards, options too were used in other ancient civilizations. Certainly, there is considerable evidence of organized options trading dating back several hundred years. Joseph de la Vega, in his delightful book "Confusion des Confusiones" published in 1688, discusses the trading of call and put options in 17th century Amsterdam. Options also played a role in the Dutch "Tulipmania" in the early 17th century. Options on common stocks were offered over a hundred years ago on the London Stock Exchange. In the US, too, options were trading on the CBoT in the 1930s although they were called "privilleges" rather than "options."

To be sure, the options market has changed dramatically over the past few decades. Volume has exploded; the Bank for International Settlements (BIS) estimates that in end-2008, the notional outstanding on options worldwide exceeded $100 trillion. The nature of the options traded has also changed. Options on equities and currencies continue to be traded in large amounts, but as with forwards and futures, a substantial chunk of the market is now occupied by *interest-rate options*, options written directly or indirectly on interest rates. Innovation has continued apace with the introduction of several new products in recent years such as credit-spread, energy, electricity, and bandwidth options.

In this first chapter on options, we begin with a review of the basic definitions and terminology, and introduce the important notion of options as a form of *financial insurance*. Then, in the centerpiece of this chapter, we examine "naked" options positions (options positions viewed in isolation) and how each naked option position corresponds to a unique combination of views on market direction and volatility. Chapter 8 builds on this material and describes various commonly-employed trading strategies that use options to reflect specific directional and/or volatility views. The appendix to this chapter describes options markets worldwide, their breakdown by marketplace (exchange-traded versus over-the-counter) and their compositions in terms of the underlying instrument (equities, currencies, etc.).

## 7.2 Definitions and Terminology

Options were defined in Chapter 1. We review the definitions here. Table 7.1 summarizes the basic terminology.

An *option* is a financial security that gives its holder the right to buy or sell a specified quantity of a specified asset (the "underlying asset" or simply the "underlying") at a specified

**TABLE 7.1** Basic Options Terminology

| Term | Meaning |
|------|---------|
| Call option | Right to *buy* the underlying asset |
| Put option | Right to *sell* the underlying asset |
| Expiration/Maturity date | Date on which the right expires |
| Strike/Exercise price | Price at which right may be exercised |
| American-style option | Right may be exercised at any point before maturity |
| European-style option | Right may be exercised only at maturity |
| Long position/Holder/Buyer | Party that holds the right in the contract |
| Short position/Writer/Seller | Party with a contingent obligation in the contract |

price on or before a specified date. The defining characteristic of an option is its "optionality": the holder has the *right* to participate in the specified trade but is not *obligated* to do so.

The underlying asset in a financial options contract is commonly one whose value depends on equity prices ("equity options"), exchange rates ("currency options"), or interest rates ("interest-rate options") but may also be a commodity (such as gold or crude oil) or other type of asset or financial variable (e.g., electricity or credit spreads).

There are two basic types of options. A *call* option gives its holder the right to *buy* the specified asset at the price specified in the contract. A *put* option gives its holder the right to *sell* the asset at the specified price. The specified price is itself referred to as the "strike price" or "exercise price" of the option.

The date by which the right must be exercised is called the "maturity" or "expiration" date of the contract. If the right is not exercised by this date, it expires. Options with infinite life spans ("perpetual options") are rare but do exist.

Options are also distinguished by *when* the right in the contract may be exercised. In an *American-style* option, the right may be exercised at any time before expiry of the contract. In a *European-style* option, the right may be exercised on only one date: the maturity date of the contract. Options that may be exercised before maturity but only on certain pre-specified dates are called *Bermudan-style* options; in this part of the book, we are concerned mainly with only European- and American-style options.

There is an important difference in terminology between forwards and options. In a forward contract, "long" and "short" refer, respectively, to the buyer and seller in the trade underlying the contract. In an option, "long" refers to the party holding the *right* in the contract; this right could be either the right to buy (if the option is a call) or the right to sell (if a put). The terms "holder" and "buyer" are used interchangeably with long position.

The party on the other side of the option contract is said to have a "short position" in the option and is also referred to as the "seller" or "writer" of the option. The option writer has a contingent *obligation* in the contract: the writer must take part in the specified trade if the option holder elects to exercise his right in the contract. (If I sell you the right to buy Microsoft shares from me at a price of $25 a share, I am obligated to sell you the shares at that price if you want to buy.)

# 7.3 Options as Financial Insurance

Insurance, in general, offers us protection from unpleasant surprises. Health insurance protects us from financial consequences of shocks to our physical well-being. Earthquake or fire insurance protects us from financial consequences of home damage due to earthquakes or fires. Options can protect us from the financial consequences of unfavorable changes in market prices.

The holder of an option has the right to participate in the trade specified in the contract but can elect not to do so. Two simple examples will illustrate how this translates into insurance.

---

**Example 7.1**

### Puts as Insurance for Sellers

Consider an investor who plans to sell Widget Corp stock in a month's time. Suppose Widget Corp's stock price is currently 95. The investor is exposed to the risk of a fall in the stock price over the month. If the investor buys a put option on Widget Corp stock with a strike of 95, then she is protected against this exposure:

- If Widget Corp's price falls below 95, she can exercise the put and sell the stock for 95.
- If Widget Corp's price rises above 95, she can let the put lapse and sell the stock at the higher price.

This one-sided protection is exactly what we think of as "insurance." Thus, a put option offers a seller insurance against a price decrease while allowing the seller to take full advantage of a price increase.
■

---

**Example 7.2**

### Calls as Insurance for Buyers

Now consider an investor who is planning to *buy* Widget Corp stock in a month's time. The investor faces the risk that Widget Corp's stock price could rise over this month. If the investor buys a call option on Widget Corp with a strike of 95, he is protected from this risk:

- If Widget Corp's price rises above 95, he can exercise the call and buy the stock for 95.
- If Widget Corp's price falls below 95, he can let the call lapse and buy the stock at the cheaper price.

Thus, a call option offers a buyer one-sided protection against a price increase; that is, it insures the buyer against a price increase while allowing the buyer to take advantage of a price decrease.
■

## The Option Price/Premium

The protection, in either case, is provided to the option holder by the option writer. In exchange for this protection, the holder pays the writer an up-front fee that is called the *option price* or the *option premium*. As with all insurance, the premium will depend on many factors including the likelihood that the insurer will have to make a payout and the size of the anticipated payout. The determination of the "fair" value of the option premium is one of the central issues we will examine in this book.

## Remark

One should not get carried away with the options-insurance analogy. If an investor has an underlying exposure (is planning to buy IBM stock or to sell Japanese yen), then using options does indeed provide insurance-style protection on this exposure. But, unlike insurance, which always presumes an underlying insurable risk, options may be used even by investors who do not have any underlying exposure; that is, options can also be used to *speculate*. It is also relevant to note that unlike most conventional forms of insurance, the risks underlying options contracts typically correspond to traded securities with observable prices (e.g., IBM stock prices or yen-dollar exchange rates). The properties of these underlying prices are key to identifying the fair prices of financial options.

# 7.4  Naked Option Positions

As the first step in our analysis, we begin with a study of "naked" options positions, i.e., options positions viewed in isolation. The material that follows forms the foundation for both the trading and risk-management strategies using options discussed in the next chapter, as well as the pricing material that follows in the succeeding several chapters.

The most important lesson that comes out of this analysis can be summarized in four words: *options react to volatility*. That is, a fundamental determinant of option payoffs and option values is the amount of uncertainty anticipated in the future price of the underlying asset. This simple observation has profound implications. From a pricing standpoint, it means that any attempt to value options must include a central role for the volatility of the underlying asset. From a risk-management standpoint, it means that options may not only be used to hedge against (or bet on) *directional views* concerning the market—for which purpose one can also use "linear" derivatives such as futures or forwards—but uniquely also on views regarding market *volatility*.

There are four basic naked option positions: (a) long call, (b) short call, (c) long put, and (d) short put. We analyze these positions in this section and show that each position can be associated with a unique combination of views on market direction and volatility. We use the following notation:

- $S$: current price of the asset underlying the options contract.
- $T$: maturity date of option.
- $S_T$: asset price at date $T$.
- $K$: strike price of option.
- $C$: current call price.
- $P$: current put price.

For specificity, we refer throughout to the asset underlying the contract as a "stock," although the analysis is unchanged if it is a bond, index, commodity, or foreign currency. We treat the option as if it is European in style, so exercise occurs at date $T$. By reinterpreting $T$ as the exercise date of the option, much of the analysis may also be extended to American-style options.

## Payoffs from Long and Short Call Positions

Consider an example. Suppose you have a call option to buy the stock of $XYZ$ corporation at a strike price of $K = 100$. What will you do on date $T$?

- If the price $S_T$ of $XYZ$ is *less* than 100, it is obviously best to let the option lapse: there is no point paying $K = 100$ for a stock that is worth less than that amount. The call is said to be *out-of-the-money* in this case.
- If $S_T = 100$, then you are indifferent between exercising the option and not exercising the option (although transactions costs, which we ignore, may push you towards not exercising). The call is said to be *at-the-money* in this case.
- Finally, if $S_T > 100$, it is very much in your interest to exercise the call: the call allows you to buy for 100 an asset that is worth $S_T > 100$. The call is said to be *in-the-money* in this case. The profit from exercising the call is $S_T - 100$; the higher is $S_T$, the greater the profits.

What about the short position who sold you the option? The short position has only a contingent *obligation* in the contract; the decision on exercise is made by you as the

**TABLE 7.2** Gross Payoffs to Long and Short Call Positions

| | $S_T$ | Long Call Payoffs | Short Call Payoffs |
|---|---|---|---|
| Out-of-the-money | 70 | 0 | 0 |
| | 80 | 0 | 0 |
| | 90 | 0 | 0 |
| At-the-money | 100 | 0 | 0 |
| In-the-money | 110 | 10 | −10 |
| | 120 | 20 | −20 |
| | 130 | 30 | −30 |

long position. So to identify the payoffs to the short, we must see when the option will be exercised by the long position and calculate the consequences to the short.

- If $S_T < 100$, then the option finishes out-of-the-money and lapses unexercised. Thus, there are no payoffs to the short either in this case.
- The same is, of course, true at-the-money.
- If $S_T > 100$, the option finishes in-the-money and *is* exercised. This means the short position sells for 100 an asset worth $S_T > 100$, so the short *loses* $S_T - 100$.

These payoffs to both long and short positions are described in Table 7.2. Of course, all these are *gross* payoffs. To obtain the net payoffs, the cost of the call $C$ must be subtracted from the payoffs of the long position and added to the payoffs of the short position.

We can also represent these payoffs in a graph. In general, when you exercise a long call with a strike of $K$, you receive for $K$ an asset worth $S_T$. Thus, the payoffs to the long position from exercise are

$$\max\{S_T - K, 0\} = \begin{cases} S_T - K, & \text{if } S_T \geq K \\ 0, & \text{if } S_T < K \end{cases} \quad \textbf{(7.1)}$$

which means the payoffs to the short call are

$$-\max\{S_T - K, 0\} = \begin{cases} -(S_T - K), & \text{if } S_T \geq K \\ 0, & \text{if } S_T < K \end{cases} \quad \textbf{(7.2)}$$

Figures 7.1 and 7.2 represent these payoffs. The payoffs are *nonlinear*. The long call has a payoff of zero when the option is out-of-the-money (i.e., $S_T < K$) and a slope of $+1$ when

**FIGURE 7.1**
Payoffs to a Long Call Position

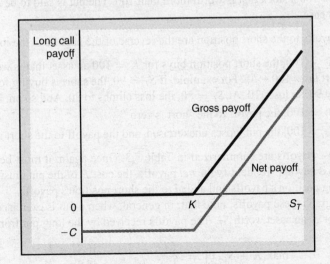

Long call payoff

Gross payoff

Net payoff

0     K     $S_T$

$-C$

**FIGURE 7.2**

Payoffs to a Short Call Position

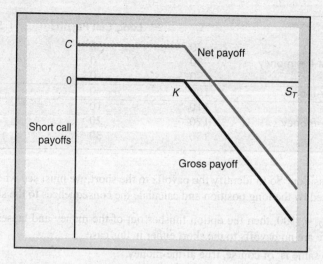

the option is in-the-money (i.e., every increase of $1 in the price above $K$ translates to an extra $1 of profit for the long position). The payoffs of the short position are the mirror image of the long call's payoffs: zero when the option is out-of-the-money and decreasing with a slope of $-1$ when the option is in-the-money.

## Payoffs from Long and Short Put Positions

The payoffs to long and short put positions are computed in an analogous fashion. Consider, for example, the payoffs to a long position in a put on $XYZ$ stock with a strike of $K = 100$.

- If the price $S_T < 100$, it is in the long position's interest to exercise the put: the put enables the long to sell for $K = 100$ an asset that is worth $S_T < 100$. The put is *in-the-money* in this case. The payoff from exercise is $100 - S_T$. The lower is $S_T$, the greater the profit from exercising the put.

- If $S_T = 100$, the long is indifferent between exercising and not exercising the put: either action leads to a payoff of zero. The put is said to be *at-the-money* in this case.

- If $S_T > 100$, it is obviously best to let the option lapse: there is no point in selling for $K = 100$ a stock that is worth more than 100. The put is said to be *out-of-the-money* in this case.

The payoffs to the short position are the reverse of the payoffs to the long:

- If $S_T < 100$, the short position buys for $K = 100$ an asset that is worth $S_T < 100$. The short *loses* $100 - S_T$. For example, if $S_T = 90$, the short is buying for 100 a stock worth only 90, so loses 10. At $S_T = 80$, the loss climbs to 20. And so on.

- If $S_T = 100$, the payoff to the short is zero.

- If $S_T > 100$, the put lapses unexercised, and the payoff to the short is once again zero.

These payoffs are summarized in Table 7.3. Once again, it must be stressed that these are *gross* payoffs. To identify the *net* payoffs, the cost $P$ of the put must be subtracted from the long position's payoffs and added to the short position's payoffs.

To graph these payoffs, note that, in general, when a put is exercised, the long position sells for $K$ an asset worth $S_T$. The payoffs received by the long put from exercise are

$$\max\{K - S_T, 0\} = \begin{cases} (K - S_T), & \text{if } S_T < K \\ 0, & \text{if } S_T \geq K \end{cases} \tag{7.3}$$

**TABLE 7.3** Gross Payoffs from Long and Short Put Positions

| | $S_T$ | Long Put Payoffs | Short Put Payoffs |
|---|---|---|---|
| | 70 | 30 | −30 |
| In-the-money | 80 | 20 | −20 |
| | 90 | 10 | −10 |
| At-the-money | 100 | 0 | 0 |
| | 110 | 0 | 0 |
| Out-of-the-money | 120 | 0 | 0 |
| | 130 | 0 | 0 |

**FIGURE 7.3**

Payoffs from a Long Put Position

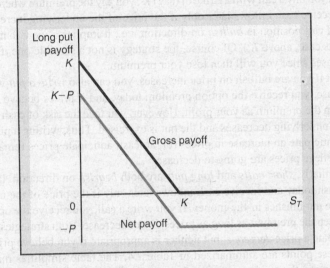

**FIGURE 7.4**

Payoffs from a Short Put Position

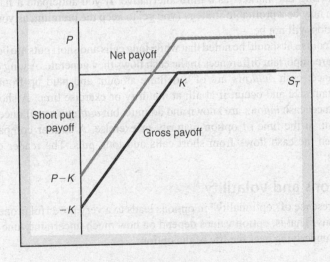

Thus, the payoffs to the short position are

$$-\max\{K - S_T, 0\} = \min\{S_T - K, 0\} \qquad (7.4)$$

Figures 7.3 and 7.4 illustrate these payoffs. The payoff to a long put has a slope of −1 for $S_T < K$ (i.e., it *decreases* by $1 for every $1 *increase* in $S_T$) and is flat for $S_T \geq K$. The payoff of the short put has a slope of +1 for $S_T < K$ (i.e., the short's losses decrease by $1 for every $1 increase in the price) and are flat for $S_T \geq K$.

# 7.5   Options as Views on Market Direction and Volatility

Each naked option position embodies a unique combination of views on market *direction* and market *volatility*. Market direction refers to the direction of prices (are prices going up or down?). Market volatility is a more nebulous concept; we define it formally later in the book. For the time being, it suffices to think of volatility as a measure of uncertainty in price movements; roughly, more volatility means that larger price swings may occur.

## Options and Directional Views

When you buy a call with a strike of (say) $K$, you pay the premium when the call is purchased and receive cash inflows later only if the price of the underlying increases above $K$. Thus, a long call position is *bullish* on direction, i.e., it implies a view that prices are going up (in this case, above $K$). Of course, the strategy is not a sensible one if you anticipate price decreases since you will then lose your premium.

But if you are bullish on price increases, you can also *write a put* with a strike of $K$. In this case, you receive the option premium today, and if prices behave as expected, you get to keep the premium as your profit. However, you face the risk of cash outflows if the price of the underlying decreases and the put is exercised. Thus, writing a put too makes sense if you anticipate an increase in prices (or, at least, anticipate prices remaining flat) but not if you believe prices are going to decrease.

Similarly, *short calls* and *long puts* are both *bearish* on direction. If you buy a put, you pay cash today and receive cash inflows later only if the price of the underlying decreases and the put finishes in-the-money. If you write a call, you receive the option premium today and keep the premium as long as prices do not decrease. Both strategies are profitable if you anticipate a price *decrease*, but neither is appropriate if you believe prices are going up.

These points are summarized in Table 7.4. The table simplifies matters a little by not considering flat markets as a third alternative. If you anticipate a flat market, writing an option may be a profitable strategy (you get to keep the premium as your profit), but buying an option will not be.

Of course, it should be noted that while long calls and short puts are both bullish strategies, there are important differences in the cash flows they generate. A long call is akin to *buying* insurance: cash *outflows* are of a definite amount and paid up-front, but *inflows* are of uncertain size and occur, if at all, at maturity or exercise time. A short put is like *selling* insurance: cash *inflows* are known and definite, but *outflows* are of uncertain size and occur, if at all, at the time of option maturity or exercise. A similar comparison can be drawn between the cash flows from short calls and long puts. The reader can easily fill in the details.

## Options and Volatility

The presence of "optionality" in options leads to a very powerful property: options react to volatility. That is, option values depend on how much uncertainty one expects in the price of the underlying over the life of the option.

**TABLE 7.4**  Naked Options and Views on Direction

| This table summarizes the implied market view on direction of the four basic naked option positions. | |
|---|---|
| **Bullish on Direction** | **Bearish on Direction** |
| Long call | Long put |
| Short put | Short call |

A simple example will help illustrate this point. Suppose we have a call option on a stock with a strike of $K = 100$. We compare option payoffs under two possible distributions for $S_T$. First, suppose that the distribution of $S_T$ is given by

$$S_T = \begin{cases} 110, & \text{with probability } 1/2 \\ 90, & \text{with probability } 1/2 \end{cases} \quad \text{(7.5)}$$

Then, the call payoffs at time $T$ are

$$C_T = \begin{cases} 10, & \text{with probability } 1/2 \\ 0, & \text{with probability } 1/2 \end{cases} \quad \text{(7.6)}$$

Now suppose the distribution (7.5) is modified to one with the same mean but more spread-out prices (i.e., with greater "volatility"):

$$S_T = \begin{cases} 120, & \text{with probability } 1/2 \\ 80, & \text{with probability } 1/2 \end{cases} \quad \text{(7.7)}$$

The option payoffs at time $T$ are then

$$C_T = \begin{cases} 20, & \text{with probability } 1/2 \\ 0, & \text{with probability } 1/2 \end{cases} \quad \text{(7.8)}$$

It is clear from comparing (7.6) and (7.8) that the greater volatility in the second distribution has been beneficial: the payoffs in (7.8) are unambiguously superior to those in (7.6). A call buyer would clearly be willing to pay more for the option if the uncertainty anticipated is given by the more volatile distribution (7.7) rather than the distribution (7.5). That is, higher volatility leads to higher call values.

Intuitively, when volatility increases, prices become more spread out; higher and lower prices both become more likely. For the holder of a call, the higher prices are good news: they result in larger payoffs when the call is exercised. But there is no corresponding downside from the lower prices since the call holder can simply elect not to exercise the call. Thus, the call holder benefits from the increased volatility.

Long *put* options also benefit from volatility. Continuing the same example, the payoffs to the holder of a put option with a strike of 100 are given by

$$P_T = \begin{cases} 0, & \text{with probability } 1/2 \\ 10, & \text{with probability } 1/2 \end{cases} \quad \text{(7.9)}$$

if the distribution of $S_T$ is given by (7.5). Whereas if the distribution of $S_T$ has the more volatile form (7.7), the payoffs to the put holder are

$$P_T = \begin{cases} 0, & \text{with probability } 1/2 \\ 20, & \text{with probability } 1/2 \end{cases} \quad \text{(7.10)}$$

Once again, the more volatile distribution translates to a superior payoff profile for the option holder. A put buyer would be willing to pay more for the put if the uncertainty anticipated was given by the distribution (7.7) rather than (7.5).

Optionality is, of course, crucial in this link. Without optionality, one cannot avoid the downside cost of increased volatility. In our example, the holder of a long forward position will enjoy the larger benefit from the price increase to 120, but will also have a larger loss from the fall to 80.

Just as increased volatility benefits the holder of an option, it makes the *writer* of an option worse off. The larger price swings imply that the option writer loses more in the event that the option is exercised but gains nothing from price moves in the other direction since the option will not be exercised. Thus, an option writer prefers low volatility.

**TABLE 7.5** Naked Options and Views on Volatility

This table summarizes the view on volatility embodied by each of the four basic naked option positions.

| Bullish on Volatility | Bearish on Volatility |
|---|---|
| Long call | Short call |
| Long put | Short put |

**TABLE 7.6** Naked Options and Views on Direction and Volatility

This table summarizes the view on direction and volatility embodied by each of the four basic naked option positions.

| | Bullish on Direction | Bearish on Direction |
|---|---|---|
| Bullish on Volatility | Long Call | Long Put |
| Bearish on Volatility | Short Put | Short Call |

## Options as Views on Volatility

These observations show that every naked option position embodies a view on *volatility*. A *long* option position, whether a long call or a long put, is necessarily a *bullish* view on volatility. Such a position increases in value when volatility increases and decreases in value when volatility decreases. Long option positions are consequently referred to as "long volatility" positions. Similarly, a *short* option position—whether a short call or a short put—is *bearish* on volatility: such a position *in*creases in value when volatility *de*creases and vice versa. Short option positions are consequently referred to as short volatility positions. Table 7.5 summarizes these observations.

Combining the information in Tables 7.4 and 7.5, we can separate the role of each naked option position from a risk standpoint. Table 7.6 presents this overall picture. It shows that each naked option position corresponds to a unique combination of views on volatility and direction. For example, while both long calls and short puts are bullish positions on direction, only one—the long call—will benefit from an increase in the volatility of the underlying. The short put loses value when volatility increases. Thus, a bullish view on both volatility and direction indicates a long call position, while a view that is bullish on direction but bearish on volatility indicates a short put. Similarly, if we are bearish on both direction and volatility, a short call position is indicated, but if we are bearish on direction but bullish on volatility, a long put position is indicated.

## Options versus Forwards/Futures/Spot

The options-volatility relationship also highlights a fundamental difference between options and positions in spot or futures. We can take advantage of views on *direction* with spot or futures also; there is nothing unique about options in this context. If we are bullish on direction, we can use a long position in spot or futures or forwards; all three will make money if prices increase. If we are bearish on direction, we can take short positions in spot or futures or forwards; all three will be profitable if prices decline.

However, there is no obvious way to incorporate views on *volatility* using spot, futures, or forwards. All three are instruments with *linear* payoffs. It is the nonlinearity of options payoffs that allow options to react to volatility. Indeed, options also permit pure volatility plays where we are neutral on direction but have a view on volatility. Portfolios such as straddles (described in Chapter 8) are examples of such strategies.

## 7.6 Exercises

1. What is the difference between an American option and a European option?

2. Explain the following terms in the context of options: long, short, call, put, American, European, in-the-money, out-of-the-money, at-the-money, strike, holder, buyer, writer, seller, expiry, premium, over-the-counter, and exchange-traded.

3. What is a "Bermudan" option?

4. Why is being long a put option somewhat analogous to being in a short stock position?

5. What is the main difference between a forward and an option?

6. What is the difference between over-the-counter (OTC) contracts and exchange-traded contracts?

7. Make a list of securities that you can think of that contain embedded options. For each embedded option, state the underlying source of risk.

8. Give an example of an option contract that is both exchange-traded and provided over-the-counter. Which of these forms is more widely in use? Explain?

9. Explain why an option is like an insurance contract. How is it different from a futures contract? Can an option, like a future, be used for hedging?

10. What position in naked options would you adopt if you believe that the price of the stock is going to drop *and* the volatility of the stock is going to decrease?

11. Why do options usually increase in value with volatility? What essential feature of the payoff diagram leads to this result?

12. Explain the difference between the payoff and price of an option. Write down the payoff formula for a call option and for a put option. What is the difference between the "gross" and "net" payoffs of an option (as widely applied in common usage)? Which concept do you think is the more useful one for valuing an option? Why?

13. Draw a gross payoff diagram for a short position in a call at strike 100. Also draw the gross payoff diagram for a long position in a put option at the same strike and maturity as the call. Overlay these plots on the same axis to get an aggregate payoff diagram for the portfolio of call and put. What other security do you know of with the same payoff diagram as this portfolio?

14. Why does a callable bond contain embedded options? Explain what kind of option this bond has. Who benefits from this option? Based on your answer, is a callable bond priced higher or lower than a noncallable bond?

15. Explain what options exist in a convertible-callable corporate bond.

16. If you hold a callable bond and the volatility of interest rates increases, what do you think usually happens to the value of your bond?

17. If you hold a convertible bond and the volatility of equity prices declines, what is the effect on bond value, assuming nothing else changes?

18. A quanto (quantity) option is one in which the option contains price risk from two sources. Quantos are discussed in the chapter on exotic options. An example is where you buy a put option on the Nikkei stock index (which is yen denominated), but the strike price of the option is stated in dollars. Explain what the different sources of risk in such an option might be. For each source of risk, state in which direction it must move for the value of the option to increase.

19. A European investor in the US equity markets wants to buy a quanto call on the S&P 500 index, where the strike is written in euros. (See the previous question for the definition of a quanto). Can you explain why the investor wants such an option? Also explain what risks the investor is hedging by buying a quanto call on the equity index rather than a plain call on the S&P 500.

20. If you are manufacturing consumer products that use oil-based chemicals as inputs, then you are subject to oil price risk. Suppose you order your oil from Saudi Arabia and usually pay for it in Saudi rials. You are now concerned that the appreciation in the rial will affect your profitability.

   (a) How would you use forward contracts to hedge the risk of your oil purchases?

   (b) What type of quanto option would you like to buy to hedge this risk? (See Question 18 for the definition of a quanto.)

21. Employee stock options have additional risk over and above standard call options in that the employee may not be able (or allowed) to cash in the option in the event of termination of the employee's job with the firm if the option is not vested. But if the option is vested, so immediate exercise in the event of termination is possible, should it be worth as much as the usual American option trading on the firm? Explain.

22. Market timers are traders who vary their allocation between equity and bonds so as to optimize the performance of their portfolios by trading off one market versus the other. Rather than physically trade in the two markets, you want to avail yourself of the best return from the bond or stock markets over the next year using an option. Suggest an option that will provide you this result. (Feel free to define the option's terms.) What factors drive the value of this option?

# Options Markets

This appendix provides a brief discussion of options markets worldwide and their characteristics. Like forwards and futures, options may be divided into two broad groups. First, there are options that are traded on organized exchanges. These are the analogs of futures contracts, and like futures contracts, come with standardized contract terms (expiration dates, strike prices, etc.) and margining requirements. Second, there are over-the-counter (OTC) options. These are the counterparts of forward contracts and are bilateral agreements that can be customized to the counterparties' requirements.

## Options Markets: Size and Composition

A snapshot picture of worldwide options and derivatives markets as of end-2008 is provided in Table 7.7. Three features of particular interest are highlighted by this table:

- The exchange-traded and OTC options markets are both large markets, but the OTC options market with a notional outstanding of $68 trillion is about 80% larger than the exchange-traded options market with its notional outstanding of $38 trillion.

- Virtually all options are written on one of three categories of underlying instruments: currencies, equities (including equity indices), and interest rates/interest-rate sensitive securities like bonds.

  – Equity options are of comparable dollar sizes in the two markets, accounting for about 11% of the exchange-traded options market and 7% of the OTC options market.

  – Currency options account for a negligible fraction of exchange-traded options but are around 15% of the OTC options market. Put differently, most currency options traded in this world are OTC.

**TABLE 7.7**
Derivatives and
Options Markets
Worldwide

This table describes the breakdown of worldwide derivatives and options markets in terms of the underlying security (currency, interest rate, equities, commodities, other) as reported in Tables 19-23 of the *BIS Quarterly Review*, June 2009. Blank entries indicate no data was provided. The numbers are in billions of US dollars and represent the notional outstandings worldwide on the respective contracts as of December 2008.

| Category | Exchange-Traded | Over-the-Counter |
|---|---|---|
| All currency derivatives | 220 | 49,753 |
| *of which:* Currency options | 125 | 10,466 |
| All equity-linked derivatives | 4,929 | 6,494 |
| *of which:* Equity-linked options | 4,273 | 4,862 |
| All interest-rate derivatives | 52,711 | 418,678 |
| *of which:* Interest-rate options | 33,979 | 51,301 |
| All commodity derivatives | — | 4,427 |
| *of which:* Commodity options | — | 1,561 |
| Other derivatives | — | 112,610 |
| Total: All derivatives | 57,860 | 591,963 |
| *of which:* Options | 38,377 | 68,190 |

- Interest-rate options take the lion's share in both markets, amounting to almost 90% of the exchange-traded options market and about 75% of the OTC options markets.
- Exchange-traded options constitute a substantial chunk (over 65%) of the notional outstanding on all exchange-traded derivatives. In contrast, OTC options account for only about 12% of the OTC derivatives markets. The most popular OTC derivatives by far are interest rate swaps, which account for over half the notional outstanding.

The remainder of this appendix discusses exchange-traded and OTC options markets in more detail, highlighting some important features and points of differences.

# Exchange-Traded Options

Options are traded on several exchanges worldwide. Some of the biggest exchanges trading options include the Chicago Board Options Exchange (CBOE), the International Securities Exchange (ISE), CME, and CBoT in the US; Eurex and Liffe in Europe; and Tokyo, Osaka, and SGX (the Singapore Exchange, formerly Simex) in Asia. Exchange-traded options are written on a variety of underlying assets including equities, currencies, and futures contracts.

## Options on Equities

Exchange-traded options on equities come in three forms. The first is options on individual stocks. For example, the CBOE offers options on over 1,500 US stocks and American depository receipts (ADRs), while Liffe offers options on over 100 British equities, and Eurex offers options on a range of individual European stocks. Options on individual stocks are almost invariably American in style.

The second is options on equity indices. Options on the S&P 100 index, the S&P 500 index, and several other indices are offered by the CBOE. Options on the FTSE-100 are traded on Liffe. Eurex has options on the Swiss, Finnish, and German stock market indices. Options on the Nikkei-225 are traded in Osaka and elsewhere. One of the world's most heavily traded derivatives contracts (in terms of number of contracts traded) is the KOSPI-200 options contract on the Korea Stock Exchange. Options on indices can be both American and European in style. For instance, the CBOE's S&P 500 index options contract is European while its S&P 100 index options contract is offered in both European and American styles.

Third, option-exposure to equities can also be taken via options on index futures. These are discussed under "Options on Futures" below.

## Options on Currencies

A number of exchanges offer options on foreign currencies. In the US, the CME offers options on a number of different currencies including the Australian dollar, the Brazilian real, the British pound, the euro, the Israeli shekel, the Swiss franc, and the Japanese yen. Options on currencies may be both European and American in style.

## Options on Futures

Options on futures have futures contracts as their underlying security and are almost invariably American in style. The holder of a *call* option on futures has the right to enter into a *long* position in the futures contract at the strike price specified in the options contract. If the right is exercised, the holder of the call receives (a) a long position in the specified futures contract and (b) a cash settlement (paid into the futures margin account) of the amount by which the current futures price exceeds the option strike price.

Similarly, the holder of a *put* has the right to take a *short* position in the futures contract at the strike price specified in the options contract. If the right is exercised, the holder of the

**TABLE 7.8**  Option Prices in *The Wall Street Journal*

| Microsoft (MSFT) | | | | | Underlying stock price*: 27.25 | | |
| --- | --- | --- | --- | --- | --- | --- | --- |
| | | | | **Call** | | **Put** | |
| **Expiration** | **Strike** | **Last** | **Volume** | **Open Interest** | **Last** | **Volume** | **Open Interest** |
| Apr | 5.00 | 22.30 | 46 | 484 | — | — | — |
| Apr | 22.50 | 4.83 | 14 | 13154 | — | — | 35087 |
| Oct | 22.50 | 5.40 | 160 | 4348 | — | — | 13500 |
| Apr | 25.00 | 2.35 | 256 | 38786 | 0.05 | 5 | 53804 |
| Jul | 25.00 | 2.70 | 21 | 20680 | 0.20 | 436 | 9302 |
| Apr | 27.50 | 0.20 | 3686 | 154002 | 0.35 | 2894 | 54901 |
| May | 27.50 | 0.50 | 14870 | 29471 | 0.65 | 7340 | 21191 |
| Jul | 27.50 | 0.90 | 954 | 96304 | 0.85 | 140 | 64638 |
| Oct | 27.50 | 1.43 | 46 | 29839 | 1.05 | 355 | 22473 |
| Apr | 30.00 | 0.05 | 4 | 122309 | 2.70 | 364 | 743 |
| Jul | 30.00 | 0.20 | 265 | 94110 | 2.70 | 981 | 7498 |
| May | 42.50 | — | — | — | 15.20 | 602 | 300 |
| May | 45.50 | — | — | — | 17.70 | 602 | 300 |

*Underlying stock price* represents listed exchange price only. It may not match the composite closing price.

put receives (a) a short position in the specified futures contract and (b) a cash settlement (paid into the futures margin account) of the amount by which the strike price exceeds the current futures price.

While any futures contract can have an option contract defined on it, most options on futures contracts in practice have as the underlying either an interest-rate/bond futures contract or an equity-index futures contract. The former are categorized and counted as interest-rate options, while the latter are included in equity-linked options. Almost all interest-rate options traded on exchanges are in the form of options on interest-rate futures or options on bond futures.

Exchange-traded options prices are routinely reported in the financial press. Table 7.8 shows the typical style of reporting of options prices. The numbers in the table are taken from the *The Wall Street Journal* website and report prices of options on Miscrosoft on April 7, 2006.

- The first and second columns report the combination of expiration months and strike prices in which options are available. For example, there were calls and puts available on Microsoft with a strike of $27.50 and expirations in April, May, July, and October.
- The third column shows the prices of calls for those strikes and expirations, while the sixth column shows the prices of the corresponding puts. For example, a call expiring in October with a strike of $27.50 has a cost of $1.43, while the price of the corresponding put is $1.05. Since each options contract is for the right to buy or sell 100 shares of Microsoft stock, this means one October call option contract with a strike of $27.50 costs $143 while one October put option contract with a strike of $27.50 costs $105.
- The fourth and seventh columns show the volume of contracts traded on that particular day. The May $27.50-strike contract has the greatest trading volume for both calls and puts with 14,870 call contracts and 7,340 put contracts. Observe that the $27.50 strike is the closest strike to the $27.25 closing share price of Microsoft that day. It is very typical for option volumes to be highest for the nearest-the-money strike at the short end of the maturity spectrum.
- Finally, the fifth and eighth columns show the total outstanding volume of contracts in each maturity-strike category.

# Over-the-Counter Options

Table 7.7 showed that OTC options account for a worldwide notional outstanding that is roughly 80% larger than the notional outstanding of exchange-traded options. OTC options too may have equities, equity indices, currencies, or interest-rate sensitive instruments as their underlyings, but there are some differences.

First, while most exchange-traded options involve "plain vanilla" calls and puts (calls and puts as we have defined above), in the OTC market, there is also a vast range of "exotic" options. Simply put, an exotic option is any option that is *not* a vanilla option. Such options may differ from vanilla options in terms of when they can be exercised and how payoffs are defined. Some exotics are significantly more complex than vanilla options; others actually have simpler forms. Exotic options are described and analyzed in Chapters 18 and 19.

Second, while interest-rate-linked options in the exchange-traded context mostly take on the form of options on interest-rate futures or bond futures, OTC interest-rate options are mostly written directly on specific interest rates such as Libor. *Caps*, for example, are packages of interest-rate options that protect the holder from rises in interest rates beyond the strike rate specified in the contract; they provide insurance to borrowers against rising interest rates. *Floors* similarly protect holders from declines in interest rates below the strike rate; they provide insurance to investors against falling interest rates. *Swaptions* are options to enter into swaps at a fixed rate. Of course, there are also a number of exotic interest-rate options.

# Embedded Options

Any discussion of options markets would be incomplete if it did not also mention the vast number of financial securities that come with "embedded" options. A typical example is a *callable bond*, a bond that gives its issuer the right to buy the bond back from the holder at a price specified in the contract. Callable bonds are used by corporations and other borrowers who wish to retain the flexibility to refinance at cheaper rates if interest rates should fall.

US mortgages offer an example of callable bonds at the household, rather than corporate, level. US home owners have the right to prepay their mortgages at any time without penalty. This right becomes valuable, and is often exercised, in a time of falling interest rates: home owners can pay back the original mortgages and take out new ones at the current cheaper rates. This means borrowers—who are the issuers of the mortgages—effectively hold call options that give them the right to buy back the loan at any time at par.

A somewhat more complex example is a *convertible bond*, a bond that gives its holder the right to convert the bond into a fixed number of shares of stock in the underlying company. Convertible bonds are very often also callable by the issuer. Thus, each side holds an option—the buyer a convert option and the issuer a call option—and the exercise of one option extinguishes the other. In addition, convertibles may also be *puttable*; that is, under specified circumstances, the bond holder may have the right to sell the bond back to the issuer at a given price. Convertible bonds and other hybrid instruments are discussed in Chapter 21.

Instruments with embedded optionalities have become increasingly common in recent years. For the most part, they can be analyzed using standard techniques drawn from option theory. A callable bond, for example, may be viewed as a package of two securities, a straight bond and a call option on the bond. The buyer of the callable bond is long the straight bond but is short the call option on the bond; the issuer of the callable bond has the opposite positions. As such, the properties of the callable bond such as its price may be ascertained from the properties of the straight bond and the option.

# Chapter 8

# Options: Payoffs and Trading Strategies

## 8.1 Introduction

The last chapter defined the basic terminology of options contracts, provided a brief description of options as "financial insurance," and highlighted the centrality of volatility to the study of options. Building on that foundation, the current chapter describes the role that options can play in incorporating views on the market into a portfolio.

In a nutshell, the contents of this chapter may be described as illustrating what is special about options from a risk-management standpoint, i.e., what can be achieved with options that cannot be (or at least cannot easily be) accomplished without options. Sections 8.2–8.5 look at several standard portfolios (or "trading strategies") that illustrate how options may be added or combined into portfolios to reflect specific outlooks on the market. Rounding off this material, we discuss the case of Barings Bank, the protagonist in one of the leading financial scandals of the 1990s.

## 8.2 Trading Strategies I: Covered Calls and Protective Puts

A "trading strategy," as the term is used in this chapter, refers to a portfolio consisting of options on a given underlying asset, possibly combined with positions in the asset itself and perhaps cash (risk-free investment/borrowing). There are a large number of standard trading strategies that use options. We examine a number of these over this section and the next two:

1. Covered calls and protective puts.
2. Spreads: bullish, bearish, butterfly, and horizontal.
3. Combinations: straddles, strangles, strips, and straps.
4. Others: collars, box spreads, ratio spreads, and condors.

This section focuses on covered calls and protective put strategies. Section 8.3 looks at spreads and Section 8.4 looks at combinations. In all cases, a central issue is how options may be incorporated into a portfolio to reflect specific market views. Put differently, the material here highlights what one can do with options that one cannot do without options.

We illustrate the use of all the trading strategies discussed in this chapter using a common example. The example concerns a hypothetical stock ($XYZ$ stock) that is currently trading at 100. There are one-month put and call options available on this stock with strike prices

**TABLE 8.1** *XYZ* Options: Illustrative Example for Options Trading Strategies

The numbers in this table are used to illustrate the various trading strategies described in this chapter. The table concerns a hypothetical stock (*XYZ* stock) that is assumed to be currently trading at 100. There are one-month calls and puts available on the stock with strike prices of 95, 100, and 105. The prices of these options are described in the table.

| Strike | Call Price | Put Price |
|--------|-----------|-----------|
| 95 | 6.29 | 0.89 |
| 100 | 3.09 | 2.67 |
| 105 | 1.21 | 5.77 |

of 95, 100, and 105. The prices of these options are taken to be as given in Table 8.1. Note that the price of the call decreases as the strike price increases (the right to buy at 95 is worth more than the right to buy at 100) while the price of the put increases as the strike increases (the right to sell at 100 is more valuable than the right to sell for 95).

## Covered Calls

A covered call is a portfolio consisting of a long position in the underlying and a short position in a call option on the underlying. The terminology derives from the observation that the long underlying position "covers" the writer of the call if the option is exercised.

To determine the payoffs from a covered call portfolio at maturity, consider two scenarios:

1. $S_T \leq K$: In this case, the call is worthless. The long position in the underlying is, of course, worth $S_T$. Therefore, the value of the covered call portfolio is just $S_T$.

2. $S_T > K$: Now the call will be exercised. The short call is worth $-(S_T - K)$. Since the long position in the underlying is worth $S_T$, the value of the covered call portfolio is $S_T - (S_T - K) = K$.

More briefly, the value of a covered call portfolio at maturity may be expressed as

$$\min\{S_T, K\} \tag{8.1}$$

Figure 8.1 graphs these payoffs. These are *gross* payoffs, i.e., they do not take into account the cost of the option. To obtain the net payoffs, we must add back the initial option cost $C$ received for writing the option.

**FIGURE 8.1** Covered Call Payoffs

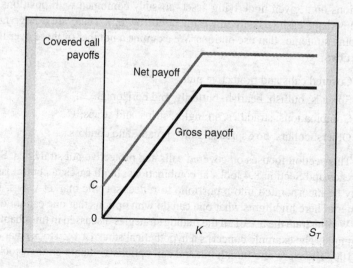

Why use a covered call portfolio? Suppose you hold the underlying and you expect the market to be flat, i.e., to remain at its current level. Then your anticipated standstill return is zero. If you write a call in this market, you receive the option premium, so the standstill return becomes positive and equal to the option premium. If your view of the market holds and the market does remain flat, you have "upped" your returns by the amount of the premium.

Nor does the portfolio do badly for small changes in price in either direction. For small falls in price, the decline in value of the long underlying position is offset by the option premium received. For small *increases* in price, you lose on the short call, but as long as this loss is covered by the option premium, you are better off.

However, a covered call is explicitly a short volatility position (indeed, its payoff is essentially similar to that of a short put position). The risk in the position is that volatility may turn out to be larger than anticipated, i.e., there may be large price swings in either direction. If prices rise by more than the amount of the premium, the portfolio is worse off for incorporating the option. If prices tumble sharply, the option premium may be insufficient to offset the loss on the long underlying position.

As an example of all of these points, consider $XYZ$ stock from Table 8.1. Suppose you hold the stock and expect it to be flat at its current price of 100 over the next month. Based on this expectation, you write a call on $XYZ$ with a strike of 100. From Table 8.1, you receive an option premium of 3.09. This premium represents your profit if your view proves correct and prices remain flat. Moreover, as long as prices move by *less* than 3.09, you are better off for having written the call. If prices fall, but by less than 3.09, the option premium makes up for the losses you suffer on the long stock position. If they rise by less than 3.09, whatever you lose by the call being exercised is made up by the premium.

However, if the price swings turn out to be substantial—that is, your view of low volatility is proved incorrect—you may lose. If prices rise sharply (say, by 6), then your premium is insufficient to cover your losses on the call (your net loss would now be $6 - 3.09 = 2.91$). Thus, you would have been better off not writing the option. If prices fall sharply (again, say by 6), the loss on the long stock position will lead to a net fall in the value of your portfolio (once again, of 2.91); in this case, you would have been better off selling the stock.

## Protective Puts

A protective put portfolio (PPP) is a portfolio consisting of a long position in the underlying and a long position in a put option on the underlying. Protective puts are the classic "insurance" use of options.

To determine the payoffs from a PPP at the time of exercise, consider two scenarios:

1. $S_T < K$: In this case, the put is in-the-money and pays $(K - S_T)$. The long underlying position is worth $S_T$. Therefore, the PPP is worth $(K - S_T) + S_T = K$.
2. $S_T \geq K$: Now, the put is worthless. The long stock position is worth $S_T$. Therefore, the PPP is worth $S_T$.

More briefly, the payoffs from a PPP at maturity can be expressed as

$$\max\{K, S_T\} \tag{8.2}$$

Figure 8.2 graphs these payoffs. As usual, these are gross payoffs. To obtain the net payoffs, we must subtract the cost $P$ of the option from these payoffs.

As the figure indicates, the protective put in the portfolio ensures a floor value for the portfolio. Intuitively, we hold the underlying, but we also hold the *right* to sell the underlying for $K$. If the price of the underlying is above $K$, we keep these upside gains. But if the price

**FIGURE 8.2**

Payoffs from a
Protective Put

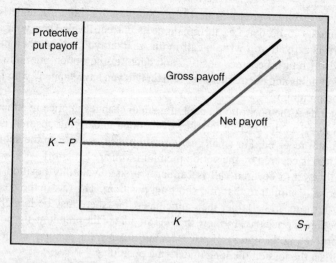

of the underlying falls below $K$, we exercise our rights in the option and receive $K$. This is the classical insurance use of options. The level of insurance obtained is the strike price $K$ of the put since this determines the floor value of the portfolio.

Of course, this insurance does not come for free since there is an up-front fee for the put. The price of the put will be higher as the strike price is larger. Consider, for instance, the $XYZ$ example from Table 8.1. If you want to ensure a floor value of 100 for $XYZ$ stock in one month's time, you need to buy a put with a strike of 100, which costs 2.67. If you are willing to accept a lower floor value of 95, the cost of the protection is only 0.89.

## 8.3 Trading Strategies II: Spreads

A *spread* is a portfolio consisting of options of the same type (either all calls or all puts). There are two basic kinds of spreads.

1. *Vertical* spreads are spreads in which the options have the same expiry date and differ in their strike prices.

2. *Horizontal* or *calendar* spreads are those in which the options have the same strike price but differ in their expiry dates.

The terminology comes from the way option prices were once reported in the financial press. The prices were presented in a grid with maturity dates listed horizontally and strike prices listed vertically. Thus, fixing a maturity and combining options of different strike prices involved moving vertically along a column on the grid while fixing a strike and combining different maturities involved moving horizontally across a row of the grid.

We first examine the three basic kinds of vertical spreads in this section: bull spreads, bear spreads, and butterfly spreads. Then we look at horizontal spreads. Each of these spreads may be set up using either calls or puts. We discuss both call spreads and put spreads in each case below.

### Bullish Vertical Spreads: The Motivation

Suppose you are bullish on $XYZ$ stock; you expect the price to increase over the next month from its current level of 100. There are two things you could do to implement this view using options:

1. You could buy a call with a strike of $K = 100$.
2. You could write a put with a strike of $K = 100$.

Either strategy will make money if prices go up as expected, but each also comes with the risk of losses. The first requires, from Table 8.1, an up-front cash payment of 3.09 that is lost if prices go down. The second has the problem of all written option strategies of substantial losses if prices move in the wrong direction, in this case if the price of *XYZ* stock falls sharply below 100.

In each case, you can limit these costs by combining the given option with another option to set up a strategy called a *bullish vertical spread* or simply a *bull spread*. Of course, you have to give up a part of the upside to achieve this. We examine how this may be done for call options first and then for put options.

## Bullish Vertical Spreads Using Calls

Consider combining your long position in the 100-strike call with a *short* position in the 105-strike call. This has two effects:

1. It reduces your up-front cost from 3.09 to $3.09 - 1.21 = 1.88$. This is the maximum loss in case your view proves wrong and prices go down.

2. It caps your maximum upside. If prices increase beyond 105, whatever you gain by holding the 100-strike call, you lose on the 105-strike call you have written.

If you estimate that a price increase above 105 is not very likely, this is a trade-off you will probably find acceptable.

The portfolio you have created is a *bullish vertical spread using calls*, or simply just a *call bull spread*. In general, in a call bull spread, you buy a call with one strike price $K_1$ and simultaneously sell another call with a *higher* strike price $K_2$. The lower strike $K_1$ is typically chosen at or close to the current stock price. This makes the portfolio bullish (you make money when the stock price goes up from its current level).

Including the $K_2$-strike call in the portfolio reflects a cost-benefit trade-off. On the one hand, the cost of the portfolio is reduced by the premium received for this call. On the other hand, the upside of the portfolio is now capped: any increase in the price of the underlying above $K_2$ means that whatever you gain on the $K_1$-strike call, you lose on the $K_2$-strike call.

Figure 8.3 graphs the payoffs from a call bull spread at maturity. The net payoffs are obtained from the gross payoffs by subtracting the cost $C(K_1) - C(K_2)$ of the portfolio. The payoff structure is intuitive:

- Until a price of $K_1$ is reached, neither call will be exercised, so the gross payoff is zero.
- Between $K_1$ and $K_2$, only the $K_1$-strike call is exercised, so the payoffs from the portfolio are just $S_T - K_1$. At $S_T = K_2$, these payoffs are $K_2 - K_1$.

**FIGURE 8.3**

Payoffs from a Bullish Vertical Spread Using Calls

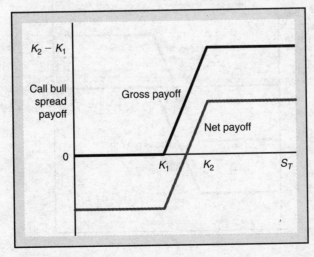

- Beyond $K_2$, both calls are exercised. Whatever is gained on the $K_1$-strike call is lost on the $K_2$-strike call, so payoffs are flat at the level $K_2 - K_1$.

## Bullish Vertical Spreads Using Puts

Now consider the strategy of writing a 100-strike put to incorporate a bullish view on $XYZ$ stock. As we saw, the danger with this strategy is that if prices move snarply down, substantial losses may be incurred on the short put position.

One way to cap this risk is to *buy* a put with a strike of (say) 95. If you do this, then your maximum danger is a price fall to 95. Beyond that, whatever you lose on the put you have written, you make up on the put you have bought. Of course, there is a cost to obtaining this cap—your initial cash inflow has been reduced from 2.67 to $2.67 - 0.89 = 1.78$.

The portfolio you have created here is a *bullish vertical spread using puts* or, simply, a *put bull spread*. In general, a put bull spread involves selling a put with a strike price $K_2$ and simultaneously buying another put with a lower strike price $K_1$. The initial cash inflow is $P(K_2) - P(K_1)$. The strike price $K_2$ is chosen to be at or near the current stock price, making the position bullish; the long $K_1$-put offers protection on the downside in case this view is wrong.

Figure 8.4 graphs the gross payoffs from a put bull spread. The payoffs are obtained using the same arguments as the call bull spread:

- If $S_T \geq K_2$, neither put is exercised. The gross payoffs are zero.
- If $S_T$ lies between $K_1$ and $K_2$, only the $K_2$-strike put is exercised, so the portfolio payoff is $-(K_2 - S_T)$. When $S_T = K_1$, the loss is $K_2 - K_1$.
- Below a price of $K_1$, both puts are exercised. Additional losses from the $K_2$-strike put are now canceled out by gains on the $K_1$-strike put, so payoffs are flat at the level $-(K_2 - K_1)$.

To obtain the net payoffs from a put bull spread, we must add back the initial cash flow of $P(K_2) - P(K_1)$.

## Bearish Vertical Spreads: The Motivation

Bearish vertical spreads are just the bearish-outlook analog of the bullish vertical spreads. Suppose you are *bearish* about $XYZ$ stock. Once again, there are two strategies open to you.

**FIGURE 8.4**

Payoffs from a Bullish Vertical Spread Using Puts

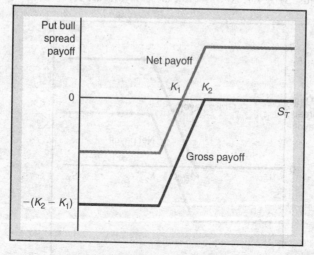

1. You could *write* a call with a strike of 100.
2. You could *buy* a put with a strike of 100.

Both strategies make money if the price decreases from the current level of 100, but each strategy comes with potential disadvantages. The first has the risk that if prices *increase*, the losses from writing a call could be very large, even unlimited. The second requires an up-front cash payment of 2.67 (from Table 8.1), which is lost entirely if prices go up; this is a nontrivial concern especially if you believe that the likelihood of prices going down below some level (say, 95) is low, so you expect only a limited upside.

Once again, in both cases, the solution is to soften these potential negative effects by combining the given options with another option to create a spread. We examine the call spread first and then the put spread.

## Bearish Vertical Spreads Using Calls

Consider combining your short position in the 100-strike call with a *long* position in a call with a *higher* strike price (say, 105). This reduces your initial cash inflow from 3.09 to $3.09 - 1.21 = 1.88$, but also limits your maximum loss: if prices rise above 105, whatever you lose on the 100-strike call you have sold, you make up on the 105-strike call that you hold.

This is a *call bear spread* or a *bearish vertical spread using calls*. In general, it involves selling a call with some strike $K_1$ (typically at- or near-the-money) and buying a call with a *higher* strike $K_2$. The short position in the $K_1$-call implies the position is essentially bearish. When combined with the long $K_2$-strike call, the initial cash inflow is reduced from $C(K_1)$ to $C(K_1) - C(K_2)$, but potential losses are capped: any loss on the short $K_1$-strike call from a price greater than $K_2$ is offset by gains on the long $K_2$-strike call.

Figure 8.5 graphs the payoffs from a call bear spread. The net payoffs are obtained by adding the initial cash inflow $C(K_1) - C(K_2)$ to the gross payoffs.

## Bearish Vertical Spreads Using Puts

As we have seen, the risk in buying a put to reflect a bearish view on direction is that the entire premium may be lost if prices increase. One way to reduce your up-front cost is to *sell* a put with a *lower* strike price, e.g., 95. This reduces your initial cost to $2.67 - 0.89 = 1.78$. In exchange, you receive no benefit for price falls below 95: whatever you gain on the 100-strike put you hold, you lose on the 95-strike put you have written.

**FIGURE 8.5**

Payoffs from a Bearish Vertical Spread Using Calls

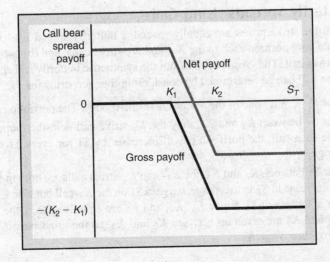

**FIGURE 8.6**

Payoffs from a Bearish
Vertical Spread Using
Puts

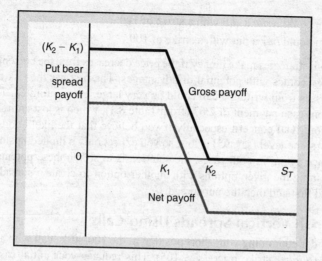

You have created a *put bear spread* or a *bearish vertical spread using puts*. This is a portfolio with a long position in a put at some strike $K_2$ and a short position in a put with a *lower* strike $K_1$. The strike $K_2$ is usually close to the money, which ensures that the position is essentially bearish. Selling the $K_1$-strike put reduces the set-up cost for the portfolio, but it also caps the upside benefit; the maximum benefit is reached when the stock price reaches $K_1$. Any gains on the $K_2$-strike put at lower stock prices are canceled by the losses on the $K_1$-strike put.

Figure 8.6 graphs the payoffs from a put bear spread.

## Butterfly Spreads

A *butterfly spread* using calls involves taking positions in calls with three strike prices $K_1 < K_2 < K_3$. The extreme strike prices $K_1$ and $K_3$ are called the "wings" of the spread. We first discuss butterfly spreads in the "symmetric" case, i.e., where the three strike prices are equally spaced so $K_2$ is the mid-point of $K_1$ and $K_3$. This is the case most commonly associated with butterfly spreads in practice. However, butterfly spreads can be set up for *any* three strike prices. We discuss the general case in Appendix 8A. Butterfly spreads too can be set up using either calls or puts. We discuss call butterfly spreads first.

## Butterfly Spreads Using Calls

When the strike prices are equally spaced, a butterfly spread is a portfolio consisting of (a) one long position each in the $K_1$- and $K_3$-strike calls, and (b) two short positions in the $K_2$-strike call. The gross payoffs from the symmetric butterfly call spread at $T$ (graphed in Figure 8.7) can be determined by considering four scenarios for $S_T$:

- For $S_T < K_1$, none of the options is in-the-money. The portfolio payoff is zero.
- For $S_T$ between $K_1$ and $K_2$, only the $K_1$-strike call is in-the-money. Since we are long one such call, the portfolio payoff increases by $1 for every $1 increase in $S_T$ in this range.
- For $S_T$ between $K_2$ and $K_3$, the $K_1$- and $K_2$-strike calls are both in-the-money. For every $1 increase in $S_T$ in this range, we gain $1 on the $K_1$-call but lose $2 on the two $K_2$-calls, for a net loss of $1. Since $K_1$, $K_2$, and $K_3$ are equally spaced, the entire gains between $K_1$ and $K_2$ are given up between $K_2$ and $K_3$, so the gross payoff from the portfolio is zero when $S_T = K_3$.

**FIGURE 8.7**

Payoffs from a Call
Butterfly Spread

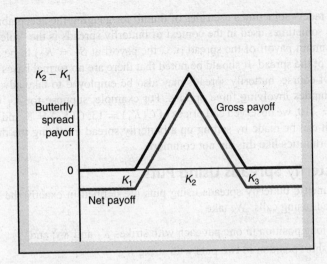

- For $S_T > K_3$, all three options are in the money. For each \$1 increase in $S_T$ in this range, we gain \$1 each on the $K_1$- and $K_3$-calls but lose \$2 on the two short $K_2$-calls, for a net gain of zero. Thus, the payoff remains flat at zero in this range.

## The Cost of a Call Butterfly Spread

The cost of setting up the butterfly spread is

$$C(K_1) + C(K_3) - 2\,C(K_2) \qquad\qquad (8.3)$$

Is this cost positive, negative, or zero? Arbitrage provides an easy answer. Figure 8.7 shows that the gross time-$T$ payoffs to a symmetric butterfly spread are always non-negative, and are strictly positive if $S_T$ lies between $K_1$ and $K_3$. That is, there is never a cash *outflow* at $T$, but there is a cash *inflow* whenever $S_T$ lies between $K_1$ and $K_3$. To avoid arbitrage, it must cost something to set up the portfolio:

$$C(K_1) + C(K_3) - 2\,C(K_2) \;>\; 0 \qquad\qquad (8.4)$$

For instance, in the $XYZ$ example, the cost of the butterfly spread is positive: from Table 8.1, the cost is

$$6.29 + 1.21 - (2 \times 3.09) \;=\; 1.32$$

Expression (8.4) offers a very powerful restriction on call prices *for any three equally-spaced strike prices*. This result is actually a special case of a general result known as *convexity* of option prices in the strike price that holds even when strike prices are not equally spaced. We state the general result in Appendix 8A.

## Why Use Butterfly Spreads?

The most common use of the butterfly spread is as a directional/volatility bet. The spread pays off maximally if $S_T$ is at $K_2$. Moreover, it decreases rapidly as $S_T$ moves away from $K_2$ in either direction, that is, it is a *short volatility* portfolio. Thus, the butterfly spread is a bet that the price will be around $K_2$ with very little volatility.

As an illustration, consider the $XYZ$ example again. Suppose you anticipate prices being flat at the current price of 100. If you set up a butterfly spread using the 95-, 100-, and 105-strike calls, the up-front cost, as we have seen, is 1.32. If the price does in fact remain flat, the payoff from the option will be 5 for a net profit of 3.68.

Traders sometimes use rules of thumb for gauging the acceptability of risky strategies. One sometimes used in the context of butterfly spreads is the "rule of 3" that requires the maximum payoff of the spread (i.e., the payoff at $S_T = K_2$) to be at least three times the cost of the spread. It should be noted that there are no formal bases for such rules.

Of course, butterfly spreads may also be employed to take advantage of arbitrage opportunities involving three options. For example, suppose for $K_1 = 90$, $K_2 = 100$, and $K_3 = 110$, we observed call prices of $C(K_1) = 13$, $C(K_2) = 8$, and $C(K_3) = 2$. A riskless profit can be made by setting up a butterfly spread involving the three options. Arbitrage opportunities like this are not common.

## Butterfly Spreads Using Puts

Symmetric butterfly spreads using puts are defined in exactly the same way as butterfly spreads using calls: We take

- a long position in one put each with strikes $K_1$ and $K_3$; and
- a short position in two puts with strike $K_2$.

The payoffs of the put butterfly spread are *identical* to those of the call butterfly spread: That is, Figure 8.7 also represents the gross payoffs from a symmetric put butterfly spread. This may be checked directly:

- For $S_T < K_1$: All three puts are in-the-money. The portfolio's payoff is

$$(K_1 - S_T) - 2(K_2 - S_T) + (K_3 - S_T) = K_1 - 2K_2 + K_3 = 0$$

- For $S_T$ lying between $K_1$ and $K_2$: The $K_2$- and $K_3$-strike puts are in-the-money, so the portfolio payoff is

$$-2(K_2 - S_T) + (K_3 - S_T) = S_T + K_3 - 2K_2$$

This is identical to the call payoff in this interval since $-(K_3 - 2K_2) = K_1$.

- For $S_T$ lying between $K_2$ and $K_3$: Only the $K_3$-strike put is in-the-money. The portfolio payoff in this case is $K_3 - S_T$. This is identical to the call payoff in this interval since $2K_2 - K_1 = K_3$.

- For $S_T \geq K_3$: All the puts are out-of-the-money, so the portfolio payoff is zero.

As a consequence, the cost of a put butterfly spread must also be strictly positive, i.e., we must have

$$P(K_1) + P(K_3) - 2P(K_2) > 0 \qquad \textbf{(8.5)}$$

## Horizontal Spreads Using Calls

Horizontal spreads use options with the same strike $K$ and two different maturities, $T_1$ and $T_2$, where $T_1 < T_2$. In a *long horizontal call spread*, the investor takes a long position in the $T_2$-maturity call (the "distant" call) and a short position in the $T_1$-maturity call (the "nearby" call). A *short horizontal call spread* is the opposite portfolio: long the nearby call and short the distant call. Long and short horizontal put spreads are defined analogously with "put" replacing "call" in the preceding definitions.

### *Payoff at $T_1$ of a Horizontal Call Spread*

Figure 8.8 shows the value of a horizontal call spread at $T_1$, the date of maturity of the nearby call, for different values of the stock price $S_{T_1}$ on this date. The payoff looks similar to a butterfly spread—it is highest at the common strike price of the options and tails off in either direction. As with a butterfly spread, the payoff of a horizontal call spread is always non-negative.

**FIGURE 8.8**

Payoffs from a
Horizontal Call Spread

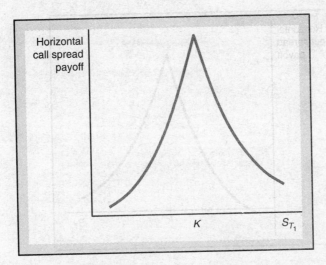

A formal derivation of the graph requires knowledge of option pricing that will be developed only over the next several chapters, but the three broad features of the graph—why it is increasing up to $K$, decreasing beyond that, and positive everywhere—are not hard to understand intuitively.

Consider $S_{T_1} < K$. The nearby call expires worthless in this case, so the value of the portfolio is just the value of the distant call, which is positive. Moreover, other things being equal, the higher is $S_{T_1}$ today, the better the chances of the $T_2$-maturity call eventually finishing in-the-money. So, the value of the horizontal call spread increases as $S_{T_1}$ increases in this range.

When $S_{T_1} \geq K$, the nearby call comes into the money and will be exercised. Thus, the value of the spread is now the value of the distant call (denoted, say, $C(K; T_2)$) minus the value of the expiring call:

$$C(K; T_2) - (S_{T_1} - K) \tag{8.6}$$

Now, a long-dated call is always worth more than a short-dated call (under almost all circumstances) for two reasons that we explore in greater detail in the coming chapters. First, the longer time to maturity gives volatility a greater time to have an impact. Second, the calls involve *paying K* to buy the stock. The longer one has to pay this $K$, the greater the interest savings. Thus, the difference (8.6) is positive, explaining why the horizontal call spread has a positive payoff everywhere.

Finally, as the call gets deeper in-the-money at $T_1$, the more likely it is that it will finish in-the-money, so the less optionality (hence, volatility) matters. Since volatility is one of the reasons the longer-dated option costs more, the diminishing impact of volatility means the difference (8.6) in option values also gets smaller, explaining why the portfolio value declines beyond $K$.

### Why Use Horizontal Call Spreads?

The value of a horizontal call spread is influenced by two factors: time and volatility. As mentioned above, a shorter-maturity call is worth less than a longer-maturity one. Put differently, this says that, *ceteris paribus*, the value of a call will decrease as maturity approaches. This is called *time-decay* in a call. The rate of decay is relatively small when an option has a long time left to maturity (the passage of one day doesn't matter that much if we still have three months left). But closer to maturity, time-decay increases rapidly (a day makes a huge difference if we have only a week to maturity).

**FIGURE 8.9**

Payoffs from a
Horizontal Put Spread

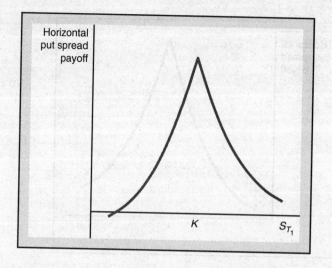

In a long horizontal call spread, we own the distant call but are short the nearby call. Other things being the same, the value of the portfolio will increase over time since the shorter-dated call will lose value faster than the long-dated one. Thus, the horizontal call spread is an attempt to profit from time-decay. However, the *ceteris paribus* qualification is important here. As the payoff diagram makes clear, the horizontal call spread is also a bet that the price will be at or in a small neighborhood of $K$.

The horizontal call spread can also be a play on the stock's *implied volatility*. Implied volatility is defined formally later in the book, but intuitively, it is just the level of volatility reflected in current option prices. If you have a view that the stock's implied volatility will go up but the stock price will not immediately change very much, then buying an at-the-money horizontal call spread may be appropriate. When implied volatility goes up, the prices of both the nearby and distant calls will increase. However, because the latter has greater maturity than the former, it will increase by more (there is more time for volatility to matter). So the value of your portfolio will go up.

### Horizontal Spreads Using Puts

As noted above, horizontal put spreads are defined in the same way as horizontal call spreads. Figure 8.9 shows the value of a horizontal put spread at time $T_1$. There is one important difference between puts and calls that is reflected in the graph. *American* puts, like European and American calls, increase in value with maturity. That is, a longer-dated American put must cost more than a short-dated one (if you don't want the extra time, you can always exercise early). However, this is not necessarily true for *European* puts, especially when they are deep in-the-money. Intuitively, if you have a deep in-the-money put and are sure to exercise it, you would rather receive the strike price $K$ earlier than later. In a long-dated European put, you are forced to wait longer for the money, and this hurts you. Thus, when the puts in the horizontal spread are both deep in-the-money, the value of the spread may become *negative*, as happens in the graph.

## 8.4   Trading Strategies III: Combinations

A *combination* is used to refer to a portfolio that involves positions in both puts and calls on a given underlying asset. It has become increasingly common, however, to refer to such portfolios too as "spreads." We retain the old-fashioned terminology in this section.

**FIGURE 8.10**

Payoffs from a Straddle

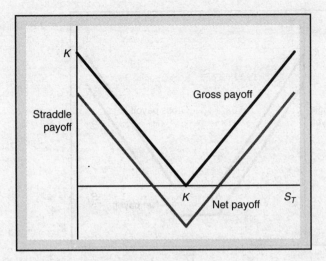

We look at four popular combination strategies: straddles, strangles, strips, and straps. Straddles and strangles are the most important of these and are among the most important of all strategies discussed in this chapter. They are quintessential options strategies in that they incorporate a view on *volatility* but not on *direction* as we explain below.

## Straddles

A *straddle* is one of the simplest and most popular of options-based trading strategies. It is a portfolio consisting of long positions in a call and a put with the same strike price and maturity. The strike is usually chosen to be at or near the current stock price. Letting $K$ denote the common strike price, the payoffs from a straddle at maturity are:

- If $S_T < K$: Only the put is in-the-money. The payoff of the straddle is $(K - S_T)$.
- If $S_T \geq K$: Only the call is in-the-money. The payoff of the straddle is $(S_T - K)$.

These payoffs are graphed in Figure 8.10.

Straddles result in a positive gross payoff at maturity *regardless of the direction in which the market moves*. Thus, they are *neutral on market direction*. Intuitively, the directional bullishness of the call is canceled by the directional bearishness of the put. However, straddles are clearly very *bullish on volatility*. The greater the price swings, the better off is the holder of a straddle.

Volatility is key here. Straddles involve purchasing multiple options, so large movements in prices are required for them to be profitable. In the $XYZ$ example, for instance, buying an at-the-money straddle with a strike of 100 costs $3.09 + 2.67 = 5.76$. Thus, the price has to move below 94.24 or above 105.76 from its current level of 100 for the strategy to be profitable. More generally, option prices reflect the market's expectation of volatility over the option's life. If high volatility is anticipated, the price of the call and put will both rise, making straddles even more expensive.

### Short Straddles

A *short straddle* is a short position in a straddle. Writing naked straddles (i.e., writing straddles and then not hedging oneself) is a bet on low volatility and is neutral on direction. This can be profitable in flat markets but is also quite obviously a very risky strategy since the potential losses from price swings (in either direction!) can be very large. This point may seem uncomplicated and obvious. Yet the massive use of naked short straddles lay behind one of the major financial scandals of the 1990s, the downfall of Barings Bank, that is described later in this chapter.

**FIGURE 8.11**

Payoffs from a Strangle

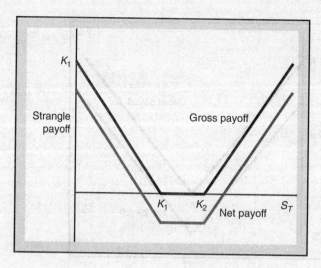

## Strangles

A *strangle* is essentially the poor cousin of a straddle. Like the straddle, it aims to be neutral on direction but bullish on volatility. The difference is that, rather than using the same strike price for the call and the put, the strangle uses a *higher* strike price for the call and a *lower* one for the put. This makes the strangle cheaper than a straddle, but it also means much larger price moves are required for the strangle to make money.

As an example, consider the prices for $XYZ$ options from Table 8.1. As we saw, the cost of a 100-strike straddle is 5.76. One inexpensive alternative is to set up a 95-105 strangle, i.e., buy a put with a strike of 95 and a call with a strike of 105. From the prices in the table, the strangle would cost only $1.21 + 0.89 = 2.10$. However, for the strangle to turn a profit after taking into account the cost of the options, the price has to be above 107.10 or below 92.90, a wider range than the corresponding one for the straddle.

The gross payoffs from a strangle are graphed in Figure 8.11. The put and call strikes are, respectively, $K_1$ and $K_2$ with $K_1 < K_2$. The payoff of the strangle is

- equal to the put payoff if $S_T < K_1$;
- zero if $S_T$ lies between $K_1$ and $K_2$; and
- equal to the call payoff if $S_T > K_2$.

The net payoffs from a strangle are obtained by subtracting the cost of the strangle from these values.

## Strips

A *strip* is a portfolio consisting of long puts and calls with the same strike and maturity but it has more puts than calls (e.g., two puts for every call). Like a straddle, a strip is a bet on volatility, but now the bet is *asymmetric*: by using more puts than calls, it is biased towards price *decreases*. Thus, a strip makes sense if one anticipates high volatility but believes that price decreases are more likely than price increases.

Figure 8.12 graphs the payoffs from a strip assuming a ratio of two puts per call and with $K$ denoting the common strike price. If $S_T < K$, only the puts are in-the-money, so the strip's payoffs are $2(K - S_T)$. If $S_T \geq K$, only the call is in-the-money, so the strip's payoff is $(S_T - K)$.

**FIGURE 8.12**

Payoffs from a Strip

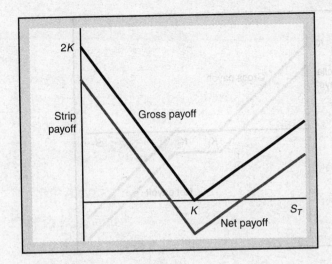

**FIGURE 8.13**

Payoffs from a Strap

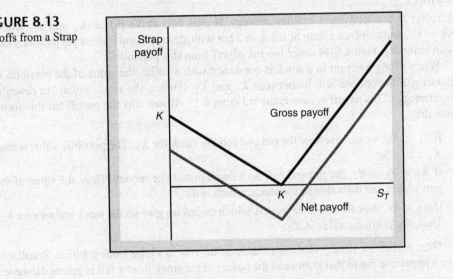

### Straps

A *strap* is the other side of a strip: it is a portfolio consisting of long positions in more calls than puts. A strap is an asymmetric bet on volatility, one that is biased towards price *increases*. Thus, a strap makes sense if one anticipates high volatility but believes that price increases are more likely than price decreases.

Figure 8.13 graphs the payoffs from a strap assuming a ratio of two calls per put. Letting $K$ denote the common strike price in the strap, the payoffs from a strap at $T$ are $(K - S_T)$ if $S_T < K$ and $2(S_T - K)$ if $S_T \geq K$.

## 8.5 Trading Strategies IV: Other Strategies

In this section, we discuss four further classes of trading strategies: collars, box spreads, ratio spreads, and condors. Box spreads and ratio spreads are related to the bull and bear spreads discussed earlier, while condors have a close resemblance to butterfly spreads.

**FIGURE 8.14**

Payoffs from a Collar

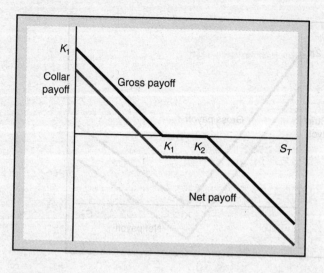

## Collars

A collar is a widely-used options strategy. It uses two strike prices $K_1$ and $K_2$ where $K_1 < K_2$, and involves a *long* position in a put with strike $K_1$ and a *short* position in a call with strike $K_2$. Figure 8.14 describes the payoff from this portfolio.

When a long position in a stock is combined with a collar, the value of the portfolio at maturity of the options will lie between $K_1$ and $K_2$. (Hence, the word "collar" to describe the strategy.) This payoff is illustrated in Figure 8.15. To see why the payoff has this form, note that:

- If $S_T < K_1$, we can exercise the put and sell the stock for $K_1$. The portfolio value is thus $K_1$.
- If $K_1 < S_T < K_2$, the put and call both finish out-of-the-money. Thus, the value of the portfolio is just the value of the stock, which is $S_T$.
- If $K_2 < S_T$, the call will be exercised, which means we give up the stock and receive $K_2$. Thus, the portfolio value is $K_2$.

Thus, collars are simply strategies that limit the risk in a long stock position. A collar is like a protective put in that it protects the holder of the stock from a fall in prices. However,

**FIGURE 8.15**

Payoffs from a Stock + Collar

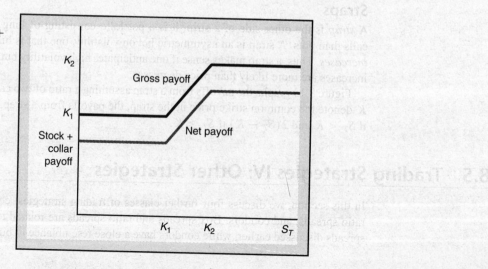

the collar also caps the upside benefit from holding the stock at $K_2$. In exchange, the up-front cost of the strategy is reduced: while the cost of a protective put would be the price $P(K_1)$ of the $K_1$-strike put, that of the collar is

$$P(K_1) - C(K_2)$$

This cost can be positive or negative depending on the option premia. Consider the $XYZ$ example of Table 8.1. If we set up a collar with the 95-strike put and the 105-strike call, the cost of the collar is

$$0.89 - 1.21 = -0.32,$$

that is, there is an initial cash *inflow* of 0.32 from the collar.

A *cashless collar* is one in which the strike prices $K_1$ and $K_2$ are chosen so that the premia cancel each other out and the collar has a zero net initial cost. Also called *zero-cost collars*, cashless collars have become especially popular with corporate executives and other investors who hold large blocks of shares in a single company and want to limit the riskiness of their exposures. Paul Allen, billionaire co-founder of Microsoft, is reputed to have protected a substantial chunk of his Microsoft holdings using cashless collars. Since the strategy involves capping the upside benefit in exchange for the downside protection, such strategies are not prohibited for executives under SEC rules and have not (or at least not yet) been the subject of lawsuits or media attacks.

## Box Spreads

Consider a portfolio in the $XYZ$ example of Table 8.1 in which you hold a 95/100 call bull spread and a 95/100 put bear spread. That is, you are long a 95-strike call and short a 100-strike call as well as long a 100-strike put and short a 95-strike put. This portfolio is called a *box spread*.

What is the payoff from this portfolio? The long 95-strike call and short 95-strike put together create a synthetic forward contract to buy the stock at 95. The short 100-strike call and the long 100-strike put together create a synthetic forward contract to sell the stock at 100. This means you are buying at 95 and selling at 100 for a flat payoff of 5 at maturity. Thus, a box spread creates a *synthetic zero-coupon bond* using options.

In general, a box spread involves a position in four options with two strike prices $K_1$ and $K_2$ with $K_1 < K_2$: (a) long the $K_1$-strike call, (b) short the $K_2$-strike call, (c) long the $K_2$-strike put, and (d) short the $K_1$-strike put. The payoff of the spread at maturity is just $K_2 - K_1$ regardless of $S_T$.

## Ratio Spreads

*Ratio spreads* are like the bull and bear spreads described above except that the number of calls bought and sold at the different strikes are not equal. A *ratio call spread* may, for example, involve buying one call with strike $K_1$ and selling *two* calls with a higher strike $K_2$. In this case, the payoff looks as in Figure 8.16. Ratio put spreads are defined similarly.

The cost of a ratio spread may be positive, negative, or zero, depending on the ratio in which the two options are combined. Consider, for instance, a ratio spread in the example of Table 8.1 using the 100- and 105-strike calls. If we use two short 105-strike calls for every long 100-strike call, the cost of the spread is

$$3.09 - (2 \times 1.21) = 0.67$$

which is positive. If we use *three* short 105-strike calls for every long 100-strike call, the cost is

$$3.09 - (3 \times 1.21) = -0.54$$

**FIGURE 8.16**

Payoffs from a Ratio Spread

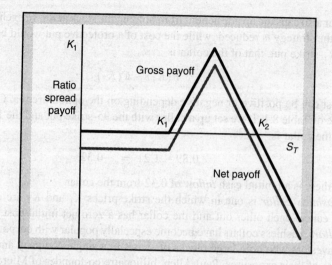

which is negative. Thus, ratio spreads may involve cash outflows or cash inflows when they are set up.

As the payoff diagram indicates, the ratio spread is essentially a bet that prices will rise but not to more than $K_2$. We can also set up *bearish* ratio spreads, which are bets that prices will fall to, but not beyond, a specified price. Consider, for instance, a portfolio in the example of Table 8.1 that is long a 100-strike put and is short two 95-strike puts. This portfolio has a payoff that is highest when $S_T = 95$ and declines on either side of this price.

## Condors

Condors are essentially like butterfly spreads except that the peak payoff occurs over an interval of prices rather than at a single price. A condor consists of options with *four* strike prices $K_1$, $K_2$, $K_3$, and $K_4$. We buy calls at the two extreme strike prices $K_1$ and $K_4$ and sell calls at the two intermediate strike prices $K_2$ and $K_3$. Put condor spreads are defined analogously.

The resulting payoff is, as Figure 8.17 shows, akin to a butterfly payoff except that the payoff is flat between $K_2$ and $K_3$. Thus, condors are bets on the price being in the band $[K_2, K_3]$.

**FIGURE 8.17**

Payoffs from a Condor

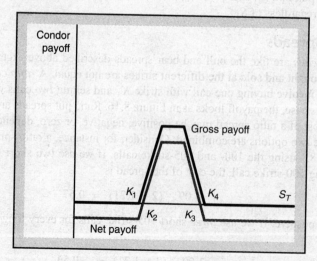

# 8.6   Which Strategies Are the Most Widely Used?

We have described a large (but not quite exhaustive) list of standard trading strategies using options. How much of options trading is accounted for by these strategies? A study by Chaput and Ederington (2003), the first of its type, offers an answer. The authors consider eurodollar options, which is one of the largest options markets in the world. They find that spreads and combinations collectively account for over 55% of large trades (those of 100 contracts or more) and are responsible for 75% of the trading volume generated by large trades.

In terms of total volume, the four most heavily used strategies are (in order) straddles, ratio spreads, vertical spreads, and strangles. Collectively, these account for two-thirds of all spread/combination trades. Strategies such as butterflies and collars are lightly traded, while trading in condors, horizontal spreads, and box spreads is rare. Overall, the authors conclude that popular trading strategies appear driven more by volatility considerations than directional ones. This finding backs the point that while there are many ways (spot, forwards, options) to take advantage of directional views, there is only one (options) to incorporate views on volatility.

# 8.7   The Barings Case

On February 27, 1995, Barings, a small but venerable British bank with a rich history, came to an ignominious end when it filed for receivership. The bank's capital of around $618 million had been comprehensively eroded by losses well in excess of $1 billion that had been incurred from trading in derivatives by a single individual, Nick Leeson, operating out of Barings' Singapore office. There were several remarkable aspects to this episode that bear highlighting, none more so than the fact that only the simplest kinds of derivatives—long futures and short straddles—whose risks are easily understood, were involved. This is a summary of the Barings saga.[1]

## What Leeson Was Supposed to Be Doing

Leeson's mandate from Barings was to do arbitrage trades that exploited short-lived differences in Nikkei 225 futures prices on the Osaka and Singapore Exchanges (OSE and SIMEX, respectively; SIMEX is now SGX) by buying the cheaper contract and simultaneously selling the more expensive one. These trades ("switching" trades in Barings' lexicon) involve very low risk: since the arbitrageur is long Nikkei futures on one exchange and short the futures on the other, there is no directional exposure. Leeson also put through trades on client orders but was not otherwise allowed to take on proprietary positions that exposed Barings to market risk.

## What He Was Actually Doing

What Leeson was actually doing bore little resemblance to his mandate. Evidence uncovered after the collapse of Barings shows that he engaged in unauthorized trading almost from the day he began in Singapore in 1992, taking on proprietary positions in both futures and options. The evidence also shows that he ran up large losses almost from the beginning. But, incredibly, his supervisors in London believed that he was making money hand over fist for them and that he had single-handedly accounted for almost 20% of the entire firm's

---

[1] The presentation below draws especially from the analysis provided by the International Financial Risk Institute on its website http://riskinstitute.ch/137550.htm.

**TABLE 8.2** The Reported and Actual Profits Generated by Nick Leeson

The table below describes the profits Barings' London office thought Leeson had made and the actual losses he was running up. The figures are in US dollars.

| Year | Reported | Actual |
|------|----------|--------|
| 1993 | +14 million | −33 million |
| 1994 | +46 million | −296 million |
| 1995 | +30 million | −1 billion |

**TABLE 8.3** The Reported and Actual Holdings of Nick Leeson

The table below describes the actual and reported holdings of Nick Leeson at the time of Barings' bankruptcy. The figures are in terms of number of SIMEX contracts. Long positions are indicated by a + and short positions by a − sign.

| Contract | Reported | Actual |
|----------|----------|--------|
| Nikkei 225 futures | +30,112 | +61,039 |
| Japanese government bond futures | +15,940 | −28,034 |
| Euroyen futures | +601 | −6,845 |
| Nikkei 225 calls | 0 | −37,925 |
| Nikkei 225 puts | 0 | −32,967 |

profits in 1993 and almost 50% in 1994. Table 8.2 describes the reported and actual profits from Leeson's trading activity.

These numbers are astonishing but no less so than the magnitude of the positions he held. In end-February 1995, against Barings' capital of a little over $615 million, Leeson's notional positions in derivatives amounted to over $33 billion, including over $6.50 billion in unhedged short options positions on the Nikkei 225 index. Once again, the gap between his actual and reported holdings is remarkable. Table 8.3 summarizes this information.

## How Did He Get Away with It?

The information gaps highlighted in the previous paragraphs suggest that Barings' operational controls must have been exceptionally poor. They were. One extraordinary feature of Barings' Singapore operations was that Leeson was not only the trader but also the back-office responsible for settling the trades. This is essentially what enabled him to withhold important information from London.

The British Board of Banking Supervision, in its postmortem of the Barings affair, highlights the "cross trade" as the single main vehicle Leeson employed to carry through the fraud. In a cross trade, a single member on the floor of the exchange is both the buyer and the seller; it is usually used to match buy and sell orders from two separate clients. There are some regulations cross trades must follow. For example, SIMEX required the transaction to be at the current market price; moreover, the member was required to declare the price at least three times and was allowed to carry out the cross trade only if no other member took the price.

In Leeson's cross trades, Barings was the counterparty to itself. The trades were entered into several accounts including an "error account" numbered 88888. After the cross trades, Leeson's staff, acting on his instructions, entered the profits into the legitimate trading accounts and the losses into account 88888.

Also under Leeson's instructions, information on account 88888 was never transmitted to London. Thus, Leeson's supervisors had no idea of the real size of his positions. As one example, in late February 1995, they believed he was *short* 30,000 Nikkei 225 futures contracts on SIMEX; in fact, he was *long* 22,000 contracts.

## Options Trading and the End of Barings

Leeson's mandate did not allow him to trade in options, but he did so anyway. He effectively sold straddles on the Nikkei 225. As we have seen earlier in this chapter, naked short straddles are extraordinarily risky positions that lose money for the writer no matter which direction prices move in. They are bets on flat prices (i.e., low volatility). Through much of the early months of Leeson's straddle positions, the Nikkei was quite flat, and he earned a substantial premium income from the positions.

In November and December of 1994, Leeson ratcheted up his options positions considerably, selling over 34,000 contracts in those two months alone. The strike prices of his options positions ranged from about 18,500 to 20,000, and the trades would have been profitable if the Nikkei had remained in a range of about 19,000–20,000. Unfortuantely for Leeson and Barings, it did not (see Figure 8.18).

On January 17, 1995, the Nikkei was at around 19,350. That day, the Kobe earthquake struck, market sentiment took a downturn, and the index closed the week at a little below 19,000. Yet, on Friday, January 20, Leeson *bought* an additional 10,800 Nikkei futures contracts expiring in March 1995. This may have been an attempt to profit from what he perceived as market overreaction to the earthquake or may have simply been an attempt to shore up the market.

The next week proved disastrous for Leeson and Barings. By Monday, January 23, the Nikkei had lost over 1,000 points and closed below 18,000 (see the downward spike on that date in Figure 8.18). Huge losses were incurred on both the long futures positions as well as the written puts. At this point, Leeson could not close out his positions and take his losses without disclosing the unauthorized trading. Moving into "double-or-nothing" mode, he increased his long futures positions massively, winding up by February 22 with over 55,000 long March 1995 futures contracts and over 5,600 June 1995 futures contracts.

None of this buying restored confidence in the markets. When the Nikkei continued its resolute downward march (Figure 8.18), margin calls on the derivatives positions revealed Barings' insolvency. The once-proud bank was finally bought by ING, a Dutch bank, for all of £1.

### FIGURE 8.18
Nikkei Index:
January–March 1995

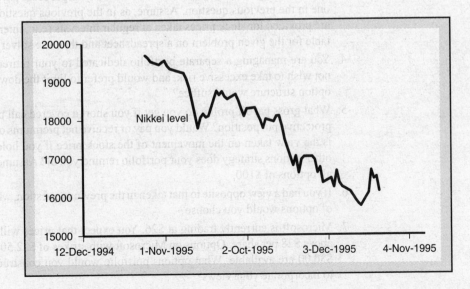

## Who Was to Blame?

Leeson was obviously a central party, and in the press, he (and "derivatives" generally) were adjudged to be the villains of the piece. More sober analysis carried out by the British Board of Banking Supervision pointed out that operational risk played a significant role in the debacle, and, therefore, that Barings management shared a substantial portion of the blame.

To begin, management ignored a fundamental banking rule in making Leeson also responsible for settling his own trades. Management were also frequently negligent; they ignored a number of queries and warnings from third parties that all was not well. Indeed, they even wired huge amounts of cash to Barings Singapore (that enabled Leeson to meet his trading losses and margin calls) without asking him for an explanation.

In the final analysis, more than anything else, the Barings episode highlights the importance of operational controls. Used sensibly and with the proper controls, derivatives can do considerable good. Used irresponsibly and in a manner that ignores their risks, they have the potential to create considerable damage.

## 8.8 Exercises

1. Draw the payoff diagram for the following portfolio of options, all with the same maturity: (a) long a call at strike 75, (b) long two calls at strike 80, and (c) long three calls at strike 85. What is the view of the stock price change consistent with this portfolio?

2. You are interested in creating the following gross payoff profile using an options portfolio:

| Stock price | 60 | 70 | 80 | 90 | 100 | 110 | 120 | 130 | 140 | 150 |
|---|---|---|---|---|---|---|---|---|---|---|
| Payoff | 10 | 30 | 20 | 10 | 0 | 10 | 30 | 10 | 0 | −10 |

What options, at what strikes, would you hold in your portfolio? Assume that the desired payoffs are zero for any stock price less than 50 or greater than 160.

3. (Difficult) Using the principles of the previous question, create a spreadsheet-based algorithm to generate an option portfolio for any target gross payoff profile, such as the one in the previous question. Assume, as in the previous question, that option payoffs are provided for stock prices taken at regular intervals (e.g., intervals of $10). Create a table for the given problem on a spreadsheet and then use solver to find the solution.

4. You are managing a separate portfolio dedicated to your retirement income. You do not wish to take excessive risk, and would prefer to limit the downside. What common option structure would suffice?

5. What gross payoff profile do you get if you short a covered call position and go long a protective put position? Would you pay or receive net premiums on this position? What is the view taken on the movement of the stock price if you hold this position? What other options strategy does your portfolio remind you of? Assume a common strike for all options of $100.

6. If you had a view opposite to that taken in the previous question, what portfolio structure of options would you choose?

7. Microsoft is currently trading at $26. You expect that prices will increase but not rise above $28 per share. Options on Microsoft with strikes of $22.50, $25.00, $27.50, and $30.00 are available. What options portfolio would you construct from these options to incorporate your views?

8. Suppose your view in the previous question were instead that Microsoft's shares will fall but a fall below $22 is unlikely. Now what strategy will you use?

9. Calls are available on IBM at strikes of 95, 100, and 105. Which should cost more, the 95–100 bullish vertical spread, or the 95–100–105 butterfly spread?

10. A bullish call spread is bullish on direction. Is it also bullish on volatility?

11. What is the directional view in a long put butterfly spread?

12. How would your answer to the previous question change if this butterfly spread were constructed using calls instead?

13. How does a horizontal spread exploit time-decay of options?

14. What is the volatility view implied by a long horizontal call spread? What about a short horizontal put spread?

15. Assume the current volatility of oil is high. What options portfolio offers you a gain from the high volatility if you do not have a view on direction?

16. You are planning to trade on the fortunes of a biotech firm that has a drug patent pending FDA approval. If the patent is approved, the stock price is expected to go up sharply. If it is not approved, the stock will drop sharply, In your view, it is unlikely to move more than 20% in either direction. Describe a portfolio combining straddles and strangles that takes advantage of your view.

17. Firm A is likely to be the target in a takeover attempt by Firm B. The stock price is likely to rise over the next few weeks as the takeover progresses, but if it fails, the stock price of A is likely to fall even more than the rise. What option strategy might exploit this information?

18. The options for Microsoft (stock price $25.84) are trading at the following prices:

| Strike | Calls | Puts |
|---|---|---|
| 22.50 | 3.40 | 0.10 |
| 25.00 | 1.25 | 0.30 |
| 27.50 | 0.15 | 1.80 |

State the trading ranges at maturity in which the *net* payoff of the following option positions is positive: (a) 25.00 straddle, (b) 22.50 strip, (c) 27.50 strap, and (d) 22.50–27.50 strangle.

19. What are collars? What is the investor's objective when using a collar?

20. Is the price of a collar positive, zero, or negative?

21. Suppose options trade at two strikes: $K_1 < K_2$. You notice that whereas $C(K_2) - P(K_2) = S - PV(K_2)$ (put-call parity) holds for the $K_2$ strike option, it does not hold for the $K_1$ strike option, specifically $C(K_1) - P(K_1) = S - PV(K_1) + \delta$, where $\delta > 0$. Show how you would use a box spread to take advantage of this situation by constructing a riskless arbitrage strategy. Assume there are no dividends.

22. What is a ratio spread? Construct one to take advantage of the fact that you expect stock prices $S$ to rise by about $10 from the current price but are not sure of the appreciation of more than $10.

23. Can the cost of a ratio spread be negative?

24. What is more expensive to buy: (a) a 100–110–120 butterfly spread using calls or (b) a 90–100–110–120 condor? Can you decompose condors in any useful way?

25. If you are long futures and long a straddle, what is your view on direction? On volatility?

26. How would your answer to the previous question change if you were short futures instead?

27. If you take the view that volatility will drop over the next three months and then increase thereafter, what options strategy would you like to execute? Would the value of this portfolio today be positive or negative?

28. Compute the gross payoffs for the following two portfolios in separate tables:
    - Calls (strikes in parentheses): $C(90) - 2C(100) + C(110)$.
    - Puts (strikes in parentheses): $P(90) - 2P(100) + P(110)$.

    What is the relationship between the two portfolios? Can you explain why?

29. Draw the payoff diagrams at maturity for the following two portfolios:
    - A: Long a call at strike $K$ and short a put at strike $K$, both options for the same maturity.
    - B: Long the stock plus a borrowing of the present value of the strike $K$. The payoff of this portfolio is the cash flow received at maturity from an unwinding of the positions in the portfolio.

    Compare your two payoff diagrams and explain what you see.

# Asymmetric Butterfly Spreads

Suppose we have three strike prices $K_1 < K_2 < K_3$ that are not necessarily equally-spaced. To set up a call butterfly spread with these strikes, we combine the calls in the ratio $w : -1 : (1 - w)$, where $w$ is a fraction defined by

$$w K_1 + (1 - w) K_3 = K_2 \qquad (8.7)$$

or, equivalently,

$$w = \frac{K_3 - K_2}{K_3 - K_1} \qquad (8.8)$$

In other words, for every short position in the $K_2$-strike call, we use (a) $w$ long positions in the $K_1$-strike call and (b) $1 - w$ long positions in the $K_3$-strike call. The use of this particular value for $w$ is dictated by a simple consideration: under this value, the payoffs from the butterfly spread at $T$ will always be:

- zero, if $S_T \leq K_1$ or $S_T \geq K_3$;
- strictly positive and increasing for $S_T$ between $K_1$ and $K_2$; and
- strictly positive and decreasing towards zero for $S_T$ between $K_2$ and $K_3$.

That is, the payoffs at $T$ will look just like Figure 8.7, although they need not, of course, be symmetric. We leave it as an exercise for the reader to draw the time-$T$ payoffs and verify these statements.

## Convexity of Option Prices in $K$

Since the payoffs of the general butterfly spread are always non-negative (and are strictly positive for $S_T$ between $K_1$ and $K_3$), the cost of the spread *must* be positive, i.e., we must have

$$w C(K_1) + (1 - w) C(K_3) > C(K_2), \quad \text{where } w = \frac{K_3 - K_2}{K_3 - K_1} \qquad (8.9)$$

Expression (8.9) is called *convexity* of the call price in the strike price. It is a very powerful restriction on call prices *for any three strike prices*. Expression (8.4) is, of course, a special case of this, corresponding to the weight $w = 1/2$.

## Put Butterfly Spreads

Asymmetric butterfly spreads using puts are defined in exactly the same way as butterfly spreads using calls. Given any three strike prices $K_1$, $K_2$, and $K_3$, we define $w$ as in (8.8). A put butterfly spread then involves

- a long position in $w$ puts with strike $K_1$,
- a long position in $(1 - w)$ puts with strike $K_3$, and
- a short position in one put with strike $K_2$.

The payoff from a put butterfly spread in the general case too is identical to the payoff from a call butterfly spread. Thus, the convexity restriction (8.9) holds for puts too:

$$w P(K_1) + (1 - w) P(K_3) > P(K_2), \quad \text{where } w = \frac{K_3 - K_2}{K_3 - K_1} \qquad (8.10)$$

# Chapter

# 9

# No-Arbitrage Restrictions on Option Prices

## 9.1   Introduction

We have seen in Chapter 7 that volatility is a major source of option value. This means we cannot "price" options without first modeling volatility, that is, without a model of how the underlying asset's price evolves over time. In Chapters 11–16, we examine how this may be done. But since any particular model of volatility and price evolution is necessarily limited, the question arises: is there anything interesting we can say about option prices without making any assumptions concerning the price behavior of the underlying?

It turns out that yes, there is quite a lot. Over this chapter and the next, we describe a number of conditions option prices *must* satisfy independent of how the underlying's prices may evolve over time. Such conditions are called "no-arbitrage restrictions" since they rely only on the minimal assumption that the market does not permit arbitrage.[1]

This chapter focuses on deriving no-arbitrage restrictions on the prices of individual options. We examine two main issues: maximum and minimum prices for options (Section 9.4) and the nature of dependence of option prices on the two key contract parameters, strike price and maturity (Section 9.6). Along the way, we use one of the results to motivate an intuitive definition of the *insurance value* of an option, a concept that we appeal to repeatedly in later chapters. Chapter 10 then looks at the implications of no-arbitrage on two key relationships: the relationship between the prices of otherwise identical calls and puts, and that between otherwise identical American and European options. The results derived over these two chapters will play a major role in later chapters in deriving and understanding properties of options.

## 9.2   Motivating Examples

To get a flavor of the kind of results we shall derive in this chapter and their usefulness, consider the following examples.

---

[1] "Only" is an exaggeration. We also make the usual smooth market assumptions: no taxes, transactions costs, restrictions on short sales, execution risk, and so on. Merton (1973) was the first paper to derive no-arbitrage restrictions on option prices and is the source of most of the results of this chapter.

**Example 9.1**
A stock is currently trading at $55. A European call with a strike of 50 and maturity of two months is trading for $3. The stock is expected to pay a dividend of $2 in one month. The yield curve is flat at 12% for all maturities (in continuously-compounded annualized terms). Is there an arbitrage?

The call is trading for $3, but its current depth-in-the-money is $5. So if this were an American option, the answer would be "yes": buy the call, exercise it immediately, and sell the stock. But since the call is European, this cannot be done. Indeed, since it cannot be exercised for two months, the call does not even look particularly underpriced since the dividend of $2 will be removed from the stock price before maturity. ∎

**Example 9.2**
A stock is currently trading at $45. A European put with a strike of 50 and maturity of two months is trading for $3. The stock is expected to pay a dividend of $1 in one month. The yield curve is flat at 12% for all maturities (in continuously-compounded annualized terms). Is there an arbitrage?

Not obvious. If the option were American, then there *is* a simple arbitrage opportunity: purchase the stock and the put, and exercise the put immediately. But since it is European, this will not work. ∎

**Example 9.3**
The current price of a given stock is $100. A three-month American call option on the stock with a strike of 95 is trading for a price of $6. The three-month rate of interest is 12% (expressed in annualized, continuously-compounded terms). No dividends are expected on the stock over this period. Is there an arbitrage?

Again, not obvious. At least, there doesn't seem to be any simple opportunity. For example, immediate exercise of the call will bring in $(100 − 95) = $5, but the call costs $6, which is greater than the profit from immediate exercise. ∎

**Example 9.4**
A stock is trading at $100. A one-month European put with a strike of 100 costs $3.25, and a one-month European put with a strike of 110 costs $14. The one-month rate of interest (in simple terms) is 1%. Is there an arbitrage?

The ordering of put prices in this question appears correct: the right to sell at 110 should clearly be worth more than the right to sell at 100. But is the difference of $14 − 3.25 = 10.75$ in put prices "too much"? How large can differences be before an arbitrage opportunity arises? ∎

**Example 9.5**
A stock is trading at $40. There are three-month European calls on the stock with strikes of 35, 40, and 45. The prices of the calls are, respectively, 5.50, 3.85, and 1.50. Is there an arbitrage?

Again, the ordering of call prices seems correct with the 35-strike call costing the most and the 45-strike call the least. Is there a deeper relationship that should link the three call prices? ∎

None of these examples has anything "obviously" wrong with it. Yet, the results we derive in this chapter show that each of them admits an arbitrage opportunity. In Section 9.7, we revisit these examples, derive the arbitrage opportunity in each of them, and explain how it may be exploited. But before this can be done, we first have to derive the no-arbitrage restrictions. We turn to this now.

# 9.3   Notation and Other Preliminaries

The properties of option prices will depend on several factors:

- Whether the option is a call or a put.
- Whether the option is American or European.
- The size of the dividend payments (if any) that are expected from the underlying asset over the life of the option.

The importance of option type (puts vs. calls) and option style (American vs. European) is evident. Dividends become important because options are typically not "payout-protected" instruments, i.e., the terms of the option (such as the strike price) are usually not adjusted when a dividend is paid on the underlying.[2] Dividend payments cause a fall in the price of the underlying asset. This hurts the holder of a call option since the call becomes "less" in-the-money, but benefits the holder of a put option since the put becomes "more" in-the-money. The absence of payout protection means that the size of the expected dividend payment will affect the amount investors are willing to pay for calls and puts: other things being equal, an increase in the expected dividend size will lower the value of a call and increase the value of a put.

From a conceptual standpoint, it helps to distinguish between the case where the underlying asset is not expected to pay any dividends over the life of the option, and where it is expected to pay dividends. We refer to the former case as one of a *non-dividend-paying* or NDP asset, and the latter as a *dividend-paying* or DP asset. Note that NDP and DP refer only to dividends that may occur *during the option's life*; any dividends that may occur after the option's expiry do not affect the option's value and so do not concern us here. Finally, when dealing with DP assets, we assume, as we did in the context of forward pricing, that the timing and size of the dividend payments are known. This is not entirely an innocuous assumption, but it is a reasonable one, especially for short-dated options.

## Notation

The notation used in this chapter is summarized in Table 9.1. We retain the notation introduced in earlier chapters for the price of the underlying and for the option's strike and maturity. Also as earlier, $C$ and $P$ will denote call and put option prices, but now we shall add subscripts $A$ and $E$ where necessary to denote American and European styles, respectively. Thus, $C_A$ will denote the price of an American call, while $P_E$ is the price of a European put. If a pricing property holds for both American and European styles of an option, we shall drop the subscripts and simply use $C$ and $P$.

Two other pieces of notation will come in handy. Let $PV(D)$ denote the present value (viewed from today) of the dividends receivable over the life of the option. And let $PV(K)$ denote the present value of an amount $K$ receivable at the maturity time $T$ of the option.

One final observation. Since we can always choose to hold an American option to maturity, such an option can never cost less than its European counterpart, so we must have:

$$C_A \geq C_E \quad \text{and} \quad P_A \geq P_E \tag{9.1}$$

[2] This is true for normal dividend payments. If dividend payments are extraordinarily high (a threshold of 10% of the stock price is commonly used), then exchanges often respond by reducing the strike price by the amount of the dividend. This was done, for example, in the case of the large Microsoft dividend in late 2004.

**TABLE 9.1**
Notation and
Terminology

| Notation | Meaning |
|---|---|
| $S$ | Current price of underlying |
| $K$ | Strike price of option |
| $T$ | Maturity date of option |
| $S_T$ | Time-$T$ price of underlying |
| $C$ | Call option (can be American or European) |
| $P$ | Put option (can be American or European) |
| $C_A, C_E$ | American and European calls, respectively |
| $P_A, P_E$ | American and European puts, respectively |
| $PV(D)$ | Present value of dividends receivable over option life |
| $PV(K)$ | Present value of an amount $K$ receivable at time $T$ |

## 9.4 Maximum and Minimum Prices for Options

We begin with call prices first, and then look at the corresponding results for puts.

### Bounds on Call Option Prices

An *upper* bound on call prices is easy to derive: the price of a call option can never exceed the current price $S$ of the underlying asset.

$$C \leq S \tag{9.2}$$

The reasoning behind (9.2) is simple: when the asset can be purchased directly today for $S$, why pay more than $S$ for the call which provides you only the right to buy the underlying asset by making a further payment of $K$?

Lower bounds are just a little bit trickier. We derive two simple lower bounds first and then a third one that involves a tad more work.

A call confers a right without an obligation. Therefore, the price of a call cannot be negative—that is, you cannot be paid to take on a right that you can throw away for free. This gives us the first lower bound:

$$C \geq 0 \tag{9.3}$$

Note that (9.3) need not hold for derivatives such as forward that involve an obligation rather than a right. For example, if you hold a long forward contract and prices have dropped sharply since you entered into the contract, the contract will have negative value for you. This means you cannot get out of the contract except at a cost.

Our second lower bound is one that holds for *American* calls. Such a call can be exercised at any time. If it is exercised immediately, the investor pays $K$ and receives an asset worth $S$; thus, the value of immediate exercise is $S - K$. In the absence of arbitrage, the price $C_A$ of the call must be at least the value of immediate exercise:

$$C_A \geq S - K \tag{9.4}$$

If (9.4) did not hold (that is, if $C_A < S - K$), an investor could make arbitrage profits by buying the call and exercising it immediately. Note that this argument will not hold for European calls, which can be exercised only at maturity. Thus, (9.4) may or may not hold for European calls.

The third lower bound holds both for European and American calls, but it helps to break up the derivation into a series of steps. We consider first the case of a European call on an NDP asset; then we bring in dividends; and finally we allow for early exercise. So

**TABLE 9.2**
Portfolios A and B:
Costs and Payoffs

| | | Cash Flows at $T$ When | |
|---|---|---|---|
| | Initial Cost | $S_T < K$ | $S_T \geq K$ |
| **Portfolio A** | $C_E$ | 0 | $S_T - K$ |
| **Portfolio B** | $S - PV(K)$ | $S_T - K$ | $S_T - K$ |

suppose we are given a European call option on an NDP asset. Consider the following two portfolios:

| **Portfolio A** | Long one call with strike $K$ and maturity $T$ |
|---|---|
| **Portfolio B** | Long one unit of the underlying |
| | Borrowing of $PV(K)$ for repayment at $T$ |

The cost and time-$T$ payoffs of each portfolio are summarized in Table 9.2. (There are no interim cash flows to worry about since the call cannot be exercised until maturity and there are no dividends.) The initial cost of Portfolio A is just the current price $C_E$ of the call, while that of Portfolio B is $S - PV(K)$. The time-$T$ values of both portfolios depend on $S_T$:

- Portfolio A, the call, expires worthless if $S_T < K$ and is worth $S_T - K$ if $S_T \geq K$.
- In Portfolio B, the long underlying position is worth $S_T$ while repayment of the borrowing leads to a cash outflow of $K$. Thus, the value of Portfolio B at maturity is $S_T - K$.

These payoffs are graphed in Figure 9.1. At maturity, Portfolio A does exactly as well as Portfolio B when $S_T \geq K$ and does strictly better when $S_T < K$. Portfolio A must therefore cost at least as much as Portfolio B. That is, we must have

$$C_E \geq S - PV(K) \tag{9.5}$$

Expression (9.5) is the desired third lower bound. In Section 9.5, we give a simple interpretation of Portfolio B that makes this lower bound seem almost obvious.

How should (9.5) be modified to account for dividend payments and early exercise? Consider dividends first. If the underlying is a DP asset, then there will be an intermediate

**FIGURE 9.1**
Payoffs of Portfolios
A and B

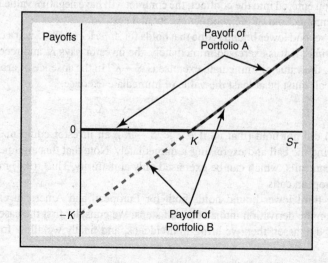

**FIGURE 9.2**

Bounds on Call Prices
When $D = 0$

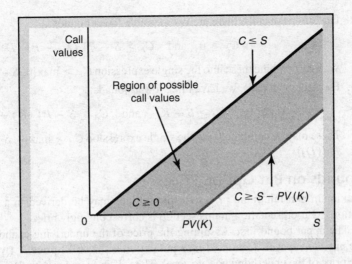

cash inflow in Portfolio B at the time the dividend is paid, but there is no corresponding cash flow in Portfolio A. To restore the comparability, all we need do is create a corresponding cash outflow in Portfolio B that cancels out the dividend cash flow. That is, consider the following modification to Portfolio B:

**Portfolio B**      Long one unit of the underlying
                       Borrowing of $PV(K)$ for repayment at $T$
                       Borrowing of $PV(D)$ for repayment on the dividend date

The initial cost of Portfolio B changes; it is now $S - PV(K) - PV(D)$. But there are no net interim cash flows in this portfolio, and its time-$T$ value remains exactly as in Table 9.2. Therefore, the same comparison we made earlier between the portfolios is valid: Portfolio A does as well or strictly better than Portfolio B at maturity. Since neither portfolio has interim cash flows, Portfolio A must cost at least as much as Portfolio B:

$$C_E \geq S - PV(K) - PV(D) \tag{9.6}$$

Expression (9.6) is the general version of (9.5) when dividends may be nonzero.

This leaves early exercise. But this is easily brought into the mix. Since we must always have $C_A \geq C_E$, the lower bound (9.6) must also hold for American calls! Thus, we obtain the third and last lower bound for calls:

$$C \geq S - PV(K) - PV(D) \tag{9.7}$$

Figure 9.2 illustrates the bounds on call prices when there are no dividends ($D = 0$). In this case, the lower bound $C \geq S - PV(K)$, which holds for both American and European options, is "tighter" than the bound $C_A \geq S - K$, so this last lower bound is ignored in the figure. Only simple changes are required to the figure when $D$ is positive; the details are left as an exercise.

## Bounds on Call Prices: Summary

To summarize the bounds on call option prices:

1. The current price of the underlying is an upper bound on the price of any call:

$$C_E \leq S \quad \text{and} \quad C_A \leq S \tag{9.8}$$

2. For European calls, there are two possible lower bounds:

$$C_E \geq 0 \quad \text{and} \quad C_E \geq S - PV(K) - PV(D)$$

We may combine these into the single expression $C_E \geq \max\{0, S - PV(K) - PV(D)\}$.

3. For American calls, we have three lower bounds:

$$C_A \geq 0, \quad C_A \geq S - K, \quad \text{and} \quad C_A \geq S - PV(K) - PV(D)$$

These may be combined into the single expression $C_A \geq \max\{0, S - K, S - PV(K) - PV(D)\}$.

## Bounds on Put Option Prices

Maximum and minimum prices for put options may be derived in a similar way to call options. Our presentation in this section is correspondingly brief.

The upper bound first. Assuming the price of the underlying cannot become negative, the *maximum* payoff from holding a put option is the strike price $K$ (which happens when the price of the underlying goes to zero). Thus, $K$ is an upper bound on the price of the put:

$$P \leq K \tag{9.9}$$

Expression (9.9) can be strengthened a little for European puts. In this case, even the maximum profit of $K$ can occur only at time $T$, so is worth only $PV(K)$ today. Thus, we must have $P_E \leq PV(K)$. But for American puts, (9.9) is the best upper bound we can get in general.

Two lower bounds for puts are easily derived. First, as options, puts have rights but no obligations, so their value must always be non-negative:

$$P \geq 0 \tag{9.10}$$

Second, the holder of an American put can always receive the payoff $K - S$ from immediate exercise. To prevent arbitrage, the put must cost at least this much:

$$P_A \geq K - S \tag{9.11}$$

Analogous to the procedure we used for calls, the third lower bound is best derived in several steps. So consider first the case of a European put on an NDP asset. Consider the following two portfolios:

**Portfolio C**   Long one put with strike $K$ and maturity $T$

**Portfolio D**   Short one unit of the underlying
Investment of $PV(K)$ for maturity at $T$

Section 9.5 gives a simple interpretation of Portfolio D when discussing this comparison further. The cost and time-$T$ payoffs of each portfolio are summarized in Table 9.3. (There are no interim cash flows to worry about since the put cannot be exercised until maturity and there are no dividends.) The initial cost of Portfolio C is just the current price $P_E$ of the

**TABLE 9.3**
Portfolios C and D: Costs and Payoffs

| | | Cash Flows at $T$ When | |
|---|---|---|---|
| | Initial Cost | $S_T < K$ | $S_T \geq K$ |
| Portfolio C | $P_E$ | $K - S_T$ | 0 |
| Portfolio D | $PV(K) - S$ | $K - S_T$ | $K - S_T$ |

call, while that of Portfolio D is $PV(K) - S$. The time-$T$ values of both portfolios depend on $S_T$:

- Portfolio C, the put, is worth $K - S_T$ if $S_T < K$ and expires worthless otherwise.
- In Portfolio D, the investment leads to a cash inflow of $K$ while covering the short underlying position costs $S_T$, so the value of Portfolio D at maturity is $K - S_T$.

So Portfolio C does exactly as well as Portfolio D at maturity when $S_T < K$ and does strictly better when $S_T \geq K$. Thus, it must cost more, and we have

$$P_E \geq PV(K) - S \qquad (9.12)$$

Extending (9.12) to the case of dividend-paying assets is straighforward. If there are dividends on the underlying, this will lead to cash outflows at dividend times in Portfolio D since the short position is responsible for dividend payments. To cancel out this cash outflow, we must have a corresponding cash inflow. To this end, we modify the definition of Portfolio D to

| **Portfolio D** | Short one unit of the underlying |
|---|---|
| | Investment of $PV(K)$ for maturity at $T$ |
| | Investment of $PV(D)$ for maturity on the dividend date |

The initial cost of Portfolio D changes to $PV(K) + PV(D) - S$. Nothing else changes: there are no net interim cash flows now, and the cash flows at $T$ are exactly as described in Table 9.3. Thus, Portfolio C continues to dominate this modified Portfolio D, which means it must cost more:

$$P_E \geq PV(K) + PV(D) - S \qquad (9.13)$$

Expression (9.13) is simply the generalization of (9.12) to the case where dividends may be nonzero.

Finally, since we must always have $P_A \geq P_E$, this lower bound (9.13) must also hold for American puts, so we finally have the general form of the third lower bound that holds for both American and European puts:

$$P \geq PV(K) + PV(D) - S \qquad (9.14)$$

Figure 9.3 illustrates the bounds on put prices when there are no dividends ($D = 0$). For simplicity, the figure does not present the additional lower bound $P_A \geq K - S$ that holds

**FIGURE 9.3**

Bounds on Put Prices When $D = 0$

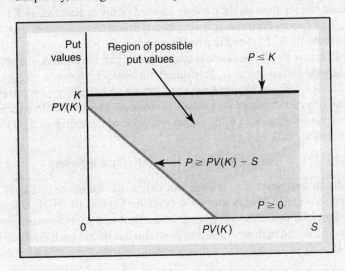

for American options. (Note that this omitted bound is actually a tighter lower bound when there are no dividends.) Once again, only simple changes are required to the figure when $D$ is positive, and the details are left as an exercise.

## Bounds on Put Prices: Summary

Summarizing the bounds on put option prices:

1. The strike price of the option is an upper bound on the price of a put:

$$P \leq K$$

For European puts, this bound can be improved to $P_E \leq PV(K)$.

2. For European puts, there are two lower bounds, which can be combined to yield

$$P_E \geq \max\{0, PV(K) + PV(D) - S\}$$

3. For American puts, there are three lower bounds, which can be be combined to yield:

$$P_A \geq \max\{0, K - S, PV(K) + PV(D) - S\}$$

# 9.5 The Insurance Value of an Option

Holding an option provides an investor with protection against unfavorable price movements. The value of this protection is called the *insurance value* of the option. In this section, we describe a measure of an option's insurance value motivated by the comparisons of the previous section.

Consider again the Portfolios A and B from Section 9.4 that were used to derive the third and last lower bound on call option values. By construction, the only difference in the portfolios' cash flows occurs at time $T$. Moreover:

- If $S_T \geq K$, then the two portfolios have the same payoff, namely, $S_T - K$.
- If $S_T < K$, then Portfolio A has a payoff of 0, but Portfolio B's payoff continues to be given by $S_T - K$, which is now negative. That is, Portfolio A is protected against a fall in the asset price below $K$, while Portfolio B is not.

Indeed, what exactly is Portfolio B? By construction, this portfolio has no net cash flows up to $T$ and has a cash flow of $S_T - K$ at time $T$. These are exactly the cash flows one would receive from holding a long forward position maturing at $T$ with a delivery price of $K$. This means Portfolio B is simply a *synthetic long forward* with a delivery price of $K$ and maturity of $T$! (See the payoffs in Figure 9.1.)

Compare Portfolios A and B again in this light. Portfolio A, the option, gives us the *right* to buy the underlying at $K$. Portfolio B, the synthetic forward, *obligates* us to buy at $K$. The difference between having a right and having an obligation is precisely what we intuitively think of as downside protection or "insurance." Thus, the difference in the costs of the two portfolios is a measure of the insurance value of the call: writing $IV(C)$ for the insurance value of the call, we have

$$IV(C) = C - [S - PV(K) - PV(D)] \tag{9.15}$$

In an analogous manner, we can define the insurance value of a put by comparing Portfolios C and D of Section 9.4. Portfolio C gives us the *right* to sell the underlying at $K$. Portfolio D, on the other hand, is identical to a *short forward* position with a delivery price of $K$ and maturity of $T$: the portfolio has no net cash flows up to $T$ and a cash flow of $K - S_T$ at $T$. Thus, the difference in the prices of the two portfolios provides us with a natural measure of the insurance value of the put:

$$IV(P) = P - [PV(K) + PV(D) - S] \qquad (9.16)$$

In the next chapter, we build further on this material to provide a decomposition of option values that is useful in understanding option risk from an intuitive standpoint and that we appeal to at several points in this book. The decompositions, as well as the definitions (9.15)–(9.16) of the options' insurance values, appear in Figlewski, Silber, and Subrahmanyam (1992).

### Remark

European options, like the synthetic forward, can be exercised only at maturity. However, American options can also be exercised prior to maturity, so the insurance values (9.15) and (9.16) of these options include not only the insurance value of the corresponding European option but also the *early-exercise premium*, i.e., the extra amount over the European price one pays for the right to exercise early. (Of course, the right to exercise early is itself a form of insurance protection.) Thus, the insurance value of an American option will typically be larger than that of its European counterpart, and the difference will increase as early exercise becomes more important. In Chapter 10, we discuss conditions that make early exercise more or less important.

## 9.6   Option Prices and Contract Parameters

The manner in which option prices depend on the contract parameters—that is, on the strike price $K$ for a fixed maturity $T$, or on the maturity $T$ for a fixed strike price $K$—are issues of some interest. In this section, we look at the implications of no-arbitrage for these relationships. We begin with the strike price $K$.

### Call Prices and the Strike Price

Our first result is a simple one: as the strike price rises, call values must fall. That is:

$$\text{If } K_1 < K_2, \text{ then } C(K_1) \geq C(K_2) \qquad (9.17)$$

where $C(K)$ is the price of call with strike $K$. Intuitively this is obvious—the right to buy at $K_2$ must be worth less than the right to buy at the cheaper price $K_1$—but here's a formal proof. Suppose we instead had $C(K_1) < C(K_2)$. Set up a bull spread: go long the $K_1$-strike call, short the $K_2$-strike call. The initial cash flow from this spread is then $C(K_2) - C(K_1) > 0$. And, of course, as Figure 8.3 shows, the cash flows from a bull spread at maturity are never negative, so this is an arbitrage opportunity.

Expression (9.17) tells us only that a call with a lower strike must be more expensive. But how much more expensive can it be? That is, what is the maximum value of the difference $C(K_1) - C(K_2)$?

To judge the answer, consider European calls first. The *maximum* additional payoff that can be realized by using the $K_1$-strike call instead of the $K_2$-strike call is evidently $K_2 - K_1$. (Compare the payoffs of calls with strikes $K_1$ and $K_2$ and look at the maximum difference in the payoffs.) However, this maximum profit can be realized only at date $T$ because the options cannot be exercised until that point. Therefore:

$$\text{If } K_1 < K_2, \text{ then } C_E(K_1) - C_E(K_2) \leq PV(K_2 - K_1) \qquad (9.18)$$

Now consider American calls. Once again, the maximum additional advantage that can be realized by using the call with strike $K_1$ instead of the call with strike $K_2$ is $(K_2 - K_1)$.

In this case, however, the calls can be exercised at any time. Therefore, this maximum additional profit may be realizable immediately in some cases, so:

$$\text{If } K_1 < K_2, \text{ then } C_A(K_1) - C_A(K_2) \leq K_2 - K_1 \qquad \textbf{(9.19)}$$

Expressions (9.18) and (9.19) place upper limits on how large the price differences can be between two calls that differ only in their strike price. Thus, they are in the nature of "slope" restrictions on call prices. In calculus terms, (9.19) is equivalent to the condition that the first derivative $dC/dK$ of the call price with respect to the strike satisfy $dC/dK \geq -1$.

Our final restriction relates any three calls that differ only in their strike prices. Let any three strike prices $K_1 < K_2 < K_3$ be given. Define

$$w = \frac{K_3 - K_2}{K_3 - K_1} \qquad \textbf{(9.20)}$$

Consider a portfolio consisting of $w$ long positions in the $K_1$-strike call, $(1 - w)$ long positions in the $K_3$-strike call, and one short position in the $K_2$-strike call. This is just the butterfly spread described in Appendix 8A. As we saw there, the payoff of the butterfly spread is strictly positive or zero, so it must have a positive cost. That is, we must have

$$wC(K_1) + (1 - w)C(K_3) \geq C(K_2) \qquad \textbf{(9.21)}$$

Expression (9.21) was also described in Appendix 8A (see (8.9)). Mathematically, this is the condition that the call price be *convex* in the strike price. Convexity is a *curvature* restriction on the call price: it is equivalent to having $d^2C/dK^2 > 0$.

To sum up, there are three restrictions on the relationship between call prices and the strike price:

1. If $K_1 < K_2$, then $C(K_1) > C(K_2)$.
2. If $K_1 < K_2$, then

$$C_E(K_1) - C_E(K_2) \leq PV(K_2 - K_1), \quad C_A(K_1) - C_A(K_2) \leq K_2 - K_1$$

3. If $K_1 < K_2 < K_3$, then, defining $w = (K_3 - K_2)/(K_3 - K_1)$,

$$wC(K_1) + (1 - w)C(K_3) \geq C(K_2)$$

## Put Prices and the Strike Price

The corresponding relationships for put options are easily obtained using similar arguments. First,

$$\text{If } K_1 < K_2, \text{ then } P(K_1) < P(K_2) \qquad \textbf{(9.22)}$$

that is, put prices must be increasing in the strike price. Intuitively, the right to sell at $K_2$ must be worth more than the right to sell at the lower price $K_1$. For a formal proof, suppose this inequality fails and we have $P(K_1) > P(K_2)$. Set up a bear spread using puts (sell the $K_1$-strike put, buy the $K_2$-strike put). This portfolio has an initial cash inflow, and, as Figure 8.6 shows, it involves non-negative cash inflows at maturity. This is an arbitrage.

Second, the maximum difference between holding the $K_2$-strike put and the $K_1$-strike put is $K_2 - K_1$ (compare the payoff diagrams of the two puts). For European puts, this payoff can be realized only at maturity, so:

$$\text{If } K_1 < K_2, \text{ then } P_E(K_2) - P_E(K_1) \leq PV(K_2 - K_1) \qquad \textbf{(9.23)}$$

For American puts, however, the difference may be realized at any time, so

$$\text{If } K_1 < K_2, \text{ then } P_A(K_2) - P_A(K_1) \leq K_2 - K_1 \qquad \textbf{(9.24)}$$

Finally, given any three strike prices $K_1 < K_2 < K_3$ and defining $w$ by (9.20), we can always set up a butterfly spread using puts as described in Section 8.9. As shown there, the payoff from the spread is non-negative at maturity and is strictly positive for $S_T$ lying between $K_1$ and $K_3$, so the initial cost of the butterfly spread must be positive, i.e.,

$$w P(K_1) + (1 - w) P(K_3) \geq P(K_2) \tag{9.25}$$

Expression (9.25) was also described in Appendix 8A (see (8.10)).

## Call Prices and the Time to Maturity

Consider two call options that differ in their time to maturity but are otherwise identical. Let $T_1$ and $T_2$ denote the maturity dates of the two options, where $T_1 < T_2$. Our aim is to examine how the values of such options are related.

If the calls in question are American, then the answer is easy to see: since the call with maturity $T_2$ can always be exercised at the same time as the call with maturity $T_1$, the former must also cost more. That is:

$$\text{If } T_1 < T_2, \text{ then } C_A(T_1) \leq C_A(T_2) \tag{9.26}$$

If the calls are European, however, the arguments leading to (9.26) do not work since the call with the longer maturity cannot be exercised at the same time as the call with shorter maturity. Nonetheless, with some work, we can show that this result holds for European call options also, *provided the underlying asset does not pay a dividend between $T_1$ and $T_2$*. We start by recalling that the price of a European call on an NDP asset satisfies (see Section 9.4)

$$C_E \geq S - PV(K)$$

Now consider two European calls, one with maturity $T_1$ and the other with maturity $T_2 > T_1$. On date $T_1$:

- The call with expiry $T_1$ is worth $\max\{0, S_{T_1} - K\}$.
- The call with expiry $T_2$ is worth *at least* $\max\{0, S_{T_1} - PV(K)\}$, where $PV(K)$ denotes the present value at time $T_1$ of an amount $K$ receivable at $T_2$.

Since $PV(K) \leq K$ always, it is the case that on date $T_1$, the call with expiry $T_2$ is always worth at least as much as the call with expiry $T_1$. Therefore, the current price of the call with maturity $T_2$ must also be larger, i.e., we must have

$$C_E(T_1) \leq C_E(T_2) \quad \text{if } T_1 < T_2 \tag{9.27}$$

However, if there is a dividend between $T_1$ and $T_2$, it lowers the value of the $T_2$-maturity call without affecting the value of the $T_1$-maturity call, so the call with the longer maturity could cost less. So (9.27) need not hold for European options on dividend-paying stocks.

## Put Prices and the Time to Maturity

The same reasoning as for American calls shows that for American puts too we must have

$$P_A(T_1) \leq P_A(T_2) \quad \text{if } T_1 < T_2 \tag{9.28}$$

However, (9.28) may fail for European puts even if there are no dividends. Here is a short indirect proof. We have seen that an upper bound on the value of a European put is $PV(K)$, the present value of an amount $K$ receivable at the put's maturity. For a perpetual $(T = \infty)$ European put, this upper bound is the present value of an amount $K$ receivable in the infinitely distant future, which must be zero under any reasonable scenario. Thus, the price of a perpetual European put must be zero. Now, suppose (9.28) did hold for European puts. Then, European put values would increase as maturity increases, so the price of the perpetual put is an *upper* bound on the price of any finite-maturity put. But this implies, absurdly, that the price of any finite-maturity put must also be zero! Thus, (9.28) cannot hold for European options even if there are no dividends.

This points to a fundamental asymmetry between call and put options. In Section 10.2 in the next chapter, we explain intuitively why European put prices may drop as maturity increases and when this is likely to happen. Several numerical examples in later chapters then provide concrete instances of situations where European put prices do, in fact, decrease as maturity increases. See, for example, the section "A Comment: The Impact of Maturity" in Chapter 12 or Section 17.5 of Chapter 17.

## 9.7 Numerical Examples

This section returns to the five examples presented in Section 9.2. We work through each example to illustrate the exploitation of the no-arbitrage restrictions on option prices derived in the previous sections.

**Example 9.1**
**Revisited**

In Example 9.1, we are given the following data: $S = 55$, $K = 50$, $T = 1/6$, $D = 2$ in one month, $r = 0.12$, and $C_E = 3$. Is there an arbitrage?

Clearly, $C_E \leq S$ and $C_E \geq 0$, so it remains to be checked that $C_E \geq S - PV(K) - PV(D)$. We have

$$PV(K) = e^{-(1/6)\times 0.12}\, 50 = 49.01 \qquad PV(D) = e^{-(1/12)\times 0.12}\, 2 = 1.98$$

This means $S - PV(K) - PV(D) = 4.01$, and the no-arbitrage bound is violated. This tells us the call is *undervalued*; that is, in the notation of Section 9.4, Portfolio A costs less than Portfolio B. To take advantage, we buy Portfolio A and sell Portfolio B. That is:

- Buy the call. Cash outflow = 3.
- Short the stock. Cash inflow = 55.
- Invest $PV(D)$ for one month. Cash outflow = 1.98.
- Invest $PV(K)$ for two months. Cash outflow = 49.01.

The initial cash flow from this strategy is $-3 + 55 - 49.01 - 1.98 = +1.01$. At the end of one month, we receive \$2 from the investment of $PV(D)$ and use this to pay the dividend due on the shorted stock. Thus, there is no net cash flow at this interim time point. At the end of two months, there are two possibilities:

- $S_T < 50$. In this case, we let the call lapse, buy the stock for $S_T$ and use it to close out the short position, and receive $K = 50$ from the two-month investment. Net cash flow: $50 - S_T > 0$.
- $S_T \geq 50$. Now, we exercise the call, buy the stock for 50, use it to cover the short position, and receive $K = 50$ from the investment. Net cash flow: 0.

With all cash flows being zero or positive, we have identified the desired arbitrage. ∎

**Example 9.2**
**Revisited**

Example 9.2 describes the following data: $S = 45$, $K = 50$, $T = 1/6$, $D = 1$ in one month, $r = 0.12$ for all maturities, and $P_E = 3$. Is there an arbitrage?

Since $P_E \leq K$ and $P_E \geq 0$, it only remains to be checked that $P_E \geq PV(K) + PV(D) - S$. An easy computation shows that $PV(K) = 49.01$ and $PV(D) = 0.99$. So $PV(K) + PV(D) - S = 5.00$, and the no-arbitrage bound is violated. This tells us the put is *undervalued*; that is, in the notation of Section 9.4, that Portfolio C costs less than Portfolio D when it should cost more. So, we buy Portfolio C and sell Portfolio D, that is, we

- Buy the put. Cash outflow = 3.
- Buy the stock. Cash outflow = 45.
- Borrow $PV(D)$ for one month. Cash inflow = 0.99.
- Borrow $PV(K)$ for two months. Cash inflow = 49.01.

The initial cash flow from this strategy is $-3 - 45 + 49.01 + 0.99 = +2.00$. At the end of one month, we pay \$1 on the borrowing of $PV(D)$ and receive \$1 in dividend from the stock for a net interim cash flow of zero. At the end of two months, there are two possibilities:

- $S_T < 50$. In this case, we exercise the put, sell the stock for 50, and repay $K = 50$ on the borrowing. Net cash flow: $50 - 50 = 0$.
- $S_T \geq 50$. Now, we let the put lapse, sell the stock for $S_T$, and repay $K$ on the borrowing. Net cash flow: $S_T - 50 \geq 0$.

With all cash flows being positive or zero, this is an arbitrage opportunity. ∎

---

**Example 9.3 Revisited**

In notational terms, in Example 9.3, we are given that $S = 100$, $K = 95$, $T = 1/4$, $r = 0.12$, and $C_A = 6$. Is there an arbitrage?

Clearly, $C_A \leq S$. The lower bounds $C_A \geq 0$ and $C_A \geq S - K$ are also clearly satisfied. Thus, it remains only to be checked if the third no-arbitrage lower bound holds. Since $D = 0$, we must check if $C_A \geq S - PV(K)$. We have

$$PV(K) = e^{-(1/4) \times 0.12} 95 \approx 92.20$$

Therefore, $S - PV(K) = 7.80$, and the third no-arbitrage bound is violated.

This means the call is *undervalued*. The arbitrage bound says it should be worth at least 7.80, whereas it is trading for only 6. To take advantage of this opportunity, we must (in the notation of Section 9.4) buy Portfolio A and sell Portfolio B, i.e.,

- Buy the call.
- Short the stock.
- Invest $PV(K)$.

This results in an initial cash inflow of $-6 + 100 - 92.20 = +1.80$. At time $T$, there are two possibilities:

- $S_T < 95$. In this case, we let the call lapse, buy the stock from the market to cover the short position, and receive $K$ from our investment. Net cash flow: $-S_T + 95 > 0$.
- $S_T \geq 95$. Now, we exercise the call and buy the stock for $K$, use the stock to close out the short position, and receive $K$ from the investment. Net cash flow: $-95 + 95 = 0$.

Since the strategy has cash inflows with no net cash outflows, we have derived an arbitrage opportunity. ∎

---

**Example 9.4 Revisited**

In Example 9.4, we are given $K_1 = 100$ and $K_2 = 110$. Since the one-month rate of interest is given to be 1% in simple terms,

$$PV(K_2 - K_1) = \frac{10}{1.01} = 9.90$$

On the other hand, we are also given $P_E(100) = 3.25$ and $P_E(110) = 14$, so $P_E(110) - P_E(100) = 10.75$. This means the no-arbitrage condition (9.23) is violated.

To take advantage of the opportunity, we buy the relatively overvalued right-hand side of (9.23) and sell the relatively undervalued left-hand side. That is, we

- Invest $PV(K_2 - K_1) = \$9.90$ for one month.
- Sell the $K_2$-strike put for \$14.
- Buy the $K_1$-strike put for \$3.25.

This creates an initial cash inflow of \$0.85. At maturity, the investment grows to \$10. If the stock price at this time is

- $S_T < 100$, both options are in-the-money. We gain $100 - S_T$ on the put we hold and lose $110 - S_T$ on the put we have sold for a net loss of 10. Combined with the receipt from the investment, this results in a net payoff of zero.
- $100 \leq S_T < 110$, the option we hold is out-of-the-money, but the one we sold finishes in-the-money. We lose $110 - S_T$ on the latter. Since this is less than the \$10 receipt from the investment, there is a net positive cash inflow.
- $S_T > 110$, both options are out-of-the-money. Thus, the net cash flow is the receipt from the investment, which is +\$10.

Since all cash flows are positive or zero, this is an arbitrage. ∎

## Example 9.5 Revisited

In Example 9.5, we are given three strike prices—$K_1 = 35$, $K_2 = 40$, and $K_3 = 45$—with respective call prices $C(35) = 5.50$, $C(40) = 3.85$, and $C(45) = 1.50$. Consider the convexity restriction (9.21). A simple calculation shows that $w = 1/2$ and that

$$\frac{1}{2} C(35) + \frac{1}{2} C(45) < C(40)$$

So the convexity condition (9.21) is violated. To take advantage of the resulting arbitrage opportunity, buy the butterfly spread; this creates a cash inflow today and a possible cash inflow at maturity. ∎

## 9.8 Exercises

1. What is meant by payout protection? Are options payout protected?
2. How does the payment of an unexpected dividend affect (a) call prices and (b) put prices?
3. As we have seen, options always have non-negative value. Give an example of a derivative whose value may become negative.
4. What are the upper and lower bounds on call option prices?
5. What are the upper and lower bounds on put option prices?
6. What is meant by the insurance value of an option? Describe how it may be measured.
7. What does the early-exercise premium measure?
8. What is meant by convexity of option prices in the strike price?
9. There are call and put options on a stock with strike 40, 50, and 55. Which of the following inequalities must hold?
   (a) $0.5C(40) + 0.5C(55) > C(50)$
   (b) $(1/3)C(40) + (2/3)C(55) > C(50)$

(c) $(2/3)C(40) + (1/3)C(55) > C(50)$

(d) $0.5P(40) + 0.5P(55) > P(50)$

(e) $(1/3)P(40) + (2/3)P(55) > P(50)$

(f) $(2/3)P(40) + (1/3)P(55) > P(50)$

Note: This question uses the general form of convexity in the strike for options:

$$wC(K_1) + (1-w)C(K_3) \geq C(K_2)$$

and

$$wP(K_1) + (1-w)P(K_3) \geq P(K_2)$$

where

$$w = \frac{K_3 - K_2}{K_3 - K_1}$$

10. There are call and put options on ABC stock with strikes of 40 and 50. The 40-strike call is priced at $13, while the 50-strike put is at $12.8. What are the best bounds you can find for (a) the 40-strike put and (b) the 50-strike call?

11. The following three call option prices are observed in the market, for XYZ stock:

| Type | Strike | Option Price |
|------|--------|--------------|
| Call | 50 | 10 |
| Call | 60 | 7 |
| Call | 70 | 2 |

Are these prices free from arbitrage? How would you determine this? If they are incorrect, suggest a strategy that you might employ to make sure profits.

12. The current price of a stock is $60. The one-year call option on the stock at a strike of $60 is trading at $10. If the one-year rate of interest is 10%, is the call price free from arbitrage, assuming that the stock pays no dividends? What if the stock pays a dividend of $5 one day before the maturity of the option?

13. The current price of ABC stock is $50. The term structure of interest rates (continuously compounded) is flat at 10%. What is the six-month forward price of the stock? Denote this as $F$. The six-month call price at strike $F$ is equal to $8. The six-month put price at strike $F$ is equal to $7. Explain why there is arbitrage opportunity given these prices.

14. The prices of the following puts $P(K)$ at strike $K$ are given to you:

$$P(40) = 2, \quad P(45) = 6, \quad P(60) = 14$$

The current stock price is $50. What is inconsistent about these prices? How would you create arbitrage profits?

15. The price of a three-month at-the-money call option on a stock at a price of $80 is currently $5. What is the maximum possible continuously compounded interest rate in the market for three-month maturity that is consistent with the absence of arbitrage?

16. The six-month continuously compounded rate of interest is 4%. The six-month forward price of stock KLM is 58. The stock pays no dividends. You are given that the price of a put option $P(K)$ is $3. What is the maximum possible strike price $K$ that is consistent with the absence of arbitrage?

17. (Difficult) Suppose there are five call options $C(K)$, i.e., $\{C(80), C(90), C(100), C(110), C(120)\}$. The prices of two of these are $C(110) = 4$, $C(120) = 2$. Find the best possible lower bound for the call option $C(80)$.

18. In the previous problem, also find the minimum prices of $C(90)$ and $C(100)$.

19. The following are one-year put option prices: the put at strike 90 is trading at $12, and the put at strike 80 is trading at $2.50. The rate of interest (continuously compounded) for one year is 10%. Show how you would construct an arbitrage strategy in this market.

20. The one-year European put option at strike 100 (current stock price = 100) is quoted at $10. The two-year European put at the same strike is quoted at $4: The term structure of interest rates is flat at 10% (continuously compounded). Is this an arbitrage?

21. Given the following data, construct an arbitrage strategy: $S = 100$, $K = 95$, $T = 1/2$ year, $D = 3$ in three months, $r = 0.05$, and $C_E = 4$.

22. Given the following data, construct an arbitrage strategy: $S = 95$, $K = 100$, $T = 1/2$ year, $D = 3$ in three months, $r = 0.05$, and $P_E = 4$.

23. We are given that $S = 100$, $K = 100$, $T = 1/4$, $r = 0.06$, and $C_A = 1$. Is there an arbitrage opportunity?

24. Given that there are two put options with strikes at 40 and 50, with prices 3 and 14, respectively, show the arbitrage opportunity if the option maturity is $T$ and interest rates are $r$ for this maturity.

25. Given the price of three calls, construct an arbitrage strategy: $C(10) = 13$, $C(15) = 8$, $C(20) = 2$.

26. A call option on a stock is trading for $1.80. The option matures in two months. The stock is currently trading for $52 and will pay a dividend of $2 in one month. The risk-free rate of interest (on investments of all maturities) is 12%. Finally, suppose that the strike price of the option is $50. Examine whether there is an arbitrage opportunity in this problem. If so, show how it may be exploited to make a riskless profit.

27. ABC stock is currently trading at 100. There are three-month American options on ABC stock with strike prices 90, 100, and 110. The risk-free interest rate is 12% per year for all maturities in continuously compounded terms. Which of the following sets of prices offers an arbitrage opportunity? How can the opportunity be exploited?

    (a) The 90 call is selling for 10 1/4.

    (b) The 90 put is at 4, and the 100 put is at 3.

    (c) The 100 call is at 12, and the 110 call is at 1.

    (d) The 90 call is 13, the 100 call is 8, and the 110 call is 1.

# Chapter 10

# Early Exercise and Put-Call Parity

## 10.1 Introduction

The previous chapter examined no-arbitrage restrictions on individual option prices. Building on this material, this chapter examines two questions: what does no-arbitrage tell us about the relationship between

1. the prices of otherwise identical European and American options?
2. the prices of otherwise identical call and put options?

Regarding the first question, any wedge between the prices of American and otherwise identical European options must be solely on account of the right to exercise early. Thus, our analysis of this issue focuses on identifying when the right to early exercise may be valuable and when it is definitely not of value.

Regarding the second question, calls and puts appear, at least at a superficial level (for instance, judging from their payoff diagrams), to be very different financial instruments. Nonetheless, it is possible to relate their prices using no-arbitrage considerations. For *European* calls and puts, this relationship is an exact one, and is called *put-call parity*. Put-call parity is one of the most important pricing relationships in all of option pricing theory. For *American* options, the relationship is an inexact one; it takes on the form of inequalities, viz., upper and lower bounds on American put prices in terms of American call prices.

## 10.2 A Decomposition of Option Prices

We begin this chapter's analysis by describing a "decomposition" of option values, first for calls and then for puts. This decomposition makes intuitive our results concerning the optimality of early exercise, which is discussed next in Section 10.3. We also appeal to this decomposition at several points in later chapters, notably in Chapter 17 in discussing the behavior of the various option "greeks." The idea of such a decomposition appears in Figlewski, Silber, and Subrahmanyam (1992).

We retain the notation of Chapter 9 (see Table 9.1). As earlier, we refer to the asset underlying the options as a "stock," although the same arguments hold for other underlying assets too.

## A Decomposition of Call Prices

In Chapter 9, we showed that call prices must satisfy

$$C \geq S - PV(K) - PV(D) \tag{10.1}$$

As we noted in Section 9.5, the right-hand side of (10.1) corresponds to the value of a long forward position that *obligates* the holder to buy the underlying for $K$, while the left-hand side, of course, gives the holder the *right* to buy the underlying for $K$. The difference between these two values provides a natural measure of the *insurance value* (IV) of an option:

$$IV(C) = C - [S - PV(K) - PV(D)] \tag{10.2}$$

Equivalently, we may write

$$C = S - PV(K) - PV(D) + IV(C) \tag{10.3}$$

Now, add and subtract $K$ to the right-hand side of this expression, and rearrange the terms to obtain:

$$C = (S - K) + (K - PV(K)) + IV(C) - PV(D) \tag{10.4}$$

Expression (10.4) motivates a simple decomposition of call prices. The expression breaks the call value into four parts.

- The first part $(S - K)$ is called the *intrinsic value* of the call and measures how deep in-the-money the call is at present. The intrinsic value can be positive, zero, or negative. Ceteris paribus, the higher is the intrinsic value (i.e., the deeper we are in-the-money today), the deeper we are likely to finish in-the-money, so the higher is call value.
- The second term $(K - PV(K))$ is what we shall call the *time value* of the call. The time value of a call is always positive (or at least non-negative). The call gives us the right to buy the underlying at a price of $K$ at time $T$. In present value terms, the strike price we pay is worth only $PV(K)$ today; the longer is the call's maturity or the higher are interest rates, the lower is this present value. The time value of the call measures the interest savings we obtain from this deferred purchase.
- The third term $IV(C)$ is the *insurance value* of the call. It measures the value of "optionality" and is always positive. The call gives us the right to buy the underlying at $K$, but we are not obligated to buy at that price. By waiting, it is possible that the price of the underlying may fall below $K$, so we are able to buy at a cheaper price. The insurance value measures the value of this downside protection.
- The last term $-PV(D)$ represents the impact of *payouts* on the underlying during the life of the call. Since payouts lower the price of the underlying, they hurt the holders of calls, so the impact of payouts on calls is always negative.

In words, we may represent this decomposition as

Call Price $=$ Intrinsic Value $+$ Time Value $+$ Insurance Value $+$ Impact of Payouts

Before discussing this decomposition and its use in greater detail, we present the corresponding decomposition of put values.

## A Decomposition of Put Prices

In Chapter 9, we showed that put prices must satisfy

$$P \geq PV(K) + PV(D) - S \tag{10.5}$$

As we noted in Section 9.5, the right-hand side of (10.5) is the value of a short forward position that *obligates* the holder to sell the underlying for $K$, while the left-hand side is an option that gives the holder the *right* to sell the underlying for $K$. The difference between the two sides provides a natural measure of the insurance value of the put:

$$IV(P) = P - [PV(K) + PV(D) - S] \qquad (10.6)$$

Rewriting (10.6), we obtain

$$P = PV(K) + PV(D) - S + IV(P) \qquad (10.7)$$

Adding and subtracting $K$ to the right-hand side, we finally arrive at a decomposition similar to that of the call:

$$P = (K - S) - (K - PV(K)) + IV(P) + PV(D) \qquad (10.8)$$

Expression (10.8) breaks the value of a put into four components:

- The *intrinsic value* of the put $K - S$.
- The *time value* of the put $-(K - PV(K))$.
- The *insurance value* of the put $IV(P)$.
- The impact of *payouts* $PV(D)$.

In words, we can express the put decomposition as:

Put Price = Intrinsic Value + Time Value + Insurance Value + Impact of Payouts

Two differences between calls and puts should be highlighted:

1. In a call, we pay the strike price upon exercise, but in a put, we receive the strike price upon exercise. So while the time value of a call is *positive* (there are interest savings from deferred purchase), that of a put is *negative* (there are interest losses from the deferred sale).
2. Payouts depress the price of the underlying, thereby hurting calls and benefiting puts. So the impact of payouts is *negative* for a call and *positive* for a put.

## Comments on the Decompositions

The intrinsic and time values of an option have simple structures. Aside from the fixed strike price $K$, intrinsic value depends on only one variable: the current price $S$ of the stock. An increase in $S$ increases the intrinsic value of a call and decreases that of a put. Time value is a function of only two factors: interest rates and the remaining time to maturity. An increase in interest rates or an increase in the option's time to maturity increases the time value of a call since it results in larger interest savings from deferred exercise; conversely, it decreases (makes more negative) the time value of a put.

Insurance value is more complex; as a measure of the impact of optionality, it is, in principle, affected by all the parameters that could affect option value. For instance, an increase in $S$ makes it less likely that a call will finish out-of-the-money. This reduces the value of optionality and so the call's insurance value. (This is why an increase of $1 in $S$ increases the call value by less than the dollar increase in intrinsic value, or the payment of a dividend affects option values by less than $PV(D)$.) Similarly, the time value $K - PV(K)$ overstates the impact of interest rates on an option; the likelihood that the interest costs/savings may not be realized because the option lapses unexercised is folded into and reflected in the option's insurance value.

But the insurance value is especially affected by *volatility* and *time*. In the absence of volatility, insurance value—the right to do something without the obligation to do it—is trivial: the option will either be exercised for sure or not be exercised for sure. As volatility increases, larger price swings become more likely, so the importance of downside protection increases. This increases the insurance value for both calls and puts. Time also matters; for a given level of volatility, a greater time to maturity allows for greater price swings and so makes insurance value more important.

## Depth-in-the-Money and the Decomposition

As option depth-in-the-money (or "moneyness") changes, the components of option value also change in relative importance. For an option that is deep in-the-money, intrinsic value is by far the most important component of option value (by definition, such options have large intrinsic values). Time value is the next most important since there is a high probability of garnering the interest savings reflected in time value. But insurance value matters relatively little. Insurance value matters primarily to the extent that optionality is important, and for a deep in-the-money option, the chances of going out-of-the-money are slight, so optionality is not very important.

Conversely, for deep out-of-the-money options, insurance value is the most important component of option value and intrinsic value the least. With negative intrinsic value, the only reason such options have positive value at all is the hope that volatility will push the option into-the-money. For options that are at- or near-the-money, time value and insurance value are both important, though, loosely speaking, insurance value will dominate since it is the likelihood of volatility pushing the option into-the-money that gives the option value in the first place.

## Using the Decomposition: A Simple Illustration

As an example of how these ideas may be used to obtain an intuitive feel for option risk, consider how the passage of time affects European option values. Suppose, for simplicity, that the options are written on a non-dividend-paying stock.

The passage of time reduces the time to maturity of the option. This affects the insurance value and time value of the option. For calls, a lower time to maturity means a lower insurance value *and* a lower time value. Ceteris paribus, this means call values decline as time passes, i.e., calls exhibit "time-decay." In the language of Chapter 17, the *theta* of the call (its reaction to the passage of time) is negative.

But for puts, the effect is ambiguous: a lower time to maturity reduces insurance value but increases time value. If the time value effect dominates (as will generally be the case for deep in-the-money puts), the put value will *increase*. If the insurance value effect dominates (as will typically be the case for near-the-money and out-of-the-money puts), put values will decrease. Thus, while the theta of a European put is generally negative, it can be positive for deep in-the-money puts.

# 10.3  The Optimality of Early Exercise

Any difference in the prices of American options and their European counterparts must come from the right to exercise the option early. We examine when this right is of value and what factors give it value. We show that under some conditions, the right to early exercise is of *no* value; in such cases, the prices of American and European options must coincide. We examine calls first.

## The Early Exercise of American Calls

When a call is exercised, the holder receives the intrinsic value of the call at that point: the holder pays $K$ and receives a stock worth $S$ for a net gain of $S - K$. Thus, the holder of an American call has three possible courses of action open to him at any point:

- he can exercise the call immediately and receive its intrinsic value $S - K$;
- he can sell the call and realize its market price $C_A$; or
- he can do nothing and retain a call worth $C_A$ in his portfolio.

The second and third alternatives have the same value at any given point in time, so we shall not treat them separately. The optimality of early exercise may be judged by comparing the first alternative to the others. Note that we always have $C_A \geq S - K$ since an American call can never trade for less than its intrinsic value. Thus, the question more precisely is whether we have (a) $C_A > S - K$, in which case early exercise is strictly suboptimal, or (b) $C_A = S - K$, in which case early exercise becomes optimal. We examine this question in two stages, first when there are no dividends on the underlying (during the option's life) and then when dividends may exist.

## American Calls on Non-Dividend-Paying Assets

When there are no dividends, the call value is given by

$$C_A = (S - K) + (K - PV(K)) + IV(C) \tag{10.9}$$

So, the difference between selling the call and exercising it immediately is

$$C_A - (S - K) = (K - PV(K)) + IV(C) \tag{10.10}$$

This difference is strictly positive since each term on the right-hand side is positive. This means *an American call on a non-dividend-paying asset should never be exercised early*. An option holder who wishes to convert the option to cash is strictly better off selling the call than exercising it.

Intuitively speaking, what drives this result? The call gives you the right to buy the underlying stock for the fixed amount $K$ at any time over the option's life. When you exercise early, you are giving up two things. One is time value, the interest lost because you could have always bought the stock for the same price $K$ later. (This is the first term on the right-hand side of (10.10).) The other is insurance value, the possibility that by waiting, the stock price may fall and you may be able to buy the stock at a cheaper price than $K$. (This is the second term on the right-hand side of (10.10).) If there are no dividends on the stock during the call's remaining life, you receive no compensating benefits. This means the call is worth more "alive" than "dead," and makes early exercise suboptimal.

Note that it is not important for these arguments that the holder of the call wishes to buy the stock to hold on to it (at least up to the option maturity date). As long as there is some investor in the market who desires to hold the stock—a necessary condition if the stock price is to be above zero—such an investor would be willing to pay strictly more for the call than its intrinsic value because of the time value and insurance value the call provides.

## American Calls on Dividend-Paying Assets

When dividends are nonzero, the call value takes the form

$$C_A = (S - K) + (K - PV(K)) + IV(C) - PV(D) \tag{10.11}$$

Thus, the difference between the value of the call and the value of immediate exercise is

$$C_A - (S - K) = (K - PV(K)) + IV(C) - PV(D) \tag{10.12}$$

The first two terms on the right-hand side of this expression are positive, but the third term is negative. Thus, we cannot assert that the call is worth strictly more "alive" than "dead." That is, early exercise of a call on a dividend-paying asset could be optimal.

It is easy to see why. Dividends offer a countervailing benefit to the loss of time and insurance value from early exercise. By exercising prior to the ex-dividend date, the holder of the option can receive the dividends, but delaying exercise past the ex-dividend date causes the dividends to be lost. Thus, there is now a trade-off between retaining time and insurance value—the first two terms on the right-hand side of (10.12)—and receiving the dividends—the last term on the right-hand side of (10.12). If the former dominates, early exercise will remain suboptimal; if the latter, it is optimal to exercise immediately.

We can further sharpen this conclusion. The *only* motive for exercising the call early is to obtain the dividends. So, if at all it is optimal to exercise early, the investor is best off by exercising the call just before the stock goes ex-dividend. Such a strategy would result in the investor's retaining the time value and insurance value as long as possible while still obtaining the dividends. This point simplifies the pricing of American calls: the optimality of early exercise does not have to be checked at every point but only at points just before the ex-dividend dates.

These observations are useful at more than just an abstract level. In Section 10.4 ("Put-Call Parity, Insurance Value, and Rules of Thumb for Early Exercise"), we explain how rules of thumb commonly used in practice to gauge the optimality of early exercise can be understood precisely in terms of the trade-off described here.

The nature of the trade-off also makes it easy to see the conditions that make early exercise more likely. For example, early exercise becomes more likely to be optimal if

- dividends are high (this increases the benefits from early exercise).
- volatility is low (this results in a low insurance value, reducing the loss from early exercise).
- interest rates are low (this results in a low time value, reducing the loss from early exercise).

For examples that illustrate the optimality of early exercise of American calls in the presence of dividends, see Chapter 12, particularly Section 12.6 and the Exercises.

## The Early Exercise of American Puts

The early-exercise analysis for puts follows similar lines to that for calls, but the results, as we shall see, are quite different. When a put is exercised, the holder receives the intrinsic value of the put at that point: the holder gives up a stock worth $S$ and receives $K$ in exchange for a net gain of $K - S$. Thus, the holder of an American put has three possible courses of action open to her at any point:

- she can exercise the put immediately and receive its intrinsic value $K - S$;
- she can sell the put and realize its market price $P_A$; or
- she can do nothing and retain a put worth $P_A$ in her portfolio.

The second and third alternatives have the same value at any given point in time, so we shall not treat them separately. The optimality of early exercise may be judged by comparing the first alternative to the others. Note that we always have $P_A \geq K - S$ since an American put can never trade for less than its intrinsic value. Thus, the question more precisely is whether we have (a) $P_A > K - S$, in which case early exercise is strictly suboptimal, or (b) $P_A = K - S$, in which case early exercise becomes optimal. Once again, we proceed in two stages, first when there are no dividends on the underlying, and then when dividends may exist.

## American Puts on Non-Dividend-Paying Assets

When there are no dividends, the value $P_A$ of the put has the decomposition

$$P_A = (K - S) - (K - PV(K)) + IV(P) \qquad (10.13)$$

Exercising the put early gives the holder its intrinsic value $K - S$. Thus, the difference between the put value and the value of immediate exercise is

$$P_A - (K - S) = -(K - PV(K)) + IV(P) \qquad (10.14)$$

The second term on the right-hand side, the insurance value of the put, is positive, but the first term on the right-hand side, the time value of the put, is negative. Thus, the right-hand side may not be strictly positive, so we cannot rule out the optimality of early exercise for the put. (Note the contrast with calls here: as we have seen, early exercise can *never* be optimal for calls on a non-dividend-paying asset.)

The intuition behind this result is itself captured in the right-hand side of (10.14). Delaying exercise of the put means receiving the strike price later, so results in a loss of interest that could otherwise have been earned on the strike price received. This negative time-value effect is the first term on the right-hand side of (10.14). On the other hand, delaying exercise results in retaining the insurance value of the put (here, retaining the possibility that the stock could be sold for a higher price later); this is the second term in (10.14). The trade-off between these effects determines whether early exercise is optimal or not. Anything that reduces the insurance value or increases time value makes early exercise more likely to be optimal. For instance, early exercise is more likely to be optimal if

- volatility is low (this reduces the insurance value lost from early exercise).
- interest rates are high (this increases the time value gained by early exercise).

For examples that illustrate the optimality of early exercise of puts on non-dividend-paying assets, see Section 12.7 and the exercises in Chapter 12. See also the discussion on the option theta in Chapter 17.

## American Puts on Dividend-Paying Assets

With nonzero dividends, the decomposition of the put price is

$$P_A = (K - S) - (K - PV(K)) + IV(P) + PV(D) \qquad (10.15)$$

The difference between the put value and the value $K - S$ of immediate exercise is

$$P_A - (K - S) = -(K - PV(K)) + IV(P) + PV(D) \qquad (10.16)$$

The first term on the right-hand side is negative, but the second and third terms are positive. Thus, we cannot assert that the difference must be positive; that is, it may be optimal to exercise the put early.

The intuitive underpinnings of the result are clear. Delaying exercise of the put means receiving the strike price later, so there is a negative time-value effect. However, by delaying exercise, the put holder retains insurance value (the possibility that the stock can be sold for a higher price later) and obtains the dividends. The trade-off between these costs and benefits of early exercise determines the optimality of exercise. For example, early exercise is more likely to be optimal if

- volatility is low (this lowers insurance value, reducing the losses from early exercise).
- interest rates are high (this results in larger time value gains from early exercise).
- dividends are low (cost of early exercise is reduced).

In the next section, these results on early exercise will be used to identify the pricing relationship between American calls and otherwise identical American puts.

# 10.4 Put-Call Parity

We now turn our attention to the relationship between calls and otherwise identical (same underlying, strike, and maturity) put options. The common strike and maturity of the options are denoted $K$ and $T$, respectively. The analysis proceeds in four steps. We look first at European options on non-dividend-paying assets; then at European options on dividend-paying assets; then at American options on non-dividend-paying assets; and finally at American options on dividend-paying assets.

## European Options on Non-Dividend-Paying Assets

Let a call and put be given. As usual, denote by $PV(K)$ the present value of an amount $K$ receivable at $T$. Consider the following portfolios:

**Portfolio A**  Long one call
Investment of $PV(K)$ for maturity at $T$

**Portfolio B**  Long one put
Long one unit of stock

The cost and payoff information from these portfolios is summarized in Table 10.1. The initial cost of Portfolio A is the cost of the call plus the amount of the investment, which is $C_E + PV(K)$. That of Portfolio B is the sum of the prices of the put and the stock, which is $P_E + S$. The time-$T$ values of the two portfolios are determined in the usual way:

- If $S_T < K$:
  - The call in Portfolio A is worthless, while the investment is worth $K$. Total value of Portfolio A: $K$.
  - The put in Portfolio B is worth $K - S_T$ and the stock is worth $S_T$. Total value of Portfolio B: $K$.
- If $S_T \geq K$:
  - The call in Portfolio A is worth $S_T - K$ and the investment is worth $K$. Total value of Portfolio A: $S_T$.
  - The put in Portfolio B is worthless, while the stock is worth $S_T$. Total value of Portfolio B: $S_T$.

Thus, the portfolios have identical values in all circumstances at time $T$. Moreover, neither portfolio has interim cash flows since there are no dividends on the stock and the options cannot be exercised early. Therefore, the initial cost of the two portfolios must also be the same. That is, we must have

$$C_E + PV(K) = P_E + S \qquad (10.17)$$

Expression (10.17) is called *put-call parity*. It provides an exact relationship between the prices of European calls and puts that are otherwise identical. Before exploring the

**TABLE 10.1**
Portfolios A and B:
Costs and Payoffs

| | | Portfolio Value at $T$ in the Event | |
|---|---|---|---|
| | Initial Cost | $S_T < K$ | $S_T \geq K$ |
| Portfolio A | $C_E + PV(K)$ | $0 + K = K$ | $S_T - K + K = S_T$ |
| Portfolio B | $P_E + S$ | $K - S_T + S_T = K$ | $0 + S_T = S_T$ |

extension of this relationship to dividends and early exercise, we first take a detour through some of the uses of this result.

## Uses of Put-Call Parity

One of the most well-known results in option pricing, put-call parity is also one of the most useful. The first and most obvious use of the result is in the valuation problem. Once we can price European calls on non-dividend-paying assets, we can derive the prices of the corresponding put options using (10.17).

Second, as an immediate consequence, put-call parity can be used to check for arbitrage opportunities resulting from relative mispricing of calls and puts. For example, if we find $C_E + PV(K) > P_E + S$, then the call is overvalued relative to the put. We can buy Portfolio B, sell Portfolio A, and make an arbitrage profit. Conversely, if we find $C_E + PV(K) < P_E + S$, the put is overvalued relative to the call. Arbitrage profits can be made by selling Portfolio B and buying Portfolio A.

Third, rearranging the put-call parity expression tells us how to create synthetic instruments from traded ones. For example, since put-call parity tells us that $P = C + PV(K) - S$, we can create a synthetic long put by buying a call, investing $PV(K)$, and shorting one unit of the underlying. Similarly, we can create a

- synthetic long call by buying the put and the stock and borrowing $PV(K)$.
- synthetic long position in the stock by buying the call, investing $PV(K)$, and shorting the put.
- synthetic long forward position by buying the call and shorting the put.
- synthetic long zero-coupon bond with face value $K$ and maturity $T$ by buying the put and the stock and shorting the call.

Of course, synthetic short positions in each of these instruments can be created simply by reversing the above portfolios.

Fourth, put-call parity may be used to judge *relative* sensitivity to parameter changes, i.e., the *difference* in the reactions of calls and puts to changes in parameter values. Rearranging put-call parity, we have

$$C_E - P_E = S - PV(K) \qquad \textbf{(10.18)}$$

Since (10.18) is an identity, the difference in the changes in call and put values caused by a parameter change must be the same as the change in the right-hand side of (10.18). So, for example, suppose $S$ changes by \$1. Denote the change this causes in call and put values by $dC$ and $dP$, respectively. The change in the left-hand side of (10.18) is then $dC - dP$, so we must have

$$dC - dP = 1$$

That is, the change in call value is a dollar more than the change in put value.

A similar procedure can be used to identify the difference in call and put sensitivities to changes in other parameters such as the maturity $T$ or the interest rate $r$. In Chapter 17 where we discuss the option greeks, we repeatedly appeal to put-call parity to explain the responses of calls and puts to changes in key parameter values.

## European Options on Dividend-Paying Assets

Modifying the put-call parity arguments to allow for dividends is easy. The only difference that dividends create is that in Portfolio B, there will be an interim cash flow when the underlying pays a dividend. There is no corresponding interim cash flow in A. Thus, if we modify the definition of Portfolio A to create an additional interim cash flow of $D$, we can use the same arguments again.

So consider the following modification in the definition of the portfolios:

| | |
|---|---|
| **Portfolio A** | Long one call |
| | Investment of $PV(K)$ for maturity at $T$ |
| | Investment of $PV(D)$ for maturity on the dividend date |
| **Portfolio B** | Long one put |
| | Long one unit of stock |

This changes the initial cost of Portfolio A to $C_E + PV(K) + PV(D)$; the initial cost of Portfolio B remains the same. The portfolios have the same value at $T$. By construction, they also have the same interim cash flows. Therefore, the initial costs of the two portfolios must be the same, so:

$$C_E + PV(K) + PV(D) = P_E + S \tag{10.19}$$

Expression (10.19) is the put-call parity relationship between the prices of European calls and puts on dividend-paying assets.

## American Options on Non-Dividend-Paying Assets

When the options concerned are American in style, it does not suffice to compare the portfolio values at maturity alone since one or both options may be exercised prior to maturity. Indeed, it becomes impossible to derive a "parity" (i.e., exact) relationship between the prices of calls and puts. However, an inequality-based relationship can still be derived, viz., that

$$C_A + PV(K) \leq P_A + S \leq C_A + K \tag{10.20}$$

To derive (10.20), consider again the following two portfolios (in the no-dividends setting), and suppose that the options are American in style:

| | |
|---|---|
| **Portfolio A** | Long one call |
| | Investment of $PV(K)$ for maturity at $T$ |
| **Portfolio B** | Long one put |
| | Long one unit of stock |

The initial cost of Portfolio A is $C_A + PV(K)$ while that of Portfolio B is $P_A + S$. Now note the following:

- An American call on a non-dividend-paying asset will never be exercised early (Section 10.3), so we must have $C_A = C_E$.
- Early exercise could be optimal for puts even on non-dividend-paying assets (Section 10.3), so in general we have $P_A \geq P_E$.

Therefore, we have

$$C_A + PV(K) = C_E + PV(K), \text{ and } P_A + S \geq P_E + S \tag{10.21}$$

Moreover, from European put-call parity,

$$C_E + PV(K) = P_E + S \tag{10.22}$$

Putting (10.22) and (10.21) together, we obtain the first inequality in (10.20):

$$C_A + PV(K) \leq P_A + S \tag{10.23}$$

We now derive the second inequality:

$$P_A + S \leq C_A + K \tag{10.24}$$

Consider the following portfolios:

**Portfolio A′**   Long one call
Investment of $K$ rolled over at the money-market rate

**Portfolio B′**   Long one put
Long one unit of stock

The initial cost of Portfolio A′ is $C_A + K$, while that of Portfolio B′ is $P_A + S$. Suppose we buy Portfolio A′ and sell Portfolio B′. Since we hold the call, we can always choose to not exercise it until $T$ (this is anyway optimal since there are no dividends). However, the put may be exercised in the interim, so there are two possibilities concerning cash flows from this strategy:

1. The put is exercised early. In this case, we pay $K$ and receive one unit of the stock. We use the stock received to close out the short stock position. The net effect: we are left with the call (and whatever interest we earned on the strike price so far) for a positive net cash flow.

2. The put is held until maturity. In this case, mimicking the arguments leading to the payoffs derived in Table 10.1 shows that the net value of our position is just the interest earned on rolling over $K$ to maturity.

Thus, the strategy outlined leaves us with a positive cash flow at maturity. To avoid arbitrage, it must have a positive cost, which is precisely the statement that (10.24) holds.

Combining (10.23) and (10.24), we obtain (10.20), the closest we can get to a parity relationship for American options.

## American Options on Dividend-Paying Assets

In the presence of dividends, early exercise of the call may also become optimal, so we cannot assume that $C_A = C_E$ as we did in the no-dividends case. So, we adopt a different tack, one that exploits the motive for early exercise of American calls. Consider a choice between the following portfolios: (a) an American call with strike $K$ and maturity $T$, or (b) a European call with strike $K$ and maturity $T$, *plus* an investment of $PV(D)$. We claim that the second portfolio must cost at least as much as the first, that is, we must have

$$C_A \leq C_E + PV(D) \tag{10.25}$$

A simple intuition underlies (10.25). As we have seen, the only motive for exercising an American call early is to receive the dividends on the stock, but early exercise also means giving up the call's insurance and time values. In the first portfolio, the investor faces this trade-off between exercising to capture the dividends and retaining the call to preserve its insurance and time values. In the second portfolio, the investor gets to receive the dividends even while retaining the call's time and insurance value up to maturity. It follows that the second portfolio must be more valuable.

If we add $PV(K)$ to both sides of expression (10.25), we obtain

$$C_A + PV(K) \leq C_E + PV(K) + PV(D) \tag{10.26}$$

Now, European put-call parity on dividend-paying stocks tells us that

$$C_E + PV(K) + PV(D) = P_E + S \tag{10.27}$$

Combining the information in (10.26) and (10.27), we obtain

$$C_A + PV(K) \leq P_E + S \tag{10.28}$$

Further, we must always have $P_A \geq P_E$. Using this on the right-hand side of (10.28), we finally get

$$C_A + PV(K) \leq P_A + S \tag{10.29}$$

Expression (10.29) is the closest we can get to a put-call parity relationship for American options on dividend-paying assets. This expression is identical to the lower bound derived for American options on non-dividend-paying assets. In particular, the dividends $D$ do not enter the expression explicitly because they have been subsumed in the value of the call; see (10.25).

As we did in the non-dividends case, we can also find an upper bound for the American put in terms of the call, namely,

$$P_A + S \leq C_A + K + PV(D) \tag{10.30}$$

The derivation of (10.30) uses similar arguments to the derivation of the no-dividends upper bound (10.24). The construction of the portfolios to support this inequality should by now be familiar to the reader. The details are left as an exercise.

## Put-Call Parity, Insurance Value, and Rules of Thumb for Early Exercise

Traders in practice often use rules of thumb for determining early exercise of American options. A typical rule for American calls, for example, runs along the following lines:

> Exercise the call on the day before the stock goes ex-dividend if the dividend on the stock is greater than the price of an otherwise identical put plus forgone interest on the strike price; otherwise do not exercise.

The first part of this rule—exercising the day before the stock goes ex-dividend—is easily justified: as we have seen in Section 10.3, if at all American calls are exercised early, they should be exercised just before the stock goes ex-dividend. A rationale for the second part of the rule—exercise if the dividend on the stock is greater than the price of an otherwise identical put plus forgone interest on the strike price—is obtained by combining put-call parity and the analysis in Section 10.3.

Recall from Section 10.3 that early exercise is optimal on a call if the value of dividends received exceeds the time value plus insurance value of the call. The time value of the call is proxied by the forgone interest on the strike price from early exercise. What about the insurance value? For the answer, compare expression (10.3) and the statement of European put-call parity (10.19). The comparison reveals that for European calls, the insurance value of the call is just the value of the corresponding European put! This is both intuitive and logical. The insurance value is the difference between the value of the call and the value of the corresponding forward. This difference is exactly the European put as a glance at their payoff diagrams reveals (see Figure 10.1). Similarly, the insurance value of a European put is the value of the corresponding European call.

Now, this identification of insurance value with the corresponding put or call does not hold exactly for American options since we do not have a parity expression for American options, but the upper and lower bounds (10.29) and (10.30) suggest it is not a bad approximation in general. If we accept it as an approximation, then the rule that early exercise is optimal

**FIGURE 10.1**
Call Minus Forward
Equals Put

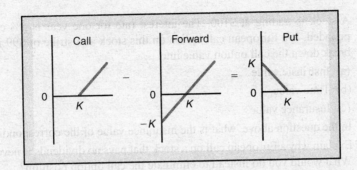

whenever dividends exceed insurance value and time value is just the rule of thumb described above.

## Put-Call Parity with a Continuous Dividend Yield

In the analysis above, we have assumed that dividend payments, if they exist, are discrete. As we have seen earlier in the book, in many cases (such as currencies or stock indices), payouts on the underlying are more naturally described as continuous yields at a rate $q$. The put-call parity expression (10.19) for European options is easily modified to handle this case.

The key step in the modification is to note the following: to end up with one unit of the underlying at date $T$, we need to buy only $e^{-qT}$ units of it today. We have seen this earlier in the book, but we repeat the arguments here:

- Suppose the underlying is a foreign currency paying a continuously-compounded interest rate of $q$. Then, one unit of the foreign currency invested at the rate $q$ will grow to $e^{qT}$ units by maturity. So $e^{-qT}$ units of the foreign currency invested today at the rate $q$ will provide us with $e^{-qT} \times e^{qT} = 1$ unit of the foreign currency by date $T$.

- Suppose the underlying is a stock index with a dividend yield of $q$. Then, reinvesting all the dividends received into buying more of the index will cause our holding of the index to grow at the rate $q$. Thus, if we start with $e^{-qT}$ units of the index today, we will end up with one unit at date $T$.

Let $r$ denote the (domestic) interest rate in continuously-compounded terms, so $PV(K) = e^{-rT}K$. Now consider the following portfolios:

**Portfolio A**    Long one European call
Investment of $e^{-rT}K$ for maturity at $T$

**Portfolio B**    Long one European put
Long $e^{-qT}$ units of the underlying

The cost of Portfolio A is $C_E + e^{-rT}K$, while that of Portfolio B is $P_E + e^{-qT}S$, where $S$ is the current price of the underlying (current price of one unit of the foreign currency or current level of the index). Neither portfolio has any net interim cash flows. By time $T$, Portfolio B has one unit of the underlying. The same arguments used to derive the payoffs in Table 10.1 show that the two portfolios have identical values at time $T$. Thus, their initial costs must be the same:

$$C_E + e^{-rT}K = P_E + e^{-qT}S \tag{10.31}$$

Equation (10.31) is the modified form of put-call parity for European options when the underlying has a continuous yield at rate $q$.

## 10.5 Exercises

1. A stock is trading at $100. The interest rate for one year is 5% continuously compounded. If a European call option on this stock at a strike of $99 is priced at $8.50, break down the call option value into
   (a) Instrinsic value.
   (b) Time value.
   (c) Insurance value.

2. In the question above, what is the insurance value of the corresponding put option?

3. Explain why a European call on a stock that pays no dividends is never exercised early. What would you do instead to eliminate the call option position?

4. Stock ABC pays no dividends. The current price of an American call on the stock at a strike of 41 is $4. The current stock price is $40. Compute the time value of the European put option if it is trading at a price of $3.

5. Stock ABC is trading at a price of $50. At a strike price of 55, there is a traded six-month American put. There are no dividends on the stock, and maturity of the option is a half year. If the half-year rate of interest is 5%, what must the minimum insurance value of the put be for the put not to be exercised?

6. Stock XYZ is trading at a price of $105. The American-style call option on XYZ with maturity one year and strike 100 is traded in the market. The term structure of interest rates is flat at 1% and there is a dividend payment in six months of $8. What is the maximum insurance value for the call at which it still makes sense to exercise it?

7. Assume that the true formula for pricing options is unknown, e.g., Black-Scholes is not applicable. Hence, you are asked to use the following approximation for the insurance value of a put option:

$$IV(P) = \exp\left(\frac{S}{K}\frac{\sigma^2}{T}\right)$$

   where $S$ is the current price of the stock, $K$ is the strike price, $\sigma$ is the volatility of the stock return, and $T$ is option maturity.

   You are given that $S = 100$, $K = 105$, and the interest rate $r = 1\%$. Option maturity is $T = 1$ year, and there are no dividends.

   What is the maximum volatility for which early exercise of the option is induced?

8. If a stock does not pay dividends, what is the relationship between call prices and interest rates for early exercise of a put to occur?

9. You are given the following data about options: $S = 60$, $K = 60$, $r = 2\%$, $T = 0.5$, $D = 0$ (dividends). If the American call is trading at a price of $5, what is the minimum price of the American put?

10. In the preceding question, refine the lower bound on the American put if there is a dividend to be received after three months of an amount of $2. Assume that the term structure is flat and the American call with dividends is worth $6.

11. Company WHY pays no dividends. Its stock price is $30. The three-month European call at strike 29 is trading at $3. The three-month interest rate is 1%. What is the price of the European put?

12. Stock ABC is trading at $43 and pays no dividends. If the six-month 50-strike call and put are equal in price, what is the six-month risk-free interest rate?

13. Stock XYZ is currently priced at $50. It pays no dividends. The one-year maturity 60-strike European call and put are trading at $10 and $12, respectively. What is the one-year forward price on the stock?

14. You observe the following European option prices in the OTC market on stock QWY, which does not pay dividends:

| T (years) | Call | Puts | Strike |
|-----------|------|------|--------|
| 0.5 | 7 | 5 | 100 |
| 1.0 | 19 | 12 | 100 |

However, the firm you work for does not subscribe to price quote services for the equity and interest rate markets. All you know is that the term structure of interest rates is flat.

You receive a call from a client wishing to buy a forward on the stock QWY for two years. What price should you quote for this contract?

15. You are working on an option trading desk in charge of arbitrage trading. The following data is presented to you on screen, and you immediately see an arbitrage. What is it, and how much money can you make risk free?

$$S = 60 \qquad T = 0.25 \qquad C_E = 5$$
$$K = 60 \qquad D = 0 \qquad P_E = 3$$
$$r = 3\%$$

16. Stock DEF is trading at $100 and is expected to pay a dividend of $3 in three months. The European call at strike 95 with half-year maturity is priced at $7. If the flat term structure of interest rates is 5%, find a lower bound on the price of the American put option.

17. Stock CBA is trading at price $50 and is not expected to pay any dividends. The following puts are traded at maturity in three months:

$$P(K = 50) = 3$$
$$P(K = 60) = 15$$

The three-month interest rate is 2%. What is the price of a (50,60) bullish call spread?

18. Stock KLM trades at $100 and pays no dividends. The one-year straddle struck at $102 is trading at a price of $10. The one-year interest rate is 2%. Find the price of the one-year European call and put.

19. An investor buys a call on ABC stock with a strike price of $K$ and writes a put with the same strike price and maturity. Assuming the options are European and that there are no dividends expected during the life of the underlying, how much should such a portfolio cost?

20. Use put-call parity to show that the cost of a butterfly spread created using European puts is identical to the cost of a butterfly spread using European calls.

21. A stock is trading at $S = 50$. There are one-month European calls and puts on the stock with a strike of 50. The call is trading at a price of $C_E = 3$. Assume that the one-month rate of interest (annualized) is 2% and that no dividends are expected on the stock over the next month.

    (a) What should be the arbitrage-free price of the put?

    (b) Suppose the put is trading at a price of $P_E = 2.70$. Are there any arbitrage opportunities?

22. A stock is trading at $S = 60$. There are one-month American calls and puts on the stock with a strike of 60. The call costs 2.50 while the put costs 1.90. No dividends are expected on the stock during the options' lives. If the one-month rate of interest (annualized) is 3%, show that there is an arbitrage opportunity available and explain how to take advantage of it.

# Chapter

# Option Pricing: An Introduction

## 11.1 Overview

The previous chapters examined option prices from two standpoints: restrictions imposed by no-arbitrage conditions (e.g., minimum and maximum prices for options) and "relative" pricing (e.g., how are call and put prices related?). Beginning with this chapter and over the next several, we move to a more difficult problem: the determination of individual option prices from information about the underlying.

The aim of this chapter is to build a strong foundation for the material to follow. A number of important concepts pertaining to option pricing and hedging are introduced and discussed here. This chapter:

- introduces the *binomial model*, which is one of the two canonical models of option pricing (the other being the Black-Scholes model);
- uses a one-period binomial model to illustrate the two general methods of identifying arbitrage-free option prices, namely *replication* and *risk-neutral pricing*;
- discusses dynamic replication strategies at an intuitive level, focusing especially on the concept of the *option delta*, its behavior, properties, and uses; and
- illustrates the idea of dynamic replication of options by presenting a case study of the dynamic hedging strategy known as *portfolio insurance*, which was immensely popular in the 1980s.

A good starting point for this material is the contrast between forward pricing and option pricing. We begin with this.

### Option Pricing Compared to Forward Pricing

As with forward, the basic idea behind pricing options is *replication*: we look to create identical payoffs to the options using positions in the underlying and investment/borrowing at the risk-free rate. However, replicating options involves complications that do not arise with forward.

With forward, there is a commitment to taking part in the trade underlying the contract. As we have seen, this makes it possible to replicate the outcome at maturity *without regard to how the price of the underlying evolves over time.*

With options, exercise occurs only if this is in the holder's interest. For European options, this depends on the underlying asset's price at maturity. For American options, it depends on the entire pattern of evolution of the asset's price since exercise may occur at any time. Thus, it is impossible to identify a "fair" price for options *without first positing a model of how the price of the underlying evolves over time.*

But we already knew this! As we observed in Chapter 8, option payoff diagrams show that *volatility*—the uncertainty anticipated in the price of the underlying—is a primary determinant of how much investors expect to make from options. This means one cannot value options without accounting for and modeling this uncertainty. This is called *model dependence*: our estimated option prices and hedging strategies will be only as good as our model of price evolution.

Over the years, a number of alternative models have been proposed in the option pricing literature. Two particularly popular ones are the *binomial model* and the *Black-Scholes model*. Both are used widely in practice for pricing options on equities, indices, exchange rates, and other underlyings. The Black-Scholes model is very well known and, indeed, is almost synonymous with option pricing, but it is somewhat technical and does not offer much intuition about option pricing and hedging. It also has some limitations; for example, it cannot easily handle early exercise.

The binomial model, in contrast, is an ideal starting point for understanding option pricing. The next section describes this model. Throughout this chapter, we refer to the underlying security as a "stock," although it could equally be an index level, exchange rate, or other price.

## 11.2   The Binomial Model

Look at the evolution of stock prices described in Figure 11.1. The current stock price is 58. After one period, the price takes on one of two values: it either moves up to 63 or down to 54. This is an example of a binomial model, more specifically, a one-period binomial model.

The general binomial model extends this to allow for several price changes. Price changes in the model occur at specified time points $t = 0, 1, 2, \ldots$. The calendar time between two time points is $h$ years, where $h$, a parameter of our choosing, can be very small (one day or less). The main assumption of the model is that given the price $S_t$ at time $t$, the price $S_{t+1}$ at time $t + 1$ takes on one of two possible values:

$$S_{t+1} = \begin{cases} u S_t, & \text{with probability } p \\ d S_t, & \text{with probability } 1 - p \end{cases} \qquad (11.1)$$

**FIGURE 11.1**
A One-Period
Binomial Model

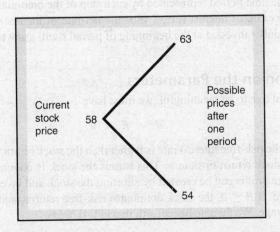

where $u > d$. The number $u$, called the "up" move, denotes the gross return on the stock over period $t$ if the price moves from $S_t$ to $uS_t$, while $d$, the "down" move, is the gross return if the stock price moves from $S_t$ to $dS_t$. In Figure 11.1, these are given, respectively, by $63/58 \approx 1.0862$ and $54/58 \approx 0.9310$.

## Is This a Bit Too Simple?

At first sight, the binomial model looks too simplistic to be taken seriously as a model of real-world price changes with price changes occurring only at specified times and only two (two!) possible prices when a change occurs. But the apparent simplicity of the model masks a rich and versatile analytical framework.

For example, the Black-Scholes model with its continuous price changes appears much more sophisticated, complex, and realistic than the binomial. Yet, as we show in Chapter 13, it is simple to choose the parameter values so that the binomial model resembles the Black-Scholes model arbitrarily closely. Thus, the binomial may be thought of as just a discrete version of the Black-Scholes model.

But this is only part of the story. The influential work of Dupire (1994), Derman and Kani (1994), and Rubinstein (1994) has shown that we can also go well beyond Black-Scholes with nonstandard binomial models. We elaborate further on this in Chapter 16.

## Volatility in the Binomial Model

Intuitively, volatility in the binomial model is related to the ratio $u/d$: the larger is this ratio, the wider are the "jaws" of the binomial model and the greater the variability of stock prices. This is made more formal in Chapter 13. In one common formulation of the binomial model we describe there, the parameters $u$ and $d$ are defined by

$$u = e^{\sigma\sqrt{h}} \qquad d = e^{-\sigma\sqrt{h}} \tag{11.2}$$

where $\sigma$ is the annualized volatility of the stock and $h$ the length in years of one period in the binomial tree. (The notion of annualized volatility is also made precise in Chapter 13.) From (11.2), the annualized volatility $\sigma$ is related to the ratio $u/d$ by

$$\sigma = \left[\frac{1}{2\sqrt{h}}\right] \ln\left(\frac{u}{d}\right) \tag{11.3}$$

## Interest Rates

To keep notation simple, we depart in two ways from our usual convention for interest rates. First, interest rates will not be in annualized terms; rather, we denote by $R$ the rate of interest applicable to the time period represented by each step of the binomial tree. Second, $R$ will denote the *gross* rate of interest (i.e., 1 plus the net rate of interest) expressed in *simple* terms. Thus, a dollar invested at the beginning of period $t$ will grow to $R$ dollars by period $t+1$.

## A Restriction on the Parameters

For the binomial tree to be meaningful, we must have

$$d < R < u \tag{11.4}$$

If $R \geq u$, then the risk-free interest rate is higher than the stock return in state $d$ and at least as high as the stock return in state $u$. This means the stock is *dominated* by the risk-free rate, so arbitrage profits can be created by shorting the stock and investing the proceeds at the risk-free rate. If $R \leq d$, the stock dominates risk-free returns, and the reverse strategy creates an arbitrage. We assume henceforth that (11.4) holds.

## What This Chapter Does

In practice, binomial models used to price options and other derivatives use at least 100 time steps (and very often more). In this first chapter on option pricing, we examine valuation and hedging in a *one-period* model. The main point of this exercise is to get an intuitive feel for the option pricing problem and for key concepts such as the option delta. Following this, Chapter 12 discusses the general multiperiod problem including considerations such as dividends and early exercise.

In both the current chapter and Chapter 12, the numbers $u$, $d$, and $p$ are taken to be known. In Chapter 13, we discuss how these values are determined.

# 11.3   Pricing by Replication in a One-Period Binomial Model

We work through a pair of examples that illustrate the mechanics of pricing by replication in the binomial setting. In both examples, we use the following parameter values:

- The initial stock price is $S = 100$.
- The price moves up by a factor of $u = 1.10$ with probability $p = 0.75$ or down by a factor of $d = 0.90$ with probability $1 - p = 0.25$.
- The risk-free rate of interest is $R = 1.02$. That is, a dollar invested at the beginning of the period grows with certainty to $1.02 at the end of the period.

Given this information, what are the prices of (a) a one-period call option with strike $K = 100$ and (b) a one-period put option with strike $K = 100$?

### Pricing the Call

The value of the call today is the present value of the payoffs it provides at maturity, so the first step is to identify these payoffs at maturity. If the up state occurs, the stock price is $uS = 110$ while the call gives us the right to buy the stock for 100; thus, the value of the stock, denoted $C_u$, is 10. In the down state, the stock price is only $dS = 90$, so the call lapses unexercised; its value $C_d$ is zero. This information is summarized in Figure 11.2.

What is the initial value $C$ of a call with these payoffs? Replication provides the answer. Consider a portfolio consisting of

- $\Delta_c$ units of stock.
- An amount $B_c$ invested at the risk-free rate $R$.

**FIGURE 11.2**

Pricing the One-Period Call

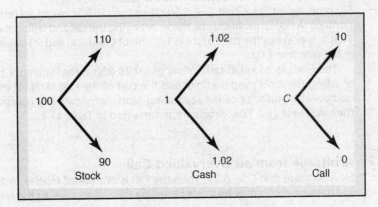

We want to choose $\Delta_c$ and $B_c$ so that the portfolio mimics the call. Both $\Delta_c$ and $B_c$ may be positive or negative. If $\Delta_c > 0$, we are buying or taking a long position in the stock; if $\Delta_c < 0$, we are selling or taking a short position in the stock. Similarly, $B_c > 0$ means we are investing at the rate $R$, while $B_c < 0$ means we are borrowing at the rate $R$.

For the portfolio to replicate the call, it must yield exactly the same payoffs as the call in *each* state. The call is worth 10 in the state $uS$. The portfolio value in this state is

$$110\,\Delta_c + 1.02\,B_c$$

since each unit of the stock is worth 110 in this state, and the risk-free rate on the borrowing/investment is $R = 1.02$. Similarly, the call is worth zero in the state $dS$, while the portfolio value in this state is

$$90\,\Delta_c + 1.02\,B_c$$

So, for the portfolio to replicate the call, two conditions must be satisfied:

$$110\,\Delta_c + 1.02\,B_c = 10 \qquad (11.5)$$

$$90\,\Delta_c + 1.02\,B_c = 0 \qquad (11.6)$$

This is a simple two-equation/two-unknown system. Subtracting the second equation from the first, we obtain $20\,\Delta_c = 10$, so

$$\Delta_c = \frac{1}{2} \qquad (11.7)$$

Substituting $\Delta_c = 1/2$ into the first equation and rearranging gives us $1.02\,B_c = -45$, so

$$B_c = -44.12 \qquad (11.8)$$

In words, the following portfolio perfectly replicates the call option: (a) a *long* position in 1/2 unit of the stock, and (b) borrowing of 44.12. Since $S = 100$, the initial cost of setting up this replicating portfolio is

$$\frac{1}{2}\,100 - 44.12 = 5.88 \qquad (11.9)$$

Thus, the price of the call must be $C = 5.88$! Any other price leads to arbitrage profits. We illustrate this by considering two scenarios.

---

### Example 11.1  Arbitrage from an Undervalued Call

Suppose, for instance, that $C = 5.50$. Then the call is *undervalued* relative to the replicating portfolio. A riskless profit may be made by buying the call and selling the replicating portfolio. That is, we (a) buy the call, (b) short 1/2 unit of the stock, and (c) invest 44.12 for one period at the rate $R = 1.02$.

This leads to an initial cash inflow of $+0.38$ (this is the difference between the proceeds of selling the replicating portfolio and the cost of the call). And, of course, there is no cash outflow at maturity since the replicating portfolio mimics (by construction) the payoffs of the call. These cash flow details are summarized in Table 11.1. ■

---

### Example 11.2  Arbitrage from an Overvalued Call

Now suppose that $C = 6.25$. Then the call is *overvalued* relative to the cost of replicating it. Arbitrage profits may be made by selling the call and selling the replicating portfolio: we

**TABLE 11.1**

Arbitrage from an
Undervalued Call

| Source | Initial Cash Flow | Cash Flow at Maturity | |
|---|---|---|---|
| | | State $u$ | State $d$ |
| Long call | −5.50 | +10.00 | 0 |
| Short 1/2 stock | +50.00 | −55.00 | −45.00 |
| Investment | −44.12 | +45.00 | +45.00 |
| Net | +0.38 | 0 | 0 |

**TABLE 11.2**

Arbitrage from an
Overvalued Call

| Source | Initial Cash Flow | Cash Flow at Maturity | |
|---|---|---|---|
| | | State $u$ | State $d$ |
| Short call | +6.25 | −10.00 | 0 |
| Long 1/2 stock | −50.00 | +55.00 | +45.00 |
| Borrowing | +44.12 | −45.00 | −45.00 |
| Net | +0.37 | 0 | 0 |

(a) sell the call, (b) buy 1/2 unit of the stock, and (c) borrow 44.12 for one period at the rate $R = 1.02$.

This leads to an initial cash inflow of +0.37 (the difference between the proceeds of selling the call and the cost of setting up the replicating portfolio). And, of course, there is no cash outflow at maturity once again since the replicating portfolio mimics the payoffs of the call. These cash flow details are summarized in Table 11.2. ∎

### What Happened to the Probability p?

Now for a question that has probably already struck the reader: why did the probability $p$ play no role in identifying the call's arbitrage-free price? The mechanical reason is that when we are replicating the option, we are re-creating its payoffs *state by state*. The probabilities of these states do not matter since we are not replicating "on average" (for example, by weighting each state by its likelihood).

A more subtle point is that information about $p$ is already embedded into the current stock price and, therefore, into the returns $u$ and $d$ on the stock. The price process represented by the binomial set-up implicitly assumes a market equilibrium that incorporates investors' degrees of risk-aversion and other factors. If we change the likelihoods of the two states, the equilibrium is upset, and the current price of the stock will change to reflect the changed equilibrium; this will, in turn, change $u$ and $d$. As an extreme example, consider what would happen if $p = 1$, that is, the stock were sure to fetch a price of 110 in one period. It is easy to see that its current price cannot then be 100; rather, it must be $110/1.02 = 107.85$. This alters $u$ (which is now equal to $R$) while $d$ becomes irrelevant.

### Pricing the Put Option

The arguments are essentially the same as the call. We begin by identifying the payoffs of the put at maturity. There are two possible prices of the security after one period: $uS = 110$ and $dS = 90$. In the state $u$, the put is valueless: you have the right to sell for 100 a security that is worth 110. In the state $d$, the put is worth $P_d = 10$. This information is summarized in Figure 11.3.

To replicate the put, consider a portfolio consisting of (a) $\Delta_p$ units of stock and (b) an investment of $B_p$. Once again, $\Delta_p$ and $B_p$ may be positive or negative with negative

**FIGURE 11.3**
Pricing the One-Period
Put

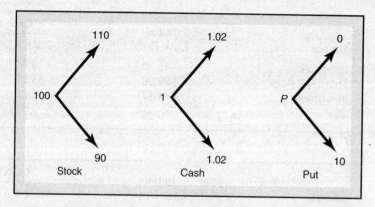

investment levels corresponding to borrowing. For the portfolio to replicate the put, it must produce the same outcome as the put in *each* state. By the same arguments used for the call, the portfolio is worth

$$110 \, \Delta_p + 1.02 \, B_p$$

in the state $u$, and

$$90 \, \Delta_p + 1.02 \, B_p$$

in the state $d$. Thus, for the portfolio to replicate the put, we must have

$$110 \, \Delta_p + 1.02 \, B_p = 0 \qquad\qquad \textbf{(11.10)}$$

$$90 \, \Delta_p + 1.02 \, B_p = 10 \qquad\qquad \textbf{(11.11)}$$

Subtracting the second equation from the first, we get $20 \, \Delta_p = -10$, or

$$\Delta_p = -\frac{1}{2}$$

Substituting this into the first equation and rearranging, we obtain $1.02 \, B_p = 55$, so

$$B_p = +53.92$$

In words, to replicate the put, we set up a portfolio consisting of (a) a *short* position in 1/2 unit of the stock and (b) an investment of 53.92. The initial cost of setting up this portfolio is

$$-\frac{1}{2}(100) + 53.92 \;=\; 3.92$$

Thus, the unique arbitrage-free price of the put is $P = 3.92$. The following two examples illustrate how any departures from this price result in arbitrage opportunities.

---

**Example 11.3**

### Arbitrage from an Undervalued Put

Suppose $P = 3.75$. Then the put is *undervalued* relative to the cost of replicating it. To create arbitrage profits, we buy the put and sell the replicating portfolio, i.e., we (a) buy the put, (b) buy 1/2 unit of the stock, and (c) borrow 53.92 for one period at the rate $R = 1.02$.

This leads to an initial cash inflow of +0.17 (the difference between the proceeds of selling the replicating portfolio and the cost of the put). There are no net cash flows at maturity

**TABLE 11.3**
Arbitrage from an
Undervalued Put

| Source | Initial Cash Flow | Cash Flow at Maturity | |
|---|---|---|---|
| | | State *u* | State *d* |
| Long put | −3.75 | 0 | +10.00 |
| Long 1/2 stock | −50.00 | +55.00 | +45.00 |
| Borrowing | +53.92 | −55.00 | −55.00 |
| Net | +0.17 | 0 | 0 |

**TABLE 11.4**
Arbitrage from an
Overvalued Put

| Source | Initial Cash Flow | Cash Flow at Maturity | |
|---|---|---|---|
| | | State *u* | State *d* |
| Short put | +4.10 | 0 | −10.00 |
| Short 1/2 stock | +50.00 | −55.00 | −45.00 |
| Investment | −53.92 | +55.00 | +55.00 |
| Net | +0.18 | 0 | 0 |

since the replicating portfolio mimics the outcome of the put. These cash flow details are summarized in Table 11.3. ∎

**Example 11.4**  **Arbitrage from an Overvalued Put**

Now suppose that $P = 4.10$. Then, the put is *overvalued* relative to the cost of replicating it. To make arbitrage profits, we sell the put and buy the replicating portfolio: (a) sell the put, (b) sell 1/2 unit of the stock, and (c) invest 53.92 for one period at the rate $R = 1.02$.

This leads to an initial cash inflow of +0.18 (the difference between the proceeds of selling the put and the cost of setting up the replicating portfolio), and there is, once again, no net cash flow at maturity. These cash flow details are summarized in Table 11.4. ∎

## 11.4  Comments

The examples above illustrate the broad mechanics of pricing options by replication. Several comments are in order here.

### 1. Pricing Options through a CAPM Approach

Once we assume a price process for the underlying stock, we can derive the payoff process for any given derivative written on that stock. Thus, it appears that an alternative way to value derivatives is to look at the cash flows generated by the derivative and discount them at an appropriate risk-adjusted rate. This is correct, although the process is a bit more complex than replication. Operationalizing this idea requires us to choose a model (such as the CAPM) for converting uncertain future cash flows into present values. Then, to implement the model, we need to identify the appropriate inputs such as the option betas.

The beauty of replication is that it does not rely on the validity of the CAPM or any such model for determining stock values. Nonetheless, options may indeed be priced in this manner; indeed, Black and Scholes (1973) provide an alternative derivation of their celebrated formula using this approach. In Chapter 15, we describe the derivation of the Black-Scholes formula using both replication and CAPM.

## 2. Leverage and Expected Returns from Options

If we look at the payoff distributions of the options in the binomial example, their arbitrage-free prices seem out of line with—or, at least, odd compared to—these distributions. The payoffs from the call and put are:

$$\text{Call Payoffs} = \begin{cases} 10, & \text{w.p. } 0.75 \\ 0, & \text{w.p. } 0.25 \end{cases} \qquad \text{Put Payoffs} = \begin{cases} 0, & \text{w.p. } 0.75 \\ 10, & \text{w.p. } 0.25 \end{cases}$$

Thus, the call's expected payoff in the example is 7.50, and the put's expected payoff is 2.50. Yet the arbitrage-free price of the call is only 5.88, which implies a large positive expected return of over 27% (compared to the 5% expected return on the stock and the 2% risk-free rate). On the other hand, the price of the put is 3.92, which vastly *exceeds* its expected payoff and implies a *negative* expected return of around −36%. These numbers appear both inflated *and* odd—why, for instance, would anyone buy a put with such a huge negative expected return?—but they are easily understood intuitively.

First, the expected returns are large in absolute value because of *leverage*. The replicating portfolio for the call is a levered long position in the call: the portfolio is long 0.50 units of the stock, which costs 50, but 44.12 of the total cost of 50 is borrowed. Put differently, the call has a price of just 5.88, or under 6% of the value of the stock, yet its holder gets full exposure to increases in the price of the stock. Similarly, the put costs 3.92, less than 4% of the value of the stock, but gives the investor full exposure to decreases in the price of the stock. In a nutshell, calls are levered bets on price increases and puts are levered bets on price decreases. The expected returns are correspondingly large.

Second, "on average," stock prices go up; loosely, the stock returns at least as much as the risk-free asset. Thus, the call, which is a bet on price increases, has a positive expected return. But the put, which is a bet on a price decrease, loses money on average. In CAPM terms, the call has a positive beta, the put a negative one.

Of course, all this is only in a cooked-up example with assumed probabilities for the up and down moves. Do options prices in reality exhibit such characteristics? The answer is "yes." A study of empirical options returns by Coval and Shumway (2001) finds that at-the-money calls on the S&P 500 index have positive expected returns of between 1.8% and 2% per week while at-the-money puts tend to *lose* between 7.7% and 9.5% per week. These returns reflect the options' betas, which are large and positive for the calls (between +21 and +55) and large and negative for the puts (between −37 and −27). They also find similar numbers for options on the S&P 100 index: here, on average, at-the-money calls gain 0.6% to 0.8% daily, while at-the-money puts lose 1.4% to 1.8% per day.

## 3. The Importance of Replicability

The importance of "replicability" should be stressed. A number of options in practice are not capable of being replicated because of limitations on the strategies that may be employed. Two important examples are employee stock options and real options. In the former case, employees receiving the options as compensation may neither trade in the option nor short the underlying stock. Since the validity of the replication-based price depends on being able to sell an overvalued call or short stock against an undervalued one, the theory is inapplicable. In the latter case, the underlying is not typically a traded variable.

In such cases, using option-pricing models or formulae (including the Black-Scholes formula) may be inappropriate and even misleading. There is no easy "out" here. Depending on the particular situation, prices obtained via the standard techniques may still be useful as a benchmark. It may also be possible to modify the model to obtain a more appropriate price. Rubinstein (1995) discusses the ways in which employee stock options deviate from standard option-pricing models and suggests potential ways to correct for these.

## 4. More Complex Models and Dynamic Replication

In the one-period binomial model, the stock price makes just a single move before the option is at maturity. Thus, replication involved a static strategy where we set up a portfolio at the beginning of the period and unwind it at the end of the period. In a more realistic setting, the stock price will move several times before maturity and there will be many more than just two possible prices at maturity. This means a static strategy will not suffice for option replication: with only two assets (the stock and risk-free investment) at our disposal, a static strategy can match option outcomes in two states but not in three or more states.

Rather, replication requires a *dynamic* strategy that adapts the composition of the replicating portfolio to changing stock prices and other factors so that the portfolio value matches the option's final outcome. For example, if a call moves deep into-the-money and is almost sure to be exercised eventually, it resembles a portfolio that is long one unit of the stock and has a borrowing with a face value of $K$. If the call moves deep out-of-the-money and so is almost sure to lapse unexercised, its replicating portfolio resembles the "null" portfolio that contains neither stock nor cash.

Dynamic replication is described in the chapters on binomial option pricing and the Black-Scholes model later in this book. To set the foundation for this material, the current chapter provides a detailed, but informal, discussion of replication and the option delta in Section 11.8. These arguments are illustrated in Section 11.9 with a case study of "portfolio insurance," a specific dynamic replication strategy that was widely blamed for exacerbating the October 1987 stock market crash.

# 11.5   Riskless Hedge Portfolios

Replication shows that we can combine the underlying stock with an appropriate amount of borrowing to create a call: we can write

$$\Delta \text{ Units of Stock} + \text{Borrowing} = \text{Long Call} \qquad (11.12)$$

If we rearrange this expression (and use the fact that a negative borrowing is an investment), we see that we can create a synthetic investment by combining the stock and the call:

$$\Delta \text{ Units of Stock} + \text{Short Call} = \text{Investment} \qquad (11.13)$$

Expression (11.13) suggests an alternative pricing procedure for identifying the call's fair value. We first choose $\Delta$ so that the stock and call combine to create a synthetic risk-free investment. Since a risk-free portfolio must earn only the risk-free rate of return, the portfolio may be valued. Finally, since the portfolio consists of only the stock and the option, we can identify the option's value from knowledge of the portfolio value and the current stock price.

This method of pricing is called using a "riskless hedge portfolio" since the riskless portfolio is created by hedging the option risk with the stock. The riskless hedge portfolio method has been used frequently to derive option prices, including in the seminal Black and Scholes (1973) and Merton (1973) papers.

Of course, this method is *completely equivalent* to the replication procedure described earlier since (11.12) and (11.13) express *exactly* the same thing. In particular, the value of $\Delta$

that will create a riskless hedge portfolio is the same as the value that is used in replication. And, like replication, maintaining a riskless hedge portfolio is a dynamic task.

In Appendix 11A, we illustrate the riskless hedge portfolio procedure on the same binomial example presented above and derive option values using this procedure.

# 11.6 Pricing Using Risk-Neutral Probabilities

Pricing via replication is the economically "correct" way of identifying the arbitrage-free price of an option. However, the actual computations can be quite cumbersome. The composition of the replicating portfolio depends on the precise characteristics of the option in question: what kind of option it is, what maturity and strike it has, and so on—and, of course, this composition alters as stock prices and other features of the environment change. This procedure can get especially difficult when we look at exotic options with more complex features than straightforward calls and puts.

So, we arrive at the question: is there an easier way to arrive at option prices? Note that this question is primarily computational. Replication is already guaranteed to give us the unique arbitrage-free price. The only issue is whether we can arrive at this same price in a quicker way.

The answer, happily, is "yes." There is a method called *risk-neutral pricing* that is *guaranteed* to result in the same option prices as replication but is computationally very much simpler. Risk-neutral pricing reduces the pricing problem to one of taking expectations of discounted option payoffs. The discounting is done at the risk-free rate and the expectations are taken with respect to a particular probability measure called the *risk-neutral probability*. Unlike the replicating portfolio, the risk-neutral probability does not depend on which derivative is being valued; it is a fixed probability that depends only on the model's "primitive" assets (e.g., the stock and the risk-free rate in the binomial model). We describe risk-neutral pricing in this section.

## A Brief Historical Note

The intellectual underpinnings of risk-neutral pricing can be traced back to a 1953 paper by Nobel Laureate Kenneth Arrow, but the first formal development of the ideas, especially in the context of option pricing, came some two decades later in Cox and Ross (1976). The ideas were then developed in great depth in a series of papers by Kreps (1982), Harrison and Kreps (1979), and Harrison and Pliska (1981), where it was also shown that risk-neutral probabilities have important applications that go well beyond just pricing. Subsequently, a number of authors have clarified and extended these applications. Collectively, the ideas in these papers have had an impact on the development of derivative-pricing theory as great as—and perhaps even greater than—the work of Black and Scholes (1973) and Merton (1973).

## Outline of Discussion

In this section, we outline the steps involved in risk-neutral pricing and illustrate the method in the context of a one-period binomial model. We also provide an intuitive explanation of why the method "works." The risk-neutral probability has two other important uses. It can be used to identify whether a model is internally consistent, i.e., whether a model admits arbitrage opportunities in its very specification. It can also be used to identify whether a given model is *complete*, that is, whether all contingent claims in the model are replicable. These two uses of risk-neutral probabilities are described in Appendix 11C. An intuitive and relatively non-technical explanation of the properties and uses of risk-neutral probabilities may be found in Sundaram (1997).

## The Steps Involved in Risk-Neutral Pricing

Risk-neutral pricing in the binomial model involves a very simple three-step procedure:

- Step 1: Compute the "probabilities" $q$ and $1 - q$ of the states $u$ and $d$ that make the expected return on the stock equal to the risk-free rate $R$.
- Step 2: Compute the expected payoff from the option at maturity *under the probabilities $q$ and $1 - q$*.
- Step 3: Discount these expected payoffs back to the current period using the risk-free rate $R$.

The final result will be precisely the arbitrage-free price of the option that is obtained by replication!

The risk-neutral pricing procedure in any general model is the same as in the binomial model but with one slight modification possibly needed. In the binomial model, we have assumed interest rates are constant. Thus, it does not matter if Steps 2 and 3 are reversed; that is, we can first discount the option's payoffs at the risk-free rate and then take expectations under $q$. In a general multiasset model—and especially if we are considering interest-rate derivatives—we might want to allow for the risk-free interest rate itself to be stochastic and to change over time depending on the "state of the world." In this case, the risk-free discount factor to be applied to each option payoff will be different since both the path of interest rates and the option payoff are stochastic and depend on the state. Thus, we discount the payoffs before taking the expectation under the risk-neutral probability.

## Risk-Neutral Pricing: Terminology

The probabilities $q$ and $1 - q$ are commonly referred to as the model's *risk-neutral probabilities*, but they are also called by other names such as *pseudo-probabilities*, *risk-adjusted probabilities*, or *martingale probabilities*. The term "pseudo-probabilities" is perhaps the most descriptive of all of these: it emphasizes the fact that these probabilities are synthetic constructs, distinct from the "true" probabilities $p$ and $1 - p$. The remaining three appellations need explanations.

First, "risk-neutral" probabilities. An investor who is neutral to risk cares only about the expected return on an asset, and not on its other characteristics. Such an investor, therefore, would be indifferent between the stock and the risk-free rate $R$ only when faced with the probabilities $q$ and $1 - q$; at all other probabilities, the investor would strictly prefer the stock or the risk-free rate. Given this unique association with risk-neutrality, these probabilities are called risk-neutral probabilities.

Why "risk-adjusted" probabilities? In the usual approach to valuation in finance, to identify the value of an uncertain cash flow, we calculate its present value (under the true probabilities) and discount this at a risk-adjusted rate. Here we are discounting at the risk-free rate, but we are calculating the expectation under the constructed probabilities rather than the true probabilities. Thus, it is as if we are applying the risk-adjustment to the probabilities instead of the discount factor.

The reason these probabilities are called "martingale probabilities" is more technical and is explained in Appendix 11D.

## Examples

We illustrate risk-neutral pricing in a one-period binomial model. We continue with the parameters employed in the earlier examples: $S = 100, u = 1.10, d = 0.90, p = 0.75$, and $R = 1.02$.

As the first step, we compute the risk-neutral probability. The stock returns $u$ in the up state and $d$ in the down state, while the riskless rate is a constant $R$. Thus, the risk-neutral probabilities $q$ and $1 - q$ must satisfy

$$q \cdot u + (1 - q) \cdot d = R \qquad \qquad \textbf{(11.14)}$$

or $q(u - d) = R - d$. This identifies the risk-neutral probability uniquely as

$$q = \frac{R - d}{u - d} \qquad \qquad \textbf{(11.15)}$$

In the present case, $u = 1.10$, $d = 0.90$, and $R = 1.02$, so we obtain $q = 0.60$.

---

**Example 11.5**

First, consider pricing a call with a strike of $K = 100$. As we have seen, the call pays 10 in state $u$ and 0 in state $d$. Therefore, its expected payoff under $q$ is

$$(0.60) \cdot 10 + (0.40) \cdot 0 = 6$$

Discounting this expected payoff at the risk-free rate, we obtain

$$\frac{6}{1.02} = 5.88$$

This is the same as the call price we derived earlier using replication techniques!   ∎

---

**Example 11.6**

Now, consider a put with a strike of 100. The put pays 0 in state $u$ and 10 in state $d$. Therefore, its expected payoff under $q$ is

$$(0.60) \cdot 0 + (0.40) \cdot 10 = 4$$

Discounting this expected payoff at the risk-free rate, we obtain

$$\frac{4}{1.02} = 3.92$$

Once again, this is the same put price derived using replication.   ∎

---

**Example 11.7**

Consider one final example. Suppose we wish to price a call with a strike of 105.

First, consider pricing this call by replication. The call pays 5 in the state $u$ and nothing in the state $d$. If the replicating portfolio holds $\Delta_c$ units of stock and has $B_c$ invested at the risk-free rate, then $\Delta_c$ and $B_c$ must satisfy

$$110\,\Delta_c + 1.02\,B_c = 5$$
$$90\,\Delta_c + 1.02\,B_c = 0$$

Solving this pair of equations gives us $\Delta_c = 0.25$ and $B_c = -22.06$. Thus, the initial cost of the replicating portfolio is

$$(100 \times 0.25) - 22.06 = 2.94$$

This means the arbitrage-free price of the call is also 2.94.

Now consider pricing the same call by risk-neutral probabilities. As we have already seen, the risk-neutral probabilities of the states $u$ and $d$ are 0.60 and 0.40, respectively. The expected payoff of the call under these probabilities is

$$(0.60)(5) + (0.40)(0) = 3$$

Discounting this payoff at the risk-free rate gives us the price of the call as

$$\frac{3}{1.02} = 2.94$$

∎

These examples show just how much easier it is to compute arbitrage-free prices using risk-neutral probabilities than replication even in the simple one-period binomial model. In more complex models, the computational advantage of risk-neutral pricing only gets enhanced.

## Why Does Risk-Neutral Pricing "Work"?

Risk-neutral pricing is one of finance's "beautifully unexpected" results, unexpected because there seems no obvious connection between replication and the risk-neutral probabilities. Why does the procedure work?

An intuitive explanation provided by Cox and Ross (1976) involves the following thought experiment. Imagine two worlds in which all securities have the same current price and the same set of possible future prices. The only difference between the two worlds is the probabilities of these different future prices. Suppose one of these worlds is risk-neutral, so the probabilities are such that all expected returns are the same. The other world is our own in which investors are generally risk averse so prices of risky assets carry a risk premium.

Consider a call option in this setting and suppose that the call can be replicated using the other securities. Since the composition and cost of the replicating portfolio do not depend on the probabilities of the different future states (as we noted earlier in this chapter), the option must have the same price in both worlds. But, as with any security in the risk-neutral world, the option's price in the risk-neutral world is just its discounted expected value.

This says precisely that we can identify the value of the option in our original, risk-averse, world by considering a risk-neutral world with the same set of future prices and seeing how much the option would cost there. This is exactly what the risk-neutral pricing procedure does!

A more technical explanation has to do with the relationship between risk-neutral probabilities and the prices of the model's "Arrow securities" (so-called after Arrow's description of them in his 1953 paper; what are sometimes also called "Arrow-Debreu securities"). This is outlined in Appendix 11B.

## Other Uses of the Risk-Neutral Probability

The risk-neutral probability is very useful as a computational tool in pricing derivatives, but its uses stretch well beyond this. Two of particular importance are in identifying inconsistently-specified models and ensuring market completeness.

Suppose we have a model with a large number of primitive assets (e.g., many stocks and/or bonds). How can we be sure that the stochastic processes we specify for each of these are consistent with no arbitrage, i.e., that it is not possible to form some complex trading strategy using these different securities that creates riskless profits? Obviously, such internal consistency is a minimal condition we want satisfied in our model.

One way to ensure this is, of course, to check through all possible trading strategies, but this is likely to be infeasible in complex models. A simpler solution, however, is available: a model is internally consistent *if and only if* it has at least one risk-neutral probability, that is, there is at least one set of probabilities on the different states of the world under which all assets in the model have the same expected returns.

A second use of risk-neutral probabilities is equally unexpected and powerful. How can we know if derivatives in a given model are capable of being replicated? In simple models (such as a one-period binomial model), we can verify this by exhausting all possible derivatives, but in a richer setting, this is impractical. Here's the answer: all derivatives in a model are capable of being replicated *if and only if* the model has a *unique* risk-neutral probability.

These two remarkable properties of risk-neutral probabilities—model consistency and market completeness—are discussed further in Appendix 11C.

## 11.7 The One-Period Model in General Notation

Consider a one-period binomial model in which the current stock price is $S$; the price goes up to $uS$ with probability $p$ and down to $dS$ with probability $1 - p$; the risk-free rate is $R$; and we are looking to price a derivative that has the value $X_u$ in state $u$ and $X_d$ in state $d$. What is the initial value of the derivative?

The risk-neutral probability $q$ of the up move in this setting is, as we have seen in (11.15) above, given by

$$q = \frac{R - d}{u - d}$$

Thus, using the risk-neutral pricing approach, the initial price of the claim is

$$X = \frac{1}{R}[qX_u + (1 - q)X_d] = \frac{1}{R}\left[\left(\frac{r - d}{u - d}\right)X_u + \left(\frac{u - R}{u - d}\right)X_d\right] \quad \textbf{(11.16)}$$

Of course, we can also derive (11.16) by replication. Suppose the replicating portfolio consists of $\Delta$ units of the stock and an amount $B$ of investment. The initial cost of the replicating portfolio is then

$$\Delta S + B \quad \textbf{(11.17)}$$

For the portfolio to replicate the derivative's outcomes, $\Delta$ and $B$ must satisfy

$$\Delta uS + RB = X_u$$
$$\Delta dS + RB = X_d \quad \textbf{(11.18)}$$

Subtracing the second equation from the first shows us that

$$\Delta = \frac{X_u - X_d}{uS - dS} \quad \textbf{(11.19)}$$

Substituting this value of $\Delta$ in (11.18) and rearranging, we obtain

$$B = \frac{1}{R}\left(\frac{uX_d - dX_u}{u - d}\right) \quad \textbf{(11.20)}$$

Finally, substituting these values of $\Delta$ and $B$ into (11.17) and doing some algebraic manipulation, we can see that the option price is precisely the expression given in (11.16).

## 11.8 The Delta of an Option

One of the most important concepts in dealing with options is that of the option *delta*. The delta is defined as the number of units of the underlying security that must be held in a portfolio that replicates (a long position in) the option. In the binomial examples for instance, the call delta was +0.50 and the put delta was −0.50. The delta is central to the pricing, hedging, and risk-management of options. Given its importance, it is helpful to have an intuitive feel for this concept before examining its role more formally. In this section, we provide such an informal description of the delta's properties and its uses.

An observation first. Recall that, as discussed in Section 11.4, replication requires a *dynamic* strategy that adapts the composition of the replicating portfolio—in particular, the option delta—to changing stock prices and other factors. Thus, the delta of an option represents a "snapshot" view: it is the number of units of the underlying required to replicate the option *at a point in time*. As information changes, the delta too will typically change with it. This point should be kept in mind throughout.

## Properties of the Delta

There are three properties call and put deltas must have.

### Property 1

The delta of a call is *positive* and that of a put is *negative*. That is, replicating a long call position requires holding a *long* position in the underlying; replicating a long put position requires a *short* position in the underlying.

It is not hard to see why. A call is a bullish instrument; it increases in value when the stock price increases. Thus, the replicating portfolio must also increase in value when the stock price increases. This is possible only if the portfolio has a long position in the underlying. Conversely, a put is a bearish instrument that gains value when the stock price decreases. The portfolio replicating the put must also then move in the opposite direction to the stock price, and this mandates a short position in the stock.

### Property 2

The delta of a call must lie between 0 and 1, while that of a put must lie between $-1$ and 0. Intuitively, the maximum benefit to the holder of a call from a $1 increase in the stock price is $1; typically, the benefit will be lower since the change may be reversed with some likelihood. So the maximum number of units of the stock that need be held in the replicating portfolio is 1. Similarly, the maximum gain to the holder of a put from a $1 fall in the stock price is $1, so the replicating portfolio will need to be short at most one unit of the stock.

### Property 3

The delta of an option depends on its depth in-the-money. Options that are deep in-the-money (i.e., that are very likely to finish in-the-money) have deltas that are close to unity in absolute value. Those that are deep out-of-the-money (i.e., are very unlikely to eventually move into-the-money) have deltas close to zero. In general, as an option moves further into-the-money, the higher is its delta in absolute terms.

To see this, suppose a call is very deep in-the-money, so the call holder is very likely to exercise the option eventually. Effectively, the call holder is then looking at paying the strike price at maturity and receiving one unit of the stock. Holding the call is therefore almost equivalent to holding a portfolio consisting of one unit of the stock and a borrowing with face value $K$. ("Almost" because there is some probability that the call might go back out-of-the-money.) This says precisely that the delta of the call is almost $+1$. An analogous argument shows that the delta of a deep in-the-money put is close to $-1$.

On the other hand, suppose a call is deep out-of-the-money, i.e., there is a very low likelihood of its being exercised. Then the replicating portfolio for the call is almost the "null" portfolio, the one that contains neither the stock nor cash. (Once again, only "almost" because there is some probability that the option might wind up in-the-money at maturity.) Thus, the delta of the call is now close to zero. The delta of a deep out-of-the-money put is similarly close to zero.

**FIGURE 11.4**

Option Deltas as Depth in-the-Money Varies

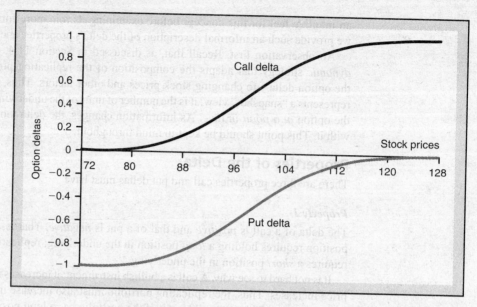

Figure 11.4 summarizes all three properties in a single picture. The figure was generated using the Black-Scholes model for European options and assumes a strike price of $K = 100$. Note that at any given stock price, the difference in the call and put deltas in the figure is exactly $+1$. We will explain later why this must hold for European options; it is a consequence of—what else?—put-call parity. The figure also shows why option replication must be dynamic: the replicating portfolio requires us to hold delta units of the underlying asset, but the delta changes when the price of the underlying stock changes.

## Uses of the Delta

The delta is perhaps the single most important number characterizing an option. First and foremost, it enables us to express option risk in terms of units of the underlying asset. For example, suppose the delta of a given call is $+0.60$. This means that the portfolio replicating the call has a long position in 0.60 units of the underlying. Since the replicating portfolio mimics the call, it is as if the call embeds 0.60 units of the underlying. That is, the risk in the option on account of the underlying is akin to the risk in a long position of 0.60 units of the underlying. This simple observation has several important implications.

### 1. Hedging Option Positions

First, the delta enables us to *hedge* option positions using the underlying. Say that we have written a call whose delta is currently $+0.70$. Then the risk in the call is the same as the risk in a long position in 0.70 units of the underlying. Since we are short the call, it is as if we are short 0.70 units of the underlying. Thus, to hedge the position, we simply buy 0.70 units of the underlying asset. This is called *delta hedging*. Of course, like replication, delta hedging too is a dynamic strategy in general: as changes in the price of the underlying cause option risk to change, we need to rebalance the delta hedge.

### 2. Aggregating Risk

The delta also enables us to *aggregate* risk across different options written on the same underlying security. As a simple example, suppose we have written 100 calls on a given stock, each with a delta of $+0.35$, and are long 100 puts on the same stock, each with a delta of −0.32. Suppose we also have 100 shares of stock. Then:

- A long position in each of the calls is akin to a long position in 0.35 units of the stock. We are *short* 100 of these calls. Thus, it is as if we are *short* $0.35 \times 100 = 35$ units of the stock.
- A long position in each of the puts is akin to being short 0.32 units of the stock. Since we are long 100 of these puts, it is as if we are short $0.32 \times 100 = 32$ units of the stock.
- We are also long 100 units of the stock.

Thus, in aggregate, the portfolio has a risk equivalent to $-35 - 32 + 100 = 33$ units of the underlying. (This aggregate is called the "portfolio delta.") Of course, we can offset this risk by delta-hedging at the portfolio level: to do this, we sell 33 units of the underlying stock.

### 3. As a Sensitivity Measure

Third, the delta is also a *sensitivity measure*: it predicts the dollar change in the value of a call for a given change in the price of the underlying. For example, suppose the delta of a call is +0.50. Then, holding the call is "like" holding +0.50 units of the stock. Thus, a change of $1 in the price of the stock will lead to a change of +0.50 in the value of the call. Of course, the sensitivity measure can be applied at the portfolio level also. If the delta of a given portfolio is (say) +315, then the portfolio increases in value by $315 for each $1 increase in the share price.

### Equivalent Ways of Defining the Delta

These three uses of the delta—in replication, in (delta-)hedging, and as a sensitivity measure—are *equivalent*. They are merely different ways of looking at the same concept. Knowing any of them is the same as knowing all of them. For example, if we know the sensitivity of the option to changes in $S$ (say, an option changes value by $0.56 for every $1 change in $S$), then we know its delta (in this example, it must be +0.56). Thus, we could have equivalently defined the delta as the number of units of the stock required to hedge a short option position; or we could have defined it as the change in option value for a $1 increase in the stock price. In the sequel, when we refer to the delta, we will appeal to any of these definitions.

### The Delta as a Probability?

It is often suggested that the (absolute value of the) delta is "like" the probability that the option will finish in-the-money. Figure 11.4 shows an intuitive basis for this: deep in-the-money options that are very likely to finish in-the-money have deltas close to 1 (in absolute value), and deep out-of-the-money options that are unlikely to finish in-the-money have deltas close to zero. Strictly speaking, this interpretation is inaccurate: despite the apparent similarity between the two concepts, there is a difference, sometimes stark, between the likelihood of an option finishing in-the-money and its delta. Nonetheless, there is also intuitive insight to be gained sometimes from viewing the delta in this way so we shall occasionally appeal to this interpretation.

### An Important Cautionary Note

The delta is clearly valuable from a number of viewpoints, but a cautionary note is relevant here. The equivalence between holding a call and holding delta units of the underlying is only "local," *that is, it is valid only for small changes in S*. This is because the delta itself changes as the stock price changes. A substantial change in the stock price will change call values differently from delta units of the stock. For example, consider the following hypothetical information on a call on XYZ stock with a strike of $30:

| Current stock price | 30 | 31 | 32 | 33 | 34 | 35 |
|---|---|---|---|---|---|---|
| Call $\Delta$ | 0.59 | 0.67 | 0.72 | 0.78 | 0.83 | 0.86 |

By how much does the call value change if the stock price jumps from $30 to $35? The delta at $S = 30$ is 0.59, suggesting that at a stock price of $30, the call value changes by $0.59 for every $1 change in $S$. If we naïvely applied this to a $5 change, we would guess that the call price would change by $5 \times 0.59 = 2.45$.

To see why this is wrong, note from the given deltas that a move in the stock price from 30 to 31 changes the call value by around $0.59; a move from 31 to 32 changes the call value by around $0.67; a move from 32 to 33 by about $0.72; and so on. Thus, a move in the stock price from 30 to 35 changes the call value by around

$$0.59 + 0.67 + 0.72 + 0.78 + 0.83 = 3.59$$

which is substantially larger than the $2.45 change predicted by naïve use of the delta at $S = 30$.

The same example also shows that delta-hedging works only for small stock price changes. Suppose we had written this call and delta-hedged by buying 0.59 units of the stock. If the price jumps to $35, the value of our short option position decreases by around $3.59 (as we have just seen) while the value of the 0.59 units of the stock we hold increases only by $2.45, which does not fully offset the lost value on the call.

Thus, we should exercise some care in interpreting the delta and working with it. However, we should not also exaggerate this shortcoming of the delta. In practice, most of the time and in most markets, prices move only by small increments, and the delta works very well in providing a hedge on option positions or in predicting sensitivity. It remains the first line of defense in managing option risk. In Chapter 17, we examine how to augment the delta with a measure called the *option gamma* and how to use the delta and gamma together for gauging the impact on option prices of large price moves as well as for hedging option risk.

# 11.9   An Application: Portfolio Insurance

Portfolio insurance[1] is a dynamic trading strategy that was devised in the late 1970s by two Berkeley professors, Hayne Leland and Mark Rubinstein. At its core, it involves a simple idea. If we want to obtain protection against a decline in the value of a portfolio we hold, we can buy a put option on the portfolio. In the late 1970s, there were few exchange-traded put options and no exchange-traded index options. Even had the latter existed, they might have been unsuitable for those managers whose portfolios did not closely resemble the index. A demand for protection nonetheless existed: with insurance, portfolio managers are protected against stock market downturns but are able to participate in upswings. Without it, many pension fund managers had withdrawn from the stock market after the decline of 1973–74 only to miss the rally of 1974–75.

Leland and Rubinstein proposed creating the required put *synthetically* by dynamic replication using a model of option pricing. This makes it possible to "customize" the synthetic option in terms of the maturity, strike price, and composition of the underlying portfolio.

---

[1] There are many sources of information on the history of portfolio insurance and its alleged role in the stock market crash of 1987. The presentation here draws especially on Leland and Rubinstein (1988) and McKenzie (2004).

Now, as we have seen, replicating a put involves taking a short position in the underlying. Here, since we are creating a put on a portfolio we already hold, we simply have to sell the appropriate number of units of the underlying portfolio. As the delta of the put changes, we either sell more of the portfolio or buy back some of it to reflect the changing delta.

Note the dynamics of this strategy. As prices decline, the delta of a put moves towards −1, so more of the portfolio has to be sold to stay replicated. As prices increase, the delta moves towards zero, so some of the portfolio has to be bought back. No, this is *not* a buy-high/sell-low strategy! Rather, the objective is to move from stocks to cash as prices go down and to move back into stocks as prices increase.

Implementing this strategy involves repeated trading in the underlying portfolio, and this may involve substantial transactions costs. The introduction of index futures in the early 1980s helped alleviate this problem. For those managers whose broadly diversified portfolios resembled the market index, index futures could be used in place of the spot asset. Since the futures and index levels move in lockstep under no-arbitrage, this gave rise to virtually the same hedge as long as arbitrageurs ensured the futures-spot link was not broken.

By 1987, portfolio insurance was a hugely popular strategy. It is estimated that the total size of the portfolios managed using portfolio insurance strategies at this time was perhaps of the order of around $90 billion, with around $50 billion under the management of LOR Associates and its licensees alone. (LOR Associates was the firm co-founded by Leland and Rubinstein with John O'Brien, an investment professional.) A large fraction of portfolio insurance strategies were being implemented using index futures contracts.

In October of that year came the stock market crash. On Friday, October 16, the Dow Jones index fell by 4.6%, a very large figure for a one-day move. But this was only a small indication of things to come. On Monday, October 19, the Dow experienced its largest ever single-day decline of 22.6%, a figure that was almost twice the size of the largest one-day decline during the 1929 crash. Many stocks, even some of the largest, simply stopped trading during the day as the NYSE's specialists were overwhelmed by the volume of sell orders. The lack of liquidity in the cash market snapped the futures-spot link. While the S&P 500 index fell around 20% that day, the S&P 500 index futures fell around 29%.

## The Role of Portfolio Insurance?

A Presidential Task Force chaired by Nicholas Brady, later Secretary of the Treasury under Presidents Reagan and George H. W. Bush, was appointed to investigate the causes for the crash. The Task Force noted that a substantial fraction of the trading volume that day (about 10% of the NYSE volume and about 40% of the S&P 500 index futures volume) was attributable to portfolio insurance strategies. Since portfolio insurance involves *selling* (either spot or futures) in the event of a price decrease, the Task Force concluded that such strategies had exacerbated the price decline and, if not responsible for the crash, had at least to share a substantial amount of blame for it.

At an intuitive level, this appears plausible. Following the price decline on Friday, October 16, portfolio insurance strategies had to sell to stay rebalanced (they sold mainly futures but also some spot). This selling put downward pressure on futures prices (so the argument goes). The falling futures prices created downward pressure on the spot as well. And, of course, as prices fell, further selling pressure resulted from these strategies, leading to further falls.

Yet reflection and subsequent study have cast much doubt on these conclusions. Portfolio insurance strategies are reactive strategies rather than informed ones—they respond to a price decline post facto but do not carry any information about anticipated future declines. Thus, investors ought not to read bad news in selling dictated by portfolio insurance considerations. Moreover, if market fundamentals had not changed but prices had declined excessively because of the selling pressures of portfolio insurance strategies, markets ought to have recovered in short order. They did not. Roll (1988) also pointed out that the crash of 1987 was an almost worldwide phenomenon with all developed markets' equity indices experiencing steep declines on the same day. Yet in most of these other markets, portfolio insurance strategies were not present or were used in a very small way.

Regardless of their role in the 1987 crash, the popularity of portfolio insurance strategies has subsequently faded. Poor performance during the crash was not likely a factor. It is estimated, for example, that over 60% of LOR's clients obtained the floor value the synthetic put was supposed to create, and most of the rest were off by only 5–7% from their floors. Rather, one reason may have been portfolio managers' reluctance to use a tainted strategy. But more generally, synthetic options strategies appear to have been replaced by exchange-traded index options and customized over-the-counter options in hedges.

## 11.10 Exercises

1. Explain intuitively why the delta of a call will lie between zero and unity. When will it be close to zero? When will it be close to unity?

2. Give an example of a derivative whose delta is positive for some ranges of the stock price and negative for others. (Use your imagination here.)

3. A stock is currently trading at 80. You hold a portfolio consisting of the following:
   (a) *Long* 100 units of stock.
   (b) *Short* 100 calls, each with a strike of 90.
   (c) *Long* 100 puts, each with a strike of 70.

   Suppose the delta of the 90-strike call is 0.45 while the delta of the 70-strike put is $-0.60$. What is the aggregate delta of your portfolio?

4. (Difficult) Compare the replication of an option in a binomial model versus replication in a trinomial model by answering the following questions:
   (a) How many securities do we need to carry out replication in each model?
   (b) Is the risk-neutral probability defined in each model unique?

5. In a binomial-tree framework, if the risk-neutral probability on the up branch is given as $p = 0.8956$, the risk-free rate per period is 2%, and the down move is the reciprocal of the up move, then, given a current stock price of $100, what are the two prices a period from now?

6. In the question above, suppose we have a one-period call option with a strike price of $100; what is the delta of the call? If the up-shift parameter $u$ is increased to 1.5, then what is the delta of the call? Is it higher or lower? Why?

7. A stock is currently trading at 80. There are one-month calls and puts on the stock with strike prices of 70, 75, 80, 85, and 90. The price and delta of each of these options are given below:

| Strike | 70 | 75 | 80 | 85 | 90 |
|---|---|---|---|---|---|
| Call price | 10.60 | 6.47 | 3.39 | 1.50 | 0.56 |
| Put price | 0.30 | 1.15 | 3.05 | 6.14 | 10.18 |
| Call $\Delta$ | 0.92 | 0.77 | 0.54 | 0.31 | 0.14 |
| Put $\Delta$ | $-0.08$ | $-0.23$ | $-0.46$ | $-0.69$ | $-0.86$ |

For each of the following portfolios, identify (i) the current value of the portfolio, and (ii) the approximate value of the portfolio following a $1 *decrease* in the stock price.

(a) Long 100 units of stock, short 100 units of the 80-strike call.

(b) Long 1000 units of the 80-strike call and 1174 units of the 80-strike put.

(c) Long 100 units of stock, long 100 units of the 75-strike put, and short 100 units of the 85-strike call.

(d) Long 100 units of the 70-strike call, long 100 units of the 90-strike call, and short 200 units of the 80-strike call.

(e) Long 100 units of the 85-strike put and short 100 units of the 75-strike put.

8. ABC stock is currently trading at 100. In the next period, the price will either go up by 10% or down by 10%. The risk-free rate of interest over the period is 5%.

(a) Construct a replicating portfolio to value a call option written today with a strike price of 100. What is the hedge ratio?

(b) Calculate the risk-neutral probabilities in the model. Value the same call option using the risk-neutral probabilities. Check that you get the same answer as in part (a).

(c) Using the risk-neutral probabilities, find the value of a put option written today, lasting one period and with an exercise price of 100.

(d) Verify that the same price for the put results from put-call parity.

9. ABC stock is currently at 100. In the next period, the price will either increase by 10% or decrease by 10%. The risk-free rate of return per period is 2%. Consider a call option on ABC stock with strike $K = 100$.

(a) Set up a replicating portfolio to value the call.

(b) Suppose the call is trading for $7. Explain how you would exploit the resulting arbitrage opportunity.

10. ABC stock is currently at 100. In the next period, the price will either increase by 5% or decrease by 5%. The risk-free rate of return per period is 3%. Consider a put option on ABC stock with strike $K = 100$.

(a) Set up a replicating portfolio to value the put.

(b) Suppose the put is trading for $2. Explain how you would exploit the resulting arbitrage opportunity.

11. Consider a one-period binomial model with the parameters $u = 1.05$, $d = 0.95$, and $r = 1.01$. Let the initial stock price be $S = 100$.

(a) Identify the price and delta of a call with strike $K = 100$.

(b) Repeat this exercise for $K = 96$, $K = 98$, $K = 102$, and $K = 104$.

(c) Use put-call parity to identify the value of the corresponding put options and the put deltas.

12. There are two stocks, A and B, both trading at price $20. Consider a one-period binomial model in which stock A's price can go to either of {35, 5}. Stock B's price can take one of the following values after one period: {36, 18}. An investment in $1.00 of bonds at the start of the period delivers a risk-free value at the end of the period of $1.10.

(a) Using replication, find the prices of call options on both stocks A and B if the calls have a strike of $20.

(b) Which call is worth more, that on stock A or on stock B? Why?

13. In a one-period setting, suppose there are three states of the world at the end of the period. Suppose there are three securities, stocks A and C, and a risk-free bond B. The

initial prices of securities A, B, and C are, respectively, 20, 1, and 10. The prices after one period are as given in the table below:

| Security | State 1 | State 2 | State 3 |
|----------|---------|---------|---------|
| A | 50 | 20 | 5 |
| B | 1.10 | 1.10 | 1.10 |
| C | 20 | 30 | 2 |

(a) Using replication, find the price of a call option on stock A at a strike price of $K = 15$.

(b) Using replication, find the price of a call option on stock B at a strike price of $K = 15$.

(c) What are state prices? Compute these for the three states in the model. (State prices are defined in Appendix 11B.)

(d) Show how you would price the two call options above using state prices.

14. The price of XYZ stock is currently at $100. After one period, the price will move to one of the following two values: {130, 80}. A $1.00 investment in the risk-free asset will return $1.05 at the end of the period.

(a) Find the risk-neutral probabilities governing the movement of the stock price.

(b) Find the state prices for each of the states in the following period.

(c) Calculate the price of a $102-strike put directly using the state prices.

15. The price of ABC stock is currently at $S = $100. After one period, the price will move to one of the following two values: {$uS, dS$}, where {$u = 1.2, d = 0.9$}. A $1.00 investment in the risk-free asset will return $1.10 at the end of the period.

(a) Find the risk-neutral probabilities governing the movement of the stock price.

(b) For a strike-100 call, find the delta of the call.

(c) For a strike-100 put, find the delta of the put.

(d) Compute the difference between the call delta and the put delta and explain the answer you get.

16. In the previous question, if the stock price rises to $110, then

(a) Recompute $\Delta_c, \Delta_p$.

(b) Explain why the deltas moved in their respective directions.

(c) Confirm that the difference in the deltas is still equal to +1.

17. The current price of a stock is $50. The one-period rate of interest is 10%. The up-move parameter for the stock movement over one period is $u = 1.5$, and the down-move parameter is $d = 0.5$.

(a) If the delta of the call at strike $K$ is 0.5, what is the strike of this option?

(b) What is the delta of the put at the same strike?

(c) What is the price of this put?

18. (Difficult) The current price of a stock is $100. After one period, this stock may move to three possible values: {150, 110, 60}. The value of $1.00 invested in the risk-free asset compounds to a value of $1.05 in one period. Find the upper and lower bounds of the call price if its strike is $100.

19. *Portfolio insurance*: The current price of the stock we are holding is $100. We want to continue to hold the stock position but modify it so that the portfolio value never drops

below $90. If the stock may move up to $130 or down to $80 after one period, how do we modify our holding of $100 so as to make sure that it is at least of $90 value at the end of the period? The rate of simple interest for the period is 10%.

20. What is a martingale measure? What is the role of the martingale measure in finance?

21. Does the delta of the option in the binomial tree depend on the risk-neutral probabilities?

22. In the binomial model, the up move of the stock is set by parameter $u$, i.e., the stock goes from $S$ at the start of the period to $uS$ at the end of the period if it moves up. Likewise, the down-move parameter for the stock is $d$. The value of 1 plus the interest rate is specified as $R$. What is the no-arbitrage relationship between $u, d, R$? Explain what happens if this relationship is violated.

23. You are given the following one-period-ahead binomial outcomes for a stock, trading at a current price of $S$ ($h$ is the length of one period measured in years):

$$\begin{cases} S\exp(\sigma\sqrt{h}) & \text{with prob } q \\ S\exp(-\sigma\sqrt{h}) & \text{with prob } 1-q \end{cases}$$

The continuously compounded interest rate is $r$. Answer the following questions:

(a) What is a martingale?

(b) If the normalized price of the stock is a martingale, then what is the probability $q$?

(c) What is the variance of the continuously compounded return on the stock in this scenario?

# Riskless Hedge Portfolios and Option Pricing

The basic ideas underlying pricing by constructing a riskless hedge portfolio are easily described. Since the option derives its value from the underlying, it "should" be possible to combine the option and the underlying in such a way as to cancel out uncertainty and create a *riskless* portfolio. Such a riskless portfolio must earn only the risk-free rate of return. Therefore, the present value of the riskless portfolio is simply its value at maturity discounted at the risk-free rate. Since the portfolio consists of only the option and the underlying, the price of the option is determined from the present value of the portfolio and the price of the underlying.

Of course, the first step in this procedure is just delta hedging—the creation of a riskless position by hedging the risk in the option with the underlying! Thus, just like replication, the identification of the option delta is also central to this method, and indeed, as we mentioned above, the two methods are virtually the same.

In particular, suppose we know the composition of the replicating portfolio for a given call (say, it involves a long position in $\Delta$ units of the underlying and borrowing of $B_c$ at the risk-free rate). We describe how to construct a riskless hedge portfolio from this, i.e., how to combine appropriate quantities of the stock and the option into a portfolio that makes the portfolio riskless.

First, note that the replication can be written as:

$$\text{Long Call} = \Delta_c \cdot \text{Stock} - B_c$$

Rearranging this expression:

$$\Delta_c \cdot \text{Stock} - \text{Long Call} = B_c$$

or, since the negative of a long position is a short position:

$$\Delta_c \cdot \text{Stock} + \text{Short Call} = B_c$$

In words, this says that if we combine a short position in the call with $\Delta_c$ units of the stock, we effectively create a riskless investment of $B_c$.

Thus, the riskless hedge portfolio can be computed from the replicating portfolio. Note, in particular, that the deltas are the same, and the value of the riskless hedge portfolio is identical to the size of the borrowing $B_c$ in the replicating portfolio.

Similarly, from knowledge of the riskless hedge portfolio, we can construct the replicating portfolio.

## A Numerical Example

An example will illustrate the close relationship between replication and riskless hedge portfolios. Consider the same parameters as earlier: $S = 100$, $u = 1.10$, $d = 0.90$, $q = 0.75$, and $R = 1.02$. Suppose we wish to price a call with a strike of $K = 100$.

We will construct a riskless hedge portfolio (without referring to the replicating portfolio) to price this call. It will be seen that the portfolio values coincide with the numbers obtained earlier from the replication arguments.

The first step in the argument is to identify the composition of the riskless hedge portfolio. So, let the hedge portfolio consist of a short position in one call option and $\Delta_c$ units of the underlying. Of course, $\Delta_c$ can be positive or negative: $\Delta_c > 0$ indicates a *long* position in the underlying while $\Delta_c < 0$ indicates a *short* position in the underlying.

The key question: for what value of $\Delta_c$ is this portfolio *riskless*? There are two possible values for this portfolio after one period:

1. If $uS$ occurs, the portfolio is worth

$$uS \cdot \Delta_c - C_u = 110 \cdot \Delta_c - 10$$

2. If $dS$ occurs, the portfolio is worth

$$dS \cdot \Delta_c - C_d = 90 \cdot \Delta_c$$

For the portfolio to be *riskless*, these values must be equal:

$$110 \cdot \Delta_c - 10 = 90\Delta_c$$

This gives us $\Delta_c = 0.50$, completing the first step of the pricing argument.

The second step is to identify the present value of the riskless portfolio we have constructed. If $\Delta_c = 0.50$, the portfolio is always worth 45 after one period regardless of which state occurs. Therefore, the present value of the portfolio is $45/1.02 = 44.12$. This completes the second step.

Finally, in the third step, we identify the fair price of the option from knowledge of the portfolio's present value and the current price of the underlying. To this end, note that the portfolio consists of 0.50 units of the underlying and a short call option. Therefore, if $C$ denotes the price of the option, the cost of this portfolio is

$$\Delta \cdot S - C = 100 \cdot (0.50) - C = 50 - C$$

Since the cost of the portfolio must equal its present value, we must have $50 - C = 44.12$, or

$$C = 50 - 44.12 = 5.88$$

This completes step 3.

Any other price for the call leads to arbitrage:

1. If $C < 5.88$, then the portfolio costs more than its present value, so an arbitrage can be made by selling the riskless hedge portfolio and borrowing.
2. If $C > 5.88$, then the portfolio costs less than its present value, so an arbitrage can be made by buying the riskless hedge portfolio and investing.

Note that the price of 5.88 obtained using a riskless hedge portfolio is the same value as obtained using replication. Indeed, so are the other quantities. The delta value $\Delta_c$ is equal to 0.50 under both methods. The present value of the riskless hedge portfolio is 44.12, which is exactly the value of the borrowing under replication.

---

**Exercise**   Price a put with $K = 100$ using a riskless hedge portfolio and verify that the answer is $P = 3.92$.

# Risk-Neutral Probabilities and Arrow Security Prices

In Section 11.6 where risk-neutral probabilities were defined, we offered an intuitive explanation of why risk-neutral pricing identifies the correct arbitrage-free price. Here we describe a more formal mathematical link between risk-neutral probabilities and the prices of a class of claims called *Arrow securities*. Arrow securities are named after Economics Nobel Laureate Kenneth Arrow who first described the use of such securities in a 1953 paper.

Arrow securities are the fundamental building blocks of all contingent claims (claims, like derivatives, whose payoffs may be contingent on future states of the world). An Arrow security is defined as a security that pays $1 in a given state and nothing otherwise. For example, in a one-period binomial model, there are two future states of the world, so there are two Arrow securities: one associated with state $u$ and one associated with state $d$. The price of an Arrow security is called a *state price*. We denote the state prices in the one-period binomial model by $\pi_u$ and $\pi_d$, respectively.

Given a model, *any* contingent claim in that model can obviously be written as a portfolio of Arrow securities. For instance, consider a call option in a one-period binomial model that pays $10 in the state $u$ and nothing in the state $d$. The call is equivalent to a portfolio consisting of (i) 10 state-$u$ Arrow securities and (ii) zero state-$d$ Arrow securities. Thus, the price of any contingent claim is simply the value of the corresponding portfolio of Arrow securities, so any claim can be priced from knowledge of the state prices.

Now here is the fundamental mathematical connection: it turns out that in any model, the model's state prices are equal to the discounted risk-neutral probabilities! This result is not hard to verify in the binomial model. Consider, for instance, the state-$u$ Arrow security. A portfolio consisting of $a$ units of the stock and an investment of $b$ at the risk-free rate will replicate this Arrow security if $a$ and $b$ are chosen to satisfy

$$a\,uS + Rb = 1$$
$$a\,dS + Rb = 0$$

Some simple calculation shows that the solutions to this pair of equations are:

$$a = \frac{1}{uS - dS} \qquad b = \frac{1}{R}\left(\frac{-d}{u-d}\right)$$

Thus, the cost of the replicating portfolio is

$$aS + b = \frac{1}{R}\left(\frac{R-d}{u-d}\right) \qquad\qquad \textbf{(11.21)}$$

But $(R-d)/(u-d)$ is the risk-neutral probability $q$ of the state $u$ in this model, so (11.21) states precisely that the state price $\pi_u$ is

$$\pi_u = \frac{q}{R}$$

An analogous set of calculations shows that the state price $d$ associated with the state $d$ is

$$\pi_d = \frac{1-q}{R}$$

This relationship between risk-neutral probabilities and state prices explains why risk-neutral pricing works. When we take a derivative's expected payoff under the risk-neutral measure and discount the result at the risk-free rate, the payoff associated with each state gets multiplied by the risk-neutral probability of that state and discounted at the rate $R$, i.e., the payoff associated with each state is multiplied by the state price! Thus, risk-neutral pricing is just pricing using state prices. Harrison and Kreps (1979) present a complete exposition of the relationship between risk-neutral probabilities and state prices.

## Appendix 11C

# The Risk-Neutral Probability, No-Arbitrage, and Market Completeness

In some models, the risk-neutral probability is uniquely defined; the binomial model is an example of this. In general, however, it is possible that a model may admit more than one risk-neutral probability, or it may admit none at all. In either case, there are important implications. A risk-neutral probability can fail to exist in a model if and only if the model is internally *inconsistent*, i.e., if it admits arbitrage opportunities in its very specification. And a model admits more than one risk-neutral probability if and only if there are contingent claims in the model that cannot be replicated. We elaborate on these two points in this section. The material of this section, as of Appendix 11D, is taken from Sundaram (1997).

## Arbitrage and the Nonexistence of Risk-Neutral Probabilities

Recall the connection between risk-neutral probabilities and state prices mentioned in the previous section. A risk-neutral probability then fails to exist if and only if it is not possible to define a set of state prices. Intuitively, the only way *no* vector of state prices results in an equilibrium is if the model itself is inconsistently specified, i.e., it admits an arbitrage.

In the binomial model, the connection between the existence of a risk-neutral probability and the internal consistency of the model is easy to see. The risk-neutral probabilities are defined here as

$$q = \frac{R - d}{u - d} \qquad 1 - q = \frac{u - R}{u - d}$$

These are "probabilities" (i.e., lie between 0 and 1) if and only if $d < R < u$. And, of course, $d < R < u$ is exactly the condition for the binomial model to be internally consistent (i.e., for the bond not to dominate the stock or vice versa).

Here is a simple example of a model that does not admit any risk-neutral probability, and therefore, permits arbitrage. Consider a binomial model with *two* risky assets and the risk-free rate. Let $S_1$ and $S_2$ denote the initial prices of the risky assets, and let their possible prices after one period be denoted by $u_i S_i$ and $d_i S_i$, $i = 1, 2$. Finally, suppose that the asset prices are perfectly correlated so that there are only two possible sets of prices after one period: $(R, u_1 S_1, u_2 S_2)$ and $(R, d_1 S_1, d_2 S_2)$.

For $q$ to be a risk-neutral probability in this setting, the expected return of both risky assets under $q$ must equal $R$, i.e., we must have

$$q u_1 + (1 - q) d_1 = R$$

as well as

$$qu_2 + (1-q)d_2 = R$$

Therefore, $q$ must satisfy

$$q = \frac{R - d_1}{u_1 - d_1} = \frac{R - d_2}{u_2 - d_2} \tag{11.22}$$

However, it is obviously possible to choose $R$, $u_i$, and $d_i$ so that the fractions in (11.22) are unequal; no risk-neutral probability can then exist.

We will now show that the model admits an arbitrage opportunity if and only if the two fractions in (11.22) are unequal. Consider a portfolio that invests $\$a$ in the bond, and $\$b$ and $\$c$, respectively, in the two risky assets. The current cost of this portfolio is

$$a + b + c \tag{11.23}$$

while its possible values at maturity are

$$\begin{cases} ar + bu_1 + cu_2 & \text{if } (u_1, u_2) \text{ occurs} \\ ar + bd_1 + cd_2 & \text{if } (d_1, d_2) \text{ occurs} \end{cases} \tag{11.24}$$

For this portfolio to generate a free lunch, there must exist a value of $(a, b, c)$ such that (11.23) is strictly negative and both values in (11.24) are zero. Such a solution exists when, and only when, the two fractions in (11.22) are unequal. This can be seen by setting the two quantities in (11.24) to zero, using them to solve for $a$ and $b$ in terms of $c$, and then substituting these solutions into (11.23). Thus, the conditions in this model that lead to the nonexistence of a risk-neutral probability are also identically the conditions that lead to the existence of an arbitrage opportunity.

## Completeness and the Uniqueness of Risk-Neutral Probabilities

A model is said to be *complete* if all contingent claims in the model may be replicated using the primitive assets. A simple test for market completeness is *uniqueness* of the risk-neutral probability. Intuitively, multiple risk-neutral probabilities can exist if and only if there are multiple state-price vectors. This means that at least one Arrow security has many possible prices consistent with no-arbitrage, and this, in turn, is possible only if the Arrow security in question is not replicable. Thus, the market must be incomplete.

This equivalence is easy to see in the binomial model. As we have seen, any claim paying $X_u$ in state $u$ and $X_d$ in state $d$ may be replicated, so the model is complete. And, of course, the risk-neutral probability in this model is unique.

Here is a simple example of a model that admits more than one risk-neutral probability and is therefore not complete. Consider a *trinomial* model in which there are three possible values for the stock price $\tilde{S}$ after one period, viz.,

$$\tilde{S} = \begin{cases} uS, & \text{with probability } p_u \\ mS, & \text{with probability } p_m \\ dS, & \text{with probability } p_d \end{cases} \tag{11.25}$$

where $u > m > d$ and $p_i > 0$ for $i = u, m, d$. Suppose also that the bond continues to return $r$ with certainty. For the vector $(q_u, q_m, q_d)$ to be a risk-neutral probability in this model, it must satisfy $q_i > 0$ for $i = u, m, d$, as well as

$$q_u u + q_d d + q_m m = r \quad \text{and} \quad q_u + q_m + q_d = 1 \tag{11.26}$$

Expressions (11.26) give us two equations in three unknowns. There are infinitely many solutions that satisfy both equations as well as $q_i > 0$ for $i = u, m, d$. Thus, there are infinitely many risk-neutral probabilities in this model.

To see that the trinomial model is also not complete, observe that a contingent claim with payoffs $(X_u, X_m, X_d)$ can be replicated by a portfolio consisting of the stock and investment at the risk-free rate if and only if there is a solution $(a^*, b^*)$ to the following system of equations:

$$a^*uS + b^*R = X_u \tag{11.27}$$

$$a^*mS + b^*R = X_m \tag{11.28}$$

$$a^*dS + b^*R = X_d \tag{11.29}$$

From (11.27) and (11.28), any such solution must satisfy

$$a^* = \frac{X_u - X_m}{uS - mS} \tag{11.30}$$

while from (11.28) and (11.29), we must also have

$$a^* = \frac{X_m - X_d}{mS - dS} \tag{11.31}$$

It is an elementary matter to choose values of $(X_u, X_m, X_d)$ such that (11.30) and (11.31) are inconsistent (for example, let $X_u = X_m = 1$ and $X_d = 0$).

# Equivalent Martingale Measures

Risk-neutral probabilities are frequently referred to as "martingale measures," or more elaborately, as "equivalent martingale measures." This section provides a brief explanation of this terminology.

The definition of a risk-neutral probability actually involves two conditions:

1. The prices that occur with positive probability under the risk-neutral probability should be identical to the prices that occur with positive probability in the original model.

2. Under the risk-neutral probability, the expected return on all assets in the model should be the same.

The first of these conditions is almost obvious, which is why we have focused on only the second one so far. As we explain below, the first condition is an "equivalence" condition and the second one a "martingale" condition.

In mathematical terminology, two probability measures are said to be *equivalent* if the set of events having positive probability under one is identical to the set having positive probability under the other. Thus, the first condition is simply the requirement that the risk-neutral probability be equivalent to the original probability. Although the requirement of equivalence is often not stated explicitly, it is an important part of the definition of a risk-neutral probability.

Second, a stochastic process is said to be a *martingale* if the expected change in the value of the process is always zero. Suppose, for example, you start with a wealth level of $100 and toss a fair coin repeatedly; each time the coin lands heads, you receive $1 and each time it lands tails, you lose $1. Then, in each round, you gain $1 with probability 1/2, and lose

$1 with probability 1/2, so the expected change in your wealth level is zero. Your wealth process in this case follows a martingale.

To see where martingales enter the discussion here, consider a "money-market account" that involves an initial investment of $1 that is rolled over at the risk-free rate. (In the binomial mode, this will grow to $R$ after one period, $R^2$ after two periods, and so on. In general, if interest rates are stochastic, the returns on the money-market account can depend on the state of the world at that point.) Consider the "discounted" asset prices that arise when asset prices at each point are divided by the price of the money-market account at that point.[2]

Since the money-market account grows at the risk-free rate, this operation simply results in the growth in all asset prices being discounted at the risk-free rate. By Condition 2 in the definition of a risk-neutral probability, the expected rate of growth in asset prices under the risk-neutral probability is equal to the risk-free rate. Therefore, the expected rate of growth in *discounted* prices under the risk-neutral probability is zero. This means Condition 2 is just the requirement that discounted asset prices be martingales under the risk-neutral probability.

---

[2] In other words, the money-market account serves as a "numeraire" asset. The choice of the money-market account as numeraire asset is customary, but not really necessary. Any asset in the model could serve as numeraire.

# Chapter 12

# Binomial Option Pricing

## 12.1 Introduction

The last chapter described the mechanics of pricing options in the context of one-period binomial models. Building on that foundation, this chapter examines the pricing of options in *multiperiod* binomial models. We begin with the simplest case, namely, two-period binomial models. Then we show how the arguments are easily extended to *n*-period binomial models. Completing this discussion, Chapter 13 describes the implementation of binomial models.

We present the analysis in this chapter in three steps. First, we look at *European* options on non-dividend-paying stock (i.e., there are no dividends on the stock during the life of the option). Then, we look at *American* options on non-dividend-paying stock. Finally, we describe the modeling of dividends in the binomial tree and the pricing of both European and American options in this case.

Because of their inherent simplicity, binomial models offer a transparent platform to see formally several characteristics of options prices and exercise policies. Dynamic replication is easily illustrated in this setting. The present chapter illustrates this and many other characteristics, including that

- It can be optimal to exercise American puts early even on non-dividend-paying stock.
- It can be optimal to exercise American calls early in the presence of dividends, though early exercise is never optimal without dividends.
- European put options can *fall* in value as maturity increases owing to the time value/insurance value trade-off. This can never happen for American options or for European calls on non-dividend-paying stock.
- In the presence of dividends, an increase in maturity can reduce European call values.
- Dividends hurt call values but benefit put values. Both American and European call values are hurt, but the former is hurt less because of the ability to exercise the option before the stock goes ex-dividend.

Several other characteristics are highlighted through the exercises at the end of this chapter.

### Notation

We retain the notation introduced in the last chapter:

- $S$ denotes the initial stock price.
- $u$ denotes an up move in the stock price, $d$ a down move.

- $p$ is the ("true") probability of an up move, $(1-p)$ that of a down move.
- $n$ is the number of steps in the binomial tree.
- $R$ is the (gross) risk-free rate of interest per period.
- $K$ denotes the strike price of the option under consideration.

## Review of the One-Period Model

The last chapter described two equivalent methods for pricing options: pricing by replication and pricing by using risk-neutral probabilities. It is useful to briefly review the main ideas in each approach in the context of a one-period binomial model.

### (A) Replication and the Option Delta

Replication looks to identify option prices by creating a portfolio of the underlying and borrowing/investment at the risk-free rate that mimics the option outcome. The option delta—the number of units of the underlying that must be held in the replicating portfolio—is a key component of option pricing and risk management; the delta's properties and uses were highlighted in the last chapter.

Consider a derivative in the one-period model that has a value of $X_u$ after an up move and $X_d$ after a down move. To replicate this derivative, we set up a portfolio consisting of $\Delta_x$ units of the underlying and an investment of $B_x$ at the risk-free rate, where

$$\Delta_x = \frac{X_u - X_d}{uS - dS} \qquad \text{(12.1)}$$

$$B_x = \frac{1}{R}\left[\frac{uX_d - dX_u}{u-d}\right] \qquad \text{(12.2)}$$

(A negative $\Delta_x$ indicates a short position in the underlying and a negative $B_x$ is a borrowing.) The initial value of the derivative is

$$X = \Delta_x S + B_x$$

Substituting for $\Delta_x$ and $B_x$ from (12.1)–(12.2) and simplifying, we obtain the derivative's price as

$$X = \frac{1}{R}\left[\left(\frac{R-d}{u-d}\right)X_u + \left(\frac{u-R}{u-d}\right)X_d\right] \qquad \text{(12.3)}$$

### (B) Risk-Neutral Pricing

In risk-neutral pricing, we identify the fair price of an option by taking expectations of its payoffs under a particular probability called the *risk-neutral probability* and discounting these expectations at the risk-free rate. This "risk-neutral price" of the option is guaranteed to coincide with its replication-based price for any option that can be priced by replication.

The risk-neutral probability is the probability under which all assets in the model have the same expected rate of return. It is a hypothetical construct and should not be confused with the "true" probabilities in the model; nor does it involve any assumptions about investors' attitudes to risk.

In the one-period binomial model, the risk-neutral probability $q$ of an up move satisfies the condition $qu + (1-q)d = R$. Therefore, $q$ is given by

$$q = \frac{R-d}{u-d} \qquad \text{(12.4)}$$

Now, suppose we have a derivative in this model that pays $X_u$ in the state $u$ and $X_d$ in the state $d$. Then, the initial value of the derivative is given by

$$X = \frac{1}{R}[qX_u + (1-q)X_d] \qquad (12.5)$$

This is, of course, the same as (12.3), the price obtained by replication.

## 12.2 The Two-Period Binomial Tree

To specify a two-period binomial tree, we must specify the up and down moves in each period. In general, the up and down moves may differ across the two periods and may even vary depending on whether the price went up in the first period or down. Consider, for the time being, the simple scenario in which the price in each period moves up or down by the same factors $u$ and $d$ with the same probabilities. Since the ratio $u/d$ is a measure of volatility, this says that volatility remains constant over the tree.

After one period, there are two possible prices for the stock, namely $uS$ and $dS$. In the second period, each of these two prices can itself go up by $u$ or down by $d$. Therefore, there are four possible *paths* that prices can take over two periods: (i) $u$ followed by $u$, (ii) $u$ followed by $d$, (iii) $d$ followed by $u$, and (iv) $d$ followed by $d$.

The path $uu$ results in the stock price $u(uS) = u^2S$, and the path $dd$ results in the stock price $d(dS) = d^2S$. However, the paths $ud$ and $du$ result in the same terminal price, namely $udS$. Thus, even though there are four distinct price paths, there are only three *distinct* terminal prices at the end of two periods, namely, $u^2S$, $udS$, and $d^2S$. Figure 12.1 summarizes this information.

### Recombination

The feature that the paths $ud$ and $du$ lead to the same price is known as *recombination* of the binomial tree. Recombination reduces the number of distinct terminal prices in the binomial tree while retaining the complexity of a large number of possible paths that lead to these prices.

In an $n$-period binomial tree, there will be $2^n$ possible price paths since the number of possible paths doubles at each stage. Without recombination, each path could result in a

**FIGURE 12.1**

The Two-Period Binomial Tree

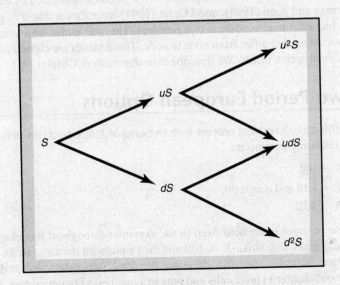

**TABLE 12.1**

Terminal Prices in an
*n*-Period Binomial
Model

| Terminal Price | Results From |
|---|---|
| $u^n S$ | $n$ up moves |
| $u^{n-1} d S$ | $(n-1)$ up moves and 1 down move |
| $u^{n-2} d^2 S$ | $(n-2)$ up moves and 2 down moves |
| $\vdots$ | $\vdots$ |
| $u d^{n-1} S$ | 1 up move and $(n-1)$ down moves |
| $d^n S$ | $n$ down moves |

different terminal price. With recombination, however, there will be only $(n + 1)$ distinct terminal prices; these are listed in Table 12.1. Even for small values of $n$ (say, $n = 30$), the difference between these numbers is significant.

Binomial models in practice routinely use a hundred or more time steps. This means the models have considerable richness in describing the pattern of evolution of asset prices (for example, with 100 time steps, there are roughly $10^{30}$ different possible time paths). However, there are only $n + 1$ distinct nodes after $n$ periods, and this eases the computational process considerably. Recombination is particularly significant for European options; since they can be exercised only at maturity, all that really matters is the set of possible terminal prices and their distribution.

### A Comment: Allowing *u* and *d* to Vary

In Chapter 13, we show that the lognormal price distribution of the Black-Scholes model may be approximated arbitrarily closely by a binomial tree with *constant* values for *u* and *d*. Thus, the binomial tree with constant parameters may be regarded as just a discrete version of the Black-Scholes model. Given the widespread use of the lognormal distribution in practice, this is a strong point in favor of using constant parameters. From an expositional standpoint too, the constant-parameter model suffices: however one draws the tree, the procedure for pricing options within the tree remains the same.

On the other hand, the lognormal distribution is inadequate in some ways in describing price evolution in many markets, a feature reflected through the model's inability to simultaneously match market prices of options of differing maturities and strikes. This point is discussed more fully in the chapter on Black-Scholes. Motivated by this, Rubinstein (1994), Derman and Kani (1994), and Dupire (1994) have shown that it is possible to generalize the binomial tree to address this problem. The tree under their construction has up and down values that differ from node to node. These values are chosen endogenously to match observed option prices. We describe their approach in Chapter 16.

## 12.3   Pricing Two-Period European Options

We illustrate the pricing process with an example. Consider a two-period binomial tree with the following parameters:

- $S = 100$.
- $u = 1.10$ and $d = 0.90$.
- $R = 1.02$.

These parameters are held fixed in the examples throughout this chapter. We first look at pricing a call with strike $K = 100$ and then a put with the same strike price.

Parenthetically, note that these are the same parameters and strike price used in the previous chapter to price calls and puts in a one-period binomial tree. Thus, the options we

**FIGURE 12.2**

Pricing Example: The
Two-Period Binomial
Tree

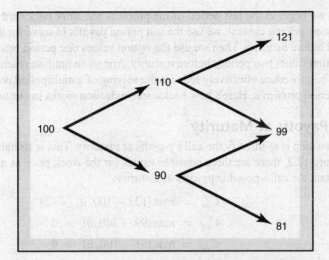

**FIGURE 12.3**

The Call Payoffs

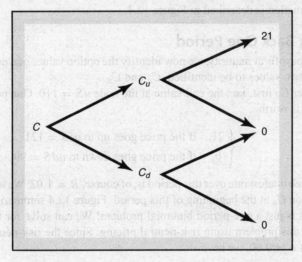

are pricing here differ from those priced earlier purely on account of maturity: they have twice the maturity of the options in the last chapter. For later reference, recall that with these parameters,

- The price of a one-period call is 5.88.
- The price of a one-period put is 3.92.

Figure 12.2 describes the two-period stock price tree for the given parameters. Note that the risk-neutral probability $q$ of an up move at any node is given by

$$q = \frac{R - d}{u - d} = 0.60$$

## Pricing the Call: General Comments

Let $C$ denote the initial value of the call. After one period, the stock price moves to either $uS = 110$ or $dS = 90$. In either case, the call price will change from its initial value. Denote the value of the call at the node $uS$ by $C_u$ and that at the node $dS$ by $C_d$. The payoffs from the call and these unknown values $C$, $C_u$, and $C_d$ are described in Figure 12.3.

To recover the values $C$, $C_u$, and $C_d$, we use a mathematical technique called *backwards induction*. Backwards induction is a procedure for solving general multiperiod problems in which we begin in the last period of the problem and work backward to the beginning. In the option-pricing context, we use the last period payoffs to solve for the option values one period before maturity. Then we use the option values one period before maturity to solve for option values two periods before maturity. And so on until we reach the beginning of the tree. The procedure effectively reduces the solving of a multiperiod problem to a family of one-period problems. Here's how backwards induction works in our two-period example.

### The Payoffs at Maturity

The first step is to identify the call's payoffs at maturity. This is straightforward. As shown in Figure 12.2, there are three possible values for the stock price at maturity. From these, we obtain the call's possible payoffs at maturity:

$$C_{uu} = \max\{121 - 100, 0\} = 21$$
$$C_{ud} = \max\{99 - 100, 0\} = 0$$
$$C_{dd} = \max\{81 - 100, 0\} = 0$$

This information is described in Figure 12.3.

### Moving Back One Period

Using the payoffs at maturity, we now identify the option values one period before maturity. There are two values to be identified: $C_u$ and $C_d$.

Consider $C_u$ first, i.e., the call value at the node $uS = 110$. One period from this point, the option is worth

$$\begin{cases} 21, & \text{if the price goes up to } u^2 S = 121 \\ 0, & \text{if the price goes down to } udS = 99 \end{cases}$$

The risk-free interest rate over this period is, of course, $R = 1.02$. We want to know the value of the option $C_u$ at the beginning of this period. Figure 12.4 summarizes this information.

But this is just a one-period binomial problem! We can solve for the initial price $C_u$ of the call in this problem using risk-neutral pricing. Since the risk-neutral probability of an up move is $q = 0.60$, we have

$$C_u = \frac{1}{1.02} [(0.60) \cdot (21) + (0.40) \cdot 0] = 12.35 \qquad (12.6)$$

In a similar manner, we identify the value $C_d$ of the call at the node $dS$. In this example, this is trivial: regardless of whether the stock price moves up to $udS = 99$ or down to $d^2 S = 81$, the call expires worthless. Thus, we must also have $C_d = 0$.

**FIGURE 12.4**

Backwards Induction at the Node $uS$

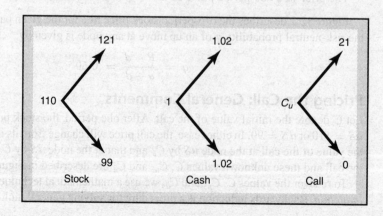

| Stock | Cash | Call |

## One More Step Back

Having identified all the prices one period from maturity, we move back one more period and idenitfy the call price $C$ at the initial node $S = 100$. We have just shown that one period from the initial node, the call will be worth

$$\begin{cases} 12.35, & \text{if the price goes up to } uS = 110 \\ 0, & \text{if the price goes down to } dS = 90 \end{cases}$$

Thus, finding the initial value $C$ of the call is the one-period problem described in Figure 12.5. Invoking the risk-neutral probability, we obtain

$$C = \frac{1}{1.02}[(0.60)\cdot(12.35) + (0.40)\cdot 0] = 7.27 \qquad \textbf{(12.7)}$$

The complete evolution of call prices in this tree is shown in Figure 12.6.

## Pricing the Call by Dynamic Replication

Rather than use the risk-neutral probabilities, we could have used replicating portfolios in the backwards induction argument. We illustrate this here.

Consider the node $uS$ first. At this point, the option holder faces the one-period problem described in Figure 12.4. From (12.1)–(12.2), the replicating portfolio at this node is

$$\Delta^u = \frac{21 - 0}{121 - 99} = 0.9545 \qquad B^u = \frac{1}{1.02}\frac{-(0.90)(21)}{1.10 - 0.90} = -92.65 \qquad \textbf{(12.8)}$$

**FIGURE 12.5**

Backwards Induction: The Last Step

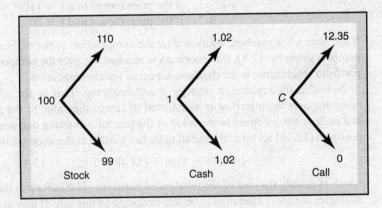

**FIGURE 12.6**

Evolution of Call Values

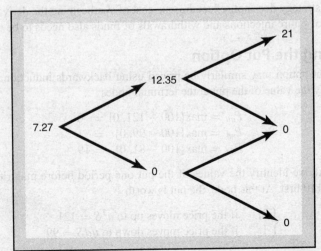

Since the stock costs 110 at this node, the cost of this replicating portfolio is

$$(0.9545)(110) - 92.65 = 12.35$$

So the call is worth 12.35 at this node. This is, of course, the same value obtained above using risk-neutral pricing.

At the node $dS$, the option is worthless—it finishes out-of-the-money regardless of whether the price goes up or down the next period. Thus, the replicating portfolio at this node is the null portfolio:

$$\Delta^d = 0 \qquad B^d = 0 \tag{12.9}$$

Finally, at the initial node $S$, the option holder faces the one-period problem described in Figure 12.5. From (12.1)–(12.2), the replicating portfolio at this node is

$$\Delta = \frac{12.35 - 0}{110 - 90} = 0.6175 \quad B^u = \frac{1}{1.02} \frac{-(0.90)(12.35)}{1.10 - 0.90} = -54.48 \tag{12.10}$$

Thus, the initial cost of the option is

$$(0.6175)(100) - 54.48 = 7.27$$

which is the same value obtained using risk-neutral pricing.

In words, the replicating strategy has the following structure. Initially, we set up a portfolio consisting of a long position in 0.6175 units of the stock and borrowing of 54.48 for one period at the risk-free rate. At the end of one period, this portfolio is worth

$$\begin{cases} 12.35, & \text{if the price moves to } uS = 110 \\ 0, & \text{if the price moves to } dS = 90 \end{cases}$$

If the node $uS$ is reached, we must alter the composition of the replicating portfolio to the numbers given by (12.8). If the node $dS$ is reached, we alter the composition to (12.9). This portfolio rebalancing is the dynamic aspect of option replication.

Note that the replication strategy is *self-financing*. That is, the rebalancing at a node never requires the injection or withdrawal of funds: the value of the rebalanced portfolio at a node is always equal to the value of the portfolio entering that node. For example, the portfolio (12.10) set up at the initial node has a value at the node $uS$ of

$$(0.6175 \times 110) - (54.48 \times 1.02) = 12.35$$

which is exactly the cost of the rebalanced portfolio (12.8) set up at this node. Replication strategies are always required to be self-financing in this way. If they are not, the initial cost of the strategy does not reflect the true cost of synthesizing the derivative since the present value of future injections and withdrawals of funds also needs to be taken into account.

## Pricing the Put Option

The put option may similarly be priced using backwards induction. As the first step, we identify the value of the put at the terminal nodes:

$$\begin{aligned} P_{uu} &= \max\{100 - 121, 0\} = 0 \\ P_{ud} &= \max\{100 - 99, 0\} = 1 \\ P_{dd} &= \max\{100 - 81, 0\} = 19 \end{aligned} \tag{12.11}$$

Next, we identify the values of the put one period before maturity. Consider the node $uS = 110$ first. At this node, the put is worth

$$\begin{cases} 0, & \text{if the price moves up to } u^2 S = 121 \\ 1, & \text{if the price moves down to } udS = 99 \end{cases} \tag{12.12}$$

**FIGURE 12.7**

Evolution of Put Prices

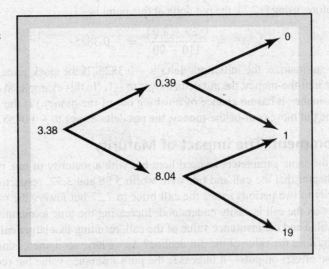

Thus, using risk-neutral pricing, the arbitrage-free price $P_u$ of the put at the node $uS$ is

$$P_u = \frac{1}{1.02}[(0.60)(0) + (0.40)(1)] = 0.39 \qquad (12.13)$$

Next, consider the node $dS = 90$. Here, the put is worth

$$\begin{cases} 1, & \text{if the price moves up to } udS = 99 \\ 19, & \text{if the price moves down to } d^2S = 81 \end{cases} \qquad (12.14)$$

Thus, the arbitrage-free price $P_d$ of the put at this node is

$$P_d = \frac{1}{1.02}[(0.60)(1) + (0.40)(19)] = 8.04 \qquad (12.15)$$

Finally, consider the initial node $S = 100$. As we have just seen, if the price goes up to $uS$, the put is worth $P_u = 0.39$; while if the price goes down to $dS = 90$, the put is worth $P_d = 8.04$. Invoking the risk-neutral probability again, the initial price $P$ of the put is

$$P = \frac{1}{r}[(0.60)(0.39) + (0.40)(8.04)] = 3.38 \qquad (12.16)$$

Figure 12.7 summarizes the evolution of put prices in this example.

## The Put Deltas

How do the put deltas change over the binomial tree? Consider the node $uS = 110$ first. The put values one period hence are given by (12.12). Therefore, using (12.1), the put delta at this point is

$$\Delta_u^p = \frac{0 - 1}{121 - 99} = -0.0455 \qquad (12.17)$$

Now consider the node $dS = 90$. Here, the put values one period hence are given by (12.14). Thus, from (12.1), the put delta at this point is

$$\Delta_d^p = \frac{1 - 18}{99 - 81} = -1 \qquad (12.18)$$

Finally, consider the initial node $S$. At this point, the stock price can go up to 110 or down to 90. The put value is 0.39 if the stock price goes up, and 8.04 if the stock price goes down.

Therefore, using (12.1), the put delta at this point is

$$\Delta^p = \frac{0.39 - 8.04}{110 - 90} = -0.3825 \qquad (12.19)$$

To summarize: the initial put delta is $-0.3825$. If the stock price declines and the put moves into-the-money, the put delta moves to $-1$. (In this example, at $dS$, the put is so deep in-the-money it has no chance of finishing out-of-the-money.) If the stock price increases and the put moves out-of-the-money, the put delta moves to $-0.0455$.

## A Comment: The Impact of Maturity

With the same parameters as used here but with a maturity of one period, we saw in the last chapter that the call and put were worth 5.88 and 3.92, respectively. The increase in maturity to two periods *raises* the call price to 7.27 but *lowers* the put value to 3.38. The impact on the call is easily understood. Increasing the time to maturity increases both the time value and the insurance value of the call, resulting in a larger call value.

Why does the value of the put decline? As we have seen, increasing maturity in general has two effects on puts—it increases the put's insurance value but reduces its time value. Whether the put value increases or decreases depends on which of these factors dominates. In the current example, once the node $dS = 90$ is reached, the two-period put is *guaranteed* to finish in-the-money. Thus, there is no insurance value left in the put at this node—insurance value matters only if optionality matters. However, there is negative time value since the put cannot be exercised for one more period. (Of course, there is some insurance value left in period 1 at the node $uS$, but the contribution of this node to the put value is relatively small.) As a consequence, the time-value effect dominates and the put value declines.

## An End-of-Tree Approach to European Option Pricing

The backwards induction procedure is an intuitive one, and it is one we shall need to price American-style options in binomial trees. For *European* options, however, there is a more direct procedure that exploits the fact that these options cannot be exercised until maturity. Specifically, we (a) find the risk-neutral probability of each terminal node, (b) multiply the option payoff at each terminal node by its risk-neutral probability, and (c) discount the result back to the beginning of the tree.

We illustrate this by applying it to our two-period example. In the example, the risk-neutral probability of an up move at any node is $q = 0.60$. There are three terminal stock prices: $u^2 S = 121$, $ud S = 99$, and $d^2 S = 81$. The risk-neutral probability of $u^2 S$ is the risk-neutral probability of two up moves, which is

$$0.60 \times 0.60 = 0.36$$

The node $ud S$ can be reached in two ways: by an up move followed by a down move or by a down move followed by an up move. Each of these has a risk-neutral probability of

$$0.60 \times 0.40 = 0.24$$

Thus, the risk-neutral probability of $ud S$ is $2 \times 0.24 = 0.48$. Finally, the node $d^2 S$ arises after two down moves, so its risk-neutral probability is

$$0.40 \times 0.40 = 0.16$$

Table 12.2 summarizes the information on the set of possible terminal stock prices, their risk-neutral probabilities, and the payoffs of the call and put options at each of these nodes. The expected payoff of the call under the risk-neutral probabilities is

$$(21 \times 0.36) + (0 \times 0.48) + (0 \times 0.16) = 7.56$$

**TABLE 12.2**
Terminal Node
Information

| Terminal Stock Prices | Risk-Neutral Probability | Terminal Payoffs Call | Put |
|---|---|---|---|
| 121 | 0.36 | 21 | 0 |
| 99 | 0.48 | 0 | 1 |
| 81 | 0.16 | 0 | 19 |

Since the payoffs occur at the end of two periods and the risk-free interest rate per period is 1.02, the payoffs should be discounted back using the two-period risk-free rate of $(1.02)^2$. This results in the initial call price

$$C = \frac{7.56}{(1.02)^2} = 7.27$$

The put may be priced similarly; its initial price $P$ is

$$P = \frac{(0 \times 0.36) + (1 \times 0.48) + (19 \times 0.16)}{(1.02)^2} = 3.38$$

Of course, these are the same prices recovered for the call and put earlier using backwards induction. This method of identifying the option prices is much quicker, but it cannot, unfortunately, be used for American-style options since it assumes there is no early exercise.

## 12.4  European Option Pricing in General $n$-Period Trees

European option prices in a general $n$-period tree may be found by either method described above: we can either use backwards induction or work directly with end-of-tree prices.

The backwards induction procedure in a general $n$-period tree follows the same steps. First, we identify all the option payoffs at maturity. Then we solve the one-period problem repeatedly to identify all the option values one period before maturity. Using these values, we "fold" the tree back one more step and identify all the option values two periods before maturity. We repeat this procedure until we reach the initial node. Of course, the process is easy to implement using a program or even a spreadsheet since it involves calling the same function (the one-period pricing function) repeatedly; for details, see Chapter 13.

Alternatively, we can use the end-of-tree prices approach. Using this procedure, it is possible to derive a general representation of European option prices in $n$-period binomial trees. The representation is of particular value because it bears considerable similarity to the Black-Scholes option pricing formula and can be used as a motivation for that formula. Of course, this resemblance is not accidental since the binomial model with a large number of periods starts resembling the Black-Scholes model. The representation is conceptually simple but involves some additional notation; we describe the details in Appendix 12A.

## 12.5  Pricing American Options: Preliminary Comments

The pricing of American options in binomial trees involves one extra degree of complication over the pricing of European options: it is necessary, in the backwards induction procedure, to allow for early exercise of the options. Some comments on the general procedure are useful.

To identify the value of an American-style option, we need to know when the cash flows are going to occur so that we can discount them back appropriately. This means we must know the *optimal early-exercise policy*, i.e., the conditions under which it is optimal to exercise the option early. Now, it is optimal to exercise at a node only if the value of immediate exercise exceeds the value of *not* exercising, i.e., of continuing. But the value of continuing depends on the option value at future nodes, which, in turn, depends on the value of stopping at those nodes or continuing further. Put differently, to identify the optimal exercise policy at a node, we need to know the optimal exercise policy at all future nodes.

This suggests a simple procedure for valuing the American option. We begin at a set of nodes where continuation is no longer an option, i.e., at the terminal nodes. The option values at these nodes can be ascertained unambiguously. Then we go back one period before maturity. If we exercise early at this stage, the value received is the intrinsic value of the option at that node. If we wait, we will be at maturity, and we know the option values that will result then. Comparing the two alternatives tells us (a) whether it is optimal to exercise early, and (b) the option value at this point.

Having identified all the option values one period before maturity, we now fold the tree back one more period. At each of the nodes that is two periods before maturity, we compare the value of exercising immediately to waiting. If we exercise immediately, we get the depth in-the-money of the option at that node. If we wait, we reach nodes that are one period from maturity, and we know the option value at each of these nodes. The higher of the two values again determines (a) whether and at which nodes it is optimal to exercise early and (b) the option value at each of these nodes.

This procedure is repeated until the initial time point of the tree is reached. The next section illustrates this using a two-period binomial example.

## 12.6   American Puts on Non-Dividend-Paying Stocks

Consider the two-period binomial tree used earlier in this chapter: $S = 100$, $u = 1.10$, $d = 0.90$, and $R = 1.02$. We look at pricing an American put in this example. The strike price is taken to be $K = 100$.

As an aside, recall that in an earlier chapter, we argued that early exercise could be optimal for an American put option even when there are no dividends. Exercising the put early results in a gain in time value but a loss in insurance value. The trade-off between these values determines the optimality of early exercise. We show that in this two-period example, the trade-off goes in favor of the time-value gain, so early exercise is optimal.

We begin, as the backwards induction procedure requires, at the end of the tree. At the terminal nodes, the payoffs from the put are the same as identified earlier in (12.11) for the European put:

$$P_{uu} = 0$$
$$P_{ud} = 1$$
$$P_{dd} = 19$$

Now we move back one period to the nodes $uS = 110$ and $dS = 90$.

### At the Node $uS = 110$

If the option is left unexercised at this node, then after one step, it pays

$$\begin{cases} 0, & \text{if the price moves to } u^2S = 121 \\ 1, & \text{if the price moves to } udS = 99 \end{cases}$$

Since the risk-neutral probability of an up move in this model is $q = 0.60$, the value of leaving the option unexercised is

$$\frac{1}{1.02}[(0.60)(0) + (0.40)(1)] = 0.392$$

The value of immediate exercise is negative: the option gives us the right to sell the stock for 100, but at this node, the stock is worth 110. Comparing these two values easily establishes that at the node $uS$:

- The value $P_u$ of the option is 0.392.
- Early exercise is *not* optimal at $uS$.

## At the Node $dS = 90$

If the option is left unexercised at $dS$, it pays:

$$\begin{cases} 1, & \text{if the price moves to } udS = 99 \\ 19, & \text{if the price moves to } d^2S = 81 \end{cases}$$

Thus, the value of leaving the option unexercised is

$$\frac{1}{1.02}[(0.60)(1) + (0.40)(19)] = 8.04$$

The value of immediate exercise at this node is $+10$ since the put gives us the right to sell for 100 a stock that is worth only 90. Comparing the two values, it is easy to see that at the node $dS$:

- The value $P_d$ of the option is 10.
- Early exercise *is* optimal at this node.

## At the Initial Node $S = 100$

We now move back a further period to the initial node $S$. If the option is not exercised immediately, it has a value after one step of, as we have just shown,

$$\begin{cases} 0.39, & \text{if the price moves to } uS = 110 \\ 10, & \text{if the price moves to } dS = 90 \end{cases}$$

Thus, the value of the option from not exercising immediately is

$$\frac{1}{1.02}[(0.60)(0.39) + (0.40)(10)] = 4.15$$

The value of immediate exercise at the node $S$ is zero since the option is at-the-money at this point. Comparing these values, we finally obtain

- The initial value of the put is $P = 4.15$.
- It is not optimal to exercise the put at the node $S$.

## What Drives Early Exercise?

Why is early exercise optimal at $dS$ in this example? A look at the option's payoffs provides the answer. As noted earlier, the put is very deep in-the-money at this node, so deep, in fact, that it is guaranteed to finish in-the-money at expiry. Under these conditions, there is no insurance value left in the put; insurance value arises only if optionality—the right to exercise (or not)—is important. However, there is still negative time value, which may be captured by exercising the option early.

## The Early-Exercise Premium

Recall that the price of the European-style put in this same example was 3.38. The American put costs significantly more at 4.15. The *early-exercise premium* (the excess price of the American put over the European) is given by $4.15 - 3.38 = 0.77$, which is over 18% of the value of the American put! The significant early-exercise premium reflects the American put holder's ability to avoid time-value loss by exercising early, while the European put holder is unable to do so.

### The Impact of Maturity

As we have seen, European put options can fall in value as maturity increases: the one-period put in this model costs 3.92, but the two-period European put costs 3.38. With American options, this is impossible since the put holder can always exercise early and avoid the negative effects of extra time. Thus, American puts will generally increase in value (or at least not decrease in value) with maturity. The present example illustrates this: while the one-period put costs 3.92, the two-period American put costs about 6% more at 4.15.

Finally, some notes about the option delta in this example. A simple calculation shows that the initial delta of the option (at the node $S$) is

$$\frac{0.39 - 10}{110 - 90} = -0.48$$

After an up move in the stock price the delta moves to

$$\frac{0 - 1}{121 - 99} = -0.045$$

After a down move in the stock price, early exercise is optimal; however, if the holder does not exercise at this stage, the delta becomes $-1$.

### Pricing American Calls

We argued in an earlier chapter that American calls on non-dividend-paying stock should never be exercised early. Thus, the price of an American call in this world must be equal to the European call. We have already seen how to price a European call in this model, so there is nothing to be added here.

It is a useful exercise for the reader to verify the non-optimality of early exercise for this example. That is, repeat the same steps we followed for the American put and show that early exercise is never optimal at any node.

## 12.7   Cash Dividends in the Binomial Tree

So far, we have ignored the possibility of dividends on the underlying asset during the life of the option. Now, we discuss how to extend the analysis to incorporate this feature.

In considering dividends on the underlying in the binomial tree, there are two possibilities to consider. The first is discrete "fixed cash" (or just "cash") dividends such as dividends on common stock. The second is a continuous dividend *yield* such as the yield on currencies or an index. The two have different implications for modeling. We examine cash dividends in this section and dividend yields later in this chapter.

The payment of discrete cash dividends causes a discontinuity in the stock price. Dividend announcements come with an *ex-dividend* date. The stockholder of record on the ex-dividend date is the one entitled to receive the dividends on the stock although the dividends are typically paid some time later. Thus, the stock price before the ex-dividend date (the "cum-dividend stock price") incorporates the dividend that will be paid on the stock, but this is not true of the stock price after the ex-dividend date (the "ex-dividend stock price").

**FIGURE 12.8**

The Binomial Tree
with Dividends

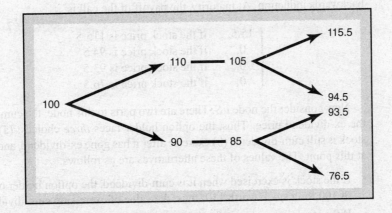

## Modifying the Binomial Tree to Incorporate Dividends

We first describe how to modify the binomial tree to incorporate the payment of dividends. Consider the same two-period model studied above: $u = 1.10$, $d = 0.90$, $R = 1.02$, and $S = 100$. Suppose now, however, that a dividend of $5 is paid after one period (i.e., period 1 is the ex-dividend date of the stock).

Then, the *cum-dividend* price following an up move in the stock price is 110. However, the *ex-dividend* price at this node is $110 - 5 = 105$. Similarly, the cum-dividend price at the node $dS$ is 90, but the ex-dividend price at $dS$ is $90 - 5 = 85$.

Since only the ex-dividend prices are relevant for further evolution of the prices, we have the following.

- The stock price following two up moves in the price is $105 \times 1.10 = 115.5$.
- The stock price after an up move followed by a down move is $105 \times 0.90 = 94.5$.
- The stock price after a down move followed by an up move is $85 \times 1.10 = 93.5$.
- The stock price following two down moves in the price is $85 \times 0.90 = 76.5$.

The resulting stock price tree is shown in Figure 12.8.

Note that in the presence of dividends, an up move followed by a down move does not lead to the same price as a down move followed by an up move: the tree fails to recombine. Recombination is, as we mentioned earlier, a desirable property from a computational standpoint; its failure makes the pricing more computationally complex. However, this added computational complexity is the only serious effect of introducing dividends; from a conceptual standpoint, the pricing of options remains quite simple, as we now see. In the next section, we see an alternative approach to modeling cash dividends that avoids the no-recombination problem.

## American Calls on Dividend-Paying Stocks

We saw in an earlier chapter that the optimality of early exercise could not be ruled out for calls on a dividend-paying stock. By exercising early, the holder of the call gives up the time value of the call and the insurance value of the call but gains the dividends on the underlying stock. The trade-off between these factors determines the optimality of early exercise; in particular, early exercise is optimal whenever the dividends are large enough to overwhelm the loss in insurance and time value.

The two-period tree described above illustrates this point. Consider an American call option with a strike of 100. We solve for the call value and the early exercise policy by backwards induction. At maturity, the payoff of the call is

$$\begin{cases} 15.5, & \text{if the stock price is } 115.5 \\ 0, & \text{if the stock price is } 94.5 \\ 0, & \text{if the stock price is } 93.5 \\ 0, & \text{if the stock price is } 76.5 \end{cases} \qquad \textbf{(12.20)}$$

Now consider the node $uS$. There are two parts to this node, the cum-dividend price and the ex-dividend price. Thus, the option holder faces *three* choices: (a) exercise when the stock is still cum-dividend, (b) exercise after it has gone ex-dividend, and (c) do not exercise at this point. The values of these alternatives are as follows:

- If the stock is exercised when it is cum-dividend, the option holder pays the strike price of 100 for a stock worth 110; thus, the value of exercising cum-dividend is $+10$.
- If the stock is exercised after it has gone ex-dividend, the option holder receives a stock worth 105 for the strike price of 100. Thus, exercising the call ex-dividend is worth $+5$.
- Finally, if the option is left unexercised, it has a value of 15.5 if the price goes up to 115.5 and a value of 0 if the price goes down to 94.5. Since the risk-neutral probability of an up move is 0.60, the value of leaving the option unexercised is

$$\frac{1}{1.02} [(0.60)(15.5) + (0.40)(0)] = 9.12$$

A comparison of these three values establishes that it is optimal to exercise the call early at the node $uS$ when the stock is still cum-dividend (i.e., just before it goes ex-dividend). Thus, the value of the option at the node $uS$ is $+10$.

The node $dS$ is easier to handle in this example. There are again the same three alternatives to consider. At the cum-dividend point, the stock price is 90, so exercising early results in a value of $-10$. At the ex-dividend point, the stock price is 85, so early exercise leads to a payoff of $-15$. If the option is not exercised early at this node, it results in a payoff of zero one period later. Thus, early exercise is not optimal at $dS$ and the value of the option here is zero.

Finally, consider the initial node $S$. Exercising the option at this node leads to a payoff of zero since the option is at-the-money. If it is left unexercised, it leads to a value in one period of

$$\begin{cases} +10, & \text{if the stock price goes up} \\ 0, & \text{if the stock price goes down} \end{cases}$$

Using the risk-neutral probability, the value of leaving the option unexercised is

$$\frac{1}{1.02}[(0.60)(10) + (0.40)(0)] = 5.88$$

Thus, the initial value of the American call option is 5.88.

What is the value of the corresponding *European*-style call? To identify the answer, we can use the end-of-tree payoffs in expression (12.20). The end-of-tree risk-neutral probability of the path

$$\begin{aligned} uu \text{ is } (0.6)(0.6) &= 0.36 \\ ud \text{ is } (0.6)(0.4) &= 0.24 \\ du \text{ is } (0.4)(0.6) &= 0.24 \\ dd \text{ is } (0.4)(0.4) &= 0.16 \end{aligned} \qquad \textbf{(12.21)}$$

So the initial value of the European call option works out to

$$\frac{1}{(1.02)^2} [(0.36)(15.5) + (0.24)(0) + (0.24)(0) + (0.16)(0)] = 5.37$$

The early-exercise premium is now $5.88 - 5.37 = 0.51$.

## Comments

The example above highlights three valuable points. The first is that dividends may make early exercise of calls optimal. In this example, this is because the dividends are high enough to make worthwhile giving up the call's time value and insurance value. In the exercises at the end of this chapter, we consider a similar setting but with lower dividends and higher volatility, and show that early exercise is no longer optimal.

Second, dividends on the stock always reduce option values. Without dividends, the American and European calls in this example are both worth 7.27. The presence of dividends hurts both: the American call falls in value to 5.88, while the European call falls to 5.37. The American call falls in value because the option holder is forced to choose between receiving the dividends and retaining the option's time and insurance value. The European call falls by even more because early exercise is not an option; the call holder takes the full brunt of the fall in stock prices on account of the dividend payment.

Third, greater time to maturity may not increase call values if there are interim dividends. The one-period call was worth 5.88, but the two-period European call is worth only 5.37: the dividend between the two periods lowers the payoffs to the holder of the longer-dated option. *American* calls cannot decline in value even if there are dividends since one can always exercise early, but they may not increase in value either: in the current example, the two-period American call is worth exactly the same as a one-period call.

### American Puts on Dividend-Paying Stocks

This is carried out exactly as in the case of an American call on a dividend-paying stock with the obvious changes. The details are left as an exercise to the reader.

1. The price of the American put is 7.15.
2. Early exercise is optimal at the node $dS$ after the stock goes ex-dividend.
3. The price of the corresponding European put is 6.38; thus, the early-exercise premium is 0.77.

# 12.8 An Alternative Approach to Cash Dividends

If we assume stock prices follow the Black-Scholes process but that there are cash dividends at discrete points in time, then the "correct" discrete-time representation of this is the binomial model described in the last section. Unfortunately, the lack of recombination of the binomial tree makes this model computationally harder to work with, especially if multiple dividend payments are involved. It is common in practice to use one of two alternatives. One is to use a different cash dividends model, described in this section, that assumes that the *net-of-dividends* stock price (rather than the cum-dividend stock price) is lognormal and may be represented by a recombining binomial tree. The other popular alternative is to represent the dividend as a *yield* (i.e., as a proportion of the stock price), in which case the tree is naturally recombining. Dividend yield models are the subject of the next section.

The first of these alternatives is introduced in Schroder (1988). In Schroder's approach, the stock price is viewed as being composed of two components: a riskless part equal to the present value of all the dividends that will be received over the option's lifetime, and a risky part representing the remainder of the stock price. The risky part is then modeled as a lognormal process (in this discrete setting, as a binomial tree). Since the risky component contains no dividend payments, the tree is recombining. We describe pricing options in this setting first in general notational terms in a binomial setting and then work through a numerical example.

## Dividends and the Stock Price Tree

Let $S_t$ denote the time-$t$ stock price, $D_t$ the cash dividend paid at time $t$, and $PV_t(D)$ the present value (viewed from time $t$ and including $D_t$) of the dividends that will be received over the option's remaining life. Note that, if $h$ denotes the time between binomial periods, then by definition,

$$PV_t(D) = D_t + \frac{1}{R} PV_{t+h}(D) \tag{12.22}$$

On the maturity date $T$ of the option, $PV_T(D)$ is just the dividends $D_T$ receivable on that date.[1]

Let $S_t^{net} = S_t - PV_t(D)$ denote the *net-of-dividends* component of the stock price. The main assumption in this approach is that this net-of-dividends component (the "net stock price") evolves according to a binomial process:

$$S_{t+h}^{net} = \begin{cases} uS_t^{net}, & \text{with probability } p \\ dS_t^{net}, & \text{with probability } 1 - p \end{cases} \tag{12.23}$$

The definition (12.23) ensures that the net stock price tree will be a recombining one. Now to obtain the total stock price tree, we simply add back the "escrowed" dividends at that point, i.e., the present value of the dividends receivable from that date to the option's maturity. For example, viewed from time $t$, the two possible values of the total stock price at $t + h$ are

$$S_{t+h}^u = uS_t^{net} + PV_{t+h}(D) \qquad \text{and} \qquad S_{t+h}^d = dS_t^{net} + PV_{t+h}(D) \tag{12.24}$$

The resulting total stock price tree will also be recombining since we are changing only the numbers at the various nodes but not the structure of the tree itself. See the example below for an illustration.

## The Risk-Neutral Probability

The risk-neutral likelihood $q$ of an up move in this setting is obtained as

$$qu + (1 - q)d = R \qquad \Longleftrightarrow \qquad q = \frac{R - d}{u - d} \tag{12.25}$$

To see that the risk-neutral probability has the form (12.25), note the following. If we buy the stock at time $t$ and hold it for one period, we receive $D_t$ at time $t$, so the net expenditure is only $S_t - D_t$. For this net outlay, we receive either $S_{t+h}^u$ or $S_{t+h}^d$ in one period. Under $q$, the expected return on the investment must be the risk-free rate $R$, i.e., $q$ must satisfy

$$\frac{qS_{t+h}^u + (1 - q)S_{t+h}^d}{S_t - D_t} = R$$

or what is the same thing,

$$qS_{t+h}^u + (1 - q)S_{t+h}^d = R(S_t - D_t) \tag{12.26}$$

---

[1] This notation allows for a dividend payment $D_t$ in each period of the binomial tree, but, of course, many of these payments may be zero.

Now, $S_t = S_t^{\text{net}} + PV_t(D)$, so, from (12.22),

$$S_t - D_t = S_t^{\text{net}} + \frac{1}{R} PV_{t+h}(D)$$

This means the right-hand side of (12.26) is

$$RS_t^{\text{net}} + PV_{t+h}(D) \qquad \qquad \textbf{(12.27)}$$

Combining (12.23) and (12.24), the left-hand side of (12.26) works out to be

$$qS_{t+h}^u + (1-q)S_{t+h}^d = [qu + (1-q)d]S_t^{\text{net}} + PV_{t+h}(D) \qquad \textbf{(12.28)}$$

Expressions (12.27) and (12.28) are equal if and only if the risk-neutral probability $q$ is given by (12.25).

## Pricing Options: The General Procedure

Given the stock price tree, options may be priced by backwards induction. Consider a call, for example. Let $C_t$ denote the value of the call at time $t$, and let $C_{t+h}^u$ and $C_{t+h}^d$ denote its possible values one period hence. If the option is European, then we have

$$C_t = \frac{1}{R}\left[qC_{t+h}^u + (1-q)C_{t+h}^d\right] \qquad \qquad \textbf{(12.29)}$$

while, at maturity $T$, the call is worth $C_T = \max\{S_T - K, 0\}$. Using (12.29), we can use backwards induction on the stock price tree to identify the initial value of the option.

If the call is American, immediate exercise at $t$ is also possible. We must distinguish between exercising the call cum-dividend and ex-dividend at this node. If the call is exercised cum-dividend, the amount received by the call holder is

$$S_t - K = S^{\text{net}} + PV_t(D) - K$$

If it is exercised ex-dividend, the amount received is

$$S_t - D_t - K = S^{\text{net}} + PV_t(D) - D_t - K$$

Putting these together, the call value is the maximum of the continuation value and the value of immediate exercise:

$$C_t = \max\left\{S_t - K, S_t - D_t - K, \frac{1}{R}\left[qC_{t+h}^u + (1-q)C_{t+h}^d\right]\right\} \qquad \textbf{(12.30)}$$

Expression (12.30) can be used to obtain the option price through backwards induction along the stock price tree. We illustrate these pricing arguments in an example.

**Example 12.1**  Consider a two-period binomial example. Let the initial price of the stock be $S = 100$. Suppose that there is only a single cash dividend over the two periods; assume this dividend is 5 in period 1. For the remaining parameters, we take $R = 1.02$, $u = 1.05$, and $d = 0.95$. Suppose that we wish to price two-period American and European calls with a strike of 100 in this setting.

In the notation introduced above, we have $D_0 = 0$, $D_1 = 5$, and $D_2 = 0$. This means $PV_0(D) = 5/1.02 = 4.90$, $PV_1(D) = 5$, and $PV_2(D) = 0$. The initial net-of-dividends price is

$$S^{\text{net}} = 100 - PV_0(D) = 100 - \frac{5}{1.02} = 95.098$$

The evolution of the net stock price from this level is determined by $u$ and $d$ as described in (12.23). The two-period net stock price tree is depicted in Figure 12.9.

**FIGURE 12.9**
Evolution of
Net-of-Dividend
Stock Prices

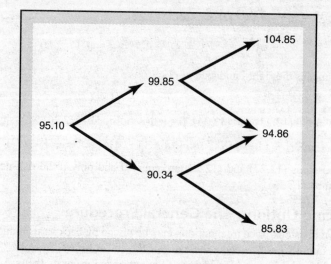

**FIGURE 12.10**
Evolution of Total
Stock Price

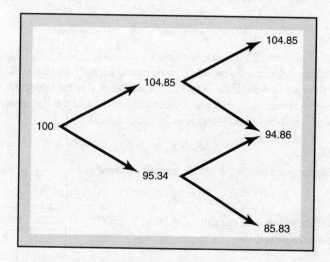

To obtain the total stock price tree from this, we simply add back $PV_t(D)$ at each date. The resulting evolution of total stock prices is depicted in Figure 12.10. Note that both the net-of-dividends tree and the total stock price tree are recombining trees.

Consider first the pricing of an American call on this tree. If the call is held to maturity, it pays $\max\{S_T - K, 0\}$; thus, the call values at the three terminal nodes are

$$C^{uu} = 4.85, \qquad C^{ud} = C^{dd} = 0$$

Using this and (12.30), we can identify the value of the option at earlier nodes. Consider the node $S_{t+h}^u$. At this point, the stock price is 104.85, while the dividend on this date is 5. Therefore, if the option is exercised cum-dividend, the holder receives

$$\max\{104.85 - 100, 0\} = 4.85$$

Exercising ex-dividend is not profitable since the ex-dividend stock price of $104.85 - 5 = 99.85$ is less than the strike price of 100. If the option is not exercised at this node, it is worth either 4.85 or zero next period, depending on whether the stock registers an up or a down move. So, using the risk-neutral probabilities, the value of not exercising is

$$\frac{1}{1.02}[(0.70)(4.85) + (0.30)(0)] = 2.28$$

**FIGURE 12.11**
Evolution of American
Call Values

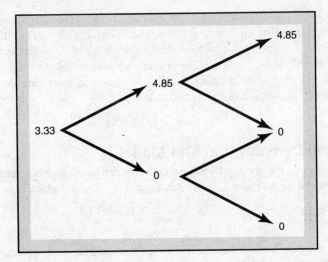

**FIGURE 12.12**
Evolution of European
Call Values

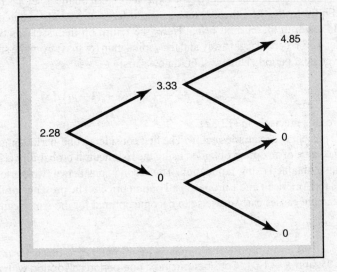

Comparing these three values establishes that the optimal action at this node is to exercise the call early and that the value of the call is 4.85. Working similarly, the rest of the tree can be filled up. Figure 12.11 describes the evolution of these prices.

The corresponding prices for the European call are similar but are easier to derive since there is no early exercise decision at each node. Figure 12.12 describes the evolution of European call values in this case. Note that there is a substantial early exercise premium of the American call in this example of $3.33 - 2.28 = 1.05$. ■

## 12.9   Dividend Yields in Binomial Trees

The notion of discrete dividends is okay for individual stocks, but payouts for some underlying assets, such as currencies and stock indices, are more naturally modeled as *yields*, i.e., as proportions of the current asset price. In this section, we describe binomial option pricing in this case. As we shall see, only minor adjustments to the theory are required.

The first step is describing the evolution of asset prices and the dividend process. We take *cum-dividend* prices to evolve on the binomial tree in the usual way as in Figure 12.1. But now we add the condition that holding the asset results in a cash flow of [$\delta \times$ the price of the asset] at each node. Thus, the asset pays a cash dividend of $\delta S$ if the current stock price is $S$; its price next period is either $uS$ or $dS$, at which point it pays a dividend of either $\delta uS$ or $\delta dS$, etc.

Chapter 13 describes how we identify the values of $\delta$, $u$, and $d$ for a stock paying a continuous dividend yield. For the present, we assume these values are given to us. Note that the presence of the dividend yield also requires us to modify the condition (11.4) for consistency of the binomial tree; rather than $d < R < u$, the condition now becomes

$$d \; < \; R(1 - \delta) \; < \; u \tag{12.31}$$

## Valuing Derivatives in This Model

The impact of the dividend yield on the valuation procedure is a remarkably simple one: the only change we make is to the risk-neutral probability, which now becomes

$$q = \frac{R(1 - \delta) - d}{u - d} \tag{12.32}$$

(If $\delta = 0$, we are back to the usual formula.) To see why the risk-neutral probability takes the form (12.32), recall that under $q$, the expected return on the asset has to equal the risk-free rate. Equivalently, the expected returns on the asset under $q$ discounted at the risk-free rate should result in the current price. Here, the return on the asset has two components, the dividend $\delta S$ received right away and the capital gain (or loss) from the stock price movement received next period. Thus, $q$ should now satisfy

$$S \; = \; \delta S + \frac{1}{R} \left[ q \, uS + (1 - q) \, dS \right]$$

This results precisely in (12.32).

We present two examples below. The first considers a one-period binomial tree and shows that the value of an option obtained using the risk-neutral probability (12.32) coincides with the value obtained using replication. The second considers a two-period binomial tree and solves for American and European call option prices. The presence of the dividend yield in the example causes early exercise to become optimal for the American option.

**Example 12.2**

Let $S = 100$ and suppose the remaining parameters are given by $u = 1.05$, $d = 0.95$, $\delta = 0.05$, and $R = 1.01$. Consider pricing a one-period call option with a strike of $K = 100$. The payoffs from the call after one period are

$$\begin{cases} 5, & \text{if the asset price moves to } 105 \\ 0, & \text{if the asset price moves to } 95 \end{cases}$$

We first price the call by risk-neutral valuation. From (12.32), the risk-neutral probability of an up move in the price is given by

$$q = \frac{R(1 - \delta) - d}{u - d} = \frac{0.0095}{0.10} = 0.095$$

Therefore, the value of the call obtained from risk-neutral valuation is

$$C = \frac{1}{1.01} \left[ (0.095)(5) + (0.905)(0) \right] = 0.4703 \tag{12.33}$$

We will show that the same call value results from replication. Consider a portfolio consisting of $\Delta$ units of the stock and $B$ in cash invested or borrowed at the rate $R$. Since the dividend on the call returns $\delta S$, the net cost of the portfolio is

$$\Delta (1 - \delta) S + B \; = \; 95 \, \Delta + B \tag{12.34}$$

After one period, the portfolio is worth $\Delta\, uS + RB$ if the asset price goes up and $\Delta\, dS + RB$ if it goes down. Substituting the values for $u$, $d$, and $\delta$, replication requires that the following equations be satisfied:

$$105\,\Delta + 1.01\,B = 5$$

$$95\,\Delta + 1.01\,B = 0$$

Solving this, we obtain $\Delta = 1/2$ and $B = -47.0297$. Substituting these values in (12.34), the initial cost of the replicating portfolio (and so the price of the call option) is

$$\left[95 \times \frac{1}{2}\right] - 47.0297 = 0.4703 \qquad \textbf{(12.35)}$$

This is, of course, the same value obtained using risk-neutral pricing. ∎

---

**Example 12.3**

Let a binomial tree be given with the following parameters: $S = 100$, $u = 1.10$, $d = 0.90$, $R = 1.02$, and $\delta = 0.05$. The cum-dividend stock price tree is the same as in earlier examples in this chapter (see Figure 12.2) and so is the interest rate. However, because of the dividend yield, the risk-neutral probability of an up move in any period is

$$q = \frac{R(1 - \delta) - d}{u - d} = \frac{0.069}{0.20} = 0.345 \qquad \textbf{(12.36)}$$

Suppose we wish to price a two-period call with a strike of 100. Consider a European call first. The payoffs from the call at maturity are exactly as described in Figure 12.3; in particular, the call has a positive payoff only if the path $uu$ occurs. Since the risk-neutral probability of two up moves is $(0.345)^2$, the price of the European call is

$$C_E = \frac{1}{(1.02)^2}\left[(0.345)^2 \times 21\right] = 2.4025 \qquad \textbf{(12.37)}$$

Now suppose the call is American. Its payoffs if left unexercised until maturity are exactly as described in Figure 12.3. We now apply backwards induction. At the node $uS$, the stock price is $uS = 110$, so early exercise of the call is worth 10. Not exercising early brings a payoff in the next period of either 21 (if the stock price moves up) or 0 (if it moves down). So the value of not exercising at $uS$ is

$$\frac{1}{1.02}[0.345 \times 21] = 7.103 \qquad \textbf{(12.38)}$$

Comparing these values, it is clear that early exercise is optimal at $uS$, so the option value at this node is 10. The option value at the node $dS$ is evidently zero. Continuing the backwards induction, the value of the American call at the initial node is

$$C_A = \frac{1}{1.02}[(0.345)(10) + (0.655)(0)] = 3.38 \qquad \textbf{(12.39)}$$

As the comparison of (12.37) and (12.39) shows, the dividend yield leads to early exercise of the American call and to a substantial early-exercise premium. ∎

## 12.10 Exercises

1. Keeping all other parameters the same, if the dividend rate on the stock increases, which option depreciates less, the American call or the European call? Why?

2. What condition is required on the movement of stock prices for the binomial tree to be recombining?

3. Why does the payment of dividends usually render the binomial tree into a nonrecombining one? What type of dividends causes the failure of recombination? What type of dividends does not?

4. Holding all else constant, if dividends increase, does the difference between American calls and puts increase or decrease? Why? What about the difference between European calls and puts?

5. How would you know from examining the risk-neutral probabilities on a binomial tree if the model is free from arbitrage?

6. Explain briefly in a heuristic manner why option replication on a binomial tree is a "dynamic" strategy.

7. Explain what is meant by a "self-financing" replicating strategy.

8. Suppose we used a trinomial tree with three replicating securities instead of a binomial tree with two securities. Would the dynamic replication be "self-financing"?

9. Suppose you have two states of the world and two assets. The prices of both assets in each of the two states are known. What conditions are needed for a derivative security that is a function of the two assets to be replicable?

10. (Difficult) In a two-period binomial tree, let the volatility at a given node (this is called the "local volatility" at that node) be given by

$$\sigma = \ln(u/d)$$

where $u$ and $d$ are the up and down moves, respectively, at that node. Given a starting stock price of \$50, suggest one way to draw a two-period *recombining* stock tree when the volatility of the first period is $\sigma = 0.20$ and in the second period $\sigma$ is 0.25.

11. You are given the following tree of stock prices. In addition, the rate of interest per period is constant at 2%. Find the risk-neutral probabilities of the stock movements from each node on the tree. Are these probabilities the same? If not, explain whether the tree is a valid one.

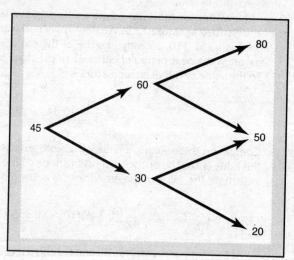

12. On the tree given in the previous problem, price the American call and the American put. Both options are assumed to be at strike $45.

13. Again, using the same tree as in the previous two questions, what is the delta of the call and the put at times 0 and 1?

14. The initial stock price is $100. The stock moves up each period by a factor of 1.3 and down by a factor of 0.8. If the simple interest rate per period is 1%, what is the risk-neutral probability of an up move in the stock price?

    Draw the stock price tree for three periods and price a European call option for three periods at strike $105.

15. The initial stock price is $100. The stock moves up each period by a factor of 1.3 and down by a factor of 0.8. If the simple interest rate per period is 1%, find the prices of three-period European and American puts, and state the early exercise premium amount.

16. When there are no dividends, the early exercise of an American put depends on a trade-off between insurance value (which comes from volatility) and time value (a function of interest rates). Thus, for example, for a given level of volatility, early exercise of the put becomes more likely if interest rates are higher. This question provides a numerical illustration.

    Consider a two-period binomial model with $u = 1.10$ and $d = 0.90$. Suppose the initial stock price is 100, and we are looking to price a two-period American put option with a strike of $K = 95$.

    (a) First, consider a "low" interest rate of $r = 1.02$. Show that early exercise of the American put is never optimal in this case.

    (b) Now consider a "high" interest rate of $r = 1.05$. Show that it now becomes optimal to exercise the put early in some circumstances. What is the early exercise premium in this case?

17. Consider a two-period example with $S = 100$, $u = 1.10$, $d = 0.90$, $r = 1.02$, and a dividend of $5 after one period. Is early exercise of a call optimal given these parameters?

18. We repeat the previous question with higher volatility and interest rates and with lower dividends. Consider a two-period binomial tree with the following parameters: $S = 100$, $u = 1.20$, $d = 0.80$, and $r = 1.10$. Suppose also that a dividend of $2 is expected after one period.

    (a) Compute the risk-neutral probability in this world.

    (b) Find the tree of prices of an American call option with a strike of 100 expiring in two periods.

    (c) What is the early-exercise premium?

19. The payment of a dividend on the underlying stock increases the value of a put option since it "lowers" the stock price distribution at maturity. This question provides a numerical illustration.

    Let a two-period binomial tree be given with the following parameters: $S = 100$, $u = 1.10$, $d = 0.90$, and $r = 1.05$. Consider a two-period American put option with a strike of 90. Note that this put is quite deep out-of-the-money at inception.

    (a) What is the value of the American put given these parameters?

    (b) Now suppose a dividend of $4 is paid at the end of the first period. What is the new price of the put?

20. In the absence of dividends, the holder of a European call always benefits from an increase in maturity since the insurance value and time value of the call both increase. However, for the holder of a European put in this case, insurance value increases but time value decreases, so the put value could increase or decrease. In general, for a given level of volatility, if interest rates are "high," the time-value effect will outweigh the insurance-value effect, so European put values will *decrease* as maturity increases; but if interest rates are "low," the insurance-value effect will dominate, so the put value will increase. This question illustrates these arguments.

Consider a binomial model with parameters $S = 100$, $u = 1.10$, and $d = 0.90$, and a European put with a strike of $K = 100$.

(a) First, consider a "high" interest rate environment where $r = 1.02$ (1 plus the interest rate). We can see that with these parameter values, a one-period put is worth 3.92, but a two-period European put is worth only 3.38. The increase in maturity hurts the put holder because the insurance-value effect is outweighed by the time-value effect.

(b) Now consider a "low" interest-rate environment where $r = 1.00$. Show that in this case, the one-period put is worth less than the two-period put.

21. Consider a binomial tree model with $u = 1.05$ and $d = 0.90$. Suppose the per-period interest rate is $r = 1.02$. Suppose the initial stock price is 100.

(a) What is the risk-neutral probability?

(b) Calculate the value of an American put option on the stock with a maturity of two periods and a strike of 95.

(c) Compute the early-exercise premium.

22. The initial stock price is $50. The up move in the stock price is modulated by factor $u = 1.2$, and the down move is $d = 0.9$. One dollar invested at the beginning of a period returns $1.05 at the end of the period.

Draw a two-period stock price tree for this stock. Then price the European call for two periods with a strike price of 50.

Find the replicating portfolio at the initial node on the tree. Show that this replicating portfolio does mimic the price of the call at both subsequent nodes at time 1 on the option tree.

23. Suppose the initial price of the stock is $100. The binomial process has an upshift $u = 1.5$ and a downshift $d = 0.6$ per period. The interest rate per period is assumed to be zero. What is the risk-neutral probability that the stock finishes above a price of $200 after six periods? What is the price of the six-period call at a strike of $200?

24. (Difficult) Using values for $u = 1.03$ and $d = 0.98$ and an initial stock price of $50, compute and plot the final risk-neutral probability distribution of the stock price after 100 periods. The interest rate is zero. What distribution does this remind you of?

25. The price today of stock XYZ is $100. Each period on a stock binomial tree is of length two months, i.e., 0.1667 of a year. The annualized risk-free rate on a continuously compounded basis is 5%. The annualized dividend rate on the stock is 2% continuously compounded. The dividend is paid as a percentage of the stock value at the *end* of period.

The up move (after adjusting for downward drift from the dividends) in the stock is driven by the factor $u = 1.167618$, and the down move (also after the effect of dividends) is modulated by $d = 0.842289$.

(a) What is the risk-neutral probability of an up move in the price?

(b) Compute the stock tree for three periods (i.e., for a six-month horizon).

(c) Based on this stock tree, compute the value of the dividends paid at the end of each period.

(d) Now compute the present value, as of time zero, of the terminal prices of the stock tree. Weight each value by its probability of occurring. What is the present value you get? Does this strike you as strange? Why or why not?

(e) Price the European call option at a strike of 100 for a maturity of six months.

(f) Price the American call option at a strike of 100 for a maturity of six months. Assume that if you exercise at a given node on the tree, you do not get the dividends for that period, but only for subsequent periods.

(g) Price the European put. Same terms as the calls.

(h) Price the American put. Same terms as the calls.

# A General Representation of European Option Prices

As mentioned in the text, we can derive a general $n$-period representation of European option prices in the binomial model that resembles the Black-Scholes formula in its structure. Consider an $n$-period binomial model with up and down moves given by $u$ and $d$, respectively. Let $S$ denote the initial stock price and $r$ the risk-free rate of interest per time step. Finally, let $K$ be the strike price of the options.

After $n$ periods, there are $n + 1$ possible distinct terminal prices as we noted at the beginning of this chapter (see Table 12.1):

- $n$ up moves, resulting in the price $u^n S$.
- $(n - 1)$ up moves and one down move, resulting in the price $u^{n-1} d S$.
- etc.
- $n$ down moves resulting in the price $d^n S$.

Denote by $C(m)$ and $P(m)$ the call and put payoffs at maturity if there have been $m$ up moves and $n - m$ down moves:

$$C(m) = \max\{u^m d^{n-m} S - K, 0\} \tag{12.40}$$

$$P(m) = \max\{K - u^m d^{n-m} S, 0\} \tag{12.41}$$

What are the risk-neutral probabilities of the various terminal nodes? A standard combinatoric exercise shows that the number of different combinations of $m$ up moves and $n - m$ down moves (i.e., of different ways in which $m$ up moves and $n - m$ down moves can happen) is

$$\frac{n!}{m!\,(n-m)!}$$

where $k!$ represents "factorial $k$," the product of all integers from 1 through $k$. (By convention, we take $0! = 1$.) Now, the risk-neutral probability of an up move in any period is given by

$$q = \frac{R - d}{u - d}$$

This means a specific combination of $m$ up moves and $n - m$ down moves has a risk-neutral probability of

$$q^m (1 - q)^{n-m}$$

Thus, the total risk-neutral likelihood of $m$ up moves and $n - m$ down moves, which we denote $Q(m)$, is

$$Q(m) = \frac{n!}{m!\,(n-m)!}\, q^m (1 - q)^{n-m}$$

Table 12.3 summarizes this notation. The expected payoff of the call at maturity under the risk-neutral probability is

$$Q(0)C(0) + \cdots + Q(n)C(n) \tag{12.42}$$

**TABLE 12.3**
Terminal Node
Information: General
$n$-Period Tree

| Stock Prices | Risk-Neutral Probability | Call Payoffs | Put Payoffs |
|---|---|---|---|
| $u^n S$ | $Q(n)$ | $C(n)$ | $P(n)$ |
| $u^{n-1}d S$ | $Q(n-1)$ | $C(n-1)$ | $P(n-1)$ |
| $\vdots$ | $\vdots$ | $\vdots$ | $\vdots$ |
| $ud^{n-1} S$ | $Q(1)$ | $C(1)$ | $P(1)$ |
| $d^n S$ | $Q(0)$ | $C(0)$ | $P(0)$ |

Discounting this back for $n$ periods using the risk-free rate $r$, we obtain the initial prices of the call and the put:

$$C = \frac{1}{R^n}[Q(0)C(0) + \cdots + Q(n)C(n)] \tag{12.43}$$

$$P = \frac{1}{R^n}[Q(0)P(0) + \cdots + Q(n)P(n)] \tag{12.44}$$

These expressions can be rewritten in a form similar to the Black-Scholes formula. Consider the call first. Since more up moves result in a higher stock price at maturity, there is a critical number of up moves $m^*$ such that the call finishes in-the-money if and only if the number of up moves $m$ satisfies $m \geq m^*$. That is:

$$C(m) = \begin{cases} 0, & \text{if } m < m^* \\ u^m d^{n-m} S - K, & \text{if } m \geq m^* \end{cases} \tag{12.45}$$

Therefore, we can rewrite (12.43) as

$$C = \frac{1}{R^n}[Q(m^*)C(m^*) + Q(m^*+1)C(m^*+1) + \cdots + Q(n)C(n)] \tag{12.46}$$

Substituting for $C(m)$ from (12.45), we have

$$C = \frac{1}{R^n}\sum_{m=m^*}^{n} Q(m)[u^m d^{n-m} S - K] \tag{12.47}$$

Breaking the right-hand side into two terms, we finally obtain

$$C = S \cdot \left(\frac{1}{R^n}\sum_{m=m^*}^{n}[Q(m)u^m d^{n-m}]\right) - \left(\frac{1}{R^n}K\sum_{m=m^*}^{n}[Q(m)]\right) \tag{12.48}$$

The second term on the right-hand side has a very simple interpretation. The first part of this term, $K/R^n$, is simply the present value of $K$ viewed from time 0. The second part of the term, $\sum_{m=m^*}^{n} Q(m)$, is, by definition of $m^*$, the risk-neutral probability that the call option will finish in-the-money. Thus, the second term measures the anticipated "cost" of exercising the option: the present value of $K$ times the probability of exercise. Similarly, the first term measures the anticipated benefit from the option (what one is going to receive times the likelihood of receiving it). The difference between the two terms must, of course, be the option value.

As we see later in this book, the Black-Scholes option pricing formula has a very similar structure to (12.48): the Black-Scholes call price too is of the form

$$[S \times \text{term 1}] - [PV(K) \times \text{term 2}]$$

where "term 2" in the Black-Scholes model is again the risk-neutral probability of the option finishing in-the-money.

The put price in the binomial model has a similar representation. The put finishes in-the-money if and only if $m < m^*$:

$$P(m) = \begin{cases} K - u^m d^{n-m} S, & \text{if } m < m^* \\ 0, & \text{if } m \geq m^* \end{cases} \qquad (12.49)$$

So, the initial price of the put may be written as

$$P = \frac{1}{R^n} \sum_{m=0}^{m^*-1} Q(m) [K - u^m d^{n-m} S] \qquad (12.50)$$

Breaking up the last term into two parts, we obtain

$$P = \frac{K}{R^n} \left( \sum_{m=0}^{m^*-1} Q(m) \right) - S \cdot \left( \frac{1}{R^n} \sum_{m=0}^{m^*-1} u^n d^{n-m} \right) \qquad (12.51)$$

The first term is the present value of $K$ times the risk-neutral probability that the put finishes in-the-money; it represents what one expects to get from the put. The second term represents the value of what one expects to give up in the put (i.e., the value of the stock given up by exercise). The difference between the terms is the value of the put.

As with the call, the Black-Scholes formula for the price of a European put has a very similar structure to (12.51); it is of the form

$$P = [PV(K) \times \text{ term 1}] - [S \times \text{ term 2}] \qquad (12.52)$$

with "term 1" being the risk-neutral probability that the put finishes in-the-money.

# Chapter 13

# Implementing the Binomial Model

## 13.1 Introduction

The last two chapters have examined the pricing of options using binomial trees, taking the parameters of the tree as given. Rounding off this material, this chapter discusses two key issues: (a) *how* these parameters are determined, and (b) computer implementation of binomial trees. In the process, we introduce one of the most useful distributions in option pricing, the lognormal distribution.

The idea behind identifying the parameters of the binomial model is a simple one. Given a horizon $T$, we choose a distribution of prices that "best" represents the possible prices of the underlying at $T$. Then we choose the parameters of the binomial tree so that the distribution of prices on the terminal nodes of the binomial tree resembles the chosen distribution as closely as possible.

For the time-$T$ distribution, we choose the lognormal distribution. The lognormal distribution is widely used in practice to represent returns on a variety of underlying assets such as equities, indices, and currencies. The lognormal is also the distribution underlying the Black-Scholes model, which we examine in the next chapter. However, there are some assets (such as bonds) for which the lognormal is not always suitable. Given its widespread use and importance, we begin with a discussion of this distribution.

## 13.2 The Lognormal Distribution

In expressing the evolution of prices on an asset, what we are describing is the process of *returns* on that asset. The lognormal distribution assumes that the log of these returns has a normal distribution.

Let $S_0$ denote the current price of the asset and $S_T$ denote its price in $T$ years. In simple terms, the gross return on the asset over this horizon is $S_T/S_0$. Let $N(m, v)$ denote the normal distribution with mean $m$ and variance $v$ (i.e., with standard deviation $\sqrt{v}$). The lognormal distribution assumes that for any $T$

$$\ln\left(\frac{S_T}{S_0}\right) \sim N(\mu T, \sigma^2 T) \qquad (13.1)$$

where $\mu$ and $\sigma$ are the two parameters of the distribution. From (13.1), the expected log-return and variance of log-returns over the $T$-year horizon are, respectively, $\mu T$ and $\sigma^2 T$:

$$E\left[\ln\left(\frac{S_T}{S_0}\right)\right] = \mu T \tag{13.2}$$

$$\mathrm{Var}\left[\ln\left(\frac{S_T}{S_0}\right)\right] = \sigma^2 T \tag{13.3}$$

In particular, by taking $T = 1$ year, we see that $\mu$ is the expected annual log-return and $\sigma^2$ is the variance of the annual log-returns.

Figure 13.1 provides plots of the lognormal returns for various parameter values. (The plots are of the lognormal probability density function. Thus, the probability of gross returns less than or equal to $x$ is the area under the curve to the left of $x$.) The horizon in the figure is

**FIGURE 13.1**

The Lognormal Density Function

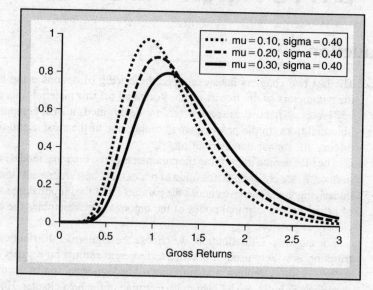

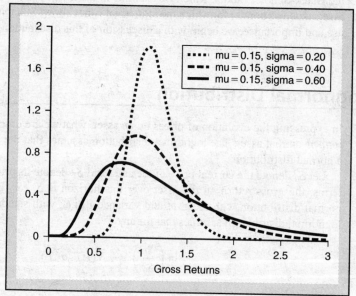

fixed at one year. As is evident from the plots, the lognormal is a skewed distribution. Unlike the normal distribution, which can take both positive and negative values, the logarithmic function $\ln x$ is defined only for positive $x$, so the lognormal distribution is defined over only the positive part of the axis.

## Log-Returns = Continuously-Compounded Returns

Suppose the realized log-return on an asset over a horizon $[0, T]$ is $x$:

$$\ln \left( \frac{S_T}{S_0} \right) = x \tag{13.4}$$

Then, this implies

$$\frac{S_T}{S_0} = e^x \tag{13.5}$$

(We have used the fact that if $\ln y = z$, then $y = e^z$.) Expression (13.5) says precisely that the continuously-compounded return on the asset over the period $[0, T]$ is also $x$. That is, log-returns and continuously-compounded returns are two names for exactly the same concept.

## The Notion of "Volatility"

The parameter $\sigma$ has a special name: it is called the asset's *volatility*. Thus, the term volatility refers to the *standard deviation of log-returns* expressed in annualized terms.

It is common in practice to express volatility in percentage terms, for example, to refer to a volatility of 35%. A volatility of 35% means that $\sigma = 0.35$. In general, while $\sigma$ must be positive, there are no natural upper bounds on how large it can be. Individual stock volatilities in the US are usually of the order of 30%–50%, although much higher volatilities (70%–100% and even more) may obtain on occasion, particularly on small-cap or technology/new economy stocks. Stock index and currency volatilities tend to be much lower, typically 20% or less.

In Appendix 13A, we discuss how to compute the volatility of an asset from information on past price observations. This is called *historical volatility*. A related but distinct notion is that of *implied volatility*, which we discuss in the chapter on Black-Scholes.

## Log-Returns and the Simple Returns $S_T/S_0$

What does the lognormal distribution imply for the simple expected returns $S_T/S_0$? Appealing to standard properties of the lognormal distribution, it can be shown that the mean and variance of simple returns are given by

$$E \left[ \frac{S_T}{S_0} \right] = e^{\mu T + \frac{1}{2}\sigma^2 T} \tag{13.6}$$

$$\text{Var} \left[ \frac{S_T}{S_0} \right] = e^{2\mu T + 2\sigma^2 T} - e^{2\mu T + \sigma^2 T} \tag{13.7}$$

For one special case, (13.6) is easily verified. When $\sigma = 0$ (there is no volatility), the lognormal assumption implies that

$$\ln \left( \frac{S_T}{S_0} \right) = \mu T \tag{13.8}$$

so that

$$\frac{S_T}{S_0} = e^{\mu T} \tag{13.9}$$

which is precisely (13.6) for this case.

While they are related, log-returns and simple returns are distinct concepts and should not be confused with each other. An example will help make this point.

---

**Example 13.1**

Suppose the returns on XYZ stock are distributed lognormally with a mean of 10% and a volatility of 40%. Then, using (13.6), the expected simple return from holding the stock for a period of one year is

$$e^{(0.10)(1)+\frac{1}{2}(0.16)(1)} = 1.197$$

so the net return is 19.7%, almost twice the expected log-return of 10%. The variance of simple returns over a one-year holding period is

$$e^{2(0.10)(1)+2(0.16)(1)} - e^{2(0.10)(1)+(0.16)(1)} = 0.249$$

or 24.9%, compared to the variance of log-returns of $(0.40)^2 = 16\%$. ∎

---

Here is one other difference. Suppose *simple* returns were normal, i.e.,

$$\frac{S_T}{S_0} \sim N(mT, s^2 T)$$

for some $m$ and $s > 0$. Then, since the outcomes of a normal distribution can assume any value between $-\infty$ and $+\infty$, simple returns may be *less* than 100%, meaning that the time-$T$ price $S_T$ may be negative. This is obviously undesirable since equity prices or exchange rates cannot turn negative. With a lognormal distribution, this is never a problem: for any realization $z$ of log-returns, $S_T/S_0$ is, from (13.1), given by $e^z$, and this must always be positive.

## The Assumption of i.i.d. Returns

The term "independently and identically distributed" (abbreviated i.i.d.) refers to a stochastic process in which

- the probability distribution of outcomes at any time is identical to that at any other time, and

- outcomes are independent over time, i.e., outcomes at time $t$ do not depend on outcomes at any point before $t$.

The assumption (13.1) of lognormal returns also involves an assumption that log-returns are i.i.d. The log-returns over any period of length $T$ years depend only on $T$ and the parameters $\mu$ and $\sigma$ of the normal distribution. Thus, the expected log-return over a two-month period is twice the expected log-return over a one-month period, etc. And, of course, returns at any point do not depend on past returns.

The assumption of i.i.d. returns makes the model technically easy to handle, but is it a good assumption from an *economic* standpoint? That is, are returns in practice (at least approximately) i.i.d.? Available data suggests perhaps not. In stock markets, sharply negative returns are often followed by increased volatility, while high returns are often succeeded by low volatility, a pattern that is sometimes called the "leverage effect." We discuss this issue further at the end of the Black-Scholes chapter.

## Working with the Lognormal Distribution

The normal distribution is mathematically one of the easiest distributions to work with. It has a number of powerful properties. For example, every normal distribution is symmetric about the mean, and in *any* normal distribution, the mean $\pm 1.96$ standard deviations covers 95% of the area. This makes it very easy to construct confidence intervals and such financial measures as Value-at-Risk.

Almost all of the properties of the normal are preserved in the lognormal. For example, to construct confidence intervals for a lognormal distribution, all we need do is construct confidence intervals using the underlying normal distribution for log-returns and then exponentiate. The following example illustrates.

**Example 13.2**

Consider a horizon of three months ($T = 1/4$), and suppose a stock has lognormal returns with $\mu = 0.10$ and $\sigma = 0.30$. Suppose also that the current price of the stock is $S = 100$. What is a 95% confidence interval for the stock price in three months?

Since $T = 1/4$, we have

$$\mu T = 0.10 \times 0.25 = 0.025, \qquad \sigma^2 T = 0.30^2 \times 0.25 = 0.0225$$

That is, $\ln(S_T/S)$ is distributed normally with a mean of 0.025 and a standard deviation of $\sqrt{0.0225} = 0.15$. For a normally distributed random variable, 95% of observations lie within 1.96 standard deviations of the mean. Thus, with probability 0.95, $\ln(S_T/S)$ will lie between

$$[0.025 - (1.96)(0.15)] = -0.269 \quad \text{and} \quad [0.025 + (1.96)(0.15)] = +0.319$$

Exponentiating both sides, it is the case that with probability 0.95, $S_T/S$ lies between

$$e^{-0.269} = 0.7641 \quad \text{and} \quad e^{+0.319} = 1.3758$$

Therefore, with probability 0.95, $S_T$ lies between

$$S \times (0.7641) = 76.41 \quad \text{and} \quad S \times (1.3758) = 137.58$$

This identifies the 95% confidence interval for $S_T$. ∎

## The Lognormal as a Model of Bond Returns?

For at least two reasons, the lognormal is inadequate as a model of bond price evolution. First, in a lognormal distribution, the uncertainty regarding future prices increases as the horizon increases—the larger is $T$, the greater is the variance of returns $\sigma^2 T$. However, absent default risk, the bond price at maturity—its face value—is known with certainty today; thus, uncertainty regarding future bond prices must go to zero as maturity approaches. Even with default risk, the bond price at maturity can vary only between zero and its face value, so the lognormal is still inappropriate. Second, a lognormal distribution of bond prices implies a normal distribution of bond yields. This means bond yields and interest rates can be negative.

## The Actual and Risk-Neutral Distributions

Since derivative prices depend only on the risk-neutral distribution of asset prices, we can use the binomial tree to approximate either the actual distribution of asset prices or the risk-neutral distribution. If we use the former, $\mu$ and $\sigma$ represent the actual annualized mean and variance of log-returns on the underlying asset. If we use the risk-neutral distribution, the asset's volatility is unaffected but its expected return must equal the risk-free rate. The expected return is, as we have seen in (13.6) above, given by

$$E\left[\frac{S_T}{S_0}\right] = e^{\mu T + \frac{1}{2}\sigma^2 T} \tag{13.10}$$

Let $r$ be the risk-free rate for a horizon of $T$ years expressed in annualized continuously-compounded terms. Then, \$1 invested for $T$ years at the rate $r$ grows to \$$e^{rT}$ in $T$ years. So, for the expected return in (13.10) to equal the risk-free rate, we must have

$$\mu T + \frac{1}{2}\sigma^2 T = rT$$

or

$$\mu = r - \frac{1}{2}\sigma^2 \qquad\qquad \textbf{(13.11)}$$

Thus, if the lognormal is to represent the risk-neutral distribution of asset returns, $\mu$ is given by (13.11).

## 13.3 Binomial Approximations of the Lognormal

Suppose we are given an asset whose returns follow a lognormal distribution with parameters $\mu$ and $\sigma$. Given a horizon of $T$ years, how do we choose binomial parameters so that the binomial tree approximates the given distribution?

In principle, we have four free binomial-tree parameters we can choose:

- $u$ and $d$, the up and down move sizes, respectively.
- $p$, the probability of an up move.
- $n$, the number of steps in the binomial tree.

Of these parameters, $n$ is usually fixed in advance. Ideally, we would like to choose $n$ as large as possible, but we would also like computational tractability of the model. The choice of $n$ reflects a compromise between these conflicting objectives. Typically, $n$ is taken to be at least 100, although far larger trees are commonly used in practice.

So, suppose $n$ is fixed at some level. Let $h = T/n$ denote the length (in years) of each step of the binomial tree. This leaves us with three parameters whose values are to be determined: $u$, $d$, and $p$. Our objective is to choose these parameters so that the distribution of prices after $n$ steps of the binomial tree resembles a lognormal distribution with parameters $\mu T$ and $\sigma^2 T$. In particular, we want the expected log-return after $n$ steps of the tree to be approximately $\mu T$, and the variance of log-returns to be approximately $\sigma^2 T$, with the approximations improving as $n$ increases.

Now, the returns on each step of the binomial tree are identical to the returns on any other step of the tree. Moreover, returns across different time steps are independent—the return realized in any step does not affect the likelihood of $u$ or $d$ in any other time step. Thus:

- The expected return over $n$ steps of the binomial tree is simply $n$ times the expected return over each step of the tree.
- The variance of returns over $n$ steps of the tree is $n$ times the variance of returns over each step.

So our first step has to be an understanding of the returns *per step* of the binomial tree. Over each step, the asset returns $u$ with probability $p$ and $d$ with probability $1 - p$. Thus, the *log-returns* in each step are

$$\begin{cases} \ln u, & \text{with probability } p \\ \ln d, & \text{with probability } 1 - p \end{cases}$$

This gives us:

Expected log-return per step $\quad = p \ln u + (1 - p) \ln d$

Variance of log-returns per step $\; = p(1 - p) [\ln u - \ln d]^2$

Summing these returns over $n$ steps,

Expected log-return over $n$ steps $\quad = n[p \ln u + (1 - p) \ln d]$

Variance of log-returns over $n$ steps $= np(1 - p) [\ln u - \ln d]^2$

To match this mean and variance with those of the lognormal, we must choose $u$, $d$, and $p$ so that the following equalities hold at least approximately:

$$n[p \ln u + (1 - p) \ln d] = \mu T \qquad (13.12)$$

$$np(1 - p)[\ln u - \ln d]^2 = \sigma^2 T \qquad (13.13)$$

Equivalently, dividing through by $n$ in both equations, we want

$$p \ln u + (1 - p) \ln d = \mu h \qquad (13.14)$$

$$p(1 - p)[\ln u - \ln d]^2 = \sigma^2 h \qquad (13.15)$$

Expressions (13.14) and (13.15) give us two equations in three unknowns. Obviously, there are multiple solutions to these equations. Two of particular interest are highlighted below.

## The Cox-Ross-Rubinstein Solution

The Cox-Ross-Rubinstein (CRR) solution to parametrizing the binomial model is to take

$$u = e^{\sigma \sqrt{h}} \qquad (13.16)$$

$$d = \frac{1}{u} = e^{-\sigma \sqrt{h}} \qquad (13.17)$$

$$p = \frac{1}{2} + \frac{1}{2} \left( \frac{\mu}{\sigma} \right) \sqrt{h} \qquad (13.18)$$

A simple calculation shows that under (13.16)–(13.18), we obtain

$$p \ln u + (1 - p) \ln d = \mu h \qquad (13.19)$$

so the requirement (13.14) is met exactly. Moreover,

$$p(1 - p) [\ln u - \ln d]^2 = \sigma^2 h - \mu^2 h^2 \qquad (13.20)$$

For large values of $n$, $h$ becomes a small fraction, so terms of the order of $h^2$ become smaller still. This means the variance requirement (13.15) is approximately met, and the approximation becomes more accurate the larger is the value of $n$. Indeed, as $n \to \infty$, the entire binomial distribution with parameters given by the CRR solution (13.16)–(13.18) converges to a lognormal distribution with mean $\mu T$ and variance $\sigma^2 T$.

The CRR solution has some properties worth emphasizing. First, the CRR tree is "centered" on $S$. Since $ud = 1$ in the CRR solution, an up move followed by a down move always brings us back to the initial price. Second, in the CRR solution, $u$ and $d$ depend only on a single parameter $\sigma$. This is important because the probability $p$ plays no role in pricing derivatives in a binomial model; only $u$ and $d$ (and the risk-free rate) matter. Thus, the CRR tree can be implemented and options priced based on knowledge of $\sigma$ alone.

## The Jarrow-Rudd Solution

The Jarrow-Rudd (JR) solution to parametrizing the binomial model is to take

$$u = e^{\mu h + \sigma\sqrt{h}} \qquad (13.21)$$

$$d = e^{\mu h - \sigma\sqrt{h}} \qquad (13.22)$$

$$p = \frac{1}{2} \qquad (13.23)$$

It is easy to check that under the JR solution, the requirements (13.14) and (13.15) are met exactly. And, indeed, once again, as $n \to \infty$, the entire binomial distribution with parameters given by the JR solution (13.21)–(13.23) converges to a lognormal distribution with mean $\mu T$ and variance $\sigma^2 T$.

A seeming disadvantage of the JR solution is that the parameters $u$ and $d$ depend on both $\mu$ and $\sigma$, so the mean expected log-return is also required to implement the tree. One way around this problem, commonly adopted in using this solution, is to approximate the *risk-neutral* distribution of the asset returns rather than the actual distribution. In this case, as we have seen in (13.11) above, $\mu$ depends on only the risk-free rate and $\sigma$.

## Other Possibilities?

Since we have two equations in three unknowns, many other solutions are, of course, possible. For example, we could choose the parameters of the tree so that the *risk-neutral probability* implied by the parameters is equal to 1/2. Recall that the risk-neutral probability is given by

$$q = \frac{R - d}{u - d} \qquad (13.24)$$

where $R$ is the gross rate of interest per step of the binomial tree. The parameter $R$ may be readily computed from knowledge of the $T$-year interest rate. For example, if the $T$-year interest rate in continuously compounded terms is $r$ (i.e., an investment of \$1 grows to $e^{rh}$ in $T$ years), then $R$ is given by

$$R = \exp\{rh\} \qquad (13.25)$$

Using the approximation $e^x \approx 1 + x$ (which is a good approximation for small values of $x$), it is easily seen that the risk-neutral probabilities under the CRR and JR solutions are, respectively,

$$q_{CRR} = \frac{1}{2} + \frac{1}{2}\frac{r}{\sigma}\sqrt{h}$$

and

$$q_{JR} = \frac{1}{2} + \frac{1}{4}\sigma\sqrt{h}$$

In each case, these probabilities converge to 1/2 as $h \to 0$. But if we want $q$ to be exactly equal to 1/2 for a given value of $h$, then we must have

$$\frac{R - d}{u - d} = \frac{1}{2}$$

which is the same thing as

$$u + d = 2R \qquad (13.26)$$

Expression (13.26) gives us a third equation in the unknowns $u$ and $d$. In conjunction with (13.14) and (13.15), this gives us a three-equation system in the three unknowns $u$, $d$, and *p*. In the solution to this three-equation system, the risk-neutral probability is guaranteed to be 1/2.

## Does It Matter Which Solution We Use?

To an extent, no. As long as all the solutions converge to the lognormal distribution, they also resemble each other for large values of *n*. However, the pace and manner of the convergence can be quite different.

Figure 13.2 illustrates this point. The upper panel of the figure considers a call option priced on a binomial tree using the CRR approximation of the lognormal. The lower panel uses the JR approximation. In either case, the lognormal distribution has a volatility of 40%, the maturity of the option is taken to be one year, the risk-free rate is 5% per year in continuously compounded terms, the initial stock price is 100, and the call is taken to be at-the-money. In both panels, the horizontal axis is the number of steps used in the binomial tree, and the vertical axis is the option price obtained from the tree.

**FIGURE 13.2**

Convergence of the
CRR and JR Solutions

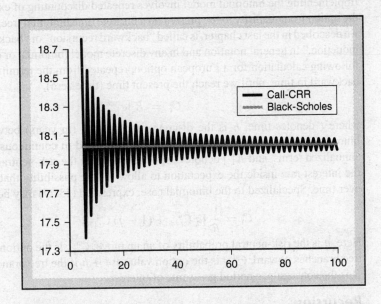

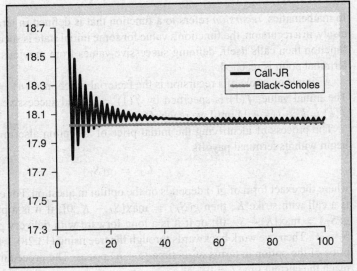

The option price in both panels converges to the Black-Scholes price, which for the given parameters, works out to marginally under 18.023. However, as the figure shows, the manner of convergence is quite different. The CRR solution oscillates between over- and under-approximations of the limit price with the oscillations gradually dampening as the number of steps in the binomial tree increases. The over- and under-approximations are almost symmetric, so their *average* converges very rapidly to the Black-Scholes price. For example, with $n = 21$ and $n = 22$, the option prices on the tree are 18.199 and 17.847, which represent significant over- and under-estimates of the Black-Scholes price. However, the average of the two is 18.023, almost exactly the limit price. The JR convergence pattern is more complex.

## 13.4 Computer Implementation of the Binomial Model

Implementing the binomial model involves repeated discounting of expected cash flows of the option from maturity to the present on a discrete time binomial tree. This process, which we described in the last chapter, is called "backward recursion" or "backward (or backwards) induction." In general notation and in any discrete model (binomial or other), it requires the following calculation for a European option, repeated from the terminal nodes on the tree, backward in time, until we reach the present time (time zero).

$$C_t = E \left[ e^{-rh} C_{t+h} \right] \qquad \text{(13.27)}$$

where $t$ denotes time, $h$ is the discrete time interval (in years) between periods on the binomial tree, $r$ is the risk-free interest rate expressed in continuously-compounded and annualized terms, and $E[\cdot]$ denotes expectations under the risk-neutral probability. We put the interest rate inside the expectation to allow for the possibility that it may be changing over time. Specialized to the binomial case, expression (13.27) may be rewritten as

$$C_t = \frac{1}{R} \left[ q\, C_{t+h}^u + (1-q)\, C_{t+h}^d \right] \qquad \text{(13.28)}$$

Here, $q$ is the risk-neutral probability of an up move, $C_{t+h}^u$ is the option value at $t + h$ if the tree branches upward, $C_{t+h}^d$ is the option value at $t + h$ if the tree branches downward, and $R$ is the constant per-period gross rate of interest.

### Recursion

In mathematics, *recursion* refers to a function that is defined in terms of itself. More precisely, in a recursion, the function's value for some initial state is specified exogenously. The function then calls itself, defining successive values from previous ones, until a specified terminal point is reached.

A simple example of a recursion is the factorial function, $f(n) = n! = 1 \times 2 \times \cdots \times n$. The initial value, $f(1)$ is specified by $f(1) = 1$, and successive values are defined by $f(k) = k \times f(k-1)$ until we reach $f(n)$.

The process of identifying the initial price of an option also involves a recursion. We begin with its terminal payoffs

$$C_T = g(S_T)$$

where the exact form of $g(\cdot)$ depends on the option in question. For example, if the security is a call with strike $K$, then $g(S_T) = \max\{S_T - K, 0\}$; if it is a put with strike $K$, then $g(S_T) = \max\{K - S_T, 0\}$; or if it is a long forward with delivery price $F$, then $g(S_T) = S_T - F$. Then, we work backwards through the tree using (13.28), which defines the time-$t$ price of the option in terms of its time-$(t + h)$ prices. The procedure terminates when we reach the current time $t = 0$.

## Implementing the Recursion

Implementing this recursion on a computer is not hard. Let the initial stock price be $S$, the annualized stock volatility be $\sigma$, the option strike price be $K$, and the number of periods on the tree be $n$. Suppose we use the CRR solution to parametrizing the binomial tree. The entire system of equations is:

$$h = \frac{T}{n}$$

$$u = \exp(\sigma\sqrt{h})$$

$$d = \exp(-\sigma\sqrt{h}) = \frac{1}{u}$$

$$R = e^{-rh}$$

$$q = \frac{R-d}{u-d}$$

$$S_0 = S$$

$$S_{t+h}^u = uS_t$$

$$S_{t+h}^d = dS_t$$

$$C_T = \begin{cases} \max[0, S_T - K] \text{ for calls} \\ \max[0, K - S_T] \text{ for puts} \end{cases}$$

$$C_t = \frac{1}{R}\left[q\,C_{t+h}^u + (1-q)\,C_{t+h}^d\right]$$

Here is Octave code to implement this recursion:

```
%Recursive program to price options
function w = crr_rec(s,k,t,v,r,pc,n);
if n==0;
        if pc==1; optval=max(0,s-k); end;
        if pc==0; optval=max(0,k-s); end;
else
        h = t/n;
        u = exp(v*sqrt(h));
        d = exp(-v*sqrt(h));
        R = exp(r*h);
        q = (R-d)/(u-d);
        optval = (q*crr_rec(s*u,k,t-h,v,r,pc,n-1) + ...
                 (1-q)*crr_rec(s*d,k,t-h,v,r,pc,n-1))/R;
end;
w = optval;
```

The tree underlying the option is represented as a recursion on the third- and fourth-last lines of the program. This line where optval is computed contains, therefore, a recursion over the option price and embeds another recursion in the underlying stock price as well. Note carefully how the boundary condition is implemented in this model. Within the recursion line is yet another (trivial) recursion in time where we count down to maturity. When there are no remaining periods (n==0), the program ignores the recursion and implements the terminal payoff conditions in lines 4–5 of the program.

As an example, we can run the program and do three things: (a) price a call, (b) price a put, and (c) check whether put-call parity holds so that we can assure ourselves that the model works. Here is the `Octave` output:

```
octave:1> callopt = crr_rec(50,52,0.5,0.3,0.03,1,10)
callopt = 3.7553
octave:2> putopt = crr_rec(50,52,0.5,0.3,0.03,0,10).
putopt = 4.9812
octave:3> callopt - putopt
ans = -1.2258
octave:4> 50 - 52*exp(-0.03*0.5)
ans = -1.2258
```

We used an initial stock price of \$50, strike of \$52, maturity of a half year, $\sigma = 0.3$, $r = 0.03$, and $n = 10$ (10 periods in the tree). Note that put-call parity holds exactly.

The implementation remains exactly the same if we choose to adopt the JR form of the binomial model. Only the definitions for $u$ and $d$ in the program would require modification.

## The Problem with Recursion

While recursion is easy to implement, it is not the most efficient way to implement the binomial tree because the recursion does not take advantage of the fact that the CRR tree is a recombining one. Think for a moment about what happens when we start the recursion. The initial node calls upon the two succeeding nodes, which in turn call upon two nodes each, and so on. Hence, after two steps, four nodes are called, even though there are only three distinct nodes after two periods in the recombining binomial tree. In a recursion, since the computational effort is proportional to the number of nodes generated in the calculation (which is $2^n$ for an $n$-period model), the computational effort can blow up. Also, from a technical point of view, recursions within a computer are held in memory (informally speaking) on a recursion stack, and there are sheer physical limitations on the size of the stack, resulting in further slowdowns.

Motivated by this, we next look at writing a program to implement binomial option pricing on a tree using a two-dimensional array representation instead of a recursion. But note that recursion is still quite an efficient approach when working with models that do not result in recombining trees.

## Recombining Tree Models

Recall that a binomial tree is said to be *recombining* if an up move followed by a down move leads to the same price as a down move followed by an up move. If $u$ and $d$ are constant and do not change over the tree, then the binomial tree will always be recombining, as we noted in Chapter 12 (see Section 12.2). Both the CRR and JR solutions lead to recombining trees.

With a recombining tree, the entire tree can be represented in a two-dimensional $(n + 1) \times (n + 1)$ lattice. We describe how to create the lattice for the evolution of stock prices, and then overlay on this another lattice for the option values.

A typical cell in the stock price lattice is denoted $S(j, t)$. The index $t$ keeps track of time. From $S(j, t)$ come two nodes at time $t + 1$:

$$S(j, t + 1) = u \times S(j, t)$$
$$S(j + 1, t + 1) = d \times S(j, t)$$

Thus, for example:

- At the initial node, there is only one possible price, so we have a single price $S(1, 1) = S$.

**FIGURE 13.3**

The Recombining Tree

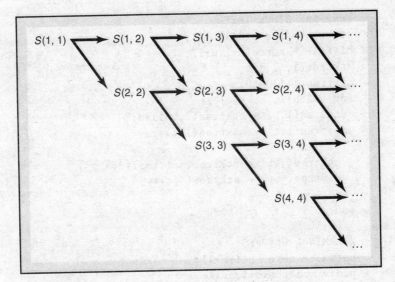

- After one period, there are two possible prices $S(1, 2) = uS(1, 1)$ and $S(2, 2) = dS(1, 1)$.
- After two periods, there are three possible prices, $S(1, 3)$, $S(2, 3)$, and $S(3, 3)$, with

$$S(1, 3) = uS(1, 2) \qquad S(2, 3) = dS(1, 2) = uS(2, 2) \qquad S(3, 3) = dS(2, 2)$$

The tree is pictured in Figure 13.3. Note that the tree uses only the upper triangle of the lattice.

Programming this tree is not difficult. The Octave code for it is shown below. The equations of motion of the model are exactly as we had in the recursion section except that in the program, we replace the forward propagation of the recursion system with backward recursion on the tree.

```
%CRR BINOMIAL TREE WITH DIVIDENDS
%s: stock price
%k: strike
%t: maturity
%v: volatility
%rf: risk free rate
%div: proportional dividend yield
%pc: call=1, put=0
%ae: american=1, european=0
%n: no of steps in the tree

function crrval = crr_div(s,k,t,v,rf,div,pc,ae,n);

%BASIC SET UP
h = t/n;
u = exp(v*sqrt(h));
d = exp(-v*sqrt(h));
r = exp(rf*h);
y = exp(div*h)-1;
q = (exp((rf-div)*h)-d)/(u-d);
```

```
%PREPARE STOCK TREE
stktree = zeros(n+1,n+1);
divtree = zeros(n+1,n+1);
stktree(1,1) = s;
divtree(1,1) = 0;
for t=2:n+1;
 stktree(1,t) = stktree(1,t-1)*u;
 divtree(1,t) = stktree(1,t)*y;
 for j=2:t;
  stktree(j,t) = stktree(j-1,t-1)*d;
  divtree(j,t) = stktree(j,t)*y;
 end;
end;


%TERMINAL PAYOFFS
optval = zeros(n+1,n+1);
pvdiv = zeros(n+1,n+1);
for j=1:n+1;
 if pc==1; optval(j,n+1)=max(0,stktree(j,n+1)-k); end;
 if pc==0; optval(j,n+1)=max(0,k-stktree(j,n+1)); end;
 pvdiv(j,n+1) = divtree(j,n+1);
end;


%PRICE OPTION BY BACKWARD RECURSION
for t=n:-1:1;
 for j=1:t;
  pvdiv(j,t) = (1/r)*(q*pvdiv(j,t+1)+(1-q)*pvdiv(j+1,t+1));
  optval(j,t) = (1/r)*(q*optval(j,t+1)+(1-q)*optval(j+1,t+1));
  if ae==1;
   if pc==1;
    optval(j,t) = max(optval(j,t),stktree(j,t)+pvdiv(j,t)-k);
    else
    optval(j,t) = max(optval(j,t),k-stktree(j,t)-pvdiv(j,t));
    end;
  end;
  pvdiv(j,t) = pvdiv(j,t) + divtree(j,t);
end;
end;
crrval = optval(1,1);
```

The program is compact and easy to decipher. If we use the same parameters as we did in the recursion example, we get precisely the same values for option prices (as indeed, we must):

```
octave:5> callopt = crr_div(50,52,0.5,0.3,0.03,0,1,0,10)
callopt = 3.7553
octave:6> putopt = crr_div(50,52,0.5,0.3,0.03,0,0,0,10)
putopt = 4.9812
octave:7> callopt - putopt
ans = -1.2258
octave:8> 50 - 52*exp(-0.03*0.5)
ans = -1.2258
```

## American Options

Both schemes described above, recursion and trees, look at European options. To extend the analysis to American options, we need to add just one additional line to the programs. In the line below the `optval` calculation, we need to check whether the value from early exercise of the option is higher than the continuation value. The following program statement in the recursion model does the trick (for calls):

```
optval = max(s-k,optval)
```

In the binomial tree, we add

```
optval(j,t) = max(s(j,t)-k,optval(j,t))
```

Analogous changes for puts are straightforward.

## Convergence

It is also easy to use the functions to examine how the model converges. As we increase $n$, the price should converge to the Black-Scholes model value. Here is a simple snippet of program code to see this.

```
for k=1:3;
    fprintf('%7.0f  %8.3f \n',10^k,crr(50,52,0.5,0.3,0.03,1,10^k));
end;
```

The code takes $n$ in powers of 10 up to 1,000 periods on the tree and prints out the results in a formatted way. Note the formatting commands; they may be useful in your working with Octave. We get

| | |
|---|---|
| 10 | 3.755 |
| 100 | 3.685 |
| 1000 | 3.690 |

The Black-Scholes option pricing formula gives the value of the option as $3.690.

## 13.5 Exercises

1. Suppose the distribution of $S_t$ is given to be lognormal:

$$\log \left( \frac{S_t}{S} \right) \sim N \left( \mu t, \sigma^2 t \right)$$

where $\mu = 0.10$ and $\sigma = 0.20$. Given that $S = 60$, calculate 95% confidence intervals for the price of $S_t$ three months from today.

2. Repeat Question 1 with $\mu = 0.10$ and $\sigma = 0.10$.

3. Suppose you wish to approximate the distribution of a stock price three months from now using a binomial tree with 100 steps. Suppose also that the stock price distribution is given to be lognormal with $\mu = 0.04$ and $\sigma = 0.40$. What values would you use for the parameters of the binomial model?

4. Repeat Question 3 but with $\mu = 0.20$ and $\sigma = 0.20$.

5. Suppose the price $S_t$ of a stock follows a lognormal distribution with $\mu = 0.07$ and $\sigma = 0.30$. What are the expected simple returns on the stock over a three-month horizon?

6. Assume the S&P 500 index follows a lognormal distribution with a volatility of 25%. Suppose the expected simple returns on the index over a one-year horizon are 8%. What is the value $\mu$ of the annual expected log-return?

7. If the continuously compounded return on a stock is normal, then why is the stock price distribution lognormal?

8. If the continuously compounded return on a stock worth $1 currently for a preset interval of time is distributed normally as follows: $r \sim N(\mu, \sigma^2) \equiv N(0.1, 0.2^2)$, then what are (a) the expected price of the stock after one interval and (b) the variance of the stock price?

9. (Technical) Suppose that the continuously compounded returns in each period are normal but are not always independent from period to period. Will the final stock price after all periods be lognormal?

10. (Technical) In binomial tree models, as we shrink the time interval on the tree, will the final return distribution of the stock price always converge to the normal distribution?

11. For a binomial tree with the probability of 0.01 of an outcome of 1 and a probability of 0.99 of an outcome of 0, what are the mean and variance of the payoff? Intuitively, what do you learn from this analysis?

12. For a binomial tree with equity returns continuously compounded with $\sigma = 0.2$ and interest rates quarterly compounded at annual rate $r = 0.03$, what is the upshift in stock price, downshift, and the risk-neutral probability of the upshift if the interval on the tree is quarterly?

13. Suppose the annualized volatility of a stock is $\sigma = 0.30$. The mean return is $\mu = 0.10$. The risk-free rate is constant for all maturities at 2%. Letting the time interval $h$ increase in monthly increments (1/12 of a year), how does the risk-neutral probability of an up move in the stock price change when using the CRR model? Why do we see this pattern?

14. If the standard deviation of daily stock returns is 2%, what is the volatility of annual stock returns?

15. What is the key assumption that supports converting weekly standard deviation into an annual standard deviation by multiplying it by $\sqrt{52}$?

16. You are constructing a 100-period binomial tree to represent a 91-day ($\approx 0.2493$-year) horizon. The risk-free rate for the given horizon is 4% in annualized continuously compounded terms. The underlying asset has a volatility of 38%. What are the parameters of the binomial tree if you use the JR solution? What is the risk-neutral probability in the constructed tree?

17. Rederive the risk-neutral probability in the JR model using general algebra. Is the probability always exactly $\frac{1}{2}$?

18. This problem will require a spreadsheet or programming effort. The initial stock price is given to be $100. We wish to price European calls and puts with strike price $100. The option maturity is $T = 1$ year, and the risk-free rate of interest is 5% per annum. If the volatility is $\sigma = 0.40$, then price the call and the put using the JR model. Assume you use a binomial tree comprising $n = 30$ periods.

19. Using the same parameters as in the problem above and the same JR tree, what are the prices of American calls and puts?

20. In Problem 18, check that your solution satisfies put-call parity exactly.

21. Rework Problem 18 with exactly the same parameters but use the CRR model instead. Compare your European put and call prices with those from the JR model. Also price the options using the Black-Scholes model and compare those prices as well.

22. You are given the following parameter values and are required to price calls using both the JR model and the CRR model for different values of $n$, the number of periods on the tree. The given values are $S = 100$, $K = 100$, $T = 1$, $\sigma = 0.4$, and $r = 0.05$. For

varying values of $n$, running from 5 to 100, plot the values of the call option obtained from the two models. How different are the convergence rates?

23. Repeat the previous question for the CRR model only, but change the strike price to $90, i.e., the call option is deep in-the-money. What happens to the plot? Then repeat this with the strike equal to $110, i.e., when the option is out-of-the-money. What happens to the plot?

24. (Technical) Prepare program code in Visual Basic for Applications (VBA) in Excel (i.e., macro programming) to price options using a recursive implementation of the binomial tree. This exercise is meant to give you some experience with recursive programming structure.

25. Is it possible to build a recombining tree if the interest rate is not constant, nor stochastic, but a deterministic function of time, i.e., $r(t)$?

# Estimating Historical Volatility

Under the assumptions of the lognormal distribution, the variance of log-returns over $T$ years is simply $T$ times the variance over one year. So, one way to estimate volatility (which is the standard deviation of annual log-returns) is to estimate the standard deviation of daily log-returns and then multiply this by the appropriate factor to convert it into an annualized form.

So, the first step in the process is to gather information on daily returns. Suppose we are given the information in Table 13.1. Let $E[\ell]$ and $E[\ell^2]$ denote, respectively, the expectation of daily log-return and the expectation of (daily log-return)$^2$, and let $V[\ell]$ and $\sigma(\ell)$ be the variance and standard deviation, respectively, of daily log-returns. We compute:

$$E[\ell] = \frac{1}{N} \sum_{i=1}^{N} \ell_i$$

$$E[\ell^2] = \frac{1}{N} \sum_{i=1}^{N} \ell_i^2$$

$$V[\ell] = E[\ell^2] - (E[\ell])^2$$

$$\sigma[\ell] = \sqrt{V[\ell]}$$

From $\sigma[\ell]$, we can obtain the annualized volatility $\sigma$. If one day denotes a fraction $\epsilon$ of a year, then, by definition we have $\sigma[\ell] = \sigma \sqrt{\epsilon}$, so finally,

$$\sigma = \sigma[\ell] \times \frac{1}{\sqrt{\epsilon}} \qquad \textbf{(13.29)}$$

One last question is important before we can take this to the data: what exactly is $\epsilon$? The question is a tricky one. If trading took place continuously throughout the year, then we could gather closing price information for every single day and simply use $\epsilon = 1/365$. However, in practice, we do have weekends and other holidays during which exchanges are closed, and we have no closing prices for those days. Moreover, empirical evidence gathered by Fama (1965), French (1980), and others suggests that markets are less volatile over holidays than over trading days (so that, for example, the variance of returns from Friday's close to Monday's close is much less than three times the volatility observed from close to close when there are no intervening holidays).

What is commonly done in practice, therefore, is to measure time in *trading days* rather than calendar days and to ignore holidays in the calculation. Thus, the gap from Friday to Monday is treated as just one day. Since there are typically around 252 trading days in a year, we estimate daily volatility and multiply this figure by $\sqrt{252}$ to get annualized volatility. An alternative would be to use *weekly* rather than daily data and to multiply the estimated weekly standard deviation by $\sqrt{52}$ to get annualized volatility, but this does not use all of the available data.

**TABLE 13.1** Daily Closing Prices and Log-Returns

| Day | Closing Price | Daily Log-Return |
|-----|---------------|------------------|
| 0 | $S_0$ | – |
| 1 | $S_1$ | $\ell_1 = \ln(S_1/S_0)$ |
| 2 | $S_2$ | $\ell_2 = \ln(S_2/S_1)$ |
| 3 | $S_3$ | $\ell_3 = \ln(S_3/S_2)$ |
| $\vdots$ | $\vdots$ | $\vdots$ |
| $N$ | $S_N$ | $\ell_N = \ln(S_N/S_{N-1})$ |

**Example 13.3**

Consider the information on closing stock prices of Cisco stock in Figure 13.4. The first seven columns represent data downloaded from `http://finance.yahoo.com`. (The full data set goes back to 1990; only the last two months are shown here.) The last column is the daily log-returns calculated from the adjusted closing prices (column 7).

Using 60 trading days' worth of data (roughly three months, so one earnings cycle will be covered), we can estimate the historical volatility of Cisco's returns. From (13.29) and setting $\epsilon = 1/252$, we obtain:

60-Day Historical Volatility = 27.08%

Of course, we can also use longer periods for the estimation. This would be particularly useful if we wish to check the "representativeness" of the 60-day period. Using other horizons results in the following numbers:

120-Day Historical Volatility = 30.10%
1-Year Historical Volatility  = 27.99%
4-Year Historical Volatility  = 28.57%

In light of these numbers, the figure of 27.08% estimated from 60 days of data looks slightly low from a longer historical perspective but not excessively so.   ∎

**FIGURE 13.4**

Estimating Historical Volatility: Data

| Date | Open | High | Low | Close | Volume | Adj Close | Log Returns |
|---|---|---|---|---|---|---|---|
| 01/26/07 | 26.16 | 26.54 | 25.76 | 26.35 | 64449600 | 26.35 | 0.00495 |
| 01/25/07 | 26.93 | 26.95 | 26.16 | 26.22 | 55317400 | 26.22 | −0.02523 |
| 01/24/07 | 26.23 | 26.95 | 26.19 | 26.89 | 63817000 | 26.89 | 0.03212 |
| 01/23/07 | 26.37 | 26.72 | 26.03 | 26.04 | 67695900 | 26.04 | −0.01864 |
| 01/22/07 | 26.75 | 26.8 | 26.15 | 26.53 | 69421400 | 26.53 | −0.00639 |
| 01/19/07 | 26.45 | 26.85 | 26.42 | 26.7 | 62266800 | 26.7 | 0.00941 |
| 01/18/07 | 27.13 | 27.15 | 26.27 | 26.45 | 80498300 | 26.45 | −0.01984 |
| 01/17/07 | 27.86 | 28 | 26.89 | 26.98 | 108858000 | 26.98 | −0.03854 |
| 01/16/07 | 28.59 | 28.59 | 28 | 28.04 | 75551500 | 28.04 | −0.03090 |
| 01/12/07 | 28.54 | 28.97 | 28.45 | 28.92 | 54588000 | 28.92 | 0.00798 |
| 01/11/07 | 28.77 | 28.99 | 28.61 | 28.69 | 54602200 | 28.69 | 0.00035 |
| 01/10/07 | 28.27 | 28.73 | 28.21 | 28.68 | 50632400 | 28.68 | 0.00735 |
| 01/09/07 | 28.72 | 28.75 | 28.31 | 28.47 | 50488300 | 28.47 | −0.00560 |
| 01/08/07 | 28.54 | 28.74 | 28.32 | 28.63 | 47936500 | 28.63 | 0.00560 |
| 01/05/07 | 28.44 | 28.57 | 28.05 | 28.47 | 62647800 | 28.47 | 0.00035 |
| 01/04/07 | 27.68 | 28.49 | 27.54 | 28.46 | 73012100 | 28.46 | 0.02598 |
| 01/03/07 | 27.46 | 27.98 | 27.33 | 27.73 | 64226000 | 27.73 | 0.01453 |
| 12/29/06 | 27.33 | 27.63 | 27.29 | 27.33 | 27125900 | 27.33 | −0.00329 |
| 12/28/06 | 27.29 | 27.58 | 27.25 | 27.42 | 34817800 | 27.42 | 0.00439 |
| 12/27/06 | 27.3 | 27.5 | 26.83 | 27.3 | 25675600 | 27.3 | 0.00404 |
| 12/26/06 | 27.04 | 27.33 | 26.85 | 27.19 | 18185700 | 27.19 | 0.00961 |
| 12/22/06 | 27.34 | 27.42 | 26.93 | 26.93 | 27400500 | 26.93 | −0.01328 |
| 12/21/06 | 27.5 | 27.6 | 27.22 | 27.29 | 32398900 | 27.29 | −0.00366 |
| 12/20/06 | 27.68 | 27.7 | 27.38 | 27.39 | 31825400 | 27.39 | −0.00872 |
| 12/19/06 | 27.47 | 27.76 | 27.3 | 27.63 | 38603100 | 27.63 | 0.00072 |
| 12/18/06 | 27.6 | 27.96 | 27.43 | 27.61 | 46255800 | 27.61 | 0.00181 |
| 12/15/06 | 27.43 | 27.77 | 27.33 | 27.56 | 66987100 | 27.56 | 0.00911 |
| 12/14/06 | 27.22 | 27.44 | 27.18 | 27.31 | 39441600 | 27.31 | 0.00220 |
| 12/13/06 | 27.34 | 27.35 | 26.93 | 27.25 | 43170100 | 27.25 | 0.00626 |
| 12/12/06 | 27.12 | 27.4 | 27.4 | 27.08 | 43065500 | 27.08 | −0.00111 |
| 12/11/06 | 26.9 | 27.48 | 26.85 | 27.11 | 43035200 | 27.11 | 0.00481 |
| 12/08/06 | 26.88 | 27.15 | 26.75 | 26.98 | 29495600 | 26.98 | 0.00371 |
| 12/07/06 | 27.2 | 27.3 | 26.88 | 26.88 | 31417900 | 26.88 | −0.00778 |
| 12/06/06 | 27.12 | 27.27 | 26.95 | 27.09 | 34092600 | 27.09 | 0.00185 |
| 12/05/06 | 27.4 | 27.44 | 27 | 27.04 | 43080300 | 27.04 | −0.00774 |
| 12/04/06 | 26.94 | 27.57 | 26.86 | 27.25 | 68450100 | 27.25 | 0.02076 |
| 12/01/06 | 26.95 | 27.08 | 26.45 | 26.69 | 47014700 | 26.69 | −0.00821 |
| 11/30/06 | 27.02 | 27.05 | 26.8 | 26.91 | 45935300 | 26.91 | −0.00630 |
| 11/29/06 | 27.05 | 27.3 | 26.9 | 27.08 | 68137400 | 27.08 | 0.00185 |
| 11/28/06 | 25.62 | 27.13 | 25.59 | 27.03 | 108606500 | 27.03 | 0.04657 |
| 11/27/06 | 26.76 | 26.89 | 25.73 | 25.8 | 63803200 | 25.8 | −0.03952 |

# Chapter 14

# The Black-Scholes Model

## 14.1 Introduction

Easily the best known model of option pricing, the Black-Scholes model is also one of the most widely used models in practice. It forms the benchmark model for pricing options on a variety of underlying assets including equities, equity indices, currencies, and futures. While not designed as a model of interest rates, a variant of the Black-Scholes model, the Black model, is nonetheless commonly used in practice to price certain interest-rate options like caps and floors.

Technically, the Black-Scholes model is more complex than the binomial or other discrete models because it is set in *continuous time*, i.e., prices in the model may change continuously rather than only at discrete points in time. Modeling continuous-time uncertainty requires the use of much more sophisticated mathematics than we have employed so far. A first question we should ask ourselves is: why bother? The binomial model is a flexible one and is transparent and easy to work with. What do we gain from the additional fancy mathematical footwork?

It turns out that there *is* a point. The Black-Scholes model provides something almost unique at the output level: option prices in the model can be expressed in *closed-form*, i.e., as particular explicit functions of the parameters. There are many advantages to having closed-forms. Most importantly, closed-forms simplify computation of option prices and option sensitivities and facilitate developing and verifying intuition about option pricing and hedging behavior.

In the initial segment of this chapter, we focus on options on equities, the context in which the Black-Scholes model was first developed. In later sections, we examine how the model may be modified to accommodate options on indices, currencies, and futures.

### The Main Assumption: Geometric Brownian Motion

The main assumption of the Black-Scholes model concerns the evolution of the price of the underlying stock.

**Assumption 1.** The stock price evolves according to *geometric Brownian motion*.

What is a "geometric Brownian motion"? A formal definition is given in Chapter 15 (see Section 15.2), but shorn of technical details, it simply requires that two conditions be satisfied:

1. Returns on the stock over any holding period have a *lognormal* distribution with mean $\mu$ and constant volatility $\sigma$: if $S_0$ denotes the current stock price and $S_T$ the price in $T$

years for some arbitrary $T$, then

$$\ln\left(\frac{S_T}{S_0}\right) \sim N(\mu T, \sigma^2 T)$$

2. Stock prices must evolve continuously; they cannot jump (the market cannot "gap").

Is this a good assumption? From an analytical standpoint, undoubtedly. As we have seen in the last chapter, the lognormal inherits many of the properties of the normal distribution that make the latter easy to work with. But from an economic standpoint, the evidence is mixed. Casual observation suggests—and formal analysis confirms—that the volatility of stocks and markets is typically not constant over time. Markets do also "gap," most often in response to unexpected good or bad news. More generally, empirical return distributions appear to deviate in systematic ways from the lognormal assumption. Of course, how important these deviations are for option prices is ultimately an empirical question. We revisit and discuss these issues further in Section 14.8 below.

## Other Assumptions

The second assumption of the Black-Scholes model concerns interest rates. In keeping with the continuous-time setting, interest rates are quoted in continuously-compounded terms. As with the binomial model, the Black-Scholes model assumes that

**Assumption 2.** The risk-free rate of interest, denoted $r$, is constant.

The assumption that stock prices must evolve continuously rules out discrete dividend payments on the stock: such dividends drive a wedge between cum-dividend and ex-dividend stock prices, and so create discontinuous stock prices. For emphasis, we state this as an explicit assumption:

**Assumption 3.** There are no dividends on the underlying stock during the life of the option.

The zero-dividend requirement is obviously a *very* restrictive one; it places a severe limitation on the stocks to which the model may be applied. Fortunately, it turns out that it is not too hard to modify the model to handle "predictable" discontinuities such as those caused by dividends. (Random jumps are another matter.) We describe the extension in Section 14.6.

Finally, the technical complication of working in continuous time makes it impossible to solve for option prices in closed-form if early exercise is permitted. Thus, the analysis in the rest of this chapter applies only to European options. Even though this is a restriction on the kinds of options that may be priced in closed-form and not a restriction on the model itself, we state it separately as an assumption to highlight its importance:

**Assumption 4.** All options are European in style with maturity date $T$ and strike price $K$.

Besides these, the model makes the usual smoothness assumptions concerning the market: no taxes, no transactions costs, no restrictions on short sales, borrowing or lending, etc.

## Notation

Table 14.1 summarizes the notation we use. Note that we denote current time by $t$ and the horizon of the model (i.e., the maturity date of the option) by $T$. Thus, the time left to maturity is $T - t$. The stock price is denoted $S$ with a time subscript; thus, $S_t$ denotes the current price and $S_T$ the price at maturity. The remaining notation is that defined above. $C$ and $P$ will denote the prices of the call and put option, respectively.

**TABLE 14.1**
Black-Scholes
Notation

| Notation | Meaning |
|----------|---------|
| $t$ | Current time |
| $T$ | Maturity date of option |
| $S_t$ | Current stock price |
| $S_T$ | Stock price at $T$ |
| $K$ | Strike price of option |
| $r$ | Riskless interest rate |
| $\mu$ | Expected log-return on stock (annualized) |
| $\sigma$ | Volatility of stock returns (annualized) |
| $C$ | Price of call |
| $P$ | Price of put |

## Order of Analysis

Through the first part of this chapter, we focus on the theoretical side of the Black-Scholes setting. We begin with the Black-Scholes formulae under the assumptions listed above. Then we discuss generalizing the formula to allow for payouts in the form of either discrete dividends (as on a single stock) or a continuous yield (as on a stock index). Using these generalizations, we describe Black-Scholes formulae for pricing options on dividend-paying stocks, stock indices, currencies, and futures.

The second part of the chapter examines empirical performance of the model. We define the important notion of *implied volatility* and describe the implied volatility *skew* that is typically observed in most financial markets. As we shall see, the skew should not exist under the Black-Scholes assumptions, so its presence raises questions about the model's empirical fit. We relate the skew to shortcomings in the model's assumptions and discuss possible resolutions and extensions.

We conclude the chapter with a discussion of the VIX and derivatives on the VIX. The VIX is an index of implied volatilities extracted from options on the S&P 500 index. The VIX has become well known as the US market's "fear index." There are futures and options available on the VIX that enable one to trade market volatility "directly" rather than indirectly using (for example) straddles on the S&P 500 index. Appendix 14B discusses two related over-the-counter products, volatility swaps and variance swaps. Volatility and variance swaps are cash-settled forward contracts on the realized volatility and the realized variance of returns, respectively.

# 14.2   Option Pricing in the Black-Scholes Setting

We can recover option prices in the Black-Scholes model by either replication or risk-neutral pricing, methods which were outlined in earlier chapters. There are also other, more exotic, approaches we could adopt. Since the lognormal model is the limit as $n$ goes to infinity of an $n$-period binomial model, we could look at the behavior of option prices obtained from $n$-period binomial models and see their limiting behavior as $n$ gets large. A fourth possibility (and one used in the original paper of Black and Scholes (1973) as an alternative derivation of their formula) is to use a CAPM-based approach.

All of these approaches are mathematically much more sophisticated than option pricing in the binomial model. The additional work is mainly technical in nature, so there is not much insight to be gained by it. Therefore, we present the details of the derivations in a separate chapter (Chapter 15, Sections 15.3–15.5). Here, we focus on the structure of the formulae and their intuitive content. We begin with a description of the formulae.

# The Black-Scholes Formulae

The arbitrage-free prices of the call and put in the Black-Scholes world are given respectively by

$$C = S_t N(d_1) - PV(K) N(d_2) \tag{14.1}$$

$$P = PV(K) N(-d_2) - S_t N(-d_1) \tag{14.2}$$

where

$$d_1 = \frac{1}{\sigma\sqrt{T-t}} \left[ \ln\left(\frac{S_t}{K}\right) + \left(r + \frac{1}{2}\sigma^2\right)(T - t) \right] \tag{14.3}$$

$$d_2 = d_1 - \sigma\sqrt{T-t} \tag{14.4}$$

$$PV(K) = e^{-r(T-t)} K \text{ is the present value of } K \text{ receivable at } T \tag{14.5}$$

and $N(\cdot)$ is the cumulative standard normal distribution, i.e., for any $x$, $N(x)$ is the probability under a standard normal distribution of an observation less than or equal to $x$.

These expressions appear menacing the first time one sees them, but their structure and composition can be intuitively understood by relating them to the replication and risk-neutral pricing approaches. The price of an option, in general, is the difference between the present value of what one expects to *receive* from exercise of the option and the present value of what one expects to *pay* on account of exercise. The price of the call in the Black-Scholes model has the form

$$C = \{S_t \times [\text{Term involving } d_1]\} - \{PV(K) \times [\text{Term involving } d_2]\}$$

- The first term in braces represents the present value of the stock the call holder expects to *receive* upon exercise. In the Black-Scholes model, this component happens to have an attractive decomposition: the replication approach shows us that $N(d_1)$ is the delta of the call option in the Black-Scholes model, so the entire term is just the value of the stock currently embedded in the call (the current price of the stock times the call delta).
- The second term in braces represents the present value of what the call holder expects to *pay* upon exercise. It too has an attractive decomposition. Exercise of the call results in a cash outflow of $K$, which viewed from today has a present value of $PV(K)$. The risk-neutral pricing approach tells us that $N(d_2)$ is the risk-neutral probability of the option finishing in-the-money, so the entire term is simply the present value of an outflow of $K$ at date $T$ times the risk-neutral probability of this outflow.

The difference between these values (what you expect to receive and what you expect to pay) is the Black-Scholes value of the call. Analogous statements hold for the put.

The material below elaborates on this by relating the Black-Scholes formula first to the replication approach and then to the risk-neutral pricing approach.

## Replication and the Black-Scholes Formula

We have seen in earlier chapters that replicating a call in general involves a long position in the underlying (of size, say, $\Delta_c$) and borrowing at the risk-free rate (an amount, say, $B_c$). Since each unit of the stock costs $S_t$ currently, the replicating portfolio costs $S_t \Delta_c - B_c$. Since this must equal the cost of the call, we can write

$$C = S_t \Delta_c - B_c \tag{14.6}$$

The structure of this general representation (14.6) is identical to that of the Black-Scholes call price (14.1). This is not a coincidence! As the comparison suggests, we do indeed have

$$\Delta_c = N(d_1) \quad \text{and} \quad B_c = PV(K)N(d_2) \tag{14.7}$$

In words, $N(d_1)$ is the delta of the call, and $PV(K)N(d_2)$ is the amount of borrowing required in a replicating portfolio.

Analogous statements are true for the put. In general, to replicate a put, we take a *short* position in the underlying and invest at the risk-free rate. Denoting the position in the underlying by $\Delta_p$ and the investment by $B_p$, we may write

$$P = B_p + S_t \Delta_p \tag{14.8}$$

Note that $\Delta_p$ is a negative number since the stock position is a short one. Comparing this general representation to the Black-Scholes formula (14.2) suggests that

$$\Delta_p = -N(-d_1) \quad \text{and} \quad B_p = PV(K)N(-d_2) \tag{14.9}$$

This is exactly correct. The Black-Scholes formula for the put is just the replicating portfolio (14.9) substituted into the general pricing expression (14.8).

The full implication of these observations is worth restating for emphasis: the Black-Scholes formula gives us a great deal more than just the option prices—it gives us the complete replicating portfolios for the call and the put.

## Black-Scholes via Risk-Neutral Probabilities

Further insight into the Black-Scholes formula can be obtained by considering the risk-neutral pricing approach. The payoffs of the call at maturity are

$$\max(S_T - K, 0)$$

To identify the call value, we must take expectation of these payoffs under the risk-neutral probability measure and discount at the risk-free rate. Let $E_t$ denote expectations under the risk-neutral probability of time-$T$ cash flows. (The subscript $t$ emphasizes dependence of these expectations on the current stock price $S_t$.) Then, the arbitrage-free price of the call is

$$C = e^{-r(T-t)} E_t [\max(S_T - K, 0)]$$

Since the call pays nothing if $S_T < K$, we can write the call price as

$$C = e^{-r(T-t)} E_t \left[ (S_T - K) \times I_{\{S_T \geq K\}} \right]$$

where $I_{\{S_T \geq K\}}$ is the indicator function that takes on the value 1 if $S_T \geq K$ and zero otherwise:

$$I_{\{S_T \geq K\}} = \begin{cases} 1, & \text{if } S_T \geq K \\ 0, & \text{otherwise} \end{cases}$$

For notational simplicity, we write just $I$ for $I_{\{S_T \geq K\}}$. Now, $(S_T - K) \times I = (S_T \times I) - (K \times I)$, and the expectation of the difference of two terms is just the difference of the expectations, so

$$C = e^{-r(T-t)} E_t [S_T \times I] - e^{-r(T-t)} E_t [K \times I] \tag{14.10}$$

The second term on the right-hand side can be simplified. Intuitively, if you have to pay out $K$ whenever $S_T \geq K$, your expected payout is simply $K$ times the likelihood that $S_T \geq K$. So we can write

$$E_t [K \times I] = K \operatorname{Prob}_t (S_T \geq K) \tag{14.11}$$

Thus, using $e^{-r(T-t)} K = PV(K)$, the call price (14.10) may be written as

$$C = e^{-r(T-t)} E_t [S_T \times I] - PV(K) \operatorname{Prob}_t (S_T \geq K) \tag{14.12}$$

From this to the Black-Scholes formula is simply a matter of grinding through the expectations, which are tedious but not otherwise difficult (see Section 15.3). Specifically, it can be shown that under the Black-Scholes assumptions,

$$e^{-r(T-t)} E_t[S_T \times I] = S_t N(d_1) \qquad \textbf{(14.13)}$$

$$\text{Prob}_t(S_T \geq K) = N(d_2) \qquad \textbf{(14.14)}$$

Equation (14.13) states that the present value of the stock that will be *received* from the call upon exercise is equal to $S_t N(d_1)$. Equation (14.14) states that the probability that the call finishes in-the-money is $N(d_2)$; it follows that the present value of the cash outflow that is *paid* upon exercise of the call is equal to $PV(K) N(d_2)$.

Analogous statements hold for the put option. In particular, $N(-d_2)$ works out to just the risk-neutral probability of the put finishing in-the-money.

### Warning

It must be emphasized that these are *risk-neutral probabilities*, not the actual probabilities. That is, they are the probabilities taking the expected return on the stock to be the risk-free rate. If the expected return on the stock exceeds the risk-free rate, then the actual probability of the call finishing in-the-money will be *higher* than the risk-neutral probability (the stock price grows faster than under the risk-neutral probability). Similarly, the actual probability of the put finishing in-the-money will be lower than the risk-neutral probability.

## 14.3 Remarks on the Formula

The Black-Scholes formulae have two remarkable features that facilitate easy implementation:

1. Option prices depend on only *five* variables: $S$, $K$, $r$, $T - t$, and $\sigma$.
2. Of these five variables, two are contract variables (strike and maturity), and two are market variables (stock price and interest rates). Only *one*—the volatility $\sigma$—is not directly observable.

In particular, option prices do not depend on the stock's expected returns, which are notoriously difficult to estimate reliably. That the option price does not depend on the stock's expected return is one of the unexpected surprises of the Black-Scholes model. Note that this should not be taken to mean that the expected returns on the option are independent of the expected returns on the stock; indeed, since the option is in many ways akin to a leveraged position in the stock (see Section 11.4), its expected returns are affected directly by the stock's expected returns.

The Black-Scholes formulae represent *arbitrage-free* option prices under the model's assumptions. Thus, they can be used to take advantage of mispricing. They can also be used to delta-hedge option positions. For example, suppose we have written a call option whose current delta, using the Black-Scholes formula, is $N(d_1)$. To hedge this position, we take a long position in $N(d_1)$ units of the underlying. Of course, dynamic hedging is required, i.e., the hedge will have to be adjusted each time the delta of the underlying has changed.

Finally, it must be stressed again that closed-form expressions of this sort for option prices are rare. Nonetheless, such closed-form expressions exist in the Black-Scholes framework only for *European*-style options. For example, closed-forms do not exist for American put options. However, as we see later in the book, it *is* possible to obtain closed-form solutions in the Black-Scholes setting for certain classes of exotic options, such as compound options, digital options, and barrier options.

# 14.4 Working with the Formulae I: Plotting Option Prices

The best way to gain familiarity with the formal and intuitive content of the Black-Scholes formula is to work with it. This section describes how to use the Black-Scholes formula to plot option prices. Such plots are particularly useful to get a feel for how option values (or the option delta) react to changes in the model's parameters. The next section discusses working with the formula algebraically.

The existence of closed-forms makes it a simple matter to plot option prices in the Black-Scholes model using a spreadsheet. Six easy steps are involved:

1. Input values for $S_t$, $K$, $r$, $T-t$, and $\sigma$.
2. Compute $d_1 = [\ln(S_t/K) + (r + \sigma^2/2)(T-t)]/[\sigma\sqrt{T-t}]$.
3. Compute $d_2 = d_1 - \sigma\sqrt{T-t}$.
4. Compute $N(d_1)$ and $N(-d_1)$.
5. Compute $N(d_2)$ and $N(-d_2)$.
6. Compute option prices.

$$C = S_t N(d_1) - e^{-r(T-t)} K N(d_2)$$
$$P = e^{-r(T-t)} K N(-d_2) - S_t N(-d_1)$$

In Excel, cumulative standard normal distribution values may be computed using the NORMSDIST function. For any $x$, $N(x)$ is given by NORMSDIST($x$). One can also use the more elaborate NORMDIST function that applies to any normal distribution (not just the standard normal). In this case, $N(x)$ is given by NORMDIST($x$, 0, 1, 1).

Figure 14.1 illustrates a plot of Black-Scholes option prices. Four parameters are held fixed in the exercise:

- The strike price is $K = 100$.
- The time-to-maturity is $T - t = 6$ months.

**FIGURE 14.1**

Black-Scholes Option Prices

This figure plots call and put prices as the underlying stock price ranges between 72 and 128. The strike price of the options is 100, the time-to-maturity is six months, the risk-free interest rate is 5%, and the volatility is 20%.

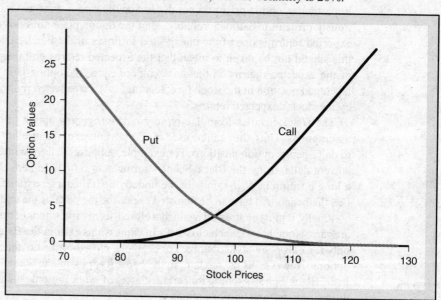

- The annualized volatility of the stock price is 20% ($\sigma = 0.20$).
- The risk-free interest rate is 5%.

The figure plots call and put prices as the fifth parameter, the current price of the stock, varies from 72 to 128. At a price of 72, the call is deep out-of-the-money, while the put is deep in-the-money. At a price of 128, the call is deep in-the-money, while the put is deep out-of-the-money.

Observe the nonlinear reaction of option prices to changes in the stock price. This is evident visually in the curvature of the option prices as $S$ varies. For example, when the call is deep out-of-the-money, it reacts very little to a dollar change in the stock price—the call pricing function is almost flat. When the call is deep in-the-money, it reacts almost one-for-one to a change in the stock price—the slope of the call pricing function is almost $+1$. (Of course, this slope of the call pricing function is just the option delta!) In the next chapter, we will examine the implications of this nonlinearity in greater detail when we look at the option "greeks."

## 14.5   Working with the Formulae II: Algebraic Manipulation

To gain a *theoretical* understanding of how the Black-Scholes model's parameters interact with each other and how they influence option prices and the option delta, it is necessary to work directly with the formulae. This section and Appendix 14A go through a number of exercises with this objective in mind. Some of the exercises are simple ones; others (notably those in Appendix 14A) are a bit more complex. In all cases, the aim is to improve the reader's "feel" for manipulating the Black-Scholes formula algebraically.

In principle, this material can be skipped without too much loss of continuity (or at least, skimming through it should suffice for the sequel). Nonetheless, we strongly encourage readers to take the effort to go through it carefully, since doing so will enhance general intuition for working with options as well as theoretical understanding of the Black-Scholes formula.

### The Functions ln and $N(\cdot)$

Despite its apparent complexity, the Black-Scholes formula is not hard to work with algebraically since it involves only two main functions: the natural log function ln and the cumulative normal distribution $N(\cdot)$. (As one might guess, this is a consequence of our assumption of lognormality of the returns distribution.) To understand the working of the formulae, it is useful to keep the following properties of these functions in mind.

First, the natural log function ln. The function $\ln x$ is defined only for positive values of $x$, and increases as $x$ increases. At $x = 0$, we have $\ln x = -\infty$; at $x = 1$, we have $\ln x = 0$; and as $x$ goes to $+\infty$, $\ln x$ also goes to $+\infty$:

$$\ln 0 = -\infty \qquad \ln 1 = 0 \qquad \ln x \to \infty \text{ as } x \to \infty$$

Figure 14.2 displays a plot of the natural log function.

Next, $N(\cdot)$. $N(x)$ is the probability under a standard normal distribution of an observation less than or equal to $x$. The standard normal distribution is the normal distribution with a mean of zero and variance of 1. Figure 14.3 displays $N(x)$ with its familiar bell-shaped curve.

Observations under a normal distribution can range from $-\infty$ to $+\infty$, so $N(x)$ is defined for all values of $x$. Since the standard normal is symmetric around its mean of zero, we have

$$N(0) = \frac{1}{2}$$

**FIGURE 14.2**
The Natural Log
Function

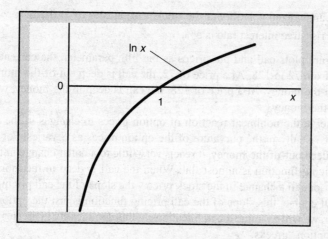

**FIGURE 14.3**
The Standard Normal
Distribution

The figure below displays the density function of the standard normal distribution. The density is symmetric around zero. The area under the curve to the left of a point $x$, denoted $N(x)$, is the likelihood of observing an outcome less than or equal to $x$. The total area under the curve is 1.

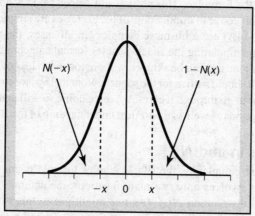

As $x$ goes to $-\infty$, the probability of an observation smaller than $x$ goes to zero, so $N(x)$ goes to zero. As $x$ goes to $+\infty$, we are looking at the probability of an observation less than $+\infty$, so $N(x)$ goes to $+1$:

$$N(-\infty) = 0 \qquad N(+\infty) = 1$$

Here is one final and useful property of $N(\cdot)$. For any $x$, we have

$$N(x) + N(-x) = 1 \qquad\qquad (14.15)$$

To see this, note that the standard normal is symmetric around its mean zero. Pick any $x$. Since $x$ and $-x$ are symmetric around the mean, the area to the *right* of $x$ (which is $1 - N(x)$) must be the same as the area to the *left* of $-x$ (which is $N(-x)$). (See Figure 14.3.) This means $1 - N(x) = N(-x)$, which is (14.15).

## Put-Call Parity and the Black-Scholes Formulae

Since the Black-Scholes formulae concern European options, the Black-Scholes put price can be derived from the call price using put-call parity. Put-call parity tells us that

$$P = C + PV(K) - S_t$$

Substituting for $C$ from the Black-Scholes formula (14.1) and rearranging, we obtain

$$P = S_t [N(d_1) - 1] + PV(K) [1 - N(d_2)] \qquad \textbf{(14.16)}$$

Using (14.15) in (14.16) gives us

$$P = -S_t N(-d_1) + PV(K) N(-d_2)$$

which is precisely the Black-Scholes put price (14.2).

## Call Behavior and Depth in-the-Money

Consider a call. Intuitively speaking:

- As $S_t$ becomes very small relative to $K$ (i.e., "as $S_t \to 0$"), the call becomes very likely to lapse unexercised, so its replicating portfolio should go to the null portfolio, the one that holds neither stock nor cash. In particular, the delta of the call should go to zero.

- As $S_t$ becomes very large relative to $K$ ("$S_t \to \infty$"), the call is almost sure to be exercised, so the call holder is looking at paying $K$ and receiving one unit of the stock at maturity. Thus, the replicating portfolio should now resemble a portfolio containing one unit of the stock and a borrowing of $PV(K)$. In particular, the delta of the call should approach $+1$.

Does the Black-Scholes call formula exhibit this behavior? First, consider what happens as $S_t$ goes to zero. In this event, the ratio $(S_t/K)$ also goes to zero. This means

$$\ln \left( \frac{S_t}{K} \right) \to -\infty$$

From the definition of $d_1$ (see (14.3)), this means $d_1$ also goes to $-\infty$. If $d_1$ goes to $-\infty$, so must $d_2$. And this finally implies that both $N(d_1)$ and $N(d_2)$ go to zero. Put into a single line, we have:

$$\frac{S_t}{K} \to 0 \;\Rightarrow\; \ln \left( \frac{S_t}{K} \right) \to -\infty \;\Rightarrow\; d_1, d_2 \to -\infty \;\Rightarrow\; N(d_1), N(d_2) \to 0$$

Since $N(d_1)$ goes to zero, the call delta goes to zero as required. Since $N(d_2)$ also goes to zero, the replicating portfolio indeed converges to the null portfolio.

Now consider what happens as $S_t \to \infty$. We obtain the following chain of effects:

$$\frac{S_t}{K} \to \infty \;\Rightarrow\; \ln \left( \frac{S_t}{K} \right) \to \infty \;\Rightarrow\; d_1, d_2 \to \infty \;\Rightarrow\; N(d_1), N(d_2) \to +1$$

Since $N(d_1)$ goes to $+1$, the delta goes to $+1$, as required. Since $N(d_2)$ also goes to $+1$, the amount of borrowing converges to just $PV(K)$. Thus, the replicating portfolio converges to a long position of one unit of the stock and borrowing of $PV(K)$.

## Put Behavior and Depth in-the-Money

What is the corresponding behavior of the put?

- As $S_t$ becomes large relative to $K$, the put becomes increasingly likely to lapse unexercised, so the replicating portfolio should resemble the null portfolio. In particular, the put delta should go to zero.

- As $S_t$ becomes very small relative to $K$, the put is almost sure to be exercised, so the put holder is looking at giving up the stock and receiving $K$ at time $T$. The replicating portfolio thus resembles one that has an investment of $PV(K)$ and a short position in the stock. In particular, the put delta goes to $-1$.

From what we have already worked out for the call, we can show that the put too meets these requirements. As $S_t$ becomes very large, we have seen that $d_1$ and $d_2$ go to $+\infty$, so $-d_1$ and $-d_2$ must each go to $-\infty$. This means $N(-d_1)$ and $N(-d_2)$ both go to zero, so (a) the delta of the put (which is $-N(-d_1)$) goes to zero, and (b) the replicating portfolio converges to the null portfolio. Put into a single line of notation:

$$\frac{S_t}{K} \to \infty \;\Rightarrow\; -d_1, -d_2 \to -\infty \;\Rightarrow\; -N(-d_1) \to 0, N(-d_2) \to 0$$

Similarly, as $S_t$ goes to zero, $d_1$ and $d_2$ go to $-\infty$, so $-d_1$ and $-d_2$ go to $+\infty$. This means the delta of the put, $-N(-d_1)$, goes towards $-1$. Moreover, $N(-d_2)$ goes to $+1$, so the replicating portfolio resembles an investment of $PV(K)$ and a short position of one unit in the stock. In notational terms:

$$\frac{S_t}{K} \to 0 \;\Rightarrow\; -d_1, -d_2 \to +\infty \;\Rightarrow\; -N(-d_1) \to -1, N(-d_2) \to +1$$

Thus, the Black-Scholes put formula behaves as intuition suggests.

## Option Values as Maturity Approaches

As maturity approaches ($T - t \to 0$), the call value should converge to $S_T - K$ if $S_T > K$, or to zero if $S_T < K$. We show that the Black-Scholes call formula meets these properties.

The term $d_1$ can be written as

$$d_1 = \frac{1}{\sigma\sqrt{T-t}} \ln\left(\frac{S_t}{K}\right) + \frac{1}{\sigma}\left(r + \frac{1}{2}\sigma^2\right)\sqrt{T-t}$$

The second component on the right-hand side always goes to zero as $T - t \to 0$. What about the first component? As maturity approaches, $S_t$ gets closer to $S_T$ (remember, there are no jumps in the price), so $\ln(S_t/K)$ converges to $\ln(S_T/K)$. Since this is divided by $\sqrt{T-t}$, the entire term goes to either $+\infty$ or $-\infty$ depending on whether $\ln(S_T/K)$ is positive or negative. Thus:

- If $S_T > K$, then $\ln(S_T/K) > 0$, so $d_1 \to +\infty$ as $T - t \to 0$.
- If $S_T < K$, then $\ln(S_T/K) < 0$, so $d_1 \to -\infty$ as $T - t \to 0$.

Now, the difference between $d_1$ and $d_2$ is $\sigma\sqrt{T-t}$, which goes to zero as maturity approaches. So $d_2$ has the same limiting values as $d_1$. Finally, note that $PV(K)$ converges to $K$ as we approach maturity. Putting these together, we have the following:

- If $S_T > K$, then $N(d_1)$, $N(d_2) \to +1$. So the call value converges to $S_T - K$.
- If $S_T < K$, then $N(d_1)$, $N(d_2) \to 0$. So the call value converges to 0.

## When Is the Black-Scholes Call Delta Equal to 1/2?

This is a commonly encountered question: when is an option delta equal to 1/2 (i.e., $+1/2$ for a call or $-1/2$ for a put)? The first instinct is to say "when the option is at-the-money," but this is easily seen to be incorrect. If a call is at-the-money, we have $S_t = K$, so $\ln(S_t/K) = 0$. This means

$$d_1 = \frac{1}{\sigma\sqrt{T-t}}\left[0 + (r + \frac{1}{2}\sigma^2)(T-t)\right] = \frac{1}{\sigma}\left[(r + \frac{1}{2}\sigma^2)\sqrt{T-t}\right]$$

so $d_1$ is strictly positive. Since $N(0) = 1/2$, this means the call delta is $N(d_1) > 1/2$.

For example, suppose we take $S = K = 50, r = 0.05, T - t = 1/4$, and $\sigma = 0.25$. Then, $N(d_1)$ works out to about 0.565, substantially different from $1/2$. Intuitively, the stock price in the risk-neutral world grows at the risk-free rate, so if the option starts out at-the-money, there is a greater-than-even chance of its finishing in-the-money.

What if we take the option to be *at-the-money-forward*, i.e., such that $S_t = PV(K)$? This cancels out the interest-rate effect, so works somewhat better. Since $PV(K) = e^{-r(T-t)}K$, $S_t = PV(K)$ implies

$$\ln\left(\frac{S_t}{K}\right) = -r(T - t)$$

so we obtain

$$d_1 = \frac{1}{\sigma\sqrt{T-t}}\left[-r(T-t) + (r + \frac{1}{2}\sigma^2)(T-t)\right] = \frac{1}{2}\sigma\sqrt{T-t}$$

This is still positive, though smaller than the corresponding value for the at-the-money delta. For example, with $K = 50, r = 0.05, T = 1/4, \sigma = 0.25$, and $S = PV(K) = 49.38$, we obtain $N(d_1) = 0.525$.

So for what values of $S_t$ (relative to $K$ and the other parameters) is the call delta equal to $1/2$ in the Black-Scholes model? That is, what must $d_1$ be for delta to be equal to $1/2$?

## The Delta and Other Parameters

Exercises such as the ones above enhance understanding of both general option behavior as well as the Black-Scholes formula. As further examples of such exercises, the reader is invited to check that the call delta satisfies the following properties. Appendix 14A describes the intuition for why these properties should hold in general, and shows that they do hold in the Black-Scholes setting.

1. *Volatility.* For deep in-the-money call options, the delta *decreases* as volatility increases. For deep out-of-the-money call options, the delta *increases* as volatility increases. Thus, delta depends on volatility through depth-in-the-money.

2. *Time-to-Maturity.* For deep in-the-money call options, the delta *decreases* as time-to-maturity increases. For deep out-of-the-money call options, the delta *increases* as time-to-maturity increases. Thus, delta depends on time-to-maturity also through depth-in-the-money.

3. *Interest Rates.* The call delta increases with an increase in the riskless interest rate.

As an aside, these properties indicate that the components of the replicating portfolio depend in complex and nonlinear ways on the underlying parameters, which is one reason closed-form expressions for option prices are rare.

## 14.6   Dividends in the Black-Scholes Model

The assumption that the underlying asset does not pay dividends is evidently very restrictive. In this section, we see how this condition may be removed. There are two cases to consider. The first is that of discrete or cash dividends such as dividends paid on individual stocks. The second is a continuous dividend yield, as is appropriate when the underlying asset is a broad equity index or a currency. We examine both possibilities here. Mathematically, the difference between the two is that cash dividends cause discontinuities in the stock price whereas continuous dividend yields do not.

In either case, we show how the "non-dividend" Black-Scholes formulae presented earlier in this chapter (expressions (14.1) and (14.2)) may be amended to incorporate the presence of dividends. For expositional simplicity, we refer to the underlying security throughout as a "stock," though the continuous dividend yield setting is more naturally applied to an index or a currency.

## Cash Dividends in the Black-Scholes Model

Suppose the underlying stock has a cash dividend (or several cash dividends) over the life of the option. A dividend is counted as falling within the option's life if the ex-dividend date occurs before date $T$. Let $PV(D)$ denote the present value (viewed from the current time $t$) of all the dividends that are expected over the option's life. Then, the stock price $S_t$ at time $t$ can be regarded as being comprised of two components:

1. A riskless "fixed income" component of $PV(D)$.
2. A risky component of $S_t - PV(D)$.

Since the ex-dividend dates occur before date $T$, the dividends are removed from the stock price before $T$. Only the risky component of the stock price (i.e., the stock price net of anticipated dividend payouts) survives to date $T$, so it is the time-$T$ distribution of this component that determines option payoffs.

These observations suggest that the option may be priced by simply replacing the term $S_t$ in the Black-Scholes formula with $(S_t - PV(D))$! That is, the Black-Scholes formulae become

$$C = (S_t - PV(D))\, N(\hat{d}_1) - PV(K)\, N(\hat{d}_2) \qquad \textbf{(14.17)}$$

$$P = PV(K)\, N(-\hat{d}_2) - (S_t - PV(D))\, N(-\hat{d}_1) \qquad \textbf{(14.18)}$$

where

$$\hat{d}_1 = \frac{1}{\sigma\sqrt{T-t}}\left[\ln\left(\frac{S_t - PV(D)}{K}\right) + (r + \frac{1}{2}\sigma^2)(T-t)\right] \qquad \textbf{(14.19)}$$

$$\hat{d}_2 = d_1 - \sigma\sqrt{T-t} \qquad \textbf{(14.20)}$$

More precisely, (14.17)–(14.18) are the option prices if the stock price net of anticipated dividend payouts is assumed to meet the Black-Scholes conditions, i.e., to follow a lognormal price process with volatility $\sigma$ and to have no jumps.[1] Implicitly, this means the only reason the stock price process may be discontinuous is on account of dividends.

Note that $\sigma$ here refers to the volatility of the net-of-dividends stock price, not of the stock price itself. The two are not quite identical; the stock price, which is larger than the net-of-dividends price, has a lower volatility. If $\sigma_S$ denotes the volatility of the stock price and $\sigma$ the volatility of the net-of-dividends price, the two are related approximately by

$$\sigma = \sigma_S \times \frac{S_t}{S_t - PV(D)}$$

Figure 14.4 illustrates the impact of dividends on Black-Scholes prices. It considers the same parameter values as the earlier plot ($K = 100$, $r = 0.05$, $\sigma = 0.20$, maturity = 1/2 year, and current stock price $S_t$ ranging from 72 to 128). The figure plots call and put values under three scenarios: (i) zero dividends ($D = 0$), (ii) low dividends ($D = 2$), and (iii) high dividends ($D = 5$). The ex-dividend date is assumed to be three months (i.e., the halfway point of the option life).

---

[1] This is the assumption underlying the Schroder (1988) binomial model, which we discussed in Section 12.8.

**FIGURE 14.4**

Cash Dividends in the Black-Scholes Model

This figure plots call and put values for the same parameter values as in Figure 14.1 but with three possible values for dividends: $D = 0$ (which corresponds to Figure 14.1), $D = 2$, and $D = 5$. The ex-dividend date is at the halfway point of the option's life.

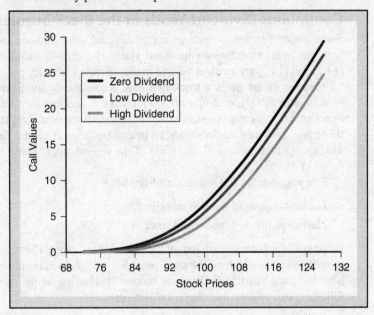

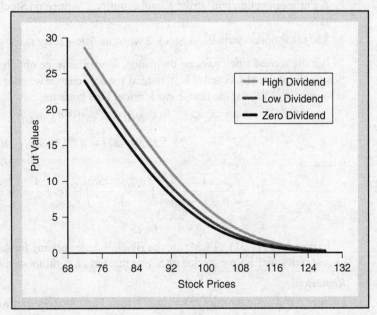

The figure shows that dividends lower call values and raise put values. This is expected. Dividends lower the price of the underlying. Thus, they push out-of-the-money calls further out-of-the-money and make in-the-money calls less in-the-money. Similarly, they push puts "more" into-the-money.

Of course, the effect is not uniform. Among calls, the impact of dividends is maximal for ones that are deep in-the-money. Such calls have a high likelihood of finishing in the money and are affected almost one-for-one by the dividend. At-the-money calls are affected less, and deep out-of-the-money calls are affected the least: such calls are anyway nearly worthless, so getting pushed further out of the money cannot have a large dollar impact. Similarly, deep in-the-money puts benefit almost one-for-one from the dividend payment, but deep out-of-the-money puts see very little dollar benefit.

## Continuous Dividend Yields in the Black-Scholes Model

Some underlying assets such as currencies and stock indices are naturally modeled as securities with a continuous dividend yield. The zero-dividend option pricing formulae (14.1) and (14.2) are easily modified to incorporate this case.

Suppose we are given a stock that pays a continuous dividend yield at rate $\delta$, and we wish to price an option on this stock with strike $K$ and maturity date $T$. Consider a second, hypothetical, stock that is equivalent to the first in all respects except that it pays no dividends. Since this stock pays no dividends, its price must grow at a rate $\delta$ *faster* than the first stock. This means that by time $T$, the price of the second stock would have grown by an extra factor of $e^{\delta(T-t)}$.

Now suppose the following conditions hold:

- The time-$t$ price of the first stock is $S_t$.
- The time-$t$ price of the second stock is $e^{-\delta(T-t)} S_t$.

By time $T$, the faster growth rate of the second stock cancels out this initial price difference, so the two stocks will have the same price $S_T$. An option maturing at date $T$ will, therefore, have the same payoff whether it is written on the first or the second stock. That is, the following two options must have the same price:

1. A European option with strike $K$ and maturity $T$ written on Stock 1 when its date-$t$ price is $S_t$.
2. The same option written on Stock 2 when its date-$t$ price is $e^{-\delta(T-t)} S_t$.

But the second stock pays no dividends, so we can price options on it using the Black-Scholes formulae (14.1) and (14.2)! Indeed, the only change we need make to those formulae is to use $e^{-\delta(T-t)} S_t$ for the time-$t$ stock price. This gives us

$$C^* = e^{-\delta(T-t)} S_t\, N(d_1^*) - e^{-r(T-t)} K\, N(d_2^*) \tag{14.21}$$

$$P^* = e^{-r(T-t)} K\, N(-d_2^*) - e^{-\delta(T-t)} S_t\, N(-d_1^*) \tag{14.22}$$

where

$$d_1^* = \frac{1}{\sigma\sqrt{T-t}} \left[ \ln\left( \frac{e^{-\delta(T-t)} S_t}{K} \right) + \left(r + \frac{1}{2}\sigma^2\right)(T-t) \right] \tag{14.23}$$

$$d_2^* = d_1^* - \sigma\sqrt{T-t} \tag{14.24}$$

Expressions (14.21)–(14.24) are the Black-Scholes pricing formulae for options written on a security with a time-$t$ price of $S_t$ and that pays a continuous dividend yield of $\delta$.

### Remark

For any $y$ and $z$, we have $\ln(yz) = \ln y + \ln z$. Therefore, we can write

$$\ln\left( \frac{e^{-\delta(T-t)} S_t}{K} \right) = \ln\left( \frac{S_t}{K} \right) + \ln\left( e^{-\delta(T-t)} \right) = \ln\left( \frac{S_t}{K} \right) - \delta(T-t)$$

Using this, the expression (14.23) for $d_1^*$ can be rewritten as

$$d_1^* = \frac{1}{\sigma\sqrt{T-t}} \left[ \ln\left( \frac{S_t}{K} \right) + \left(r - \delta + \frac{1}{2}\sigma^2\right)(T-t) \right] \tag{14.25}$$

In the sequel, we use the representation (14.25) for $d_1^*$.

**FIGURE 14.5**
Dividend Yields in the
Black-Scholes Model

This figure plots call and put values for the same parameter values as in Figure 14.1 but with three possible values for the annualized dividend yield on the underlying: $\delta = 0$ (which corresponds to Figure 14.1), $\delta = 0.025$, and $\delta = 0.10$.

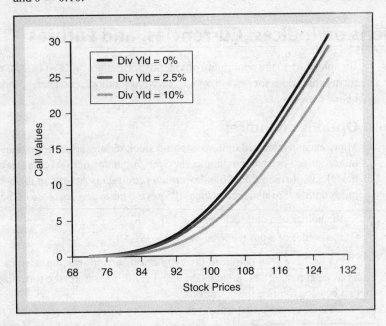

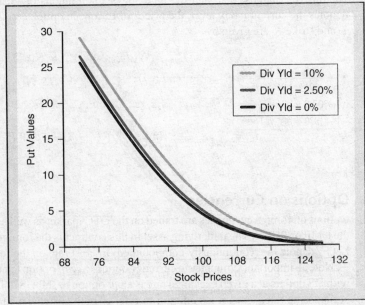

Figure 14.5 illustrates the impact of a continuous dividend yield on Black-Scholes option values. It considers the same range of parameter values as in Figure 14.1 but allows for three possible values for the annualized dividend yield on the underlying: (i) zero (which corresponds to Figure 14.1), (ii) 2.50%, and (iii) 10%.

The higher the dividend yield, the lower the growth rate of the stock price. Thus, a higher dividend yield $\delta$ implies lower call prices and higher put prices. As with cash dividends, the impact is once again maximal for deep in-the-money options and least for deep out-of-the-money options.

# 14.7 Options on Indices, Currencies, and Futures

By appealing to the continuous-dividends formulae (14.21)–(14.25), we can obtain closed-form expressions for pricing options on equity indices, currencies, and futures. The material below explains.

## Options on Indices

Many exchange-traded options exist on stock indices. Both European- and American-style index options exist. For example, the S&P 500 index options contract in the US is European in style, while the S&P 100 index options contract is American in style. Like index futures, index options are also *cash settled*. If $S_T$ is the index level at close of the last trading day, then

- the holder of a call receives $\max\{S_T - K, 0\}$.
- the holder of a put receives $\max\{K - S_T, 0\}$.

As we have seen earlier in the chapter on forward pricing, a stock index can be treated as an asset paying a continuous dividend yield. Therefore, the formulae (14.21) and (14.22) can be used to price index options.

That is, suppose that index returns follow a geometric Brownian motion with constant volatility $\sigma$. Suppose also that the index pays a continuous dividend yield at rate $\delta$. If $S_t$ denotes the current index level, the prices of European options on the index with maturity $T$ and strike $K$ are given by

$$C^* = e^{-\delta(T-t)} S_t \, N(d_1^*) - e^{-r(T-t)} K \, N(d_2^*) \qquad \textbf{(14.26)}$$

$$P^* = e^{-r(T-t)} K \, N(-d_2^*) - e^{-\delta(T-t)} S_t \, N(-d_1^*) \qquad \textbf{(14.27)}$$

where

$$d_1^* = \frac{1}{\sigma\sqrt{T-t}} \left[ \ln\left(\frac{S_t}{K}\right) + (r - \delta + \frac{1}{2}\sigma^2)(T-t) \right]$$

$$d_2^* = d_1^* - \sigma\sqrt{T-t}$$

## Options on Currencies

Options on foreign currencies are traded on the OTC market as well as on exchanges such as the CME or PHLX. The underlying asset in this contract is the foreign currency in question. Let $r_f$ denote the (continuously-compounded) interest rate on the foreign currency.

Note an important symmetry in currency options: a *call* option to purchase British pounds with US dollars at a given exchange rate is a *put* option to sell US dollars for British pounds at that same rate. Thus, it is common to refer to both currencies in identifying the option (e.g., dollar-call/yen-put or euro-call/dollar-put).

The formulae (14.21)–(14.22) can be used to price options on currencies with the foreign interest rate $r_f$ playing the role of the dividend yield $\delta$. For specificity, suppose that the US dollar is the domestic currency. Suppose further that:

- $S_t$ denotes the current exchange rate (dollars per unit of foreign currency).

- The exchange rate follows a geometric Brownian motion with constant volatility $\sigma$.
- $r$ and $r_f$ denote the risk-free rates in, respectively, dollars and the foreign currency.

Then, the prices of call and put options on the foreign currency with a strike price of $K$ (i.e., $K$ dollars per unit of the foreign currency) and maturity date of $T$ are given by

$$C^* = e^{-r_f(T-t)} S_t N(d_1^*) - e^{-r(T-t)} K N(d_2^*) \qquad \textbf{(14.28)}$$

$$P^* = e^{-r(T-t)} K N(-d_2^*) - e^{-r_f(T-t)} S_t N(-d_1^*) \qquad \textbf{(14.29)}$$

where

$$d_1^* = \frac{1}{\sigma\sqrt{T-t}} \left[ \ln\left(\frac{S_t}{K}\right) + \left(r - r_f + \frac{1}{2}\sigma^2\right)(T-t) \right]$$

$$d_2^* = d_1^* - \sigma\sqrt{T-t}$$

## Options on Futures

Options on futures are defined somewhat differently from options on spot. A call option on futures with a strike of $K$ gives the holder the right to take a *long* position in the futures contract at a futures price of $K$. A put option on futures with a strike of $K$ gives the holder the right to take a *short* position in the futures contract at a futures price of $K$.

Clearly, one can take a futures position only at the prevailing futures price. Therefore, upon exercise of a call, the holder receives a long position in the futures contract with the difference between the prevailing futures price and the strike price of the contract credited to the margin account. The exercise of a put is handled similarly.

The key to pricing futures options lies in the relationship between spot and futures prices. Suppose the current (time-$t$) spot price of the asset underlying the futures contract is $S_t$. Suppose too that the underlying asset does not pay any dividends. (We will examine the consequences of dropping this assumption shortly.) Let $T_f$ denote the maturity date of the futures contract. Then, the arbitrage-free futures price at $t$ is

$$F_t = e^{r(T_f - t)} S_t \qquad \textbf{(14.30)}$$

On date $T_f$, spot and futures prices coincide:

$$F_{T_f} = S_{T_f} \qquad \textbf{(14.31)}$$

Equations (14.30) and (14.31) show that the relation between the futures price $F_t$ and the spot price $S_t$ is analogous to that between Stock 1 and Stock 2 in the discussion on continuous dividend yields in Section 14.6: the futures price starts at a higher level at date $t$, but the prices coincide by date $T_f$. Thus, the futures price grows at a rate $r$ *slower* than the spot price, so it is "as if" the futures pays a continuous dividend yield of $r$.

Using this observation, the price of a European option on futures can be found using the formulae (14.21) and (14.22) with $S_t$ replaced by the futures price $F_t$, and with $r$ playing the role of the continuous dividend yield $\delta$. Specifically, suppose that the futures price follows a geometric Brownian motion with constant volatility $\sigma$. Then, the price of call and put options on the futures contract with maturity date $T$ ($T < T_f$) and strike $K$ are given by

$$C^* = e^{-r(T-t)} [F_t N(d_1^*) - K N(d_2^*)] \qquad \textbf{(14.32)}$$

$$P^* = e^{-r(T-t)} [K N(-d_2^*) - F N(-d_1^*)] \qquad \textbf{(14.33)}$$

where

$$d_1^* = \frac{1}{\sigma\sqrt{T-t}}\left[\ln\left(\frac{F_t}{K}\right) + \frac{1}{2}\sigma^2(T-t)\right]$$

$$d_2^* = d_1^* - \sigma\sqrt{T-t}$$

The assumption that the asset underlying the futures pays no dividends is not always reasonable (e.g., for futures on stock indices). But it turns out this assumption is irrelevant! The formulae (14.32)–(14.33) remain valid even if the asset has a continuous dividend yield at rate $\delta$. To see this, note that in this case, the time-$t$ futures price is related to the time-$t$ spot price $S_t$ via

$$F_t = e^{(r-\delta)(T_f-t)}S_t \tag{14.34}$$

On the maturity date $T_f$ of the futures contract, spot and futures prices must still coincide:

$$F_{T_f} = S_{T_f} \tag{14.35}$$

Thus, it is "as if" the futures contract pays a continuous dividend yield at the rate $r - \delta$ relative to the underlying spot asset. But the spot asset itself pays dividends at rate $\delta$, so relative to a non-dividend-paying equivalent, it is as if the futures pays dividends at rate $r$. So formulae (14.32)–(14.33) remain valid in this case too.

An alternative way to see this is to consider the behavior of futures prices under the risk-neutral measure. Futures contracts are marked-to-market every day, so the value of the contract is reset to zero each day. Let $F_t$ denote the date-$t$ futures price, and let $F_{t+1}$ be the futures price on date $t + 1$. Let $h$ denote the length of time between $t$ and $t + 1$ (so cash flows occurring at time $t + 1$ are discounted by $e^{-rh}$ to get time-$t$ present values). If $E_t[\cdot]$ denotes time-$t$ expectations under the risk-neutral measure, then we must have

$$E_t\left[e^{-rh}(F_{t+1} - F_t)\right] = 0 \tag{14.36}$$

The quantity $(F_{t+1} - F_t)$ is just the cash flow that results on date $t + 1$ from resettlement of the futures contract. By definition, the discounted expectation (under the risk-neutral measure) of this cash flow must equal the present value of the futures contract. But this present value is zero, since the value of the futures contract is reset to zero every day. This gives us (14.36). Note that this holds regardless of the dividend yield rate on the asset underlying the futures contract (we have made no assumption about this).

Now, the discount factor $e^{-rh}$ is a known quantity at time $t$, so can be taken out of the expectation, which results in $e^{-rh} E_t[F_{t+1} - F_t] = 0$, so $E_t[F_{t+1} - F_t] = 0$. But $F_t$ is also known at time $t$ and can be taken out of the expectation, which finally yields

$$E_t[F_{t+1}] = F_t \tag{14.37}$$

Expression (14.37) states the fundamental result that the futures price follows a martingale under the risk-neutral measure: its expected value tomorrow (under the risk-neutral measure) is equal to today's price. Equivalently, this says that the futures price has zero drift under the risk-neutral measure. (Note again that this is true regardless of the dividend yield rate on the asset underlying the futures contract.) But, in general, the drift of a security's price under the risk-neutral measure is equal to $r - \delta$ where $r$ is the risk-free rate (with respect to which the risk-neutral measure is defined) and $\delta$ is the dividend yield on the security. Thus, a zero drift for the futures price implies an implicit dividend yield at rate $r$. And this results in the prices (14.32)–(14.33) for options on the futures contract.

## 14.8  Testing the Black-Scholes Model: Implied Volatility

The Black-Scholes formula tells us how to identify option prices *given* the volatility of the underlying. However, volatility is unobservable, while we often observe prices of options. This motivates the reverse question: given an option price, what level of volatility is implied by the observed price? This level is called the *implied volatility*. Formally, implied volatility is the level of volatility that would make observed option prices consistent with the Black-Scholes formula given values for the other parameters.

For example, suppose we are looking at a call on a non-dividend-paying stock. Let $K$ and $T - t$ denote the call's strike and time-to-maturity, and let $\widehat{C}$ be the observed call price. Let $S_t$ be the stock price and $r$ the interest rate. Then, the implied volatility is the level $\sigma$ for which

$$C^{bs}(S, K, T-t, r, \sigma) = \widehat{C}$$

where $C^{bs}$ is the Black-Scholes call option pricing formula.

Implied volatility is always uniquely defined. That is, given an observed call price $\widehat{C}$, there is at most one value of $\sigma$ such that the Black-Scholes formula will give rise to the observed value $\widehat{C}$. This is a consequence of the fact that the Black-Scholes price is increasing in $\sigma$.

In a general sense, implied volatility represents the market-wide average perception of volatility anticipated over the option's lifetime. As such, it is a *forward looking* concept. In contrast, historical volatility is *backward looking*; it describes the uncertainty in the stock price evolution that was experienced in the past.

### The Volatility Smile/Skew

Fix an underlying asset. If the Black-Scholes model were an accurate description of the returns process for that asset, the arbitrage-free price of *any* option on the asset (i.e., any strike $K$ and maturity date $T$) must be determined by the Black-Scholes formula. This means implied volatility inferred from any option on the asset should be the same as implied volatility inferred from any other option—they should all be equal to the "true" underlying volatility. The requirement that implied volatilities should be constant across different strikes and maturities offers an indirect test of the Black-Scholes model.

In practice, in virtually every market, the Black-Scholes model fails this test. When maturity is held constant and implied volatilities are plotted against strikes, two patterns are commonly witnessed. In equity index markets, implied volatilities for "low" strikes (corresponding to out-of-the-money puts) tend to be higher than implied volatilities for at-the-money or in-the-money puts. This is called the *volatility skew*. In currency markets, the graph is more symmetric: implied volatilities for out-of-the-money and in-the-money puts tend to be roughly identical and higher than implied volatilities of at-the-money options, so we obtain what is called a *volatility smile*. Implied volatilities on individual equities too tend to exhibit greater symmetry than implied volatilities on indices.

Figures 14.6 and 14.7 provide examples of implied volatility skews on the S&P 500 index options and on US dollar/British pound currency options. Each figure is a screenshot taken from the website www.pmpublishing.com. All the screenshots pertain to data on April 7, 2004. The two panels of Figure 14.6 describe implied volatility skews on the S&P 500 index options expiring in June and September, respectively. The two panels of Figure 14.7 represent implied volatility smiles on the USD/GBP options expiring in May and June, respectively.

**FIGURE 14.6**
Implied Volatility
Skews on S&P 500
Index Options

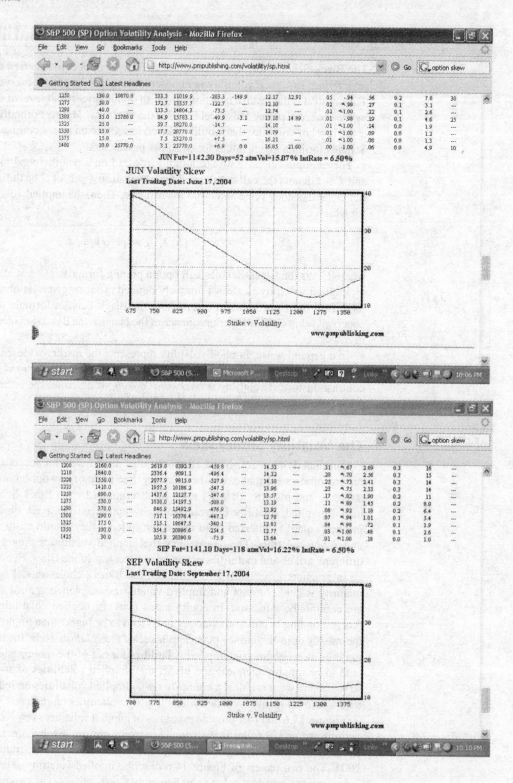

www.pmpublishing.com

**FIGURE 14.7**
Implied Volatility
Skews on USD/GBP
Currency Options

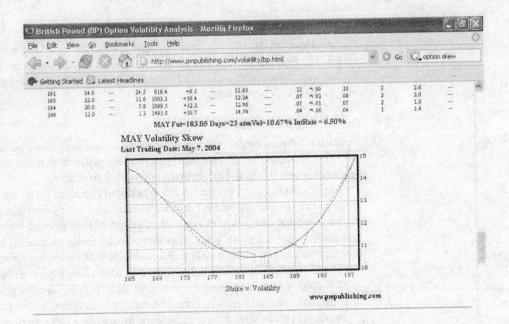

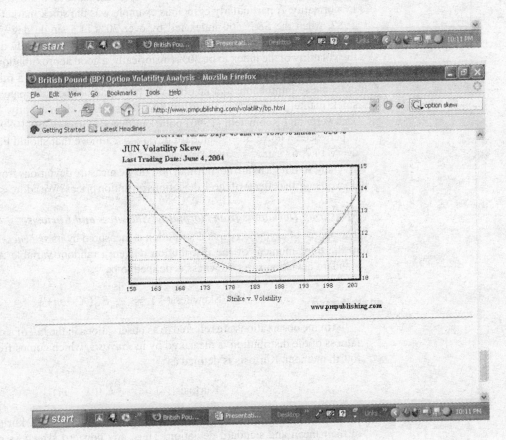

# The Source of the Volatility Skew

The existence of the skew is evidence that something is wrong with the Black-Scholes model. The first question to ask, therefore, is: what? Once we identify where the problem lies, we can think about ways of adjusting the model and its assumptions so that we get a better match with observations.

## *Deviations from Normality*

The Black-Scholes model assumes log-returns are *normally* distributed. However, in virtually every financial market, empirical plots and estimates from historical returns and options markets suggest this is not an accurate description of reality.

Two deviations from normality are particularly visible. First, the normal distribution is symmetric around its mean. Empirically estimated return distributions, especially from equities markets, often exhibit *skewness*. Second, of fundamental importance, extreme observations occur far more often than they should under normality. For example, in any normal distribution, there is only a 5% probability of observing an outcome that is more than 1.645 standard deviations below the mean, which means that on average only 1 outcome in 20 should fall into this category. Similarly, there is only a 0.50% probability (1 outcome in 200) of an observation more than 2.58 standard deviations below the mean.

In practice, such extreme price moves tend to take place far more frequently than predicted by normality. A particularly egregious example was the stock market crash of October 19, 1987, when the S&P 500 index fell by over 20% in a single day while S&P 500 index futures declined by 29%. Assuming index returns are lognormally distributed and taking the volatility of the index to be 20% (historically, a good approximation), Rubinstein (1998) points out that the likelihood of a 29% move in a single day is a microscopic $10^{-160}$, an outcome so improbable that he observes, "it would not be anticipated to occur even if the stock market were to last for 20 billion years." Less dramatically, but no less tellingly, Jackwerth and Rubinstein (1996) point out that on October 13, 1989, the S&P 500 index experienced a move of $-5$ standard deviations, a move that should be expected only once every 14,756 years.

Okay, so if returns are not normal, how do we measure deviations from normality and how do we gauge the effects of these deviations on option prices? We address these questions now.

## *Measuring Deviations from Normality: Skewness and Kurtosis*

The degree of asymmetry in a distribution is measured by its *skewness*. Skewness is related to the third moment of the distribution. Given a random variable $X$ with mean $m$ and standard deviation $s$, its skewness is defined to be

$$\text{Skewness}(X) \;=\; \frac{1}{s^3}\, E\left[(X - m)^3\right]$$

Extreme observations are referred to as observations in the *tail* of a distribution. The tail-fatness of the distribution is measured by its *kurtosis*, which comes from the distribution's fourth moment. Kurtosis is defined as

$$\text{Kurtosis}(X) \;=\; \frac{1}{s^4}\, E\left[(X - m)^4\right]$$

Normal distributions always have a skewness of zero and a kurtosis of 3 *regardless* of their mean and standard deviation. Thus, any nonzero skewness or kurtosis different from 3 involves a departure from normality. A distribution is said to have "fat tails" or to exhibit *leptokurtosis* if its kurtosis exceeds 3; conversely, it is said to have thin tails or to exhibit *platykurtosis* if its kurtosis is less than 3. Empirical returns distributions are typically fat-tailed or leptokurtic. The "excess kurtosis" in a distribution is the amount by which its kurtosis exceeds 3. The larger is the excess kurtosis, the more likely are extreme observations compared to the normal's predictions.

### Skewness, Kurtosis, and the Volatility Skew

To undestand the impact of leptokurtosis on implied volatilities, suppose that you are writing an out-of-the-money put option on the S&P 500 index. For specificity, suppose that the index is currently at 1140 and the put has a strike of 1075. You estimate implied volatility from at-the-money options. Using this volatility, you then find that under lognormality, the probability of a 65-point fall in the index level (which is needed for the put to come into the money) is so unlikely, the Black-Scholes model assigns a near-zero value to this put. Should you accept this value?

Clearly not. Lognormality understates the likelihood of extreme moves, so the probability of the put coming into the money is larger than that predicted by the Black-Scholes model. This means the Black-Scholes model *underprices* the out-of-the-money put relative to those at-the-money. You would, therefore, charge a higher price than the Black-Scholes model suggests. But this means the implied volatility inferred from your price for the out-of-the-money put would be higher than the at-the-money implied volatility, so a volatility skew results!

Thus, volatility skews are a natural and rational consequence of leptokurtosis in the returns distributions. If, further, returns are negatively skewed and left tails are fatter than right tails, we expect an asymmetric volatility skew. This is typically the case in equity index markets. However, if the return distribution is more symmetric and left and right tails tend to matter more equally, we would expect to see a more symmetric smile, which is the typical case in currency markets and markets for many individual equities.

### Potential Sources of Skewness and Kurtosis

Several potential (and nonexclusive) hypotheses have been advanced to explain the presence of negative skewness and kurtosis in equity returns distributions, and, thereby, the shape of the implied volatility skew. We mention two here.

In a hypothesis termed "crash-o-phobia," Rubinstein (1994) suggests that fears of a major stock market crash akin to that of October 1987 are taken into account by traders pricing out-of-the-money puts. The possibility of a crash creates leptokurtosis in the returns distribution since the crash is, by definition, a tail event. Moreover, since a crash is a *left*-tail event, its incorporation in the returns distribution also creates negative skewness. Thus, crash-o-phobia offers a potential explanation of both the presence and shape of the implied volatility curve in equity markets.

Empirical investigation has found some support for this hypothesis. Its plausibility is also enhanced by the observation that in the electricity options market, where the fear is that of a sudden *spike* in electricity prices, the implied volatility skew is reversed (i.e., out-of-the-money calls have higher implied volatilities than at- or in-the-money calls) exactly as crash-o-phobia would suggest.

An alternative source of negative skewness and leptokurtosis in equity markets is the relationship between equity returns and equity volatility. Negative returns in equity markets are often accompanied by increased volatility, while positive returns are accompanied by lower volatility. This pattern has itself been attributed to a possible "leverage" effect. The story goes that declining equity prices raise the debt-equity ratio, making equity riskier and leading to higher equity volatility; while conversely, positive equity returns lower the debt-equity ratio, making equity less risky and reducing its volatility. Whatever the driver, this returns-volatility relationship leads both to leptokurtosis and to negative skewness in returns, and offers another potential explanation of the typical implied volatility skew.

These hypotheses have been adduced in the context of equity markets, but they have analogs for other markets too. The fear of sharp exchange-rate moves (perhaps on account of intervention) creates leptokurtosis analogous to crash-o-phobia. Similarly, randomly changing volatility can create tail-fatness in exchange-rate or other returns distributions.

## Other Explanations for the Skew

It is often suggested that the volatility skew or smile is caused by the effects of demand for protection. Investors are net long equities, so the demand for cheap protection (out-of-the-money puts on the equities) raises the demand for these puts relative to those at-the-money, resulting in the volatility skew. In currency markets, the implied volatility plot is more symmetric because investors are net long both currencies. Since a put on one currency is a call on the other, demand for protection on the currencies raises the implied volatility levels in either direction away from-the-money, resulting in the volatility smile.

These explanations appear plausible, but they are incomplete. They cannot, in isolation, explain observed skews; rather, they must be combined with some market friction(s). In a smooth environment such as that assumed by Black-Scholes, replicating an out-of-the-money option is as easy as replicating an at-the-money option, so merely the fact that there is a demand for out-of-the-money puts cannot create a volatility skew. In contrast, non-normality in returns such as excess kurtosis will result in a volatility skew regardless of the presence of market frictions.

## Generalizing or Replacing Black-Scholes

If the Black-Scholes model exhibits systematic departures from the market, why not generalize it or replace it with distributions that allow for skewness and leptokurtosis? There may even be a "natural" generalization. The Black-Scholes model makes two uncomfortable assumptions:

1. There are no jumps in the returns process.
2. The volatility of the returns process is constant over time.

Empirical observation suggests there is a strong case for dropping both these assumptions. Indeed, the explanations discussed above implicitly indicate this. The "leverage effect" suggests that constant volatility should be replaced with a model in which volatility is stochastic and negatively correlated with the returns process. "Crash-o-phobia" assumes large negative jumps may occur in the returns distribution. If jumps are added to the log-normal model or if volatility is allowed to be stochastic, the model can be made to exhibit both fat tails and skewness.

Over the last several years, a vast number of models have been proposed as generalizations or alternatives to Black-Scholes. These models typically involve a substantially greater degree of complexity than the Black-Scholes model; Chapter 16 reviews several of them. Despite its empirical shortcomings, however, the Black-Scholes model has continued to retain immense popularity and remains the benchmark model for pricing options. This may partly be a recognition that any model is likely to be fallible. But it is also likely a reflection of a preference for working with simple and elegant models whose shortcomings are readily understood and, therefore, more easily compensated for.

# 14.9   The VIX and Its Derivatives

US investors have become accustomed to hearing about the "fear index," or the VIX, the market's proxy for the degree of risk borne in the equity markets. The VIX is the Chicago Board Option Exchange's "near-term" volatility index. It is a forward-looking estimate of the

**FIGURE 14.8**

The CBOE Volatility Index (VIX): Jan 1990–Mar 2009

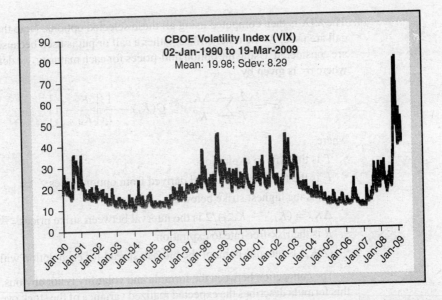

CBOE Volatility Index (VIX)
02-Jan-1990 to 19-Mar-2009
Mean: 19.98; Sdev: 8.29

annualized volatility of the S&P500 over the next 30 calendar days. There are VIX futures (inception May 2004, traded on the CBOE Futures Exchange) as well as exchange-traded VIX options (inception February 2006, traded on the CBOE). Figure 14.8 shows the evolution of the VIX since 1990. The mean level of the VIX is around 20% with a standard deviation of about 8%–9%. The time series is characterized by quiet periods interjected by sporadic epochs of high volatility when the VIX spikes to as much as three times its normal value.

The VIX is computed on a real-time basis throughout the day. It was introduced and developed by Whaley (1993). (The notion of a volatility index had also been proposed earlier in Brenner and Galai (1989); see also Brenner and Galai (1993).) The underlying index for the VIX is the S&P 500 index (SPX). This was not always the case. When the VIX was first introduced, the S&P 100 index (OEX) was used as the volume in options was limited to the top few names in the S&P. Today SPX options volume far surpasses that of the OEX and the VIX is based on the volatility of the former index. Moreover, SPX options are European style whereas OEX ones are American, making valuation of the SPX options easier. In any event, the SPX and OEX indexes are close substitutes, and from 1986 to 2008, the correlation between the two index returns was 99% (see Whaley, 2008).

Since September 2003, the VIX has been a measure of SPX 30-day volatility. It is implied from options of various strikes on the SPX, so incorporates the skew. The VIX uses nearby and second nearby options with at least 8 days left to expiration and then weights them to yield a constant, 30-day measure of the expected volatility of the S&P 500 index. The options used are the ones that are at-the-money (ATM) and OTM, both puts and calls. The procedure is as follows:

1. For each maturity (next-term and near-term), the ATM forward strike is first identified. This is done by choosing the strike at which the difference in price between the call and put options is the least. Denote this strike $K_0$.

2. For puts: All options for ATM/OTM strikes ($K_i \leq K_0$) are selected for which the bid price is nonzero. The process stops selecting further strikes when two consecutive zero bid prices are encountered as one goes more out-of-the-money.

3. For calls: All options for ATM/OTM strikes ($K_i \geq K_0$) are selected for which the bid price is nonzero. The process stops selecting further strikes when two consecutive zero bid prices are encountered.

4. The VIX is then computed using all these selected options. Note that at $K_0$, a put and a call are used. At the other strikes, either a call or put is used because only OTM options are considered. Using the option mid-prices for each maturity, we define VIX $= \sigma \times 100$, where $\sigma^2$ is given by

$$\sigma^2 = \frac{2}{T} \sum_i \frac{\Delta K_i}{K_i^2} e^{RT} Q(K_i) - \frac{1}{T} \left[ \frac{F}{K_0} - 1 \right]^2 \qquad \textbf{(14.38)}$$

where

- $T$ is the time to expiration.
- $F$ is the forward index level derived from option prices.
- $K_0$ is the highest strike below $F$.
- $\Delta K_i = (K_{i+1} - K_{i-1})/2$ is the interval between strike prices.
- $R$ is the risk-free rate to expiration.
- $Q(K_i)$ is the mid-point of the bid-ask spread for each option with strike $K_i$.

The connection between the formula and volatility is not obvious, but it turns out that this formula describes the expected realized variance of the stock over the horizon $[0, T]$ as implied by option prices. A derivation of this result is presented in Appendix 14B in the context of describing volatility and variance swaps (see the discussion towards the end of the material on variance swaps).

5. Since this calculation is undertaken for the near-term and next-term maturities, we get two values, denoted $\sigma_1^2$ and $\sigma_2^2$. These are then combined to get the 30-day weighted average as follows:

$$VIX = 100 \times \sqrt{\left( T_1 \sigma_1^2 \left[ \frac{N_{T_2} - N_{30}}{N_{T_2} - N_{T_1}} \right] + T_2 \sigma_2^2 \left[ \frac{N_{30} - N_{T_1}}{N_{T_2} - N_{T_1}} \right] \right) \times \frac{N_{365}}{N_{30}}} \qquad \textbf{(14.39)}$$

where $N_T$ is the number of minutes to time $T$

As is evident from this description, the VIX is calculated using transparent rules. Further details and examples are available at the CBOE website.

Volatility indexes have been developed for other broad equity markets. We have the Dow Jones volatility index (VXD), the NASDAQ 100 volatility index (VXN), the Russell 2000 volatility index (RVX), and the S&P 500 three-month volatility index (VXV). Volatility indexes are being developed for many European indexes such as the DAX, FTSE 100, and the CAC 40.

## Trading Volatility via the VIX

There are various ways in which volatility may be traded. One is to purchase options and delta-hedge them, leaving only amplitude risk. A second is to buy a straddle (and delta-hedge it, if necessary). Finally, there is the trading of pure volatility using the VIX.

Trades may be made on volatility direction by using the futures on VIX (ticker: VX). The contract size is $1000 times the VIX. The CBOE may list futures for trading up to nine near-term serial months and five months on the February quarterly cycle for the VIX futures contract. So it is easy to inject volatility positions into standard portfolios using VIX futures.

VIX futures may be a good way to enhance returns on a portfolio as well as manage its risk. What makes adding a position in volatility to an equity portfolio particularly attractive is that volatility moves are generally negatively correlated with equity returns. Indeed, the return on VIX futures in 2008 was a massive 81%, even as equity markets suffered sharp declines. The CBOE estimated that a 15% allocation to VIX in a well-diversified portfolio would have resulted in a −13.08% return in 2008 (or +5.07% four-year average, standard deviation 1.93%) versus the same portfolio earning −20.99% in 2008 (−3.87% four-year average, standard deviation 3.03%) without any VIX component.

VIX options (ticker: VRO) may be used to trade the volatility of volatility. However, options on the VIX are generally quite expensive because the volatility of volatility is very high, usually much more than the volatility of equity. In 2007, for example, the volatility of the VIX was 132% whereas that of the SPX was only 16%.

Since July 2008, it has also been possible to trade in binary options on the VIX (ticker: BVZ). Offered by the CBOE first in the form of binary calls and later as binary puts, these options are structured so that if the options are in-the-money at expiration, the payoff is $100.

## 14.10 Exercises

1. Explain why the Black-Scholes model is inappropriate if the stock can gap.

2. Is assuming a constant (nonstochastic) interest rate in the Black-Scholes model a major deficiency of the model?

3. The Black-Scholes model assumes constant volatility. How serious a shortcoming is this?

4. Compute the three-month ($T = 1/4$) forward price $F$ of a stock currently trading at $40 when the risk-free rate for this period is $r = 4\%$. Then, set the strike price $K = F$ and calculate call and put values from the Black-Scholes model if the volatility is $\sigma = 0.4$, assuming the stock pays no dividends. What can you say about the call and put prices you just computed?

5. (We repeat the previous question allowing for nonzero dividends). Assume a stock has a dividend yield of $d = 2\%$. Compute the three-month ($T = 1/4$) forward price $F$ of a stock currently trading at $40 when the risk-free rate for this period is $r = 4\%$. Then, set the strike price $K = F$ and calculate call and put values from the Black-Scholes model if the volatility is $\sigma = 0.4$. What can you say about the call and put prices you just computed?

6. Plot the price of a Black-Scholes call for a range of volatility from 5% to 40%. Use the following parameters: $S = 30$, $K = 33$, $T = 1/3$, $r = 0.03$, and $d = 0$. Does the function appear concave or convex?

7. Plot the price of a Black-Scholes call for declining maturity from three years to zero years. Does the function appear concave or convex? Use the following parameters: $S = 30$, $K = 33$, $\sigma = 0.3$, $r = 0.03$, and $d = 0$.

8. Plot the price of a Black-Scholes call for a range of interest rates from 1% to 20%. Use the following parameters: $S = 30$, $K = 33$, $T = 3$, $\sigma = 0.3$, and $d = 0$.

9. On December 1, the S&P 500 index (SPX) is trading at 1396.71. The prices of call options on the index expiring on March 16 (i.e., in a bit over three months) are as follows:

| Strike $K$ | Call Prices |
|---|---|
| 1300 | 116.80 |
| 1350 | 73.70 |
| 1400 | 41.00 |

Assuming the interest rate for that period is 4.88% and the annual dividend rate on the SPX is 1.5%, compute the implied volatility for each of the SPX options using the Black-Scholes formula. Are these volatilities the same? Explain.

10. (Repeat for puts) On December 1, the S&P 500 index (SPX) is trading at 1396.71. The prices of put options on the index expiring on March 16 (i.e., a little over three months) are as follows:

| Strike $K$ | Put Prices |
|---|---|
| 1300 | 11.20 |
| 1350 | 17.30 |
| 1400 | 30.50 |

Assuming the interest rate for that period is 4.88%, and the annual dividend rate on the SPX is 1.5%, compute the implied volatility for each of the options using the Black-Scholes formula. Are these volatilities the same? Explain. Also, are these volatilities the same as that obtained from the previous question? Should they be? Explain.

11. Show that the delta of an at-the-money European call option in the Black-Scholes model is at least 1/2. What about the delta of an at-the-money put?

12. What happens to the delta of an at-the-money call as the time-to-maturity declines? What about a put?

13. Let $S = K = 100$, $\sigma = 0.25$, and $T - t = 1$ month. Create a spreadsheet to value a call and a put for the following values of $r$:
    (a) $r = 0.08$.
    (b) $r = 0.06$.
    (c) $r = 0.04$.

14. Microsoft stock is currently trading at $24.35. Consider call and put options with a strike of $25.00 expiring in 12 days ($= 0.0476$ years). Suppose that the volatility of Microsoft stock is 40% and that the interest rate is 3%. What are the Black-Scholes prices of the call and the put? What are the option deltas?

15. GE stock is currently trading at $26.15. A call option with a strike of $25.00 and 12 days ($= 0.0476$ years) to expiry costs $1.56. Assuming an interest rate of 3%, what is the implied volatility?

16. The S&P 500 index is currently at 1101. A call option with a strike of 1075 and 17 days ($= 0.067$ years) to maturity costs 36.20. Assume an interest rate of 3%. For simplicity, assume also that the dividend yield on the index is zero.
    (a) What is the implied volatility?
    (b) If implied volatility went up to 20%, what would happen to the call's value?
    (c) If the other parameters remained the same, what would the option value be after one week (i.e., with 12 trading days or 0.0476 years left to maturity)?
    (d) Finally, how would your answer to part (a) change if the dividend yield were taken to be 2% instead of zero?

17. The spot USD-EUR exchange rate is USD1.24/EUR. Consider a one-month ($= 0.083$ years) put option on the EUR with a strike of USD1.25/EUR. Assume that the volatility of the exchange rate is 12%, the one-month interest rate on the USD is 3.1%, and the one-month interest rate on the EUR is 3.7%, both in continuously-compounded terms.
    (a) What is the Black-Scholes price of the put?
    (b) If you had written this put on EUR 10 million, what would you do to delta-hedge your position?

18. The spot USD-EUR exchange rate is USD1.50/EUR. Consider a six-month (= 0.5 years) call option on the EUR with a strike of USD1.50/EUR. Suppose the volatility of the exchange rate is 20%, the six-month interest rate on the USD is 1.5%, and the six-month interest rate on the EUR is 2.5%, both in continuously-compounded terms.

    (a) What is the Black-Scholes price of the call?

    (b) If you had written this call on EUR 100 million, what would you do to delta-hedge your position?

19. The spot USD-EUR exchange rate is USD1.50/EUR. Price a one-month straddle with an *at-the-money-forward* (ATMF) strike. The ATMF strike price is defined to be that value of $K$ which equals the forward exchange rate for that maturity, i.e., for which $Ke^{-rT} = Se^{-qT}$. Assume that the volatility of the exchange rate is 20%, the six-month interest rate on the USD is 1.5%, and the six-month interest rate on the EUR is 2.5%, both in continuously-compounded terms.

20. An option on a stock is said to be *at-the-money-forward* (ATMF) if the strike price equals the forward price on the stock for that maturity. Assume there are no dividends, so the ATMF strike $K$ satisfies $S_t = PV(K) = e^{-r(T-t)}K$. Show that the value of an ATMF call in the Black-Scholes world is given by

$$S_t [2N(\hat{d}_1) - 1] \qquad \textbf{(14.40)}$$

    where $\hat{d}_1 = [\sigma\sqrt{T-t}]/2$.

21. Show that the at-the-money-forward call price (14.40) is approximately equal to

$$S_t \frac{1}{\sqrt{2\pi}} \sigma\sqrt{T-t} \qquad \textbf{(14.41)}$$

    *Remark*: Expression (14.41) gives us a quick method for calculating the prices of ATMF calls. Two interesting points about expression (14.41):

    (a) It depends on only three parameters ($S_t, \sigma$, and $T-t$) and the constant $\pi$; in particular, the cumulative normal distribution function $N(\cdot)$ is not involved.

    (b) It shows that the prices of at-the-money-forward calls are approximately *linear* in $\sigma$.

    These features make the formula above very easy to use in practice not only to obtain prices of ATMF options, but also to obtain quick estimates of implied volatility of such options. The next two questions illustrate these points.

22. Using (14.41), identify the approximate price of an at-the-money-forward call with the following parameters:

    (a) $S = 50$, $T - t = 1$ month, and $\sigma = 0.15$.

    (b) $S = 70$, $T - t = 2$ months, and $\sigma = 0.25$.

23. Suppose an at-the-money-forward call with one month to maturity is trading at a price of $C = 0.946$ when the stock price is $S_t = 54.77$.

    (a) Using the approximation (14.41), what is the implied volatility on the call?

    (b) What if the call were trading at $C = 1.576$ instead?

24. A stock index is currently at 858. A call option with a strike of 850 and 17 days (= 0.047 years) to maturity costs 23.50. Assume an interest rate of 3%. For simplicity, assume also that the dividend yield on the index is zero.

    (a) What is the implied volatility?

    (b) If implied volatility went up to 28%, what would happen to the call's value?

    (c) If all the other parameters remained the same, what would the option value be after one week (i.e., with 10 days or 0.027 years left to maturity)?

# Further Properties of the Black-Scholes Delta

In Section 14.5, we outlined a number of properties satisfied by call deltas. This appendix provides both the general intuition for these properties and the confirmation that they hold in the Black-Scholes setting.

## Behavior of Option Deltas in $\sigma$

In general, how would one expect the delta of a call to change as $\sigma$ increases? By using the analogy between the call delta and its likelihood of finishing in-the-money (see Section 11.8), we can get some intuition for the anticipated behavior. (The analogy is not quite pristine, but as we mentioned there, it is very useful from an intuitive standpoint.)

Consider a situation where $S_t$ is very large relative to $K$, so the call is deep in-the-money. With very low volatility, the call is almost sure to finish in-the-money, so the delta will be close to $+1$. With high volatility, on the other hand, there is a greater likelihood of being thrown out-of-the-money (the depth-in-the-money measured in terms of standard deviation is smaller now). Thus, the delta will be smaller.

Conversely, suppose $S_t$ is very small relative to $K$, so the call is deep out-of-the-money. With low volatility, the chances of moving back into-the-money are low, so the delta of the call will be close to zero. With higher volatility, there is a greater chance of being thrown into-the-money (the number of standard deviation moves required of the stock price is smaller), which raises the option delta.

Taken together, these arguments indicate that the behavior of the delta should depend on depth in-the-money of the call:

- When $S_t$ is large relative to $K$, the delta should *decrease* as $\sigma$ increases.
- When $S_t$ is small relative to $K$, the delta should *increase* as $\sigma$ increases.

The Black-Scholes formula exhibits this behavior. The term $d_1$ in the call price can be rewritten as

$$ d_1 = \frac{1}{\sigma\sqrt{T-t}}\left[\ln\left(\frac{S_t}{K}\right) + r(T-t)\right] + \frac{1}{2}\sigma\sqrt{T-t} $$

For small values of $S_t$, the term $\ln(S_t/K)$ is negative, so an increase in $\sigma$ raises $d_1$, as required. If $S_t \geq K$, then $\ln(S_t/K)$ is positive, so the first term above decreases when $\sigma$ increases. The second term always increases with $\sigma$. If $S_t$ is large relative to $K$, the first effect dominates, so $d_1$ decreases. All of this may be seen more formally by differentiating $d_1$ with respect to $\sigma$, which results in

$$ -\frac{1}{\sigma^2\sqrt{T-t}}\left[\ln\left(\frac{S_t}{K}\right) + r(T-t)\right] + \frac{1}{2}\sqrt{T-t} $$

If $S_t$ is sufficiently smaller than $K$, the negative term $\ln(S_t/K)$ outweighs the positive term $r(T-t)$, so the entire expression above becomes positive. Thus, if the call is sufficiently deep out-of-the-money, the delta increases as volatility increases. If $S_t$ is suitably large relative to $K$, the last term above, which is positive, is dominated by the earlier expression, which is negative, so delta decreases as volatility increases.

# Behavior of Option Deltas in $T - t$

The intuitive behavior of the delta in time-to-maturity is very similar to that in volatility. For a deep in-the-money call, a short time-to-maturity implies the option is almost sure to finish in-the-money, so the delta is close to $+1$. A longer time-to-maturity increases the odds of the option finishing out-of-the-money, so reduces the delta. Conversely, for a deep out-of-the-money call, a short time to maturity makes it virtually certain the option finishes out-of-the-money, so the delta is close to zero. Increasing the time-to-maturity improves the prospects for finishing in-the-money, raising the delta. Thus, we have:

- When $S_t$ is large relative to $K$, the delta should *decrease* as $T - t$ increases.
- When $S_t$ is small relative to $K$, the delta should *increase* as $T - t$ increases.

Verifying that the Black-Scholes formula meets these conditions is analogous to the process for $\sigma$ above. The term $d_1$ can be rewritten as

$$d_1 = \frac{1}{\sigma \sqrt{T - t}} \left[ \ln \left( \frac{S_t}{K} \right) \right] + \frac{1}{\sigma} \left[ r + \frac{1}{2} \sigma^2 \right] \sqrt{T - t}$$

The second term always increases when $T - t$ increases. If $S_t \geq K$, the first term decreases when $T - t$ increases, but if $S_t < K$, then $\ln(S_t/K)$ is negative, so it increases when $T - t$ increases. Formally, differentiating $d_1$ with respect to $T - t$, we obtain

$$-\frac{1}{2\sigma(T - t)^{3/2}} \left[ \ln \left( \frac{S_t}{K} \right) \right] + \frac{1}{2\sigma \sqrt{T - t}} \left[ r + \frac{1}{2} \sigma^2 \right]$$

This term is positive if $S_t$ is smaller than $K$, and is negative if $S_t$ is sufficiently larger than $K$, as required.

# Behavior of Option Deltas in $r$

An increase in interest rates increases the risk-neutral drift of the stock and so makes it more likely that a call will finish in-the-money and a put will finish out-of-the-money. This raises call deltas and reduces put deltas in absolute value (i.e., the put delta becomes less negative). It is not hard to see these effects in the Black-Scholes setting. We have

$$d_1 = \frac{1}{\sigma \sqrt{T - t}} \left[ \ln \left( \frac{S_t}{K} \right) + (r + \frac{1}{2} \sigma^2)(T - t) \right]$$

so $d_1$ clearly increases as $r$ increases. This means $N(d_1)$, the call delta, increases (it becomes more positive) while $-N(-d_1)$, the put delta, also increases (towards zero, i.e., it becomes less negative).

**Appendix 14B**

# Variance and Volatility Swaps

Variance and volatility swaps are forward contracts on the realized variance and volatility, respectively, of an underlying security. Introduced in the 1990s in over-the-counter markets, they offer an alternative to futures on the VIX for trading volatility. We begin our discussion with variance swaps.

# Variance Swaps

Variance swaps are *forwards* on the square of realized volatility over a prespecified period $(t, T)$. These swaps are handy securities with which to trade pure volatility separately from directional movements in the underlying. One could also trade volatility through positions in vanilla options, but these trades mix volatility risk with the directional risk of the underlying equity as well, and in order to get a pure volatility trade, we need to hedge away the directional risk.

The payoff on a variance swap is given by

$$N \times (\sigma_R^2 - K_2) \qquad (14.42)$$

where $N$ is the contract notional amount, $K_2$ is the annualized variance strike, and $\sigma_R^2$ is the annualized realized variance over the contract period. Likewise, the payoff on a volatility swap is given by $N \times (\sigma_R - K_1)$ where $K_1$ is the strike volatility. Interestingly, as we will see, variance swaps are theoretically more tractable than volatility swaps; they also trade in greater volume in the marketplace.

Neuberger (1990) and Demeterfi, Derman, Kamal, and Zou (1999) demonstrate how variance swaps might be replicated using forwards and options on the underlying. Briefly put, the expectation of realized variance may be written as the value of a portfolio of forwards and vanilla calls and puts (all under the risk-neutral measure). Thus, variance swaps are priced under a de facto replication/hedging argument. We describe the derivation here. The derivation is based on a continuous-time setting using stochastic calculus; the basics of stochastic calculus are described in Chapter 15.

Referring to equation (14.42), we see that a variance swap is a forward contract on realized variance. No money changes hands between the counterparties at inception, so the fair value at inception of a variance swap must be zero. This means the following must hold:

$$E[N \times (\sigma_R^2 - K_2)] = 0 \qquad (14.43)$$

where the expectation is taken using risk-neutral probabilities. That is, $K_2$ must be chosen so that

$$K_2 = E(\sigma_R^2) = E\left[\frac{1}{\tau} \int_0^\tau \sigma_t^2 \, dt\right] \qquad (14.44)$$

The pricing of a variance swap requires computing $K_2$.

In the generalized Black-Scholes modeling environment, where geometric Brownian motion describes the movement of stock prices, the stock price process in the risk-neutral setting is given by

$$dS_t = rS_t \, dt + \sigma_t S_t \, dz_t \qquad (14.45)$$

where $r$ is the risk-free rate and $z_t$ is a standard Brownian motion. Using Ito's lemma (see Chapter 15), we obtain

$$d(\ln S_t) = \left(r - \frac{1}{2}\sigma^2\right) dt + \sigma_t \, dz_t \qquad (14.46)$$

Taking the difference of the above two equations gives

$$\frac{dS_t}{S_t} - d(\ln S_t) = \frac{1}{2}\sigma_t^2 \, dt \qquad (14.47)$$

Seeing that the right-hand side (RHS) is the variance we want, we may write

$$E(\sigma_R^2) = \frac{1}{\tau}E\left[\int_0^\tau \sigma_t^2 \, dt\right] = \frac{2}{\tau}E\left[\int_0^\tau \frac{dS_t}{S_t} - \ln \frac{S_\tau}{S_0}\right] \qquad (14.48)$$

If we replicate the RHS of equation (14.48), we replicate the variance and, hence, can get the fair strike $K_2 = E(\sigma_R^2)$. The RHS has two terms:

- The first term is simple. It is the accumulated value of a *dynamic* position from rebalancing a stock position that is always long $\$1/S_t$ of stock. Its expectation under the risk-neutral measure is $E[\int_0^\tau dS/S] = r\tau$.

- The second term is not so simple. It is a *static* short position in a contract that pays the log return at maturity. This may be replicated with available forwards, calls, and puts. The replicated payoff at maturity is shown by Demeterfi, Derman, Kamal, and Zou (1999) to be as follows:

$$-\ln \frac{S_\tau}{S_0} = -\frac{S_\tau - S_0}{S_0} \tag{14.49}$$

$$+ \int_0^{S_0} \frac{1}{K^2} \max[0, K - S_\tau]\, dK + \int_{S_0}^\infty \frac{1}{K^2} \max[0, S_\tau - K]\, dK$$

The replication involves a forward contract at forward price $S_0$ and a weighted sum of puts and calls where the weights are inversely proportional to the square of the strike price of the option.

How does one arrive at equation (14.49)? The mathematical details are beyond the scope of this book, but we can demonstrate that the log contract may be replicated as stated with a simple example. The result in equation (14.49) is general enough to apply to any underlying behavior of the stock price as long as there are no jumps. When the underlying process is continuous, perfect replication is possible with an infinite set of strikes, but with jumps, perfect replication is lost because higher moments are introduced, and pricing error is introduced. However, Carr and Wu (2009) show that this error is very small.

Figure 14.9 shows the payoff function for varying terminal stock price using the left-hand side (LHS) of equation (14.49) (the solid line) and the RHS of the same equation (the circles)

**FIGURE 14.9**

Payoff of the Log Contract at Maturity

The plot shows the payoff function for varying terminal stock price using the LHS of equation (14.49) (the solid line) and the RHS of the same equation (the circles) for $S_0 = 100$ and various $S_\tau$ on the x-axis. The strikes used are spaced $dK = \$5$ apart so that the approximation to the RHS of the equation is reasonably sparse yet shows a very high accuracy in replication.

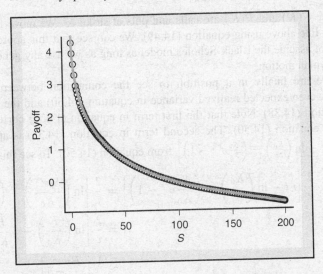

for $S_0 = 100$ and various $S_T$ on the x-axis. The strikes used are spaced $dK = \$5$ apart so that the approximation to the RHS of the equation is given by

$$\text{RHS of equation (14.49)} = -\frac{S_\tau - S_0}{S_0}$$

$$+ \sum_{K=5}^{S_0} \frac{1}{K^2} \max[0, K - S_\tau] \, dK$$

$$+ \sum_{K=S_0}^{2S_0} \frac{1}{K^2} \max[0, S_\tau - K] \, dK$$

We see from Figure 14.9 that the two lines almost coincide. They are even more coincident when the interval between strikes more closely approximates the integral in equation (14.49), for example, when $dK = \$1$.

We can use equations (14.48) and (14.49) to write down the fair value of the expected realized variance with time $\tau$ remaining. In practice, instead of centering the break point between the puts and calls at $S_0$, it is better to center it at the strike price closest to the ATMF level, which we will denote $K_0$. In this case, the expression in equation (14.48) above becomes

$$
\begin{aligned}
K_2 &= \frac{2}{\tau} E\left[\int_0^\tau \frac{dS_t}{S_t}\right] - \frac{2}{\tau} E\left[\ln\left(\frac{S_\tau}{S_0}\right)\right] \\
&= \frac{2}{\tau}(r\tau) - \frac{2}{\tau} E\left[\ln\left(\frac{S_\tau}{K_0}\right) + \ln\left(\frac{K_0}{S_0}\right)\right] \\
&= \frac{2}{\tau}\left[r\tau - \ln\left(\frac{K_0}{S_0}\right) - E\left(\frac{S_\tau - K_0}{K_0}\right) + P + C\right] \\
&= \frac{2}{\tau}\left[r\tau - \ln\left(\frac{K_0}{S_0}\right) - \left(\frac{S_0}{K_0}e^{r\tau} - 1\right) + P + C\right] \quad \textbf{(14.50)}
\end{aligned}
$$

$$P = e^{r\tau} \int_0^{K_0} \frac{1}{K^2} P(K) \, dK$$

$$C = e^{r\tau} \int_{K_0}^{\infty} \frac{1}{K^2} C(K) \, dK$$

where $C(K)$ and $P(K)$ are calls and puts at strike $K$. We move from the second to the third line above using equation (14.49). We can see that this approach works even if we do not assume the Black-Scholes model as long as we use any general form of geometric Brownian motion.

We are finally in a position to see the connection between the formula for the break-even expected realized variance in equation (14.50) and the VIX index formula in equation (14.38). Note that the first term in equation (14.38) corresponds to $\frac{2}{\tau}(P + C)$ from equation (14.50). The second term in equation (14.38) is approximately equal to $\frac{2}{\tau}\left[r\tau - \ln\left(\frac{K_0}{S_0}\right) - \left(\frac{S_0}{K_0}e^{r\tau} - 1\right)\right]$ from equation (14.50). To see this, note that

$$
\begin{aligned}
\frac{2}{\tau}\left[r\tau - \ln\left(\frac{K_0}{S_0}\right) - \left(\frac{S_0}{K_0}e^{r\tau} - 1\right)\right] &= \frac{2}{\tau}\left[\ln\left(\frac{S_0 e^{r\tau}}{K_0}\right) - \left(\frac{S_0}{K_0}e^{r\tau} - 1\right)\right] \\
&= \frac{2}{\tau}\left[\ln\left(\frac{F}{K_0}\right) - \left(\frac{F}{K_0} - 1\right)\right] \\
&\approx \frac{1}{\tau}\left[\frac{F}{K_0} - 1\right]^2
\end{aligned}
$$

when the forward price $F$ and the approximate forward price $K_0$ are very close to each other.

## Volatility Swaps

Volatility swaps do not have the same connection to the log contract as variance swaps. This is because there is no direct replication possible for the realized standard deviation of returns using forwards, calls, and puts as there is for the variance. Recall that the payoff per dollar notional on a volatility swap is $(\sigma_R - K_1)$ whereas that on a variance swap is $(\sigma_R^2 - K_2)$. Since it is possible to replicate the latter and get the fair value of $K_2$ exactly, it is, of course, tempting to assume that we could express the payoff on a volatility swap as a function of the payoff on a variance swap and thereby replicate it. However, this is only possible approximately and results in a bias.

Demeterfi, Derman, Kamal, and Zou (1999) suggest the following approximation.

$$\sigma_R - K_1 \approx \frac{1}{2K_1}(\sigma_R^2 - K_1^2) \qquad (14.51)$$

which works well when $\sigma_R \approx K_1$. But even then, we end up with a bias because the LHS of the equation above is linear in $\sigma_R$ whereas the RHS is not, i.e.,

$$\text{Bias} = \frac{1}{2K_1}(\sigma_R^2 - K_1^2) - (\sigma_R - K_1) = \frac{1}{2K_1}(\sigma_R - K_1)^2 \qquad (14.52)$$

This is known as the convexity bias. Therefore, even if we assume that $K_1 = \sqrt{K_2}$, we end up with the payoff being replicated in error. These replication difficulties with volatility swaps have probably resulted in variance swaps becoming the instrument of choice for trading pure volatility.

# Chapter 15

# The Mathematics of Black-Scholes

## 15.1 Introduction

In this chapter, we offer a more formal mathematical treatment of the Black-Scholes model and the derivation of the Black-Scholes formula. We begin with a description of Brownian motion and Ito processes to put the Black-Scholes model into mathematical context. Then we offer three ways of deriving the Black-Scholes formula: by replication, by risk-neutral pricing, and using the capital-asset pricing model (CAPM). A fourth way of deriving the Black-Scholes formula, through the limit of option prices in binomial models, is presented in Hsia (1983).

## 15.2 Geometric Brownian Motion Defined

A stochastic process is a sequence of random variables $(X_t)$ indexed by time. In a *discrete-time* stochastic process, observations on the stochastic process are made at discrete points in time $t = 0, 1, 2, \ldots$. For example, $X_t$ could be the outcome of the $t$-th roll of a die.

In a *continuous-time* stochastic process, time is a continuous index, and the process is observed at every instant $t$. For example, $X_t$ could be the price of a stock at time $t$. The path $X_t$ then traces the random evolution of the price as time moves.

### Wiener Processes

The fundamental stochastic process in continuous time is called a *standard Brownian motion* or a *Wiener process*. A Wiener process, denoted $(W_t)$, is a stochastic process defined for all $t \geq 0$ and satisfying four properties:

1. The process starts at 0: $W_0 = 0$.
2. The process has independent increments: the change $W_t - W_s$ in the value of the process between two points in time $s$ and $t > s$ is independent of *how* the process got to its time-$s$ value.
3. The increments are normally distributed: given the value of $W_s$ at time $s$, the difference $W_t - W_s$ is distributed normally with mean 0 and variance $t - s$.
4. The process evolves continuously: $W_t$ is a continuous function of $t$.

If we take $s = 0$ in Condition 3, then, since $W_0 = 0$, $W_t - W_0$ is just equal to $W_t$. Hence, Condition 3 says that we have $W_t \sim N(0, t)$ for every $t$.

The "differential" notation $dW_t$ is often used as a shorthand for the instantaneous change in the process $W_t$ at time $t$. Roughly, we can think of $dW_t$ as the change in the value of the process between $t$ and $t + dt$ for a small $dt$; Condition 3 then implies that $dW_t \sim N(0, dt)$.

## Introducing Drift and Variance

Since $W_t - W_s$ has a mean of zero, Wiener processes have no "drift" (on average, the change in the process is zero). We can easily create processes that build on Wiener processes and have nonzero drift. For instance, given a constant $a$, define

$$Y_t = at + W_t \tag{15.1}$$

Then a simple computation using the properties of $W_t$ shows that we have

$$Y_t \sim N(at, t)$$

so the value of the $Y_t$ process grows at the rate $a$ per unit time. We can also change the variance of the $Y_t$ process per unit time. For $b > 0$, define

$$Y_t = at + bW_t \tag{15.2}$$

Now we have

$$Y_t \sim N(at, b^2 t)$$

so the $Y_t$ process now has a variance of $b^2$ per unit time.

We can also express the process $(Y_t)$ given by (15.2) in differential form. Interpret $dY_t$ as the change in the process between times $t$ and $t + dt$ for some small $dt$. Then,

$$
\begin{aligned}
dY_t &= Y_{t+dt} - Y_t \\
&= [a(t + dt) + b\,W_{t+dt}] - [at + b\,W_t] \\
&= [a(t + dt) - at] + [b\,W_{t+dt} - b\,W_t] \\
&= a\,dt + b\,dW_t
\end{aligned}
$$

The final line is called the "stochastic differential equation" for the process $Y_t$:

$$dY_t = a\,dt + b\,dW_t \tag{15.3}$$

In words, the change in the process between $t$ and $t + dt$ is composed of two parts: the change on account of the mean growth rate of the process (which is $a\,dt$) and a random component (which is $b\,dW_t$). The term $a$ is called the "drift" of the $Y_t$ process. There is no one name for the term $b$, but it is common to call it the "diffusion" component.

## Ito Processes and Ito's Lemma

The process $Y_t$ described in (15.3) is a special case of an *Ito process*. An Ito process is a function of a Wiener process, but in which, more generally, the drift and diffusion components may change over time. That is, we write

$$dY_t = a_t\,dt + b_t\,dW_t \tag{15.4}$$

Both the drift $a_t$ and diffusion $b_t$ at time $t$ may depend on the value of $t$ as well as on the past evolution of $Y_t$ up to that point. Some technical conditions must be met by these terms to ensure the stochastic process $Y_t$ is properly defined, but these are quite general and need not concern us here.

A central result in the study of continuous-time stochastic processes is *Ito's lemma*. Roughly speaking, Ito's lemma says that any function of an Ito process is itself an Ito process; it describes how to get from the differential form of a given Ito process to the differential form for a function of that process.

**Proposition 15.1 (Ito's lemma)** *Let $Y_t$ be an Ito process with the differential form (15.4). Suppose $X_t = f(Y_t, t)$ where $f$ is twice-continuously differentiable in its first argument and once-continuously differentiable in its second argument. Then, $X_t$ is itself an Ito process with differential form*

$$dX_t = \alpha_t \, dt + \beta_t \, dW_t \qquad (15.5)$$

*where $\alpha_t$ and $\beta_t$ are given by*

$$\alpha_t = a_t \frac{\partial f}{\partial y} + \frac{\partial f}{\partial t} + \frac{1}{2} \frac{\partial^2 f}{\partial y^2} b_t^2 \qquad (15.6)$$

$$\beta_t = \frac{\partial f}{\partial y} b_t \qquad (15.7)$$

### Remark

In standard notation, the terms $\partial f / \partial y$, etc. refer to the partial derivatives of $f$. As is implicit in the description above, these derivatives are evaluated at $(Y_t, t)$, but to keep notation simple, we suppress these arguments of the function.

## A Heuristic Motivation of Ito's Lemma

While a formal proof of Ito's lemma is well beyond the scope of this book, the result itself may be motivated as follows. In ordinary calculus, suppose we have a function $x = f(y, t)$. Suppose $y$ and $t$ change by small amounts $dy$ and $dt$, respectively. Then, the change in $x$ is given by

$$dx = \frac{\partial f}{\partial y} dy + \frac{\partial f}{\partial t} dt + \frac{1}{2} \frac{\partial^2 f}{\partial y^2} (dy)^2 + \frac{\partial^2 f}{\partial y \partial t} dy \, dt + \frac{1}{2} \frac{\partial^2 f}{\partial t^2} (dt)^2 + \cdots \quad (15.8)$$

For small $dy$ and $dt$, terms of the form $(dy)^2$, $dy \, dt$, etc., are small compared to the first-order terms $dy$ and $dt$ so they can be ignored in a first approximation, and we may write

$$dx = \frac{\partial f}{\partial y} dy + \frac{\partial f}{\partial t} dt \qquad (15.9)$$

But when $y$ represents an Ito process $Y_t$, we have $dY_t = a_t \, dt + b_t \, dW_t$, so

$$(dY_t)^2 = a_t^2 (dt)^2 + 2a_t b_t \, dt \, dW_t + b_t^2 (dW_t)^2 \qquad (15.10)$$

The first and second terms on the right-hand side of (15.10) can be ignored because they are second-order terms. However, this is not true of the term $(dW_t)^2$. Recall that $dW_t \sim N(0, dt)$, that is, the variance of $dW_t$ is $dt$. Since the variance of $dW_t$ is the expectation of $(dW_t)^2$, this means that $(dW_t)^2$ is itself of order $dt$—that is, it is a first-order term! Therefore, this term cannot be ignored, so we must amend (15.9) to

$$dx = \frac{\partial f}{\partial y} dy + \frac{\partial f}{\partial t} dt + \frac{1}{2} \frac{\partial^2 f}{\partial y^2} b_t^2 \, dt \qquad (15.11)$$

Substituting for $dy$ from (15.4), this is exactly what Ito's lemma says.

**Example 15.1**

Suppose $a_t = 0$ and $b_t = b$, where $b > 0$ is a constant. Then the Ito process $Y_t$ is just $bW_t$, so its differential form is

$$dY_t = b\,dW_t$$

Consider the process $X_t$ defined by

$$X_t = Y_t^2$$

The function $f$ here is $f(y, t) = y^2$, so it has the partial derivatives

$$\frac{\partial f}{\partial y} = 2y, \qquad \frac{\partial^2 f}{\partial y^2} = 2, \qquad \frac{\partial f}{\partial t} = 0$$

Therefore, from (15.6)–(15.7), we have

$$\alpha_t = \frac{1}{2}\,2b^2 = b^2$$

$$\beta_t = 2bY_t = 2b\sqrt{X_t}$$

So $X_t$ is the Ito process with differential form

$$dX_t = b^2\,dt + 2b\sqrt{X_t}\,dW_t$$

∎

## Geometric Brownian Motion

Let $\mu$ and $\sigma > 0$ be given, and let $S_0$ denote the initial level of a stock price. Define the evolution of the stock price by the process $S_t$ where

$$S_t = S_0\,e^{\mu t + \sigma W_t} \qquad\qquad (15.12)$$

The process (15.12) is called a *geometric Brownian motion* or GBM and is the stock price process assumed by the Black-Scholes model. As we noted in the text, GBM has two properties: (i) it implies a lognormal returns distrbution, and (ii) it implies continuous price movements (no jumps).

The second of these properties follows from the requirement that $W_t$ be continuous (this is the fourth requirement in the definition of a Wiener process). To see the lognormality implication, note that

$$\frac{S_t}{S_0} = e^{\mu t + \sigma W_t}$$

so

$$\ln\left(\frac{S_t}{S_0}\right) = \mu t + \sigma W_t$$

This tells us precisely that

$$\ln\left(\frac{S_t}{S_0}\right) \sim N(\mu t, \sigma^2 t)$$

so returns are lognormal with annual expected log-returns of $\mu$ and volatility of $\sigma$.

What is the stochastic differential form of $S_t$? Let $Y_t = \mu t + \sigma W_t$, so $Y_t$ has the differential form

$$dY_t = \mu\,dt + \sigma\,dW_t$$

The stock price is obtained from $Y_t$ by defining

$$S_t = S_0 e^{Y_t}$$

In the notation of Ito's lemma, we have $f(y, t) = S_0 e^y$, so the partial derivatives are given by

$$\frac{\partial f}{\partial y} = S_0 e^y, \qquad \frac{\partial^2 f}{\partial y^2} = S_0 e^y, \qquad \frac{\partial f}{\partial t} = 0$$

Therefore, from (15.6)–(15.7), we have

$$\alpha_t = \mu S_0 e^{Y_t} + \frac{1}{2} \sigma^2 S_0 e^{Y_t} = (\mu + \frac{1}{2} \sigma^2) S_t$$

$$\beta_t = \sigma S_0 e^{Y_t} = \sigma S_t$$

Thus, the stochastic differential representation of the GBM process (15.12) is given by

$$dS_t = (\mu + \frac{1}{2} \sigma^2) S_t \, dt + \sigma S_t \, dW_t \qquad \textbf{(15.13)}$$

Let $\alpha = \mu + \frac{1}{2} \sigma^2$. Sometimes this stochastic differential equation is expressed in "proportional-change" form as

$$\frac{dS_t}{S_t} = \alpha \, dt + \sigma \, dW_t \qquad \textbf{(15.14)}$$

The left-hand side of this expression represents the instantaneous returns on the stock. The right-hand side expresses these returns as composed of a drift of $\alpha$ and a variance of $\sigma^2$.

## 15.3   The Black-Scholes Formula via Replication

This section derives the Black-Scholes formula using replication arguments. We focus on the call price. The put price is obtained using analogous arguments.

### The Security Prices

Suppose the stock price $S_t$ follows a geometric Brownian motion as described in Section 15.2. In stochastic differential form, we write

$$dS_t = \alpha S_t \, dt + \sigma S_t \, dW_t \qquad \textbf{(15.15)}$$

Let $r$ denote the continuously compounded interest rate. Since $r$ is constant, an initial investment of $1 grows by time $t$ to $B_t = e^{rt}$. The rate of growth of this "money-market account" is given by

$$\frac{dB_t}{dt} = r e^{rt} = r B_t$$

Hence, in differential form (but this time as an ordinary differential equation), we write

$$dB_t = r B_t \, dt \qquad \textbf{(15.16)}$$

### The Call

Let a call option with maturity $T$ and strike $K$ be given. Denote by $C(S_t, t)$ the value of the call at time $t$, given a stock price of $S_t$ at that point. For notational simplicity, we use $C_S$, $C_t$, and $C_{SS}$ to denote, respectively, the partial derivatives with respect to $S$ and $t$, and the second partial with respect to $S$. We are assuming that the call price is differentiable in this manner, but this will be justified in the solution.

## The Procedure

In a continuous time setting, we cannot use the backwards induction procedure we did in the binomial model (Section 12.3). Rather, the replicating portfolio and the option price have to be identified using indirect techniques. So here's how we proceed.

We assume that a replicating portfolio $(\Delta_\tau, b_\tau)$ exists for the call, where $\Delta_\tau$ and $b_\tau$ are, respectively, the number of units of the stock and the bond held at time $\tau$ (these quantities may, of course, depend on all information available at time $\tau$). Then, using Ito's lemma on the call pricing function $C$ in conjunction with the replicating portfolio, we show that the call price must meet a certain condition. This condition is the famous *fundamental partial differential equation* of the Black-Scholes model: it specifies a restriction on the partial derivatives of $C$. Solving this partial differential equation enables us to identify simultaneously the call price function $C$ (which, of course, turns out to be the Black-Scholes call formula) as well as the values $\Delta_\tau$ and $b_\tau$.

A parenthetical comment. Recall from the discussion of dynamic replication in Section 12.3 that the replication strategy for an option is also required to be self-financing. That is, all changes to the composition of the portfolio have to be financed using purchases or sales of other parts of the portfolio. To avoid excessive technical detail, we do not deal with self-financing here, but it can be shown that the replication strategy we identify does meet this requirement.

## Obtaining the Fundamental Partial Differential Equation

Given the differential form (15.15) for the stock price process $S_t$, Ito's lemma implies

$$dC = \left[\alpha S_t C_S + C_t + \frac{1}{2} C_{SS}\sigma^2 S_t^2\right] dt + \sigma S_t C_S \, dW_t \qquad (15.17)$$

On the other hand, the call value at each point in time is equal to the value of the replicating portfolio (by definition), so it must also satisfy

$$C(S_t, t) = \Delta_t S_t + b_t \qquad (15.18)$$

Using $db_t = rb_t \, dt$ and expressing (15.18) in differential form,

$$dC = \Delta_t \, dS_t + db_t = [\Delta_t \alpha S_t + rb_t] dt + \Delta_t \sigma S_t \, dW_t \qquad (15.19)$$

Compare (15.17) and (15.19). Since both represent the evolution of the call price, they have to be identical. Therefore, the coefficients of the $dt$ and $dW_t$ terms must coincide in the two equations. Equating the coefficients of the $dW_t$ terms gives us

$$\sigma S_t C_S = \Delta_t \sigma S_t \iff C_S = \Delta_t \qquad (15.20)$$

Equating the coefficients of the $dt$ terms gives us

$$\alpha S_t C_S + C_t + \frac{1}{2} C_{SS} \sigma^2 S_t^2 = \Delta_t \alpha S_t + rb_t \qquad (15.21)$$

Since $\Delta_t = C_S$ from (15.20), the first term on either side drops out, so we obtain

$$b_t = \frac{1}{r} \left[C_t + \frac{1}{2} C_{SS} \sigma^2 S_t^2\right] \qquad (15.22)$$

Equations (15.20) and (15.22) give us expressions for $\Delta_t$ and $b_t$ in terms of $C$ and its partial derivatives. Substituting these expressions into (15.18) results in

$$C = C_S S_t + \frac{1}{r} \left[ C_t + \frac{1}{2} C_{SS} \sigma^2 S_t^2 \right] \qquad \textbf{(15.23)}$$

Multiplying through by $r$ and rearranging, we finally obtain

$$r C_S S_t + C_t + \frac{1}{2} C_{SS} \sigma^2 S_t^2 - rC = 0 \qquad \textbf{(15.24)}$$

Equation (15.24), which is called the *fundamental partial differential equation* of the model, must be satisfied by the call pricing function $C(S_t, t)$ for any $S_t \geq 0$ and $t < T$.

Here's an important point: so far, we have not used the fact that the option is a call, so *any* European option (actually any derivative including forwards and even unexercised American options) in the Black-Scholes model must satisfy this fundamental pde. Where the features of the call come in is in the boundary conditions. At time $T$, the call must also satisfy

$$C(S_T, T) = \max(S_T - K, 0) \qquad \text{for any } S_T \geq 0 \qquad \textbf{(15.25)}$$

Thus, we arrive at our final condition: the call price $C(S_t, t)$ must be a solution to the partial differential equation (15.24) subject to the boundary condition (15.25).

## The Black-Scholes Solution

There are standard techniques in mathematics for identifying solutions to partial differential equations, but it may be verified through direct calculation that if we define $C(S_t, t)$ as in the Black-Scholes formula (14.1), namely

$$C(S_t, t) = S_t N(d_1) - PV(K) N(d_2) \qquad \textbf{(15.26)}$$

with $d_1$ and $d_2$ defined by (14.3) and (14.4), then the conditions (15.24)–(15.25) are satisfied. In particular, the relevant derivatives turn out to be

$$C_S(S_t, t) = N(d_1) \qquad \textbf{(15.27)}$$

$$C_{SS}(S_t, t) = \frac{1}{\sigma S_t \sqrt{T-t}} N'(d_1)) \qquad \textbf{(15.28)}$$

$$C_t(S_t, t) = S_t N'(d_1) \left[ \frac{-\sigma}{2\sqrt{T-t}} \right] - re^{-r(T-t)} K N(d_2) \qquad \textbf{(15.29)}$$

For a proof of (15.27)–(15.29), see Appendix 17A. Substituting the expressions (15.26)–(15.29) in (15.24) shows that the partial differential equation is satisfied.

## The Replicating Portfolio

Substituting from (15.27)–(15.29) into the expressions for $\Delta_t$ and $b_t$ in (15.20) and (15.22), we obtain the following values for $\Delta_t$ and $b_t$:

$$\Delta_t = N(d_1) \qquad \textbf{(15.30)}$$

$$b_t = -PV(K) N(d_2) \qquad \textbf{(15.31)}$$

Note that we have $\Delta_t S_t + b_t = C(S_t, t)$ as required at all $t$, so (15.30)–(15.31) is, in fact, the composition of the replicating portfolio.

# 15.4   The Black-Scholes Formula via Risk-Neutral Pricing

In Section 14.2, we showed that the risk-neutral pricing method leads to the call price $C$ given by

$$C = e^{-r(T-t)} E_t[S_T \times I_{\{S_T \geq K\}}] - PV(K) \operatorname{Prob}_t(S_T \geq K) \qquad (15.32)$$

where $I_{\{S_T \geq K\}}$ is the indicator function that takes on the value 1 if $S_T \geq K$ and zero otherwise, and expectations are taken under the risk-neutral probability. To proceed further, we must identify the risk-neutral distribution of $S_T$ explicitly. This distribution is given by

$$\ln\left(\frac{S_T}{S_t}\right) \sim N\left((r - \frac{1}{2}\sigma^2)(T - t), \sigma^2(T - t)\right) \qquad (15.33)$$

Note that the expected return under (15.33) is

$$E\left[\frac{S_T}{S_t}\right] = e^{(r - \frac{1}{2}\sigma^2)(T-t) + \frac{1}{2}\sigma^2(T-t)} = e^{r(T-t)} \qquad (15.34)$$

as required. (See expression (13.6) for the expected value of a lognormal.) Note, too, that going from the actual distribution to the risk-neutral one affects only the mean return, not the volatility $\sigma$. For a formal derivation of the risk-neutral distribution, see Duffie (1996) or the simplified exposition in Sundaram (1997).

Under (15.33), $\ln S_T$ has a mean of

$$\ln S_t + (r - \frac{1}{2}\sigma^2)(T - t)$$

and a variance of $\sigma^2(T - t)$. To simplify lengthy expressions in the derivation, we define some new variables:

$$\tau = T - t \qquad (15.35)$$

$$\eta = \ln S_t + (r - \frac{1}{2}\sigma^2)(T - t) \qquad (15.36)$$

In this notation, $\ln S_T$ is normally distributed with a mean of $\eta$ and a variance of $\sigma^2 \tau$. Thus, the density function for $S_T$ is

$$\frac{1}{S_T \sigma \sqrt{\tau}} \frac{1}{\sqrt{2\pi}} \exp\left\{-\frac{1}{2}\left(\frac{\ln S_T - \eta}{\sigma \sqrt{\tau}}\right)^2\right\}$$

## The First Term

Consider the first term $e^{-r(T-t)} E_t[S_T \times I_{\{S_T \geq K\}}]$. We will show that this equals $S_t N(d_1)$. Throughout this derivation, we write " exp " for the exponential function $e$ to avoid lengthy superscripts. Writing out the expectation in full, this term is

$$\int_K^\infty \exp\{-r\tau\} S_T \frac{1}{S_T \sigma \sqrt{\tau}} \frac{1}{\sqrt{2\pi}} \exp\left\{-\frac{1}{2}\left(\frac{\ln S_T - \eta}{\sigma \sqrt{\tau}}\right)^2\right\} dS_T \qquad (15.37)$$

The first two $S_T$ terms in the integral may be canceled. To simplify the expression further, we perform a change of variable. Define

$$z = \frac{\ln S_T - \eta}{\sigma \sqrt{\tau}} \qquad (15.38)$$

Note then that $S_T = \exp\{\eta + z\sigma\sqrt{\tau}\}$. Therefore, we obtain

$$dS_T = \exp\{\eta + z\sigma\sqrt{\tau}\}\sigma\sqrt{\tau}\,dz \qquad (15.39)$$

Finally, note also that $S_T \geq K$ implies $\ln S_T \geq \ln K$, so

$$z \geq \frac{\ln K - \eta}{\sigma\sqrt{\tau}} \qquad (15.40)$$

Denote the right-hand side of (15.40) by $a$. Using (15.38)–(15.40) in the integral (15.37) and canceling common terms, we get

$$\int_a^\infty \exp\{-r\tau\}\,\frac{1}{\sqrt{2\pi}}\,\exp\{\eta + z\sigma\sqrt{\tau}\}\exp\left\{-\frac{1}{2}z^2\right\}\,dz \qquad (15.41)$$

Now, look at the first two exponential terms in this integral. By substituting for $\eta$, we obtain

$$\begin{aligned}
\exp\{-r\tau\}\exp\{\eta + z\sigma\sqrt{\tau}\} &= \exp\left\{-r\tau + \ln S_t + r\tau - \tfrac{1}{2}\sigma^2\tau + z\sigma\sqrt{\tau}\right\} \\
&= \exp\left\{\ln S_t - \tfrac{1}{2}\sigma^2\tau + z\sigma\sqrt{\tau}\right\} \\
&= S_t \exp\left\{-\tfrac{1}{2}\sigma^2\tau + z\sigma\sqrt{\tau}\right\}
\end{aligned}$$

Substituting this in (15.41), we obtain

$$S_t \int_a^\infty \frac{1}{\sqrt{2\pi}}\,\exp\left\{-\frac{1}{2}\sigma^2\tau + z\sigma\sqrt{\tau} - \frac{1}{2}z^2\right\}\,dz \qquad (15.42)$$

which can be rewritten as

$$S_t \int_a^\infty \frac{1}{\sqrt{2\pi}}\,\exp\left\{-\frac{1}{2}(z - \sigma\sqrt{\tau})^2\right\}\,dz \qquad (15.43)$$

We do a final change of variable. Define $y = z - \sigma\sqrt{\tau}$. Then, $dy = dz$. Moreover,

$$z \geq a \quad\Longleftrightarrow\quad y \geq a - \sigma\sqrt{\tau}$$

Now

$$\begin{aligned}
a - \sigma\sqrt{\tau} &= \tfrac{1}{\sigma\sqrt{\tau}}\left[\ln K - \eta - \sigma^2\tau\right] \\
&= \tfrac{1}{\sigma\sqrt{\tau}}\left[\ln K - \ln S_t - r\tau + \tfrac{1}{2}\sigma^2\tau - \sigma^2\tau\right] \\
&= \tfrac{1}{\sigma\sqrt{\tau}}\left[\ln K - \ln S_t - r\tau - \tfrac{1}{2}\sigma^2\tau\right] \\
&= -d_1
\end{aligned}$$

where $d_1$ is exactly the quantity (14.3) used in the Black-Scholes formula. Therefore, the integral (15.43) can be written as

$$S_t \int_{-d_1}^\infty \frac{1}{\sqrt{2\pi}}\,\exp\left\{-\frac{1}{2}y^2\right\}\,dy \qquad (15.44)$$

The integral is just that of a standard normal density from $-d_1$ to $+\infty$, so is equal to $1 - N(-d_1)$. Since $N(x) + N(-x) = 1$ for any $x$ (see (14.15)), it is also equal to $N(d_1)$. Thus, we have shown that the first term of (15.32) is equal to $S_t\,N(d_1)$.

## The Second Term

Now consider the second term

$$PV(K)\,\text{Prob}_t(S_T \geq K) \qquad (15.45)$$

The probability that $S_T \geq K$ is the same as the probability that $\ln S_T \geq \ln K$. Now, $\ln S_T$ is normally distributed with mean $\eta$ and variance $\sigma^2 \tau$, so this probability is given by

$$\int_{\ln K}^{\infty} \frac{1}{\sigma \sqrt{\tau}} \frac{1}{\sqrt{2\pi}} \exp\left\{ -\frac{1}{2} \left( \frac{\ln S_T - \eta}{\sigma \sqrt{\tau}} \right)^2 \right\} d[\ln S_T] \qquad \textbf{(15.46)}$$

Again, we use a change of variable. Define

$$w = \frac{\ln S_T - \eta}{\sigma \sqrt{\tau}}$$

Then, $\ln S_T = w\sigma\sqrt{\tau} + \eta$, so $d[\ln S_T] = \sigma\sqrt{\tau}\, dw$. Finally, $S_T \geq K$ implies

$$w \geq \tfrac{1}{\sigma\sqrt{\tau}} [\ln K - \eta]$$
$$= \tfrac{1}{\sigma\sqrt{\tau}} [\ln K - \ln S_t - r\tau + \tfrac{1}{2}\sigma^2\tau]$$
$$= -d_2$$

where $d_2$ is the quantity used in the Black-Scholes formula (14.4). Using this change of variable, the integral (15.46) can be rewritten, after canceling common terms and simplifying, as

$$\int_{-d_2}^{\infty} \frac{1}{\sqrt{2\pi}} \exp\left\{ -\frac{1}{2} w^2 \right\} dw \qquad \textbf{(15.47)}$$

This is just $1 - N(-d_2)$, or equivalently, $N(d_2)$. Thus, we have shown that the second term (15.45) is just $PV(K)\,N(d_2)$, completing the derivation of the Black-Scholes formula.

## 15.5   The Black-Scholes Formula via CAPM

In their original paper, Black and Scholes (1973) give two derivations of their celebrated formula. One is the replication/hedging approach described in Section 15.3 above. The other is by using the capital-asset pricing model (CAPM). In this section, we describe the latter derivation.

The capital-asset pricing model is a general method for discounting under uncertainty. That is, it identifies the appropriate discount rate to apply to an asset so that its present value may be obtained from knowledge of its terminal value (or value at some horizon $T$). This discount rate is the expected return on the asset.

The CAPM describes the relation between an asset's expected return and its risk. More specifically, the expected return on an asset is a linear function of its "beta" (denoted $\beta$), where $\beta$ is the covariance of the asset return with the market return divided by the variance of the market return.

Consider a call option with strike $K$ and maturity $T$. Suppose that the beta of the underlying stock is denoted $\beta_S$. Denote, as usual, the call value today by $C(S_t, t)$, where $S_t$ is the current price of the stock and $t$ is the current date. As in Section 15.3, let $C_S$, $C_{SS}$, and $C_t$ denote, respectively, the partial derivatives $\partial C/\partial S_t$, $\partial^2 C/\partial S_t^2$, and $\partial C/\partial t$. From Ito's lemma (Proposition 15.1), we have

$$dC = C_S\, dS_t + \frac{1}{2} C_{SS}\sigma^2 S_t^2\, dt + C_t\, dt \qquad \textbf{(15.48)}$$

Now, the instantaneous return on the option is $dC/C$, while the instantaneous return on the stock is $dS_t/S_t$. From (15.48), therefore, the covariance of the option return $dC/C$ with the market return is $S_t C_S/C$ times the covariance of the stock return $dS_t/S_t$ with the market return. That is, if $\beta_C$ denotes the beta of the call option, then

$$\beta_C = S_t \frac{C_S}{C} \beta_S \tag{15.49}$$

Let $m$ denote the expected excess return on the market (i.e., the expected return on the market less the risk-free rate $r$). Under the CAPM, the expected return on the stock and the option are then given by

$$E\left[\frac{dS_t}{S_t}\right] = [r + \beta_S m]\,dt \tag{15.50}$$

$$E\left[\frac{dC}{C}\right] = [r + \beta_C m]\,dt \tag{15.51}$$

Multiplying both sides of (15.51) by $C$ and using (15.49) to express $\beta_C$ in terms of $\beta_S$, we obtain

$$E[dC] = [rC + mS_t C_S \beta_S]\,dt \tag{15.52}$$

On the other hand, by taking expectations in (15.48) and using (15.50) for the expected returns on the stock, we also have

$$E[dC] = C_S[rS_t + \beta_S m S_t]\,dt + \frac{1}{2}C_{SS}\sigma^2 S_t^2\,dt + C_t\,dt \tag{15.53}$$

Equating (15.52) and (15.53), and canceling the common term $m S_t C_S \beta_S$, we obtain

$$rC = rC_S S_t + \frac{1}{2}C_{SS}\sigma^2 S_t^2 + C_t \tag{15.54}$$

which is exactly the fundamental partial differential equation (15.24) obtained earlier through the replication argument. Thus, the CAPM-based pricing approach leads to the same price as the replication approach. Of course, the weakness of this approach to pricing options is that it depends on the validity of the CAPM; the replication and risk-neutral pricing methods place no requirement in this regard.

## 15.6 Exercises

1. If $x_t = at + bW_t$ where $W_t$ is a Wiener process and $W_0 = 0$, then write down the equation in differential form.
2. If $x_t = at + bW_t$, and $y = e^x$ (time subscripts suppressed), what is the differential process for $y$?
3. In the previous question, what is the expected value of $y$ at time $t$?
4. If $dr = k(\theta - r)\,dt + \eta\,dz$ and $P(r, t)$ is a given function, then what is $dP$?
5. If $dx = a\,dt + b\,dW$ and $y = \ln(x)$, find $dy$.
6. Show that, in the Black-Scholes model, stock prices are lognormal.
7. (Requires Numerical Analysis) (a) Write down the probability density function of the terminal distribution of returns for stocks in the Black-Scholes model. (b) Then write down the expression for the value of a call option on a stock in integral (expectation) form under the risk-neutral probability measure. (c) For the following parameter values, undertake the integration using Octave and price the call option: $S = 100$, strike $K = 102$, volatility $\sigma = 0.3$, risk-free rate $r = 0.02$, and maturity $T = 0.5$. There are no dividends.

8. In the previous question, if $\mu = 0.20$ and $\sigma = 0.40$, what is the expected value of the stock price after two years if the current price is $100? What is the standard deviation of the stock price value after two years?

9. Given that stock prices follow a risk-neutral geometric Brownian motion, i.e., $dS = rS\,dt + \sigma S\,dz$, write down the volatility for a put option's return. Denote the put as a function $P(S, t)$.

10. From the solution to the preceding question what can you say about the volatility of a put option when the stock price increases?

11. Intuitively, by inspection, in relation to the previous questions, what is the formula for the volatility of a call? Does the volatility of a call increase or decrease as the stock price increases?

12. Suppose you start with the risk-neutral stochastic differential equation for the stock, which is

$$dS = rS\,dt + \sigma S\,dW$$

Note here that the drift is now the risk-free rate $r$. Suppose you want to price a derivative security $V(S, t)$, which is a function of the stock price and time. (a) Write down the process for $dV$ using Ito's lemma. (b) Take the expectation $E(dV)$. (c) Under risk neutrality, what should this expectation be equal to? (d) Setting $E(dV)$ to the correct expected value, re-arrange the equation, and explain your result.

13. Suppose $x \sim N(0, 1)$. Let a value $K$ be given. Define $x_K^+$ by $x_K^+ = x \times I_{x \geq K}$, where $I_{x \geq K}$ is, as usual, the indicator function that takes on the value 1 if $x \geq K$ and is zero otherwise.

   (a) Compute $E[x_K^+]$ symbolically.

   (b) What might you imagine is the use of this calculation from an option pricing standpoint?

14. In this chapter, we developed the following approaches to solving the option pricing problem:

   (a) The PDE approach: In this method, we found that the call option value was the solution to the following differential equation:

$$rV = \frac{\partial V}{\partial S}\,rS + \frac{1}{2}\frac{\partial^2 V}{\partial S^2}\sigma^2 S^2 + \frac{\partial V}{\partial t}$$

   subject to $V(T) = \max(0, S_T - K)$.

   (b) The risk-neutral approach: In this method, we solved for the option price by taking the following expectation (under the risk-neutral measure):

$$V = e^{-rT}E[V(T)].$$

   The answer to both these methods was found to be the same. Is this always true?

15. Suppose the beta of a stock is 1.2, and the stock price is $S = 40$. Let the volatility be $\sigma = 0.4$, the risk-free rate be $r = 0.04$, and assume no dividends are paid. What is the beta of a put option with maturity one year and strike $K = 40$?

16. Suppose the beta of a stock is 1.2, and the stock price is $S = 40$. Let the volatility be $\sigma = 0.4$, the risk-free rate be $r = 0.04$, and assume no dividends are paid. What is the beta of a call option with maturity one year and strike $K = 40$?

17. From the previous two questions, can you derive the relationship between the betas of call, put, and stock?

18. (Cash-or-Nothing Option) What is the value of an option that pays $100 if the stock price exceeds a prespecified strike at maturity? Assume that the initial stock price is $100, maturity is one year, volatility is 50%, and the strike is $110. Assume also that the risk-free rate of interest is zero.

19. (Corridor Options) What is the price of an option that has a maturity of 60 days and pays $1 for each day that the stock price lies in the range (50,60)? The current stock price is $S = 55$, volatility $\sigma = 0.4$, interest rate $r = 0.03$, and dividends $d = 0$.

20. (Extension of Previous Question) Consider an option that is the same as the above except that the option pays off $1 for each day only when the stock is outside the range (50,60). What is the price of this option?

21. Which is higher, the expected return on a stock or that of a call option on a stock? Assume the CAPM model governs returns in the real world.

# Chapter 16

# Options Modeling: Beyond Black-Scholes

## 16.1 Introduction

The Black-Scholes model assumes that the price of the underlying asset follows a geometric Brownian motion, or GBM. This assumption has two implications:

- Log-returns over any horizon are normally distributed with constant volatility $\sigma$.
- The stock price evolution is continuous, i.e., there are no market "gaps."

These conditions are commonly violated in practice: empirical returns typically exhibit fatter tails than a normal distribution, volatility is not constant over time, and markets do sometimes gap. The volatility "smile" or "skew" discussed in Section 14.8 arises as a consequence. The existence of the volatility skew means that if Black-Scholes volatility is chosen to match the prices of at-the-money options, then away-from-the-money options will be mispriced by the model, perhaps substantially.

Motivated by this, a number of models have looked to generalize or modify the Black-Scholes model in order to better fit observed option prices. Important classes of these models include the following.

### Jump-Diffusion Models

One of the earliest generalizations of Black-Scholes is Merton (1976). Merton's approach assumes that stock returns are composed of two parts: a "normal" part that evolves according to the GBM process of Black-Scholes and an "extraordinary" part that causes unexpected jumps in the stock price. The likelihood of jumps and the distribution of the jump size now enter as additional variables in the option pricing problem. The occurrence of jumps results in fat tails in the returns distribution (and also in skewness if the distribution of the jump size is not symmetric); and, of course, jumps *are* market gaps. We examine jump-diffusions and their implications in Section 16.2 below.

### Stochastic Volatility Models

A second generalization of Black-Scholes is the class of models known as "stochastic volatility" models. An early and influential paper in the development of these models is Heston (1993). Volatility in these models is not taken to be a constant but is itself a random variable that evolves over time. With volatility being random, the correlation between changes in volatility and returns enters as another important variable. While stock prices are still continuous in these models (markets do not gap), returns are no longer normally distributed: stochastic volatility results in fat tails, while nonzero correlation between volatility and returns generates skewness. Stochastic volatility models are discussed in Section 16.3.

### ARCH/GARCH Models

A third class of models, related to the second, are those in which volatility may not be separately random but may change over time in a manner that may be dependent on the movement of the stock price. One form of this class of models, known as ARCH (Auto-Regressive Conditional Heteroskedasticity), was developed by Engle (1982). An extension, known as Generalized ARCH or GARCH models, was developed by Bollerslev (1986). ARCH and GARCH models have proved highly influential in economics and finance, and for his pioneering work, Engle shared the Nobel Prize in 2003. Duan (1995) and others have developed option pricing theory for these models. GARCH models are the subject of Section 16.4.

### "Non-Normal" Models

Among the other approaches that have been proposed to better fit observed option prices are those that directly posit non-normal returns distributions (rather than start with a normal distribution and then modify it). These include the log-stable models of Carr and Wu (2003) and McCulloch (2003), and the variance-gamma model of Madan, Carr, and Chang (1998). These are discussed briefly in Section 16.5.

### Implied Binomial Trees

Implied binomial trees (or "local volatility models") were developed by Derman and Kani (1994), Dupire (1994), and Rubinstein (1994). While they may be viewed as a general form of stochastic volatility models, in practice they are used more with a financial engineering bent. The approach takes the entire implied volatility surface—observed implied volatilities across all strikes and maturities—as an input. In a common version of this approach, a binomial or trinomial tree is then constructed whose option prices are consistent with the observed input option prices. In the special case where the input prices are all generated from the same lognormal process (i.e., where all the implied volatilities are the same), the "implied binomial tree" will just be a standard binomial tree with constant up and down moves. The construction of implied binomial trees is the subject of Section 16.6.

## The Presentation in This Chapter

This chapter discusses the classes of models described above in greater detail. Our objective is to give the student a "feel" for these models, what each of them contributes, and how this contribution is reflected in option prices. Many of these models are technical in nature, certainly more so than the Black-Scholes model they seek to generalize. So, wherever this is appropriate, we first use simplified discrete-time formulations to convey the flavor of the setting before describing the more complex continuous-time model. At various points in the chapter, we also provide code in the Octave programming language for implementing the models we present, so that students may generate on their own the tables and figures used in this chapter or work further with the models to improve their understanding.

## 16.2   Jump-Diffusion Models

A market gap is a discontinuous price move. That is, you will not be able to draw the stock price graph on a piece of paper without lifting your pen off the page. The Black-Scholes model does not admit such discontinuities, but casual observation appears to suggest that markets do gap, notably when unexpected good or bad information hits the market. So, in 1976, Robert Merton suggested modifying the Black-Scholes model by adding a "jump" process to it. A jump process is exactly what the name suggests: it is a process that remains constant between jumps, and changes (by a possibly random amount) at jump times. Jumps cause discontinuities in the instantaneous movement of the stock price.

The stock price process in Merton's framework thus consists of two processes—one based on a GBM process and the other on a jump process. The two are intended to match, respectively, the smooth and discontinuous movement of equity prices. Because they are combinations of Brownian diffusion processes and jump processes, such models are called "jump-diffusions." To specify a jump-diffusion, we must specify (a) the GBM process including its volatility, (b) the likelihood or frequency of jumps, and (c) the distribution of the jump size when jumps do occur.

This section aims to develop an understanding of the impact of introducing jumps into our pricing models. We present the formal models that are used along with brief program code. But first we present a simpler setting by extending the familiar discrete-time binomial model to include jumps and illustrating the effect this has on option prices. Impatient readers may proceed straight to the segment on the Poisson distribution with no loss of continuity.

## Depicting Jumps in Binomial Models

The notion of a jump in discrete-time models is somewhat slippery because every price change in a discrete-time model is effectively a jump. After all, in a typical binomial model, the price jumps from its current level $S$ to one of two possible levels $uS$ or $dS$ next period. So what exactly do we mean by a "jump" in this setting?

Here's one way to think about it. The standard binomial model is not "really" a jump process because it is an approximation of the GBM; that is, as the time interval between price moves shrinks, the size of the up and down moves too shrink, in such a manner that the process ultimately starts resembling the continuous GBM process. By a jump, we mean intuitively a price move that does *not* vanish in the limit, i.e., that remains a discontinuous price move even as the time-interval $h$ between price changes shrinks to zero.

Operationally, what this means is that to implement a jump-diffusion model in a discrete-time setting, we may begin with a binomial model that approximates the GBM component of prices. Then we tack additional price moves on to this that capture the jump process. We illustrate this idea with a specific jump process called a "jump-to-default."

## An Illustration: Binomial Trees with Jump-to-Default

Suppose that the stock price evolves according to the usual binomial model, moving from $S$ to either $uS$ or $dS$ at each point. But suppose, however, there is also a third possibility at each node—that the stock price can drop to zero. Suppose also that once the stock price reaches zero, it remains there forever. The dropping of the stock price to zero is meant to capture the likelihood that there may be a sudden, unexpected default by the company, making its stock worthless. An early "jump-to-default" model of this sort was studied by Paul Samuelson (see Merton, 1976); later versions include Davis and Lischka (1999), Das and Sundaram (2007), and Carr and Linetsky (2006).

Each step of a binomial tree with jump-to-default looks like Figure 16.1. Let $\lambda$ denote the (risk-neutral) probability of the jump at each node. The remaining probability $(1 - \lambda)$ is apportioned between the nondefault nodes. Let $q(1 - \lambda)$ and $(1 - q)(1 - \lambda)$ denote, respectively, the risk-neutral probabilities of an up and down move. When $\lambda = 0$, this is the standard binomial tree.

**FIGURE 16.1**

Binomial Tree with
Jump-to-Default

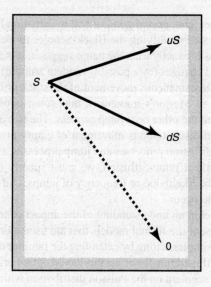

## A One-Period Example

Consider a simple one-period example in which the single period represents $h = 0.50$ years. Suppose the initial stock price is $S = 100$ and the volatility of the GBM component of the stock price is $\sigma = 0.40$. Then, using the CRR parametrization (Chapter 13), the up and down moves of the binomial tree are given by

$$u = \exp\{\sigma\sqrt{h}\} = 1.3269 \qquad d = \exp\{-\sigma\sqrt{h}\} = 0.7536$$

Finally, let the risk-free interest rate in continuously-compounded terms be $r = 0.05$, so the per-period gross interest rate on the tree is $R = e^{rh} = 1.0253$.

Under the risk-neutral probabilities, the expected return on the stock must equal $R$. Since the stock price is $uS$ with probability $q(1 - \lambda)$, $dS$ with probability $(1 - q)(1 - \lambda)$, and zero with probability $\lambda$, this means we must have

$$R = (1 - \lambda)qu + (1 - \lambda)(1 - q)d$$

For any given value of $\lambda$, this expression can be solved to obtain

$$q = \frac{[R/(1 - \lambda)] - d}{u - d} \qquad\qquad (16.1)$$

Consider a call option with a strike of $K = 100$ maturing in one period. The call pays $uS - K = 32.69$ in state $u$ but nothing in the other two states. So its initial value is $q(1 - \lambda) \times 32.69$. The call values that result from different values of $\lambda$ are described in the second column of Table 16.1. Observe that call values increase as $\lambda$ increases. We return to these numbers in a short while.

## A Multiperiod Example

It is a simple matter to extend this example to a multiperiod setting. The upper panel of Table 16.2 shows the evolution of stock prices over a five-period tree assuming the same values of $u$ and $d$ as above. The table does not show the third branch from each node that represents the jump and that drops the stock value to zero, but it is implicit that such a branch exists at each node.

The lower panel of the table prices, by the usual backwards induction argument, a call option with a strike of $K = 100$ and maturing in five periods. The value of $\lambda$ used in this

**TABLE 16.1**
The Effect of Jump-to-Default in a One-Period Model

| Default Probability $\lambda$ | Call Option Values in | |
|---|---|---|
| | One-Period Model | Five-Period Model |
| 0.000 | 15.11 | 30.71 |
| 0.005 | 15.32 | 31.68 |
| 0.010 | 15.53 | 32.65 |
| 0.025 | 16.16 | 35.63 |
| 0.050 | 17.21 | 40.73 |
| 0.100 | 19.30 | 51.23 |

**TABLE 16.2**
Binomial Option Pricing with Jump-to-Default

Option prices when the binomial model is enhanced with a probability of $\lambda$ of a jump to zero. The upper and lower panels present stock prices and call values, respectively, in a five-period tree when $\lambda = 0.10$. The remaining parameters are described in the text.

**Stock Price Evolution: $\lambda = 0.10$**

| Maturity | 0.5 | 1 | 1.5 | 2 | 2.5 |
|---|---|---|---|---|---|
| | | | | | 411.33 |
| | | | | 309.99 | |
| | | | 233.62 | | 233.62 |
| | | 176.07 | | 176.07 | |
| | 132.69 | | 132.69 | | 132.69 |
| 100.00 | | 100.00 | | 100.00 | |
| | 75.36 | | 75.36 | | 75.36 |
| | | 56.80 | | 56.80 | |
| | | | 42.80 | | 42.80 |
| | | | | 32.26 | |
| | | | | | 24.31 |

**Call Option Prices: $\lambda = 0.10$**

| Maturity | 0.5 | 1 | 1.5 | 2 | 2.5 |
|---|---|---|---|---|---|
| | | | | | 311.33 |
| | | | | 222.21 | |
| | | | 156.57 | | 133.62 |
| | | 109.02 | | 88.29 | |
| | 75.09 | | 57.67 | | 32.69 |
| 51.23 | | 37.33 | | 19.30 | |
| | 23.97 | | 11.40 | | 0.00 |
| | | 6.73 | | 0.00 | |
| | | | 0.00 | | 0.00 |
| | | | | 0.00 | |
| | | | | | 0.00 |

table is $\lambda = 0.10$; the remaining risk-neutral probabilities needed for pricing are obtained using (16.1). As the table shows, the initial price of the call is 51.23. Carrying out similar computations, the last column of Table 16.1 reports call values for some other values of $\lambda$.

## The Bias from Ignoring Jumps

Suppose that the true stock price follows a GBM process with jump-to-default. If the stock has not yet defaulted, an observer who looks at a sufficiently long history of stock prices and computes the stock volatility would arrive at the estimate $\sigma = 0.40$. Representing this in a binomial tree with $h = 0.50$ would result precisely in the values $u$ and $d$ we have used in the trees above.

Suppose now that this observer ignores the possibility of the default branch, i.e., effectively sets $\lambda = 0$. As Table 16.1 shows, the resulting price would then be biased, in some cases quite severely. In the five-period model, even a 0.5% chance of default ($\lambda = 0.005$) creates a pricing error of over 3%. Moreover, the bias is always in terms of an *under*estimation of the correct price; that is, the more likely is default, the more the call is undervalued when we ignore default.[1]

Of course, in general, both the impact of jump risk and the direction of the bias introduced by ignoring it will depend on the stock return distribution under the jump; the example uses a very special form for this distribution. So, the next step in our analysis is to look at option pricing when the likelihood of jumps and the jump distribution have more general forms. To this end, the next segment introduces the *Poisson distribution*, which will be used to describe the frequency of jumps. Following that, we describe the essential content of the Merton (1976) jump-diffusion model.

## The Poisson Distribution

The Poisson distribution is frequently used in practice to represent random arrivals, such as, for example, the number of customers arriving at a bank counter during a specified time. So, a Poisson-distributed random variable $N$ takes on the values $k = 0, 1, 2, \ldots$. The distribution is described by a single parameter $\lambda > 0$. The probabilities of the outcomes are defined by

$$\mathrm{Prob}(N = k) = \frac{e^{-\lambda} \lambda^k}{k!}$$

Here, $k!$ refers to "factorial $k$," i.e., the product of the first $k$ integers. By convention, $0! = 1$. Thus, for example, the probability that $N = 0$ is just $e^{-\lambda}$, while the probability that $N = 3$ (say) is $[e^{-\lambda}\lambda^3]/6$. The single parameter $\lambda$ of the Poisson distribution is both the mean and the variance of the distribution:

$$E(N) = \sum_{k=0}^{\infty} [k \times \mathrm{Prob}(N = k)] = \lambda \qquad \textbf{(16.2)}$$

$$\mathrm{Var}(N) = E(N^2) - [E(N)]^2 = \lambda \qquad \textbf{(16.3)}$$

In our context, the Poisson distribution will be used to describe the number of jumps in the stock price. Intuitively, the continuous portion of the stock price corresponds to "normal" price changes that occur because of, for instance, demand-supply imbalances or portfolio rebalancing, while the jumps correspond to price changes that occur because of the arrival of important new information, perhaps stock- or industry-specific news.

---

[1] It may appear counterintuitive that call values *increase* when default is more likely, but the reason is simple. When we keep the current stock price constant but increase the probability of the stock price going to zero next period, we must compensate by increasing the likelihood of the up move also. (Otherwise, the current stock price will not be the discounted expected value of future stock prices.) Expression (16.1) shows precisely how the likelihood of an up move is related to the jump-to-default probability. This creates an upward skew that pushes up the call price.

## The Jump-Diffusion Returns Specification

Consider a $t$-year horizon denoted $[0, t]$. Let $S$ denote the current (time-0) price and $S_t$ the price at time $t$. Let $R_t = \ln(S_t/S)$ be the log-returns over $[0, t]$, and let $Z_t$ denote a normally-distributed random variable with mean $\alpha t$ and variance $\sigma^2 t$. Under the Black-Scholes model, we have

$$R_t = Z_t$$

In a jump-diffusion model, the return $R_t$ is the sum of $Z_t$ and the outcomes of each of a random number of jumps. We want to represent the number of jumps by a Poisson distribution, but we need to "scale" the distribution with the length of the horizon since jumps should become more likely over a longer horizon. So we assume that the number of jumps over the interval $[0, t]$ is determined by a Poisson distribution with parameter $\lambda t$ where $\lambda > 0$. That is, if we let $N_t$ denote the number of jumps in the interval $[0, t]$, then

$$\text{Prob}(N_t = k) = \frac{e^{-\lambda t}(\lambda t)^k}{k!}, \quad k = 0, 1, 2, \ldots \tag{16.4}$$

The jump process is presumed to be independent of the diffusion process driving the continuous portion of the stock returns. From (16.2), the expected number of jumps over $[0, t]$ is $\lambda t$. Taking $t = 1$ year gives us a simple interpretation of $\lambda$: it is the *expected number of jumps per year*.

We must also specify how the jump returns are distributed. Following Merton (1976), we assume that each jump return is normally distributed and that jump outcomes are independent of each other. So let $(H_k)$ denote a sequence of independent and identically distributed random variables, each of which is normal with mean $\mu$ and variance $\gamma^2$. Then, conditional on there being $k$ jumps in the interval $[0, t]$, the returns $R_t$ under a jump-diffusion are given by

$$R_t = \begin{cases} Z_t, & \text{if } k = 0 \\ Z_t + H_1 + H_2 + \cdots + H_k, & \text{if } k \geq 1 \end{cases} \tag{16.5}$$

Together with the distribution (16.4) of $k$, this specifies the jump-diffusion return process. We first point out some implications of this distribution and then turn to option pricing.

## Moment Implications of Jump-Diffusions

If $k$ were fixed and not random, then the return $R_t$ in (16.5), as the sum of normal random variates, would also be normally distributed. However, since $k$ is random, $R_t$ is no longer normal. Das and Sundaram (1999) show that the first four moments of $R_t$ are

$$\text{Mean} = (\alpha + \lambda\mu)t \tag{16.6}$$

$$\text{Variance} = [\sigma^2 + \lambda(\mu^2 + \gamma^2)]t \tag{16.7}$$

$$\text{Skewness} = \frac{1}{\sqrt{t}}\left[\frac{\lambda(\mu^3 + 3\mu\gamma^2)}{(\sigma^2 + \lambda(\mu^2 + \gamma^2))^{3/2}}\right] \tag{16.8}$$

$$\text{Kurtosis} = 3 + \frac{1}{t}\left[\frac{\lambda(\mu^4 + 6\mu^2\gamma^2 + 3\gamma^4)}{(\sigma^2 + \lambda(\mu^2 + \gamma^2))^2}\right] \tag{16.9}$$

Every normal distribution is symmetric and so has a skewness of zero. Expression (16.8) shows that the skewness of the jump-diffusion is zero if, and only if, the jump component itself has a mean of zero (i.e., $\mu = 0$). If $\mu > 0$, the jump-diffusion has positively skewed returns, while if $\mu < 0$, returns are negatively skewed.

More interesting is the kurtosis. Every normal distribution has a kurtosis of exactly 3. Any distribution with kurtosis greater than 3 is said to be "leptokurtic" or "fat-tailed"; intuitively, extreme outcomes are more likely in such a distribution than in a normal distribution. As (16.9) shows, the kurtosis of the jump-diffusion always exceeds 3, so the jump-diffusion is fat-tailed.

These observations have important implications for option prices. In Section 14.8, we noted that one reason for the implied volatility skew is that the empirical returns distributions exhibit greater kurtosis than the Black-Scholes model and sometimes also exhibit skewness. By allowing for both skewness and kurtosis in the returns distribution, the jump-diffusion aims to address these shortcomings. Of course, how well it does so is ultimately an empirical question. We address this question after taking a look at option pricing formulae under jump-diffusions.

## The Merton (1976) Option Pricing Formula

Suppose the stock price follows a jump-diffusion as just described. Let $S$ be the current (time-0) stock price and $r$ be the risk-free rate of interest (expressed, as usual, in continuously-compounded terms). Consider a European call option maturing in $T$ years and with strike $K$. Merton (1976) describes a formula for pricing this option.

To describe Merton's formula concisely, some additional notation will help. Let $g$ be the expected proportional change in the stock price caused by a jump. In terms of the notation introduced above, $g = \exp\{\mu + \frac{1}{2}\gamma^2\} - 1$.[2] Now, define the following variables:

$$\xi = \lambda(1 + g)$$

$$\nu = \ln(1 + g)$$

Next, for $k = 0, 1, 2, \ldots$, let $\sigma_k^2$ and $r_k$ be given by

$$\sigma_k^2 = \sigma^2 + \frac{1}{T} k\gamma^2$$

$$r_k = r - \lambda g + \frac{1}{T} k\nu$$

Finally, let $C^{BS}(S, K, T, \eta, \rho)$ denote the Black-Scholes price of a call option with strike $K$ and $T$ years to maturity when the current stock price is $S$, the stock volatility is $\eta$, and the riskless interest rate is $\rho$. Then, Merton shows that the price of the call option under the jump-diffusion, denoted $C^{JD}$, is

$$C^{JD} = \sum_{k=0}^{\infty} \frac{e^{-\xi T}(\xi T)^k}{k!} C^{BS}(S, K, T, \sigma_k, r_k) \qquad \textbf{(16.10)}$$

The price $P^{JD}$ of the corresponding put option can be determined from the call price using put-call parity.

It should be noted that the derivation of this formula is not quite as straightforward as the Black-Scholes formula. Merton notes that with a jump-diffusion, it is not possible to set up a portfolio that continuously replicates the option. Replication aims to use positions in the stock to mimic changes in the value of the option. If the stock price can register

---

[2] To see why this is the case, suppose that the jump causes a gross proportional change of $Y$ in the stock price, i.e., the stock price changes from $S$ to $SY$ on account of the jump. Then, the log-return on account of the jump is just $\ln(Y)$, which under our assumptions is normally distributed with mean $\mu$ and variance $\gamma^2$. From the standard properties of the lognormal, it follows that $E(Y) = \exp\{\mu + \frac{1}{2}\gamma^2\}$. The expected proportional change is $E(Y) - 1$.

unexpected jump moves of a random size, then, since the position in the stock responds linearly to changes in the stock price but the option responds nonlinearly, replication becomes impossible.

Merton's approach is to assume that jump-risk is diversifiable and so is not priced. Under this assumption, Merton derives a mixed partial differential-difference equation that option prices must satisfy. The option pricing formula (16.10) is derived from this equation.

## The Implied Volatility Skew under Jump-Diffusions

An important motivation behind the development of the jump-diffusion model is the presence of the implied volatility skew in options markets. So one question of interest is: for plausible parameter values, what kinds of implied volatility skews is the jump-diffusion theoretically capable of generating? Are they similar to the shapes observed in practice?

Appendix 16A describes program code in Octave for implementing the Merton jump-diffusion formula (16.10). Using this, we identify option prices under the jump-diffusion for the following set of parameters:

| Variable | Value |
| --- | --- |
| Initial stock price | $S = 100$ |
| Option maturity | $T = 0.50$ years |
| Interest rate | $r = 0.03$ |
| Diffusion volatility | $\sigma = 0.30$ |
| Jump frequency | $\lambda = 0.50$ |
| Jump mean | $\mu = -0.10, 0, +0.10$ |
| Jump standard deviation | $\gamma = 0.50$ |

Since $\lambda = 0.50$, jumps take place on average once every two years. When $\mu = 0$, there is no skewness in the stock's return distribution (see (16.8)); skewness is positive when $\mu = +0.10$ and is negative when $\mu = -0.10$. From the option prices, we back out the implied volatilities at various strike prices. (Recall that implied volatility is defined as that level of volatility that would make the Black-Scholes formula consistent with a given option price.) The results are presented in Figure 16.2. The range of strike prices used is symmetric around the current level of the stock price, ranging from \$50 to \$150.

The figure shows that away-from-the-money options under jump-diffusions generally have higher implied volatilities than at-the-money options, i.e., there is an implied volatility skew. This is on account of the excess kurtosis ("fat tails") under the jump-diffusion (see (16.9)). When $\mu = 0$, there is no skewness and the implied volatility skew is symmetric (i.e., is a "smile"); this is the shape typically observed in currency options markets. When $\mu < 0$, the negative skewness in the returns distribution skews the implied volatility curve so that out-of-the-money puts register higher implied volatilities than at-the-money options or out-of-the-money calls. To an extent, this is similar to the shape found in equity index option markets, although empirical skews are typically less U-shaped. Similarly, for $\mu > 0$, the positive skewness means that the implied volatility curve is skewed to the right with higher implied volatilities for out-of-the-money calls than for at-the-money options or for out-of-the-money puts. Thus, theoretically speaking, jump-diffusions are capable of generating a variety of shapes for the implied volatility skew.

## The Pricing Bias from Ignoring Jumps

A related question of interest is the pricing bias introduced by ignoring jumps. That is, consider an observer who assumes the stock follows a geometric Brownian motion when

**FIGURE 16.2**

Option Smiles in a
Jump-Diffusion Model

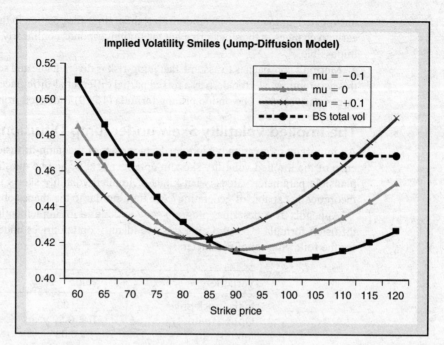

it really follows the Merton jump-diffusion process. If the observer uses the stock's price history to estimate the stock's volatility (and has available to her a sufficiently long history of stock prices), she will arrive at the return variance estimate (16.7). That is, the stock's volatility $\psi$ will be calculated to be

$$\psi = \left[\sigma^2 + \lambda(\mu^2 + \gamma^2)\right]^{1/2} \tag{16.11}$$

So our question is: how does the Black-Scholes price computed using (16.11) as the volatility compare to the jump-diffusion price given $(\lambda, \mu, \gamma)$?

For specificity, we consider the case $\mu = 0$. Figure 16.3 plots jump-diffusion and Black-Scholes options prices for this case. The remaining parameters are the same as used in Figure 16.2. The figure shows that the Black-Scholes model overprices at- and near-the-money options relative to the jump-diffusion but underprices away-from-the-money options.[3] Merton (1976) shows that this is a consequence of the curvature properties of the Black-Scholes option pricing formula combined with the fact that the jump-diffusion price (16.10) is a probability weighted convex combination of Black-Scholes prices.

## Calibration of the Model and Its Empirical Performance

One approach to calibrating any model is to take the prices of traded options and to search over the model's parameter values so as to best match the prices of the options. This is the "implied" parameter approach. In the simple case of the Black-Scholes model, the only unobserved parameter—the volatility—can be backed out of the price of a single option. In

---

[3] This effect can also be seen using the implied volatility plot in Figure 16.2. For $\mu = 0$, (16.11) implies a volatility of about 0.46. As can be seen from Figure 16.2, this is greater than the near-the-money implied volatility, but less than the away-from-the-money implied volatility, of the jump-diffusion. However, the implied volatility figure does not enable us to compute the dollar pricing error, which is what Figure 16.3 describes.

**FIGURE 16.3**

Comparison of
Jump-Diffusion and
Black-Scholes Prices

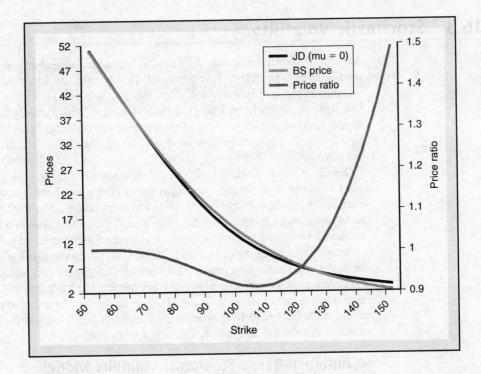

the more complex case of the local volatility model studied later in this chapter, the tree is "fitted" using the prices of a larger set of chosen options.

In the jump-diffusion model, there are four unobserved parameters that need to be fit: the volatility of the diffusion ($\sigma$), the jump probability ($\lambda$), the mean of the jump ($\mu$), and the variance of the jump ($\gamma^2$). Using a cross-section of option prices, we can identify the "best-fit" parameter values by, for instance, minimizing the sum of squared deviations between the model-implied prices and the observed prices. Alternatively, using a time series of stock and/or option prices and the probability functions that drive the jump-diffusion process, we may, for example, fit the parameters econometrically using maximum-likelihood methods or by the method of moments.

Empirically, the evidence in favor of jump-diffusions is mixed. Jorion (1988) and Bates (1996), among others, have found some support for the model in equity and currency markets. The ability of the model to generate skewness and excess kurtosis means that it is typically able to match observed option prices, particularly at short maturities, under reasonable parametrizations. However, as Das and Sundaram (1999) show, the skewness and, especially, excess kurtosis dissipate very rapidly as maturity increases (see (16.8) and (16.9)), so returns become approximately normal as maturity increases (Backus, Foresi, Li, and Wu (1997)). As a result, the implied volatility smile under a jump-diffusion becomes flat very rapidly, much faster than observed in practice.[4] These results all suggest that the ability of jump-diffusions to match observed options prices at long maturities (or simultaneously at different maturities) may be limited.

[4] There is even a question about whether the implied volatility smile in practice flattens out at all. Using an extensive data set of options with maturities out to five years and across several countries, Foresi and Wu (2005) provide strong evidence that the option smile remains steep even at very long maturities. See also Carr and Wu (2003).

## 16.3   Stochastic Volatility

As with jump-diffusions, the stochastic volatility model makes a single, but important, modification to the Black-Scholes model. In this case, the Black-Scholes condition that volatility is constant is dropped. Rather, volatility is allowed to evolve over time according to a separate stochastic process. The time-varying volatility creates fat tails in the returns distribution and so addresses one of the principal shortcomings of the Black-Scholes model. However, price paths are continuous in stochastic volatility models; that is, market gaps are not admitted.

Specifying a stochastic volatility model means specifying three things: (a) the underlying stock return process, (b) the stochastic process governing changes in volatility, and (c) the correlation between changes in volatility and stock returns. The third requirement enables us to capture such things as the "leverage effect" commonly observed in practice in equity markets where sharp negative returns are associated with increased volatility.

Many different stochastic volatility models have been proposed in the literature. All of these are continuous-time models that are technically more complex than Black-Scholes. So before presenting a description of these models, we work our way through a discrete-time version that captures the main ideas; in particular, the example explains how prices under stochastic volatility compare to Black-Scholes prices and how the correlation between changes in volatility and returns affects this relationship.

### A Binomial-Based Stochastic Volatility Model

In the typical CRR parametrization of the binomial model (Chapter 13), the up and down moves on the binomial tree are given by $u = e^{\sigma\sqrt{h}}$ and $d = e^{-\sigma\sqrt{h}}$, respectively, where $\sigma$ is the stock's volatility and $h$ the length of one period in the tree measured in years. So, given $S_t$, the two possible values of $S_{t+h}$ are

$$S_{t+h} = \begin{cases} S_{t+h}^u = e^{\sigma\sqrt{h}}S_t \\ S_{t+h}^d = e^{-\sigma\sqrt{h}}S_t \end{cases} \qquad \textbf{(16.12)}$$

It is easy to modify this specification to allow for volatility to change in a *deterministic* manner from period to period. For example, suppose that the volatility between time points $t$ and $t + h$ is $\sigma_t$. Then, we simply allow the up and down moves to change from period to period. That is, we define the possible values of $S_{t+h}$ by

$$S_{t+h} = \begin{cases} S_{t+h}^u = e^{\sigma_t\sqrt{h}}S_t \\ S_{t+h}^d = e^{-\sigma_t\sqrt{h}}S_t \end{cases} \qquad \textbf{(16.13)}$$

But what about *randomly*-changing volatility? In this case, we must first specify the stochastic process for the evolution of volatility over time and then use this to build the tree. A simple discrete-time process for the evolution of volatility may be developed as follows. As we explain shortly, this formulation is simply a discrete-time version of the model of Heston (1993) and captures many of the key characteristics associated with stochastic volatility models.

Let $\sigma_t$ denote the *realized* period-$t$ volatility, and let $\kappa$, $\theta$, and $\eta$ be positive terms with $0 < \kappa < 1$. We model the evolution of the variance $V_t = \sigma_t^2$. Suppose that the time-$(t + h)$ variance can take on two possible values given by

$$V_{t+h} = \begin{cases} V_{t+h}^u = V_t + \kappa(\theta - \sigma_t)h + \eta\sqrt{V_t h} \\ V_{t+h}^d = V_t + \kappa(\theta - \sigma_t)h - \eta\sqrt{V_t h} \end{cases} \qquad \textbf{(16.14)}$$

This binomial process for the variance should be thought of as a discrete-time approximation of a continuous-time diffusion process. Expression (16.14) effectively expresses the difference $V_{t+h} - V_t$ between the values of variance at times $t + h$ and $t$ as composed of two terms:

- The term $\kappa(\theta - \sigma_t)h$, called the *drift* of the process.
- The term $\eta\sqrt{V_t h}$, which represents the randomness in the evolution since it enters with a positive sign in one case and a negative sign in the other.

Consider the drift $\kappa(\theta - \sigma_t)$. The parameter $\theta$ represents the *mean long-run variance*: if current variance is less than this level, the drift increases the variance, while if current variance is greater than this level, the drift pushes it down. That is:

- If $V_t < \theta$, the drift is positive, increasing $V_t$ from its time-$t$ value.
- If $V_t > \theta$, the drift is negative, dragging $V_{t+h}$ down.
- If $V_t = \theta$, the drift is zero.

In a nutshell, we say that this specification for $V_t$ exhibits "mean-reversion." The term $\kappa$ is the coefficient of mean-reversion: it controls the speed with which variance reverts to its mean. The higher is $\kappa$, the faster is variance pushed towards its mean level $\theta$.

Finally, the parameter $\eta$ is called the "volatility of volatility." If $\eta = 0$, there is no randomness in the volatility process since the noise term $\eta\sqrt{V_t h}$ disappears. And as $\eta$ increases, the difference between the two possible values of $V_{t+h}$ becomes larger, increasing the swings in volatility.

As noted, this volatility process is just a discrete-time version of Heston's (1993) continuous-time model (see below for the description of Heston's model). The model has three key characteristics: a long-term mean level around which volatility evolves, a coefficient of mean-reversion, and a volatility-of-volatility term that determines the size of volatility swings. A similar model in continuous time has also been studied by Stein and Stein (1991) and others. Nonetheless, this discrete-time model is meant only for illustrative purposes; for instance, we have not added constraints to prevent variance from becoming negative, which it could under (16.14), a situation that is easily ruled out in the continuous-time formulation.

The stock price process meanwhile evolves exactly as in (16.13) but with $\sigma_t = \sqrt{V_t}$ given by the *realized* volatility in period $t$. Since both the stock price and volatility can go up or down, there is a total of four possible outcomes at time $t + h$:

$$(S_{t+h}^u, V_{t+h}^u), (S_{t+h}^u, V_{t+h}^d), (S_{t+h}^d, V_{t+h}^u), \text{ and } (S_{t+h}^d, V_{t+h}^d)$$

Thus, we have the quadrinomial model pictured in Figure 16.4 in each period. The probability of the stock price registering an up move is the sum of the probabilities of the top two nodes. Similarly, the probability of $V$ moving to $V_{t+h}^u$ is the sum of the probabilities of the first and third nodes. The correlation between changes in volatility and stock returns is precisely the quantity $\rho$ in the figure.

## Option Prices in the Model

Appendix 16B describes code in `Octave` for implementing the stochastic model described above. It is a simple matter to modify the code to incorporate other stochastic processes for volatility. We use this implementation to obtain option prices under stochastic volatility. We want to compare these prices to Black-Scholes prices, which, in this discrete setting, are just prices in a binomial model with constant volatility. The comparison highlights not just the role of stochastic volatility but also that of the correlation $\rho$ between changes in volatility and returns.

**FIGURE 16.4**

The Quadrinomial
Stochastic Volatility
Tree

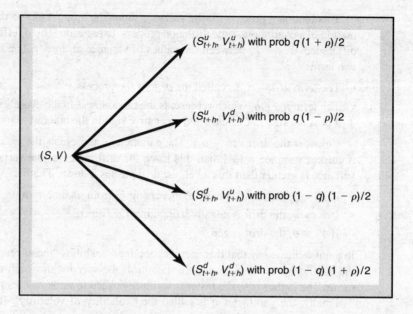

Table 16.3 presents the prices of a call with strike $K = 100$ under stochastic volatility for three values of the correlation ($\rho = -0.50, 0, +0.50$) and for a range of strike prices. The table also presents Black-Scholes prices. The following parameter values are used to generate these numbers:

| Variable | Value |
|---|---|
| Initial stock price | $S = 100$ |
| Risk-free interest rate | $r = 0$ |
| Option maturity | $T = 0.50$ |
| Initial volatility | $V = 0.09$ |
| Volatility mean | $\theta = 0.09$ |
| Volatility of volatility | $\eta = 0.30$ |
| Mean reversion rate | $\kappa = 0.10$ |

The Black-Scholes/binomial values are computed using the initial level of volatility—which is also the long-run mean $\theta$—as the fixed level of volatility. That is, we just set $\kappa = \eta = 0$. The Black-Scholes values do not, of course, depend on $\rho$, but note that the stochastic volatility values in Table 16.3 do change with $\rho$.

## Comparison of Stochastic Volatility and Black-Scholes Option Prices

Before discussing the numbers in Table 16.3, we first talk about *how* stochastic volatility should matter. Stochastic volatility creates excess kurtosis (fat tails) in the return distribution. Moreover, nonzero correlation between returns and volatility induces skewness into the returns distribution.

• Negative correlation results in negative skewness. Loosely, with negative correlation, higher volatility levels are associated with more negative stock returns, which means bigger moves on the downside. And when volatility decreases, there is a greater chance that stock price changes will be positive but small since volatility has declined to a smaller value.

**TABLE 16.3**

Call Prices under the Stochastic Volatility and Black-Scholes Models

Call option prices from the stochastic volatility and Black-Scholes models based on the program code in Appendix 16B. The values are computed by pricing the option with trees of six and seven steps and then averaging the two values. The table below presents call values for three values of the correlation $\rho$ between volatility changes and stock returns and for a range of strike prices.

| Strike Price | Black-Scholes Price | Call Prices under Stochastic Volatility | | |
|---|---|---|---|---|
| | | $\rho = -0.5$ | $\rho = 0.0$ | $\rho = +0.5$ |
| 60 | 40.005 | 40.047 | 40.024 | 40.008 |
| 70 | 30.306 | 30.354 | 30.284 | 30.214 |
| 80 | 21.554 | 21.508 | 21.396 | 21.280 |
| 90 | 13.740 | 14.194 | 14.092 | 13.989 |
| 100 | 8.874 | 8.475 | 8.469 | 8.475 |
| 110 | 4.332 | 4.716 | 4.829 | 4.939 |
| 120 | 2.739 | 2.324 | 2.470 | 2.605 |
| 130 | 1.146 | 1.098 | 1.235 | 1.367 |
| 140 | 0.507 | 0.425 | 0.548 | 0.671 |

- Conversely, when correlation $\rho$ is positive, there is positive skewness in the stock return distribution.
- Finally, with zero correlation, there is no skewness in the returns distribution.

These patterns of skewness and kurtosis are reflected in the numbers in Table 16.3.

- When $\rho < 0$, negative skewness in returns makes call option prices at lower strikes relatively higher. That is, option prices at lower strike ranges are higher for $\rho = -0.5$ than for the other values of $\rho$. Moreover, the negative skewness implies that the left tail is fat, so options with low strike prices have higher values under stochastic volatility than under Black-Scholes. However, option values at high strike prices are lower.
- Conversely, with positive correlation, option values in the stochastic volatility model are relatively higher at higher strikes for $\rho = +0.5$ than for the other values of $\rho$. Moreover, since the right tail is now the fat one, high strike option prices from the stochastic volatility model exceed those of the Black-Scholes model, but the lower-strike option prices are lower.
- When $\rho = 0$, both tails are fat. This leads to higher prices under stochastic volatility than under Black-Scholes for away-from-the-money options in either direction.

These results can be expressed succinctly in terms of the implied volatility smiles. Recall that the smile is generated by computing the implied volatility from the Black-Scholes model using the prices at various strikes obtained from the stochastic volatility model. Figure 16.5 presents smoothed implied volatility smile curves using the option prices from Table 16.3.

When the correlation is negative, the smile is skewed to the left. This is the case commonly seen in equity indices; of course, equity index markets do commonly exhibit negative correlation between volatility and returns. When the correlation is zero, the smile is symmetric. This is typical of currency options markets and to a lesser extent for options on individual stocks. When correlation is positive, the smile is right skewed. Thus, depending on the degree of skewness and kurtosis, a variety of shapes can be generated for implied volatility smiles under stochastic volatility.

**FIGURE 16.5**

Implied Volatility Smiles in the Stochastic Volatility Model

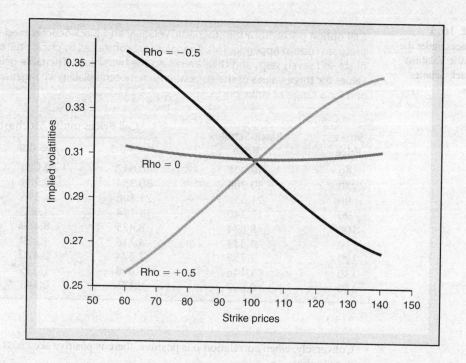

## Continuous-Time Stochastic Volatility Models

Several different continuous-time formulations of stochastic volatility have been proposed. We focus in this segment on perhaps the most popular and best known, the model of Heston (1993). We also briefly touch upon other formulations. Technically, there are three equations that go into a stochastic volatility model description, one for the evolution of stock prices, one for the evolution of volatility, and the final one describing the relation between the first two.

Let $\sigma_t$ denote the instantaneous volatility at time $t$. The first equation in Heston's model is similar to the Black-Scholes expression for the evolution of the price of the underlying (see Chapter 15) but with $\sigma_t$ replacing the constant $\sigma$:

$$dS_t = \alpha S_t\, dt + \sigma_t S_t\, dW_t^1 \qquad \textbf{(16.15)}$$

$(W_t^1)$ is the Brownian motion process driving the stock price process, and $\alpha$ is the drift of the stock price process. To this stock return process, we append a second stochastic process, this one for the evolution of volatility. Letting $v_t = \sigma_t^2$ be the instantaneous variance, the second equation in Heston's model is

$$dv_t = \kappa(\theta - v_t)\, dt + \eta \sqrt{v_t}\, dW_t^2 \qquad \textbf{(16.16)}$$

where $\kappa, \theta$, and $\eta$ are all positive. As in the discrete-time formulation, $\theta$ is the long-run mean of the instantaneous variance, $\kappa$ the coefficient of mean-reversion, and $\eta$ the volatility of volatility. The process (16.16) for $v_t$ is guaranteed to remain positive as long as $\kappa\theta > \frac{1}{2}\eta^2$. The third and final equation connects the first two by specifying the correlation between the Brownian processes $W_t^1$ and $W_t^2$:

$$E[dW_t^1\, dW_t^2] = \rho\, dt \qquad \textbf{(16.17)}$$

In equity markets, where we often witness increased volatility associated with sharp negative returns, we would expect $\rho$ to be negative. In general, though, the model does not require any particular sign of $\rho$. Equations (16.15)–(16.17) complete the description of Heston's model.

Kurtosis in stock returns in this model is created by random changes in volatility. Nonzero correlation between changes in volatility and returns results in skewness. The behavior of skewness and kurtosis in this model is described in Das and Sundaram (1999) who give closed-form solutions for these moments. One important property they derive is that kurtosis is hump-shaped in the horizon: excess kurtosis is close to zero at very low maturities, rises to a maximum, and tapers away to zero again at long maturities. Intuitively, at low maturities, changing volatility has not had enough time to create excess kurtosis, while at long maturities, mean-reversion eliminates excess kurtosis. A higher value of $\kappa$ causes volatility to revert to its mean value faster, so kills kurtosis more quickly. Since excess kurtosis is needed to generate an implied volatility skew, $\kappa$ also kills the skew unless it is small in size.

Other models of stochastic volatility proposed in the literature include Hull and White (1987), Wiggins (1987), Stein and Stein (1991), and Amin and Ng (1992), among several others. Hull and White (1987) examine a model in which the volatility process (16.16) itself takes the form of geometric Brownian motion:

$$dv_t \;=\; \varphi v_t\, dt + \zeta v_t\, dW_t^2 \qquad\qquad \textbf{(16.18)}$$

Under this specification, there is no mean reversion, so expected volatility either diverges to infinity or converges to zero depending on the value of $\varphi$. Hull and White also assume that the stock and volatility process are uncorrelated, which implies a symmetric volatility smile in their model.

Stein and Stein (1991) study a model with mean-reversion as in Heston's model, but model the behavior of instantaneous volatility rather than instantaneous variance. Instantaneous volatility in their model follows a mean-reverting Gaussian process, i.e., (16.16) is replaced by

$$d\sigma_t \;=\; \kappa(\theta - \sigma_t)\, dt + \alpha\, dW_t^2 \qquad\qquad \textbf{(16.19)}$$

This is called the Ornstein-Uhlenbeck, or O-U, process. Stein and Stein also allow for arbitrary correlation between the volatility and return processes as in equation (16.17). Schöbl and Zhu (1999) study a similar model.

## Option Pricing under Stochastic Volatility

When volatility and returns are uncorrelated, Hull and White show that option prices in a stochastic volatility model may be expressed as a function of Black-Scholes prices. Specifically, let $\overline{V}$ denote the average variance over the life of the option. $\overline{V}$ will clearly depend on the particular path of realized variances, so let $h(\overline{V})$ denote the probability density function of $\overline{V}$. Also, let $C^{BS}(\overline{V})$ be the Black-Scholes call price given $\overline{V}$, i.e., for a volatility of $\sqrt{\overline{V}}$. Then, if $C^{SV}$ denotes the call price under stochastic volatility, Hull and White show that

$$C^{SV} \;=\; \int_0^\infty C^{BS}(\overline{V}) h(\overline{V}) d\overline{V}$$

The general case where volatility and returns may be correlated is much harder and was solved in closed form in Heston's (1993) paper. Heston's paper had a significant impact on option pricing because it opened up an entirely new technical approach to obtaining closed-form solutions for option models, one that extended the basic setting of the Black-Scholes formula and allowed for rapid computation of option prices in extended models. The option formulae retain the basic structure of Black-Scholes; for example, the call pricing formula is the difference of two components, one of which is the present value of the stock price when the option ends up in-the-money (the general counterpart of the term $SN(d_1)$ in the Black-Scholes call-pricing formula), and the other of which is the present value of the strike price for all in-the-money outcomes (the counterpart of the term $Ke^{-rT}N(d_2)$).

As we saw in Chapter 15, there are two ways we can derive option prices in a continuous-time setting. One is by using arbitrage arguments to reduce the option pricing problem to the solution to a partial difference equation (pde). The other is by taking expectations under the risk-neutral measure. The former approach, in most cases, defies closed-form solutions. The latter involves solving for the expectation of the call payoff $\max\{S_T - K, 0\}$ under the risk-neutral probability and discounting this back to the present time. That is, denoting by $r$ the (constant) risk-free interest rate and by $f$ the risk-neutral stock-price density at $T$ conditional on current information, the call price is

$$C = e^{-rT} \int_K^\infty (S_T - K) f(S_T) dS_T \qquad\qquad \textbf{(16.20)}$$

The key innovation in Heston's paper was showing that this option price could be solved for under stochastic volatility by solving two pdes, one each for the analogs of $N(d_1)$ and $N(d_2)$. The details behind Heston's derivation are technically quite complex. We describe a heuristic motivation of the basic ideas in Appendix 16C.

## Calibration and Empirical Performance of the Stochastic Volatility Model

There are five unknown and unobserved variables in the Heston model: $\sigma_0$, $\kappa$, $\theta$, $\eta$, and $\rho$. One procedure for identifying these values is to find the parameters that minimize the sum of squared differences between the fitted implied volatilities and those observed in market prices. Note that there are also non-negativity constraints on all the parameters except $\rho$.

Other metrics may also be employed. One is to minimize the sum of absolute deviations of model and market implied volatilities. Weighted sums may be used. Fitting may also be based on option prices rather than implied volatilities; then the procedure aims to minimize the percentage differences in prices. However, this may be unstable because the value of out-of-the-money options is often too small, resulting in blowing up the difference and overweighting those options.

Empirically, as with jump-diffusions, the evidence in favor of stochastic volatility models is mixed. Varying degrees of support of such models have been found in different markets (e.g., Bates, 1996). The model's ability to generate skewness and excess kurtosis enables it to better fit observed option prices than the Black-Scholes model. However, stochastic volatility models imply a hump-shaped pattern of excess kurtosis (see Das and Sundaram, 1999). Intuitively, at low maturities, changing volatility has not had enough time to create excess kurtosis, while at long maturities, mean-reversion eliminates excess kurtosis. Consequently, for reasonable parametrizations, stochastic volatility models have only limited impact on short-dated option prices. And the evidence that the option smile in equities markets remains steep even at very long maturities (Foresi and Wu, 2005) suggests that these models may not do well at matching the data unless other factors (e.g., jumps) are also included in the models.

# 16.4   GARCH Models

GARCH (generalized autoregressive conditional heteroskedasticity) models are popular discrete-time alternatives to stochastic volatility models. Developed as ARCH models by Engle (1982) and extended to generalized ARCH (or GARCH) models by Bollerslev (1986), the setting has been found to be very good at depicting stock price processes and return behavior. Option pricing for GARCH models was developed in the 1990s (see, especially, Duan, 1995).

Unlike the jump-diffusion and stochastic volatility approaches, each of which required the addition of a second stochastic process to augment the underlying GBM process of the Black-Scholes model, the GARCH approach does not necessitate introducing any additional random variables. GARCH models are also essentially discrete-time models with the changes in volatility occurring at fixed time points $t, t + h, t + 2h$, and so on. However, it is possible to define a different GARCH process for each $h$ such that as $h$ goes to zero, the GARCH processes converge to a limiting continuous-time diffusion process. For details, the reader may refer to Nelson (1990) or Duan (1995).

## The GARCH Process: A Description

Let the discrete time-points of the process be denoted $t, t + 1, t + 2, \ldots$, where the gap between any two successive time-points is fixed at $h$ years (for example, $h$ could be one day). Let $R_t = \ln(S_t/S_{t-1})$ denote the log-return over period $t$. Conditional on all the information $F_{t-1}$ available up to period $(t - 1)$, let $\alpha_t$ denote the expected return: $\alpha_t = E(R_t \| F_{t-1})$. Then, we may write $R_t$ as

$$R_t = \alpha_t + \epsilon_t \tag{16.21}$$

where $\epsilon_t = R_t - \alpha_t$ denotes the unexpected portion of the returns. By definition, $\epsilon_t$ has mean zero. Let $\sigma_t^2$ denote the variance of $\epsilon_t$ conditional on all information available up to $(t - 1)$: $\sigma_t^2 = \text{Var}(\epsilon_t \| F_{t-1})$. The basic and most popular version of the GARCH model, known as the GARCH (1,1) model, represents the evolution of $\sigma_t^2$ as a function of the immediate past values of $\epsilon$ and $\sigma$:

$$\sigma_t^2 = \beta + \gamma \sigma_{t-1}^2 + \zeta \epsilon_{t-1}^2 \tag{16.22}$$

Two conditions must be met for (16.22) to be meaningful: (i) $\beta$, $\gamma$, and $\zeta$ are all nonnegative; and (ii) $\gamma + \zeta < 1$. The first condition is required to ensure that variance does not become negative, while the second condition ensures volatility does not explode. Given this condition, the long-run mean level of variance is $\overline{\sigma}^2 = \beta/(1 - \gamma - \zeta)$.

The specification (16.22) implies that a large return "shock" will result in a persistent spike in volatility. A large value of $\epsilon$ today will, via (16.22), increase volatility tomorrow, and through that volatility in all subsequent periods. But since $\gamma < 1$, this effect on future volatilities decays geometrically.

## Variants and Extensions of GARCH (1,1)

Several variants on the GARCH (1,1) model have been studied in the literature. Here are a few examples:

### ARCH (q)

The earliest version of GARCH was the ARCH model introduced in Engle (1982). In ARCH models, persistence arises only from the shock terms $\epsilon_t$ and not from previous values of variance. The ARCH $(q)$ model is defined by

$$\sigma_t^2 = \beta + \sum_{i=1}^{q} \zeta_i \epsilon_{t-i}^2 \tag{16.23}$$

The effect of a return shock $m$ periods ago ($1 \leq m \leq q$) depends on the parameter $\zeta_m$. The higher is this parameter, the more an earlier return shock continues to matter. In general, we would expect to have $\zeta_1 \geq \zeta_2 \geq \cdots \geq \zeta_q$, so recent shocks to return matter more. In an ARCH $(q)$ model, shocks to returns that occurred more than $q$ periods ago have no impact at all on current variance.

### GARCH $(p, q)$

The ARCH $(q)$ model was generalized to the GARCH $(p, q)$ model by Bollerslev (1986). Here, $\sigma_t^2$ depends not only on lagged values of the $\epsilon$'s but also on lagged values of variance:

$$\sigma_t^2 = \beta + \sum_{i=1}^{p} \gamma_i \sigma_{t-i}^2 + \sum_{i=1}^{q} \zeta_i \epsilon_{t-i}^2 \qquad (16.24)$$

The GARCH $(p, q)$ model is an infinite-order ARCH model: a shock to returns today affects variance tomorrow and through the variance, affects variance the day after, and so on infinitely. The GARCH $(1, 1)$ model defined earlier is the special case of (16.24) in which $p = q = 1$ and is the most popular version of the GARCH $(p, q)$ model.

### GJR GARCH

Glosten, Jagannathan, and Runkle (1993) introduced a variant of GARCH designed to capture asymmetry. In GARCH $(1,1)$ form, their model is

$$\sigma_t^2 = \beta + \gamma \sigma_{t-1}^2 + \zeta \epsilon_{t-1}^2 + \delta I_{t-1} \epsilon_{t-1}^2 \qquad (16.25)$$

where $I_{t-1}$ is an indicator variable that takes the value 1 if $\epsilon_{t-1} < 0$, and is zero otherwise. The parameter $\delta > 0$ is designed to capture the asymmetric behavior of markets where volatility rises as markets fall (the "leverage effect"). In the specification (16.25), $\epsilon_{t-1} < 0$, which may be thought of as "bad news," has a greater impact on time-$t$ volatility than "good news" ($\epsilon_{t-1} \geq 0$). The GJR GARCH model offers an excellent example of the flexibility afforded the modeler by the GARCH setting, in this case, the ability to build in the market's asymmetric responses into the volatility process.

### Asymmetric GARCH

Asymmetric GARCH or AGARCH was introduced in Engle (1990). In GARCH $(1,1)$ form, his specification is

$$\sigma_t^2 = \beta + \gamma \sigma_{t-1}^2 + \zeta (\epsilon_{t-1} - c)^2 \qquad (16.26)$$

If $c$ is positive, then negative shocks $\epsilon_{t-1} < 0$ will have a greater impact on period-$t$ variance $\sigma_t^2$ than positive shocks $\epsilon_{t-1} \geq 0$. This builds in an asymmetric response along the lines of the "leverage effect."

### Exponential GARCH

Exponential GARCH or EGARCH was introduced in Nelson (1991). The EGARCH model has subsequently been adopted and studied in many forms. The EGARCH $(1,1)$ model has the specification

$$\ln[\sigma_t^2] = \beta + \gamma \ln[\sigma_{t-1}^2] + \zeta \frac{\epsilon_{t-1}}{\sqrt{h_{t-1}}} + \psi \left[ \frac{|\epsilon_{t-1}|}{\sqrt{h_{t-1}}} - \sqrt{\frac{2}{\pi}} \right] \qquad (16.27)$$

By running the equation in the logarithm of the variance, the system results in a nonlinear form of the GARCH model.

## GARCH Models and Option Pricing

GARCH models have found favor with modelers for many reasons. They have been found to describe empirical stock price series very well. The model is parsimonious in the number of parameters and so does not lead to very complex process formulations. Yet it is a flexible one; for example, in its asymmetric forms, it provides for both the skewness and kurtosis distortions that have been documented in empirical returns. Estimation of GARCH models is made simple in part by the fact that GARCH increments are conditionally normal, making the transition density functions for the process easy to write down.

Duan (1995) describes option pricing under GARCH processes. A key step lies in identifying the risk-neutral GARCH process. In the case of the Asymmetric GARCH (1,1) model, the risk-neutral evolution of the stock price over the interval $[t, t + 1]$ may be described as follows. Let $\eta_t \sim N(0, 1)$ be a series of i.i.d. variables, and let $v_t = \sigma_t^2$ denote the variance over the period $[t - 1, t]$. Then, the following pair of equations describes the model:

$$S_t = S_{t-1} \exp\left[\left(r - \frac{1}{2}v_t\right) + \sqrt{v_t}\eta_t\right] \qquad (16.28)$$

$$v_t = \beta + \gamma v_{t-1} + \zeta v_t(\epsilon_{t-1} - k)^2 \qquad (16.29)$$

where $r$ is the risk-free interest rate over the interval and $k$ is a constant. ($k = 0$ corresponds to the GARCH (1,1) model.) Note that the variance equation has four parameters: $\beta, \gamma, \zeta$, and $k$.

Implementing a GARCH option pricing model comprises two steps: (a) estimating the parameters of the model, and (b) using the estimated process to compute option values. Estimation involves calibrating five parameters, i.e., $\{\beta, \gamma, \zeta, k, v_0\}$, where $v_0$ is the initial volatility. Computing option values may be done by Monte Carlo simulation or by building an approximating lattice model as in Ritchken and Trevor (1999).

## Calibration and Simulation of a GARCH Process

If we denote the logarithm of the stock price as $x_t = \ln(S_t)$, then $x_t$ is conditionally normally distributed with

$$E(x_t) = \mu_t = x_{t-1} + r - \frac{1}{2}v_t \qquad (16.30)$$

$$Var(x_t) = v_t = \sigma_t^2 \qquad (16.31)$$

Given this, the conditional probability density of each transition of the process is

$$f[x_t|x_{t-1}] = \frac{1}{\sqrt{2\pi \eta_t^2}} \exp[-0.5(x_{t+1} - \mu_t)^2/\eta_t^2]$$

Then, given a series of log stock prices, $x_0, x_1, \ldots, x_T$, we may estimate the parameters by maximizing the log-likelihood of the time series, i.e.,

$$\max_\theta \ln \left[\prod_{t=0}^{T-1} f[x_t|x_{t-1}]\right] \equiv \max_\theta \sum_{t=0}^{T-1} \ln f[x_t|x_{t-1}]$$

where $\theta$ is the parameter set $\{\beta, \gamma, \zeta, k, v_0\}$.

A simpler approach to the calibration problem is as follows. From equation (16.28), we may write the error term as

$$\eta_t = \frac{1}{\sqrt{v_t}}\left[\ln(S_t/S_{t-1}) - r + \frac{1}{2}v_t\right]$$

Since this is conditionally normal in distribution, we may write down the log-likelihood estimator as

$$\max_{\theta} \sum_{t=0}^{T-1} \ln\{\phi(\epsilon_{t+1})\}$$

where $\phi(.)$ is the function for the density of the standard normal.

Once the parameters are obtained, equations (16.28) and (16.29) may be used to generate sample paths for the stock price. Based on these sample paths, a simulated estimator of option value is easily computed. This is considered in detail in Chapter 36, where we take up the topic of simulation and deal with particular examples of GARCH processes.

Barone-Adesi, Engle, and Mancini (2004) propose a method for computing option prices based on GARCH models in which volatility of the pricing process (i.e., in the risk-neutral world) is not the same as volatility of the asset returns. Despite the growth in popularity of GARCH models, Duan, Ritchken, and Sun (2005) argue that such models alone cannot fit observed option prices well unless the process is also enhanced by jumps.

# 16.5   Other Approaches

This is a technical section that may be skipped without loss of continuity. Its purpose is to introduce two further classes of models, log-stable models and variance-gamma models.

The continuous-time models we have looked at thus far all take as their foundation Brownian motion processes or Poisson processes. Brownian motions and Poisson processes (as also their combination, jump-diffusion processes) are special cases of a general class of processes known as Levy processes. A Levy process $L_t$ is a right-continuous process that

1. Begins at zero: $L_0 = 0$.
2. Has stationary increments: for $t > s$, the distribution of $L_t - L_s$ depends only on $t - s$.
3. Has independent increments: for $t > s$, the distribution of $L_t - L_s$ is independent of how the process got to $L_s$.
4. Satisfies stochastic continuity: for all $s \geq 0$ and $a > 0$, the probability that $|L_{t+s} - L_s| > a$ goes to zero as $t \to s$.

A Levy process has characteristic function

$$F(\phi) = E[e^{i\phi L_t}] = \exp\left[t\left(i\alpha\phi - \frac{1}{2}\sigma^2\phi^2 + \int_{\mathbb{R}}[e^{i\phi x} - 1 - i\phi x \mathbf{1}_{|x|<1}]\,v(dx)\right)\right].$$

Here, $\alpha$ and $\sigma$ are real constants, and $v(\cdot)$ is a measure on $\mathbb{R}$ that satisfies

$$\int \min\{1, x^2\}v(dx) < \infty$$

The triple $(\alpha, \sigma, v)$ characterizes a Levy process. Brownian motion is the special case of a Levy process with $\alpha = 0$, $\sigma = 1$, and $v = 0$. Levy processes also admit other forms outside the jump-diffusion class. Two examples are "stable" processes, which underlie the log-stable models proposed by Carr and Wu (2003) and the variance-gamma model proposed by Madan, Carr, and Chang (1998).

## Log-Stable Models

As noted earlier in this chapter, the excess kurtosis in jump-diffusion models goes to zero very rapidly as the horizon expands so that returns become nearly normal and the volatility skew becomes almost flat. This is in contrast to empirical observations that indicate that the volatility skew remains quite steep even at very long maturities (Carr and Wu (2003), Foresi and Wu (2005)). Stochastic volatility processes too have the problem that excess kurtosis goes to zero as the horizon increases, although the pattern is different from jump-diffusions; here, the excess kurtosis is hump-shaped, increasing from zero to a maximum and then back to zero again.

To handle this problem, Carr and Wu (2003) develop a model of option pricing using stable processes. Since they posit that the logarithm of the stock price follows a stable process, they call their model "log-stable." This model has one distinguishing feature that separates it from the jump-diffusion model—namely that the shape (in particular, tail fatness) of the terminal distribution of the stock price does not attenuate with horizon.

Stable distributions have the unfortunate property that their moments need not be finite. Even worse, the expected payoffs (functions of the underlying variable) are also not finite. Carr and Wu develop their model using a single exceptional case, that of maximally negative skewness. McCulloch (2003), however, shows that the restrictions of Carr and Wu (2003) are not necessary. He develops a model with finite payoff expectations that may be applied for a wide range of parameters.

### Variance-Gamma Models

Another approach to better calibration of option smiles that also lies within the Levy process class is the variance-gamma (or VG) model (cf. Madan, Carr, and Chang, 1998). The VG process is one where stock price changes occur at random times, and the time interval between changes is governed by a gamma distribution. This distribution is well suited to modeling random times. The amplitude of the stock price change is obtained by observing the increment of a Brownian motion at the random times. Since movements in the stock are permitted only at these random times, the process is unlike a Brownian motion in that it is not continuous but is instead very much like a jump process. However, unlike a Poisson process, where the number of jumps is finite in any time interval, here there may be an infinite number of jumps.

The VG process may be intuitively thought of as a pure jump process where small jumps arrive with very high frequency and large jumps occur rarely. In addition to the diffusion variance (from the underlying observed Brownian motion), the drift of the Brownian motion and the variance of the gamma process allow calibration of the skewness and kurtosis in stock returns. The available evidence suggests that this model may be effective in matching option price smiles even at longer maturities.

## 16.6   Implied Binomial Trees/Local Volatility Models

Local volatility models are, in one sense, a form of stochastic volatility models with a general specification for the evolution of volatility in which volatility may be both time- and state-dependent. In applications, however, such models are used more with a financial engineering bent: the objective is typically to set up a pricing model whose option prices match observed option prices simultaneously at all strikes and maturities. More precisely, we aim to identify the evolution path $\sigma(t, S_t)$ for volatility as a function of future time $t$ and time-$t$ stock price $S_t$ such that the model with this form of stochastic volatility results in option prices that match empirically observed prices for all combinations of strikes $K$ and maturities $T$. The term "local volatilities" refers to the quantities $\sigma(t, S_t)$ unearthed in this procedure.

One implementation of local volatility models involves constructing a binomial tree whose implied option prices match observed levels. In this context, such models are also— and perhaps more descriptively—called "implied binomial trees." We describe the construction of implied binomial trees in this section.

To motivate what implied binomial trees are, imagine first that the standard Black-Scholes model applies and there is no volatility skew (i.e., all options have the same implied volatility). Suppose we wish to construct a binomial tree to match all option prices. There is only a single unknown parameter to be identified, viz., the volatility underlying the tree. We can pick any single option and undertake a simple numerical search and find that value of volatility that causes the price implied by the tree to match the observed option price. Since all options have the same implied volatility, the tree will also match the prices of all other options at any strike and maturity. This is the simplest kind of "implied binomial tree."

The general procedure aims to do this even when the Black-Scholes model may be invalid, so a volatility skew may be present at every maturity. We can no longer use just a single option; the binomial tree must use information from all options since each may have a different implied volatility. To allow for the best match possible, we must allow the size of the up and down moves and the probabilities of these moves to vary from period to period and from node to node within a period. (The sizes of the up and down moves at a node define precisely the "local volatility" at that node.) It is the construction of such trees that we examine in this section.

The first exposition of implied binomial trees came in three separate papers published in the same year: Derman and Kani (1994), Dupire (1994), and Rubinstein (1994). Our description below essentially follows Derman and Kani.

As an aside, it should be noted that an analytical formula for local volatilities was described by Dupire (1994) and generalized by Andersen and Brotherton-Ratcliffe (1997). Suppose there are sufficiently many traded call options that the observed *market* prices can be represented as a smooth function $C(T, K)$ of strike and maturity. Let $C_T(T, K)$ and $C_K(T, K)$ denote the partial derivatives of $C$ with respect to $T$ and $K$, respectively, and let $C_{KK}(T, K)$ denote the second partial derivative with respect to $K$. Then, the local volatilities are given by

$$\sigma(T, K) = \frac{2}{K^2 C_{KK}(T, K)} \left[ C_T(T, K) - (r - q)C + K(r - q)C_K(T, K) \right] \quad \textbf{(16.32)}$$

Anderson and Brotherton-Ratcliffe describe the implementation of (16.32) using the implicit finite-difference method. Finite-difference methods are described in Chapter 35.

## A Word of Advice

A word of advice to the reader may be appropriate here. The technique of implied binomial trees is not a difficult one to follow, but it is also not a trivial extension of the standard binomial tree construction. There is no better way for the reader to understand the fitting procedure than to work through the approach alongside the text using pencil and paper, i.e., one needs to dirty one's hands with the material to truly "get it." The original papers on which this section is based do provide some detail, but they are written for financial engineers rather than for beginners. Hence, our development is intentionally copious, allowing the reader to follow each single calculation that goes into the development of the tree. The example developed here extends over many periods so that a full exposition is provided. In the final analysis, it is probably true that the best way to learn these models is to write program code for their implementation. The more adventurous students who decide to go that route will certainly find the end result greatly satisfying.

## Notation and Preliminaries

There are two goals to the tree-building procedure on which we are about to embark:

1. To build a tree that fits the prices of all observed options on a maturity ($T$) and strike ($K$) grid.

**FIGURE 16.6**
The Stock Price Tree

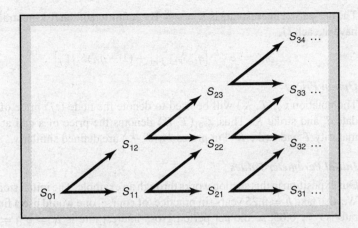

2. To ensure the tree is recombining. This ensures that the numerical procedure will run fast and will calibrate rapidly.

Since the implied binomial tree approach aims to match observed option prices, these observed prices—or equivalently the entire volatility surface (the plot of implied volatilities against strikes and maturities)—are taken as an input. By interpolating between the implied volatilities of different traded strikes and maturities, we can "fill in" the entire surface, so we may assume in the construction of the tree that we know the price of an option with any desired strike and maturity. (While we do not describe the filling-in procedure here, we note that it can be a non-trivial exercise to get a smooth surface from the given data points. Even single "bad" data points can create problems.) We also assume that put-call parity holds, so calls and puts with a given strike and maturity have the same implied volatilities.

### *Stock Prices*

Since the size of up and down moves may differ from node to node, we will need a convenient notation to represent stock price evolution on the tree. We use the notation pictured in Figure 16.6. A typical node is denoted $tj$, with $S_{tj}$ denoting the stock price at node $tj$. The first subscript stands for the time period and the second for the node number at that period. Higher values of $j$ denote higher stock prices. Specifically, note that in a recombining tree, there are $(t + 1)$ distinct nodes at the end of $t$ periods. These nodes are numbered $S_{t,1}, \ldots, S_{t,t+1}$ in our scheme with

$$S_{t,1} \; < \; S_{t,2} \; < \cdots < \; S_{t,t+1}$$

Thus, the initial stock price is $S_{01}$. After one period, the price can register a "down" move to $S_{11}$ or an "up" move to $S_{12}$. More generally, from any price $S_{tj}$, the price can either move down to $S_{t+1,j}$ or up to $S_{t+1,j+1}$. The implicit up- and down-move sizes at the node $tj$ are just

$$u_{tj} \;=\; \frac{S_{t+1,j+1}}{S_{tj}} \qquad d_{tj} \;=\; \frac{S_{t+1,j}}{S_{tj}}$$

In general, these up and down moves could vary across $t$ and $j$. To keep unnecessary notation to a minimum, we will not refer to the quantities $u_{tj}$ and $d_{tj}$ in the remainder of this section, and rely on the stock price notation alone instead.

### *Other Tree Notation*

The risk-neutral probability of an up move at node $tj$ is denoted $q_{tj}$, so $1 - q_{tj}$ is the probability of a down move. As usual, $h$ will denote the length of one period in the binomial tree measured in years, and $r$ the interest rate expressed in continuously-compounded terms.

The per-period interest rate is $R = e^{rh}$. By definition of the risk-neutral probability, we must have at each $tj$,

$$S_{tj} = e^{-rh} \left[ q_{tj} S_{t+1,j+1} + (1 - q_{tj}) S_{t+1,j} \right] \qquad \textbf{(16.33)}$$

### Option Prices

The notation $C_{tj}(T, K)$ will be used to denote the node-$(tj)$ price of a call with maturity date $T$ and strike $K$. Thus, $C_{01}(T, K)$ denotes the price of a call at the initial date with maturity $T$ and strike $K$. Put prices $P_{tj}(T, K)$ are defined similarly.

### Initial Parameter Values

Our exposition in this section works through an example. The initial stock price is $S_{01} = 100$. We also take $h = 0.25$ years (in practice, of course, one would use a finer tree). The interest rate is $r = 0.05$, so the per-period gross interest rate is $R = e^{rh} = 1.0126$. Finally, the initial price of a one-period at-the-money call, $C_{01}(h, S_{01})$ in the notation defined above, is taken to be 5. Further option prices will be introduced as we go along.

## How We Proceed

The construction of an implied binomial tree proceeds by a form of forward induction. We first build a one-period tree, then a two-period tree on top of that, then a three-period tree on top of the two-period tree, and so on. We provide a description of the general procedure here and then specialize this procedure to building the first three periods of the tree in the numerical example.

Suppose we have built the $(t - 1)$-period tree. That is, we know all the nodes up to the end of time $(t - 1)$ and all the (risk-neutral) probabilities of up and down moves to this point. In the next step, we have to determine a total of $2t + 1$ variables: (a) the $(t + 1)$ prices that can occur at the end of $t$ periods (i.e., the prices $S_{t,1}, \ldots, S_{t,t+1}$) and (b) the $t$ probabilities of an "up" move, one at each of the $t$ nodes at the end of the $(t - 1)$-period tree. We require a total of $2t + 1$ equations to solve for these variables.

Our first step is to eliminate one of these by a "centering" condition analogous to that used in the CRR binomial model:

- If $t$ is even—that is, if there are an odd number of nodes at the end of $t$ periods—we set the middle node equal to the initial price $S_{01}$.
- If $t$ is odd, so there are an even number of prices at the end of $t$ periods, we let $S_{t,m_1}$ and $S_{t,m_2}$ denote the two middle prices, and impose the condition $S_{t,m_1} S_{t,m_2} = (S_{01})^2$.

This centering condition is an engineering imposition, not an economic one, but it has the benefit of balancing out the tree. It provides us with one of the $2t + 1$ conditions we need. A further set of $t$ conditions is provided by the risk-neutral pricing condition (16.33): at each of the $t$ nodes at the end of $t - 1$ periods, we must have

$$S_{t-1j} = e^{-rh} \left[ q_{t-1,j} S_{t,j+1} + (1 - q_{t-1,j}) S_{t,j} \right], \qquad j = 1, \ldots, t \quad \textbf{(16.34)}$$

The final $t$ conditions are obtained by considering the prices of $t$ options maturing at the end of period $t$. Of course, we may use any $t$ options for this purpose, but we choose a specific set of $t$ options to make both exposition and computation simple: namely, options with strikes equal to the $t$ terminal prices at the end of $t - 1$ periods, $S_{t-1,1}, \ldots, S_{t-1,t}$. The reason is just that when viewed from the node $S_{t-1,j}$, the option with strike $S_{t-1,j}$ will finish in-the-money at only one of the two terminal nodes that arise next period, and this makes computing its price simple. For strike prices that lie at or above the initial stock price, we use call options, while for strikes that lie below the stock price, we use put options.

**FIGURE 16.7**   The Completed Local Volatility Model Tree

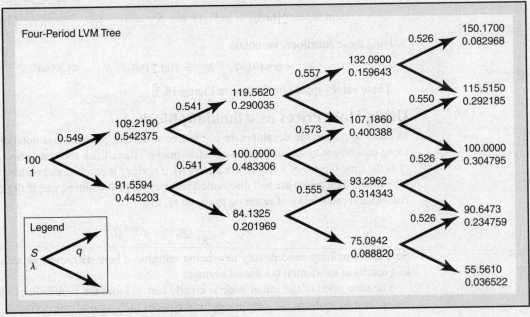

Note that the construction of the $t$-th period of the binomial tree uses $t$ options maturing in $t$ periods. This means that the constructed binomial tree can match up to $t$ points on the volatility skew of $t$-period options. Thus, for example, if each period in the binomial tree represents one trading day and we take a month to have 22 trading days, the model can match the implied volatilities of 22 different one-month options.

This, then, is the general procedure. A detailed example follows. The entire final tree depicting the results of the computations is presented in Figure 16.7. This diagram will be referenced repeatedly as we work through the example below.

### Calibrating the First Period

The first step in the construction of the tree is to solve for the values at the end of one period on the tree. There are three variables to be solved for: the prices $S_{11}$ and $S_{12}$ at the end of one period, and the probability $q_{01}$ of an "up" move in the first period. One condition on these three objects is given by the risk-neutral pricing condition (16.34); specialized to period 0, this is

$$S_{01}e^{rh} = q_{01}S_{12} + (1 - q_{01})S_{11} \tag{16.35}$$

Observe that the left-hand side is just the one-period forward price of the stock at the node 01. (This follows from the usual forward pricing arguments; see Chapter 3.) Writing $F_{01}$ for this forward price, (16.35) may equivalently be written as

$$F_{01} = q_{01}S_{12} + (1 - q_{01})S_{11} \tag{16.36}$$

For the second condition, consider a one-period call option with a strike of 100. Suppose that the initial price of this call is 5. Then the call finishes in-the-money if the stock price goes up to $S_{12}$ but not if it goes down to $S_{11}$, so the risk-neutral call pricing condition is

$$5 = e^{-rh}\left[q_{01}(S_{12} - 5) + (1 - q_{01}) \cdot 0\right] \tag{16.37}$$

For the third condition, we impose the "centering" condition mentioned above:

$$\ln S_{01} = \frac{1}{2}[\ln S_{11} + \ln S_{12}] \quad \Leftrightarrow \quad S_{01}^2 = S_{11} \cdot S_{12} \qquad \textbf{(16.38)}$$

Solving these equations, we obtain

$$q_{01} = 0.549197, \quad S_{12} = 109.2190, \quad S_{11} = 91.5594$$

These values appear on the tree in Figure 16.7.

## Using State Prices as a Building Block

In order to pursue the development of the tree to further periods, it is notationally much more convenient to use the notion of "state prices." Recall that the state price $\lambda_{tj}$ at node $tj$ is the time-0 price of a security that pays \$1 if node $tj$ is reached and nothing otherwise. Obviously, state prices are just discounted risk-neutral probabilities, i.e., if $Q_{tj}$ denotes the risk-neutral probability of reaching the node $tj$, then

$$\lambda_{tj} = \frac{1}{R^t} Q_{tj} = e^{-rth} Q_{tj}$$

So there is nothing conceptually new being introduced here. However, as we see shortly, this results in substantial notational savings.

The state price of the initial node is clearly just 1. From the probabilities identified so far, we can write down the state prices for the nodes at the end of one period:

$$\lambda_{01} = 1.000000$$

$$\lambda_{12} = 0.542375 = e^{-0.05h}(0.549197)$$

$$\lambda_{11} = 0.445203 = e^{-0.05h}(1 - 0.549197)$$

Thus, there are three numbers that characterize a node $tj$: the stock price $S_{tj}$, the probability of an up move at that node $q_{tj}$, and the state price $\lambda_{tj}$:

$$\boxed{\text{Node } (t,j): \{S_{tj}, q_{tj}, \lambda_{tj}\}}$$

To avoid legitimate confusion, we stress the following:

- $q_{tj}$ is the probability of an up move *from* node $tj$.
- $\lambda_{tj}$ is the time-0 state price of node $tj$, i.e., it is the risk-neutral probability of *reaching* node $tj$ discounted at the risk-free rate back to the initial node.

In this format, the tree so far appears as follows (depicting the available information as we have at the current stage of development of the tree):

$$\text{Node } (0, 1): \quad \{100, 0.549197, 1.00\}$$

$$\text{Node } (1, 2): \quad \{109.2190, q_{12}, 0.542375\}$$

$$\text{Node } (1, 1): \quad \{91.5594, q_{11}, 0.445203\}$$

The probabilities $q_{11}$ and $q_{12}$ are, as yet, undetermined. They will be identified once we solve for the second period of the tree. We turn to this now.

## The Second Period

To complete the tree for the second period, we need to solve for the three stock prices that are consistent with the prices of two-period options. These three stock prices are $S_{21}$, $S_{22}$, and $S_{23}$. We also need to determine the likelihoods of up moves from the two first-period nodes, $q_{12}$ and $q_{11}$. This gives us a total of five unknowns.

We begin by setting the middle node $S_{22} = S_{01} = 100$. This "centers" the tree around the initial price as in the CRR solution for the simple binomial tree and removes one unknown from the analysis. To identify the remaining two stock prices, $S_{23}$ and $S_{21}$, and the risk-neutral probabilities $q_{12}$ and $q_{11}$, we use options. Specifically, for the upper node, we use a call option with strike $S_{12}$, and for the lower node, we use a put option with strike $S_{11}$. Note that the call is out-of-the-money at the initial node $S_{01}$, as is the put. Suppose the initial prices of these two options are 3 and 1.50, respectively.

We proceed in two stages:

1. We first solve for the upper half of the tree using the call price. This gives the values of $S_{23}$ and $q_{12}$.

2. Next we solve for the lower half of the tree using the put price. This gives the values of $S_{21}$ and $q_{11}$.

### (A) Upper Half of Period 2 Tree

To find $q_{12}$ and $S_{23}$, we need two equations. One is given by the usual forward price condition: letting $F_{12} = e^{rh}S_{12}$, we have

$$F_{12} = q_{12}S_{23} + (1 - q_{12})S_{22} \qquad (16.39)$$

The second is given by the call-pricing equation. Since the call has a strike of $S_{12}$, it finishes in-the-money if the stock price goes up to $S_{23}$ but out-of-the-money if the price goes down to $S_{22}$. Thus, the value of the call at the stock price $S_{12}$ is given by

$$e^{-rh}q_{12}(S_{23} - S_{12})$$

Now, a dollar of payoffs at node $(1, 2)$ has a time-0 value of $\lambda_{12}$. Thus, the time-0 value of the call is

$$C = \lambda_{12}e^{-rh}q_{12}(S_{23} - S_{12}) \qquad (16.40)$$

The call value is given to be 3. Substituting for the other known values and solving (16.39)–(16.40), we obtain

$$q_{12} = 0.541476, \quad S_{23} = 119.5620$$

Refer to Figure 16.7 for the upper half of the second-period tree.

### (B) Lower Half of Period 2 Tree

In the lower half of the tree, we apply the same arguments using the chosen put instead of the call. The first equation is again the forward pricing equation:

$$F_{11} = q_{11}S_{22} + (1 - q_{11})S_{21}$$

The second is the put pricing equation. The put has a strike of $S_{11}$, so it finishes in-the-money if the stock price goes down to $S_{21}$ and out-of-the-money if the stock price goes up to $S_{22}$. So we have:

$$P = \lambda_{11}e^{-rh}(1 - q_{11})(S_{11} - S_{21})$$

The put value is given to be 1.50. Substituting this and other known values in the two equations, we can solve for $q_{11}$ and $S_{21}$:

$$q_{11} = 0.540638, \quad S_{21} = 84.1325$$

Refer to the lower half of the tree, which appears in Figure 16.7.

### State Prices after Two Periods

Along with the three stock prices at the end of the second period, given that we have also solved for the branching probabilities, we can also compute the state prices. These are as follows:

$$\lambda_{23} = e^{-rh}\lambda_{12}q_{12} = 0.290035$$
$$\lambda_{22} = e^{-rh}[(1 - q_{12})\lambda_{12} + q_{11}\lambda_{11}] = 0.483306$$
$$\lambda_{21} = e^{-rh}(1 - q_{11})\lambda_{11} = 0.201969$$

This completes the development of the tree for the second period.

## The Third Period

In the third period on the tree, we are to determine four stock prices ($S_{31}$, $S_{32}$, $S_{33}$, and $S_{34}$), and three risk-neutral probabilities ($q_{21}$, $q_{22}$, and $q_{23}$). Since there are now two middle nodes, the "centering" condition takes the form it did in the first period. We carry out the tree building scheme in three steps:

1. Solve for the two middle nodes. For this, we will use a call with strike $S_{22}$, whose initial (time-0) price is taken to be 8.
2. Solve for the upper half of the tree. For this, we will use a call with strike $S_{23}$, whose initial price is taken to be 2.
3. Solve for the lower half of the tree. For this, we will use a put with strike $S_{21}$, whose initial price is taken to be 1.

### (A) Solving for the Middle Nodes

The two middle nodes are $S_{33}$ and $S_{32}$. To solve for these, we will set this up as a solution of three equations to solve for $q_{22}$, $S_{33}$, and $S_{32}$. These equations are as follows:

- A symmetry equation, centering the two stock prices around the initial stock price, i.e.,

$$S_{22}^2 = S_{33} \cdot S_{32}$$

- The forward pricing equation, i.e.,

$$F_{22} = e^{rh}S_{22} = q_{22}S_{33} + (1 - q_{22})S_{32}$$

- One call-pricing equation for the ATM (i.e., $S_{22}$) strike:

$$C(3h, S_{22}) = e^{-rh}(S_{33} - S_{22})\, q_{22}\,\lambda_{22}$$
$$+ e^{-rh}(S_{33} - S_{22})(1 - q_{23})\,\lambda_{23}$$
$$+ e^{-rh}(S_{34} - S_{22})\, q_{23}\,\lambda_{23}$$

This equation may be rewritten as follows:

$$e^{rh}C(3h, S_{22}) = \lambda_{22}q_{22}(S_{33} - S_{22})$$
$$+ \lambda_{23}[q_{23}S_{34} + (1 - q_{23})S_{33} - S_{22}]$$
$$= \lambda_{22}q_{22}(S_{33} - S_{22}) + \lambda_{23}[F_{23} - S_{22}] \quad \textbf{(16.41)}$$

Note that $F_{23}$ is just $e^{rh}S_{23}$. Solving for these three equations, we obtain

$$q_{22} = 0.573221, \quad S_{33} = 107.1860, \quad S_{32} = 93.2962$$

The middle segment of the third period of the tree may be read from Figure 16.7.

### (B) Solving for the Upper Node

With $S_{33}$ known, we can recover the remaining upper part of the stock price tree, i.e., $S_{34}$. For this, we use the price of a call with strike $S_{23}$, which, as mentioned, we take to be 2. To find $q_{23}$ and $S_{34}$, we solve the usual two equations, one the forward pricing equation, and the other the option-pricing equation:

$$F_{23} = e^{rh} S_{23} = q_{23} S_{34} + (1 - q_{23}) S_{33}$$
$$C(3h, S_{23}) = q_{23}(S_{34} - S_{23}) \, e^{-rh} \, \lambda_{23}$$

Since $C(3h, S_{23})$ is given to be 2, we can easily solve these equations to obtain

$$q_{23} = 0.557351, \quad S_{34} = 132.0900$$

### (C) Solving for the Lower Node

Using the value of $S_{32}$, we can recover the remaining lower part of the stock price tree, i.e., $S_{31}$. We begin by using the following put option price as given

$$P(3h, S_{21}) = C(0.75, 84.1325) = 1$$

To find $q_{21}$ and $S_{31}$, we solve the following two equations (again, the forward price equation and the option pricing equation):

$$F_{21} = e^{rh} S_{21} = q_{21} S_{32} + (1 - q_{21}) S_{31}$$
$$P(3h, S_{21}) = q_{21}(S_{21} - S_{31}) \, e^{-rh} \, \lambda_{21}$$

Substituting for the known values and solving, we obtain

$$q_{21} = 0.554697, \quad S_{31} = 75.0942$$

Finally, we can compute the four state prices, which are:

$$\lambda_{34} = \lambda_{23} \, q_{23} \, e^{-rh} = 0.159643$$
$$\lambda_{33} = [(1 - q_{23})\lambda_{23} + q_{22} \, \lambda_{22}]e^{-rh} = 0.400388$$
$$\lambda_{32} = [(1 - q_{22})\lambda_{22} + q_{21} \, \lambda_{21}]e^{-rh} = 0.314343$$
$$\lambda_{31} = (1 - q_{21})\lambda_{21} \, e^{-rh} = 0.088820$$

## Recap of the Local Volatility Approach

The three-period tree is sufficient to demonstrate all the mechanics required for building the stock price so as to be consistent with the local volatility surface. Repetition of the same ideas to subsequent periods extends the tree as far out as is required. An extension of the same tree to four periods is presented in Appendix 16E. The reader may wish to attempt building the fourth period and then check the results against those in the appendix. The appendix provides somewhat more general mechanics that may be skipped unless the reader wishes to undertake a full-blown implementation of the model. It does not provide any new conceptual developments over what has been covered in this section already.

At each stage of the model, we invoked the necessary at-the-money (ATM) option price (call or put) as was required. These ATM strikes are determined as we build the tree, i.e., as we determine subsequent stock prices. There is no reason for options with exactly these strikes to be actually traded in the market. Hence, in the tree-building procedure, we need to interpolate the prices of options from neighboring ones that have traded prices.

To recap, we used the prices of calls and puts of different strikes and maturities to calibrate the stock price tree. The options used are presented in Figure 16.8. The options used at each stage of the calibration are presented at the node where they are used.

**FIGURE 16.8**

The Option Prices
Used for Calibration

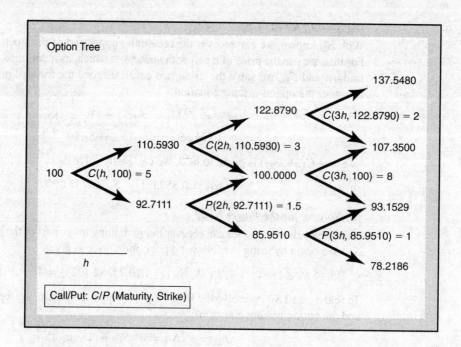

Option Tree

137.5480

122.8790        $C(3h, 122.8790) = 2$

110.5930    $C(2h, 110.5930) = 3$        107.3500

100    $C(h, 100) = 5$        100.0000    $C(3h, 100) = 8$

92.7111        $P(2h, 92.7111) = 1.5$        93.1529

85.9510    $P(3h, 85.9510) = 1$

*h*        78.2186

Call/Put: *C/P* (Maturity, Strike)

We use calls to calibrate the upper portion of the tree, and puts for the lower portion. We summarize some of the mechanics one more time:

1. The calibration procedure is a bootstrapping one. We start with the one-period option and subsequently use for each period longer maturity options. The options used vary in strike and maturity, i.e., represent discrete points on the local volatility surface. The usual approach is to determine the upper prices on the stock tree using calls and the lower prices using puts.

2. In each period, there are either an even or an odd number of stock prices to be determined. If the number is odd, then the middle stock price is set to the current price of the stock. Then a series of equations is used to determine the upper stock prices, and, likewise, a separate system of equations is used for the lower stock prices. The usual system of equations comprises the following:

   • An equation for the forward price of the stock.

   • An equation for the ATM call or put price.

   • An additional equation if required, usually an imposition of symmetry on the lattice, which is nothing but another form of interpolation between stock prices. However, it does provide a necessary additional identification condition for fixing stock prices on the tree.

3. If the number of stock prices is even, then the two middle prices are determined initially using a system of equations (three types as described previously). Once these are known, the upper half of the tree is calibrated separately, and so is the lower half. The procedure followed is the same.

The approach of fitting implied binomial trees is a practical one since it is based on relative pricing and the uncovering of the stock price process that is consistent with the prices of options across a range of strikes and maturities. Once the lattice in stock prices is uncovered, it may be examined to infer what type of stochastic process equity prices may be following or, more simply, to what extent the evolution of the stock price deviates from the assumptions of the Black-Scholes model, essentially in that returns are not normal or constant at all points in time.

## 16.7   Summary

Empirical asset price return distributions tend to depart from normality in important ways. The presence of non-normality results in the option smile, which is one diagnostic of the extent to which option prices in the market deviate from prices that would arise in a Black-Scholes model. Several variants and alternatives to the Black-Scholes model have been proposed to capture these departures from normality.

In this chapter, we have looked at a selection of these alternatives: jump-diffusion models, stochastic volatility models, GARCH models, and implied tree models. Each of these classes of models is motivated by a specific shortcoming of the Black-Scholes approach: discontinuities in observed price processes (jump-diffusions), non-constant volatility with persistence in volatility (stochastic volatility and GARCH), and the presence and variations in the shape of implied volatility smiles (local volatility models).

Each class of models obtains some improvement over Black-Scholes, but none is also a completely satisfactory resolution of the non-normality problem. This has led to the proposal of several further, and technically more sophisticated, alternatives such as the variance-gamma model and the "log-stable" model, as well as models based on stable-Paretian and inverse-Gaussian processes. The last word on this topic is far from written.

## 16.8 Exercises

1. What are the shortcomings of the geometric Brownian motion for stock prices that underlies the Black-Scholes option pricing model? For each deficiency, state what modification to the model is likely to provide an improvement.

2. (Difficult) In a jump model for returns, what determines the skewness and kurtosis of the statistical distribution?

3. In a model of stock returns with geometric Brownian motion, where the volatility is assumed to be stochastic, what determines the type of skewness that emerges? What determines the kurtosis?

4. (Very Difficult) Suppose you want to model stock returns $r$ as being driven purely by jumps. The jumps arrive at rate $\lambda = 0.1$ per time interval. When they do arise, they are normally distributed with mean $\mu = -0.05$ and variance $\gamma^2 = 0.50^2$. What is the variance, skewness, and kurtosis of returns?

5. What is the option smile? Why does it arise from fat-tailed stock return distributions?

6. A skewed implied volatility smile occurs more often than a symmetric smile. Why? What model feature is needed to generate this skew?

7. Suppose the S&P index options demonstrate a left-skewed smile. You are an options trader and believe that the smile is steeper than it should be because the market has overestimated the extent of crash risk. You believe that the market will correct its view within the next month. What options trading strategy would you adopt?

8. Suppose the index option smile is symmetric, but you expect it to steepen on both sides. What option strategy would you adopt?

9. (Requires Writing Code) Using the following parameters, price call options for a range of seven strike prices with the Merton jump model.

```
S = 100
K = {70, 80, 90, 100, 110, 120, 130}
T = 0.5 years
rf = 3%
sigma = 0.30
mu = -0.05
gamma = 0.50
lambda = 0.5
```

Now with the seven option prices (one for each strike price), find out what the implied volatility is in the Black-Scholes model. You will need to write program code to find the implied volatility.

Once you have the seven corresponding implied volatilities, plot them against the strike prices. What shape does your options smile have?

10. (Requires Writing Code) Write a program to simulate monthly returns for two years from a process where returns $r$ are drawn from a normal distribution with mean 10% p.a. and standard deviation $\sigma_t$, which follows the risk-neutral process:

$$\sigma_{t+1} = \sigma_t e^{\eta x}, x \sim N(0, 1)$$

The initial stock price is $100 and the initial $\sigma_0 = 0.15$. Each month the stock price grows as follows:

$$S_{t+1} = S_t e_t^r, \quad r_t \sim N(0.10, \sigma_t)$$

(a) Price call options for strikes: 90, 100, 110 with $\eta = 0.1$. Assume the interest rate is zero.

(b) Now set $\eta = 0$ and reprice the options for these strikes. Compare your results with those in (a) and comment.

11. (Requires Writing Code) Write a program to implement the Derman-Kani model for $n$ periods. The inputs are the current stock price and a volatility surface. Your output will be the Derman-Kani tree of stock prices.

12. For a negatively skewed stock return process, what GARCH model would you use? Why?

13. (a) What happens empirically to the option smile with increasing maturity? (b) How is the smirk typically different from the smile? (c) Which markets are characterized by smiles, and which ones display smirks? (d) What is the volatility surface?

14. (Requires Writing Code) Does put-call parity hold in the extended Black-Scholes models? Explain.

15. (Requires Writing Code) Can GARCH models develop an option smile? Simulate option prices (puts and calls) for a maturity of a half year and an initial stock price of $50; let the initial volatility equal 30% per annum. Choose various strike prices and parameter values for the volatility process such that you are able to generate a left skew of implied volatility where the implieds are generated from the Black-Scholes model after prices are generated by the GARCH model.

16. What is the leverage effect? How does it impact option prices? How would you account for the leverage effect in a stochastic volatility equity option model? In a jump-diffusion model?

17. (Requires Writing Code) Using Octave, write a short recursive program to implement the Cox-Ross-Rubinstein model. Run this out six periods. Use the following parameters: initial stock price of $100, strike price of $101, risk-free rate of 5%, volatility is 25%

per annum, and maturity of 1/2 year.

(a) Make sure that the program provides reasonably accurate prices by checking your results against the Black-Scholes formula (the prices will be within the ballpark of the correct prices even though there are very few periods in the model). Use both puts and calls in your validation. Report your results.

(b) Extend the program to allow for an extra negative jump in stock returns of 20% per jump. This jump occurs with probability of 5% (risk neutral). (Now you have three branches emanating from each node.) For the calls and puts reported in the previous question, also report the prices from the jump-enhanced model. What can you say from your comparisons about the effect of jumps?

(c) Now extend the basic program in (a) to incorporate switching volatility. This is a simple volatility process where the volatility can take just one of two values, i.e., 10% or 40%, with equal risk-neutral probability. Volatility is not correlated with the stock price movement. With this addition, there will now be four branches emanating from each node. What can you say from your comparisons about the effect of stochastic volatility? Start with the initial volatility of 25% and then let it switch between 10% and 40%.

(d) Run your program from the previous question with volatility at levels 20% and 30%. Start with initial volatility of 25%. How do prices change in comparison? Explain why. *Note*: Make sure that in each question, you set up the risk-neutral probabilities correctly. You will need to calculate it differently for each of the subparts of this problem.

18. State at least three reasons why the Black-Scholes model has warranted extension in the past decades. What is the impact of these extensions on the stock return distribution. What impact does this have on the prices of calls and puts?

19. In the jump-diffusion model, what parameter needs to be set to develop a sharp negative smirk (asymmetric skew)? What is your answer to this question in the case of the stochastic volatility model?

20. The stock price of Microsoft (MSFT) on December 22 is $26.95. The traded option prices for calls and puts maturing on January 21, February 18, and April 15 (i.e., in one, two, and four months) are as follows:

| Maturity ($T$) | Strike ($K$) | Calls | Puts |
|---|---|---|---|
| January 21 | 27 | 0.45 | 0.35 |
| February 18 | 25 | 2.15 | 0.15 |
| | 27.5 | 0.50 | 0.95 |
| | 30 | 0.05 | NA |
| April 15 | 19.5 | 7.80 | 0.05 |
| | 22 | 5.20 | 0.05 |
| | 24.5 | 2.85 | 0.25 |
| | 27 | 1.10 | 0.95 |
| | 27.5 | 0.80 | 1.25 |
| | 29.5 | 0.25 | 2.61 |
| | 32 | 0.09 | 5.10 |

Use this information to build a three-period implied binomial tree that fits this set of options as best as possible. Each period will be for one calendar month.

Use linear interpolation between option prices as needed. If these prices admit arbitrage, i.e., there is a violation of no-arbitrage relationships among option prices, assume that the closer-to-the-money option is more accurate. As required, decide whether to use calls or puts.

Your tree will have an initial stock price node and three periods thereafter. Since the tree is recombining, you will have altogether 10 nodes on your tree. At each node, show the stock price, the state price, and the branching probability.

21. One of the early extensions to the Black-Scholes model was the constant elasticity of variance (CEV) model for equities. The CEV model assumes the following form of stochastic process for the stock price:

$$dS = \mu S\, dt + \sigma S^\beta\, dZ$$

where the parameters are defined as usual except that $0 < \beta \leq 1$ is the CEV parameter.

(a) What parameter value for $\beta$ results in the Black-Scholes model?

(b) As $\beta$ declines, does the riskiness of the stock increase or decrease?

(c) Explain the linkage of this model to the leverage effect.

## Appendix 16A

# Program Code for Jump-Diffusions

In this section, we describe program code in Octave for implementing the Merton jump-diffusion formula (16.10). The formula involves the infinite sum of Black-Scholes prices. In the program, the sum is truncated to 20 terms, but this may be modified as desired.

```
%Program to compute option values in Merton's 1976 jump-diffusion model
%BASIC INPUTS
%s0 = 100    %Initial stock price
%X = 101     %Strike price
%r = 0.10    %Risk free rate
%sig = 0.25  %Diffusion coefficient
%mu = 0      %Mean jump
%gam = 0.50  %Jump standard deviation
%lambda = 0.1 %Jump arrival frequency per year
%t = 0.25    %Option maturity in years

function u = merton76(s0,X,t,sig,r,lambda,mu,gam)


%INTERMEDIATE VALUES
g = exp(mu + 0.5*gam^2) - 1;
xi = lambda*(1+g);

%COMPUTE OPTION VALUE
optval = 0;
totpoiss = 0;
for k=0:20;     %Assuming that k=20 is large enough for interval t
    eta = sqrt(sig^2 + k*gam^2/t);
    rf = r - lambda*g + k*log(1+g)/t;
    c_bs = bs73(s0,X,t,eta,rf,0,1);
    optval = optval + c_bs*exp(-xi*t)*(xi*t)^k/prod(1:k);
    totpoiss = totpoiss + exp(-xi*t)*(xi*t)^k/prod(1:k);
end;
%printf('totpoiss = %10.4f \n',totpoiss);
u = optval;
```

For the given parameters, the price of the call option is obtained as 6.1366. Note that the program calls the Black-Scholes model function. The code for this function is:

```
%Black-Scholes 1973 model
%s: stock price
%x: exercise price
%t: maturity
%v: volatility
%r: risk free interest rate
%q: dividend rate
%pc: flag, call=1, put=0

function u = bs73(s,x,t,v,r,q,pc);
d1 = (log(s/x)+(r-q+v^2/2)*t)/(v*sqrt(t));
```

```
d2 = d1 - v*sqrt(t);
if pc==1;
    u = s*exp(-q*t)*normal_cdf(d1) - x*exp(-r*t)*normal_cdf(d2);
else
    u = -s*exp(-q*t)*normal_cdf(-d1) + x*exp(-r*t)*normal_cdf(-d2);
end;
```

Here is the program code using the ideas in the Newton-Raphson algorithm to find Black-Scholes implied volatilities.

```
%Program to price a call option using Merton 76 model
% and then use BS 73 to back out the implied vol

function u = jump_ivol(s0,X,t,sig,r,lambda,mu,gam);

jcall = merton76(s0,X,t,sig,r,lambda,mu,gam);
diff = 9999;
ivol = sqrt(sig^2 + lambda*gam^2);
dv = 0.0001;
while diff > 0.00001;
    bspr = bs73(s0,X,t,ivol,r,0,1);
    bspr1 = bs73(s0,X,t,ivol+dv,r,0,1);
    ivol = ivol + (jcall - bspr)/(bspr1 - bspr)*dv;
    diff = abs(jcall - bspr);
end;
u = ivol;
```

## Appendix 16B

# Program Code for a Stochastic Volatility Model

In this section, we describe program code in Octave for implementation of the discrete stochastic volatility model outlined in Section 16.3. The code is in recursive form. Recursion is not always the most optimized implementation approach but it is often the most parsimonious in terms of the amount of code that needs to be written. Simple modification of the code can be carried out to incorporate other stochastic forms for the evolution of volatility.

The main element of the program is the generation of four nodes from a starting node. The recursive program code comprises a function that generates four subsequent nodes as in Figure 16.4. These nodes are fed into the function, which generates another four nodes for each node, and so on. Hence, one can rapidly build up a tree. Note, however, that recursion inherently generates nonrecombining trees, and is thus not always efficient for large trees. The program code must include a stopping rule, i.e., how many steps or nested calls are to be undertaken before the program calls a halt. When it reaches this point, it does not call any more nodes and returns a value based on the nodes where it is.

```
%Program to compute stochastic volatility based option prices
%Uses a recursive algorithm
%s: stock price
%v: initial volatility
%k: strike price
```

```
%T: maturity
%r: risk free interest rate
%kappa: volatility mean reversion
%theta: long run mean volatility
%sigv: volatility of volatility
%rho: correlation of stock change to volatility change
%h: time step
%n: no of periods on the tree

%FUNCTION SVREC
function u = svrec(s,v,k,T,r,kappa,theta,sigv,rho,h,n);
u = exp(v*sqrt(h));
d = 1/u;
s_u = s*u; s_d = s*d;
v_u = v + kappa*(theta - v)*h + sigv*sqrt(v*h); v_u = abs(v_u);
v_d = v + kappa*(theta - v)*h - sigv*sqrt(v*h); v_d = abs(v_d);
p = (exp(r*h) - d)/(u - d);
p_uu = (1+rho)/2*p;
p_ud = (1-rho)/2*p;
p_du = (1-rho)/2*(1-p);
p_dd = (1+rho)/2*(1-p);

%RECURSIVE SEGMENT
if (n*h >= T);
    u = max(0,s-k);
else
    u = (p_uu * svrec(s_u,v_u,k,T,r,kappa,theta,sigv,rho,h,n+1) +
            p_ud * svrec(s_u,v_d,k,T,r,kappa,theta,sigv,rho,h,n+1) +
            p_du * svrec(s_d,v_u,k,T,r,kappa,theta,sigv,rho,h,n+1) +
            p_dd * svrec(s_d,v_d,k,T,r,kappa,theta,sigv,rho,h,n+1)) *
            exp(-r*h);
end;
```

The recursive program is parsimonious. Note the last few lines of the program where the function calls itself four times, once for each of the subsequent nodes. Note also the four lines of code that generate the probabilities for the branches from a node in the quadrinomial tree. These probabilities contain the variable $\rho$ (rho), the correlation between the stock return and the volatility.

The next step is to generate prices from this model. For this, we call the option pricing function defined above from the following "main" program. This main program (as may be seen from the code below) uses the following parameters:

| | |
|---|---|
| Stock price | $s = 100$ |
| Volatility | $v = 0.3$ |
| Risk-free interest rate | $r = 0$ |
| Option maturity | $T = 0.5$ |
| Volatility mean-reversion rate | $\kappa = 0.1$ |
| Volatility mean | $\theta = 0.3$ |
| Volatility of volatility | $\eta = \sigma_v = 0.3$ |
| Correlation of stock and volatility | $\rho = 0$ |
| Time step | $h = 0.1$ |

```
%Program to generate prices for SV model versus Black-Scholes
%Computes the difference between the Black-Scholes and the SV models
clear all;

s = 100;
v = 0.3;
r = 0;
T = 0.5;
kappa = 0.1;
theta = 0.3;
sigv = 0.3;
rho = -0.5;
h = 0.1;

k = [50:10:150]';
lenk = length(k);
bsval = zeros(lenk,1);
svval = zeros(lenk,1);

for j=1:lenk;
        bsval(j) = svrec(s,v,k(j),T,r,0,theta,0,rho,h,0);
        svval(j) = svrec(s,v,k(j),T,r,kappa,theta,sigv,rho,h,0);
end;

plot(k,svval-bsval,";SV-BS;");

[k  svval  bsval]
```

This program computes option prices under both stochastic volatility and the Black-Scholes model. Note how the Black-Scholes model values are computed as special cases of the SV model by setting the mean-reversion parameter $\kappa$ and the volatility of volatility parameter $\eta$ to zero. The program is run for a maturity of half a year ($T = 0.5$) so each step in the tree represents $h = 0.1$ years.

---

**Appendix 16C**

# Heuristic Comments on Option Pricing under Stochastic Volatility

To understand option pricing under stochastic volatility heuristically, we will revisit the concepts studied in the chapter on the mathematics of the Black-Scholes equation. Recall that the Black-Scholes formula can be derived as the solution to a partial differential equation (pde) containing time $t$ and the stock price $S$ as variables. The solution to this pde comes from applying the boundary condition for the payoff of the option that is being valued. This pde is also known as the "fundamental pde." Given the Brownian motion for the stock price $S$, defining the option pricing function as $F(S, t)$, we use Ito's lemma to derive the process for the evolution of $F$, i.e., for $dF$. Then applying the martingale property that $E(dF) = rF\,dt$, we exploit one of the different approaches by which we may arrive at the fundamental pde.

Now, to price an option without solving the fundamental pde (which, barring some simple cases, defeats solution), we might instead wish to compute the expected payoff of the option and take its present value. For a call option, this calculation is as follows:

$$F = e^{-rT} \int_0^\infty \max(0, S_T - K) f(S_T) dS_T$$

where $f(S_T)$ is the probability function of the terminal stock price. Of course, for extended models, we would now need to know the function $f(S_T)$. It turns out that this probability may also be obtained by solving a pde very similar to the fundamental pde.

Suppose the function $F$ above were not the option price but a probability function. Then by the principle of conservation of probability, the expected change in a probability function is zero; therefore, by setting $E(dF) = 0$, we obtain the pde for the probability of the stock price at any time. Recognizing this, Heston was able to solve for the probability function over terminal stock prices even when the stock's volatility is stochastic. More important, Heston showed that, rather than solve the pde for the option price itself, it was in fact easier to solve two pdes, for each of the probability functions, analogous to $N(d_1)$ and $N(d_2)$ in the Black-Scholes model.

Therefore, there are two aspects to the insight of Heston's approach. First, the recognition that every standard option contract, even when based on a more complex stochastic process than Black-Scholes, can be decomposed into two parts, each with a probability function. The second is the realization that it is often easier to solve the pdes for the probability function than for the option price itself. (Technically speaking, the ease comes partly because the boundary condition for the probability function leads to more tractable mathematics than that for the option.) Heston's model spawned a spate of solutions to other option pricing situations, many of which were subsequently recognized as populating the same class of problems. The precise technical details are certainly beyond the scope of this book. The interested reader may refer to a generalized presentation of this entire framework in the paper by Duffie, Pan, and Singleton (2000).

To illustrate how we may derive the probability function quite easily, let's look at a simple example. Suppose we are interested in the probability of the variable $S$'s value after time $t$ where $S$ is governed by the following stochastic process:

$$dS_t = \alpha \, dt + \sigma \, dW_t, \quad S_0 = 0$$

You may recognize this as the familiar arithmetic Brownian motion process. Let's say the probability function is denoted $F(S_t)$. Applying Ito's lemma, we write down the differential process for $F$, i.e.,

$$dF = F_s(\alpha \, dt + \sigma \, dW_t) + \frac{1}{2} F_{ss} \sigma^2 dt + F_t \, dt$$

where the subscripts denote the partial derivative with respect to the variable in the subscript. If we let time run backward, i.e., replace $\tau = -t$, then we have

$$dF = F_s(\alpha \, dt + \sigma \, dW_t) + \frac{1}{2} F_{ss} \sigma^2 dt - F_\tau \, dt$$

where $\tau$ denotes time to maturity or horizon. As one may imagine, this is useful when working with option pricing problems. Since $F$ is a probability function, we have $E(dF) = 0$, and with some minor simplification, this results in the following pde:

$$0 = \alpha F_s + \frac{1}{2} \sigma^2 F_{ss} - F_\tau \qquad \textbf{(16.42)}$$

We solve for a special type of probability function, namely the characteristic function of $S$. The characteristic function of a random variable $S$ is defined as

$$F(S, \tau; \phi) = E[\exp(i\phi S)] \qquad \textbf{(16.43)}$$

where $i = \sqrt{-1}$. Here $\phi$ is known as the characteristic function (CF) variable. Since the CF is an expectation, notice that it is implicitly related to the probability governing $S$. There are several useful properties of the CF such as the fact that it always exists for random variables and that we can recover the probability function for $S$ by an *inversion* of the CF. Hence, our goal is to solve the pde for the CF and then invert it to get the probability function. Another useful property of the CF is that we may obtain the moments (mean, variance, etc.) of the random variable directly from the CF. The $k$-th moment of $S$ is computed as follows:

$$E[S^k] = \frac{1}{i^k} \left[ \frac{\partial^k F}{\partial \phi^k} \right]_{\phi=0}$$

We are now ready to solve the pde for the CF. First, we will need to define the boundary condition for the pde. At maturity, the stock price is known for certain; hence, we have

$$F(S, \tau = 0; \phi) = \exp(i\phi S)$$

Second, we guess a solution. With some experience in these problems, guessing becomes easier! Our guess in this case is

$$F(S, \tau; \phi) = \exp[i\phi S + A(\tau)]$$

We need to solve for the function $A(\tau)$ and once we do, we will have the entire CF. Let's take derivatives of the guessed function to obtain:

$$F_s = i\phi F$$
$$F_{ss} = -\phi^2 F$$
$$F_\tau = A_\tau F$$

We substitute these values into equation (16.42), and we find that $F$ drops out so that we obtain:

$$\alpha i\phi - \frac{1}{2}\sigma^2\phi^2 - A_\tau = 0$$

This is an ordinary differential equation (ode) with a boundary condition $A(\tau) = 0$, which follows from the boundary condition for the pde in equation (16.42). This is an easy ode to solve as simple integration will suffice, and we get the following solution:

$$A(\tau) = \alpha i\phi\tau - \frac{1}{2}\sigma^2\phi^2\tau$$

Substituting this back into our guessed solution, we have

$$F(S, \tau; \phi) = \exp\left[ i\phi S + \alpha i\phi\tau - \frac{1}{2}\sigma^2\phi^2\tau \right] \qquad \textbf{(16.44)}$$

The inversion formula to get the probability density function is

$$f(S) = \frac{1}{2\pi} \int_{-\infty}^{\infty} \text{Re}[e^{-i\phi S}] F(S, \tau; \phi) dS$$

As a cross-check, let's compute the mean (first moment, $k = 1$) of the stock price $S$. We take the solution in equation (16.44) and differentiate it.

$$E(S) = \frac{1}{i}\left[\frac{\partial F}{\partial \phi}\right]_{\phi=0}$$

$$= \frac{1}{i}\left[F(iS + \alpha i\tau - \sigma^2\phi\tau)\right]_{\phi=0}$$

$$= S_0 + \alpha\tau$$

Hence, we have seen how deriving the characteristic function allows us to derive the moments of the stock price as well as obtain the probability density function by inversion of the characteristic function. It is also possible to invert the characteristic function to get the cumulative probability. This is precisely what Heston did in his innovative model for pricing options with stochastic volatility.

## Appendix 16D

# Program Code for Simulating GARCH Stock Prices Distributions

The following Octave program code simulates the stock price distribution for the asymmetric GARCH process of Engle (1990). For a standard GARCH (1,1) process, we simply set $c = 0$.

```
%Program to simulate the nonlinear asymmetric GARCH process
% Assumed that the time interval is daily
% Inputs are on a daily metric (not annualized)
%Simulation is for one year on a daily interval
clear all;

%INPUTS
n = 260;                    %No of trading days in a year
s0 = 100;                   %Initial stock price
sigsq0 = 0.25^2/n;          %Initial Daily variance
r = 0.10/n;                 %Daily interest rate
beta0 = 6.5 * 10^(-6);      %Constant in variance equation
beta1 = 0.92;               %Autoregressive coefficient
beta2 = 0.04;               %Coefficient on innovation term
c = 0.5;                    %Asymmetry parameter (more vol on downside)
m = 50000;                  %No of simulation paths

%SIMULATION
s = s0*ones(m,1);           %Initialize all paths
sigsq = sigsq0*ones(m,1);   %Initialize variance
for t = 1:n;
        shock = randn(m,1);
        sigsq = beta0 + beta1*sigsq + beta2*sigsq.*((shock - c).^2);
        s = s.*exp(r - 0.5*sigsq + sqrt(sigsq).*shock);
end;
```

```
%PLOT HISTOGRAM OF STOCK RETURNS
rets = log(s/s0);
hist(rets,100)
```

```
%COMPUTE THE MOMENTS OF THE RETURNS
[mean(rets)  std(rets)  skewness(rets)  kurtosis(rets)]
```

The simulation program has been optimized using vectorization, and, hence, the reader will find that there is only one loop (over time) and no loop over stock price paths. It should be easy to see the two lines of code with the return equation that propagates the stock price and the volatility equation that propagates volatility.

The program runs 50,000 simulation paths. By setting $c > 0$, we inject negative skewness into the return distribution, and the fatter tails imply that there will be positive excess kurtosis. The simulation run resulted in the following moments of the return distribution (for annual returns).

| | |
|---|---|
| Mean | −0.002273 |
| Standard deviation | 0.252241 |
| Skewness | −0.254104 |
| Excess kurtosis | 0.230780 |

The skewness is negative, and the excess kurtosis is positive as predicted. If we had stipulated that $c < 0$, skewness would be positive.

The same program can also be used to compute the price of a call with a strike price of $X = 101$, using one more line of code as follows:

```
X = 101; exp(-r*n)*mean(max(0,s-X))
```

We ran this piece of code and obtained a call price of 10.003.

# Local Volatility Models: The Fourth Period of the Example

In this appendix, we extend the implied trees (local volatility) model of Section 16.6 to another period and use this analysis to undertake the exposition in more general form.

Here to shorten the exposition, we introduce a simple notation scheme to depict *recombining binomial trees*. These trees have one stock price at the root of the tree. At the end of each period $t$, there will then be $(t + 1)$ nodes.

Recall also that for implied volatility trees, we depict each node as a 3-tuple of the stock price $(S)$, the up branch probability $(p)$, and the state price $(\lambda)$. Hence, a characterization of the $N$-period tree in quasi-diagrammatic form is used in this appendix. Stock prices are highest at the top nodes and lowest at the bottom nodes.

$$S_{01}, q_{01}, \lambda_{01} \rightarrow \ldots \rightarrow \begin{cases} S_{t,t+1}, q_{t,t+1}, \lambda_{t,t+1} \\ \vdots \\ \vdots \\ S_{t,1}, q_{t,1}, \lambda_{t,1} \end{cases} \rightarrow \ldots \rightarrow \begin{cases} S_{N,N+1} \\ \vdots \\ S_{N,k} \\ \vdots \\ S_{N,1} \end{cases}$$

In the section on implied binomial trees, we completed building the tree out to the end of three periods. Using the new diagrammatic notation described above, we may depict the tree at the end of the second and third periods as follows (we also show the unknown stock prices at the end of the fourth period).

$$\rightarrow \begin{cases} 119.2190,\ 0.557351,\ 0.290035 \\ 100.0000,\ 0.573221,\ 0.483306 \\ 84.1325,\ 0.554697,\ 0.201969 \end{cases} \rightarrow \begin{cases} 132.0900,\ q_{34},\ 0.159643 \\ 107.1860,\ q_{33},\ 0.400388 \\ 93.2962,\ q_{32},\ 0.314343 \\ 75.0942,\ q_{31},\ 0.088820 \end{cases} \rightarrow \begin{cases} S_{45} \\ S_{44} \\ S_{43} \\ S_{42} \\ S_{41} \end{cases}$$

We now proceed to solve for the stock prices at the end of the fourth period. There are now an odd number of stock prices to be determined, and so we can set $S_{43} = S_{01} = 100$. As before, we now solve separately for the prices on the upper portion of the tree and the lower portion of the tree.

## Stock Prices on the Upper Portion of the Tree

This involves determining stock prices $S_{44}$ and $S_{45}$ as well as probabilities $q_{33}$, $q_{34}$. Fortunately, this can be done two at a time and does not require finding a solution to all four values simultaneously.

Let's start with the call option at a strike price of $S_{33}$, i.e., $C(4h, S_{33})$. Suppose the value of this option is $6. As before, we develop two equations for our solution of probability $q_{33}$ and stock price $S_{44}$.

- The forward price equation:

$$F_{33} = e^{rh}\ S_{33} = q_{33}S_{44} + (1 - q_{33})S_{43}$$

- The call pricing equation (the reader may refer to previous use of this equation, which is the same):

$$e^{rh}\ C(4h, S_{33}) = \lambda_{33}\ q_{33}[S_{44} - S_{33}] + \sum_{j=4}^{4} \lambda_{3,j}(F_{3,j} - S_{33})$$

$$= \lambda_{33}\ q_{33}[S_{44} - S_{33}] + \lambda_{34}(F_{34} - S_{33})$$

From the first equation, we have that

$$q_{33} = \frac{F_{33} - S_{43}}{S_{44} - S_{43}}$$

Next, substituting $q_{33}$ into the second equation, and rearranging, we get

$$S_{44} = \frac{S_{43}[e^{rh}\ C(4h, S_{33}) - \sum_{j=4}^{4} \lambda_{3,j}(F_{3,j} - S_{33})] - \lambda_{33}\ S_{33}[F_{33} - S_{43}]}{[e^{rh}\ C(4h, S_{33}) - \sum_{j=4}^{4} \lambda_{3,j}(F_{3,j} - S_{33})] - \lambda_{33}\ [F_{33} - S_{43}]} \quad \textbf{(16.45)}$$

$$= \frac{S_{43}[e^{rh}\ C(4h, S_{33}) - \lambda_{34}(F_{34} - S_{33})] - \lambda_{33}\ S_{33}[F_{33} - S_{43}]}{[e^{rh}\ C(4h, S_{33}) - \lambda_{34}(F_{34} - S_{33})] - \lambda_{33}\ [F_{33} - S_{43}]}$$

Every term on the right-hand side of the equation above is already known and, hence, we can retrieve the value of $S_{44}$. This is then used to solve for $q_{33}$. Solving, we have

$$S_{44} = 115.5150, \quad q_{33} = 0.550038$$

These values for $q_{33}$, $S_{44}$ may be used to solve for $q_{34}$, $S_{45}$. Again, we have two equations:

$$F_{34} = e^{rh}\, S_{34} = q_{34}\, S_{45} + (1 - q_{34})\, S_{44}$$

$$C(4h, S_{34}) = e^{-rh}\, q_{34}[S_{45} - S_{34}]\, \lambda_{34}$$

Suppose that $C(4h, S_{34}) = 1.5$. Solving, we have

$$S_{45} = 150.1700, \qquad q_{34} = 0.526245$$

## Stock Prices in the Lower Portion of the Tree

This involves determining stock prices $S_{42}$ and $S_{41}$ as well as probabilities $q_{32}$, $q_{31}$. Again, this can be done two at a time and does not require finding a solution to all four values simultaneously.

Let's start with the put option at a strike price of $S_{32}$, i.e., $P(4h, S_{32})$. Suppose the value of this option is $2. As before, we develop two equations for our solution of probability $q_{32}$ and stock price $S_{42}$.

- The forward price equation:

$$F_{32} = e^{rh}\, S_{32} = q_{32} S_{43} + (1 - q_{33}) S_{42}$$

- The put pricing equation:

$$e^{rh}\, C(4h, S_{32}) = \lambda_{32}\, (1 - q_{32})\, [S_{32} - S_{42}] + \sum_{j=1}^{1} \lambda_{3,j}(S_{32} - F_{3,j})$$

$$= \lambda_{32}\, (1 - q_{32})\, [S_{32} - S_{42}] + \lambda_{31}(S_{32} - F_{31})$$

From the first equation we have that

$$q_{32} = \frac{F_{32} - S_{42}}{S_{43} - S_{42}}$$

or

$$1 - q_{32} = \frac{F_{32} - S_{43}}{S_{42} - S_{43}}$$

Next, substituting $(1 - q_{32})$ into the second equation and rearranging, we get

$$S_{42} = \frac{S_{43}[e^{rh}\, P(4h, S_{32}) - \sum_{j=1}^{1} \lambda_{3,j}(S_{32} - F_{3,j})] + \lambda_{32}\, S_{32}[F_{32} - S_{43}]}{[e^{rh}\, P(4h, S_{32}) - \sum_{j=1}^{1} \lambda_{3,j}(S_{32} - F_{3,j})] + \lambda_{32}\, [F_{32} - S_{43}]} \qquad \textbf{(16.46)}$$

$$= \frac{S_{43}[e^{rh}\, P(4h, S_{32}) - \lambda_{31}(S_{32} - F_{31})] + \lambda_{32}\, S_{32}[F_{32} - S_{43}]}{[e^{rh}\, P(4h, S_{32}) - \lambda_{31}(S_{32} - F_{31})] + \lambda_{32}\, [F_{32} - S_{43}]}$$

Every term on the right-hand side of the equation above is already known and, hence, we can retrieve the value of $S_{42}$. This is then used to solve for $q_{32}$. Solving, we have

$$S_{42} = 90.6473, \qquad q_{32} = 0.408693$$

These values for $q_{32}$, $S_{42}$ may be used to solve for $q_{31}$, $S_{41}$. Again, we have two equations:

$$F_{31} = e^{rh}\, S_{31} = q_{31}\, S_{42} + (1 - q_{31})\, S_{41}$$

$$P(4h, S_{31}) = e^{-rh}\, q_{31}[S_{31} - S_{41}]\, \lambda_{31}$$

Suppose that $P(4h, S_{34}) = 1$. Solving, we have

$$S_{41} = 55.5610, \quad q_{31} = 0.583640$$

As before, we proceed on to compute the state prices as of the end of the fourth period:

$$\lambda_{45} = \lambda_{34}\, q_{34}\, e^{-rh} = 0.082968$$

$$\lambda_{44} = [(1 - q_{34})\lambda_{34} + q_{33}\, \lambda_{33}]e^{-rh} = 0.292185$$

$$\lambda_{43} = [(1 - q_{33})\lambda_{33} + q_{32}\, \lambda_{32}]e^{-rh} = 0.304795$$

$$\lambda_{42} = [(1 - q_{32})\lambda_{32} + q_{31}\, \lambda_{31}]e^{-rh} = 0.234759$$

$$\lambda_{41} = (1 - q_{31})\lambda_{31}\, e^{-rh} = 0.036522$$

Hence, the tree in the last two periods now looks as follows (in $[S, p, \lambda]$ space):

$$\rightarrow \begin{cases} 132.0900,\ 0.526245,\ 0.159643 \\ 107.1860,\ 0.550038,\ 0.400388 \\ 93.2962,\ 0.408693,\ 0.314343 \\ 75.0942,\ 0.583640,\ 0.088820 \end{cases} \rightarrow \begin{cases} 150.1700,\ q_{45},\ 0.082968 \\ 115.5150,\ q_{44},\ 0.292185 \\ 100.0000,\ q_{43},\ 0.304795 \\ 90.6473,\ q_{42},\ 0.234759 \\ 55.5610,\ q_{41},\ 0.036522 \end{cases}$$

# The General Solution Form

As noticed, the stock prices on the upper and lower segments of the tree were computed in closed-form via an iterative procedure. The formulae for the upper and lower sections were somewhat different, although this is hard to notice in the example. To summarize, we present the general form of these equations.

## Upper Tree Stock Prices

This equation is a generalization of equation (16.45):

$$S_{t+1,i+1} = \frac{S_{t+1,i}[e^{rh}\, C((t+1)h, S_{t,i}) - \sum_{j=i+1}^{t+1} \lambda_{t,j}(F_{t,j} - S_{t,i})] - \lambda_{t,i}\, S_{t,i}[F_{t,i} - S_{t+1,i}]}{[e^{rh}\, C((t+1)h, S_{t,i}) - \sum_{j=i+1}^{t+1} \lambda_{t,j}(F_{t,j} - S_{t,i})] - \lambda_{t,i}\, [F_{t,i} - S_{t+1,i}]}$$

and

$$q_{t,i} = \frac{F_{t,i} - S_{t+1,i}}{S_{t+1,i+1} - S_{t+1,i}}$$

## Lower Tree Stock Prices

This equation is a generalization of equation (16.46):

$$S_{t+1,i} = \frac{S_{t+1,i+1}[e^{rh}\, C((t+1)h, P_{t,i}) - \sum_{j=1}^{i-1} \lambda_{t,j}(S_{t,i} - F_{t,j})] + \lambda_{t,i}\, S_{t,i}[F_{t,i} - S_{t+1,i+1}]}{[e^{rh}\, P((t+1)h, S_{t,i}) - \sum_{j=1}^{i-1} \lambda_{t,j}(S_{t,i} - F_{t,j})] + \lambda_{t,i}\, [F_{t,i} - S_{t+1,i+1}]}$$

and

$$q_{t,i} = \frac{F_{t,i} - S_{t+1,i}}{S_{t+1,i+1} - S_{t+1,i}}$$

# Chapter **17**

# Sensitivity Analysis:
# The Option "Greeks"

## 17.1 Introduction

Option pricing models value options given information *at a point in time*. As time passes, changes in the underlying parameter values—the remaining maturity, the price of the underlying, perhaps volatility and interest rates—will cause option values to change. For a trader or risk-manager or investor holding a portfolio of options, the question is: by how much? How sensitive are option prices to different factors? How much will option prices change for a $1 change in the price of the stock? for a 1% change in volatility? How much will the portfolio lose or gain from just the passage of time?

*Sensitivity analysis* provides the answers to these and related questions. It looks at the four main factors that influence option values: the underlying price $S$, the time to maturity $T - t$ of the option, the volatility $\sigma$, and the interest rate $\rho$. Corresponding to these factors, it defines five sensitivity measures that are collectively known as the option "greeks." These are

1. The delta, denoted $\Delta$.
2. The gamma, denoted $\Gamma$.
3. The theta, denoted $\Theta$.
4. The vega, denoted $\mathcal{V}$.
5. The rho, denoted $\rho$.

This chapter describes the option greeks and their interpretation, uses, and properties. A comment on notation first. While $\Delta$, $\Gamma$, $\Theta$, and $\rho$ are actually letters in the Greek alphabet, vega is not—in fact, it is not a letter in any alphabet of which the authors are aware—so there is no standard notation for it. We use the calligraphic form $\mathcal{V}$ to represent it, but readers should be aware that other authors may use different notation.

## 17.2 Interpreting the Greeks: A Snapshot View

What does it mean for option sensitivity if the delta of a call is $+0.75$ or its vega is 12.25? As we explain below (and elaborate on in the rest of this chapter), the option greeks are very easy to interpret.

## The Option Delta

The option delta provides a linear representation of how option prices change in response to a change in the price of the underlying:

$$\text{Change in Option Value} = \Delta \times \text{Change in } S \qquad (17.1)$$

Thus, a delta of $+0.75$ means that a $+\$1$ change in the price of the underlying will change the option value by $+75$ cents. A delta of $-0.30$ means that the option price decreases by 30 cents for every $\$1$ increase in the price of the underlying.

## The Option Theta

The option theta provides a similar representation of how option values change in response to a change in the option's time to maturity $T - t$. If time to maturity declines by an amount $dt$ (measured in years), then

$$\text{Change in Option Value} = \Theta \times dt \qquad (17.2)$$

The change $dt$ is typically taken to be one trading day $= 1/252$ years $\approx 0.004$ years. For example, suppose that a call has a theta of $-13.50$. Then, all else being equal, the passage of one trading day will cause a change in option value of

$$-13.50 \times 0.004 = -0.054$$

That is, the call value will *decline* by $\$0.054$.

## The Option Vega

In the same vein, the option vega describes the option's price response to changes in the volatility $\sigma$. If volatility changes by an amount $d\sigma$, then

$$\text{Change in Option Value} = \mathcal{V} \times d\sigma \qquad (17.3)$$

For example, if an option's vega is $\mathcal{V} = 9.80$ and volatility falls by 1% (so $d\sigma = -0.01$), then the change in the option value is

$$9.80 \times -0.01 = -0.098$$

That is, the option value falls by 9.8 cents.

## The Option Rho

The option rho measures sensitivity to interest rates. If interest rates change by amount $dr$, then

$$\text{Change in Option Value} = \rho \times dr \qquad (17.4)$$

For instance, suppose an option's rho is $\rho = 5.40$ and interest rates increase by 1% ($dr = +0.01$). Then the option value changes by

$$5.40 \times 0.01 = 0.054$$

that is, it increases by 5.4 cents.

## It's That Simple?

If you think all of this looks a bit too simple and too neat, you are partly right. The changes in option value described in equations (17.1)–(17.4) are only approximately correct.[1] Option prices are nonlinear functions of the parameters, while the descriptions (17.1)–(17.4) treat the option price as if it were linear in the individual parameters. However, these linear approximations work excellently for "small" changes in the values of the factors, and in practice, the greeks provide a very useful snapshot summary of option sensitivity.

But for large changes, the simple approximations provided by these formulae do not always do well and sometimes may even do very poorly. This is a matter of particular concern in evaluating the impact of stock price changes on option values since the underlying price can change very sharply very abruptly. This is where the option gamma comes in.

## The Option Gamma

Perhaps the most complex greek to understand, the gamma performs two roles. First, it measures the change in the option *delta* for a given change in the price of the underlying. That is, we have

$$\text{Change in } \Delta \ = \ \Gamma \times \text{Change in } S \qquad \textbf{(17.5)}$$

How sensitive delta is to changes in $S$ is of concern, for example, to a trader who is delta-hedging an option portfolio. A large value of gamma implies that the delta will change substantially even for a relatively small change in $S$, so the portfolio needs to be rebalanced to keep it delta-hedged. But if gamma is small, then portfolio rebalancing need not be undertaken as often.

Second, the gamma provides a "curvature correction" to the change in option price predicted by the delta: we modify (17.1) by writing

$$\text{Change in Option Price} \ = \ [\Delta \times \text{Change in } S] + [\tfrac{1}{2} \Gamma \times (\text{Change in } S)^2] \quad \textbf{(17.6)}$$

Equation (17.6) is always more accurate than (17.1) as a predictor of the change in option value for a given change in $S$.[2] For small changes in $S$, the gain in accuracy is minimal since the change in $S$ enters with a squared term (e.g., if $S$ changes by \$0.05, then the term (Change in $S$)$^2$ is only 0.0025), so we usually ignore the correction term and use only (17.1). But for large changes in $S$, the improved performance is significant as we see later in this chapter.

## Why Do We Need the Greeks?

At this point, a legitimate question has probably entered the reader's mind: why do we need these sensitivity measures at all? If we want to find out how much the option price will respond to a change in (say) the price of the underlying, why not simply compute the new value using the model and compare it to the old value? This way the computed impact on option prices will be exact rather than approximate.

We can always do this, but the greeks are still of huge value for risk-management for several reasons. First, they package a great deal of information regarding option sensitivity into something that can be absorbed virtually at a glance. When we see an option with a delta of +0.85, for example, we know that it will react very sharply to changes in the price

---

[1] For readers accustomed to thinking in calculus terms, the option greeks correspond to the first-order Taylor-series expansions of the option pricing function.

[2] Once again, for readers accustomed to thinking in calculus terms, (17.6) is a *second-order* Taylor-series expansion in $S$, which is, of course, always more accurate than a first-order expansion.

of the underlying, whereas an option with a delta of $-0.05$ will be almost unresponsive. Similarly, from knowing the vega of a call, we can estimate how much the call will respond to changes in volatility even if this estimate is only approximate.

Second, the magnitudes of these changes can be compared and used to offset each other, i.e., to create portfolios that are *hedged* against changes in particular factors. For example, suppose we have two options on the same stock whose vegas are (say) 12.0 and 6.0. Then the first option is twice as sensitive to changes in volatility as the second one. If a long position in the first option is combined with two short positions in the second, we will have created a portfolio that is insensitive to volatility changes, i.e., that is *vega-hedged*.

Finally, the greeks are easily extended to entire portfolios on a given underlying rather than just individual instruments. The greek of a portfolio is just the sum of the greeks of each individual item in the portfolio. This makes it simple to gauge portfolio sensitivity at a glance and to do hedging and risk-management at the portfolio level.

## Outline of This Chapter

The rest of this chapter describes the option greeks in more detail, beginning with the delta, and then working through the gamma, theta, vega, and rho.

In each case, we first look at the definition of the greek and discuss how it is computed. Then we examine general properties of the greek such as: is the greek positive or negative in sign (that is, does an increase in the underlying parameter increase or decrease option values)? When is it largest in value? Why does it exhibit this sensitivity? How do the greeks of otherwise identical calls and puts compare? And so on. Lastly, we discuss the use/interpretation of the greek using numerical examples.

A final section describes how to extend the definitions to cover a *portfolio* of options on a given underlying. The end-of-chapter exercises apply the ideas to several standard option portfolios such as those discussed in Chapter 8.

## The Black-Scholes Setting and a Running Example

Whenever we refer to the Black-Scholes setting, we use the notation introduced in the Black-Scholes chapter: $S_t$ will denote the current (time-$t$) price of the underlying, $\sigma$ its volatility, $K$ the strike price of the option, $T - t$ the remaining time to maturity, and $r$ the risk-free rate of interest. $N(\cdot)$ will denote the cumulative standard normal distribution, i.e., $N(x)$ is the probability under a standard normal distribution of an observation less than or equal to $x$.

Each of the greeks can be represented in closed-form (i.e., using a formula) in the Black-Scholes setting. We use these formulae in numerical examples throughout this chapter to illustrate the material. All the examples use the baseline parameters described in Table 17.1. In each example, one of the parameters is varied from its baseline level to illustrate sensitivity to that parameter (for example, the volatility is varied to illustrate the vega).

**TABLE 17.1**  A Common Example

| The numerical examples presented in this chapter are all based on a Black-Scholes setting with the following baseline parameters. | |
|---|---|
| **Parameter** | **Value** |
| Current stock price $S_t$ | 100 |
| Strike price $K$ | 100 |
| Time to maturity $T - t$ | 0.50 |
| Risk-free rate $r$ | 0.05 |
| Volatility $\sigma$ | 0.20 |

# 17.3 The Option Delta

The delta, which measures the sensitivity of option prices to changes in the price of the underlying, is unquestionably the single most important sensitivity measure for an option. Intuitively speaking, the delta may be thought of as a ratio:

$$\Delta = \text{Change in option value per \$1 change in } S \qquad (17.7)$$

The mathematical definition puts this more formally: delta is the rate of change (i.e., the *slope*) of the option price with respect to $S$:

$$\Delta_C = \frac{\partial C}{\partial S} \qquad \Delta_P = \frac{\partial P}{\partial S} \qquad (17.8)$$

To obtain the informal definition (17.7) from this, view $\partial C$ and $\partial P$ as the changes in the option values caused by a small change $\partial S$ in the stock price, and take $\partial S = \$1$.

## Computing the Delta

In models such as Black-Scholes where we have a formula for the option price, we can apply the definition (17.8) directly to get a formula for the option delta. Appendix 17A shows that in the Black-Scholes model,

$$\Delta_C = N(d_1) \qquad \Delta_P = -N(-d_1) \qquad (17.9)$$

where

$$d_1 = \frac{1}{\sigma\sqrt{T-t}}\left[\ln\left(\frac{S_t}{K}\right) + (r + \frac{1}{2}\sigma^2)(T-t)\right]$$

In discrete models such as the binomial, we lack formulae for describing option prices. To calculate the delta, we need to "discretize" (17.8). Let $C$ and $P$ be the option prices at the initial price $S$. Consider a nearby price[3] $S'$. Rerun the model from the initial price $S'$, and compute the new option prices $C'$ and $P'$. The change in the underlying price is $dS = S' - S$, while the changes in the call and put prices are, respectively,

$$dC = C' - C \quad \text{and} \quad dP = P' - P$$

The delta is given by the change in option value divided by the change in $S$:

$$\Delta_C = \frac{C' - C}{S' - S} \qquad \Delta_P = \frac{P' - P}{S' - S} \qquad (17.10)$$

## Properties of the Delta

We identified the main properties of the delta in Chapter 11. We restate the properties briefly here.

First, calls gain value when the price of the underlying increases but puts lose value in this case. So the delta of a call is positive and that of a put is negative.

Second, the delta of a call is less than $+1$ because the call cannot increase by more than one dollar for a dollar increase in the value of the underlying. Similarly, the delta of a put is always greater than $-1$: a dollar decrease in the price of the underlying cannot cause more

---

[3] There is no hard-and-fast definition of "nearby." For a stock trading at a price of (say) $90, a change of $1 may be considered small, but not for a stock trading at a price of $9. Common sense should be the guide here.

than a dollar increase in the value of the put. Combining the first two properties,

$$0 \leq \Delta_C \leq 1 \qquad -1 \leq \Delta_P \leq 0$$

Third, the size of the delta depends on the option's *depth-in-the-money*. Deep in-the-money options are the most responsive to changes in the price of the underlying, while deep out-of-the-money options are the least responsive. In more detail:

- The delta of a call is close to zero when the call is deep out-of-the-money. It increases as the price $S$ of the underlying increases, and goes towards $+1$ as the call moves deep in-the-money.

- The delta of a put is close to $-1$ when the put is deep in-the-money. It decreases in absolute value as $S$ increases, and goes towards 0 as the put moves deep out-of-the-money.

Finally, for otherwise identical *European* calls and puts, we have

$$\Delta_C - \Delta_P = 1 \qquad \qquad \textbf{(17.11)}$$

(The relation (17.11) need not hold for American options.) To obtain this result, differentiate both sides of the put-call parity expression with respect to $S$:

$$C - P = S - PV(K) - PV(D) \qquad \qquad \textbf{(17.12)}$$

More informally, suppose $S$ changes by \$1 causing changes in $C$ and $P$ of $\Delta_C$ and $\Delta_P$, respectively. Then, the total change in the left-hand side of (17.12) is $\Delta_C - \Delta_P$, while the change in the right-hand side is \$1. These two changes must be equal since put-call parity must always hold.

Figure 17.1 plots the delta in a Black-Scholes setting using the formulae (17.9). The baseline values are those given in Table 17.1. The graphs plot call and put deltas as $S$ varies from 72 to 128. The figure illustrates all the properties of option deltas listed above.

**FIGURE 17.1**

Option Deltas as $S$ Changes

This figure describes the behavior of call and put deltas as the price of the underlying varies. The details of the calculation are given in the text.

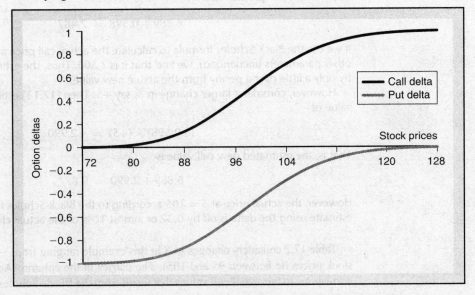

## Using the Option Delta

The delta as a measure of option sensitivity has a simple interpretation. If the underlying price changes by a small amount $dS$, the delta predicts a change in the option price of $\Delta \times dS$.

$$dC = \Delta_C \times dS \qquad dP = \Delta_P \times dS \qquad (17.13)$$

**Example 17.1**  Suppose that a put is trading at $P = 8.45$ and that the delta of the put is $-0.70$. Suppose the underlying price increases by $0.50. The delta estimates a change in the put price of

$$(-0.70) \times (+0.50) = -0.35$$

So the new put price should be $8.45 - 0.35 = 8.10$.  ∎

## Unfortunately ...

While simple, (17.13) represents only an approximation to the actual change in the option price. The approximation is extremely good for small changes in the price of the underlying, but becomes progressively less accurate as the changes in $S$ increase in size. For a large abrupt change in $S$, the estimate can fare quite poorly.

To illustrate these points and gain more insight into this problem, a numerical example is helpful. We use the Black-Scholes model for this purpose. Since we have closed-forms for both option prices and option deltas in this model, we can calculate the changes predicted by the delta and compare them to the actual changes resulting from the formula.

**Example 17.2**  Consider the baseline parameter values given in Table 17.1. For these parameters, applying the Black-Scholes formula yields

$$C = 6.889 \qquad \Delta_C = 0.598$$

Suppose $S$ changes by $1. Then equation (17.13) estimates a change in call value of $+0.598$, i.e., the new call price should be

$$6.889 + 0.598 = 7.487$$

If we use the Black-Scholes formula to calculate the actual call price at $S = 101$ (leaving the other parameters unchanged), we find that it is 7.500. Thus, the estimated new value is off by only a little over a penny from the actual new value.

However, consider a larger change in $S$, say $+5$. Then (17.13) estimates a change in call value of

$$(+0.598) \times (+5) = +2.990$$

That is, the estimated new call value is

$$6.889 + 2.990 = 9.877$$

However, the actual price at $S = 105$ according to the Black-Scholes formula is 10.201. The estimate using the delta is off by 0.32 or almost 10% of the actual change in call value.  ∎

Table 17.2 considers changes in $S$ in this example ranging from $-5$ to $+5$ (i.e., the new stock prices lie between 95 and 105). The entries in the column "Actual New Call Price" correspond to the actual call values that result from the Black-Scholes formula at these new

**TABLE 17.2** Using the Delta to Approximate Call Value Changes

This table compares the actual call prices that result from changes in $S$ to the estimates of new call values obtained using the delta. The original value of $S$ is 100, while $S_{new}$ denotes the new value. The details of the computations are explained in the text.

| New Stock Price | Actual New Call Price | Delta Approximation | Error |
|---|---|---|---|
| 95 | 4.255 | 3.900 | 0.355 |
| 96 | 4.723 | 4.498 | 0.225 |
| 97 | 5.222 | 5.096 | 0.126 |
| 98 | 5.749 | 5.693 | 0.056 |
| 99 | 6.305 | 6.291 | 0.014 |
| 100 | 6.889 | 6.889 | – |
| 101 | 7.500 | 7.487 | 0.013 |
| 102 | 8.138 | 8.084 | 0.054 |
| 103 | 8.801 | 8.682 | 0.119 |
| 104 | 9.489 | 9.280 | 0.209 |
| 105 | 10.201 | 9.877 | 0.324 |

values of $S$. The entries in the column "Delta Approximation" correspond to the values obtained by using the formula (17.13), i.e.,

$$\text{Estimated New Call Price} = \text{Old Call Price} + [\Delta \times \text{Change in } S]$$
$$= 6.889 + [0.598 \times (S_{new} - 100)] \qquad \textbf{(17.14)}$$

As the table shows, the delta approximation to the actual change is very good for small changes in $S$ but becomes progressively less accurate as the size of the change in $S$ increases.

## The Importance of Curvature

What causes the error to behave in this fashion? In a word, *curvature*. When we estimate the change in option price using the formula

$$\text{Change in call value} = \Delta \times \text{Change in } S$$

we are implicitly treating the call price as if it is *linear* in $S$. A \$2 change in $S$ causes twice the change in the option price that a \$1 change causes; a \$1 change in $S$ has twice the impact of a \$0.50 change; and so on. However, as we saw in the Black-Scholes chapter, the option pricing function has *curvature*: it is emphatically not linear in $S$.

The consequences are illustrated in Figure 17.2, which is just a graphic representation of the information in Table 17.2, but over a wider price range. The gray line in the figure represents the new call values estimated using the delta, i.e., it is a plot of equation (17.14). This plot is just a straight line with a slope of 0.598.

The black line in the figure represents the actual new option prices in the example computed using the Black-Scholes formula. The slope of this line at any $S$ is the delta at that value of $S$. The slope increases as $S$ changes, indicating the function's curvature. At $S = 100$, the slope is 0.598, so the gray line is tangent to the option pricing function at this point.

When we estimate option price changes using (17.13), we are moving along the gray line, whereas actual price changes occur along the black line. The two lines lie close to each other for small changes in $S$. But as $S$ changes by a large amount, the tangent begins to move away from the curved option pricing function, and the difference between them becomes

**FIGURE 17.2**

The Impact of Curvature

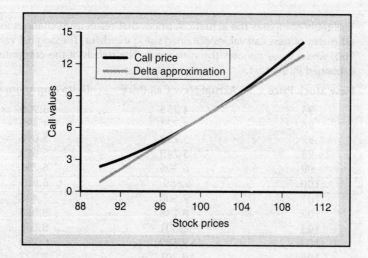

large. Note that because option prices have positive curvature (i.e., they are *convex* in *S*), the delta always *under*predicts the amount of the actual change.

The error in the estimate from using the delta clearly depends on the extent of curvature in the option pricing function at the initial price. A lower curvature means that the black and gray lines will be closer together and the error will generally be small. How do we quantify and account for this curvature in measuring option sensitivity? The answer: the option gamma, to which we now turn.

## 17.4 The Option Gamma

There are two equivalent ways to think about the option gamma. The first is as a measure of the change in the option delta for a given change in *S*. Intuitively,

$$\Gamma = \text{Change in option delta per \$1 change in } S$$

More formally, gamma is the slope of delta with respect to *S*:

$$\Gamma_C = \frac{\partial \Delta_C}{\partial S} \qquad \Gamma_P = \frac{\partial \Delta_P}{\partial S} \qquad \textbf{(17.15)}$$

Now, delta is itself the slope of the option pricing function, so gamma measures the *change* in this slope as *S* changes. The change in a function's slope is its *curvature*. This gives us the second interpretation of gamma: as a measure of the curvature of the option price in *S*. In calculus notation, gamma is then the second derivative of the option pricing function with respect to *S*:

$$\Gamma_C = \frac{\partial^2 C}{\partial S^2} \qquad \Gamma_P = \frac{\partial^2 P}{\partial S^2} \qquad \textbf{(17.16)}$$

### Computing the Gamma

In models where we know the option pricing formula, either of the equivalent definitions (17.15) or (17.16) can be applied directly to the option price to obtain a formula for the option gamma. In the Black-Scholes setting, Appendix 17A shows that the gamma is given by

$$\Gamma_C = \Gamma_P = \frac{1}{\sigma S_t \sqrt{T - t}} N'(d_1) \qquad \textbf{(17.17)}$$

where, for any $x$, $N'(x)$ is given by

$$N'(x) = \frac{1}{\sqrt{2\pi}} e^{-x^2/2} \qquad \textbf{(17.18)}$$

In models such as the binomial where there are no closed-form representations of option prices, we discretize (17.16). For specificity, consider a call (puts are handled analogously). Let $C(S)$ denote the call value at the initial price $S$. Pick a small change in price $b$ and rerun the model to compute the call values from the initial price $S - b$ and $S + b$. Denote these call values by $C(S - b)$ and $C(S + b)$, respectively. Then, the discretized form of (17.16), which may be used to compute the call gamma at $S$, is given by

$$\Gamma = \frac{C(S+b) + C(S-b) - 2C(S)}{b^2} \qquad \textbf{(17.19)}$$

## Properties of the Gamma

As we have seen, call and put deltas both *increase* as $S$ increases. This means that the gamma is *positive* for both calls and puts:

$$\Gamma_C > 0 \qquad \Gamma_P > 0 \qquad \textbf{(17.20)}$$

In mathematical terminology, the property (17.20) of positive curvature is called *convexity*: option prices are said to be *convex* in $S$.

When is gamma large and when is it small? Look at a plot of option prices as $S$ varies. When an option (either a call or a put) is deep out-of-the-money, the option pricing function is almost flat. There is very little curvature, implying that the gamma of deep out-of-the-money options is small.

Similarly, when an option is deep in-the-money, it responds almost one-for-one to changes in $S$. The option pricing function is again almost a straight line with very little curvature. So the gamma of deep out-of the-money options is also small.

When an option is at- or near-the-money, however, the option pricing function displays considerable curvature: its slope (which is the option delta) changes rapidly as $S$ changes. Thus, the gamma is highest in this region.

Summarizing, the gamma of an option is

- least when the option is deep out-of-the-money or deep in-the-money; and is
- highest when the option is near-the-money.

A final property holds only for European options. For otherwise identical European calls and puts,

$$\Gamma_C = \Gamma_P \qquad \textbf{(17.21)}$$

(Alert readers would have noted in (17.17) that call and put gammas coincide in the Black-Scholes setting.) This equality is again a consequence of—what else?—put-call parity. As we have seen, put-call parity implies that for European options,

$$\Delta_C - \Delta_P = 1$$

If we differentiate both sides with respect to $S$, we obtain $\Gamma_C - \Gamma_P = 0$ or $\Gamma_C = \Gamma_P$. More informally, when $S$ changes by \$1, the left-hand side changes by $\Gamma_C - \Gamma_P$ but the right-hand side does not change (it is a constant and does not depend on $S$). This gives us $\Gamma_C - \Gamma_P = 0$.

Figure 17.3 plots the option gamma in a Black-Scholes setting using the formula (17.17). The baseline values are those from Table 17.1. The graph plots the gamma as $S$ varies from 76 to 124. The figure illustrates the properties described above.

**FIGURE 17.3**
The Option Gamma

This figure plots call gammas in a Black-Scholes setting as the price of the underlying varies. The details of the computations are given in the text.

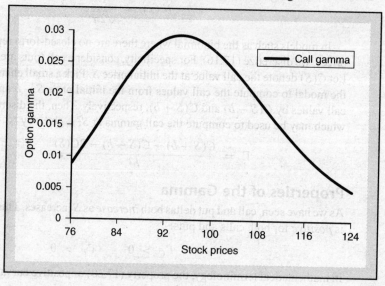

## Using the Option Gamma

The gamma has many important uses, formal and informal, in risk-management. We examine several of these in the material that follows.

### (A) Gamma as a Curvature Correction

As we saw earlier, the delta underestimates the impact of large price changes on option values because it ignores curvature. The gamma can be used to correct for curvature.

Consider a change of $a$ in $S$. When using the delta alone, the estimated change in option price is

$$\text{Change in option value} = \Delta a$$

A much more accurate estimate is obtained by augmenting this with the gamma:

$$\text{Change in option value} = \Delta a + \frac{1}{2} \Gamma a^2 \tag{17.22}$$

For small changes $a$, the improvement is also small, but for large $a$, the improvement is very substantial.

**Example 17.3**

Consider the Black-Scholes setting of Table 17.1. As we have seen, the call price and delta with these parameters are

$$C = 6.889, \qquad \Delta = 0.598$$

Applying the formula (17.17) for the gamma in this model, we obtain

$$\Gamma = 0.0274$$

Consider a change of $a = +5$ in the stock price $S$. We saw in the last section that using the delta alone leads to a large error of over $0.32 in estimating the change in call value.

Using the curvature correction (17.22), the new price estimate is

$$6.889 + (0.598)(5) + \frac{1}{2}(0.0274)(25) = 10.219$$

This is within $0.02 of the actual Black-Scholes price of 10.201.  ∎

### Why Does This Correction Formula "Work"?

Table 17.2 and Figure 17.2 show that (a) the delta systematically *under*estimates the impact of changes in $S$ on the option price, and (b) because of curvature in the option price, the extent of underestimation becomes larger as the change in $S$ increases.

Both issues are addressed by the curvature correction (17.22). First, $\Gamma$ is always positive, as is the term $a^2$ for any change $a$ (positive or negative) in the underlying price. This means $\frac{1}{2}\Gamma a^2 > 0$, so we are adding a *positive* term to the delta estimate. This addresses the first problem. Second, the $a^2$ term adds curvature to the estimate, addressing the second problem.

### But, a Warning …

Although using the gamma as a curvature correction provides a better estimate of the impact of a large price change than using the delta alone, it must be stressed that the gamma too is only an approximation. For very large changes in $S$, even the estimate provided by the gamma can be substantially off. For example, consider a sudden change of $a = -10$ in the stock price in the setting of Table 17.1. Using the curvature correction (17.22), the new estimated call value is

$$6.889 + (0.598)(-10) + (0.0274)(100) = 3.649$$

However, the actual call value at $S = 90$ is only about 2.349.

## (B) Curvature and Delta-Hedging

Since the gamma of an option is always positive, the holder of an option is said to be "long gamma," but the writer of the option is said to be "short gamma" or to have a negative gamma position. One of the most important—and for option writers, most unpleasant—implications of gamma comes in the delta-hedging of written option positions. Delta-hedging involves offsetting the risk in the written option position by using a position in the underlying. The problem is that options have curvature while stock payoffs do not—the stock reacts by exactly $1 for every $1 change in its price, so is a zero-gamma instrument.

To see the consequences of this, suppose you are short a call and have delta-hedged yourself by holding $\Delta$ units of the stock. Suppose the underlying stock price registers an unanticipated move of $a$. What is the impact on your portfolio?

The change in value of the $\Delta$ units of stock held is just $\Delta a$. From (17.22), the change in option value is approximately

$$\Delta a + \frac{1}{2}\Gamma a^2$$

Since you are *long* delta units of stock and *short* the call, the change in your portfolio value is approximately

$$\Delta a - \left[\Delta a + \frac{1}{2}\Gamma a^2\right] = -\frac{1}{2}\Gamma a^2$$

This is negative *regardless of a*! This result is worth emphasizing:

*A delta-hedged position in which an investor is short the option will lose money from an unanticipated change in prices regardless of the direction in which the price moves. The loss is approximately $-\frac{1}{2}\Gamma a^2$, where a is the change in price.*

This observation explains why rookie option traders are often told to avoid negative gamma positions. Note that the larger the gamma, the larger is this loss for any given *a*.

---

**Example 17.4**

Consider the Black-Scholes setting of Table 17.1. As we have seen, we then have

$$C = 6.889 \qquad \Delta = 0.598 \qquad \Gamma = 0.0274$$

Suppose we hold a delta-hedged portfolio that is short one call and long 0.598 units of the stock. What is the impact on the portfolio of a $2 change in the price?

First, consider a $2 *increase* in the price to $S = 102$. In this case, the Black-Scholes option value increases by +1.250 (see Table 17.2). The value of the 0.598 shares held increases by $0.598 \times 2 = 1.196$. Since we are short the option, the net change in portfolio value is

$$1.196 - 1.250 = -0.054$$

which is approximately $-\frac{1}{2}\Gamma a^2$ (recall that $\Gamma = 0.0274$).

Now consider a $2 *decrease* in the price to $S = 98$. In this case, the option value declines by 1.140 (Table 17.2). The value of the 0.598 shares decreases by 1.196. Therefore, the net change in portfolio value is

$$-1.196 + 1.140 = -0.056$$

Again, this is approximately $-\frac{1}{2}\Gamma a^2$. ∎

---

Conversely, of course, a delta-hedged position in which we are long the option will make money regardless of the direction in which the price moves. Figure 17.4 illustrates. The figure describes the change in the value of a delta-hedged portfolio in which we are long

**FIGURE 17.4**
Curvature and
Delta-Hedging

This figure plots the change in value of a portfolio consisting of a long call position delta-hedged with the stock when the underlying price registers an unexpected move.

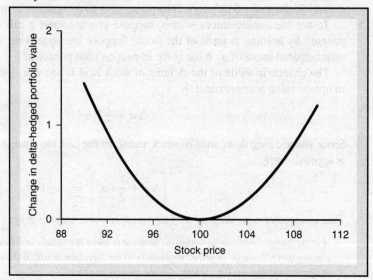

a call and short $\Delta$(call) units of the stock.[4] The setting and initial parameters are those of Table 17.1. Any move in the price from its initial level of $S = 100$ results in a gain in portfolio value.

## (C) Gamma as a View on Jump Risk/Volatility

The behavior of delta-hedged portfolios in response to changes in the price of the underlying explains why gamma is associated with a view on volatility (particularly, the risk of jumps in the price). If you are long the option and delta-hedged, you benefit from the curvature regardless of the direction in which the price moves. And, of course, the higher the gamma, the more the curvature, and so the greater your benefit from large price swings. Conversely, if you are short an option and delta-hedged, you lose from price moves in either direction, and the greater the gamma, the greater the curvature, so the greater your losses from price swings.

The association between gamma and jump risk can also be understood from the standpoint of an *unhedged* option position. Because of curvature, an option provides its holder with an *asymmetric* response to price changes. The holder of a call benefits more from a price increase than he loses from a corresponding price decrease; the difference between the changes is approximately $\Gamma a^2$ where $a$ is the change in the underlying price. A put holder similarly gains more from a price decrease than she loses from a corresponding price increase.

---

**Example 17.5**

Consider the Black-Scholes setting of Table 17.1. Table 17.2 shows that a $1 increase in price to $S = 101$ causes a gain in the call value of

$$7.500 - 6.889 = 0.611$$

On the other hand, a $1 *decrease* in price to $S = 101$ causes the option value to decrease by the smaller amount

$$6.889 - 6.305 = 0.584$$

The difference between these changes is 0.027, which is approximately $\Gamma a^2$.

As is easily verified from the table, a similar degree of asymmetry results from any change $\pm a$ in $S$. Figure 17.5 illustrates the asymmetry for a change of $\pm 4$. ∎

---

This asymmetric exposure is desirable if you expect large price swings: you will benefit more on the upside than you lose on the downside. Thus, a positive gamma position is regarded as a *bullish* view on jump risk (or, more generally, on volatility), while a *negative* gamma position (corresponding to a short option position) is regarded as a bearish view on jump risk/volatility.

## (D) Gamma as a Predictor of Changes in Delta

From its very definition (17.15), gamma can be used to predict changes in delta caused by changes in $S$. Writing $d\Delta_C$ for the change in $\Delta_C$ caused by a small change $dS$ in the stock price, a rewriting of (17.15) gives us

$$d\Delta_C = \Gamma_C \times dS \qquad \textbf{(17.23)}$$

That is,

$$\text{Change in } \Delta = \Gamma \times \text{Change in } S$$

Informally, we can think of $\Gamma$ as the change in $\Delta$ per $1 change in $S$.

---

[4] Note that, by put-call parity, the same figure also describes the change in value of a portfolio in which we are long the put and long $\Delta$(put) units of the stock.

**FIGURE 17.5**
Curvature and Jump
Risk

This figure illustrates the asymmetric response of call values to price increases
and decreases as a result of curvature.

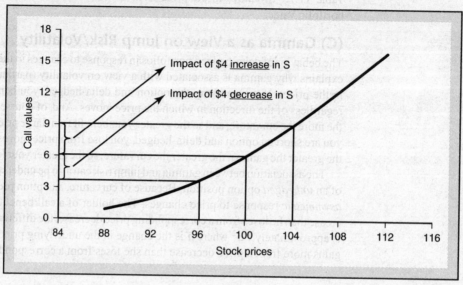

**Example 17.6**

Take the Black-Scholes setting of Table 17.1. At $S = 100$, we have $\Delta_C = 0.598$ and $\Gamma_C = 0.0274$. Consider changes in $S$ of $+4$ and $-4$. Expression (17.23) estimates the values of delta at $S = 96$ and $S = 104$ to be

$$\Delta(96) = 0.598 + (0.0274)(-4) = 0.489$$

and

$$\Delta(104) = 0.598 + (0.0274)(+4) = 0.707$$

The actual values, computed using the formula for the delta, are $\Delta(96) = 0.484$ and $\Delta(104) = 0.700$. Thus, despite the relatively large changes in $S$, (17.23) estimates the change in $\Delta$ quite accurately.    ■

## (E) Gamma as an Indicator of Hedge Rebalancing

As a measure of the sensitivity of delta to changes in $S$, the gamma is an indicator of the frequency with which a delta hedge needs to be rebalanced. If the gamma of an option is small (close to zero), this means that the delta will not change much for changes in $S$. Thus, a delta-hedged position will remain approximately delta-hedged even as $S$ changes. However, if the gamma is large, then even a small change in $S$ can create a nontrivial change in the option delta. Thus, a delta-hedged position may become risky following changes in $S$ and the hedge will have to be rebalanced more frequently to maintain delta-neutrality. Such positions need to be monitored carefully.

## 17.5    The Option Theta

Options are *finitely-lived* instruments, so the time remaining to maturity plays a major role in determining option values. The option *theta* measures the impact of the passage of time on option values. It is often referred to as the *time-decay* in an option for reasons we will see shortly.

Theta is the rate of change of option values with respect to a small move forward in current time (equivalently, a small *reduction* in the time to maturity):

$$\Theta_C = \frac{\partial C}{\partial t} \qquad \Theta_P = \frac{\partial P}{\partial t} \qquad (17.24)$$

Appendix 17A shows that in the Black-Scholes model, applying the definition (17.24) results in the following expressions for call and put thetas:

$$\Theta_C = -\frac{1}{2\sqrt{T-t}}\,\sigma S_t N'(d_1) - re^{-r(T-t)}KN(d_2) \qquad (17.25)$$

$$\Theta_P = -\frac{1}{2\sqrt{T-t}}\,\sigma S_t N'(-d_1) + re^{-r(T-t)}KN(-d_2) \qquad (17.26)$$

In models where we lack closed-forms, we must discretize (17.24). Let $C$ and $P$ denote the option values given the current maturity $\tau = T - t$. Consider a small reduction (e.g., one day) in the time to maturity. Denote the new maturity by $\tau'$, and the resulting call and put values by $C'$ and $P'$, respectively. Then, the option thetas are given by

$$\Theta_C = \frac{C - C'}{\tau - \tau'} \qquad \Theta_P = \frac{P - P'}{\tau - \tau'} \qquad (17.27)$$

## Sign of the Option Theta

For American options, a longer time to maturity is unambiguously good since a longer-dated option can always be exercised at the same time as a shorter-dated option (the option holder can simply choose to throw away the extra time). Thus, American option values increase with greater time to maturity, or what is the same thing, they decrease in value as time to maturity falls. This means theta is *negative* for American options. The decline in option values as maturity approaches is expressed as saying that the options are subject to *time decay*.

This is also true for European call options on non-dividend-paying stock: as time to maturity declines, the time value and insurance value of the option both fall, so the call value falls. Figure 17.6 plots Black-Scholes call values for different times to maturity and illustrates this point.

**FIGURE 17.6**

Impact of Time to Maturity on Call Values

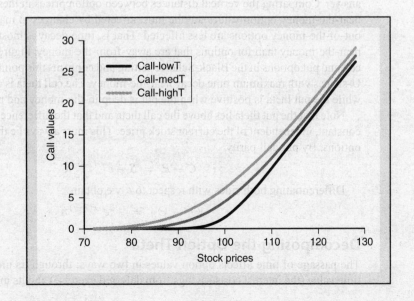

**FIGURE 17.7**
Impact of Time to
Maturity on Put Values

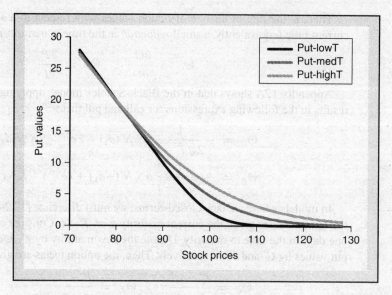

For European put options, however, there is ambiguity. A lower time to maturity reduces the put's insurance value since volatility has less time to have an impact, but it increases the put's time value since the put holder receives money from the put's exercise earlier. Thus, in some cases, put values may increase as time to maturity shrinks, i.e., theta may become positive. This is particularly likely for deep in-the-money puts since insurance value is minimal for such puts (the put is almost sure to be exercised), but time value is very important.

Figure 17.7 illustrates such a situation using the Black-Scholes setting. At low stock prices in the figure (i.e., when the put is deep in-the-money), the short-dated put is actually worth more than the longer-dated puts. Thus, theta becomes positive.

## Theta and Depth-in-the-Money

How does option theta depend on depth-in-the-money? Figures 17.6 and 17.7 suggest the answer. Comparing the vertical distances between option prices in these graphs shows that near-the-money option values are the most affected by changes in maturity, while in- and out-of-the-money options are less affected. That is, time decay is most for options that are near-the-money than for options that are away-from-the-money. Figure 17.8 plots thetas of call and put options in the Black-Scholes setting and confirms this point: the plots both have U-shapes with maximum time decay near-the-money. The call theta is negative throughout, while the put theta is positive when the put is deep in-the-money and negative otherwise.

Note that the put theta lies above the call theta and that the difference between the two is a constant, independent of the current stock price. This must always be the case for European options. By put-call parity,

$$C - P = S - e^{-r(T-t)}K$$

Differentiating both sides with respect to $t$, we obtain

$$\Theta_C - \Theta_P = -re^{-r(T-t)}K \qquad \textbf{(17.28)}$$

## Decomposing the Option Theta

The passage of time affects option values in two ways: through its impact on the option's time value (the interest costs/savings from deferred exercise) and its impact on the option's

**FIGURE 17.8**
Option Thetas

This figure plots call and put option thetas in a Black-Scholes setting. The baseline parameters are those of Table 17.1.

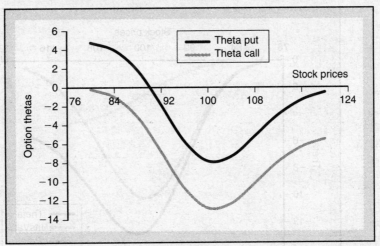

insurance value (volatility has less time to have an impact).[5] Greater insight into the behavior of the theta can be obtained by decomposing it along these lines.

Consider the Black-Scholes formulae for call and put thetas (17.25) and (17.26). The second term in each formula represents the net time-value effect (i.e., the change in time value multiplied by the likelihood of eventual exercise). This is negative for a call but positive for a put. The first term in each case captures the insurance value effect of a reduction in the time to maturity. This effect is negative for both calls and puts.

Figure 17.9 presents the decomposition of the call theta of Figure 17.8; Figure 17.10 does the same for the put theta. In both cases, the time-value component becomes more important with depth-in-the-money. For puts, this component is positive and becomes more positive as the put is deeper in-the-money. For calls, it is negative and becomes more negative the deeper in-the-money is the call. This is what one would expect since the anticipated interest savings/cost from deferred exercise increases with the likelihood of the option's eventual exercise.

The insurance value impact, on the other hand, is U-shaped and negative in both figures. The maximum impact is near-the-money. The impact tails away as the option moves away from the money in either direction. Again, this is expected. For deep out-of-the-money options, insurance value is *relatively* a large part of the option's value; however, the dollar value of the option is itself small, so the dollar impact of a change in time to maturity on the option's insurance value is also small. For deep in-the-money options, most of the option's value comes from *intrinsic* value. Insurance value is almost irrelevant since the option is very likely to finish in-the-money. For an option that is near-the-money, however, optionality and insurance value are very important since the possibility that volatility will push the option into the money accounts for a substantial portion of the option's value.

---

[5] The time value component of the theta is closely related to the idea of the option rho. The former measures the effect of a reduction in the time to maturity for a given interest rate; the latter measures the impact of a change in interest rates for a given time to maturity. In particular, the Black-Scholes formulae for the two have similar structures; see below for details. The same comments apply to the insurance value component of theta and the notion of the option vega.

**FIGURE 17.9**
Decomposition of the Call Theta

This figure decomposes the call theta of Figure 17.8 into its insurance value and time value components as explained in the text.

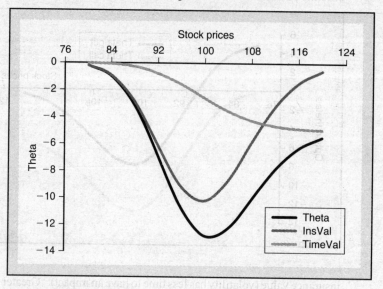

## Using the Option Theta

For a given change $dt$ in current time (i.e., for a given reduction $dt$ in the time to maturity), the impact $dC$ and $dP$ on option values may be estimated from the option thetas by rewriting (17.24):

$$dC = \Theta_C \times dt \qquad dP = \Theta_P \times dt \qquad (17.29)$$

It is common in practice to take $dt = 1$ trading day $\approx 0.004$ years and to express theta in dollar terms as the rate of decay per day. For example, for the baseline parameters of

**FIGURE 17.10**
Decomposition of the Put Theta

This figure decomposes the put theta of Figure 17.8 into its insurance value and time value components as explained in the text.

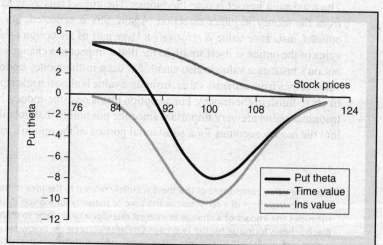

Table 17.1, the theta of a call works out to $-8.116$. Taking $dt$ to be one trading day, the decay in call value is roughly

$$-8.116 \times 0.004 = -0.032$$

That is, the call theta, expressed in dollar terms as the decay per day, is 0.032 or 3.2 cents. Note the severity of time decay: even with six months left to maturity, the passage of a single day causes a fall of over 46 basis points in option value.

For the same parameters but with a time to maturity of only one week ($\approx 0.0192$ years), the call value drops to 0.714, but its theta rises to $-19.246$. Thus, the passage of a trading day will now cost the option about 7.7 cents, or almost 11% of its value.

### The Gamma-Theta Trade-Off

The gamma of an option is positive, but the theta is (typically) negative. So if you want to profit from volatility, you must incur time decay. A *short* option position has negative time decay, but it also has negative convexity. This, in a nutshell, is the gamma-theta trade-off: to have convexity in your favor, you must pay in time.

The gamma-theta trade-off is most important for options that are at- or near-the-money, since this is where gamma and theta are both highest in absolute terms. Moreover, the trade-off for ATM options becomes particularly acute as maturity approaches since theta and gamma both rise.

Figure 17.11 illustrates these points. The upper panel of the figure plots option gammas at different maturities, while the lower panel plots call thetas. The gamma and theta of near-the-money options both rise as maturity approaches.

A more formal mathematical connection linking the delta, gamma, and theta is provided by the fundamental partial differential equation (15.24) that option prices must satisfy. The terms $C_S$, $C_{SS}$, and $C_t$ in that equation are simply the delta, gamma, and theta of the option, respectively. Therefore, the option price must obey

$$r S_t \, \Delta + \Theta + \frac{1}{2} \sigma^2 S_t^2 \, \Gamma = r \times \text{Current option value} \qquad \textbf{(17.30)}$$

The gamma-theta trade-off is easy to see here: other things being equal, if $\Gamma$ increases, then $\Theta$ must become more negative for equality to continue holding in (17.30). Expression (17.30) must also hold for portfolios of options on a given underlying (with "Current portfolio value" replacing "Current option value"). Section 17.8 discusses how to compute the greeks of a portfolio.

## 17.6 The Option Vega

Volatility is a primary determinant of option value. Many option pricing models treat volatility as constant for computational simplicity. In reality, however, volatility frequently changes. The option *vega*, denoted $\mathcal{V}$, measures the effect on option values of a change in volatility. The vega is defined as:

$$\mathcal{V}_C = \frac{\partial C}{\partial \sigma} \qquad \mathcal{V}_P = \frac{\partial P}{\partial \sigma} \qquad \textbf{(17.31)}$$

In continuous models such as Black-Scholes where we have formulae for option prices, we can directly apply (17.31) to get the formulae for option vegas. Appendix 17A shows that in the Black-Scholes model, the vegas are given by

$$\mathcal{V}_C = \mathcal{V}_P = \sqrt{T - t} \, S_t N'(d_1) \qquad \textbf{(17.32)}$$

**FIGURE 17.11**

Gamma and Theta as Maturity Approaches

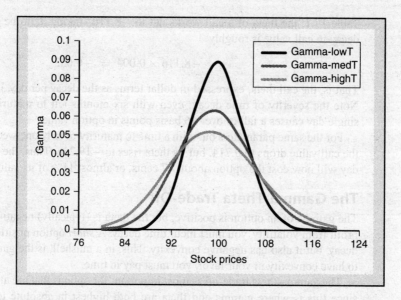

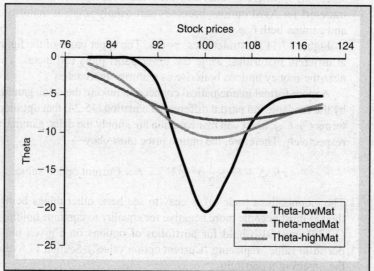

In models where we lack closed-forms, we must discretize (17.31). Let $C$ and $P$ represent call and put prices at the original volatility $\sigma$, and let $C'$ and $P'$ be the option values if volatility changes to a nearby value $\sigma'$ (e.g., $\sigma' = \sigma \pm 0.01$). Then, the option vegas are given by

$$\mathcal{V}_C = \frac{C - C'}{\sigma - \sigma'} \qquad \mathcal{V}_P = \frac{P - P'}{\sigma - \sigma'} \qquad (17.33)$$

## Properties of the Vega

The option vega measures the dollar impact on the option of a change in volatility. Higher volatility always increases option values as illustrated in Figure 17.12, so the vega is always *positive* for both calls and puts.

How does the option vega depend on depth-in-the-money? That is, which options experience the greatest dollar change in value when volatility changes? Figure 17.12 suggests an answer: the impact is greatest near-the-money and least away-from-the-money.

**FIGURE 17.12**

The Impact of
Volatility on Call
Values

This figure plots call values for a range of strike prices as volatility changes.

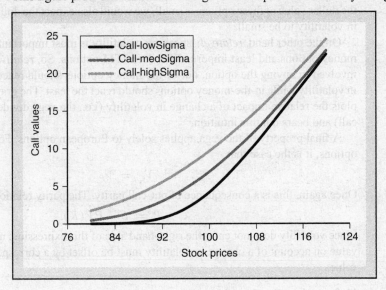

Figure 17.13 confirms this observation. The black line in the figure is a plot of call vegas in a Black-Scholes setting computed using the formula (17.32).

This behavior of the vega is intuitive. A change in volatility affects the option's *insurance value*. For deep in-the-money options, most of the option value comes from intrinsic value. Insurance value is not a big component of overall value since optionality is unimportant: the option is very likely to be exercised. Vega will therefore be small. For options that are near-the-money, optionality is central; such options derive a substantial part of their value from the possibility that volatility will push them into-the-money. Thus, they react very quickly to changes in volatility, i.e., their vegas are large. For options that are deep

**FIGURE 17.13**

The Call Vega

The black line in this figure plots call vegas as the stock price varies. The remaining parameters are as in Table 17.1. The gray line plots the *relative* impact of a change in volatility: it is the vega divided by the price of the call.

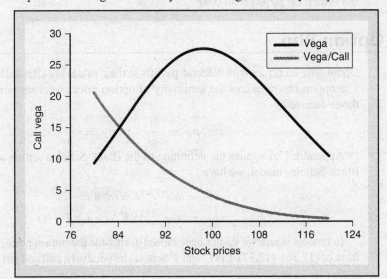

out-of-the-money, insurance value is *relatively* a large component of overall value, but since the dollar value of these options is small, we would also expect the dollar impact of a change in volatility to be small.

On the other hand, *relatively* speaking, volatility is most important for deep out-of-the-money options and least important for deep ITM options. So, *relative* to the dollar outlay involved in buying the option, out-of-the-money options should react the most to changes in volatility while in-the-money options should react the least. The gray line in Figure 17.13 plots the relative impact of a change in volatility (i.e., the vega divided by the price of the call) and bears out this intuition.

A final property of the vega applies solely to European options. For otherwise identical options, it is the case that

$$\mathcal{V}_C = \mathcal{V}_P \qquad (17.34)$$

Once again, this is a consequence of put-call parity. The parity relationship says that

$$C - P = S - PV(K)$$

Since volatility does not enter the right-hand side of this expression, any change in the call value on account of a change in volatility must be offset by a corresponding change in put value.

### Using the Option Vega

Suppose volatility changes by an amount $d\sigma$. Then, given the vegas, the estimated impact on option values is, from rewriting (17.31),

$$dC = \mathcal{V}_C \times d\sigma \qquad dP = \mathcal{V}_P \times d\sigma$$

**Example 17.7**

Consider the Black-Scholes setting of Table 17.1. The call price for these parameters is 6.889 and the vega (computed using the formula (17.32)) is 25.36. Consider a change $d\sigma = +0.01$ (i.e., volatility increases from its original value of 20% to 21%). Then, the estimated change in call value is

$$25.36 \times +0.01 = 0.2536$$

That is, the estimated new call value is $6.889 + 0.2536 = 7.143$. The actual call value when $\sigma = 0.21$, calculated from the Black-Scholes formula, is 7.162, so the estimate provided by the vega is off by less than 0.02.  ∎

## 17.7  The Option Rho

Options are securities with deferred payoffs so their values are affected by the rate of interest. The option *rho* measures the sensitivity of option prices to changes in interest rates. The rho is defined by

$$\rho_C = \frac{\partial C}{\partial r} \qquad \rho_P = \frac{\partial P}{\partial r} \qquad (17.35)$$

Appendix 17A applies the definition to the Black-Scholes setting and shows that in the Black-Scholes model, we have

$$\rho_C = e^{-r(T-t)} K N(d_2)(T - t) \qquad (17.36)$$

$$\rho_P = -e^{-r(T-t)} K N(-d_2)(T - t) \qquad (17.37)$$

In models where we do not have closed-forms for the option price, we use a discretized form of (17.36)–(17.37). Let $C$ and $P$ denote, respectively, call and put prices at the original

**FIGURE 17.14**
The Impact of Interest
Rates on Call Values

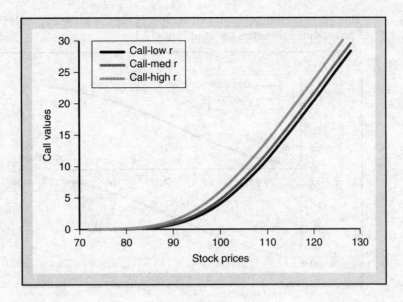

interest rate $r$. Consider a small (e.g., 10 basis points) change in interest rates to $r'$ and let $C'$ and $P'$ denote the call and put prices at the interest rate $r'$. Then, we have

$$\rho_C = \frac{C - C'}{r - r'} \qquad \rho_P = \frac{P - P'}{r - r'}. \qquad \textbf{(17.38)}$$

## Properties of the Rho

The time value of a call is positive: when interest rates rise, the holder of a call benefits since potential interest savings from deferred exercise increases. However, the time value of a put is negative: the put holder loses from an increase in interest rates since the present value of the strike price that will be *received* upon exercise declines. Figures 17.14 and 17.15 plot

**FIGURE 17.15**
The Impact of Interest
Rates on Put Values

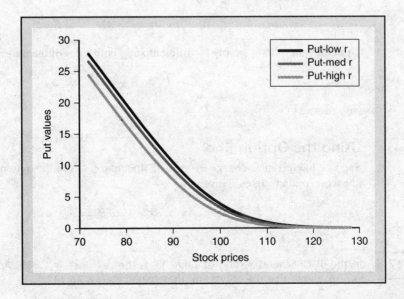

**FIGURE 17.16**
Call and Put Rhos

This figure plots the rhos of call and put options in a Black-Scholes setting. The baseline parameters are as in Table 17.1.

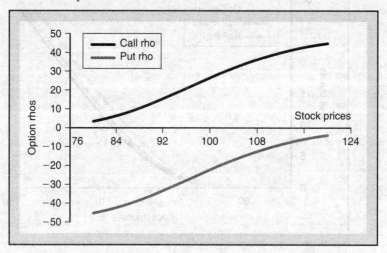

call and put values at different interest rates to illustrate these points. Thus,

$$\rho_C > 0 \qquad \rho_P < 0 \qquad\qquad (17.39)$$

How does the rho depend on depth-in-the-money? A change in interest rates primarily affects the option's time value. Time value is most important for in-the-money options since the probability of ultimate exercise is highest here. For calls, this should mean the rho increases as depth-in-the-money increases. For puts, it should mean that the rho becomes more negative as the put moves deep into-the-money. Figure 17.16 plots call and put rhos in the Black-Scholes setting; the figure is as anticipated.

The final property of the option rhos holds only for European options (and is apparent in Figure 17.16): the difference between the rhos of a call and an otherwise identical put is a constant:

$$\rho_C - \rho_P = (T - t)e^{-r(T-t)}K \qquad\qquad (17.40)$$

This equation follows simply by differentiating both sides of the put-call parity equation

$$C - P = S - e^{-r(T-t)}K$$

with respect to $r$.

## Using the Option Rho

Suppose interest rates change by a small amount $dr$. Given the option rhos, the estimated impact on option values is given by

$$dC = \rho_C \times dr \qquad dP = \rho_P \times dr$$

**Example 17.8**

In the Black-Scholes setting of Table 17.1, the call price is 6.889. Applying the formula (17.36) shows that the call rho for these parameters is 26.44.

Consider an increase of 25 basis points in interest rates from 5% to 5.25% (so change in interest rates = +0.0025). Given the call rho, the estimated change in the call value is

$$26.44 \times +0.0025 = +0.0661$$

Thus, the estimated new call value is $6.889 + 0.0661 = 6.955$. This estimate is accurate to three decimal places: as can be checked using the Black-Scholes formula, the actual new call price at an interest rate of 5.25% is 6.955. ∎

# 17.8  Portfolio Greeks

The greeks are easily extended from individual options to portfolios consisting of options and the underlying asset. The greek of a portfolio is simply the sum of the greeks of the items in the portfolio. The material below elaborates and explains with examples.

To describe the general expressions, we use the following notation. We consider a portfolio of options written on a given underlying. The portfolio is taken to consist of $n_1$ positions in option 1, $n_2$ positions in option 2, etc., where $n_i > 0$ indicates a long position and $n_i < 0$ indicates a short position. (Each category of option is distinguished by its strike, maturity, and whether it is a call or a put.) The portfolio may also have a position in the underlying of size $n$. Once again, $n > 0$ implies a long position and $n < 0$ a short position (of course, $n$ may also be zero).

### The Position Delta

Let $\Delta_1$ denote the delta of option 1, $\Delta_2$ the delta of option 2, etc. The delta of the underlying is, of course, $+1$. The aggregate delta of the portfolio (called the *position delta*) is defined as

$$\Delta \text{pos} = n + n_1 \Delta_1 + n_2 \Delta_2 + \cdots \qquad \textbf{(17.41)}$$

For example, suppose we have a portfolio consisting solely of calls and puts on a given stock. Assume the portfolio is long 100 calls, each of which has a delta of $+0.75$, and long 150 puts each with a delta of $-0.40$. Then, the position delta is

$$\Delta \text{pos} = (100 \times 0.75) + (150 \times -0.40) = 15$$

The position delta has exactly the same interpretation as the individual option delta: it measures the sensitivity of the portfolio value to changes in the price of the underlying. More informally, it measures the dollar change in portfolio value for a $1 change in the price of the underlying. So, for instance, in our example, a position delta of 15 says that the portfolio value changes by $15 for every $1 change in the stock price.

It is not hard to check that this is correct (and why). Consider a $1 increase in the stock price. Each call in the example has a delta of 0.75. Therefore, each call increases by $0.75 when the stock price increases by $1. So the 100 calls in the portfolio collectively increase by $75. On the other hand, each put has a delta of $-0.40$, so each put decreases by $0.40 when the underlying increases by $1. This means the 150 puts collectively decrease by $60. The net change in the portfolio is precisely an increase of $15.

As a measure of portfolio sensitivity to the stock price, the position delta implies a directional view for the portfolio. If the position delta is positive, the portfolio is bullish on direction. If the position delta is negative, the portfolio is bearish on direction. And if the position delta is zero, the portfolio is neutral on direction. A portfolio with a position delta of zero is said to be a *delta-neutral* portfolio.

The position delta can be changed in many ways: by adding calls, by adding puts, or by taking positions in the underlying. In our example, for instance, the portfolio can be made delta neutral by taking a short position in 15 units of the underlying stock; or by taking a short position in 20 of the calls; or by taking an additional long position in about 38 of the puts; or, finally, by bringing in other calls and puts on the same underlying stock.

## The Position Gamma

Let $\Gamma_1$ denote the gamma of option 1, $\Gamma_2$ the gamma of option 2, etc. Then, the aggregate gamma of the portfolio (called the *position gamma*) is

$$\Gamma\text{pos} = n_1\Gamma_1 + n_2\Gamma_2 + \cdots \qquad (17.42)$$

Note that positions in the underlying do not affect the position gamma since the underlying has a gamma of zero (its delta is always equal to +1).

To illustrate, consider the same portfolio used as an example in the position delta. Suppose that each of the calls has a gamma of +0.02 and each of the puts has a gamma of +0.03. Then, the position gamma is

$$\Gamma\text{pos} = (0.02 \times 100) + (0.03 \times 150) = 6.50$$

The position gamma is the portfolio analog of the individual option gamma: it is an aggregate measure of portfolio curvature. In particular, it can be used to estimate (a) the impact of large price movements on aggregate portfolio value, and (b) the impact on the position delta of a change in the underlying price.

To illustrate the first use, suppose the underlying in the example changes by $5. Then applying the curvature correction, the change in portfolio value should be around

$$(\Delta\text{pos} \times 5) + (\tfrac{1}{2}\Gamma\text{pos} \times 5^2) = (15 \times 5) + (\tfrac{1}{2}6.50 \times 25)$$
$$= +156.25$$

We can check that this is correct by checking the impact of the $5 increase on each individual option and then aggregating the effects. First note that following a $5 increase in the stock price, each call in the portfolio will change in value by

$$(0.75 \times 5) + (\frac{1}{2}0.02 \times 25) = +4.00$$

so the 100 calls will collectively increase in value by $400. Each put in the portfolio will change in value by

$$(-0.40 \times 5) + (\frac{1}{2}0.03 \times 25) = -1.625$$

so the 150 puts collectively fall in value by $150 \times 1.625 = 243.75$. Therefore, the net change in portfolio value is

$$400 - 243.75 = +156.25$$

which is exactly the value identified above.

To illustrate the second use of the option gamma, suppose the stock price in our example decreases by $1. Then, the estimated change in the position delta is

$$6.50 \times -1 = -6.50,$$

i.e., the new position delta should be $15 - 6.50 = +8.50$. Again, this can be verified by considering the changes at the individual option level. A decrease of $1 in the stock price changes the delta of each call by $-0.02$, so the new delta of each call is $+0.73$. It also changes the delta of each put by $-0.03$, so the new delta of each put is $-0.43$. Thus, the new position delta is

$$(100 \times 0.73) + (150 \times -0.43) = 73 - 64.50 = +8.50$$

which is the value we identified above.

As the portfolio equivalent of individual option gammas, the position gamma inherits all the uses/interpretations of the individual option gamma. In particular, a portfolio with a positive position gamma is considered one that is bullish on jump risk/volatility; a position with a negative position gamma is bearish on jump risk/volatility; and a portfolio with a zero position gamma (a "gamma-neutral" portfolio) is neutral on jump risk/volatility.

Since only options have curvature, the position gamma can be altered only by adding options to the portfolio. Adding positions in the underlying will affect the position delta but not the position gamma. Suppose, for instance, we want to make the portfolio in our example gamma neutral using only the calls. Since the current gamma is 6.50 and the gamma of each call is $+0.02$, we need a short position in

$$\frac{6.50}{0.02} = 325$$

calls to offset the existing gamma and make the portfolio gamma neutral. Note that adding this short position in 325 calls will also affect the position delta: the new position delta is now

$$15 + (-325 \times 0.75) = 15 - 243.75 = -228.75$$

What if we wanted to make the portfolio both delta neutral *and* gamma neutral? Simple. We first choose the options we want to use to make the portfolio gamma neutral. Then, we compute the new position delta after adding these options positions. Finally, we make the position delta neutral by adding positions in the underlying. Since the underlying does not affect the position gamma, the portfolio is now both delta neutral and gamma neutral.

## The Position Theta

The *position theta* measures the time-decay of the portfolio. It is simply the sum of the thetas of the individual options in the portfolio. Suppose $\Theta_1$ denotes the theta of option 1, $\Theta_2$ that of option 2, and so on. Then, the position theta is given by

$$\Theta\text{pos} = n_1\Theta_1 + n_2\Theta_2 + \cdots \qquad \textbf{(17.43)}$$

Positions in the underlying do not affect the position theta since the theta of the underlying is zero.

For an example, we continue with the portfolio used to illustrate the position delta and gamma. Suppose that the theta of each call is $-12.50$ and the theta of each put is $-9.40$. Then, the position theta is

$$\Theta\text{pos} = (100 \times -12.50) + (150 \times -9.40) = -2660$$

So the passage of each trading day ($\approx 0.004$ years) will cause a change in the portfolio value of around

$$-2660 \times 0.004 = -10.64$$

That is, the portfolio will lose value at roughly $10.64 over the next trading day. It is easy to verify that this aggregate effect is correct by looking at the impact on each option individually and then aggregating them.

## The Position Vega

The *position vega* measures the portfolio's sensitivity to volatility. Let $V_1$ be the vega of option 1, $V_2$ the vega of option 2, etc. Then, the position vega is defined by

$$V_{pos} = n_1 V_1 + n_2 V_2 + \cdots \qquad (17.44)$$

Once again, positions in the underlying have no impact on the position vega since the vega of the underlying is zero.

To illustrate, we continue with the example. Suppose each call in the portfolio has a vega of 18.50, and each put in the portfolio has a vega of 21.90. Then, the position vega of the portfolio is given by

$$V_{pos} = (100 \times 18.50) + (150 \times 21.90) = 5135$$

We interpret the position vega as the portfolio extension of the individual option vega. In our example, the vega of 5135 means that a change of 1% in the volatility ($d\sigma = 0.01$) will change the portfolio value by

$$5135 \times 0.01 = 51.35$$

It is easy to verify that this is correct by considering the effect of the volatility change on each individual option and then aggregating the effects.

## The Position Rho

The *position rho* measures the portfolio's sensitivity to interest rates. For the general expression, let $\rho_1$ be the rho of option 1, $\rho_2$ that of option 2, etc. Then the position rho is given by

$$\rho_{pos} = n_1 \rho_1 + n_2 \rho_2 + \cdots \qquad (17.45)$$

Suppose, for instance, that in our example, each call has a rho of $+28.70$ and each put has a rho of $-17.40$. Then, the position rho is given by

$$\rho_{pos} = (100 \times 28.70) + (150 \times -17.40) = +260$$

Thus, a change of 25 basis points in the interest rate ($dr = 0.0025$) will change the portfolio value by

$$260 \times 0.0025 = 0.65$$

## 17.9 Exercises

1. What is the sign of the delta of (a) a call and (b) a put?
2. What is the sign of the gamma of (a) calls and (b) puts?
3. What is the sign of the theta for (a) calls and (b) puts?
4. What is the sign of the vega for (a) calls and (b) puts?
5. What is the sign of the rho for (a) calls and (b) puts?
6. You are given two puts on the same stock but with strikes $K_1$ and $K_2$. If their individual gammas are $\Gamma_1$ and $\Gamma_2$, what is the gamma of the portfolio consisting of both options?
7. Why is the gamma of an ATM option that is about to expire large in magnitude?
8. If the delta of a European call is 0.6, what is the delta of the European put for the same strike and maturity?

9. Can you derive the delta of a European call from the delta of the corresponding European put with no knowledge of the strike price?

10. Is it possible to determine the strike price of a pair of a call and a put on the same stock with the same strike if you know the deltas of both the call and the put? Assume the options are European. [*Note*: You are not given the option pricing model underlying the option prices and deltas.]

11. If the gamma of a European call is 0.03, what is the gamma of the corresponding European put at the same strike and maturity?

12. In the Black-Scholes model, what is higher, the delta of a one-year call or that of a two-year call on the same stock if the respective strikes are at-the-money forward? Show the result algebraically and then discuss the intuition.

13. Does your answer to the preceding question change if the call is deep out-of-the-money (OTM)? What about if it is deep in-the-money (ITM)?

14. In the Black-Scholes model, how does the delta of an ATM call change as volatility increases?

15. Intuitively speaking, how does the delta of a deep OTM call change as volatility increases?

16. Intuitively speaking, how does the delta of a deep ITM call change as volatility increases?

17. For an at-the-money-forward (ATMF) call in the Black-Scholes model, how does $\Delta_C$ change when interest rates rise?

18. Intuitively speaking, how does the delta of a call option change for constant strike $K$ when interest rates rise?

19. Intuitively speaking, how does the delta of a put (at fixed strike) change when interest rates rise?

20. For European options, what is the relationship of the interest-rate sensitivity of the call delta to that of the put delta?

21. How does the gamma of an OTM option behave as we approach maturity? What about the gamma of an ITM option? Derive the answers in the context of the Black-Scholes model and explain the intuition.

22. How does the vega of an OTM option behave as we approach maturity? What about the vega of an ITM option? Derive the answers in the context of the Black-Scholes model and explain the intuition.

23. Gamma is often thought of as representing a view on volatility, while vega measures the dollar impact on option values of a change in volatility. Do they measure the same thing? Is it possible for gamma to increase and vega to decrease simultaneously?

24. How does the theta of an OTM option behave as we approach maturity? What about the theta of an ITM option? Derive the answers in the context of the Black-Scholes model and explain the intuition.

25. Suppose a stock is currently trading at 100. An at-the-money call with a maturity of three months has the following price and greeks:

$$
\begin{aligned}
C &= \phantom{-}5.598 \\
\Delta &= \phantom{-}0.565 \\
\Gamma &= \phantom{-}0.032 \\
\Theta &= -12.385 \\
V &= \phantom{-}19.685 \\
\rho &= \phantom{-}12.71
\end{aligned}
$$

(a) If the stock price moves to $S = 101$, what is the predicted new option price (using the delta alone)?

(b) If the stock price moves to $S = 101$, what is the predicted new call delta?

(c) Repeat these questions assuming the stock price moves to 98 instead.

(d) If the stock price registers a large jump increase to 120, what is the new call value predicted by the delta alone? By the delta and gamma combined?

(e) Go back to the original parameters. If the time to maturity falls by 0.01, what is the new call value predicted by the theta?

(f) Repeat the last question if the time to maturity falls by 0.05.

(g) Go back to the original parameters. If the volatility increases by 1%, what is the predicted new value of the call? What if volatility fell by 2%?

(h) Go back to the original parameters. If interest rates should rise by 50 basis points, what is the new call value predicted by the rho?

26. A stock is currently trading at 55. You hold a portfolio of the following instruments:
   - Long 200 shares of stock.
   - Long 200 puts with a strike of 50 and maturity of three months.
   - Short 200 calls with a strike of 60 and maturity of three months.

You are given the following information:

| Instrument | Price | Delta | Gamma | Vega | Theta | Rho |
|---|---|---|---|---|---|---|
| Call with $K = 50$ | 6.321 | 0.823 | 0.038 | 7.152 | −5.522 | 9.730 |
| Put with $K = 50$ | 0.700 | −0.177 | 0.038 | 7.152 | −3.053 | −2.615 |
| Call with $K = 55$ | 3.079 | 0.565 | 0.057 | 10.827 | −6.812 | 6.993 |
| Put with $K = 55$ | 2.396 | −0.435 | 0.057 | 10.827 | −4.096 | −6.586 |
| Call with $K = 60$ | 1.210 | 0.297 | 0.050 | 9.515 | −5.513 | 3.779 |
| Put with $K = 60$ | 5.465 | −0.703 | 0.050 | 9.515 | −2.551 | −11.035 |

(a) What is the current value of your portfolio?

(b) What is the delta of your portfolio? the gamma? the vega? the theta? the rho?

(c) Suppose you want to make your portfolio gamma neutral. What is the cost of achieving this using the 55-strike call? What is the theta of your new position?

(d) What is the cost if you used the 55-strike put? What is the theta of the new position?

27. Using the same information as in Question 26, calculate the following quantities:

(a) The delta and gamma of a covered call portfolio with $K = 55$ (i.e., a portfolio where you are long the stock and short a call with a strike of 55).

(b) The delta and gamma of a protective put portfolio with $K = 50$ (long the stock and long a put with a strike of 50).

(c) The delta and gamma of a bull spread using calls with strikes of 55 and 60 (long a 55-strike call, short a 60-strike call).

(d) The delta and gamma of a butterfly spread using calls with strikes of 50, 55, and 60 (long a 50-strike call, long a 60-strike call, and short two 55-strike calls).

(e) The delta and gamma of a collar with strikes 50 and 60 (long position in the stock, long a 50-strike put, short a 60-strike call).

28. You hold a portfolio that is short 2,000 puts, each with a delta of $-0.63$. What would you do to delta-hedge the portfolio?

29. A stock has a volatility of 40%. An at-the-money call on the stock has a vega of $+21.45$. By how much will the call value change if volatility falls to 39%? Assuming the options are European, what about the corresponding put?

30. The theta of a put with 23 days left to maturity is $-17.50$. Other things being equal, by how much does the value of the put change if a day passes?

31. You hold two types of calls and two types of puts on a given stock. The deltas and gammas of the respective types are $(+0.40, +0.03)$, $(+0.55, +0.036)$, $(-0.63, +0.028)$, and $(-0.40, +0.032)$. You have a long position in 1,000 of the first type of call, a short position in 500 of the second type of call, a long position in 1,000 of the first type of put, and a short position in 500 of the second type of put.

    (a) What is the aggregate delta of your portfolio? The aggregate gamma?

    (b) Suppose you decide to gamma hedge your portfolio using only the first type of call. What is the resulting delta of the new portfolio? What position in the underlying is now required to create a delta-neutral gamma-neutral portfolio?

32. You hold a portfolio that is short 800 calls, each with a rho of $+21.50$, and long 800 puts, each with a rho of $-16.70$. By how much does your portfolio value change if interest rates move down by 20 basis points?

33. A stock is currently trading at $22.50. The delta of an at-the-money call on the stock is $+0.56$ and the gamma is $+0.035$. If the stock price were to change to $22.25, by how much would the call price change (using the delta alone)? What is the approximate new value of the call delta?

# Deriving the Black-Scholes Option Greeks

The Black-Scholes option pricing formulae are:

$$C = S_t\, N(d_1) - PV(K)\, N(d_2)$$
$$P = PV(K)\, N(-d_2) - S_t\, N(-d_1) \tag{17.46}$$

where

$$PV(K) = e^{-r(T-t)}K$$

$$d_1 = \frac{1}{\sigma\sqrt{T-t}}\left[\ln\left(\frac{S_t}{K}\right) + \left(r + \frac{1}{2}\sigma^2\right)(T-t)\right]$$

$$d_2 = d_1 - \sigma\sqrt{T-t}$$

and $N(\cdot)$ is the cumulative standard normal distribution. For any $x$, note that the density of the standard normal distribution is

$$N'(x) = \frac{1}{\sqrt{2\pi}}\, e^{-\frac{1}{2}x^2} \tag{17.47}$$

## An Important Preliminary Result

We begin with a result to which we will appeal repeatedly in the rest of this appendix. Namely, we shall show that

$$S_t\, N'(d_1) - PV(K)\, N'(d_2) = 0 \tag{17.48}$$

To prove (17.48), we must show that

$$S_t\, \frac{1}{\sqrt{2\pi}}\, e^{-\frac{1}{2}d_1^2} = PV(K)\, \frac{1}{\sqrt{2\pi}}\, e^{-\frac{1}{2}d_2^2}$$

or, after rearranging terms and simplifying, that

$$\frac{S_t}{PV(K)} = e^{\frac{1}{2}(d_1^2 - d_2^2)} \tag{17.49}$$

Take the natural log of both sides of (17.49). Using $\ln AB = \ln A + \ln B$, we may write the natural log of the left-hand side as

$$\ln\left(\frac{S_t}{e^{-r(T-t)}K}\right) = \ln\left(\frac{S_t}{K}\right) + \ln\left(\frac{1}{e^{-r(T-t)}}\right)$$

$$= \ln\left(\frac{S_t}{K}\right) + \ln\left(e^{r(T-t)}\right) \tag{17.50}$$

$$= \ln\left(\frac{S_t}{K}\right) + r(T-t)$$

The natural log of the right-hand side of (17.49) is

$$\ln\left(e^{\frac{1}{2}(d_1^2 - d_2^2)}\right) = \frac{1}{2}\left(d_1^2 - d_2^2\right) = \frac{1}{2}(d_1 - d_2)(d_1 + d_2) \tag{17.51}$$

Substituting in the definitions of $d_1$ and $d_2$, the last term of (17.51) expands as

$$\frac{1}{2}\sigma\sqrt{T-t}\left[\frac{2}{\sigma\sqrt{T-t}}\left\{\ln\left(\frac{S_t}{K}\right)+(r+\frac{1}{2}\sigma^2)(T-t)\right\}-\sigma\sqrt{T-t}\right] \qquad \textbf{(17.52)}$$

which after simplification and elimination of common terms becomes just

$$\ln\left(\frac{S_t}{K}\right)+r(T-t) \qquad \textbf{(17.53)}$$

From (17.50) and (17.53), the natural logarithms of the left- and right-hand sides of (17.49) coincide. Therefore, the key result, expression (17.48), holds. We shall use this to derive each of the Black-Scholes greeks. Throughout, the partial derivative of a function $f$ with respect to an argument $x$ is written $\partial f/\partial x$.

## The Black-Scholes Delta

The delta is the partial derivative of the option pricing function with respect to $S$. Differentiating the call pricing formula with respect to $S_t$,

$$\Delta_C = N(d_1)+S_t\,N'(d_1)\frac{\partial d_1}{\partial S_t}-PV(K)\,N'(d_2)\frac{\partial d_2}{\partial S_t} \qquad \textbf{(17.54)}$$

Since $d_1 - d_2 = \sigma\sqrt{T-t}$, we have

$$\frac{\partial d_1}{\partial S_t}=\frac{\partial d_2}{\partial S_t}$$

Using this in (17.55), we obtain

$$\Delta_C = N(d_1)+[S_t\,N'(d_1)-PV(K)\,N'(d_2)]\frac{\partial d_1}{\partial S_t} \qquad \textbf{(17.55)}$$

But, as we have seen in (17.48), $S_t N'(d_1) - PV(K)N'(d_2) = 0$. This means the delta reduces to just

$$\Delta_C = N(d_1)$$

as required. The Black-Scholes put delta may be derived from this using put-call parity (see expression (17.11)).

## The Black-Scholes Gamma

The gamma is the derivative of delta with respect to $S_t$. Since we have shown that the call delta is just $N(d_1)$, the call gamma is

$$\Gamma_C = \frac{\partial\Delta_C}{\partial S_t}=N'(d_1)\frac{\partial d_1}{\partial S_t} \qquad \textbf{(17.56)}$$

Direct computation shows that

$$\frac{\partial d_1}{\partial S_t}=\frac{1}{\sigma\sqrt{T-t}}\frac{1}{S_t}$$

so that

$$\Gamma_C = \frac{1}{\sigma S_t\sqrt{T-t}}N'(d_1) \qquad \textbf{(17.57)}$$

as claimed in the text. From put-call parity, the gammas of otherwise identical call and put European options coincide (see expression (17.21)), so this is also the gamma of the Black-Scholes put.

## The Black-Scholes Theta

The theta is the derivative of the option pricing function with respect to current time $t$. Applying this definition to the Black-Scholes call formula,

$$\Theta_C = S_t N'(d_1) \frac{\partial d_1}{\partial t} - PV(K) N'(d_2) \frac{\partial d_2}{\partial t} - re^{-r(T-t)} K N(d_2) \qquad \textbf{(17.58)}$$

Since $d_1 = d_2 + \sigma \sqrt{T - t}$, we have

$$\frac{\partial d_1}{\partial t} = \frac{\partial d_2}{\partial t} - \frac{\sigma}{2\sqrt{T - t}}$$

Therefore, we may rewrite (17.58) as

$$\begin{aligned} \Theta_C = &[S_t N'(d_1) - PV(K)N'(d_2)] \frac{\partial d_2}{\partial t} \\ &- \frac{1}{2\sqrt{T - t}} \sigma S_t N'(d_1) - re^{-r(T-t)} K N(d_2) \end{aligned} \qquad \textbf{(17.59)}$$

which from (17.48) is just

$$\Theta_C = -\frac{1}{2\sqrt{T - t}} \sigma S_t N'(d_1) - re^{-r(T-t)} K N(d_2) \qquad \textbf{(17.60)}$$

From put-call parity, European call and put thetas differ by the constant amount $-re^{-r(T-t)}K$ (see expression (17.28)). The Black-Scholes put theta may be derived from (17.60) using this observation.

## The Black-Scholes Vega

The vega is the derivative of the option pricing function with respect to $\sigma$. Applying this to the Black-Scholes call pricing formula,

$$\mathcal{V}_C = S_t N'(d_1) \frac{\partial d_1}{\partial \sigma} - PV(K)N'(d_2) \frac{\partial d_2}{\partial \sigma} \qquad \textbf{(17.61)}$$

Now, $d_1 = d_2 + \sigma \sqrt{T - t}$, so

$$\frac{\partial d_1}{\partial \sigma} = \frac{\partial d_2}{\partial \sigma} + \sqrt{T - t}$$

Substituting this into (17.61), we obtain

$$\mathcal{V}_C = [S_t N'(d_1) - PV(K)N'(d_2)] \frac{\partial d_2}{\partial \sigma} + S_t N'(d_1) \sqrt{T - t} \qquad \textbf{(17.62)}$$

From (17.48), this becomes just

$$\mathcal{V}_C = S_t N'(d_1) \sqrt{T - t} \qquad \textbf{(17.63)}$$

From put-call parity, European call and put vegas coincide (see expression (17.34)), so this is also the expression for the Black-Scholes put vega.

## The Black-Scholes Rho

The rho is the derivative of the option pricing function with respect to $r$. Applying this to the Black-Scholes call pricing formula,

$$\rho_C = S_t N'(d_1) \frac{\partial d_1}{\partial r} - PV(K)N'(d_2) \frac{\partial d_2}{\partial r} + (T - t)e^{-r(T-t)}KN(d_2) \quad \textbf{(17.64)}$$

Now, $d_1 = d_2 + \sigma\sqrt{T - t}$, so

$$\frac{\partial d_1}{\partial r} = \frac{\partial d_2}{\partial r}$$

Substituting this into (17.64), we obtain

$$\rho_C = [S_t N'(d_1) - PV(K)N'(d_2)] \frac{\partial d_2}{\partial r} + (T - t)e^{-r(T-t)}KN(d_2) \quad \textbf{(17.65)}$$

From (17.48), this becomes just

$$\rho_C = (T - t)e^{-r(T-t)}KN(d_2) \quad \textbf{(17.66)}$$

From put-call parity, European call and put rhos differ by the constant amount $(T - t)e^{-r(T-t)}K$ (see expression (17.40)). Using this in (17.66), the Black-Scholes put rho may be derived.

# Chapter 18

# Exotic Options I: Path-Independent Options

## 18.1 Introduction

An *exotic option* is an option whose payoffs or exercise features are different from those of standard ("plain vanilla") calls and puts. An immense variety of exotic options trades in the over-the-counter market. The list includes forward starts, binaries, compounds, lookbacks, choosers, cliquets, shouts, Asians, Bermudans, barriers, quantos, and many, many others.

"Different" does not always mean more complex. Some exotics, such as lookbacks and Asians, do involve more complex payoffs than plain vanilla options, but others, such as binary options, have very simple payoff structures. Nor should the word "exotic" be taken to imply that these options are rare; to the contrary, some exotics, like barrier options, have become commonplace in the market.

Exotic options provide richer and more targeted payoff patterns than can be obtained from vanilla options. For example, an Asian option addresses a specific kind of hedging need—exposure to the average—more efficiently than vanilla options; a chooser option is a cheaper version of a volatility instrument like a straddle; a knock-out barrier option provides greater speculative potential than its vanilla counterpart in taking directional bets; and so on. This chapter and the next discuss the uses, pricing, and hedging of several types of exotic options.

### Path-Independent and Path-Dependent Exotics

There are two broad categories of exotic options. The first is *path-independent exotics*. These are exotic options whose payoff at the time of exercise may depend on the price of the underlying at that point, but not on *how* that price was reached, i.e., not on the *past* behavior of prices. In this chapter, we examine six classes of path-independent exotics: forward starts, binaries, compounds, choosers, exchange options, and quantos. We also examine several variants on the exchange option theme such as rainbow options and options on the maximum or minimum of several assets.

In the next chapter, we examine the class of exotic options called *path-dependent exotics*. In a path-dependent exotic, the payoffs from the option at the time of exercise may depend not only on the price of the underlying at that time but also on some or all of the entire *path*

**TABLE 18.1**
Notation When Using the Black-Scholes Setting

| Notation | Meaning |
|---|---|
| $T$ | Maturity date of option/Time left to maturity |
| $S$ | Current stock price |
| $S_T$ | Stock price at $T$ |
| $K$ | Strike price of option |
| $r$ | Riskless interest rate |
| $\sigma$ | Volatility of stock returns |
| $\delta$ | Dividend yield on stock |
| $C(S, K, T)$ | Price of vanilla European call with maturity $T$ and strike $K$ |
| $P(S, K, T)$ | Price of vanilla European put with maturity $T$ and strike $K$ |

of prices leading to that terminal price. This path could matter in simple ways (e.g., did the price ever cross a critical level $S^*$?) or in more complex ways (e.g., what was the *average* price observed over the option's life?). We examine five classes of path-dependent exotics: cliquets, barriers, Asians, lookbacks, and shouts.

## The Framework

Throughout the discussion on exotics, we take the underlying security to be a stock. With obvious modifications, the same arguments extend to other underlying securities. We use the Black-Scholes and/or binomial framework to describe the pricing and hedging of exotics.

The Black-Scholes framework is used when there are closed-form solutions available for describing option prices. For this purpose, we use the notation introduced in Chapter 14 but with one simplification: the current time is normalized to $t = 0$, so $T$ denotes both the maturity date and the remaining time to maturity of the option. The notation is summarized in Table 18.1.

The binomial framework is used when there are no closed-forms available (and sometimes, to illustrate special points, even when they are). When using the binomial framework, a specific two-period model is employed for illustration. The initial stock price is $S = 100$; the up and down moves are $u = 1.10$ and $d = 0.90$; and the risk-free rate of interest per period is $R = 1.02$. The two-period tree is described in Figure 18.1. For later use, note that

**FIGURE 18.1**
Stock Price Tree for Binomial Illustrations

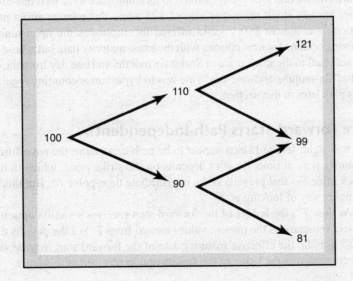

with these parameters, the risk-neutral probability $q$ of an up move is given by

$$q = \frac{R - d}{u - d} = 0.60$$

### Two Common Themes

Two common themes run through this material. The first is to do with pricing. The price of an exotic option is the fair value of the payoffs it generates. Conceptually, identifying this value is a straightforward application of risk-neutral valuation: we find the payoffs of the option and take the discounted expectations of these payoffs under the risk-neutral probability. Computationally, the process can be quite hard. This is especially the case for path-dependent exotics such as barriers or Asians.

The second concerns hedging, and more generally, the exotic greeks. As we have seen, vanilla option greeks exhibit an intuitive and consistent pattern of behavior. Call deltas are positive and put deltas negative, the gammas of both are always positive and maximal near-the-money, and so on. With exotics, one or more of these properties may fail. For example, for certain exotics, vega can be negative, meaning the option value *decreases* as volatility increases; or gamma can be negative, meaning the option delta decreases as the option moves into-the-money. None of this means that the behavior of exotics is conceptually complicated. The behavior of each exotic is, as we shall see, intuitive given its payoff structure. But it does imply that vanilla option behavior should not be extrapolated to exotics.

# 18.2   Forward Start Options

A forward start option is a particularly simple type of exotic option. It is one that comes to life at a specified point $T^*$ in the future and has a life of $\tau$ years (measured from $T^*$). The strike price $K$ of the forward start is not specified at the outset; rather, it is determined at time $T^*$ as $K = \alpha S_{T^*}$, where $S_{T^*}$ is the stock price at $T^*$ and $\alpha$ is a prespecified number. In the "typical" case, we have $\alpha = 1$, meaning the forward start option is at-the-money when it comes to life.

A noteworthy example of a forward start option is a plan offered by Sprint to its employees in November 2000. Following a steep decline in its stock price, many of the stock option awards Sprint had previously granted to its employees were well out-of-the-money. (At the time, Sprint's stock price was around $25 while the average strike price of the affected options was almost $60.) Sprint offered its employees the opportunity to trade in their existing options for new options with the same maturity date but whose strike prices would be set equal to the stock price of Sprint six months and one day from the date of the trade-in. (The "six-months-and-one-day" rule was to bypass an accounting regulation.) We return to this plan later in this section.

### Are Forward Starts Path-Independent?

At first sight, forward starts appear to be path-*dependent*: the payoff from the option at its maturity (i.e., at time $T^* + \tau$) depends on the strike price, which in turn depends on the stock price $S_{T^*}$ that prevails at the intermediate time-point $T^*$. But this is an unnecessarily complex way of looking at it.

At time $T^*$, the holder of the forward start receives a vanilla option whose value completely summarizes the present value (viewed from $T^*$) of the payoffs that will be received at $T^* + \tau$. So the effective maturity date of the forward start may be viewed as $T^*$ and its effective payoffs the value of the vanilla option received at this point.

Looking at it this way makes the forward start path-independent: the value of the option received at $T^*$ depends on stock prices only through $S_{T^*}$. It also makes the pricing problem quite simple as we shall see shortly. A preliminary result is required first.

## Option Prices and "Homogeneity of Degree 1"

The pricing of forward starts is considerably simplified by a strong property of vanilla option prices called "homogeneity of degree 1 in $(S, K)$." This property is almost an obvious one, certainly one that is very intuitive.

To motivate this property, consider an example. Suppose the stock of a given company is currently trading at $S = 100$, and you have options on the stock struck at $K = 92$. Suppose the company goes through a 4-for-1 stock split, so the post-split price of the stock is 25. What change in the option contract would leave its value unchanged?

The instinctive guess is the right answer: the strike price should also be reduced to one-fourth of its original level (i.e., to 23) and the number of options should be increased fourfold. Intuitively, when the stock price and strike price are both divided by 4, it takes four new options to make up each old option. This is exactly the statement that option prices are homogeneous of degree 1 in $(S, K)$.

To put this in notational terms, let $C(S, K, T)$ denote the value of an option (say, a call) with current stock price $S$, strike price $K$, and remaining maturity $T$. Suppose $S$ and $K$ are each multiplied by a factor $m > 0$. Then, as we have seen, the new call value $C(mS, mK, T)$ should be just $m$ times the old call value:

$$C(mS, mK, T) = m\, C(S, K, T) \qquad \textbf{(18.1)}$$

Expression (18.1) is the mathematical statement that *option prices are homogeneous of degree 1 in $(S, K)$.*

## Pricing Forward Starts

We describe the pricing of forward start calls here. Puts are handled identically. We assume the underlying stock pays a continuous dividend yield at the rate $\delta$ (which could be zero).

Let $C^{FS}(S, T^*, \tau, \alpha)$ denote the current price of a forward start call, where $S$ is the current (date 0) stock price and the parameters $(T^*, \tau, \alpha)$ define the forward start. For a vanilla call with strike $K$ and maturity $T$, the current call price is denoted $C(S, K, T)$.

At time $T^*$, the holder of the option receives a vanilla option with a strike of $\alpha S_{T^*}$ and $\tau$ years to maturity. This option is worth $C(S_{T^*}, \alpha S_{T^*}, \tau)$. From the homogeneity property (18.1),

$$C(S_{T^*}, \alpha S_{T^*}, \tau) = S_{T^*}\, C(1, \alpha, \tau) \qquad \textbf{(18.2)}$$

Of course, $C(1, \tau, \alpha)$ is just the price of a vanilla call with current stock price $S = 1$, strike $K = \alpha$, and maturity $\tau$.

Now, the price $C^{FS}(S, T^*, \tau, \alpha)$ of the forward start is the expectation under the risk-neutral probability of its time-$T^*$ payoffs (18.2) discounted back to the current time at the risk-free rate $r$. So if $E[\cdot]$ denotes expectation under the risk-neutral probability, we have:

$$C^{FS}(S, T^*, \tau, \alpha) = e^{-rT^*}\, E\left[S_{T^*}\, C(1, \alpha, \tau)\right] \qquad \textbf{(18.3)}$$

Since $C(1, \alpha, \tau)$ is a constant that does not depend on $S_{T^*}$, it can be pulled out of the expectation, which means we have

$$C^{FS}(S, T^*, \tau, \alpha) = C(1, \alpha, \tau)\, e^{-rT^*}\, E[S_{T^*}] \qquad \textbf{(18.4)}$$

The term $e^{-rT^*} E[S_{T^*}]$ measures the present value of receiving the (random) payment $S_{T^*}$ at time $T^*$, i.e., of receiving one unit of the stock at $T^*$. This payoff can be replicated by buying $e^{-\delta T^*}$ units of the stock today and reinvesting all the dividends in buying more of the stock. (This will result in a holding of one unit of the stock at time $T^*$.) Thus, we have

$$e^{-rT^*} E[S_{T^*}] = e^{-\delta T^*} S \qquad (18.5)$$

Substituting (18.5) into (18.4), we obtain

$$C^{FS}(S, T^*, \tau, \alpha) = e^{-\delta T^*} S C(1, \alpha, \tau) \qquad (18.6)$$

Applying the homogeneity property again (this time in reverse) to the right-hand side of (18.6), we finally get:

$$C^{FS}(S, T^*, \tau, \alpha) = e^{-\delta T^*} C(S, \alpha S, \tau) \qquad (18.7)$$

Expression (18.7) is the general expression for the price of a forward start option when the underlying has a continuous dividend yield of $\delta$. In words, it says that the value of the forward start is the value of $e^{-\delta T^*}$ units of a vanilla option with the same characteristics as the forward start (maturity $\tau$ and strike equal to $\alpha$ times the current stock price). Note that:

- If $\delta > 0$, a higher $T^*$ lowers the value of the option. Intuitively, the more one has to wait, the greater the proportion of the current stock price that has been paid out as dividends, so the lower the value of the option that is received.
- If $\delta = 0$, then $T^*$ does not affect the option value! What matters is only the remaining maturity of the option measured from $T^*$.

## The Sprint Repricing Scheme

The forward start valuation expression (18.7) can be used to highlight the essential trade-offs in a Sprint-type repricing scheme. One simplifying assumption is required: that executive stock options can be treated as vanilla options and valued using risk-neutral procedures.[1] Let $K^o$ denote the strike price of the original option, $T^o$ its remaining maturity in years, $S$ the current price of the stock, and $C(S, K^o, T^o)$ the value of the original option.

Under Sprint's scheme, option holders can trade these options for forward starts coming to life in six months and one day, with $\alpha = 1$ and a remaining maturity $\tau$ that is $T^o$ years minus six months and a day. Ignoring dividends, the forward starts are worth $C(S, S, \tau)$. The trade-in is worthwhile if

$$C(S, S, \tau) > C(S, K^o, T^o) \qquad (18.8)$$

Expression (18.8) summarizes the essence of the scheme: the original option (the right-hand side of (18.8)) has a higher strike but also a longer maturity. For the option holder weighing the trade-in, the question is whether the lower strike price $S$ on the new option compensates for the reduction in time to maturity. For the stock holder worried about the cost of the scheme, the extra compensation cost is the difference between the left-hand and right-hand sides of (18.8).

## Hedging Forward Starts

From (18.5), the value of the forward start at any current stock price $S$ is just $e^{-\delta T^*} S \times C(1, \alpha, \tau)$. This means the forward start has very simple greeks. Its delta is a constant:

$$\Delta^{FS} = e^{-\delta T^*} C(1, \alpha, \tau) \qquad (18.9)$$

[1] This is not an innocuous assumption. Unlike normal options, executive options cannot be freely traded nor can their holders short the stock of their companies. Rubinstein (1995) discusses the possible valuation impact of these and other deviations from the assumptions underlying risk-neutral valuation procedures.

Since the delta is constant, the gamma is zero. The remaining greeks are just the greeks of the $(1, \alpha, \tau)$-vanilla call multiplied by $e^{-\delta T^*} S$.

# 18.3  Binary Options

The term *binary* (or *digital*) option is used to refer to any option with a *discontinuous* payoff structure. While several examples of such options exist, by far the most prominent, and the canonical example of binary options, is the *cash-or-nothing* option. A cash-or-nothing option is simply a straight bet on the market: the option holder receives a fixed amount of cash (say, $M$) if the stock price finishes above the strike price $K$ at maturity $T$ of the option, and nothing otherwise. The payoffs at maturity of the cash-or-nothing option are graphed in the left panel of Figure 18.2. There is a discontinuity in the payoffs at $K$.

A variant on this theme is the *asset-or-nothing* option in which the holder of the option receives one unit of the asset if the option finishes in-the-money ($S_T \geq K$) and nothing otherwise. The payoff from such an option is graphed in the right panel of Figure 18.2. Once again, there is a discontinuity in the payoffs at $K$.

A third example of a binary option is a *gap* option. In a gap option, the holder is long an asset-or-nothing option and short a cash-or-nothing option. Two special cases of a gap option are of interest. First, when $M = K$ in the cash-or-nothing option, the gap option reduces to a vanilla call (see the paragraph leading to (18.11) below). Second, when $M$ and $K$ are chosen so that the value of the asset-or-nothing option equals that of the cash-or-nothing option, we obtain what is called a *pay later* option. In this case, no money exchanges hands at inception; the only possible cash flows to either party are at maturity.

Our discussion of binary options in this chapter concentrates mainly on cash-or-nothing options.

## Pricing Cash-or-Nothing Options

Let $C^{C\text{-}or\text{-}N}$ denote the price of a cash-or-nothing option. Since the payoff from the option is a constant $M$, the fair price of the option is simply the present value of $M$ times the risk-neutral likelihood the option finishes in-the-money (i.e., the risk-neutral likelihood that $S_T \geq K$).

As we have seen in Chapter 14, the risk-neutral probability that $S_T \geq K$ in the Black-Scholes setting is $N(d_2)$, where $N(\cdot)$ is the cumulative standard normal distribution and $d_2$

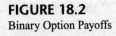

**FIGURE 18.2**
Binary Option Payoffs

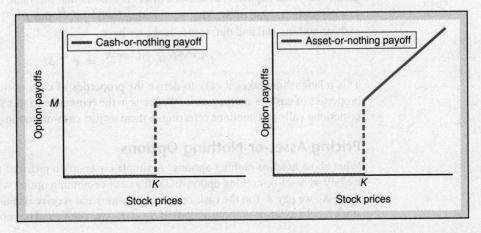

**FIGURE 18.3**
Binary Option Values
at Different Maturities

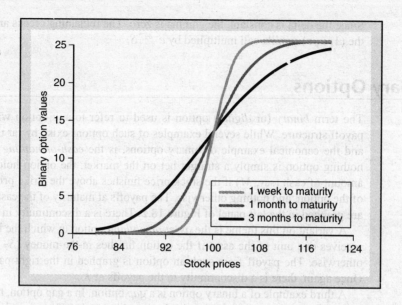

is defined by

$$d_2 = \frac{1}{\sigma\sqrt{T}} \left[ \ln\left(\frac{S}{K}\right) + \left(r - \delta - \frac{1}{2}\sigma^2\right) T \right]$$

Thus, the price of the cash-or-nothing option in the Black-Scholes setting is

$$C^{C\text{-}or\text{-}N} = e^{-rT} M N(d_2) \tag{18.10}$$

Figure 18.3 plots binary option values in a Black-Scholes setting. The parameters used are $S = K = 100$, $M = 25$, $\sigma = 0.20$, and $r = 0.05$. Three maturities are used: one week, one month, and three months. As the option approaches maturity, its value converges to the discontinuous payoff in Figure 18.2.

A final comment. What we have defined here as a cash-or-nothing option is more commonly called a cash-or-nothing *call*: it pays off only if the strike price finishes *above* a specified strike level $K$. We can also define cash-or-nothing *put* options. In this case, the option pays $M$ if $S_T < K$ and nothing otherwise. Cash-or-nothing calls and cash-or-nothing puts are intimately related—if we hold both of them, we are guaranteed a payoff of $M$ regardless of what happens to the stock price. It follows that the value of such a portfolio is just the present value of $M$. That is, denoting by $C^{C\text{-}or\text{-}N}$ and $P^{C\text{-}or\text{-}N}$ the prices of the cash-or-nothing call and put, respectively, we have

$$C^{C\text{-}or\text{-}N} + P^{C\text{-}or\text{-}N} = e^{-rT} M$$

This relationship makes it easy to derive the properties of cash-or-nothing puts from the properties of cash-or-nothing calls. We focus in the remainder of this section only on cash-or-nothing calls and continue referring to them as just cash-or-nothing options.

## Pricing Asset-or-Nothing Options

What about asset-or-nothing options? A simple observation provides the answer. Suppose we buy an asset-or-nothing option and sell a cash-or-nothing option with $M = K$. Then, if $S_T \geq K$, we pay $K$ (on the cash-or-nothing option) and receive one unit of the underlying stock (on the asset-or-nothing option); if $S_T < K$, we receive and pay nothing. These payoffs are exactly the same as a vanilla call. So, if $C^{A\text{-}or\text{-}N}$ denotes the price of the asset-or-nothing option and $C$ the price of a vanilla call, we have

$$C^{A\text{-}or\text{-}N} - C^{C\text{-}or\text{-}N} = C \qquad (18.11)$$

Substituting for $C^{C\text{-}or\text{-}N}$ and $C$ in the Black-Scholes setting, this gives us

$$C^{A\text{-}or\text{-}N} = e^{-\delta T} S\, N(d_1) \qquad (18.12)$$

where $d_1$ is defined by

$$d_1 = \frac{1}{\sigma\sqrt{T}}\left[\ln\left(\frac{S}{K}\right) + \left(r - \delta + \frac{1}{2}\sigma^2\right)T\right]$$

## Binary Option Greeks

Since (18.11) is an identity, we can calculate the greeks of the asset-or-nothing option from knowledge of the greeks of vanilla and cash-or-nothing options. (That is, $\Delta^{A\text{-}or\text{-}N} = \Delta^{Vanilla} - \Delta^{C\text{-}or\text{-}N}$, $\Gamma^{A\text{-}or\text{-}N} = \Gamma^{Vanilla} - \Gamma^{C\text{-}or\text{-}N}$, etc.) So we focus on the greeks of cash-or-nothing options in the rest of this section.

## Hedging Cash-or-Nothing Options: The Delta

When a cash-or-nothing option is deep out-of-the-money, a small change in the stock price leaves it deep out-of-the-money. The option is almost sure to pay zero in this case and is not very sensitive to changes in the stock price. That is, its delta is close to zero.

But this is also true if the cash-or-nothing option is deep *in*-the-money! In this case, the option's payoff is fixed at $M$ regardless of how deep in-the-money the option moves. Thus, small changes in the stock price of a deep in-the-money option have a negligible effect, so the delta is again close to zero.

Both effects are visible in Figure 18.3—the slope of the option pricing function goes to zero as the option moves out-of-the-money and as it moves into-the-money. Figure 18.4 plots these slopes. The deltas are bell-shaped, reaching their maximum values at the money and tailing away to zero as the option moves away from the money in either direction.

**FIGURE 18.4**

Binary Option Deltas at Different Maturities

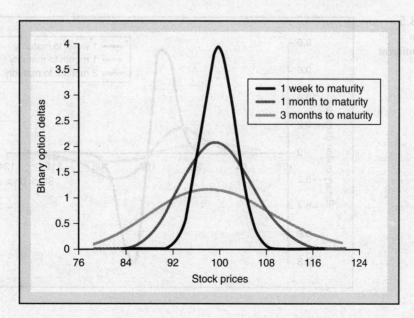

## Cash-or-Nothing Options: The Gamma and Other Greeks

Cash-or-nothing options offer an excellent illustration of how different exotic options can be from vanilla options in terms of their sensitivities. Cash-or-nothing call options resemble vanilla call options in that they make money if prices go up and have a zero payoff if they go down. Yet we have already seen that cash-or-nothing deltas differ dramatically from call deltas. The same is true for the other greeks as well.

The gamma first. Since the delta increases as the option goes from being out-of-the-money to at-the-money, the gamma is *positive* in this range. However, since the delta declines as the option moves from at- to into-the-money, the gamma becomes *negative*. Thus, a long binary option position can have either positive or negative gamma depending on depth in-the-money.

Figure 18.5 plots the option gammas for the same parameter values as the earlier plots. As the option gets closer to maturity, its payoff more closely resembles the discontinuous final payoff of Figure 18.2, so the delta rises sharply at-the-money and falls away steeply on either side. Thus, the gamma blows up at-the-money, being large and positive on one side and large and negative on the other. As maturity approaches, the gamma at-the-money is undefined: it goes to $+\infty$ on one side and to $-\infty$ on the other.

The vega next. For a deep out-of-the-money cash-or-nothing option, an increase in volatility is unambiguously good because it increases the likelihood of the option finishing in the money. So the vega is positive. However, when the cash-or-nothing option is deep *in*-the-money, volatility is a bad thing: it cannot *increase* payoffs since these are capped at $M$, but it can *decrease* them by pushing the option out-of-the-money. Thus, vega becomes *negative*, which can never happen for a long vanilla position. Figure 18.6 plots cash-or-nothing vegas for the same parameter values as in the earlier graphs.

Third, the theta. For a vanilla call, the theta is always negative. For a cash-or-nothing option, it can be negative or positive. When the option is out-of-the-money, a lower time to maturity hurts and theta is negative. But if the option is in-the-money, there is no further upside benefit possible in a longer maturity, so theta is positive. Figure 18.7 illustrates.

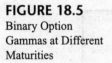

**FIGURE 18.5**
Binary Option Gammas at Different Maturities

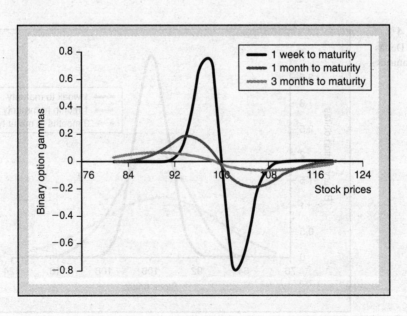

**FIGURE 18.6**
Binary Option Vegas at
Different Maturities

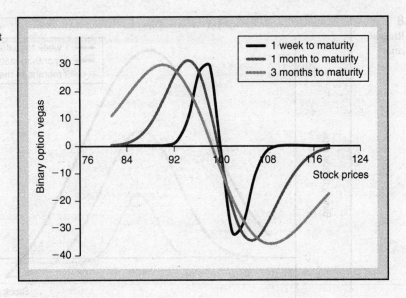

**FIGURE 18.7**
Binary Option Thetas
at Different Maturities

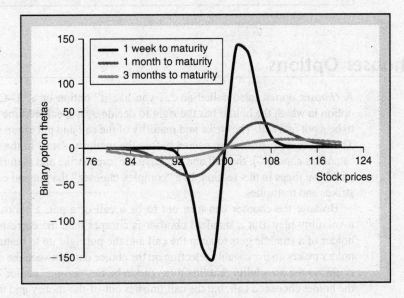

Finally, the rho. Vanilla calls always have a positive rho; moreover, the rho increases with depth-in-the-money. Neither property is true for cash-or-nothing options. In a cash-or-nothing option, the holder *receives* cash upon exercise, so higher interest rates lower the present value of what is received. On the other hand, higher interest rates also result in a higher risk-neutral drift of the stock price. When the option is out-of-the-money, the second factor dominates, so the rho is positive. However, as the option goes deep into-the-money, the first factor becomes more important, and the rho turns negative. Figure 18.8 describes this behavior.

**FIGURE 18.8**
Binary Option Rhos at
Different Maturities

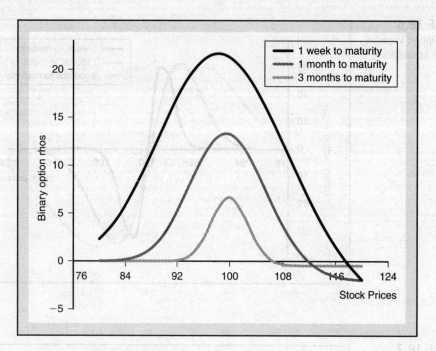

## 18.4 Chooser Options

A *chooser option* (also called an "as-you-like-it" option or a "U-Choose" option) is an option in which the holder has the right to decide by a specified time whether the option is to be a put or a call. The strike and maturity of the call and put are specified in the contract. The choice date, of course, occurs before the maturity dates. In the typical case (called a "standard chooser"), the call and put have the same strike and maturity; this is the case on which we focus in this section. In a "complex chooser," the put and call may have different strikes and maturities.

Because the chooser can turn out to be a call or a put, a chooser, like a straddle, is a volatility play. But a standard chooser is cheaper than the corresponding straddle. The holder of a straddle gets to keep the call and the put right up to maturity. In a chooser, the holder makes an irrevocable selection on the choice date between the call and the put. There is always the possibility that this turns out to be the "wrong" choice ex post (for example, the holder chooses a call, but the call finishes out-of-the-money and the put finishes in-the-money at maturity), leading to a lower value for the chooser vis-à-vis a straddle.

The closer the choice date and maturity date are, the lower the likelihood of a wrong choice, so the more closely the chooser resembles a straddle. In the limit, as the choice date and maturity date coincide, the chooser becomes identical to the straddle.

Indeed, it is possible to relate the price of a chooser precisely to the price of the corresponding straddle using put-call parity. We do this prior to discussing the pricing and hedging of choosers.

### The Relationship between Choosers and Straddles

Let $K$ and $T$ denote the common strike price and maturity date of the call and put in a standard chooser, and let $\tau$ be the choice date ($\tau < T$).

Suppose $S_\tau$ is the stock price on date $\tau$. At this point, the options have a further maturity of $T - \tau$; denote their values by $C(S_\tau, K, T - \tau)$ and $P(S_\tau, K, T - \tau)$, respectively. The holder of the chooser will obviously choose the more valuable of the two options. So the value of the chooser at $\tau$ is:

$$\max\{C(S_\tau, K, T - \tau), P(S_\tau, K, T - \tau)\} \qquad \textbf{(18.13)}$$

Now, by put-call parity, the call and put prices on date $\tau$ are related by

$$P(S_\tau, K, T - \tau) = C(S_\tau, K, T - \tau) + PV_\tau(K) - e^{-\delta(T-\tau)}S_\tau \qquad \textbf{(18.14)}$$

where $PV_\tau(K) = e^{-r(T-\tau)}K$. Substituting this in (18.13), the time-$\tau$ value of the chooser is

$$\max\{C(S_\tau, K, T - \tau), C(S_\tau, K, T - \tau) + PV_\tau(K) - e^{-\delta(T-\tau)}S_\tau\} \qquad \textbf{(18.15)}$$

Pulling the common term $C(S_\tau, \tau, K, T)$ out of the braces, we obtain

$$C(S_\tau, K, T - \tau) + e^{-\delta(T-\tau)} \max\{0, e^{-(r-\delta)(T-\tau)}K - S_\tau\} \qquad \textbf{(18.16)}$$

The second term in (18.16) is simply the payoff from $e^{-\delta(T-\tau)}$ put options on the stock with strike $e^{-(r-\delta)(T-\tau)}K$ and maturing at $\tau$. Thus, (18.16) shows that the chooser is equivalent to a portfolio consisting of

- A call option with strike $K$ and maturity $T$.
- $e^{-\delta(T-\tau)}$ put options with strike $e^{-(r-\delta)(T-\tau)}K$ and maturity $\tau$.

The corresponding straddle consists of

- A call option with strike $K$ and maturity $T$.
- A put option with strike $K$ and maturity $T$.

The difference in value between the straddle and the chooser is just the difference in price of the respective puts. In particular, when $\delta = 0$, it is as if a chooser consists of the same call as a straddle but has a put with a *lower* strike and a *shorter* maturity.

## Pricing Choosers

The decomposition (18.16) of the chooser suggests an easy way to price a standard chooser. The value $V^{ch}$ of the chooser is simply the sum of the prices of a vanilla call with strike $K$ and maturity $T$, and $e^{-\delta(T-\tau)}$ vanilla puts with strike $e^{-(r-\delta)(T-\tau)}K$ and maturity $\tau$:

$$V^{ch} = C(S, K, T) + e^{-\delta(T-\tau)}P(S, e^{-(r-\delta)(T-\tau)}K, \tau) \qquad \textbf{(18.17)}$$

The required call and put values are easily calculated in a given model. In a Black-Scholes setting, we can represent chooser values in closed-form by using the closed-forms for the call and the put.

Figure 18.9 plots straddle and chooser values for various values of the current stock price $S$. At low and high values of $S$ (i.e., when the put or call moves deep into-the-money), the difference between the two becomes small. It is maximal when the options are near-the-money.

## Hedging Choosers

The greek of the chooser is just the sum of the greeks on (a) a call with strike $K$ and maturity $T$, and (b) $e^{-\delta(T-\tau)}$ puts with strike $e^{-(r-\delta)(T-\tau)}K$ and maturity $\tau$. So, for instance, the chooser delta in a Black-Scholes setting is just

$$N(d_1) - e^{-\delta(T-\tau)} N(-\hat{d}_1) \qquad \textbf{(18.18)}$$

**FIGURE 18.9**

Straddle and Chooser
Values

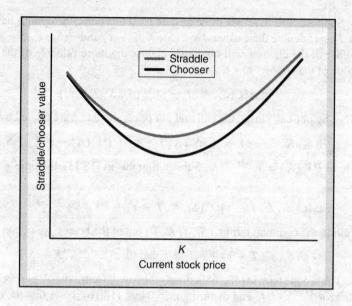

where $N(\cdot)$ is the cumulative standard normal distribution and $d_1$ and $\hat{d}_1$ are given by

$$d_1 = \frac{1}{\sigma\sqrt{T}}\left[\ln\left(\frac{S}{K}\right) + \left(r - \delta + \frac{1}{2}\sigma^2\right)T\right] \tag{18.19}$$

$$\hat{d}_1 = \frac{1}{\sigma\sqrt{\tau}}\left[\ln\left(\frac{S}{e^{-(r-\delta)(T-\tau)}K}\right) + \left(r - \delta + \frac{1}{2}\sigma^2\right)\tau\right] \tag{18.20}$$

Figure 18.10 plots the chooser delta as the current stock price $S$ varies. At low stock prices, the chooser behaves much like a put, so the delta goes towards $-1$. At high stock prices, the chooser behaves much like a call and the delta goes towards $+1$. The other greeks are derived similarly.

**FIGURE 18.10**

Straddle and Chooser
Deltas

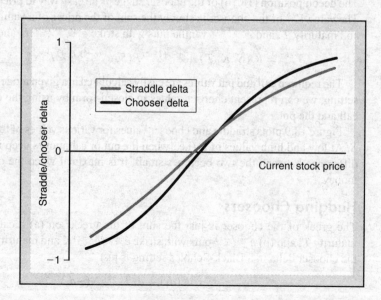

# 18.5  Compound Options

A *compound option* is simply an option written on an option, i.e., one in which the underlying asset is itself an option written on another asset. The strike price in a compound option is the price at which the holder of the option may purchase or sell the underlying option. To distinguish between the two options' strike prices, the strike price of the compound option is sometimes referred to as the "front fee" while that on the underlying option is the "back fee."

Since the compound can be a call or a put and the underlying option can be a call or a put, there are four basic kinds of compound options: (i) a call option on a call option, (ii) a call option on a put option, (iii) a put option on a call option, and (iv) a put option on a put option.

Loosely speaking, compound options enable the holder to lock in a price for insurance while postponing the decision on whether to obtain that insurance. Suppose, for example, that an investor is debating whether to buy a put option to obtain protection against a decrease in the price of XYZ stock. Suppose the investor finds current option prices high. If the investor does not buy the put and the price of XYZ stock does in fact decline, then the price of the put option will go up even further. That is, the very circumstances in which insurance becomes more valuable to the investor are the ones in which insurance becomes even more expensive.

To guard against this eventuality, the investor can buy a compound option, in this case, a call on the put. By doing so, the investor locks in the price at which the put option may be purchased if asset prices do decline and the put becomes more expensive. Of course, there is no free lunch here; in particular, if asset prices do not decline sufficiently to make exercising the compound option attractive, the amount paid as premium is lost.

## Payoffs from Compound Options

Denote the strike and time to maturity of the underlying option by $K$ and $T$, respectively, and the strike price and time to maturity of the compound option by $k$ and $t$, respectively. Consider a call on a call first. At maturity $t$, the holder of this option has the right to buy the underlying vanilla call at a price of $k$. So given a time-$t$ stock price $S_t$, the payoff from the call on call is

$$\max\{C(S_t, K, T-t) - k, 0\}$$

Here, $C(S_t, K, T-t)$ is the time-$t$ value of the underlying vanilla call (which now has $T-t$ years left to maturity). The key variable determining whether each of these options finishes in- or out-of-the-money is the time-$t$ value of the stock price $S_t$. As $S_t$ increases, the call value $C(S_t, K, T-t)$ also increases, so there is a critical value $S_t^*$ such that

$$\begin{aligned} C(S_t, K, T-t) &< k, \quad \text{if } S_t < S_t^* \\ C(S_t, K, T-t) &> k, \quad \text{if } S_t \geq S_t^* \end{aligned} \tag{18.21}$$

Thus, the payoff to the holder of the call-on-call compound is

$$\begin{cases} 0, & \text{if } S_t < S_t^* \\ C(S_t, K, T-t) - k, & \text{if } S_t \geq S_t^* \end{cases}$$

Similarly, the payoffs at maturity $t$ from a put on a call is

$$\max\{k - C(S_t, K, T-t), 0\} = \begin{cases} k - C(S_t, K, T-t), & \text{if } S_t < S_t^* \\ 0, & \text{if } S_t \geq S_t^* \end{cases}$$

The upper panels of Figure 18.11 describe the payoffs from these two options.

**FIGURE 18.11**
Payoffs from
Compound Options

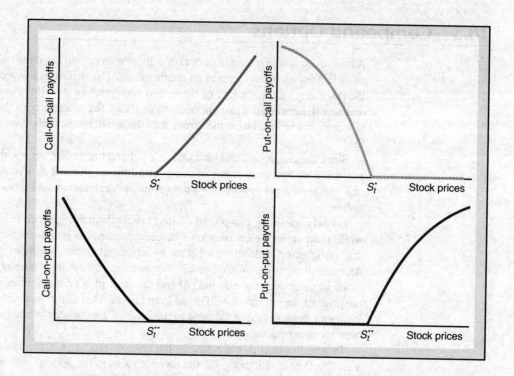

What about options on puts? The value $P(S_t, K, T-t)$ of the vanilla put at $t$ is decreasing in $S_t$. Therefore, there is $S_t^{**}$ such that the put value exceeds $k$ when and only when $S_t < S_t^{**}$. This means the payoffs of a call on a put and a put on a put can be expressed as, respectively,

$$\max\{P(S_t, K, T-t) - k, 0\} = \begin{cases} P(S_t, K, T-t) - k, & \text{if } S_t < S_t^{**} \\ 0, & \text{if } S_t \geq S_t^{**} \end{cases}$$

$$\max\{k - P(S_t, K, T-t), 0\} = \begin{cases} 0, & \text{if } S_t < S_t^{**} \\ k - P(S_t, K, T-t), & \text{if } S_t \geq S_t^{**} \end{cases}$$

The lower panels of Figure 18.11 describe these two payoffs.

## Pricing Compound Options: A Binomial Example

Although closed-form expressions exist for compound options in a Black-Scholes setting, the expressions are complex and not particularly informative. So, before describing these closed-forms, we begin with a simple binomial example that better explains the mechanics of the pricing process.

The compound option is taken to be a call on a put. The put is written on the stock whose price process is described in Figure 18.1. The put is taken to be European and to have a maturity of two periods and a strike of $K = 100$. The put price evolves as shown in Figure 18.12.

Suppose that the compound option (the call on the put) has a strike of $k = 4$ and a maturity of one period. That is, at the end of one period, the holder of the compound has the right to buy the underlying put at a price of 4. At the end of one period, there are two possibilities:

- The stock price has gone up to 110. In this case, the underlying put is worth only 0.39, so the call on the put lapses unexercised.

**FIGURE 18.12**
Put Price Evolution in
the Binomial Example

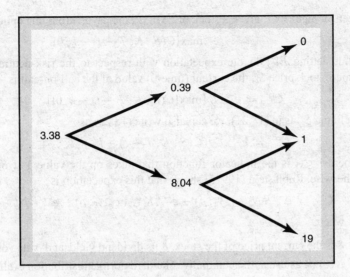

**FIGURE 18.13**
Call on a Put in the
Binomial Example

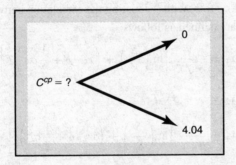

- The stock price has gone down to 90. Now the underlying put is worth 8.04. It is optimal to exercise the compound option. This results in a profit of $(8.04 - 4.00) = 4.04$.

This information is summarized in Figure 18.13. The price $C^{cp}$ of the compound option (the superscript $cp$ stands for call-on-put) is just the expected value of its payoffs under the risk-neutral probability discounted at the risk-free rate. Since the risk-neutral probability of an up move is 0.60, we have

$$C^{cp} = \frac{1}{R} \left( pC_u^{cp} + (1-p)C_d^{cp} \right) = 1.58 \qquad (18.22)$$

## Compounds as Installment Options

The example above provides a nice illustration of the flexibility a compound option provides. The investor can buy the underlying put directly at the initial time point at a price of 3.38. The compound offers the alternative of buying the same put on an "installment" plan. The investor makes a smaller initial outlay of 1.58. Then, at the end of one period, the investor can, if he wishes, make a further payment of 4 and take possession of the put.

## Pricing Formulae for Compound Options

Rubinstein (1991a) showed that closed-form solutions can be obtained for the prices of compound options in a Black-Scholes setting. Consider a call on a call first. As we have seen, at maturity $t$, given a stock price of $S_t$, the payoff from this option is

$$\max\{C(S_t, K, T - t) - k, 0\}$$

Thus, letting $E[\cdot]$ denote expectation with respect to the risk-neutral distribution of the time-$t$ stock price $S_t$, the current (time-0) value of the call-on-call is

$$C^{cc} = e^{-rt} E\left[\max\{C(S_t, K, T - t) - k, 0\}\right] \qquad \textbf{(18.23)}$$

Defining $S_t^*$ as in (18.21), we can also write (18.23) as

$$C^{cc} = e^{-rt} E\left[(C(S_t, K, T - t) - k) \times I_{S_t > S_t^*}\right] \qquad \textbf{(18.24)}$$

where $I_{S_t > S_t^*}$ is the indicator function that takes on the value 1 if $S_t > S_t^*$, and is zero otherwise. Rubinstein (1991a) shows that this expectation is

$$C^{cc} = e^{-\delta t} S\, N_2(x_1, y_1; \rho) - e^{-rT} K\, N_2(x_2, y_2; \rho) - e^{-rt} k\, N(y_2) \qquad \textbf{(18.25)}$$

where:

- $S$ is the current price of the stock, $\delta$ its dividend yield, and $\sigma$ its volatility.
- $N(z)$ is, as usual, the cumulative standard normal distribution evaluated at $z$.
- $N_2(a, b; \xi)$ is the area under a bivariate standard normal distribution covering the region from $-\infty$ to $a$ and $-\infty$ to $b$, with $\xi$ denoting the correlation between the variables.
- $x_1, x_2, y_1, y_2$, and $\rho$ are defined as follows:

$$x_1 = \frac{1}{\sigma\sqrt{T}}\left[\ln\left(\frac{S}{K}\right) + \left(r - \delta + \frac{1}{2}\sigma^2\right)T\right] \qquad \textbf{(18.26)}$$

$$x_2 = x_1 - \sigma\sqrt{T} \qquad \textbf{(18.27)}$$

$$y_1 = \frac{1}{\sigma\sqrt{t}}\left[\ln\left(\frac{S}{S_t^*}\right) + \left(r - \delta + \frac{1}{2}\sigma^2\right)t\right] \qquad \textbf{(18.28)}$$

$$y_2 = y_1 - \sigma\sqrt{t} \qquad \textbf{(18.29)}$$

$$\rho = \sqrt{\frac{t}{T}} \qquad \textbf{(18.30)}$$

In a similar way, the value of the other three compound options can be expressed in closed-form. To simplify matters and permit the description of all four compound option formulae at one go, define the variables $\eta$ and $\phi$ by

$$\eta = \begin{cases} +1, & \text{if the underlying option is a call} \\ -1, & \text{if the underlying option is a put} \end{cases} \qquad \textbf{(18.31)}$$

$$\phi = \begin{cases} +1, & \text{if the compound is a call} \\ -1, & \text{if the compound is a put} \end{cases} \qquad \textbf{(18.32)}$$

Then, the value of the general compound option may be written as

$$X = H_1 - H_2 - H_3 \qquad \textbf{(18.33)}$$

where $x_1, x_2, y_1, y_2$, and $\rho$ are defined as above, and

$$H_1 = \phi\eta e^{-\delta T} S\, N_2(\eta x_1, \phi\eta y_1; \phi\rho) \qquad \textbf{(18.34)}$$

$$H_2 = \phi\eta e^{-rT} K\, N_2(\eta x_2, \phi\eta y_2; \phi\rho) \qquad \textbf{(18.35)}$$

$$H_3 = \phi e^{-rt} k\, N(\phi\eta y_2) \qquad \textbf{(18.36)}$$

Allowing $\phi$ and $\eta$ to each roam over its two possible values, we get pricing expressions for all four basic compound options; (18.25) is then the special case corresponding to $\eta = \phi = +1$.

## Hedging Compound Options: The Delta

While the instrument underlying a compound option is a vanilla option, the "real" driver of compound option values is the *stock* on which the vanilla option is written. Compound options are thus typically hedged directly with the underlying stock. The delta of a compound option measures the sensitivity of the compound's value to changes in the price of the stock.

While closed-form expressions for the delta are messy to derive, the qualitative behavior of the delta is not hard to describe. As Figure 18.11 shows:

- The payoffs from calls-on-calls and puts-on-puts increase as the stock price increases, so both have *positive* deltas.
- The payoffs from calls-on-puts and puts-on-calls move inversely with the stock price, so their deltas are *negative*.

A simple intuition underlies these signs. Consider a call on a call, for example. The compound call increases in value when its underlying, the vanilla call, increases in value; and the vanilla call increases in value when *its* underlying, the stock price, increases. Thus, an increase in the stock price leads to an increase in the value of the call-on-call, implying a positive delta. A similar argument can be used to explain the signs of the other deltas.

## Behavior of the Delta and the Compound Gamma

The behavior of the delta as $S$ varies, and therefore of the gamma, exhibits interesting properties. We illustrate with two cases.

For a call on a call, the delta behaves much like a vanilla call. As the stock price increases, the underlying call moves "more" into-the-money, so becomes more sensitive to the stock price. But as the vanilla call price increases, the call-on-call too moves "deeper" into-the-money, so it becomes more sensitive to the vanilla call price. Combining these statements, the call-on-call becomes more sensitive to the stock price as the stock price increases, meaning its delta increases (so the gamma of a call-on-call is always positive). At very high stock prices, this delta is close to $+1$ since both options are deep in-the-money and respond almost one-for-one to their respective underlyings. At very low stock prices, the delta is close to zero since both options are deep out-of-the-money and almost unresponsive to the respective underlyings.

But for a put on a put, the delta is bell-shaped, first increasing as $S$ increases, then decreasing back towards zero. To see why, note that at very low values of $S$, the underlying put is deep-in-the-money and so is near its maximum value. This means the compound put is deep out-of-the-money and so not very responsive to changes in the price of its underlying put. As a consequence, the delta of the compound is close to zero. As $S$ increases, the value of the underlying put falls, so the compound put moves more into-the-money and becomes more responsive to changes in its underlying, decreasing as the value of the underlying increases. This means the delta of the compound put with respect to $S$ is positive. But at very high levels of $S$, the underlying put is deep out-of-the-money and almost unresponsive to $S$. Since the value of *its* underlying is unresponsive to $S$, the compound too will be unresponsive to $S$, so its delta with respect to $S$ again approaches zero. Finally, from the behavior of the delta, it follows that the gamma of a put-on-put can be positive or negative.

## 18.6 Exchange Options

An exchange option involves two risky assets, for example, two stocks. It gives the holder the right to exchange one of the assets (say, asset 2) for the other (asset 1) at the option's maturity. Obviously, the option will be exercised only if asset 1 is worth more than asset 2 at maturity. Thus, the payoff at maturity to the holder is given by

$$\max\left\{0, S_T^{(1)} - S_T^{(2)}\right\} \qquad \textbf{(18.37)}$$

where $S_t^{(1)}$ and $S_t^{(2)}$ denote, respectively, the two assets' time-$t$ prices. Exchange options are also referred to as "outperformance options" or as "spread options."

### Pricing Exchange Options

Exchange options were first considered in Margrabe (1978) who gave a closed-form formula for such options in a Black-Scholes setting. Suppose that the asset returns are log-normally distributed. Let $S^{(1)}$, $S^{(2)}$ denote the current (time-0) prices of the two assets, $\sigma_1$, $\sigma_2$ their volatilities, and $\delta_1$, $\delta_2$ their respective dividend yields. Finally, let $\rho$ denote the correlation of returns. Then the price of the exchange option at time 0 is given by

$$V^{exch} = e^{-\delta_1 T} S^{(1)} N(\tilde{d}_1) - e^{-\delta_2 T} S^{(2)} N(\tilde{d}_2) \qquad \textbf{(18.38)}$$

where $\tilde{d}_1$ and $\tilde{d}_2$ are defined by

$$\tilde{d}_1 = \frac{1}{\sigma\sqrt{T}}\left[\ln\left(\frac{S^{(1)}}{S^{(2)}}\right) + \left(\delta_2 - \delta_1 + \frac{1}{2}\sigma^2\right)T\right] \qquad \textbf{(18.39)}$$

$$\tilde{d}_2 = \tilde{d}_1 - \sigma\sqrt{T} \qquad \textbf{(18.40)}$$

and $\sigma$ is given by

$$\sigma^2 = \sigma_1^2 + \sigma_2^2 - 2\rho\sigma_1\sigma_2 \qquad \textbf{(18.41)}$$

Some intuition for this pricing expression can be obtained by comparing it to the Black-Scholes formula for a call. A call is also an exchange option, albeit a particularly simple one: it gives us the right to exchange the strike price $K$ for asset 1. The strike price may be viewed as an asset that is always worth $K$. The yield on holding this asset is the risk-free return $r$ one can make from investing in it, and, of course, the asset has no volatility since its "price" is always $K$. So if we set $S^{(2)} = K$, $\delta_2 = r$, and $\sigma_2 = 0$ in (18.38), we should recover the Black-Scholes call price, and it is easy to check that we do. Thus, (18.38) is just a generalization of the Black-Scholes formula.

Put a bit more formally, note that the payoff from the exchange option at maturity can be written as

$$S_T^{(2)} \max\left\{\frac{S_T^{(1)}}{S_T^{(2)}} - 1, 0\right\} \qquad \textbf{(18.42)}$$

If we use the price of the second asset as a numeraire and express all payoffs and prices in units of the second asset, then this payoff, normalized by the numeraire, is

$$\max\left\{\frac{S_T^{(1)}}{S_T^{(2)}} - 1, 0\right\} \qquad \textbf{(18.43)}$$

This is just a standard call option on the normalized asset $S_t^{(1)}/S_t^{(2)}$ with a strike price of 1. If $S_t^{(1)}/S_t^{(2)}$ follows a geometric Brownian motion with constant volatility $\sigma$, then we can price this option using the standard Black-Scholes formula. Note that in this process, the risk-free rate will be the dividend yield $\delta_2$ on the numeraire asset while $\delta_1$ remains the dividend rate on the normalized asset $S_t^{(1)}/S_t^{(2)}$. Multiplying this Black-Scholes price by the time-0 price $S^{(2)}$ of the numeraire asset then provides us with the time-0 price of the exchange option. The result is exactly the formula (18.38).

One final point is worth noting. As the preceding argument shows, all that is really needed for the Margrabe exchange option formula to hold is that $S_t^{(1)}/S_t^{(2)}$ follow a geometric Brownian motion with constant volatility $\sigma$. This is implied by the assumptions we have made (viz., that $S_t^{(1)}$ and $S_t^{(2)}$ each individually follow geometric Brownian motions with constant volatilities $\sigma_1$ and $\sigma_2$, etc.), but these assumptions are stronger than required.

## Hedging Exchange Options

Since an exchange option's payoffs depend on the prices $S^{(1)}$ and $S^{(2)}$ of *two* risky assets, hedging it involves hedging two risks, those of changes in either price. That is, there are two deltas: the delta $\Delta^{(1)}$ with respect to asset 1 and the delta $\Delta^{(2)}$ with respect to asset 2. In a Black-Scholes setting, these deltas are

$$\Delta^{(1)} = e^{-\delta_1 T} N(\tilde{d}_1) \qquad (18.44)$$

$$\Delta^{(2)} = -e^{-\delta_2 T} N(\tilde{d}_2) \qquad (18.45)$$

In words, to hedge a *short* position in an exchange option, we take a long position in $e^{-\delta_1 T} N(\tilde{d}_1)$ units of asset 1 and a short position in $e^{-\delta_2 T} N(\tilde{d}_2)$ units of asset 2.

Expressions (18.44) and (18.45) actually identify the *entire* replicating portfolio for an exchange option. That is, the replication of an exchange option requires holding only $\Delta^{(1)}$ units of asset 1 and $\Delta^{(2)}$ units of asset 2. No holding in cash is required. This should not be surprising. As we have pointed out above, asset 2 plays the role of the strike price here, so the position in asset 2 is the analog of the cash holding.

## Euler's Theorem and the Replicating Portfolio

We sketch the arguments here for why the replicating portfolio for an exchange option consists only of positions in the two assets. Suppose the replicating portfolio consists of $\Delta^{(1)}$ units of asset 1, $\Delta^{(2)}$ units of asset 2, and $B$ in cash. Then, the value of the option can be written as

$$V^{exch} = [\Delta^{(1)} \times S^{(1)}] + [\Delta^{(2)} \times S^{(2)}] + B \qquad (18.46)$$

Now examine again the exchange option payoff (18.37). If we multiply the price of both asset 1 and asset 2 by a constant $m$, the payoff from the exchange option becomes $m$ times the payoff from the original option:

$$\max\{0, mS_T^{(1)} - mS_T^{(2)}\} = m \times \max\{0, S_T^{(1)} - S_T^{(2)}\} \qquad (18.47)$$

This means that exchange option payoffs are *homogeneous of degree 1* in $(S^{(1)}, S^{(2)})$. A result in mathematics known as *Euler's Theorem* states that if a function $f(y, z)$ is homogeneous of degree 1 in $(y, z)$, then the following equality must hold:

$$f(y, z) = \left[ y \times \frac{\partial f}{\partial y}(y, z) \right] + \left[ z \times \frac{\partial f}{\partial z}(y, z) \right] \qquad (18.48)$$

Therefore, the price $V^{exch}$ of the exchange option must satisfy

$$V^{exch} = \left[ S^{(1)} \times \frac{\partial V^{exch}}{\partial S^{(1)}} \right] + \left[ S^{(2)} \times \frac{\partial V^{exch}}{\partial S^{(2)}} \right] \qquad (18.49)$$

The term $\partial V^{exch}/\partial S^{(i)}$ measures the sensitivity of option value to changes in the price of asset $i$. This is just the option's delta with respect to the $i$-th asset. So we can write (18.49) in simpler form as

$$V^{exch} = [S^{(1)} \times \Delta^{(1)}] + [S^{(2)} \times \Delta^{(2)}] \qquad (18.50)$$

Comparing (18.46) and (18.50) indicates that we must have $B = 0$ in the replicating portfolio, while comparing (18.38) and (18.50) suggests that the deltas do have the forms (18.44) and (18.45).

## 18.7  Quanto Options

*Quanto options* are cross-currency options in which the option is written on a security that trades in one currency but the payoff is translated into a different currency in a prespecified manner. To motivate these options, consider an example.

Suppose a US-based investor wishes to buy a call option on a French company whose shares trade in Paris in euros. Then, since the option trades in euros, the investor must bear currency risk at the end of the transaction: if the call finishes in-the-money, the profit from the call is realized in euros and must be converted back to US dollars at the then-prevailing exchange rate. If the investor does not want to bear this exchange-rate risk, she can buy an option in which the euros are converted back into US dollars at a fixed, prespecified exchange rate. Such an option is a *quanto*.

To put this in general notational terms, suppose, for specificity, that the US dollar (USD) is the local currency. We use a superscript $f$ to denote a quantity in the foreign currency. Let $S^f$ denote the price of a foreign security and $K^f$ the strike price of an option on that security. For specificity, suppose the option is a call. Then, the payoff from the option at maturity (in units of the foreign currency) is

$$\max\left\{0, S_T^f - K^f\right\} \qquad (18.51)$$

If $\zeta$ denotes some arbitrary fixed rate for converting the payoffs from the foreign currency into USD, the payoff received in USD by the holder of a quanto is

$$\zeta \times \max\left\{0, S_T^f - K^f\right\} \qquad (18.52)$$

In general, the fixed rate $\zeta$ at which cash flows are converted back into the domestic currency need not have any relationship to the actual exchange rate.

The NYSE Arca Japan Index Option traded on the erstwhile American Stock Exchange (now part of NYSE Euronext) is an example of a quanto. The index underlying the contract is constructed using 210 stocks traded on the Tokyo Stock Exchange. The index value is computed using the yen prices of the respective stocks. At maturity, the holder of this option receives $100 times the depth-in-the-money of the option. For example, if the strike price is 110 and the index closes at 114 on the last trading day, the holder of a call receives $(100 \times 4) = \$400$.

### Pricing Quantos

The pricing of quantos is discussed in James (2003). Here is one way to think about how one might approach the problem of pricing quantos. Suppose $X_t$ denotes the time-$t$ price of USD 1 in the foreign currency. Then, consider the quantity

$$X_T \times \zeta \max\left\{0, S_T^f - K^f\right\} \qquad (18.53)$$

This is just the payoff from the quanto converted back into the foreign currency. We can rewrite this quantity as

$$\zeta \, \max \left\{ 0, \, X_T S_T^f - X_T K^f \right\} \qquad \textbf{(18.54)}$$

If we define $A_T = X_T S_T^f$ and $B_T = X_T K^f$, we obtain

$$\zeta \, \max\{0, \, A_T - B_T\} \qquad \textbf{(18.55)}$$

This is just $\zeta$ units of Margrabe's exchange option: the option to exchange $B_T$ for $A_T$! So we can apply the exchange-option pricing formula (18.38) to obtain the fair price of the quanto. Of course, this fair price will be in the foreign currency; we must convert it into USD using the current exchange rate.[2]

If we take $X_T$ and $S_T^f$ to have lognormally-distributed returns, so does $A_T$, their product. We have

$$\ln A_T \, = \, \ln \left( X_T S_T^f \right) = \ln X_T + \ln S_T^f$$

so, if $\ln X_T$ and $\ln S_T^f$ are normal, so is $\ln A_T$. Thus, technically, the problem can be put into Margrabe's exchange-option setting. The resulting price of the quanto option is

$$V^{quanto} \, = \, [e^{-\delta_A T} A_0 \, N(\Lambda_A) - e^{-\delta_B T} B_0 \, N(\Lambda_B)] \times \zeta \qquad \textbf{(18.56)}$$

where

$$\Lambda_A = \frac{1}{\sigma \sqrt{T}} \left[ \ln \left( \frac{A_0}{B_0} \right) + \left( \delta_B - \delta_A + \frac{1}{2} \sigma^2 \right) T \right]$$

$$\Lambda_B = \Lambda_A - \sigma \sqrt{T}$$

$$\sigma^2 = \sigma_A^2 + \sigma_B^2 - 2\rho(A, B) \sigma_A \sigma_B$$

$$\delta_A = \delta^f + r - r^f - \rho(S^f, X) \sigma_{S^f} \sigma_X$$

$$\delta_B = r$$

The price (18.56) is in the foreign currency since the payoffs (18.55) are in that currency. To find the USD price of the quanto, we must divide through by the time-0 exchange rate $X_0$.

This pricing expression can be simplified. Observe that

$$\frac{A_t}{B_t} \, = \, \frac{X_t S_t^f}{X_t K^f} \, = \, \frac{S_t}{K^f}$$

This means also that $\sigma$, which is the volatility of $A/B$, is just $\sigma_{S^f}$, the volatility of the underlying security. Using these simplifications, we obtain

$$V^{quanto} \, = \, X_0 \left[ e^{-\delta_A T} S_0^f \, N(\Lambda_1) - e^{-rT} K^f \, N(\Lambda_2) \right] \times \zeta \qquad \textbf{(18.57)}$$

---

[2] Note that $A_T$ and $B_T$ are not themselves prices. $A_T$, for example, is the product of two prices: the price of USD 1 in the foreign currency multiplied by the price of the underlying security in the foreign currency.

where $\delta_A$ is as defined above and

$$\Lambda_1 = \frac{1}{\sigma_{S^f}\sqrt{T}} \left[ \ln\left(\frac{S_0^f}{K}\right) + [r^f - \delta^f + \rho(S^f, X)\sigma_{S^f}\sigma_X + \frac{1}{2}\sigma_{S^f}^2]T \right]$$

$$\Lambda_2 = \Lambda_1 - \sigma_{S^f}\sqrt{T}$$

The price (18.57) is in units of the foreign currency. To obtain the price in USD, simply divide through by $X_0$ to obtain

$$\text{USD } V^{quanto} = \left[ e^{-\delta_A T}S_0^f N(\Lambda_1) - e^{-rT}K N(\Lambda_2) \right] \times \zeta \qquad (18.58)$$

## 18.8 Variants on the Exchange Option Theme

There are several exotic options that are variants on the exchange options considered by Margrabe (1978). These include options paying the maximum or minimum of two assets (considered by Stulz, 1982) and rainbow options (considered by Rubinstein, 1991c), among others. We consider several of these variants in this section and present pricing formulae for them. The usual assumption of lognormally distributed returns is maintained throughout.

### Variation 1: Maximum of Two Assets

Consider an option whose time-$T$ payoff is $\max\{S_T^{(1)}, S_T^{(2)}\}$. Such an option was considered by Stulz (1982). The payoff from the option can be re-expressed as

$$\max\left\{S_T^{(1)}, S_T^{(2)}\right\} = S_T^{(2)} + \max\left\{S_T^{(1)} - S_T^{(2)}, 0\right\} \qquad (18.59)$$

Thus, the maximum-of-two-assets option is equivalent to holding an exchange option and receiving the value of asset 2 at time $T$. The current (time-0) price of the option is just the sum of the prices of these components. To describe the pricing formula, we use the notation of Section 18.6.

The first term $S_T^{(2)}$ in (18.59) has a time-0 present value of $e^{-\delta_2 T}S^{(2)}$. Intuitively, if we buy $e^{-\delta_2 T}$ units of asset 2 at time 0 and reinvest all the dividends, our holding of asset 2 will grow at the rate $\delta_2$ so that we have exactly one unit at date $T$. The second term's present value is the expression (18.38) for the price of an exchange option. Combining these terms, the time-0 price of the maximum-of-two-assets option is

$$V^{max} = e^{-\delta_2 T}S^{(2)} + [e^{-\delta_1 T}S^{(1)} N(\tilde{d}_1) - e^{-\delta_2 T}S^{(2)} N(\tilde{d}_2)] \qquad (18.60)$$

Using the relationship $N(x) + N(-x) = 1$ for any $x$, this may be rewritten as

$$V^{max} = e^{-\delta_1 T}S^{(1)} N(\tilde{d}_1) + e^{-\delta_2 T}S^{(2)} N(-\tilde{d}_2) \qquad (18.61)$$

It is also possible to express (18.61) in a more aesthetically-pleasing "symmetric" form. Define the term $\Lambda_{i,j}$ by

$$\Lambda_{i,j} = \frac{1}{\sigma\sqrt{T}} \left[ \ln\left(\frac{S^{(i)}}{S^{(j)}}\right) + \left(\delta_j - \delta_i + \frac{1}{2}\sigma^2\right)T \right] \qquad (18.62)$$

A simple check shows that $\tilde{d}_1 = \Lambda_{1,2}$ and $-\tilde{d}_2 = \Lambda_{2,1}$. So we may write

$$V^{max} = e^{-\delta_1 T}S^{(1)} N(\Lambda_{1,2}) + e^{-\delta_2 T}S^{(2)} N(\Lambda_{2,1}) \qquad (18.63)$$

## Variation 2: Minimum of Two Assets

What if the option paid the *minimum* of $S_T^{(1)}$ and $S_T^{(2)}$? (This case is also considered in Stulz, 1982). The payoff from this option can be rewritten in terms of the maximum-of-two-assets option:

$$\min\left\{S_T^{(1)}, S_T^{(2)}\right\} = S_T^{(1)} + S_T^{(2)} - \max\left\{S_T^{(1)}, S_T^{(2)}\right\} \qquad (18.64)$$

The time-0 present values of the first two terms in (18.64) are $e^{-\delta_1 T} S^{(1)}$ and $e^{-\delta_2 T} S^{(2)}$, respectively, while that of the last is $V^{max}$ as given in (18.63). So we have

$$V^{min} = e^{-\delta_1 T} S^{(1)} + e^{-\delta_2 T} S^{(2)} - V^{max} \qquad (18.65)$$

## Variation 3: Maximum of Two Assets and Cash

A more interesting and complex variation is the maximum of two assets and cash: the option holder receives the payoff

$$\max\left\{S_T^{(1)}, S_T^{(2)}, K\right\} \qquad (18.66)$$

where $K$ is a fixed amount of money. The current (time-0) price of the option is the present value of its time-$T$ payoffs:

$$
\begin{aligned}
V^{max\text{-}or\text{-}cash} = {} & PV\left[S_T^{(1)} \mid S_T^{(1)} \geq S_T^{(2)}, S_T^{(1)} \geq K\right] \\
& + PV\left[S_T^{(2)} \mid S_T^{(2)} > S_T^{(1)}, S_T^{(2)} > K\right] \\
& + PV\left[K \mid K > S_T^{(1)}, K > S_T^{(2)}\right]
\end{aligned} \qquad (18.67)
$$

To express this in closed-form, define $\sigma$ and $\Lambda_{i,j}$ as in (18.41) and (18.62), respectively. Let $\Lambda_1, \Lambda_2, \rho_1,$ and $\rho_2$ be given by

$$\Lambda_1 = \frac{1}{\sigma_1 \sqrt{T}}\left[\ln\left(\frac{S^{(1)}}{K}\right) + \left(r - \delta_1 + \frac{1}{2}\sigma_1^2\right)T\right] \qquad (18.68)$$

$$\Lambda_2 = \frac{1}{\sigma_2 \sqrt{T}}\left[\ln\left(\frac{S^{(2)}}{K}\right) + \left(r - \delta_2 + \frac{1}{2}\sigma_2^2\right)T\right] \qquad (18.69)$$

$$\rho_1 = \frac{\rho\sigma_2 - \sigma_1}{\sigma} \qquad \rho_2 = \frac{\rho\sigma_1 - \sigma_2}{\sigma} \qquad (18.70)$$

Finally, let $N_2(x, y; \xi)$ denote the area under a standard bivariate normal with correlation $\xi$ covering the region between $-\infty$ and $x$, and $-\infty$ and $y$. Then, the value of the maximum-or-cash option is

$$
\begin{aligned}
V^{max\text{-}or\text{-}cash} = {} & e^{-\delta_1 T} S^{(1)}[N(\Lambda_{1,2}) - N_2(-\Lambda_1, \Lambda_{1,2}; \rho_1)] \\
& + e^{-\delta_2 T} S^{(2)}[N(\Lambda_{2,1}) - N_2(-\Lambda_2, \Lambda_{2,1}; \rho_2)] \\
& + e^{-rT} K\, N_2(-\Lambda_1 + \sigma_1\sqrt{T}, -\Lambda_2 + \sigma_2\sqrt{T}; \rho)
\end{aligned} \qquad (18.71)
$$

## Variation 4: Options on the Maximum or Minimum

Suppose we have an option that gives us the right to purchase either of two assets at $T$ for a strike of $K$. The time-$T$ payoff of this option is

$$\max\left\{0, \max\left(S_T^{(1)}, S_T^{(2)}\right) - K\right\} \qquad (18.72)$$

This is one version of a *rainbow* option and was first studied in Rubinstein (1991b). By adding and subtracting $K$, the payoff (18.72) can be rewritten as

$$\max \left\{ S_T^{(1)}, S_T^{(2)}, K \right\} - K \tag{18.73}$$

Thus, the value of this option, denoted $V^{max\ call}$, is given by

$$V^{max\ call} = V^{max-or-cash} - e^{-rT} K \tag{18.74}$$

where $V^{max-or-cash}$ is given by (18.71).

While rainbow call options as defined above are the most common types of rainbow options in practice, we can also find the prices of other rainbow options from this result. The price of a *put* on the maximum of two options can be found from the call price (18.74) using a variant of put-call parity. Let $P(\max(S_T^{(1)}, S_T^{(2)}))$ and $C(\max(S_T^{(1)}, S_T^{(2)}))$ denote the payoffs at $T$ from a put and call, respectively, on the maximum of two assets. A straightforward computation verifies that

$$P\left( \max \left( S_T^{(1)}, S_T^{(2)} \right) \right) + \max \left( S_T^{(1)}, S_T^{(2)} \right) = C\left( \max \left( S_T^{(1)}, S_T^{(2)} \right) \right) + K \tag{18.75}$$

Substituting for the value of the call from (18.74) and rearranging,

$$V^{max\ put} = V^{max\ call} - V^{max} \tag{18.76}$$

where $V^{max}$ is given by (18.63).

Finally, calls and puts on the *minimum* of two prices can also be computed using the above expressions using the following relationships (the terms $C(S^{(1)})$, $P(S^{(1)})$, etc., below refer to vanilla calls and puts on the underlying asset):

$$C\left( \min \left( S_T^{(1)}, S_T^{(2)} \right) \right) = C\left( S_T^{(1)} \right) + C\left( S_T^{(2)} \right) - C\left( \max \left( S_T^{(1)}, S_T^{(2)} \right) \right) \tag{18.77}$$

$$P\left( \min \left( S_T^{(1)}, S_T^{(2)} \right) \right) = P\left( S_T^{(1)} \right) + P\left( S_T^{(2)} \right) - P\left( \max \left( S_T^{(1)}, S_T^{(2)} \right) \right) \tag{18.78}$$

## Variation 5: Maximum of Three Assets

An obvious extension of the earlier case is where the option pays the maximum of *three* assets: the option's payoff at time $T$ is

$$\max \left\{ S_T^{(1)}, S_T^{(2)}, S_T^{(3)} \right\} \tag{18.79}$$

The current (time-0) value of this option, denoted say $V^{3-max}$, is the present value of its time-$T$ payoffs:

$$\begin{aligned} V^{3-max} = \ & PV\left[ S_T^{(1)} \mid S_T^{(1)} \geq S_T^{(2)}, S_T^{(1)} \geq S_T^{(3)} \right] \\ & + PV\left[ S_T^{(2)} \mid S_T^{(2)} > S_T^{(1)}, S_T^{(2)} > S_T^{(3)} \right] \\ & + PV\left[ S_T^{(3)} \mid S_T^{(3)} > S_T^{(1)}, S_T^{(3)} > S_T^{(2)} \right] \end{aligned} \tag{18.80}$$

This can be expressed in closed-form. Some notation first. Define

$$\sigma_{i,j}^2 = \sigma_i^2 + \sigma_j^2 - 2\rho_{ij}\sigma_i\sigma_j$$

$$\Lambda_{i,j} = \frac{1}{\sigma_{i,j}\sqrt{T}} \left[ \ln \left( \frac{S^{(i)}}{S^{(j)}} \right) + \left( \delta_j - \delta_i + \frac{1}{2}\sigma_{i,j}^2 \right) T \right]$$

$$\rho_{i,j,k} = \frac{1}{\sigma_{i,k}\sigma_{j,k}} \left[ \sigma_i\sigma_j\rho_{ij} - \sigma_i\sigma_k\rho_{ik} - \sigma_j\sigma_k\rho_{jk} + \sigma_k^2 \right]$$

Finally, let $N_2(x, y, \rho)$ denote the area under a bivariate standard normal distribution with correlation $\rho$ covering the region between $-\infty$ and $x$, and $-\infty$ and $y$. Then, the value (18.80) of the option is

$$V^{3-max} = S^{(1)} N_2(\Lambda_{1,2}, \Lambda_{1,3}, \rho_{2,3,1}) + S^{(2)} N_2(\Lambda_{2,1}, \Lambda_{2,3}, \rho_{1,3,2})$$
$$+ S^{(3)} N_2(\Lambda_{3,1}, \Lambda_{3,2}, \rho_{1,2,3}) \qquad \textbf{(18.81)}$$

## 18.9 Exercises

1. What is the sign of the delta of a call option on a put option? Why? What about a put on a call?

2. Why does a call on a put cost less than the put?

3. Find the price of a binary cash-or-nothing put option in a binomial tree with the following parameters: $S = 100$, $u = 1.10$, $d = 0.90$, $R = 1.02$, and $K = 100$. Assume that the binary pays a flat amount of $10 if $S_T \leq 100$, and nothing otherwise.

4. Consider a digital call option, i.e., one that pays a dollar if at maturity the stock price $S_T$ is greater than the strike $K$.
   (a) What is the sign of the delta of this option?
   (b) When will the delta of this option be the highest?

5. You are given a three-period binomial tree with the following parameters: $S = 100$, $R = 1.02$, $u = 1.10$, and $d = 0.90$. Consider a claim whose payoff at maturity is given by $S^{max} - S^{min}$ where $S^{max}$ and $S^{min}$ are, respectively, the highest and lowest stock prices observed during the option's life (including the initial price of $S = 100$). What is the initial price of this claim?

6. Are ordinary American-style options path-independent?

7. Consider a stock with current price $S = 50$ whose price process can be represented by a binomial tree with parameters $u = 1.221$ and $d = 0.819$. Suppose the per-period gross interest rate is $R = 1.005$.
   (a) Find the value of a two-period European put option with a strike of $K = 50$.
   (b) Using backwards induction on the tree, find the value of a forward start put option that comes to life in one period, is European, has a further life of two periods, and will be at-the-money when it comes to life.
   (c) Verify that your answers to parts (a) and (b) coincide.
   (d) Suppose the puts had been American. What are the answers to parts (a) and (b)? Do they still coincide?

8. Consider a stock currently trading at $S = 80$ whose price evolution can be represented by a binomial tree with parameters $u = 1.226$ and $d = 0.815$. Suppose the per-period gross rate of interest is $R = 1.005$.
   (a) Price a one-period call option on the tree with a strike of $K = 76$.
   (b) Using backwards induction, find the price of a forward start call option that comes to life in one period, has a further life of one period, and has a strike equal to 95% of the stock price when it comes to life. Verify that it is the same as your answer to (a).
   (c) Find the initial delta of the forward start.
   (d) Now assume that the initial stock price is $S = 1$. Assuming the same parameters for the binomial tree, find the price of a one-period call with strike $K = 0.95$. How does this price compare to the delta you identified in part (c)? Why?

9. This question deals with a Sprint-like repricing situation (see Section 18.2 for details of the Sprint scheme). Assume that the current stock price is $S = 24$, the volatility of the stock price is 45%, and the risk-free rate is 4%. Use the Black-Scholes model to answer the following questions.

   (a) Consider an option with a strike price of $K = 32$ and six years left to maturity. Ignoring dividends, would you trade it in for a forward start call specified as in Sprint's scheme?

   (b) What if the option had only one year to maturity?

10. A stock is currently trading at $24. Assume that its volatility is 35% and the term-structure of interest rates is flat at 6%.

    (a) What is the price of a forward start call option with $T^* = 1$ year, $\tau = 1$ year, and $\alpha = 1.10$? Note that $T^*$ is maturity of the forward start period, and $\tau$ is the maturity of the option once started. Also, $\alpha$ is the strike multiplier, i.e., strike $K = \alpha\, S_{T^*}$.

    (b) What is the delta of this option?

11. Consider the binomial tree of Figure 18.14. Suppose that the per-period interest rate is $R = 1.02$.

    (a) Show that the price of a call on a put in this model with a strike of $k = 4$ and a maturity of one period is 1.58.

    (b) Show that the delta of the call on the put in the binomial example is $-0.202$. (Use the usual formula for a binomial delta.)

    (c) Verify that a position consisting of a short position in the option and a short position in 0.202 units of the stock is perfectly riskless over the compound option's one-period life.

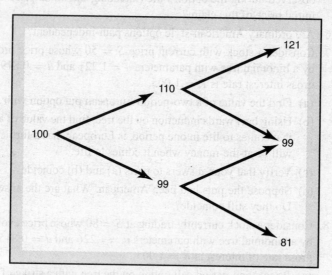

**FIGURE 18.14**   Stock Price Tree for Binomial Illustrations

12. Describe a put-call parity relationship for compound options, i.e., one that connects calls-on-calls to puts-on-calls (or calls-on-puts to puts-on-puts).

13. Consider a stock currently trading at $45. Suppose its price evolution can be represented by a binomial tree with $u = 1.05$ and $d = 0.95$. The riskless rate per period is $R = 1.01$. Calculate the following:

    (a) The price of a two-period European call option with $K = 43$.

    (b) The price of a one-period call on the two-period call with a strike of $K = 2$.

(c) The price of a one-period put on the two-period call with a strike of $K = 0.50$.

(d) The price of a forward start option beginning in one period with a further life of one period that will be at-the-money when it starts.

14. Consider a two-period cash-or-nothing binary option in the binomial example of Figure 18.14 with $K = 90$ and $M = 10$. Assume that the per-period interest rate is $R = 1.02$.

(a) Show that the initial value of the option is $C^{C\text{-}or\text{-}N} = 8.07$.

(b) What is the value of an asset-or-nothing option in this case?

(c) What is the value of a vanilla option? Verify that the following equation holds.

$$C^{A\text{-}or\text{-}N} - \frac{K}{M} C^{C\text{-}or\text{-}N} = C$$

15. Consider a cash-or-nothing option in the binomial tree setting of Figure 18.14 with $K = 90$ and $M = 10$. Let $\Delta^b$ denote the initial delta of the option, $\Delta^b_u$ the delta following an up move in the stock price, and $\Delta^b_d$ the delta following a down move. Show that $\Delta^b_u < \Delta^b$ even though the option has moved into-the-money.

16. Let $C^{C\text{-}or\text{-}N}$ denote a cash-or-nothing option that pays $M$ if $S_T \geq K$. Let $P^{C\text{-}or\text{-}N}$ be a "put" version of this cash-or-nothing option, i.e., it pays $M$ if $S_T < K$ and nothing otherwise. What is the relation between the prices of these two options?

17. Consider two-period European options with a strike of 100 in the binomial model of Figure 18.14. Assume the per-period interest rate is $R = 1.02$.

(a) Find the value of a straddle in this model.

(b) Find the value of a chooser where the holder must decide between the call and put at the end of one period.

(c) Why is the difference in values between the straddle and chooser so small?

(d) What are the deltas of the straddle and the chooser?

18. Price a chooser option using the Black-Scholes formula with the following inputs: $S = 100$, $K = 100$, the maturity at which the option holder has to opt for a call or a put is $\tau = 1$ year, the final maturity of the option is $T = 2$ years, risk-free rate $r = 0.10$, and dividends $\delta = 0.03$.

19. Using the same input values as in the previous question, compute the value of the straddle. Compare the price of the straddle with that of the chooser. Which is greater? Why?

20. You are asked to price a quanto option on the DAX index. The DAX is currently trading at a value of 5000. Price a one-year maturity ATM option on one unit of the DAX given that the current exchange rate is $0.8/€. The volatility of the DAX is 50%, and that of the exchange rate is 20%. The correlation between the DAX return and exchange rate is +0.25. The US risk-free rate is 1%, and the euro interest rate is 2%. Dividends on the DAX are 1%.

21. Using the same parameters as in the previous question, price the quanto when the correlation between the DAX stock index and the $/€ exchange rate is $-0.25$ instead of $+0.25$. What happens to the price of the quanto? Explain.

22. Consider an option that pays the holder the amount

$$\max\{(S_T - K)^2, 0\} \qquad (18.82)$$

at maturity where $S_T$ is the terminal price of the stock and $K$ the option's strike price. Such an option is one example of a *power option*. Consider a binomial tree with initial stock price $S = 60$ and parameters $u = 1.20$ and $d = 0.833$. Suppose the per-period gross rate of interest is $r = 1.01$. Value a power option of the form (18.82) that has a maturity of two periods and a strike of $K = 70$.

23. Another example of a power option is one that pays the amount

$$\max\{S_T^2 - K^2, 0\} \qquad (18.83)$$

(a) Show that the payoffs of this option may be written in terms of (18.82) and a vanilla call with strike $K$. [*Hint:* Expand the term $(S_T - K)^2$ and rearrange.]

(b) Price the option (18.83) using the same binomial tree as in Question 23.

24. Consider a Black-Scholes setting with volatility $\sigma$ and dividend yield $q$. Show that a closed-form expression for the price of a power option of the form (18.83) is obtained simply by using the Black-Scholes vanilla call option formula with

(a) A strike of $K^2$.

(b) A volatility of $2\sigma$.

(c) A dividend yield of $2q - (r + \sigma^2)$.

25. This question generalizes Question 24. Consider a power option with payoff

$$\max\{S_T^\alpha - M, 0\} \qquad (18.84)$$

If we take $\alpha = 2$ and $M = K^2$, this is (18.83). Consider a Black-Scholes setting with volatility $\sigma$ and dividend yield $q$. Show that the closed-form solution for this option's price is the vanilla call price with

(a) A strike of $M$.

(b) A volatility of $\alpha\sigma$.

(c) A dividend yield of $\alpha q - (\alpha - 1)(r + \frac{1}{2}\alpha\sigma^2)$.

26. A *corridor option* is one that pays a fixed sum $M$ if the price at maturity lies between two specified levels $K_1$ and $K_2$ but nothing otherwise. Consider a two-period binomial tree with parameters $u = 1.10$ and $d = 0.91$. Suppose the initial stock price is $S = 100$ and $r = 1.01$.

(a) Find the initial value and the value at all points on the tree of a corridor option that pays $M = 10$ if the price lies between $K_1 = 90$ and $K_2 = 110$ (both prices inclusive), and nothing otherwise.

(b) Find the deltas of the corridor option at all points in the tree. Intuitively, why is the delta positive in parts of the tree and negative in others?

27. Find a closed-form expression for the price of a corridor option in a Black-Scholes setting. [*Hint:* Show that a corridor is just a combination of two binary cash-or-nothing options.]

28. Given the following parameters, price a gap call option: $S = 100$, $K = 100$, $T = 1$, $\sigma = 0.3$, $r = 0.10$, and $M = 90$. Dividends are $\delta = 0.02$. Remember, $K$ is the strike of the asset-or-nothing call, and $M$ is the strike of the cash-or-nothing call option.

29. Let the following Black-Scholes parameters be given: $S = 100$, $K = 100$, $T = 1$, $\sigma = 0.3$, $r = 0.10$, and $\delta = 0.02$. Consider a pay-later option (see Section 18.3 for the definition of the option). Find the strike $M$ of the cash-or-nothing call. Remember, $K$ is the strike of the asset-or-nothing call.

30. Consider a Margrabe exchange option. Suppose the initial prices of the two stocks are $S_1 = S_2 = 100$ and $\sigma_1 = 0.40$. Suppose also that the returns on the stocks are uncorrelated. Assume no dividends.

(a) Using the closed-form expressions for the price of these options, identify the price of the exchange option when $\sigma_2 = 0$, $\sigma_2 = 0.20$, $\sigma_2 = 0.40$, and $\sigma_2 = 0.60$.

(b) Is there a trend in the price? Intuitively, why is this the case?

31. What is the value of a one-year option on the maximum of two assets when both assets are trading at $100 each, their volatilities are 50% and 40%, and the correlation between their returns is +0.30? Both assets pay no dividends.

32. What is the value of a one-year option on the maximum of two assets when both assets are trading at $100 each, their volatilities are 50% and 40%, and the correlation between their returns is −0.30? Both assets pay no dividends. Compare the value against the case where the correlation is positive +0.3. Explain your result intuitively.

33. What is the value of a one-year option on the minimum of two assets when both assets are trading at $100 each, their volatilities are 50% and 40%, and the correlation between their returns is +0.30? Both assets pay no dividends.

# Chapter 19

# Exotic Options II: Path-Dependent Options

## 19.1 Path-Dependent Exotic Options

Building on the foundations laid in the last chapter, this chapter looks at the class of *path-dependent exotic options*. These are options whose payoffs upon exercise depend not only on the price of the underlying at that point but also on some or all of the entire *path* of prices leading to that terminal price.

In general, path dependence makes both the pricing and hedging of exotics more complex. Pricing becomes computationally more involved because we have to treat each path of prices separately even if they lead to the same end price. Hedging is complicated by the fact that the delta measures only the sensitivity of option value to changes in the *current* price of the stock (since we can only hedge with stock purchased at the current price), whereas the option payoffs may depend on *past* prices as well.

Once again, we use the Black-Scholes setting to describe closed-form solutions where these are available, and the binomial setting to illustrate the mechanics of pricing when they are not. Pricing in the binomial framework will be illustrated using the two-period example of Figure 18.1, which is reproduced here as Figure 19.1 for convenience. We examine five classes of path-dependent exotics in this chapter: barriers, Asians, lookbacks, cliquets, and shouts.

## 19.2 Barrier Options

*Barrier options* are among the most important of all classes of exotic options. In a nutshell, they are options that either cease to exist ("knock-out" options) or come to life ("knock-in" options) when the asset price breaches a prespecified barrier level during the life of the option.

For example, a *knock-out put option* with barrier $H$ is a put option that gets knocked out (i.e., ceases to exist) if the stock price crosses the level $H$ during the option's life. If the barrier is not breached at any point during the option's life, the option payoff is the same as

**FIGURE 19.1**
Stock Price Tree for
Binomial Illustrations

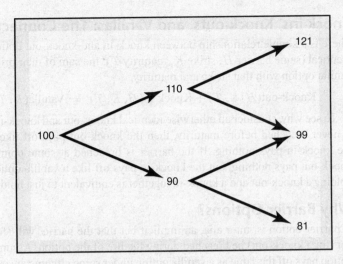

that from a vanilla put. Thus, given a strike $K$ and maturity $T$, its payoff at maturity is

$$\begin{cases} 0, & \text{if the stock price crosses } H \text{ before date } T \\ \max\{K - S_T, 0\}, & \text{if the stock price does not cross } H \text{ before date } T \end{cases}$$

As a second example, a *knock-in call option* with barrier $H$ is a call option that comes to life only if the asset price crosses the barrier $H$ at some point before the expiry of the option. If the barrier is never breached, the option expires worthless. The payoff from the option at maturity $T$ is, therefore,

$$\begin{cases} 0, & \text{if the stock price does not cross } H \text{ before date } T \\ \max\{S_T - K, 0\}, & \text{if the stock price crosses } H \text{ before date } T \end{cases}$$

As a general matter of classification, we distinguish between barrier options on whether they are knock-out or knock-in ("out-versus-in" options), and whether the barrier lies above or below the initial stock price ("up-versus-down" options). Thus, there are four basic kinds of barrier options:

- up-and-out options, where the barrier lies above the stock price and the option gets knocked out if the barrier is breached.
- up-and-in options, where the barrier lies above the stock price and the option gets knocked in only if the barrier is breached.
- down-and-out options, where the barrier lies below the stock price and the option gets knocked out if the barrier is breached.
- down-and-in options, where the barrier lies below the stock price and the option gets knocked in only if the barrier is breached.

Each of these catgories can be further broken down into whether the concerned option is a call or a put (it could even be a binary or other exotic option).

Barrier options may also involve a *rebate* paid by the seller to the option holder if the barrier is breached. Rebates are associated with knock-out options and are effectively a consolation prize in the event of the knock-out. The rebate may be paid either at the time of knock-out or at maturity. Of course, the possibility and size of the rebate payment will be reflected in the original barrier price. Knock-outs trade more often without rebates than with rebates. We focus on barriers without rebates in the rest of this section.

## Knock-ins, Knock-outs, and Vanillas: The Connection

There is a simple relationship between knock-in and knock-out options that are otherwise identical (same barrier $H$, strike $K$, maturity $T$): the sum of their prices must be equal to a vanilla option with that strike and maturity.

$$\text{Knock-out}(H, K, T) + \text{Knock-in}(H, K, T) = \text{Vanilla}(K, T) \qquad \textbf{(19.1)}$$

To see why, consider an otherwise identical knock-out and knock-in option. If the barrier is never breached before maturity, then the knock-out pays off like a vanilla option, but the knock-in pays nothing. If the barrier is breached at some point before maturity, the knock-out pays nothing, but the knock-in pays off like a vanilla option. So, in either case, holding a knock-out and a knock-in together is equivalent to just holding the vanilla option.

## Why Barrier Options?

A barrier option is, inter alia, an implicit bet that the barrier will (for a knock-in) or will not (for a knock-out) be breached during the life of the option. Assuming a zero rebate, the option pays off the same as a vanilla option under some circumstances but has a zero payoff under others, so it must cost less than its vanilla counterpart.

As such, barrier options offer a cheaper way of taking a directional bet than vanilla options. Consider, for example, a currency trader who expects the US dollar (USD) to rise against the euro (EUR). One way for her to speculate on these beliefs is to buy a USD call/EUR put. But if she is very confident about direction, she could lower her costs by buying a knock-out barrier option that ceases to exist if the dollar depreciates more than a certain amount against the euro.

Alternatively, consider an investor who is bullish about a stock. The investor can buy a call to bet on this belief. If the investor is further confident that the stock will not appreciate more than a given amount, he can lower his costs by buying an up-and-out call that gets knocked out if the stock price appreciates beyond a point.

## Pricing Barrier Options: A Binomial Example

While closed-form expressions exist for barrier options in a Black-Scholes setting, it helps to go through a binomial example to get a feel for the mechanics of the pricing process. So consider the two-period tree of Figure 19.1. Suppose we want to price an up-and-out put option in this setting with a strike price of $K = 100$ and a barrier of $H = 105$.

As Figure 19.2 shows, the price breaches the barrier in the two-period model only if it moves up in the first period. In all other circumstances, the barrier is not touched over the two-period horizon. Path-dependence in the tree is reflected in the fact that a terminal stock price of $udS = 99$ results in a zero payoff if the stock price went up and then came down, but in a payoff of $+1$ if the price went down first and then up.

In pricing a barrier option on the tree, we have to treat each price path separately and check whether the barrier is breached or not. If the barrier is not breached, we identify the payoffs from the option in the usual way. This results in the payoffs shown in Figure 19.3.

Once we have identified the barrier's payoffs from each path, we can use the risk-neutral probabilities to price the option. In this particular example, recall that the risk-neutral probability of an up move is $p = 0.60$, and the risk-free rate per period is $r = 1.02$. Working directly with the end-of-tree payoffs, this means the initial value of the option is

$$p^{knock\text{-}out} = \frac{1}{(1.02)^2} \left[ (0.36)(0) + (0.24)(0) + (0.24)(1) + (0.16)(19) \right]$$

$$= 3.15 \qquad \textbf{(19.2)}$$

**FIGURE 19.2**
Binomial Stock Price
Tree with Barrier

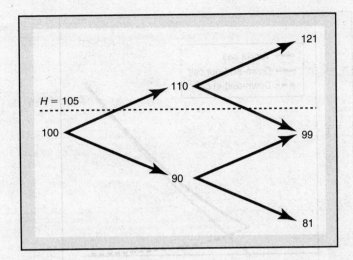

**FIGURE 19.3**
Barrier Option Payoffs
in Binomial Tree

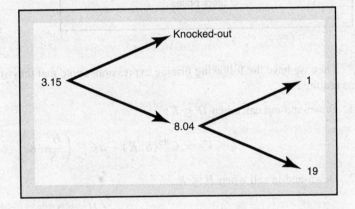

As expected, this value is smaller than the price of the corresponding vanilla put, which is 3.38.

## Barrier Option Pricing Formulae

Reiner and Rubinstein (1991) derive closed-form expressions for barrier options in a Black-Scholes setting. To describe these formulae, we use the notation described in the last chapter (see Table 18.1). As above, we denote the barrier by $H$. Finally, given $S$ and $K$ (and values for the other parameters), denote the Black-Scholes prices of a vanilla call and put by $C^{BS}(S, K)$ and $P^{BS}(S, K)$.

The expressions for two barrier options—down-and-in calls and down-and-out calls for the case where the barrier $H$ lies at or below the strike $K$—have relatively simple forms. We present them here. The others have more complex forms and are described in Appendix 19A. Define $\gamma$ and $a$ by

$$\gamma = \frac{2r}{\sigma^2} \tag{19.3}$$

$$a = \left(\frac{H}{S}\right)^{\gamma-1} \tag{19.4}$$

**FIGURE 19.4**

Down Calls when
$H < K$

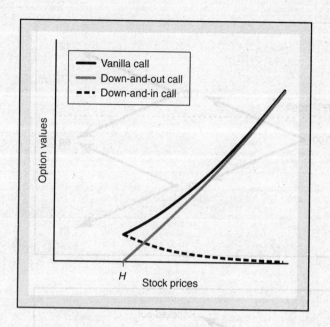

Then we have the following pricing expressions (note that they sum to the vanilla call, as required):

1. Down-and-out call when $H \leq K$:

$$V = C^{BS}(S, K) - a\, C^{BS}\left(\frac{H^2}{S}, K\right)$$

2. Down-and-in call when $H \leq K$:

$$V = a\, C^{BS}\left(\frac{H^2}{S}, K\right)$$

Figure 19.4 plots "down" call option prices for the case $H < K$ as the current stock price $S$ varies. Only values $S \geq H$ are considered since these would not be "down" options for $S < H$. As $S$ increases, the value of a down-and-in option decreases to zero since the probability of the stock price hitting the barrier declines; but the value of a down-and-out call increases towards the vanilla call since the likelihood of the option getting knocked out goes to zero as $S$ increases.

Figure 19.5 similarly plots "up" put options for the case $H > K$ using the formulae presented in Appendix 19A. Only values $S \leq H$ are considered since these are "up" options. As the stock price decreases, the value of the up-and-in put goes to zero since the likelihood of the option coming to life becomes small, but the value of the up-and-out put becomes correspondingly large, converging towards the price of the vanilla put.

## Barrier Options and Volatility

Barrier options have one peculiarity not shared by vanilla options (or, indeed, by even most other exotic options). For a vanilla option, an increase in volatility is unambiguously a good thing. For a knock-*out* option, an increase in volatility is a mixed blessing. On the one hand, it increases upside payoffs at maturity if the option is not knocked out. On the other, by making prices more disperse, it also increases the probability of the option getting knocked out.

**FIGURE 19.5**
Up Put Values when
$H > K$

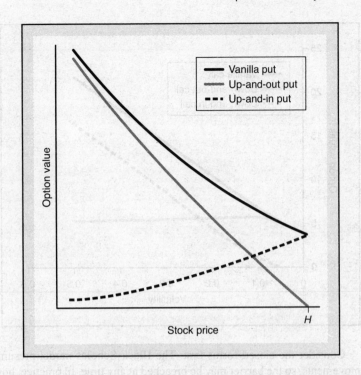

**TABLE 19.1**
Barrier Options and
Volatility

| Volatility | Black-Scholes Value | Knock-Out Value | Knock-In Value |
|---|---|---|---|
| 0.10 | 6.81 | 5.69 | 1.12 |
| 0.20 | 10.45 | 5.63 | 4.82 |
| 0.30 | 14.23 | 5.50 | 8.73 |
| 0.40 | 18.02 | 5.40 | 12.62 |
| 0.50 | 21.79 | 5.33 | 16.46 |

Thus, an increase in volatility may actually *lower* the value of a knock-out option, that is, the option may have negative vega. Put differently, a *long* knock-out position may be a *short* volatility position.

For a numerical example, consider a down-and-out call option with $S = K = 100$ and barrier $H = 95$. Let the maturity be $T = 1$ year and the interest rate be $r = 0.05$. Using the formulae for the prices, we can calculate the reaction of vanilla and knock-out option values to changes in volatility. Table 19.1 presents option values as volatility changes for these parameters. Figure 19.6 presents this information in a picture.

On the other hand, knock-*in* options benefit doubly from increases in volatility. An increase in volatility increases the likelihood of the option getting knocked in, and, of course, a higher level of volatility is a good thing once the option is knocked in. The numbers in Table 19.1 confirm this: proportional to their initial value, knock-in options gain more from an increase in volatility than do even vanilla options.

## Comments on Barrier Option Pricing

The pricing of barrier options is not quite as straightforward as suggested by either the binomial example or the closed-form solutions for barrier option prices. There are subtle problems that arise in each case.

**FIGURE 19.6**
Barrier Options and
Volatility

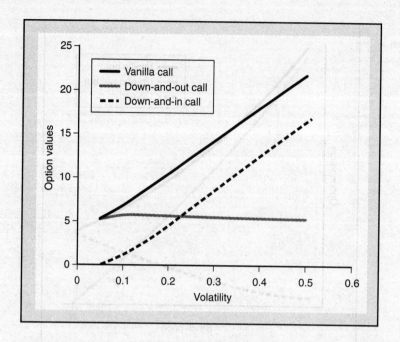

Consider the closed-forms first. The Black-Scholes model presumes *continuous* price movements, so the barrier may be breached at any time. In practice, however, intraday price movements are usually ignored in checking whether the barrier has been breached; rather, close-of-day (or, perhaps, close-of-week) prices are used. Thus, we should ignore barrier crossings that occur during the day. Since the model fails to do so, it allows "too many" breaches of the barrier and so *under*estimates knock-out option values and *over*estimates knock-in option values.

It turns out that there is no quick fix: we cannot get closed-form solutions if observations on the barrier being breached are taken only discretely. Happily, however, we *can* obtain very good approximations. One, proposed by Broadie, Glasserman, and Kou (1997), is to continue to use the closed-form solutions provided above (and in the appendix) but with the given barrier $H$ in the pricing formulae replaced with an adjusted barrier $\widehat{H}$. If $h$ is the time-interval between observations, then this adjusted barrier is defined by

$$\widehat{H} = e^{\beta \sigma \sqrt{h}} H \qquad\qquad (19.5)$$

if the barrier option is an "up" option or by

$$\widehat{H} = e^{-\beta \sigma \sqrt{h}} H \qquad\qquad (19.6)$$

if the barrier option is a "down" option, where $\beta \approx 0.5826$. Intuitively, to compensate for the excessive frequency of the barrier being breached when observations are continuous, we want to push the barrier away from the initial stock price; this is what (19.5)–(19.6) do.

Using discrete-time models (such as the binomial) for pricing purposes is also problematic albeit for different reasons. It turns out that in such models, the option price is very sensitive to the placement of the nodes of the tree around the barrier level. Since the barrier may not actually pass through any nodes on the binomial tree, the *effective* barrier (the "outer barrier" as it is sometimes called) is the set of nodes on the tree that lies immediately above the barrier (for an up option) or immediately below the barrier (for a down option). Figure 19.2 is a simple, if somewhat crude, illustration of this point. The effective barrier in the figure is the node $uS = 110$. A more detailed illustration is in Figure 19.7.

**FIGURE 19.7**

Inner, Outer, and True Barriers in a Binomial Tree

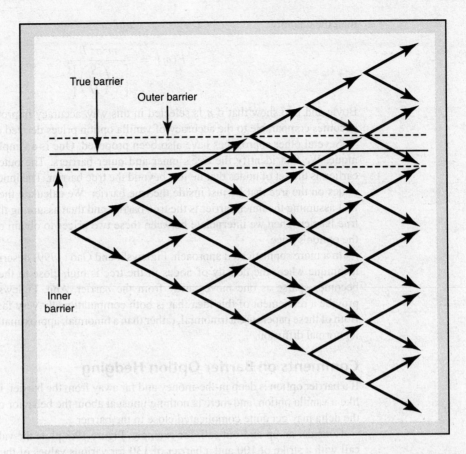

In general, the closer is the effective barrier to the true barrier, the more accurate the estimate of the barrier option price provided by the binomial tree. But this points to a problem. When we increase the number of time steps in the binomial tree, we change the positioning of the nodes, so it is possible that the effective barrier may actually move away from the true barrier. That is, merely increasing the number of time steps does *not* guarantee increased accuracy of barrier option prices obtained via the binomial tree. This was first pointed out in Boyle and Lau (1994).

Boyle and Lau show that the accuracy of option prices from the binomial tree can be improved substantially by choosing the number of steps $n$ in the tree with care. They use a Cox-Ross-Rubinstein (CRR) parametrization of the binomial tree (see Chapter 13). In this case, the up and down moves on the tree are defined by

$$u = e^{\sigma\sqrt{T/n}} \qquad d = e^{-\sigma\sqrt{T/n}}$$

where $T$ is the horizon of the tree in years and $n$ is the number of steps in the tree. For specificity, consider a down option. For any given parametrization, there will exist $m$ such that the barrier lies between the price after $m$ down moves and the price after $m+1$ down moves:

$$d^m S > H > d^{m+1} S$$

We want to choose the binomial tree so that the barrier is close to, and just above, a layer of nodes on the tree. This means we must select $n$ to be the largest integer that is smaller than the quantity

$$F(m) = \frac{m^2\sigma^2 T}{\left[\ln\left(\frac{S}{H}\right)\right]^2}$$  (19.7)

Boyle and Lau show that if $n$ is selected in this way, accuracy improves substantially and becomes comparable to the accuracy of vanilla option prices derived on the tree.

Several other approaches have also been proposed. One is a simple interpolation technique. We first identify the tree's inner and outer barriers. The outer barrier, as defined earlier, is the set of nodes that lie just beyond the true barrier. The inner barrier is the set of nodes on the tree that lie just inside the true barrier. We calculate the barrier option price first assuming the inner barrier is the true barrier and then assuming the outer barrier is the true barrier. Then we interpolate between these two prices to obtain our approximation of the option's price.

In a more sophisticated approach, Figlewski and Gao (1999) describe an *adaptive mesh* technique where the density of nodes in the tree is high close to the barrier but the tree becomes sparse as one moves away from the barrier. Ahn, Figlewski, and Gao (1999) provide a refinement of this idea that is both computationally very fast and very accurate. Both of these papers use a trinomial, rather than a binomial, approximation of the continuous lognormal diffusion.

## Comments on Barrier Option Hedging

If a barrier option is deep in-the-money and far away from the barrier, it behaves very much like a vanilla option, and there is nothing unusual about the behavior of its delta. However, the delta may get quite complicated close to the barrier.

Consider an up-and-out call, for example. Figure 19.8 plots the value of an up-and-out call with a strike of 100 and a barrier of 130 for various values of the current stock price. As the stock price is far from the barrier, the option resembles a vanilla call, but as it gets close to the barrier, the likelihood of the option getting knocked out increases, so the option value goes to zero. At the peak of the option price, the delta switches sign from positive to negative. Close to maturity, this peak becomes very pronounced, and the gamma

**FIGURE 19.8**

Behavior of an
Up-and-Out Call

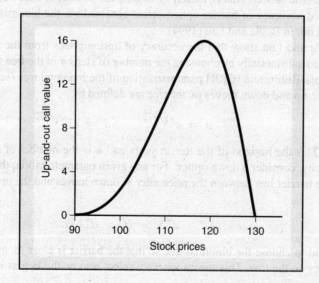

becomes very large and negative. Writing such options involves considerable delta-hedging risk.

As a different example, consider the down-and-in call in Figure 19.4. Prior to knock-in, the option value is a declining function of the stock price: the higher the stock price, the lower the probability of the option getting knocked in. Thus, the delta is negative. But if the option gets knocked in, it becomes a vanilla call, so has a positive delta. In this case, the delta changes sign at the barrier. The hedging problem presented in this case is, however, less severe than the previous one: the option value is small close to the barrier because even if the option gets knocked-in, it is out-of-the-money at the time of knock-in.

# 19.3 Asian Options

Asian options are options in which the payoff to the holder of the option depends on the *average price* of the underlying over the life of the contract. The period over which this average is taken is specified in the contract. It may, for example, be the average daily closing price over the entire life of the option. Alternatively, it may be the average daily closing price only over the last month of the option's life. It may even involve averaging only over two or three specified time points.

Let $\overline{S}$ denote this average price. The most common variety of Asian options is *average-price* options. In these options, a strike price $K$ is specified in the option contract. At maturity of the option, the option holder's payoff is calculated as in a vanilla option but with $\overline{S}$ playing the role of $S_T$. That is, the holder of an Asian average-price call receives the payoff

$$\max\{\overline{S} - K, 0\} \qquad (19.8)$$

while the holder of an Asian average-price put receives

$$\max\{K - \overline{S}, 0\} \qquad (19.9)$$

There is also a class of less popular Asian options called *average-strike* options in which the averaging is applied to the strike price instead. That is, $\overline{S}$ plays the role of the strike price in these options, so the holder of an Asian average-strike call receives the payoff

$$\max\{S_T - \overline{S}, 0\} \qquad (19.10)$$

while the holder of an Asian average-strike put receives

$$\max\{\overline{S} - S_T, 0\} \qquad (19.11)$$

Since average-price options are far more common, we focus on these in the remainder of this section. We also drop the qualifier "average price" and refer to these simply as Asian options.

## Why Asian Options I: Exposure to the Average

Perhaps the most important aspect of Asian options is that they address a particular kind of hedging need: exposure to the *average*. That is, for investors who anticipate repeated transactions in a given underlying (a typical example is an exporter who receives foreign currency on a regular basis), Asian options offer a cost-efficient way of obtaining a cap or floor on cash flows.

Consider, for example, a company that makes oil purchases on a regular basis (say, monthly) and wishes to insulate itself against oil price fluctuations. Specifically, suppose the company wishes to cap its total cost on the purchases over a given horizon (say, one year).

There are two ways to achieve this. First, the company can buy a strip of vanilla call options on oil, one expiring each month, each with the same strike of $K$. Then, in no month will the company spend more than $K$ on oil, so overall costs are capped at $12K$.

As an alternative, the company can buy the oil spot each month and purchase 12 Asian call options expiring in a year's time and with a strike of $K$. If the average price over the year is greater than $K$, the company receives the difference between the average and $K$ on each option. Thus, the company's total net expenditure works out to just $12K$. If the average is less than $K$, the company receives nothing from the options, but, of course, it has spent, on average, less than $K$ each month. Thus, this method too provides a cap.

Of the two methods, Asians offer the cheaper way of obtaining the desired cap. Intuitively, Asian calls cost less because the volatility of the *average* is less than the volatility of the price itself. Of course, this cheaper protection is not an "arbitrage"! Asian calls cost less precisely because they offer protection only on average, not on each individual price spike as would vanilla calls. That is, it is possible that some of the vanilla calls finish in-the-money and others finish out-of-the-money, but the average price is sufficiently low that all the Asians finish out-of-the-money. Nonetheless, a company whose objective is only to control average costs might find it worthwhile to trade off the larger upside of the vanilla options for the lower cost and easier administration of the Asian calls.

## Why Asian Options II: Smoothing the Data

A fundamental aspect of Asian options is that they "smooth" the data. Because prices are averaged over the life of the option, Asian option payoffs are less sensitive to "spikes" in the price of the underlying at maturity. This has at least two important consequences.

First, it means that manipulating Asian options' payoffs by manipulating the price of the underlying is a lot harder than is the case for vanilla options. This is a feature of interest to investors operating in thin markets.

Second, Asian options may be of interest to investors whose concern regarding vanilla options may be that the options may spend most of their lives in-the-money only to plunge out-of-the-money at maturity. For example, an investor who anticipates that the price of a stock will be higher in six months will be less concerned about prices spiking down close to maturity if she buys an Asian option that takes the average price over (say) the last month in determining the option's payoff.

On the other hand, Asian options are *not* as useful as vanilla options in taking directional bets. When prices rise, the average will climb slower than the price itself, so an Asian call option is of less value to an investor with bullish market views than is a vanilla call option. Similarly, an investor with bearish views will find greater payoffs in using a vanilla put than an Asian put.

## Can Asian Options Be Used for Speculation?

For the reasons described in the last paragraph, Asian options are viewed primarily as instruments for *hedging* rather than *speculation*. Nonetheless, it would be wrong to conclude (as is sometimes done) that Asian options cannot be used for speculation.

A case in point is the episode involving China Aviation Oil (Singapore) Corporation, an overseas arm of China's main jet fuel supplier. In December 2004, the company announced that it had run up trading losses of over $500 million, a substantial chunk of which was derivatives related. One of the trades (detailed in *The Wall Street Journal*, December 3, 2004) was with J. Aron, a subsidiary of Goldman Sachs, and involved Asian put options.

The contract involved jet fuel as the underlying asset and was for 100,000 barrels. Under the contract, which was entered into on September 1, 2004, CAO Singapore sold Asian calls to J. Aron with a strike of $37 a barrel. The payoff from the calls was to be calculated by averaging the spot price during October 2004. Thus, CAO Singapore was betting that the average spot price in October would be below $37. They were wrong and by a wide margin. Over October, jet fuel prices averaged $61.25 a barrel, leading to losses for CAO Singapore of over $2.4 million on this trade alone.

## Arithmetic and Geometric Averages

So far, we have been silent on the question of what we mean by the "average." Suppose we have price observations $S_1, \ldots, S_n$ over the life of the option that we are to average. There are two ways in which we could define this "average" (actually, there are many ways, but these are two popular ones):

1. *The arithmetic average:* $\bar{S}^a = \dfrac{1}{n}(S_1 + \cdots + S_n)$.
2. *The geometric average:* $\bar{S}^g = (S_1 \times \cdots \times S_n)^{1/n}$.

Both arithmetic and geometric averages are used in financial markets, although the use of arithmetic averages is far more common. One example of the geometric average is the Value Line Geometric Index published by Value Line. (Value Line has also published an arithmetic index since 1988.) From the standpoint of pricing Asian options, the geometric average has a significant technical advantage as we explain shortly. A brief digression first.

## Put-Call Parity for Asian Options

A version of put-call parity can be derived for Asian average-price options (whether based on arithmetic or geometric averaging). Let $C_t^{\text{ave}}$ and $P_t^{\text{ave}}$ denote, respectively, the time-$t$ prices of otherwise identical call and put average-price options (whether arithmetic or geometric). Using the subscript $T$ to denote values at maturity and $\bar{S}$ to denote the average price of the underlying at $T$, we have

$$C_T^{\text{ave}} - P_T^{\text{ave}} = \bar{S} - K$$

The present value at any earlier time $t$ is the discounted risk-neutral expectation of these payoffs. Letting $E[\cdot]$ denote the risk-neutral expectation, we obtain

$$C_t^{\text{ave}} - P_t^{\text{ave}} = e^{-r(T-t)}E[\bar{S}] - e^{-r(T-t)}K$$

For both geometric and arithmetic averaging, expressions for $E[\bar{S}]$ can be calculated exactly (see, for example, Chapter 17 and Appendix A13 of James, 2003). So, put prices can be obtained via call prices and vice versa.

## Pricing Asian Options on the Geometric Average

Suppose we are taking observations every $h$ years, and there are $N + 1$ observations in all: the initial price $S_0 = S$, the $N - 1$ interim observations $S_1, S_2, \ldots, S_{N-1}$ taken at the time points $h, 2h, \ldots, (N - 1)h$, and the terminal price $S_N$ taken at maturity $T$. The geometric average is then

$$S^g = (S_0 \times S_1 \times \cdots \times S_N)^{1/(N+1)} \tag{19.12}$$

Now, note that

$$\ln\left(\frac{S^g}{S_0}\right) = \ln\left[\left(\frac{S_0 \times S_1 \times \cdots \times S_N}{S_0 \times S_0 \times \cdots \times S_0}\right)^{1/(N+1)}\right]$$

so that, by the usual properties of the logarithm,

$$\ln\left(\frac{S^g}{S_0}\right) = \frac{1}{N+1}\left[\ln\left(\frac{S_0}{S_0}\right) + \ln\left(\frac{S_1}{S_0}\right) + \cdots + \ln\left(\frac{S_N}{S_0}\right)\right] \tag{19.13}$$

Under the usual Black-Scholes assumptions, the returns $\ln(S_n/S_0)$ are normally distributed for each $n \geq 1$. Therefore, so is their sum. This means the geometric-average return is itself lognormally distributed, so we can use the Black-Scholes formula to price options on the geometric average! From (19.13), it can be shown that the volatility $\sigma_g$ and dividend yield $\delta_g$ of the geometric average are given by

$$\sigma_g = \frac{\sigma^2}{3}\frac{2N+1}{2N+2} \tag{19.14}$$

$$\delta_g = \frac{1}{2}\left(r + \delta + \frac{1}{6}\sigma^2\right) \tag{19.15}$$

Using (19.14)–(19.15) in the Black-Scholes pricing formula (14.21)–(14.22), we obtain the prices of Asian options on the geometric-average price.

## Pricing Arithmetic-Average Price Options

Unfortunately, the pricing formulae for Asian geometric-average price options are of limited use. In practice, it is the arithmetic, and not the geometric, average that is used to determine the payoffs of Asian options. The arithmetic average is much less mathematically tractable since the arithmetic average of lognormal prices is not itself lognormal. In particular, closed-form solutions are not available for Asian option prices.

One common solution to this problem is to use numerical techniques such as Monte Carlo simulation to identify the option price. In addition, several techniques have also been proposed that look to approximate the option's price analytically. We describe some of these below. We focus on call options; put prices can be obtained from call prices using put-call parity. We use $C^g$ to denote the price of a geometric-average-price call, and $C^a$ for the arithmetic-average-price call.

Vorst (1992) derives upper and lower bounds for the arithmetic-average-price option in terms of the geometric-average-price option. The lower bound is simple to derive. Mathematically, one can show that the arithmetic average of a set of positive numbers must always exceed their geometric-average, so:

$$\bar{S}^a \geq \bar{S}^g$$

This means the payoff at maturity on a geometric-average-price call will always be less than that on an otherwise identical arithmetic-average-price call. It follows that the arithmetic-average option must cost at least as much as the geometric-average option:

$$C^a \geq C^g$$

For the upper bound, Vorst (1992) notes that since $\bar{S}^a \geq \bar{S}^g$, it is the case that

$$\max\{0, S^a - K\} - \max\{0, S^g - K\} \leq S^a - S^g$$

that is, the difference in maturity payoffs is less than the difference between the arithmetic and geometric averages. It follows by taking present values in the above expression that

$$C^a - C^g \leq e^{-rT}E[S^a - S^g] \tag{19.16}$$

where $T$ denotes the remaining time to maturity and $E[\cdot]$ is the risk-neutral expectation. (As noted earlier, exact expressions may be derived for $E[S^a]$ and $E[S^g]$.) Expression (19.16) gives us an upper bound on arithmetic-average-price call options in terms of their geometric counterparts. Combining the upper and lower bounds, we may write

$$C^g \leq C^a \leq C^g + e^{-rT}E[S^a - S^g] \tag{19.17}$$

Vorst (1992) also provides an approximation of the arithmetic-average call's price in terms of the geometric-average call. He shows that the price of an arithmetic-average call with strike $K$ is roughly equal to that of a geometric-average call with strike $K - E[S^a - S^g]$:

$$C^a(K) \approx C^g(K - E[S^a - S^g]) \tag{19.18}$$

An alternative approach sometimes used is to assume that the arithmetic-average price $S^a$ is lognormally distributed. We calculate exact values for the first two moments of the arithmetic-average price and use these as the parameters of the lognormal distribution. Turnbull and Wakeman (1991) describe an extension of this approach. In their approximation, the distribution of $S^a$ is assumed to be approximately, but not exactly, lognormal. They show how Edgeworth expansions may then be used to approximate the true distribution via the lognormal. A different approach is proposed in Curran (1994) which involves pricing the arithmetic-average option through conditioning on the geometric mean. Table 17.1 of James (2003) presents a comparison of these approximation approaches; the numbers in this table indicate that the two best approaches are a sophisticated version of the Turnbull-Wakeman method that makes use of higher moments as well, and the geometric conditioning of Curran. Both approximate the Monte Carlo results very well, although Curran's approach does slightly better overall in almost every case.

## Pricing Asian Options: A Binomial Example

A simple binomial example can be used to illustrate several useful points about Asian options. Consider the two-period binomial tree of Figure 19.1. Suppose we are averaging over the observations at times 1 and 2 (but not including the initial observation) and we are looking to price an Asian call option with a strike of $K = 100$.

The average stock price from each of the four possible paths and the resulting payoff of the Asian call are shown in Table 19.2. The risk-neutral probabilities are calculated on the basis of the gross risk-free interest rate per period of 1.02. The initial value of the Asian call is

$$C^{Asian} = \frac{1}{(1.02)^2}[(0.36)(15.5) + (0.24)(4.5)] = 6.40 \tag{19.19}$$

In contrast, the corresponding vanilla call costs much more at 7.27.

## Hedging Asian Options: Comments

The binomial example also provides a nice illustration of the behavior of the Asian delta. The deltas are easily computed using the standard rules for binomial trees. The delta

- at the initial node $S = 100$ is 0.55.

**TABLE 19.2** Asian Call Option Payoffs in the Binomial Tree

| Path | Average Price | Call Payoff | Risk-Neutral Probability |
|------|---------------|-------------|--------------------------|
| uu | 115.5 | 15.5 | 0.36 |
| ud | 104.5 | 4.5 | 0.24 |
| du | 94.5 | 0 | 0.24 |
| dd | 85.5 | 0 | 0.16 |

- at the node $uS = 110$ is 0.50.
- at the node $dS = 90$ is zero.

Two interesting points are highlighted by these numbers. First, a vanilla call that is guaranteed to finish in-the-money has a delta of $+1$. The Asian call in this example is guaranteed to finish in-the-money if the node $uS = 110$ is reached, yet its delta at this point is only 0.50, which is very far from $+1$. Second, the delta of a vanilla call increases when the call moves deeper into-the-money. The Asian call in this example moves deeper into-the-money when the stock price moves up to $uS = 110$ from the initial price of $S = 100$, but nonetheless, its delta *falls* from 0.55 to 0.50.

Why is this the case? Both phenomena have a common explanation: the delta measures only the sensitivity of the option value to changes in the *current* price of the stock. However, the option payoff depends on the *average* price that has been observed since inception. The more time has passed, the less influence changes in the current price have on the average price. (For instance, suppose that after 99 observations, the average price works out to 50. Then, even if the 100th observation is a very high value of 150, the average moves only from 50 to 51.) This means the delta becomes less sensitive to changes in the underlying as maturity approaches.

## Asian versus Vanilla Puts

Finally, an important point. It is often missed in treatments of Asian options that Asian puts, unlike Asian calls, can sometimes be worth *more* than their vanilla counterparts. Averaging produces a dampening effect resulting in a lower growth rate *and* a lower volatility. For a call, each of these features works to reduce the value of the Asian call compared to its vanilla counterpart. But for a put, the lower growth rate of the average works to increase the Asian put's payoff, while the lower volatility works to reduce it. Depending on which effect dominates, the Asian put may be worth more or less than its European counterpart.

For an example of a situation in which the Asian put is worth more, consider the binomial example again. As we have seen, a two-period vanilla European put in this setting with a strike of 100 has a price of 3.38. Consider a two-period Asian put with $K = 100$ in which the price is averaged over nodes 1 and 2. The average prices from the four possible paths, the consequent Asian put payoffs, and the risk-neutral likelihoods of the different outcomes are summarized in Table 19.3. The initial price of the Asian put is

$$\frac{1}{1.02} \left[ (0.24)(5.5) + (0.16)(14.5) \right] = 3.57$$

which exceeds the value of the vanilla put.

Here is a very simple proof that Asian puts are more valuable than their vanilla counterparts when volatility is suitably low. The argument is based on the analysis of Ye (2005). Suppose a security is currently trading at $S$. First consider the case in which the volatility of the security's returns is zero. Let $r$ denote the risk-free rate of interest, so the time-$T$ price of the security is just $S_T = e^{rT} S_0$. Now compare two put options, one vanilla, one Asian, both with strike $K$ and maturity $T$.

- The vanilla has the payoff $\max\{K - S_T, 0\}$.

**TABLE 19.3** Asian Put Option Payoffs in the Binomial Tree

| Path | Average Price | Put Payoff | Risk-Neutral Probability |
|------|---------------|------------|--------------------------|
| uu | 115.5 | 0 | 0.36 |
| ud | 104.5 | 0 | 0.24 |
| du | 94.5 | 5.5 | 0.24 |
| dd | 85.5 | 14.5 | 0.16 |

- The Asian considers the average price $\overline{S}$ between time 0 and time $T$ (where the average is computed with respect to some $n$ observations taken at prespecified times) and gives the holder the payoff $\max\{K - \overline{S}, 0\}$.

Since the price of the asset is trending up at the risk-free rate $r$, the average price $\overline{S}$ must be less than the time-$T$ price $S_T$. This implies that the Asian put's payoff is strictly higher than the vanilla put's for $K > \overline{S}$, while both have zero payoffs for $K \leq \overline{S}$. Therefore, for $K > \overline{S}$, the Asian put must cost strictly more than the vanilla put.

Now suppose volatility may be nonzero. Let $P(\sigma)$ and $P^A(\sigma)$ denote the values of the vanilla and Asian puts when volatility is $\sigma$. We have just shown that $P^A(0) > P(0)$. Therefore, assuming the underlying equilibrium is continuous in $\sigma$ (which does not appear to be a strong assumption), we must also have $P^A(\sigma) > P(\sigma)$ for suitably small $\sigma$, completing the proof.

## 19.4   Lookback Options

Lookback options are options in which the holder may "look back" at maturity and choose the most favorable price for determining the payoffs. Obviously, which price is the most favorable depends on whether we are holding a call or a put. In addition, the payoffs are defined differently depending on whether we are looking at *floating-strike* lookback options or *fixed-strike* lookback options.

The more common version of lookback options is the floating-strike option (also sometimes called the "lookback strike" option). In this case, the strike price for a lookback call is set equal to the lowest price $S^{\min}$ that was observed during the life of the option. Thus, the payoff at time $T$ to the holder of a floating-strike lookback call is

$$\max\{S_T - S^{\min}, 0\} \qquad \textbf{(19.20)}$$

Note that the "max" is really superfluous since $S_T - S^{\min}$ cannot be less than zero. Analogously, for the holder of a floating-strike lookback put, the strike is set equal to the highest price that was observed during the life of the option. This results in a payoff at maturity of

$$\max\{S^{\max} - S_T, 0\} \qquad \textbf{(19.21)}$$

The other kind of lookback options has a fixed strike price and is also called "lookback price" options (or, sometimes, "lookforward") options. In this case, the holder of a call receives at maturity the payoff

$$\max\{S^{\max} - K, 0\} \qquad \textbf{(19.22)}$$

while the holder of a put receives

$$\max\{K - S^{\min}, 0\} \qquad \textbf{(19.23)}$$

### Why Lookbacks?

Lookback options combine, in a sense, the best features of American and European options. The holder of an American option can take advantage of favorable prices prior to maturity by exercising the option early. However, since future prices cannot be forecast perfectly, early exercise necessarily leaves the door open for regret: an even more favorable price may occur subsequently. Lookbacks eliminate this ex-post regret. As such, they offer considerably more protection to the holder than do vanilla options. But by the same token, they are typically very expensive, perhaps why, despite their obvious appeal, they are not very heavily traded.

## Pricing and Hedging Lookbacks: A Binomial Example

Closed-form solutions do exist for lookback options in a Black-Scholes setting, but they involve complex forms that lack an easy intuitive interpretation. It is instructive to first examine a simple binomial model. The example below illustrates how much more expensive the lookbacks can be compared to the vanilla options. It also illustrates some aspects of the lookback delta.

Consider fixed-strike lookbacks with a strike of 100 in the stock price tree of Figure 19.1. Since lookbacks are path-dependent options, computing their prices involves looking at each possible path of asset prices and identifying the most favorable price for the option holder along that path. There are four possible price paths in this tree. The maximum prices they lead to, and the payoffs of the option at these points, are listed in Table 19.4. Path-dependence of the lookbacks is implicit in the fact that the nodes $ud$ and $du$ lead to different payoffs.

Recall that the gross interest rate per time step in this example is 1.02, so the risk-neutral probability of an up move in each step is 0.60. Applying this to the terminal payoffs, the initial prices of the fixed-strike lookback call and put are, respectively,

$$C^{\text{FiSt}} = \frac{1}{(1.02)^2} [(0.36)(21) + (0.24)(10) + (0.24)(0) + (0.16)(0)] \quad \textbf{(19.24)}$$

$$= 9.57$$

$$P^{\text{FiSt}} = \frac{1}{(1.02)^2} [(0.36)(0) + (0.24)(1) + (0.24)(10) + (0.16)(19)] \quad \textbf{(19.25)}$$

$$= 5.46$$

These values are considerably higher than the vanilla European call and put prices of 7.27 and 3.38, respectively.

This binomial tree can also be used to illustrate one other simple, but interesting, point: that the delta of a lookback will not necessarily increase with the stock price. Using the usual arguments, it is simple to verify that the delta of the call option

- at the initial node is 0.81.
- at the node $uS$ is 0.50.
- at the node $dS$ is zero.

Note that at the node $uS$, the call is guaranteed to finish in-the-money yet has a delta substantially less than $+1$. Moreover, as the stock price *increases* from $S = 100$ to $uS = 110$, the delta of the lookback call *falls* from 0.81 to 0.50.

It is not difficult to see why this happens. The delta measures the sensitivity of option value to changes in the *current* price of the underlying asset. However, the option payoff here depends on only the *maximum* price observed over the life of the option. Thus, the *current* price influences option values only insofar as it influences the maximum price. Along some paths, very high prices may have already been observed, and this reduces the

**TABLE 19.4**
Lookback Option Payoffs in the Binomial Tree

| Path | Maximum Price | Minimum Price | Call Payoff | Put Payoff |
|------|---------------|---------------|-------------|------------|
| *uu* | 121 | 100 | 21 | 0 |
| *ud* | 110 | 99 | 10 | 1 |
| *du* | 100 | 90 | 0 | 10 |
| *dd* | 100 | 81 | 0 | 19 |

option's sensitivity to the current price. Thus, its delta will not necessarily increase even if asset prices do so.

## Pricing Formulae for Lookbacks

Rather than describe how to identify the option price at time 0 alone, we will describe more generally how to identify the lookback's price at any time $t$ during the option's life. Let $S_t$ denote the time-$t$ stock price, and let $S_H$ and $S_L$ denote the highest and lowest prices that have been observed thus far in the option's life, i.e., between times 0 and $t$. If we are at the beginning of the option's life, then $S_H = S_L = S$, where $S$ is the time-0 stock price.

Let $S_t^{\max}$ and $S_t^{\min}$ denote the maximum and minimum prices, respectively, observed between time $t$ and maturity. Viewed from time $t$, these are random quantities. Define $M_t$ and $m_t$ by

$$M_t = E\left[\max\{S_H, S_t^{\max}\}\right] \tag{19.26}$$

$$m_t = E\left[\min\{S_L, S_t^{\min}\}\right] \tag{19.27}$$

The expectations are under the risk-neutral distribution of $S_t$. We provide closed-form expressions for $M_t$ and $m_t$ further below. But first, we describe pricing formulae for lookbacks in terms of $M_t$ and $m_t$.

## (A) Floating-Strike Lookback Options

Pick any time $t$ and define $S_H$ and $S_L$ as above. The fair value at time $t$ of a floating-strike lookback call is the expectation of its time-$T$ payoff under the risk-neutral measure discounted back to $t$ at the risk-free rate:

$$
\begin{aligned}
C_t^{\text{FlSt}} &= e^{-r(T-t)} E\left[S_T - \min\{S_L, S_t^{\min}\}\right] \\
&= e^{-r(T-t)} E[S_T] - e^{-r(T-t)} E[\min\{S_L, S_t^{\min}\}] \\
&= e^{-\delta(T-t)} S_t - e^{-r(T-t)} m_t
\end{aligned}
\tag{19.28}
$$

Similarly, the time-$t$ price of a floating-strike lookback put is

$$
\begin{aligned}
P_t^{\text{FlSt}} &= e^{-r(T-t)} E\left[\max\{S_H, S_t^{\max}\} - S_T\right] \\
&= e^{-r(T-t)} E[\max\{S_H, S_t^{\max}\}] - e^{-r(T-t)} E[S_T] \\
&= e^{-r(T-t)} M_t - e^{-\delta(T-t)} S_t
\end{aligned}
\tag{19.29}
$$

## (B) Fixed-Strike Lookback Options

For fixed-strike lookback options, closed-forms can be easily derived if the options are issued at-the-money (as is commonly the case in practice). In this case, $K$ is just the time-0 price $S$, so the payoffs of a call are

$$\max\{S^{\max} - K, 0\} = S^{\max} - S \tag{19.30}$$

while the payoffs from a put are

$$\max\{K - S^{\min}, 0\} = S - S^{\min} \tag{19.31}$$

Viewed from time $t$ and continuing with the notation introduced above, these payoffs are given respectively by

$$\max\{S_H, S_t^{\max}\} - S \tag{19.32}$$

$$S - \min\{S_L, S_t^{\min}\} \tag{19.33}$$

Thus, the time-$t$ value of a fixed-strike lookback call and put are, respectively,

$$C_t^{\text{FiSt}} = e^{-r(T-t)} E\left[\max\{S_H, S_t^{\max}\} - S\right]$$

$$= e^{-r(T-t)} E[\max\{S_H, S_t^{\max}\}] - e^{-r(T-t)} S \qquad (19.34)$$

$$= e^{-\delta(T-t)} M_t - e^{-r(T-t)} S$$

$$P_t^{\text{FiSt}} = e^{-r(T-t)} E\left[S - \min\{S_L, S_t^{\min}\}\right]$$

$$= e^{-r(T-t)} S - e^{-r(T-t)} E[\min\{S_L, S_t^{\min}\}] \qquad (19.35)$$

$$= e^{-r(T-t)} S - e^{-r(T-t)} m_t$$

## (C) $M_t$ and $m_t$

To complete the closed-form descriptions, we give closed-form representations for $M_t$ and $m_t$. These take the form

$$M_t = S_H\left[N(\beta_1) - \frac{\sigma^2}{2(r-\delta)} e^Y N(-\beta_3)\right] + e^{(r-\delta)(T-t)} S_t \left[1 + \frac{\sigma^2}{2(r-\delta)}\right] N(-\beta_2)$$

$$(19.36)$$

and

$$m_t = S_L\left[N(\alpha_2) - \frac{\sigma^2}{2(r-\delta)} e^X N(\alpha_3)\right] + e^{(r-\delta)(T-t)} S_t \left[1 + \frac{\sigma^2}{2(r-\delta)}\right] N(-\alpha_1)$$

$$(19.37)$$

where

$$\beta_1 = \frac{1}{\sigma\sqrt{T-t}} \left[\ln\left(\frac{S_H}{S_t}\right) - (r - \delta - \tfrac{1}{2}\sigma^2)(T-t)\right] \qquad (19.38)$$

$$\beta_2 = \beta_1 - \sigma\sqrt{T-t} \qquad (19.39)$$

$$\beta_3 = \frac{1}{\sigma\sqrt{T-t}} \left[\ln\left(\frac{S_H}{S_t}\right) + (r - \delta - \tfrac{1}{2}\sigma^2)(T-t)\right] \qquad (19.40)$$

$$Y = \frac{1}{\sigma^2} \left[2(r - \delta - \tfrac{1}{2}\sigma^2) \ln\left(\frac{S_H}{S_t}\right)\right] \qquad (19.41)$$

$$\alpha_1 = \frac{1}{\sigma\sqrt{T-t}} \left[\ln\left(\frac{S_t}{S_L}\right) + (r - \delta + \tfrac{1}{2}\sigma^2)(T-t)\right] \qquad (19.42)$$

$$\alpha_2 = \alpha_1 - \sigma\sqrt{T-t} \qquad (19.43)$$

$$\alpha_3 = \frac{1}{\sigma\sqrt{T-t}} \left[\ln\left(\frac{S_t}{S_L}\right) - (r - \delta - \tfrac{1}{2}\sigma^2)(T-t)\right] \qquad (19.44)$$

$$X = \frac{1}{\sigma^2} \left[2(r - \delta - \tfrac{1}{2}\sigma^2) \ln\left(\frac{S_t}{S_L}\right)\right] \qquad (19.45)$$

# 19.5 Cliquets

Cliquets (also known as "ratchets") generalize the idea of forward-start options. Let time 0 and time $T$ denote the start date and maturity date of the cliquet. The specification of a cliquet also involves $n$ intermediate "reset dates" $\tau_1, \ldots, \tau_n$ satisfying

$$0 < \tau_1 < \cdots < \tau_n < T$$

For example, the final maturity could be one year from the current time, and the reset dates could be quarterly. At each reset date, the holder of the cliquet receives the payout from a call option whose strike is equal to the stock price at the previous reset date. That is, on the first reset date $\tau_1$, the holder of the option receives a payout equal to

$$\max\{0,\, S_{\tau_1} - S\} \qquad\qquad \textbf{(19.46)}$$

where $S$, in our usual notation, denotes the price at time 0. On the second reset date $\tau_2$, the holder receives a payout

$$\max\{0,\, S_{\tau_2} - S_{\tau_1}\} \qquad\qquad \textbf{(19.47)}$$

And so on until the final maturity date of $T$, when the holder receives the payment

$$\max\{0,\, S_T - S_{\tau_n}\} \qquad\qquad \textbf{(19.48)}$$

The payouts (19.46)–(19.48) may also be made in a single lump sum at time $T$. In common variants, there may also be a cap on the cliquet payoff in any sub-period and/or a cap on total payoffs from the cliquet and/or a floor payment different from zero.

The payoffs (19.46)–(19.48) show that a cliquet is just a series of forward-starting call options coming to life at times $0, \tau_1, \ldots, \tau_n$, and maturing at times $\tau_1, \tau_2, \ldots, T$, respectively. Each forward start in the cliquet is at-the-money when it comes to life. The total payoff from the cliquet is path-dependent since it depends on the intermediate stock prices $S_{\tau_1}, \ldots, S_{\tau_n}$. The path-dependence is even more apparent if the cliquet comes with a cap on overall payoffs.

## Why Cliquets?

Cliquets offer protection against stock price spikes close to maturity. An investor who is worried that the stock price may exceed a vanilla option's strike during the option's life but crash below it close to maturity may find the intermediate payments locked-in via a cliquet to be an attractive proposition. More generally, a cliquet is a bet that the underlying will have at least some periods of positive returns.

One alternative to a cliquet is to buy at-the-money calls at each reset date, but this has the problem that future volatility is unknown. Using a cliquet eliminates this uncertainty by implicitly locking in a volatility level. If volatility turns out to be higher than implied in the cliquet price, the cliquet holder benefits, but of course he loses if it turns out to be lower.

## Pricing Cliquets

To price a cliquet, we price each forward start in the cliquet and add them up. Let $C(S, K, \tau)$ denote the price of a vanilla call with strike $K$ and time to maturity $\tau$ given the current stock price of $S$. As usual, let $q$ denote the dividend yield on the underlying. As we saw in the last chapter, the price of a forward start that comes to life at $\tau_i$ and matures at $\tau_{i+1}$ is just

$$e^{-\delta \tau_i} C(S, S, \tau_{i+1} - \tau_i)$$

Thus, the initial price of the cliquet is

$$V^{cliquet} = C(S, S, \tau_1) + e^{-\delta \tau_1} C(S, S, \tau_2 - \tau_1) + \cdots + e^{-\delta \tau_n} C(S, S, T - \tau_n) \quad \textbf{(19.49)}$$

## Hedging Cliquets

Since a cliquet is just a portfolio of forward starts, hedging the cliquet too is just an issue of hedging the forward starts in the portfolio. As we saw in the last chapter, the delta of a forward start that comes to life at $\tau_i$ and matures at $\tau_{i+1}$ is

$$e^{-\delta \tau_i} C(1, 1, \tau_{i+1} - \tau_i)$$

The delta of the cliquet is the sum of the deltas of these forward starts.

### Reverse Cliquets

A reverse cliquet, like a cliquet, involves $n$ reset dates $\tau_1, \ldots, \tau_n$. In a typical version, a coupon rate is specified on the underlying investment. The coupon is payable at maturity. However, if between two reset dates the underlying stock or index has experienced negative returns, these negative returns are subtracted from the coupon due at maturity. Thus, a reverse cliquet is a view that the market price of the underlying will *not* fall during any subperiod.

For example, suppose a coupon of 10% is specified on a one-year reverse cliquet with quarterly resets. Suppose that during the four quarters, the observed returns on the underlying are $+4\%, -1.4\%, -2.1\%$, and $+1.2\%$. Then, the negative returns in the middle two quarters are removed from the coupon payment, so the net coupon paid at maturity is $10 - (1.4 + 2.1) = 6.50\%$.

## 19.6   Shout Options

A shout option is like a vanilla European option except that the holder is allowed to "shout" at one point in the option's life. At maturity, the holder receives the greater of the intrinsic value at the shout time or at maturity. That is, if the holder of a shout call option shouts at time $t$, the payoff received at maturity is

$$\max\{0, S_t - K, S_T - K\} \qquad \textbf{(19.50)}$$

Similarly, the payoff to the holder of a shout put option who shouts at $t$ is

$$\max\{0, K - S_t, K - S_T\} \qquad \textbf{(19.51)}$$

### Why Shout Options?

A shout option is a combination of an American and a European option. The shout time in a shout option is analogous to the early exercise time in an American option. The difference is that in an American option, the option is extinguished upon early exercise and the holder only receives the intrinsic value at exercise time. In a shout, the final payoff may exceed the intrinsic value at shout time if the stock price moves favorably. Thus, a shout will be particularly attractive to investors who may want to take advantage of possible price spikes prior to maturity without giving up the optionality.

### Pricing Shout Options: A Binomial Example

Shout option prices cannot be expressed in closed-form, but they are not difficult to evaluate on a binomial tree. The usual backwards induction procedure applies. We illustrate using a shout call with strike $K = 100$ in the three-period binomial tree of Figure 19.9. This tree uses the same up and down moves ($u = 1.10$ and $d = 0.90$) as in Figure 19.1. Once again, we assume the risk-free gross rate of interest is 1.02, so the risk-neutral probability of an up move is 0.60.

The usual backwards induction procedure applies. At the end of the tree, if we have not shouted up to that point, we simply receive the value of exercise at that point. Thus, we receive:

- $C_{uuu}^S = 33.1$ at the node $u^3 S = 133.1$.
- $C_{uud}^S = 8.9$ at the node $u^2 dS = 108.9$.

**FIGURE 19.9**

A Three-Period
Binomial Example

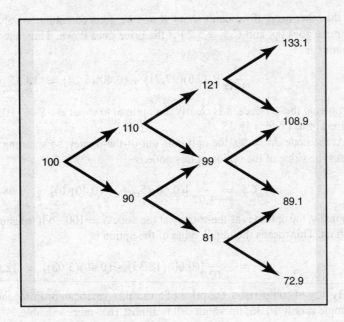

- $C^S_{udd} = 0$ at the node $ud^2S = 89.1$.
- $C^S_{ddd} = 0$ at the node $d^3S = 72.9$.

Now roll back the tree by one period. At the node $u^2S = 121$, we have the option of shouting or not shouting. If we shout, we receive at least 21 at maturity or more if the option finishes deeper in the money. If we do not shout, we receive only the depth in the money at maturity. Clearly, it is optimal to shout, resulting in a value of the option at this node of

$$C^S_{uu} = \frac{1}{1.02} [0.60 \times \max(33.1, 21) + 0.40 \times \max(8.9, 21)] = 27.71$$

At the nodes $udS = 99$ and $d^2S = 81$, there is no point in shouting because the option is out-of-the-money. Thus, the option value at these nodes is just

$$C^S_{ud} = \frac{1}{1.02} [(0.60)(8.9) + (0.40)(0)] = 5.24$$

$$C^S_{dd} = \frac{1}{1.02} [(0.60)(0) + (0.40)(0)] = 0$$

Now we roll the tree one period further back. Consider the node $uS = 110$. If we shout at this node, we receive a minimum payoff of $110 - 100 = 10$. This means we get a payoff of

- $\max(33.1, 10) = 33.1$, if the final price is $u^3S = 133.1$.
- $\max(8.9, 10) = 10$ if the final price is $u^2dS = 108.9$.
- $\max(0, 10) = 10$ if the final price is $ud^2S = 89.1$.

These are the only three terminal prices possible from the node $uS$; their risk-neutral probabilities (viewed from $uS$) are, respectively, 0.36, 0.48, and 0.16. Thus, the value of shouting at $uS$ is

$$\frac{1}{(1.02)^2} [(0.36)(33.1) + (0.48)(10) + (0.16)(10)] = 17.60$$

On the other hand, if we don't shout at $uS$, we get a continuation value of $C_{uu} = 27.71$ if the price goes up, and $C_{ud} = 5.24$ if the price goes down. Thus, the present value of not shouting is

$$\frac{1}{1.02}[(0.60)(27.71) + (0.40)(5.24] = 18.35$$

Comparing these values, it is clearly not optimal to shout at $uS = 110$. The value $C_u$ of the option at this node is 18.35.

At the node $dS = 90$, the option is out-of-the-money, so shouting is not optimal. This means the value of the option at this node is

$$C_d^S = \frac{1}{1.02}[(0.60)(5.24) + (0.40)(0)] = 3.08$$

Finally, the option is at-the-money at the node $S = 100$, so it is again clearly not optimal to shout. This means the initial value of the option is

$$C^S = \frac{1}{1.02}[(0.60)(18.35) + (0.40)(3.08)] = 12.00$$

By way of comparison, the price of a vanilla (American or European) call option in this example is only 10.36; the shout call is almost 16% more valuable.

## 19.7 Exercises

1. What makes an exotic option path-dependent? Think of an example of such an option that is not covered in this chapter. Explain why you consider it path-dependent.

2. If an option is path-dependent, do we need to use a nonrecombining binomial tree for pricing it?

3. Are American options path-dependent? Why or why not?

4. Why are Asian options popular? State some uses of Asian options.

5. Is an Asian option cheaper or more expensive than a plain vanilla option? Why? Is this always true?

6. Explain the difference between an Asian average-price option and an Asian average-strike option.

7. Distinguish between a lookback *price* option and a lookback *strike* option.

8. Consider an initially at-the-money knock-out put option with the knock-out price $H$ set above the strike $K$. Will the price of the put be greater, smaller, or equal to that of a vanilla put? Why?

9. Why does a knock-out call cost less than the corresponding vanilla call?

10. If you want to invest in the upside potential of a stock but are afraid of overpaying for options that favor your view, suggest two ways in which you may buy a single barrier option that implements your view more cheaply.

11. You are the holder of an up-and-out put option. Now you want to replace it with a plain vanilla put at the same strike and maturity. What option should you purchase to achieve this?

12. Which has greater value, an arithmetic-average-price Asian option or a geometric-average-price one?

13. What is the sign of the delta of an up-and-out call option? Explain how the delta depends on the closeness of the current stock price to the barrier.

14. Suppose you are given a two-period binomial tree with the following parameters: $S = 100$, $R = 1.01$, $u = 1.04$, and $d = 0.96$. Consider a two-period Asian call option where the averaging is done *over all three prices observed*, i.e., the initial price, the price after one period, and the price after two periods.

    (a) Suppose the option is an average-price option with a strike of 100. What is its initial price?

    (b) Suppose the option is an average-strike option. What is its initial price?

15. Consider a two-period binomial tree with the following parameters: $S = 100$, $u = 1.10$, $d = 0.90$, and $R = 1.03$. Find the prices of:

    (a) A knock-out call option with a strike of 95 and a barrier of 90.

    (b) A knock-in call option with a strike of 95 and a barrier of 90.

    (c) A vanilla call option with a strike of 95.

16. Suppose you are given a two-period binomial tree with the following parameters: $S = 100$, $R = 1.01$, $u = 1.05$, and $d = 0.95$. Consider an option with a strike of $K = 95$ whose payoff at maturity is

$$X_T = \begin{cases} (S_T - K)^2, & \text{if } S_T \geq K \\ 0, & \text{if } S_T < K \end{cases}$$

What is the initial price of this option?

17. There have been many instances where companies have "backdated" their employee option grants to especially favorable dates, namely dates when the stock price was low so as to set low strikes on their issued call options relative to current prices. What exotic option does this practice resemble? Are there any differences between this exotic option and the backdated option grant?

18. How does a fixed-strike lookback option's value change when the lookback period increases?

19. A floating-strike lookback option has two periods in it: (i) the maturity of the option itself, i.e., $T$, and (ii) the lookback period $\tau \leq T$. How does the value of the option change when

    (a) Maturity $T$ increases, keeping $\tau$ fixed?

    (b) Holding $T$ fixed, the lookback period $\tau$ increases (but does not exceed $T$)?

    (c) Maturity $T$ decreases, but $\tau$ increases (but does not exceed $T$)?

    (d) Maturity $T$ decreases, and $\tau$ increases (but does not exceed $T$)?

20. Employee stock options are often reset in their strike when the stock price of the company has declined over a period of time. Why do you think companies reset their employee option strikes? What path-dependent option have you learned about that most closely resembles this practice?

21. Using a three-period binomial tree, value a down-and-out call option. The parameters you are given are the following: the initial stock price is $100, the strike price is $105, the barrier is $90, the risk-free rate per-period is 5%, the option maturity is three years, and the volatility of the stock is 40%. Use the CRR method to construct the binomial tree.

22. In the above question, what would we do to the model to make it default to a vanilla call option? Would the vanilla call be worth more or less than the barrier option?

23. (Requires Writing Code) The same barrier option pricing problem in the last two questions may be solved using the recursive programming approach developed in Chapter 13.

Reprogram the pricing model using such an approach. Check that the barrier option price is the same. Use the same parameter values.

24. A reverse cliquet with quarterly resets pays an annual coupon of 15% less the return during any quarter in which the return is negative. The index is at 1000 at the beginning of the year and takes values of 900, 1000, 1100, and 1050 at the end of each of the succeeding quarters. What is the final payoff of this option for each of the end-of-quarter values of the index?

25. What has higher value for options of strike $K$ that are at-the-money at inception:
    (a) A cliquet option with maturity $T = 1$ year and a single reset at $T = 1/2$ year?
    (b) A one-shout shout option with maturity $T = 1$ year?

26. (Requires Writing Code) (a) Write a program to price a down-and-in barrier call option with the following parameters: $S = 50$, strike $K = 50$, an annual risk-free rate $r = 3\%$, volatility $\sigma = 0.3$, and barrier $H = 45$. Use a CRR pricing tree with a time step of one year for each period. The maturity of the option is six years.
    (b) Modify the program to price the down-and-in put.
    (c) Does European put-call parity hold for barrier options? Why?

27. (a) Price a ten-year down-and-in barrier call option with the following parameters: $S = 100$, strike $K = 102$, annual risk-free rate $r = 2\%$, volatility $\sigma = 0.4$, and barrier $H = 90$. Use a time step of one year on the CRR tree for this problem.
    (b) Price the down-and-out barrier call with the same parameters.
    (c) Price the vanilla call with the same parameters.
    (d) Verify that the sum of the prices you obtain in parts (a) and (b) equals the price you obtain in part (c).

28. Consider a shout option with strike K. One way to price the option is as follows. If at some point in time prior to maturity you shout when the stock price is $S > K$, then you capture the profits $S - K$ (to be paid at maturity) and the original shout call option held is replaced with a new vanilla call option with a strike of $S$ for the remaining maturity.
    (a) Explain how you would use a binomial tree to price this option.
    (b) Will the tree be recombining?
    (c) Is the option path-dependent?

29. Price a ten-year Asian option with an initial stock price of $50, strike $50, annual risk-free rate $r = 10\%$, and volatility $\sigma = 0.35$. Price the call and the put, and see whether put-call parity holds. Use a pricing tree with a time step of one year per period.

30. (Requires Writing Code) For the same parameters as in the previous question, price a *lookback price* call and put.

31. (Requires Writing Code) Implement the formula in the chapter appendix for up-and-out calls, and value the option for the following parameters: $S = 102$, $K = 100$, $r = 5\%$ p.a., barrier $H = 130$, and maturity $T = 0.25$. Annualized volatility is $\sigma = 40\%$. Program a tree model to do the same and report the value. Compare the tree model to the closed-form answer.

32. In the preceding question, what is the effect of increasing the maturity of the up-and-out call? Keep the parameters the same but vary the maturity to take the following values (in years): 0.1, 0.2, 0.3, 0.5, and 1.0.

33. Consider a more complex form of barrier option, the double barrier knock-out call. For this option, using any method of your choosing, price the option for the following parameters: $S = 100$, $K = 100$, lower barrier 80, upper barrier 120, maturity 0.25

years, risk-free rate of 6% p.a., zero dividends, and volatility of 35%. Answer the following questions:

(a) What is the price of this option?

(b) What is the price at $S = 95$ and at $S = 105$?

(c) What is the price at a volatility of 50%? What does this tell you about the sign of the vega?

(d) What is the delta of the option at stock prices 95, 100, and 105?

34. Using the formulae in the chapter appendix, price the up-and-in put option with the following parameters: $S = 100$, $K = 100$, barrier $H = 110$, rebate of 50, maturity of one year, annual risk-free interest rate of 3%, and stock volatility of 40%. There are no dividends.

(a) What is the price of the option?

(b) What is the option price if the stock rises to 105?

(c) What is the option price if the stock rises to 109?

(d) What can you say about the sign of the delta and the gamma?

35. The current stock price is $100. Price a half-year average strike Asian call option if the stock volatility is 30%, and the annual risk-free rate is 10%. Use a tree model with six monthly steps. Compare the price you arrive at with the price of an otherwise identical average price Asian call at a strike of $100. State intuitively why the prices are different.

36. Using the same parameters as in Question 35, calculate the prices of Asian puts of both types, average price and average strike. Compare the prices. Explain why one is higher than the other.

37. Repeat Question 35 but for a stock price of $90, leaving all other parameters unchanged. Value the average-price and average-strike options and compare their prices.

38. The current stock price is $100. Price a half-year floating strike lookback call option if the stock volatility is 30%, and the annual risk-free rate is 10%. Use a tree model with six monthly steps. Also price the lookback put.

# Barrier Option Pricing Formulae

Recall the basic notation: $S$ is the current (time-0) stock price, $K$ is the strike and $T$ the maturity of the option, $r$ is the risk-free interest rate, $\sigma$ is the volatility of the stock, and $H$ the barrier. The Black-Scholes prices of a vanilla call and put are denoted by $C^{BS}(S, K)$ and $P^{BS}(S, K)$, respectively. The quantities $\gamma$ and $a$ are defined by

$$\gamma = \frac{2r}{\sigma^2} \tag{19.52}$$

$$a = \left(\frac{H}{S}\right)^{\gamma-1} \tag{19.53}$$

Now define $b$ and $d_1, d_2, \ldots, d_8$ by the following:

$$b = \left(\frac{H}{S}\right)^{\gamma+1} \tag{19.54}$$

$$d_1 = \frac{1}{\sigma\sqrt{T}}\left[\ln\left(\frac{S}{K}\right) + \left(r + \frac{1}{2}\sigma^2\right)T\right] \tag{19.55}$$

$$d_2 = \frac{1}{\sigma\sqrt{T}}\left[\ln\left(\frac{S}{K}\right) + \left(r - \frac{1}{2}\sigma^2\right)T\right] \tag{19.56}$$

$$d_3 = \frac{1}{\sigma\sqrt{T}}\left[\ln\left(\frac{S}{H}\right) + \left(r - \frac{1}{2}\sigma^2\right)T\right] \tag{19.57}$$

$$d_4 = \frac{1}{\sigma\sqrt{T}}\left[\ln\left(\frac{S}{H}\right) + \left(r + \frac{1}{2}\sigma^2\right)T\right] \tag{19.58}$$

$$d_5 = \frac{1}{\sigma\sqrt{T}}\left[\ln\left(\frac{S}{H}\right) - \left(r + \frac{1}{2}\sigma^2\right)T\right] \tag{19.59}$$

$$d_6 = \frac{1}{\sigma\sqrt{T}}\left[\ln\left(\frac{S}{H}\right) - \left(r - \frac{1}{2}\sigma^2\right)T\right] \tag{19.60}$$

$$d_7 = \frac{1}{\sigma\sqrt{T}}\left[\ln\left(\frac{SK}{H^2}\right) - \left(r - \frac{1}{2}\sigma^2\right)T\right] \tag{19.61}$$

$$d_8 = \frac{1}{\sigma\sqrt{T}}\left[\ln\left(\frac{SK}{H^2}\right) - \left(r + \frac{1}{2}\sigma^2\right)T\right] \tag{19.62}$$

The prices for a down-and-out call and a down-and-in call when $H \leq K$ were given in the text in the section on barrier options. Here are the pricing expressions for the remaining barrier options:

1. Up-and-out call:

$$S\left[N(d_1) - N(d_3) - bN(d_6) + bN(d_8)\right]$$
$$-PV(K)\left[N(d_2) - N(d_4) - aN(d_5) + aN(d_7)\right]$$

2. Up-and-in-call:

$$S\left[N(d_3) + bN(d_6) - bN(d_8)\right] - PV(K)\left[N(d_4) + aN(d_5) - aN(d_7)\right]$$

3. Down-and-out call, $K > H$:

$$S\left[N(d_1) - bN(-d_8)\right] - PV(K)\left[N(d_2) - aN(-d_7)\right]$$

4. Down-and-out call, $K < H$:

$$S\left[N(d_3) - bN(-d_6)\right] - PV(K)\left[N(d_4) - aN(-d_5)\right]$$

5. Down-and-in call, $K > H$:

$$S\,bN(-d_8) - PV(K)\,aN(-d_7)$$

6. Down-and-in call, $K < H$:

$$S\left[N(d_1) - N(d_3) + bN(-d_6)\right] - PV(K)\left[N(d_2) - N(d_4) + aN(-d_5)\right]$$

7. Down-and-out put:

$$PV(K)\left[N(d_4) - N(d_2) - aN(d_7) + aN(d_5)\right]$$
$$-S\left[N(d_3) - N(d_1) - bN(d_8) + bN(d_6)\right]$$

8. Down-and-in put:

$$PV(K)\left[1 - N(d_4) + aN(d_7) - aN(d_5)\right] - S\left[1 - N(d_3) + bN(d_8) - bN(d_6)\right]$$

9. Up-and-in put, $H > K$:

$$PV(K)\,aN(d_7) - S\,bN(d_8)$$

10. Up-and-in put, $H < K$:

$$PV(K)\left[N(-d_3) - aN(d_6)\right] - S\left[N(-d_4) - bN(d_5)\right]$$

11. Up-and-out put, $H > K$:

$$PV(K)\left[N(-d_2) - aN(d_7)\right] - S\left[N(-d_1) - bN(d_8)\right]$$

12. Up-and-out put, $H < K$:

$$PV(K)\left[N(-d_2) - N(-d_3) + aN(d_6)\right] - S\left[N(-d_1) - N(-d_4) + bN(d_5)\right]$$

# Chapter 20

# Value-at-Risk

## 20.1 Introduction

All portfolio management is about *risk* and *return*. "Return" is an unambiguous and self-explanatory concept, but "risk" is a harder concept to pin down. In equity markets, we can think of risk in terms of volatility or betas or factor loadings; in fixed-income markets, we have the notions of volatility, duration, and convexity; while in the context of options, there are the delta, gamma, theta, and other greeks.

In the 1990s, a new tool emerged for measuring portfolio risk called *Value-at-Risk* or VaR, which was explicitly geared towards gauging the adequacy of capital held to meet losses on risky portfolios. The first prominent mention of VaR occurs in a 1993 report of the Group of Thirty titled "Derivatives: Practices and Principles," which recommended the use of VaR and stress-testing to evaluate the riskiness of portfolios. But perhaps the most important factor in encouraging the use of VaR was the introduction of J.P. Morgan's RiskMetrics system in 1994. VaR is today the single most popular measure of portfolio risk for gauging capital adequacy.

This chapter examines VaR and related ideas. We begin in Section 20.2 with an analysis of VaR, discussing its definition and uses, the different methods for computing VaR, and the advantages and disadvantages of each method. Then, building on this foundation, Section 20.3 develops the idea of *risk budgeting*. A final section on "coherent" risk measures is more abstract: it describes a set of conditions that have been proposed as necessary for a "good" risk measure to satisfy.

VaR and risk budgeting are topics that have received several book-length treatments in recent years. Our exposition in this chapter is, of course, briefer. Readers wishing to delve more into the areas of portfolio risk-management are directed to the many available books in this area such as Pearson (2002) on which we have based especially our discussion of risk budgeting.

## 20.2 Value-at-Risk

The concept of VaR is best motivated with an example. Say we have a portfolio that is currently worth $100 and that will be worth $100 + X$ in one year, where $X \sim N(5, 10^2)$, i.e., $X$ is distributed normally with a mean of 5 and a standard deviation of 10. Suppose that we are interested in estimating the riskiness of this portfolio in terms of "tail outcomes," that is, in terms of how much we could lose on the portfolio and with what probability.

One way to gauge this risk is to ask a question such as: what is the probability $p$ that the one-year return on the portfolio will be less than some dollar amount $m$? For example, we may want to know the probability that the returns over the year will be less than −10, i.e., that the portfolio will lose at least 10% of its current value of 100.

This is not hard to do. We need to identify the probability of an observation $x \leq -10$ from a return distribution that is normal with mean 5 and standard deviation 10. Consulting a normal distribution table (or using the function NORMDIST in Excel) we see that the answer is 6.68%.

Value-at-Risk poses this problem the other way around. Rather than fix a dollar amount $m$ and ask what is the probability $p$ of falling below that, it fixes a probability $p$ and asks: what is the amount $m$ such that the likelihood of an outcome worse than $m$ is no more than $p$? This number $m$ is called the $(1 - p)$ VaR because with probability at least $1 - p$, the outcome will be better than $m$. For instance, if $p$ is taken to be 1% (a typical value), $m$ is called the 99% VaR.

In our example, the 99% VaR is the number $m$ such that the probability of an observation $x \leq m$ from an $N(5, 10^2)$ distribution is 0.01. To identify this number, recall that in any normal distribution, if we take a distance 2.33 standard deviations from the mean, then there is about 1% of mass remaining in each tail. Since our attention is on the *left* tail of the portfolio, we compute the quantity

$$\text{mean} - (2.33 \times \text{standard deviation}) \qquad\qquad \textbf{(20.1)}$$

This is the required number $m$. For the numbers in the example, the 99% VaR works out to

$$m = 5 - (2.33 \times 10) = -18.30$$

Thus, there is a 1% probability that the returns on the portfolio will be worse than −18.30. Equivalently, there is a 99% probability that the portfolio value at the end of one year will be at least $100 − 18.30 = 81.70$.

As this example indicates, there are three components to VaR: a probability $p$, a dollar amount $m$, and a horizon $h$ over which the VaR is computed. In reporting VaR, the probability $p$ is typically taken to be 0.01 or 0.05 (1% or 5%). The horizon varies depending on the reporting purpose. Portfolio managers often use VaR based on a horizon of one day. Banks' capital requirements are calculated using a horizon of one year.

## A Note on VaR Signs

Since the left tail of portfolio returns will usually involve losses, the VaR as we have defined it above will typically be a negative number. In practice, it is common to drop the negative sign when reporting VaR. Implicitly, this means we are interpreting VaR as *losses* on the portfolio. (Thus, for instance, the 99% VaR in the numerical example above would be reported as 18.30 rather than −18.30.)

We will follow this convention in this chapter. A higher VaR then means a more risky portfolio. A *negative* VaR in this convention means that returns on the portfolio will be positive with the given confidence level. For example, a 95% VaR of −3 million means that the probability that the portfolio will make a return of less than +3 million is 0.05.

## VaR as a Risk Measure: Some Comments

One of the most important aspects of VaR as a risk measure is that VaR provides a summary picture of *capital adequacy*. That is, it quantifies, in a probabilistic manner, how safe the firm is from events leading to bankruptcy. For example, suppose a firm has equity capital of $10 million and a 95% one-year VaR of $12 million. This implies that there is at least a 5% chance of the firm losing more money over the coming year than it holds in equity capital. If the firm wishes to reduce the probability of ruin, there are essentially only two options. It can elect to hold more capital (say, increase the capital to $15 million), or it can lower the tail risk in its portfolio by altering the portfolio's composition.

By capturing a portfolio's downside risk with a single number, VaR also facilitates comparison across portfolios. For example, suppose we have two $10 million portfolios. Suppose that the first portfolio will be worth $10 + X_1$ million at the end of one year, while the second portfolio will be worth $10 + X_2$ million. By comparing the VaRs of these portfolios at a given confidence level (say, 99%), we can identify which has greater tail risk.

For example, suppose $X_1$ and $X_2$ are both normally distributed with $X_1 \sim N(1, 1^2)$ and $X_2 \sim N(0.8, 0.7^2)$. The first portfolio has a higher expected return than the second portfolio but also a higher standard deviation, so it is not immediately apparent which has the lower tail risk. Using (20.1), the one-year 99% VaR of the first portfolio (in millions of $) is 1.33 since

$$1 - (2.33 \times 1) = -1.33$$

Similarly, that of the second portfolio is 0.83:

$$0.80 - (2.33 \times 0.7) = -0.83$$

Thus, under 99% VaR, the second portfolio involves less tail risk than the first.

Third, as an aggregate forward-looking measure, VaR facilitates *decomposition* of risk into sources such as asset class, manager, or risk factor. Such decompositions may be used to reallocate assets, set limits, or monitor asset allocations/portfolio managers. This collective process is called *risk budgeting* and is the subject of Section 20.3 below.

Fourth, VaR simply involves identifying the point in the tail of the returns distribution beyond which a given mass of the distribution lies. It involves no distributional assumptions concerning returns and can be used on both continuous and discrete returns distributions. The "historical simulation" method of calculating VaR described below makes use of this agnosticism concerning the actual returns distribution.

The simplicity of VaR combined with these features has led to its widespread use as a measure of portfolio risk. Nonetheless, VaR is not a summary measure of everything that we associate with "portfolio risk." We highlight now some features of VaR to emphasize what it does *not* do.

## Limitations of VaR

First, as is evident from the definition, VaR is solely a measure of *downside risk*, i.e., of losses that could happen in the *left tail* of the returns distribution. It does not pay any attention to the shape of the return distribution outside this tail and should not be treated as a general measure of portfolio risk. For a simple example that illustrates this point, consider the two possible outcome distributions given in Table 20.1. The 99% VaR for both distributions is 0: in either case, there is a probability of 0.99 of an outcome of zero or better. Yet the distributions are obviously very different.

Not only does VaR not pay attention to what happens outside the left tail of the distribution, but also it does not even say much about how returns behave *in* the left tail. Two

**TABLE 20.1**

| Outcome | Distribution 1 Probability | Distribution 2 Probability |
|---------|---------------------------|----------------------------|
| −10 | 0.01 | 0.01 |
| 0 | 0.90 | 0.09 |
| +10 | 0.09 | 0.90 |

**TABLE 20.2**

| Outcome | Distribution 1 Probability | Distribution 2 Probability |
|---------|----------------------------|----------------------------|
| −50     | 0.025                      | 0.000                      |
| −10     | 0.035                      | 0.060                      |
| +10     | 0.940                      | 0.940                      |

distributions could have very different left tails yet have similar VaRs at a given confidence level. For instance, consider the two returns distributions in Table 20.2. In each case, the 95% VaR is seen to be −10, so the 95% VaR would rank the distributions on par in terms of tail risk. However, it is evident that the first distribution has more tail risk than the second.

A third, and important, shortcoming of VaR is highlighted later in this chapter. An example in Section 20.4 shows that VaR might fail to respect the benefits of diversification, i.e., a portfolio's VaR could go up even while it becomes more diversified and (intuitively speaking) less risky. This is obviously undesirable in a risk measure. All of these points indicate that VaR should be interpreted and used with care.

## Methods of Calculating VaR

There are many ways to calculate the VaR of a portfolio. Each approach has advantages and disadvantages; no one way is best. It is important to note too that different methods can provide different VaR. Three popular ways of computing VaR in practice are:

- The delta-normal method.
- Historical simulation.
- Monte Carlo simulation.

Each method is based to some extent on parameters derived from historical data. We describe each below.

## Estimating VaR I: The Delta-Normal Method

In the delta-normal approach, asset returns are assumed to be *normally* distributed. Thus, there are two main inputs into the model: the vector of expected returns on each asset and the variance-covariance matrix of these returns. Using these inputs, we compute the mean and variance of the portfolio's returns. Using the assumption of normality, the portfolio's VaR is now easily computed.

In notational terms, suppose there are $n$ assets in the portfolio, indexed by $i = 1, \ldots, n$. Let:

- $w_i$ denote the dollar investment in asset $i$.
- $\mu_i$ be the expected return on asset $i$.
- $\sigma_{ij}$ be the covariance of returns between assets $i$ and $j$. When $i = j$, this is the covariance of asset $i$'s returns with itself, which is just the variance $\sigma_i^2$ of asset $i$'s returns.

To avoid legitimate confusion, we stress two points about this notation. First, the investments $w = (w_1, \ldots, w_n)$ are stated in *dollar* terms, not as proportions of portfolio value invested in the different assets. Thus, the sum of the $w_i$'s gives us the total dollar amount invested in the portfolio. Second, the returns on the individual assets (i.e., the terms $\mu_i$ and $\sigma_i^2$) are, as usual, in terms of returns per dollar invested in these assets. The total *dollar return* on the portfolio will depend on the number of dollars invested in each asset. We use the following notation here and in the rest of this chapter:

- The expected dollar return on the portfolio is denoted $\mu_P(w)$. Where $w$ is understood, we simplify notation by writing just $\mu_P$. This expected return is given by

$$\mu_P = \sum_{i=1}^{n} \mu_i w_i \qquad \qquad \textbf{(20.2)}$$

- The variance of dollar returns on the portfolio is denoted $\sigma_P^2(w)$, or, where $w$ is understood, as just $\sigma_P^2$. This variance is given by

$$\sigma_P^2 = \sum_{i,j=1}^{n} w_i w_j \sigma_{ij} \qquad \qquad \textbf{(20.3)}$$

Since all asset returns are normally distributed (by assumption) and since the sum of normal distributions is normal, the portfolio (dollar) returns are themselves normal with mean $\mu_P$ and variance $\sigma_P^2$.

Suppose that we wish to calculate the 99% VaR of the portfolio. This is the quantity $-m$, where $m$ is defined by

$$m = \mu_P - (2.33 \times \sigma_P)$$

If we wish to calculate the 95% VaR instead, we replace the number 2.33 in the equation above with 1.645. The following example illustrates the procedure.

## Example 20.1    Calculating the Delta-Normal VaR

Suppose we have two assets whose returns are jointly normally distributed with expected returns and variance-covariance matrix given by the following:

$$\begin{bmatrix} \mu_1 \\ \mu_2 \end{bmatrix} = \begin{bmatrix} 0.20 \\ 0.12 \end{bmatrix}, \qquad \begin{bmatrix} \sigma_1^2 & \sigma_{12} \\ \sigma_{21} & \sigma_2^2 \end{bmatrix} = \begin{bmatrix} 0.04 & 0.02 \\ 0.02 & 0.03 \end{bmatrix}$$

Suppose we have a portfolio with an investment of $w_1 = 5$ in the first asset and $w_2 = 5$ in the second asset. Using (20.2) and (20.3), the expected return and variance of returns on the portfolio are seen to be

$$\mu_P = 1.60 \qquad \sigma_P^2 = 2.75$$

So portfolio returns are normally distributed with a mean of 1.60 and a variance of 2.75 (i.e., a standard deviation of approximately 1.658). Suppose now that we wish to compute the 95% VaR. We have

$$\mu_P - (1.645 \times \sigma_P) = 1.60 - (1.645 \times 1.658) = -1.128$$

Thus, the 95% VaR is 1.128 or 11.28% of the portfolio's initial value. That is, there is a 95% chance that returns on the portfolio will be no worse than $-11.28\%$. It is left to the reader as an exercise to verify that the 99% VaR in this example is 2.264 or 22.64% of the initial portfolio value. Note that if we are using the VaR to gauge capital adequacy, the 99% VaR requires a little over double the capital of the 95% VaR.    ∎

### Pros and Cons of the Delta-Normal Approach

There are some obvious advantages to the delta-normal approach. It is easy to understand and communicate, and requires nothing more than knowledge of the normal distribution and basic linear algebra. It is not computationally intensive, and, in particular, does not require any simulation. Also, it can easily build in dependence on recent data and trends.

Weighing against these are two principal disadvantages. First, where options are present in the portfolio, the delta-normal approach uses the options' deltas to convert the option exposures into equivalent units of the underlyings. (This is where the "delta" in the name of the approach comes from.) The problem is that this approach assumes linear exposure to underlying prices, which, as we have seen in the chapter on option greeks, is not a good assumption. In particular, if the portfolio has a positive gamma, VaR based on linearity will overstate possible losses on the portfolio; with a negative gamma, losses are underestimated.

The second shortcoming of the delta-normal approach comes from the "normal" part. Returns in practice are often non-normal, even conditionally, and the non-normality often takes the form of fatter tails than that of a normal distribution. This means that assuming a normal distribution most often results in an *under*statement of risk, which is a serious concern for a risk measure that focuses on the tail.

## Estimating VaR II: Historical Simulation

The second approach to computing VaR, *historical simulation*, uses actual historic data to evaluate risk. The implicit presumption is that the future will mirror the past distribution of returns. So we take the *current* portfolio and subject it to the *actual* returns on the assets in the portfolio over a chosen period in the past.

For example, suppose we are interested in the one-day VaR of a given portfolio, and we wish to estimate this quantity via historical simulation using data from the preceding 1000 days. We look at the dollar returns the portfolio would have had on each of those 1000 days and rank the outcomes from worst to best. If we want the 95% VaR, we then pick the 50th worst outcome (5% of the one-day returns actually observed over the past 1000 days are at or below this level while 95% are better). Similarly, if we want the 99% VaR, we pick the 10th worst of the 1000 outcomes, and so on.

### Advantages and Disadvantages of Historical Simulation

There are two main advantages to historical simulation as a means of estimating VaR. First, the approach is very easy to understand and explain since it involves no technical details. It is similar to backtesting—we just go back in time and run our portfolio through history and see what it tells us about the return distribution. Second, non-normality and nonlinearity are not issues. Since we use actual historical data, we automatically capture the true empirical distribution.

Balancing this are some disadvantages. Historical simulation is a "lazy" method; it does not force the risk manager to think critically about the future. The implicit assumption that the future will mirror the past may be inaccurate (even wildly so—think, for instance, of the Thai baht circa 1997). Relying on the past may be an especially poor idea when volatility is unstable. A sudden spike in volatility will cause a small change in a lengthy historical time series as it affects only the newest observations. This will result in historical VaR understating actual risk. Conversely, a sharp drop in volatility means that the historical simulation approach will overstate risk.

Historical simulation is also a very data-intensive approach. For each asset in our portfolio, we need to maintain a time series of returns. However, with modern computing resources, this is becoming less of a problem every day. Nonetheless, observe that most of the data contributes very little to the analysis: since we are interested only in the bottom few observations that form the data's left tail, the structure of the remainder of the distribution matters little. In contrast, a statistical approach assuming an underlying distribution of returns links the tails of the distribution to the central observations. When the parameters of the distribution change affecting the central observations, so do the tails.

## Estimating VaR III: Monte Carlo Simulation

This is the third approach to computing VaR and a commonly used one in practice. It is similar to historical simulation in that the portfolio is revalued repeatedly under various scenarios for returns. The difference is that the scenarios are not based on historical data but on Monte Carlo simulation using an assumed joint distribution for the returns.

The advantages of this approach are that it handles non-normality well and that there is great freedom in choosing the form of the joint distribution. It is also far easier to include options in the analysis since nonlinearity is not an issue. The main disadvantage is that it is computationally very expensive.

## An Assessment of VaR

VaR is now very widely used and has formed the basis for many new and improved risk measures. It has several plus points including the following:

- It is intuitive and captures well a commonplace notion of "extreme" risk. Loosely speaking, it corresponds to the safety-first criterion as a portfolio objective.

- By focusing on the tails of return distributions, it serves as a good measure of capital adequacy. As such, it is of particular value to financial-market regulators and has become the linchpin of system-wide risk management.

- Since VaR reduces all portfolios to a single number, it facilitates comparisons across portfolios and across markets and enables aggregation across business units.

- VaR is a one-sided measure (it looks only at the left tail of the return distribution) and so avoids the symmetry in measures such as standard deviation.

But VaR is by no means a perfect measure. Many of the problems with it are related to implementation. For instance, normality of returns distributions and payoff-linearity are often assumed. These assumptions become questionable as portfolios become more complex and utilize nonlinear securities such as options. Implementation in this method (or with Monte Carlo simulation) also requires knowledge of the correlation in returns between the different assets in the portfolio, something that is hard to measure accurately. On a similar note, volatility is well known to be nonconstant over time, yet most VaR systems as used in practice assume it to be constant over the computing horizon; this becomes problematic in gauging portfolio risk over long horizons such as one year. Likewise, most VaR systems ignore jump risk so that tail assessments may be off substantially. Stress-testing of portfolios—calculating portfolio values under an assumed extreme scenario for prices—is often used to tackle this issue.

These shortcomings of VaR focus on statistical issues. However, as noted earlier, VaR also has an important conceptual shortcoming. In Section 20.4, we show that diversifying a portfolio might result in an increase in its VaR rather than a decrease.

In the final analysis, it is likely that almost any risk measure will suffer from some shortcomings. Overall, VaR seems to apply well across most portfolios and is almost surely worth the attention it receives, especially in the regulatory realm. The important thing to keep in mind is that VaR is only an indicative risk measure and not a comprehensive or foolproof one; that is, a high VaR is likely a sign of trouble, but a low VaR should not, in itself, be interpreted as a sign that all is well.

# 20.3   Risk Decomposition

The total *return* on a portfolio is just the sum of the returns on the individual assets in the portfolio (see (20.2)). Thus, it is a simple matter to decompose a portfolio's returns and identify what portion of return comes from each component of the portfolio. In notational terms, if we have $w_i$ invested in each asset $i = 1, \ldots, n$, and the expected returns on asset $i$ are given by $\mu_i$, then the portfolio's returns are just

$$\mu_P = \sum_{i=1}^{n} \mu_i w_i$$

So the fraction of total portfolio returns contributed by the position in asset $i$ is just

$$\frac{\mu_i w_i}{\mu_P}$$

*Risk decomposition* attempts similarly to decompose the total *risk* in a portfolio and identify the contribution of each individual position in the portfolio to the total portfolio risk. Risk decomposition is of interest for a number of reasons. It provides an understanding of which components of the portfolio account for much of the portfolio's risk, a question of concern for risk managers. Second, when incrementally adding positions to the portfolio, we gain an understanding of the marginal risk contributions of the new components, which facilitates computing the amount of additional capital that will be required for regulatory purposes. Third, in a setting where several business units contribute to the overall risk of the portfolio (for example, in the case of many trading desks in a large dealing room), knowing the risk of each unit also enables an assessment of the risk-adjusted return of each trading unit and so for an appropriate provision of ex ante incentives and ex post rewards for each unit.

## Why Is Risk Decomposition a Challenge?

Risk decomposition is a nontrivial task because risk, unlike return, is not additive: the total risk of a portfolio is, in general, not the sum of the individual risks of each position in the portfolio. We illustrate this statement here for a two-asset setting with normally distributed returns.

So suppose we have a portfolio with $w_1$ invested in asset 1 and $w_2$ in asset 2. Suppose too that the returns on the assets are jointly normal with expected returns $(\mu_1, \mu_2)$ and variance-covariance matrix

$$\Sigma = \begin{bmatrix} \sigma_1^2 & \sigma_{12} \\ \sigma_{12} & \sigma_2^2 \end{bmatrix}$$

The expected (dollar) return on the portfolio, $\mu_P$, and the variance of dollar returns, $\sigma_P^2$, are given by

$$\mu_P = w_1 \mu_1 + w_2 \mu_2 \qquad (20.4)$$

$$\sigma_P^2 = w_1^2 \sigma_1^2 + w_2^2 \sigma_2^2 + 2 w_1 w_2 \sigma_{12} \qquad (20.5)$$

Suppose that our measure of risk is 99% VaR. Then, the portfolio's risk is given by $-m$, where

$$m = \mu_P - (2.33 \times \sigma_P) \qquad (20.6)$$

Now, the $w_1$ invested in asset 1 generates normally distributed returns with a mean of $w_1 \mu_1$ and a variance or $w_1^2 \sigma_1^2$, so the risk (i.e., the 99% VaR) of the investment in asset 1 is given by $-m_1$, where

$$m_1 = w_1\mu_1 - (2.33 \times w_1\sigma_1) \tag{20.7}$$

Similarly, the risk of the position in asset 2 is $-m_2$, where

$$m_2 = w_2\mu_2 - (2.33 \times w_2\sigma_2) \tag{20.8}$$

From the definitions of $\mu_P$ and $\sigma_P$, it is apparent that the total portfolio risk (20.6) is not, in general, equal to the sum of the individual risks (20.7)–(20.8). Specifically, while the portfolio's mean return is the sum of the individual mean returns, the portfolio standard deviation is not just the sum of the individual standard deviations except in one trivial case: where $\sigma_{12} = \sigma_1 \times \sigma_2$, i.e., where the assets are perfectly correlated. Thus, one cannot decompose portfolio VaR into the sum of the VaRs of the individual positions in the portfolio.

## What about an "Incremental" Approach?

One way of getting around the additivity problem is to try an *incremental risk* approach. That is, first compute the risk of the position $w_1$ in asset 1 alone and use this as the contribution of asset 1 to portfolio risk. Then compute the risk of the portfolio $(w_1, w_2)$, and take the change in risk as the marginal contribution of asset 2. Next, compute the risk of the portfolio $(w_1, w_2, w_3)$ and take the new net increase in risk to be the marginal contribution of asset 3, etc.

This approach has the virtue that—by construction!—the risk of the portfolio is equal to the sum of the risks contributed by each position. But it suffers from a rather obvious and severe flaw: the order in which assets are introduced affects their risk-contributions. For example, since the ordering of assets is arbitrary, we could have started with asset 3 first, then considered assets 1 and 3, then assets 1, 2, and 3, and so on. But this will provide us with different marginal contributions compared to the previous ordering. Here is a simple example.

**Example 20.2**

Consider again the two-asset setting used in Example 20.1. The returns are jointly normal with expected return vector and variance-covariance matrix given by

$$\begin{bmatrix} \mu_1 \\ \mu_2 \end{bmatrix} = \begin{bmatrix} 0.20 \\ 0.12 \end{bmatrix}, \quad \begin{bmatrix} \sigma_1^2 & \sigma_{12} \\ \sigma_{21} & \sigma_2^2 \end{bmatrix} = \begin{bmatrix} 0.04 & 0.02 \\ 0.02 & 0.03 \end{bmatrix}$$

The portfolio has an investment of 5 in each asset: $w_1 = 5$ and $w_2 = 5$. As we have seen, the expected return and variance of returns on the portfolio are then

$$\mu_P = 1.60 \qquad \sigma_P^2 = 2.75$$

Returns from the $5 investment in asset 1 are normally distributed with expected return and variance given by

$$\mu_1(w_1) = 1.00 \qquad \sigma_1^2(w_1) = 1.00$$

Similarly, returns from the $5 investment in asset 2 are normally distributed with expected return and variance given by

$$\mu_2(w_2) = 0.60 \qquad \sigma_2^2(w_2) = 0.75$$

Suppose that our measure of risk is 99% VaR. The total portfolio risk is then, as we have seen, 2.264. Using the incremental approach, we obtain the following risk-contributions:

- If we begin with asset 1 first, the risk-contribution of asset 1 is $-m_1$, where

$$m_1 = 1 - (2.33 \times 1) = -1.33$$

Thus, asset 1 contributes a fraction $1.33/2.26 = 59\%$ of total risk, while asset 2 contributes the remaining 41%.

- If we begin with asset 2 first, then the risk-contribution of asset 2 is $-m_2$, where

$$m_2 = 0.60 - (2.33 \times \sqrt{0.75}) = -1.418$$

Thus, asset 2 now contributes a fraction 1.418/2.264 or over 62% of the total risk, while asset 1 contributes only the balance 38%.   ∎

As these widely-differing numbers show, the incremental approach fails to identify risk-contributions uniquely.

## The Key Properties: Linear Homogeneity and Euler's Theorem

A superior way to identify the risk contribution of each position is provided by a mathematical property called *linear homogeneity* (or *homogeneity of degree 1*). Linear homogeneity is a property we have seen earlier in the book in the context of option prices. It was used in the pricing of forward start options earlier in this book (see Chapter 18). To recall the definition, a function $f(x_1, \ldots x_k)$ is said to be linearly homogeneous in the variables $(x_1, \ldots, x_k)$ if for any $m > 0$, we have

$$f(mx_1, \ldots, mx_k) = m \times f(x_1, \ldots, x_k)$$

A result known as *Euler's Theorem* describes a powerful mathematical property of linearly homogeneous functions. Euler's Theorem was also described in Chapter 18 (see the segment "Euler's Theorem and the Replicating Portfolio"). Writing $x$ for the vector $(x_1, \ldots, x_k)$, Euler's Theorem states that if $f(x)$ is linearly homogeneous in $x$, then

$$f(x) = \left[ x_1 \times \frac{\partial f(x)}{\partial x_1} \right] + \cdots + \left[ x_n \times \frac{\partial f(x)}{\partial x_n} \right] \qquad (20.9)$$

where, as usual, the term $\partial f(x)/\partial x_i$ refers to the partial derivative of the function $f(x)$ with respect to $x_i$.

## Linear Homogeneity and Risk Measures

The VaR of a portfolio is linearly homogeneous in the portfolio weight vector $w = (w_1, \ldots, w_n)$. That is, if we scale up the investment in each asset by a factor of $m$ (i.e., to the vector $m \cdot w = (mw_1, \ldots, mw_n)$), the VaR of the scaled portfolio is just $m$ times the VaR of the original portfolio:

$$\text{VaR}(m \cdot w) = m \times \text{VaR}(w) \qquad (20.10)$$

Property (20.10) is an intuitive one: if I double all my positions in my portfolio, then the dollar value in the 1% left tail of the distribution should also double.

VaR is not the only risk measure to possess the property of linear homogeneity. The standard deviation has this property too:

$$\sigma_P(m \cdot w) = m \times \sigma_P(w) \qquad (20.11)$$

Again, this is easy to see. When we scale up all our positions by a factor of $m$, the portfolio variance increases by a factor of $m^2$, so the standard deviation increases by a factor of $m$.

Other left-tail-based risk measures, such as expected shortfall, also satisfy linear homogeneity. Indeed, linear homogeneity is listed by Artzner, Delbaen, Eber, and Heath (1999) as one of the four desirable conditions any risk measure should satisfy (see Section 20.4).

## Decomposing Risk

Applying Euler's Theorem to the VaR of the portfolio $w = (w_1, \ldots, w_n)$, we obtain

$$\text{VaR}(w) = \left[ w_1 \times \frac{\partial \text{VaR}(w)}{\partial w_1} \right] + \cdots + \left[ w_n \times \frac{\partial \text{VaR}(w)}{\partial w_n} \right] \qquad (20.12)$$

The left-hand side of (20.12) is the total risk in the portfolio $w$. The right-hand side breaks down this total risk into $n$ terms, one corresponding to each component of the portfolio. The $i$-th component of this breakdown is

$$w_i \times \frac{\partial \text{VaR}(w)}{\partial w_i} \qquad (20.13)$$

This quantity has a natural interpretation as the *risk-contribution* of the $i$-th asset: it measures the impact on overall risk of proportional changes in the allocation $w_i$. For example, suppose $w_i$ changes by a small proportion $\xi_i$ (i.e., from $w_i$ to $w_i(1 + \xi_i)$); then, from (20.12), the change in total portfolio risk is approximately

$$\left[ \frac{\partial \text{VaR}(w)}{\partial w_i} w_i \right] \times \xi_i$$

Observe that if (20.13) is the risk-contribution of asset $i$, then, because of the identity (20.12), the sum of the risk-contributions equals the total risk in the portfolio. Thus, we have achieved the desired breakdown of total portfolio risk into risk attributable to individual components. The *percentage* risk-contribution of asset $i$ is

$$\% \text{ Risk-Contribution of } i = \frac{1}{\text{VaR}(w)} \left[ \frac{\partial \text{VaR}(w)}{\partial w_i} w_i \right]$$

Note too that the risk-contribution of asset $i$ depends (through the term $\text{VaR}(w)$) on all the other assets in the portfolio and the covariance of asset $i$ with these terms. This dependence can be made explicit in the delta-normal method, as we explain below.

Finally, observe that this method of computing the risk-contribution can be applied to any measure that satisfies linear homogeneity; there is nothing special about VaR in this regard. In particular, it can be applied to the portfolio standard deviation if that is our measure of portfolio risk or to the left-tail measure known as expected shortfall.

## Example 20.3    Calculating Risk-Contributions

Consider, once again, the two-asset setting used in Example 20.1. We have $w_1 = w_2 = 5$. Returns are jointly normal with the expected return vector and the variance-covariance matrix given by

$$\begin{bmatrix} \mu_1 \\ \mu_2 \end{bmatrix} = \begin{bmatrix} 0.20 \\ 0.12 \end{bmatrix} \qquad \begin{bmatrix} \sigma_1^2 & \sigma_{12} \\ \sigma_{21} & \sigma_2^2 \end{bmatrix} = \begin{bmatrix} 0.04 & 0.02 \\ 0.02 & 0.03 \end{bmatrix}$$

As we have seen earlier, the 99% VaR of this portfolio is 2.264. What is the contribution of each asset to this total portfolio risk? To answer this question, note that the portfolio value is normally distributed with a mean of $\mu_P(w)$ and a standard deviation of $\sigma_P(w)$, where

$$\mu_P(w) = \mu_1 w_1 + \mu_2 w_2$$

$$\sigma_P(w) = \left[ \sigma_1^2 w_1^2 + \sigma_2^2 w_2^2 + 2\sigma_{12} w_1 w_2 \right]^{1/2}$$

By definition, the 99% VaR is given by

$$\text{VaR}(w) = -[\mu_P(w) - 2.33 \times \sigma_P(w)]$$

Differentiating $\mu_P$ and $\sigma_P$ with respect to $w_1$ and $w_2$, we obtain:

$$\frac{\partial \mu_P(w)}{\partial w_1} = \mu_1 \qquad \frac{\partial \mu_P(w)}{\partial w_2} = \mu_2$$

$$\frac{\partial \sigma_P(w)}{\partial w_1} = \frac{1}{\sigma_P(w)}\left[w_1\sigma_1^2 + w_2\sigma_{12}\right]$$

$$\frac{\partial \sigma_P(w)}{\partial w_2} = \frac{1}{\sigma_P(w)}\left[w_1\sigma_{12} + w_2\sigma_2^2\right]$$

Now, by definition of the VaR, we have

$$\frac{\partial \text{VaR}(w)}{\partial w_i} = -\left(\frac{\partial \mu_P(w)}{\partial w_i} - 2.33\,\frac{\partial \sigma_P(w)}{\partial w_i}\right)$$

Expanding this, we obtain the final expressions for the risk-contributions:

$$w_1\,\frac{\partial \text{VaR}(w)}{\partial w_1} = w_1 \times \left[-\mu_1 + 2.33 \times \frac{1}{\sigma_P(w)}\left(w_1\sigma_1^2 + w_2\sigma_{12}\right)\right]$$

$$w_2\,\frac{\partial \text{VaR}(w)}{\partial w_2} = w_2 \times \left[-\mu_2 + 2.33 \times \frac{1}{\sigma_P(w)}\left(w_1\sigma_{12} + w_2\sigma_2^2\right)\right]$$

Substituting for the various parameter values, these risk-contributions are seen to be 1.1076 and 1.1563, respectively. In percentage terms, the first asset contributes

$$\frac{1.1076}{2.264} = 49\%$$

of the portfolio risk. The second asset contributes the remaining 51%.    ∎

## Risk-Contributions in the Delta-Normal Method

In the delta-normal method, the VaR has the form

$$\text{VaR}(w) = -(\mu_P(w) - k\,\sigma_P(w)) \tag{20.14}$$

for some $k$ that depends on the significance level of the VaR. (For example, if we are computing 99% VaR, then $k = 2.33$.) The terms $\mu_P$ and $\sigma_P$ are, of course, given by (20.2) and (20.3), respectively.

Taking the relevant partial derivatives in (20.14), a little algebra shows that the risk-contribution of the $i$-th position works out to

$$w_i\,\frac{\partial \text{VaR}(w)}{\partial w_i} = w_i\left[-\mu_i + k \times \frac{1}{\sqrt{\sigma(w)}}\sum_{j=1}^{n} w_j\sigma_{ij}\right] \tag{20.15}$$

Expression (20.15) highlights a central point: the risk-contribution of a position depends on its covariance with the rest of the portfolio. In particular:

- The higher (more positive) this covariance, the higher the risk-contribution. This is intuitive. To the extent that an incremental position does not correlate strongly with the other components of the portfolio, we do not bump up overall risk substantially.

- If the covariance is negative, then the risk-contribution is reduced and can even become negative (i.e., the position serves as a hedge).

## Computing Risk-Contribution in Other Methods

The risk-contribution denominated in VaR may be computed for the other methods similarly, not just for the delta-normal approach. The only complication is that the partial derivative $\partial \text{VaR}/\partial w_i$ cannot be computed explicitly since we do not have a formula for VaR under historical simulation or the Monte Carlo method. But it is easy to compute this quantity numerically so the risk decomposition is always feasible. This is because the linear homogeneity property of the VaR function does not depend on the method used to compute VaR.

## Uses of the Risk Decomposition

The risk decomposition we have just described has uses in identifying (a) the risk-minimizing trades or "best hedges"; (b) the "implied views" in a portfolio; and (c) "optimal" portfolio allocations. We elaborate on each of these below. Our description below is based on Pearson (2002); for a more detailed development of the ideas, we refer the reader to this book.

### (A) Risk Decomposition and Hedging

Suppose we are interested in reducing the overall risk of a given portfolio (say, because it exceeds some target level). If we decide to do this using some asset (say, asset $i$), how large is the trade size required to achieve this? Risk decomposition helps address this question.

Let the initial dollar allocations be $w = (w_1, \ldots, w_n)$. Pick any $i$. Suppose we change the investment in asset $i$ from $w_i$ to $w_i(1 + \Delta_i)$ where $\Delta_i$ could be positive or negative. From the risk decomposition (20.12), portfolio risk changes by approximately

$$\left[ \frac{\partial \text{VaR}(w)}{\partial w_i} w_i \right] \times \Delta_i \tag{20.16}$$

If we want the change in portfolio risk to be a given amount, then, using (20.16), we can identify for each $i$ the size $\Delta_i$ of the trade in $i$ that would be required to achieve the desired reduction. For example, if we wish to reduce portfolio risk by an amount $A$, the proportional change $\Delta_i$ that is required is

$$\Delta_i = A \Big/ \left[ \frac{\partial \text{VaR}(w)}{\partial w_i} w_i \right]$$

This observation carries the benefit that we can now manage the risk of the portfolio at an individual asset level by using individual risk decompositions to determine how much we need to tweak the holdings of each asset. That is, risk decomposition facilitates managing aggregate risk at an individual level.

**Example 20.4**

We continue with the two-asset example introduced in Example 20.1. In this setting, the total VaR is 2.264, and, as we showed above, the risk-contributions of assets 1 and 2 are, respectively, 1.1076 and 1.1563. Suppose we want to reduce the total VaR to 2.0. If this change is to be effected by changing the investment in asset 1, the size of the required trade in asset 1 is

$$\Delta_1 = \frac{2.0 - 0.2639}{1.1076} = -0.2382$$

which is a reduction of 23.8% in the position. Likewise, if the reduction is to be made in asset 2, we have

$$\Delta_2 = \frac{2.0 - 0.2639}{1.1563} = -0.2282$$

implying a reduction of 22.8% in the position.   ∎

### (B) Risk Decomposition and Portfolio Optimization

A second use of the risk decompositions is in optimizing portfolio holdings. Intuitively speaking, we want the return of each asset to be commensurate to its risk-contribution. If an asset contributes more return than risk, we want to increase its holding in the portfolio. If it contributes more risk than return, we want to reduce our holding of the asset. More formally, the mathematical expression of this optimality requirement is that for all distinct assets $i$ and $j$, the following condition should hold:

$$\frac{\mu_i w_i}{\text{Risk-contribution of } i} = \frac{\mu_j w_j}{\text{Risk-contribution of } j}$$

If the left-hand side is greater than the right-hand side, then we could reallocate a small amount from $j$ to $i$ and improve portfolio performance; if the left-hand side is smaller, then moving resources from $i$ to $j$ improves matters. Knowing how to measure portfolio risk-contributions enables us to optimize in this fashion.

### (C) Risk Decomposition and "Implied Views"

In an "optimal" portfolio, the contribution of a position to returns is proportional to its contribution to risk. Therefore, given a particular portfolio at a point in time, one can ask: under what vector of expected returns is this portfolio optimal? These expected returns are known as the portfolio's *implied views*. The implied views can be used to judge the reasonableness of a portfolio's allocations. For example, if we find that for a given allocation to be optimal, a particular asset's expected returns have to be 43%, and we think this expected return is unreasonable, then the given allocation is not optimal.

## 20.4   Coherent Risk Measures

To judge the acceptability or "goodness" of any given risk measure, it helps to have a set of criteria to which we can appeal. Artzner et al. (1999) (henceforth ADEH) propose such a set of criteria. They call "coherent" a risk measure that meets their conditions. This section discusses their criteria and, particularly, their finding that VaR is *not* a coherent risk measure.

At the outset, it should be stressed that a fundamental motivation behind the ADEH paper is the estimation of capital adequacy. Thus, their focus is explicitly on "left-tail" measures such as VaR.

Let $\mathcal{R}$ denote a generic risk measure. Given a portfolio $w$, we denote the risk of $w$ under the measure $\mathcal{R}$ by $\mathcal{R}(w)$. ADEH propose four conditions that $\mathcal{R}$ should meet:

**Linear Homogeneity**   If all positions are scaled by a factor of $m$, then the risk measure should also scale by $m$: $\mathcal{R}(m \cdot w) = m \, \mathcal{R}(w)$ for any $m > 0$. Intuitively, if a capital level of $K$ is required for the portfolio $w$, then a level of $mK$ is required for the portfolio $mw$ since tail risk has changed by the factor $m$. As we have noted, VaR satisfies this condition.

**Montonicity**   Any portfolio that "dominates" another should result in a lower risk measure. A portfolio is said to dominate another if it does at least as well or strictly better than the second portfolio in all states of the world. This requirement is intuitive: if $w$ dominates $\tilde{w}$, then—by definition—$w$ has lower left-tail risk than $\tilde{w}$. It is also easy to see that VaR meets this condition.[1]

**Subadditivity**   Diversification should reduce risk, and our risk measure should reflect this. That is, the risk of a combination of portfolios should be less than the sum of risks of the individual portfolios. In mathematical terms, if $P1$ and $P2$ are any two portfolios, then subadditivity is the condition that the risk measure satisfy

$$\mathcal{R}(P1 + P2) \leq \mathcal{R}(P1) + \mathcal{R}(P2)$$

The failure of this condition may lead a risk manager to reject diversification when, in fact, he should be encouraged to do just that. Such failure also has consequences for regulators and others who rely on left-tail measures for gauging capital adequacy. Futures exchanges, for example, set margin requirements based on tail-event considerations. If the risk measure they use for this purpose violates subadditivity, they would require lower margins from a customer who opened two positions under different accounts than from one who opened the positions under the same account. Remarkably, VaR does not satisfy the subadditivity property. This is a sufficiently important failing that we illustrate it separately with two examples below.

**Translation Invariance**   If we add a risk-free asset to the portfolio with an expected return of $r$, the risk of the portfolio should come down by the extent of this risk-free addition. It is apparent that VaR meets this condition.

ADEH provide a number of examples in their paper on the failure of commonly-used risk measures to satisfy these conditions. We present below two examples taken from their paper that highlight the shortcomings of VaR. The first example shows that VaR may fail subadditivity. The second shows that VaR may fail to recognize concentration of risk in the tails. In the example, VaR awards a lower risk to a portfolio with highly concentrated tail risk than to one with more diversified risk.

---

**Example 20.5**

## VaR and the Failure of Subadditivity

Consider a portfolio consisting solely of binary cash-or-nothing options on a stock, with payoff $M > 0$ if the options finish in-the-money. There are two kinds of options:

1. Type-$U$ options: The options pay $M$ if $S_T > K_u$, and nothing otherwise. The initial price of these options is $P_u$.
2. Type-$D$ options: The options pay $M$ if $S_T < K_d$, and nothing otherwise. The initial price of these options is $P_d$.

The strikes $K_u$ and $K_d$ are chosen so that $\text{Prob}(S_T > K_u) = \text{Prob}(S_T < K_d) = 0.008$. The riskless rate is taken to be zero. Note that we must have $K_d < K_u$; and, of course, we must also have $P_u, P_d < M$. We further assume that $M > P_u + P_d$. Given the miniscule probabilities of the options finishing in-the-money, this is reasonable.

The risk measure in this example is 99% VaR with a horizon of $T$ where $T$ is the maturity date of the options. Consider three portfolios:

---

[1] Not all risk measures satisfy monotonicity. Even a simple risk measure like the portfolio standard deviation violates it. For an example, suppose that there are four equiprobable states of the world. The first portfolio, Portfolio P1, has payoffs in these four states given by the vector {1, 2, 4, 5}. The second portfolio, Portfolio P2, has the payoff vector {1, 2, 3, 4}. It is apparent that P1 dominates P2 and should not be ranked by any reasonable risk measure as worse than P2. But if we compare the two portfolios' standard deviations, we obtain $\sigma(P1) = 1.83$, and $\sigma(P2) = 1.29$.

- **Portfolio A** Short one Type-$U$ option, investment of $P_u$ at the riskless rate for maturity at $T$.
- **Portfolio B** Short one Type-$D$ option, investment of $P_d$ at the riskless rate for maturity at $T$.
- **Portfolio C** Short one Type-$U$ option and one Type-$D$ option; investment of $P_u + P_d$ at the riskless rate for maturity at $T$.

Each portfolio has a value of zero today. At $T$, the first portfolio is worth $P_u$ if $S_T \leq K_u$, and $-M + P_u$ if $S_T > K_u$, so its payoff distribution is

$$\begin{cases} P_u - M, & \text{with probability } 0.008 \\ P_u, & \text{with probability } 0.992 \end{cases}$$

It follows that the 99% VaR of Portfolio A is $-P_u$. Note that the VaR is *negative* since with probability at least 0.99, the portfolio is not expected to lose money. Similarly, the 99% VaR of Portfolio B is $-P_d$. If capital adequacy were based on 99% VaR, neither portfolio would be deemed to require any extra capital.

Portfolio C, on the other hand, has the following payoffs at $T$:

$$\begin{cases} P_u + P_d - M, & \text{if } S_T < K_d \\ P_u + P_d, & \text{if } S_T \in [K_d, K_u] \\ P_u + P_d - M, & \text{if } S_T > K_u \end{cases}$$

Thus, its payoff distribution is

$$\begin{cases} P_u + P_d - M, & \text{with probability } 0.016 \\ P_u + P_d, & \text{with probability } 0.984 \end{cases}$$

Since Portfolio C loses money with a total likelihood of 1.6% (0.8% on either option), the 99% VaR of Portfolio C is $M - P_u - P_d$, so it is *positive*. It follows that the 99% VaR risk measure will rank Portfolio C as having more risk than the sum of the risks of Portfolios A and B. This says precisely that VaR fails the subadditivity condition. ∎

---

### Example 20.6  VaR and Concentrated Tail Risks

This example is also based on the ADEH paper and is attributed by them to Claudio Albanese. Suppose that there are 100 different corporate bonds. Each bond costs 100 today and will provide a payoff of 102 on a common maturity date if there is no default and nothing otherwise. The likelihood of default on each bond is 0.01, and default is independent across bonds. The risk-free rate of interest is zero. The risk measure is 95% VaR with a horizon equal to that of the bonds' maturity.

Consider, first, the following highly concentrated portfolio. You borrow 1 million at the risk-free rate and invest the entire sum in the bonds of a single company (say Company 1). The payoff received at maturity is

$$\begin{cases} 20,000, & \text{if there is no default} \\ -1,000,000, & \text{otherwise} \end{cases}$$

Since the probability of default is 0.01, the 95% VaR of the portfolio is negative and equal to $-20,000$.

Now consider the alternative of investing 10,000 in each of the 100 bonds. The payoff at maturity will depend on how many bonds default. The likelihood of $k$ defaults ($k = 0, 1, 2, \ldots, 100$), denoted $\pi_k$, can be found using the usual binomial formula:

$$\pi_k = \frac{100!}{k!(100-k)!} (0.01)^k (0.99)^{100-k} \qquad (20.17)$$

The payoffs received at maturity in the event of $k$ defaults are

$$(10,200 \times (100 - k)) - 1,000,000 \qquad (20.18)$$

It is easily checked from (20.17) that the probability of two or fewer defaults is about 0.92 while the probability of three or fewer defaults is about 0.98. Thus, the 5% VaR of this portfolio corresponds to the payoffs received from exactly two defaults. From (20.18), the 5% VaR is 400.

Thus, VaR indicates that diversifying by putting an equal amount into each of the 100 bonds is *worse* than (and requires more capital than) putting all our money into the bonds of a single company, a patently absurd conclusion. ∎

To the extent that one accepts the axiom of subadditivity as a desirable one, these examples are obviously damaging to the notion of VaR as a risk measure. Mitigating this are two factors. First, if returns are jointly normally distributed, then the resulting VaR measure will always satisfy subadditivity. This means if we use the delta-normal method to compute VaR (as is commonly done in practice), the possible failure of subadditivity is not a concern. Second, even its most ardent advocates do not view VaR as a "stand-alone" risk measure that summarizes everything relevant about tail risk. Complementing VaR with other measures of tail risk can greatly improve our understanding of overall portfolio risk. Two such measures of tail risk are worst-case scenario analysis and expected shortfall.

## Worst-Case Scenario Analysis and Expected Shortfall

VaR has the disadvantage that it has nothing to say about what could happen *in* the tail of the distribution. For example, knowing the 99% VaR does not tell us what could happen in the 1% tail, i.e., how big might losses be in that region. The potential magnitude of tail loss is obviously important. *Worst-case scenario* (WCS) analysis and *expected shortfall* (ES) have been proposed as complements to VaR for this purpose.

WCS, proposed by Boudoukh, Richardson, and Whitelaw (1995), explores the properties of the tail of the VaR distribution. Effectively, it asks: how bad can things get in the tail? More precisely, it examines the distribution of the loss over the worst trading period over a given horizon. (For example, the worst day in a horizon of 250 trading days. Observe that a "worst" period always exists over any horizon.) In notational terms, if we let $r_1, r_2, \ldots, r_N$ denote the returns on the portfolio over $N$ trading periods, then WCS looks at the distribution of $\min\{r_1, \ldots, r_N\}$. Boudoukh et al. compare VaR and WCS numerically and conclude that the expected loss during the worst period is much larger than the corresponding VaR.

We can also look at the tail with a different focus and ask how bad things can become in the tail *on average*. That is, conditional on losses exceeding the VaR limit, what is the average loss? This measure is called *expected shortfall*. ES is known to be a coherent measure of risk, one factor that has led to its popularity. For a description of the properties of ES, see, e.g., Acerbi, Nordio, and Sirtori (2001) or Acerbi and Tasche (2002).

**20.5 Exercises**   1. What is Value-at-Risk (VaR)? What is the minimal information you need to compute VaR? What are its advantages and its limitations?

2. What are the three different approaches to computing VaR? State some advantages and disadvantages of each method. State two attributes of these three methods that you think are the most important, and then assess which of them satisfies your attributes best.

3. How is Value-at-Risk (VaR) different as a measure of risk than the variance of return?

4. What, if any, is the relationship of variance and VaR?

5. Which moments of the return distribution are measures of risk? State some of them, and explain what the nature of the risk measure is, and what insight one might be aiming for with your chosen measure of risk.

6. If the mean, variance, and skewness remain the same, but the kurtosis of returns on a portfolio increases, will the VaR increase or decrease, keeping all else the same?

7. If the mean and variance remain the same but the skewness of returns on a portfolio becomes more negative than before, what do you think will happen to the VaR of the portfolio?

8. Compare VaR and kurtosis as risk measures for a portfolio.

9. What is the relationship of the trading horizon used for calculating VaR and the level of VaR? What do you think is an optimal horizon for VaR calculations?

10. Is it feasible to compute the risk contribution of individual assets to the total risk of a portfolio under the VaR measure if the distribution of returns is not normal and the delta-normal approach is not available?

11. VaR has been criticized for not being a "coherent" risk measure. Why is this?

12. Suppose the average profit of FOF Inc. is $1 million per week. The standard deviation of profits per week is $1 million as well. Calculate the 1% and 10% VaR for FOF. Assume profits are normally distributed.

13. In the preceding problem, suppose the distribution of returns is not normal but Student's $t$ with 5 degrees of freedom. What is the 1% VaR under the new assumption? What happens to the VaR when the $t$ distribution has 20 degrees of freedom instead? Explain the difference in results.

14. Consider a portfolio that has equal amounts of $10 invested in two assets. Suppose returns on the two assets are jointly normally distributed. The annual expected returns and variance of returns on the first asset are given by

$$\mu_1 = 0.10 \quad \sigma_1^2 = 0.04$$

and those on the second asset are given by

$$\mu_2 = 0.05 \quad \sigma_2^2 = 0.03$$

Consider three cases:
(a) The correlation between the returns is $\rho = 0$.
(b) The correlation between the returns is $\rho = +0.50$.
(c) The correlation between the returns is $\rho = -0.50$.

For each case, identify the 1% Value-at-Risk of the portfolio. Explain the pattern of dependence of VaR on the correlation.

15. Consider the same parameters as in the previous problem, but consider now only the case $\rho = -0.50$. The total portfolio risk in this case is given by the VaR amount you have computed above. What are the risk contributions of the two assets?

16. You are given a portfolio of three assets with mean vector and covariance matrix of returns as follows:

$$\begin{bmatrix} 0.10 \\ 0.15 \\ 0.05 \end{bmatrix} \quad \begin{bmatrix} 0.08 & 0.05 & 0.05 \\ 0.05 & 0.06 & 0.05 \\ 0.05 & 0.05 & 0.07 \end{bmatrix}$$

Compute the 5% VaR for a portfolio that is invested in $1 in each asset using the delta-normal method.

17. Repeat the previous exercise using Monte Carlo simulation and compare your solution to the analytical value from the delta-normal method.

18. Repeat the previous Monte Carlo problem assuming instead that the random numbers are drawn from a Student's $t$ distribution with 5 degrees of freedom. Compare the VaR values with that from the normal distribution.

19. You are managing a portfolio that tracks the S&P 500 index. You consider two ways in which you might calculate the VaR:

    (a) Using the delta-normal approach by calibrating the mean and variance of the portfolio to the historical data.

    (b) Using historical simulation based on the same data.

    Which one would you expect to provide a riskier picture of the portfolio?

20. You are given a portfolio of three assets whose returns are jointly normally distributed with the following mean vector and covariance matrix:

$$\begin{bmatrix} 0.20 \\ 0.10 \\ 0.15 \end{bmatrix} \quad \begin{bmatrix} 0.08 & 0.02 & 0.02 \\ 0.02 & 0.06 & 0.03 \\ 0.02 & 0.03 & 0.07 \end{bmatrix}$$

    (a) Compute the 5% VaR for the portfolio if we invest $1 in the first asset, $2 in the second asset, and $3 in the third asset.

    (b) How much does each asset's holding contribute to the overall VaR risk?

21. Examine the following plots of bivariate return distributions closely. Pay special attention to the values on the axes. Both plots are joint distributions of returns of stocks. The first

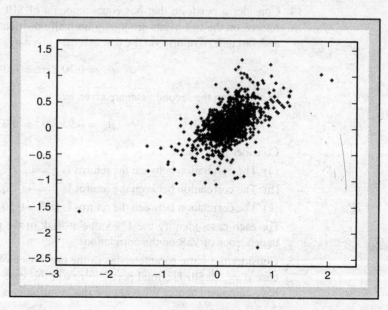

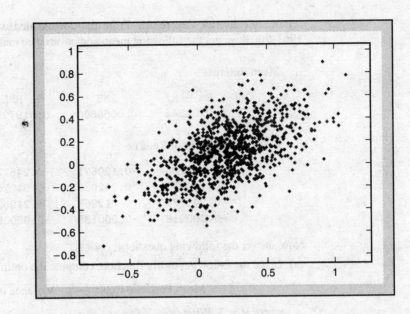

plot is from a Student's *t* distribution and the second one from a normal distribution. Both have the same means and covariance matrices. Explain which joint return distribution is likely to be riskier in terms of VaR. Why are they different in risk even though the means, variances, and covariances are the same?

22. You are given a portfolio of two assets whose returns are jointly normally distributed with the following mean vector and covariance matrix:

$$\begin{bmatrix} 0.20 \\ 0.10 \end{bmatrix} \quad \begin{bmatrix} 0.08 & 0.04 \\ 0.04 & 0.06 \end{bmatrix}$$

(a) Compute the 5% VaR of the portfolio if $1 is invested in the first asset and $1 is invested in the second.

(b) Compute the risk-contribution of each asset to the VaR.

(c) Is the current portfolio weighting optimal? If not, suggest a better one.

23. (Requires Writing Code) You are given a portfolio of two assets with mean vector and covariance matrix of returns over the VaR horizon as follows:

$$\begin{bmatrix} 0.20 \\ 0.10 \end{bmatrix} \quad \begin{bmatrix} 0.08 & 0.04 \\ 0.04 & 0.06 \end{bmatrix}$$

(a) The joint distribution of the securities is assumed to be Student's *t* with 5 degrees of freedom. Compute the 5% VaR of the portfolio if $100 is invested in the first asset and $200 is invested in the second. Assume that the returns are continuously compounded. Use Monte Carlo simulation for this question. Present your Octave program code with solutions.

(b) Redo part (a) using a Student's *t* distribution with 20 degrees of freedom. Comment on how your results compare to the first part.

24. (Difficult) The following asset-pricing factor returns are downloaded from the Fama-French database: the excess market return, the SMB portfolio return, the HML portfolio

return, and the risk-free return. From the downloaded data, which is for the period 1963–2003, we get the following mean and covariance matrix:

Mean Returns

| Rm – Rf | SMB | HML | Rf |
|---|---|---|---|
| 0.0204244 | 0.0065800 | 0.0197292 | 0.0231443 |

Covariance Matrix of Returns

| | | | |
|---|---|---|---|
| 0.805756 | −0.120621 | −0.245771 | −0.000218 |
| −0.120621 | 0.242035 | −0.012267 | −0.000135 |
| −0.245771 | −0.012267 | 0.212526 | 0.000086 |
| −0.000218 | −0.000135 | 0.000086 | 0.000109 |

Now answer the following questions:

(a) Given the following utility function, compute the optimal portfolio weights:

$$U = \text{Mean Portfolio Return} - \gamma \cdot \text{Variance of Portfolio Return}$$

where $\gamma = 3$. What is $\gamma$?

(b) For the given portfolio weights, compute the 1% VaR of the optimal portfolio.

(c) Compute the risk decomposition of the portfolio, and allocate the risk across the four asset classes. Which asset class contributes the most risk?

(d) Now choose some random weights different from the optimal ones you just computed. Recompute the VaR. Is the risk measure higher or lower? Why?

(e) If you had to double the proportions of just one of the assets, which one would you choose? Why?

25. This question talks about adjustments you may need to make in the computation of VaR.

(a) In a historical simulation algorithm for VaR, suppose the portfolio's historical mean return is anticipated to be understated by 2%. What adjustment would you make in the simulation for determining the VaR in a new simulation run? Explain this in detail with the specific steps you would use.

(b) In addition, suppose that the portfolio variance in the future is anticipated to be 1.5 times what it was in the past. Again, explain the specific modification to the simulation algorithm required to accommodate this feature.

# Chapter 21

# Convertible Bonds

## 21.1  Introduction

A convertible bond is a corporate bond with an embedded option that allows its holder to convert the bond into equity at a fixed price. Convertibles possess characteristics of both equity and corporate debt, but they are more than just a package of these securities. Their complexity comes from the interplay of their equity and debt components and the fact that convertibles very often have other optionalities embedded in them such as callability by the issuer. Their values depend on multiple risk factors including equity risk of the issuing company, interest-rate risk, and credit risk of the issuing company. In this chapter, we examine the main features of convertible bonds, looking especially at the factors that affect the prices of these bonds and how these factors could matter.

Convertibles are attractive to both investor and issuer for a variety of reasons. By providing bondholders with a conversion option, convertibles offer protection from risk-shifting actions by management that benefit equity holders at the expense of bondholders. (Green (1984) develops a theoretical model that highlights the features of convertible bonds that make them preferable to conventional bonds.) For fixed-income investors, convertibles offer the opportunity to participate in the equity upside of the company. For equity investors, the bond floor limits their downside risk compared to an investment in straight equity.

Convertible bonds vary widely in their characteristics, sufficiently so that there is really no such thing as a "typical" convertible. We begin with some terminology and then list the main features of convertible bonds.

## 21.2  Convertible Bond Terminology

A convertible bond is a fixed-income obligation of a company that gives the bondholder the right to convert the bond into a fixed number of shares. This fixed number of shares is called the *conversion ratio*. For example, a conversion ratio of 2.5 means that each convertible bond may be exchanged for 2.5 shares of equity. The *conversion price* is the face value of the bond divided by the conversion ratio:

$$\text{Conversion Price} = \frac{\text{Face Value}}{\text{Conversion Ratio}}$$

The conversion price is that price of equity at which the bondholder would be indifferent between converting to equity or receiving the bond's face value.

Unlike warrants, no money changes hands at conversion time. When the bonds are exchanged for equity, investors forfeit future interest payments and redemption of principal on the bond. Typically, the conversion right may be exercised at any time (i.e., it is an

American-style option). At maturity, if the security has not been converted into equity, it will be redeemed by the issuer like a straight bond.

## Parity and Premium

The market value of the shares in a convertible bond (henceforth, CB) is called *parity*:

$$\text{Parity} = \text{Conversion Ratio} \times \text{Market Price/Share}$$

The *premium* for a convertible bond is the excess of the market price of the CB over parity:

$$\text{Premium} = \text{Price of CB} - \text{Parity}$$

Thus, the premium is the value of the bond over and above its immediate conversion value. At issue, the premium reflects the anticipated net value of the various embedded options within the convertible bond.

There are two equivalent ways to think about convertible bonds, either as a package of a fixed number of shares, or on a per-share basis. The latter is more intuitive, but the CB market uses the former. Of course, we may translate from one to the other using the conversion ratio. Prices in the CB market are quoted in "points," i.e., as percentages of nominal value.

**Example 21.1**    Consider the following information about a convertible bond:

- Face value: $5,000.
- Issue price: $5,200.
- Conversion ratio: 500.
- Current share price: $9.50.

Table 21.1 summarizes the three ways of looking at this information. Given a conversion ratio of 500, the conversion price is equal to the face value of the bond divided by the conversion ratio, i.e., $10. Parity is the conversion ratio times the current market price of equity, which equals $4,750. Since the bond is trading at $5,200, the premium is $450.  ∎

## 21.3  Main Features of Convertible Bonds

There are some features that are common across convertible bonds (such as callability) and some dimensions along which convertibles exhibit considerable variability (such as the coupon structure or other embedded optionalities). This section lists the main features of covertible bonds.

**TABLE 21.1**
Convertible Bond Terminology

|  | Cash Value | Value/Share | Market Quote |
|---|---|---|---|
| Conversion ratio | 500 | | |
| Face value | $5,000 | $10.00 | 100.00 |
| Conversion price | $5,000 | 10.00 | 100.00 |
| CB price | $5,200 | $10.40 | 104.00 |
| Parity | $4,750 | 9.50 | 95.00 |
| Premium | $450 | $0.90 | 9.00 |
| Premium % | 9.47% | 9.47% | 9.47% |

## Callability and Call Protection

Convertible bonds are, almost invariably, *callable* by the issuer, that is, the issuer has the right to buy the bond back from the holder at a prespecified price, typically par. Thus, both the issuer and the holder of the convertible hold options, and the exercise of one option affects the life of the other. The exercise of the convert option by the bondholder extinguishes the call held by the issuer. If the call is exercised by the issuer, then the convert option is not extinguished immediately, but its life is shortened sharply: the bondholder may convert the bond to equity within a fixed period of time from the date of the call (e.g., 30 days), failing which the bond is surrendered to the issuer for the call consideration. The call feature is commonly invoked by issuers to force conversion.

To maintain a balance between the issuer's rights and those of the investor, some protection against callability is commonly provided to the investor. This protection takes on one or both of two forms:

- **"Hard" Protection**  The bond cannot be called for a specified length of time (typically, two to four years from the issue date).
- **Provisional ("Soft") Protection**  The share price must be trading at a minimum specified premium to the conversion price (often 30%–50%) when it is called.

## Maturity and Coupon Structure

Convertibles range in maturity from 3 to 30 years, and some convertibles even come with no maturity date (see the segment below on "Convertible Preferreds"). The coupon structure in convertibles too varies widely. In traditional "cash-pay" convertibles, the coupon is set so that the bond initially trades at par; thus, the coupon equals the yield-to-maturity (ytm) on the instrument. In "original issue discount" or OID convertibles, the coupon is lower than the ytm, and the convertible trades below par at inception; part of the return to the investor is received in the form of capital appreciation as the bond accretes to par at maturity. Zero-coupon or "deep-discount" convertibles pay no coupon at all; the entire return is from capital appreciation.

When coupons are paid, the coupon may be fixed, or it may be a variable coupon with reset clauses; in the latter case, the coupon can be floating, based on an interest-rate index, or set to vary for different periods in the life of the bond. Multicurrency convertibles also exist with the principal and interest in different currencies; sometimes the investor is allowed to choose the currency in which to receive the coupon.

## Convertible Preferreds

Convertible securities are most often coupon-paying bonds as we have described above, but convertibles may also be dividend-paying preferred stock that may be converted to common stock at the fixed conversion ratio specified in the contract. Convertible preferred stock typically has no maturity date. An important exception is the class of "mandatory convertibles." A mandatory convertible is convertible preferred stock with a fixed maturity date (typically three years from the date of issue) on which the preferred stock mandatorily converts to common stock. Mandatory convertibles are usually not callable. In a mandatory convertible, the number of units of common stock received per unit of preferred share is typically variable and depends on the value of the underlying common stock at maturity.

## Puttability and Other Features

Convertible bonds may also be puttable: that is, the investor may have the right to put the bond back to the company at specified points in time. The put option is used to make the convertible more attractive to the investor and so to lower the coupon paid on the bond. Puts are particularly common in zero-coupon convertibles where the put option may be exercised at specified intervals (e.g., every five years) at the accreted value of the bond.

More exotic features may also be present in convertibles. For example, in "reset convertibles" (a.k.a. "death-spiral convertibles"), the conversion ratio depends on the behavior of the stock price: an initial conversion ratio is specified, but the conversion ratio is increased if the stock price drops below specified trigger levels. The objective is to offer some protection to convertible bond investors against a loss in value following a sharp drop in the stock price. Reset convertibles were issued in large numbers by Japanese banks in the 1990s.

## The Attractions of Convertibles

Convertibles combine features of both debt and equity. As such, they have many attractive features for issuers. The presence of the convert option means that the coupon on CBs will be lower than that on straight debt. Moreover if the bond is eventually converted to equity, then this future injection of equity will have come at a premium to the current equity price.[1] Management may also use the convertible bond issue for signaling purposes. In particular, the convert feature acts as a guarantee that management will not pursue actions that benefit equity holders at the cost of bondholders since CB investors can always convert and cash in on gains in equity value resulting from such "risk-shifting."

Convertibles also offer several advantages to the investor. For equity investors, they have the attraction of a lower risk profile: unlike equity, CBs offer greater downside protection. For fixed-income investors, they offer a degree of upside participation if equity prices should increase. Of course, these advantages come at a price; there is no "best of both worlds" argument. For equity investors, owing equity via a convertible provides a bond floor but the convertible also involves a premium over the parity value of equity. For fixed-income investors, the potential upside advantage is paid for in the form of a lower coupon on the convertible than could be obtained on a straight bond.

# 21.4   Breakeven Analysis

Breakeven analysis is a simple approach to analyzing the convertible premium. It focuses on the extra income that the investor receives over a specified horizon from owning the convertible instead of an equivalent amount of equity. The implicit assumption in this analysis is that the CB will be converted into equity with certainty at the end of the horizon. The calculations for breakeven analysis then focus on figuring the time to "breakeven," which determines the fair premium.

Plain vanilla convertibles usually yield more than the dividend yield on the underlying shares, so the extra income from owning the convertible instead of equity is positive. The *breakeven* is the measure of time required to recover the conversion premium through the higher income received from the convertible. We compare two quantities:

- The cash premium an investor pays to own stock indirectly via a convertible.

- The additional annual income the convertible provides versus an investment of an equivalent amount directly in the equity.

---

[1] To be sure, these post-hoc justifications do not imply the superiority of convertibles over straight debt or equity. For example, if equity prices do not ever rise to the point where conversion becomes optimal, then it is true that the convertible works out, ex-post, to be cheaper than straight debt, but issuing straight equity would have been cheaper still.

The breakeven period (measured in years) is the premium divided by the annual income advantage. This breakeven is compared to the number of years the convertible is guaranteed to remain in existence. It is common to use the first call date for this purpose. From the investor's point of view, a shorter breakeven is better.

If the breakeven is within the noncall period, this is viewed as a case where investors are "guaranteed" to recover the conversion premium through the income advantage alone. Any further income is considered "free." If the breakeven lies beyond the noncall period, then the interpretation is that recovery of the conversion premium is not guaranteed, so the premium is viewed as excessive.

| | |
|---|---|
| **Example 21.2** | Suppose that we are given the following information about a convertible bond and its issuer's equity. |

- Face value: $5,000.00.
- Issue price: $5,000.00.
- Parity: $4,500.00.
- Coupon: 3% (semiannual).
- Dividend yield: 1%.
- Premium: $500.00 = 10 points.

The annual income from the convertible is $0.03 \times 5{,}000 = 150$. Given the dividend yield of 1%, the annual income from investing $5,000 in equity instead works out to $0.01 \times 5{,}000 = 50$. Thus, the extra annual income from the convertible is $100. Therefore,

$$\text{Breakeven} = \frac{\text{Cash Premium}}{\text{Excess Annual Income}} = \frac{500}{100} = 5 \text{ years}$$

∎

Breakeven analysis offers a useful first glance at the fair value of a CB. However, it has some obvious and serious shortcomings. It ignores the time value of money in its calculations. It fails to take into account the different risk characteristics of different securities. For instance, it ignores the optionality in the convertible and so gives no value either to the bond floor present in the convertible or to such factors as equity volatility and the equity upside. To obtain more insight about the risk characteristics of convertibles, one must use a more sophisticated approach. We discuss this next.

# 21.5 Pricing Convertibles: A First Pass

A convertible is often likened to a package of two securities: a straight bond and a warrant. There are obvious similarities, and indeed there is considerable intuitive insight to be gained from thinking of convertibles as possessing a "bond" component and a "warrant" or "optionality" component. But there are also important differences. In a bond-cum-warrant package, exercise of the warrant requires payment of the strike price but leaves the bond undisturbed. In a convertible, there is no cash payment when conversion occurs, but the bond is given up. CBs also have callability features, and the exercise of the call feature on the bond shortens the life of the convert option.

In general, there is a large list of features we need to take into account in identifying the fair price of a convertible bond. These include:

- **Equity Characteristics** The current level of the stock price and its volatility are obvious important determinants of the CB price. So, too, is the dividend yield anticipated on the equity: ceteris paribus, a higher dividend yield results in a lower growth rate of the stock price which affects the convertible option.

- **Interest Rates** Changes in interest rates affect both the bond component of the CB as well as the optionality component. The former works through changing the present values of the coupons and principal payments that remain. The latter effect is similar to the effect of interest-rate changes on equity call option values.
- **The Issuer's Credit Risk** The issuer's credit risk affects both the bond and optionality components of the CB. Default results in lost coupons on the bond and a recovery below the face value due at maturity. Since the likelihood of default also affects equity characteristics, the warrant component of the CB is also affected.
- **The Convertible Structure** This includes such factors as the size of coupons, the presence of other optionalities in the convertible such as callability by the issuer, puttability by the holder, etc.

All this means that the pricing of convertibles by no-arbitrage methods must involve more complex models than the pricing of equity options. But if, as a first approximation, we ignore interest-rate and credit-risk considerations, then the pricing of convertibles becomes considerably simplified. We may then think of the convertible as a straight bond-cum-warrant package, but one in which the strike price on the warrant at any time is the value of the bond at that point. Exploiting this idea, we can price convertibles using binomial models. We examine this approach in the remainder of this section. The next section discusses introducing credit risk into the modeling process.

Even with equity risk alone, there is a wide range of factors that affect CB prices. Rather than build a model that simultaneously incorporates all of these factors, we adopt a "building-blocks" approach. We begin with a look at the valuation of convertibles in a simple one-period binomial model. The ideas developed here are easily generalized to many-period binomial models in the obvious way. Then, we discuss in turn adding coupons, dividends, and call and put features to the model.[2] The analysis is done on a per-share basis.

## Valuation in a One-Period Binomial Model

Let $S = 100$ denote the current price of the equity underlying the CB. Suppose that after one period, the stock will return either $+10\%$ or $-10\%$. Thus, the two possible prices after one period are $uS = 110$ and $dS = 90$. Let the one-period interest rate be 2%. Consider valuing in this framework a one-period convertible bond with a face value of $E = 100$.

After one period, the bond is at maturity. If the state $uS = 110$ has been reached, it is optimal to convert the bond to equity. Thus, the value $CB_u$ of the convertible in this state is 110. If the state $dS = 90$ is reached, it is optimal to receive the par value of 100. Thus, $CB_d = 100$. This information is summarized in Figure 21.1.

We can use replication arguments to price the convertible bond. Consider a portfolio of $\Delta$ units of the stock and $B$ of cash invested/borrowed at the 2% rate. This portfolio will perfectly mimic the CB after one period if

$$110 \Delta + 1.02 B = 110$$
$$90 \Delta + 1.02 B = 100$$

Solving, we get:

$$\Delta = 0.50 \qquad B = 53.92$$

---

[2] The pricing of convertibles in binomial trees has been undertaken by many authors. For example, Carayannopoulos and Kalimipalli (2003) and Das and Sundaram (2007) develop versions that also incorporate default and interest-rate risk. Our building-blocks exposition in this section adopts the simpler didactic approach of Connolly (1998).

**FIGURE 21.1**
One-Period Pricing
Model

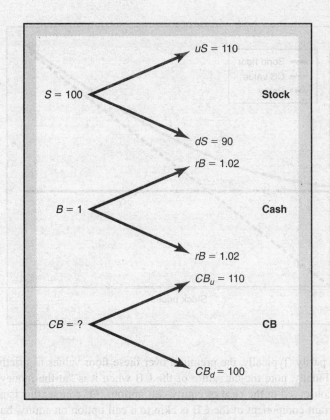

In words, the following portfolio perfectly mimics the behavior of the CB: a *long* position in 0.50 units of the stock and investment of 53.92. Since the portfolio perfectly replicates the CB, the fair price of the CB must be equal to the cost of the portfolio:

$$CB = \Delta S + B = 103.92$$

Thus, the arbitrage-free price of the convertible may be determined from knowledge of the characteristics of the issuer's equity.

## Generalizing to Many Periods

This pricing argument may be generalized in the obvious way to many period binomial models along the lines described in Chapters 12 and 13 for equity options. We do not repeat the details here. Constructing a CRR binomial tree as described in Chapter 13 and carrying out the pricing procedure for several different values of the initial stock price results in a graph of convertible bond prices as described in Figure 21.2.

The shape of the CB price curve in the figure accords well with intuition. The value of the CB increases as the stock price increases. At very high levels of the stock price, the CB is almost sure to be converted to equity, so increases almost one-for-one with the stock price. At very low levels of the stock price, there is almost no chance of conversion, so the CB is very much like debt. The price of the CB thus converges to the price of a straight bond with the CB's coupon and maturity structure.

The bond floor forms one lower bound for the price of the CB. The other lower bound is the value of the equity in the CB, i.e., parity. The CB can always be converted to equity but the holder of the CB, unlike the owner of straight equity, is protected by the bond floor if stock prices were to decrease sharply. As a consequence, the CB must always be worth

**FIGURE 21.2**
Convertibles, Parity, and the Bond Floor

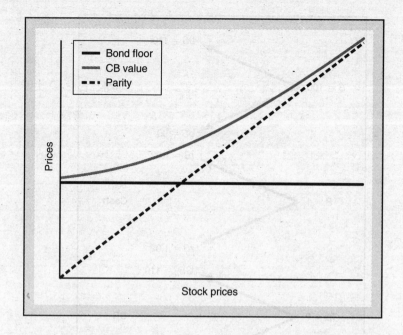

at least parity. Typically, the premium over these floor values is strictly positive as in the figure. Finally, note the curvature of the CB when it is "at-the-money." This mimics the feature observed in the case of equity call options. Of course, this is not surprising since the warrant component of the CB is akin to a call option on equity, but it does mean that CBs, like options, have gamma risk.

To be sure, Figure 21.2 is a little simplistic. Among other things, the figure takes the bond floor to be constant regardless of the level of stock prices. But very low stock prices may indicate the company is in distress and close to default, so the bond values will correspondingly fall. The next section discusses how to extend the model to incorporate credit risk. But first we discuss some simpler, but equally important, extensions such as adding coupons and dividends and including such features as callability of the CB in the pricing analysis.

## Adding Coupons

Coupons are an important motivation for fixed-income investors, and convertibles are no different in this regard. Indeed, techniques such as breakeven analysis reflect the centrality of coupons in the convertible structure. Adding coupons to the pricing model is simple if we are using a lattice framework such as the binomial. Conditional on the CB not having been converted so far, in each period in the tree where a coupon occurs, we add the coupon to the value of the CB at that point. For example, if the amount due at maturity is the face value $F$ plus the final coupon $c$, and the CB has not been converted so far, then at the last node, the value of the CB is

$$\max\{F + c, S\}$$

where $S$ is the equity price at this point. Figure 21.3, adapted from Connolly (1998), illustrates the pricing procedure (compare the top and bottom panels).

Holding all else constant, the ultimate impact of adding coupons is that the CB value goes up. The increase can be quite substantial even with small coupons. (Compare the upper and lower panels in Figure 21.3, for example.) When does the CB benefit the most? The coupons operate through the bond component of the convertible. When stock prices

**FIGURE 21.3** Coupons in the Binomial Tree

## CB Pricing without Coupons

**Input Parameters**

| | |
|---|---|
| No. of Periods | 10 |
| Equity Volatility | 0.15 |
| Annual Interest Rate | 0.04 |
| Interest Rate per Period | 0.0202 |
| Maturity of CB | 5.00 |
| Face Value of CB | 100.00 |
| Initial Stock Price | 95.00 |
| Coupon (paid annually) | 0.00 |

**Binomial Tree Parameters**

| | |
|---|---|
| u (up move) | 1.1119 |
| d (down move) | 0.8994 |
| Risk-Neutral Prob of u | 0.5686 |
| Risk-Neutral Prob of d | 0.4314 |

Stock Price = 95.00   CB Value = 101.37

Stock Price (bold) tree — by Period, nodes top → bottom:

| Period | Stock Prices |
|---|---|
| 1 | 105.63, 85.44 |
| 2 | 117.45, 95.00, 76.84 |
| 3 | 130.59, 105.63, 85.44, 69.11 |
| 4 | 145.20, 117.45, 95.00, 76.84, 62.15 |
| 5 | 161.45, 130.59, 105.63, 85.44, 69.11, 55.90 |
| 6 | 179.52, 145.20, 117.45, 95.00, 76.84, 62.15, 50.27 |
| 7 | 199.60, 161.45, 130.59, 105.63, 85.44, 69.11, 55.90, 45.21 |
| 8 | 221.94, 179.52, 145.20, 117.45, 95.00, 76.84, 62.15, 50.27, 40.66 |
| 9 | 246.77, 199.60, 161.45, 130.59, 105.63, 85.44, 69.11, 55.90, 45.21, 36.57 |
| 10 | 274.39, 221.94, 179.52, 145.20, 117.45, 95.00, 76.84, 62.15, 50.27, 40.66, 32.89 |

CB Value (italic) tree — by Period, nodes top → bottom:

| Period | CB Values |
|---|---|
| 0 | 101.37 |
| 1 | 109.68, 95.16 |
| 2 | 119.72, 101.60, 91.13 |
| 3 | 131.64, 109.61, 95.80, 89.24 |
| 4 | 145.56, 119.46, 101.76, 92.43, 89.21 |
| 5 | 161.52, 131.35, 109.38, 96.47, 91.42, 90.48 |
| 6 | 179.52, 145.36, 119.03, 101.78, 93.99, 92.31, 92.31 |
| 7 | 199.60, 161.45, 130.97, 108.88, 97.20, 94.18, 94.18, 94.18 |
| 8 | 221.94, 179.52, 145.20, 118.34, 101.50, 96.08, 96.08, 96.08, 96.08 |
| 9 | 246.77, 199.60, 161.45, 130.59, 107.74, 98.02, 98.02, 98.02, 98.02, 98.02 |
| 10 | 274.39, 221.94, 179.52, 145.20, 117.45, 100.00, 100.00, 100.00, 100.00, 100.00, 100.00 |

Period: 1 2 3 4 5 6 7 8 9 10

## CB Pricing with Coupons

**Input Parameters**

| | |
|---|---|
| No. of Periods | 10 |
| Equity Volatility | 0.15 |
| Annual Interest Rate | 0.04 |
| Interest Rate per Period | 0.0202 |
| Maturity of CB | 5.00 |
| Face Value of CB | 100.00 |
| Initial Stock Price | 95.00 |
| Coupon (paid annually) | 4.00 |

**Binomial Tree Parameters**

| | |
|---|---|
| u (up move) | 1.1119 |
| d (down move) | 0.8994 |
| Risk-Neutral Prob of u | 0.5686 |
| Risk-Neutral Prob of d | 0.4314 |

Stock Price = 95.00   CB Value = 117.32

Stock Price (bold) tree — identical to the panel above:

| Period | Stock Prices |
|---|---|
| 1 | 105.63, 85.44 |
| 2 | 117.45, 95.00, 76.84 |
| 3 | 130.59, 105.63, 85.44, 69.11 |
| 4 | 145.20, 117.45, 95.00, 76.84, 62.15 |
| 5 | 161.45, 130.59, 105.63, 85.44, 69.11, 55.90 |
| 6 | 179.52, 145.20, 117.45, 95.00, 76.84, 62.15, 50.27 |
| 7 | 199.60, 161.45, 130.59, 105.63, 85.44, 69.11, 55.90, 45.21 |
| 8 | 221.94, 179.52, 145.20, 117.45, 95.00, 76.84, 62.15, 50.27, 40.66 |
| 9 | 246.77, 199.60, 161.45, 130.59, 105.63, 85.44, 69.11, 55.90, 45.21, 36.57 |
| 10 | 274.39, 221.94, 179.52, 145.20, 117.45, 95.00, 76.84, 62.15, 50.27, 40.66, 32.89 |

CB Value (italic) tree — by Period, nodes top → bottom:

| Period | CB Values |
|---|---|
| 0 | 117.32 |
| 1 | 125.59, 111.93 |
| 2 | 135.57, 118.31, 108.75 |
| 3 | 143.40, 122.14, 109.35, 103.60 |
| 4 | 157.30, 131.79, 115.14, 106.84, 104.18 |
| 5 | 169.26, 139.45, 118.42, 106.75, 102.51, 101.79 |
| 6 | 187.36, 153.34, 127.68, 111.76, 105.14, 103.85, 103.85 |
| 7 | 203.53, 165.37, 135.19, 114.30, 104.19, 101.86, 103.85, 101.86 |
| 8 | 225.94, 183.52, 149.20, 123.06, 108.10, 103.92, 103.92, 103.92, 103.92 |
| 9 | 246.77, 199.60, 161.45, 130.59, 109.44, 101.94, 101.94, 101.94, 101.94, 101.94 |
| 10 | 274.39, 221.94, 179.52, 145.20, 117.45, 104.00, 104.00, 104.00, 104.00, 104.00, 104.00 |

Coupon 2   Coupon 4   Coupon 6   Coupon 8   Coupon 10

Period: 1 2 3 4 5 6 7 8 9 10

## FIGURE 21.4
CB and Coupons

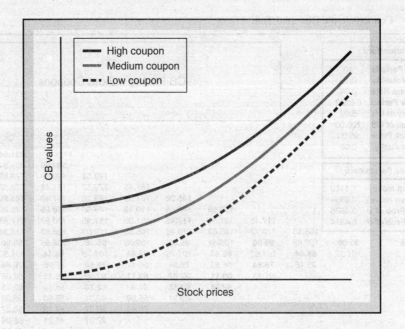

are low and the convertible is deep out-of-the-money (OTM), the bond component is the main determinant of convertible values, and this is when coupons have the most effect. As the convertible moves more into-the-money, the bond component becomes steadily less important, and the effect of coupons declines. Figure 21.4 illustrates these points. Note that even at very high stock prices, the effect does not go to zero because there is still some residual bond component until the CB is actually converted to equity.

## Adding Dividends

Dividends may be added to the binomial tree using the approaches discussed in Chapter 12. One effect of dividends on valuation is that they increase the possibility of early exercise. It is well known that a call option on a non-dividend-paying stock should never be exercised early. Intuitively, without dividends, early exercise has no benefits but has costs since one is giving up the optionality and time-value components. A similar argument applies to convertibles also.

But with large dividends, the countervailing effect of dividends can outweigh the loss in insurance and time values, and early exercise can become optimal. It should be noted, however, that exercising to capture the dividends means giving up the coupons on the bond. Since dividends may be small relative to the coupons, this may not be an important consideration.

How do dividends affect the value of the CB? Dividends affect the warrant component of the convertible. The payment of dividends lowers the price of the stock, and, in the long run, lowers the rate of growth of the stock price. This reduces the value of CBs. In-the-money CBs suffer the most and out-of-the-money CBs the least from dividends. Figure 21.5 illustrates. The figure shows that as dividends increase, holding all else constant, the value of the CB falls for all levels of the stock price.

## The Call Feature

As we have noted, CBs are almost invariably callable by the issuer, typically at par, but the CB holder also has some protection from callability in the form of hard protection

**FIGURE 21.5**
CB and Dividends

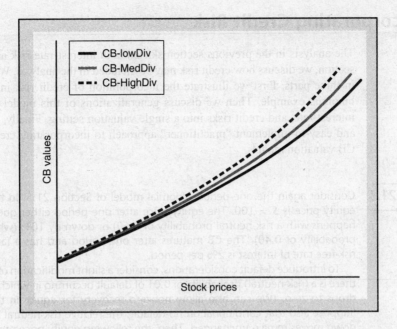

that forbids calling the bond during an initial period and/or soft protection in the form of requiring the stock price to be at a minimum premium to the conversion price.

Call considerations are easily incorporated in the lattice. First, we use the call-protection restrictions to identify the set of nodes where it is permissible to call the CB. Then, at each node where the calling is feasible, the bond is called if its value exceeds the call price. The payoff received by the CB holder at the node is then the maximum of the call price and parity at that node.

Callability reduces the potential life of the instrument. CBs trade at a premium to the market price of the share because of the warrant component. If there is a possibility that the CB could be called and this optionality extinguished, the premium will fall. So, callability reduces the value of the CB.

Which CBs suffer the most from callability? The effect of callability is minimal when the share price is very high or very low. In the former case, the intrinsic value of the option determines its value; optionality has little value since there is not much probability of the option moving out-of-the-money. In the latter case, optionality again has little value since the CB is trading near its bond floor. Therefore, the effect of callability is maximal when the CB is at- or near-the-money.

## The Put Feature

Convertibles often come with put features. The put option may be exercised at specified times at specified prices. Put considerations are simple to incorporate in the pricing lattice. At each node where the CB may be put, putting is optimal for the CB holder if the value of the CB is less than the put consideration.

The put option is particularly valuable when rising interest rates have pushed down bond prices. In general, the presence of the put will raise CB values because the investor can recover the put value even when the price of the CB drops. Out-of-the-money (OTM) convertibles will benefit the most, and in-the-money (ITM) the least from the presence of the put option.

# 21.6 Incorporating Credit Risk

The analysis in the previous section skirted both interest-rate risk and credit risk. In this section, we discuss how credit risk may be included in the analysis. We present the material in three parts. First we illustrate the incorporation of credit risk in a simple one-period binomial example. Then we discuss generalizations of this model that combine equity, interest-rate, and credit risks into a single valuation setting. Finally, we examine a simple and easy-to-implement "practitioner" approach to incorporating credit risk in tree-based CB valuation models.

**Example 21.3**

Consider again the one-period binomial model of Section 21.5. In this setting, the initial equity price is $S = 100$. The equity price after one period either goes up by 10% (which happens with a risk-neutral probability of 0.60) or down by 10% (which has a risk-neutral probability of 0.40). The CB matures after one period and has a face value of 100. The risk-free rate of interest is 2% per period.

To introduce default considerations, consider a slight modification of this setting. Suppose there is a (risk-neutral) probability of 0.01 of default occurring in which case the equity price drops to zero. (We can also allow nonzero recovery for equity in the event of default.) Suppose also that conditional on no-default, the relative risk-neutral likelihoods of up and down moves remain unchanged. Then, the following equity price process results:

$$\text{Equity price after one period} = \begin{cases} uS, & \text{with probability } 0.594 \\ dS, & \text{with probability } 0.396 \\ 0, & \text{with probability } 0.010 \end{cases}$$

Note that this is not a trinomial model of equity price evolution since the third branch leads to an "absorbing" state: once default occurs, no further moves in equity prices result. This is a simple example of a "jump-to-default" model in which default is represented by a jump to an absorbing state. The class of "reduced-form models" of credit risk, described later in the book, utilizes a general form of such a process.

Returning to our example, if default does not occur, the holder of the CB will convert to equity if the stock price moves up to 110, and will opt to receive the face value and forgo conversion if the stock price drops to 90. Suppose that in the event of default, CB holders recover 40% of the face value, which is a typical recovery amount on senior unsecured corporate claims in the US. This means the payoffs from the CB after one period are:

$$\text{Convertible values after one period} = \begin{cases} 110, & \text{with probability } 0.594 \\ 100, & \text{with probability } 0.396 \\ 40, & \text{with probability } 0.010 \end{cases}$$

A simple computation shows that the initial value of the CB is

$$\frac{1}{1.02} [(0.594)(110) + (0.396)(100) + (0.01)(40)] = 103.27$$

This value is lower by 0.65 (or by about 0.63%) than the 103.92 value of the CB when default was not considered. ∎

Generalizations of this simple model, both in discrete- and continuous-time settings, have been the focus of a number of papers. The next segment discusses some of these.

## Generalizations of the Jump-to-Default Binomial Model

Models combining equity processes with jump-to-default (and, in many cases, also interest-rate risk) have been developed in a number of papers. Samuelson (1972, 1973) are early examples. Later papers include Davis and Lischka (1999), Carayannopoulos and Kalimipalli (2003), Carr and Linetsky (2006), and Das and Sundaram (2007). The Samuelson papers look at the pricing of call options on defaultable equity, while Carr and Linetsky study the pricing of equity and credit derivatives in a single consistent setting. The remaining papers have as their objective the development of a framework for the pricing and hedging of hybrid securities such as convertibles that depend on multiple sources of risk.

We describe below the structure of the Das and Sundaram model. The model combines a constant elasticity of variance (CEV) process for equity and a Heath-Jarrow-Morton (HJM) process for interest rates with an "endogenous" jump-to-default specification in which default intensities may depend on equity and interest-rate values as well as other information. The other papers are variants of this setting:

- The off-default equity process in Samuelson, Davis and Lischka, and Carayannopoulos and Kalimipalli is geometric Brownian motion (GBM), a special case of the CEV model. Carr and Linetsky use the CEV model.

- Interest rates are nonstochastic in Samuelson, Caryannopoulos and Kalimipalli, and Carr and Linetsky. Davis and Lischka use the Vasicek (1977) model's Ornstein-Uhlenbeck process.

- The default intensity process in Samuelson is constant. The remaining papers all use an endogenous default intensity approach but with some differences. For example, Davis and Lischka take the intensity to be perfectly correlated with the equity process.

Finally, while Das and Sundaram develop and work with a discretized version of the underlying continuous-time model, the other papers work in the continuous-time setting directly.

## The Das and Sundaram (2007) Model

The Das and Sundaram model has the following characteristics:

### Equity Process

Until default occurs, equity prices in the model follow a constant elasticity of variance, or CEV, process. (After default, equity prices are absorbed at zero.) In continuous time, the evolution of the CEV process is described by

$$dS_t = \mu S \, dt + \sigma S^\gamma \, dW_t \qquad (21.1)$$

where $0 < \gamma \leq 1$. In the special case of $\gamma = 1$, the CEV process is just the lognormal process of Black-Scholes. The CEV process has the attractive feature that for $\gamma < 1$, it implies a negative relationship between equity prices and equity volatility; this relationship, which is called the "leverage effect," has been documented empirically and is a common feature of equity markets. (The leverage effect is not present in geometric Brownian motion.) A further attractive feature of the CEV specification is that for $\gamma < 1$, the process can also be absorbed at zero; this means that the Das-Sundaram model admits both "drift-to-default" and jump-to-default.

### Interest-Rate Process

Interest rates in the Das-Sundaram model are stochastic and follow a one-factor Heath-Jarrow-Morton process. The Heath-Jarrow-Morton framework is described in Chapter 30. Any other interest-rate process could be used in its stead, although the flexibility of the HJM process makes it a natural choice.

### Default Process

In general, one could take default to be a third stochastic process in the model, but this makes the model quite complex in implementation. Das and Sundaram instead use an "endogenous default" approach. They take the instantaneous probability of jump-to-default $\lambda_t$ at each node on the tree to be a function of the available information at that point, including stock prices $S_t$ and interest rates $r_t$ at that node. More precisely, $\lambda_t = 1 - \exp\{-\xi_t h\}$, where $h$ is the length of one period in the binomial tree (in years), and

$$\xi_t = \exp\{a_0 + a_1\, t + a_2\, r_t\} S_t^{-a_3}$$

Assuming $a_3 > 0$, the jump-to-default likelihood under this specification is inversely related to the level of stock prices (and so, is positively related to equity volatility). In particular, as is easily checked, the likelihood of default goes to 1 as $S_t \to 0$, and to zero as $S_t \to \infty$.

Nelson and Ramaswamy (1990) show how to discretize the CEV process on a recombining binomial tree. Das and Sundaram expand on their approach and create a recombining lattice that incorporates the CEV process and the interest-rate process with arbitrary correlation between the two processes. This lattice is then calibrated to information from equity, interest-rate, and credit default swap markets. In Appendix 21B, we describe Octave code for a simplified version of their model in which (a) interest rates are constant, (b) the stock price follows a geometric Brownian motion, and (c) the jump-to-default probability is constant at each node.

Das and Sundaram show that the effect of increasing credit risk on convertible bonds can be quite subtle. An increase in credit risk affects both the bond and warrant components of a convertible, and in the case of callable-convertible bonds (convertibles which are also callable), it also affects the call component. The ultimate impact on convertible value depends on the net effect over the three components. For instance, Das and Sundaram show that, depending on the situation, an increase in default risk may narrow or widen the price difference between callable-convertibles and noncallable, non-convertible bonds.

## A Practitioner Approach Using Blended Discount Rates

Straight bonds issued by a company trade at a spread to the risk-free rate. The spread is meant to compensate investors for the credit risk present in the bond. The higher the default risk of the company, the higher, ceteris paribus, is the size of the spread. A simple practitioner approach to incorporating credit risk into CB valuation models, but without explicitly modeling the default event as part of the tree, uses the credit spread on straight bonds in the valuation process. We discuss the approach below after first motivating its theoretical basis.

Fix a tree of equity price evolution (without default considerations) and the corresponding risk-neutral probabilities. Let $s$ denote the size of the credit spread on a company's straight bonds. By definition, this means that the current market price of the straight bond results when the bond's promised cash flows are discounted back at the risk-free rate plus $s$. Now consider pricing this bond using risk-neutral pricing on the tree. Since the tree does not include default, the bond returns its promised face value at maturity with probability one. And since standard risk-neutral pricing discounts promised cash flows at the risk-free rate, the resulting "price" of the bond will be that of a default-risk-free bond with zero spread. That is, standard risk-neutral pricing methods employed on a tree that does not incorporate default will overvalue defaultable bonds.

One way to handle this problem is to incorporate default into the tree as we did in the binomial model with jump-to-default. An alternative way is to discount the promised cash flows in the tree not at the risk-free rate but at the risk-free rate plus the spread $s$. This way, we are guaranteed that the value of the straight bond obtained from the tree will be its market price. A framework developed by Duffie and Singleton (1999a) formalizes and validates a general version of this approach. The precise details of the Duffie-Singleton theory are presented in Chapter 33, but, roughly speaking, the authors show that risk-neutral pricing arguments can be applied to defaultable claims also provided the claim's promised payoffs are discounted at a rate that depends on the credit-risk characteristics *of that claim*. A security that is free from default is simply discounted at the risk-free rate, while one that is subject to default is discounted at a rate that takes into account the likelihood of default and the loss-given-default.

An informal practitioner approach to valuing convertible bonds (that predates Duffie and Singleton) bases itself on a similar line of reasoning. Here is the argument. When a CB is far out-of-the-money, it resembles a straight bond issued by the company, so its value at such nodes on the tree should be obtained by discounting its future cash flows at the risk-free rate plus $s$. On the other hand, as a CB moves deep into-the-money and resembles straight equity, its value on the tree should be obtained by discounting at the risk-free rate. Now, in general, a CB is part bond and part equity, so it appears that the "correct" rate of discount to employ at each point in the tree should be a blend of the risk-free rate and the risk-free rate plus the spread, where the blend depends on how much like a bond or equity the CB looks *at that node*. This approach is described in Bardhan, Berger, Derman, Dosembet, and Kani (1994).

Central to the implementation of this idea is the choice of weights to use in the blend of discount factors. The CB delta is commonly used for this purpose, that is, the discount rate used at a node is

$$\Delta \cdot r + (1 - \Delta) \cdot (r + s) \qquad\qquad \textbf{(21.2)}$$

where $r$ denotes the risk-free rate. When the CB is deep in-the-money, its $\Delta$ is close to 1, so the discount rate is close to the risk-free rate as required. When the CB is deep out-of-the-money, its $\Delta$ is close to zero, so the discount rate is close to the risk-free rate plus $s$, again as required. Such simple blended-discount factor models are easy to implement in a tree structure. In Appendix 21A, we provide an implementation in `Octave` of a callable-convertible pricing program with credit spreads.

Unfortunately, while easy to implement, the theoretical foundations of the blended discount approach (e.g., of the form (21.2)) are unsound. Under the Duffie-Singleton theory, the correct rate of discount to employ at a node depends on the credit risk characteristics of the CB viewed from that node. It will rarely be the case that this discount rate will be a simple blend (weighted by the CB delta or some other similar characteristic) of the risk-free rate and the risk-free rate plus the spread on straight bonds. And the use of the wrong discount factor results in prices that are not arbitrage-free.

As an illustration, it is instructive to compare the prices for convertibles that result from this blended discount rates model for otherwise identical parameters. In Appendix 21A, we describe the output from the blended discount rates model for a specific choice of parameters. The output obtained is:

```
cb_credit(100,0.3,0.03,6,100,0.03,5,20)
ans = 106.71
```

Using a recovery rate of 50% and otherwise the same parameters, we obtain the following output value in the simplified Das-Sundaram model (see Appendix 21B):

```
cb_dassundaram(100,0.3,0.03,6,100,0.03,5,0.5,20)
ans = 102.25
```

which is a substantially different price. Two other aspects of the blended discount factor are worth noting:

1. The model does not explicitly specify the recovery rates on default since it works through the spreads directly.
2. The blended discount rate assumes that the credit spread is fixed at all levels of the stock price in these models. Of course, the total discount rate reflects default risk levels through the moneyness of the warrant component of the convertible, but it is likely that the spread itself is increasing when the stock price falls.

A popular and widely-used variant of the blended discount factor approach was developed by Tsiveriotis and Fernandes (1998). They regard the convertible as composed of two securities, a "warrant component" entitled to the equity on conversion and a "cash-only component" entitled to the bond-based cash flows (coupons, subject to the call feature in the event of an issuer call). Since both components are dependent on the value of equity, the model is solved using the same fundamental partial differential equation (pde) approach underlying the Black-Scholes model, as explained in Chapter 15. There are now two linked pdes, one for each of the components of the convertible bond. Three sets of boundary conditions apply: (a) for the values of both components at maturity, (b) for the values of both components when the stock price becomes very high ("goes to infinity"), and (c) for the values of both components when the stock price goes to zero. The pde for the cash-only component uses a discount rate that equals the risk-free rate $r$ plus the credit spread $s$, and the equity component uses the risk-free rate $r$. Therefore, by splitting the pricing pde of the convertible bond into two component pdes with different discount rates, an implicit blended rate is implemented.

The attractive feature of the Tsiveriotis and Fernandes (1998) model, compared to blended discount models such as (21.2), is that the blend is determined by the boundary conditions to both the component pdes. The model may be implemented on binomial or trinomial trees, or by direct numerical solution of the pdes. The model assumes constant interest rates and credit spreads; some later versions have sought to relax these restrictions. We note here that making interest rates stochastic in convertible bond pricing models is easier in the alternative class of jump-to-default models such as those by Davis and Lischka (1999) and Das and Sundaram (2007).

## 21.7   Convertible Greeks

The convertible greeks are sensivity measures that seek to quantify the impact of a change in a relevant parameter on CB values. There are five basic convertible greeks:

- The delta, denoted $\Delta$, which measures sensitivity of CB prices to changes in the price of the issuer's equity.
- The gamma, denoted, $\Gamma$, which measures the sensitivity of the delta to changes in the underlying equity price.
- The theta, denoted $\Theta$, which measures the impact of the passage of time on CB values.
- The vega, denoted $\mathcal{V}$, which measures the sensitivity of CB values to changes in the volatility of the issuer's equity.
- The rho, denoted $\rho$, which measures the sensitivity of CB values to changes in interest rates.

Some of these greeks (like the vega) are similar in behavior to the greeks of equity call options since they work primarily through the warrant component of the CB. Others, like the theta, exhibit very different behavior since the underlying parameter affects both the bond and warrant components. In addition to these, other greeks can also be defined with respect to the many other parameters that affect CB values such as the volatility of interest rates and credit-risk-related measures. Two of these—the CB omicron and the CB upsilon—are at the end of this section.

## The Convertible Delta

The (equity) *delta* of a CB measures the sensitivity of CB values to changes in the price of the underlying equity. In calculus terms, the CB delta is the slope of the CB price function in Figure 21.2:

$$\Delta = \frac{\partial CB}{\partial S}$$

More informally, the CB delta may be thought of as the change in CB values per \$1 change in $S$. That is, if the stock price changes by an amount $dS$ (i.e., it changes from $S$ to $S+dS$), then the estimated change in CB values, based on the delta, is

$$\Delta \cdot dS \qquad\qquad\qquad\qquad (21.3)$$

Put differently, a position that is long the CB and short delta units of the underlying equity is "neutral" to equity risk. Of course, such delta hedging is only approximate. CB values have curvature as shown in Figure 21.2, and, as we saw in Chapter 17, this means that even after delta-hedging with the stock, the position has residual gamma risk. Such gamma risk is largest near-the-money since curvature is maximal in this area.

In terms of its properties, the CB delta is similar to the behavior of equity call option deltas as described in Chapters 11 and 17. It is positive, lies between 0 and 1, and increases as the equity price increases. Figure 21.6 illustrates.

For exotic convertibles, the behavior of the delta could be much more complex than this. In the case of reset convertibles, for example, as the stock price falls and reaches a trigger point, the conversion ratio increases. The initial part of the stock price decline will

**FIGURE 21.6**
The CB Delta

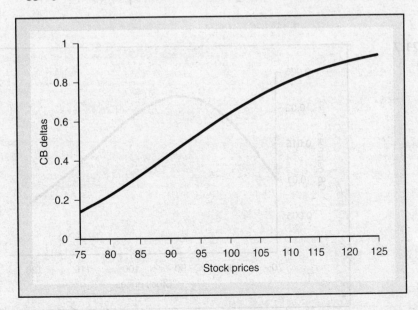

**FIGURE 21.6**
The CB Delta

be accompanied by a falling delta, but as the stock price approaches the trigger point, the likelihood of the increased conversion ratio kicking in will result in the delta increasing. Thus, the gamma of reset convertibles will have both positive and negative segments.

## The Convertible Gamma

The CB gamma measures the change in the CB delta for a given change in $S$. In calculus terms, gamma is the derivative of delta with respect to $S$:

$$\Gamma = \frac{\partial \Delta}{\partial S}$$

More informally, gamma may be thought of as a ratio:

$$\Gamma = \text{Change in CB Delta per \$1 change in } S$$

Since delta itself measures the slope of the CB pricing function, gamma measures the change in the slope, i.e., it measures the *curvature* of the CB pricing function:

$$\Gamma = \frac{\partial^2 CB}{\partial S^2}$$

As Figure 21.6 shows, the delta of a CB increases as $S$ increases. Therefore, the gamma of a CB is *positive*. In mathematical terms, CB prices are *convex* in $S$. As with equity calls, the gamma is least when the CB is deep OTM or deep ITM (there is little curvature in the CB pricing function in either case) and is highest for balanced CBs. Figure 21.7 illustrates.

The CB gamma can be used both as a curvature correction and to estimate the impact on delta of a change in $S$. If the equity price changes by $S$, a better estimate than (21.3) of the change in CB values is:

$$\Delta \cdot dS + \frac{1}{2} \Gamma (dS)^2$$

The change $dS$ also causes a change in the CB delta of roughly

$$\Gamma \cdot dS$$

**FIGURE 21.7**
CB Gamma

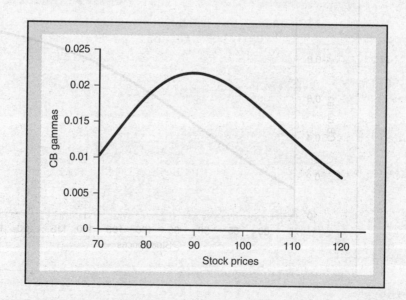

For example, suppose that the price of a CB is 101.50, its delta is 0.55, and its gamma is 0.06. Then a change of $dS = -0.80$ in the stock price causes a change of roughly

$$(0.55)(-0.80) + \frac{1}{2}(0.06)(-0.80)^2 = -0.44 + 0.0192 \approx -0.42$$

in the CB price, and a change of roughly

$$(0.06)(-0.80) = -0.048$$

in the CB delta. That is, the new CB price is approximately 101.08, and the new CB delta is approximately 0.502.

## The Convertible Theta

Most CBs are finitely lived. Thus, the remaining time to maturity plays a major role in determining CB values. The CB theta measures the impact of the passage of time on CB values. In calculus terms, the theta is the derivative of the CB value with respect to the current time $t$:

$$\Theta = \frac{\partial CB}{\partial t}$$

More informally, theta may be thought of as a ratio:

$$\Theta = \text{Change in CB Value for a one-day reduction in time to maturity}$$

Time affects the CB value in two ways. On the one hand, the warrant component—which is akin to a call—loses value as the maturity date draws closer. On the other hand, the bond component may accrete in value as the maturity date nears (think, for example, of a zero-coupon structure), so the bond component may have a positive theta. Whether the overall theta is positive or negative depends on which of these effects dominates. When the CB is out-of-the-money, the bond component dominates, so the theta may be positive. When the CB is in-the-money, the warrant component dominates, and the theta will be negative. Figure 21.8 graphs the behavior of the CB theta.

Note the contrast with equity call option thetas here. Unlike the CB theta, the call theta is always negative; it is maximally negative near-the-money and tails away in either direction away-from-the-money.

**FIGURE 21.8**
CB Theta

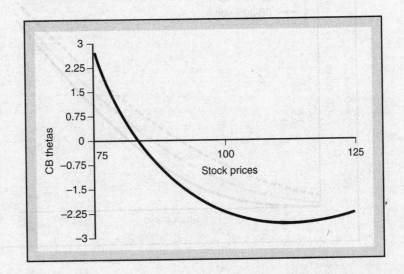

## The Convertible Vega

Equity volatility is a primary determinant of the CB value, operating mainly through the warrant component of the CB. The CB *vega* measures the effect of a change in equity volatility on CB prices.

We denote the vega of a CB by $\mathcal{V}$. In calculus terms, the vega is defined by:

$$\mathcal{V} = \frac{\partial CB}{\partial \sigma}$$

More informally, vega may be thought of as a ratio:

$$\mathcal{V} = \text{Change in CB Value for a 1\% change in volatility}$$

(The 1% change in the above definition is an absolute change, i.e., a change in volatility from (say) 23% to 24%. It is not a relative 1% change in volatility from 23% to 23.23%.)

The vega of a CB is generally positive. An increase in equity volatility increases the value of the warrant component of the CB, and this increases CB value. Figure 21.9 plots CB prices for three values of volatility: 10%, 15%, and 20%. Intuitively, higher volatility means both higher and lower equity prices. The higher equity prices are good news for the CB holder, but the lower prices are not correspondingly bad news because of the bond floor.

As the figure also illustrates, deep in-the-money (ITM) and out-of-the-money (OTM) convertibles are not as affected by volatility increases as "balanced" convertibles, i.e., those that are at- or near-the-money. For deep ITM convertibles, exercise is almost sure, so optionality is unimportant and the effect of volatility is minimal. Deep OTM convertibles are like the bond floor; there is a low probability of finishing in-the-money, and while the increased volatility may improve these prospects, in dollar terms the effect remains small. It is for balanced convertibles that optionality and volatility are most important.

Thus, the depth in-the-money is a determinant of the CB vega. The vega is small for deep ITM and deep OTM convertibles and maximal for balanced convertibles. Figure 21.10 illustrates.

**FIGURE 21.9**
CB Values and Volatility

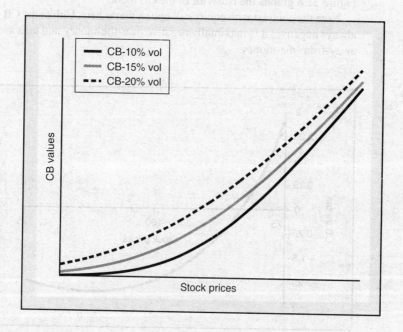

**FIGURE 21.10**
CB Vega

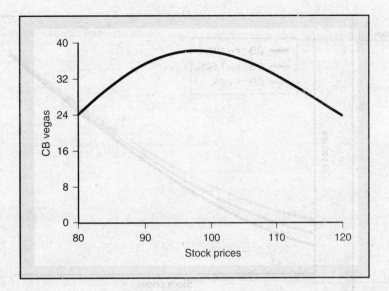

Finally, a caveat. Increased equity volatility may be associated with or arise on account of increased credit risk of the issuing company. In this case, the increased volatility is not necessarily beneficial. The increased credit risk lowers the bond floor of the CB and so could lower CB values. Thus, the effects of increased volatility could be much more complex than captured in Figure 21.9.

## The Convertible Rho

CB values are affected by interest rates in two ways: through the bond component and through the warrant component. The CB *rho* measures the sensitivity of CB prices to changes in interest rates. In calculus terms, the rho is defined by

$$\rho = \frac{\partial CB}{\partial r}$$

More informally, rho may be thought of as a ratio:

$$\rho = 100 \times \text{Change in CB Value for a 100 bps increase in } r$$

Interest rates affect both the bond and warrant components of the convertible. The bond component always reacts negatively to interest rates, declining as interest rates increase. The warrant component reacts like equity call options, increasing with interest rates; intuitively, the present value of the bond being given up on exercise is lower as interest rates increase. Thus, the net effect on the convertible depends on which of these effects is larger. In general, the bond component will dominate the warrant component (for the bond, interest rates are a first-order and primary determinant of values), so the overall effect of an interest-rate increase on the CB is likely to be negative. That is, the rho of a CB is generally negative.

Which CBs (in terms of moneyness) are likely to be most affected? The bond component is most important for deep OTM convertibles, so this is where the effect is likely to be maximal. As the convertible moves towards becoming balanced and then deep ITM, the bond component plays an increasingly smaller role and the warrant component an increasingly larger one. Thus, the overall effect on CB prices should become smaller.

Figure 21.11 illustrates the effect of changing interest rates on CB values. As the intuitive argument suggests, convertibles drop in value when interest rates increase, and the effect is most for deep OTM convertibles.

**FIGURE 21.11**
CB and Interest Rates

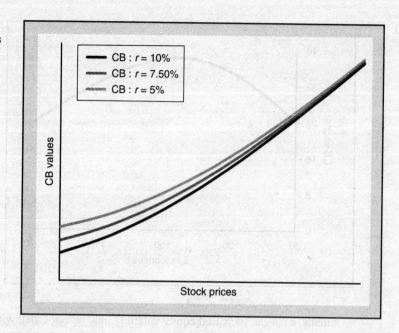

**FIGURE 21.12**
CB Rho

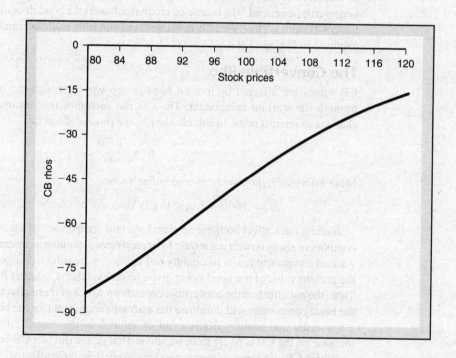

Expressing all of this in terms of the rho, the rho of a CB is generally negative. It is most negative for deep OTM CBs, less negative for balanced CBs, and least negative for ITM CBs. This behavior of the rho is illustrated in Figure 21.12.

Finally, it must once again be noted that the effect of interest rates can be more subtle than described here. For one thing, we have ignored any possible correlation between interest-rate changes and changes in the underlying firm value or equity prices. It may also be the case that an increase in interest rates affects the present value of the firm's debt and so affects its default likelihood. While Figure 21.11 is indicative, it should not be taken as definitive.

## Credit-Risk-Related CB Greeks

The handling of credit risk raises the issue of sensitivity of the convertible bond to various default risk inputs. Two measures of default risk are the credit spread $s$ and the recovery rate $\phi$. Sensitivities with respect to these are denoted omicron ($o$) and upsilon ($\upsilon$), respectively, in the convertible markets.

### The CB Omicron

The CB $o$ measures the sensitivity of CB prices to changes in credit spreads. In calculus terms, the omicron is defined by

$$o = \frac{\partial CB}{\partial s}$$

More informally, omicron may be thought of as a ratio:

$$o = 100 \times \text{Change in CB Value for a 1\% Increase in Spreads}$$

The bond component of a CB typically dominates the option component insofar as the effect of spreads is concerned. The bond component falls in value as spreads increase. Therefore, CB values will typically fall in value as spreads increase, i.e., $o < 0$. The CBs that are most affected are OTM CBs, which are most like the bond floor. Balanced CBs are less affected, and ITM CBs are least sensitive to changes in credit spreads.

There is another way to understand why ITM CBs have low omicron. Spreads are a function of default probabilities $\lambda$ and recovery rates $\phi$. Logically, if the stock price is high (i.e., the CB is ITM), then the corresponding default probability must be low and spreads will be low as well. Given that there is low default risk, the sensitivity of the CB to spreads will be low.

Quantitatively, the omicron of a CB has the same interpretation as the other greeks. If the omicron of a CB is $o$ and spreads change by an amount $\epsilon$, the omicron-based estimate of the change in CB value is $o \cdot \epsilon$. For example, suppose we are given that the current price of a CB is 102.25 and that the omicron of the CB is $-15$. If spreads increase by 100 basis points ($\epsilon = +0.01$), then the estimated change in CB value is $(-15)(0.01) = -0.15$. Thus, the predicted new CB price is $102.25 - 0.15 = 102.10$.

### CB Upsilon

The CB upsilon ($\upsilon$) measures the sensitivity of CB prices to changes in recovery rates ($\phi$). In calculus terms, the upsilon is defined by

$$\upsilon = \frac{\partial CB}{\partial \phi}$$

The upsilon is very low unless the convertible is distressed, in which case it becomes very relevant. Small changes in anticipated recovery rates can change the value of the CB substantially. After the convertible has defaulted, the upsilon approaches unity, i.e., $\upsilon \to 1$.

The reader can see very easily also that $\upsilon > 0$; as expected recovery rates rise, so will the price of the CB. This is a direct effect when the convertible is distressed, but it also operates indirectly through the equity price when the convertible is far from default. Finally, it is easily seen that as the stock price increases and default is remote, $\upsilon$ becomes very small.

## 21.8   Convertible Arbitrage

*Convertible arbitrage* is a strategy which aims to unlock "cheap" volatility in a convertible bond. The starting point of most convertible arbitrage strategies is the identification of convertibles in which the convert option is considered undervalued by the convertible arbitrageur. The arbitrageur then buys the convertible bond and goes short $\Delta$ units of the underlying stock.

There are three key characteristics to the convertible arbitrageur's position. First, the short equity position provides immunity to the convertible against small price moves in the underlying equity (similar to a delta-hedged call option position). Second, there is "gamma capture": since the convertible has positive gamma, going long the convertible and delta-hedging with equity leaves the arbitrageur with net positive curvature with all the attendant advantages of such a position. Finally, since the coupon on the convertible will typically comfortably exceed the dividends due on the short equity position, the overall position involves positive "carry," i.e., it generates net cash inflows to the holder.

It should be noted that strategies of this form eliminate only the directional equity risk in a convertible bond. Since convertibles are affected by a host of other factors, there remain many other risks in the position which must be monitored and managed. Interest-rate risk is one. An increase in interest rates will lower the value of the convertible (through the bond component) while having a smaller effect on the equity position. Thus, the position is vulnerable to a sharp upward move in interest rates. Call risk is another. Most convertibles are also callable by the issuer and the exercise of the call provision extinguishes the convert option whose putative underpricing motivated the strategy in the first place. Credit risk is a third. The vast majority of convertibles in the US are sub-investment-grade issues or are unrated. If there is a sudden credit event (e.g., a jump-to-default), the convertible will lose value. Of course, equity prices will also crash in this situation, so, depending on the hedge ratio employed, this may be partially, or even fully, made up on the short equity position. In recent years, it has become popular to use credit-default swaps to hedge out credit risk that remains uncovered by the equity position. Then, there is liquidity risk; for instance, equity market liquidity is essential to delta-hedge the convertible. Finally, there is model risk. Convertibles are complex instruments with values affected by many factors. To the extent that the models may be unreliable or may not be able to take all relevant factors into account, perceived arbitrages may not exist or incorrect hedge ratios may be employed.

Less conventionally, convertible arbitrage also takes on the opposite form to the strategy described above: that is, convertible arbitrageurs short convertibles they find overvalued and delta-hedge the position by going long the underlying equity. Called a "reverse hedge," this is a negative carry strategy since the cash outflows required on the shorted convertible will typically exceed the dividends received on the long equity position. It is also a short gamma position, though the short bond component of the convertible position mitigates this to some extent. (As we explain in Chapter 32 in discussing "structural" credit-risk models, an increase in the volatility of a firm's assets hurts bondholders and benefits equity holders. Thus, a short position in a firm's bonds is a long position in the firm's asset volatility.) Reverse hedges are usually short-term positions employed by hedge funds and other market participants when temporary demand or volatility factors make convertibles appear overpriced.

## 21.9   Summary

Convertible bonds are among the most important of all hybrid instruments. They combine features of debt and equity, and are attractive to both issuers and investors for a variety of reasons. From a pricing standpoint, they are very complex to model because they depend on all possible factors that could affect equity and debt values: equity risk (equity volatility, dividends), interest-rate risk (changes in the risk-free interest rate, interest-rate volatility, coupon rates), and credit risk (risk of default, recovery in the event of default), in addition to liquidity risk and other market factors.

This chapter has undertaken an introduction to the modeling of convertibles. The presentation was intentionally gentle: while we have discussed how to incorporate features of equity risk and credit risk in the valuation exercise, the inclusion of interest-rate risk was not discussed in any level of detail. For a more comprehensive treatment of the modeling process and a deeper understanding of the effect of various factors on convertible values, we refer the reader to the technical papers in this area, many of which have been cited earlier in this chapter.

## 21.10 Exercises

1. Define and quantify the following terms related to convertible bonds: (a) *conversion ratio,* (b) *callability,* (c) *fair premium,* (d) *parity,* (e) *breakeven,* and (f) *dilution.*

2. You are given the following input information:

| | |
|---|---|
| Face value of the CB | $100 |
| Issue price of the CB | $120 |
| Equity price | $ 10 |
| Conversion ratio | 11 |

   (a) What is the parity value per bond?
   (b) What is the premium over parity per bond?
   (c) Express the same results on a per-share basis.

3. In the previous question, you computed the value of parity and premium over parity. Suppose the coupon rate on the convertible was 5% and the dividend yield on the equity is 1%. What is the extra income from the convertible relative to equity? What is the breakeven for the convertible?

4. What are the different types of embedded options within a convertible bond? Explain whether they benefit the investor or the issuer.

5. What incentive issue has been commonly resolved by the issuance of a convertible bond by the management of a firm?

6. The face value of a convertible bond is $100, and the issue price is $150, with a conversion ratio of 5. The market price of the equity shares is $25. Compute the (a) conversion price, (b) parity, and (c) premium of the bond.

7. XYZ Co. has issued convertibles with face value $100, and the issue price is $100. The market price per share is $20 and the conversion ratio is 4. The bond pays a coupon of 5%, and the dividend rate on equity is 1%. What is the premium on the bond? What is the breakeven period to recover the premium?

8. Assume the current stock price is $100. Next period it can take a value of either 120 or 80. If the return on $1 invested today for one period is 3%, then how much will a zero-coupon convertible bond be worth today if the conversion ratio is 1?

9. (Convertible Arbitrage) Assume the current stock price is $100. Next period it can take a value of either 130 or 90. If the return on $1 invested today for one period is 5%, then how much will a 6% coupon convertible bond be worth today if the conversion ratio is 1? Can you construct an arbitrage in this situation that delivers risk-free profit if the CB is trading at $105?

10. Assume the current stock price is $100. Next period it can take a value of either 1.2 or 0.8 times the stock price. If the return on $1 invested today for one period is 2%, then how much will a zero-coupon convertible bond (face value $1000) be worth today if the conversion ratio is 10? What are the parity value and premium on this bond? Compute the (a) price, (b) parity, and (c) premium for the bond at the following levels of the stock price: 80, 90, 100, 110, and 120.

11. Using a semiannual CRR binomial tree, price a convertible bond with a face value of $100, conversion ratio of 1, and a coupon rate of 10%. The maturity of the bond is three years. Assume that the stock volatility is 25%. The risk-free rate of interest is 4%. All calculations may be based on continuous compounding.

12. In the preceding question, assume that the convertible bond is also callable at a price of $110 (cum-coupon). Rework the price of the convertible bond. Explain your answer.

13. Using the program you wrote for the callable-convertible bond, modify it to compute the delta of the bond for a range of stock prices from 80 to 120. Let the coupon rate be 10%, the risk free rate be 4%, and the volatility 25%. The call strike is $100. Explain your results.

14. (Advanced Question; Goes beyond Text) Think of five trading strategies that you may wish to implement using convertible bonds. For each of these ideas, what risks would you need to eliminate from the bonds in order to implement your trading views?

15. The current equity price of firm XYZ is $10. The equity trades at a volatility of 20%. The firm issues a five-year convertible bond at a face value of $100 and a coupon of 6%. This bond may be converted into eight shares of equity at any time in the next five years. The risk-free interest rate in the market is 3%. The bond may also be called after two years at a call price of $105. Build a 20-period model to value this convertible bond, assuming that the equity price follows a binomial process. Make sure you account correctly for call and conversion features. Given the price, what is the premium on the bond? Also calculate the breakeven.

16. A convertible bond is sensitive to both stock price movements and interest-rate changes. Which of the following scenarios is likely to result in the greatest price increase of a convertible?

    (a) Stock price rises; interest rates fall.

    (b) Stock price rises; interest rates rise.

    (c) Stock price falls; interest rates fall.

    (d) Stock price falls; interest rates rise.

    If you think your answer must be qualified, add the necessary qualifications.

17. Which of the following scenarios is most likely to result in the greatest increase in the price of a convertible bond?

    (a) Stock volatility increases; interest-rate volatility increases.

    (b) Stock volatility increases; interest-rate volatility declines.

    (c) Stock volatility declines; interest-rate volatility increases.

    (d) Stock volatility declines; interest-rate volatility declines.

18. What is the expected impact of an increase in maturity on convertible bond values, holding all other conditions the same?

## Appendix 21A

# Octave **Code for the Blended Discount Rate Valuation Tree**

This appendix presents the Octave code for the blended discount rate "practitioner model" described in Section 21.6.

```
%Function to build a CRR tree and price a callable convertible bond.
%Specialized to handle credit spreads
%Specify the call strike cum-coupon
%Note that rf below is also the drift of the stock.

function cbval = cb_credit(s0,sig,rf,cpnpa,callstr,spread,T,n);
h = T/n;
u = exp(sig*sqrt(h)); d = 1/u; R = exp(rf*h);
q = (R-d)/(u-d);

stktree = zeros(n+1,n+1);
stktree(1,1) = s0;
for i=2:n+1;
        stktree(1,i) = stktree(1,i-1)*u;
        for j=2:i;
                stktree(j,i) = stktree(j-1,i-1)*d;
        end;
end;

cb = zeros(n+1,n+1);
cbdelta = zeros(n,n);
for j=1:n+1;
        cb(j,n+1) = max(stktree(j,n+1),100+cpnpa*h);
end;

for i=[n:-1:2];
        for j=1:i;
                cbdelta(j,i) =  (cb(j,i+1) - cb(j+1,i+1))/ ...
                                (stktree(j,i+1) - stktree(j+1,i+1));
                discrate = cbdelta(j,i)*rf + (1-cbdelta(j,i))*(rf+spread);
                R = exp(discrate*h);
                cb(j,i) = (q*cb(j,i+1) + (1-q)*cb(j+1,i+1))/R+cpnpa*h;
                if cb(j,i)>callstr;
                        cb(j,i) = max(callstr,stktree(j,i));
                else;
                        cb(j,i) = max(cb(j,i),stktree(j,i));
                end;
        end;
end;
i=1; j=1;
cbdelta(j,i) =  (cb(j,i+1) - cb(j+1,i+1))/(stktree(j,i+1) - stktree(j+1,i+1));
```

```
discrate = cbdelta(j,i)*rf + (1-cbdelta(j,i))*(rf+spread);
R = exp(discrate*h);
cb(j,i) = (q*cb(j,i+1) + (1-q)*cb(j+1,i+1))/R;
cbval = cb(1,1);
```

For a simple example of using this function, we price a five-year 6% convertible bond, where the initial stock price is $100, the equity volatility is 30% per annum, risk-free rate of interest is 3%, the credit spread on the bond is 3%, the call strike is $100. We assume the CB has a five-year maturity and we set the number of periods in the tree to be 20. The program run is as follows:

```
cb_credit(100,0.3,0.03,6,100,0.03,5,20)
ans = 106.71
```

## Octave Code for the Simplified Das-Sundaram Model

This appendix describes Octave code for implementation of the simplified Das-Sundaram model described in Section 21.6. The off-default stock price is taken to follow a geometric Brownian motion, and recovery is specified according to the recovery of market value (RMV)—see Chapter 33—convention.

```
%Function to build a CRR tree and price a callable convertible bond.
%This is the Das-Sundaram model
%Specify the call strike cum-coupon
%Note that rf below is the drift of the stock.

function cbval = cb_dassundaram(s0,sig,rf,cpnpa,callstr,spread,phi,T,n);
h = T/n;
lambda = spread/(1-phi);
u = exp(sig*sqrt(h)); d = 1/u; R = exp(rf*h);
q = (R/(1-lambda*h)-d)/(u-d);

stktree = zeros(n+1,n+1);
stktree(1,1) = s0;
for i=2:n+1;
        stktree(1,i) = stktree(1,i-1)*u;
        for j=2:i;
                stktree(j,i) = stktree(j-1,i-1)*d;
        end;
end;

cb = zeros(n+1,n+1);
cbdelta = zeros(n,n);
for j=1:n+1;
        cb(j,n+1) = max(stktree(j,n+1),100+cpnpa*h);
end;
```

```
for i=[n:-1:2];
        for j=1:i;
                cbdelta(j,i) =  (cb(j,i+1) - cb(j+1,i+1))/ ...
                                (stktree(j,i+1) - stktree(j+1,i+1));
                cb(j,i) = (q*cb(j,i+1) + (1-q)*cb(j+1,i+1))/R+cpnpa*h;
                if cb(j,i)>callstr;
                        cb(j,i) = max(callstr,stktree(j,i));
                else;
                        cb(j,i) = max(cb(j,i),stktree(j,i));
                end;
                cb(j,i) = cb(j,i)*(1-lambda*h*(1-phi));  %Accounts for default
        end;
end;
i=1; j=1;
cbdelta(j,i) =  (cb(j,i+1) - cb(j+1,i+1))/(stktree(j,i+1) - stktree(j+1,i+1));
cb(j,i) = (q*cb(j,i+1) + (1-q)*cb(j+1,i+1))/R;
cbval = cb(1,1);
```

# Chapter 22

# Real Options

## 22.1 Introduction

The term "real option" is used to connote the value of optionality embedded within an investment project. Real options are distinguished from "financial options," which are options present or embedded in financial instruments and which have concerned us so far in the book. Real options arise on account of choices that need to be made at specified times during the life of an investment project and that affect the nature of cash flows from the project. The availability of these choices confers additional value on the project and needs to be taken explicitly into account in valuing the project.

Real options arise naturally in almost all investment settings. Here is a simple example. Suppose a firm is planning to invest in developing a new technology, the superwidget, and plans to be the pioneer in the field. The entrepreneur has done all the required homework and has a detailed business plan with the costs and production details of the project. Unfortunately, the value of the technology is uncertain and will be determined only later by market forces. The entrepreneur makes an estimate of the mean price per superwidget after two years, the time when the product is anticipated to roll out. He is also able to make a good guess at the distribution of possible prices as well as the future evolution of this price. These prices represent the major source of risk in the project: if they end up at the lower end of the range, then the firm will fail to be profitable. By running various plausible scenarios, the entrepreneur calculates the probability of each scenario as well as the profitability under each one.

In a "standard" discounted cash-flow (DCF) valuation setting, the entrepreneur would choose an appropriate risk-adjusted discount rate for the cash flows of the project. This is often a tricky exercise requiring considerable subjective judgment. Then, using the probability and profitability scenarios to determine the expected cash flow, the entrepreneur determines a present value of the project.

The real options approach views the valuation problem from a different angle. It involves the explicit consideration of project choices that may influence the scenarios that may evolve. In so doing, it transforms the valuation exercise from an essentially *static* one to one that is *dynamic*.

For instance, here is a basic question the entrepreneur will have to confront: should the superwidget project get under way right now, or is there some value in waiting to learn more information about the final selling price of the product? If by waiting six months, the entrepreneur would get a clearer picture of the value of the new technology, then the option of "waiting to invest" (one of the most common forms of real options) has value that must be taken into account. Of course, procrastination may be risky too since it may result in the entrepreneur getting "scooped" by a rival, and this possibility too needs to be taken into account. Other real options facing the entrepreneur may include the option to abandon (that of shutting down the project if it proves non-viable down the road) and the option to expand (that of increasing project scale should it be profitable) among many others. As these examples suggest, real options valuation is project valuation enhanced by a consideration of the value of *path-dependent* choices that need to be handled in an optimal manner.

To be sure, much of this is easier said than done. The option valuation models we have considered so far in the book have assumed that the underlying drivers of option value are traded in a liquid market, thereby allowing for valuation by replication. For financial options, particularly in developed financial markets, such an assumption is fine. But in investment projects, it is often invalid. The absence of a properly observable underlying value process is often the biggest difference between real and financial options. It makes the calibration of project uncertainty and/or the identification of risk-neutral probabilities hard. Later in this chapter, we discuss a possible approach to working through these issues. But for the moment, these are caveats that must be kept in mind when going through the analysis.[1]

## Types of Real Options

There are many kinds of real options. Categories of particular interest include the following:

**Waiting to Invest**  Often as important as finding a good investment is the timing of the investment decision. The option to wait before investing reduces timing risk since more information usually becomes available as one waits. However, it may also create new risks—the investment cost might increase, and new competition may materialize. The trade-off of these risks determines the value of this real option.

**Abandonment**  In a sense, this is the converse of the waiting-to-invest option. Having invested and then discovered that the market is weaker than anticipated, the owner of the project has the option to abandon the project to prevent further capital losses. Taking this into account increases the ex ante value of the project.

**Switching**  After commencement of the project, there may be opportunities to switch to other technologies should they become value-enhancing. To the extent possible, such scenarios for future cost-reduction should be included in the prior assessment of the project or else the value will be understated.

**Expansion of Scale**  Project structures are often flexible enough to allow a scale expansion at an intermediate stage. A project may have a high up-front fixed cost and permit a smaller investment later to scale up its size with no delay. If the expansion enhances the future profitability of the project, it is a real option that should be included in ex ante value. An esoteric example of this type of option is a right to movie sequels. By paying a premium up front, the producer of the first movie is able to expand scale to a second movie if the series catches on with motion picture audiences.

**Maturity Adjustments**  The structure of some projects is such that they may be completed over flexible time frames. It may be possible to complete the project faster than scheduled if production time scales with input. (This may not always be possible, of course. Think of wine making.) For instance, it is possible to shorten the time taken to build a bridge if more resources are added to the project, and it may sometimes be advantageous to do so. If the project funding is, say, on a floating-rate basis, it is better

---

[1] Of course, the DCF problem faces analogous problems in generating the required input information (realistic possible scenarios with their probabilities) or identifying the the correct discount rate to be used.

to scale up the project if there is a sharp drop in interest rates. Likewise, it may be advantageous to scale down when rates shoot up, although this would depend on the costs of project delay as well.

**Stop/Restart**   Investment projects may be affected by market cycles, being profitable in some periods but not in others. If the project can be shut down in the low-performance epochs, then there is a real option of material value embedded in it. A typical example of this class of options arises in mining; mining companies often shut down mines during periods in which output prices are low.

This list is indicative but not even close to exhaustive. Since real options pertain to project choices that must be made over time, there are effectively as many types of real options as there are types of path dependencies. Each real option concerns an ex post choice (one made after the project has been accepted) but one whose consequences need to be taken into account ex ante (in the evaluation of the project and the decision on whether to accept it).

## 22.2   Preliminary Analysis and Examples

Real options analysis aims to value correctly the current business of a firm taking into account the value of its investment and project optionalities, both current and future. In a sense, a real option comprises a call option on a business opportunity that may be invested in at a given future date. In this section, we present a series of examples, some simple, some more elaborate, of various types of real options.

### A Setting with Stochastic Cash Flows

Oil companies confront real options in almost all their activities. In the simplest case, they pay for exploration, and after the exploration period, they extract oil for refining, resulting in revenues.

Here is a simplified model. An oil company is considering exploring and developing an oil field. For the moment, assume there is no quantity uncertainty, so the up-front fixed cost of exploration/development can be expressed in per-barrel terms, say, $K_1$ per barrel. This initial phase takes time; a period of time $T$ must elapse after beginning exploration before the company can start refining and selling oil. The risk the company faces is that the price per barrel $P$ of the oil that will prevail at time $T$ is uncertain, and the cost of refining oil per barrel, say $K_2$, is fixed. If the price of oil turns out to be low, losses result.

The firm faces the decision as to whether to explore for oil at all. In a simple "expected value" approach to this problem, we would compare the expected price $E(P)$ to the total cost $K_1 + K_2$ and choose to explore only if $E(P) > K_1 + K_2$. The real options framework takes a more sophisticated approach. We note first that the oil company need only choose to proceed with refining if the price of oil is higher than that of the unit cost of refining, i.e., $P > K_2$. Hence, the decision to refine is akin to holding a call option on the price of oil with a strike price of $K_2$ and a maturity of $T$. We denote the value of this call by $C(P, K_2, T)$.

Given $C$, the decision on whether to proceed with exploration is easily resolved: the company should proceed with exploration only if the real option value is greater than the cost of exploration, i.e., if $C(P, K_2, T) > K_1$.

---

**Example 22.1**   Suppose the price of oil is currently $40 per barrel, and that oil price volatility (annualized) is 30%. If the exploration cost is $K_1 = \$5$ per barrel and the refining cost is $K_2 = \$30$ per barrel, should the firm proceed with exploiting the oil well? Assume that the exploration period lasts one year, the risk-free rate is 3%, and the convenience yield for oil is 1%.

We can solve this problem using the Black-Scholes model where the dividend yields in the model are replaced with the convenience yield. The strike price is $30. Plugging these values in gives us the price of a call option on the price of oil with a maturity of one year:

$$C(P, K_2, T, \sigma, r_f, q) = 11.29$$

Since this is larger than $K_1 = 5$, it is worth carrying out the exploitation of the oil well. ∎

## A Potential Problem: Quantity Risk

What happens in this setting if the amount of oil discovered after exploration is uncertain? For specificity, suppose that in the numerical example there are two (ex ante equiprobable) quantity outcomes, either 1 million or 2 million barrels of oil. Suppose too that the total fixed cost of exploration is $15 million. Should the company now proceed with exploration?

We have already determined that the net benefit per barrel of oil after refining costs is the value of the call option, which is $11.29. This means that if the field contains 2 million barrels of oil, the venture is profitable:

$$\text{Expected Profit} = 2,000,000 \times \$11.29 - 15,000,000 = \$7,580,000$$

However, if the field contains only 1 million barrels of oil, then a loss results:

$$\text{Expected Profit} = 1,000,000 \times \$11.29 - 15,000,000 = -\$3,710,000$$

From an ex ante standpoint, it appears that the right decision would be to apply the probabilities of each outcome to these profits and to explore the field only if the average profit is positive. (In the current example, this average is indeed positive at $1,935,000.) However, these equal probabilities are the real-world probabilities of the quantity outcomes, not risk-neutral ones. The "correct" valuation requires us to use risk-neutral probabilities. As we have seen in earlier examples in this book (for instance, Section 11.3), the risk-neutral probability of the good outcome may be much smaller than the outcome's actual probability.

But where do we get the correct risk-neutral probabilities? In the first example, where there was only price risk and where the parameters of this price risk could be gauged since the underlying asset (refined oil) was traded, the model's parameters, its risk-neutral probabilities, and the option price could all be determined in accordance with the Black-Scholes model. But now, with quantity risk, the underlying uncertainty is not traded, so there is no direct source of risk-neutral probabilities. This example highlights an important issue that arises in the analysis of real options, namely that replication-based option pricing may be infeasible because the underlying source of uncertainty is not traded. In a later section, we will consider a possible solution to this problem.

## A "Waiting-to-Invest" Setting

Optonium is a (fictitious) metal with a price process that evolves according to a binomial process. The time-0 price per gram of optonium is denoted $p_0$. In each period $t \geq 1$, the price is realized according to the binomial distribution

$$p_{t+1} = \begin{cases} u\, p_t, & \text{with probability } q \\ d\, p_t, & \text{with probability } 1 - q \end{cases}$$

where $q$ is the risk-neutral probability of an "up" move in the price. The risk-free (gross) rate of interest per period is $R = qu + (1 - q)d$.

An investor holds the rights to operate an optonium mine. The mine will produce 1 gram of optonium in the period it is opened, and production thereafter decays by a factor $\delta < 1$. That is, the mine produces $\delta$ grams in the next period, $\delta^2$ grams the period after that, and so on. The investor's option gives her the right to open the mine over any of the next $n$ periods by investing an amount $M$ at that point; if the right is not exercised over the $n$ periods, it lapses. There are no costs to extracting optonium, so if the mine is opened in period $t$, the investor receives cash flows from the optonium sales of $p_t, \delta p_{t+1}, \delta^2 p_{t+2}, \ldots$ into the indefinite future. How much are the rights worth to the investor?

In a typical DCF approach to this problem, we would look at the expected cash flows from opening the mine today and operating it forever. Note that these expected cash flows would have to be calculated under the actual probabilities, not the risk-neutral probabilities described above. Then we would identify an appropriate cost of capital for the project and use this to discount the expected cash flows.

The real options approach takes additional contingencies into account. For example, since the investor has the right to operate the mine beginning not just now but any time over the next $n$ periods, the real options approach looks to value the mine by identifying the *optimal* point for opening it over the $n$ periods. This means there are two related questions of interest: (a) when should the investor optimally exercise her right? and (b) what is the consequent value of the rights she holds?

The first step to answering these questions is to identify the present value of the cash inflows the investor receives by exercising the option in any period $t$ given the price $p_t$ at that point. (We are interested in these cash flows only for $t \leq n$, but a general expression is just as easy to define.) This present value may be identified by taking expectations of all future cash flows under the risk-neutral measure and discounting them back to the present. The discount factor per period is denoted $\beta = 1/R$. In Appendix 22A, we show that this present value is just

$$V(p_t) = \frac{p_t}{1 - \delta} \qquad (22.1)$$

Expression (22.1) is intuitive; we can actually arrive at it without the formal calculations of Appendix 22A Under the risk-neutral measure, the price grows at the risk-free rate, so the discounted expected value of the future price is always the current price. Since production decays at the rate $\delta$, the expected sequence of cash flows from opening the mine in period $t$ is just $(p_t, \delta p_t, \delta^2 p_t, \ldots)$, which sums precisely to $p_t/(1 - \delta)$.

The remainder of the problem is easy to solve since it is akin to an American option problem with the "strike price" being the initial investment $M$ required to open the mine. The optimal starting time is obtained by backwards induction as explained in Chapter 12 (see Section 12.5). We begin at the "end" of the tree, i.e., in the last period in which the mine may be opened. Let $p_n$ denote the period-$n$ price. Then, the value of the option to undertake the project given $p_n$, denoted $J^*(p_n)$, is

$$J_n^*(p_n) = \max\{V(p_n) - M, 0\}$$

Conditional on the project not having been undertaken so far, the investor's optimal action is to undertake the project at those values of $p_n$ for which $J_n^*(p_n) > 0$.

Now we fold the tree back one period. Given a value $p_{n-1}$ for the price in period $n - 1$, the value of the investor's option from $p_{n-1}$ on, denoted $J_{n-1}^*(p_{n-1})$, is

$$J_{n-1}^*(p_{n-1}) = \max\{V(p_{n-1}) - M, \beta[q \cdot J_n^*(up_{n-1}) + (1 - q) \cdot J_n^*(dp_{n-1})]\}$$

In words, the investor has the option of starting the project right away at the node $p_{n-1}$, in which case she receives the net value $V(p_{n-1}) - M$, or of waiting for one more period, in which the continuation value depends on which of the two possible states results from $p_{n-1}$. Conditional on the project not having been undertaken so far, the investor's optimal action is to begin the project right away in period $n - 1$ if $J_{n-1}^*(p_{n-1}) = V(p_{n-1}) - M$.

Continuing in a similar vein, we can identify the optimal action for the investor to undertake at each point as well as the initial value $J_0^*(p_0)$ of the original option.

---

**Example 22.2**

Consider a specific parametrization of the above setting in which $p_0 = 1$, $u = 1/d = 1.30$, $q = 1/2$, and $\delta = 10/11$. The risk-free rate implied by these parameter values is $R = 1.0346$ (so $\beta = 0.9665$). Suppose $M = 10$ and $n = 1$, that is, the mine can be opened right away or in period 1 at a cost of 10.

From (22.1), the present value of all cash flows from period 0 on is $V_0 = 11$, so if the mine is opened in period 0, the net value received by the investor is $11 - 10 = 1$. If the investor waits one period, the present value of all future cash flows from period 1 onwards moves to either $V_1 = 14.30$ (which happens if the period 1 price is $up_0$) or to $V_1 = 8.4615$ (if the period 1 price is $dp_0$).

Conditional on not starting the project in period 0, it is optimal to start the project in period 1 if and only if the "high" price occurs in period 1, in which case the net value of the project is $14.30 - 10 = 4.30$. Therefore, the time-0 present value of not starting the project in period 0 is

$$(0.9665)[(1/2)(4.30) + (1/2)(0)] = 2.078$$

Thus, the optimal action for the investor is to wait one period and then to begin the project if and only if the high state occurs. The value of the option held by the investor is 2.078.  ∎

### Further Readings on the Waiting-to-Invest Option

This notion of waiting to invest was developed in several papers by various authors and still forms the essential motivation for a real options approach to investment choice. Interested readers may reference the books and papers by Kester (1984), Brennan and Schwartz (1985), McDonald and Siegel (1986), Majd and Pindyck (1987), Majd and Pindyck (1989), Paddock, Siegel, and Smith (1988), Dixit (1989), Pindyck (1991, 1993), Trigeorgis (1993a, 1993b), Capozza and Li (1994), and Chance and Peterson (2002).

## "Open and Shut" Options

In this final example of real options, we modify the waiting-to-invest setting by adding an operating cost.

---

**Example 22.3**

Consider the setting of Example 22.2, but with several modifications. First, suppose that the cost of operating the mine per period is $c = 1.10$. Second, assume that once the mine is opened, it can be shut and re-opened without any cost.

Third, assume there is no decay in production, so $\delta = 1$. This means the mine produces 1 gram of optonium each period that it is open. Finally, suppose that the investor has the right to operate the mine over the next 10 periods; during each of these periods, the investor can choose whether to keep the mine open (and produce 1 gram of optonium) or shut. After the 10 periods, the right lapses. The remainder of the example (the price process, interest rates, etc.) is unchanged.

We are interested in the answer to two questions. First, if the investor behaves optimally, what is the value of the mine? Second, what is the value of the mine if we ignore the option the investor holds to open and shut the mine, i.e., if we assume that the mine must remain open for the full 10 periods?

The second question is easy to answer. Given the initial price of $p_0 = 1$, the present value of the cash inflows from keeping the mine open for 10 periods is just $10\,p_0 = 10$. To see this, recall that the price grows at the risk-free rate in the risk-neutral world, so the discounted expected value of future prices is always the current price. Since we have production of 1 gram per period for 10 periods, the present value of the total revenue received is just 10 times the current price. The present value of the costs incurred on the other hand is the present value of an outflow of 1.10 in each period for 10 periods. Netting these out, we see that the value of the mine if it is kept open for 10 periods is about 0.834.

What about the value if we do not ignore the option to shut the mine during unprofitable periods and re-open it when desired? In each period, the mine owner effectively has a call option with a strike price of $c = 1.10$. If the price of optonium that period is greater than $c$, it is worthwhile opening the mine that period, or else it is best to shut the mine. This is a simple valuation problem. Solving for the values of these options on the binomial tree, we find a total value for the mine of 2.686. Thus, including the values of the optionalities increases the value of the mine more than threefold.   ∎

# 22.3   A Real Options "Case Study"

In this section, we present a case study of a fictitious company and analyze it in several steps. The case involves more than one real option (the option to wait and the option to abandon) in the same setting. Perhaps most important, the case also illustrates how risk-neutral probabilities (or "state prices") may be determined for real options by considering a set of securities that spans the uncertainty in the fundamental driver of the project. This spanning idea is revisited in the next section of this chapter where we go through a more technical description of the general procedure that is involved.

## Case Study

Greasy Oil Company (GOC) has been awarded a government license to exploit an oil well that supports an annual production of 3075 barrels of oil and has a total productive life of two years, after which all the oil will be sluiced out. Licenses granted must be used within one year. For simplicity, we assume time is discrete with periods of one year length. This means there are two scenarios that are open to GOC:

1. Drill right away, i.e., at time $t = 0$, and sell the output over the first two years.
2. Wait one year and start drilling at time $t = 1$, and sell the output over the next two years, i.e., years 2 and 3.

We assume further that the output in a year is sold at the end of the year at the prices known at the beginning of the year. The current price of oil is $17 per barrel. We also assume that the new oil price realized at the end of the first year remains the same for the next two years. These are all simplifications to aid the exposition; the ideas are easily extended to handle more complex settings.

The choice between drilling right away or waiting for a year depends on the expected price of oil in one year. If the price is expected to increase, GOC may wish to wait a year, especially if the price appreciation outweighs the time-value loss of receiving revenues a year later. GOC's chief economist Oyl Slyck has provided a quad of possible oil prices a year ahead. Slyck, who is unfortunately given to punning, calls this her "four"-cast:

| Scenario | Oil Price ($) | Probability |
|---|---|---|
| 1 | 14 | 0.1658 |
| 2 | 13.08 | 0.1530 |
| 3 | 20 | 0.2904 |
| 4 | 25 | 0.3908 |
| Current | 17 | |

The probabilities provided are the actual, not risk-neutral, ones. Note that there is a greater chance of the price of oil rising than falling. If GOC were to start drilling right away, then the first year's oil production would have to be sold at the current price of $17 per barrel. On the one hand, this means relinquishing gains from a possible rise in the price of oil after one year; but prices may also be lower at year's end, and waiting a year means passing up on locking in revenues for the first year at the current price.

Therefore, GOC's management begins to consider the broader business environment. Slyck gives them additional forecasts relating to her scenarios. Corresponding to the oil prices, she has computed the likely value of the traded stock market index for each of the four oil price scenarios. She has also forecast the corresponding risk-free interest rates (the current interest rate is 6%; all interest rates in this study are in annualized terms with annual compounding). These are presented in the following table:

| Variable | End of Year-1 Scenarios | | | |
|---|---|---|---|---|
| | 1 | 2 | 3 | 4 |
| Stock index ($S$) | 1500 | 1170.40 | 900 | 500 |
| Oil price ($X$) | 14 | 13.08 | 20 | 25 |
| Interest rate ($r$) | 0.08 | 0.06 | 0.04 | 0.03 |

The table shows that the oil price is negatively correlated to the stock market index and the interest-rate level. Given the probabilities of the four scenarios from the previous table, there appears to be a greater than even chance of a recession driven by high oil prices, where interest rates are low and the stock index does poorly.

The following additional information is also provided about GOC, the project, and the market environment.

| | |
|---|---|
| Current value of stock index | 960 |
| Fixed cost of drilling oil per year (paid at the start of the year) | $50,000 |
| One-year risk-free interest rate | 6.00% |
| Price of two-year Treasury discount bond | $0.8966 |

## Analysis of the Case: The Steps

Our analysis of GOC's decision problem proceeds in several steps. In the first step, we show how to compute the *risk-neutral* probabilities of the four scenarios using the given information. Then using these risk-neutral probabilities, we compute the value of the project if it is begun right away. We arrive at a project value of $2,046.23.

There are two optionalities ignored in this first step. One is the option to wait, i.e., to begin the project in a year's time (at $t = 1$). The second is to abandon the project a year after it is begun if the environment is unprofitable (because oil prices have fallen). In Step 2, we consider the first of these options. We show that including this option in the analysis causes a sharp increase in the project value to $5,546.35.

In Step 3, we assume the project is begun at $t = 0$ but include the option to abandon the project costlessly after a year if the climate is unsuitable. We show that this option too has a huge impact on project value: the project value is now $7,820.79.

Finally, in Step 4, we look at starting the project at $t = 1$, but allowing for abandoning it after a year. To show how such considerations are easily incorporated into the analysis, we further assume in this case that there is a cost of abandonment. The project value is sharply higher than when the project is begun at this point but there is no abandonment allowed: the project value is now $7,136.26.

Comparing all these numbers, we see that the optimal course of action is for GOC to begin the project right away but to abandon it after a year under the right circumstances.

## Project Value if Commenced at $t = 0$

To identify the risk-neutral value of the project if it is commenced at $t = 0$ (but without including any optionalities), the first step is to identify the risk-neutral probabilities of the four scenarios. To accomplish this, we use four securities that span the state space at the end of year 1. The four securities that will be used are the stock market index, oil, and the one- and two-year riskless discount bonds. The current price of the stock index is 960, oil is at $17 a barrel, and the one-year interest rate is 6%. Therefore, the current price of the one-year riskless bond (assuming a face value of $1) is $1/(1.06) = 0.9434$. The price of the two-year discount bond as given before is $0.8966. We write the price of the four securities at time $t = 0$ as a vector:

$$P(t = 0) = \begin{bmatrix} S(0) \\ X(0) \\ B_1(0) \\ B_2(0) \end{bmatrix} = \begin{bmatrix} 960 \\ 17 \\ 0.9434 \\ 0.8966 \end{bmatrix}$$

Next, we write down the scenario space of prices of these securities at time $t = 1$:

$$P(t = 1) = \begin{bmatrix} S(1) \\ X(1) \\ B_1(1) \\ B_2(1) \end{bmatrix} = \begin{bmatrix} 1500 & 1170.4 & 900 & 500 \\ 14 & 13.08 & 20 & 25 \\ 1 & 1 & 1 & 1 \\ 0.9259 & 0.9434 & 0.9615 & 0.9709 \end{bmatrix}$$

Each row comprises the prices of each security across the four scenarios. Now, let the risk-neutral probability vector be $Q$,

$$Q = \begin{bmatrix} q_1 \\ q_2 \\ q_3 \\ q_4 \end{bmatrix}$$

where $q_i$ denotes the risk-neutral probability of scenario $i$. Note that we must have $q_1 + q_2 + q_3 + q_4 = 1$.

Under the risk-neutral probability, the expected value of an asset's price discounted at the risk-free rate must equal the current price. That is, we must have

$$P(t = 0) = \frac{1}{1 + r} P(t = 1) Q$$

Since $P(t = 0)$, $P(t = 1)$, and $r$ are known, we can use this to solve for $Q$. We obtain

$$Q = P(t = 1)^{-1} P(t = 0)[1 + r]$$

$$= \begin{bmatrix} 1500 & 1170.4 & 900 & 500 \\ 14 & 13.08 & 20 & 25 \\ 1 & 1 & 1 & 1 \\ 0.9259 & 0.9434 & 0.9615 & 0.9709 \end{bmatrix}^{-1} \begin{bmatrix} 960 \\ 17 \\ 0.9434 \\ 0.8966 \end{bmatrix} (1 + 0.06)$$

$$= \begin{bmatrix} 0.25 \\ 0.25 \\ 0.25 \\ 0.25 \end{bmatrix}$$

We can now use these risk-neutral probabilities to value the future cash flows of the company if the project is begun at $t = 0$.[2] Note that all discounting must now be done at the risk-free rate.

In the first year of the project, there is a cash outflow at the beginning of the year of $50,000 and a cash inflow at the end of the year from the sale of 3,075 barrels of oil at $17 per barrel. The present value of this year's cash flows is

$$\text{NPV of first year} = \frac{3075 \times 17}{1 + 0.06} - 50,000 = -683.96$$

In the second year, the cost incurred is again $50,000, and the revenue received at the end of year 2 depends on the four possible prices of oil in that period. Therefore, the four possible present values at time $t = 0$ are:

$$\text{Scenario 1: NPV} = \left( \frac{14 \times 3075}{1 + 0.0.08} - 50,000 \right) / (1 + 0.06)$$

$$\text{Scenario 2: NPV} = \left( \frac{13.08 \times 3075}{1 + 0.06} - 50,000 \right) / (1 + 0.06)$$

$$\text{Scenario 3: NPV} = \left( \frac{20 \times 3075}{1 + 0.04} - 50,000 \right) / (1 + 0.06)$$

$$\text{Scenario 4: NPV} = \left( \frac{25 \times 3075}{1 + 0.03} - 50,000 \right) / (1 + 0.06)$$

Weighting these four outcomes by the risk-neutral probabilities $Q$, we obtain the expected net present value of the cash flows from the project's second year of operation. This equals an amount of $2,730.19.

Summing up the project's two years of operations results in a net total present value of $2,046.23.

---

[2] Note that the risk-neutral probabilities lie between 0 and 1, and sum to 1 as required. If our solution for $Q$ had resulted in elements that were either less than 0 or greater than 1, it would have meant the presence of an arbitrage in the prices of the four securities used to span the state space of the project.

## Project Value if Commenced at $t = 1$

We now assess the time-0 value of the project if the project is begun after waiting for one year, i.e., at time $t = 1$. We do this to examine whether the trade-off between risky oil prices and possibly higher revenues from price increases makes it more lucrative on the whole to wait and begin drilling for oil after one year. Note that since oil revenues are received only at the end of the year, the cash inflows in this case are received at the end of years 2 and 3.

Our case study has assumed that the price outcomes at the end of the first year will hold for two years. Therefore, we need be concerned only with the state space at the end of the first year. This is already known and has been defined as the matrix $P(t = 1)$.

The project may be valued by considering the four possible cash-flow scenarios at the end of one year based on which expected present value may be computed using risk-neutral probabilities and discounting at the risk-free rate of interest. The following table summarizes the cash flows.

| | Cash Flow Present Values at $t = 1$ | | | |
| Scenario | $t = 1$ | $t = 2$ | $t = 3$ | Total |
| --- | --- | --- | --- | --- |
| 1 | −50000 | −6435.19 | 36908.44 | −19526.75 |
| 2 | −50000 | −9225.47 | 35796.55 | −23428.92 |
| 3 | −50000 | 11057.69 | 56860.21 | 17917.90 |
| 4 | −50000 | 26092.23 | 72462.06 | 48554.29 |

The $t = 1$ entry corresponds to the fixed cost of operating the project in the first year. This is paid at the beginning of the year.

The $t = 2$ entry is the present value (as of $t = 1$) of the cash inflow received from the sale of the first period's output at the end of the first year as well as the cash outflow of $50,000 at the beginning of the second year required to keep the project operational for the second year. For example, in the first scenario, this is

$$\frac{-50000 + 3075(14)}{1 + 0.08} = -6,435.19$$

The $t = 3$ cash flows correspond to the present value (as of $t = 1$) of the cash inflows received from the second year of oil sales in the project. In scenario 1, for example, the present value at $t = 1$ of the cash flow from the second year of oil sales is

$$\frac{3075(14)}{(1 + 0.08)^2} = 36,908.44$$

The last column of the table sums these present values in each scenario.

The present value of the project as of $t = 0$ is simply the expectation of these four present values under the risk-neutral probabilities, discounted back to time 0. Carrying out this operation provides a final present value of $5,546.35. This is greater than the expected present value of the project begun at $t = 0$, i.e., $2,046.23. Thus, we see that it is advantageous to begin the project after one year to take advantage of the greater than even probability of increases in the price of oil.

## Beginning at $t = 0$ and Allowing for Abandonment

As mentioned earlier, there is a second option available to the company: that of abandoning operations in the second year of the project should continuing the project become unprofitable. In this segment, we look at the value of the project if it is begun at $t = 0$ and the abandonment option is available. In the next segment, we complete the analysis by looking at the case where the project is begun at $t = 1$ and there is an abandonment option. Here, we assume that the project may be abandoned costlessly. Adding a cost to abandon the project is an easy extension, and we do this in the next segment.

If the project is begun at time $t = 0$, the analysis of the first year of the project is the same as earlier and has present value of −$683.96 as before.

In the second year, abandonment becomes the optimal action when oil prices have dropped at time $t = 1$. In scenarios 1 and 2, oil prices are $14 and $13.08, respectively. At these prices, operating the oil field does not result in revenues that cover the fixed costs of $50,000: as is easily checked, the present values (as of $t = 1$) of the cash inflows from the four scenarios are, respectively, 39,861.11, 37,944.34, 59,134.62, and 74,635.92. Note that in scenarios 3 and 4, the oil price is sufficiently high to make continued production worthwhile.

The expected average present value at $t = 0$ is obtained by weighting these values from optimal continuation with the risk-neutral probabilities and discounting back to period 0:

$$\frac{1}{1 + 0.06} \times 0.25 \times (0 + 0 + 9134.62 + 24635.92) = 7{,}964.75$$

Adding this value to that of the first period results in a net present value overall of $7,280.79. This may be compared to starting the project at $t = 0$ and not allowing for abandonment, which amounts to an expected project value of only $2,046.22. Thus, the abandonment option has substantial value.

## Beginning at $t = 1$ and Allowing for Abandonment

Finally, we will look at the case where the project may be abandoned after starting at time $t = 1$. Just to illustrate how costs of abandonment may be incorporated into the analysis, we add an extra wrinkle to the problem here. We assume that the government penalizes licensees who abandon the project after only one year of production by fining them $7,500; to keep the earlier numbers in the analysis unchanged, assume that this fine is levied only if the company exploits both options (the option to wait and the option to abandon), so it applies only to the present setting and not the earlier ones.

The first step in the analysis is to determine whether to continue with the project at time $t = 2$, the starting point for the second year of operation. Viewed at time $t = 2$, the present value in each scenario (indexed by $k$) may be computed as follows:

$$\text{NPV}_k(t = 2) = \max\left[-7500, \ \frac{3075 \times X_k}{1 + r_k} - 50{,}000\right]$$

(Here, in obvious notation, $X_k$ is the price of oil in scenario $k$, and $r_k$ is the risk-free rate in that scenario.) In words, if the present value of continuing is lower than $-7,500$, the project is abandoned and the fine of $7,500 is paid. Based on this, the present values as of $t = 2$ in each of the four scenarios is:

| | Net Present Value at $t = 2$ | |
|---|---|---|
| Scenario | No Abandonment | With Abandonment |
| 1 | −10,138.89 | −7,500.00 |
| 2 | −12,055.66 | −7,500.00 |
| 3 | 9,134.62 | 9,134.62 |
| 4 | 24,635.92 | 24,635.92 |

With these values in hand for the second year of project operation (or non-operation), we compute the present value of the first year of operation. The net present value at time $t = 1$ of the first year of project operation is equal to (for each scenario $k$):

$$\frac{3075 \times X_k}{1 + r_k} - 50{,}000$$

To this quantity, we must add the present value as of $t = 1$ of the second period continuation cash flows. The sum total of these two values at time $t = 1$ in each of the four scenarios is summarized below:

| Scenario | Net Present Value at $t = 1$ |
|---|---|
| 1 | −17, 083.33 |
| 2 | −19, 131.13 |
| 3 | 17, 917.90 |
| 4 | 48, 554.29 |

Finally, these four values are weighted by the risk-neutral probabilities and discounted back to time $t = 0$, resulting in a time-0 present value of $7,136.26. This may be compared to the net present value of starting at time $t = 0$ with the option to abandon with an overall NPV of $7,280.79. The burden of the cancellation penalty has shifted the decision against waiting to invest.

## 22.4   Creating the State Space

In this section, we will look at two interesting extensions of the state-space approach. Both features are useful for developing the state space itself. So far in this chapter, we have assumed that the state space is exogenously given. However, it is possible to use quantitative techniques to develop the state space using the mathematics of linear algebra. This will help in reducing the element of individual judgment required.

Before we develop these ideas, it is useful to note that the generation of scenarios is an important aspect of either method, be it the DCF or state-space approach. Therefore, the ideas presented in this section are useful even when the DCF model is used. After all, cash-flow forecasts are required in any valuation exercise.

The material in this section is technically more advanced than in earlier sections and may be skipped without any loss of continuity.

### Generating a Parsimonious State Space

It is possible by using simple tools in linear algebra to create a very parsimonious state space of outcomes for evaluating any security that is a function of assets within the state space. If we have $N$ securities, then our method generates a state space with $N + 1$ scenarios. This is as parsimonious as one would like. Recall that, when we were using the binomial tree to price stock options, the state space comprised just two scenarios because the stock was permitted to take on only one of two values at a time. Hence, we were able to complete the state space by adding to it the risk-free bond, thereby resulting in two securities (stock and bond) that spanned the two scenarios in the model.

To demonstrate the state-space generation procedure, let us take a simple example. Assume that we have four random variables (i.e., assets), all of which have mean zero. (Assuming that the mean values are zero is without loss of generality since after we generate scenarios, we may add back the means of each variable.) Let us also assume that the covariance matrix for these random variables is the following:

$$\begin{bmatrix} 2 & 1 & 2 & 1 \\ 1 & 3 & 1 & 1 \\ 2 & 1 & 4 & 2 \\ 1 & 1 & 2 & 5 \end{bmatrix}$$

Using a tool called the Gram-Schmidt decomposition from linear algebra, we can convert this $4 \times 4$ covariance matrix into a scenario space comprising five scenarios, each with values of the four random variables. The scenarios are of equal probability, i.e., in this case, the probability equals 0.2 each.

This procedure literally "decomposes" the summary covariation information in the covariance matrix into a set of actual scenarios. The main component of the decomposition procedure consists of a $QR$-decomposition, which is a matrix decomposition of the form $A = QR$, where $R$ is an upper triangular matrix and $Q$ is an orthogonal matrix, i.e., $Q'Q = I$, $I$ being the identity matrix. The $A$ matrix we use below is essentially an enhanced identity matrix (see the program code that follows). The $R$ matrix from this procedure is combined with the Cholesky decomposition of the covariance matrix to obtain the state space. This may be illustrated with some simple Octave program code:

```
%Input the covariance matrix
covmat = [2  1  2  1;
          1  3  1  1;
          2  1  4  2;
          1  1  2  5];

%Get dimension and also create a reverse index for later use
n = length(covmat);
idx = [n:-1:1]';

%Identity matrix
uMat = eye(n)

%Extended identity matrix
vMat = [uMat, -1*ones(n,1)]

%QR Decomposition
[q, r, p] = qr(vMat)

%Create (0,1) variable state space
x = -1 * sqrt(n+1) * r;
x(1,:) = x(1,:)/(-sqrt(n+1));
x = x(idx,:)

%Cholesky decomposition of covariance matrix
coeffmat = chol(covmat)

%Combine (0,1) state space with decomposed covariances
%to obtain the final scenario space (s)
s = coeffmat' * x
```

We ran this program, and it generated the following matrix of scenarios. To interpret this matrix, note that each row comprises one random variable; each column is for a scenario. Thus, there are $N = 4$ rows and $N + 1 = 5$ columns.

$$s = \begin{bmatrix} 0 & 0 & 0 & -2.23607 & 2.23607 \\ 0 & 0 & 2.88675 & -2.56141 & -0.32534 \\ 0 & 2.73861 & -0.91287 & -3.14894 & 1.32320 \\ 3.94968 & 0.38189 & -0.86651 & -2.85057 & -0.61450 \end{bmatrix}$$

Recall that each scenario occurs with equal probability. Let us check whether this procedure has correctly generated an acceptable state space. We first check that each random variable is mean zero. This may be done by hand, but the following code confirms that averaging the values in each row of the scenario space results in an outcome of zero.

```
check_mean = mean(s')
```

Next, we check that we can recover the covariance matrix. Since the variables are mean zero and each scenario is equiprobable, the covariance matrix is given by $E(s\,s') = (s\,s')/(N+1)$. The code snippet is as follows:

```
check_cov = (s*s')/(n+1)
```

The reader should check that this provides exactly the $4 \times 4$ covariance matrix we started out with above.

Finally, it is natural to ask where the covariance matrix comes from (in this example, it was exogenously provided). Since the state space is generated using traded securities, the random variables we use are all observable, and historical time-series data on these variables will be available. The covariance matrix may be computed from this data. However, this assumes that the data from the past is a good indication of the future. If this is unpalatable, forward-looking covariance matrices may be generated using some procedure (for example, there are vendors in the equity space who provide such forecasts).

At a broader level, this approach to generating scenarios connotes a shift in modeling practice, going from judgmental forecasts of cash-flow scenarios to statistically-generated ones.

## Cash-Flow Generation Using a Factor Approach

In the previous subsection, it was assumed that the securities (random variables) that defined the scenario space were already known. How do we come up with a set of securities to span the state space?

Essentially, the choice of state variables is driven by applying one's judgment and selecting a set of variables that are related to the business environment in which the project resides. As we saw earlier in our case study of Greasy Oil Company (GOC), which involved oil extraction, we use the traded price of oil as one of the state variables. In addition, we use the stock market index, which is correlated with almost any business undertaking. The other state variables are the prices of bonds, again a natural choice, since they are intricately tied to the time value of money, an essential element in any evaluation of cash flows over time.

How many state variables should be used? Again, this is a judgment call. Usually, a small well-chosen set of variables, that are intuitively related to the factors in the economy driving the project cash flows, will suffice. More generally, we aim to choose a set of factors that explains a large portion of the variation in a firm's cash flows.

Once specific state variables have been chosen, we may conduct statistical analyses to determine the efficacy of this choice. One can develop a cash-flow forecasting model based on the chosen state variables. This is also required when cash flows are forecast for DCF valuations. For instance, in the case of GOC, we might specify cash flows as a function of three of the state variables in the model, i.e., the stock index $S$, the price of oil $X$, and the risk-free interest rate $r_f$. We can write this as a cash-flow function $C(S, X, r_f)$. Then, it remains to specify this function using a model and to estimate it using data. If time-series data is available on cash flows and the state variables, then the function could be fit using econometric techniques, which might range from simple linear or nonlinear regressions to vastly more complex systems of equations. The goodness-of-fit of the model may be assessed, thereby validating (or negating) the judgment calls made in choosing the number and type of state variables.

The fitting approach notwithstanding, we would end up with a parametrized cash-flow function, which would directly identify cash flows in each of the scenarios of our valuation model. Thus, in our numerical example above, we have five scenarios, and the cash-flow function would be applied across the four random variable values in each scenario to arrive at a cash-flow value for each scenario.

Notice how the state-space approach automatically provides a basis for generating cash-flow forecasts in each scenario. Calibration of the system directly leads to a forecast because the state-variables-based scenarios are provided using the Gram-Schmidt decomposition technique described earlier. Contrast this with the DCF approach in which an economic model is required but is not always forced to conform to market prices of traded securities, nor does it provide a basis for scenario generation.

## 22.5   Applications of Real Options

We wrap up this chapter with a survey of settings in which real options analysis is applicable and valuable.

Real options may come in the form of tax opportunities for multinational corporations (MNCs). MNCs can switch revenues, production, and product lines across regions depending on variations in tax regimes, moving revenues to low-tax regimes from high-tax regimes. For example, MNCs move production when tax breaks are given for various forms of joint ventures. For a detailed analysis of the real options embedded in tax regimes, see Muralidhar (1992).

A second example of real options comes from the movie business. When the rights to the movie are purchased, there is no guarantee that the movie will be ultimately produced. The rights provide a real option to eventually invest in the movie, but there is a chance too that the project will be abandoned.

Similarly, the development of a movie sequel is a valuable right and is a real option in which a choice to expand scale may be exercised. The trade-off lies in deciding to make the original movie and its sequels all at the same time (as in the case of *The Lord of the Rings*) or to develop them serially and play a waiting game (as with *The Godfather*). The former approach results in the cheaper development of all the movies, whereas the latter approach prevents over-investment in case the results of the first film release turn out to be weaker than anticipated.

Real options analysis is also widely used in the drug industry. Investment in pharmaceutical development is vast, and a better assessment of real options makes it feasible for these firms to allocate their research funds in the most effective manner. Merck was among the first firms to apply real options analysis to their project choices. Many firms followed suit, and such analyses are now routine in this industry.

Earnings management is also a form of real option. Firms do have and often exercise their ability to undertake window dressing, so as to smooth earnings to manage share values. See the paper by DeGeorge, Patel, and Zeckhauser (1999).

As in oil exploration, the exploitation of natural resources is a common setting in which real options emerge. An interesting and unusual setting is highlighted in the case of the Peruvian copper mine Antamina, the subject of a study by Moel and Tufano (1997). The right to develop the copper mine was offered by the Peruvian government as part of the country's privatization program. The mine had a valuable real options component in the form of the right to develop the mine after completing exploration, and this right was analyzed using Monte Carlo methods. The novel aspect of the transaction was the type of bid requested by the Peruvian government, requiring bidders to state both the exercise price they would set and the premium they would pay for the real option. This structure gives rise to various incentive issues, affecting the amount that firms offer, their preferences between the premium and exercise price, the identity of the bidders, the likelihood of ultimate development and possible ex post renegotiation of the contract.

Finally, an important generator of real options is regulation. Classic examples come from the electricity and telecommunications industries. The uncertainties of any industry in the midst of deregulation change the evaluation of projects dramatically as the number and complexity of project options increase, perhaps sharply. The need for a flexible and easy-to-implement real options framework becomes paramount.

## 22.6    Summary

It is important to carefully evaluate optionality within a project-choice setting. In the examples developed in this chapter, we have shown how ignoring real options leads to suboptimal project choices. There are many real-world instances in which the methods of analysis developed in this chapter are applicable.

The real options approach has some advantages over the discounted cash-flow (DCF) technique. The cost of capital is not required for discounting cash flows; only the risk-free rate is used. It values projects relative to the prices of the securities spanning the project's uncertainty and so provides an arbitrage-free approach to project valuation. Most important, it becomes possible to take into account several optionalities at once (even interacting optionalities) in the valuation exercise; such optionalities are routinely ignored in the DCF approach leading to (perhaps considerable) mis-valuation. Perhaps the biggest disadvantage of the real options approach is the need to identify the risk-neutral probabilities accurately or, equivalently, to identify a set of traded securities that spans the project's uncertainty. This is always nontrivial and sometimes infeasible. Computationally too, the method often proves quite demanding.

Early courses in finance emphasize the time value of money and how to use it to value projects. It is apposite then to conclude this chapter with the words of Stephen Ross, who described real options as being about the "money value of time."

## 22.7  Exercises

1. Why does traditional NPV analysis break down in the presence of real options within an investment opportunity?

2. State three different forms of real options and discuss possible real-world cases in which such options are likely to be manifest.

3. You have the option to invest in a project at any time in the future. If the riskiness of the project increases, does it increase or decrease the average waiting time to making the investment?

4. The option to wait to invest in a risky project is a valuable one. The risk of waiting to invest is a possible loss in market share to other early movers into the market. How would you use the option pricing framework to model the possible loss of market share? What parameter in the option model gives you the ability to represent loss of market share?

5. What does the option of waiting to invest do to the following features of the project versus making a project choice based on NPV alone? (a) riskiness of the project, (b) effective hurdle rate for the project, and (c) probability that the project will be undertaken.

6. Shining Metal Inc. has invested in a gold mine. The company needs to decide whether to drill for gold at the beginning of the year or wait until next year. Gold drilled this year will be sold at end-of-year market prices. The mine generates 15,000 ounces of gold per year. The current price of gold is $400 per ounce, and the volatility of gold returns is 40% per year. The risk-free rate of interest is 2%. The variable cost of extracting and marketing gold is $300 per ounce. The fixed costs of operating the mine are $2,000,000 a year. Assume no convenience yields and decide whether it is worth drilling for gold this year or it is better to shut the mine down and wait for one year.

7. In a gold mine, the price of gold is a major determinant of the value of the project.
   (a) When the price of gold drops, what real option in the mine may be exercised?
   (b) When the price of gold rises, what real option in the mine may be exercised?
   (c) If the volatility of gold increases and all else remains the same, is it more or less likely for a closed gold mine to reopen?
   (d) If the volatility of gold increases and all else remains the same, is it more or less likely for an open gold mine to close?
   (e) Given that gold production has both fixed and variable costs, which of these is more important in assessing real option value? What are the option analogs to these two types of costs?

8. In real options analysis, what discount rate should be used in the model for valuing the option?

9. You invest in an oil exploration project with a public company. What are the two main risks you face? How do you hedge these risks?

10. Based on real options analysis, would you expect to see more or less oil exploration as oil price volatility increases?

11. The current price of silver is $7 per ounce. You are a maker of silver jewelry and wish to obtain a guaranteed supply of silver at the end of the year at a maximum price of $8 per ounce. If the volatility of silver is 20%, how much would you be willing to pay for the guarantee? The risk-free interest rate is 3%.

12. You are the purchasing manager of a major health provider. A certain generic drug is selling at a price of $10 per unit. To ensure that costs for this drug do not exceed $12 per unit the following year, you arrange a guaranteed maximum price with the supplier for a commitment fee of $0.15 per unit. The growth rate of the drug price is normally distributed at 30% with a standard deviation of 10%. The risk-free rate of interest is 1%. Is the commitment fee priced appropriately to offer your firm a reasonably priced hedge against escalating health care costs?

13. How does the option of waiting to invest impact project values? When is it worth the wait? What is the implicit effect of the option of waiting to invest on the project's hurdle rate?

14. How is the option of waiting to invest different from the option to abandon the project? What exotic options are these optionalities analogous to?

15. Contrast the state-space approach to valuing real options with the traditional discounted cash-flow approach. Highlight three advantages of the state-space approach over the DCF one. What are the possible disadvantages?

16. A project generates annual cash flows $C_t$, received at the end of the year. The cash flow is based on market conditions and changes from year to year as follows:

$$C_{t+1} = 2 + 0.8C_t + 20\epsilon_{t+1}$$

where $\epsilon \sim N(0, 1)$ is drawn randomly from a normal distribution with zero mean and unit variance. This cash-flow-generating process continues year after year even if the plant is closed. You have to decide when to keep the plant open.

The first year's cash flow is 10. The project is such that one can start and stop it in any year. Find a rule of the following form: find triggers $a$, $b$ within which the project will operate. The limit $a$ is such that if the project is not in progress, it will start when the cash-flow level crosses above $a$. The level $b$ is the stop limit, i.e., if the project is in progress, it is worthwhile to stop it when the cash-flow level drops below $b$. The goal is to find a rule that maximizes the average cash flow over time. [*Hint:* Think of a way to solve this problem using Monte Carlo simulation.]

17. In this problem, you will download market data and generate a state space for valuation purposes. Please carry out the following set of steps:

   (a) Download five years of monthly stock price data from the web. You may use a convenient source such as Yahoo! Finance. Do this for 10 stocks.

   (b) Convert the stock price data into returns.

   (c) Compute the mean stock returns for each stock and the covariance matrix of returns for all the stocks.

   (d) Use the covariance matrix and mean returns to generate the state space of stock returns using the Gram-Schmidt decomposition technique.

   (e) Price an option that pays off $1 million when the stock return exceeds 10% on more than five stocks.

   (f) Into which business decision might this option pricing problem provide you an insight?

18. You have current wealth of $100. You are offered a venture in which you may with equal probability double your money or halve it. If your utility is the square root of your wealth, would you take this venture?

19. You have developed a new material called gossamer, which has demand characteristics closely related to the markets for gold and silver. The prices of these commodities at the end of the year are forecast to be as follows:

| Material | Low Demand Prices | High Demand Prices |
| --- | --- | --- |
| Gold | 300 | 400 |
| Silver | 4 | 8 |
| Gossamer | 50 | 80 |

The input raw materials to make gossamer cost $65. Do you think this is a project you would be interested in pursuing?

20. (Difficult) A project once a year generates cash flows $C_t$ received at the end of the year. The cash flow is equal to $100y$, where $y$ is an index of business conditions. Each year's cash flow is related to that of the previous year based on the following scheme:

$$y_{t+1} = \begin{cases} y_t x & \text{with prob } 1/3 \\ y_t & \text{with prob } 1/3 \\ y_t/x & \text{with prob } 1/3 \end{cases}$$

The first year's cash flow is 100, and let $x = 1.4$. The project is such that one can start and stop it any year. However, starting the project requires a commitment to operate the project for at least three years. Stopping the project prevents restarting the project for three years. Find a rule of the following form: find a range $(a, b)$ within which the project will continue. The upper limit $a$ is such that if the project is not in progress, it will start when the cash-flow level crosses $a$. The level $b$ is the stop limit, i.e., if the project is in progress, it is useful to stop it when the cash-flow level drops below $b$. [*Hint:* Think of a way to solve this problem using Monte Carlo simulation.]

# Derivation of Cash-Flow Value in the "Waiting-to-Invest" Example

We use the notation introduced in the "Waiting-to-Invest" setting of Section 22.2. The objective is to derive equation (22.1).

Suppose the period $t$ price observed is $p_t$ and the mine is opened at this point. The distribution of future prices from this point on depends only on $p_t$, so the present value of the cash inflows received from opening the mine in period $t$ depends only on $p_t$. Denote this present value by $V(p_t)$. Let $E(p_{t+\tau}|p_t)$ denote the expected price (under the risk-neutral measure) at time $t + \tau$ given the time-$t$ price $p_t$. The expected cash flow from optonium sales in period $t + \tau$ is $\delta^\tau E(p_{t+\tau}|p_t)$. Therefore,

$$V(p_t) = \sum_{\tau=0}^{\infty} \beta^\tau \delta^\tau E(p_{t+\tau}|p_t) \tag{22.2}$$

We can express $V(p_t)$ in a more useful form that links the present values of future cash flows from times $t$ and $t + 1$:

$$V(p_t) = p_t + \delta\,[q\delta V(up_t) + (1-q)\delta V(dp_t)] \tag{22.3}$$

Equation (22.3) has a simple interpretation. The value of cash flows from time $t$ onward is the period-$t$ cash flow $p_t$ plus the discounted value of all future cash flows from period $t+1$ on. Now in period $t+1$, the "state of the world" can be either $up_t$ or $dp_t$. In the former case, the present value of continuation cash inflows is $\delta V(up_t)$ (since a decay of delta has occurred since period $t$ in the mine's production). In the latter case, it is $\delta V(dp_t)$. Taking expectations over these continuation values under $q$, we obtain (22.3).

We can use (22.3) to solve for an explicit form for the function $V(\cdot)$. One way to do this is to guess a form for $V(\cdot)$ and identify the relevant parameters. Suppose we try $V(p_t) = kp_t$ for some fixed $k$. We substitute this form for $V(p_t)$ in (22.3) and see if we can solve for $k$. (If we cannot, the posited form of $V(\cdot)$ is wrong.) In the present case, the substitution results in

$$kp_t = p_t + \beta\,[q\delta\,kup_t + (1-q)\delta\,kdp_t]$$

Canceling the common term $p_t$, this expression may be solved for $k$:

$$k = [1 - \beta\delta(qu + (1-q)d)]^{-1} \tag{22.4}$$

Since $\beta(qu + (1-d)d) = 1$, we obtain the simpler expression $k = (1-\delta)^{-1}$. This finally gives us

$$V(p_t) = \frac{p_t}{1-\delta}$$

which is exactly equation (22.1).

# Part 3

# Swaps

# Chapter 23

# Interest Rate Swaps and Floating-Rate Products

## 23.1 Introduction

A *swap* is a periodic exchange of cash flows under specified rules. In an interest rate swap, the exchanged cash flows are determined by the level of interest rates. With over $300 trillion in notional outstanding worldwide in 2007,[1] interest rate swaps are among the most important classes of derivatives. This chapter examines a variety of interest rate swaps, beginning with "plain vanilla" fixed-for-floating swaps. Non-interest rate swaps, such as equity swaps, commodity swaps, currency swaps, and credit swaps, are examined in later chapters.

Interest rate swaps are intimately related to forward-rate agreements or FRAs, which we examined in Chapter 6. Two other classes of instruments that are closely related to FRAs and interest rate swaps are caps and floors. The defining feature of caps and floors is *optionality*. Caps are akin to a portfolio of call options on the interest rate, while floors are like a portfolio of puts. A portfolio that is long a cap and short a floor is just an interest rate swap (or, equivalently, just a portfolio of FRAs). FRAs, interest rate swaps, and caps and floors, as also their exchange-traded cousin, eurodollar futures, constitute by far the most important classes of floating-rate derivative products.

We begin this chapter with a brief review of floating-rate bond mathematics.

## 23.2 Floating-Rate Notes

Floating-rate notes or FRNs are coupon bonds in which the coupon paid by the bonds depends on a pre-specified interest rate or index. The most popular floating-rate notes are those indexed to Libor.

As an illustration, take a five-year maturity, semiannual pay $1 FRN indexed to six-month Libor. That is, the underlying instrument is a five-year FRN with semiannual coupons and a face value of $1, whose coupon is equal to the six-month Libor rate at the previous reset date. At time 0 (the issuance date of the FRN), the first coupon, due in six months, is fixed

---

[1] BIS report available at http://www.bis.org/publ/rpfxf07t.htm.

depending on the six-month Libor rate at time 0. Suppose this Libor rate is 6%. Then, on the first coupon date, a coupon of

$$(0.06) \times \frac{d_1}{360}$$

will be paid, where $d_1$ denotes the actual number of days in the first six-month period. Simultaneously, the six-month Libor rate observed on the first payment date is then used to determine the size of the second coupon payment (due in twelve months from issuance of the bond). If this rate is (say) 6.25%, then the coupon received at the end of twelve months is

$$(0.0625) \times \frac{d_2}{360}$$

where $d_2$ denotes the actual number of days in the second six-month period. And so on until maturity when the principal is also repaid.

Note that only the first coupon is known at the time of issuance, The remaining cash flows that may arise from the FRN are not known until the relevant reset dates. Nonetheless, the FRN is easy to value as we explain next.

## Valuation of FRNs: A No-Arbitrage Approach

Suppose we have an FRN with a face value of $1 and $N$ remaining payment dates $t_1, t_2, \ldots, t_N$. Let $t$ denote the current date and let $t_0$ denote the last reset date, i.e., the date on which the coupon due at $t_1$ was determined. Let $\ell_0$ denote the Libor rate fixing at $t_0$ and $d_0$ the actual number of days between $t_0$ and $t_1$. Then, the coupon due at $t_1$ is

$$\ell_0 \frac{d_0}{360}$$

Now, the value of the FRN at time $t$ is the sum of two quantities: (a) the present value of this coupon due at $t_1$, and (b) the present value of all future cash flows (coupons and principal) due beyond $t_1$ from the FRN. Of these, the quantity (a) is easily identified since the cash flow due at $t_1$ is known at time $t$. If $B(t, t_1)$ is the time-$t$ present value of $1 receivable at time $t_1$, then the present value of the first coupon is[2]

$$B(t, t_1) \times \ell_0 \frac{d_0}{360}$$

However, future cash flows beyond $t_1$ are not known at time $t$, so how do we ascertain the quantity (b)? The answer is simplicity itself as the following proposition shows:

**Proposition 23.1** *On any reset date, the value of the FRN (which is the present value of all future cash flows due from the FRN) is equal to par.*

**Proof** Consider date $t_1$ (the argument is the same for any reset date). Suppose the value of the FRN at time $t_1$ exceeds par, i.e., $V > 1$. Then, the following strategy generates arbitrage profits:

- Short the FRN and invest $1 at Libor. Net cash inflow: $V - 1$.

---

[2] Recall from Chapter 6 that the discount factors $B$ are determined from the Libor rates $\ell$. For example, $B(t, t_1)$ is given by

$$B(t, t_1) = \left(1 + \ell(t, t_1) \frac{d(t, t_1)}{360}\right)^{-1}$$

where $\ell(t, t_1)$ is the Libor rate observed at $t$ for maturity $t_1$ and $d(t, t_1)$ is the actual number of days between $t$ and $t_1$.

- At each payment date $t_2, \ldots, t_{N-1}$, use the interest obtained from the Libor investment to pay the coupon due on the FRN. Roll the \$1 investment forward at Libor for one more period. Net cash flow: 0.
- At date $t_N$, receive \$1 + interest on the Libor investment and use this to retire the FRN. Net cash flow: zero.

Conversely, if the value of the FRN at $t_1$ is $V < 1$, then reversing the above strategy provides an arbitrage. ■

Summing up, the FRN is equivalent to receiving a cash flow at time $t_1$ of \$1 + the coupon due at $t_1$. Thus, the time-$t$ present value of the FRN is

$$B(t, t_1) \times \left(1 + \ell_0 \frac{d_0}{360}\right) \tag{23.1}$$

Expression (23.1) is also called the "short form" approach to FRN valuation since the present values of all cash flows from date $t_2$ onwards are subsumed in the par value of \$1 at time $t_1$ that is used in the valuation expression.

## Valuation of FRNs: The "Forward Method"

An alternative method that is sometimes used to value FRNs is called the *forward* method. The forward method "fills in" amounts for the unknown future cash flows from the FRN by using the relevant forward interest rates. For example, suppose that the forward interest rate at time $t$ for borrowing or investment over the period $(t_{k-1}, t_k)$ is 5%. Then, in the forward method, we calculate the interest received at time $t_k$ as if the realized Libor rate on the reset date $t_{k-1}$ were in fact 5%. Having projected cash flows at all payment dates in this fashion, we take the present value of the cash-flow stream to obtain the value of the FRN.

Although the forward method sounds different from the no-arbitrage result—and also sounds less satisfactory because it appears to make specific assumptions about uncertain future cash flows—it is easy to show that the two methods are in fact mathematically equivalent, so the forward method is actually a no-arbitrage approach to valuation.

Note that in both approaches, the coupon at payment date $t_1$ is known. Thus, to show the equivalence between the approaches, we need to show that the time-$t$ present values of the cash-flow stream from and including date $t_2$ on are equal. As we have seen above, this present value in the no-arbitrage approach is $B(t, t_1)$: the present value viewed from $t_1$ of all future cash flows is par or \$1, and $B(t, t_1)$ is the time-$t$ present value of \$1 receivable at $t_1$. We show that the same value results under the forward method also.

The first step is to identify precisely the projected coupon amounts on each payment date. Consider any coupon date $t_k \geq t_2$. Let $B(t, t_k)$ represent the time-$t$ present value of \$1 due at $t_k$. As we showed in Chapter 6 (see the arguments leading to equation (6.13)), the forward rate at time $t$ for an investment or borrowing between $t_{k-1}$ and $t_k$, expressed in terms of the discount factors $B$, is

$$f(t, t_{k-1}, t_k) = \frac{B(t, t_{k-1}) - B(t, t_k)}{B(t, t_k)} \times \frac{360}{d_k} \tag{23.2}$$

where $d_k$ is the actual number of days between $t_{k-1}$ and $t_k$. Using the forward rate, the projected coupon received at time $t_k$ in the forward method is

$$f(t, t_{k-1}, t_k) \times \frac{d_k}{360} = \frac{B(t, t_{k-1}) - B(t, t_k)}{B(t, t_k)} \tag{23.3}$$

The time-$t$ present value of this coupon flow is just $B(t, t_k)$ times the right-hand side of (23.3), which is

$$B(t, t_{k-1}) - B(t, t_k) \tag{23.4}$$

Summing (23.4) over $k$ (from $k = 2$ to $k = N$), the present value of all the coupon cash flows from date $t_2$ on works out to

$$B(t, t_1) - B(t, t_2) + B(t, t_2) - B(t, t_3) + \cdots + B(t, t_{N-1}) - B(t, t_N)$$

which simplifies to

$$B(t, t_1) - B(t, t_N)$$

In addition, on the final payment date, the principal of $1 is also received; this has a time-$t$ present value of $B(t, t_N)$. Adding this to the present value of the coupon cash flows, the present value of all cash flows from $t_2$ on works out to just $B(t, t_1)$, which is exactly what we were looking to show.

---

**Example 23.1**

Suppose that we are given the following information. An FRN has four remaining payment dates: in $t_1 = 100$ days, $t_2 = 283$ days, $t_3 = 465$ days, and $t_4 = 649$ days, respectively. The coupon rate for the first payment date is 5.25%, and the number of days between the last reset date and the first coupon date is 182 days. The Libor rates viewed from today for maturities of 100 days, 283 days, 465 days, and 649 days are, respectively, 5.15%, 5.21%, 5.36%, and 5.84%. The FRN has a face value of $1. What is its value using the short-form method? Using the forward method?

**Short-Form Method**

The size of the first coupon due on the FRN is

$$\text{Coupon at } t_1 = (0.0525) \times \frac{182}{360} = 0.0265$$

In addition, the present value (viewed from $t_1$) of all future coupons due on the FRN is just par, which is $1. Thus, the FRN is equivalent to receiving a cash flow of $1 + 0.0265$ on date $t_1$. To "present value" this quantity, we must identify the discount factor $B(t, t_1)$.

The Libor rate viewed from today for maturity on date $t_1$ is 5.15%. Thus, the discount factor for cash flows due in 100 days is

$$B(t, t_1) = \left(1 + (0.0515)\frac{100}{360}\right)^{-1} = 0.9859$$

It follows that the current value of the FRN is

$$(0.9859)(1 + 0.0265) = 1.01201$$

**Forward Method**

We begin by identifying the discount factors $B(t, t_k)$ and thence the forward rates $f(t, t_{k-1}, t_k)$ using (23.2). We have

$$B(t, t_2) = \left(1 + (0.0521)\frac{283}{360}\right)^{-1} = 0.9607$$

$$B(t, t_3) = \left(1 + (0.0536)\frac{465}{360}\right)^{-1} = 0.9352$$

$$B(t, t_4) = \left(1 + (0.0584)\frac{649}{360}\right)^{-1} = 0.9047$$

From (23.2), the forward rates for the coupon periods ending at times $t_2$, $t_3$, and $t_4$ are:

$$f(t, t_1, t_2) = \frac{B(t, t_1) - B(t, t_2)}{B(t, t_2)} \times \frac{360}{183} = 0.0517$$

$$f(t, t_2, t_3) = \frac{B(t, t_2) - B(t, t_3)}{B(t, t_3)} \times \frac{360}{182} = 0.0537$$

$$f(t, t_3, t_4) = \frac{B(t, t_3) - B(t, t_4)}{B(t, t_4)} \times \frac{360}{184} = 0.0660$$

Using these forward rates, the projected coupons at times $t_2$, $t_3$, and $t_4$ are, respectively:

$$\text{Coupon at } t_2 = 0.0517 \times \frac{183}{360} = 0.0263$$

$$\text{Coupon at } t_3 = 0.0537 \times \frac{182}{360} = 0.0272$$

$$\text{Coupon at } t_4 = 0.0660 \times \frac{184}{360} = 0.0337$$

Thus, the present value of the coupon inflows from the FRN is

$$\sum_{k=1}^{4}[B(t, t_k) \times \text{Coupon at } t_k] = 0.1073$$

In addition, the principal of $1 is received on the final payment date $t_4$. This principal has a present value of $B(t, t_4) \times 1 = 0.9047$. Adding this to the present value of the coupon inflows gives us a total value for the FRN of $0.1073 + 0.9047 = 1.0120$. Except for the minor rounding-induced difference, this is exactly the same value obtained by the short-form method. ∎

## 23.3  Interest Rate Swaps

Interest rate swaps are bilateral agreements between two counterparties to exchange interest payments in a common currency calculated using specified rules on a given notional principal. The principal itself is not exchanged in the swap (hence "notional" principal). The currency in which both payments are made is the same in an interest rate swap. Swaps in which the two legs make interest payments in different currencies are called *cross-currency swaps* (or simply currency swaps) and are the subject of a later chapter.

The most common kind of interest rate swap is the "plain vanilla" *fixed-for-floating swap*. Here, one counterparty makes payments computed under a fixed interest rate specified in the contract in exchange for receiving floating payments according to some specified index (typically Libor). For example, a corporation may enter into a five-year pay-fixed receive-floating swap with semiannual payments on a notional principal of $100,000,000, in which the corporation agrees to

- make six-monthly interest payments at a fixed rate of (say) 7% computed on the $100,000,000 principal, and
- receive six-month Libor on the same notional principal every six months until maturity.

In practice, two separate interest payments are not made; rather, only the net interest amount is exchanged.

Importantly, the payment frequency of the two sides need not be the same. It is common to have the floating-side payment frequency correspond to money-market practices and the fixed-side payments correspond to corporate bond market practice. In the US, the floating payments are made quarterly and linked to three-month Libor, while the fixed payments are made semiannually. In the euro-zone, floating payments are semiannual and linked to six-month Euribor, while fixed payments are made annually.

There are a number of common variations on the basic fixed-for-floating swap. These include:

- Above/below market rate swaps, also known as off-market swaps, in which the fixed rate in the swap differs from that of the standard market swap.
- Zero-coupon swaps, in which one side of the swap makes no payments until maturity of the swap, but the other side makes periodic payments.
- Swaps with changing fixed rates, in which the fixed rate on the swap varies according to a specified schedule.
- Spread-to-Libor swaps, where the floating payments consist of Libor plus or minus a fixed spread.
- Forward-starting swaps, in which the swap is entered into today, but the swap itself commences only at some specified date in the future.
- Amortizing/accreting/roller-coaster swaps, in which the notional principal amount is not fixed but varies over time in a prespecified manner (decreasing in an amortizing swap and increasing in an accreting swap; in a roller-coaster swap, as the name suggests, the principal amount can move both up and down).

We examine these variants after first studying the vanilla fixed-for-floating swap. We begin by highlighting some of the uses of swaps in risk-management. Following this, we work through the cash flows from a fixed-for-floating swap and discuss the valuation and pricing of fixed-for-floating swaps. Then, we discuss pricing and other aspects of more exotic swaps including all the variants listed above.

## 23.4   Uses of Swaps

One reason that the swaps market has reached its immense size is that more and more applications of swaps are discovered (invented may be a better word) each year. We list and discuss some of the many uses of swaps in this section.

### Comparative Advantage

The notion of comparative advantage in economics is over two centuries old and goes back to the work of David Ricardo on the rationale underlying international trade. Comparative advantage is the idea that even if one party can do everything more efficiently than another, it may still pay each of the parties to specialize in the respective areas in which they are *relatively* more efficient (or less inefficient) and then to trade. As a simple analogy, a doctor may be better at managing her records and running her office than her office manager, but she nonetheless finds it worthwhile to employ the office manager because it enables her to concentrate on medicine in which her advantage over the office manager is far greater.

In the context of financial markets, comparative advantage arises in the difference between borrowing rates in fixed- and floating-rate markets. While higher-rated borrowers can borrow at a cheaper rate in both markets, it often turns out that the difference in borrowing rates between high- and low-rated borrowers is higher in the fixed-rate market than in the floating-rate market. This enables a Pareto-improving ("everyone benefits") situation via a swap. The following simple numerical example illustrates the point.

**Example 23.2**

Consider two corporations, A and B. A, a high-quality borrower, wishes to raise $50 million in five-year floating-rate funding. The company can borrow fixed-rate at 5% and floating-rate at Libor − 0.50%. B, a lower-rated company, wishes to raise $50 million in five-year fixed-rate funding. B finds it can borrow fixed at 7% and floating at Libor + 0.50%. The borrowing rate information is represented in the following table ($L$ represents Libor):

| Type of Borrowing | Company A | Company B |
|---|---|---|
| Fixed | 5% | 7% |
| Floating | $L - 0.50\%$ | $L + 0.50\%$ |

Absent the availability of swaps, A would borrow floating and pay Libor − 0.50%, while B would borrow fixed and pay 7%. Note, however, that A has a comparative advantage in the fixed-rate markets: although it can borrow cheaper in both markets, it can borrow 2% cheaper in fixed-rate markets and only 1% cheaper in floating-rate markets. So comparative advantage would suggest that A should borrow fixed and B floating. The use of a swap then completes the Pareto-improvement. Here are the details:

- Company A borrows funds from the fixed-rate markets at 5%.
- Company B raises money in the floating-rate markets at $L + \frac{1}{2}\%$.
- The two parties enter into a swap in which A pays B a floating rate of $L$ (i.e., Libor flat) while B pays A a fixed rate of 7%−y basis points.

What are the net funding costs that result? Company A pays 5% fixed on its borrowing, receives 7%−y basis points from B, and pays $L$ to B. The net outflow for A is

$$L - 2\% + y \quad \text{basis points}$$

As long as $y < 1.50\%$, A finds this method of obtaining floating-rate funding preferable to borrowing directly from floating-rate markets. What about B? The net cash outflow to B from the proposed strategy is

$$7.50\% - y \quad \text{basis points}$$

As long as $y > 0.50\%$, this is a preferable way for B to obtain fixed-rate funding than borrowing directly in fixed-rate markets.

A range of values is possible for $y$ that satisfies these inequalities. For example, consider the halfway point, $y = 1.0\%$. In this case,

- A borrows fixed at 5%, pays B the floating payment of $L$, and receives from B the fixed payment of 6%. The net cost to A is a floating-rate payment of $L − 1\%$, which is 50 basis points cheaper than accessing floating-rate funding directly in the market.
- B borrows floating at $L + 0.50\%$, pays A a fixed-rate of 6%, and receives from A a floating rate of $L$. The net cost to B is a fixed rate of 6.50%, which is a 50-basis point saving over accessing funds directly in the fixed-rate market.

The total funding cost savings (50 basis points + 50 basis points = 1%) is exactly the "gains from trade." That is, by having each participant borrow in the market in which they have a comparative advantage, the total borrowing costs are 5% + ($L + 0.50\%$) = $L + 5.50\%$, which is 1% less than if A borrowed floating (at $L − 0.50\%$) and B fixed (at 7%). It is this 1% savings that is allocated to the participants via the swap.

Of course, many other solutions could have been chosen as well; these would assign the 1% gain differently. As two examples:

- If we choose $y = 0.50\%$, then A ends up with a net funding cost of $L − 1.50\%$ while B's funding cost is 7%, so all the gains from trade go to A.
- Conversely, if we choose $y = 1.50\%$, A's net funding cost works out to $L − 0.50\%$ and B's to 6%, so B now gets all gains from trade. ∎

## Analyzing Funding Costs with Swaps

Swaps are useful devices for comparing different types of financing. Firms are often faced with a choice between fixed-rate and floating-rate forms of finance. From a purely funding cost standpoint, it is not clear how one should make this comparison. For instance, how do you compare a 10-year loan at a fixed rate of 10% versus a 10-year floating-rate note at 1-year Libor + 0.75% when the current 1-year Libor rate is 5%? That the Libor alternative is cheaper now does not mean it will be so in the future too. If interest rates escalate sharply, then the FRN may end up being more expensive than the fixed-rate loan.

The swap market, it turns out, provides us with exactly the right vehicle to make this comparison. Suppose, for example, that the company faced with these funding choices finds that the current fixed rate versus one-year Libor being offered to it in the swap market is 9.125%. It is easy to show that the floating-rate note then dominates the fixed-rate borrowing. Consider the following:

- Raise money in the floating-rate market at $L + 0.75\%$.
- Enter into a pay-fixed, receive-floating swap in which the company pays 9.125% and receives one-year Libor.

The net result is a fixed-cost borrowing at 9.875%, or 0.125% cheaper than directly borrowing in the fixed-rate market at 10%.

## Risk/Maturity Management

Swaps can be used to manage the risk of both individual positions and balance sheets. For example, consider a bank that has fixed-rate assets and floating-rate liabilities. The bank is vulnerable to an increase in interest rates. One solution is to enter into a swap where the bank pays fixed and receives floating. Both sides of the balance sheet are now based on floating rates. This is depicted in Figure 23.1.

## Speculation and Other Uses

Swaps can also be used to speculate without any prior underlying exposure. An investor who has the view that rates will increase can enter into a pay-fixed/receive-floating swap. If the investor's view holds and rates increase, the floating-rate receipts will be higher in the future, and the swap can be unwound profitably (its marked-to-market value will be positive). Similarly, an investor whose view is that interest rates are going to decrease can enter into a pay-floating/receive-fixed swap.

**FIGURE 23.1**

Managing Balance
Sheet Risk

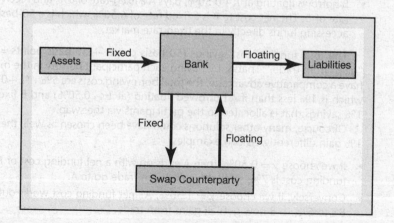

Swaps also offer financial-planning flexibility. For example, a company that is currently raising money and wishes to raise fixed-rate funding but has the view that rates will go down in the future can raise floating-rate financing now and swap into fixed when rates decrease.

# 23.5    Swap Payoffs

This section discusses the cash flows generated by vanilla fixed-for-floating swaps.[3] The mechanics are similar to that of FRAs, but there are some minor differences. In an FRA, the cash flows from both legs are computed using the money-market day-count convention, In a swap, the cash flows on the floating side use the money-market day-count convention while those on the fixed side use what is called the swap-market convention.

Consider a swap entered into on date $t_0$ with notional principal $A$. For simplicity, we assume that the two legs of the swap have the same payment frequency and occur on the payment dates $t_1, t_2, \ldots, t_N$. (Handling different frequencies is conceptually trivial but notationally cumbersome since it would require us to distinguish between payment dates for the floating and fixed sides.) We look at the payoffs to a *long* swap position, i.e., the side that pays fixed and receives floating. We denote the fixed rate in the swap by $k$ and take the floating payments to be Libor flat.

### Floating Payments

For each reset date $t_n$, let $\ell_n$ denote the Libor rate observed at $t_n$ for the period $(t_n, t_{n+1})$, $n = 0, 1, \ldots, N - 1$. The rate $\ell_n$ is used to calculate floating payments due at $t_{n+1}$. Note that $\ell_0$ is known at the time of entering into the swap, but $\ell_1, \ldots, \ell_{N-1}$ are observed only on dates $t_1, \ldots, t_{N-1}$, respectively.

In calculating the floating payments due on the swap, the money-market day-count convention is commonly used. In general, let $m_n$ denote the day-count fraction applicable to the period $(t_n, t_{n+1})$ in the relevant convention. For example, in the Actual/360 convention (which is what we use in the numerical examples below), the fraction $m_n$ is given by

$$m_n = \frac{d_n}{360}$$

where $d_n$ is the actual number of days between $t_n$ and $t_{n+1}$.

### Fixed Payments

For calculating the fixed payments, the swap-market convention is used. Let $s_n$ denote the day-count fraction applicable to the period $(t_n, t_{n+1})$ in this convention. For example, if the swap-market convention is 30/360 (as in US dollar and euro swaps), then $s_n$ is given by

$$s_n = \frac{30}{360} \times \text{Number of months between } t_n \text{ and } t_{n+1}$$

## Cash Flows on the First Payment Date

Since $\ell_0$ is known at the time of entering into the swap, the first set of payments in a swap is known at the outset. On date $t_1$, the floating payment due is computed using $\ell_0$ as

$$\text{Floating payment}_1 = (\ell_0 \times m_0) \times A$$

The fixed payment is computed using the contract swap-rate $k$:

$$\text{Fixed payment}_1 = (k \times s_0) \times A$$

[3] Our presentation of swap payoffs and pricing (Sections 23.5 and 23.6) follows closely the class notes on this material developed by Marti Subrahmanyam at New York University.

Thus, the net payment received by the long swap position is

$$(\ell_0 m_0 - k s_0) \times A$$

## Cash Flows on Subsequent Payment Dates

These are calculated exactly in the same manner as on the first payment date. If $\ell_n$ is the realized Libor rate on date $t_n$, then the floating payment due at $t_{n+1}$ is

$$\text{Floating payment}_{n+1} = (\ell_n \times m_n) \times A$$

The fixed payment due at $t_{n+1}$ is computed using the rate $k$:

$$\text{Fixed payment}_{n+1} = (k \times s_n) \times A$$

Thus, the net payment received by the long swap position is

$$(\ell_n m_n - k s_n) \times A$$

## Differing Payment Frequencies

In the presentation above, it was assumed that the payment frequencies of the fixed and floating sides are the same, but this is trivial to drop. On the dates that fixed payments are due, the payments are calculated exactly as above with the day-count fraction using the period between the fixed-payment dates. Similarly, on the dates floating payments are due, the payments are calculated exactly as above with the day-count fraction referring to the period between floating-payment dates.

**Example 23.3**

Consider a three-year swap with parameters as in Table 23.1. Note that "Year 1" refers to the year in which the swap is initiated. Note too that the example assumes a common payment frequency for the fixed and floating sides.

## Payoffs on the First Payment Date

We compute the cash flows to the holder of the long swap (pay fixed/receive floating). Suppose the six-month Libor rate on the inception date of the swap is 6.50%. Then this rate is used to determine the floating payments on the first payment date, December 11 of Year 1, written 11-Dec-Year 1. Note that there are 183 days between June 11 and December 11. So the floating payment due on 11-Dec-Year 1 is:

$$(100,000,000) \times \left( 0.065 \times \frac{183}{360} \right) = 3,304,167$$

The fixed payment is, of course, determined using the swap rate $k$ and the 30/360 day-count convention. The fixed payment due on 11-Dec-Year 1:

$$(100,000,000) \times \left( 0.060 \times \frac{180}{360} \right) = 3,000,000$$

**TABLE 23.1** Swap Payoffs Example: The Input Data

| | |
|---|---|
| Principal amount | $100,000,000 |
| Spot date | June 11, Year 1 |
| Term | 3 years |
| Interest-rate index | 6-month Libor |
| Reset interval | 6 months |
| Swap rate ($k$) | 6% |
| Initial Libor rate | 6.50% |
| Payment frequency (fixed) | 6 months |
| Payment frequency (floating) | 6 months |

Therefore, net receipts of the long position on 11-Dec-Year 1:

$$3,304,167 - 3,000,000 = 304,167$$

## Payoffs on the Second Payment Date

The floating payment on the second payment date (June 11 of Year 2, written 11-Jun-Year 2) depends on the six-month Libor rate observed on 11-Dec-Year 1. Suppose, for example, this rate is 7.00%. Assuming 182 days between 11-Dec-Year 1 and 11-Jun-Year 2 (i.e., assuming Year 2 is not a leap year), the floating payment due on 11-Jun-Year 2 is determined as:

$$(100,000,000) \times \left(0.07 \times \frac{182}{360}\right) = 3,538,889$$

The fixed payment due on 11-Jun-Year 2 is simpler to compute:

$$(100,000,000) \times \left(0.060 \times \frac{180}{360}\right) = 3,000,000$$

Therefore, the net receipts of the long position on 11-Jun-Year 2:

$$3,538,889 - 3,000,000 = 538,889$$

Figure 23.2 describes the payoffs from the swap on the second payment date for a range of possible values of the Libor rate on the reset date 11-Dec-Year 1. The payoff is linear in the Libor rate observed on the reset date. Note that when the floating rate equals the swap rate, the payoff is slightly positive since the two legs use different day-count conventions.

## Payoffs on Subsequent Payment Dates

Payoffs on subsequent dates are computed in exactly the same manner based on the Libor rates observed on the relevant reset dates. Table 23.2 fills in hypothetical values for these Libor rates and describes the payoffs that result from the swap. ∎

### FIGURE 23.2

Swap Payoffs on the
Second Payment Date

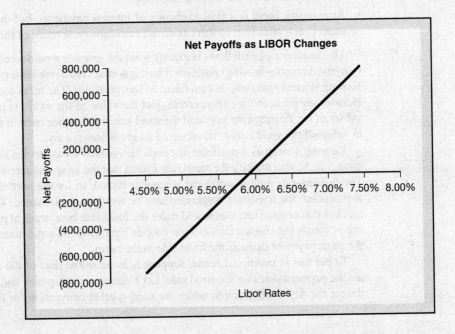

**TABLE 23.2**    Swap Payoffs Example: Hypothetical Outcomes

| Date | Days from Last Reset | Libor at Last Reset | Swap Rate | Fixed Cash Flow | Floating Receipt | Net |
|------|---------------------|--------------------|-----------|-----------------|------------------|-----|
| 11-Dec-Year 1 | 183 | 6.50% | 6.00% | −3,000,000 | 3,304,167 | 304,167 |
| 11-Jun-Year 2 | 182 | 7.00% | 6.00% | −3,000,000 | 3,538,889 | 538,889 |
| 11-Dec-Year 2 | 183 | 6.50% | 6.00% | −3,000,000 | 3,304,167 | 304,167 |
| 11-Jun-Year 3 | 182 | 6.25% | 6.00% | −3,000,000 | 3,159,722 | 159,722 |
| 11-Dec-Year 3 | 183 | 5.75% | 6.00% | −3,000,000 | 2,922,917 | −77,083 |
| 11-Jun-Year 4 | 183 | 5.25% | 6.00% | −3,000,000 | 2,668,750 | −331,250 |

## 23.6    Valuing and Pricing Swaps

Let a fixed-for-floating swap with swap rate $k$ and specified payment dates be given. From an analytical standpoint, the swap may be decomposed into a portfolio of a fixed-rate bond and a floating-rate note with specific maturity and coupon characteristics. If the payment frequencies of the fixed and floating sides are the same, it may also be decomposed into a portfolio of FRAs. Either approach makes the valuation of existing swaps or the pricing of new swaps simple. We discuss each approach in turn.

### The Principal Method: Swaps as a Portfolio of Bonds

Consider an investor who is (a) short a fixed-rate bond with coupon $k$, and (b) long a floating-rate note indexed to Libor. Suppose the bond and note have the same maturities, have face values equal to the notional principal of the swap, and have respective coupon dates that coincide with the fixed and floating payment dates on the swap. What are the cash flows to the investor from this portfolio?

- On the respective coupon dates, the investor makes fixed-rate payments at the rate $k$ on the short position in the fixed-rate bond and receives floating-rate Libor payments from the long position in the floating-rate note.

- At maturity, there is a final exchange of interest payments, but the principal amounts cancel each other out, so there is no net cash flow on account of the principals.

This sequence of cash flows is *exactly* what the investor would receive from a long swap (pay-fixed/receive-floating) position. Thus, ignoring credit risk issues, a pay-fixed/receive-floating interest rate swap is equivalent to this portfolio. The mark-to-market value of the swap at any point in time (henceforth, just the value of the swap) is just the difference in values of the floating-rate note and the fixed-rate bond. Since each of these objects is easy to value off the yield curve, valuation of swaps becomes easy.

Viewing a swap as a portfolio of bonds also makes it easy to see how to "price" a new swap, i.e., how to identify the *swap rate* $k$ such that the swap has zero value to both parties. The floating-rate note is worth par when it is issued, so for the portfolio to be worth zero at inception, the fixed-rate bond must also be worth par at issuance. This means the swap rate $k$ is that coupon rate that would make the fixed-rate bond trade at par. That is, the swap rate is simply the coupon rate on a par coupon bond with the same maturity as the swap and the same payment dates as the fixed side in the swap.

To put this in notational terms, suppose $t_0$ is the initial date of the swap and $t_1, \ldots, t_N$ are the payment dates for the fixed side. Let $k$ denote the swap rate, and, as earlier, let (a) $s_n$ denote the day-count fraction under the swap-market convention for the period $(t_n, t_{n+1})$, and (b) $B(t, t_n)$ denote the time-$t$ present value of \$1 receivable at time $t_n$. The value at inception of a fixed-rate bond with principal \$1, coupon $k$, maturity $t_N$, and coupon dates $t_1, \ldots, t_N$ is

$$[ks_0 B(t_0, t_1) + ks_1 B(t_0, t_2) + \cdots + ks_{N-1} B(t_0, t_N)] + B(t_0, t_N)$$

At inception of the swap, this must be worth par, so we have

$$1 = k \times [s_0 B(t_0, t_1) + s_1 B(t_0, t_2) + \cdots + s_{N-1} B(t_0, t_N)] + B(t_0, t_N)$$

The swap rate is, therefore,

$$k^* = \frac{1 - B(t_0, t_N)}{s_0 B(t_0, t_1) + s_1 B(t_0, t_2) + \cdots + s_{N-1} B(t_0, t_N)}$$

In particular, if, as in the US, the swap market uses the 30/360 convention and fixed payments are made semiannually, then the payment dates are separated by six months each, so $s_n = 1/2$ for all $n$, and the swap rate is

$$k^* = \frac{1 - B(t_0, t_N)}{\frac{1}{2}[B(t_0, t_1) + B(t_0, t_2) + \cdots + B(t_0, t_N)]} \tag{23.5}$$

If, as in euro swap contracts, the swap market uses the 30/360 convention and fixed payments are made annually, then the payment dates are one year apart, and $s_n = 1$ for all $n$. The swap rate in this case works out to

$$k^* = \frac{1 - B(t_0, t_N)}{B(t_0, t_1) + B(t_0, t_2) + \cdots + B(t_0, t_N)} \tag{23.6}$$

A final comment is important. In establishing the equivalence between the swap and the portfolio, we have ignored credit risk issues. This caveat must be kept in mind since the credit risk profiles of the swap and the portfolio are not the same. In the portfolio, the principal amounts are themselves subject to credit risk. If there is default on the long floating-rate note held by the investor, the investor still has to make the fixed-rate payments on the short bond. In the swap, since the principal amount is purely notional, the credit risk exposure is much smaller.

## The Swap Spread and the Swap Curve

The *swap spread* at a given maturity refers to the difference between the swap rate for that maturity and the yield on a government bond of the same maturity. The *swap curve* refers to a plot of swap spreads against maturities.

Swap rates are generally higher than Treasury yields with corresponding maturities, so the swap curve typically lies above the Treasury curve. The size of the swap spread is affected by several factors, including supply and demand considerations and liquidity, but the predominant factor that it reflects is the creditworthiness of the major banks that provide swaps and participate in this market.

The swap curve and the level of swap spreads are key indicators of the conditions in fixed-income markets. Today, it is the swap curve, and not the Treasury curve, that is the benchmark for pricing corporate bonds, mortgages, and other private sector obligations.

## The Forward Method: Swaps as a Portfolio of FRAs

The second approach to valuing swaps is to treat them as a collection of forward-rate agreements. If the fixed and floating sides of the swap have the same payment dates, then each payment date is exactly like an FRA. For example, if we consider a five-year, semiannual swap with floating payments based on Libor and a fixed rate of 10%, the swap is equivalent to a portfolio consisting of 10 FRAs, each with an FRA rate of 10%, and maturing at six-month intervals. The only difference between an FRA and the payments in a swap is that the former is settled in discounted form while the latter are not, but this is unimportant and does not affect the valuation. Note too that unlike the principal method, credit-risk considerations are less important here since FRAs too do not involve an exchange of principals.

Here is one other subtle difference that needs to be taken into account in the valuation and pricing mechanics. In an FRA, cash flows from both legs are computed using the money-market day-count convention. In a swap, the fixed leg uses the swap-market convention. Thus, if $k$ denotes the swap rate, the swap corresponds to a portfolio of FRAs with fixed rate $\widehat{k}$, where $\widehat{k}$ and $k$ are related by

$$\widehat{k} = k \left(\frac{s}{S}\right) \left(\frac{M}{m}\right)$$

## Example 23.4   Valuing an Existing Swap

On August 13 of Year 1 (written 13-Aug-Year 1), a bank has a swap contract on its books with the characteristics listed in Table 23.3. What is the current value of the swap?

The first step in the valuation exercise is to obtain the discount factors to be used for cash flows occurring on the payment dates. Suppose the discount factors are as follows:

| Payment Date | Days from Present | Discount Factor |
|---|---|---|
| 11-Dec-Year 1 | 120 | 0.984009 |
| 11-Jun-Year 2 | 302 | 0.957735 |
| 11-Dec-Year 2 | 485 | 0.929581 |
| 11-Jun-Year 3 | 667 | 0.900683 |
| 11-Dec-Year 3 | 850 | 0.871945 |

With these discount factors in hand, we value the swap in the principal method. In this approach, the swap is viewed as a portfolio consisting of a short position in a fixed-rate bond and a long position in a floating-rate note designed to mimic the cash flows of the swap. The calculations are summarized in Table 23.4.

First consider valuing the floating-rate note. The note has a face value of 100,000,000, is indexed to six-month Libor, and the Libor at the last reset date was 6.50%. The next coupon is due on 11-Dec-Year 1, and there are 183 days between the last reset date and 11-Dec-Year 1. Thus, the coupon due on 11-Dec-Year 1 is

$$0.065 \times \frac{183}{360} \times 100,000,000 = 3,304,167$$

**TABLE 23.3** Swap Valuation Example: Input Data

| | |
|---|---|
| Fixed payment dates | 11-Dec-Year 1, 11-Jun-Year 2, 11-Dec-Year 2, 11-Jun-Year 3, and 11-Dec-Year 3 |
| Floating payment dates | Same as fixed payment dates |
| Swap rate | 6% |
| Floating rate | 6-month Libor |
| Libor at last reset | 6.50% |
| Notional principal | $100,000,000 |
| Pay | Fixed |
| Receive | Floating |

**TABLE 23.4**  Example: Valuing the Swap by the Principal Method

| Payment Date | Discount Factor | Floating Cash Flow | PV(Floating Cash Flow) | Fixed Cash Flow | PV(Fixed Cash Flow) |
|---|---|---|---|---|---|
| 11-Dec-Year 1 | 0.984009 | 103,304,167 | 101,652,230 | 3,000,000 | 2,952,027 |
| 11-Jun-Year 2 | 0.957735 | | | 3,000,000 | 2,873,205 |
| 11-Dec-Year 2 | 0.929581 | | | 3,000,000 | 2,788,743 |
| 11-Jun-Year 3 | 0.900683 | | | 3,000,000 | 2,702,049 |
| 11-Dec-Year 3 | 0.871945 | | | 103,000,000 | 89,810,335 |
| Totals | | | 101,652,230 | | 101,126,359 |

On the coupon date, the floating-rate note resets to par, so the floating-rate note is equivalent to receiving par + interest on 11-Dec-Year 1, i.e., to receiving 103,304,167. Since the discount factor applicable to 11-Dec-Year 1 is 0.984009, the present value of the floating-rate note, as of August 13, is

$$0.984009 \times 103,304,167 = 101,652,230$$

Now consider the fixed-rate bond. The bond carries a coupon equal to the swap rate of 6%, has a face value of 100,000,000, makes coupon payments on the payment dates of the swap, and has the same maturity as the swap. Given the 30/360 day-count convention, this means the bond pays a coupon of

$$0.06 \times \frac{180}{360} \times 100,000,000 = 3,000,000$$

every six months. In addition, the principal of 100,000,000 is repaid at maturity, i.e., on 11-Dec-Year 3. Since we know the discount factors applicable to each of these payment dates, the present values of each of these cash flows is easily computed. Adding them up gives us a value of 101,126,359 for the fixed-rate bond (see Table 23.4).

The value of the long (i.e., pay-fixed/receive-floating) swap is the value of the floating-rate note minus the value of the fixed-rate bond, which is

$$101,652,230 - 101,126,369 = 525,861$$  ∎

---

**Example 23.5  Pricing a New Swap**

Suppose we wish to price a new swap, say a three-year swap commencing on 18-June-Year 1, and with semiannual payment dates for both the fixed and floating sides. The payment dates are 18-Dec-Year 1, 18-Jun-Year 2, 18-Dec-Year 2, 18-Jun-Year 3, 18-Dec-Year 3, and 18-Jun-Year 4.[4]

The swap rate is then determined by (23.5). Thus, we first need to identify the discount factors associated with cash flows occurring on the payment dates of the swap. Suppose

---

[4] In reality, some of the payment dates may fall on weekends or holidays in which case we have to use the convention specified in the contract to determine the payment dates. Commonly-used conventions are the next-business-day convention in which the payment date simply becomes the next business day; and the modified-next-business-day convention in which the payment date becomes the next business day unless the next business day happens to be in a different calendar month, in which case it becomes the preceding business day.

these discount factors are given by the numbers in the following table:

| Date | Discount Factor |
|------|-----------------|
| 18-Dec-Year 1 | 0.975369 |
| 18-Jun-Year 2 | 0.948236 |
| 18-Dec-Year 2 | 0.920011 |
| 18-Jun-Year 3 | 0.890677 |
| 18-Dec-Year 3 | 0.861854 |
| 18-Jun-Year 4 | 0.832676 |

Once we have the discount factors, we can obtain the swap rate from (23.5):

$$\text{Three-year swap rate} = 0.0616429$$

&#9632;

## 23.7 Extending the Pricing Arguments

The pricing and valuation methodology is easily extended to many nonstandard swaps. We look at several examples in this section, all of which require only minor modifications of the procedure described in the previous section. The classes of swaps we look at here include:

- Swaps at above/below market rates ("off-market swaps").
- Zero-coupon swaps.
- Swaps with changing fixed rates (e.g., step-up or step-down swaps).
- Swaps whose floating rates are at a spread to Libor.
- Forward-starting swaps.
- Amortizing/accreting/roller-coaster swaps.

### Off-Market Swaps

In an off-market rate swap, the fixed rate on the swap is set above or below the market swap rate for that maturity. By definition, therefore, the initial value of the swap is different from zero. The valuation of the swap is carried out in the same way. We decompose the swap into a floating-rate note and a fixed-rate bond. The present values of each of these legs is identified in the usual way. Since the initial value is different from zero, there will be an up-front payment equal to the positive or negative NPV of the swap.

Table 23.5 illustrates the pricing mechanics in an example. The example uses a three-year swap with the same payment dates and discount factors as used in Example 23.5. Recall that the market swap rate with these parameters is 0.0616 = 6.16%. The example in Table 23.5 considers a fixed rate of 6%. With semiannual coupons and the 30/360 convention, this means the fixed side makes a payment of 3,000,000 on each payment date.

Since the fixed rate is less than the market swap rate of 6.16%, the value of the long swap (pay fixed/receive floating) is positive. As Table 23.5 shows, the value of the swap is 445,931.

### Zero-Coupon Swaps

Zero-coupon swaps are, as the name suggests, swaps in which the fixed side resembles a zero-coupon bond. That is, the fixed-side makes no payments until maturity and a single lump-sum payment at maturity. The price is stated in terms of the single maturity payment (i.e., as a simple percentage of the notional principal).

**TABLE 23.5**  Example: Valuing Off-Market Swaps

| Payment Date | Discount Factor | Floating Cash Flow | Fixed Cash Flow | PV(Floating Cash Flow) | PV(Fixed Cash Flow) |
|---|---|---|---|---|---|
| 18-Jun-Year 1 | 1.000000 | 100,000,000 | | 100,000,000 | |
| 18-Dec-Year 1 | 0.975369 | | 3,000,000 | | 2,926,107 |
| 18-Jun-Year 2 | 0.948236 | | 3,000,000 | | 2,844,708 |
| 18-Dec-Year 2 | 0.920011 | | 3,000,000 | | 2,760,033 |
| 18-Jun-Year 3 | 0.890677 | | 3,000,000 | | 2,672,031 |
| 18-Dec-Year 3 | 0.861854 | | 3,000,000 | | 2,585,562 |
| 18-Jun-Year 4 | 0.832676 | | 103,000,000 | | 85,765,628 |
| Totals | | | | 100,000,000 | 99,554,069 |
| Value of long swap | | | | | 445,931 |

The valuation and pricing of these swaps is simple. We decompose the swap into a floating-rate note and a bond with a single coupon at maturity, each with a face value equal to the swap's notional. The single-coupon bond has only a single cash flow, so is straightforward to value. The initial fair price of the swap is that size of the single coupon (as a percentage of the swap's notional principal) which would make the bond trade at par.

Table 23.6 illustrates the pricing mechanics. It takes the same payment dates and discount factors as in Example 23.5. With these parameters, the fair price of a three-year zero-coupon swap turns out to be 20.095%.

## Changing Fixed Rates

Here, the fixed rate changes during the life of the swap in accordance with a specified schedule. This causes no complications for pricing. We decompose the swap into a floating-rate note and a bond with coupons equal to the changing fixed rates. (We continue calling this the "fixed-rate bond.") Since the rate changes are pre-specified, the fixed-rate bond has known cash flows, so its present value is easily calculated. The initial value of the swap (which need not be zero) is the difference between the values of the fixed-rate bond and the floating-rate note, or what is the same thing, between the value of the fixed-rate bond and par.

Table 23.7 illustrates the valuation exercise assuming the same payment dates and discount factors as in Example 23.5, and assuming a changing fixed-rate pattern as specified in the table. The initial value of the pay-fixed/receive-floating swap is 524,373.

**TABLE 23.6**  Example: Pricing a Zero-Coupon Swap

| Payment Date | Discount Factor | Floating Cash Flow | Fixed Cash Flow | PV(Floating Cash Flow) | PV(Fixed Cash Flow) |
|---|---|---|---|---|---|
| 18-Jun-Year 1 | 1.000000 | 100,000,000 | | 100,000,000 | |
| 18-Dec-Year 1 | 0.975369 | | | | |
| 18-Jun-Year 2 | 0.948236 | | | | |
| 18-Dec-Year 2 | 0.920011 | | | | |
| 18-Jun-Year 3 | 0.890677 | | | | |
| 18-Dec-Year 3 | 0.861854 | | | | |
| 18-Jun-Year 4 | 0.832676 | | 120,094,731 | | 100,000,000 |
| Totals | | | | 100,000,000 | 100,000,000 |

**TABLE 23.7** Example: Valuing a Swap with Changing Fixed Rates

| Payment Date | Discount Factor | Fixed Rate | Floating Cash Flow | Fixed Cash Flow | PV(Floating Cash Flow) | PV(Fixed Cash Flow) |
|---|---|---|---|---|---|---|
| 18-Jun-Year 1 | 1.000000 | | 100,000,000 | | 100,000,000 | |
| 18-Dec-Year 1 | 0.975369 | 5.00% | | 2,500,000 | | 2,438,423 |
| 18-Jun-Year 2 | 0.948236 | 5.50% | | 2,750,000 | | 2,607,649 |
| 18-Dec-Year 2 | 0.920011 | 6.00% | | 3,000,000 | | 2,760,033 |
| 18-Jun-Year 3 | 0.890677 | 6.50% | | 3,250,000 | | 2,894,700 |
| 18-Dec-Year 3 | 0.861854 | 6.50% | | 3,250,000 | | 2,801,026 |
| 18-Jun-Year 4 | 0.832676 | 6.50% | | 103,250,000 | | 85,973,797 |
| Totals | | | | | 100,000,000 | 99,475,627 |
| Value of long swap | | | | | | 525,373 |

## Spread to Libor

In many swaps, the floating-rate payer pays Libor plus or minus a fixed spread rather than Libor flat. The spread may reflect the credit-riskiness of the floating-rate counterparty, but if not, or if we set aside credit-risk issues (perhaps because they are handled by collateral-posting), then pricing of such swaps is easily handled in this case by extending the earlier arguments. We decompose the swap into a fixed-rate bond and a floating-rate note, where the floating-rate note pays Libor plus the fixed spread. The fixed side is valued as usual. To value the floating side, we use the observation that receiving Libor + $x$ basis points (bps) is the same thing as receiving Libor flat and receiving $x$ bps fixed. We calculate the value of the floating leg by calculating separately the values of a floating-rate note paying Libor flat (which is par) and a coupon stream of $x$ bps. To price the swap, we identify the fixed rate that makes the swap value zero.

Table 23.8 illustrates the pricing of a swap with a spread to Libor. The same payment dates and discount factors are used as in the earlier examples. It is assumed that the floating side pays Libor + 30 bps. The fixed rate required to make the initial value of this swap zero is 6.4673%.

## Forward-Starting Swaps

These swaps are similar to a standard swap except that the swap begins only at a specified date in the future. Thus, it is identical to a plain vanilla swap except that payment dates

**TABLE 23.8** Example: Pricing a Spread-to-Libor Swap

| Payment Date | Discount Factor | Fixed Cash Flow | Floating Cash Flow | Spread Cash Flow | PV(Fixed Cash Flow) | PV(Floating Cash Flow) |
|---|---|---|---|---|---|---|
| 18-Jun-Year 1 | 1.000000 | | 100,000,000 | | | 100,000,000 |
| 18-Dec-Year 1 | 0.975369 | 3,233,655 | | 152,500 | 3,154,007 | 148,744 |
| 18-Jun-Year 2 | 0.948236 | 3,233,655 | | 149,589 | 3,066,268 | 141,846 |
| 18-Dec-Year 2 | 0.920011 | 3,233,655 | | 152,500 | 2,974,998 | 140,302 |
| 18-Jun-Year 3 | 0.890677 | 3,233,655 | | 149,589 | 2,880,142 | 133,236 |
| 18-Dec-Year 3 | 0.861854 | 3,233,655 | | 152,500 | 2,786,939 | 131,433 |
| 18-Jun-Year 4 | 0.832676 | 103,233,655 | | 152,500 | 85,960,187 | 126,983 |
| Totals | | | | | 100,822,543 | 100,822,543 |

**TABLE 23.9**   Example: Pricing a Forward-Starting Swap

| Payment Date | Discount Factor | Floating Cash Flow | Fixed Cash Flow | PV(Floating Cash Flow) | PV(Fixed Cash Flow) |
|---|---|---|---|---|---|
| 18-Dec-Year 1 | 0.975369 | 100,000,000 | | 97,536,900 | |
| 18-Jun-Year 2 | 0.948236 | | 3,193,907 | | 3,028,578 |
| 18-Dec-Year 2 | 0.920011 | | 3,193,907 | | 2,938,430 |
| 18-Jun-Year 3 | 0.890677 | | 3,193,907 | | 2,844,740 |
| 18-Dec-Year 3 | 0.861854 | | 3,193,907 | | 2,752,682 |
| 18-Jun-Year 4 | 0.832676 | | 3,193,907 | | 2,659,490 |
| 18-Dec-Year 4 | 0.807344 | | 103,193,907 | | 83,312,982 |
| Totals | | | | 97,536,900 | 97,536,900 |

are different. Forward-starting swaps can be decomposed into the difference of two vanilla swaps. For example, a three-year pay-fixed/receive-floating swap starting after one year is the same as the following portfolio of two plain vanilla swaps with the same fixed rate:

- A pay-fixed/receive-floating four-year swap.
- A receive-fixed/pay-floating one-year swap.

Table 23.9 illustrates the pricing of forward-starting swaps. The same payment dates and discount factors are used as in the previous examples except that the swap starts only after six months, so an extra payment date is added at the end. The fixed rate that makes this swap have zero initial value today is 6.3878%.

### Amortizing/Accreting/Roller-Coaster Swaps

In these swaps, the notional principal amount changes during the life of the swap in a prespecified manner. Common versions of these include:

1. **Amortizing Swaps**  The principal decreases over time in a specified manner.
2. **Accreting Swaps**  The principal increases over time in a specified manner.
3. **Roller-Coaster Swaps**  The principal changes over time in a specified manner, increasing in some periods and decreasing in others.

Swaps with varying principal of this sort are required to better hedge loans whose principal outstanding may vary over time. Consider, for example, an amortizing loan on the books of a corporation. If the company is using a swap to change the nature of interest-rate risk on this loan, the notional principal in the swap must vary in a similar way to the loan, so an amortizing swap is required. More generally, the swap may be used to hedge an entire book of loans with principal repayments due at different times.

## 23.8   Case Study: The Procter & Gamble–Bankers Trust "5/30" Swap

The 1990s was a decade that abounded in derivatives scandals and blowups (Barings, Metallgesellschaft, Sumitomo, Orange County, Federal Paper Board, Gibson Greetings, LTCM, . . . ). In this section, we describe one of the most notorious of these cases, an exotic interest rate swap purchased by the consumer-products giant Procter & Gamble (P&G) from

**FIGURE 23.3**
The Bankers
Trust–Procter &
Gamble Swap

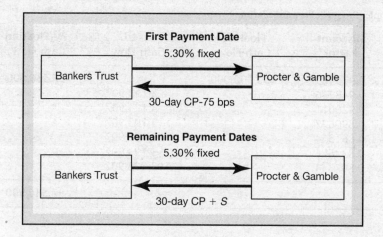

Bankers Trust (BT) in late 1993.[5] The swap involved a relatively small notional principal of $200 million. Nonetheless, such extraordinary leverage was built into the swap payoffs that by the time it was unwound just a few months later, P&G had lost over $100 million on the transaction, and the matter wound up in court.

## The "5/30" Swap: Payoffs

On November 2, 1993, P&G entered into a receive-fixed/pay-floating five-year interest rate swap with BT. The swap had a notional principal of $200 million with semiannual payments on both legs. The payoff structure of the swap is summarized in Figure 23.3. The fixed payment was specified as 5.30%. The floating side was specified in a manner analogous to the spread-to-Libor swaps that we looked at in Section 23.7 but with some unusual twists. For one thing, the benchmark floating rate used was not Libor but the daily average 30-day commercial paper (CP) rate. More interesting is the way the spread over this floating rate was defined. This spread was fixed at −75 basis points for the first payment date, and at

$$S = -75 \text{ basis points } + \max\{0, \xi\} \qquad \textbf{(23.7)}$$

for the nine remaining payment dates thereafter, where $\xi$ was a value that would be determined on the first payment date of the swap, May 4, 1994. The formula determining $\xi$ was specified as

$$\xi = \frac{1}{100} \left[ \left( \frac{98.5}{5.78} \times \text{CMT}_5\% \right) - P_{30} \right] \qquad \textbf{(23.8)}$$

where

- $\text{CMT}_5\%$ was the *yield* (expressed as a percentage) on a five-year constant maturity Treasury (CMT) note, as reported by the Federal Reserve on May 4, 1994.

- $P_{30}$ was the *price* on the same day of a specific 30-year Treasury bond, namely, the 6.25% Treasury bond that would be maturing in August 2023.

It was this dependence on the 5-year and 30-year Treasury rates that gave the swap its "5/30" moniker. Note that $\xi$ depends on the 5-year Treasury's *yield* and the 30-year Treasury's *price*.

[5] Our description and analysis of the P&G–BT swap draws substantially on Smith (1994).

## Analyzing the Swap Payoff

The payoff from this swap looks somewhat complex at first blush, but a closer look reveals a structure that is not hard to understand. The floating rate P&G is required to pay on the swap is

$$30\text{-day CP rate } - 75 \text{ basis points } + \max\{0, \xi\}$$

The last of these terms resembles an option's payoff. As $\xi$ increases and this option finishes in-the-money, P&G's floating-rate payment increases. Thus, P&G is effectively short this option to BT.

What exactly is this option? The value of $\xi$ depends on the *difference* between (a multiple of) the 5-year CMT yield and the price of the 30-year Treasury bond. So the option can be interpreted as an exchange or "Margrabe" option (see Chapter 18) in which the holder has the option to give up (pay) the 30-year bond price in exchange for receiving a multiple of the 5-year CMT yield. Alternatively, the optionality can be described in terms of a call or a put, albeit with a stochastic strike:

- As a *call* option on a multiple of the 5-year CMT yield with a strike price equal to the 30-year bond price.
- As a put option on the 30-year bond price with a strike price equal to a multiple of the 5-year CMT yield.

Of course, all these ways of describing the option are equivalent. A formal valuation of the option $\max\{0, \xi\}$ is not difficult to carry out using a term-structure model (see Part 4 of the book for descriptions of several term-structure models). But with even less effort, it is possible to gain a good idea of what risks it is that P&G is taking on and what movements in the term-structure could hurt or help P&G.

To begin, we note the following. At inception of the swap, the 5-year CMT yield was 5.02%, and the 30-year bond price was 102.57811. Plugging these into the definition of $\xi$, we get $\xi = -0.1703$. This means $\max\{0, \xi\} = 0$, so the option was out-of-the-money at inception.

What could cause it to move into-the-money? This is easy. An increase in either the 5-year CMT yield or the yield of the 30-year bond (which would lower its price) both increases the value of $\xi$, so pushes the option towards the money. An increase in both yields simultaneously has a sharp effect on $\xi$. So P&G is primarily exposed to upward shifts in interest rates, and especially to upward shifts in the entire yield curve.

To gauge the quantitative effects of such an increase, consider the following exercise. At inception of the swap, the 5-year CMT yield was, as mentioned, 5.02%, while the price of the 30-year bond implied a yield of 6.06%. What would happen if both yields were to increase by roughly 100 basis points, to 6% and 7%, respectively, at maturity? From Table 23.10, the resulting value of $\xi$ would be 0.1155, or 11.55%. That is, P&G would now be making

**TABLE 23.10** The P&G–BT Swap: The Values of $\xi$

| | 30-Year Treasury Yields | | | |
|---|---|---|---|---|
| This table describes the values of $\xi$ for different values of the 5-year CMT yield and the 30-year bond yield. Source: Smith (1994). | | | | |
| **5-Year Yields** | **6.00%** | **6.50%** | **7.00%** | **7.25%** |
| 5.00% | −0.1821 | −0.1152 | −0.0549 | −0.0270 |
| 5.50% | −0.0969 | −0.0300 | +0.0303 | +0.0582 |
| 6.00% | −0.0117 | +0.0552 | +0.1155 | +0.1434 |
| 6.50% | +0.0735 | +0.1404 | +0.2007 | +0.2286 |

a floating payment of

$$30\text{-day CP} - 0.0075 + 0.1155 = 30\text{-day CP} + 10.80\%$$

Since P&G is receiving only 5.30% fixed on the swap's other leg, such a movement in yields would evidently be disastrous for P&G (but correspondingly very profitable for BT).

Table 23.10 also shows the spreads that would result for some other values of the 5-year CMT and 30-year bond yields. The numbers in the table show that there is some protection for P&G against the yield curve steepening (specifically, against the 30-year rate alone increasing while the 5-year rate remains stationary); in this case, $\xi$ increases but remains negative even with a 1% move in the 30-year yield. There is also some protection against the yield curve inverting (specifically, the 5-year yield increasing while the 30-year yield stays constant). But an increase in both rates hurts P&G.

The table also shows that the realizations of $\xi$ are more sensitive to changes in the 5-year CMT yield than to changes in the 30-year bond's yield. Smith (1994) derives an expression that makes this point succinctly; he shows that *changes* in the value of $\xi$ from its value at inception are approximately equal to

$$[0.170415 \times \Delta(\text{CMT}_5)] + [0.136442 \times \Delta(\text{YLD}_{30})]$$

where $\Delta(\text{CMT}_5)$ and $\Delta(\text{YLD}_{30})$ are the changes in the 5-year CMT yield and 30-year bond yield (both expressed as percentages), respectively, from their initial values. This means that a 1% change in the 5-year CMT yield changes $\xi$ by over 0.17 or 17% while a 1% change in the yield of the 30-year bond changes $\xi$ by the smaller, but still impressive, amount of over 0.13, or 13%. A simultaneous change of 1% in the two yields increases $\xi$ by over 0.30 or an astonishing 30%.

The asymmetric impact of interest rates in the payoffs is to be emphasized. Once we have $\xi < 0$, the option $\max\{0, \xi\}$ is out-of-the-money and any further decreases in interest rates that lower $\xi$ further have no impact on the swap's payoffs. So P&G faces enormous risk from interest-rate increases without a corresponding benefit from interest-rate decreases. None of this is hard to see—indeed, most of the work that is required is the tedious but straightforward job of converting 30-year bond yields into prices, so that all the arguments can be expressed in terms of yields rather than prices. Yet, oddly, one of the complaints made by P&G in the lawsuit that it brought against BT was that BT had not adequately explained the complexity of the swap to P&G.

## The Outcome

In January 1994, the terms of the swap were altered in two ways. First, the date for fixing the spread was changed from May 4 to May 19. This change greatly increased the uncertainty concerning the final interest rates because of a Federal Open Market Committee meeting scheduled for May 17, 1994, at which important monetary policy decisions could potentially be made. The increased volatility in interest rates on this account combined with the increased maturity greatly increased the value of the option that BT held and that P&G was short. As compensation, the floating-rate payment was reduced by 13 basis points to

$$30\text{-day CP rate} - 88 \text{ basis points} + \max\{0, \xi\}$$

At this point, interest rates were only slightly higher than they had been in November, and the option was still well out-of-the-money. If interest rates had remained unchanged from this point on, P&G would have found itself locked into an extremely favorable swap in which it would have received a fixed rate of 5.30% in exchange for paying the daily average 30-day CP rate less 88 basis points.

Unfortunately for P&G, they did not. In February 1994, the Federal Reserve tightened monetary policy, causing a sharp upward movement in the interest rates. By mid-February, both the 5-year and 30-year yields had increased by about 60 basis points each. When interest rates continued climbing in March, P&G decided to lock in a value for the spread rather than take the risk of even higher interest rates. The lock in was done in phases and by the time it was complete, the value of $\xi$ agreed to was 15%; that is, P&G would pay

$$30\text{-day CP rate } - 88 \text{ basis points } + 15\% = 30\text{-day CP rate } + 14.12\%$$

in exchange for receiving 5.30% fixed. Present-valuing the cash-flow streams based on the then-prevailing interest rates, Smith (1994) reports that the swap had a negative value to P&G of over $106 million, or an amazing 53% of the swap principal of $200 million.

As it happens, waiting until May would have made the situation much worse. Interest rates continued to climb, and by May 19 (the fixing date for the spread), the 5-year rate was around 6.60% and the 30-year yield was at around 7.40%, each around 80–100 basis points higher than in March. This would have resulted in P&G having to make a floating-rate payment of the 30-day CP rate plus around 27%!

### The Inevitable Lawsuit

P&G had also entered into a second swap with BT, this one a leveraged swap referencing the Deutsche mark rate. The "DM swap," as it came to be known, also turned into a huge loss for P&G. The loss suffered on the two swaps combined amounted to almost $200 million.

In late 1994, P&G sued BT alleging that BT had misled it with respect to the risk involved in the transaction. BT countered that it was just a counterparty to P&G and was not acting in a fiduciary role. But by this time, two other clients of BT, Gibson Greetings and Air Products and Chemicals, who too had suffered losses of several million dollars in derivatives transactions with BT, had also filed suit. The lawsuits alleged that BT had taken advantage of their relative lack of financial experience, particularly with respect to complex derivative transactions. BT found itself in the hot seat in terms of public perception when tapes were released to the media in which BT employees were recorded discussing the lack of financial sophistication of their clients.

P&G and BT ultimately reached an out-of-court settlement in 1996, with P&G reporting a net gain of $78 million in this context in its quarterly reports. BT also settled its suit with Air Products and Chemicals, and paid a fine to the SEC for misleading Gibson Greetings. By the time the dust settled, BT, a leader in derivatives innovation and risk-management in the 1990s, had suffered a near-irreparable loss of reputation. A short while later, following considerable losses in 1998 after the Russian default crisis, it was taken over by Deutsche Bank.

## 23.9  Case Study: A Long-Term Capital Management "Convergence Trade"

Long-Term Capital Management (LTCM) was a hedge fund founded in 1994 by John Merriwether, former head of fixed-income trading at Salomon Brothers.[6] It rapidly became the most glamorous and well-known institution of its kind. Among its other founding

---

[6] The general material of this section draws on many sources including David Shirreff's "Lessons from the Collapse of Hedge Fund, Long-Term Capital Management," available at `http://riskinstitute.ch/146480.htm`. The description of the convergence trade is taken from the London Business School class notes of Viral Acharya, and was attributed by him to Tim Johnson.

partners were star Wall Street traders, luminaries from academia (including the soon-to-be Nobel laureates Robert Merton and Myron Scholes), and senior government officials (such as David Mullins, former vice-chairman of the US Federal Reserve). The fund placed a hefty minimum investment threshold for investors of $10 million. It also charged a 2-and-25 fee structure (2% of the assets under management, 25% of profits), much steeper than the 1-and-20 structure prevalent at that time. Despite all this, the fund raised a then-record initial investment of $1.25 billion.

Leveraging its star power and contacts, the fund obtained trading and margin terms from Wall Street banks that were far more favorable than those available to typical hedge funds. Its first full years in operation, 1995 and 1996, brought eye-popping returns to investors of 43% and 41%, respectively, far outperforming market indices such as the S&P 500. But 1997 was a quieter year: the fund returned a respectable 17% but was substantially beaten by the 31% return on the S&P 500.

Finding fewer investment opportunities in its traditional areas of operations, the fund started moving increasingly into newer areas like risk-arbitrage and emerging markets but also returned $2.7 billion to investors. It entered 1998 with about $4.8 billion under management.

## Relative Value and Convergence Trades

The bread-and-butter of LTCM's trading strategies were relative value and convergence trades, trades in which the prices of two securities or assets were viewed as out of kilter relative to each other and in which the price difference was therefore expected to narrow or even to converge to zero. By buying one security and selling the other, profits could be racked up when (or, more accurately, if) the relative prices moved as predicted.

One simple example of a relative value trade involves on-the-run versus off-the-run Treasuries. Newly-issued US Treasury securities (those "on-the-run") tend to have higher prices (so lower yields) than older ("off-the-run") ones; the lower prices of the off-the-run securities compensate their holders for their lower liquidity. Not all off-the-run securities are identical; those that were more recently on-the-run tend to be more liquid, so to have lower yields, than those more distantly on-the-run although the differences are dwarfed by those between on-the-run and off-the-run securities.

To take a hypothetical example, suppose that the difference in yields (the "spread") between the on-the-run 30-year Treasury bond and the previously on-the-run bond is typically 15 basis points (0.15%) and that between the previously on-the-run bond and *its* predecessor is typically 5 basis points (0.05%). This means that while the current difference between the on-the-run bond and its predecessor is 15 basis points, we can expect this difference to narrow to 5 basis points when the current on-the-run bond goes off-the-run. So by going short the on-the-run security and long the previously on-the-run security, we expect to make 10 basis points regardless of the direction of interest rates—provided our anticipations concerning the spreads work out.

LTCM used many such relative value/convergence trades, often betting on convergence or a narrowing of spreads between liquid Treasury or other G-10 government securities on the one hand and other, more illiquid, and sometimes more complex, instruments on the other.

## Leverage

While it may be profitable, the profits from such relative value/convergence trades are very small (possibly as low as just a few basis points), so a significant degree of leverage is required to generate decent returns. LTCM's leverage levels were simply enormous. At the time of the fund's collapse in late 1998, it had assets on its books of over $125 billion supported by its capital of only \$4.8 billion, a leverage ratio exceeding 25:1. In addition, the fund had over \$1 *trillion* in notional principal in off-balance-sheet instruments, mainly swaps with various counterparties. (This figure should not be taken too literally. LTCM frequently offset existing swaps by entering into new swaps with new counterparties rather than unwinding the existing swap. Since the swaps were covered by ISDA netting agreements, LTCM's actual exposure was likely much smaller than the notional \$1 trillion figure.)

## The Summer of 1998

In July 1998, Salomon Brothers closed its bond arbitrage unit and began unwinding its positions. LTCM apparently had many positions similar to those of Salomon because when Salomon began selling its positions, LTCM took a substantial hit. In all, the fund dropped almost 10% that month. But this was nothing compared to the storm that was about to hit.

On August 17, Russia declared a moratorium on payments on its rouble debt and its dollar-denominated local debt. Panic hit the world's financial markets, and investments fled to the safety of G-10 government securities. Spreads between these and non-sovereign or emerging market instruments widened sharply, and spreads between even on-the-run and off-the-run Treasuries widened.

LTCM had huge positions in several exotic convergence trades around the world, many of which had bet on the relevant spreads narrowing. These trades registered massive losses. The year-to-date losses on a marked-to-market basis exceeded \$2.5 billion (or a stunning 52% of the capital of \$4.8 billion at the beginning of the year), with losses of \$2.1 billion in August alone. At this point, these were still only paper losses, not realized ones; nonetheless, LTCM estimated that it needed fresh capital of \$1.5 billion to stay afloat through the market turmoil.

But the fund had lost the confidence of investors by now. It found it impossible to raise the required capital, and by mid-September, Bear Stearns, its clearing agent, demanded an extra collateral of \$500 million to continue clearing LTCM's trades. Attempts to sell the portfolio to a single buyer went nowhere; the few offers that came, including a \$250 million offer from Warren Buffet's Berkshire Hathaway, were rejected by the fund's partners. In the end, a massive bailout was orchestrated by the New York Federal Reserve that involved 14 large international banks. The banks contributed a combined sum of \$3.625 billion in exchange for a 90% stake in the fund. The fund survived for another several months, even reporting a return after fees and expenses of 10% in 1999, before finally being liquidated in 2000.

## An LTCM Convergence Trade

One of the convergence trades implemented by LTCM, and one that lost it over a billion dollars, had the following four components:

1. Receive fixed on five-year forward fixed-for-floating British pound (GBP) swaps.
2. Short gilts (bonds issued by the UK government, the UK analog of US Treasuries).
3. Pay fixed on five-year forward fixed-for-floating Deutsche mark (DEM) swaps.[7]
4. Long bunds (the German analog of gilts).

The positions were calibrated to reflect, in totality, a specific market view concerning the behavior of the *difference* between UK and German swap spreads, specifically, that this difference would *narrow*.

---

[7] The German currency at the time of this transaction was still the DEM. The German (DEM) floating rate was the Frankfurt Interbank Offered Rate or Fibor.

To understand this implied view, consider first the vanilla fixed-for-floating GBP swap. Since LTCM is receiving fixed and paying floating on this swap, it gains if GBP swap rates generally decrease. Thus, this leg is profitable if

- gilt yields decrease even while the spread between GBP swap rates and gilts remains the same; or
- the spread between GBP swap rates and gilts declines even while gilt yields stay the same.

(Of course, the position also makes money in some other cases, e.g., if both gilt yields and GBP swap spreads decline.) On the other hand, the second component of the portfolio involves a short position in gilts, so *loses* money if gilt yields go down. The two positions were calibrated so that the effect of a movement in gilt yields alone was offsetting. Thus, the combined position is effectively one in GBP swap spreads: it is profitable if spreads narrow and loses money if spreads widen.

By the same argument, the third and fourth legs of the portfolio reflect in combination a position in DEM swap spreads. In this case, because the portfolio involves *paying* fixed on the swap and a *long* position in bunds, it is analogous to holding a position that makes money when German (DEM) swap spreads widen and loses money when they narrow.

Combining all four positions now, the overall portfolio involves a view not separately on UK swap spreads or German swap spreads, but on the *difference* between the two. As long as UK swap spreads fell *relative to* German swap spreads, the position would be profitable. The bet was really one of *convergence*. At the time, quoted UK swap spreads were wider than German swap spreads. LTCM was speculating that this difference would narrow. In part, this was a bet that the UK would also join the euro zone, so GBP-Libor and DEM-Fibor would both become the same rate, what is now called the Euribor rate.

Unfortunately for LTCM, things went horribly wrong. Following the Russian default, the gap between GBP-Libor and DEM-Fibor widened even further. LTCM lost considerable money on a marked-to-market basis. Closing out of similar positions by other banks widened the difference between the spreads even further and led to counterparties demanding extra collateral. In all, as mentioned above, LTCM lost around a billion dollars on this strategy.

## 23.10    Credit Risk and Credit Exposure

As with all derivatives, two major sources of risks in swaps come from changes in the value of the underlying driving variable (in this case, interest rates; this is "market risk") and from counterparty default ("credit risk").

Interest-rate changes affect the fixed and floating sides of the swap differentially. Since the fixed leg involves fixed future cash flows, a change in interest rates has a greater effect on it than on the floating leg, where only the next payment is fixed. Interest-rate risk can also take on other forms. For example, in certain classes of swaps such as basis swaps, each leg of the swap is indexed to a floating rate. In this case, the swap holder also faces the risk of changes in the basis.

The other potential source of risk is credit risk. Credit risk in swaps differs from that in bonds. In interest rate swaps, the principal is "notional" in that it is used to calculate interest payments, but the principal amount is itself never exchanged. So, unlike bonds, there is no principal risk in a swap. Moreover, if the current value of a swap is negative, there is no loss from the swap being terminated on account of counterparty default (in fact, there is a gain), so there is no credit risk concern. It is only when the value of the swap is positive that credit risk exists.

The level of credit risk in a swap is affected by many factors. Counterparty creditworthiness at the time of entering into the swap and changes in creditworthiness over the life of the swap are of obvious importance. So too are deal size, maturity, and other terms of the contract. For example, mismatches in payment dates have credit-risk implications. If the floating side pays quarterly and the fixed side semiannually, the floating payer is exposed to default from the fixed payment for longer periods of time.

Market risk changes can also have a credit-risk impact. A sharp change in interest rates can lead to a severe worsening of the position of the counterparty in a swap leading to increased credit risk. Finally, netting agreements in place matter for credit risk. Most swap agreements between counterparties are undertaken within the ambit of a broader master agreement that provides for netting losses in case there are many swap contracts between the same parties. Hence, the losses in one contract may offset the gains on another, mitigating the possible loss from failure of a counterparty.

The *credit exposure* in a swap is a measure of the maximum potential loss from the swap. Credit exposure is divided into two parts: current exposure and future exposure. Current exposure is the loss that would occur were the counterparty to default immediately, so is the maximum of the current mark-to-market value of the swap and zero. (There is no current exposure if the mark-to-market value of the swap is negative.) Future exposure measures the potential losses that could occur over the remaining life of the swap. To compute this exposure, we first choose a model of interest-rate movements and identify, with a given confidence level (say, 95%), the maximum extent to which rates could move against the counterparty. We calculate the amount the counterparty would owe at those levels. This is the future exposure.

Credit exposure changes over the life of a swap. In general, credit exposure has an inverted U-shape, increasing from zero as time moves on and then decreasing towards zero again. The exposure at the beginning of the swap is zero since the swap itself has zero value at that time. As the swap approaches maturity, the credit exposure again goes to zero since the number of remaining cash flows at risk falls.

# 23.11   Hedging Swaps

The main source of risk in swaps is changes in interest rates. An increase in interest rates raises the value of the swap to fixed-rate payers and lowers it for the floating-rate payer; vice versa if interest rates decrease.

Interest-rate exposure could be hedged by using an offsetting position in another swap with identical dates, etc. However, this may not be feasible for non-standard swaps or at the level of a portfolio of swaps. Therefore, other means of managing interest-rate risk in swaps are usually called for. There are several alternatives:

- Hedge using a different swap.
- Hedge using bonds.
- Hedge using futures and FRAs.

The ideas behind these hedges are simple. We match the interest-rate sensitivity of the swap with other instruments that are inversely sensitive in the same magnitude to the risk from the swap. The three choices above are very popular routes to a hedging strategy.

Of course, there will always be some residual basis risk. (Recall that basis risk arises when the hedge used does not perfectly track the underlying risk). However, using portfolios of these instruments usually helps in keeping basis risk to a minimum. The absolute amount of basis risk depends on two important aspects of the risk in question:

- The correlation of the hedge with swap cash flows.
- The size of the hedged position.

Setting up the hedge begins with the ascertainment of the delta of the swap position. Note that this is not the same delta as computed for equity options. Here delta measures sensitivity with respect to interest-rate risk and is defined as the change in the value of the swap for a 1 bps increase in interest rates.

- If the delta is positive, swap value increases when interest rates increase.
- If the delta is negative, swap value decreases when interest rates decrease.

The delta is positive when the swap is viewed from the viewpoint of the payer of the fixed leg in the swap. When rates rise, the fixed payer does not pay out more but instead receives higher interest on the floating leg. Hence, the value of the swap for the fixed payer rises when interest rates increase, implying that delta is positive.

We may extend the concept of delta to that of a *delta vector*. This is defined as the change in value of a portfolio of swaps for an independent 1 bps increase in each interest rate (of all maturities). This notion takes heed of the fact that the swap is sensitive to changes in the entire term structure of interest rates, not a single rate. To operationalize the computation of the delta vector, we split the portfolio into "buckets" of different maturities. The idea is to create an equivalent portfolio that has the same delta vector as the one being hedged. The cash flows of the original swap (or book of swaps) are assigned to these buckets. Each bucket is then treated as a stand-alone security with a single cash flow at the maturity of the bucket. The delta of each bucket may then be computed with respect to the interest rate for only the maturity of that bucket, as we now explain.

## Allocating Cash Flows to Buckets

Bucketing of cash flows involves collapsing the given cash flows onto a finite set of points in time. We begin by choosing the time points that act as the "buckets" to which all swap cash flows will be allocated. For example, if we have a book of swaps going out to 10 years, we may use 40 evenly-spaced buckets to represent the horizon, so there is one bucket per quarter. Our objective is to allocate all cash flows from the given swaps to the chosen time buckets in some reasonable way. Intuitively, we want the bucketed portfolio to look "like" the original portfolio. There is no formal definition of what it means for one portfolio to look like another, but here are two plausible criteria:

1. **Value Preservation** The present value of the cash flows should not change.
2. **Risk Preservation** The riskiness of the cash flows should not change.

To illustrate, suppose we wish to allocate a given cash flow $c$ that occurs at a given time $t$ to the buckets. Identify the two time points $t_1$ and $t_2$ in the bucket that "bracket" $t$, i.e., which are the nearest points in the bucket such that

$$t_1 < t < t_2$$

Denote the allocation to $t_1$ and $t_2$ by $c_1$ and $c_2$, respectively. The first criterion says that $c_1$ and $c_2$ should satisfy

$$PV(c_1) + PV(c_2) = PV(c)$$

**FIGURE 23.4**
Allocation of a Single
Cash Flow to
Adjoining Buckets

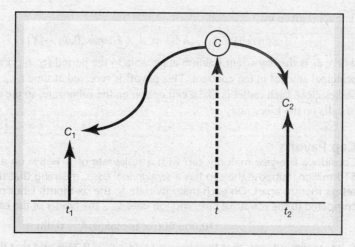

For example, suppose the interest rates in continuously-compounded terms for times $t_1$, $t$, and $t_2$ are, respectively, $r_1$, $r$, and $r_2$. Then, we obtain

$$e^{-r_1 t_1} c_1 + e^{-r_2 t_2} c_2 = e^{-rt} c$$

This gives us one equation in two unknowns. For a second equation, we use the second criterion. For this, we need to define "risk." We take the risk of a cash flow to be measured by its PVBP, i.e., by the change in the present value of the cash flow for a one basis point change in interest rates. This gives us the second equation as

$$PVBP(c_1) + PVBP(c_2) = PVBP(c)$$

In the case of continuously-compounded interest rates, this works out to

$$e^{-r_1 t_1} t_1 c_1 + e^{-r_2 t_2} t_2 c_2 = e^{-rt} ct$$

Solving the two equations, we get the desired break-up of the cash flow $c$. In this way, all the cash flows of the swap book may be allocated to the different buckets.

See Figure 23.4 for a diagrammatic description of the procedure. We note that doing an allocation like this for each individual swap will not save us any computation since it involves calculating the present value of each cash flow anyway. However, if we take all the swaps in the trading book and aggregate cash flows on each date before allocating the cash flows to the surrounding pair of dates, then a substantive speedup of the procedure is obtained.

## 23.12   Caps, Floors, and Swaptions

The products we have discussed so far in the chapter have not contained optionality features. We examine in this segment some of the most popular classes of interest-rate options: caps, floors, and swaptions. We begin with caps and floors. Swaptions—options on swaps—are discussed further down in this section.

A *cap* is a portfolio of options, each called a *caplet*. The caplets have maturity dates $t_1, \ldots, t_n$ that are equally spaced (e.g., quarterly or semiannually). All caplets share the same strike $X$, which is referred to as the strike of the cap. Let $\ell_k$ denote the Libor rate observed at $t_k$ for the period $(t_k, t_{k+1})$. Then, the payoff from the $k$-th caplet (i.e., the one with maturity date $t_k$) is given by

$$A \times \max\{0, \ell_k\delta_k - X\delta_k\} = A \times \delta_k \max\{0, \ell_k - X\} \qquad \text{(23.9)}$$

where $\delta_k$ is the day-count fraction applicable to the period $(t_k, t_{k+1})$ and $A$ is the notional principal amount in the contract. This payoff is received at time $t_{k+1}$. As the payoff (23.9) makes clear, each caplet is like a call option on the Libor rate, so the cap is just a portfolio of calls on the Libor rate.

## Example 23.6   Cap Payoffs

Consider a five-year maturity cap with a strike rate of $X = 8\%$ on a principal amount of $10 million. Suppose the cap has a *semiannual basis*, meaning that the dates $t_1, t_2, \ldots$ are set six months apart. On each maturity date $t_k$, the six-month Libor rate $\ell_k$ at that point is compared to the 8% strike rate, and, on date $t_{k+1}$, the holder of the cap receives the payoff

$$10{,}000{,}000 \times \delta_k \max\{0, \ell_k - 0.08\}$$

Suppose, for instance, that the observed rate is $\ell_k = 9.25\%$ and that the day-count fraction is 183/360. Then, on date $t_{k+1}$, the holder of the cap receives the payoff

$$10{,}000{,}000 \times \frac{183}{360} \times \max\{0, 0.0925 - 0.08\} = 63{,}541.67 \qquad \blacksquare$$

Two points bear emphasizing. First, note that the payoff that is determined at each reset date $t_k$ is paid out only on date $t_{k+1}$. Second, conventionally, there is no exchange of cash flows on the first reset date in a cap. In principle, any exchange of payments on the first reset date $t_1$ would be based on the prevailing Libor rates at the time the cap is purchased and so would be fully known at the outset. This is analogous to the situation in swaps where the payments in the first exchange are known at the time of entering into the swap. However, unlike in swaps, the practice in the caps/floors markets is not to exchange these first payments. Thus, for example, in a five-year cap with a semiannual basis, there are nine exchanges of cash flows in all (in months 12, 18, 24, ... 54, and 60, corresponding to the Libor rates observed in months 6, 12, 18, ..., 48, and 54).

## Floors

The complement of a cap is called a *floor*. Floors correspond to *put options* on the interest rate. A floor, like a cap, is a portfolio of options with the same strike $X$, and expiring at successive equally-spaced maturity dates $t_1, \ldots, t_n$. If the Libor rate on date $t_k$ is $\ell_k$, then on date $t_{k+1}$, the holder of the floor receives the payoff

$$A \times \delta_k \max\{0, X - \ell_k\} \qquad \text{(23.10)}$$

where $A$ and $\delta_k$ have been defined above.

## Uses of Caps and Floors

One important purpose of a cap is in hedging, in particular, to enable floating-rate borrowers to lock-in a ceiling rate they have to pay on their borrowing. For example, a floating-rate borrower who wishes to hedge against the risk of interest rates exceeding 9% can buy a 9%-strike cap. If interest rates remain below 9%, the caps expire worthless, but the borrower achieves the objective of keeping interest payments below 9%. If interest rates exceed 9% on any maturity date, the appropriate caplet compensates the holder for the amount by which Libor exceeds 9%, so the net payment made by the borrower is exactly 9%. Shortly, we present an example that illustrates this use of caps in controlling financing costs. Just as a cap provides a ceiling on interest rates, a floor provides a lower bound that is particularly useful for floating-rate investors.

Of course, caps and floors can also be used for speculative purposes. For instance, speculators wishing to bet on increasing interest rates can buy caps. Often, in both hedging and speculation, the purchase of a cap is done in tandem with selling floors so as to subsidize the cost of the caps. A contract of this sort (the simultaneous purchase of a cap and sale of a floor) is called a "collar." The opposite contract is a short collar and can be undertaken if a bet on dropping interest rates is being made. In a collar, the cap strike rate is higher than the floor strike rate. It is always possible to set the strike rates on the cap and floor in such a way that the premium paid on the cap is exactly offset by the premium received on the floor. This is known as a "zero-cost collar."

## Controlling Financing Costs with Caps and Floors

As with swaps, caps and floors may be used to compare different financing options. The use of caps and floors in conjunction with floating-rate borrowing often allows firms to raise cheaper financing. The following pair of examples illustrate. The first example looks at caps alone and the second includes caps and floors.

### Example 23.7

Consider a hypothetical company that wishes to raise two-year financing. In discussions with their bankers, the company is presented with two alternatives. One is to obtain a semiannual pay two-year loan at a fixed interest rate of 9%. The alternative is to issue a floating-rate note (FRN) at six-month Libor plus 10 basis points. Suppose that the current rate for six-month Libor is 8%. A two-year 8%-strike cap (semiannual basis) is trading at a premium of $1.55 for every $100 notional. What should the company do?

To address this question, we compute the financing cost of the floating-rate route and compare it with the fixed-rate cost of 9%. At time 0, the company can raise $100 through issuance of the FRN and simultaneously purchase the two-year semiannual basis cap for $1.55, resulting in a net cash inflow at time 0 of $98.45. Note that the first interest payment, due at the end of six months, is already determined by the current level of six-month Libor.

The financing cost varies with the six-month Libor rate, so consider first the *worst-case* cash flows in this case. If the rate drops and remains below 8%, the caplets expire worthless, but the financing cost remains below the desired 8% level. If the rate rises and exceeds 8%, then the FRN coupons are higher but this is offset by the cap. So, at worst, the rate paid is 8% plus the 10 basis points spread on the floating-rate borrowing. Therefore, assuming for simplicity that the six-month day-count fraction is 0.50, the *maximum* cash outflow for coupon payments is $4.05 (half of 8.10%) in months 12, 18, and 24 per $100 of notional principal. For the first payment in six months, the rate is already fixed at Libor + 10 bps, i.e., at 8.10%, meaning a cash outflow of $4.05 in month 6. Finally, at maturity, there is the final payment of principal of $100 as well. These cash flows are summarized in the following table:

| Month | Worst-Case Cash Flow |
| --- | --- |
| 0 | 98.45 |
| 6 | −4.05 |
| 12 | −4.05 |
| 18 | −4.05 |
| 24 | −104.05 |
| Internal rate of return | 0.08964 |

The "all-in cost" of the strategy is the internal rate of return (IRR) on these cash flows, i.e., the discount rate such that the NPV of the cash flows is zero. For the given cash flows, the

IRR works out to 8.964%. This is the worst-case cost of the combined FRN-plus-cap strategy. Even this worst case is superior to the 9% cost of fixed-rate financing, so the company is evidently better off going in for floating-rate borrowing combined with the interest-rate caps than fixed-rate borrowing.   ∎

---

**Example 23.8**

We extend Example 23.7 by introducing floors. Suppose that a two-year floor (semiannual basis) is trading at a premium of $0.40. The company might wish to sell this floor to subsidize the cost of the cap they bought. Of course, the cost of selling the floor is that the company no longer benefits if interest rates drop below 6%, so this strategy makes sense especially if the company believes that interest rates are unlikely to drop below 6% over the next two years.

Once again, we begin by identifying the all-in cost of the worst-case scenario. In this case, the time-0 cash flows are equal to $98.85, i.e., the issue of the FRN at $100 less the cost of the cap ($1.55) plus the inflow from the sale of the floor ($0.40). The cash flows after time 0 remain the same as in the previous table. (Introducing the floor doesn't affect the worst-case interest payments.) For the modified inflow and other cash flows, the internal rate of return works out to 8.739% as shown in the following table.

| Month | Worst-Case Cash Flow | Best-Case Cash Flow |
|-------|----------------------|---------------------|
| 0     | 98.85                | 98.85               |
| 6     | −4.05                | −4.05               |
| 12    | −4.05                | −3.05               |
| 18    | −4.05                | −3.05               |
| 24    | −104.05              | −103.05             |
| IRR   | 0.08739              | 0.07255             |

What about the *best-case* cash flows? Without a position in the floor, the best-case scenario is that the six-month Libor rate drops to zero for the payments due in months 12, 18, and 24. (Note that the first payment due in six months is not affected since that rate is already determined.) In this case, the cash outflow in months 12, 18, and 24 would just be the 10 basis points spread. As a consequence, the all-in cost would work out to a measly 0.68%.

But with the floor also present, the best-case scenario in months 12, 18, and 24 is that the floor payment is made in each period. Since the floor strike is 6%, this means an interest rate of 6.10% including the 10 basis points spread, or a cash outflow of $3.05 per $100 of principal. These best-case cash flows are also shown in the table above. The best-case all-in cost works out to 7.255%. The use of the collar means that the final realized all-in cost will lie in the band between 7.255% and 8.964%.

The choice the company ultimately makes will depend on the directional views held. If the company were of the opinion that the six-month Libor rate could fall below 6% with a high probability, it would be better off going in for the cap alone. Conversely, if the view is that rates are unlikely to fall below 6%, use of the floor to subsidize the purchase of the cap is a good idea. In either case, comparison of the fixed-rate financing route with its synthetic counterpart, manufactured using an FRN and caps/floors, is a comparison of a point with a range. Such analyses are routine and result in close linkages between the fixed- and floating-rate markets.   ∎

## Put-Call Parity Revisited

Since caps are akin to calls on the interest rates and floors to puts, a version of put-call parity can be derived in this market. The parity relationship links caps and floors to swaps.

Consider a cap and floor with identical notional principals, bases and payment dates, and a strike of $X$. Suppose we are long the cap and short the floor. Then, on each caplet/floorlet maturity date $t_k$, there are two possibilities:

- If the relevant Libor rate $\ell_k$ exceeds $X$, the caplet is in-the-money and has a payoff of $(\ell_k - X)\delta_k$ on date $t_{k+1}$. The floorlet lapses unexercised.
- If $\ell_k < X$, then the floorlet is in-the-money, and the cash flow to the short position is $-(X - \ell_k)\delta_k = (\ell_k - X)\delta_k$. The caplet lapses unexercised.

Thus, in either case, the cash flow from the portfolio is $(\ell_k - X)\delta_k$ and this payoff is received at date $t_{k+1}$.

Now, consider a vanilla fixed-for-floating swap with fixed rate $X$ and reset dates identical to the maturity dates of the caplets but with two modifications. First, suppose that the swap has no exchange of payments on the first reset date $t_1$. Second, assume that both legs of the swap use the same day-count convention, so $\delta_k$ is the day-count fraction that applies to both legs of the swap for payments at $t_{k+1}$. The date-$t_{k+1}$ cash flows (for $k \geq 1$) from receiving floating and paying fixed on this swap are

$$(\ell_k \delta_k - X\delta_k) = (\ell_k - X)\delta_k$$

These cash flows are identical to the cash flows from the long cap-short floor portfolio. It follows that the value of this swap (denoted Swap[Receive $L$, Pay $X$]) is identical to the value of the portfolio:

$$\text{Swap[Receive } L, \text{Pay } X] = \text{Cap}(X) - \text{Floor}(X) \qquad \textbf{(23.11)}$$

Expression (23.11) is the promised put-call parity relationship.

We can express this in slightly different form. For this, recall that a long swap position is identical to being long a floating-rate note and short a fixed-rate bond:

$$\text{Swap[Receive } L, \text{Pay } X] = \text{FRN}[L] - \text{Fixed-Rate Bond}[X] \qquad \textbf{(23.12)}$$

(Note that such a decomposition of the swap can be derived even after incorporating the modifications to the swap mentioned above, although, of course, the fixed- and floating-rate bond structures have to be modified slightly for this purpose. In particular, we require that neither bond has a coupon on date $t_1$, and they use the same day-count convention.) Using this in (23.11), we obtain

$$\text{Cap}(X) - \text{Floor}(X) = \text{FRN}[L] - \text{Fixed-Rate Bond}[X] \qquad \textbf{(23.13)}$$

The fixed-rate bond here plays the role of the present value of the strike price, while the floating-rate note plays the role of the price of the underlying. Expressed thus, the relationship has a form that is similar to the put-call parity relationship for equity options.

## Swaptions

Recall that a forward-starting swap is an interest rate swap with given fixed rates but where the swap begins only at a specified point in the future. In a forward-starting swap, both parties are obligated to enter into the underlying swap. A *swaption* (or "swap option") introduces optionality into this process. In a *receiver swaption*, the long position in the option has the right, but not the obligation, to enter into a swap in which she receives the fixed cash flows and pays floating. In a *payer swaption*, the long position has the right to pay the fixed cash flows and receive floating.

For example, the underlying swap may be a three-year fixed-for-floating swap with semiannual resets beginning in one year's time and with a fixed rate of 8%. The first exchange of cash flows in this swap will take place 6 months after the swap begins, i.e., in 18 months. The cash flows due from the fixed side are computed using the fixed rate of 8%. The holder of a receiver swaption on this swap can decide in one year whether to enter into the swap. The exercise decision will depend on the swap rate prevailing in one year for a three-year swap with semiannual resets. If the swap rate at that time is less than 8%, then it is obviously in the holder's interest to exercise the option, while if it is greater than 8%, it is better to let the option lapse unexercised.

Swaptions are closely related to caps and floors. A cap is a portfolio of call options on the interest rate, while a payer swaption is effectively an option on the portfolio of forward exchanges represented by the long swap. That is, in a cap, one can compare each Libor rate to the strike on the reset date and decide on the exercise decision caplet by caplet. In a payer swaption, once it has been exercised, the investor is committed to paying fixed and receiving floating on each reset date. Hence, the cap must be worth at least as much as a payer swaption with fixed rate equal to the strike rate in the cap. Similarly, a floor must be worth at least as much as a receiver swaption with fixed rate equal to the strike rate in the floor.

# 23.13    The Black Model for Pricing Caps, Floors, and Swaptions

Black (1976) developed a model for the pricing of options on futures. It is common market practice to use the Black model (often referred to in this context as the "market model") in pricing caps, floors, and swaptions. We elaborate on this approach here. Since caps and floors involve options on interest rates while the Black formula concerns options on futures, it is necessary to first draw a link between the two. We proceed in several steps beginning with Black's option pricing formula.

## The Black (1976) Formula

The Black option pricing formula was originally developed for options on futures contracts when interest rates are constant (or, more generally, deterministic). With constant or deterministic interest rates, futures and forward prices coincide (as we noted in Chapter 3), which means Black's formula also applies to options on forward contracts. Indeed, even more is true. It turns out that Black's formula remains valid for pricing options on forwards even if interest rates are stochastic. Our use of the Black formula here is in the context of pricing options on forwards (with possibly stochastic interest rates), so we present it in that form.

Let $S_t$ denote the time-$t$ price of some asset, and let $F(t, T^*)$ denote the time-$t$ forward price on the asset for a contract maturing at $T^*$. Let $B(t, T^*)$ denote the time-$t$ price of a zero-coupon bond that pays \$1 at $T^*$. Consider call and put options on the forward contract with a maturity of $T \leq T^*$ and a strike of $K$.

Options on forwards are defined in exactly the same way as options on futures. That is, a call option on a forward gives the holder the right, on the maturity date $T$ of the call, to enter into a long position in the forward contract with a delivery price equal to the call's strike $K$. A put option gives the right to enter into a short position in the forward contract with a delivery price of $K$. To gauge the payoffs from such options, consider the call for specificity. On date $T$, exercise of the call gives the holder a long position in a forward contract with a delivery price of $K$. Offsetting this with a short position in the forward at the prevailing market price of $F(T, T^*)$, the holder realizes the cash flow $[F(T, T^*) - K]$ on date $T^*$, or, equivalently, the amount $\{B(T, T^*) \times [F(T, T^*) - K]\}$ on date $T$. Thus, the call will be exercised if and only if $F(T, T^*) \geq K$, and its effective payoff may be taken to be

$$\max\{0, B(T, T^*) [F(T, T^*) - K]\}$$

on date $T$. Similarly, the payoff from the put is the amount

$$\max\{0, B(T, T^*)[K - F(T, T^*)]\}$$

on date $T$.

Now suppose that the forward price evolves according to a geometric Brownian motion process:

$$dF(t, T^*) = \mu F(t, T^*)\,dt + \sigma F(t, T^*)\,dW_t$$

where $\sigma$ is a constant. Black's formula then gives the time-$t$ prices of call and put options on the forward contract as:

$$C(t; T, K) = B(t, T^*)\left[F(t, T^*)\,N(d_1^F) - K\,N(d_2^F)\right]$$

$$P(t; T, K) = B(t, T^*)\left[K\,N(-d_2^F) - F(t, T^*)\,N(-d_1^F)\right]$$

where

$$d_1^F = \frac{1}{\sigma\sqrt{T-t}}\left[\ln\left(\frac{F(t, T^*)}{K}\right) + \frac{1}{2}\sigma^2(T-t)\right]$$

$$d_2^F = d_1^F - \sigma\sqrt{T-t}$$

## Expressing Cap/Floor Payoffs as Options on Forwards

To be able to exploit the Black formula, we must express caplet and floorlet payoffs as payoffs on a specific forward contract on some asset. In the forms they are written (see (23.9) and (23.10)), caplet and floorlet payoffs are options on the Libor rate, but the interest rate is not itself a traded variable.

As a first step in re-expressing cap and floor payoffs, we show that the component $\ell_k \delta_k$ in caplet and floorlet payoffs ((23.9) and (23.10), respectively) can be generated using traded assets, specifically, using zero-coupon bonds maturing on the reset dates. Consider the following strategy:

- Go long a $t_k$-maturity zero-coupon bond with a face value of \$1, and short a $t_{k+1}$-maturity zero-coupon bond with a face value of \$1. At time $t_k$, invest \$1 at Libor for maturity at $t_{k+1}$.

There is no net cash flow from this strategy at time $t_k$ because the \$1 received from the zero-coupon bond is reinvested at Libor for maturity at $t_{k+1}$. If $\ell_k$ denotes the realized Libor rate at $t_k$, then at $t_{k+1}$, we receive the amount $1 + \ell_k \delta_k$ from the investment and owe \$1 on the short $t_{k+1}$-maturity zero for a net cash flow of

$$(1 + \ell_k \delta_k) - 1 = \ell_k \delta_k$$

We have shown, as desired, that there is a portfolio that generates the quantity $\ell_k \delta_k$ as its payoff at time $t_{k+1}$.

Let $S_t$ denote the time-$t$ value of this "replicating" portfolio. We have

$$S_t = \begin{cases} B(t, t_k) - B(t, t_{k+1}), & \text{if } t < t_k \\ B(t, t_{k+1}) \times \ell_k \delta_k, & \text{if } t_k \le t \le t_{k+1} \end{cases} \qquad \textbf{(23.14)}$$

To see (23.14), note that until time $t_k$, the value of the portfolio is simply the difference in the values of the two zero-coupon bonds underlying the portfolio. At time $t_k$, the Libor rate determining payoffs gets fixed, so the value of the portfolio is simply the present value of the certainty payoff receivable at time $t_{k+1}$.

Now, consider a forward contract on $S_t$ maturing at time $t_{k+1}$. What is the time-$t$ forward price $F_t$? The "asset" represented by $S_t$ is a non-dividend-paying asset, so from the arguments in Chapter 3, its forward price obeys the rule

$$PV(\text{Forward price}) = \text{Spot price}$$

This means we have

$$B(t, t_{k+1})F_t = S_t$$

so, from (23.14),

$$F_t = \begin{cases} [B(t.t_k)/B(t, t_{k+1})] - 1, & \text{if } t < t_k \\ \ell_k \delta_k, & \text{if } t_k \le t \le t_{k+1} \end{cases} \qquad \textbf{(23.15)}$$

Note that $F_{t_k} = \ell_k \delta_k$. Define a call option on the forward contract $F_t$ expiring at time $t_k$ with strike $X\delta_k$. The payoff from exercising this contract at time $t_k$ is

$$B(t_k, t_{k+1}) \times (F_{t_k} - X\delta_k) = B(t_k, t_{k+1}) \times \delta_k(\ell_k - X)$$

which means the option's payoff at time $t_k$ can be written as

$$B(t_k, t_{k+1}) \times \delta_k \max\{0, \ell_k - X\} \qquad \textbf{(23.16)}$$

From (23.9), this is *exactly* the time-$t_k$ present value of the payoff received from the caplet expiring at $t_k$. (Note that the payoff in (23.9) is received at $t_{k+1}$. Bringing it back to $t_k$ results precisely in (23.16).) Thus, we have shown that the caplet's payoff can be represented as a call option on the forward contract whose price process is represented by (23.15). Considering a put option on the forward contract with a strike of $\delta_k X$ establishes the analogous result for the corresponding floorlet.

We are now in a position to exploit the Black formula to represent caplet prices. To do so, we have to assume that the forward prices $F_t$ are lognormally distributed with constant volatility. One final result will make the interpretation of this assumption easier.

## The Forward Contract as Forward Libor Rates

Let $f(t, t_k, t_{k+1})$ represent the *forward Libor rate* at time $t$ $(t \le t_k)$ for an investment or borrowing over the period $(t_k, t_{k+1})$. We will show that in the absence of arbitrage, we must have

$$\delta_k f(t, t_k, t_{k+1}) = \frac{B(t, t_k)}{B(t, t_{k+1})} - 1 \qquad \textbf{(23.17)}$$

To see (23.17), consider the following two alternative strategies:

- **Strategy 1** Buy a zero-coupon bond maturing on date $t_{k+1}$ with a face value of $1.
- **Strategy 2** Buy a zero-coupon bond maturing on date $t_k$ with a face value of $(1 + \delta_k f(t, t_k, t_{k+1}))^{-1}$. Simultaneously, enter into a commitment to invest the proceeds from $t_k$ to $t_{k+1}$ at the forward rate $f(t, t_k, t_{k+1})$.

Both strategies ensure winding up with a certain dollar at time $t_{k+1}$; therefore they must have the same cost. The cost of the first strategy is $B(t, t_{k+1})$, while that of the second strategy is

$$\frac{1}{1 + f(t, t_k, t_{k+1})\delta_k} B(t, t_k)$$

Equating these costs results in (23.17).

Expression (23.17) means that for $t \leq t_k$, the forward price $F_t$ in (23.15) is just the forward Libor rate $f(t, t_k, t_{k+1})$ times the day-count fraction $\delta_k$. In particular, this means that if the *volatility* of $F_t$ is constant, so is the volatility of the forward Libor rate. Thus, the assumption that $F_t$ is lognormally distributed with constant volatility is equivalent to the assumption that forward Libor rates are lognormally distributed with constant volatility.

## Cap and Floor Prices Using Black's Model

Combining all of the above, we have the following: suppose that for $t \leq t_k$, the forward Libor rate $f(t, t_k, t_{k+1})$ is lognormally distributed with constant volatility $\sigma$. Then:

1. The time-$t$ price of a caplet maturing at $t_k$ and paying $\max\{0, \ell_k \delta_k - X \delta_k\}$ at time $t_{k+1}$ is

$$B(t, t_{k+1}) \times [f(t, t_k, t_{k+1}) \delta_k N(d_1) - X \delta_k N(d_2)] \qquad \textbf{(23.18)}$$

where $d_1$ and $d_2$ are defined by

$$d_1 = \frac{1}{\sqrt{t_k - t}} \left[ \ln \left( \frac{f(t, t_k, t_{k+1})}{X} \right) + \frac{1}{2} \sigma^2 (t_k - t) \right]$$

$$d_2 = d_1 - \sigma \sqrt{t_k - t}$$

and $t_k - t$ is the time between $t$ and $t_k$ measured in years.

2. The time-$t$ price of a floorlet maturing at $t_k$ and paying $\max\{0, X \delta_k - \ell_k \delta_k\}$ at time $t_{k+1}$ is

$$B(t, t_{k+1}) \times [X \delta_k N(-d_2) - f(t, t_k, t_{k+1}) \delta_k N(-d_1)] \qquad \textbf{(23.19)}$$

where $d_1$ and $d_2$ are as defined in the caplet pricing formula.

The price of a cap is just the sum of the prices of all the caplets in the cap, and the price of a floor is the sum of all the floorlets in the floor. So expressions (23.18) and (23.19) may be used to identify cap and floor prices under the assumption that forward Libor rates of various maturities are each lognormally distributed with a constant volatility.

## The Black Model for Swaptions

Upon exercise of a payer swaption, the holder receives a long position (pay fixed, receive floating) in a swap with a fixed rate $X$ as specified in the swaption contract. Let $T$ denote the maturity date of the swaption, $t_0$ denote the initial date of the swap (with $t_0 \geq T$), and $t_1, \ldots, t_n$ the remaining reset or payment dates on the swap. We take the notional principal of the swap to be \$1.

Viewed from any date $t \leq T$, the cash flows from the floating leg of the swap can be replicated at a cost of

$$B(t, t_0) - B(t, t_n)$$

i.e., by buying a $t_0$-maturity zero with face value \$1 and selling a $t_n$-maturity zero with face value \$1. To see this, note that if we re-invest the \$1 received at $t_0$ at the Libor rate up to $t_1$, then re-invest \$1 at $t_1$ at the Libor rate up to $t_2$ and so on, we will re-create the floating-rate Libor cash flows in each period $t_1, \ldots, t_n$. At the final time point $t_n$, we also receive the principal amount of \$1, but this is canceled out by the short position in the $t_n$-maturity zero.

Identifying the present values of the fixed cash flows, given the fixed rate of $X$, is easier. This is just

$$\sum_{k=1}^{n} B(t, t_k) X \delta_k$$

where $\delta_k$ denotes the day-count fraction applicable to the fixed side for the period $(t_{k-1}, t_k)$.

Putting these together, the value of the pay-fixed/receive-floating swap, viewed from time $t$, is

$$S_t^{(1)} - S_t^{(2)}$$

where

$$S_t^{(1)} = B(t, t_0) - B(t, t_n) \quad \text{and} \quad S_t^{(2)} = \sum_{k=1}^{n} B(t, t_k) X \delta_k$$

The payoff of the payer swaption at maturity is, therefore,

$$\max\{0, S_T^{(1)} - S_T^{(2)}\}$$

This is just an exchange option as described by Margrabe (1978) (see Chapter 18). As noted in Section 18.6, the Margrabe formula can be used to price these options provided that $S_t^{(1)}/S_t^{(2)}$ follows a geometric Brownian motion with constant volatility $\sigma$. But this last requirement is the same as the requirement that the *forward swap rate* (i.e., the arbitrage-free rate for the swap as seen from time $t$) follow a geometric Brownian motion with constant volatility. To see this, note that the forward swap rate at $t$ is that value $X_t^f$, which is such that the value of the swap viewed from time $t$ is zero, i.e., such that

$$B(t, t_0) - B(t, t_n) = \sum_{k=1}^{n} B(t, t_k) X_t^f \delta_k$$

This identifies the forward swap rate as

$$X_t^f = \frac{B(t, t_0) - B(t, t_n)}{\sum_{k=1}^{n} B(t, t_k) \delta_k} \qquad \text{(23.20)}$$

Now, from the definitions of $S_t^{(1)}$ and $S_t^{(2)}$, we have

$$\frac{S_t^{(1)}}{S_t^{(2)}} = \frac{B(t, t_0) - B(t, t_n)}{X \sum_{k=1}^{n} B(t, t_k) \delta_k}$$

so, substituting for $B(t, t_0) - B(t, t_n)$ from (23.20), we obtain

$$\frac{S_t^{(1)}}{S_t^{(2)}} = \frac{X_t^f \sum_{k=1}^{n} B(t, t_k) \delta_k}{X \sum_{k=1}^{n} B(t, t_k) \delta_k} = \frac{X_t^f}{X}$$

Thus, the assumption that $S_t^{(1)}/S_t^{(2)}$ follows a geometric Brownian motion with constant volatility is equivalent to the assumption that the forward swap rate $X_t^f$ follows a geometric Brownian motion with constant volatility.

Putting all this together, we have the following: if the forward swap rate follows a geometric Brownian motion with constant volatility $\sigma$, then the date-$t$ value of a payer swaption is

$$S_t^{(1)} N(d_1) - S_t^{(2)} N(d_2)$$

where

$$d_1 = \frac{1}{\sigma \sqrt{T-t}} \left[ \ln \left( \frac{S_t^{(1)}}{S_t^{(2)}} \right) + \frac{1}{2} \sigma^2 (T-t) \right]$$

$$d_2 = d_1 - \sigma \sqrt{T-t}$$

By similar argument, the time-$t$ value of a receiver swaption is given by

$$S_t^{(2)} N(-d_2) - S_t^{(1)} N(-d_1)$$

## 23.14   Summary

This chapter has looked at some of the most important classes of floating-rate interest derivatives including interest rate swaps, caps, floors, and swaptions. Swaps are akin to forward-rate agreements with multiple exchanges, but they can also be viewed as an exchange of fixed- and floating-rate bonds. The latter point of view is particularly advantageous from an analytical standpoint, as we have seen in this chapter. Caps, floors, and swaptions, all closely related to interest rate swaps, bring optionality into the process. Caps and floors are akin to swaps in which on a leg-by-leg basis the holder has the option of participating in the exchange of cash flows required by that leg. Swaptions are options on a swap with fixed terms that begins some time in the future.

We have also examined in this chapter the pricing of caps, floors, and swaptions using the Black and Margrabe models. (These are sometimes called the "market models" for pricing these instruments, but they are perhaps more accurately, described as market practice.) These models are incomplete in the sense that they specify the behavior of specific individual rates separately without discussing how the yield curve as a whole evolves over time. In later chapters on term-structure modeling, we examine this broader question and introduce several different term-structure models.

## 23.15   Exercises

1. Explain why a swap is a collection of forward rate agreements (FRAs).

2. Show that a swap in which one receives fixed and pays floating is equivalent to a portfolio of caps and floors. Present the specific relationship.

3. What is the relationship of a swap to fixed- and floating-rate bonds?

4. What is the duration of a floating-rate note (FRN)?

5. You hold a Libor FRN with a coupon rate that is capped at 10%. Explain whether the price is increasing or decreasing as a function of Libor.

6. A swaption is an option on a swap. A cap is a portfolio of options on FRAs. Given that swaps are portfolios of FRAs, what has greater value, (a) a swaption or (b) a cap?

7. What is the impact on the value of a swap if, ceteris paribus, the volatility of interest rates rises?

8. The six-month Libor rate is given to be 3% and the twelve-month rate to be 4%. The $6 \times 12$ FRA is trading at 4.2%. Show how you would construct a sure arbitrage to take advantage of these market rates. Assume the first six-month period is 181 days and the second is 184 days. The interest-rate convention is Actual/360.

9. Consider a long position in a $6 \times 12$ FRA contract at a fixed rate of 4.2% Compute the payoff to this contract for a range of interest rates from 1% to 10%. Is the slope of this payoff function positive or negative? Explain. Assume the first half of the year is 181 days and the second half is 184 days. The interest-rate convention is Actual/360.

10. For the previous question, compute the payoffs for two conventions: (a) in discounted form (at maturity of the FRA) and (b) in arrears (settlement at maturity of the underlying borrowing). Are both lines linear or nonlinear? Explain the differences between the two payoffs. The interest-rate convention is Actual/360.

11. The $6 \times 12$ FRA is trading at a fixed rate of 4%. The $12 \times 18$ FRA is at 5%, and the $18 \times 24$ FRA is at 6%. What should you quote on the $12 \times 24$ FRA? Express your answer in rate per annum, given that the consecutive six-month periods are of 182, 183, 181, and 184 days, respectively. The interest-rate convention is Actual/360.

12. Rework the previous question with continuous compounding, treating every six-month period as half a year. Can you provide a simplified algebraic expression for all problems of this type? Is it harder to do this with continuous compounding? Explain why or why not.

13. You are able to borrow on a floating basis at a rate of Libor + 100 bps for two years. In addition, you can contract on a $6 \times 12$ FRA in which you can exchange Libor for a fixed rate of 3%. Similarly, you can contract on a $12 \times 18$ FRA at 3.5% and the $18 \times 24$ FRA at 4%. Assume the money market convention of Actual/360. The first four semiannual periods contain 181, 184, 182, and 183 days, respectively. The current six-month Libor rate is 2%. Given no credit arbitrage in the market, what should be the fair value of your borrowing at a fixed rate for two years? Assume interest payments are made in equal amounts for each half year.

14. You have an FRA to borrow at 5% that has six months to run until maturity and is for the period (6,12) containing 183 days. The current forward rate for the period (6,12) is 5.2%. What is the mark-to-market value of the FRA? What is the PVBP of this contract? Explain the sign of the PVBP. Assume the standard Actual/360 money market convention.

15. What is the price of a five-year floating-rate note that has coupons at the rate of Libor + 100 bps when the current yield curve is flat at 6%? Assume that the conventions in the market are 30/360 for coupons and discounting instead of the usual Actual/360.

16. Two firms X and Y are able to borrow funds as follows:

    A: Fixed-rate funding at 4% and floating rate at Libor − 1%.

    B: Fixed-rate funding at 5% and floating rate at Libor + 1%.

    Show how these two firms can both obtain cheaper financing using a swap. What swap would you suggest to the two firms if you were an unbiased advisor?

17. Firm A can borrow fixed rate at 10%. It can also borrow floating at Libor + 1%. The market swap rate at the bid is Libor versus 8.9% and is Libor versus 9.1% at the ask (i.e., the firm can enter into a swap by paying fixed at 9.1% or receiving at 8.9%). Find the cheapest form of financing for the firm if it wishes to be in floating-rate debt.

18. The student loan association raises floating-rate financing and makes loans of maturity 5–10 years at fixed rates. Can you describe the nature of the risks on the balance sheet? What financial contract should the association undertake to mitigate these risks?

19. You are given the following data on Libor yields at six monthly intervals.

| Maturity Dates | Annualized Yields (%) |
|---|---|
| 19-May-04 | |
| 19-Nov-04 | 1.06 |
| 19-May-05 | 1.23 |
| 19-Nov-05 | 1.44 |
| 19-May-06 | 2.06 |
| 19-Nov-06 | 2.66 |
| 19-May-07 | 3.10 |
| 19-Nov-07 | 3.20 |
| 19-May-08 | 3.49 |

The current date is 19-May-04. All swaps in this question have a four-year maturity and a notional principal of 100,000. Assume the fixed-rate side of the swap is on a 30/360 basis, and the floating side is on an Actual/360 basis. The zero-coupon yields above may be converted into discount factors using the following formula:

$$d = \frac{1}{1 + (z \times D/360)}$$

where $z$ is the zero-coupon rate and $D$ is the number of days to the payment from inception.

(a) Find the price of a fixed-for-floating interest-rate swap that pays Libor on the floating leg.

(b) Find the price of a fixed-for-floating interest-rate swap that pays Libor + 25 bps on the floating leg. The notional principal is 100,000.

(c) Find the price of a zero-coupon swap against floating Libor.

(d) If the fixed rate on the swap is 3%, what is the spread over Libor on the floating leg to make this a fair swap?

20. You are given the following table for the next eight half-year periods.

| Period | Days in Period | Libor |
|--------|----------------|-------|
| 1 | 182 | 3.00 |
| 2 | 183 | 3.25 |
| 3 | 182 | 3.75 |
| 4 | 183 | 4.00 |
| 5 | 182 | 4.24 |
| 6 | 183 | 4.50 |
| 7 | 182 | 5.00 |
| 8 | 183 | 5.50 |

The zero-coupon rates are converted into discount factors with the following formula:

$$d = \frac{1}{1 + (z \times D/360)}$$

where $z$ is the zero-coupon rate and $D$ is the number of days to the payment from inception. Find the fixed rate at which a four-year swap with half-year payments should be quoted if the swap is fair. The fixed side also uses the Actual/360 convention.

21. Who bears more credit risk in a five-year fixed-for-floating interest rate swap when the yield curve is upward sloping, the fixed rate payer or receiver? Assume that both parties have the same credit quality.

22. How would you hedge a portfolio of swaps using zero-coupon swaps? Explain the logic you would follow to set up the appropriate set of swaps.

23. There is a cash flow of $125 at time 1.68 years to be allocated to two time points: 1.5 years and 2 years. The zero-coupon rates for these two points are 3% and 4%, and compounding is continuous. Find the allocation that preserves value and risk.

24. Major investor Iwan Itall has a portfolio of 100 million USD two-year semiannual floating-rate notes, based on six-month Libor. This is a standard floating-rate note with coupons being set every six months. He wants to ensure that he receives a minimum Libor yield of 6.00% in the future. The current market quotes (one-time premiums

defined in basis points of the face value of the option) for caps and floors on six-month Libor as are follows:

| Strike | Caps (bps) 2 Year | Floors (bps) 2 Year |
|--------|-------------------|---------------------|
| 4.00%  |                   | 7                   |
| 4.50%  |                   | 12                  |
| 5.00%  | 133               | 24                  |
| 5.50%  | 91                | 48                  |
| 6.00%  | 55                | 60                  |
| 6.50%  | 40                |                     |
| 7.00%  | 20                |                     |

[*Note:* For simplicity, assume that option premiums are amortized straight line over time.] For example the two-year cap at 6.50% costs 40 basis points up front, i.e., 20 basis points per annum.

(a) What option should Iwan Itall purchase to ensure that his gross yield (before the cost of the option) does not drop below 6.00% per annum? Depict his gross payoffs per coupon payment (before options costs) and net payoffs (after options costs) on suitable diagrams. Label the diagrams correctly. Make use of the simplifying assumption in the note above.

(b) If you think the options cost of the strategy in (a) above is too high, what would you advise Iwan to do to subsidize the cost? Iwan has told you that he is willing to bear the risk that Libor will not cross 7.00%. Once again, provide the appropriate payoff diagrams.

(c) Can you help Iwan devise a zero-cost options strategy such that he can meet his objective of a minimum gross per annum yield of 6.00%?

(d) From the information provided, what is the approximate two-year fixed rate of interest?

25. An inverse floater is a security that is an FRN where the coupon rate varies inversely to the indexed rate. An example of an inverse floater is as follows. Consider a three-year semiannual pay FRN where the coupon rate equals:

$$\text{Coupon Rate } (c) = 12\% - \ell$$

where $\ell$ is the six-month Libor rate. The further condition on this note is that if $\ell > 12\%$, then $c = 0\%$. Using various parity relationships, reduce and express this inverse floater as the simplest possible combination of "basic" securities, such as straight bonds, caps, floors, etc.

# Chapter 24

# Equity Swaps

## 24.1 Introduction

Equity swaps are products that facilitate the creation or transfer of equity risk. In its generic form, an equity swap is a bilateral financial contract in which

- one counterparty pays returns on a specified equity index applied to a given principal amount, and
- the other pays a given interest rate applied to the same principal amount.

An example would be a swap of six-month returns on the S&P 500 for six-month Libor. That is, every six months, one counterparty pays the other the returns on the S&P 500 index applied to a given principal amount while the other pays six-month Libor applied to the same principal amount. The principal itself is never exchanged (hence, the term "notional" principal).

The generic swap described above exchanges equity risk for interest-rate risk. For example, a bond-portfolio manager who receives equity returns in exchange for interest-rate payments is effectively converting his interest-rate exposure to equity exposure. An equity-portfolio manager who does the opposite transaction is exchanging equity exposure for interest-rate exposure.

There are several variations on the basic theme. For example, the interest-rate leg may involve a fixed rate rather than a floating rate. The principal in the swap may vary in size depending on the returns on the index (i.e., the swap may have a "variable notional principal"). The two streams of payments may be made in different currencies ("cross-currency equity swap"), as for example when a US-based investor is swapping US dollar Libor payments for returns on a foreign index. The accompanying currency risk may be hedged in the swap or left unhedged.

Other variants include "two index" or "relative performance" equity swaps in which the returns on one equity index (or basket of equities) are swapped for the returns on another equity index (or basket of equities); "outperformance swaps," where the equity leg may involve the maximum of two or more indices or baskets of equities; and "rainbow swaps," in which the equity leg involves a blended index.

Simple to define, equity swaps are a useful and analytically interesting class of products. Uses of equity swaps are described in Section 24.2 below. The payoffs from various categories of equity swaps are discussed in Section 24.3. Section 24.4 then examines the pricing and valuation of a large class of equity swaps.[1]

---

[1] The literature on equity swaps is somewhat sparse. Chance (2003), Marshall and Yuyuenyonwatana (2000), and the Cooper and Lybrand (1992) self-study guide are some useful references. The material in this chapter draws on these sources among others.

A good place to begin our analysis is by contrasting equity swaps with their better-known cousins, interest rate swaps.

## Equity Swaps and Interest Rate Swaps

Recall that a generic ("plain vanilla, fixed-for-floating") interest rate swap is a bilateral contract in which one counterparty pays a fixed rate of interest applied to a given notional principal, and the other pays a floating rate of interest (e.g., Libor) applied to the same principal. There are some strong connections between equity swaps and interest rate swaps. The most important one concerns pricing. Consider

- An equity swap involving a swap of equity returns for a fixed rate of interest.
- A plain vanilla interest rate swap involving a swap of a floating rate for a fixed rate of interest.

At inception, the fixed rate in either swap is chosen so that the swap has zero value. Later in this chapter, we show that in the absence of arbitrage, these fixed rates must be the same. Furthermore, this common fixed rate is determined entirely by the discount function and does not depend on such features as equity volatility.

This result may appear a little surprising, at least at first glance, since equity swaps and interest rate swaps have some differences. For example, the net payment in an equity swap is not known until the end of the payment period since equity returns over the period are known only at that point. In an interest rate swap, the interest rates (e.g., Libor) that apply to a particular period are determined at the beginning of the period, although payments take place at the end of the period. In addition, equity returns can be negative, meaning that one party may be making both payments in an equity swap. Nonetheless, the result is an intuitive one, as we explain in Section 24.4.

## 24.2 Uses of Equity Swaps

The essential purpose of an equity swap is to create (or transfer) equity exposure *synthetically*, i.e., without actually owing (or transferring) the equities. In this context, equity swaps offer several advantages. They

- offer a low-cost way to obtain this exposure.
- can be structured in a tax-advantaged manner.
- may enable getting around regulatory restrictions on investments.
- simplify rebalancing and, more generally, portfolio management.
- offer a useful vehicle for obtaining exposure to foreign equity or foreign equity indices (particularly, emerging markets); this exposure can be structured without currency risk if this is desired.

The material below provides specific settings illustrating these uses.

### Index Tracking

Equity swaps provide synthetic multiyear exposure to a (possibly customized) equity index. Obtaining the same exposure via the cash market would necessitate replicating the index perfectly with the cash equities, and rebalancing the portfolio when index composition changes. In an equity swap, we obtain the total returns on the index—without slippage—in exchange for making money-market-linked payments.

### Cross-Country Investing

Consider a domestic (e.g., US) fund manager diversifying into foreign (e.g., British) equities who wishes to track an index in that foreign country (say, the FTSE-100 or some customized index). One way to do this is to carry out actual cash purchases of the relevant basket of British stocks. Among other disadvantages (administrative, legal, etc.) of this method is the dividend withholding tax levied by many countries on dividends paid to foreign investors: a 15% tax on a 2% dividend yield has the immediate effect of reducing returns by 30 basis points. Equity swaps offer an efficient alternative. The US manager can enter into an equity swap in which she pays (for example) S&P 500 returns and receives returns on the FTSE-100. The currency risk in the swap can also be hedged within the swap itself using a hedged cross-currency equity swap as described in Section 24.3 below.

### Emerging Market Equity Investments

A problem confronting investors who wish to invest in emerging markets equities is that of illiquidity. Illiquidity makes it difficult to get in and out of positions nimbly and becomes a particular problem during market crises when flexibility is important. Equity swaps offer several advantages here. The fund manager can get into and out of the market quickly and obtain exposure to the market and basket of securities desired with fewer liquidity constraints. Credit exposure is limited to the swap counterparty, and this may be superior to buying local equities guaranteed by local brokerages. And finally, as mentioned earlier, the equity swap can be structured so as to limit the exposure to changes in the exchange rates by having all cash flows denominated in USD.

### Regulatory Considerations

Equity swaps can also help investors overcome regulatory restrictions in some cases. The website http://www.finpipe.com/equityswaps.htm describes a particularly interesting case in this regard, that of the Canadian Registered Retirement Savings Plan (RRSP). RRSP participants are not allowed to invest more than 20% of their accounts in non-Canadian assets. This is an unwelcome restriction from the standpoint of diversification, especially during periods in which Canadian markets are outperformed by foreign (e.g., US) markets, as was the case in the 1990s.

Equity swaps enabled an end-run around this regulation. Mutual funds that used equity swaps purchased from Canadian banks were deemed to be invested in Canadian investment products and so were RRSP-eligible. The equity swaps paid the funds the total return on US equities, thus delivering US equity returns to participants in the RRSP who invested in these funds.

### Diversification without Stock Sales

Corporate executives are often heavily invested in their own stock. An executive whose share price has appreciated considerably may wish to lock-in at least a part of the gains, but to do so requires selling shares, which entails its own costs including capital gains taxes as well as a loss of voting rights. The transaction would, moreover, have to be reported to the shareholders, and this may trigger a negative reaction in share price.

Equity swaps provided a solution to many executives in this position in the 1990s. The executive enters into an equity swap in which he pays the total returns on his own stock to his counterparty, in exchange receiving a money-market-linked payment such as Libor or the returns from a broad market index such as the S&P 500.

One example of such a transaction is described in Bolster, Chance, and Rich (1996). It involved the CEO, Lorne Weil, of a manufacturer of computerized wagering equipment, Autotote Inc. In 1994, Mr. Weil's holding of Autotote shares had climbed in value to almost $23 million, more than seven times their value of two years earlier. These were paper gains; converting them to realized gains would have required selling at least a part of the shareholding, resulting in a large tax bill. So Mr. Weil entered into a five-year equity swap with Banker's Trust (BT) in which he agreed to pay BT the total return on 500,000 shares (worth about $13.4 million at the time of the transaction) in exchange for receiving Libor minus 2.125% on an alternative investment of $13.4 million.

BT advertised the strategy widely. A full-page advertisement in *Barron's* in July 1994 asked "Too much money in just one stock?" "Get rid of the risk, not the stock," it went on, adding that investors could "diversify your risk—without selling the stock. Without owing capital-gains taxes. And without sacrificing your voting rights."

In retrospect, this publicity may not have been a good idea. Regulatory authorities argued successfully that the equity swaps were economically equivalent to a sale and should be taxed as such. The Taxpayer Relief Act of 1997 included rules requiring recognition of gains when the transactions were functionally equivalent to a sale. Agreeing with this position, the SEC required that transactions functionally equivalent to a sale be reported to shareholders. Two major advantages of equity swaps over outright sales were erased.

### Equity-Linked Deposits

Marshall and Yuyuenyonwatana (2000) offer another use of equity swaps, this one in equity-linked deposits. Equity-linked bank deposits became popular in the US in the 1990s. In these contracts, banks offer accounts that guarantee principal and a fraction of the return on the S&P 500 index. The bank then uses off-balance-sheet derivatives—a combination of equity swaps and options (to guarantee the floor)—to generate these returns on its asset side. Equity-linked deposits are then issued against these returns.

## 24.3 Payoffs from Equity Swaps

In this section, we illustrate the payoffs from equity swaps. Understanding the payoff streams is important to clarifying both the motivation for the use of and the risk in the swap. We consider four broad types of equity swaps here:

- Equity for Libor with a fixed notional principal.
- Equity for Libor with a variable notional principal.
- Cross-currency equity swaps with unhedged currency risk.
- Cross-currency equity swaps with hedged currency risk.

In all cases, we consider a three-year swap with six-monthly exchanges of cash flows. The floating rate is taken to be six-month Libor. The spot date of the swap is taken to be June 11 of some calendar year that we call "Year 1"; we write this date as 11-Jun-Year 1. The first exchange of payments takes place on December 11, Year 1 (written 11-Dec-Year 1), and the sixth and last one on 11-Jun-Year 4. The hypothetical Libor realizations applying to these six dates are assumed to be as in Table 24.1. The initial notional principal is taken to be $100 million throughout, and the payments in each case are computed from the standpoint of an investor who is paying USD Libor in exchange for receiving the equity returns.

### (A) Equity for Libor with a Fixed Notional Principal

Consider the first payment date, 11-Dec-Year 1. The floating payment due on this date is calculated according to the Libor rate that prevailed on 11-Jun-Year 1, which we have taken to be 6.50%. The floating payments are computed using the money market convention (Actual/360). Assuming 183 days between the dates, the floating payment due is

$$0.065 \times \left(\frac{183}{360}\right) \times 100,000,000 = 3,304,167$$

**TABLE 24.1**
Assumed Libor Rates on Reset Dates

| Date | Six-Month Libor |
|------|-----------------|
| 11-Jun-Year 1 | 6.50% |
| 11-Dec-Year 1 | 7.00% |
| 11-Jun-Year 2 | 6.50 % |
| 11-Dec-Year 2 | 6.25% |
| 11-Jun-Year 3 | 5.75% |
| 11-Dec-Year 3 | 5.25% |

The equity receipts due on 11-Dec-Year 1 depend on the returns on the equity index between 11-Jun-Year 1 and 11-Dec-Year 1. Suppose this return is 8.74%. Then, the receipts on the equity leg are

$$(0.0874) \times 100,000,000 = 8,740,000$$

Note that there is no day-count adjustment in computing payments on the equity leg. Thus, the net receipt on 11-Dec-Year 1 is

$$8,740,000 - 3,304,167 = 5,435,833$$

The second payment date is 11-Jun-Year 2. The floating payment on this date depends on the six-month Libor rate on 11-Dec-Year 1, which has been taken to be 7.00%. Assuming 183 days in this six-month period, the floating payment due is

$$(0.07) \times \left(\frac{183}{360}\right) \times 100,000,000 = 3,558,333$$

Now suppose that the equity returns between 11-Dec-Year 1 and 11-Jun-Year 2 are 6.74%. Then, the receipts from the equity leg are:

$$(0.0674) \times 100,000,000 = 6,740,000$$

The net receipt on 11-Jun-Year 2 is, therefore, $6,740,000 - 3,558,333 = 3,181,667$.

Proceeding in this way, we can identify all the payoffs. Assuming hypothetical values for the equity returns, Table 24.2 describes the payoffs that result.

**TABLE 24.2**   Equity Swaps Payoffs with a Fixed Notional Principal

| | Three-Year Equity Swap: Receive Equity Returns, Pay Libor Floating Rate: Six-Month Libor, Notional Principal = $100,000,000 | | | | | |
|---|---|---|---|---|---|---|
| Time | Days from Last Reset | Libor at Last Reset | Equity Returns | Equity Receipts | Floating Payments | Net Receipts |
| 11-Dec-Year 1 | 183 | 6.50% | 8.74% | 8,740,000 | 3,304,167 | 5,435,833 |
| 11-Jun-Year 2 | 183 | 7.00% | 6.74% | 6,740,000 | 3,558,333 | 3,181,667 |
| 11-Dec-Year 2 | 183 | 6.50% | −5.23% | −5,230,000 | 3,304,167 | −8,534,167 |
| 11-Jun-Year 3 | 182 | 6.25% | −7.84% | −7,840,000 | 3,159,722 | −10,999,722 |
| 11-Dec-Year 3 | 183 | 5.75% | 1.80% | 1,800,000 | 2,922,917 | −1,122,917 |
| 11-Jun-Year 4 | 182 | 5.25% | 13.40% | 13,400,000 | 2,668,750 | 10,731,250 |
| Totals | | | | 17,610,000 | 18,918,056 | −1,308,056 |

## (B) Equity for Libor with a Variable Notional Principal

We first explain the concept of a "variable" notional principal. In an equity swap with a variable notional principal, the principal amount that applies to each payment period beyond the first is the notional principal at the last reset date multiplied by 1 plus the returns on the equity index since that date. For example, say that the initial notional principal is $100,000,000. Also assume that by the first payment date, the total returns on the index are 5.33%. Then the notional principal amount for the second payment period is reset to

$$100,000,000 \times (1 + 0.0533) = 105,330,000$$

Suppose that between the first and second payment dates, the index falls by 3.23%. Then, the notional principal that will apply to the third payment date is

$$105,330,000 \times (1 - 0.0323) = 101,927,841$$

And so on . . .

### Why a "Variable" Notional Principal?

It is often argued that equity swaps with variable notional principals better synthesize a long-term equity investment than those with a fixed notional principal. To see the argument, consider a simple example. We invest $100 in an equity index. Suppose the index goes up by 5% during the first payment period and by 10% during the second payment period. Then, the value of our initial investment is

$$100 \times 1.05 \times 1.10 = 115.50$$

This means we have a capital gain of $15.50. Suppose we aim to obtain these returns synthetically using an equity swap on this index. First, consider a *fixed* notional principal of $100. In this case, the receipts from the equity leg would be $100 \times 0.05 = 5$ in the first payment period and $100 \times 1.10 = 10$ in the second payment period for a total return of only

$$\$(5 + 10) = \$15$$

against the $15.50 of the cash investment in the index. Suppose, however, our equity swap had a *variable* notional principal. In this case, the notional principal for the second payment would be $100 \times 1.05 = 105$, so the second-period payment is $105 \times 0.1 = 10.50$ for a total return of

$$\$(5 + 10.50) = 15.50$$

This argument is less persuasive than it appears. With the cash investment, the total returns are $15.50 *only if* the $5 returns of the first period are reinvested for the second period. With a fixed notional principal, this can be exactly re-created simply by investing the $5 receipts on the first payment date into the index, generating an additional $0.50 in returns on the second payment date. As in the cash investment case, this now results in no cash flows on the first payment date and a single realization of gains of $15.50 on the second payment date. Thus, the fixed-principal equity swap mimics the cash investment perfectly.

On the other hand, the variable notional principal "overreplicates" the cash investment. It provides a return of $5 on the first payment date and $10.50 on the second payment date. Since the receipts of the first payment date can be reinvested (whether in the index or in some other investment), the "forward value" of the cash flows on the second payment date is greater than $15.50.

### Cash Flows with a Variable Notional Principal

Consider the same pattern of Libor rates and equity returns as assumed in Table 24.2. The mechanics of computing the cash flows with a variable notional principal are exactly the same as with a fixed notional principal except that we must take care to change the notional principal amount from one payment date to the next. For example, if the equity returns in the first period are 8.74% as we assumed in the case of the fixed notional principal, then the principal amount applicable to the second payment date is

$$100,000,000 \times 1.0874 = 108,740,000$$

Now, equity returns are assumed to be 6.74% during the second payment period, so the receipts on the equity leg on the second payment date are

$$0.0674 \times 108,740,000 = 7,329,076$$

Similarly, the Libor rate on the first reset date has been assumed to be 7.00%, so the payment due on the floating leg is

$$0.07 \times \left( \frac{182}{360} \right) \times 108,740,000 = 3,869,332$$

Finally, the notional principal applicable to the third payment date is now reset to

$$108,740,000 \times 1.0674 = 116,069,076$$

Table 24.3 illustrates the entire pattern of cash flows from the swap assuming a variable notional principal.

## (C) Unhedged Cross-Currency Equity Swaps

In a cross-currency equity swap, the investor receives the returns on a foreign index in exchange for interest-rate payments (which we continue to assume is Libor). This leaves the investor vulnerable to currency risk.

To understand why, consider a US-based investor who enters into an equity swap to receive the returns on the ASX 200, an Australian equity index. As above, let the principal amount in US dollars (USD) be 100,000,000. This amount has to first be converted to

**TABLE 24.3** Equity Swaps Payoffs with a Variable Notional Principal

| | | | | | | | |
|---|---|---|---|---|---|---|---|
| **Three-Year Equity Swap: Receive Equity Returns, Pay Libor** | | | | | | | |
| **Floating Rate: Six-Month Libor, Initial Notional Principal = $100,000,000** | | | | | | | |
| **Time** | **Days from Last Reset** | **Libor at Last Reset** | **Equity Returns** | **Equity Receipts** | **Floating Payments** | **Net Receipts** | **Reset Principal** |
| 11-Dec-Year 1 | 183 | 6.50% | 8.74% | 8,740,000 | 3,304,167 | 5,435,833 | 108,740,000 |
| 11-Jun-Year 2 | 182 | 7.00% | 6.74% | 7,329,076 | 3,869,332 | 3,459,744 | 116,069,076 |
| 11-Dec-Year 2 | 183 | 6.50% | −5.23% | −6,070,413 | 3,835,116 | −9,905,528 | 109,998,663 |
| 11-Jun-Year 3 | 182 | 6.25% | −7.84% | −8,623,895 | 3,475,652 | −12,099,547 | 101,374,768 |
| 11-Dec-Year 3 | 183 | 5.75% | 1.80% | 1,824,746 | 2,963,100 | −1,138,354 | 103,199,514 |
| 11-Jun-Year 4 | 182 | 5.25% | 13.40% | 13,828,735 | 2,739,087 | 11,089,648 | 117,028,249 |
| **Totals** | | | | 17,028,249 | 20,186,453 | −3,158,205 | |

Australian dollars (AUD) to get the size of the investment in the ASX 200. Suppose that at inception of the swap (i.e., on 11-Jun-Year 1), the exchange rate is USD 1 = AUD 1.50. (Again, this number and all the other numbers used in this illustrative exercise are fictitious.) Then the initial notional principal is AUD 150,000,000. This is the size of the investment in the ASX 200.

Now suppose that by the first payment date (11-Dec-Year 1), the returns on the ASX 200 are 8.91%. The value of the original investment is then

$$AUD\ 150,000,000 \times 1.0891 = AUD\ 163,365,000$$

for a gain of AUD 13,365,000. This amount must be converted back to USD *at the exchange rate prevailing on 11-Dec-Year 1*. Since this exchange rate will differ from the original rate when the swap commenced, the amount the investor receives is subject to fluctuations in the exchange rate.

Suppose, for example, that the exchange rate on 11-Dec-Year 1 is USD 1 = AUD 1.52. Then, in USD, the investor's receipts translate to

$$USD\ \left(13,365,000 \times \frac{1}{1.52}\right) = USD\ 7,476,974$$

Thus, the investor receives USD 7,476,974 from the equity leg of the swap. The payments due from the investor are calculated from the Libor rate using the usual money-market rules. Since this rate was 6.50%, the amount due on the principal of $100 million is easily calculated. If the relevant day count is 183 days, the payment due from the investor is

$$USD\ 100,000,000 \times \left(\frac{183}{360}\right) \times 0.065 = USD\ 3,304,167$$

The difference between the two legs represents the investor's net receipts. Thus, on the first payment date, the investor receives

$$USD\ (7,476,974 - 3,304,167) = USD\ 4,172,807$$

If a variable notional principal is used, the principal amounts for the next set of payment dates are adjusted using the ASX 200 returns: the new principal amounts are AUD 163,365,000 = USD 107,476,974.

Table 24.4 provides a list of possible payments from an unhedged currency swap building on this example and using hypothetical Libor rates and ASX 200 returns.

## (D) Hedged Cross-Currency Equity Swaps

Hedged cross-currency equity swaps function exactly like unhedged swaps except that the initial contract specifies a fixed exchange rate at which all cash flows may be converted back into the investor's currency, and which will also be used to convert notional principals. Thus, the investor is fully hedged against all exchange-rate changes. Table 24.5 revisits the earlier example but assuming the swap is hedged with a given exchange rate of AUD 1.52/USD.

**TABLE 24.4**  Payoffs from Unhedged Cross-Currency Equity Swap

Unhedged Cross-Currency Equity Swap, Receive ASX 200, Pay Six-Month USD Libor
Initial Principal = USD 100,000,000 = AUD 150,000,000

| Date | Day Count | Libor at Last Reset | Returns on ASX | AUD/USD Rate | Equity Receipts | Floating Payments | Net Receipts | Reset Principal Values in AUD | in USD |
|---|---|---|---|---|---|---|---|---|---|
| 11-Jun-Year 1 | | | | 1.5000 | | | | 150,000,000 | 100,000,000 |
| 11-Dec-Year 1 | 183 | 6.50% | 8.91% | 1.5200 | 7,476,974 | 3,304,167 | 4,172,807 | 163,365,000 | 107,476,974 |
| 11-Jun-Year 2 | 183 | 7.00% | 6.53% | 1.4900 | 9,323,519 | 3,824,389 | 5,499,130 | 174,032,735 | 116,800,493 |
| 11-Dec-Year 2 | 182 | 6.50% | −0.93% | 1.4800 | −304,392 | 3,838,194 | −4,142,586 | 172,414,230 | 116,496,101 |
| 11-Jun-Year 3 | 183 | 6.25% | −1.81% | 1.5050 | −4,008,704 | 3,701,178 | −7,709,883 | | |
| Totals | | | | | 12,487,397 | 14,667,928 | −2,180,531 | | |

**TABLE 24.5**  Payoffs from a Hedged Cross-Currency Equity Swap

Hedged Cross-Currency Equity Swap, Receive ASX 200, Pay Six-Month USD Libor
Initial Principal = USD 100,000,000 = AUD 150,000,000
Fixed Exchange Rate = AUD 1.5250 per USD

| Date | Day Count | Libor at Last Reset | Returns on ASX | AUD/USD Rate | Equity Receipts | Floating Payments | Net Receipts | Reset Principal Values in AUD | in USD |
|---|---|---|---|---|---|---|---|---|---|
| 11-Jun-Year 1 | | | | 1.5000 | | | | 152,500,000 | 100,000,000 |
| 11-Dec-Year 1 | 183 | 6.50% | 8.91% | 1.5250 | 8,910,000 | 3,304,167 | 5,605,833 | 166,087,750 | 108,910,000 |
| 11-Jun-Year 2 | 183 | 7.00% | 6.53% | 1.5250 | 7,111,823 | 3,875,381 | 3,236,442 | 176,933,280 | 116,021,823 |
| 11-Dec-Year 2 | 182 | 6.50% | −0.93% | 1.5250 | −1,079,003 | 3,812,606 | −4,891,609 | 175,287,801 | 114,942,820 |
| 11-Jun-Year 3 | 183 | 6.25% | −1.81% | 1.5250 | −2,080,465 | 3,651,829 | −5,732,294 | | |
| Totals | | | | | 12,862,355 | 14,643,983 | −1,781,628 | | |

# 24.4 Valuation and Pricing of Equity Swaps

In this section, we consider the pricing and valuation of several classes of equity swaps. A no-arbitrage-based approach to the pricing of equity swaps is presented in Chance and Rich (1995). At first glance, it appears that these prices may depend on the behavior of equity returns and equity volatility. This is indeed the case for variable notional equity swaps, but, as we will see, fixed notional equity swaps are a lot easier to handle: such swaps may be priced without knowledge of or assumptions regarding equity return behavior. As a matter of terminology, "valuation" refers to identifying the present value of an existing swap, while "pricing" refers to the problem of finding the swap rate in a new swap (i.e., the fixed rate that would make a swap have zero value).

The initial principal $A$ in the equity swap is normalized to \$1 for simplicity. The remaining notation we employ is the following. The current date is $t$, and the remaining payment dates are $T_1, \ldots, T_N$. When we are looking to price a new swap, we take $t$ to be the inception date and denote it by $T_0$. Equity returns over the period $[T_{k-1}, T_k]$ are denoted $z_k$, $k = 1, \ldots, N$, and the Libor rate applicable to the period $[T_{k-1}, T_k]$ is denoted $r_k$. (Note that $r_k$ is observed and may be locked-in at $T_{k-1}$.) Let $d_k$ denote the Libor day-count fraction (e.g., Actual/360) for the period $[T_{k-1}, T_k]$; thus, the amount of interest per \$1 of principal invested over this period is $r_k d_k$. $B(s, \tau)$ will denote the time-$s$ value of \$1 receivable on date $\tau$. Finally, $S_\tau$ and $V_\tau$ will denote, respectively, the time-$\tau$ value of the underlying equity portfolio and the time-$\tau$ value of the swap. This notation is summarized in Table 24.6.

Note that no restriction has been placed on the nature of the equity portfolio involved in the swap. It could be an individual equity, a basket of equities, or a standardized or customized equity index. The results described below are valid for all these cases.

Finally, an assumption regarding dividends. As always, our pricing arguments are based on replication, in this case replicating the equity swap cash flows with investments in the equity portfolio and cash. Now, returns in the equity swap are computed and paid only at the payment dates $T_1, \ldots, T_N$; thus, any dividends paid between $T_k$ and $T_{k+1}$ are treated as if they are received only at $T_{k+1}$. To avoid timing mismatches, we pretend the same condition holds for the underlying equity portfolio too; alternatively, we may assume that $S_\tau$ be interpreted as a traded total return index on the equity portfolio. Either condition is trivially satisfied if there are no dividends on the underlying equity during the life of the swap.

**TABLE 24.6**
Notation Used in This Chapter

| Notation | Meaning |
|---|---|
| $A$ | Initital principal (normalized to \$1) |
| $T_0$ | First index date |
| $T_1, \ldots, T_N$ | Remaining payment dates |
| $t$ | Current date |
| $z_k$ | Equity returns over $[T_{k-1}, T_k]$ |
| $r_k$ | Libor rate for $[T_{k-1}, T_k]$ (observed at $T_{k-1}$) |
| $d_k$ | Libor day-count fraction for $[T_{k-1}, T_k]$ |
| $B(s, \tau)$ | Time-$s$ present value of \$1 receivable at time $\tau$ |
| $S_\tau$ | Value of equity portfolio on date $\tau$ |
| $V_\tau$ | Value of swap on date $\tau$ |

# (A) Pricing a Fixed Notional Swap, Equity for Libor

Valuing any equity swap involves present-valuing its cash flows. Consider an investor who receives equity returns and pays Libor plus a spread in an equity swap. Denote the spread over Libor by $s$. Then, the net payment the investor receives on each payment date $T_k$, $k = 1, \ldots, N$, is given by $z_k - (r_k + s)d_k$, or, equivalently, by

$$[1 + z_k] - [1 + (r_k + s)d_k]$$

To price the swap, we must find the value of $s$ for which this swap has zero value at time $T_0$, i.e., the value of $s$ for which the time-$T_0$ present value of the equity returns stream equals the time-$T_0$ present value of the floating-interest payments. We show that this value of $s$ is just $s = 0$! That is, an exchange of equity returns for Libor flat has zero net present value at inception.

The formal proof of this result is not difficult (see below), but the economic intuition is even more straightforward. In economic equilibrium, investors must be indifferent between different assets in risk-return terms; if not, investors will buy assets with superior risk-adjusted returns and short assets with inferior risk-adjusted returns. Thus, in risk-adjusted terms, an investment in Libor or an investment in an individual equity or an investment in an equity index must all be the same. This means a swap of Libor flat for equity returns is a fair one; so, for that matter, is a swap of returns on one equity for returns on another, or returns on an individual equity for returns on an equity index.

For the proof, consider Table 24.7. The second column of the table presents the gross equity cash flows at the payment time points $T_1, \ldots, T_N$. The third column does likewise for the interest payments assuming $s = 0$. We will show that the time-$T_0$ present values of these gross cash flows are the same for each time point $T_k$.

So consider time $T_1$. The equity cash flow $1 + z_1$ at time $T_1$ can be generated by a \$1 investment at time $T_0$ in the equity portfolio; this means the time-$T_0$ present value of this cash flow is just \$1. Similarly, the Libor cash flow $1 + r_1 d_1$ at time $T_1$ can also be generated by an investment of \$1 at time $T_0$ at the Libor rate $r_1$; so its time-$T_0$ present value is also \$1. The information on present values is in the last two columns of Table 24.7.

Now consider the cash flows at $T_2$. The equity cash flow $1 + z_2$ can be generated by an investment of \$1 in the equity portfolio at time $T_1$; the time-$T_0$ present value of this required investment is $B(T_0, T_1)$. Similarly, the interest cash flow of $1 + r_2 d_2$ can be generated by an investment of \$1 at time $T_1$ at the Libor rate $r_2$, so it too has a time-$T_0$ present value of $B(T_0, T_1)$.

Proceeding in a similar vein, the equity cash flow $1 + z_k$ at time $T_k$ can be generated by an investment of \$1 in the equity portfolio at time $T_{k-1}$, which has a time-$T_0$ present value of $B(T_0, T_{k-1})$. And the interest cash flow of $1 + r_k d_k$ at $T_k$ can be generated by an investment of \$1 at the Libor rate $r_k$ at time $T_{k-1}$, which too has a time-$T_0$ present value of $B(T_0, T_{k-1})$.

**TABLE 24.7**  Payoffs from a Fixed Notional Swap, Equity Returns for Libor

| | Note: PV Refers to Present Value as of Time $T_0$ | | | |
|---|---|---|---|---|
| **Time** | **Equity Return** | **Interest Payment** | **PV(Equity Return)** | **PV(Interest Payment)** |
| $T_1$ | $1 + z_1$ | $1 + r_1 d_1$ | 1 | 1 |
| $T_2$ | $1 + z_2$ | $1 + r_2 d_2$ | $B(T_0, T_1)$ | $B(T_0, T_1)$ |
| $T_3$ | $1 + z_3$ | $1 + r_3 d_3$ | $B(T_0, T_2)$ | $B(T_0, T_2)$ |
| $\vdots$ | $\vdots$ | $\vdots$ | $\vdots$ | $\vdots$ |
| $T_N$ | $1 + z_N$ | $1 + r_N d_N$ | $B(T_0, T_{N-1})$ | $B(T_0, T_{N-1})$ |

Since each set of equity and interest cash flows has the same time-$T_0$ present value, it follows that the present value of the entire equity cash-flow stream is equal to the interest cash-flow stream. We have shown that the "price" of the equity-for-floating-interest swap is just Libor flat.

These arguments may be summarized concisely by simply observing that if we are, say, paying equity and receiving Libor in an equity swap, we can replicate these payoffs by periodically borrowing at Libor and investing in the cash equity or equity index.

## (B) Valuing a Fixed Notional Swap, Equity for Libor

Suppose an investor has entered into a swap of equity returns for Libor. What is the value of the swap on a given date $t$ when the remaining payment dates are $T_1, \ldots, T_N$?

Take any date $T_k$ for $k \geq 2$. The equity returns of $1 + z_k$ at this time may be replicated by a \$1 investment in the equity portfolio at time $T_{k-1}$, and this has a time-$t$ present value of $B(t, T_{k-1})$. And the Libor returns of $1 + r_k d_k$ may be replicated by a \$1 investment at Libor at time $T_{k-1}$, which too has a time-$t$ present value of $B(t, T_{k-1})$. Thus, viewed from date $t$, all the cash flows at dates $T_2$ and beyond have a zero net present value.

So the value of the swap depends only on the present value of the net cash flows receivable at time $T_1$, i.e., letting $PV_t$ denote the present value as of time $t$, it is

$$PV_t(1 + z_1) - PV_t(1 + r_1 d_1)$$

Now, the interest rate $r_1$ is known and locked-in at date $T_0$, so the cash flow $1 + r_1 d_1$ is a certainty cash flow receivable at time $T_1$. Its time-$t$ present value is just $B(t, T_1)(1 + r_1 d_1)$.

With the equity returns, we must use a different argument since the realized returns will not be known until time $T_1$. Recall that $1 + z_1$ is simply the gross return received from an investment of \$1 in the equity portfolio at time $T_0$, i.e., from purchasing $1/S_{T_0}$ units of the portfolio at time $T_0$. The time-$t$ cost of these $1/S_{T_0}$ units is $S_t \times (1/S_{T_0}) = S_t/S_{T_0}$. So the time-$t$ present value of the equity return $1 + z_1$ is $S_t/S_{T_0}$.

Putting these together, the time-$t$ value of the equity swap is

$$V_t = \frac{S_t}{S_{T_0}} - B(t, T_1)(1 + r_1 d_1) \tag{24.1}$$

Note that when $t = T_0$, this value is zero as required since $S_t = S_{T_0}$ and, by definition, $B(T_0, T_1) = 1/(1 + r_1 d_1)$.

## (C) Pricing a Fixed Notional Swap, Equity for Fixed Interest Rate

Suppose we have an equity swap of equity returns for a fixed interest rate $r$. What is the value of $r$ for which the swap has zero value at time $T_0$?

Let $d_k$ continue to denote the day-count fraction applicable to the period $[T_{k-1}, T_k]$ for the fixed rate $r$. (Despite our use of common notation, it is important to note that this fraction may be different from the floating-rate day-count fraction if the fixed- and floating-rate markets use different conventions. For example, the fixed-interest-rate payments may use a 30/360 convention while the floating-rate markets may use an Actual/360 convention.) The gross equity returns and interest payments are given by the second and third columns of Table 24.8.

The time-$T_0$ present value of the equity returns stream is exactly the same as in Table 24.7. For example, to replicate the returns of $1 + z_k$ at time $T_k$, we need an investment of \$1 in the equity portfolio at time $T_{k-1}$, and this investment has a time-$T_0$ present value of $B(T_0, T_{k-1})$.

The interest-rate stream is different from Table 24.7, but since it involves only certainty cash flows, it is easy to present value. On each payment date $T_k$, the gross interest payment is $1 + r d_k$. This certainty cash flow has a time-$T_0$ value of $B(T_0, T_k)(1 + r d_k)$.

**TABLE 24.8**  Payoffs from a Fixed Notional Swap, Equity Returns for Fixed Rate

| | | Note: PV Refers to Present Value as of Time $T_0$ | | |
| --- | --- | --- | --- | --- |
| **Time** | **Equity Return** | **Interest Payment** | **PV(Equity Return)** | **PV(Interest Payment)** |
| $T_1$ | $1 + z_1$ | $1 + rd_1$ | 1 | $B(T_0, T_1)(1 + rd_1)$ |
| $T_2$ | $1 + z_2$ | $1 + rd_2$ | $B(T_0, T_1)$ | $B(T_0, T_2)(1 + rd_2)$ |
| $T_3$ | $1 + z_3$ | $1 + rd_3$ | $B(T_0, T_2)$ | $B(T_0, T_3)(1 + rd_3)$ |
| $\vdots$ | $\vdots$ | $\vdots$ | $\vdots$ | $\vdots$ |
| $T_N$ | $1 + z_N$ | $1 + rd_N$ | $B(T_0, T_{N-1})$ | $B(T_0, T_N)(1 + rd_N)$ |

Putting these together, the time-$T_0$ value of the swap for any given fixed rate $r$ is

$$[1 + B(T_0, T_1) + \cdots + B(T_0, T_{N-1})]$$
$$-[B(T_0, T_1)(1 + rd_1) + \cdots + B(T_0, T_N)(1 + rd_N)] \quad \text{(24.2)}$$

which, after some simplification, works out to

$$1 - B(T_0, T_N) - r[d_1 B(T_0, T_1) + d_2 B(T_0, T_2) + \cdots + d_N B(T_0, T_N)] \quad \text{(24.3)}$$

The fixed rate $r$ must be chosen so that the value of the swap at time $T_0$ is zero. This means the fixed $r$ must be

$$r = \frac{1 - B(T_0, T_N)}{d_1 B(T_0, T_1) + d_2 B(T_0, T_2) + \cdots + d_N B(T_0, T_N)} \quad \text{(24.4)}$$

There are two points of interest regarding this swap price (24.4):

- The swap rate depends *only* on the term-structure of interest rates and not on any properties of equity returns. In particular, equity returns and volatility play no role.
- The swap rate is exactly the same as the swap rate in a fixed-for-floating plain vanilla swap (assuming the same day-count conventions for the fixed sides of the two swaps).

Both points are simple consequences of the fact that there are two ways in which we may swap equity returns into fixed rates. One is through an equity swap. The other is by first swapping equity returns for Libor flat (which, as we have seen, is a fair swap) and then by swapping Libor for a fixed rate through a vanilla interest rate swap. To prevent arbitrage, these fixed rates must be the same.

## (D) Valuing a Fixed Notional Swap, Equity for Fixed Interest Rate

Suppose an investor has entered into a swap of equity returns for a fixed rate $r$. What is the value of the swap on a given date $t$ when the remaining payment dates are $T_1, \ldots, T_N$?

The arguments employed in the pricing segment show that the interest payments cash-flow stream has the same time-$t$ present value as identified in Table 24.8 except that (i) $t$ replaces $T_0$ and (ii) the day-count fraction $d_1$ is replaced by $d_1(t)$, the day-count fraction applicable to the period $[t, T_1]$. That is, the time-$t$ value of this stream is

$$B(t, T_1)(1 + rd_1(t)) + B(t, T_2)(1 + rd_2) + \cdots + B(t, T_N)(1 + rd_N) \quad \text{(24.5)}$$

On the equity side, all the cash flows at date $T_2$ and beyond have the same present values as identified in the fourth column of Table 24.8 except once again that $t$ replaces $T_0$. For example, the equity return $1 + z_2$ may be generated by an investment of \$1 in the equity portfolio at time $T_1$, and this investment has a time-$t$ present value of $B(t, T_1)$. This leaves just one term in the equity returns stream to be identified: the time-$t$ present value of the first equity return $1 + z_1$. This present value, as we saw in the course of valuing the equity-for-Libor swap, is $S_t/S_{T_0}$. So summing up, the time-$t$ value of the equity stream is

$$\frac{S_t}{S_{T_0}} + B(t, T_1) + \cdots + B(t, T_{N-1}) \tag{24.6}$$

The time-$t$ value of the swap $V_t$ is the difference between (24.6) and (24.5). Canceling common terms and simplifying, this value is

$$V_t = \frac{S_t}{S_{T_0}} - B(t, T_N) - r[d_1(t)B(t, T_1) + d_2 B(t, T_2) + \cdots + d_N B(t, T_N)] \tag{24.7}$$

When $t = T_0$ (so $d_1(t) = d_1$), this is just expression (24.3).

## (E) Other Fixed Notional Swaps

Other fixed notional swaps can be priced and valued along the same lines. Here are two examples.

### Same Currency Two-Equity Swaps

Consider an equity-for-equity (rather than equity-for-interest-rate) swap. Suppose the equities are denominated in the same currency. For instance, the swap could involve an exchange of S&P 500 returns for Nasdaq 100 returns or a swap of IBM for General Electric. Let $S_\tau^1$ and $S_\tau^2$ denote, respectively, the time-$\tau$ values of the two equity portfolios; assume the investor is receiving the returns on the first portfolio and paying the returns on the second.

The pricing and valuation of such two-equity swaps require only simple modifications of the arguments used in Parts (A) and (B) above in pricing and valuing equity-for-Libor swaps. A simple modification of the arguments in Part (A) shows that a straight swap of one equity portfolio for the other is a fair swap, so there is nothing to "price" here. A second simple modification, this time of the arguments in Part (B), shows that the value of the swap at time $t$ (lying between $T_0$ and $T_1$, say) is given by

$$V_t = \frac{S_t^1}{S_{T_0}^1} - \frac{S_t^2}{S_{T_0}^2} \tag{24.8}$$

### Cross-Currency Two-Equity Swaps

What if the two-equity swap also involved currency risk, say, the investor pays S&P 500 returns and receives FTSE 100 returns? Let $E_\tau$ be the exchange rate (units of domestic currency per unit of foreign currency) at time $\tau$. Let $S_\tau^d$ and $S_\tau^f$ denote, respectively, the values of the domestic and foreign indices.

The investor's receipts from the equity swap are calculated as follows. At time $T_0$, if the notional principal amount is converted into the foreign currency and invested in the foreign equity portfolio, the number of units of this portfolio purchased would be $1/[E_{T_0} S_{T_0}^f]$. By time $T_1$, this investment is worth $S_{T_1}^f/[E_{T_0} S_{T_0}^f]$. Converting this back into the domestic currency, we obtain $[E_{T_1} S_{T_1}^f]/[E_{T_0} S_{T_0}^f]$. The investor also pays the return on the domestic index, which is $S_{T_1}^d/S_{T_0}^d$. So the investor's net payoff from the equity swap at time $T_1$ is

$$\frac{S_{T_1}^f E_{T_1}}{S_{T_0}^f E_{T_0}} - \frac{S_{T_1}^d}{S_{T_0}^d} \tag{24.9}$$

The payoffs at each payment point $T_k$ take on the same form, with $T_k$ and $T_{k-1}$ replacing $T_1$ and $T_0$, respectively, in (24.9).

It is not hard to modify the arguments of Part (A) to show that this straight exchange of the domestic returns for the foreign returns is a fair one, that is, the replication costs of the two streams of cash flows are identical. For example, to reproduce the first term of the cash flow (24.9) requires an investment of one unit of the domestic currency at time $T_0$, which is the same investment required to reproduce the second term of (24.9). A similar modification of the arguments in Part (B) also shows that the time-$t$ value of this swap (for $t$ lying between $T_0$ and $T_1$, say) is

$$\frac{S_t^f E_t}{S_{T_0}^f E_{T_0}} - \frac{S_t^d}{S_{T_0}^d} \qquad (24.10)$$

Identical arguments may be used to price and value the unhedged cross-currency swaps described in Part (C) of Section 24.3. Indeed, the only change required in expressions (24.9)–(24.10) is replacing the second terms (the domestic equity returns) with the appropriate floating-rate interest payment.

## (F) Equity Swaps with Variable Notionals

In some cases, variable notional swaps may be handled in a similar fashion to fixed notional equity swaps with minor modifications to take care of the periodic resetting of the principal amount. Consider, for example, the equity-for-Libor swap of Part (A). With a variable notional principal, the principal amount applicable to the payoffs at time $T_k$, denoted $A_k$, depends on the equity return realizations up to the time-point $T_{k-1}$ and is given by

$$A_k = \prod_{i=1}^{k-1}(1 + z_i)$$

(The term $\prod$ stands for "product.") Thus, the net cash flow received by the investor at time $T_k$ is

$$A_k(1 + z_k) - A_k(1 + r_k d_k) \qquad (24.11)$$

To replicate the first term in this payoff, invest \$1 in the equity portfolio at time $T_0$ and roll it over at each payment time-point $T_1, \ldots, T_{k-1}$. To replicate the second term in this payoff, invest \$1 in the equity portfolio at time $T_0$ and roll it over at each point up to and including $T_{k-2}$. At time $T_{k-1}$, move the entire principal amount into an investment at the prevailing Libor rate $r_k$. Since the time-$T_0$ present values of these cash flows are the same, a swap of equity for Libor remains a fair one even with a variable notional principal.

The replication argument, however, becomes much harder in a swap of equity-for-fixed interest rate. The arguments of Part (C) do not extend easily to this case. On the first payment date $T_1$, the payoffs are identical to those from a fixed notional swap and are given by

$$(1 + z_1) - (1 + rd_1)$$

(Here, $d_1$ is the day-count fraction applicable to the fixed-interest-rate payment $r$, which may differ from the day-count fraction for floating-rate payments.) The present value of this cash flow may be identified in the usual way described in Part (C) above. Thus far, there are no problems. However, this is not true of the cash flows that occur from $T_2$ to $T_N$. Consider the period $T_2$ net cash flow. This is based on a principal of $1 + z_1$, so amounts to

$$(1 + z_1)[(1 + z_2) - (1 + rd_2)] = (1 + z_1)(1 + z_2) - (1 + z_1)(1 + rd_2)$$

The first term on the right-hand side can be replicated by investing \$1 in the equity portfolio at $T_0$ and rolling it over at $T_1$. However, there is no obvious way to replicate the second term. If we invest \$1 in the equity portfolio at time $T_0$, we will have $1 + z_1$ at time $T_1$, but there is no way to guarantee that this can be invested at a fixed rate $r$ at that point. Nor is there a way to replicate this payment by locking-in the interest rate at time $T_0$ (using, for example, a forward-rate agreement): in this case, the problem is we can guarantee the locked-in interest rate but we do not know the principal amount $1 + z_1$ to which this interest rate is to be applied until time $T_1$. Thus, simple replication-based pricing breaks down here.

It is possible to still develop a pricing and valuation theory for variable notional equity swaps, but we have to make assumptions regarding movements in equity prices. For example, we could use a binomial tree approach. Simplified models are possible if we assume that the correlations between two equity indexes (in a two-equity swap) or between interest rates and equity (in an equity versus interest rate swap) are zero. For details, we refer the reader to Chance and Rich (1995).

# 24.5 Summary

Equity swaps are akin to basis swaps in that each leg is tied to a floating return. The difference is that at least one leg in an equity swap is tied to the price of an equity or to an equity index. The "generic" equity swap involves an exchange of equity returns for a floating interest rate such as Libor. There are also several variants on this theme such as a swap of equity returns for a fixed interest rate, the swap of one equity return for another, and swaps involving foreign equities. The notional principal in an equity swap may be "fixed" or "variable"; in the latter case, the principal is periodically reset to reflect realized equity returns.

Equity swaps enable the creation and transfer of synthetic equity exposure, i.e., without owning or transferring the cash equity or equity index. As such, they enable the conversion of interest-rate risk into equity risk (or vice versa) or of one form of equity risk into another. Cross-currency equity swaps further enable equity exposure to be assumed or transferred across countries. The resulting efficiency gains comprise a major reason for the growing popularity of these products.

From a pricing standpoint, variable notional equity swaps are somewhat tricky, but fixed notional equity swaps are easily handled using principles similar to that employed in the pricing and valuation of interest rate swaps.

# 24.6 Exercises

1. Describe the standard features of an equity swap contract. What are the differences between an equity swap and an interest rate swap?

2. If you were a fund manager with special expertise in the mortgage markets but were advertising yourself as an equity index fund, explain how you might be able to generate extra returns (alpha) for the fund from your expertise in mortgage trading.

3. A market timer switches between stock and cash (i.e., Libor) depending on which market is expected to perform better. If you are a market-timing investment manager, explain how you would use equity swaps to time the market.

4. Why are cash flows from equity swaps more volatile than from interest rate swaps?

5. What is the interest-rate sensitivity of an equity-for-Libor swap?

6. How would you synthesize an equity swap using bonds and futures?

7. State one example of a case when you would want to implement

    (a) A fixed interest rate versus equity swap.

    (b) A floating interest rate versus equity swap.

8. Explain why, in a floating interest rate versus equity swap with a fixed notional principal, all cash flows on the equity side of the swap after the next settlement date have no risk.

9. Suggest two different ways in which equity swaps are useful to traders and hedgers.

10. A plain vanilla equity swap comprises the exchange of equity return for the return stipulated by Libor. What particular types of risk are borne by the parties to the contract?

11. On a $100,000 notional equity swap contract, your firm is the receiver of equity return and the payer of Libor interest. The swap is settled every half year. At the end of the current six-month interval, the equity had appreciated over the past half year by 7.6%, and the six-month Libor rate was set at 5.3% at the beginning of the period. What is your net payment under this swap? The half-year period in question has 181 days.

12. If you anticipate that the equity market will beat the bond market for the next five years, what swap would you find attractive to contract upon?

13. Assuming that you anticipate that the equity markets will outperform the bond markets in the period three years from today for another three years, what swap is appropriate?

14. You wish to implement a life cycle investment plan in your retirement portfolio using a special equity swap. Currently, your portfolio comprises 100% equities. Your financial advisor has suggested that over time you slowly move your money into less risky instruments, so that over the life cycle you balance off risk versus income adequately. What type of equity swap structure would you find appropriate in this case?

15. Suppose you wish to maintain a portfolio that is exactly 80% in equities and 20% in cash at the end of each quarter. What equity swap structure will enable you to do this?

16. You currently own a portfolio that is invested in broad equities and is worth $120,000. You wish to diversify some of the equity risk going forward and maintain a portfolio that is only 70% equity and 30% cash (Libor) for the next three years. Hence, you add a variable notional equity swap to the portfolio such that the portfolio is rebalanced every half year. The following table gives the annualized returns on equity and the Libor rates for the next three years. Prepare a table showing the value of the portfolio, the notional principal of the swap, and the payments made or received under the swap contract. Assume, for simplicity, that all payments including Libor are made on a 30/360 basis. The net portfolio each period is computed after taking the asset value into account as well as the net payments on the swap.

| Time (years) | Equity Return | Six-Month Libor |
|---|---|---|
| 0 | 4.00 | 4.00 |
| 0.5 | 3.50 | 5.00 |
| 1.0 | 3.00 | 6.00 |
| 1.5 | 2.50 | 7.00 |
| 2.0 | 3.50 | 6.00 |
| 2.5 | 4.00 | 5.00 |
| 3.0 | 3.75 | 5.50 |

The equity return at time *t* stands for the rate of appreciation over the past six months ending at time *t*. The Libor rate at time *t* stands for the Libor rate at time *t* and, hence, applies to the next half year.

17. You are the asset manager for an international fund. Suppose you enter into an unhedged currency swap in which you receive the return on the Euronext 100 index and pay the Libor rate. The swap is on a half yearly basis for three years and is unhedged, i.e., payments will reflect current exchange rates. The following is the experience of the

Libor rates as well as the returns on the Euronext 100 index. (These are not the returns from real data.)

| Date | Libor | Euronext 100 (index value) | $ per Euro |
|---|---|---|---|
| 11-Nov-2002 | 1.47 | 300 | 1.0132 |
| 11-May-2003 | 1.22 | 350 | 1.1502 |
| 11-Nov-2003 | 1.23 | 400 | 1.1494 |
| 11-May-2004 | 1.58 | 450 | 1.1857 |
| 11-Nov-2004 | 2.62 | 600 | 1.2897 |
| 11-May-2005 | 3.53 | 650 | 1.2874 |
| 11-Nov-2005 | 4.03 | 700 | 1.2095 |

Assume that the convention on the interest rates is Actual/360 and the swap has a variable notional principal. Prepare a table showing the payments and receipts on this swap. The notional principal at inception is $100,000.

18. Repeat the previous question but allow for the payments to be made on a hedged currency basis. The fixed currency rate is stipulated to be 1.20 $/euro. (Note that this is different from the initial exchange rate.) Prepare the table of receipts and payments under this swap.

19. Consider a five-year semiannual pay fixed notional equity swap in which you receive Libor and pay the equity index return. The current period is of 182 days, and the swap has run exactly 91 days into the period. The six-month Libor rate on the previous reset was 7% and the equity index was at 1050. The current value of the equity index is 1060. Three-month Libor is currently trading at 6%. What is the value of the swap per dollar? (Use an Actual/360 convention for calculating interest payments.)

20. Consider a five-year semiannual pay fixed notional equity swap from which you receive a fixed interest rate of 6% and pay the equity index return. The number of days in the first semiannual period is 182. The current time $t$ is precisely halfway between the inception date and the first payment date. The equity index was at 1000 at inception. The current value of the equity index is 1080. Three-month Libor is currently trading at 6%. What is the value of the swap per dollar if the yield curve is flat? (Use the Actual/360 convention for interest payments.)

21. The current yield curve is flat at 6% p.a. The equity index is at 1123. We are quoting on a new equity swap. What should the fixed interest rate on a fixed notional equity swap be to make it a fair swap at inception?

22. Consider a cross-currency equity swap in which the returns on the S&P 100 (in dollars) are received and exchanged for a payment of returns on the Euronext 100 (in euros). The swap is on a half-yearly basis, and we are at some point in time between inception and the first payment date on the swap. At inception, the S&P 500 was trading at 1000 and the Euronext 100 at 720. Today the S&P 500 is at 1100 and the Euronext 100 at 800. At inception, the spot exchange rate was 1.25 $/euro and now it is 1.20 $/euro. What is the current value of this swap?

# Chapter

# 25

# Currency and Commodity Swaps

## 25.1 Introduction

Building on the analysis of interest rate swaps and equity swaps in the last two chapters, this chapter examines two further categories of swaps, currency swaps and commodity swaps. Other classes of swaps of importance include those that enable the transfer of credit risk between counterparties (such as total return swaps and credit default swaps); these are described later in the book in the context of a broader presentation of credit derivatives (see Chapter 31).

Currency swaps and commodity swaps share some similarities but also have important points of differences. Currency swaps are a natural extension of interest rate swaps and are often undertaken for financing reasons. Commodity swaps, like equity swaps, are often undertaken for reasons of risk-management and hedging. The pricing methodologies too exhibit differences. Currency swaps, like interest rate swaps, may be viewed as the exchange of two bonds and priced accordingly. Commodity swaps are often priced off the relevant forward or futures curve.

We examine currency swaps first. Since all swaps may be represented as a collection of forwards, we open with a review and description of forward contracts in currency markets. We then describe how currency swaps may be used to compare financing alternatives available to corporate treasurers. The analysis in this segment provides a technical link of interest between currency and interest-rate markets beyond that normally embedded in the standard interest-rate parity theories.

Then we move on to commodity swaps. We begin once again with a review of commodity forwards, emphasizing the role of the convenience yield in commodity forward pricing and the differing characteristics of commodity storage. We look at the use of commodity swaps and the pricing of such swaps off the commodity forward/futures curve.

## 25.2 Currency Swaps

Currency swaps are a natural extension of interest rate swaps. While interest rate swaps involve an exchange of interest payments in the same currency, currency swaps involve an exchange of interest payments in *different* currencies. These interest payments may be fixed-fixed (i.e., at fixed rates in both currencies), fixed-floating (fixed rate in one currency, floating in the other), or floating-floating (floating rates in both currencies). Most currency swaps are of the fixed-floating form in which a fixed payment in the foreign currency is exchanged for a floating payment in the domestic currency.

A critical difference between interest rate swaps and commodity swaps is the role of the principal. In interest rate swaps, the principal is a notional one that is not actually exchanged. In a currency swap, there is an exchange of principals in the two currencies at inception and again at maturity of the swap contract. Since changes in exchange rates affect the relative values of the principal amounts, this injects an additional source of market risk into the swap. The impact of exchange rate movements in many cases may even swamp the risk of varying interest rates.

Currency swaps originated in an environment of exchange controls in the 1970s. When corporate borrowing in foreign currencies was restricted, currency swaps made access to foreign funding sources achievable. Their role has changed over the years as exchange controls have vanished in many countries and diminished in others. By providing greater liquidity at long maturities than foreign exchange forwards, currency swaps have become a key instrument of cross-border financing arbitrage. We examine the nature and mechanics of these financing transactions in this chapter. As a first step to examining the role of currency swaps in cross-border financing options, we look at currency forward contracts.

## Spot and Forward Foreign Exchange

Foreign exchange (or "FX") contracts are agreements to exchange one currency for another at a specified date at a specified exchange rate. If the contract is for immediate delivery, it is a "spot FX" contract; if for delivery at a date in the future, it is a "forward FX" contract. Spot and forward FX contracts are traded in over-the-counter (OTC) markets where rates are set by active trading between major international banks.

The quoting convention in FX markets is important. When quoting the price of a stock or commodity, it is customary to give a price per unit of the underlying (e.g., euros per share of stock, dollars per barrel of oil, or cents per bushel of wheat). Similarly, in quoting an exchange rate, it is usual to provide it in terms of $x$ units of one currency per unit of the other currency. The latter currency is referred to for obvious reasons as the "stock" or "commodity" currency since it plays the role of the underlying. The former is called the "medium of exchange" or the "unit of account." Thus, for example, in a quote of JPY 135/USD (JPY = Japanese yen, USD = US dollar), USD is the stock or commodity currency and JPY the medium of exchange.

## FX Forward Pricing

As we have seen in Chapter 3, the forward FX rate can be determined using replication arguments from knowledge of three things: the spot FX rate, the rate of interest in the domestic currency, and the rate of interest in the foreign currency. We briefly review the pricing formula here and present the same arbitrage arguments in slightly different form.

Consider JPY-USD forward rates for specificity. In the discussion that follows, the current time is taken to be time 0 and the maturity date of the forward contract to be time $T$; note that the time to maturity is also $T$ years. Let $F_T$ denote the forward price in JPY of USD 1. Let the $T$-year USD interest rate be $r_d$, and the $T$-year JPY interest rate be $r_y$, both in continuously-compounded terms. Let $S$ denote the spot JPY/USD rate. Then, the forward price $F_T$ is given by

$$F_T = S \times \frac{e^{r_y T}}{e^{r_d T}} = S e^{(r_y - r_d)T} \qquad (25.1)$$

Note that the *medium of exchange* currency's interest rate enters the formula in the numerator and the *commodity* currency's interest rate enters the denominator. How does (25.1) obtain? We have offered one derivation based on replication in Chapter 3. Here is another. A US-based investor has two alternative investment routes to investing $1 for $T$ years.

- She can invest it at the domestic interest rate $r_d$. In this case, she will receive USD $e^{r_d T}$ at maturity.
- Alternatively, she can convert her dollar into yen today, invest the yen at the yen interest rate for $T$ years, and enter into a forward contract today for reconverting the yen received in $T$ years back into USD. If she does this, she receives JPY $S$ today, which grows to JPY $Se^{r_y T}$ by time $T$. Converting this back to USD at the forward rate $F_T$, she receives USD $Se^{r_y T} \times (1/F_T)$ at time $T$.

To preclude arbitrage, these amounts must be the same. That is, we must have

$$e^{r_d T} = Se^{r_y T} \times \frac{1}{F_T}$$

which is precisely (25.1).

---

**Example 25.1**

Suppose $S = 135$, $r_y = 0.01$, and $r_d = 0.03$. Assume interest rates are in continuously-compounded terms. Then, the one-year forward rate is

$$F_1 = 135 \times e^{(0.01-0.03)} = 132.3268$$  ∎

While the spot FX rate in our example is JPY 135/USD, the arbitrage-free forward rate is only JPY 132.3268/USD. Why is it lower? Intuitively, because the lower yield on the yen must be made up by a capital gain on currency conversion. That is, since yen interest rates are lower than dollar interest rates, the forward conversion rate must be attractive enough to make up for the lower interest rate. For more dollars to be received when converting yen, the JPY/USD rate must be lower. We summarize this formally:

### Rule

*The currency with higher interest rates trades at a discount in forward markets, while the currency with lower interest rates trades at a premium.*

### Question

Suppose interest rates are instead quoted in simple terms with annualized compounding (i.e., USD 1 grows to USD $(1 + r_d)^T$ in $T$ years). Show that (25.1) then takes the form

$$F_T = S \times \frac{(1+r_y)^T}{(1+r_d)^T}$$

What is $F_T$ if $T = 1, S = 135, r_y = 0.01$, and $r_d = 0.03$?

## Bid and Offer Rates

FX rates, both spot and forward, are quoted in two-way markets, i.e., banks quote both bid and offer prices. Bid prices reflect the price at which the bank is willing to buy the commodity currency, and offer prices are those at which the bank will sell the commodity currency. Offer prices are also called "ask" prices.

The difference in bid and offer/ask prices is called the "bid-offer" or "bid-ask" spread. Ceteris paribus, FX dealers stand to gain from widening bid-ask spreads since they make the difference between the bid and ask prices on every round-trip trade. However, competition in the foreign currency markets is severe, so bid-ask spreads in practice are minuscule.

As mentioned, banks make two-way quotes in the FX market, i.e., they always post bid and ask prices. A customer approaching a bank for a quote is not required to reveal whether he is buying or selling, which is one reason for the bid-ask spread. Banks may skew the spreads if they wish to take one side more than the other. Consider the following quotes from the JPY/USD market, for example (the prices refer to bid/ask):

Median price = 134.350 / 134.370

Minimum price = 134.060 / 134.110

Maximum price = 134.990 / 135.070

The median price indicates a tight bid-ask spread of just 0.02 yen per dollar. However, there is almost a 1 yen difference between the maximum and minimum quotes in the market. Banks that wish to sell dollars for yen will skew their bid-ask quotes downwards (as in the "minimum price" above). This makes it attractive for customers to sell yen to them (you can get a dollar for just 134.06 yen) but not to buy yen from them (you receive only 134.11 yen per dollar, which is less than the median ask price). Likewise, banks wishing to buy dollars and sell yen will skew their quotes upwards (as in the "maximum price" above). How should a bank skew its quotes if it does not wish to trade?

## Forward Points

Forward FX rates are usually expressed as "points." Points are the difference between the spot and forward FX rates. For example, if $S = 135$ and $F(T) = 132.3786$, then the point difference equals 2.6214. Markets may quote points rather than forward FX rates. That is, the spot FX rate is quoted as JPY 135/USD, but the forward is quoted in terms of the point differential from the spot FX rate.

Table 25.1 provides an example of a forward FX rate table. The forward FX mid rates in the table were obtained by using a spot FX mid rate of 135 JPY/USD and then using an interest differential of 2% between the USD and JPY markets (USD 3% and JPY 1%) to arrive at the forward rates. Reasonable bid-offer spreads were then added around these mid rates.

Forward rates are declining in the table because US interest rates are higher. This is all one needs to ascertain when deciding whether to add or subtract forward points to the spot rate to obtain the forward rate. If the stock currency has the higher interest rate, then the forward points should be subtracted from the spot exchange rate to arrive at the forward exchange rate. Conversely, if the stock currency has the lower interest rate, then forward points should be added to the spot exchange rate to arrive at the forward exchange rates.

## Hedging Cross-Currency Borrowing

With this introductory material behind us, we now turn to the central issue of interest: the use of forward FX and currency swap markets to access the cheapest source of financing.

**TABLE 25.1**
Forward FX and Points Table

| Maturity (Years) | FX Rates | | Points | |
|---|---|---|---|---|
| | Bid | Offer | Bid | Offer |
| 0 | 134.9595 | 135.0405 | | |
| 1 | 132.2871 | 133.3268 | 2.6724 | 2.7137 |
| 2 | 129.6407 | 129.7065 | 5.3188 | 5.3340 |
| 3 | 127.0582 | 127.1382 | 7.9013 | 7.9023 |
| 4 | 124.5315 | 124.6206 | 10.4280 | 10.4199 |
| 5 | 122.0574 | 123.1530 | 12.9021 | 12.8875 |

It is often advantageous for a company to borrow in a currency other than that in which it maintains its books. For example, a US company might find that Japanese investors are willing to lend to it on favorable terms.[1] In this case, the company may prefer to borrow in yen and then remove the currency risk by hedging forward. Taken in conjunction with forward FX markets, this may provide the company with a superior funding opportunity to borrowing in the domestic market. Consider the following example.

## Example 25.2

A company wishes to borrow dollars for five years. It can borrow in dollars for five years in the fixed-rate US dollar markets at a rate of 4.90%. It can also borrow in yen for five years in the fixed-rate yen market at 2.50%. Can the company reduce its cost of borrowing by borrowing in yen?

Borrowing in yen has associated currency risk that may more than offest the benefit of the lower yen interest rate. For example, if the yen appreciates substantially after the loan is taken, every interest payment will cost more in dollars since more dollars will be needed to buy yen to pay off the loan interest. This makes the yen cost of borrowing non-comparable with the dollar cost. One way to restore comparability is for the company to lock-in the dollar cost of the loan using forward FX markets.

Suppose that the spot and forward FX rates faced by the company are those in Table 25.1. Then the company can book five forward FX contracts, one for each of the cash outflows associated with the loan. The complete strategy and resulting cash flows are the following:

- Borrow JPY for five years at 2.50%. Assuming an equivalent amount of USD 100 borrowed, this results in a JPY bond with the cash flows shown in Table 25.2.

- Since the borrowed yen have to be converted to dollars at time 0, we have used the spot offer rate to identify the amount to be borrowed. The initial borrowing at time 0 is signed positive since it is an inflow of yen 13,504.05. At the end of years 1 through 4, the cash flows are signed negative since they are interest payments, so constitute outflows. Each of these is for 2.50% of 13,504.05, or an amount of JPY 337.60. The final cash flow at the end of year 5 is for interest plus the repayment of principal.

- Convert the JPY cash flows into USD by entering into a series of FX forward contracts. The initial JPY 13,504.05 received is converted into USD at the spot rate. The remaining cash flows are hedged by buying JPY and selling USD and, hence, are converted at the bid rates in Table 25.1. Applying these rates, we obtain dollar cash outflows shown in Table 25.3.

**TABLE 25.2**  JPY Cash Flows in the Example

| Maturity | 0 | 1 | 2 | 3 | 4 | 5 |
|---|---|---|---|---|---|---|
| JPY | 13,504.05 | −337.60 | −337.60 | −337.60 | −337.60 | −13,841.65 |

**TABLE 25.3**  USD Cash Flows in the Example

| Maturity | 0 | 1 | 2 | 3 | 4 | 5 |
|---|---|---|---|---|---|---|
| USD | 100 | −2.55 | −2.60 | −2.66 | −2.71 | −113.40 |

[1] Japanese interest rates have been very low for more than two decades. Hence, borrowing in yen is often attractive if currency risk can be managed. The example in this section is a fictitious example of the canonical trade undertaken by US firms in hedged yen borrowing. The interested reader may refer to several well-known real cases exemplifying this transaction. See, for example, "Currency Swaps" (HBS case 286-073); "The Walt Disney Company's Yen Financing" (HBS case 287-058); "IBM Japan" (HBS case 286-074); HBS is the Harvard Business School. The last named looks at some innovative forms of financing, including so-called "sushi" bonds and dual-currency bonds. These are not taken up here but may be evaluated using the concepts in this chapter.

The initial yen loan has thus been transformed into a dollar loan. The cost of this borrowing is the internal rate of return (IRR) of these dollar cash flows, i.e., the discount rate at which these combined cash flows have a present value of zero. This IRR works out to 4.59%. This is a significant reduction of 31 basis points from the 4.90% fixed cost of borrowing directly in USD. ∎

As this example shows, a "synthetic" home currency borrowing can be created by combining FX forward transactions with foreign currency borrowing. If the synthetic borrowing costs less than straight borrowing in the home currency, financing savings result. In this example, the combination of the yen loan and FX forwards creates a synthetic dollar loan that saves the company 0.31% per year in financing costs.

Why might such exploitable differences exist? Do they indicate an inefficiency in the international credit markets? This form of "credit arbitrage" may arise because the concerned US company (or "name") is treated more favorably in the Japanese credit markets than in the US domestic market. In the absence of sufficient high-quality credits in Japan, investors there may wish to consider bonds issued by high-quality US companies. This allows such US firms to get away with lower coupon rates on their bonds. Not all US firms have access to this arbitrage. Favorable financing terms are usually available to firms that have substantial brand name recognition.

The next segment examines how currency swaps may be used in place of the FX forwards to manufacture synthetic home currency financing from foreign currency borrowing.

## Using Currency Swaps

A currency swap is really nothing more than a collection of forward FX contracts, so the mechanism of converting foreign borrowing into a home currency loan using currency swaps is not conceptually very different from the example above. However, currency swap markets are often more liquid than forward currency markets, so an improvement of the credit-arbitrage may be achieved by processing it in currency swap markets.

Currency swap markets are also two-way markets, i.e., they post both bid and offer prices. The usual quoting convention in these markets is to quote a fixed rate in the foreign currency against floating home currency (e.g., fixed-rate yen versus USD Libor). At each settlement date, the parties to the contract then exchange the fixed payment in a foreign currency for a payment based on a floating rate in the home currency. Less frequently, both sides of the currency swap may be floating. In such a case, the currency swap is called a *basis currency swap*.

The least common versions of currency swaps are those that involve an exchange of a fixed rate in the foreign currency for a fixed rate in the domestic currency; but, of course, such "fixed-fixed" swaps may be constructed simply by combining a fixed-floating currency swap with a vanilla floating-fixed interest rate swap in the domestic currency. Our next example uses precisely such a construction.

| | |
|---|---|
| **Example 25.3** | We continue with Example 25.2. Suppose now that the company also has open to it the option of using the JPY/USD currency swap market. The quotes in this market for a five-year swap (fixed yen versus one-year USD Libor) are 2.90–3.00%. That is, if the company wishes to receive fixed yen against paying floating dollar, it receives 2.90% fixed on the yen against paying dollar Libor, and if it wishes to pay fixed yen and receive floating dollar, then it pays 3.00% fixed on the yen and receives dollar Libor.<br><br>Using the currency swap enables converting a yen fixed-rate borrowing into a floating-rate dollar Libor loan in the obvious manner: the company borrows yen fixed and then enters into a receive fixed yen–pay floating-dollar currency swap. To further convert this into a fixed-rate dollar borrowing, an interest rate swap must be used to convert the floating USD Libor into a fixed payment. So suppose further that the quote for a five-year interest |

**TABLE 25.4**
Currency Swaps
Example: The Cash
Flows

| Maturity | 1 | 2 | 3 | 4 | 5 |
|---|---|---|---|---|---|
| JPY cash flows | 54 | 54 | 54 | 54 | 54 |
| USD cash flows | −0.4082 | −0.4164 | −0.4248 | −0.4334 | −0.4422 |

rate swap (fixed versus floating one-year USD Libor) is 4.80–4.88%. That is, the company can enter into a pay fixed–receive floating swap in which it pays a fixed rate of 4.88% or into a receive fixed–pay floating swap in which it receives a fixed rate of 4.80%.

Here then is the complete strategy.

- Issue a bond in yen and raise fixed-rate yen financing at 2.50% as before.
- Use a currency swap to convert the fixed-rate yen loan into a floating-rate dollar loan using the currency swap described above. On the swap, the company receives 2.90% fixed yen and pays dollar Libor.
- Use a vanilla interest rate swap to convert the floating-rate dollar loan into a fixed-rate one. In the interest rate swap, the company pays 4.88% fixed and receives dollar Libor.

The combination of the two swaps creates a fixed-fixed currency swap. In yen, the company pays 2.50% on its borrowing but receives 2.90% from the currency swap for a net inflow of 0.40% of the borrowed amount of JPY 13,504.05. In dollars, the company pays 4.88%. Thus, its net fixed cost is USD 4.88% − JPY 0.40%. Of course, this is already cheaper than the 4.90% fixed cost of straight US dollar borrowing, but to enable comparison with the strategy that locks-in a fixed rate using FX forwards, we must convert this net cost into purely dollar terms. For this, we need to convert the yen return of 0.40% into dollar terms. We note that the yen difference we receive is 0.4% of JPY 13,504.05, which is JPY 54.

Since we receive an excess of JPY 54 each year, we may convert it into USD by selling it forward. This is the same as buying USD, and so the FX rate we would face is the offer rate (see Table 25.1). Converting these JPY cash flows into USD cash flows, we obtain the numbers in Table 25.4.

The amount of JPY 54 is received every year. Using the forward FX rates, we convert this amount for each year into dollars, i.e., we hedge these JPY receipts forward. By adding USD 100 in principal as initial and final principal to the cash flows in USD so as to mimic a bond, we compute the internal rate of return for the cash flows. The IRR equals 0.42%. Hence, the equivalent USD is 42 basis points.

Combining this with the 4.88% fixed cost in dollars, the net fixed cost of borrowing in dollars using the currency swap markets is equal to 4.88% − 0.42% = 4.46%. This is cheaper than the 4.59% fixed rate using FX forwards, and, of course, significantly cheaper than the 4.90% fixed cost of borrowing outright in the USD market. ■

An obvious question arises: why are the currency swap markets better than using FX forwards? Because of liquidity: bid-ask spreads in the currency swap markets are narrower than those in the FX forward markets at long maturities since they are more liquid than long-dated FX contracts.

To summarize, currency swaps may be used to convert a fixed-rate borrowing in a foreign currency into a floating-rate borrowing in the domestic currency. A plain vanilla interest rate swap can then be used to convert the floating-rate home currency borrowing into a fixed-rate home currency borrowing. The higher liquidity of currency swaps than FX forwards in general makes them attractive as arbitrage instruments in the cross-currency financing market.

## Currency Swaps versus Forward FX: Is There an Arbitrage?

The presence of cheaper synthetic borrowing (achieved by borrowing in JPY and swapping into USD) allows the company to access a credit arbitrage. Therefore, forward currency-hedged borrowing is cheaper than direct USD fixed-rate borrowing. However, there is also a

**TABLE 25.5** Arbitraging CCY Swaps vs. FX Forwards: Case 1

| Maturity | Receive USD | Pay JPY | Conversion Rate | USD | Net USD | PV Net USD |
|---|---|---|---|---|---|---|
| 0 | 100.0000 | 13504.0500 | 135.0405 | 100.0000 | 0.0000 | 0.0000 |
| 1 | 4.8000 | −405.1215 | 132.2871 | −3.0624 | 1.7376 | 1.6862 |
| 2 | 4.8000 | −405.1215 | 129.6407 | −3.1250 | 1.6750 | 1.5775 |
| 3 | 4.8000 | −405.1215 | 127.0582 | −3.1885 | 1.6115 | 1.4728 |
| 4 | 4.8000 | −405.1215 | 124.5315 | −3.2532 | 1.5468 | 1.3719 |
| 5 | 104.8000 | −13909.1715 | 122.0574 | −113.9560 | −9.1560 | −7.8806 |
|  |  |  |  |  | NPV | −1.7722 |

difference in the all-in-cost of borrowing when hedging using FX forwards versus currency swaps. This raises the following question: is it possible to construct an arbitrage between the forward FX markets and the currency swap markets?

In our setting, if there is an arbitrage opportunity, then we should be able to construct a portfolio comprising the currency swap and FX forwards with positive NPV. We construct a portfolio as follows:

- Enter into a currency swap with principal amounts of USD 100 and JPY 13,504.05. We will receive on the USD leg of the swap and pay on the JPY leg. Such a swap is not really available directly, but we may construct it as follows: (i) enter into a currency swap to pay 3% in JPY and receive USD Libor and (ii) enter into an interest rate swap in which we receive 4.80% in USD and pay USD Libor. The net of these is a currency swap for which we pay JPY 3.0% and receive USD 4.80%.

- Hedge out, using currency forwards, all JPY payments. This will result in USD payments.

- Finally, net off these USD payments against the USD leg of the original currency swap. This results in a stream of pure USD payments. If the NPV of this stream is positive, then we have captured some value from the relative mispricing of the currency swap and the forward FX markets, which has not been wiped out by losses from trading against the bid-ask spreads in the various currency and swap markets.

We show the results of this analysis in Table 25.5. The second and third columns of the table contain the cash flows of the currency swap. The fourth column simply restates the conversion rates we derived earlier. The fifth column contains the USD equivalent of the JPY leg of the swap, i.e., the JPY cash flows FX-hedged into USD, conversion undertaken at the appropriate bid rate as required. The sixth column shows the difference between the USD side of the currency swap and the JPY leg converted into USD. Finally, the seventh column contains the present values of the USD differences, assuming as before a USD interest rate of 3%. We see that the NPV is USD −1.7722. Hence, the trade is not favorable.

However, this is only one of the trades that may be undertaken. What if we instead went the other way, i.e., we set up a currency swap for which we pay USD and receive JPY? Reversing trades from the previous example, we have the following steps:

- Enter into a currency swap with principal amounts of USD 100 and JPY 13,495.65 in which we pay fixed on the USD leg of the swap and receive fixed on the JPY leg. We construct such a swap in the usual way: (i) enter into a currency swap to receive 2.90% in JPY and pay USD Libor, and (ii) enter into an interest rate swap for which we pay 4.88% in USD and receive USD Libor. The net of these is a currency swap for which we receive JPY 2.9% and pay USD 4.88%.

- Hedge out, using currency forwards, all JPY receipts. This will result in USD receipts.

**TABLE 25.6**  Arbitraging CCY Swaps vs. FX Forwards: Case 2

| Maturity | Pay USD | Receive JPY | Conversion Rate | USD | Net USD | PV Net USD |
|---|---|---|---|---|---|---|
| 0 | 100 | 13495.95 | 134.9595 | 100.0000 | 0.0000 | 0.0000 |
| 1 | −4.88 | 391.38255 | 132.3268 | 2.9577 | −1.9223 | −1.8655 |
| 2 | −4.88 | 391.38255 | 129.7065 | 3.0174 | −1.8626 | −1.7541 |
| 3 | −4.88 | 391.38255 | 127.1382 | 3.0784 | −1.8016 | −1.6465 |
| 4 | −4.88 | 391.38255 | 124.6206 | 3.1406 | −1.7394 | −1.5427 |
| 5 | −104.88 | 13887.33255 | 123.1530 | 112.7649 | 7.8849 | 6.7866 |
| | | | | | NPV | −0.0222 |

- Finally, net off these USD receipts against the USD leg of the original currency swap. This results in a stream of pure USD payments.

We show the results of this analysis in Table 25.6.

Once again, we see that the NPV is negative, i.e., USD −0.0222. Therefore, the discrepancy between the currency swap and forward FX markets is not arbitrageable. Bid-ask spreads eat away any possible gains.

## Pricing of Currency Swaps

How are the rates on the fixed leg of a currency swap determined? The short answer is: these rates must be chosen so that the net present value of the cash flows from the swap is equal to zero at the inception of the swap. Identifying this fixed rate is not hard. The procedure is essentially identical to that followed by interest rate swaps, with simple modifications to account for the feature that the cash flows occur in different currencies.

We begin by noting that the currency swap is, in effect, an exchange of bonds in two currencies, a fixed-rate bond in one currency for a floating-rate bond in the other. Each bond may be valued separately in its own currency using the relevant forward rates to discount future cash flows. (Actually, only the fixed-rate bond needs to be valued. The price of the floating-rate bond at inception is, by definition, par.) Then the fixed-rate bond is converted into the other currency at the current spot exchange rate. We identify the fixed rate so that, after conversion, this bond is worth par too. This is the swap rate.

# 25.3  Commodity Swaps

A commodity swap, like a vanilla interest rate swap, involves the exchange of a fixed payment for a floating one. The floating payment in a typical commodity swap is linked to the price of a commodity (e.g., the spot price of a barrel of oil), while the fixed payment is a given dollar amount (e.g., $40). Of course, only the net payment—the difference between the floating and fixed payments—is exchanged in practice. A less common version of commodity swaps involves a floating-for-floating exchange in which one floating leg is tied to the price of a commodity and the other to an interest rate (e.g., Libor). Other variants on the basic theme are described at the end of this section.

Commodity swaps based on oil prices are the most common in practice, but swaps based on many other commodities are also feasible. The floating side of the commodity swap contract is usually indexed to the spot or futures price of a commodity. The fixed side is determined at inception in a manner that makes the swap a fair one. We discuss the determination of the fixed side later in this section.

Commodity swaps provide natural hedges against price changes for consumers and producers. For a consumer who periodically purchases the commodity at its spot price, being the fixed payer in a commodity swap enables locking-in a price for the commodity: the consumer continues to buy the commodity at the spot price but also receives from the swap the difference between the spot price and the fixed payment in the swap, leading to a net cash outflow of just the fixed payment. Similarly, for a producer of the commodity, being the floating payer in the swap provides a hedge against spot price changes.

This section examines the pricing of commodity swaps off the futures or forward price curve. We begin with a review of forward pricing for commodities.

## Commodity Forward Pricing: A Review

In Chapter 3, we described the cost-of-carry method of identifying forward prices. As we showed there, the forward price of an asset depends in general on the costs of holding or "carrying" that asset from now to the maturity date of the forward contract. These holding costs may be positive (e.g., storage, insurance) or negative (e.g., dividends received from holding the asset). If $M_\tau$ denotes the present value of the net holding costs (holding costs minus holding benefits) up to time $\tau$, then the forward price $F_\tau$ for maturity $\tau$ is given by

$$F_\tau = e^{r_\tau \tau}(S + M_\tau) \qquad \textbf{(25.2)}$$

Here, $S$ denotes, as usual, the current (time-0) price of the asset, and $r_\tau$ is the rate of interest applicable to a horizon of length $\tau$ expressed in continuously-compounded terms. Expression (25.2) takes holding costs and benefits to be expressed in dollar terms. In many cases, these are better expressed in yield terms. For instance, the dividend benefit from holding an index is naturally expressed in terms of the dividend yield on the index. If we let $q_\tau$ denote the dividend yield from holding the underlying (expressed in continuously-compounded terms) over the horizon $[0, \tau]$, the forward price takes the form

$$F_\tau = e^{(r_\tau - q_\tau)\tau} S \qquad \textbf{(25.3)}$$

As we discussed in Chapter 4, expressions (25.2) and (25.3) generally work very well for financial assets. As a consequence, the forward price for these assets depends only on observable quantities (spot price, holdings costs/benefits, interest rates) and may be identified ex ante from knowledge of these quantities. There is no more information in forward prices than is already embedded in these observable inputs into the formula.

For commodities, the story is somewhat different. The dividend $q_\tau$ here takes the form of a "convenience yield" that is unobservable. As noted in Chapter 4, an important difference between physical commodities and financial assets is that the former are used in production and are consumed in the process. Producers and others hold inventories of commodities because this gives them the flexibility to alter production schedules or as insurance against a shortage of supply in the spot market. The convenience yield measures the value of the option to consume the commodity out of storage. The convenience yield depends on a variety of factors, notably anticipated demand-supply imbalances. If the current supply of a commodity is large relative to its consumption demand, the convenience yield will generally be low. But the convenience yield may change, even drastically, with news and events in the marketplace.

The forward/futures prices observed for commodities reflect the market consensus concerning the unobserved convenience yields; the implied $q_\tau$ may be backed out from observed forward/futures prices using (25.3). Since $F_\tau$ and $q_\tau$ cannot be identified ex ante but only through trading, the process is referred to as one of "price discovery."

Of course, regardless of whether holdings costs and benefits are observable, the pricing expressions (25.2) and (25.3) are valid only for assets that can be stored. For non-storable underlyings such as electricity, the cost-of-carry model simply does not apply since the asset cannot be "carried" to maturity. In such cases, the forward price is simply a reflection of anticipated future spot prices, perhaps plus or minus a risk premium.

## Valuing and Pricing Commodity Swaps

Since the convenience yields are unobservable, we cannot price commodity swaps from "first principles" (i.e., from just spot price and interest-rate information) the way we could for interest rate or equity swaps. However, if futures or forward prices are available, then we can infer the convenience yields from these and use them in the pricing process. Equivalently, we may just directly price the commodity swap in terms of the forward prices, as we describe here.

The intuition behind the pricing process is simple. The swap is simply a collection of forwards, one for each payment date in the contract. Hence, the risk in the swap can be eliminated by taking offsetting positions in a series of forward contracts. The resulting portfolio has riskless cash flows, so it may be valued from knowledge of the term-structure of interest rates. The swap rate is the fixed price in the swap that makes the value of this portfolio zero.

We first describe this in terms of notation, and then work through an example. Let:

- $P$ denote the fixed payment in the swap.
- $T_1, \ldots, T_N$ be the remaining payment dates in the swap. As usual, the current date is date 0.
- $S$ be the current price of the commodity, and $S_1, \ldots, S_N$ be the (currently unknown) spot prices on the payment dates.
- $F_1, \ldots, F_N$ be the forward prices today for delivery of one unit of the commodity on dates $T_1, \ldots, T_N$, respectively.
- $B_1, \ldots, B_N$ denote the discount factors for identifying the present value of certainty cash flows on dates $T_1, \ldots, T_N$, respectively. (That is, the present value today of $1 receivable on date $T_k$ is $B_k$.)

Suppose an investor has a pay fixed–receive floating position in the commodity swap. On each payment date $T_k$, she receives a cash flow of

$$S_k - P \qquad\qquad (25.4)$$

Viewed from date 0, these cash flows are risky since the future spot prices $S_k$ are currently unknown. But suppose that on date 0, the investor also enters into a series of short forward contracts with delivery dates $T_1, \ldots, T_N$. On date $T_k$, she delivers a unit of the asset worth $S_k$ and receives the delivery price $F_k$. So, the net cash flow from the forward contract on date $T_k$ is

$$F_k - S_k \qquad\qquad (25.5)$$

Adding (25.4) and (25.5), the cash flow on date $T_k$ from the combined portfolio of the commodity swap and the series of forward contracts is

$$F_k - P \qquad\qquad (25.6)$$

For each $k$, this is a certainty cash flow whose time-0 present value may be identified simply by discounting it by the factor $B_k$. Adding up these present values over $k$, the time-0 present value of the combined portfolio is just

$$\sum_{k=1}^{N} B_k(F_k - P) = \sum_{k=1}^{N} B_k F_k - P \sum_{k=1}^{N} B_k \qquad\qquad (25.7)$$

**TABLE 25.7**
Commodity Swap
Pricing: Input
Information

| Maturity (years) | Spot Interest Rate | Forward Price |
|---|---|---|
| 1 | 0.0100 | 44.66 |
| 2 | 0.0125 | 44.78 |
| 3 | 0.0200 | 43.67 |
| 4 | 0.0300 | 43.24 |
| 5 | 0.0350 | 41.75 |

At time 0, each forward contract has zero present value by definition. So equation (25.7) is the time-0 value of the commodity swap. Pricing the swap is an easy matter now. At inception of the swap, its value must be zero. So the fair price $P$ of the swap must be

$$P = \frac{\sum_{k=1}^{N} B_k F_k}{\sum_{k=1}^{N} B_k} \tag{25.8}$$

Equation (25.8) is the promised expression that identifies the fair price of the swap in terms of the forward prices and risk-free interest rates.

**Example 25.4**

Suppose we are given the information in Table 25.7 on current spot interest rates and forward prices for delivery of oil for the next five years. The interest rates are in continuously-compounded terms, and the forward prices are dollars per barrel of oil. What is the swap rate on a five-year oil swap with payment dates $T = 1, 2, 3, 4, 5$?

As a first step, we identify the discount factors $B_1, \ldots, B_5$. Since the interest rates are in continuously-compounded terms, we have

$$B_1 = e^{-0.01 \times 1} = 0.9900$$
$$B_2 = e^{-0.0125 \times 2} = 0.9753$$
$$B_3 = e^{-0.02 \times 3} = 0.9418$$
$$B_4 = e^{-0.03 \times 4} = 0.8869$$
$$B_5 = e^{-0.035 \times 5} = 0.8395$$

Thus, we have

$$\sum_{k=1}^{5} B_k F_k = 202.4146$$

$$\sum_{k=1}^{5} B_k = 4.6335$$

Substituting these in (25.8), the swap rate in the five-year oil swap (i.e., the fixed price in the swap) is

$$P = \frac{202.4146}{4.6335} = 43.6850 \qquad \blacksquare$$

## Further Comments on Commodity Swaps

Commodity prices tend to be very volatile, much more so than equity prices, interest rates, or exchange rates. Volatilities of around 100% and even higher are not unknown. This is an important factor in creating hedging demand, in particular, for commodity swaps.

Commodity markets also exhibit several distinct features compared to the markets for financial securities. Some of these relate to the cost of hedging, institutional differences, high levels of illiquidity in some commodities, and seasonality in production. Credit risk too tends to be a factor of importance.

Our description above has focused on fixed-for-floating commodity swaps in which the floating side is indexed to the spot price of a commodity. A variant on this design is one in which the floating side is the *average* spot price witnessed over some specified reference period. Typically, the reference period is the period between payment dates and the arithmetic average of daily prices over this period is used. Such swaps are called *Asian* commodity swaps.

There are other variants too on the basic theme. These include:

- Fixed-for-floating swaps in which the floating side is linked to an index of commodity prices (for example, the Goldman Sachs Commodity Index or a property index) rather than the price of a single commodity.

- Floating-for-floating commodity swaps in which one leg is indexed to a commodity price and the other to an interest rate such as Libor. In principle, such swaps ought to be of interest for producers of the commodity as a simultaneous hedge against the commodity price risk and their interest-rate liabilities.

- Floating-for-floating commodity swaps in which the two legs are linked to closely related products (for example, Light Sweet crude oil and West Texas Intermediate crude oil). Such swaps are called commodity basis swaps and have much in common with the interest-rate basis swaps.

- Floating-for-floating commodity swaps in which the two legs relate to different sides of the production process (for example, one leg is tied to a particular crude oil price and the other to a particular refined oil price). These are called commodity spread swaps.

The pricing of many of these contracts is complicated by the unobservability of convenience yields and further by the possibility that the convenience yields, spot prices, and interest rates may all be correlated. Where replication is not feasible, risk-premia need to be incorporated into the pricing process. For a discussion of the pricing of commodity contracts, see Casassus and Collin-Dufresne (2005).

## 25.4 Summary

Foreign exchange (FX) trading volume outstrips that of any other market. Most FX trading occurs in OTC markets. The same is true for currency swaps.

A currency swap is effectively the exchange of bonds, one in each currency. Equivalently, it may be viewed as a portfolio of forward FX contracts. Currency swaps are perhaps the most useful of instruments in cross-border financing. They permit companies to access financing in other markets and enable the choice of fixed versus floating funding as desired. Cross-currency financing risk may be managed with currency swaps, which are superior on account of their greater liquidity to hedging with a portfolio of forwards.

Commodity swaps too may be viewed as a portfolio of forward contracts and valued accordingly. However, commodity forward valuation is generally more complex than for financial assets because of the presence of an unobserved convenience yield or because the commodity is not storable. Commodity swaps, however, may be priced relative to forward or futures prices if such prices are available.

## 25.5 Exercises

1. What is covered interest-rate parity?

2. If the US dollar is trading at a discount to the yen in the forward currency markets, what can you say about the relationship of the dollar and yen interest rates?

3. If the yen/dollar exchange rate is 130 and the dollar/euro rate is 1.20, what is the yen/euro exchange rate?

4. As a currency trader, what would you do to your quoted foreign exchange rates in the $/€ market if you wanted to sell down your position in euros? Assume that the current bid-ask in $/€ is 1.20–1.25.

5. In the previous question, what do you do to the bid-ask spread to induce more trading volume in your $/€ currency book?

6. If the spot $/€ rate is 1.20 and the interest rates are $r_\$ = 0.03$ and $r_€ = 0.05$ for $T = 1$ year (in continuously compounded terms), then what are the forward points for one year?

7. What is more appropriate to use to hedge a borrowing in euros for two years: a currency forward or a currency swap?

8. What type of commodity swap is ideal for a hedge fund that invests heavily in commodities if it wishes to diversify into the equities market?

9. The gas-electricity swap is one that receives the return on electricity prices and pays the return on natural gas prices. What business entity does this swap mimic?

10. Explain how you would construct multiple maturity forward contracts in oil if all you could trade were oil-equity swaps (i.e., a swap in which you exchange the return on oil prices for the equity index return) and stock market futures.

11. The spot exchange rate between the euro and the dollar is $1.2/€. If the dollar interest rate is 2% for two years, the euro rate is 3% for the same maturity, and both rates are annually compounded, what is the two-year forward FX rate?

12. In the previous question, if rates are continuously compounded and the forward exchange rate is $1.10/€, then what is the interest differential between the two currencies?

13. The bid-offer spot exchange rate is $1.31/€–$1.34/€. The one-year dollar interest rates are (bid-offer) 3.1–3.2% (simple interest basis). The one-year euro interest rates are (bid-offer) 3.9–4.0%. Find the bid-ask bounds on the forward FX rate.

14. The following table presents the zero-coupon term structures for the dollar and the euro.

| Maturity (years) | $r_\$ (\%)$ | $r_€ (\%)$ |
|---|---|---|
| 1 | 1.0 | 2.1 |
| 2 | 1.4 | 2.3 |
| 3 | 1.7 | 2.9 |
| 4 | 1.8 | 3.5 |
| 5 | 2.0 | 4.0 |

The spot exchange rate is $1.20-1.30/€. Compounding is annual.

(a) Plot the forward exchange rate bid and ask curves.

(b) Present a table showing the bid and ask points. Are the bid points higher than the ask? Explain.

(c) If the fixed cost of five-year financing is 2.5% in dollars and 3.5% in euros, how should you borrow cheapest if you want to hold your liabilities in dollars?

15. In the preceding problem, suppose you can also access floating-rate financing as follows:
    - Dollar financing at: one-year $-Libor + 50bps.
    - Euro financing at: one-year €-Libor + 100 bps.

    Also traded in the market are the following two swaps:
    - Interest rate swap: fixed $2.0-2.2% vs. floating one-year $-Libor.
    - Currency swap: fixed €3.0-3.2% vs. floating one-year $-Libor.

    Now find the cheapest form of dollar financing.

16. Using the forward FX curve from the preceding problem, convert an annual five-year stream of 75 basis points received in dollars into a similar stream received in euros. You need to express your answer in a number of euro basis points.

17. Given the forward FX curve from the previous example, and the USD interest-rate swap rates, what is the fixed rate on a fair pay-fixed € versus receive-floating one-year $-Libor swap? The swap has a five-year maturity, i.e., five annual payments.

18. Download the term structure for the euro from a website of your choice. [For example, see http://epp.eurostat.cec.eu.int/.] Also download the yield curve for the dollar from any source. Again try:

    http://www.ustreas.gov/offices/domestic-financeurodollarebt-management/

    Convert both curves into annual maturity plots by interpolation. Then, using the current spot $/€ FX rate, determine the forward FX curve. Which currency is at a discount? Is this always true for all maturities?

19. How do you replicate a currency swap by trading foreign exchange options?

20. The following is a table of noncallable US government bond prices and cash flows (in US dollars, i.e., $). Assume that the current date is January 1, 2005.

| Bond | Price | Cash Flows July 1, 2005 | January 1, 2006 | July 1, 2006 |
|------|-------|-------------------------|-----------------|--------------|
| U1 | 97.50 | 100.00 | | |
| U2 | 100.50 | 3.00 | 103.00 | |
| U3 | 101.00 | 3.20 | 3.20 | 103.20 |

The following table depicts noncallable German government bond prices and cash flows (in euros).

| Bond | Price | Cash Flows July 1, 2005 | January 1, 2006 | July 1, 2006 |
|------|-------|-------------------------|-----------------|--------------|
| G1 | 96.00 | 100.00 | | |
| G2 | 99.50 | 5.00 | 105.00 | |
| G3 | 100.20 | 6.00 | 6.00 | 106.00 |

The spot exchange (FX) rate today is $1.5/€. Find the forward FX rates for the next three half-year maturities.

21. ABC Inc., a US incorporated firm with business in the US and Germany, needs to fund an expansion of its business and wishes to raise funding immediately. It can raise 18-month debt in the US market at par by paying a coupon of 8% per annum (semiannual

pay on a 30/360 basis) at a cost of 1% in underwriting fees and commissions on the issued amount. If the company borrows in the German market, a par issue with 2% underwriting costs requires a coupon of 14% per annum (semiannual pay on a 30/360 basis). Using the FX rates from the previous problem, answer the following question: if the spot FX rate is 1.5 $/€, in which market should the company borrow?

22. The following table presents the spot rates from the risk-free interest-rate market. The spot price of gold is $425 per ounce. If the storage cost of gold is 0.15% per year and the convenience yields are flat at 1% per year, complete the table below for forward prices of gold and commodity swap rates.

| Maturity ($t$) | Spot Rate ($r_t$) | Forward Price | Swap Rate |
|---|---|---|---|
| 1 | 0.030 | | |
| 2 | 0.035 | | |
| 3 | 0.040 | | |
| 4 | 0.043 | | |
| 5 | 0.045 | | |

23. Explain with examples the circumstances under which forward-looking market information may be present in commodity forward/futures markets. When is there no information in the forward price?

# Part 4

# Interest Rate Modeling

# Chapter 26

# The Term Structure of Interest Rates: Concepts

## 26.1 Introduction

The "term structure of interest rates" or the "yield curve" refers to the way interest rates depend on maturities. This chapter and the next develop the basic analytics required to model the yield curve. In this chapter, we introduce and discuss fundamental concepts such as the discount function, zero-coupon rates, spot rates, and forward rates. In the next chapter, we discuss implementation, i.e., how the yield curve may be constructed from bond price data.

Our focus in this segment of the book is on bonds that are free of the risk of default (i.e., sovereign obligations). Subsequent chapters in the book look at instruments that are also subject to default or credit risk (e.g., corporate bonds) and examine the modeling and estimation of this risk.

So what is the "yield curve" and why is it a useful concept? It is instructive to begin with a discussion of what it is *not*.

## 26.2 The Yield-to-Maturity

It is not uncommon to plot the yield-to-maturity (or "gross redemption yield") against maturity for a set of bonds and call this a yield curve. Such a plot is conceptually misleading. It is also of limited value from a pricing standpoint.

The yield-to-maturity (ytm) is the internal rate of return on a bond. That is, it is that number $y$ such that when all the cash flows from the bond are discounted at the rate $y$ and added up, we obtain the current price of the bond. In expressing the ytm, we must first choose a compounding frequency. (Of course, any frequency may be chosen.) Readers unfamiliar with the notion of different compounding frequencies should first read Appendix 3A which also describes how to convert interest rate quotes under one frequency to interest rate quotes under another.

Consider a bond with a cash flow of $c_i$ in $t_i$ years, $i = 1, \ldots, n$. If the ytm is expressed with annual compounding, it is the value of $y$ that satisfies

$$P = \sum_{i=1}^{n} \frac{c_i}{(1+y)^{t_i}} \qquad (26.1)$$

More generally, if we use a convention in which we compound $k$ times a year, the ytm is that value of $y$ that satisfies

$$P = \sum_{i=1}^{n} \frac{c_i}{(1 + y/k)^{kt_i}} \qquad (26.2)$$

Semiannual compounding ($k = 2$) is the convention used in the US Treasury markets and some other sovereign markets. (A compounding convention is also commonly referred to as a "basis." Thus, for example, a semiannual compounding convention is also called a semiannual basis.) In this case, (26.2) becomes

$$P = \sum_{i=1}^{n} \frac{c_i}{(1 + y/2)^{2t_i}} \qquad (26.3)$$

Another popular convention is that of *continuous compounding* ($k = \infty$). For technical reasons, continuous compounding is particularly useful in modeling the yield curve. Taking the limit as $k \to \infty$ in (26.2), the ytm under continuous compounding is the value of $y$ that satisfies

$$P = \sum_{i=1}^{n} c_i e^{-y\,t_i} \qquad (26.4)$$

The compounding frequency under which ytm is expressed is very important. For example, consider a bond with cash flows of $5 in six months and $105 in one year. Suppose the current price of the bond is $101. If we express the bond's ytm under semiannual compounding, its ytm is the value of $y$ that satisfies

$$101 = \frac{5}{1 + y/2} + \frac{105}{(1 + y/2)^2}$$

which is roughly 8.93%. However, if we express the bond's ytm under continuous compounding, its ytm is the value of $y$ that satisfies

$$101 = 5e^{-y/2} + 105e^{-y}$$

which is about 8.74%. Thus, in translating financial data on ytm's into bond prices, it is important to know the compounding frequency under which the ytm's have been computed.

## Problems with the YTM

The ytm has important conceptual shortcomings. One is the implicit assumption in the definition of the ytm that all coupons received from the bond are reinvested at the ytm until maturity of the bond, which is unrealistic. A more important one, as the following example shows, is that the ytm is of limited use from a pricing standpoint. The example considers bonds with a face value of 100 paying semiannual coupons and uses a semiannual compounding convention (the convention described in (26.3) above).

**Example 26.1**   Consider a bond with a 5% coupon maturing in six months. This bond will result in a single cash flow of $(100 + 5/2) = 102.5$ in six months. Suppose the ytm on the bond is 5%. What is its price? This is an easy question. The bond's coupons are the same as its ytm. Thus, if the coupons are discounted at the ytm, the result must be par. Formally, from the price-ytm relationship,

$$P = \frac{102.5}{1 + y/2} = \frac{102.5}{1.025} = 100$$

Now suppose there is a second bond of maturity one year and a coupon of 6%. This bond has two cash flows, $3 at the half-year point and $103 at the one-year point. Suppose this bond too trades at par. What is its ytm? Again, this is an easy question. Since the bond is trading at par, its ytm must equal its coupon rate, i.e., $y = 0.06$. Formally, we have:

$$100 = \frac{3}{1 + y/2} + \frac{103}{(1 + y/2)^2}$$

solving which we obtain $y = 0.06$.

Here is a trickier question. Given this information, what is the price of a third bond with maturity also equal to one year but with a coupon of 8%? Intuition might suggest discounting the cash flows from this third bond at the ytm of 6% of the other one-year bond. This leads to a price of

$$P = \frac{4}{1.03} + \frac{104}{(1.03)^2} = 101.9135$$

We will show that this price is incorrect in a fundamental sense—it is arbitrageable. Specifically, we show that the third bond's cash flows can be perfectly replicated by a portfolio consisting of the other two bonds and that the cost of this replicating portfolio is *not* 101.9135.

Consider a portfolio consisting of $x_1$ units of the half-year maturity bond and $x_2$ units of the one-year maturity bond. Since both bonds are trading at par, the price of this portfolio is

$$100\, x_1 + 100\, x_2$$

For the portfolio to perfectly replicate the 8% coupon bond, it must generate a cash flow of 4 after six months and 104 after one year. This means we must have

$$102.5\, x_1 + 3\, x_2 = 4$$
$$103\, x_2 = 104$$

Solving these simultaneous equations gives us

$$x_1 = 0.009471939 \qquad x_2 = 1.009708738$$

Thus, the cost of the replicating portfolio is

$$100\, x_1 + 100\, x_2 = 101.9181$$

which is different from the price obtained by using the ytm of the 6% bond. The replication-based price is, of course, the correct price for the bond.  ■

A pricing error results even if the third bond in this example is "close" to the one-year 6% coupon bond (i.e., has similar but not identical characteristics). For example, suppose the third bond has a one-year maturity and a 6.1% coupon. Discounting its cash flows at the ytm of 6% results in a "price" of 100.0957, while the correct replication-based price is 100.0959. The error is smaller the more similar are the two bonds, but it will not usually be zero. Thus, knowing the ytm of one bond does not allow us to price another bond.

# 26.3   The Term Structure of Interest Rates

If the ytm has pricing limitations, what does one do in order to value large portfolios of bonds? It turns out that there is a simple solution to this problem. Actually, there are three simple solutions:

• The first is to use the *discount function*. The discount function measures, for each $t$, the present value of $1 receivable in $t$ years.

- The second is to use the *spot rate* or *zero-coupon rate*. The spot rate specifies for each $t$ the ytm on a *zero-coupon bond* with face value $1 and maturity in $t$ years.[1]
- The last is to use the *forward rate*. The forward rate provides, for each pair of dates $t_1$ and $t_2$ in the future, the rate that can be locked in today for an investment or borrowing over the period $[t_1, t_2]$.

A plot of spot rates against maturities is referred to variously as the *spot(-rate) curve*, the *zero-coupon yield curve*, or simply the *yield curve*. The phrase *forward(-rate) curve* is similarly used to denote a plot of forward rates against maturities.

The discount function, spot curve, and forward curve are *equivalent* concepts. That is, each discount function corresponds to a unique zero-coupon rate curve and a unique forward-rate curve, etc. Given this equivalence, we use the phrase "term structure of interest rates" to refer interchangeably to any of them, although the phrase is commonly used to mean the spot curve. The next three sections examine each of these concepts in turn.

## 26.4 Discount Functions

The discount function specifies, for each $t$, the present value of $1 receivable in $t$ years. It is, therefore, a *price*: it specifies the price of a zero-coupon bond with maturity in $t$ years and face value of $1. Let $d(t)$ denote the discount function. Note that since the discount function is the present value of a unit cash flow, it must satisfy $0 \leq d(t) \leq 1$.

Once the discount function is known, any bond may be priced using it. Suppose a bond pays a series of cash flows $c_i$ in $t_i$ years, $i = 1, \ldots, n$. This bond is equivalent to (i.e., can be perfectly replicated by) a portfolio of zero-coupon bonds in which we hold $c_i$ units of the zero-coupon bond maturing at time $t_i$, $i = 1, \ldots, n$. Thus, the current price of the bond must be

$$P = \sum_{i=1}^{n} c_i d(t_i). \qquad (26.5)$$

Of course, we may price entire portfolios of bonds using the same argument—there is no reason why the cash flows $c_i$ in (26.5) must come from a single bond.

From where do we obtain the discount function? In principle, the discount function may be recovered from the prices of traded bonds using a procedure known as *bootstrapping*. Bootstrapping and its limitations (as well as alternatives to bootstrapping) are discussed in detail in the next chapter. Here, we provide a simple illustration of the technique using the two bonds introduced in Example 26.1.

**Example 26.2**

Consider the two bonds of Example 26.1, each of which is trading at par: (a) a half-year bond with a ytm of 5% and (b) a one-year bond with a ytm of 6%. Coupon payments are taken to be semiannual. We shall use this data to derive the half-year and one-year discount functions. These will be denoted $d(0.5)$ and $d(1)$, respectively.

From (26.5) and since the bonds are each trading at par, we have the following two expressions ($P(t)$ denotes the price of the $t$-maturity bond):

$$P(0.5) = 102.5\, d(0.5) \qquad = 100$$
$$P(1) = 3\, d(0.5) + 103\, d(1) = 100$$

---

[1] A zero-coupon bond, or simply a "zero," is, as the name suggests, a bond that pays no coupons and repays the principal amount at maturity. Such a bond will usually trade at a discount to the face value due at maturity, so is also called a "pure discount bond."

These equations are easily solved for $d(0.5)$ and $d(1)$:

$$d(0.5) = 0.97561 \qquad d(1) = 0.942458$$

We can use these values to price any bond that has cash flows at $t = 0.5$ and $t = 1$. For example, the price of a one-year 8% coupon bond is

$$4\,d(0.5) + 104\,d(1) = 101.9181$$

which is exactly the price we obtained by replication in Section 26.2.  ∎

## 26.5   Zero-Coupon Rates

The *zero-coupon* rate or *spot rate* is an alternative way of representing the same information as the discount function. The zero-coupon rate associated with a maturity $t$ is the ytm of a zero-coupon bond with maturity $t$ years from the present. We shall write zcr for zero-coupon rate, with zcrs denoting the plural.

Unlike the discount function, the zcr is a yield and not a price, so it depends on the compounding convention we use. Suppose we use the convention that rates are compounded $k$ times a year. Denote the zcr for a given maturity $t$ by $r^{(k)}(t)$. By definition, the price $d(t)$ of the $t$-maturity zero is related to its ytm $r^{(k)}(t)$ via

$$d(t) = \frac{1}{(1 + (r^{(k)}(t)/k))^{kt}} \tag{26.6}$$

From (26.6), $r^{(k)}(t)$ may be written in terms of $d(t)$ as

$$r^{(k)}(t) = k \times ([d(t)]^{-1/kt} - 1) \tag{26.7}$$

Thus, for example, under annual compounding ($k = 1$), we have

$$r^{(1)}(t) = [d(t)]^{-1/t} - 1 \tag{26.8}$$

while under semiannual compounding ($k = 2$),

$$r^{(2)}(t) = [d(t)]^{-1/2t} - 1 \tag{26.9}$$

In the limit, as $k = \infty$, we get the continuous-compounding representation of the zcr

$$r^{(\infty)}(t) = -\frac{1}{t}\,\ln[d(t)] \tag{26.10}$$

Two points are important here: First, fixing a compounding convention, expressions (26.6)–(26.10) show that there is a one-to-one relationship between the discount function and spot rates: each discount function corresponds to a unique spot rate and vice versa.

Second, it is also immediate from these expressions that a rate under one convention can always be converted to the rate under another. If we are given the zcr $r^{(k)}(t)$ corresponding to a compounding frequency of $k$ times a year and wish to express this in terms of a compounding frequency of $\ell$ times a year, we can first convert the zcr $r^{(k)}(t)$ into a discount function value $d(t)$ using (26.6) and then identify the zcr $r^{(\ell)}(t)$ using (26.7). This means we can choose whatever compounding convention is most convenient for our purposes. For example, in modeling interest rates, it turns out that the most useful convention is continuous compounding since this is technically the most advantageous.

The curve $\{r^{(k)}(t)\,|\,t \geq 0\}$ is called the *spot curve*, *zero-coupon yield curve*, or simply the *yield curve*. In practice, the yield curve is typically upward sloping, i.e., zcrs increase as maturity increases. This is referred to as a *normal* yield curve. Sometimes, however, short-term yields exceed long-term yields, and the yield curve is downward sloping. This is referred to as an *inverted* yield curve.

## Pricing Bonds Using the Yield Curve

Knowledge of the yield curve enables us to identify the present value of any payoff $x$ occurring at any given time $t$ in the future. In turn, this means any bond or portfolio of bonds may be valued using the yield curve.

For example, suppose we have a portfolio of bonds with cash flows of $c_i$ at times $t_i$, $i = 1, \ldots, n$. This portfolio is equivalent to a portfolio consisting of $c_i$ zero-coupon bonds with face value 1 and maturity $t_i$, $i = 1, \ldots, n$. Using the yield curve, we can value each of these zero-coupon bonds, and, hence, the entire portfolio.

**Example 26.3** Consider the same information as provided in Example 26.2. There are two bonds each trading at par, one with a maturity of six months and a coupon of 5% and the other with a maturity of one year and a coupon of 6%. As we saw in Section 26.4, the discount function derived from this information is

$$d(0.5) = 0.97561 \qquad d(1) = 0.942458$$

We can use these discount rates to identify the zcrs by appealing to (26.6)–(26.10). For instance, suppose we use a semiannual compounding convention. Then, the zcrs are

$$r^{(2)}(0.5) = 2[d(0.5)^{-1} - 1] = 0.05$$
$$r^{(2)}(1) = 2[d(1)^{-1/2} - 1] = 0.060151$$

Let us use these zcrs to value a one-year bond with a coupon of 8%. The bond has two cash flows: a cash flow of 4 after six months and a cash flow of 104 after one year. Given the zcrs, the present values of these cash flows are

$$\frac{4}{1 + r^{(2)}(0.5)/2} = \frac{4}{1.025} = 3.9024$$

and

$$\frac{104}{(1 + r^{(2)}(1)/2)^2} = \frac{104}{(1.030075)^2} = 98.0157$$

Adding these values, we obtain 101.9181, which is exactly the bond value obtained by replication or using the discount functions. ∎

Intuitively, if we think of the individual cash flows of any bond as atoms, then the bond itself comprising all its coupons may be thought of as a molecule. One may always price any bond (i.e., molecule) by splitting it into its elements or atoms and then using zcrs to price each atom separately. Since the price of a bond must equal the sum of prices of its cash flows, we can price the atoms and aggregate their values to price the bond.

## 26.6 Forward Rates

Consider a period $(t_1, t_2)$ beginning $t_1$ years in the future and ending $t_2$ years in the future where $t_2 > t_1$. The *forward rate* for the period $(t_1, t_2)$ refers to the rate we can lock in today for borrowing or lending over this time period.

Since the forward rate is an interest rate, we must associate a compounding frequency with it. Assume that forward rates are quoted in continuously compounded terms (we deal with other compounding conventions a bit further down) and denote the forward rate for the period $(t_1, t_2)$ by $f(t_1, t_2)$. Then, for each $1 borrowed or invested at time $t_1$, the amount to be returned at time $t_2$ is

$$e^{f(t_1,t_2)(t_2-t_1)} \tag{26.11}$$

The forward rate is intimately related to the discount function and the spot rate. To see the connection, consider the following strategy (all bonds have a face value of $1):

1. Buy a zero-coupon bond with maturity $t_1$.
2. Sell $d(t_1)/d(t_2)$ units of a zero-coupon bond with maturity $t_2$.

Buying the $t_1$-maturity bond involves a cash outflow of $d(t_1)$, while selling $d(t_1)/d(t_2)$ units of the $t_2$-maturity bond results in a cash inflow of

$$\frac{d(t_1)}{d(t_2)} \times d(t_2) = d(t_1)$$

Thus, there is no net initial cash flow. At time $t_1$, there is a cash inflow of $1, while at time $t_2$, there is a net cash outflow of

$$\frac{d(t_1)}{d(t_2)} \tag{26.12}$$

These cash flows imply that the strategy is akin to a borrowing of $1 at time $t_1$ for a repayment of (26.12) at time $t_2$. That is, the strategy is simply a synthetic forward borrowing over the period $(t_1, t_2)$.

Now, suppose the forward rate is such that (26.11) is greater than (26.12). Then the actual forward rate is greater than the synthetic forward rate implied by (26.12). Thus, there are arbitrage profits to be made by borrowing forward synthetically and lending it out at the forward rate $f(t_1, t_2)$. This will result in no net cash flows up to time $t_2$ and a cash inflow at time $t_2$ of the difference between (26.11) and (26.12).

Similarly, the forward rate cannot be such that (26.11) is less than (26.12) or reversing the strategies of the previous paragraph will lead to an arbitrage. Thus, we must have (26.11) equal to (26.12), i.e.,

$$e^{f(t_1,t_2)(t_2-t_1)} = \frac{d(t_1)}{d(t_2)} \tag{26.13}$$

or, what is the same thing,

$$f(t_1, t_2) = \frac{1}{t_2 - t_1} \ln\left(\frac{d(t_1)}{d(t_2)}\right) = \frac{\ln d(t_1) - \ln d(t_2)}{t_2 - t_1} \tag{26.14}$$

Equation (26.14) describes the relationship between forward rates and discount functions. This relationship can also be expressed in terms of forward rates and zcrs. From (26.10), the discount function $d(t)$ is related to the (continuously-compounded) zcr $r(t)$ via

$$\ln d(t) = -t\, r(t)$$

Thus, we can rewrite (26.14) in terms of forward and spot rates as

$$f(t_1, t_2) = \frac{t_2 r(t_2) - t_1 r(t_1)}{t_2 - t_1} \tag{26.15}$$

where $r(t)$ is the continuously-compounded zcr for maturity $t$.

Expressions (26.13)–(26.14) show the unique correspondence between discount functions, spot rates, and forward rates. Thus, the three concepts—discount functions, spot rates, and forward rates—are perfectly equivalent ways of describing the term structure of interest rates.

One final concept is important. The *instantaneous forward rate* $f(t)$ refers to the forward rate $f(t, t + h)$ for a very small time period $h$. Formally, we write

$$f(t) = \lim_{h \downarrow 0} f(t, t + h) \tag{26.16}$$

For future reference, note that by taking limits in (26.14), the instantaneous forward rate is related to the discount function via

$$f(t) = -\frac{1}{d(t)} d'(t) \tag{26.17}$$

The curve $\{f(t) \mid t \geq 0\}$ is called the *forward curve*.

## Other Compounding Conventions

Of course, we may also express forward rates with other compounding frequencies and derive expressions analogous to (26.13)–(26.14). Suppose forward rates are quoted with a compounding frequency of $k$ times a year. Then for every \$1 borrowed at $t_1$, the amount to be returned at $t_2$ is

$$\left[1 + \frac{f^{(k)}(t_1, t_2)}{k}\right]^{k(t_2 - t_1)} \tag{26.18}$$

Since this must be equal to (26.12), we have

$$\left[1 + \frac{f^{(k)}(t_1, t_2)}{k}\right]^{k(t_2 - t_1)} = \frac{d(t_1)}{d(t_2)} \tag{26.19}$$

Equivalently, we may write

$$f(t_1, t_2) = \left[\left(\frac{d(t_1)}{d(t_2)}\right)^{1/[k(t_2 - t_1)]} - 1\right] \times k \tag{26.20}$$

Expressions (26.19)–(26.20) describe the correspondence between discount functions and forward rates for general compounding frequencies.

# 26.7 Yield-to-Maturity, Zero-Coupon Rates, and Forward Rates

There are three different curves we have defined: ytm (which may be regarded as the raw market data), zero-coupon rates or zcrs, and forward rates. The earlier analysis has examined the mathematical relationship between these concepts. Here, we present a simple geometric relationship between them.

Consider first the relationship between the ytm and zcr curves. Suppose the zcr is increasing in maturity. How will the ytm curve behave?

Intuitively speaking, the ytm represents an "average" yield for a bond taking into account its cash flows across different maturities, while the zcrs are yields for specific maturities. Thus, the ytm is like an average of the zcrs (albeit a somewhat complex weighted average). If the zcr curve is increasing, longer maturities have higher yields. So as maturity increases, the weighted-average yield for the bond will also increase, so the ytm curve will also increase with maturity. Of course, this weighted average will increase slower than the zcrs themselves because it is averaging out lower and higher zcrs. This means the ytm curve will lie *below* the zcr curve.

Similarly, if the zcr curve is *decreasing* with maturity, the ytm curve will also decrease with maturity. However, because it is averaging out the higher yields of the short maturities and the lower yields of the long maturities, it will decrease more slowly than the zcr curve. To summarize:

1. If the zcr curve is increasing, the ytm curve will also be increasing and will lie below the zcr curve.

2. If the zcr curve is decreasing, the ytm curve will also be decreasing and will lie above the zcr curve.

A similar relationship can be derived between the zcr and forward curves. Intuitively speaking, viewed from the present, investors must be indifferent between two strategies:

- Investing for $t_2$ years.
- Investing for $t_1$ years and rolling the proceeds forward at the forward rate $f(t_1, t_2)$ that can be locked-in now.

If the zcr curve is *increasing* in maturity, the forward curve must lie *above* the zcr curve because the forward rate $f(t_1, t_2)$ has to "make up" for the lower spot rate received over the first $t_1$ years. Similarly, if the zcr curve is *decreasing* in maturity, then the forward curve must lie *below* the zcr curve.

This relationship is also easy to see formally. From (26.15) and (26.16), the forward curve and zcr curve have a simple mathematical relationship:

$$f(t) = r(t) + t\,r'(t) \qquad\qquad (26.21)$$

If $r(t)$ is increasing, then $r'(t) > 0$. Thus, we must have $f(t) > r(t)$. Similarly, if $r(t)$ is decreasing with maturity, then we must have $r'(t) < 0$, so $f(t) < r(t)$, and the forward curve lies *below* the zcr curve. To summarize:

1. If the zcr curve is increasing, the forward curve must lie above the zcr curve.

2. If the zcr curve is decreasing, the forward curve must lie below the zcr curve.

In practice, one of the most common "issues" that arises with empirical forward curves is that they appear excessively jagged or wavy. Intuitively, this happens because forward rates have sometimes to increase or decrease very substantially to maintain the indifference between the alternatives of a single long-term investment versus a shorter-term investment that is rolled over at the forward rate. This has led to the development of various "smoothing" techniques, an issue we will discuss in detail in the next chapter.

# 26.8   Constructing the Yield-to-Maturity Curve: An Empirical Illustration

To illustrate the concepts introduced in this chapter and to highlight the geometric relationship described in the previous section, this section describes the construction of ytm curves from data on Treasury yields taken from *The Wall Street Journal*. The construction of zero-coupon yield curves from similar data is the subject of the next chapter.

The data describes the prices and yields-to-maturity (ytms) for Treasury notes and bonds as of the close of August 27, 2003. The full data is provided in the table in Appendix 26A. In the table, there are three types of instruments. First, there are notes (Type n), which run out to a maximum maturity of 10 years. Second, there are inflation-indexed issues (Type i). The remaining issues are Treasury bonds, with a maximum maturity of 30 years. The second-to-last column of the table provides the approximate time to maturity in months.

In order to obtain a visual feel for the data, the ytms for the notes alone are plotted against maturity in Figure 26.1. The ytms for bonds alone are plotted in Figure 26.2.

**FIGURE 26.1**

Ask Yields for Treasury Notes, August 27, 2003

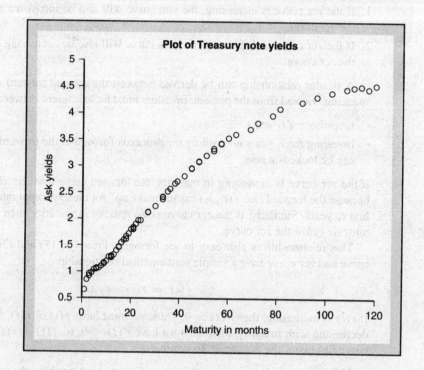

**FIGURE 26.2**

Ask Yields for Treasury Bonds, August 27, 2003

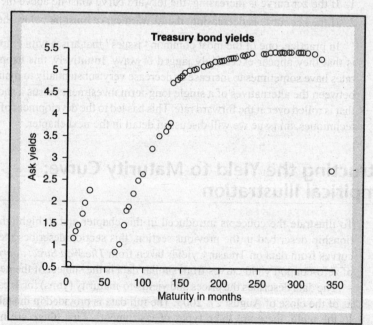

**FIGURE 26.3**

Spliced Notes and
Bonds Yield Curve

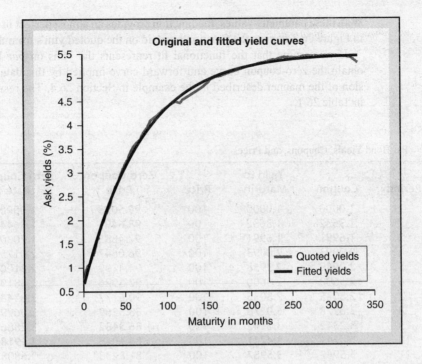

As we can see, the plot for Treasury notes returns a smooth graph of the ytm curve. However, the same cannot be said for the plot of Treasury bond ytm's against maturity. These appear to come from two distinct sets of bonds, some with higher ytm's than the rest. In particular, the medium maturity bonds appear to be trading at lower ytms. In order to obtain one smooth ytm curve, we splice the notes curve up to a maturity of 120 months onto the bonds curve for maturities greater than 120 months. This results in a single curve that is very smooth. The plot of this combined ytm curve is provided in Figure 26.3.

Next we try to fit a function that best describes this ytm curve. With $t$ denoted in months, the functional form we choose for this purpose is

$$\text{ytm}(t) \;=\; \beta_0 + \beta_1 \exp\left(-\frac{t}{\theta}\right) + \beta_2 \left(\frac{t}{\theta}\right) \exp\left(-\frac{t}{\theta}\right)$$

This particular functional form is motivated by the Nelson and Siegel (1987) function described in detail in the next chapter. The Nelson-Siegel formulation and especially its extension, the Nelson-Siegel-Svensson formulation (see Svensson, 1994), are commonly used in practice by central banks to model the *forward* curve. An important reason for this, as we note subsequently, is that the specification is very flexible and can accommodate a variety of shapes for the curve despite using only a limited set of parameters.

In the current case, there are four parameters ($\beta_0$, $\beta_1$, $\beta_2$, and $\theta$) to be estimated in fitting this curve to the given ytm data. The values of the parameters that provide the best fit to the data are:

$$\beta_0 = 5.481692$$
$$\beta_1 = -4.87414$$
$$\beta_2 = -1.10606$$
$$\theta = 55.4536$$

With these parameter values, the function provides an almost perfect fit to the data. The plot in Figure 26.3 depicts the function overlaid on the quoted ytm's from the market.

If we assume that the functional fit represents the ytms on *par* bonds, we can also obtain the zero-coupon curve and forward curve implied by this data by using an extension of the manner described in the example in Section 26.4. The results are summarized in Table 26.1.

**TABLE 26.1** Par Bond Yields, Coupons, and Prices

| Years | Period | Coupon | Yield to Maturity | Price | Zero-Coupon Price | Zero-Coupon Rate | Forward Rate |
|-------|--------|--------|-------------------|-------|-------------------|------------------|--------------|
| 0.5 | 1 | 1.0000 | 1.0000 | 100 | 99.5025 | 1.0000 | 1.0000 |
| 1.0 | 2 | 1.3632 | 1.3632 | 100 | 98.6494 | 1.3644 | 1.7296 |
| 1.5 | 3 | 1.6991 | 1.6991 | 100 | 97.4885 | 1.7030 | 2.3817 |
| 2.0 | 4 | 2.0093 | 2.0093 | 100 | 96.0647 | 2.0175 | 2.9642 |
| 2.5 | 5 | 2.2958 | 2.2958 | 100 | 94.4199 | 2.3100 | 3.4840 |
| 3.0 | 6 | 2.5600 | 2.5600 | 100 | 92.5926 | 2.5819 | 3.9470 |
| 3.5 | 7 | 2.8035 | 2.8035 | 100 | 90.6177 | 2.8348 | 4.3586 |
| 4.0 | 8 | 3.0278 | 3.0278 | 100 | 88.5269 | 3.0699 | 4.7236 |
| 4.5 | 9 | 3.2342 | 3.2342 | 100 | 86.3482 | 3.2886 | 5.0463 |
| 5.0 | 10 | 3.4241 | 3.4241 | 100 | 84.1066 | 3.4918 | 5.3304 |
| 5.5 | 11 | 3.5987 | 3.5987 | 100 | 81.8238 | 3.6808 | 5.5797 |
| 6.0 | 12 | 3.7592 | 3.7592 | 100 | 79.5189 | 3.8563 | 5.7971 |
| 6.5 | 13 | 3.9065 | 3.9065 | 100 | 77.2082 | 4.0193 | 5.9858 |
| 7.0 | 14 | 4.0417 | 4.0417 | 100 | 74.9055 | 4.1706 | 6.1483 |
| 7.5 | 15 | 4.1658 | 4.1658 | 100 | 72.6226 | 4.3111 | 6.2870 |
| 8.0 | 16 | 4.2795 | 4.2795 | 100 | 70.3692 | 4.4413 | 6.4043 |
| 8.5 | 17 | 4.3838 | 4.3838 | 100 | 68.1535 | 4.5619 | 6.5023 |
| 9.0 | 18 | 4.4793 | 4.4793 | 100 | 65.9818 | 4.6737 | 6.5827 |
| 9.5 | 19 | 4.5668 | 4.5668 | 100 | 63.8593 | 4.7771 | 6.6474 |
| 10.0 | 20 | 4.6469 | 4.6469 | 100 | 61.7899 | 4.8727 | 6.6980 |
| 10.5 | 21 | 4.7201 | 4.7201 | 100 | 59.7766 | 4.9611 | 6.7360 |
| 11.0 | 22 | 4.7872 | 4.7872 | 100 | 57.8215 | 5.0426 | 6.7628 |
| 11.5 | 23 | 4.8485 | 4.8485 | 100 | 55.9257 | 5.1178 | 6.7795 |
| 12.0 | 24 | 4.9045 | 4.9045 | 100 | 54.0901 | 5.1871 | 6.7875 |
| 12.5 | 25 | 4.9557 | 4.9557 | 100 | 52.3146 | 5.2509 | 6.7876 |
| 13.0 | 26 | 5.0024 | 5.0024 | 100 | 50.5991 | 5.3095 | 6.7810 |
| 13.5 | 27 | 5.0451 | 5.0451 | 100 | 48.9427 | 5.3634 | 6.7684 |
| 14.0 | 28 | 5.0841 | 5.0841 | 100 | 47.3447 | 5.4128 | 6.7507 |
| 14.5 | 29 | 5.1197 | 5.1197 | 100 | 45.8037 | 5.4580 | 6.7287 |
| 15.0 | 30 | 5.1522 | 5.1522 | 100 | 44.3183 | 5.4994 | 6.7030 |
| 15.5 | 31 | 5.1818 | 5.1818 | 100 | 42.8872 | 5.5372 | 6.6742 |
| 16.0 | 32 | 5.2088 | 5.2088 | 100 | 41.5085 | 5.5716 | 6.6429 |
| 16.5 | 33 | 5.2334 | 5.2334 | 100 | 40.1806 | 5.6030 | 6.6095 |
| 17.0 | 34 | 5.2558 | 5.2558 | 100 | 38.9018 | 5.6315 | 6.5745 |
| 17.5 | 35 | 5.2763 | 5.2763 | 100 | 37.6703 | 5.6574 | 6.5384 |
| 18.0 | 36 | 5.2949 | 5.2949 | 100 | 36.4843 | 5.6808 | 6.5014 |
| 18.5 | 37 | 5.3119 | 5.3119 | 100 | 35.3421 | 5.7019 | 6.4638 |
| 19.0 | 38 | 5.3273 | 5.3273 | 100 | 34.2419 | 5.7209 | 6.4260 |
| 19.5 | 39 | 5.3414 | 5.3414 | 100 | 33.1820 | 5.7380 | 6.3882 |
| 20.0 | 40 | 5.3542 | 5.3542 | 100 | 32.1608 | 5.7533 | 6.3505 |

**FIGURE 26.4**

Smooth Curves
Derived from the
Nelson-Siegel Fit

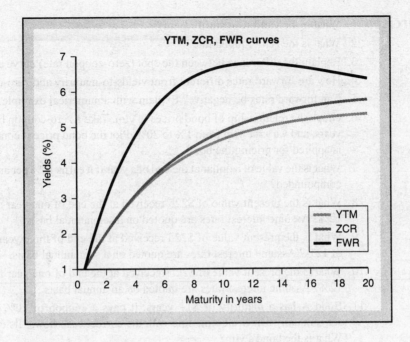

Figure 26.4 plots the derived zero-coupon rates (the curve denoted ZCR in the figure), forward rates (the curve denoted FWR), and ytms (the curve denoted YTM) as functions of maturity. The plot illustrates the geometric relationship highlighted in the previous section. In particular, the zero-coupon curve is increasing with maturity and lies above the ytm curve (as we said it should when both curves are increasing). The forward curve similarly lies above the zero-coupon curve (also as we noted it should when the latter increases with maturity).

## 26.9    Summary

The starting point for any analysis of interest-rate derivatives is the yield curve. In contrast to equity derivatives where the driving variable of value is the stock price, an interest-rate option may be affected by the co-movement of several yields at different maturities. For example, the value of a bond option is sensitive to the many cash flows of the bond, all of which are affected by different maturity rates. Modeling the co-movement of these rates is the goal of the succeeding chapters.

As we will see, interest-rate derivative models come in many flavors. Some of them take as input the yield curve, but some popular models require the forward rate curve as input. In this chapter, we defined the various ways of representing this information and the relationships between them. In the next chapter, we develop techniques for obtaining "good" curves of all types from available market quotes. Obtaining "smooth" curves is a prerequisite to modeling options, and we explore several techniques that achieve this goal. Quite apart from the options analysis of interest-rate-dependent derivatives, the derived market curves also allow easy computation of price sensitivity for bonds.

## 26.10 Exercises

1. What is the yield-to-maturity (ytm)?

2. What is the zero-coupon rate?

3. Explain the difference between the spot (zero-coupon rate) curve and the yield curve.

4. How are forward rates different from yields-to-maturity and zero-coupon rates?

5. Can forward rates be negative? Explain with a numerical example.

6. Graph the relationship of bond prices to ytm. Take a zero-coupon bond of maturity 0.1 years, and vary the ytm from 1% to 20%. Plot the bond price if continuous discounting is applied for pricing the bond.

7. What is the value of a dollar at the end of a year if it earns 10% per annum, semiannually compounded?

8. What is the present value of $225 received at the end of one year at a discount rate of 12%? Assume interest rates are quoted on a semiannual basis.

9. What is the present value of $225 received at the end of three years at a discount rate of 12%? Assume interest rates are quoted on a semiannual basis.

10. What is the present value of $225 received at the end of one year at a discount rate of 12%? Assume interest rates are quoted on an annual basis.

11. Bond A has a maturity of $1\frac{1}{2}$ years. It pays a coupon of 10% with coupons paid semiannually. Draw the time line with the correct cash flows. Its current price is $99. What is the bond's ytm?

12. Bond B has maturity one year. Its coupon is 8% per annum. The ytm is 8.5%. What is the correct price of the bond if the semiannual convention is followed?

13. Coupon Bond P (with semiannual coupons) has maturity $\frac{1}{2}$ year. Its ytm (semiannual basis) is 10%. What is the zero-coupon rate (ZCR) for $\frac{1}{2}$ year?

14. Coupon Bond Q trades at par. It has a maturity of one year. Its ytm (semiannual basis) is 11%. What is the coupon rate of this bond?

15. Using the information about bonds P and Q above, determine the zero-coupon rate for one-year maturity.

16. Using the information from the questions about bonds P and Q, determine the price of a bond R that pays a cash flow of $50 in six months and another cash flow of $50 at the end of one year.

17. Bond W has a coupon of 12% (semiannual basis) and a maturity of one year and is trading at $99.25. If the one-year zero-coupon rate is 13%, what is the half-year zero-coupon rate?

18. Consider a bond currently trading at $102. The bond has one year left to maturity and a coupon of 8% on a face value of $100. Suppose coupons are paid semiannually. What is the ytm of the bond expressed with semiannual compounding? With continuous compounding?

19. A bond is currently trading at $99.50. The bond has nine months left to maturity and carries a coupon of 3%. Coupons are paid semiannually (so the first coupon is due in three months). If the bond's face value is $100, what is its ytm expressed with semiannual compounding? With continuous compounding?

20. Consider a bond that pays annual coupons of 7% on a face value of $100. The bond has two years to maturity. If the ytm of the bond (expressed with annual compounding) is 6.80%, what is its current price? What is the bond's ytm under continuous compounding?

21. A six-month zero-coupon bond is trading at $98, while a one-year 6% coupon bond is trading at $99. Assume coupons are paid semiannually and that both bonds have a face value of $100. What are the six-month and one-year discount functions implied by these prices?

22. A six-month zero-coupon bond has a ytm of 5%, while a one-year 5% coupon bond has a ytm of 5.50%. Assume ytm's are expressed with semiannual compounding, coupons are paid semiannually, and the face value of the bonds is $100.

    (a) What are the six-month and one-year discount functions implied by these prices?

    (b) What is the price of a one-year 4.50% coupon bond?

23. Suppose six-month and one-year discount functions are 0.9804 and 0.96, respectively. What are the corresponding zero-coupon rates? What is the forward rate $f(0.50, 1)$? (Assume all rates are expressed with continuous compounding.)

24. You are given the following information: the one-year spot rate is 5.50%, the forward rate $f(1, 2)$ is 6.0%, and the forward rate $f(2, 3)$ is 7%. All rates are expressed in continuously-compounded terms.

    (a) What are the two- and three-year spot rates?

    (b) What are the discount function values for one-, two-, and three-year maturities?

25. You are given the following information: the one-year spot rate is 6.50%, the forward rate $f(1, 2)$ is 7.50%, and the forward rate $f(1, 3)$ is 9%. All rates are expressed in continuously-compounded terms.

    (a) What are the two- and three-year spot rates?

    (b) What is the forward rate $f(2, 3)$?

    (c) What are the discount function values for one-, two-, and three-year maturities?

26. If the (continuously-compounded) yield curve is flat at a rate of 5%, answer the following questions:

    (a) Price a 10-year semiannual pay bond, with a 5% coupon.

    (b) Compute the duration of this bond.

    (c) What is the convexity of this bond?

27. When interest rates are continuously compounded, the price of a unit zero-coupon bond is defined by the following equation: $P(t) = e^{-z_t t}$ where $z_t$ is the zero-coupon rate for maturity $t$. We also saw that the price of a coupon bond could be represented as the sum of the prices of the individual components $c_t$ (cash flows) of the bond, i.e. $P = \sum_t e^{-z_t t} c_t$. Therefore, the price of the coupon bond is said to be "additive" in its components.

    (a) Is the duration of the coupon bond also additive in its components? Why? Write down the expression for the duration of the coupon bond using the notation provided above in this question to justify your answer.

    (b) Is convexity additive? Again, provide the algebraic expression for the convexity.

    (c) Would your answers to the previous questions change if the compounding basis was semiannual instead of continuous compounding?

# The Raw YTM Data

The table below describes the data from *The Wall Street Journal* used in Section 26.8.

| as of August 27, 2003, *The Wall Street Journal* | | | | | | |
|---|---|---|---|---|---|---|
| Coupon | Month | Year | Ask Price | Type | T (months) | Ask YTM |
| 2.75 | 9 | 2003 | 100.06 | n | 1 | 0.66 |
| 2.75 | 10 | 2003 | 100.1 | n | 2 | 0.85 |
| 4.25 | 11 | 2003 | 100.22 | n | 3 | 0.96 |
| 3 | 11 | 2003 | 100.17 | n | 3 | 0.92 |
| 11.875 | 11 | 2003 | 102.13 | | 3 | 0.56 |
| 3.25 | 12 | 2003 | 100.24 | n | 4 | 0.98 |
| 3 | 1 | 2004 | 100.26 | n | 5 | 1.04 |
| 4.75 | 2 | 2004 | 101.22 | n | 6 | 1.06 |
| 5.875 | 2 | 2004 | 102.07 | n | 6 | 1.07 |
| 3 | 2 | 2004 | 100.31 | n | 6 | 1.05 |
| 3.625 | 3 | 2004 | 101.16 | n | 7 | 1.07 |
| 3.375 | 4 | 2004 | 101.16 | n | 8 | 1.11 |
| 5.25 | 5 | 2004 | 102.29 | n | 9 | 1.15 |
| 7.25 | 5 | 2004 | 104.1 | n | 9 | 1.17 |
| 3.25 | 5 | 2004 | 101.18 | n | 9 | 1.15 |
| 12.375 | 5 | 2004 | 107.3 | | 9 | 1.16 |
| 2.875 | 6 | 2004 | 101.12 | n | 10 | 1.2 |
| 2.25 | 7 | 2004 | 100.28 | n | 11 | 1.28 |
| 2.125 | 8 | 2004 | 100.27 | n | 12 | 1.28 |
| 6 | 8 | 2004 | 104.16 | n | 12 | 1.27 |
| 7.25 | 8 | 2004 | 105.22 | n | 12 | 1.3 |
| 13.75 | 8 | 2004 | 111.28 | | 12 | 1.32 |
| 1.875 | 9 | 2004 | 100.19 | n | 13 | 1.32 |
| 2.125 | 10 | 2004 | 100.27 | n | 14 | 1.4 |
| 5.875 | 11 | 2004 | 105.09 | n | 15 | 1.46 |
| 7.875 | 11 | 2004 | 107.22 | n | 15 | 1.46 |
| 2 | 11 | 2004 | 100.21 | n | 15 | 1.47 |
| 11.625 | 11 | 2004 | 112.06 | | 15 | 1.46 |
| 1.75 | 12 | 2004 | 100.08 | n | 16 | 1.55 |
| 1.625 | 1 | 2005 | 100.01 | n | 17 | 1.6 |
| 7.5 | 2 | 2005 | 108.15 | n | 18 | 1.62 |
| 1.5 | 2 | 2005 | 99.24 | n | 18 | 1.67 |
| 1.625 | 3 | 2005 | 99.27 | n | 19 | 1.72 |
| 1.625 | 4 | 2005 | 99.23 | | 20 | 1.8 |
| 6.5 | 5 | 2005 | 107.28 | | 21 | 1.8 |
| 6.75 | 5 | 2005 | 108.09 | | 21 | 1.81 |
| 1.25 | 5 | 2005 | 98.31 | | 21 | 1.84 |
| 12 | 5 | 2005 | 117.09 | | 21 | 1.72 |
| 1.125 | 6 | 2005 | 98.19 | n | 22 | 1.9 |
| 1.5 | 7 | 2005 | 99.03 | n | 23 | 1.97 |
| 6.5 | 8 | 2005 | 108.22 | | 24 | 1.97 |
| 10.75 | 8 | 2005 | 116.27 | | 24 | 1.97 |
| 5.75 | 11 | 2005 | 107.25 | n | 27 | 2.13 |
| 5.875 | 11 | 2005 | 108.02 | n | 27 | 2.12 |
| 5.625 | 2 | 2006 | 108.02 | n | 30 | 2.24 |
| 9.375 | 2 | 2006 | 116.3 | | 30 | 2.26 |
| 2 | 5 | 2006 | 99.01 | n | 33 | 2.37 |
| 4.625 | 5 | 2006 | 105.25 | n | 33 | 2.41 |
| 6.875 | 5 | 2006 | 111.2 | n | 33 | 2.42 |
| 7 | 7 | 2006 | 112.12 | n | 35 | 2.52 |

| Coupon | Month | Year | Ask Price | Type | T (months) | Ask YTM |
|---|---|---|---|---|---|---|
| 2.375 | 8 | 2006 | 99.14 | n | 36 | 2.57 |
| 6.5 | 10 | 2006 | 111.13 | n | 38 | 2.67 |
| 3.5 | 11 | 2006 | 102.13 | n | 39 | 2.71 |
| 3.375 | 1 | 2007 | 108.04 | i | 41 | 0.93 |
| 6.25 | 2 | 2007 | 111.08 | n | 42 | 2.81 |
| 6.625 | 5 | 2007 | 112.26 | n | 45 | 2.95 |
| 4.375 | 5 | 2007 | 104.3 | n | 45 | 2.96 |
| 3.25 | 8 | 2007 | 100.18 | n | 48 | 3.09 |
| 6.125 | 8 | 2007 | 111.09 | n | 48 | 3.08 |
| 3 | 11 | 2007 | 99.06 | n | 51 | 3.2 |
| 3.625 | 1 | 2008 | 109.27 | i | 53 | 1.31 |
| 3 | 2 | 2008 | 98.2 | n | 54 | 3.33 |
| 5.5 | 2 | 2008 | 109.04 | n | 54 | 3.29 |
| 2.625 | 5 | 2008 | 96.16 | n | 57 | 3.43 |
| 5.625 | 5 | 2008 | 109.17 | n | 57 | 3.42 |
| 3.25 | 8 | 2008 | 98.23 | n | 60 | 3.53 |
| 4.75 | 11 | 2008 | 105.13 | n | 63 | 3.6 |
| 8.75 | 11 | 2008 | 101.22 | | 63 | 0.85 |
| 3.875 | 1 | 2009 | 111.17 | i | 65 | 1.62 |
| 5.5 | 5 | 2009 | 109.06 | n | 69 | 3.7 |
| 9.125 | 5 | 2009 | 105.24 | | 69 | 1.03 |
| 6 | 8 | 2009 | 111.17 | n | 72 | 3.82 |
| 10.375 | 11 | 2009 | 110.21 | | 75 | 1.47 |
| 4.25 | 1 | 2010 | 114.07 | i | 77 | 1.87 |
| 6.5 | 2 | 2010 | 114.12 | n | 78 | 3.96 |
| 11.75 | 2 | 2010 | 114.1 | | 78 | 1.8 |
| 5.75 | 5 | 2010 | 109.31 | n | 81 | 4.09 |
| 10 | 5 | 2010 | 113.19 | | 81 | 1.89 |
| 12.75 | 11 | 2010 | 122.22 | | 87 | 2.19 |
| 3.5 | 1 | 2011 | 109.26 | i | 89 | 2.06 |
| 5 | 2 | 2011 | 105.01 | n | 90 | 4.21 |
| 13.875 | 5 | 2011 | 129.22 | | 93 | 2.49 |
| 5 | 8 | 2011 | 104.2 | n | 96 | 4.31 |
| 14 | 11 | 2011 | 134.24 | | 99 | 2.64 |
| 3.375 | 1 | 2012 | 108.27 | i | 101 | 2.21 |
| 4.875 | 2 | 2012 | 103.13 | n | 102 | 4.39 |
| 3 | 7 | 2012 | 105.29 | i | 107 | 2.26 |
| 4.375 | 8 | 2012 | 99.13 | n | 108 | 4.46 |
| 4 | 11 | 2012 | 96.09 | n | 111 | 4.49 |
| 10.375 | 11 | 2012 | 128 | | 111 | 3.22 |
| 3.875 | 2 | 2013 | 95.05 | n | 114 | 4.51 |
| 3.625 | 5 | 2013 | 93.15 | n | 117 | 4.46 |
| 1.875 | 7 | 2013 | 95.29 | i | 119 | 2.34 |
| 4.25 | 8 | 2013 | 97.24 | n | 120 | 4.53 |
| 12 | 8 | 2013 | 138.12 | | 120 | 3.51 |
| 13.25 | 5 | 2014 | 149.1 | | 129 | 3.62 |
| 12.5 | 8 | 2014 | 146.15 | | 132 | 3.73 |
| 11.75 | 11 | 2014 | 143.18 | | 135 | 3.81 |
| 11.25 | 2 | 2015 | 157.06 | | 138 | 4.73 |
| 10.625 | 8 | 2015 | 152.19 | | 144 | 4.8 |
| 9.875 | 11 | 2015 | 145.28 | | 147 | 4.85 |
| 9.25 | 2 | 2016 | 140.09 | | 150 | 4.89 |
| 7.25 | 5 | 2016 | 121.13 | | 153 | 4.96 |
| 7.5 | 11 | 2016 | 123.27 | | 159 | 5.01 |

| Coupon | Month | Year | Ask Price | Type | T (months) | Ask YTM |
|---|---|---|---|---|---|---|
| 8.75 | 5 | 2017 | 136.17 | | 165 | 5.03 |
| 8.875 | 8 | 2017 | 138 | | 168 | 5.05 |
| 9.125 | 5 | 2018 | 141.06 | | 177 | 5.11 |
| 9 | 11 | 2018 | 140.13 | | 183 | 5.14 |
| 8.875 | 2 | 2019 | 139.06 | | 186 | 5.16 |
| 8.125 | 8 | 2019 | 131.06 | | 192 | 5.22 |
| 8.5 | 2 | 2020 | 135.27 | | 198 | 5.23 |
| 8.75 | 5 | 2020 | 138.26 | | 201 | 5.24 |
| 8.75 | 8 | 2020 | 139 | | 204 | 5.25 |
| 7.875 | 2 | 2021 | 129.05 | | 210 | 5.29 |
| 8.125 | 5 | 2021 | 132.07 | | 213 | 5.3 |
| 8.125 | 8 | 2021 | 132.1 | | 216 | 5.31 |
| 8 | 11 | 2021 | 131.04 | | 219 | 5.31 |
| 7.25 | 8 | 2022 | 122.06 | | 228 | 5.37 |
| 7.625 | 11 | 2022 | 126.29 | | 231 | 5.36 |
| 7.125 | 2 | 2023 | 120.25 | | 234 | 5.39 |
| 6.25 | 8 | 2023 | 110.03 | | 240 | 5.42 |
| 7.5 | 11 | 2024 | 126.06 | | 255 | 5.41 |
| 7.625 | 2 | 2025 | 127.3 | | 258 | 5.41 |
| 6.875 | 8 | 2025 | 118.1 | | 264 | 5.44 |
| 6 | 2 | 2026 | 107.03 | | 270 | 5.45 |
| 6.75 | 8 | 2026 | 117.01 | | 276 | 5.44 |
| 6.5 | 11 | 2026 | 113.25 | | 279 | 5.45 |
| 6.625 | 2 | 2027 | 115.17 | | 282 | 5.44 |
| 6.375 | 8 | 2027 | 112.09 | | 288 | 5.45 |
| 6.125 | 11 | 2027 | 108.3 | | 291 | 5.45 |
| 3.625 | 4 | 2028 | 113.31 | i | 296 | 2.83 |
| 5.5 | 8 | 2028 | 100.21 | | 300 | 5.45 |
| 5.25 | 11 | 2028 | 97.08 | | 303 | 5.45 |
| 5.25 | 2 | 2029 | 97.09 | | 306 | 5.45 |
| 3.875 | 4 | 2029 | 119.01 | i | 308 | 2.83 |
| 6.125 | 8 | 2029 | 109.16 | | 312 | 5.44 |
| 6.25 | 5 | 2030 | 111.22 | | 321 | 5.42 |
| 5.375 | 2 | 2031 | 101 | | 330 | 5.3 |
| 3.375 | 4 | 2032 | 112.03 | | 344 | 2.76 |

# Chapter 27

# Estimating the Yield Curve

## 27.1  Introduction

In the last chapter, we defined three equivalent representations of the term-structure of interest rates: as a *discount function*, as a *zero-coupon (or yield) curve*, and as a *forward curve*. Building on this material, the current chapter examines estimation of the yield curve from market data.

We first examine a simple and intuitively appealing method known as *bootstrapping*, which extends the ideas presented in Sections 26.4–26.5 of the last chapter (see especially Example 26.3). Bootstrapping can, in principle, be used to identify the yield curve, but it also suffers from some important drawbacks in implementation. One of two alternatives is, therefore, used in practice.

The first, a method called *splining*, was proposed originally by J. Huston McCulloch in the early 1970s as a method of estimating the discount function (see McCulloch, 1971, 1975). Splining attempts to identify different segments of the yield curve and then to "knot" them together at the common maturity points. Splining is the methodology used by the US and Japanese central banks to compute their respective treasury yield curves.

The second method was proposed in a paper by Charles Nelson and Alex Siegel in 1987 and extended by Lars Svensson in 1994. The combined model is known variously as the Nelson-Siegel-Svensson (NSS) model, the extended Nelson and Siegel (1987) model, or the Svensson (1994) model; we shall refer to it as the NSS model. The NSS model posits a single functional form for the entire yield curve (actually, the forward rate curve) and looks to estimate the parameters of this function using regression analysis. The model has been adopted widely around the world; it is used by the UK, Canada, and most central banks in Europe to identify treasury yield curves.

## 27.2  Bootstrapping

Section 26.4 presented a simple example involving two bonds and showed how the values of the discount function at two points in time could be recovered from the prices of these bonds. The natural generalization of that procedure is known as "bootstrapping." In bootstrapping, we use the shortest maturity bonds to identify the discount function for short maturities and then use the discount function identified thus far together with longer maturity bonds to identify the discount function at longer maturities. An example will explain the procedure.

**Example 27.1**

Consider a market with four bonds each with a face value of $1 at maturity. Assume that coupons are paid semiannually. Suppose we are given the following information about their prices:

| Bond | Price |
|---|---|
| 6-month zero | 0.95959 |
| 1-year zero | 0.91851 |
| 18-month 8% coupon | 0.98857 |
| 24-month 9% coupon | 1.00127 |

By definition, the discount function $d(t)$ is equal to the price of a zero-coupon bond with maturity $t$ and face value $1. Thus, the given data already contains information on the values of the discount function for $t = 0.5$ and $t = 1$:

$$d(0.50) = 0.95959 \qquad d(1) = 0.91851 \qquad (27.1)$$

The 18-month 8% bond has cash flows of 0.04 at the six-month and one-year points and a cash flow of 1.04 at the 18-month point. Expressing its price in terms of these cash flows and the discount function, we have

$$0.98857 = (0.04)\, d(0.50) + (0.04)\, d(1) + (1.04)\, d(1.50) \qquad (27.2)$$

Substituting for $d(0.50)$ and $d(1)$ from (27.1), and solving for $d(1.50)$, we obtain

$$d(1.50) = 0.87831 \qquad (27.3)$$

Finally, the 24-month 9% coupon bond has cash flows of 0.045 at the six-month, one-year, and 18-month points, and a cash flow of 1.045 in 24 months. Thus, we have

$$1.00127 = (0.045)\, d(0.50) + (0.045)\, d(1) + (0.045)\, d(1.50) + (1.045)\, d(2) \qquad (27.4)$$

Substituting for $d(0.50)$, $d(1)$, and $d(1.50)$ from (27.1) and (27.3), and solving for $d(2)$, we find that

$$d(2) = 0.83946 \qquad (27.5)$$

Thus, we obtain four points on the discount function:

$$
\begin{aligned}
d(0.50) &= 0.95959 \\
d(1.00) &= 0.91851 \\
d(1.50) &= 0.87831 \\
d(2.00) &= 0.83946
\end{aligned}
\qquad (27.6)
$$

These values may alternatively be expressed in terms of the spot yield (say, with semiannual compounding). As we saw in the previous chapter (see equation (26.9)), semiannually compounded spot yields $r^{(2)}$ are related to the discount function via

$$r^{(2)}(t) = [d(t)]^{-1/2t} - 1 \qquad (27.7)$$

Using this in (27.6), we obtain four points on the yield curve:

$$
\begin{aligned}
r^{(2)}(0.50) &= 0.084223 \\
r^{(2)}(1.00) &= 0.086835 \\
r^{(2)}(1.50) &= 0.088402 \\
r^{(2)}(2.00) &= 0.089440
\end{aligned}
\qquad (27.8)
$$

∎

The bootstrapping procedure is even quicker than the above description suggests since the discount function may be obtained from the bond prices and cash-flow information through a process involving a single matrix inversion, a calculation that takes no time at all on modern computers. Appendix 27A elaborates on this.

## Problems with Bootstrapping

Bootstrapping is an excellent method in principle, but it suffers from several drawbacks in application. There are several issues that complicate matters in practice.

One is that the bonds used in the bootstrapping procedure must all have cash flows on the same set of dates. Moreover, the bonds with these common payment dates must be linearly independent so that matrix inversion may be performed. Neither condition is easy to ensure in practice. Further compounding these problems is that in most markets there is only a limited set of bonds that are liquid and possess high information content and from which the bonds used in bootstrapping should ideally be chosen.

Secondly, knowing the values of the discount function at the time points $t_1, \ldots, t_n$ does not tell us how to value cash flows occurring between these dates. For instance, in Example 27.1, we identified the discount function at six-month intervals from six months to two years. There is no direct way to obtain from this information the present value of a cash flow of $100 occurring, say, eight months and three days from the present. For this, some interpolation method (e.g., linear or cubic schemes) must be used.

Finally, it turns out in practice that the discount functions obtained by bootstrapping are sensitive to *which* bonds are actually used as inputs. Changing the basis set of bonds tends to alter the estimated discount functions. One reason is that different bonds are affected to different extents by such factors as liquidity, and the impact of these factors is reflected in their prices.

Ideally, we would like a methodology that uses the information present in *all* available bonds regardless of their cash-flow dates and whether these dates coincide or not. The two methods we discuss in the following sections are each motivated by these considerations.

## 27.3  Splines

If we want to use all the information in the set of bonds available for estimating the yield curve, a regression-based procedure is the natural way to proceed. That is, we specify a functional form for the yield curve and then use regression analysis to identify the curve's parameters. This will identify the discount function that most closely prices the bonds, i.e., that minimizes the pricing error taken over all the bonds.

Splines offer one way to achieve this end. The splining procedure may be summarized as follows. Let $[0, T]$ be the horizon over which we wish to estimate the discount function; that is, 0 is the current time and $T$ is the maturity date of the longest-maturity bond. The first step in the procedure is to divide the interval $[0, T]$ into $N + 1$ subintervals

$$[T_0, T_1], [T_1, T_2], \ldots, [T_N, T_{N+1}]$$

where $T_0 = 0$ and $T_{N+1} = T$. The intermediate points $T_1, \ldots, T_N$ are called "knot points" for reasons that will become clear shortly. Over each subinterval $[T_n, T_{n+1}]$, we specify a parametric form $g_n(t)$ for the discount function. The functions $g_n(\cdot)$ are functions solely of time $t$ and are called "splines." Thus, the overall discount function has the form

$$d(t) = \begin{cases} g_0(t), & \text{if } t \in [T_0, T_1) \\ \vdots & \vdots \\ g_k(t), & \text{if } t \in [T_k, T_{k+1}) \\ \vdots & \vdots \\ g_N(t), & \text{if } t \in [T_N, T_{N+1}] \end{cases} \tag{27.9}$$

Over different subintervals, we may use different functions $g_k(\cdot)$; this is an important part of the flexibility of the splining procedure. However, to ensure that the entire discount function is continuous and smooth, we must impose constraints at the end-points of the intervals. For example, consider the value of the discount function at the time-point $T_k$. The point $T_k$ is the lower end-point of the interval $[T_k, T_{k+1})$. On this interval, the discount function is given by the function $g_k$. Thus, the value of the discount function at this point is

$$g_k(T_k)$$

However, $T_k$ is also the upper end-point of the time interval $[T_{k-1}, T_k)$, and on this interval, the discount function is specified by $g_{k-1}(\cdot)$. Thus, the discount function at $T_k$ may also be taken to be

$$g_{k-1}(T_k)$$

With a continuous yield curve, these values should coincide, so we must have

$$g_{k-1}(T_k) = g_k(T_k) \tag{27.10}$$

Thus, the functions $g_{k-1}$ and $g_k$ must be "knotted" together at their common end-points, which explains the term "knot-points" to describe $T_1, \ldots, T_N$.

Once we have specified functional forms for the splines $g_0, \ldots, g_N$, we estimate the parameters of these functions using regression analysis.

The choice of mathematical function for the splines usually devolves into two popular forms. In a *polynomial spline*, each of the functions $g_k$ is a polynomial function of time $t$. In an *exponential spline*, each function is an exponential function of time. The following sections examine each of these in greater detail and discuss their implementation.

## 27.4   Polynomial Splines

In a polynomial spline, each function $g_k$ is taken to be a polynomial function of time of order $\ell$. Thus, for example, if $\ell = 1$, we have *linear splines*: each $g_k$ is of the form

$$g_k(t) = a_k + b_k t$$

If $\ell = 2$, we have *quadratic splines*: each $g_k$ is of the form

$$g_k(t) = a_k + b_k t + c_k t^2$$

If $\ell = 3$, we have *cubic splines*: each $g_k$ is of the form

$$g_k(t) = a_k + b_k t + c_k t^2 + d_k t^3$$

By far the most commonly used form in practice is cubic.

## Parameters to Be Estimated

In a polynomial spline of degree $\ell$, the total number of unknown parameters is $(\ell+1)(N+1)$ since there are $(\ell+1)$ parameters associated with each $\ell$-th degree polynomial spline $g_k$ and there are $(N+1)$ splines in all. Thus, in principle, there are $(\ell+1)(N+1)$ parameters to be estimated in the regression analysis. However, as we have seen, some restrictions have to be imposed on the splines at the knot points. Here are four standard restrictions imposed in practice:

1. *Condition 0:*  The present value of \$1 due immediately is just \$1. Thus, we should have $d(0) = 1$, which means

$$g_0(0) = 1 \qquad (27.11)$$

2. *Condition 1: Continuity of the Discount Function*  This requires, as we have seen, that at the knot points we must have

$$g_k(T_{k+1}) = g_{k+1}(T_{k+1}), \quad k = 1, \ldots, N \qquad (27.12)$$

This places $N$ restrictions on the parameters.

3. *Condition 2: Continuity of the Forward Curve*  From equation (26.17), the instantaneous forward rate is related to the discount function via

$$f(t) = -\frac{1}{d(t)} d'(t)$$

Thus, if we want a *continuous* forward curve, we need $d'(\cdot)$ to be continuous. Thus, the values of $d'(\cdot)$ also need to be equated at the knot points. That is, we must have:

$$g_k'(T_{k+1}) = g_{k+1}'(T_{k+1}), \quad \text{for } k = 1, \ldots, N \qquad (27.13)$$

This places a further $N$ restrictions on the parameters.

4. *Condition 3: Smoothness of the Forward Curve*  Further, if we want the forward curve to be smooth and not jagged, we also need $f'(\cdot)$ to be continuous. This means the second-derivative $d''(\cdot)$ of the discount function must be continuous. Equating these second derivatives at the knot points, we obtain

$$g_k''(T_{k+1}) = g_{k+1}''(T_{k+1}), \quad \text{for } k = 1, \ldots, N \qquad (27.14)$$

This too places $N$ restrictions on the parameters.

These four conditions give us a total of $3N+1$ restrictions on the parameters. Thus, the number of free parameters is only $(\ell+1)(N+1) - (3N+1)$. For example, if we use linear splines, the number of parameters to be estimated is $2(N+1) - (N+1) = N+1$. (With linear splines, there are only $N+1$ restrictions since Conditions 2 and 3 do not apply. The reader should think about why.) With quadratic splines, the number of free parameters to be estimated is $3(N+1) - (2N+1) = N+2$. (In this case, Condition 2 is also relevant but Condition 3 is not. Again, the reader should think about why.) With cubic splines, or splines of a higher order than 3, all the conditions are relevant, and the number of parameters to be estimated is $4(N+1) - (3N+1) = N+3$.

## A Reduced-Form Representation of the Discount Function

Once we have identified the parameters to be estimated, the actual estimation can be carried out via ordinary least squares or OLS. The first step in this procedure is to represent the discount function in terms of the unknown parameters *after* incorporating the four restrictions discussed above. (We call this the "reduced-form discount function.") We describe this first step here.

For simplicity, we look at the case of a single interior knot point denoted $\tau$. It is a simple matter to extend the arguments to the case of $n$ knot points. We also take the polynomials to be cubic which is, as mentioned earlier, the most commonly used case in practice.

Let the single knot point be denoted $\tau$. The discount function is then of the form

$$d(t) = \begin{cases} g_0(t), & t \in [0, \tau) \\ g_1(t), & t \in [\tau, T^*] \end{cases} \qquad \textbf{(27.15)}$$

where

$$\begin{aligned} g_0(t) &= a_0 + b_0 t + c_0 t^2 + d_0 t^3 \\ g_1(t) &= a_1 + b_1 t + c_1 t^2 + d_1 t^3 \end{aligned} \qquad \textbf{(27.16)}$$

In shorthand notation, we can write the discount function as

$$d(t) = g_0(t) + I_{t \geq \tau}(g_1(t) - g_0(t)) \qquad \textbf{(27.17)}$$

where $I_{t \geq \tau}$ is the *indicator function* on $t \geq \tau$, i.e., the function that takes on the value 1 if $t \geq \tau$, and is zero otherwise. Writing the full forms of $g_0$ and $g_1$, this is

$$\begin{aligned} d(t) &= a_0 + b_0 t + c_0 t^2 + d_0 t^3 \\ &+ I_{t \geq \tau} \left[ (a_1 - a_0) + (b_1 - b_0) t + (c_1 - c_0) t^2 + (d_1 - d_0) t^3 \right] \end{aligned} \qquad \textbf{(27.18)}$$

There are eight parameters in total: $(a_0, b_0, c_0, d_0)$ and $(a_1, b_1, c_1, d_1)$. However, there are four restrictions imposed on these parameters as described above:

- *Condition 0* $d(0) = 1$. This means $g_0(0) = 1$ so, from (27.16), we must have $a_0 = 1$.
- *Condition 1* At the knot point $\tau$, we must have $g_0(\tau) = g_1(\tau)$. Substituting for $g_0$ and $g_1$ from (27.16), this results in

$$(a_1 - a_0) + (b_1 - b_0)\tau + (c_1 - c_0)\tau^2 + (d_1 - d_0)\tau^3 = 0 \qquad \textbf{(27.19)}$$

- *Condition 2* At the knot point $\tau$, we must also have $g_0'(\tau) = g_1'(\tau)$. From expression (27.16),

$$g_i'(t) = b_i + 2c_i t + 3d_i t^2, \qquad i = 1, 2$$

so this means

$$(b_1 - b_0) + 2(c_1 - c_0)\tau + 3(d_1 - d_0)\tau^2 = 0 \qquad \textbf{(27.20)}$$

- *Condition 3* Finally, at the knot point $\tau$, we must also have $g_0''(\tau) = g_1''(\tau)$. From expression (27.16),

$$g_i''(t) = 2c_i + 6d_i t, \qquad i = 1, 2$$

so

$$(c_1 - c_0) + 3(d_1 - d_0)\tau = 0 \qquad \textbf{(27.21)}$$

Solving (27.19)–(27.21), we obtain:

$$a_1 - a_0 = -(d_1 - d_0)\tau^3 \qquad \textbf{(27.22)}$$

$$b_1 - b_0 = 3(d_1 - d_0)\tau^2 \qquad \textbf{(27.23)}$$

$$c_1 - c_0 = -3(d_1 - d_0)\tau \qquad \textbf{(27.24)}$$

Now, let $e_0 = d_1 - d_0$. Substituting (27.22)–(27.24) into the expression (27.18) for the discount function, the discount function may then be written

$$d(t) = a_0 + b_0 t + c_0 t^2 + d_0 t^3 + e_0 I_{t \geq \tau} (t - \tau)^3 \qquad \textbf{(27.25)}$$

Expression (27.25) is the reduced-form representation of the discount function.

### Estimating the Parameters by OLS

Given a discount function, the predicted price of a bond is simply the sum of the cash flows from the bond weighted by the appropriate discount factors. Consider a bond that has cash flows of $\xi_t$ at times $t$. With the discount function given by (27.25), the theoretical price of such a bond is

$$\widehat{P} = \sum_t \xi_t \, d(t)$$
$$= \sum_t \xi_t [1 + b_0 t + c_0 t^2 + d_0 t^3 + e_0 \, I_{(t \geq \tau)} (t - \tau)^3] \qquad \textbf{(27.26)}$$

Rearranging, we obtain

$$\widehat{P} - \sum_t \xi_t = b_0 X_1 + c_0 X_2 + d_0 X_3 + e_0 X_4 \qquad \textbf{(27.27)}$$

where

$$X_1 = \sum_t \xi_t t$$
$$X_2 = \sum_t \xi_t t^2$$
$$X_3 = \sum_t \xi_t t^3$$
$$X_4 = \sum_t \xi_t I_{(t \geq \tau)} (t - \tau)^3$$

The four free parameters $b_0, c_0, d_0$, and $e_0$ may now be estimated by regressing $(P - \sum \xi_t)$ on $X_1, X_2, X_3$, and $X_4$. This is a simple OLS regression. Note that we will obtain one equation for each bond that is traded in the market and that we choose to include in our analysis. Stacking up all the bonds in the regression and then estimating the parameters by OLS fits the entire spline model. This fitted model may then be used to obtain the discount function $d(t)$ for any maturity. Therefore, the spline model allows us to rapidly price any set of cash flows, irrespective of the date on which the cash flow materializes.

## 27.5  Exponential Splines

Exponential splines use exponential functions of time as drivers. In an exponential spline, each function $g_k$ takes on the form

$$g_k(t) = a_k + b_k(1 - e^{-mt}) + c_k(1 - e^{-2mt}) + d_k(1 - e^{-3mt}) + \cdots \qquad \textbf{(27.28)}$$

Here, $m > 0$ is an additional free parameter. This last parameter has a nice interpretation: if $f(t)$ denotes the forward curve generated by the splined discount function (27.28), then it turns out that

$$m = \lim_{t \to \infty} f(t)$$

so $m$ is the "long forward rate." Once again, the most popular form is *cubic* exponentials, i.e., to have each $g_k$ of the form

$$g_k(t) = a_k + b_k(1 - e^{-mt}) + c_k(1 - e^{-2mt}) + d_k(1 - e^{-3mt}) \qquad \textbf{(27.29)}$$

The implementation procedure for exponential splines works in a similar way to polynomial splines with the same restrictions but there are a few differences (notably, the presence of the parameter $m$). The details are presented in Appendix 27B.

## 27.6 Implementation Issues with Splines

Implementation detail always complicates good theory, and splines are no exception. Among the issues that come up are how many knot points should be employed and where they should be placed. The main trade-off here lies in balancing smoothness of the function versus the fit of the function. With a larger number of knot points, there is greater flexibility in the shape of the discount function, so evidently the fit to bond prices is improved. But the greater the number of disparate splines that have to be knotted together, the more jagged are the resulting spot and, especially, forward curves. A common choice is to use a larger number of knot points in regions in which data is plentiful (typically at the short end of the curve) and to use fewer knot points where the data gets relatively sparse. As always, there is no substitute for good judgment.

In practice, to operationalize these concerns, the splined discount function is often estimated with an additional penalty function. The penalty is an increasing function of the number of knot points. Hence, the higher the penalty, the greater smoothness being sought in the fitting procedure. One widely-used example of implementing spline calibration with a penalty is to minimize a function comprising the sum of (i) the penalty value and (ii) the average mean squared error between the fitted curve and the empirical one.

The second aspect that needs to be kept in mind is that there are often issues with the input data. The quality of the bond price data used to fit the discount functions is highly variable. All bonds may not be adequately liquid. Usually, short maturity bonds tend to be more liquid than longer bonds although this may not be true in all markets. For instance, in Japan, the ten-year bonds tend to be most liquid and play the role of being the "benchmark" for the rest of the curve. Bond prices may need to be adjusted for coupon effects since there may be non-standard coupons on many of the bonds. Tax issues, embedded options, etc., are all issues that come into play and need to be cleansed in the data before it is taken to a splining model.

## 27.7 The Nelson-Siegel-Svensson Approach

In contrast to the spline methods, the Nelson and Siegel (1987) approach (and its extension by Svensson, 1994) model the *forward* curve rather than the discount function or spot yield curve. Moreover, rather than break the curve into segments as splining does, the NSS technique aims to fit the entire curve with a single function. We describe the Nelson-Siegel model first and then the extension proposed by Svensson.

Nelson and Siegel (NS) suggested the following parametric form for the forward curve:

$$f(t) = \beta_0 + \beta_1 \exp\left(-\frac{t}{\theta}\right) + \beta_2 \left(\frac{t}{\theta}\right) \exp\left(-\frac{t}{\theta}\right) \qquad \textbf{(27.30)}$$

The spot rate curve implied by the forward curve (27.30) is given by

$$r(t) = \beta_0 + (\beta_1 + \beta_2)\left(\frac{1 - \exp(-t/\theta)}{t/\theta}\right) - \beta_2\left(\exp(-t/\theta)\right) \qquad \textbf{(27.31)}$$

There are four parameters in the Nelson-Siegel function (27.30): $\beta_0$, $\beta_1$, $\beta_2$, and $\theta$. As the parameters vary, the shape of the curve changes. Overall, four possible patterns may be generated by the Nelson-Siegel function: increasing, decreasing, flat, and humped/U-shaped. The parameters have attractive interpretations in this context:

- $\beta_0$: As $t \to \infty$, the forward rate $f(t)$ given by (27.30) goes to $\beta_0$. Thus, $\beta_0$ is just the long forward rate. Moreover, a change in $\beta_0$ results in a parallel shift in the forward curve. Hence, $\beta_0$ is also called the "level" parameter.

- $\beta_1$: At $t = 0$, the forward rate $f(t)$ under (27.30) is equal to $\beta_0 + \beta_1$. Thus, $\beta_0 + \beta_1$ is the short forward rate. This means $\beta_1$ is the difference between the short and long forward rates. This is called the "slope" of the curve.

- $\beta_2$: This determines the magnitude and direction of the hump in $f(t)$. If $\beta_2 > 0$, then the $f(t)$ curve has a hump at $\theta$. If $\beta_2 < 0$, then the $f(t)$ curve has a U-shape at $\theta$. As such, $\beta_2$ is sometimes referred to as the "curvature" parameter.

- $\theta$: This determines the location of the hump or U-shape. The last term of the NS function has two countervailing terms, $(t/\theta)$, which increases in $t$, and $\exp(-t/\theta)$, which decreases in $t$. As $t$ increases (provided $\theta > 0$), the curve rises initially on account of the first part that increases in $t$, and then the exponential decay of the second part gathers greater influence and drives the curve downward. Where this crossover occurs depends on the size of $\theta$ and, hence, it determines the location of the hump.

The Nelson-Siegel model cannot generate more complex forms (e.g., combination of U-shaped and humped). Motivated by this, Svensson (1994) proposed extending (27.30) by using two additional parameters and defining

$$f(t) = \beta_0 + \beta_1 \exp(-t/\theta) + \beta_2 [t/\theta] \exp(-t/\theta)$$
$$+ \beta_3 [t/\nu] \exp(-t/\nu) \qquad \textbf{(27.32)}$$

This six-parameter model is variously referred to as the Nelson-Siegel-Svensson (NSS) model, the Svensson model, or the extended Nelson-Siegel model. The implied spot rate in this model is given by

$$r(t) = \beta_0 + \beta_1 \{[1 - \exp(-t/\theta)]/[t/\theta]\}$$
$$+ \beta_2 (\{[1 - \exp(-t/\theta)]/[t/\theta]\} - \exp(-t/\theta)) \qquad \textbf{(27.33)}$$
$$+ \beta_3 (\{[1 - \exp(-t/\nu)]/[t/\nu]\} - \exp(-t/\nu))$$

The first four parameters have the same interpretation as earlier. The two new parameters $\beta_3$ and $\nu$ are the obvious analogs of $\beta_2$ and $\theta_2$: they allow for a second hump or U-shape with $\nu$ determining whether this is a hump or U-shape and $\beta_3$ determining its location.

## Implementing the Nelson-Siegel-Svensson Model

Implementing the NSS model involves finding the forward curve that best prices the bonds in the data set. The typical procedure involves the following steps:

1. Select a vector of starting parameters. This is the initial guess before the numerical search for the best parameters can begin.

2. Compute the spot rate curve and discount function corresponding to these initial parameters.

3. Using the discount function, determine theoretical (or model) coupon bond prices (i.e., prices under chosen parameters).

4. Compute the difference between predicted and actual prices.

5. Minimize the squared difference using a numerical procedure.

The NSS model is a very flexible one, making it widely applicable. By its very definition, the model results in smooth forward curves unlike the jagged curves that often result under splines. Moreover, studies looking at changes in yield curves using principal component analysis have identified three key factors that seem to drive changes in the term structure: the level, slope, and curvature. The parameters of the NSS model are directly identifiable with these factors, increasing its appeal.

However, there are some drawbacks to the NSS approach as well. The nonlinearity in $\theta$ and $\nu$ may create complications. Frequently, there are multiple local maxima and/or minima, so several different sets of starting parameters need to be tried. But with six parameters, specifying $k$ different starting values for each parameter results in a total of $k^6$ starting values, considerably increasing the required computation.

# 27.8   Summary

The last chapter introduced the foundational concepts needed to build models for the pricing of interest-rate derivatives. Most models used in practice take as input the current yield curve in either the form of the zero-coupon yield curve or the form of the forward curve.

Although the yield curve is a vital input into term-structure modeling and risk-management and although it is commonplace in financial analysis to refer to "the" yield curve, the actual construction of the yield curve from the prices of traded bonds is a complex and sensitive exercise. This chapter has described the two most popular methods used to construct yield curves: the method of splines, introduced by McCulloch, and the Nelson-Siegel-Svensson approach. Each approach has its advantages and disadvantages, and each has its adherents. Virtually all central banks the world over base their Treasury yield curve construction on one of these two methods.

The following three chapters build on this foundation and describe how to model in an arbitrage-free manner the evolution of the yield curve to be used for the pricing of interest-rate derivatives and, more generally, for interest-rate risk management.

## 27.9 Exercises

1. Write down the Nelson-Siegel model for fitting the forward rate curve. Explain what the intuition is for each of the parameters of the model.

2. If the yield curve is monotonically increasing with maturity, will the forward curve increase as well?

3. What are more variable across maturity: zero-coupon rates or forward rates? Explain.

4. The Neslon-Siegel (NS) model was extended by the Nelson-Siegel-Svensson (NSS) model. What additional feature was provided by the NSS model over the NS model?

5. Using the following data on bond prices, bootstrap the spot rate curve for each half-year. Assume that the semiannual compounding convention is followed.

| Maturity (years) | Bond Price (per $100) | Bond Coupon (% p.a.) |
| --- | --- | --- |
| 0.5 | 100.12 | 3.02 |
| 1.0 | 99.87 | 3.44 |
| 1.5 | 100.40 | 4.00 |
| 2.0 | 98.67 | 4.20 |

6. Given two spot rates six months apart, 3% and 4%, interpolate the spot rate four months after the first spot rate, assuming that each month is uniformly 1/12 of a year. Use three

different interpolation schemes to do so, and present your answer under each one:

(a) Linear interpolation.

(b) Exponential interpolation.

(c) Logarithmic interpolation.

Each of these schemes is based on an interpolation function that is linear, exponential, or logarithmic between known spot rates.

7. Which interpolation scheme (linear, exponential, or logarithmic) gives the highest interpolated rates? Why? Can you explain the relative ordering of the interpolation schemes in your answer to the previous question?

8. In practice, bond prices are never available at conveniently spaced intervals. Some interpolation scheme is called for. However, by making an assumption of constant forward rates between non-standard maturities, we can develop a spot rate curve even for unequal time intervals. In this question, you will undertake a simple exercise of this type.

You are given the following discount bond prices at times $t$:

| $t$ | Discount Bond Price |
|-----|---------------------|
| 0.70 | 0.9754 |
| 1.32 | 0.9256 |
| 2.11 | 0.8777 |

All compounding and discounting are in continuous time.

(a) Assuming that forward rates are constant between these dates, find these forward rates.

(b) Price a two-year $100 face value bond that pays 10% p.a. semiannually.

9. In the previous question, what type of interpolation scheme is being effectively used: linear, exponential, or logarithmic?

10. This question requires you to develop zero-coupon and forward rate curves using real-world data from the US government debt markets. Proceed by implementing the following steps:

(a) Collect data for any one recent date on bond prices and yields. There are many sources for such data, such as *The Wall Street Journal*, Bloomberg screens, etc. *The Wall Street Journal* is the easiest. You will obtain a set of maturities and yields. You need to get enough data for up to seven years of maturity. Anything from 20 bonds or more would be appropriate. Arrange them on a spreadsheet in two columns: (1) Maturity in Years (fractions allowed) from Today and (2) Yield to Maturity (ytm). Call this Table 1.

(b) Plot the points with maturity on the x-axis and ytm on the y-axis (a scatter plot). Call this Plot 1.

(c) Fit a curve through the plot. We leave this to your imagination, and you are free to choose some way to fit a smooth line through this data. Spreadsheets usually provide a tool to do this. Remember that a straight line is probably not the best way to do this. Call this curve Plot 2.

On the same plot, fit a curve through the coupon rates and through the bond prices. Now you have three interpolated curves for yields, coupons, and prices.

(d) With your fitted line for yields, generate a new table of ytms, coupon rates, and prices, each observation being six months apart. Hence, if your last maturity bond is of seven years, you will have 14 periods of a half year each. Call this Table 2.

Remember that your fitted line gives you yield as a function of maturity. Hence, for maturities $t = 0.5, 1, 1.5, 2, \ldots, 6.5, 7.0$, you will compute matching yields.

(e) Using this table of ytms, prices, and coupons, compute (a) the zero-coupon rates and (b) forward rates for all maturities in the table. Call this Table 3.

(f) Present plots of the (a) ytm curve, (b) zero-coupon rate curve, and (c) forward rate curve on the same graph. Call this Plot 3.

(g) Now, as an alternative, show how you can use Table 1 with a regression method to derive discount factors and zero-coupon rates. Feel free to make any simplifying assumptions here. Create a table of zero-coupon rates spaced half a year apart. Call this Table 4.

(h) Plot the zero-coupon curve from Table 3 versus the one from Table 4, and comment. Call this Plot 4.

Be creative!

11. If you receive a cash flow of $100 at time 1.25 years, explain how you would allocate this cash flow into two cash flows, $A$ received at one year, and cash flow $B$ received at 1.5 years. Assume that the zero-coupon rate for 1 year is 6% and that for 1.5 years is 6.5%. Assume continuous compounding.

12. Using a cubic splines scheme, fit the following discount factors using just one knot point at $t = 0.5$ years.

| $t$ | $d(t)$ |
|-----|--------|
| 0.1 | 0.9934 |
| 0.2 | 0.9845 |
| 0.6 | 0.9456 |
| 0.8 | 0.9267 |

Find the function that describes the entire discount function for any maturity $t$.

13. In the previous question, what would your solution be if you were given the following larger set of points:

| $t$ | $d(t)$ |
|-----|--------|
| 0.1 | 0.9934 |
| 0.2 | 0.9845 |
| 0.3 | 0.9778 |
| 0.6 | 0.9456 |
| 0.7 | 0.9389 |
| 0.8 | 0.9267 |

14. Fit a cubic splines framework to the following discount function values assuming two knot points at $t = 0.5$ and $t = 1$ years.

| $t$ | $d(t)$ |
|------|--------|
| 0.35 | 0.97 |
| 0.70 | 0.93 |
| 1.05 | 0.88 |
| 1.40 | 0.82 |
| 1.75 | 0.75 |

Explain your equations and the number of parameters you need to find.

15. Write a short Octave program to generalize the solution in the previous question to any prespecified number of knots points (more than two).

16. Write a general program to compute the coefficients of an exponential cubic spline fitting model given a parameter $m$. Then apply this program to a fitting of the following discount functions with knot points at $t = 0.5, 1.0$.

| $t$ | $d(t)$ |
|------|--------|
| 0.35 | 0.97 |
| 0.70 | 0.93 |
| 1.05 | 0.88 |
| 1.40 | 0.82 |
| 1.75 | 0.75 |

Refit the discount functions to the model and compare your answers against the original values. Explain.

17. You are provided the following discount function data. Fit it to a cubic exponential system with knot points every half year until and including $t = 4.5$ years.

| $t$ | $d(t)$ |
|------|---------|
| 0.25 | 0.97092 |
| 0.50 | 0.95886 |
| 0.75 | 0.94881 |
| 1.00 | 0.94160 |
| 1.25 | 0.93464 |
| 1.50 | 0.92902 |
| 1.75 | 0.92497 |
| 2.00 | 0.91828 |
| 2.25 | 0.91395 |
| 2.50 | 0.90934 |
| 2.75 | 0.90569 |
| 3.00 | 0.90124 |
| 3.25 | 0.89710 |
| 3.50 | 0.89220 |
| 3.75 | 0.89058 |
| 4.00 | 0.88761 |
| 4.25 | 0.88480 |
| 4.50 | 0.88296 |
| 4.75 | 0.87922 |
| 5.00 | 0.87592 |

18. The table below presents the forward curve for a range of maturities. Fit the Nelson-Siegel-Svensson model to this forward curve.

| $t$ (in years) | $f(t)$ (in % p.a.) |
|----------------|---------------------|
| 1/12 | 1.39 |
| 1/2  | 3.02 |
| 1.0  | 3.77 |
| 2.0  | 3.94 |
| 3.0  | 4.10 |
| 5.0  | 4.23 |
| 7.0  | 4.46 |
| 10.0 | 4.58 |

# Bootstrapping by Matrix Inversion

The procedure of bootstrapping to recover the discount function from bond prices and cash flows was described in Section 27.2. A quicker way to obtain the discount function than by the method described there is to use *matrix inversion*. We describe the general procedure first, and then apply it to the data in the example in Section 27.2. This section requires knowledge of basic matrix algebra.

Suppose we have $n$ time points $t_1, \ldots, t_n$ and wish to identify the values of the discount function $d(t_1), \ldots, d(t_n)$ at these points using $n$ bonds. We assume, of course, that as in Section 27.2, the cash flows of the bonds occur only at the time points $t_1, \ldots, t_n$.

Denote the time-$t_i$ cash flow from the $k$-th bond by $c_i^k$. Let $P^k$ denote the current price of the $k$-th bond. We have, for each $k$,

$$P^k = \sum_{i=1}^{n} c_i^k d(t_i)$$

In matrix notation, this can be written as

$$\begin{bmatrix} P^1 \\ \vdots \\ P^n \end{bmatrix} = \begin{bmatrix} c_1^1 & \cdots & c_n^1 \\ \vdots & \vdots & \vdots \\ c_1^n & \cdots & c_n^n \end{bmatrix} \begin{bmatrix} d(t_1) \\ \vdots \\ d(t_n) \end{bmatrix}$$

or, in the obvious matrix shorthand, as

$$P = C \cdot d$$

It follows from this expression that the $n$ required points are given by

$$d = C^{-1} \cdot P$$

To apply this matrix methodology to the numerical example of Section 27.2, note that in that example we have

$$P = \begin{bmatrix} 0.95959 \\ 0.91851 \\ 0.98857 \\ 1.00127 \end{bmatrix} \quad C = \begin{bmatrix} 1 & 0 & 0 & 0 \\ 0 & 1 & 0 & 0 \\ 0.04 & 0.04 & 1.04 & 0 \\ 0.045 & 0.045 & 0.045 & 1.045 \end{bmatrix} \quad d = \begin{bmatrix} d(0.50) \\ d(1.00) \\ d(1.50) \\ d(2.00) \end{bmatrix}$$

Inverting the matrix $C$, we obtain

$$C^{-1} = \begin{bmatrix} 1 & 0 & 0 & 0 \\ 0 & 1 & 0 & 0 \\ -0.0385 & -0.0385 & 0.9615 & 0 \\ -0.0414 & -0.0414 & -0.0414 & 0.9569 \end{bmatrix}$$

so

$$d = \begin{bmatrix} 1 & 0 & 0 & 0 \\ 0 & 1 & 0 & 0 \\ -0.0385 & -0.0385 & 0.9615 & 0 \\ -0.0414 & -0.0414 & -0.0414 & 0.9569 \end{bmatrix} \begin{bmatrix} 0.95959 \\ 0.91851 \\ 0.98857 \\ 1.00127 \end{bmatrix} = \begin{bmatrix} 0.95959 \\ 0.91851 \\ 0.87831 \\ 0.83946 \end{bmatrix}$$

which is, of course, the same set of values we obtained earlier in Section 27.2.

This is a very easy method to implement on a computer. The only things needed as inputs are the cash-flow matrix $C$ and the price vector $P$. The matrix approach enables us to collapse the step-by-step bootstrapping approach to a single matrix computation, which on modern computers is conducted in an instant.

To illustrate, we implement this approach in the Octave mathematical programming language. The commands that are required are as follows:

```
octave:1> P = [0.95959; 0.91851; 0.98857; 1.00127]
P =

   0.95959
   0.91851
   0.98857
   1.00127

octave:2> C = [1 0 0 0; 0 1 0 0; 0.04 0.04 1.04 0; 0.045 0.045 0.045 1.045]
C =

   1.00000   0.00000   0.00000   0.00000
   0.00000   1.00000   0.00000   0.00000
   0.04000   0.04000   1.04000   0.00000
   0.04500   0.04500   0.04500   1.04500

octave:3> d = inv(C)*P
d =

   0.95959
   0.91851
   0.87831
   0.83946
```

Since matrix inversion is feasible over exceedingly large cash-flow matrices, undertaking bootstrapping with linear algebra on a computer is exceedingly fast. Hence, the procedure may be undertaken several times a day on a trading desk with almost no computational burden.

# Implementation with Exponential Splines

Since the implementation procedure for exponential splines is similar to the procedure we have already visited for polynomial splines, our exposition here is correspondingly brief. Once again, we proceed by first describing the reduced-form discount function that obtains when all restrictions have been factored in, and then we discuss estimation by least squares. As with our exposition of polynomial splines, we keep things simple by assuming a single knot point $\tau$. The ideas are easily extended to the general case of $N$ knot points.

# Obtaining the Reduced-Form Discount Function

With a single knot point given by $\tau$, the discount function has the form

$$d(t) = \begin{cases} g_0(t), & t \in [0, \tau) \\ g_1(t), & t \in [\tau, T^*] \end{cases} \tag{27.34}$$

where for $i = 0, 1$, we have

$$g_i(t) = a_i + b_i(1 - e^{-mt}) + c_i(1 - e^{-2mt}) + d_i(1 - e^{-3mt}) \tag{27.35}$$

There are nine parameters in all: $(a_0, b_0, c_0, d_0)$, $(a_1, b_1, c_1, d_1)$, and $m$. Applying the same conditions as in the polynomial case results in the following equations:

- *Condition 0* $g_0(0) = 1$. This implies $a_0 = 1$.
- *Condition 1* $g_0(\tau) = g_1(\tau)$. This gives us

$$(a_1 - a_0) + (b_1 - b_0)(1 - e^{-m\tau}) + (c_1 - c_0)(1 - e^{-2m\tau}) \\ + (d_1 - d_0)(1 - e^{-3m\tau}) = 0 \tag{27.36}$$

- *Condition 2* $g_0'(\tau) = g_1'(\tau)$. This results in

$$(b_1 - b_0) + 2(c_1 - c_0)\,e^{-m\tau} + 3(d_1 - d_0)\,e^{-2m\tau} = 0 \tag{27.37}$$

- *Condition 3* $g_0''(\tau) = g_1''(\tau)$. This leads to

$$(b_1 - b_0) + 4(c_1 - c_0)\,e^{-m\tau} + 9(d_1 - d_0)\,e^{-2m\tau} = 0 \tag{27.38}$$

From Conditions 2 and 3, we can solve for $b_1 - b_0$ and $c_1 - c_0$ in terms of $d_1 - d_0$. Substituting these into Condition 1 gives us $a_1 - a_0$ also in terms of $d_1 - d_0$. Summarizing the results, we obtain the following:

$$a_1 - a_0 = (d_1 - d_0)[e^{-3m\tau} - 3e^{-2m\tau} + 3e^{-m\tau} - 1] \\ = (d_1 - d_0)[e^{-m\tau} - 1]^3 \tag{27.39}$$

$$b_1 - b_0 = 3(d_1 - d_0)\,e^{-2m\tau} \tag{27.40}$$

$$c_1 - c_0 = -3(d_1 - d_0)\,e^{-m\tau} \tag{27.41}$$

Define $e_0 = d_1 - d_0$. Since $a_0 = 1$, there are, then, only five unknown free parameters: $b_0, c_0, d_0, e_0$, and $m$:

The discount function (27.34) can be written as

$$d(t) = g_0(t) + I_{t \geq \tau}\,(g_1(t) - g_0(t))$$

where, as earlier, $I_{t \geq \tau}$ is the indicator function that takes on the value 1 if $t \geq \tau$ and 0 otherwise. Substituting for $g_0$ and $g_1$ and utilizing the restrictions derived above, we obtain the desired reduced-form of the discount function:

$$d(t) = a_0 + b_0\,(1 - e^{-mt}) + c_0\,(1 - e^{-2mt}) + d_0\,(1 - e^{-3mt}) \\ + e_0\,I_{t \geq \tau}\,(e^{-3m\tau} - 3e^{-m\tau - 2mt} - 3e^{-2m\tau - mt} - e^{-3mt}) \\ = 1 + b_0(1 - e^{-mt}) + c_0(1 - e^{-2mt}) + d_0(1 - e^{-3mt}) \\ + e_0 I_{t \geq \tau}\,(e^{-\tau} - e^{-t})^3 \tag{27.42}$$

Intuition suggests a further restriction that $\lim_{t \to \infty} d(t) = 0$ or

$$1 + b_0 + c_0 + d_0 + e_0 e^{-3\tau} = 0$$

We can impose this as an additional constraint on the parameters if we wish. In reduced notation, we can now rewrite (27.42) as

$$d(t) = 1 + b_0 Y_{1t} + c_0 Y_{2t} + d_0 Y_{3t} + e_0 Y_{4t} \tag{27.43}$$

where

$$Y_{1t} = (1 - e^{-mt})$$
$$Y_{2t} = (1 - e^{-2mt})$$
$$Y_{3t} = (1 - e^{-3mt})$$
$$Y_{4t} = I_{t \geq \tau} (e^{-\tau} - e^{-t})^3$$

## Estimating the Parameters

We use bond prices to extract the required parameter values. Consider a bond that has cash flows of $\xi_t$ at time $t$. Under the splined discount function, the theoretical price of such a bond is

$$\widehat{P} = \sum_t \xi_t \, d(t)$$
$$= \sum_t \xi_t \left[ 1 + b_0 Y_{1t} + c_0 Y_{2t} + d_0 Y_{3t} + e_0 Y_{4t} \right] \tag{27.44}$$

Rearranging, we obtain

$$\widehat{P} - \sum_t \xi_t = b_0 X_1 + c_0 X_2 + d_0 X_3 + e_0 X_4 \tag{27.45}$$

where

$$X_1 = \sum \xi_t Y_{1t}$$
$$X_2 = \sum \xi_t Y_{2t}$$
$$X_3 = \sum \xi_t Y_{3t}$$
$$X_4 = \sum \xi_t Y_{4t}$$

The estimation procedure with exponential splines is somewhat more complex than with polynomial splines on account of the additional parameter $m$. Since $m$ enters the pricing equations in a nonlinear way, simple regression techniques cannot be used. The following procedure may be employed as a solution:

- Fix a "reasonable" initial value of $m$. (Use the fact that $m = \lim_{t \to \infty} f(t)$ to get a ballpark initial value.)
- For any fixed value of $m$, the four free parameters $b_0$, $c_0$, $d_0$, and $e_0$ may be estimated by regressing $P - \sum \xi_t$ on $X_1$, $X_2$, $X_3$ and $X_4$.
- Optimize over the choice of $m$.

The criterion for optimizing over $m$ may be quite simple; for example, pick that $m$ for which the fit of the regression is high.

# Chapter 28

# Modeling Term-Structure Movements

## 28.1 Introduction

Modeling and pricing interest-rate derivatives requires us to first model the movements in the underlying driver, the yield curve. The earliest models of term-structure dynamics were developed in the mid- to late-1970s, but it was only in the 1980s that interest-rate modeling really took off. The succeeding decades have seen the development of a large number of models, and, importantly, different approaches to modeling itself.

In this context, this chapter has three immediate objectives. One is to discuss what exactly is different about term-structure modeling, in particular, what differentiates it from the modeling of stock price movements. As a corollary, this discussion will also highlight the kinds of features that are desirable in a good interest-rate model. Second, the chapter looks to lay the foundation for the detailed study of term-structure modeling under different approaches that occupy the next two chapters. To this end, we work our way through a simple example of a one-factor term-structure model in Section 28.4. Third, in Section 28.5, we introduce and discuss some of the terminology commonly used in this literature, such as the distinction between the "equilibrium" and "no-arbitrage" classes of term-structure models.

## 28.2 Interest-Rate Modeling versus Equity Modeling

To appreciate the differences between equity and term-structure modeling, it is instructive to begin with an examination of why the Black and Scholes (1973) model of stock price behavior, one of the most widely used models to represent equity and currency dynamics, is inadequate as a description of bond-price dynamics. Recall that the Black-Scholes model involves the following three critical assumptions (among others):

1. The price $S_t$ of the underlying security follows a lognormal distribution.
2. The interest-rate $r$ is known and constant.
3. The volatility $\sigma$ of the security's returns is constant.

Each of these assumptions is inconsistent with the requirements of a term-structure model. The assumption of a lognormal diffusion implies that the price of the underlying grows indefinitely over time on average. Bond prices, however, cannot grow indefinitely since they must revert to par at maturity. For a default-free bond, there are two points in time where its price is known with certainty: today and at maturity. The lognormal diffusion fails to capture this key feature.

Second, the assumption of a constant interest rate is obviously problematic, even paradoxical, in the context of an interest-rate derivatives model, especially if the derivatives we are looking to price are those like caps and floors, which are directly dependent on interest rates themselves. Constant interest rates are, of course, also inconsistent with bond prices being stochastic.

Third, the assumption that volatility is constant means that uncertainty in a stock's future price distribution grows with time. But since a bond's price must revert to par at maturity, the bond price *cannot* have constant volatility.

As this comparison suggests, term-structure modeling must be built on a different foundation from that of equities or currencies. Even the choice of the fundamental underlying variable is an open one. In practice, rather than model the behavior of bond prices directly (which would be the analog of modeling equity prices), it is far more popular to model the underlying drivers of bond prices—the interest-rate processes. This enables the pricing, hedging, and risk-management of various interest-rate and bond derivatives within a single encompassing framework. Modeling interest rates directly rather than bond prices has a number of advantages; interest rates can, for example, have constant volatilities.

But while modeling interest rates is more attractive than modeling bond prices directly, it also introduces some complications. One concerns the dimensionality of the pricing lattice. In modeling stock prices (or bond prices or exchange rates), we are modeling a single variable, but in modeling interest rates, we are modeling the entire yield curve. In discrete-time models, for instance, rather than a single price at each node, we have an entire vector of interest rates. This means extra care must be taken to keep the models internally consistent and free of arbitrage. In the next section, we describe a simple example of how inconsistency could arise in model specification.

## 28.3 Arbitrage Violations: A Simple Example

In modeling equity prices, we had only one variable—the stock price—to keep track of. In modeling interest rates, we have the entire yield curve, so there are as many variables as there are different maturities. To keep the resulting model of stochastic dynamics tractable, modelers typically assume there are only a small number of "factors" that influence all interest rates. These factors are also referred to as the model's *state variables*. We posit processes for the evolution of these factors over time and use this to derive term-structure movements.

The process sounds simple, yet care must be taken to ensure that the model remains arbitrage-free. In this section, we present a very simple example to illustrate how seemingly innocuous assumptions could lead to models that permit arbitrage.[1] The example combines two commonly used frameworks. The first is the approach of the binomial model; adapted here, it means that either the entire term structure moves "up" (all rates increase) or the entire term structure moves "down" (all rates decrease). This is a particular case of a one-factor model; a single underlying factor either increases all interest rates or decreases all of them. The second is the notion of a parallel shift in the yield curve. Parallel shifts in the yield curve are commonly assumed in risk management exercises such as computing the duration of a portfolio of bonds.

[1] Marti Subrahmanyam showed us this example.

**Example 28.1**

Time is discrete and periods are spaced one year apart. The yield curve consists of one-year, two-year, and three-year zero-coupon yields. The initial yield curve is given by

$$Z_0 = \begin{pmatrix} 0.10 \\ 0.11 \\ 0.12 \end{pmatrix}$$

After one year, if the yield curve registers an up move, all yields increase by 100 basis points, so the new yield curve is:

$$Z_u = \begin{pmatrix} 0.11 \\ 0.12 \\ 0.13 \end{pmatrix}$$

while if the yield curve moves down, all yields drop by 100 basis points:

$$Z_d = \begin{pmatrix} 0.09 \\ 0.10 \\ 0.11 \end{pmatrix}$$

We will show that this marriage of the binomial model to parallel yield-curve shifts results in an internally inconsistent model. Assume zero-coupon bonds have a face value of 100 and consider the following strategy. Buy a two-year zero-coupon bond (a two-year "zero") today. Finance this purchase by borrowing the required amount for one year at the one-year rate. At the end of one year, sell the two-year zero and repay the loan.

Under this strategy, there are no net cash flows at inception. After one year, the two-year zero has become a one-year zero. At this point, the one-year yield, according to the model, will be either 11% (if all interest rates have gone up) or 9% (if all interest rates have gone down). Thus, the price of the two-year zero at this point will be either

$$\frac{100}{1.11} = 90.10$$

or

$$\frac{100}{1.09} = 91.74$$

Now, the initial price of the two-year zero is

$$\frac{100}{1.11^2} = 81.16$$

Therefore, the amount borrowed at inception under the strategy is 81.16. This is a one-year borrowing and so takes place at the one-year rate of 10%. At the end of one year, the amount to be repaid is

$$81.16 \times 1.10 = 89.276$$

Since this is less than either possible price of the two-year zero at the end of one year (90.10 or 91.74), the strategy leads to a cash inflow at the end of one year with no outflows. That is, the model specification admits arbitrage. ∎

If even this simple model results in arbitrage, the question arises as to how we can define term-structure dynamics in an arbitrage-free manner in more general settings. We see this in more detail over the next two chapters but present in the next section a simple example of such an arbitrage-free development.

# 28.4 A Gentle Introduction to No-Arbitrage Modeling

In this section, we work through a simple discrete-time example to illustrate both term-structure modeling and option pricing in term-structure models. The example involves a one-factor model and a binomial structure: in each period, either all interest rates go up in response to the single factor, or all interest rates go down in response to the factor. As is the common practice in such models, we take the single factor to be the "short rate," i.e., the interest rate for the lowest maturity. (This is without any loss of generality. Since all rates move up or down together, changes in the rates are perfectly correlated over each time period. So any one of the rates may be taken to be representative of the driving factor.) Since we use a discrete-time framework, the short rate is the one-period rate. A principal objective of the exercise is to show how, from the movements in the short rate, the movements in bond prices of all maturities may be extracted in an arbitrage-free manner.

Thus, we take as given an initial yield curve and a description of the dynamics of the model's sole factor, the short rate. Using these inputs, we answer two questions: (a) How do we define the arbitrage-free evolution of the prices of bonds of different maturities? (b) How do we use the tree of bond prices to price options on bonds? The main question is, of course, the first one; the second is straightfoward once the trees have been constructed and the risk-neutral probabilities identified.

An unanswered question in this process is from where the short-rate dynamics come. There are many possible answers. The Vasicek and Cox-Ingersoll-Ross (CIR) models, discussed in the next chapter, posit specific continuous-time processes for the short rate, the former an Ornstein-Uhlenbeck process and the latter a square-root diffusion. In principle, the parameters of these processes may be estimated from historical data; alternatively, the parameters of the processes under the risk-neutral measure may be estimated from derivatives prices. The Black-Deman-Toy (BDT) model, also discussed in the next chapter, assumes a lognormal short-rate process and derives the risk-neutral short-rate process from the term structure of yield volatilities.

Here, we do not concern ourselves with this question. Rather, our objective is to explain the arbitrage-free derivation of movements in the yield curve from movements in the short rate. In a sense, the simple model presented here is complementary to the BDT model. In that model, as we will see, the probabilities of up and down moves are fixed, and the task is to determine the values of the short rate at the nodes in the binomial tree. Here, the values of the short rate in the tree are fixed and the objective is to determine the risk-neutral probabilities consistent with this short-rate tree.

## Input Information

We consider a three-year horizon. The time steps on our tree are also spaced one year apart.

We take the current term structure to be as follows: the yields on one-year, two-year, and three-year zero-coupon bonds are 10%, 11%, and 12%, respectively. Suppose also that the short-rate tree evolves according to the information provided in Figure 28.1. That is, one year from now, the one-year yield will be either 15% or 8.5%; and two years from now, the one-year yield will be either 18% or 15% (if the yield a year from now is 15%), or it will be either 15% or 6% (if the one-year yield a year from now is 8.5%).

We will use this input information to identify the arbitrage-free values of bond prices in the future. More precisely, we will construct

1. A tree of prices for a two-year zero-coupon bond with a face value of 100.

**FIGURE 28.1**

Interest-Rate Tree

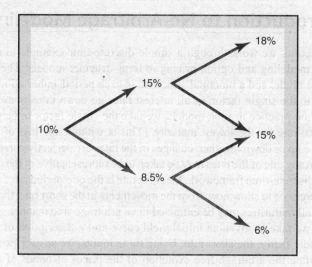

2. A tree of prices for a three-year zero-coupon bond with a face value of 100. From the prices of the three-year bond a year out, we know what the possible values are for the two-year rate a year from now.

We will also describe how to use these trees to value options and other derivatives and, in particular, how to compute risk-neutral probabilities. The arbitrage-free evolution of bond prices on the interest-rate tree implies a set of risk-neutral probabilities, which we will extract in our example. Once we have these probabilities, we will use them to price interest-rate options.

## The Two-Year Zero

Deriving the tree of values for a two-year zero in this model is simplicity itself. The initial price of the two-year zero is

$$\frac{100}{(1.11)^2} = 81.162$$

After one year, the two-year zero becomes a one-year zero. The possible one-year yields at this time are 15% and 8.5%. Therefore, the possible values of a two-year zero after one year are

$$\frac{100}{1.15} = 86.956 \quad \& \quad \frac{100}{1.085} = 92.165$$

The tree of values for a two-year zero is presented in Figure 28.2.

## Risk-Neutral Probabilities

The next step is to identify the model's risk-neutral probabilities. By definition, these probabilities must be such that the expected returns on all assets are the same. Thus, we must identify the probabilities of the up and down moves on the tree to ensure this condition.

In the model described, there are three "primitive" (as opposed to derivative) assets: the one-year, two-year, and three-year zeros. A one-year zero yields 10% in all circumstances. After one year, a two-year zero is worth either 86.956 (if the one-year rate moves to 15%) or 92.165 (if the one-year rate moves to 8.5%).

**FIGURE 28.2**

Bond-Price Tree for a
Two-Year Zero

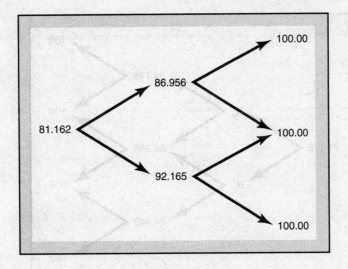

Therefore, the return from investing in a two-year zero for one year is either

$$\frac{86.956 - 81.162}{81.162} = 7.14\%$$

which obtains if there is an up move in the one-year rate (to 15%), or

$$\frac{92.165 - 81.162}{81.162} = 13.56\%$$

if the one-year rate moves down to 8.5%. Let $p_1$ be the risk-neutral probability of an up move in the one-year rate, so $(1 - p_1)$ is the risk-neutral probability of a down move in the one-year rate. Thus, the expected returns on the one- and two-year bonds are the same if and only if

$$p_1(0.0714) + (1 - p_1)(0.1356) = 0.10$$

Solving this equation yields

$$p_1 = 0.55$$

Thus, the risk-neutral probability of the one-year rate moving up in the first period is 0.55, so the risk-neutral probability of the rate moving down in the first period is 0.45.

## The Three-Year Zero

The initial price of a three-year zero is directly computed to be

$$\frac{100}{(1.12)^3} = 71.178$$

After two years, the three-year zero is a one-year zero. At this time, there are three values of the short rate: 18%, 15%, and 6%. The possible values of the three-year zero after two years are

$$\frac{100}{1.18} = 84.746, \quad \frac{100}{1.15} = 86.956, \quad \frac{100}{1.06} = 94.340$$

Thus, we obtain the following partial tree of prices for the three-year zero represented in Figure 28.3.

**FIGURE 28.3**
Three-Year Zero Tree

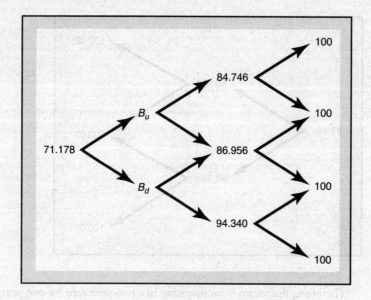

As shown in Figure 28.3, we denote the two unknown values of the three-year zero after one year by $B_u$ and $B_d$. Let $p_2$ denote the risk-neutral probability of an up move in the short rate after one year. That is, if the short rate after one year is 15%, $p_2$ is the risk-neutral probability it goes up to 18%, and $(1 - p_2)$ is the probability it remains at 15%. Similarly, if the short rate after one year is 8.5%, $p_2$ is the risk-neutral probability that it goes up to 15% while $(1 - p_2)$ is the risk-neutral probability it goes down to 6%.

Thus, the short-rate tree now has more periods and is depicted in Figure 28.4. We now describe how to solve for $B_u$, $B_d$, and $p_2$.

First, note that since (a) all bonds must yield the same return over the first year under the risk-neutral probability $p_1$, (b) $p_1 = 0.55$, and (c) the one-year bond yields 10%, we must have

$$(0.55)\left(\frac{B_u - 71.178}{71.178}\right) + (0.45)\left(\frac{B_d - 71.178}{71.178}\right) = 0.10 \qquad \textbf{(28.1)}$$

**FIGURE 28.4**
Short-Rate Tree with
Risk-Neutral
Probabilities

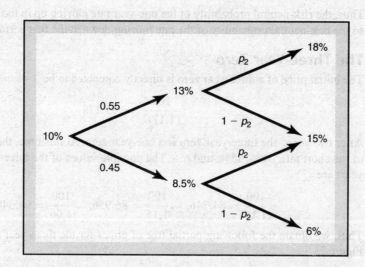

Next note that in the up state where the short rate is 13%, the three-year zero yields a return of either

$$\frac{84.746 - B_u}{B_u} \quad \text{or} \quad \frac{86.956 - B_u}{B_u}$$

Since the expected return (under the risk-neutral probability) on all bonds must be equal and a one-year zero yields 15%, we must have

$$(1 - p_2)\left(\frac{84.746 - B_u}{B_u}\right) + p_2\left(\frac{86.956 - B_u}{B_u}\right) = 0.15 \qquad \textbf{(28.2)}$$

Exactly the same argument applied to the down state (where the short rate is 8.5%) yields

$$(1 - p_2)\left(\frac{86.956 - B_d}{B_d}\right) + p_2\left(\frac{94.340 - B_d}{B_d}\right) = 0.085 \qquad \textbf{(28.3)}$$

Combining (28.1)–(28.3), a simple numerical search yields:

$$B_u = 74.502$$
$$B_d = 83.013$$
$$p_2 = 0.58$$

The tree of values for the three-year zero and the tree of risk-neutral probabilities are then depicted in Figures 28.5 and 28.6.

## Valuing Options: Examples

The basic set-up for the pricing of options is the tree with interest rates at each node and risk-neutral probabilities on each branch. On this tree, we may price interest-rate options. The tree may also be used to generate bond-price trees, which may then be used along with the risk-neutral probabilities to price bond options. The following examples illustrate the technique.

**FIGURE 28.5**

Three-Year Zero Tree

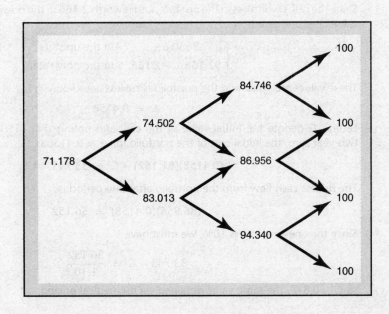

**FIGURE 28.6**
Short-Rate Tree with
Risk-Neutral
Probabilities

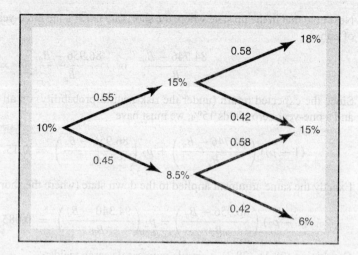

**Example 28.2**

Consider an option to buy a one-year zero for 90.00 one year from now. The asset underlying this option is a *two-year* zero since a two-year zero will become a one-year zero after one year. The values of a one-year zero a year from now will be either 86.956 (in the up state, where the short rate moves to 15%), or 92.166 (in the down state where the short rate moves to 8.5%). Therefore, the payoff from the option is zero in the up state, and is 2.166 in the down state.

Since the risk-neutral probability of the up state is 0.55, and the one-year rate is 10%, the value of the option is obtained by discounting its expected risk-neutral payoffs:

$$\frac{1}{1.10}[(0.55)(0) + (0.45)(2.166)] = 0.878$$

The same value for the option could also have been obtained by using replication or, equivalently, the riskless hedge portfolio method we examined in Chapter 11. Consider the following portfolio:

Short position in the option, position in $\Delta$ units of a two-year zero ($\Delta > 0$ implies long position, $\Delta < 0$ implies short position).

Since the call is worthless in the up state, and is worth 2.166 in the down state, the portfolio's value after one year is

$$\begin{cases} 86.956\Delta, & \text{in the up state} \\ 92.166\Delta - 2.166, & \text{in the down state} \end{cases}$$

These values are equal and the portfolio is riskless if and only if

$$\Delta = 0.4158$$

Letting C denote the initial value of the call, and noting that 81.162 is the cost of the two-year zero, the initial cost of the portfolio for $\Delta = 0.4158$ is

$$(0.4158)(81.162) - C = 33.743 - C$$

The riskless cash flow from the portfolio after one period is

$$(86.956)(0.4158) = 36.152$$

Since the one-year rate is 10%, we must have

$$33.743 - C = \frac{36.152}{1.10}$$

so C = 0.878, the same value obtained via risk-neutral pricing.

**Example 28.3**    Consider a European option to buy a one-year zero at the end of two years for 90.00.

The asset underlying this option is a *three*-year zero since a three-year zero will be a one-year zero after two years. From the tree of three-year zero prices, we see that the option's value at expiration is

- Zero if the short rate moves up twice.
- Zero if it moves up and then down, or down and then up.
- 4.340 if it moves down twice.

Let $C$ denote the initial value of this option, $C_u$ the option value if the short rate moves up in the first period, and $C_d$ the option value if the short rate moves down.

We identify $C_u$ first. Note that the short rate at this point is 15%. If the short rate moves up again in the second period, the option is worth zero, while if it moves down, the option is also worth zero. So, $C_u$ is obviously also 0.

Similar arguments yield:

$$C_d = \frac{1}{1.085}[(0.58)(0) + (0.42)(4.340)] = 1.686$$

Finally, since the risk-neutral probability in the first period is 0.55 and the short rate in the first period is 10%, we obtain:

$$C = \frac{1}{1.10}[(0.55)(0) + (0.45)(1.686)] = 0.683$$

∎

# 28.5   "No-Arbitrage" and "Equilibrium" Models

It is common in the term-structure literature to distinguish between the "no-arbitrage" class of term-structure models and the "equilibrium" class of models. This section discusses the origin of this terminology and its evolution, looking, in particular, at the distinction between the no-arbitrage and equilibrium *approaches* to term-structure modeling (as those terms were historically used) and the no-arbitrage and equilibrium *classes* of models (as those terms are currently used). The section concludes that the demarcation often made between the equilibrium and no-arbitrage classes of models is not really a useful or even meaningful one.[2]

## The No-Arbitrage Approach

Early models of the term-structure in finance (Vasicek (1977), Richard (1978), Brennan and Schwartz (1979), and others) followed Black and Scholes (1973) in adopting a "no-arbitrage" approach to modeling. Broadly speaking, the no-arbitrage approach works by (a) identifying portfolios of securities that are equivalent, (b) imposing the condition that their costs should be the same (or else arbitrage would result), and (c) deriving the consequences of this condition for security prices. For example, in the context of the Black-Scholes model, we construct a portfolio of the underlying stock and the risk-free asset that perfectly replicates the option being priced. Under no-arbitrage, the replicating portfolio and the option must have the same cost, and this leads to a partial differential equation (pde) that option prices must obey (see Section 15.3 for details). The option price is determined by solving this pde.

---

[2] The material of this section is taken from notes on term-structure modeling developed by the first author in the 1990s for his PhD class at NYU. Related discussions of this terminology also appear in Back (1996), Pelsser (2000), and elsewhere.

Section 29.4 explains the working of this approach in the context of term-structure modeling. Broadly, the procedure is the same: a comparison of portfolios is employed to obtain a pde that all bond prices must obey. For example, Vasicek (1977) studies a model in which a single factor drives all changes in the yield curve. This means (as in the one-factor example we presented earlier in this chapter) that any two bonds can be used to replicate a third bond. Using this observation, one may derive a restriction on the risk premia of bonds of different maturities; this is the so-called *market price of risk* associated with the model's single factor (see Appendix 29A for the technical details). From this comes the pde that must be obeyed by all bond prices. To solve the pde for bond prices, some assumption concerning the form of the market price of risk is necessary; in his paper, Vasicek takes it to be a constant. Once such an assumption has been made, the pde is solved to obtain the bond prices.

## The Equilibrium Approach

The no-arbitrage approach works through identifying *necessary* conditions for the absence of arbitrage, that is, conditions that are the consequence of assuming arbitrage is not present. But necessary conditions do not, in themselves, ensure that the models are internally consistent, i.e., that the prices obtained from the model are free of arbitrage.[3] For that, we need *sufficient* conditions, conditions whose satisfaction guarantees the absence of arbitrage. One such sufficient condition, as we saw in Section 11C, is that the model possess at least one risk-neutral measure.

Motivated by this shortcoming of the no-arbitrage approach (among other things), Cox, Ingersoll, and Ross (1985) proposed a different approach to term-structure modeling that was based on constructing a full dynamic general equilibrium model in which the prices of all assets in the model were simultaneously determined. Since a set of prices cannot represent an equilibrium if arbitrage is possible, their approach guaranteed the absence of arbitrage (that is, it was *sufficient* for no-arbitrage). To distinguish this from the no-arbitrage approach of Vasicek, Brennan and Schwartz, and others, and since it was based on construction of an underlying economic equilibrium, this was called the "equilibrium approach" to term-structure modeling.[4]

## No-Arbitrage versus Equilibrium Models

Somewhere in the mid-1980s and especially following the publication of the Ho and Lee (1986) paper (which is discussed in the next chapter), the use of the terms "no-arbitrage" and "equilibrium" began to change from characterizing approaches to term-structure modeling to characterizing groups of models with certain properties.

---

[3] Here is a simple example of a necessary condition whose satisfaction does not ensure the model is free of arbitrage. Consider the following situation. Suppose we have two risky stocks each following a binomial process (with parameters $(u_1, d_1)$ and $(u_2, d_2)$, respectively), and one riskless asset with return $1 + r$. Then, it is *necessary* for the absence of arbitrage that we have $d_i < 1 + r < u_i$ for $i = 1, 2$, or a trivial arbitrage arises between one of the risky assets and the riskless asset. But this is clearly not *sufficient*. As we saw in Appendix 11C, arbitrage will still exist in this setting as long as condition (11.22) identified there is not satisfied.

[4] Although this is not immediately apparent, the CIR equilibrium approach is equivalent to risk-neutral pricing. Harrison and Kreps (1979) and others have demonstrated in various contexts that if a system of prices is free of arbitrage, then it is an equilibrium for some specification of endowments and preferences, while conversely an equilibrium is always free of arbitrage. Thus, a model that does not permit arbitrage is exactly the same thing as an equilibrium model. Modulo some technical issues, the absence of arbitrage is equivalent to the existence of a risk-neutral measure, so the equilibrium approach and risk-neutral pricing are the same thing.

The Ho-Lee paper was the first paper to construct an arbitrage-free model of term-structure movements that was also consistent with any given initial term structure, i.e., whose model-implied bond prices agreed with the initial prices of these bonds for bonds of all maturities. This was significant because existing models of the term structure then were not capable of generating prices to match the entire yield curve. In the Vasicek model, for example, there are only four free model parameters: the long-run mean of the short rate $\theta$, the speed of reversion $\kappa$ to this long-run mean, the volatility $\sigma$ of the fluctuations in the short rate, and the market price of risk $\lambda$ associated with the model's single factor. With only four free parameters, the model can match the initial prices of only four bonds, or equivalently only four points on a given initial yield curve. For anyone using the model to trade, this is not a desirable feature: If the model does not price correctly even the current set of available bonds, any predictions about the future values of these bonds or estimates of the prices of options on these bonds must evidently be taken with a pinch of salt.

Following the publication of the Ho-Lee paper, a number of other papers followed that too exactly matched the given initial yield curve by construction. Such models came to be known as the class of no-arbitrage models. In contradistinction, models such as Vasicek, CIR, and others that did not match the entire initial yield curve were called equilibrium models.

From a conceptual standpoint, how important or meaningful is the distinction between equilibrium and no-arbitrage models? Here is a hint: if an equilibrium model such as Vasicek is capable of matching only four points on the yield curve because it has only four free parameters, and the Ho-Lee model is capable of matching the entire yield curve, then the Ho-Lee model must have a very large number of free parameters. This is, in fact, the case. No-arbitrage models "work" by adding a large number of free parameters to a given model, sufficiently many to be able to match any given initial yield curve. These parameters are typically added in the market price(s) of risk associated with the model's factor(s), although other parameters of the model may be made time dependent as well. A pair of examples, using two of the best-known members of the no-arbitrage class of models, the Ho-Lee and Hull-White models, will help illustrate this point. The examples use the continuous-time notation and terminology introduced in Chapter 15 (see especially Section 15.2).

---

**Example 28.4**  **The Merton and Ho-Lee Models**

An early model of the term structure was described in Merton (1973). In Merton's model, the process for the model's single factor, the short rate, evolves according to an arithmetic Brownian motion process as

$$dr_t = \alpha\, dt + \beta\, dW_t \qquad (28.4)$$

where $W_t$ is a Wiener process and $\alpha$ and $\beta$ are constants. If $\lambda$ denotes the market price of risk associated with the model's single factor, then it can be shown that the risk-neutral short-rate process in Merton's model[5] is given by

$$dr_t = (\alpha - \beta\lambda)\, dt + \beta\, d\widehat{W}_t \qquad (28.5)$$

where $\widehat{W}_t$ is a Wiener process under the risk-neutral measure. Suppose we take $\lambda$ to be a constant as in the Vasicek model. Then with only three free parameters ($\alpha$, $\beta$, and $\lambda$), we can match at most three points on a given arbitrary initial yield curve. This is the typical dilemma that equilibrium term-structure models face.

---

[5] See Section 29.4 for a general representation of the risk-neutral short-rate process in one-factor models.

The continuous-time version of the Ho-Lee model is also a single factor model with exactly the process (28.4) for the short rate. But rather than assuming that the market price of risk $\lambda$ is a constant, we assume that $\lambda$ is a deterministic function of time $\lambda_t$. The drift of $r_t$ under the risk-neutral measure now becomes $\alpha_t = \alpha - \beta\lambda_t$, so (28.5) is replaced by

$$dr_t = \alpha_t\, dt + \beta\, d\widehat{W}_t \qquad (28.6)$$

Equation (28.6) provides us with the extra requisite number of free parameters $\lambda_t$ to fit any given initial yield curve. Specifically, remember that the price of any security is the discounted expectation (under the risk-neutral measure) of its payoff. Therefore, the price of a zero-coupon bond that pays \$1 at time $t$ is simply $E[\beta_T \cdot 1]$, where $\beta_T$, the discount factor for horizon $T$, is given by

$$\beta_T = \exp\left\{-\int_0^T r_t\, dt\right\} \qquad (28.7)$$

Each $\beta_t$ depends on the values of $\lambda_s$, $0 \leq s \leq t$. By beginning at the lowest maturities and working our way up, we can identify the $\lambda_t$'s required to match the model implied prices to the actual prices.

Thus, the Ho-Lee model, which is a member of the no-arbitrage class of models, is identical to the Merton model, a member of the equilibrium class, except for the specifications concerning the market prices of risk. ∎

---

### Example 28.5    The Vasicek and Hull-White Models

The Vasicek model uses as its single factor a short-rate process that evolves according to the specification

$$dr_t = \kappa(\theta - r_t)\, dt + \sigma\, dW_t \qquad (28.8)$$

Here, $\theta$ is the long-run mean of the short-rate process. If $r_t < \theta$, then the drift of the short-rate process is positive and the short rate increases towards $\theta$; if $r_t > \theta$, then the drift of the short rate is negative and the short rate decreases towards $\theta$. The speed with which the rate reverts to its long-term mean is regulated by the parameter $\kappa$. (All subsequent factor models of the term structure follow Vasicek in using a mean-reverting drift term of this form.) The parameter $\sigma$ represents the noise in the evolution of the short-rate process.

When risk-neutralized, the market price of risk $\lambda$ enters the process. The risk-neutral short-rate process in the Vasicek model has the form

$$dr_t = (a - \kappa r_t)\, dt + \sigma\, d\widehat{W}_t \qquad (28.9)$$

where $a = \kappa\theta - \sigma\lambda$. If we assume $\lambda$ is a constant, then there are only four free parameters—$\kappa$, $\theta$, $\sigma$, and $\lambda$—with which to match the yield curve, so at most four points on the curve can be matched exactly.

Hull and White (1990) propose taking $\lambda$ to be a deterministic function of time, $\lambda_t$. This results in the risk-neutralized short-rate process having the form

$$dr_t = (a_t - \kappa r_t)\, dt + \sigma\, d\widehat{W}_t \qquad (28.10)$$

(Actually, Hull and White directly propose the risk-neutral process (28.10) but this follows from (28.8) only if the market price of risk is a deterministic function of time.) The model now has the requisite number of extra free parameters to fit any given initial yield curve; the $\lambda_t$'s that achieve this are identified precisely as explained in Example 28.4. ∎

As these two examples demonstrate, there is not really a useful distinction between no-arbitrage and equilibrium models of the term structure. Every equilibrium model has its no-arbitrage counterpart. In particular, that no-arbitrage models fit the term structure exactly is nothing more than the consequence of the fact that they use a very much larger set of free parameters, and does not indicate their superiority to equilibrium models. Finally, it should be noted that when no-arbitrage models are fit to a given initial yield curve each day, there is no reason to expect that the $\lambda_t$'s identified on one day will be the same the next day. That is, the model may change in inconsistent ways from one day to the next. This is an undoubted shortcoming of the no-arbitrage class of models but one that we must tolerate if we wish to fit yield curves exactly.

## 28.6 Summary

This chapter has sought to meet three objectives: (a) to discuss the extra subtleties that enter into interest rate modeling that are not present in modeling equity or currency derivatives, (b) to introduce term-structure modeling in the context of a simple one-factor example, and (c) to discuss some commonly-used terminology in this literature, such as the distinction between the equilibrium and no-arbitrage classes of models.

Regarding (b), the example we worked through in Section 28.4 took the movements in the short rate (the model's sole factor) as given and worked out the risk-neutral probabilities that were consistent with these movements. In practice, the alternative of fixing the risk-neutral probabilities and working out the drifts (and, therefore, future values of the short rate) that are consistent with these probabilities is more popular. We illustrate this alternative in the next chapter by studying two of the best-known discrete-time one-factor models: Ho and Lee (1986) and Black, Derman, and Toy (1990).

## 28.7 Exercises

1. Why is the Black-Scholes model inappropriate for pricing options on bonds?

2. You are given a two-period tree of zero-coupon interest rates with each period on the tree of half-year and a semiannual compounding convention applies in the model. Find the initial (at $t = 0$) yield-to-maturities for half- and one-year maturities if the current half-year spot rate is 6%. The half-year spot rate in a half-year is expected to be either 6.5% or 5.5% with equal probability. The one-year bond has a coupon of 6.3%.

3. In the previous question, find the initial curve of zero-coupon rates and of the forward rates for periods of one-half year and one year.

4. Given the tree of spot rates and probabilities, is it possible to find the entire tree of forward rates or is additional information required?

5. Explain why modeling the movement of the term structure is different than modeling the movement of equity prices.

6. You are a trader in a bond fund. The current yield curve is flat at 6%. Assume you decide to model the yield curve movement as a discrete annual process. Hence, at the end of one year, the yield curve moves up or down. Your in-house economist tells you that the yield curve will become either a flat 8% or a flat 3% with equal risk-neutral probabilities. Based on these numbers, just as you are about to make a trade, the young quant you hired to bring you sandwiches at lunch suddenly says that there is a huge problem with the economist's view. Is he right?

7. Is it possible that from some node on a binomial tree of interest rates the ensuing two nodes both have higher interest rates than the current node? Construct an example to show that this is possible or explain why it is impossible.

8. On a binomial tree of interest rates, the two-year zero-coupon bond after one year has prices 94.30 (up node) and 98.10 (down node). The one-year rate at $t = 0$ is 4%. If the one-year cap option (with a notional of $100) on the interest rate with a strike of 3% sells for $1, what is the price of the two-year zero-coupon bond? Assume simple annual compounding.

9. If the initial rate at any node at time $t$ on a binomial interest rate tree is $r_1$ and the two ensuing nodes after time $h = 1$ year are $r_u$ (with probability $p$) and $r_d$ (with probability $1 - p$), then given that the two-period zero-coupon rate is $r_2$, write down the analytic expression for the probability $p$ assuming simple compounding for each period.

10. The current one-year and two-year spot rates are 6% and 7%, respectively. Compounding is annual. The model you are using prescribes that in a risk-neutral setting, the next period's one-year interest rates will be either 8% or 5%. No risk-neutral probabilities are given. Does the modeling situation present an arbitrage? Why?

11. The initial spot rate curve (annual compounding) for three years is given as

$$0.060$$
$$0.065$$
$$0.070$$

After an assessment of volatilities and interest rate propagation in the future, your quant team provides the following tree of spot rates at times 0, 1, 2 years:

| 0.06 | 0.08 | 0.11 |
|------|------|------|
|      | 0.05 | 0.07 |
|      |      | 0.03 |

This means that from a starting rate of 6%, one-year spot rates will move up to 8% or down to 5%. From 8%, the move will be to 11% or 7%, etc.

What risk-neutral probabilities should be put on the tree so that the tree is free from arbitrage? You are given one restriction, i.e., the probability of an up move in rates may be different in each time period but is the same across all nodes in any given time period.

12. Based on the computations in the previous problem, what general scheme for computing risk-neutral probabilities at each period can you think of?

13. Can you explain what happens to the tree model in the previous two questions if we lift the restriction that $p_t$ must be the same at all nodes in time period $t$? This means that we do not require $p(t, j) = p_t$ for all nodes $j$. Does this result in an arbitrage violation?

14. You are given the following annual step, discrete-time interest rate tree, where all branches on the tree occur with probability of one-half.

| 0.04 | 0.06 | 0.08 |
|------|------|------|
|      | 0.03 | 0.05 |
|      |      | 0.01 |

Find the initial spot rate curve for three years.

15. A popular equilibrium model of interest rates is the Cox, Ingersoll, and Ross (1985) model:

$$dr_t = \kappa(\theta - r_t)\,dt + \sigma\sqrt{r_t}\,dZ_t$$

Answer the following questions:

(a) How many free parameters are available to fit the model to the term structure of interest rates?

(b) As a trader, would this model be suitable for yield curve arbitrage?

16. In the Cox, Ingersoll, and Ross (1985) model (see the previous question), what adjustment is required to make the model exactly fit the entire term structure of interest rates?

17. Can the mean-reversion rate $\kappa$ in an interest-rate model be

(a) Less than 0?

(b) Greater than 1?

# Chapter 29

# Factor Models of the Term Structure

## 29.1 Overview

This chapter has two parts to it that are largely independent of each other. The first part presents in some detail two discrete-time one-factor models of the term structure, expanding greatly on the example in Section 28.4. The second part describes general factor models of the term structure in a continuous-time setting, introducing as special cases of the setting the classic models of Vasicek (1977) and Cox, Ingersoll, and Ross (1985), among others.

Early models of the term structure were developed in continuous-time settings. Discrete-time tree-based models were first studied only in the mid-1980s. The two models that occupy the first part of this chapter are two of the earliest and best-known discrete-time models. The first is the "BDT model," the one-factor lognormal short-rate model developed by Black, Derman, and Toy (1990). The second is the model of Ho and Lee (1986), which was not just the first detailed tree-based interest-rate model but also the first representative of what came to be called the no-arbitrage class of models (to which BDT also belongs; see Section 28.5 for the definition of this class of models).

While the BDT and Ho-Lee models are of limited use in practice today, we provide detailed presentations of them for two reasons, both pedagogical. First, they illustrate well and in relatively simple contexts how factor models recursively build interest-rate trees in an arbitrage-free fashion. Second, they show how the risk-neutral pricing arguments introduced earlier in the book in the context of equity options are extended to term-structure models and the pricing of bond options. As with equity trees, the interest-rate trees we build in this chapter will be recombining binomial trees. Of course, dimensionality is an important difference between interest-rate trees and equity trees. Whereas the equity tree depicted the movement of a single stock price, in the case of interest rates, the entire term structure of interest rates is modeled on the tree.

Readers not interested in the mechanics of tree-construction may proceed directly to the second part of this chapter beginning with Section 29.4. This second part is more general and more technical, and focuses on a continuous-time setting. We begin by looking at general *one-factor* models and discuss solving for bond prices in these models using both a partial differential equation (pde) approach and a risk-neutral valuation approach. Closed-form solutions for specific models are also described here. Following this, we look at *multifactor* term-structure models. The chapter concludes with the important result of Duffie and Kan (1996) on *affine factor* models.

# 29.2 The Black-Derman-Toy Model

The BDT paper aims to develop an arbitrage-free interest-rate model that is consistent with the current term structure of interest rates and volatilities. The no-arbitrage condition is satisfied by showing the presence of a risk-neutral measure in the model. Indeed, the BDT model, like the Ho-Lee model, works directly in the risk-neutral world and develops the interest-rate tree under this measure. Since the developed tree is, by construction, consistent with a risk-neutral measure, arbitrage cannot exist. The challenge is to ensure the tree is consistent with the given term structure of rates and volatilities.

To this end, BDT posit a *single-factor, discrete-time* model of the interest-rate process. Since the model is driven by a single factor, all bond price movements are perfectly correlated over each period; in particular, all yields go up together or they all go down together. The model's single factor is identified with the short rate, as it is in virtually all one-factor models.

The short rate itself is assumed to follow a lognormal distribution on a binomial tree. If $\sigma$ denotes the volatility of the short rate at the current node in the binomial tree and if $r_u$ and $r_d$ denote the two possible values of the short rate one period hence, then the volatility is related to $r_u$ and $r_d$ by

$$\sigma = \frac{1}{2} \ln \left( \frac{r_u}{r_d} \right) \tag{29.1}$$

Why this particular form? Because if we assume that the probabilities of the up and down moves are each equal to 1/2 (as we shall in the risk-neutral world), then the standard deviation of the log of one-period-hence short rates is provided precisely by (29.1). We shall refer to (29.1) as the "volatility equation."

While reminiscent of the Cox-Ross-Rubinstein binomial model for equities, there is one important difference between the BDT lognormal short-rate model and the CRR lognormal model for equities. In the latter, volatility was constant over the tree. In the BDT model, the term structure of zero-coupon rates has a corresponding term structure of volatilities and short maturity rates may have different volatilities than longer maturity rates. Therefore, the branching process in the tree can differ from node to node. Of course, the lognormal assumption ensures that interest rates can never become negative.

The evolution of interest rates in the BDT binomial tree is determined using the current term structure of interest rates and volatilities as inputs in a manner described below.

## Building the Interest-Rate Tree: The Procedure

Under the risk-neutral probabilities, all assets must earn the same expected rate of return over each period, which is equal to the short rate over that period. We set the risk-neutral probability of an up move in the interest rate at any node to be equal to 1/2, and identify the tree of short rates that is consistent with these probabilities as well as the other input information on current rates and volatilities.

A recursive procedure is required to build up the pricing lattice in short rates. The maturity of this lattice extends to that of the longest underlying bond on which an option may be priced. Using the short-rate volatilities and the risk-neutral probabilities, a bootstrapping procedure is employed to recover the short rate tree. Specifically:

- The initial short rate $r$ and a two-year zero-coupon bond are used to determine the possible short rates $r_u$ and $r_d$ after one period.
- The rates $r$, $r_u$, and $r_d$ are used with a three-year zero-coupon bond to determine the possible short rates $r_{uu}$, $r_{ud}$, and $r_{dd}$ after two periods.

- Inductively, the procedure is completed with each step relying on all the previous steps and the price and yield volatility of an appropriate-maturity zero-coupon bond.

An important additional extra assumption that is used in this process is that volatilities depend on time but not on state. That is, the volatility at any node in a given time period is the same as at any other node in that same time period. The procedure is illustrated below in a numerical example that is taken from the original BDT paper.

## Building the Tree: An Example

We will illustrate the BDT procedure in a three period example in which each period represents one year. Consider the following data:

| Maturity (Years) | Zero-Coupon Rate (%) | Volatility (%) |
|---|---|---|
| 1 | 10 | 20 |
| 2 | 11 | 19 |
| 3 | 12 | 18 |

This data is the first three years of the five-year input data used in the original BDT paper. We use this data to construct the tree out to three years. Interest rates in the model are quoted in discrete terms with annual compounding.

As a first step, we use the zero-coupon rates to calculate the prices of zero-coupon bonds of various maturities. The current price of a one-year zero-coupon bond is

$$\frac{100}{1.10} = 90.909$$

The current price of a two-year zero is

$$\frac{100}{(1.11)^2} = 81.162$$

The current price of a three-year zero is

$$\frac{100}{(1.12)^3} = 71.178$$

The following notation is used to denote the evolution of the short rate: $r$ will denote the initial short rate; $r_u$ and $r_d$ will denote the possible values of the short rate one year hence and $r_{uu}$, $r_{ud}$, and $r_{dd}$ possible values of the short rate two years hence. We are given $r = 10\%$. The remaining values are to be identified.

## Step 1: Identifying $r_u$ and $r_d$

After one year, a two-year zero becomes a one-year zero. Its value at this time is the face value of 100 discounted back by the prevailing one-year rate at this point (which is either $r_u$ or $r_d$):

$$\frac{100}{1 + r_u} \quad \text{and} \quad \frac{100}{1 + r_d}$$

Therefore, the gross expected return (under the risk-neutral probabilities) from investing in a two-year zero for one year is

$$1 + \text{return} = \frac{1}{81.162}\left[\frac{1}{2}\left(\frac{100}{1+r_u}\right) + \frac{1}{2}\left(\frac{100}{1+r_d}\right)\right]$$

This must equal the one-year risk-free rate of 10%, so:

$$1.10 = \frac{1}{81.162}\left[\frac{1}{2}\left(\frac{100}{1+r_u}\right) + \frac{1}{2}\left(\frac{100}{1+r_d}\right)\right]$$

This is one equation in the two unknowns $r_u$ and $r_d$. A second equation is required. For this, we use the information given that the two-year yield volatility is 19%. A two-year zero is a one-year zero after one year. At this point, its yield is either $r_u$ or $r_d$. Therefore, its yield volatility is $\frac{1}{2}\ln(r_u/r_d)$, and we obtain as our second equation:

$$\frac{1}{2}\ln\left(\frac{r_u}{r_d}\right) = 0.19$$

Solving the two equations, we obtain

$$r_u = 14.32\% \quad \text{and} \quad r_d = 9.79\%$$

## Step 2: Identifying $r_{uu}$, $r_{ud}$, and $r_{dd}$

In the second step, we use $r$, $r_u$, and $r_d$ with a three-year zero-coupon bond to identify $r_{uu}$, $r_{ud}$, and $r_{dd}$. As a first step, we compute the value of the three-year bond after two years. At this point, the three-year zero has become a one-year zero, so its possible values are

$$B_{uu} = \frac{100}{1+r_{uu}}$$

$$B_{ud} = \frac{100}{1+r_{ud}}$$

$$B_{dd} = \frac{100}{1+r_{dd}}$$

A year before this, the original three-year zero was a two-year zero. Let $B_u$ and $B_d$ denote its two possible values at this stage. From the risk-neutral pricing principle, these values are the discounted expectation of its future values, so:

$$B_u = \frac{1}{1+r_u}\left(\frac{1}{2}B_{uu} + \frac{1}{2}B_{ud}\right)$$

$$B_d = \frac{1}{1+r_d}\left(\frac{1}{2}B_{ud} + \frac{1}{2}B_{dd}\right)$$

Taking expectations of these values under the risk-neutral probability and discounting back at the risk-free rate of 10%, we should obtain the initial price of the three-year zero:

$$71.178 = \frac{1}{1.10}\left[\frac{1}{2}B_u + \frac{1}{2}B_d\right]$$

We can now substitute (a) first for $B_u$ and $B_d$ in terms of $B_{uu}$, $B_{ud}$, and $B_{dd}$ from the earlier expressions, and then (b) for $B_{uu}$, $B_{ud}$, and $B_{dd}$ in terms of $r_{uu}$, $r_{ud}$, and $r_{dd}$, to obtain a single (large and unwieldy) expression involving the three unknowns $r_{uu}$, $r_{ud}$, and $r_{dd}$:

$$71.178 = \frac{1}{1.10} \left\{ \frac{1}{2} \left[ \frac{1}{2} \left( \frac{1}{2} \cdot \frac{100}{1+r_{uu}} + \frac{1}{2} \cdot \frac{100}{1+r_{ud}} \right) \right] \right.$$

$$\left. + \frac{1}{2} \left[ \frac{1}{2} \left( \frac{1}{2} \cdot \frac{100}{1+r_{ud}} + \frac{1}{2} \cdot \frac{100}{1+r_{dd}} \right) \right] \right\}$$

We need two more equations to identify the three unknowns. For a second equation, we appeal again to the volatility equation. Consider the three-year zero again. If state $u$ occurs after one period, the three-year zero is worth $B_u$. At maturity, it is worth 100. Therefore, the yield of the three-year zero in state $u$ will be

$$y_u = \left[ \sqrt{(100/B_u)} \right] - 1$$

The square root is used since there are still two periods remaining on the three-year bond at this point.

Similarly, the yield of the three-year zero in state $d$ is

$$y_d = \left[ \sqrt{(100/B_d)} \right] - 1$$

Since the current volatility of the three-year yield is given to be 0.18, we obtain our second equation:

$$\frac{1}{2} \ln \left( \frac{y_u}{y_d} \right) = 0.18$$

Finally, recall the assumption that the volatility of the short rate can at most depend on time. This means we must have

$$\frac{1}{2} \ln \left( \frac{r_{uu}}{r_{ud}} \right) = \frac{1}{2} \ln \left( \frac{r_{ud}}{r_{dd}} \right)$$

This provides us with our final equation in the three unknowns:

$$(r_{ud})^2 = r_{dd} \cdot r_{uu}$$

Solving these equations, we finally obtain

$$r_{uu} = 19.42\%$$

$$r_{ud} = 13.77\%$$

$$r_{dd} = 9.76\%$$

Summing up, we have the interest-rate tree in Figure 29.1.

## Bond Price Trees

The evolution of the prices of bonds of different maturities may be easily obtained from the tree of short rates. Figure 29.2 presents the price tree for the one-year zero-coupon bond. Figures 29.3 and 29.4 present the price trees for the two-year and three-year zero-coupon bonds, respectively.

**FIGURE 29.1**
The Interest-Rate Tree
in the BDT Model

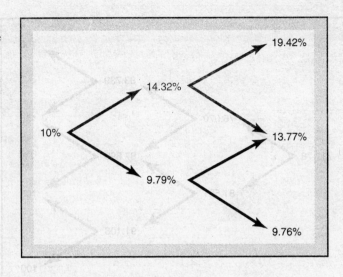

**FIGURE 29.2**
Price Tree for the
One-Year
Zero-Coupon Bond

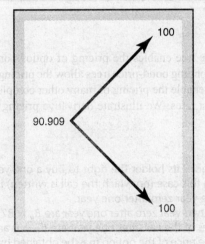

**FIGURE 29.3**
Price Tree for the
Two-Year
Zero-Coupon Bond

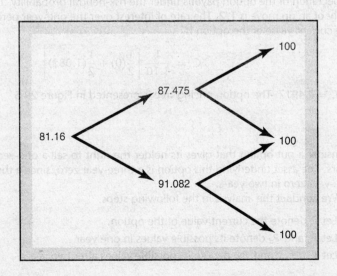

**FIGURE 29.4**
Price Tree for the
Three-Year
Zero-Coupon Bond

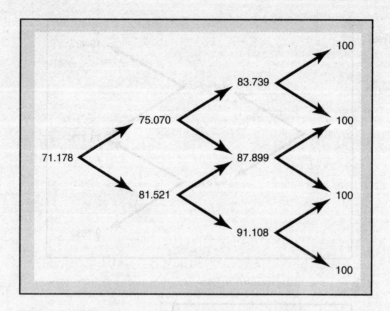

## Pricing Options

Establishing the interest-rate tree enables the pricing of options on interest rates such as caps and floors. The corresponding bond-price trees allow the pricing of call and put options on bonds. Both sets of trees enable the pricing of many other complex derivatives based on the term structure of interest rates. We illustrate derivative pricing on the tree with some simple examples.

**Example 29.1**

Consider a call option that gives its holder the right to buy a one-year zero in one year for $90. The underlying asset in this case (on which the call is written) is a two-year zero since a two-year zero will be a one-year zero after one year.

The possible prices of the two-year zero after one year are $B_u = 87.475$ and $B_d = 91.082$. Therefore, the possible values of the call after one year are $C_u = 0$ and $C_d = 1.082$.

As usual, the arbitrage-free price of the option may be obtained by taking the discounted expectation of the option payoffs under the risk-neutral probability. The risk-neutral probability of an up move is 1/2. The rate of interest over the one-year period is 10%. Therefore, the current value of the option is

$$C = \frac{1}{1.10}\left[\frac{1}{2}(0) + \frac{1}{2}(1.082)\right]$$

or $C = 0.4917$. The option pricing tree is presented in Figure 29.5.   ∎

**Example 29.2**

Consider a put option that gives its holder the right to sell a one-year zero for $90 in two years. The asset underlying this option is a three-year zero, since a three-year zero will be a one-year zero in two years.

We conduct the analysis in the following steps.

- Let $P$ denote the current value of the option.
- Let $P_u$ and $P_d$ denote its possible values in one year.
- Let $P_{uu}$, $P_{ud}$, and $P_{dd}$ denote its possible values after two years.

**FIGURE 29.5**

Pricing Tree for a
Bond Call Option

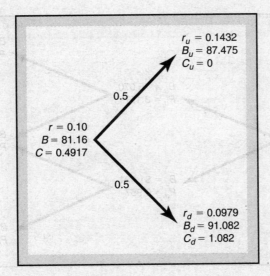

$r_u = 0.1432$
$B_u = 87.475$
$C_u = 0$

$r = 0.10$
$B = 81.16$
$C = 0.4917$

0.5

0.5

$r_d = 0.0979$
$B_d = 91.082$
$C_d = 1.082$

After two years, the possible prices of the three-year zero are

$$B_{uu} = 83.739$$
$$B_{ud} = 87.899$$
$$B_{dd} = 91.108$$

Therefore, the option values at the end of two years are

$$P_{uu} = 6.261$$
$$P_{ud} = 2.101$$
$$P_{dd} = 0.0$$

By the usual risk-neutral pricing arguments, we must have

$$P_u = \frac{1}{r_u}\left[\frac{1}{2}P_{uu} + \frac{1}{2}P_{ud}\right]$$

$$P_d = \frac{1}{r_d}\left[\frac{1}{2}P_{ud} + \frac{1}{2}P_{dd}\right]$$

Substituting for $r_u$, $r_d$, $P_{uu}$, $P_{ud}$, and $P_{dd}$, we obtain

$$P_u = 3.157 \quad P_d = 0.957$$

Finally, we must also have

$$P = \frac{1}{r}\left[\frac{1}{2}P_u + \frac{1}{2}P_d\right]$$

Substituting for $r$, $P_u$, and $P_d$, we finally obtain

$$P = 1.435$$

The pricing tree for this put option is depicted in Figure 29.6.

**FIGURE 29.6**

Pricing Tree for a Put
Option on a Bond

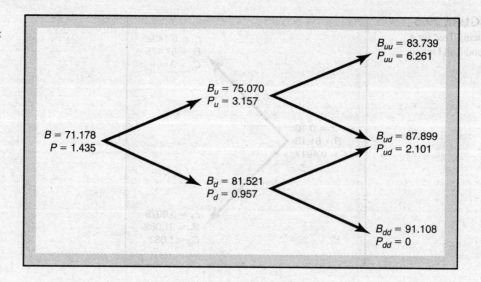

$B = 71.178$
$P = 1.435$

$B_u = 75.070$
$P_u = 3.157$

$B_d = 81.521$
$P_d = 0.957$

$B_{uu} = 83.739$
$P_{uu} = 6.261$

$B_{ud} = 87.899$
$P_{ud} = 2.101$

$B_{dd} = 91.108$
$P_{dd} = 0$

**Example 29.3**

Many bonds in the marketplace are callable at the option of the issuer. These bonds are usually coupon paying as well. For this third example in the BDT setting, we consider a three-year bond with a coupon rate of 10%. Let's say that this bond is callable at the end of the second year at par, i.e., the issuer can repay the bond at a price of 100.

In order to price this callable bond, we need to overlay its prices on the interest-rate tree, previously depicted in Figure 29.1. We begin by generating the pricing tree for the noncallable coupon bond, and subsequently, we modify it for the call feature. At the end of three years, the cash flow on this bond is 110, which is the principal plus the coupon. Therefore, we may write:

$$B_{uuu} = B_{uud} = B_{udd} = B_{ddd} = 110$$

Using the rates on the tree, we can obtain the prices of this bond at the end of year two. As before, we discount the expected future value of the bond (based on the risk-neutral probabilities) using the three interest rates that may transpire at the end of two years. The calculations are as follows:

$$B_{uu} = \frac{1}{1.1942}\left[\frac{1}{2}100 + \frac{1}{2}100 + 10\right] = 92.113$$

$$B_{ud} = \frac{1}{1.1377}\left[\frac{1}{2}100 + \frac{1}{2}100 + 10\right] = 96.689$$

$$B_{dd} = \frac{1}{1.0976}\left[\frac{1}{2}100 + \frac{1}{2}100 + 10\right] = 100.219$$

Note that the pricing equation accounted for the principal and the interest received at the end of the third year.

These three prices depict the values of the bond *before* the receipt of the coupon interest at the end of year two. In order to compute the bond prices at the end of year one, we add the coupon interest to these prices before discounting their value back to the previous period. At the end of year one, the bond may take two values:

$$B_u = \frac{1}{1.1432}\left[\frac{1}{2}92.113 + \frac{1}{2}96.689 + 10\right] = 91.325$$

$$B_d = \frac{1}{1.0979}\left[\frac{1}{2}96.689 + \frac{1}{2}100.219 + 10\right] = 98.782$$

**FIGURE 29.7**

Price Tree for a
Noncallable Coupon
Bond

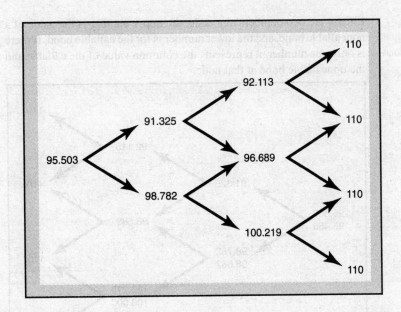

Again, notice that the coupon is added to the expected cash flow before discounting. Finally, these values may be discounted back to the start of the tree, i.e.,

$$B = \frac{1}{1.10}\left[\frac{1}{2}\,91.242 + \frac{1}{2}\,98.864 + 10\right] = 95.503$$

The tree for this bond is presented in Figure 29.7.

Note that this coupon bond does not trade at par even though at inception, the coupon rate equals the short rate. This is because the interest-rate tree tends to be skewed upwards over time, resulting in a discounting of the bonds' cash flows at rates higher than the coupon rate. The upward bias in interest rates comes from the lognormal assumption of the BDT model; unlike most other one-factor models, the BDT model does not impose mean reversion on the drift term of the short rate.

In order to price the bond with the call strike price at par (ex-coupon), we examine the tree period by period and ascertain at which nodes the price of the bond is greater than 100. By ex-coupon strike, we mean that the price of the bond *without* the current coupon is compared to the strike price of the call. It is at these nodes that the issuer will call the bond. From Figure 29.7, it is clear that these nodes reside at the lower end of the tree where bond prices are highest because interest rates are low. In this example, at the end of two years, there is only one tree node at which the bond trades above par, i.e., at $B_{dd} = 100.219$. Since the issuer will call the bond at this node, we reset the value of this node to 100.

We then proceed to discount prices back to the end of year one in the usual way. The price in the upper node at the end of the first year remains at $B_u = 91.325$, but the price in the lower node changes to $B_d = 98.682$, which is lower than that of the noncallable bond since the investor conceded some value to the issuer on account of the call feature. Finally, the price of the bond at the beginning of the tree also changes to be:

$$B = \frac{1}{1.10}\left[\frac{1}{2}\,91.325 + \frac{1}{2}\,98.682 + 10\right] = 95.458$$

The price tree for the callable bond is presented in Figure 29.8. If there are two numbers at a node, the number at the top is the old number before allowing for callability, and the lower number is the one after permitting callability.

The difference in price between the noncallable bond and the callable one represents the value of the call feature. Subtraction tells us that this is worth $95.503 - 95.458 = 0.045$. ∎

**FIGURE 29.8**
Price Tree for the
Callable Coupon Bond

If there are two numbers at a node, the upper number is the value of a noncallable bond, and the lower number is for the callable bond. If there is only one number, it represents the common value of the callable and the noncallable bond at that node.

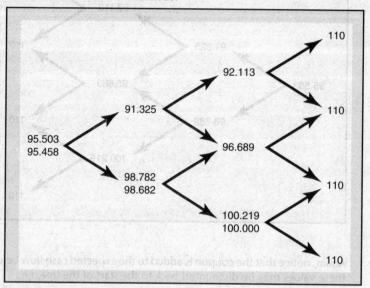

## 29.3 The Ho-Lee Model

The Ho-Lee model was among the earliest models developed for the pricing of bond options using tree methods. We present the Ho-Lee tree-building algorithm here. Our exposition follows the original paper as closely as possible yet is kept simple by avoiding excessive notation and retaining a partiality towards a numerical exposition. The development of the model is a little more complex than that of BDT; hence, our decision to present it after the BDT model even though this reverses the chronological order of the papers.

Ho and Lee (1986) called their model an "AR" model, which stands for "arbitrage-free rates" model. This initiated the class of no-arbitrage models of the term structure. We refer to the Ho-Lee model in this section as the HL model.

Rather than construct a tree of zero-coupon rates as in the BDT model, the HL approach directly models zero-coupon bond prices on the tree. Compared to the BDT model, this is quite parsimonious. Whereas the BDT model requires computation of zero-coupon bond prices on the tree as intermediate steps to the tree of zero-coupon rates, the HL model uses these discount bonds as the primitives themselves.

We develop the exposition of the model using the same data as in the previous sections and work with a three-period model. The table of zero-coupon interest rates and discount bond prices is as follows.

| T | Zero-Coupon Rates | Discount Bond Prices |
|---|---|---|
| 1 | 0.10 | 0.9091 |
| 2 | 0.11 | 0.8116 |
| 3 | 0.12 | 0.7118 |

HL described their recombining binomial tree of discount bonds using the variable $P_i^n(T)$ where $n$ denotes the time period on the tree, $i$ depicts the node on the tree at time $n$, and

$T$ the remaining maturity of the discount bond $P$ at time $n$. We clarify this notation using the prices from the table above as an example. The current time is $n = 0$. Since there is only one node at time 0, there is but one state, and $i = 0$ (numbering in the HL model was chosen to begin at 0). Finally, there are three bonds, and hence, $T = \{1, 2, 3\}$. Therefore, the initial node on the tree comprises a vector of discount bond prices that are as follows:

$$P_0^0(1) = 0.9091$$
$$P_0^0(2) = 0.8116$$
$$P_0^0(3) = 0.7118$$

We write this vector as $P_0^0(.)$.

At the end of the first period on the tree, i.e., at time $n = 1$, there will be two nodes on the tree. These two nodes comprise zero-coupon bond prices for the remaining two maturities. We may write the node values in the up state as follows:

$$P_1^1(1)$$
$$P_1^1(2)$$

and in the down state we have

$$P_0^1(1)$$
$$P_0^1(2)$$

Indeed, in general, the bifurcation from any vector $P_i^n(.)$ comprising a node on the tree may be represented in an evolution to two other vectors, an up node $P_{i+1}^{n+1}(.)$ and a down node $P_i^{n+1}(.)$. It is obvious by now that each node on the tree is indexed by $(n, i)$, i.e., by the time period $n$ and the state $i$ in each period.

As in any tree model, we may assign probabilities to the upshift on the tree and to the downshift on the tree. In the HL model, the up move occurs with probability $\pi$, and the down move with probability $(1 - \pi)$. These probabilities are held to be constant across the entire tree, and in our numerical example, we set $\pi = 0.5$.

Next the lattice upshifts and downshifts need to be imposed, and the extent of divergence between the up and down moves reflects the volatility in the model. We multiply each element of the current zero-coupon price curve by an upshift "perturbation" function denoted $h(T)$, i.e., a vector of values for each maturity. The downshift perturbation is denoted $h^*(T)$. Since we wish to have positive interest rates in the model, it is necessary that $h(T) > 0$, and $h^*(T) > 0$. The relative difference in these two values is a function of the volatility of the term structure.

Suppose we are at time $n$ on the tree and in state $i$. Also assume that the interest rate volatility is zero. Then the up and down nodes in the next period will coincide, and the perturbation functions will be equal, i.e., $h(T) = h^*(T)$ for all $T$. In this case, the zero-coupon bond prices in the next period $(n+1)$ are simply the forward prices of the bonds, i.e.,

$$P_{i+1}^{n+1}(T) = P_i^{n+1}(T) = \frac{P_i^n(T + 1)}{P_i^n(1)}$$

But if volatility is positive, then the prices in the up and down nodes will be perturbed values of the forward price: for all $T$, we have

$$P_{i+1}^{n+1}(T) = \frac{P_i^n(T + 1)}{P_i^n(1)} \, h(T) \qquad \text{(29.2)}$$

$$P_i^{n+1}(T) = \frac{P_i^n(T + 1)}{P_i^n(1)} \, h^*(T) \qquad \text{(29.3)}$$

We have not stated as yet what the perturbation functions look like, but they must be chosen such that the expected discounted value on the tree equals current prices, i.e.,

$$P_i^n(T) = P_i^n(1)[\pi P_{i+1}^{n+1}(T-1) + (1-\pi)P_i^{n+1}(T-1)]$$

or, after simplification,

$$\pi h(T) + (1-\pi)h^*(T) = 1$$

HL show that this implies a particular functional form for the perturbation function with an additional parameter $\delta$:

$$h(T) = \frac{1}{\pi + (1-\pi)\delta^T}$$

$$h^*(T) = \frac{\delta^T}{\pi + (1-\pi)\delta^T}, \quad T \geq 0$$

The parameter used to tune the volatility is denoted $\delta < 1$. It is easy to see that as $\delta$ decreases, the divergence between $h(T)$ and $h^*(T)$ widens, i.e., volatility increases.

We now take these simple equations into account while developing our numerical example. We have already set $\pi = 0.5$. We now also specify the volatility by setting $\delta = 0.98$. This makes it straightforward to compute the perturbation functions, which are purely functions of $\pi$ and $\delta$. First we compute $h(T)$.

$$h(1) = \frac{1}{0.5 + (0.5)(0.98)} = 1.010101$$

$$h(2) = \frac{1}{0.5 + (0.5)(0.98^2)} = 1.020200$$

$$h(3) = \frac{1}{0.5 + (0.5)(0.98^3)} = 1.030295$$

Likewise, we compute $h^*(T)$.

$$h^*(1) = \frac{0.98}{0.5 + (0.5)(0.98)} = 0.989899$$

$$h^*(2) = \frac{0.98^2}{0.5 + (0.5)(0.98^2)} = 0.979800$$

$$h^*(3) = \frac{0.98^3}{0.5 + (0.5)(0.98^3)} = 0.969705$$

We note that since these remain the same across the tree, recombination is facilitated. Armed with $h(T)$ and $h^*(T)$, we may obtain the values of the price vectors in the next period as follows. First, we compute the up node using equation (29.2).

$$P_1^1(1) = \frac{P_0^0(2)}{P_0^0(1)}h(1) = 0.901803$$

$$P_1^1(2) = \frac{P_0^0(3)}{P_0^0(1)}h(2) = 0.798774$$

Next we compute the down node using equation (29.3).

$$P_0^1(1) = \frac{P_0^0(2)}{P_0^0(1)}h^*(1) = 0.883767$$

$$P_0^1(2) = \frac{P_0^0(3)}{P_0^0(1)}h^*(2) = 0.767143$$

This leaves the final period on the tree for which we need prices that reside at the end of period 2, i.e., $n = 2$. These are obtained from similar calculations that we had before and are done for all three nodes of the tree at the end of period 2. At each of these three nodes, there is only one remaining zero-coupon bond price for the last period on the tree. We compute each of these here.

$$P_2^2(1) = \frac{P_1^1(2)}{P_1^1(1)}h(1) = 0.894699$$

$$P_1^2(1) = \frac{P_1^1(2)}{P_1^1(1)}h^*(1)$$

$$= \frac{P_0^1(2)}{P_0^1(1)}h(1) = 0.876806$$

$$P_0^2(1) = \frac{P_0^1(2)}{P_0^1(1)}h^*(1) = 0.859269$$

We can see that the middle node may be computed either as being reached by a downward branch from $P_1^1(.)$ or via an upward branch from $P_0^1(.)$. This confirms the recombination of the tree. The complete tree is presented in Figure 29.9.

As a final check on the procedure enunciated above, we reprice the two- and three-year zero-coupon bonds on the HL lattice. At the end of two years the two-year zero-coupon bond pays 100. We discount this back to the time point at the end of one year where there are two nodes, using the one-year discount price available at the two nodes at the end of one year.

$$100 \times 0.901803 = 90.1803$$

$$100 \times 0.883767 = 88.3767$$

**FIGURE 29.9**
The Ho-Lee Tree

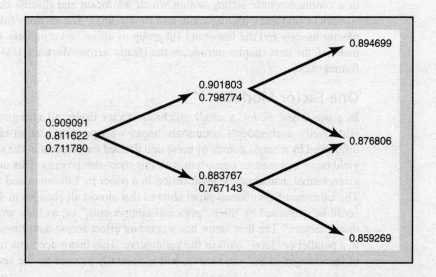

Finally, the current price of this bond will be obtained by taking the expected value of the two prices above and discounting them back to time zero.

$$\left[\frac{1}{2}90.1803 + \frac{1}{2}88.3767\right] \times 0.909091 = 81.1622$$

which coincides exactly (as it should) with the price computed earlier.

We also reprice the three-year zero-coupon bond on the lattice. We first obtain its three possible values at the end of two years by discounting the face value from maturity, i.e., 100 back to time 2. These prices are calculated as follows:

$$100 \times 0.894699 = 89.4699$$
$$100 \times 0.876806 = 87.6806$$
$$100 \times 0.859269 = 85.9269$$

From these prices, we compute the two prices at the end of one year.

$$\left[\frac{1}{2}89.4699 + \frac{1}{2}87.6806\right] \times 0.901803 = 79.8774$$

$$\left[\frac{1}{2}87.6806 + \frac{1}{2}85.9269\right] \times 0.883767 = 76.7143$$

The price at time zero then is

$$\left[\frac{1}{2}79.8774 + \frac{1}{2}76.7143\right] \times 0.909091 = 71.1780$$

Any other payoff patterns may be priced in exactly the same way. Options and other derivatives written as a function of interest rates may be easily and directly priced using this tree.

# 29.4 One-Factor Models in Continuous Time

The Ho-Lee and BDT models are two examples of the broader class of one-factor models. In this section, we provide an introduction to the general family of one-factor models in a continuous-time setting within which we locate and discuss the classic models of Vasicek (1977) and Cox, Ingersoll, and Ross (1985). The sections following discuss multifactor models and the important subgroup of affine factor models. Complementing this material, the next chapter introduces the Heath-Jarrow-Morton (HJM) and Market Model frameworks.

## One-Factor Models

In a *one-factor model*, a single stochastic factor drives all changes in the yield curve. Historically, such models commonly began with positing a short-rate process that was influenced by a single source of noise and derived movements in the remaining part of the yield curve in a manner consistent with this short-rate process. This modeling process was given formal mathematical justification in a paper by Litterman and Scheinkman (1991). The Litterman-Scheinkman paper showed that almost all changes in Treasury bond yields could be explained by three "principal components," or, as they are commonly termed, three "factors." The first factor has a constant effect across maturities and so corresponds to a parallel or "level" shift in the yield curve. This factor accounts for around 80%–90% of the changes in the yield curve, and is naturally proxied by the short rate. The second factor's effect increases monotonically with maturity, so corresponds to a "slope" factor that affects the steepness of the yield curve. This factor accounts for about 80% of the variation unexplained by the first factor. The third factor corresponds to a convexity or "curvature" effect that explains a further 2%–3% of yield curve variations.

Consider a continuous-time setting. A general one-factor model is one in which the short rate $r_t$ (i.e., the rate on an instantly-maturing bond) evolves according to the process

$$dr_t = \alpha(t, r_t)\, dt + \beta(t, r_t)\, dW_t \qquad (29.4)$$

where $\alpha(\cdot)$ and $\beta(\cdot)$ denote, respectively, the drift and diffusion component of the short rate, and $W_t$ is a standard Brownian motion process. Three special cases of (29.4) of interest are the Merton/Ho-Lee, Vasicek, and CIR models.

## The Merton/Ho-Lee Model

The Merton (1973) model, which is also the continuous-time limit of the Ho-Lee model described earlier in this chapter, uses

$$\alpha(t, r_t) = \bar{\alpha} \qquad \beta(t, r_t) = \bar{\beta} \qquad (29.5)$$

where $\bar{\alpha}$ and $\bar{\beta}$ are positive constants. This model is mostly of historical interest. Short rates in the model follow an arithmetic Brownian motion process, so carry unreasonable implications. They can drift off to arbitrarily high values and can become negative.

## The Vasicek Model

Vasicek (1977), the first detailed no-arbitrage modeling in finance of the term structure of interest rates, introduces the Ornstein-Uhlenbeck or O-U process for representing changes in the short rate. In the O-U process, the terms $\alpha(\cdot)$ and $\beta(\cdot)$ are given by

$$\alpha(t, r_t) = \kappa(\theta - r_t) \qquad \beta(t, r_t) = \bar{\beta} \qquad (29.6)$$

where $\kappa$, $\theta$, and $\bar{\beta}$ are all positive constants. This is now simply called the "Vasicek model" in the finance literature.

The drift term $\kappa(\theta - r_t)$ in the Vasicek model exhibits *mean reversion*. If the current rate $r_t$ is greater than its long-term mean $\theta$, then the drift is negative and the rate is pulled down towards $\theta$. If $r_t < \theta$, then the drift is positive and the rate is pulled up towards $\theta$. The constant $\kappa$ controls the rate at which reversion to the mean occurs. A large $\kappa$ means that reversion is rapid. Mean reversion is a common requirement imposed in modern term-structure models.

The diffusion component in the Vasicek model is a constant $\bar{\beta}$. This implies short rates have a Gaussian (i.e., normal) distribution with mean and variance given by

$$E[r_t \mid r_0] = \theta + e^{-\kappa t}(r_0 - \theta)$$

$$\mathrm{Var}(r_t \mid r_0) = \frac{1}{2\kappa} \bar{\beta}^2 (1 - e^{-2\kappa t})$$

As in Merton/Ho-Lee, the Gaussian implication means short rates can become negative. The constant $\bar{\beta}$ assumption is also in conflict with the casual observation that rates tend to become more volatile at higher levels. Despite these undesirable features, the Vasicek model has remained a popular one because it is parsimonious, easy to calibrate, and lends itself to tractable models of option pricing.

## The CIR Model

Cox, Ingersoll, and Ross (1985) introduce a mean-reverting square-root diffusion process for the short rate $r_t$:

$$\alpha(t, r_t) = \kappa(\theta - r_t) \qquad \beta(t, r_t) = \bar{\beta}\sqrt{r_t} \qquad \textbf{(29.7)}$$

where $\kappa$, $\theta$, and $\bar{\beta}$ are all positive constants. This is now simply called the "CIR model" in the finance literature.

The drift term $\kappa(\theta - r_t)$ in the CIR model exhibits mean reversion, as in the Vasicek model. The form of the diffusion component $\bar{\beta}\sqrt{r_t}$ implies that short rates follow a noncentral chi-square distribution with

$$E[r_t \mid r_0] = \theta + e^{-\kappa t}(r_0 - \theta)$$

$$\text{Var}(r_t \mid r_0) = \frac{1}{\kappa}\bar{\beta}r_0^2(e^{-\kappa t} - e^{-2\kappa t}) + \frac{1}{2\kappa}\theta\bar{\beta}^2(1 - e^{-\kappa t})^2$$

In the CIR model, short rates are guaranteed to be positive as long as $2\kappa\theta > \bar{\beta}^2$. It is also the case that volatility increases with interest-rate level from the very form of the specification. Thus, both shortcomings of the Vasicek model are overcome.

## Other One-Factor Models

Many other one-factor models have been studied in the literature. Table 29.1, based on Chan, Karolyi, Longstaff, and Sanders (1992) and other sources, presents in summary form the drift and diffusion components of some of these. The entries $\bar{\alpha}$, $\bar{\beta}$, etc., in the table are scalar constants.

## Solving One-Factor Models I: The PDE Approach

The "one factor" assumption in a one-factor model is that the evolution of all bond prices in the model depends only on the evolution of the model's single factor. That is, if $P(t, T)$ denotes the time-$t$ price of a zero-coupon bond maturing at $T$, then

$$P(t, T) = P(t, T, r_t) \qquad \textbf{(29.8)}$$

Let $r(t, T)$ denote the yield on this bond:

$$r(t, T) = -\frac{1}{T - t} \ln P(t, T) \qquad \textbf{(29.9)}$$

Since a single factor drives all changes in the yield curve, changes in bond prices of any two maturities must be perfectly instantaneously correlated. We can use this observation to

**TABLE 29.1**
One-Factor Interest
Rate Models

| Model | Drift $\alpha(t, r_t)$ | Diffusion $\beta(t, r_t)$ |
|---|---|---|
| Merton (1973) | $\bar{\alpha}$ | $\bar{\beta}$ |
| Vasicek (1977) | $\kappa(\theta - r_t)$ | $\bar{\beta}$ |
| Dothan (1978) | $0$ | $\bar{\beta}$ |
| Brennan and Schwartz (1979) | $\bar{\alpha}_0 + \bar{\alpha}_1 r_t$ | $\bar{\beta}r_t$ |
| Cox, Ingersoll, and Ross (1985) | $\kappa(\theta - r_t)$ | $\bar{\beta}\sqrt{r_t}$ |
| Chan, Karolyi, Longstaff, and Sanders (1992) | $\bar{\alpha}_0 + \bar{\alpha}_1 r_t$ | $\bar{\beta}r_t^{1.5}$ |
| Geometric Brownian motion | $\bar{\alpha}r_t$ | $\bar{\beta}r_t$ |
| Constant elasticity of variance (CEV) | $\bar{\alpha}r_t$ | $\bar{\beta}r_t^{\gamma}$ |

show (see Appendix 29A for a proof) that the ratio

$$\frac{\mu(t, T, r_t) - r_t}{\sigma(t, T, r_t)} \tag{29.10}$$

must be independent of $T$ where $\mu(\cdot)$ and $\sigma(\cdot)$ denote, respectively, the drift and volatility of the bond, i.e., where we write the bond-price process as

$$dP(t, T) = \mu(t, T, r_t)P(t, T)\,dt + \sigma(t, T, r_t)P(t, T)\,dW_t \tag{29.11}$$

Let the ratio (29.10) be denoted by $\lambda(t, r_t)$. $\lambda$ is called the "market price of risk" associated with the model's single factor.

From this, we can derive the *fundamental partial differential equation* (pde) that bond prices must follow. To describe this pde, some notational simplification will help. Write $\alpha$ for $\alpha(t, r_t)$, $\lambda$ for $\lambda(t, r_t)$, etc. Let $P$ denote the bond price $P(r, t, T)$, and let $P_r$ and $P_t$ denote the partial derivatives of $P$ with respect to the short rate $r$ and current time $t$, respectively, and let $P_{rr}$ denote the second partial with respect to $r$. In Appendix 29A, we show that in the absence of arbitrage, bond prices must satisfy the pde

$$(\alpha - \beta\lambda)\,P_r + P_t + \frac{1}{2}\beta^2 P_{rr} - rP = 0 \tag{29.12}$$

Bond prices are obtained by solving this pde subject to the boundary condition $P(T, T) = 1$.

The principal complication in solving for bond prices in this approach is that the form of $\lambda$ is unknown: $\lambda$ is defined through the drift and volatility of the unknown bond prices. Introducing a functional form for $\lambda$ is necessary to be able to solve this pde. Below, we examine the solutions in two specific cases.

### Bond Prices in the Vasicek Model

Vasicek (1977) makes the assumption that $\lambda(t, r_t)$ is a constant $\lambda$. Using this in conjunction with the forms of $\alpha$ and $\beta$ (expressions (29.6)), he solves the pde to obtain the following expressions for bond prices in his model:

$$P(t, T, r_t) = \exp[A(\tau) - r_t B(\tau)] \tag{29.13}$$

where $r_t$ is the current (time-$t$) short rate, $\tau = T - t$ is the time left to maturity on the bond, and

$$B(\tau) = \frac{1}{\kappa}[1 - \exp(-\kappa\tau)] \tag{29.14}$$

$$A(\tau) = [B(\tau) - \tau]R(\infty) - \frac{\sigma^2}{4\kappa^3}[1 - \exp(-\kappa\tau)]^2 \tag{29.15}$$

$$R(\infty) = \theta + \frac{\lambda\sigma}{\kappa} - \frac{\sigma^2}{2\kappa^2} \tag{29.16}$$

### Bond Prices in the CIR Model

CIR develop a general equilibrium model and derive the form $\lambda(t, r_t) = \lambda\sqrt{r_t}$ for the market price of risk in their model. Using this with the forms for $\alpha(\cdot)$ and $\beta(\cdot)$ in (29.7), CIR solve the fundamental pde to obtain the following closed-form solutions for bond prices in their model:

$$P(t, T, r_t) = \exp[A(\tau) - r_t B(\tau)] \tag{29.17}$$

where $r_t$ is the current (time-$t$) short rate, $\tau = T - t$ is the time left to maturity on the bond, and

$$A(\tau) = \ln\left\{\left[\frac{2\gamma e^{(\kappa + \lambda + \gamma)\tau/2}}{(\gamma + \kappa + \lambda)(e^{\gamma\tau} - 1) + 2\gamma}\right]^{2\kappa\theta/\sigma^2}\right\} \qquad \textbf{(29.18)}$$

$$B(\tau) = \frac{2(e^{\gamma\tau} - 1)}{(\gamma + \kappa + \lambda)(e^{\gamma\tau} - 1) + 2\gamma} \qquad \textbf{(29.19)}$$

$$\gamma = \sqrt{(\kappa + \lambda)^2 + 2\sigma^2} \qquad \textbf{(29.20)}$$

Observe the similarity of the structures of the bond-pricing equations (29.13) and (29.17) in the Vasicek and CIR models. This is not accidental. The Vasicek and CIR models are each special cases of the general category of affine one-factor models, and, as we show in Section 29.6 below, all one-factor affine factor models must have solutions of this form.

### Bond Price Behavior

The Vasicek and CIR solutions are easy to implement, indeed simpler even than Black-Scholes because they do not involve constructs such as cumulative normal distributions. To illustrate, we implement the Vasicek model with sample parameters to examine the effect of various inputs on the bond price. See Figure 29.10 for the discount bond price as maturity increases.

In Figure 29.11, we see that the price of the bond declines as the mean-reversion rate ($\kappa$) increases. Note that, since the bond is convex in the interest rate, it gains from volatility through the convexity effect. Mean reversion dampens the effect of volatility and accordingly also reduces the value of the bond. Based on the same reasoning, holding all else constant, increases in volatility will raise bond prices. This is shown in Figure 29.12.

## Solving One-Factor Models II: The Risk-Neutral Approach

An alternative way to solving for bond prices in factor models is to use the risk-neutral pricing approach. We have already studied the risk-neutral valuation approach when pricing equity options. The extension to term-structure modeling is straightforward.

**FIGURE 29.10**
Vasicek Discount Bond Price with Changing Maturity

The input parameters are $\kappa = 0.2$ (mean reversion), $\theta = 0.1$ (long-run mean), $\sigma = 0.01$ (volatility), and $\lambda = 0.1$ (market price of risk).

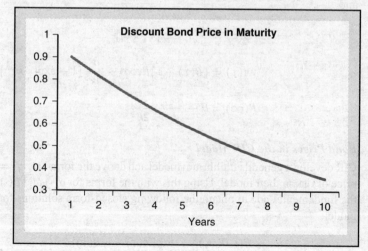

**FIGURE 29.11**
Vasicek Discount Bond
Price with Changing
Mean-Reversion Rate

The input parameters are $\kappa = \{0.1, \ldots, 1\}$ (mean reversion), $\theta = 0.1$ (long-run mean), $\sigma = 0.1$ (volatility), $\lambda = 0.1$ (market price of risk), and $T = 5$ years (maturity).

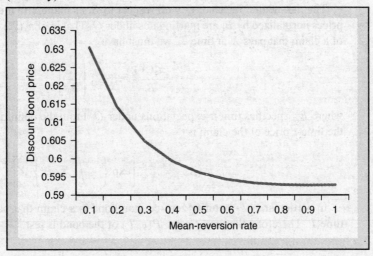

**FIGURE 29.12**
Vasicek Discount
Bond Price with
Changing Volatility

The input parameters are $\kappa = 0.2$ (mean reversion), $\theta = 0.1$ (long-run mean), $\sigma = \{0.05, \ldots, 0.14\}$ (volatility), $\lambda = 0.1$ (market price of risk), and $T = 5$ years (maturity).

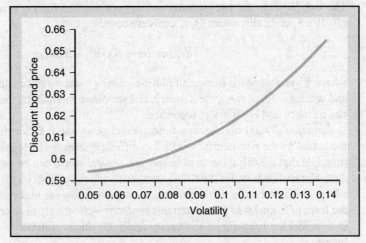

Suppose that the short rate follows the process

$$dr_t = \alpha(t, r_t) \, dt + \beta(t, r_t) \, dW_t \tag{29.21}$$

under the actual (a.k.a. "physical" or "statistical") measure. The first step in using risk-neutral pricing is to define a numeraire asset. While any bond may be used for this purpose, the most common choice in term-structure models is to use a "money market account" in which an initial investment of \$1 is rolled over continuously at the short rate $r_t$. Let $B_t$ denote the value of this account at time $t$:

$$B_t = \exp\left\{ \int_0^t r_s \, ds \right\}$$

Normalizing asset prices by the money market account is the natural extension to stochastic interest rates of the discount factor $e^{-rt}$ under constant interest rates. That is, if $r_t = r$ for all $t$, then dividing asset prices by $B_t$ is exactly the same thing as discounting by $e^{-rt}$.

The risk-neutral measure $Q$ with respect to $B_t$ as numeraire must be such that all asset prices normalized by $B_t$ are martingales under $Q$. That is, if $\pi_t(X)$ denotes the time-$t$ price of a claim that pays $X$ at time $T$, we must have

$$\frac{\pi_t(X)}{B_t} = E_Q^t \left[ \frac{X}{B_T} \right]$$

where $E_Q^t$ specifies time-$t$ expectations under $Q$. From the definition of $B_t$, it follows that the time-$t$ price of the claim is

$$\pi_t(X) = E_Q^t \left[ \exp \left\{ - \int_t^T r_s \, ds \right\} X \right]$$

In particular, a $T$-maturity zero-coupon bond is a claim that pays \$1 with certainty at time $T$. Therefore, the time-$t$ price $P(t, T)$ of the bond is just

$$P(t, T) = E_Q^t \left[ \exp \left\{ - \int_t^T r_s \, ds \right\} \right] \qquad \textbf{(29.22)}$$

To compute this expectation, we must identify the behavior of $r_t$ under the risk-neutral measure $Q$. Expression (29.21) specifies the behavior of $r_t$ only under the statistical measure. The link between the two, it turns out, is precisely the market price of risk $\lambda$ defined by (29.10). Specifically, under $Q$, $r_t$ evolves according to

$$dr_t = (\alpha - \beta\lambda) \, dt + \beta \, d\widehat{W}_t \qquad \textbf{(29.23)}$$

where $\widehat{W}_t$ is a standard Brownian motion under $Q$ and we have suppressed the arguments and written $\alpha$ for $\alpha(t, r_t)$, etc. Given $\lambda$ and the other parameters, the expectation in (29.22) can be taken and bond prices identified.

Equation (29.23) highlights a fundamental point about factor models. In moving from the actual to the risk-neutral world, the diffusion term $\beta$ is not affected, which means in principle that the diffusion term in the risk-neutral world can be estimated from historical data. Not so, however, for the risk-neutral drift, which depends on the unknown market price of risk $\lambda$. To proceed with the pricing, we need to know (or make some assumption about) the form of $\lambda$. One way to sidestep this problem—effectively to sweep it under the carpet— is to model the behavior of $r_t$ directly under $Q$; this is commonly done in the theoretical literature.

This point also provides the chief motivation for the Heath-Jarrow-Morton class of models developed in the next chapter. In the HJM class of models, as we will see, the drifts of the forward rates in the risk-neutral world are functions of their volatilities, and the latter do not change in going from the actual to the risk-neutral world.

## 29.5   Multifactor Models

One-factor models are empirically insufficiently rich to capture yield-curve movements. Beginning with Brennan and Schwartz (1979), a number of authors have proposed models with two or more factors driving the yield curve. Suggested second factors include **the long** rate, the rate of inflation, the mean of the short rate, the volatility of the short rate, and many others.

In an $n$-factor model, there are $n$ factors that affect changes in the yield curve. We may model each of these factors separately (for example, in a two-factor model, we may specify the short-rate and long-rate processes explicitly), then solve for the market prices of risk associated with each factor, and use this to price the bonds using, say, the $n$-factor version of the pde approach.

Alternatively, as equation (29.22) implies, to price bonds we need to know the behavior of the short rate only under the risk-neutral measure $Q$. So, we may begin directly with a specification of how the $n$ factors affect the behavior of the short rate under $Q$ and then use (29.22) to price the bonds. We illustrate this process here since it is commonly used in the theoretical literature.

For a general $n$-factor model, we begin with an $n$-dimensional process of the form

$$dX_t = \mu(X_t)\,dt + \sigma(X_t)\,d\widehat{W}_t$$

where (a) $X = (X_1, \ldots, X_n)$ is the vector of $n$ factors driving the term structure; (b) $(\widehat{W}_t)$ is an $n$-dimensional Brownian motion under an equivalent martingale measure $Q$ (with respect to the money-market account); (c) $\mu(\cdot)$ is an $n$-dimensional vector that specifies the drift of the $X_t$ process under $Q$; and (d) $\sigma(\cdot)$ is an $n \times n$ matrix that is the diffusion component under $Q$ of the $X_t$ process.

From the usual risk-neutral pricing arguments, the time-$t$ price of a $T$-maturity zero-coupon bond is

$$P(t, T) = E_Q\left[\exp\left\{-\int_t^T r_s\,ds\right\}\right] \qquad \textbf{(29.24)}$$

As observed earlier, zero bond prices only depend on the behavior of the short rate $r_t$ under $Q$. So we posit $r_t = R(X_t)$ for some function $R(\cdot)$. Then, the triple $(\mu(\cdot), \sigma(\cdot), R(\cdot))$ completely specifies the $n$-factor model.

Expression (29.24) describes bond prices using the martingale measure. Bond prices can also be described in terms of a pde in this model (i.e., using the risk-neutral specification). For simplicity, we describe the pde in the one-dimensional model here; the extension to $n$-dimensions is obvious. We have

$$dP = P_X\,dX + P_t\,dt + \tfrac{1}{2}\,P_{XX}\sigma^2\,dt$$
$$= [\mu P_X + P_t + \tfrac{1}{2}\,P_{XX}\sigma^2]\,dt + \sigma P_X\,d\widehat{W}_t$$

But under the risk-neutral measure, we must also have

$$dP = rP\,dt + \sigma P\,d\widehat{W}_t$$

So equating the drift terms on the right-hand sides, we obtain

$$rP = P_t + \mu P_X + \frac{1}{2}\,P_{XX}\sigma^2 \qquad \textbf{(29.25)}$$

Equation (29.25) is the fundamental pde. With $X$ equal to the short-rate $r$, this pde is identical to the one (29.12) derived earlier except that the earlier expression used the drift of $r$ under $P$ and the market price of risk whereas this one directly uses $\mu$, the drift of $r$ under $Q$. Of course, the two approaches are equivalent.

---

**Example 29.4**

## A Multifactor Example

Consider a two-factor version of the CIR model where the short rate is the sum of two independent square root diffusions:

$$r_t = x_{1t} + x_{2t}$$

where

$$dx_{it} = \kappa_i(\theta_i - x_{it})\,dt + \sigma_i\sqrt{x_{it}}\,dW_{it}, \quad i = 1, 2$$

In this setting, the bond price inherits its form directly from the single-factor model and is as follows:

$$P(t, T, x_{1t}, x_{2t}) = \left(\prod_{i=1,2} A_i(\tau)\right) \times \left(\exp\left[-\sum_{i=1,2} x_{it}\,B_i(\tau)\right]\right)$$

$$\tau = T - t$$

$$A_i(\tau) = \left[\frac{2\gamma_i\,e^{(\kappa_i+\lambda_i+\gamma_i)\tau/2}}{(\gamma_i + \kappa_i + \lambda_i)(e^{\gamma_i\tau} - 1) + 2\gamma_i}\right]^{2\kappa_i\theta_i/\sigma_i^2}$$

$$B_i(\tau) = \frac{2(e^{\gamma_i\tau} - 1)}{(\gamma_i + \kappa_i + \lambda_i)(e^{\gamma_i\tau} - 1) + 2\gamma_i}$$

$$\gamma_i = \sqrt{(\kappa_i + \lambda_i)^2 + 2\sigma_i^2}$$

$$i \in \{1, 2\}$$

∎

## 29.6 Affine Factor Models

The concept of affine factor models was introduced in Duffie and Kan (1996). Affine factor models are factor models with a certain affine property in their structure as we explain below. Duffie and Kan show that such models possess remarkable analytical tractability. We confine our presentation of their analysis to factor models driven by Brownian motion processes. For an extension that also allows for jumps, see Das and Foresi (1996) or the Duffie-Kan paper. We state the Duffie-Kan result in this section and prove a simplified version of the result.

Consider a typical *n*-factor model in which the evolution of the factors $X = (X_1, \ldots, X_n)$ under the risk-neutral measure is given by

$$dX_t = \mu(X_t)\,dt + \sigma(X_t)\,d\widehat{W}_t$$

where $\mu(X_t)$ is an $n \times 1$ vector and $\sigma(X_t)$ is an $n \times n$ matrix. Suppose also that the time-*t* short rate is specified as $R(X_t)$. The three functions $\mu(\cdot)$, $\sigma(\cdot)$, and $R(\cdot)$, of course, fully specify the model. In an *affine factor model*, $R$, $\mu$, and $\sigma\sigma'$ are all required to be affine functions of the factors $X$:

$$
\begin{aligned}
R(X) &= a + b \cdot X \\
\mu(X) &= c + d \cdot X \\
\sigma(X)\sigma(X)' &= e + f \cdot X
\end{aligned}
\tag{29.26}
$$

Many of the well-known models in the finance literature, including the Merton/Ho-Lee model, the Vasicek model, and the CIR model, are affine factor models. From (29.23), the general representation of the risk-neutral short-rate process in all three cases is

$$dr_t = (\alpha - \beta\lambda)\,dt + \beta\,d\widehat{W}_t \tag{29.27}$$

where $\alpha$ and $\beta$ in the three cases are specified by (29.5), (29.6), and (29.7), respectively. The market price of risk, $\lambda$, is a constant $\bar{\lambda}$ in the Merton/Ho-Lee and Vasicek models, while in the CIR model, it has the form $\bar{\lambda}\sqrt{r_t}$.

### The Merton/Ho-Lee Model

Combining (29.5) and (29.27), the risk-neutral process followed by the short rate in this model is

$$dr_t = (\bar{\alpha} - \bar{\beta}\bar{\lambda})\,dt + \bar{\beta}\,d\widehat{W}_t$$

This corresponds to an affine factor model in which $R(X) = X$ and the remaining parameters of (29.26) are given by

$$c = \bar{\alpha} - \bar{\beta}\bar{\lambda};\ d = 0;\ e = \bar{\beta}^2;\ f = 0$$

### The Vasicek Model

In this case, combining (29.6) and (29.27), the risk-neutral short-rate process follows

$$dr_t = (\kappa\theta - \bar{\beta}\bar{\lambda} - \kappa r_t)\,dt + \bar{\beta}\,d\widehat{W}_t$$

This corresponds to an affine factor model in which $R(X) = X$ and the remaining parameters of (29.26) are given by

$$c = \kappa\theta - \bar{\beta}\bar{\lambda};\ d = -\kappa;\ e = \bar{\beta}^2;\ f = 0$$

### The CIR Model

From (29.7) and (29.27), the risk-neutral short-rate process here is given by

$$dr_t = [\kappa\theta - (\bar{\beta}\bar{\lambda} + \kappa)r_t]\,dt + \bar{\beta}\sqrt{r_t}\,d\widehat{W}_t$$

This corresponds to an affine factor model in which $R(X) = X$ and the remaining parameters of (29.26) are given by

$$c = \kappa\theta;\ d = -(\bar{\beta}\bar{\lambda} + \kappa);\ e = 0;\ f = \bar{\beta}^2$$

An example of a short-rate process that is *not* of the affine form is geometric Brownian motion. The risk-neutral version of this process is:

$$dr_t = (\alpha_0 + \alpha_1 r_t)\,dt + \sigma r_t\,d\widehat{W}_t$$

In this case, the diffusion term fails the affinity test.

## The Main Result

A factor model is said to have *affine yields* if for all $(t, T)$, we have

$$r(t, T) = \frac{1}{\tau}[\zeta(\tau) + \eta(\tau) \cdot X_t]$$

where $\tau = T - t$, and $\zeta(\cdot)$ and $\eta(\cdot)$ are $C^1$ functions.[1] If a model has affine yields, then bond prices in the model are "exponential-affine" functions of the factors:

$$P(t, T) = \exp\{-\zeta(T - t) - \eta(T - t)X_t\}$$

---

[1] $C^1$ stands for continuously differentiable. In general, a function that is $k$-times continuously differentiable is said to be of class $C^k$.

As we have seen, both the Vasicek and CIR models have bond prices of this form. Duffie and Kan (1996) prove the powerful result that

**Proposition 29.1 (Duffie-Kan)** *A model has affine yields if and only if it is an affine factor model.*

The Duffie-Kan result, in fact, identifies the functions $\zeta(\cdot)$ and $\eta(\cdot)$ in terms of the parameters $(a, \ldots, f)$ up to a pair of partial differential equations. We derive the Duffie-Kan result for $n = 1$ here. The general proof follows similar lines.

### Proof of Duffie-Kan When $n = 1$

Let $X$ denote the sole factor in the model. We assume, without loss of generality, that $R(X) = X$, so the sole factor is the short rate. We first derive a preliminary result:

**Lemma 29.2** *If a model has affine yields, it must satisfy*

$$\zeta'(\tau) + [1 - \eta'(\tau)]X = \eta(\tau)\mu(X) + \frac{1}{2}\eta^2(\tau)\sigma^2(X) \qquad (29.28)$$

*where $\tau = T - t$.*

### Proof of Lemma

Suppose the model has affine yields. By definition, we have

$$P(t, T) = \exp\{\zeta(\tau) + \eta(\tau)X\}$$

This gives us the following expressions for the partial derivatives of $P$:

$$P_X = \eta(\tau)P$$
$$P_{XX} = \eta(\tau)^2 P$$
$$P_t = -[\zeta'(\tau) + \eta'(\tau)X] P$$

Substituting these into the fundamental pde (29.25), we get

$$XP = -[\zeta'(\tau) + \eta'(\tau)X] P + \mu(X)\eta(\tau)P + \frac{1}{2}\eta^2(\tau)\sigma^2(X)P$$

Eliminating the common term $P$, this becomes

$$X = \eta(\tau)\mu(X) - [\zeta'(\tau) + \eta'(\tau)X] + \frac{1}{2}\eta^2(\tau)\sigma^2(X)$$

which is precisely (29.28). This establishes the lemma. ∎

Returning to the proof of the proposition, suppose now that yields are affine in $X$:

$$r(t, T) = \frac{1}{\tau}[\zeta(\tau) + \eta(\tau)X]$$

We shall show that the model must be an affine factor model, i.e., that $\mu(\cdot)$ and $\sigma(\cdot)$ must have the forms

$$\mu(X) = c + dX, \qquad \sigma^2(X) = e + fX$$

for some constants $c, d, e, f$. Pick any $T_1, T_2$ and let $\tau_1 = T_1 - t, \tau_2 = T_2 - t$. Define the $2 \times 2$ matrix

$$B(\tau_1, \tau_2) = \begin{bmatrix} \eta(\tau_1) & \dfrac{1}{2}\eta^2(\tau_1) \\[2ex] \eta(\tau_2) & \dfrac{1}{2}\eta^2(\tau_2) \end{bmatrix}$$

Then from (29.28), we have

$$B(\tau_1, \tau_2) \begin{bmatrix} \mu(X) \\[1ex] \sigma^2(X) \end{bmatrix} = \begin{bmatrix} \zeta'(\tau_1) + [1 + \eta'(\tau_1)]X \\[1ex] \zeta'(\tau_2) + [1 + \eta'(\tau_2)]X \end{bmatrix}$$

If $B$ is invertible, then

$$\begin{bmatrix} \mu(X) \\[1ex] \sigma^2(X) \end{bmatrix} = B^{-1} \cdot \begin{bmatrix} \zeta'(\tau_1) + [1 + \eta'(\tau_1)]X \\[1ex] \zeta'(\tau_2) + [1 + \eta'(\tau_2)]X \end{bmatrix}$$

which says precisely that $\mu(\cdot)$ and $\sigma^2(\cdot)$ are affine as required.

Conversely, suppose now that $\mu$ and $\sigma$ are affine:

$$\mu(X) = c + dX, \qquad \sigma^2(X) = e + fX.$$

We have shown that if an affine yield exists, it must satisfy (29.28). Substituting for $\mu(\cdot)$ and $\sigma(\cdot)$ into (29.28), we obtain

$$\zeta'(\tau) + [1 + \eta'(\tau)]X = \eta(\tau)[c + dX] + \frac{1}{2}\eta^2(\tau)[e + fX] \qquad \textbf{(29.29)}$$

Each side is linear in $X$. Equating the coefficients of $X$, we have

$$1 + \eta'(\tau) = d \cdot \eta(\tau) + \frac{1}{2} f \cdot \eta^2(\tau)$$

or

$$\eta'(\tau) = d\eta(\tau) + \frac{1}{2}f\eta^2(\tau) - 1 \qquad \textbf{(29.30)}$$

Equations of the form (29.30) are called Riccati equations (named after the mathematician J. F. Riccati). Solving this Riccati equation delivers us the function $\eta(\cdot)$. That leaves the function $\zeta(\cdot)$. Equating the constant terms in (29.29), we obtain

$$\zeta'(\tau) = c\eta(\tau) + \frac{1}{2}e\eta^2(\tau) \qquad \textbf{(29.31)}$$

Expression (29.31) can be solved for $\zeta(\cdot)$. This completes the proof.

## 29.7  Summary

This chapter has explored the factor model approach to the modeling of interest-rate movements. The material covered has three components to it. The first was an exploration of discrete-time one-factor models, in particular, the mechanics of tree-building, using as bases for illustration the models of Black, Derman, and Toy (1990) and Ho and Lee (1986).

The second was a presentation of general continuous-time factor models and their solutions using partial differential equations (pdes) or risk-neutral pricing; special cases of these models include the classic models of Vasicek (1977) and Cox, Ingersoll, and Ross (1985). The last part was the discussion of affine factor models and the key result of Duffie and Kan (1996).

The next chapter builds on this material and examines one of the most popular classes of models, that introduced by Heath et al. (1990). The HJM class will be seen to provide many engineering improvements over its predecessors. We will also see how the single-factor HJM framework is extended to more than one factor. Then, rounding off our discussion of term-structure models, we present the class of Libor Market Models that provide a theoretical justification for common market pricing of interest-rate options such as caps and floors.

## 29.8 Exercises

1. What are some essential differences between pricing equity options on trees versus pricing interest-rate options on trees?

2. In the Black-Derman-Toy model, explain why negative interest rates are not feasible on the tree.

3. In the BDT model, why are all probabilities chosen to be the same across the tree at every time point?

4. For the tree in the BDT model to recombine, is it necessary that the volatilities be the same across all nodes in any period on the tree?

5. For the tree in the HL model to recombine, is it necessary that the probabilities be the same across all nodes in any period on the tree?

6. Given an initial spot rate for one period of 12%, a two-period spot rate of 14%, and a volatility of 5% for the spot rate over a period, what should the two possible values of the spot rate be after one period? (Assume the BDT model applies.)

7. Assume the same parameters as in the previous question, but change the method of discounting from linear to exponential, i.e., assume that discounting is on a continuous basis. Rework the problem and assess the impact on the solution.

8. Suggest two alternate volatility functions for the BDT model that do not impact any of the essential features of the model. Your answer will demonstrate that the model is not specifically tied to the volatility function provided in the original model by Black, Derman, and Toy.

9. Explain what happens to (a) feasibility and (b) computational burden as the number of periods in the BDT tree increases.

10. Is it possible to have a bond price of value zero on the HL tree?

11. In the BDT model, what is the relation between the level of interest rates and the absolute size of changes in interest rates on the tree? Is this behavior consistent with the real observed behavior of interest rates in the economy?

12. You are given the following data for three periods, in which each period is one year.

| T | Zero-Coupon Rate | Price | $\sigma$ |
|---|---|---|---|
| 1 | 0.11 | 90.0901 | — |
| 2 | 0.13 | 78.3147 | 0.20 |
| 3 | 0.14 | 67.4972 | 0.15 |

Use the BDT model to draw the tree of spot rates for three years. Compute the prices of the following securities on the tree:

(a) Two-year zero-coupon bond prices.

(b) Three-year zero-coupon bond prices.

(c) Three-year 13% coupon bond prices, expressed as including interest on the date of valuation.

(d) A two-year call option on a three-year 13% bond with a cum-coupon strike price of $110.

13. Use the same inputs as the previous problem, i.e.,

| T | Zero-Coupon Rate | Price | $\sigma$ |
|---|---|---|---|
| 1 | 0.11 | 90.0901 | — |
| 2 | 0.13 | 78.3147 | 0.20 |
| 3 | 0.14 | 67.4972 | 0.15 |

What is the price of a three-year 13% coupon bond that is callable by the issuer on coupon dates at an ex-coupon strike price of $100?

14. Instead of zero-coupon rates, as modeled by BDT, what comprises the tree in the Ho-Lee model? What are the pros and cons of the approach?

15. What are $h(T)$ and $h^*(T)$ in the HL model? What is their relationship to the parameter $\delta$? What happens to $h(T)$ and $h^*(T)$ when $\delta$ increases? What can you say about the role of $\delta$ in the model?

16. Given the following information, prepare the HL bond price tree for three dates, $t = 0, 1, 2$. The parameter $\pi = \frac{1}{2}$, and $\delta = 0.8$.

| T | Zero-Coupon Rate |
|---|---|
| 1 | 0.06 |
| 2 | 0.07 |
| 3 | 0.08 |

17. Bond pricing in the Vasicek (1977) model: assume an interest rate process

$$dr = k(\theta - r)\, dt + \sigma\, dB$$

where base parameter levels are $r = k = \theta = \sigma = 0.1$, $T = 1$, and $dB$ is a standard Brownian motion. Assume also that the market price of risk $\lambda = 0$. In each of the following three cases, compute the bond price for each value of the given parameter holding the other parameters at their base levels.

For each of the three cases, explain the direction in which the bond price changes. That is, provide an economic explanation for why the bond price increases or decreases with the given parameter, holding the other parameters at their base levels.

(a) $k = \{0.1, 0.2, 0.4\}$.

(b) $\theta = \{0.05, 0.10, 0.15\}$.

(c) $\sigma = \{0.05, 0.10, 0.20\}$.

18. (Extending the Model) In this problem we extend the Vasicek model to allow the mean rate $\theta$ to become stochastic. Think of a situation in which the Federal Reserve

makes minor adjustments to short-term market rates to manage the temperature of the economy. The model comprises the following two equations:

$$dr = k(\theta - r)\, dt + \sigma\, dB$$

$$d\theta = \eta\, dB$$

The Brownian motion $dB$ is the same for both the interest rate $r$ and its mean level $\theta$. Answer the following questions:

(a) Given the bond price function $P(r, \theta, T)$, write down the process for $dP$ using Ito's lemma. $T$ denotes the time to maturity. $t$ may be used to denote current time.

(b) Suppose the market price of risk is zero for both stochastic variables $r$ and $\theta$. Then the bond's instantaneous return will be given by $E(dP) = rP\, dt$. Using this identity, derive the pde for the price of the discount bond, stating clearly the boundary condition for the bond price.

(c) Guess a functional form for the solution of the pde. Use the guess to derive a closed-form expression for the price of the bond.

(d) Will bond prices be higher or lower in this model versus a model in which $\eta = 0$ where the mean rate is constant?

19. Write a function in Octave for the Cox, Ingersoll, and Ross (CIR 1985) model and price the bond when the values are $r = k = \theta = \sigma = \lambda = 0.10$, and $T = 5$ years.

20. In the CIR model, compute the yield curve from 1 to 10 years when $r = k = \theta = \sigma = \lambda = 0.10$.

21. Find a set of parameters in the CIR model such that the yield curve from 1 to 10 years is of upward-sloping shape.

# Deriving the Fundamental PDE in Factor Models

In this section, we derive the fundamental pde (29.12) in one-factor term-structure models. In the process, we show that the market price of risk defined in (29.10) is independent of $T$ as claimed in the text.

Let the short-rate process be given by

$$dr_t = \alpha(t, r_t)\, dt + \beta(t, r_t)\, dW_t \qquad (29.32)$$

Since we are in a one-factor model, the prices of all bonds depend only on the $r_t$ process: We have $P(t, T) = P(t, T, r_t)$. By Ito's lemma (see Chapter 15),

$$
\begin{aligned}
dP(t, T) &= P_t\, dt + P_r\, dr + P_{rr}\, \tfrac{1}{2}\beta^2\, dt \\
&= \left[ P_t + \alpha P_r + \tfrac{1}{2}\beta^2 P_{rr} \right] dt + \beta P_r\, dW_t \\
&= \mu P\, dt + \sigma P\, dW_t
\end{aligned}
$$

where

$$\mu = \frac{1}{P}\left[ P_t + \alpha P_r + \frac{1}{2}\beta^2 P_{rr} \right] \qquad \sigma = \frac{1}{P}[\beta P_r]$$

Pick any two maturities $T_1$ and $T_2$. For notational ease, let $P_1 = P(t, T_1), \mu_1 = \mu(t, T_1)$, etc. Consider a portfolio consisting of

- 1 unit of the $T_1$-maturity zero-coupon bond.
- $\gamma_t$ units of the $T_2$-maturity zero-coupon bond.

The portfolio value at $t$ is $V = P_1 + \gamma_t P_2$. We have

$$dV = (\mu_1 P_1 + \gamma_t \mu_2 P_2)\, dt + (\sigma_1 P_1 + \gamma_t \sigma_2 P_2)\, dW_t$$

Suppose we choose $\gamma_t = -\sigma_1 P_1 / \sigma_2 P_2$. Then, the $dW_t$ term has a coefficient of zero, so the portfolio is locally riskless. This means it must locally return the same as the short rate, so we must have

$$\mu_1 P_1 + \gamma_t \mu_2 P_2 = r_t V = r_t(P_1 + \gamma_t P_2)$$

Substituting for $\gamma_t$, this means

$$\mu_1 P_1 - \frac{\sigma_1 P_1}{\sigma_2 P_2}\mu_2 P_2 = r_t\left( P_1 - \frac{\sigma_1 P_1}{\sigma_2 P_2} P_2 \right)$$

Rearranging this, we obtain the condition

$$\frac{\mu_1 - r_t}{\sigma_1} = \frac{\mu_2 - r_t}{\sigma_2} \qquad (29.33)$$

Since $T_1$ and $T_2$ were arbitrary, (29.33) must hold for all $T_1$ and $T_2$. This means the ratios cannot depend on $T_1$ and $T_2$. So if we define $\lambda(t, r_t)$ by

$$\lambda(t, r_t) = \frac{\mu(t, T) - r_t}{\sigma(t, T)} \qquad (29.34)$$

then $\lambda(t, r_t)$ is independent of $T$. This establishes (29.10).

Now, by definition, we have

$$\mu = \frac{1}{P}\left[P_t + \alpha P_r + \frac{1}{2}\beta^2 P_{rr}\right] \qquad \sigma = \frac{1}{P}[\beta P_r]$$

Since $\lambda\sigma = \mu - r$, we have

$$\frac{1}{P}\lambda\beta P_r = \frac{1}{P}\left(P_t + \alpha P_r + \frac{1}{2}\beta^2 P_{rr}\right) - r$$

Rearranging this, $\lambda\beta P_r = P_t + \alpha P_r + \frac{1}{2}\beta^2 P_{rr} - rP$, or

$$(\alpha - \lambda\beta)P_r + P_t + \frac{1}{2}\beta^2 P_{rr} - rP = 0 \qquad\qquad \textbf{(29.35)}$$

Expression (29.35) is the *fundamental partial differential equation* of one-factor term-structure models and appears in the text as expression (29.12).

# Chapter 30

# The Heath-Jarrow-Morton and Libor Market Models

## 30.1    Overview

The framework of Heath, Jarrow, and Morton (1990, 1992b), hereafter HJM, marks a significant advance in the modeling of term-structure movements and the pricing of interest-rate derivatives. Unlike factor models that work by modeling the dynamics of certain points on the yield curve (e.g., the short rate) and deriving the movements in the rest of the curve in an arbitrage-free manner, the HJM framework works directly with the entire yield curve and models simultaneously the changes in rates of all maturities. By construction then, the HJM approach is consistent with any given initial yield curve. Implementation requires only two pieces of information: the initial yield curve itself and the volatilities of forward rates of different maturities.

Since its introduction, the HJM framework has proved a popular one for modeling securities dependent on interest-rate risk in financial markets worldwide. Further enrichment of the field came in the mid 1990s with the class of so-called Market Models. In this chapter, we present first the HJM framework and then describe one category of Market Models, the Libor Market Models, or LMMs. The other class of market models, Swap Market Models, or SMMs, are conceptually similar to LMMs but are calibrated to swap market data rather than Libor market data; we provide a brief review of SMMs towards the end of this chapter.

In their most general forms, the models studied in this chapter are technically quite complex. Our aim is to convey the essence of these models in as transparent a setting as possible, so we focus on the simplest forms of these models. Full-blown expositions of these models may be found in advanced fixed-income modeling books, such as Brigo and Mercurio (2001), Pelsser (2000), and Rebonato (2002a).

## 30.2    The HJM Framework: Preliminary Comments

Our presentation of the HJM framework begins in this section with a broad discussion of the approach and the technical advantages it offers.

At the outset, a comment. It is common in the literature to refer to the HJM "model." This is something of a misnomer in that HJM is not a specific model in the sense in which, say,

Black, Derman, and Toy (1990) is. Rather, the HJM framework offers a general approach to modeling interest-rate movements that considers movements in rates of all maturities simultaneously and describes how to model these movements in an arbitrage-free manner. The number of noise sources that drive these movements is a choice made by the modeler. Thus, we can have a one-factor HJM setting in which the entire yield curve moves in response to a single factor, a two-factor HJM setting, or, more generally, a $k$-factor HJM setting for any desired $k$. In contrast, specific factor models are explicitly tied down to the modeled number of factors. Vasicek (1977), Cox, Ingersoll, and Ross (1985), and Black, Derman, and Toy (1990) are all necessarily one-factor models, Brennan and Schwartz (1979) is necessarily a two-factor model, and so on. Similarly, the manner in which the factors matter is fixed in these papers; in Vasicek, the single factor obeys an Ornstein-Uhlenbeck process, in CIR a square root process, in BDT a lognormal process, and so on. In HJM, the choice of how the factors matter is also left to the modeler. Thus, HJM describes a general framework rather than a specific model. Nonetheless, we bow to popular terminology and refer to the framework as the HJM model.

There are two distinguishing features of the HJM approach when compared to factor models. One is the yield curve that is modeled. In factor models, it is the *spot* yield curve that is the focus of the modeling exercise. HJM models the *forward* rate curve instead. Of course, the forward and spot curves are equivalent representations, but the HJM papers show that modeling forwards has significant technical advantages.

The second distinguishing feature is a technical one and is one of the advantages of the HJM approach. As we noted in Chapter 29 (see the discussion following equation (29.23)), in a factor model, the drift of the short rate in the risk-neutral world depends on the (often unknown) market price of risk. In the HJM setting, it turns out that the risk-neutral drifts of the forward rates are functions solely of the volatilities. In principle, this facilitates implementation of the model using historical data alone.

To expand further on this point, we use the context of a continuous-time setting; the arguments here concerning factor models are essentially those that were made in Chapter 29. Readers uncomfortable with continuous-time mathematics may skip this material without loss of continuity since the main result (the relation between risk-neutral drifts and volatilities in an HJM model) is derived further below in this chapter in a discrete-time setting.

Consider the Vasicek (1977) model as a specific example. The model posits a short-rate process of the form

$$dr_t = \kappa(\theta - r_t)\, dt + \sigma\, dW_t$$

where $\theta$ is the long-run mean of the short rate, $\kappa$ is the rate of mean reversion, and $\sigma$ is the volatility of the short rate. As noted in Section 29.4, under the risk-neutral measure, this process has the form

$$dr_t = (a - \kappa r_t)\, dt + \sigma\, d\widehat{W}_t \tag{30.1}$$

where $a = \kappa\theta - \sigma\lambda$ and $\lambda$ is the market price of risk. Thus, the behavior of $r_t$ under the risk-neutral measure—in particular, the drift of $r_t$—depends on the market price of risk.

Why does this dependence on $\lambda$ matter? Recall that the price of any claim is the discounted expectation of its payoffs under the risk-neutral measure. That is, if $X_T$ denotes the payoffs of the claim at time $T$, then its value at time 0 is just

$$E[\beta_T X_T] \tag{30.2}$$

where expectations are taken under the risk-neutral measure and $\beta_T$, the discount factor, is determined from the short-rate process as

$$\beta_T = \exp\left\{-\int_0^T r_s \, ds\right\} \tag{30.3}$$

From (30.2)–(30.3), pricing the claim requires knowledge of the behavior of $r_t$ under the risk-neutral measure. But from (30.1), the drift of $r_t$ under the risk-neutral measure depends on $\lambda$, so the pricing of derivatives cannot be carried out without some assumption concerning the market price of risk. (Note here that unlike the drift, the volatility of $r_t$ is the same under the original and risk-neutral measures.)

In the HJM framework, the risk-neutral drifts of the forward rates are functions of the volatilities of these rates. Since volatilities do not change in going from the original to the risk-neutral world, this means the model can be implemented without assumptions concerning the market prices of risk. Indeed, in principle, the model can be implemented and derivatives priced on the basis of historical data alone. Technically and conceptually, this is a significant leap forward over the factor model approach.

In summary, the HJM model owes its popularity to a number of features. The model is consistent with any given initial term structure. It is tractable in both discrete- and continuous-time settings. The model admits great flexibility in its specification since both the number of factors that affect the yield curve as well as the manner in which they matter are choice variables for the modeler. Lastly, the risk-neutral drifts of interest rates in the model are solely functions of the volatilities, so no assumptions concerning the forms of the market prices of risk are needed to price derivatives.

The material to follow develops these points in greater detail. We focus on the discrete-time version of HJM as described in Heath et al. (1990). The continuous-time version of Heath et al. (1992b) is more extensive and comprehensive but is also technically more demanding. The discrete-time model suffices to describe the model's main features and its working.

## 30.3   A One-Factor HJM Model

Consider an $n$-period model with time-points numbered $t = 0, 1, 2, \ldots, n$. Each period is of length $h$ years each, so the horizon $T$ of the model is equal to $nh$ years.

The forward rate at time $t$ for a *one-period* borrowing or investment at time $s$ (where $s \geq t$ and $s \leq n - 1$) is denoted $f(t, s)$. Note that $f(t, s)$ is quoted at time $t$ but applicable to the period from $s$ to $s + 1$. All interest rates are quoted in continuously compounded and annualized terms. Since the time interval between $s$ and $s + 1$ is $h$ years, this means \$1 invested at time $s$ at the rate $f(t, s)$ will grow by time $s + 1$ to

$$\exp\{f(t, s) \cdot h\}$$

In this discrete-time setting, the forward curve at time 0 is composed of $n$ forward rates: $f(0, 0), f(0, 1), f(0, 2), \ldots, f(0, n-1)$. At time 1, we are a step closer to the horizon of the model, so the forward curve has only $(n-1)$ forward rates $(f(1, 1), f(1, 2), \ldots f(1, n-1))$. Note that the rate $f(t, t)$ at any $t$ denotes the spot rate at that point.

Let $P(t, s)$ denote the time-$t$ price of a zero-coupon bond maturing at time $s$ and with a face value of \$1. The usual spot-forward parity arguments (see Section 26.14) tell us that we must have

$$P(t, s) = \exp\left\{-\sum_{i=t}^{s-1} f(t, i) \cdot h\right\} \tag{30.4}$$

## A Numerical Example

To help exposition of the HJM setting, we shall work in parallel with a numerical example. The example takes $h = 1$ year. It involves a horizon of five years. The following is the initial input information used:

| $T$ | Forward Rate | Value |
|---|---|---|
| 0 | $f(0, 0)$ | 0.10 |
| 1 | $f(0, 1)$ | 0.11 |
| 2 | $f(0, 2)$ | 0.12 |
| 3 | $f(0, 3)$ | 0.13 |
| 4 | $f(0, 4)$ | 0.14 |

The prices of zero-coupon bonds of all maturities may be identified from this data. For example, the time-0 price of a zero-coupon bond maturing at the end of five years is

$$P(0, 5) = \exp\left[-\sum_{i=0}^{4} f(0, i) \times 1\right] = 0.548812$$

## Evolution of the Forward Curve

Our initial exposition will remain within a one-factor model in which the forward curve evolves on a binomial tree. If we use the bold-face notation $\mathbf{f}(t, T)$ to denote the forward curve at time $t$, then the forward curve $\mathbf{f}(t + 1, T)$ at time $t + 1$ can take one of two values: $\mathbf{f}_u(t + 1, T)$, corresponding to an "up" move in the forward curve, and $\mathbf{f}_d(t + 1, T)$ corresponding to a "down" move in the forward curve:

$$\mathbf{f}_u(t + 1, T) = \begin{bmatrix} f_u(t+1, t+1) \\ f_u(t+1, t+2) \\ \vdots \\ f_u(t+1, n-1) \end{bmatrix} \qquad \mathbf{f}_d(t + 1, T) = \begin{bmatrix} f_d(t+1, t+1) \\ f_d(t+1, t+2) \\ \vdots \\ f_d(t+1, n-1) \end{bmatrix}$$

To complete the specification of the model, we must explain how the curves $\mathbf{f}_u$ and $\mathbf{f}_d$ are related to $\mathbf{f}$. Let $X$ be a random variable that takes on the value $+1$ with probability $q$ and $-1$ with probability $1 - q$. Then, for each $s$, we assume that

$$f(t + 1, s) = f(t, s) + \alpha(t, s)h + \sigma(t, s)X\sqrt{h}$$

This means that for each $s$, we have

$$f_u(t + 1, s) - f(t, s) = \alpha(t, s)h + \sigma(t, s)\sqrt{h}$$
$$f_d(t + 1, s) - f(t, s) = \alpha(t, s)h - \sigma(t, s)\sqrt{h}$$

The probabilities $q$ and $1 - q$ represent the risk-neutral probabilities of up and down moves in the model. For convenience, we choose $q = \frac{1}{2}$. This is what HJM also assume, but the assumption is for expositional simplicity only and is not analytically necessary.

This evolution of forward rates is expressed graphically in Figure 30.1. Note that the forward rate change for each fixed $s$ is comprised of two components. The first is the *drift* term $\alpha$. The second is a shock or *volatility* term $\sigma$. (The reason these are called the drift and volatility terms will become clear shortly.) The drift and volatility terms may depend on current time $t$, the specific maturity $s$ to which they relate, and other information such

**FIGURE 30.1**

Evolution of Forward Rates

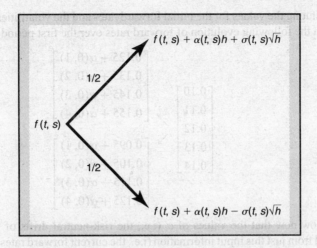

as the current level of forward rates; this dependence on additional information has been suppressed in the description above to save notation.

Given this evolution, we can compute for each pair $(t, s)$, the expected change $E_t$ and variance $V_t$ of the forward rate change:

$$E_t[f(t+1, s)|f(t, s)] = f(t, s) + \alpha(t, s)h$$

$$V_t[f(t+1, s)|f(t, s)] = \sigma(t, s)^2 h$$

Since rates change on average by $\alpha(t, s)h$, it is natural to call $\alpha$ the (risk-neutral) *drift* of the $(t, s)$-forward rates. And consistent with our usual definition of this term, the standard deviation of the change, $\sigma(t, s)\sqrt{h}$, is the *volatility* of (the change in) forward rates. Note that $\alpha$ and $\sigma$ are both in annualized terms (hence, the adjustment by $h$ and $\sqrt{h}$, respectively).

Adapting this evolution structure to the specific context of our numerical example, we have $h = 1$, so the forward curve after one period in the up state is:

$$\mathbf{f}_u(t+h, T) = \begin{bmatrix} f_u(1, 1) \\ f_u(1, 2) \\ f_u(1, 3) \\ f_u(1, 4) \end{bmatrix} = \begin{bmatrix} f(0, 1) + \alpha(0, 1) + \sigma(0, 1) \\ f(0, 2) + \alpha(0, 2) + \sigma(0, 2) \\ f(0, 3) + \alpha(0, 3) + \sigma(0, 3) \\ f(0, 4) + \alpha(0, 4) + \sigma(0, 4) \end{bmatrix} \qquad \textbf{(30.5)}$$

while in the down state we have

$$\mathbf{f}_d(t+h, T) = \begin{bmatrix} f_d(1, 1) \\ f_d(1, 2) \\ f_d(1, 3) \\ f_d(1, 4) \end{bmatrix} = \begin{bmatrix} f(0, 1) + \alpha(0, 1) - \sigma(0, 1) \\ f(0, 2) + \alpha(0, 2) - \sigma(0, 2) \\ f(0, 3) + \alpha(0, 3) - \sigma(0, 3) \\ f(0, 4) + \alpha(0, 4) - \sigma(0, 4) \end{bmatrix} \qquad \textbf{(30.6)}$$

We shall make the following very simple assumption concerning the volatility structure in this example:

$$\sigma(t, s) = 0.015 \qquad \text{for all } (t, s)$$

This is solely for expositional convenience. As the workings below will make clear, it is a trivial matter to allow for more complex volatility functions.

Substituting the values for the initial forward rates and the volatilities into (30.5)–(30.6), we obtain the following evolution of forward rates over the first period in the example:

$$
\begin{bmatrix} 0.10 \\ 0.11 \\ 0.12 \\ 0.13 \\ 0.14 \end{bmatrix}
\begin{array}{c} \nearrow \\ \searrow \end{array}
\begin{bmatrix} 0.125 + \alpha(0,1) \\ 0.135 + \alpha(0,2) \\ 0.145 + \alpha(0,3) \\ 0.155 + \alpha(0,4) \end{bmatrix}
$$

$$
\begin{bmatrix} 0.095 + \alpha(0,1) \\ 0.105 + \alpha(0,2) \\ 0.115 + \alpha(0,3) \\ 0.125 + \alpha(0,4) \end{bmatrix}
$$

We show now that the values of $\alpha$ (i.e., the risk-neutral drifts of the model) may be recovered from just this input information (i.e., the current forward rates and the volatilities) by appealing to no-arbitrage.

## Identifying the Risk-Neutral Drifts

There are four risk-neutral drifts to be determined. We begin with $\alpha(0,1)$ and solve for the others in turn by repeated appeal to the no-arbitrage condition.

To determine $\alpha(0,1)$, we use the price of a two-year zero-coupon bond. Assuming, as usual, a face value of \$1, the initial price of this bond may be obtained from the forward curve as

$$P(0,2) = \exp[-(0.10 + 0.11)] \tag{30.7}$$

But we may also price this bond using risk-neutral methods off the forward-rate evolution lattice: we discount the terminal payoff at the end of year 2 back to the end of year 1, and then further discount back to time zero. At the end of year 1, there are two possible values of the short rate. If the forward curve has moved up, then the short rate is

$$f_u(1,1) = 0.125 + \alpha(0,1)$$

The corresponding value of the bond after one year is

$$P_u(1,2) = \exp[-(0.125 + \alpha(0,1))]$$

where $P(1,2)$ denotes the time $t = 1$ price of the bond maturing at $T = 2$. Likewise, if the forward curve has moved down, then the short rate is

$$f_d(1,1) = 0.095 + \alpha(0,1)$$

The corresponding value of the bond after one year is

$$P_d(1,2) = \exp[-(0.095 + \alpha(0,1))]$$

Since the risk-neutral probabilities of the up and down moves have been assumed to be 1/2 each, we can obtain the time-0 price of this bond by weighting the up and down prices equally and discounting the expected value back to time zero:

$$P(0,2) = \exp(-0.10) \times \frac{1}{2}[P_u(1,2) + P_d(1,2)]$$

$$= \exp(-0.10) \times \frac{1}{2} \{\exp[-(0.125 + \alpha(0,1))] + \exp[-(0.095 + \alpha(0,1))]\}$$

Equating this expression to (30.7), we obtain a single equation in the unknown quantity $\alpha(0, 1)$. Solving, we get

$$\alpha(0, 1) = 0.000112$$

Plugging this back into the tree, we can restate the one-period evolution as follows

$$\begin{bmatrix} 0.10 \\ 0.11 \\ 0.12 \\ 0.13 \\ 0.14 \end{bmatrix} \nearrow \begin{bmatrix} 0.125112 \\ 0.135 + \alpha(0, 2) \\ 0.145 + \alpha(0, 3) \\ 0.155 + \alpha(0, 4) \end{bmatrix}$$
$$\searrow \begin{bmatrix} 0.095112 \\ 0.105 + \alpha(0, 2) \\ 0.115 + \alpha(0, 3) \\ 0.125 + \alpha(0, 4) \end{bmatrix}$$

We now move on to solving for $\alpha(0, 2)$. To do this, we use a three-year zero-coupon bond. After one year, the price of this bond takes one of two values, depending on whether we are in the up state or down state. In the up state, the price of the bond is

$$P_u(1, 3) = \exp[-(0.125112 + (0.135 + \alpha(0, 2)))]$$

And in the down state, the price is

$$P_d(1, 3) = \exp[-(0.095112 + (0.105 + \alpha(0, 2)))]$$

At time zero, this bond's price must be

$$P(0, 3) = \exp(-0.10) \times \frac{1}{2} (P_u(1, 3) + P_d(1, 3))$$
$$= \exp(-0.10) \times \frac{1}{2}(\exp[-(0.125112 + (0.135 + \alpha(0, 2)))]$$
$$+ \exp[-(0.095112 + (0.105 + \alpha(0, 2)))])$$

which should be equal to

$$P(0, 3) = \exp[-(0.10 + 0.11 + 0.12)]$$

Solving for $\alpha(0, 2)$, we obtain

$$\alpha(0, 2) = 0.000337$$

Plugging this into the tree, we get the revised forward curve evolution

$$\begin{bmatrix} 0.10 \\ 0.11 \\ 0.12 \\ 0.13 \\ 0.14 \end{bmatrix} \nearrow \begin{bmatrix} 0.125112 \\ 0.135337 \\ 0.145 + \alpha(0, 3) \\ 0.155 + \alpha(0, 4) \end{bmatrix}$$
$$\searrow \begin{bmatrix} 0.095112 \\ 0.105337 \\ 0.115 + \alpha(0, 3) \\ 0.125 + \alpha(0, 4) \end{bmatrix}$$

Our procedure here is a "bootstrapping" one. We first solved for $\alpha(0, 1)$ and then used this value to solve for $\alpha(0, 2)$. We then proceed by using the values of $\alpha(0, 1)$ and $\alpha(0, 2)$ to solve for $\alpha(0, 3)$ in the same way. Thus, maturity after maturity, we solve for the risk-neutral drifts in each period of the model. Rather than repeat the same calculations again, we simply state the solutions for the remaining alphas:

$$\alpha(0, 3) = 0.000562$$
$$\alpha(0, 4) = 0.000787$$

This finalizes the first period evolution on the HJM tree, which is represented as follows:

$$
\begin{bmatrix} 0.10 \\ 0.11 \\ 0.12 \\ 0.13 \\ 0.14 \end{bmatrix}
\nearrow
\begin{bmatrix} 0.125112 \\ 0.135337 \\ 0.145562 \\ 0.155787 \end{bmatrix}
$$
$$
\searrow
\begin{bmatrix} 0.095112 \\ 0.105337 \\ 0.115562 \\ 0.125787 \end{bmatrix}
$$

## Extending to Multiple Periods

We have completed most of the heavy lifting for the model. The procedure just outlined for the evolution of the forward curve over one period may be repeated for ensuing periods.

At the end of the first period, we obtained two forward curves, one for the upshift state $\mathbf{f}_u(1, T)$ and the other for the downshift $\mathbf{f}_d(1, T)$. Starting with the upshifted curve as the initial curve, and the same volatilities, we can compute the two curves that evolve from this one. Likewise, starting with the downshifted curve as the initial one, we can compute two curves in the next period. This results in a total of four forward curves on the tree after two periods. However, this assumes that the tree *does not* recombine. If it did, then the forward curve that evolved from a down move of $\mathbf{f}_u$ would coincide with the one that evolved from an up move of $\mathbf{f}_d$, and there would be only three forward curves at the end of period 2. We will examine the conditions for recombination shortly. First, we compute the tree as it emanates from the upper node at the end of time 1. We denote this as the "upper" subtree.

## The Upper Subtree

Let us deal with the upshifted forward curve as the initial one. Starting from here, the one-period evolution of the "subtree" from period 1 to period 2 may be depicted as follows (note that there are three remaining periods in the model after time 2, and so the two forward curves generated as the upper subtree will contain three elements each):

$$
\begin{bmatrix} 0.125112 \\ 0.135337 \\ 0.145562 \\ 0.155787 \end{bmatrix}
\nearrow
\begin{bmatrix} 0.150337 + \alpha(1) \\ 0.160562 + \alpha(2) \\ 0.170787 + \alpha(3) \end{bmatrix}
$$
$$
\searrow
\begin{bmatrix} 0.120337 + \alpha(1) \\ 0.130562 + \alpha(2) \\ 0.140787 + \alpha(3) \end{bmatrix}
$$

We manipulate this "triple" of forward curves in exactly the same way as before to compute $\alpha(1)$, $\alpha(2)$, and $\alpha(3)$. Even though we are aware that this triple applies to the time period between year 1 and year 2, we simply treat it as if it were for a new model beginning at the start of year 1. Therefore, even though we are building the subtree starting at $t = 1$ and we are interested in computing the forward rate curves at time $t = 2$ years, we operate as if the root node of the tree is $\mathbf{f}_u$, which will make the computations identical to that for the prior subperiod. One more time, we solve for $\alpha(1)$. The price of a two-year bond will be

$$P(1, 3) = \exp[-(0.125112 + 0.135337)]$$

which will also be equal to pricing on the tree, i.e.,

$$P(1, 3) = \exp(-0.125112) \times \frac{1}{2}[P_u(2, 3) + P_d(2, 3)]$$

where

$$P_u(2, 3) = \exp[-(0.150337 + \alpha(1))]$$
$$P_d(2, 3) = \exp[-(0.120337 + \alpha(1))]$$

Solving for $\alpha(1)$, we obtain

$$\alpha(1) = 0.000112$$

Bootstrapping, we can also solve for the remaining alpha values. The reader may wish to check the computations, which are left as an exercise. The solutions are

$$\alpha(2) = 0.000337$$
$$\alpha(3) = 0.000562$$

Plugging these into the subtree, we get the following:

$$\begin{bmatrix} 0.125112 \\ 0.135337 \\ 0.145562 \\ 0.155787 \end{bmatrix} \quad \nearrow \begin{bmatrix} 0.150449 \\ 0.160899 \\ 0.171349 \end{bmatrix} \\ \searrow \begin{bmatrix} 0.120449 \\ 0.130899 \\ 0.141349 \end{bmatrix}$$

## The Lower Subtree

Now we take up the evolution of the tree taking the downshifted forward curve as the initial one. Starting from here (i.e., at $\mathbf{f}_d$), the one-period evolution of the "subtree" from period 1 to period 2 may be depicted as follows:

$$\begin{bmatrix} 0.095112 \\ 0.105337 \\ 0.115562 \\ 0.125787 \end{bmatrix} \quad \nearrow \begin{bmatrix} 0.120337 + \alpha(1) \\ 0.130562 + \alpha(2) \\ 0.140787 + \alpha(3) \end{bmatrix} \\ \searrow \begin{bmatrix} 0.090337 + \alpha(1) \\ 0.100562 + \alpha(2) \\ 0.110787 + \alpha(3) \end{bmatrix}$$

We omit the usual calculations here and simply state the computed alpha values.

$$\alpha(1) = 0.000112$$
$$\alpha(2) = 0.000337$$
$$\alpha(3) = 0.000562$$

And we may then depict the finalized lower subtree here

$$
\begin{bmatrix} 0.095112 \\ 0.105337 \\ 0.115562 \\ 0.125787 \end{bmatrix}
\begin{matrix} \nearrow \\ \searrow \end{matrix}
\begin{matrix}
\begin{bmatrix} 0.120449 \\ 0.130899 \\ 0.141349 \end{bmatrix} \\
\\
\begin{bmatrix} 0.090449 \\ 0.100899 \\ 0.111349 \end{bmatrix}
\end{matrix}
$$

The upshift forward curve here coincides with the downshifted curve from the previous subsection, i.e., *recombination* of the tree is attained. For completeness, we now present the entire tree over two periods.

$$
\begin{bmatrix} 0.10 \\ 0.11 \\ 0.12 \\ 0.13 \\ 0.14 \end{bmatrix}
\begin{matrix} \nearrow \\ \searrow \end{matrix}
\begin{matrix}
\begin{bmatrix} 0.125112 \\ 0.135337 \\ 0.145562 \\ 0.155787 \end{bmatrix} \\
\\
\begin{bmatrix} 0.095112 \\ 0.105337 \\ 0.115562 \\ 0.125787 \end{bmatrix}
\end{matrix}
\begin{matrix} \nearrow \\ \searrow \\ \nearrow \\ \searrow \end{matrix}
\begin{matrix}
\begin{bmatrix} 0.150449 \\ 0.160899 \\ 0.171349 \end{bmatrix} \\
\begin{bmatrix} 0.120449 \\ 0.130899 \\ 0.141349 \end{bmatrix} \\
\begin{bmatrix} 0.090449 \\ 0.100899 \\ 0.111349 \end{bmatrix}
\end{matrix}
$$

## Tree Recombination

Our current numerical example of tree building in the HJM model resulted in a recombining tree. After two periods on the tree, we ended up with three different unique states (forward rate curves). Indeed, it is easy to show that with this particular chosen volatility function, the entire tree for $n$ periods will always recombine, no matter how large $n$ may be chosen to be; and, of course, after $n$ periods, there will be $(n + 1)$ states or nodes, each of which contains a forward rate curve.

What conditions do we need to impose on the model to ensure a recombining tree? The answer lies in the way we specify the volatility function for forward rates, i.e., the form of $\sigma(t, s)$. There are two cases in which the tree is recombining.

1. $\sigma(t, s) = \sigma_0$ for all $s$. That is, the volatility is constant and identical across all maturities of forward rates. This is exactly the case considered so far in our numerical example.

2. $\sigma(t, s) = \sigma(s)$ for all $s$. That is, the volatility may be different for each forward maturity $s$, but it should not depend on current time $t$ or any other factor. Note that case 1 is simply a special form of case 2.

On the other hand, if the volatility function depends on current time $t$ or on the level of current forward rates $f(t, s)$, then the tree is not guaranteed to be recombining.

**Example 30.1**

We use the two-period arbitrage-free tree we computed to illustrate interest-rate derivative pricing. We shall price options on a five-year coupon bond with a coupon of 13% per year. In particular, we price the one-year call option on this bond at a strike (ex-coupon) of 100.

In order to price this option, we need to determine the price of the five-year bond at the end of one year. There are two states at the end of one year, and at each node there is a forward curve with four rates, one for each of the remaining years. These forward curves may be used to price the bond at the end of one year. In the up state, the forward curve is

$$\begin{bmatrix} 0.125112 \\ 0.135337 \\ 0.145562 \\ 0.155787 \end{bmatrix}$$

The price of the bond (coupon = 13%) is obtained by discounting all coupons and the final principal (remember that $h = 1$):

$$P_u = 13\exp[-(0.125112)]$$
$$+13\exp[-(0.125112 + 0.135337)]$$
$$+13\exp[-(0.125112 + 0.135337 + 0.145562)]$$
$$+113\exp[-(0.125112 + 0.135337 + 0.145562 + 0.155787)]$$
$$= 94.58296$$

Since this price is less than the call strike of 100, the call will not be exercised, and its value in the up state is zero.

An identical calculation may be undertaken for the down state price, which turns out to be

$$P_d = 104.5823$$

In this state, the call option is in-the-money and generates a payoff of 4.5823. The time-0 price of the option may now be easily computed by taking expected values (when $q = \frac{1}{2}$) and discounting back to the beginning of year 1,

$$\text{Call price} = \exp(-0.10)\left[\frac{1}{2} \times 0 + \frac{1}{2} \times 4.5823\right] = 2.0731$$

∎

## An HJM Advantage over Spot-Rate Models

At this juncture, it is useful to point out the advantage of building a tree with the entire forward curve at each node (compared to a tree with only the short rate at each node, as for example, in the Black-Derman-Toy (BDT) model). In the BDT model, in order to price the option on the five-year bond, we would need to build the tree for five years, i.e., out to the maturity of the bond. Using this tree, we would discount back cash flows to the end of year 1 to assess the option's value. However, in the HJM model, we needed only to build the tree to a maturity of one year, i.e., out to the maturity of the option even though the underlying bond was for a longer maturity. This is because there is enough information in the entire forward curve available at the end of one year to price the five-year bond and thus compute payoffs on interest-rate options.

If we regard the discrete binomial model as an approximation to the continuous time model, the more periods that are imposed on the tree, the more accurate is the discrete model relative to the continuous time one. Since the HJM model requires extending the tree only to the maturity of options, not to that of the underlying bonds, it can accommodate many more time steps within a given fixed maturity, thereby allowing for far higher model accuracy.

## 30.4 A Two-Factor HJM Setting

In the one-factor model described in the last section, all rate changes are driven by a common factor so the changes are perfectly correlated. In the binomial example, this meant that all rates move up or all rates move down. (The one-factor model also permits any rate to move always in the opposite direction to the others as well, meaning that it is perfectly negatively correlated to the other rates. In the binomial model, this may be accomplished by simply reversing the sign of $\sigma$ for that rate.)

If we introduce a second factor, then each rate is affected by two shocks, one for each factor. This makes it easy to introduce imperfect correlation in the changes and more interesting interest-rate dynamics. We illustrate this with an example. The example has three periods with each period having a length of $h = 1$ year. The initial forward curve is given by

$$f(0, 0) = 0.10$$
$$f(0, 1) = 0.11$$
$$f(0, 2) = 0.12$$

Motivated by Heath, Jarrow, and Morton (1990a), we posit the following two-factor trinomial-tree process for the evolution of forward rates: for each $(t, s)$,

$$f(t + 1, s) = \begin{cases} f(t, s) + \alpha(s)h + \sigma_1(s)\sqrt{h} + \sigma_2(s)\sqrt{h} & \text{with prob } 1/3 \\ f(t, s) + \alpha(s)h + \sigma_1(s)\sqrt{h} - \sigma_2(s)\sqrt{h} & \text{with prob } 1/3 \\ f(t, s) + \alpha(s)h - \sigma_1(s)\sqrt{h} - \sigma_2(s)\sqrt{h} & \text{with prob } 1/3 \end{cases} \quad \textbf{(30.8)}$$

Finally, $\sigma_1(\cdot)$ and $\sigma_2(\cdot)$ are specified by

$$\sigma_1(1) = 0.010 \qquad\qquad \sigma_2(1) = -0.001$$
$$\sigma_1(2) = 0.009 \qquad\qquad \sigma_2(2) = -0.002$$

This is, of course, a particular example of how a two-factor model may be specified. It does not purport to be a general specification of such models. The shock factors $\sigma_1$ and $\sigma_2$ in this specification depend only on the maturity date $s$ of the forward rates, not on the current time or on the current level of forward rates as they may in general.

Nonetheless, there are several interesting features of this specification. Observe that the impact of the factors is sometimes specified to be negative. This simple device permits the two $\sigma$ functions to work in opposite directions to each other. Second, the value of $\sigma_1$ decreases as the maturity of the forward rate increases. This is motivated by the empirically observed relationship between maturities and forward rate volatilities and occurs because of mean reversion of yields. Third, the volatility function $\sigma_2$ has different signs for different maturity dates with the long volatility being negatively signed and the short volatility positively signed. This means the second factor drives the short forward rates in the opposite direction to the long forward rate. This may be interpreted as a "slope" factor, one that tends to drive the short end up and the long end down or vice versa. This feature actually introduces a twist in the yield curve and is an important feature if you do not wish to assume parallel shifts in the term structure of interest rates.

From this input information, we show how to build out the full three-period tree of forward rates, identifying along the way the risk-neutral drifts of the rates.

### Building the Trinomial Tree: The First Period

Using the specification of the $\sigma$ functions, the forward-rate evolution over the first period may be represented as a trinomial branching tree as in Figure 30.2. For simplicity, we have written $\alpha_1$ and $\alpha_2$ for the drift terms $\alpha(0, 1)$ and $\alpha(0, 2)$.

**FIGURE 30.2**

Initial Two-Factor
HJM Tree

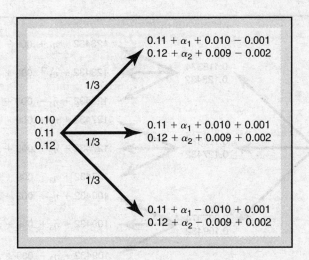

We solve for $\alpha_1$ and $\alpha_2$ in two steps. First, using the two-period bond, we solve for the value of $\alpha_1$. Then, using a three-period bond and the value of $\alpha_1$, we solve for the value of $\alpha_2$. We undertake the first step in the following equation.

$$\exp[-(0.10)] \times \exp[-(0.11)] = \exp[-(0.10)] \times \frac{1}{3} \times \exp[-(0.11 + \alpha_1 + 0.010 - 0.001)]$$

$$+ \frac{1}{3} \times \exp[-(0.11 + \alpha_1 + 0.010 + 0.001)]$$

$$+ \frac{1}{3} \times \exp[-(0.11 + \alpha_1 - 0.010 + 0.001)]$$

The equation above arises simply from the fact that the discounted expected value of the two-year zero must equal its current price when expectations are taken under the risk-neutral measure. Note that on each side of the equation, we could have eliminated the discounting back to time zero since this calculation is the same on both sides and is redundant. The solution to this equation is

$$\alpha_1 = -0.00362614$$

We now carry out the second step. The value of $\alpha_2$ comes from the following equation:

$$\exp[-(0.11 + 0.12)]$$

$$= \frac{1}{3} \times \exp[-(0.11 + \alpha_1 + 0.010 - 0.001)] \ \exp[-(0.12 + \alpha_2 + 0.009 - 0.002)]$$

$$+ \frac{1}{3} \times \exp[-(0.11 + \alpha_1 + 0.010 + 0.001)] \ \exp[-(0.12 + \alpha_2 + 0.009 + 0.002)]$$

$$+ \frac{1}{3} \times \exp[-(0.11 + \alpha_1 - 0.010 + 0.001)] \ \exp[-(0.12 + \alpha_2 - 0.009 + 0.002)]$$

Here, discounting back to time zero has been eliminated from both sides of the equation above. Given that we already know the value of $\alpha_1$, this equation contains only one unknown value, $\alpha_2$. The solution to this equation is:

$$\alpha_2 = -0.00356759$$

Substituting these values $\{\alpha_1, \alpha_2\}$ back into the tree results in the updated tree in Figure 30.3.

**FIGURE 30.3**
Two-Factor Tree with
Completed First Period

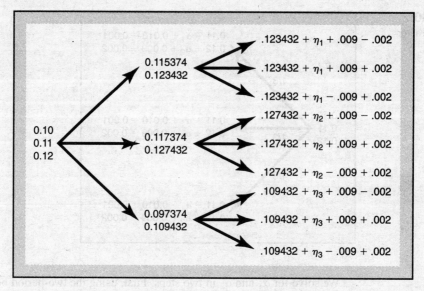

## Building the Trinomial Tree: The Second Period

We now proceed to solving for the forward rates in the second period of the model. We set the drift values to be $\eta_1$ in the uppermost subtree, $\eta_2$ in the middle subtree, and $\eta_3$ in the lowest subtree. (See Figure 30.3.) There is only one maturity drift term to be solved for in each case as there is only one year left in the horizon at this point. Therefore, there is only one equation required in each subtree.

For the upper-most subtree, we solve for $\eta_1$ using the by-now familiar approach. The equation to be solved is

$$\exp[-0.123432] =$$
$$\exp[-(0.123432 + \eta_1 + 0.009 - 0.002)] \times 1/3$$
$$+ \exp[-(0.123432 + \eta_1 + 0.009 + 0.002)] \times 1/3$$
$$+ \exp[-(0.123432 + \eta_1 - 0.009 + 0.002)] \times 1/3$$

The solution is $\eta_1 = -0.00363685$.

Similar calculations may be done for the remaining two subtrees. Carrying them out, the three values are

$$\eta_1 = -0.00363685$$
$$\eta_2 = -0.00363685$$
$$\eta_3 = -0.00363685$$

The three drift terms are identical because the stochastic process that evolves from each of the three nodes at the end of the first period is the same across the nodes. Substituting these values back into the tree, we get the final tree of forward rates, depicted in Figure 30.4.

Observe that while there is partial recombination, the tree fails to be fully recombining. (There is one node in common between the upper and middle thirds of the tree after two periods. Similarly, there is one node in common between the middle and lower thirds of the tree after two periods as well.) Recombination is lost even though all forward rate volatilities are constant over time. This happens because the model has two factors. This is a useful fact to remember about most interest-rate tree models: recombination is hard to achieve.

**FIGURE 30.4**
Final Two-Factor Tree

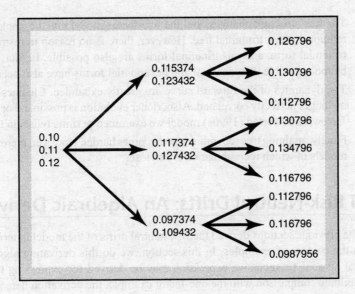

However, fairly accurate pricing is still possible even on trees with few periods, using techniques that vary the length of the time step across the tree. These ideas are described in Heath, Jarrow, Morton, and Spindel (1992).

**Example 30.2**

Consider a coupon bond with a maturity of three years and a coupon of 12%. We price a one-year call option on this bond at a strike price of 100. The strike price is the ex-coupon strike, i.e., we compare the call strike price with the value of the bond excluding the coupon.

Using the tree, we compute the possible values of the underlying bond at the end of one year. There are two remaining cash flows at the end of one year, and the forward curve may be used to determine the prices. The three nodes at time 1 give us the following three values:

$$12\exp[-(0.115374)] + 112\exp[-(0.115374 + 0.123432)] = 98.8999$$
$$12\exp[-(0.117374)] + 112\exp[-(0.117374 + 0.127432)] = 98.3509$$
$$12\exp[-(0.097374)] + 112\exp[-(0.097374 + 0.109432)] = 101.962$$

Finally the option value is computed.

$$\text{Option Value} = \left[\frac{1}{3}\max(0, 98.8999 - 100) + \frac{1}{3}\max(0, 98.3509 - 100)\right.$$
$$\left. + \frac{1}{3}\max(0, 101.962 - 100)\right]\exp[-0.10]$$
$$= 0.591898$$

■

## One-Factor versus Two-Factors: Summary

Summarizing this entire discussion, the main lessons from extending the one-factor model to two-factors are as follows:

• The basic idea of no arbitrage remains unchanged and is applied in the same way as before. Discounting zero-coupon bond values under risk-neutral probabilities allows solving for the drift terms and thus enables building the tree period by period.

- The tree structure changes, and the two-factor model may be implemented most parsimoniously on a trinomial tree. However, there is no reason to restrict the structure to a trinomial form, and quadrinomial forms are also possible. In fact, this form may even be more flexible. Pentanomial and hexanomial forms have also been used in practice.
- The dynamics of the forward curve are greatly expanded. Changes in forward rates are no longer perfectly correlated. Also, richer evolution is possible. For example, the Heath, Jarrow, and Morton (1990a) model we examined permits twists in the curve.
- Finally, attaining tree recombination becomes harder. However, there are many two-factor models in which recombination is not lost.

## 30.5   The HJM Risk-Neutral Drifts: An Algebraic Derivation

The previous sections derived the risk-neutral drifts of the model in terms of the volatilities in the context of examples. In this section, we do this derivation algebraically and show that an analytic recursive expression may be derived for expressing this relationship. To facilitate comparison with the one-factor example, the derivation here is in the context of a one-factor binomial model with equiprobable up and down moves; we also use a volatility specification that is a simple generalization of that used in the one-factor example. For a full-blown algebraic derivation of this result in a general setting, see Appendix 30A.

We restrict attention to a three-period model; as will become apparent, the derivation is easily generalized. The initial forward rate curve is given by the vector $[f(0, 0), f(0, 1), f(0, 2)]$. As in our examples, we assume that the volatilities $\sigma(t, s)$ depend only on $s$; this too is easily generalized, although the expressions for the drifts will not then look as neat.

We begin with the risk-neutral drifts over the first period. There are two forward rates left at the end of this period. Writing $\sigma_1$ for $\sigma(1)$, etc., the up state forward curve is:

$$\begin{bmatrix} f(0, 1) + \alpha_1 h + \sigma_1 \sqrt{h} \\ f(0, 2) + \alpha_2 h + \sigma_2 \sqrt{h} \end{bmatrix}$$

The down state forward curve is

$$\begin{bmatrix} f(0, 1) + \alpha_1 h - \sigma_1 \sqrt{h} \\ f(0, 2) + \alpha_2 h - \sigma_2 \sqrt{h} \end{bmatrix}$$

We solve for $\alpha_1$ and $\alpha_2$ exactly as we did in the numerical examples. Starting with the two-period \$1 zero-coupon bond as the basis, we compute its two possible prices at the end of the first period, i.e., in the up state and down state. These prices are, respectively,

$$\exp[-(f(0, 1) + \alpha_1 h + \sigma_1 \sqrt{h})h]$$
$$\exp[-(f(0, 1) + \alpha_1 h - \sigma_1 \sqrt{h})h]$$

We take expected values and discount this value to inception to obtain the price of the bond

$$P(0, 2) = \exp[-(f(0, 0) + f(0, 1))h] \cdot \frac{1}{2} \left( \exp[-(\alpha_1 h + \sigma_1 \sqrt{h})h] + \exp[-(\alpha_1 h - \sigma_1 \sqrt{h})h] \right)$$

This should equal the current price of the bond priced directly off the initial forward curve, i.e.,

$$P(0, 2) = \exp[-(f(0, 0) + f(0, 1))h]$$

Equating these expressions provides an analytic relationship between the drift $\alpha_1$ and $\sigma_1$,

$$1 = \frac{1}{2}\left(\exp[-(\alpha_1 h + \sigma_1 \sqrt{h})h] + \exp[-(\alpha_1 h - \sigma_1 \sqrt{h})h]\right)$$

which may be rewritten as

$$\alpha_1 = \frac{1}{h^2}\ln\left[\frac{1}{2}\left(\exp[\sigma_1\sqrt{h}h] + \exp[-\sigma_1\sqrt{h}h]\right)\right]$$

$$= \frac{1}{h^2}\ln\left[\frac{1}{2}\left(\exp[\sigma_1 h^{\frac{3}{2}}] + \exp[-\sigma_1 h^{\frac{3}{2}}]\right)\right]$$

$$= \frac{1}{h^2}\ln\left[\cosh\left(\sigma_1 h^{\frac{3}{2}}\right)\right]$$

where cosh is the hyperbolic cosine function defined by $\cosh(x) = (\exp(x) + \exp(-x))/2$. This simple expression relates the arbitrage-free drift term for the one-period maturity to the corresponding volatility of the same maturity. The expression for the second period drift is similar; we undertake the derivation in full again for completeness.

This time, we start with the three-period \$1 zero-coupon bond as the basis, and we compute its two possible prices at the end of the first period, i.e., in the up state and down state. These two prices are, respectively,

$$\exp[-(f(0,1) + \alpha_1 h + \sigma_1\sqrt{h} + f(0,2) + \alpha_2 h + \sigma_2\sqrt{h})h]$$
$$\exp[-(f(0,1) + \alpha_1 h - \sigma_1\sqrt{h} + f(0,2) + \alpha_2 h - \sigma_2\sqrt{h})h]$$

The usual calculation gives the price of the bond at the initial time point

$$P(0,3) = \exp[-f(0,0)h] \times$$
$$\frac{1}{2}\left(\exp[-(f(0,1) + \alpha_1 h + \sigma_1\sqrt{h} + f(0,2) + \alpha_2 h + \sigma_2\sqrt{h})h]\right.$$
$$\left. + \exp[-(f(0,1) + \alpha_1 h - \sigma_1\sqrt{h} + f(0,2) + \alpha_2 h - \sigma_2\sqrt{h})h]\right)$$

This should equal the current price of the bond priced directly off the initial forward curve:

$$P(0,3) = \exp[-(f(0,0) + f(0,1) + f(0,2))h]$$

Equating these expressions provides a relationship between the drifts $\alpha_1$ and $\alpha_2$ and the volatilities $\sigma_1$ and $\sigma_2$.

$$1 = \frac{1}{2}\left(\exp[-(\alpha_1 h + \alpha_2 h + \sigma_1\sqrt{h} + \sigma_2\sqrt{h})h] + \exp[-(\alpha_1 h + \alpha_2 h - \sigma_1\sqrt{h} - \sigma_2\sqrt{h})h]\right)$$

which may be rewritten as

$$\alpha_1 + \alpha_2 = \frac{1}{h^2}\ln\left[\frac{1}{2}\left(\exp[\sigma_1\sqrt{h}h + \sigma_2\sqrt{h}h] + \exp[-\sigma_1\sqrt{h}h - \sigma_2\sqrt{h}h]\right)\right]$$

$$= \frac{1}{h^2}\ln\left[\frac{1}{2}\left(\exp[(\sigma_1 + \sigma_2)h^{\frac{3}{2}}] + \exp[-(\sigma_1 + \sigma_2)h^{\frac{3}{2}}]\right)\right]$$

$$= \frac{1}{h^2}\ln\left[\cosh\left((\sigma_1 + \sigma_2)h^{\frac{3}{2}}\right)\right]$$

This expression generalizes in the obvious way. If there are $T$ periods in the model, then the general form of this equation for the sum of $T$ drifts is

$$\sum_{t=1}^{T} \alpha_t = \frac{1}{h^2} \ln \left[ \cosh \left( \left( \sum_{t=1}^{T} \sigma_t \right) h^{\frac{3}{2}} \right) \right] \tag{30.9}$$

Here is the Octave program code to generate the forward rate curves one period ahead. By calling this program recursively, one can generate the entire tree of forward rates.

```
% hjm(f0,sig0,h)
% Program to generate the HJM Tree
% The program takes in a fwd curve and vol curve and returns
% the next periods up and down fwd curves
%f0 : initial forward rate curve
%sig0 : forward rate volatilities (for this node)

function u = hjm(f0,sig0,h);
    n = length(f0);
    m = n-1;
    fu = f0(2:n);
    fd = f0(2:n);
    sigma = sig0(2:n);
    alpha = zeros(m,1);
    for j=[1:m];
        if (j==1);
            alpha(j) = log(0.5*(exp(-sigma(j)*h*sqrt(h)) + ...
                exp(sigma(j)*h*sqrt(h))))/h^2;
        end;
        if (j>1);
            alpha(j) = log(0.5*(exp(-sum(sigma(1:j))*h*sqrt(h)) + ...
                exp(sum(sigma(1:j))*h*sqrt(h))))/h^2-sum(alpha(1:j-1));
        end;
    end;
    fu = fu+alpha*h+sigma*sqrt(h);
    fd = fd+alpha*h-sigma*sqrt(h);
    u = [fu fd];
```

In order to illustrate the implementation, here is a snippet of the results from running the program above in the Octave programming language:

```
octave:1> f0 = [0.10; 0.11; 0.12; 0.13; 0.14];
octave:2> sig0 = 0.015*ones(5,1);
octave:3> h=1;
octave:4> hjm(f0,sig0,h)
ans =

    0.125112   0.095112
    0.135337   0.105337
    0.145562   0.115562
    0.155787   0.125787
```

We can see that these results are precisely those we developed earlier through the process of bootstrapping. Note that this is the program code (function) for a single node on the HJM tree. Repeatedly calling this function spawns the full tree in complete generality because we may choose a different volatility vector at each node.

As noted at the top of this section, a general derivation of the relation between risk-neutral drifts and volatilities in the context of discrete-time HJM models is presented in Appendix 30A.

## 30.6   Libor Market Models

Market Models were developed by Brace, Gatarek, and Musiela (1997) and Jamshidian (1997). Other versions of these models were developed around this time, but the main credit for popularizing these models has been ascribed to these two papers. For an analysis of pricing derivatives in closed form in this framework, see the paper by Miltersen, Sandmann, and Sondermann (1997).

We have seen in the previous sections that HJM offers a general framework in which many types of term-structure evolution may be accommodated. An appealing feature of HJM models is that the risk-neutral drifts for interest-rate stochastic processes may be expressed completely in terms of forward rate volatilities as in equation (30.9). Since these volatilities may be implied from the prices of interest-rate derivatives, the entire HJM model is, in principle, based on observables. The information in the term structure of forward rates is coupled with information from the term structure of volatilities to develop a lattice of forward rates admitting no arbitrage on which interest-rate derivatives may be priced. The HJM framework is widely used.

Libor Market Models (or LMMs) represent a natural development from the HJM class of models. They too are based on forward rates and volatilities. As we will see, they are much more particular in form than HJM models. One may well ask that if HJM models are so general and widely used, then what is the need for the more particular class of LMMs? Rather than model instantaneous forward rates as in the HJM model, in the LMM, observable Libor rates are modeled directly. Their volatilities are also extracted directly from the prices of traded options. This makes it much easier to link the LMM to the prices of commonly traded products.

To understand the evolution of LMMs, we note that market practice has been to model forward Libor rates using a lognormal distribution. This assumption ensures that rates remain positive at all times. Also, lognormal rates deliver closed-form option pricing formulae for caps and floors that are similar to those obtained in the Black-Scholes model. LMMs are based on lognormal forward rates so that the pricing and calibration of simple derivatives on forward rates may be analytically tractable. Indeed, we have examined the pricing of caps and floors already using the Black (1976) model (see Chapter 23).

Within a cap option, each caplet is usually based on consecutive but non-overlapping Libor rates. The total price of the cap does not require imposing correlation assumptions on the various forward Libor rates. This is because the price of each caplet may be computed separately from the others using the Black model since each underlying forward rate applies to one and only one caplet. Further, risk-neutral pricing of derivatives on single forward Libor rates may be undertaken under different martingale measures for each rate.[1]

---

[1] This is analogous to pricing each stock option on a separate binomial tree for each stock. In all cases a martingale probability measure is used but there is no restriction imposed to keep all probability measures the same.

Each caplet's market price may be used to directly extract the implied volatility of each forward Libor rate. This is done using the closed-form Black pricing equation. This makes calibration easy and simple.

Interest rate derivatives that are written on more than one forward Libor rate need to be priced using the same probability measure for rates of all maturities. The heart of the LMM approach lies in transforming all Libor rates so as to bring them under the same probability measure under which all discounted (normalized) asset prices will be martingales.

Accordingly, in the ensuing sections, we will revisit the concept of martingales as well as that of change of measure. We will learn how to adjust the drifts of the stochastic processes for forward Libor rates so as to bring them under a unified measure. The setup in which this is done is known as the "Market Model" framework.

Before proceeding, we note that there are two main classes of markets to which these models are calibrated, Libor markets (using caps and floors) and swap markets (using swaptions). Hence, we get two types of market models, the Libor Market Model (LMM) and the Swap Market Model (SMM). In this chapter, we focus on the former, using it to illustrate concepts that are important for understanding this class of models.

We turn now to a description of the LMM. After revisiting martingale concepts, we present a simple version of the model so the basic ideas may be easily understood. We elaborate each step so that the reader may find it easy to implement the model if needed. Following this description, we undertake a brief presentation of the related class of SMMs. Extensive derivations and details for the more technically inclined reader may be obtained in the book by Brigo and Mercurio (2001). A survey of both the theory and the empirical validity of the model may be found in Rebonato (2002b).

# 30.7   Mathematical Excursion: Martingales

We undertake a short diversion here to review martingales. This mathematical concept has taken center stage in the pricing of derivative securities since the papers by Harrison and Kreps (1979) and Harrison and Pliska (1981). In this section we review their ideas in brief.

A random variable $X$ is said to be a martingale if its expected value in the future is equal to its value today. For a simple example of a martingale, consider a coin toss where heads wins you a dollar and tails loses a dollar. Assuming a fair coin (heads and tails are equally likely), the expected value of this gamble is zero. In fact, the expected value of your wealth after $t$ tosses is equal to zero. More generally, suppose your wealth after $t$ tosses is $S_t$. Then,

$$E[S_k|\mathcal{F}_t] = S_t, \quad k \geq t \qquad \textbf{(30.10)}$$

In words, (30.10) says that *viewed from time t* and conditional on all information $\mathcal{F}_t$ available at time $t$ (including the past realizations of tosses and the wealth level $S_t$ reached by time $t$), the expected wealth at time $k > t$ is the same as the value at time $t$.

The condition (30.10) is the defining condition in probability theory for $S_t$ to be a martingale. Note the implicit dependence of this condition on the probability measure with respect to which future wealth is calculated. It was only because the coin is a fair one (Prob($H$) = Prob($T$) = 0.50) that ($S_t$) is a martingale. If, for instance, we had Prob($H$) = 0.60, then you are more likely to win a dollar than to lose one, so your expected wealth *increases* over time; the process is now called a *sub*martingale. If we had Prob($H$) = 0.40, then your expected wealth would *decrease* over time, that is, it would be a *super*martingale.

The significance of martingales for derivative pricing was described in the simplified setting of Chapter 11 (see Appendix 11). Briefly, given a setting with $n$ security price processes, pick any one security to act as a "numeraire." Express all other securities prices in terms of units of the numeraire security; that is, divide all security prices by the price of the numeraire security. These prices are called the "normalized" or "discounted" security prices. In notational terms, if $S_{kt}$ denotes the time-$t$ price of security $k$, and security $\ell$ has been chosen to be the numeraire, then the discounted price of security $k$, denoted, say, $Z_{kt}$, is given by

$$Z_{kt} = \frac{S_{kt}}{S_{\ell t}}$$

Note that the discounted price $Z_{\ell t}$ of the numeraire security $\ell$ itself is always equal to 1.

The fundamental connection between martingales and derivatives pricing is the following: if there exists a set of probabilities (i.e., a probability "measure," denoted, say, $Q$) under which all discounted securities prices are *martingales*, then (a) the model is free of arbitrage, and (b) the "correct" arbitrage-free price of any derivative can be identified by taking the expectation *under $Q$* of the discounted payoffs of the derivative. Following Harrison and Kreps (1979), the probability measure that makes discounted securities prices martingales is called a "martingale measure." Modulo some technical conditions, the converse is also true that if a model is free of arbitrage, then a martingale measure exists for any choice of numeraire.

Note that the martingale measure depends on the choice of numeraire security, i.e., the security with respect to which the discounted security prices are defined. If we change the numeraire, there is no reason to expect the new discounted prices will remain a martingale. Thus, to be complete, we should really say that (for example) "$Q$ is a martingale measure with respect to the numeraire $\ell$." Change the numeraire asset, and you need to change the probabilities to make discounted security prices martingales.

As one may guess, there are many combinations of numeraires and their associated martingale probabilities. The accumulated money market account (described by rolling over a dollar at the risk-free rate) is a common choice of numeraire in practice. This is the numeraire security we have used so far in this book to derive the risk-neutral probabilities. The risk-neutral measure for this choice of numeraire is called the "spot" martingale measure.

Sometimes it is more convenient to use a numeraire that is the price of a $T$-maturity discount bond $P(t, T)$ instead of the money market account. In this case, as we move ahead in time, i.e., as $t$ increases, the price of the bond rises until it reaches unity at $t = T$, i.e., $P(T, T) = 1$. To distinguish the martingale measure with respect to $P(t, T)$ as numeraire from the "spot" one, such martingale measures are denoted as "forward measures." In the following sections, we will be working with forward measures, and we will see why they are more convenient than spot measures for pricing Libor-based interest-rate derivatives. The appendix also contains some additional results on forward measures that the reader may refer to for additional insights.

## 30.8 Libor Rates: Notation

The LMM is a model that (a) has forward Libor rates moving continuously but has (b) discrete periods over which Libor rates are defined. The model is implemented on a time line with discrete intervals, each assumed to be of $\delta$ years. Let time 0 be the initial time point of the model. Subsequently, at any current time $t$, define "end-of-period" times measured from $t$ as the time points

$$T_1 = t + \delta, \quad T_2 = t + 2\delta, \quad \ldots \quad , T_N = t + N\delta$$

Given we are at time $t$, time $T_1$ is the end of the first period thereafter. Likewise, $T_2$ is the end of the second subsequent period, and so on. Next, let $L_i$ be the forward Libor rate at time $t$ for the period of length $\delta$ ending in $T_i$. For example, $L_1$ is the Libor rate for the forward period ending in $T_1$. Between time $T_{i-1}$ and $T_i$, an invested dollar earning Libor will become $(1 + \delta L_i)$.[2] The following diagram reflects this timing convention.

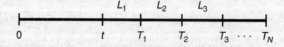

Our exposition of the LMM assumes that the source of uncertainty for $L_i$ is a Brownian motion $(W_i)$. We assume the following lognormal stochastic process for Libor rates $L_i$:

$$dL_i(t) = \mu_i(t)L_i(t)\,dt + \sigma_i L_i(t)\,dW_i(t), \qquad i = 1, \ldots, N$$

It is useful to keep in mind that the subscript $i$ refers to the end of the period over which a given forward Libor rate applies, and $t$ represents the current calendar time.

We first look at the connection between Libor rates and discount bonds. Define $P(t, T_i)$ as the time-$t$ price of the zero-coupon bond maturing at time $T_1$ and paying a certain dollar at that point. It is easily checked that the following consistency relationships exist between discount bonds:

$$P(t, t) = P(t, T_1)[1 + \delta L_1]$$
$$P(t, T_1) = P(t, T_2)[1 + \delta L_2]$$
$$P(t, T_2) = P(t, T_3)[1 + \delta L_3]$$
$$\vdots$$
$$P(t, T_{i-1}) = P(t, T_i)[1 + \delta L_i]$$
$$\vdots$$
$$P(t, T_{N-1}) = P(t, T_N)[1 + \delta L_N]$$

Rearranging these expressions, we get in general:

$$\delta L_i = \frac{P(t, T_{i-1})}{P(t, T_i)} - 1, \quad \text{for all } i$$

Suppose we take $P(t, T_i)$ as the numeraire asset and assume that there exists a probability measure $Q_i$ such that, under $Q_i$, the discounted price $P(t, T_{i-1})/P(t, T_i)$ is a martingale. Examining the equation above, we see that this implies that the Libor rate $L_i$ is also a martingale under $Q_i$ with respect to numeraire $P(t, T_i)$. This immediately implies that the evolution of the Libor rate will be arbitrage-free under $Q_i$, which is thence known as a "forward martingale measure."

This creates an unusual situation. Since each Libor rate $L_i$ has its own numeraire bond $P(t, T_i)$, each rate is a martingale with respect to a *different* measure $Q_i$, $i = 1 \ldots N$. We thus have a set of martingale measures, one for each $i$, with numeraires $P(., T_i)$ respectively. But to have a consistent pricing system, all Libor rates must be governed by the same probability measure. Fixing one martingale measure for a chosen Libor rate, we will undertake a change

---

[2] Since the Libor market uses the Actual/360 convention, the day-count fractions $\delta$ will not all be the same even if each period represents, say, three months. Some three-month periods may have 91 days in them, so $\delta$ will be 91/360. Others may have 92 days, so we have $\delta = 92/360$. For simplicity, to avoid introducing further notation, we assume this away and use the same day-count fraction for all periods.

of measure for the other Libor rates to bring them under one measure. We will derive this common measure in the next section.[3]

Finally, note that caps and floors are options on Libor rates. Since Libor rates are not traded assets, we need to be sure that we can replicate them using discount bonds. This is easy to show. Suppose we are interested in locking in an investment at time $t$ at rate $L_i$ for the period $(T_{i-1}, T_i)$. We may replicate this as follows:

- **At time $t$** Short 1 unit of the bond $P(t, T_{i-1})$ and use the proceeds to buy $\frac{P(t,T_{i-1})}{P(t,T_i)}$ units of the bond maturing at $T_i$. The net cash flow at $t$ is zero.
- **At time $T_{i-1}$** Buy back the short position in the bond maturing at time $T_{i-1}$. Since this is a discount bond the net cash flow is $-1$.
- **At time $T_i$** Sell the position in the bond maturing at $T_i$, resulting in a cash flow of $\frac{P(t,T_{i-1})}{P(t,T_i)}$. This amount is equal to $(1 + \delta L_i)$.

We have created a replicating portfolio that results in a cash flow of $-1$ at time $T_{i-1}$ and another cash flow of $(1 + \delta L_i)$ at time $T_i$. This is exactly analogous to investing in an asset at time $T_{i-1}$ at a return rate of $L_i$ for the interval $(T_{i-1}, T_i)$.

Before proceeding, let us recap. We have defined a model, based on lognormal forward Libor rates. In the HJM model, discounted bond prices are martingales under a "spot" martingale measure—the one that takes the money market account as numeraire. The LMM model has rates based on a "forward" martingale measure, one in which the numeraire asset is the price of a bond maturing in the future. The LMM may be summarized as a model framework in which an entire family of forward rates is modeled under a common forward measure such that consistency with caplet prices is maintained.

Next we develop the mechanics for implementing the change of measure needed to bring all forward Libor rates under the same probability measure while retaining their connection to traded caps and floors.

## 30.9    Risk-Neutral Pricing in the LMM

We now derive the risk-neutral process for all Libor rates. This is undertaken in two steps. First, we choose a numeraire bond. Second, we determine the drifts $\mu_i$ of all Libor rates such that they are transformed to be governed by a common probability measure.

As before, Libor rates are assumed to be lognormally distributed, i.e.,

$$\frac{dL_i}{L_i} = \mu_i \, dt + \sigma_i \, dW_i, \qquad i = 1, \ldots, N$$

It is simplest to choose the discount bond of maturity $T_N$ as the numeraire asset. Based on this, we will compute the drift terms $\mu_1, \mu_2, \ldots, \mu_N$ such that $\frac{L_1}{P(t,T_N)}, \frac{L_2}{P(t,T_N)}, \ldots, \frac{L_N}{P(t,T_N)}$ are martingales with respect to a probability measure over correlated Brownian motions $W_1, W_2, \ldots, W_N$. The numeraire is no longer a money market account as in the case of the HJM model. Instead, it is a bond maturing in the future, and, hence, the probability measure is known as the "forward" measure. From a nomenclature point of view, pricing in the HJM model is undertaken under the "spot" measure.

The calculation of risk-neutral drifts in the LMM is less than trivial, and, hence, with a view to keeping the exposition gentle, we will work with only a three period model, i.e.,

---

[3] We might say, "One Measure to rule them all, One Measure to find them, One Measure to bring them all and in no-arbitrage bind them," (adapted from *Lord of the Rings* with apologies to J.R.R. Tolkein).

$N = 3$. The results developed for three periods generalize easily to as many periods as are necessary. Thus, there are three Libor rates in our model, $\{L_1, L_2, L_3\}$, corresponding to periods $(t, T_1), (T_1, T_2)$, and $(T_2, T_3)$. Our numeraire is $P(t, T_3)$. The martingale probability measure is $Q_3$. The current point in time is denoted $t$.

### Deriving the Martingale Process for $L_3$

We begin with Libor rate $L_3$ and determine its martingale process when the numeraire is $P(t, T_3)$. From the previous section, we restate the functional form for $L_3$

$$\delta \cdot L_3 = \frac{P(t, T_2)}{P(t, T_3)} - 1$$

The right-hand side of the equation contains an expression for the price of the two-period bond $P(t, T_2)$ normalized by numeraire $P(t, T_3)$. By assumption, this must be a martingale under the probability measure based on the Brownian motion $W_3$. The expected change of the right-hand side of the equation is therefore zero. Given this, the expected change of the left-hand side is also zero, implying that $L_3$ is a martingale. Hence, if $L_3$ is already a martingale, its drift must be zero, i.e., $\mu_3 = 0$. We may then specify the stochastic process for $L_3$ as follows:

$$dL_3 = \sigma_3 L_3 \, dW_3$$

Note that $L_3$ is lognormal and it is a martingale.

### Deriving the Martingale Process for $L_2$

Turning to $L_2$, we write down its relation to discount bonds:

$$\delta \cdot L_2 = \frac{P(t, T_1)}{P(t, T_2)} - 1 = \frac{P(t, T_1) - P(t, T_2)}{P(t, T_2)}$$

Since the normalizing asset on the right-hand side of the equation is $P(t, T_2)$, not the numeraire $P(t, T_3)$, the process for $L_2$ is not a martingale with respect to the required numeraire, and, hence, we need to make a change of probability measure to convert it into a process with respect to the chosen numeraire, $P(t, T_3)$. To do this, multiply both sides of the equation by $P(t, T_2)$ and divide both sides by $P(t, T_3)$. This results in the following:

$$\delta \cdot L_2 \times \frac{P(t, T_2)}{P(t, T_3)} = \frac{P(t, T_1) - P(t, T_2)}{P(t, T_3)}$$

In the absence of arbitrage, all assets of any shape or form, normalized by $P(t, T_3)$, must be martingales. Hence, looking at the left-hand side of the equation above, the asset $L_2 P(t, T_2)$ normalized by $P(t, T_3)$ is also a martingale with respect to $Q_3$. On the right-hand side of the equation above, an asset defined as the difference of two bonds, i.e., $P(t, T_1) - P(t, T_2)$ normalized by $P(t, T_3)$ is also, by construction, a martingale. Defining $Z_2 \equiv \frac{P(t, T_2)}{P(t, T_3)}$, we have

$$\delta \cdot L_2 Z_2 = \frac{P(t, T_1) - P(t, T_2)}{P(t, T_3)}$$

Let $A_2 = L_2 Z_2$. Applying Ito's lemma to $A_2$, we get (via an extension of the product rule)

$$dA_2 = L_2 \, dZ_2 + Z_2 \, dL_2 + dZ_2 \, dL_2$$

Dividing both sides by $A_2$, we get

$$\frac{dA_2}{A_2} = \frac{dZ_2}{Z_2} + \frac{dL_2}{L_2} + \frac{dZ_2}{Z_2} \frac{dL_2}{L_2}$$

$A_2$ is a martingale, as is $Z_2$, an asset normalized by the numeraire. Therefore, taking expectations on both sides with respect to the martingale probability measure results in

$$0 = 0 + E\left[\frac{dL_2}{L_2}\right] + E\left[\frac{dZ_2}{Z_2}\frac{dL_2}{L_2}\right]$$

Noting that $E\left[\frac{dL_2}{L_2}\right] = \mu_2\,dt$, we get, via a series of simplifying steps, the expression for the drift that makes $L_2$ a martingale with respect to the chosen numeraire.

$$\mu_2\,dt = -E\left[\frac{dZ_2}{Z_2}\frac{dL_2}{L_2}\right]$$

$$= -E\left[dZ_2\frac{dL_2}{L_2}\right]\frac{1}{Z_2}$$

$$= -\frac{1}{Z_2}E\left[d(1+\delta L_3)\frac{dL_2}{L_2}\right]$$

$$= -\frac{\delta L_3}{Z_2}E\left[\frac{dL_3}{L_3}\frac{dL_2}{L_2}\right]$$

$$= -\frac{\delta L_3}{Z_2}E\left[\sigma_2\sigma_3\,dW_2\,dW_3\right]$$

$$= -\frac{\delta L_3}{Z_2}\rho_{23}\sigma_2\sigma_3\,dt$$

$$= -\frac{\delta L_3}{1+\delta L_3}\rho_{23}\sigma_2\sigma_3\,dt$$

Note that in lines 3 and 7 of the derivation above, we exploited the fact that

$$Z_i = \frac{P(t, T_i)}{P(t, T_{i+1})} = 1 + \delta L_{i+1}, \quad \forall i$$

Thus, we have derived the drift term for Libor rate $L_2$ to make it a martingale with respect to numeraire $P(t, T_3)$. The final result is

$$\mu_2 = -\frac{\delta L_3}{1+\delta L_3}\rho_{23}\sigma_2\sigma_3$$

### Deriving the Martingale Process for $L_1$

The calculations for $L_1$ are only slightly more complicated and lead on directly to the general case of many periods. Therefore, it is instructive to work through this last period of the model in detail.

Turning to $L_1$, we write down its relation to discount bonds:

$$\delta \cdot L_1 = \frac{P(t, t)}{P(t, T_1)} - 1 = \frac{P(t, t) - P(t, T_1)}{P(t, T_1)}$$

Since the normalizing asset on the right-hand side of the equation is $P(t, T_1)$, not the numeraire $P(t, T_3)$, the process for $L_1$ is not a martingale with respect to the required numeraire, and, hence, we need to make a change in the equation to convert it into a process with respect to the chosen numeraire, $P(t, T_3)$. To do this, multiply both sides of the equation by $P(t, T_1)$ and divide both sides by $P(t, T_3)$. This results in the following

$$\delta \cdot L_1 \times \frac{P(t, T_1)}{P(t, T_3)} = \frac{P(t, t) - P(t, T_1)}{P(t, T_3)}$$

We modify the left-hand side of the equation a little bit as follows:

$$\delta \cdot L_1 \times \frac{P(t, T_1)}{P(t, T_2)} \frac{P(t, T_2)}{P(t, T_3)} = \frac{P(t, t) - P(t, T_1)}{P(t, T_3)}$$

which may also be written as

$$\delta \cdot L_1 Z_1 Z_2 = \frac{P(t, t) - P(t, T_1)}{P(t, T_3)}$$

Let $A_1 = L_1 Z$ where $Z = Z_1 Z_2$ and using Ito's lemma, we get the following:

$$dA_1 = Z \, dL_1 + L_1 \, dZ + dL_1 \, dZ$$

Dividing both sides by $A_1$, we have

$$\frac{dA_1}{A_1} = \frac{dL_1}{L_1} + \frac{dZ}{Z} + \frac{dL_1}{L_1} \frac{dZ}{Z}$$

Because $A_1$ and $Z$ are martingales, we must have that, after taking expectations on both sides,

$$0 = E\left[\frac{dL_1}{L_1}\right] + 0 + E\left[\frac{dL_1}{L_1} \frac{dZ}{Z}\right]$$

Noting that $Z = Z_1 Z_2$ and that Ito's lemma gives $\frac{dZ}{Z} = \frac{dZ_1}{Z_1} + \frac{dZ_2}{Z_2} + \frac{dZ_1}{Z_1} \frac{dZ_2}{Z_2}$, the equation above may be written as

$$0 = \mu_1 \, dt + 0 + E\left[\frac{dL_1}{L_1}\left(\frac{dZ_1}{Z_1} + \frac{dZ_2}{Z_2} + \frac{dZ_1}{Z_1} \frac{dZ_2}{Z_2}\right)\right]$$

Simplifying, and noting that the third power term $dL_1 \, dZ_1 \, dZ_2 = 0$, we get

$$\mu_1 \, dt = -E\left[\frac{dL_1}{L_1} \frac{dZ_1}{Z_1} + \frac{dL_1}{L_1} \frac{dZ_2}{Z_2}\right] = -E\left[\frac{dL_1}{L_1} \frac{dZ_1}{Z_1}\right] - E\left[\frac{dL_1}{L_1} \frac{dZ_2}{Z_2}\right]$$

Let's simplify each term on the right-hand side separately.

$$-E\left[\frac{dL_1}{L_1} \frac{dZ_1}{Z_1}\right] = \frac{1}{1 + \delta L_2} E\left[d(1 + \delta L_2)\frac{dL_1}{L_1}\right]$$

$$= -\frac{\delta L_2}{1 + \delta L_2} E\left[\frac{dL_2}{L_2} \frac{dL_1}{L_1}\right]$$

$$= -\frac{\delta L_2}{1 + \delta L_2} \sigma_1 \sigma_2 E(dW_1 \, dW_2)$$

$$= -\frac{\delta L_2}{1 + \delta L_2} \rho_{12} \sigma_1 \sigma_2 \, dt \qquad \textbf{(30.11)}$$

$$-E\left[\frac{dL_1}{L_1} \frac{dZ_2}{Z_2}\right] = \frac{1}{1 + \delta L_3} E\left[d(1 + \delta L_3)\frac{dL_1}{L_1}\right]$$

$$= -\frac{\delta L_3}{1 + \delta L_3} E\left[\frac{dL_3}{L_3} \frac{dL_1}{L_1}\right]$$

$$= -\frac{\delta L_3}{1 + \delta L_3} \sigma_1 \sigma_3 E(dW_1 \, dW_3)$$

$$= -\frac{\delta L_3}{1 + \delta L_3} \rho_{13} \sigma_1 \sigma_3 \, dt \qquad \textbf{(30.12)}$$

Combining both terms (30.11) and (30.12), we get the following final result:

$$\mu_1 = -\left[\frac{\delta L_2}{1 + \delta L_2}\,\rho_{12}\sigma_1\sigma_2 + \frac{\delta L_3}{1 + \delta L_3}\,\rho_{13}\sigma_1\sigma_3\right]$$

By simple analogy, we may write down the result for the general case immediately:

$$\mu_i = -\sum_{j=i+1}^{N}\left[\frac{\delta L_j}{1 + \delta L_j}\,\rho_{ij}\sigma_i\sigma_j\right], \quad \forall i < N \qquad \textbf{(30.13)}$$

and when $i = N$, $\mu_i = 0$. Equation (30.13) is the main result of the Libor market model derivation above and may be then used in all further computations. It provides the drift terms that are then substituted back into the stochastic processes for Libor rates. The risk-neutral Libor dynamics under which no-arbitrage pricing may be undertaken with respect to numeraire $P(t, T_N)$ may now be stated as follows:

$$\frac{dL_i}{L_i} = -\sum_{j=i+1}^{N}\left[\frac{\delta L_j}{1 + \delta L_j}\,\rho_{ij}\sigma_i\sigma_j\right]\,dt + \sigma_i\,dW_i, \quad \forall i < N \qquad \textbf{(30.14)}$$

As in the HJM model, we note that the risk-neutral drifts of the LMM Libor processes are also functions of the volatilities and correlations. If instead of separate Brownian motions $W_i$, we have a simple one-factor LMM model, then $\rho_{ij} = 1$ in the equation above.

## 30.10 Simulation of the Market Model

In market models, pricing is usually undertaken by simulating Libor rates. If there are $N$ rates, then we need to simulate rates $L_1, L_2, \ldots, L_N$ jointly with the correct correlation among the rates. The $N$ Brownian motions $W_i$, $i = 1, \ldots, N$ have volatility coefficients $\sigma_i$ and pairwise correlations between $W_i$ and $W_j$ equal to $\rho_{ij}$.

Our procedure is as follows. At each point in time, we generate $N$ standard normal random numbers $W_i$ with correlation matrix $\{\rho_{ij}\}$. Each $W_i$ has a mean of 0 and a variance of 1. Assuming a simulation time interval denoted by $h$, we generate the next period's Libor rates using the following discrete-time version of equation (30.14):

$$L_i(t + h) = L_i(t)\exp\left[\left(-\sum_{j=i+1}^{N}\left[\frac{\delta L_j}{1 + \delta L_j}\,\rho_{ij}\sigma_i\sigma_j\right] - \frac{1}{2}\sigma_i^2\right)h + \sigma_i\sqrt{h}\cdot W_i\right], \quad \forall i$$

$$\textbf{(30.15)}$$

We are able to derive this expression directly since we have already encountered it previously in the case of the Black-Scholes model where stock prices are lognormal as are Libor rates here.

## 30.11 Calibration

One of the main advantages of the LMM class of models over others is ease of calibration to market prices. We explore this feature here. We begin with developing the pricing equation for cap options. A cap is a collection of caplets, and its value is the sum of the values of caplets.

Recall that options on forwards are priced using Black (1976)'s formula. The formula for options on forwards is based on two assumptions: one, that the process for the underlying forward variable is lognormal and, two, that the volatility is nonstochastic, i.e., a constant or a deterministic function of time. Caplets are options on Libor forward rates $L_i$. As long as the volatilities $\sigma_i$ are nonstochastic, Black's formula applies directly. In the case of our exposition here where we have assumed $\sigma_i$ to be constant, we meet the conditions for Black's model and obtain a closed-form pricing equation for caps and floors.

Consider a caplet with strike $X$ and maturity $T_i$. The option is therefore written on the forward Libor rate $L_{i+1}$ for the period $(T_i, T_{i+1})$. Applying Black (1976)'s model, we have the solution for the option:

$$C_0 = P(0, T_i) \, [L_{i+1}(0) \, N(d_1) - X \, N(d_2)] \, \delta$$

where

$$d_1 = \frac{1}{\sigma_{i+1}\sqrt{T_i}} \left[ \ln\left(\frac{L_{i+1}(0)}{X}\right) + \frac{1}{2}\sigma_{i+1}^2 \, T_i \right]$$

and

$$d_2 = d_1 - \sigma_{i+1}\sqrt{T_i}$$

where $\sigma_{i+1}$ is the volatility for the Libor rate $L_{i+1}$.

A similar argument shows that the price of a floorlet on $L_{i+1}$ with maturity $T_i$ and strike $K$ is

$$F_0 = P(0, T_i) \, [-L_{i+1}(0) \, N(-d_1) + X \, N(-d_2)] \, \delta$$

where $d_1$ and $d_2$ are as defined above. This is obtained by making the usual sign changes to terms in the equations for caps.

This closed-form model makes calibration simple. All we need to do is compute the value of $\sigma_{i+1}$, which matches the model price to that of the caplet for maturity $T_i$. Doing so for all strikes and maturities results in the volatility surface for caps and floors.

We have looked at a very simple model in which the volatility of the Libor rates was taken to be constant. The generalizations to time-varying Libor volatility are quite easy. As with the case of time-varying volatility derived by Merton (1973), all we need do is replace the volatility term in the equation above with the integrated time-varying volatility, i.e., replace the term $\sigma_{i+1}\sqrt{T_i}$ with the following

$$\sqrt{\int_0^{T_i} \sigma_{i+1}^2(t) \, dt}$$

The reader will find sufficient further detail in the original paper by Brace et al. (1997).

## 30.12   Swap Market Models

In this section, we briefly review swap market models (SMMs). As with LMMs, one of the advantages of SMMs is that direct calibration to the swap and swaptions market is possible. Since a full development of LMMs has already been undertaken, the main principles and concepts have been covered. However, it is instructive to focus on the differences between LMMs and SMMs as well as the relation between these two approaches.

Our comparison of LMMs and SMMs focuses on the following three main points:

1. **Numeraires** Recall that under the forward probability measure, Libor rates are martingales. The $i$-th Libor rate, $L_i(t)$, has the following relationship to zero-coupon bond

prices:

$$\delta L_i(t) = \frac{P(t, T_{i-1})}{P(t, T_i)} - 1 \qquad (30.16)$$

where $\delta$ is the time interval covered by each period in the swap, and we have assumed that $T_0 \equiv t$. The rate $L_i$ is a martingale with respect to the measure $Q_i$ if

$$E_{Q_i}\left[\frac{P(t, T_{i-1})}{P(t, T_i)} - 1\right] = E_{Q_i}\left[\frac{P(t, T_{i-1}) - P(t, T_i)}{P(t, T_i)}\right] = 0$$

In other words, in the LMM setting, Libor rates are martingales with respect to numeraire $P(t, T_i)$.

A swap comprises an exchange of fixed-for-floating payments. Each floating payment is of the amount $\delta L_i$ and at time $T_i$ has the following present value:

$$\delta\, L_i(T_{i-1})\, P(T_{i-1}, T_i) = P(T_{i-1}, T_{i-1}) - P(T_{i-1}, T_i)$$

This is obtained by rearranging equation (30.16) and setting $t = T_{i-1}$. A swap is nothing but a collection of such floating payments in exchange for fixed payments. We focus on the floating payment first. Since Libor rates are martingales, we can see that the present value at time $t$ of any floating payment is simply obtained by moving the equation above to time $t$ so that the expected present value of the entire floating side of the swap is

$$\sum_{i=1}^{N} \delta\, L_i(t)\, P(t, T_i) = \sum_{i=1}^{N} [P(t, T_{i-1}) - P(t, T_i)] = P(t, T_1) - P(t, T_N)$$

$$(30.17)$$

The present value of the fixed side of the swap is the present value of payments made at the fixed rate $S$:

$$\delta S \sum_{i=1}^{N} P(t, T_i) \qquad (30.18)$$

Equating (30.17) and (30.18), we see that the fair swap rate $S$ is written as

$$S(T_1, T_N) = \frac{P(t, T_1) - P(t, T_N)}{\delta \sum_{i=1}^{N} P(t, T_i)}$$

where $S \equiv S(T_1, T_N)$ is written to indicate that the swap covers the cash-flow periods that end in the range $(T_1, T_N)$. From equation (30.16), it follows that because $[P(t, T_1) - P(t, T_N)]$ is a martingale, then $S$ is a martingale with respect to the numeraire

$$\sum_{i=1}^{N} P(t, T_i)$$

which is the present value of the sum of unit payments each swap period. Compare this to the numeraire in the LMM, which is just $P(t, T_i)$. Thus, the essential difference between the LMM and SMM models boils down to a specification of numeraire.

2. **Incompatibility** The LMM model assumes that Libor rates are lognormal. From equation (30.16), it follows that the change in zero-coupon bond prices is also lognormal. The numeraire in the SMM is the sum of discount bond prices and is therefore not lognormal when Libor rates are lognormal.

Practitioners make a choice as to which market they should calibrate to, the Libor market or the swap market. If they choose to calibrate to the swap market (and swaptions prices), they assume that swap rates are lognormal and then directly apply the SMM. From the preceding paragraph, it is clear that choosing the SMM with lognormal swap rates must imply that another model that assumes lognormal Libor rates cannot be consistent with it. It is not possible for both models to simultaneously assume lognormal rates and still remain compatible with each other. Because of this inherent inconsistency between the models, a trading room needs to pick one of the models and stick to it.

3. **Model choice** The quandary posed by the incompatibility problem begs the question as to which model is the better choice, the LMM or the SMM. As always, model choice is based on two important attributes: *calibration* and *hedging*. Depending on the predominant business of a trading desk, traders will usually calibrate their models either to Libor futures and caplets or swaps and swaptions. Also, they will use the same instruments for hedging. This choice determines which of the two variants of market model is chosen.

Without doubt, trading practice is the most important determinant of model choice. But it also raises the natural question about cross-model error. Suppose one opts for the LMM. Then what is the extent of mispricing of swaps and swaptions? Conversely, one would like to know how biased caplet prices are if the underlying model is calibrated to swap markets. There is limited empirical analysis of this issue. The question was assessed in a paper by DeJong, Driessen, and Pelsser (2001). They found that calibrating the LMM to caplets resulted in lower pricing error for swaptions than the calibration of the SMM (to swaptions) for pricing the caplets. Much of the mispricing can be traced to a tendency to overfit these models to the data so that the in-sample fit is extremely good, but the out-of-sample performance of these models deteriorates significantly.

## 30.13 Swaptions

The SMM may be used to obtain swaption prices in closed form in much the same way in which the LMM rendered closed-form equations for caps and floors. We define the values of the floating and fixed side of the swap using equations (30.17) and (30.18) as follows:

$$\text{Floating side: } A = \sum_{i=1}^{N} \delta \, L_i(t) \, P(t, T_i) \qquad \textbf{(30.19)}$$

$$\text{Fixed side: } B = \delta S \sum_{i=1}^{N} P(t, T_i) \qquad \textbf{(30.20)}$$

where $S$ is the fixed rate that is set on the swap that underlies the swaption. As swap rates change in the market, the fair swap rate $S$ will always be such that floating and fixed sides are equal, i.e., that $\sum_{i=1}^{N} \delta \, L_i(t) \, P(t, T_i) = \delta S \sum_{i=1}^{N} P(t, T_i)$. The ratio of the fair-price floating-side value to the fixed side value is

$$\frac{A}{B} = \frac{\delta S \sum_{i=1}^{N} P(t, T_i)}{\delta S \sum_{i=1}^{N} P(t, T_i)} = \frac{S}{S}$$

Since $S$ is constant, if we assume that $S$ is lognormal with volatility $\sigma$, then we are in the setting of the Black and Scholes (1973) model. If the ratio $A/B$ is lognormal, then the swaption that is the option to exchange the floating side (receive) in return for the fixed side (pay) will be an option to exchange one side for the other and may be valued using the well-known formula of Margrabe (1978). The value of a swaption at time $t$ to receive floating Libor and pay fixed-rate $S$ for maturity $T \leq T_1$ is as follows:

$$\text{Swaption(receive floating, pay fixed)} = A\, N(d_1) - B\, N(d_2)$$

$$d_1 = \frac{\ln(A/B) + \frac{1}{2}\sigma^2 T}{\sigma\sqrt{T}}$$

$$d_2 = d_1 - \sigma\sqrt{T}$$

Correspondingly, the value of the swaption to pay floating and receive fixed is as follows:

$$\text{Swaption(pay floating, receive fixed)} = B\, N(-d_2) - A\, N(-d_1)$$

$$d_1 = \frac{\ln(A/B) + \frac{1}{2}\sigma^2 T}{\sigma\sqrt{T}}$$

$$d_2 = d_1 - \sigma\sqrt{T}$$

A final point to note is that nothing in the derivation above was particular to the market model framework. The same derivation applies to models such as HJM and to other interest-rate models where the underlying swap rates are assumed to be lognormal.

## 30.14 Summary

This chapter has examined two of the most important classes of term-structure models. The first is the Heath-Jarrow-Morton (HJM) model. The HJM approach works by modeling movements in the entire forward curve. It has some important advantages over the factor model approach. In particular, drifts of the forward-rate processes under the risk-neutral measure are functions of the volatilities. The framework is also a very general one, admitting any desired number of driving factors each of which could matter in different ways.

The second class of models examined is the so-called "Market Models," viz., the Libor Market Model (LMM) and the Swap Market Model (SMM). The lognormality of these models achieves (even in multifactor settings) solutions that are analogous to those of the Black and Scholes (1973) and Black (1976) models and offers solutions that are available in closed form. This makes the calibration of model volatilities similar to backing out implied volatilities. The LMM class of models has become a popular tool for the pricing of interest rate derivatives.

## 30.15 Exercises

1. State at least three differences between the HJM model and the model of Black-Derman-Toy (BDT).

2. Denote the forward rates in the HJM model by $f(t, T)$, where $t$ is current time, and the forward rate is for the future period $[T, T + h]$, where $h = 1$ year is the discrete time interval. Suppose you are given the following binomial evolution of forward rates:

$$f(t + h, T) = f(t, T) + \alpha(T)h \pm \sigma\sqrt{h}$$

Finally, suppose you are also provided the following data:

$$f(0, 0) = 0.06, \quad f(0, 1) = 0.07$$

If the price of a one-year call option on a two-year zero-coupon bond at a strike of $90 is $4, then what is the value of the parameter $\sigma$?

3. Assume the following process for HJM forward rates:

$$f(t + h, T) = f(t, T) + \alpha(T)h \pm \sigma(T)\sqrt{h}$$

Let the current forward curve be given by

$$f(0, 0) = 0.08$$
$$f(0, 0.5) = 0.09$$
$$f(0, 1) = 0.10$$

Finally suppose that

$$\sigma(0.5) = 0.03, \quad \sigma(1) = 0.02$$

Derive the arbitrage-free forward curves one period from now.

4. (Requires writing code) Develop the program code for the HJM model where, given an initial forward curve, volatility curve, and the length of the time step, you provide a function to generate the two forward curves for the next period. (This problem generalizes the procedures you followed in the previous two problems.) Present the results of the model for three years where the time step in the model is $h = 1/2$. Assume that the initial forward curve is flat at 6% and that the volatility curve is also flat with $\sigma = 0.05$. Program this model in Octave.

5. (Requires writing code) Redo the previous problem using Excel VBA.

6. There are six half-year periods on a forward curve. The curve is currently flat at 6%, and you are given the following declining volatility curve:

0.06
0.05
0.04
0.03
0.02
0.01

(a) What feature of interest rates might result in the volatility curve declining so sharply?

(b) Solve for the two forward curves a half-year ahead, and plot each of them. What effect does the declining volatility have on the two curves in the next period?

7. Suppose that the time interval on an HJM tree is $h$ and the forward rate process is binomial:

$$f(t + h, T) = f(t, T) + \alpha h \pm \sigma \sqrt{h}$$

Show that for $T = t + h$

$$\alpha = \frac{1}{h^2} \ln[\cosh(\sigma h^{3/2})]$$

8. In the previous question, what can you say about the expression for the drift in terms of its representation of the interest-rate risk premium? What is it uniquely a function of?

9. The following table summarizes the initial forward curve for three half-year periods and the initial volatility curve at $t = 0$. Compute the two forward curves at time $t = 0.5$ and the three forward curves at time $t = 1$.

| $(0, T)$ | $f(0, T)$ | $\sigma(T)$ |
|---|---|---|
| $(0,0)$ | 0.04 | — |
| $(0,0.5)$ | 0.045 | 0.015 |
| $(0,1)$ | 0.05 | 0.012 |

10. Based on the same input parameters as the previous question, price a cap option contract with exercise dates at $t = 0.5$ and $t = 1$, at a strike rate of the half-year interest rate of 5%. Assume the notional on the contract to be $100.

11. (Requires writing code) Using Excel VBA develop a spreadsheet to create trees in the HJM model, where you present the tree of one-period spot rates.

    (a) As an example, taking the time step $h = 1/2$, show the five-period tree when the initial forward curve is

    $$f_0$$
    $$0.09$$
    $$0.10$$
    $$0.11$$
    $$0.12$$
    $$0.13$$

    and the volatility function is given by

    $$\sigma(T) = 0.005 \exp[-2\lambda(T - 0.5)]$$

    where $\lambda = 0.2$ is the coefficient of mean reversion.

    (b) Increase $\lambda = 0.5$ and show the new tree of spot rates. What can you say about the effect of $\lambda$ on the tree?

12. In this question you will use programming to implement the Heath-Jarrow-Morton model. The model will be implemented for a non-recombining tree because the volatility function in the model will be based on a volatility matrix instead of a simple vector of volatilities. Assume that the tree you build will be for ten periods of a half year each. Hence, the model extends to a maturity of five years. The initial term structure of forward rates will be as follows:

$$f = \begin{bmatrix} 0.020 \\ 0.022 \\ 0.023 \\ 0.030 \\ 0.035 \\ 0.040 \\ 0.045 \\ 0.050 \\ 0.044 \\ 0.042 \end{bmatrix}$$

The volatility function, which also defines the volatility matrix, is simply that the volatility of each forward rate at each point in time $t$ is equal to $0.05 \times f(t, T)$ for each forward rate of maturity $T$. This effectively defines a different volatility at each node of the tree for each forward rate. Or in other words, it defines a volatility matrix. Please note that the volatilities will be different at each node of the tree.

You should write your program code to generate the tree and then price a $100 notional cap comprised of 10 caplets (one for each half year). The strike rate for all the caps is 3%. What is the price of the entire cap?

*Hint*: Write the program using recursion and you will find that there is very little programming involved. To make sure it is working, test it on fewer periods, say three, which will allow you to run more tests. Also write the code so that you can pass the program a forward curve ($f$), the time step ($h$), and the volatility function, so that it is completely general to all numbers of time periods (you can infer how many periods there are in the model from the length of the forward rate curve that you pass into the program).

13. What claimed deficiencies of the HJM model are ameliorated by using the Libor Market Model (LMM)?

14. What is the "forward" measure? Explain its importance in the pricing of interest rate derivatives.

15. (Requires writing code) Given a flat term structure of interest rates at 6% and a flat volatility term structure of 10%, use a one-factor Libor Market Model to price a one-year cap at a strike rate of 7%. Write program code in Octave. Use a monthly time step. You will need to simulate the movement of rates in the LMM to arrive at the solution.

# Risk-Neutral Drifts and Volatilities in HJM

In this section, we derive formally the connection between the risk-neutral drifts and the volatilities in a general discrete-time HJM model. For the most part, we confine attention to a one-factor model, although, as we explain towards the end of this appendix, extending the arguments to multiple factors is more intensive only algebraically, not conceptually. For the original paper on which this appendix is based, see Heath, Jarrow, and Morton (1990).

To keep the appendix self-contained, we redefine the notation. The model is set in a time line beginning at time $t = 0$. There are $n$ periods in the model, each of length $h$ years. The last time point is $nh$.

A general forward rate in this setting is denoted by $f(t, T)$ where $f(t, T)$ is the rate quoted (seen) at time $t$ for borrowing or investment over the interval $[T, T + h]$. At each $t$, there is, therefore, one forward rate for each time-point $T \geq t$. Forward rates are observed at the times $t = (ih)$, where $i = 0, 1, \dots, n$.

After one period, the forward rate $f(t, T)$ for maturity at $T$ becomes $f(t + h, T)$. The change in the forward rate over the interval $[t, t + h]$ is then

$$f(t + h, T) - f(t, T), \quad \forall T$$

This change is assumed to be composed of a deterministic component (the "drift," denoted $\alpha(t, T)$) and a random component (the "volatility," denoted $\sigma(t, T)$):

$$f(t + h, T) = f(t, T) + \alpha(t, T)h + \sigma(t, T)X_1\sqrt{h}, \quad \forall T \geq t \qquad \textbf{(30.21)}$$

Here $X_1$ is a random variable with mean zero and variance 1 (e.g., a standard normal variate). It is easy to see that the expected change in the forward rate is $\alpha(t, T)h$ and the standard deviation of the change is $\sigma(t, T)\sqrt{h}$.

The one-period spot rate of interest at any time $t$ is just the instantaneous forward rate $f(t, t)$. This one-period spot rate (or the "short rate") is known at time 0, but at this time, future values of the short rate are unknown. These random values will be the sums of the deterministic components of changes in the rates and the random components. This is expressed in the following equation:

$$r(t) = f(t, t) = f(0, t) + \sum_{j=0}^{\frac{t}{h}-1}[\alpha(jh, t)h + \sigma(jh, t)X_1(j)\sqrt{h}] \qquad \textbf{(30.22)}$$

The $X_1(j)$'s are i.i.d. random variables each with the distribution of $X_1$. We may also express this short rate process as

$$r(ih) = f(0, ih) + \sum_{j=0}^{i-1}[\alpha(jh, ih)h + \sigma(jh, ih)X_1(j)\sqrt{h}] \qquad \textbf{(30.23)}$$

More generally, we can write down an equation describing the law of motion for the one-period forward rate beginning at time $ih$:

$$f(t, ih) = f(0, ih) + \sum_{j=0}^{t/h-1}(\alpha(jh, ih)h + \sigma(jh, ih)X_1(j)\sqrt{h}) \qquad \textbf{(30.24)}$$

Note that $f(t, ih)$ as seen at time 0 is also a random variable.

We will use these laws of motion of the short rate (equation 30.22) and forward rate (equation 30.24) to determine the risk-neutral drifts of this model as functions of the volatilities. We begin by writing out the price of a zero-coupon bond paying \$1 at time $t$ with maturity $T$. The price of this bond may be computed by discounting at the sum of forward rates over the life of the bond:

$$P(t, T)$$

$$= \exp\left[-\sum_{i=\frac{t}{h}}^{\frac{T}{h}-1} f(t, ih)h\right]$$

$$= \exp\left(-\sum_{i=\frac{t}{h}}^{\frac{T}{h}-1}\left[f(0, ih) + \sum_{j=0}^{t/h-1}(\alpha(jh, ih)h + \sigma(jh, ih)X_1\sqrt{h})\right]h\right) \quad \textbf{(30.25)}$$

In the second line of the equation above, we have inserted the expression for the forward rate from equation (30.24). Again, as seen from time 0, the price of the zero-coupon bond is a random variable.

Martingale pricing ideas were presented in Chapter 11. We know that the absence of arbitrage implies that the prices of all *normalized* securities are martingales under the risk-neutral probabilities. Normalization is usually undertaken by means of a *numeraire* asset. Assuming the existence of a riskless money market account $B(t)$ as the numeraire for pricing bonds, this account accumulates *random* value at the short rate of interest as follows:

$$B(t) = \exp\left[\sum_{i=0}^{\frac{t}{h}-1} r(ih)h\right]$$

$$= \exp\left(\sum_{i=0}^{\frac{t}{h}-1}\left[f(0, ih) + \sum_{j=0}^{i-1}(\alpha(jh, ih)h + \sigma(jh, ih)X_1\sqrt{h})\right]h\right) \quad \textbf{(30.26)}$$

The term $1/B(t)$ then represents the discount function for all assets over the time interval $[t, t+h]$.

Recall that when we price options on trees (as we did earlier in this chapter), in each period we are discounting the expected future value of the asset. In the special case of a binomial tree with an up-branch probability $p$ and a down-branch probability $(1-p)$, we would, at each time $t$, write the value of a zero-coupon bond as follows:

$$P(t, T) = p\frac{P^u(t+h, T)}{B^u(t+h)} + (1-p)\frac{P^d(t+h, T)}{B^d(t+h)}$$

where $P^u(t+h, T)$ and $P^d(t+h, T)$ are the values of the bond in the up and down states one period ahead. Likewise, $B^u(t+h)$ and $B^d(t+h)$ are the corresponding values of the money market account in each state. Note that all of these values are random variables since at time $t$, they are seen one period ahead. The present value at time $t$ of the bond in any state is the price of the bond divided by the accumulated money market account. Hence, the ratios $P^u(t+h, T)/B^u(t+h)$ and $P^d(t+h, T)/B^d(t+h)$ in the expression above. More generally, when there are many states, we may write the same expression simply as

$$P(t, T) = E_t\left[\frac{P(t+h, T)}{B(t+h)}\right]$$

where the subscript $t$ indicates that the risk-neutral expectation $E_t[.]$ is taken at time $t$. Noting that at time $t$, $B(t) = 1$, we may also write this as

$$\frac{P(t, T)}{B(t)} = E_t \left[ \frac{P(t+h, T)}{B(t+h)} \right]$$

Now we define the normalized zero-coupon bond prices as

$$Z(t, T) = \frac{P(t, T)}{B(t)}, \quad Z(t+h, T) = \frac{P(t+h, T)}{B(t+h)}$$

Under the risk-neutral measure, the discounted prices of assets must follow martingales, and this is exactly the expression we have here, that is,

$$Z(t, T) = E_t[Z(t+h, T)]$$

or stated differently,

$$E_t \left[ \frac{Z(t+h, T)}{Z(t, T)} \right] = 1 \qquad (30.27)$$

This mathematical expression simply says that if the normalized asset $Z(t)$ is a martingale, then the ratio of succeeding values of the asset in expectation must be unity. Making the necessary substitutions from equations (30.25) and (30.26) into the no-arbitrage condition (30.27) above, we can solve for the values of the drifts that satisfy this condition. The calculations are long and tedious and are as follows. First, we compute $Z(t, T)$:

$$Z(t, T) = \frac{P(t, T)}{B(t)}$$

$$= \exp\left( - \sum_{i=0}^{T/h-1} f(0, ih)h \right)$$

$$\times \exp\left( - \sum_{i=t/h}^{T/h-1} \sum_{j=0}^{t/h-1} (\alpha(jh, ih)h + \sigma(jh, ih)X_1\sqrt{h})h \right)$$

$$\times \exp\left( - \sum_{i=0}^{t/h-1} \sum_{j=0}^{i-1} (\alpha(jh, ih)h + \sigma(jh, ih)X_1\sqrt{h})h \right)$$

Analogously, we get the value of $Z(t+h, T)$:

$$Z(t+h, T) = \frac{P(t+h, T)}{B(t+h)}$$

$$= \exp\left( - \sum_{i=0}^{T/h-1} f(0, ih)h \right)$$

$$\times \exp\left( - \sum_{i=t/h+1}^{T/h-1} \sum_{j=0}^{t/h} (\alpha(jh, ih)h + \sigma(jh, ih)X_1\sqrt{h})h \right)$$

$$\times \exp\left( - \sum_{i=0}^{t/h} \sum_{j=0}^{i-1} (\alpha(jh, ih)h + \sigma(jh, ih)X_1\sqrt{h})h \right)$$

To make the notation simpler, we define

$$A(jh, ih) = (\alpha(jh, ih)h + \sigma(jh, ih)X_1\sqrt{h})h$$

Then we have the following calculation:

$$\frac{Z(t+h, T)}{Z(t, T)}$$

$$= \frac{\exp\left(-\sum_{i=t/h+1}^{T/h-1}\sum_{j=0}^{t/h} A(jh, ih)\right)\exp\left(-\sum_{i=0}^{t/h}\sum_{j=0}^{i-1} A(jh, ih)\right)}{\exp\left(-\sum_{i=t/h}^{T/h-1}\sum_{j=0}^{t/h-1} A(jh, ih)\right)\exp\left(-\sum_{i=0}^{t/h-1}\sum_{j=0}^{i-1} A(jh, ih)\right)}$$

$$= \frac{\exp\left(-\sum_{i=t/h+1}^{T/h-1}\sum_{j=0}^{t/h} A(jh, ih)\right)}{\exp\left(-\sum_{i=t/h}^{T/h-1}\sum_{j=0}^{t/h-1} A(jh, ih)\right)}\exp\left(-\sum_{j=0}^{t/h-1} A(jh, t)\right)$$

$$= \frac{\exp\left(-\sum_{i=t/h+1}^{T/h-1}\left[\sum_{j=0}^{t/h-1} A(jh, ih) + A(t, ih)\right]\right)}{\exp\left(-\sum_{j=0}^{t/h-1} A(jh, t) - \sum_{i=t/h+1}^{T/h-1}\sum_{j=0}^{t/h-1} A(jh, ih)\right)}\exp\left(-\sum_{j=0}^{t/h-1} A(jh, t)\right)$$

$$= \frac{\exp\left(-\sum_{i=t/h+1}^{T/h-1}\left[\sum_{j=0}^{t/h-1} A(jh, ih) + A(t, ih)\right]\right)}{\exp\left(-\sum_{i=t/h+1}^{T/h-1}\sum_{j=0}^{t/h-1} A(jh, ih)\right)}$$

$$= \exp\left(-\sum_{i=t/h+1}^{T/h-1} A(t, ih)\right)$$

Based on equation (30.27), we have

$$E\left[\exp\left(-\sum_{i=t/h+1}^{T/h-1} A(t, ih)\right)\right] = 1$$

or

$$E\left[\exp\left(-\sum_{i=t/h+1}^{T/h-1} (\alpha(t, ih)h + \sigma(t, ih)X_1\sqrt{h})h\right)\right] = 1$$

Rearranging, we get the solution for the drift terms $\alpha(t, ih)$:

$$\sum_{i=\frac{t}{h}+1}^{\frac{T}{h}-1} \alpha(t, ih) = \frac{1}{h^2} \log E\left(\exp\left[-h\sum_{i=\frac{t}{h}+1}^{\frac{T}{h}-1} \sigma(t, ih)X_1(t)\sqrt{h}\right]\right), \quad \forall i \qquad \textbf{(30.28)}$$

Note that the expression for $A(t, ih) = (\alpha(t, ih)h + \sigma(t, ih)X_1\sqrt{h})h$ is for the one-factor version of the HJM model. However, we may write it more generally as $A(t, ih) = \left(\alpha(t, ih)h + \sum_{k=1}^{m} \sigma_k(t, ih)X_k\sqrt{h}\right)h$ and obtain an $m$-factor model instead.

By substituting the drift $[\alpha(.)]$ into the original process in equation (30.21), we obtain the risk-neutral evolution of the term structure. This transformed process can then be used to carry out the valuation of any contingent claim written on stochastic interest rates.

Equation (30.28) is a *recursive* equation. It provides the value of each maturity drift term (maturities are indexed by $i$). The left-hand side of the equation is presented as a sum of drift terms. What this means is that the drifts need to be bootstrapped. First solve for the drift of the shortest maturity forward rate. Then we may solve for the sum of the first and second drifts; since we know the value of the first drift, we can deduce that of the second. Next, using equation (30.28), we solve for the sum of the first three drifts. And so on. Even though this equation looks vastly more complex than that encountered before, it is clearly not any different technically or intuitively from that presented in the prior numerical examples in this chapter.

# Part 5

# Credit Risk

# Chapter 31

# Credit Derivative Products

## 31.1 Introduction

Conventionally, finance has distinguished between two kinds of risk, *market risk* and *credit risk*. Market risk is the risk of changes in prices of various sorts: changes in equity prices, commodity prices, interest rates, bond prices, exchange rates, index levels, and so on. Conventional derivatives such as futures, forwards, options, and swaps may be used to position and realign such risk.

*Credit risk* is the risk that promised payments on an obligation (e.g., a bond or a loan) will not materialize. It has two components to it: the occurrence of *default* on the underlying obligation and the risk of incomplete *recovery* in the event of default. As compensation for bearing this risk, the holder of such an obligation typically receives a higher yield than could be obtained on similar instruments with lower credit risk. The *credit spread* is a measure of the extra yield on a credit-risky asset over a benchmark risk-free rate.

In the derivatives industry, credit risk is an area that came into prominence in the early 1990s. Derivatives on credit risk ("credit derivatives") were first proposed in 1992 at the conference of the International Swaps and Derivatives Association (ISDA). Such derivatives enable stripping and transferring the credit risk of a security separately from its other risks, so facilitate trading in solely the credit risk attributes of an instrument. In principle, such derivatives can promote efficiency gains from at least two sources. First, loan and bond markets are very often illiquid, making it difficult, if not impossible, to take short positions in an underlying credit (i.e., in the credit risk of an issuer). Credit derivatives facilitate such shorting: the derivative may be used to achieve the desired profile synthetically rather than achieving it through the underlying cash instrument. Second, the unbundling and separate trading of risks in an instrument means that each attribute of a security will be held by the market participant who values it maximally.

This chapter describes the vast range of credit derivative products. While we make a few remarks concerning the pricing of these instruments (particularly in the context of credit default swaps), the focus of this chapter is mainly on the characteristics of the products and their uses. Different approaches to the pricing of credit risk are presented in the succeeding chapters.

### Why Only in the 1990s?

Since credit risk is an aspect of economic activity that is almost as old as economic activity itself and since derivatives for handling market risks have been around for centuries, one may legitimately ask: why did credit derivatives come into prominence only recently? Several contributory factors may be identified.

Banks, which are the primary agents of lending in almost every country, traditionally handled credit risk through two techniques. The first was simple diversification, commonly operationalized by limiting the maximum exposure to any single entity. The second was to control default risk at the level of the individual borrower by undertaking lending based on relationships and the so-called 3 C's of banking: judging the repayment risk by a borrower's character, collateral, and capacity to repay the borrowed funds.

As quantitative techniques of portfolio management became popular in the finance industry, such techniques attracted the attention of the holders of loan and bond portfolios too. However, the implementation of portfolio optimization solutions presupposes a traded market in the underlying risks: without this, one cannot get from the portfolio one currently holds to the portfolio one wishes to hold. The notorious illiquidity of loan markets meant that other tools had to be employed to create the required long and short positions synthetically. Credit derivatives were able to meet this role.

Other factors also contributed. Worldwide, there has been a huge increase in the size of debt markets. For instance, S&P rated a total of only 8 sovereigns in 1970, but by 1996, this had grown to 62 sovereigns, and the figure almost doubled by 2007 to 116. The increased sovereign, corporate, and retail debt worldwide lowered average credit quality.

Alongside came other pressures from the banking system. While banks were traditionally the main lenders in all countries, they have been steadily disintermediated in recent times, particularly in the advanced economies. On the one hand, new lenders have emerged in the form of finance companies, insurance companies, and others, offering competition to banks. On the other hand, capital markets have become increasingly accessible to firms, particularly in the advanced economies where thousands of firms routinely access the commercial paper market to obtain short-term funding. The consequence of this has been that banks have largely been left with smaller and weaker credits, with thinner margins on account of the increased competition, worsening the risk-return trade-off. Using derivatives to shed unwanted loan risks and to achieve portfolio diversification has an obvious attraction under these circumstances.

Finally, as in many other cases, regulatory considerations—in this case, the capital adequacy requirements specified by the Basle (or Basel) Accords—played an important role. We highlight this in some of the examples we provide below. It should be emphasized, however, that these regulations themselves are likely targets for modification in the wake of the financial crisis that erupted in 2008, so this incentive for the use of credit derivatives may cease to be a factor of importance going forward.

## Terminology: "Credit Risk" and "Protection"

A terminological point is important at the outset. Suppose an investor (say, a bank) uses a credit derivative to transfer the credit risk in a loan to a second investor (say, a hedge fund). The first investor, the bank, is then *selling credit risk*, while the second investor, the hedge fund, is *buying credit risk*. In credit derivatives markets, an alternative terminology is popular. Since the hedge fund is assuming the credit risk through the derivative, it has effectively undertaken to compensate the bank in the event of any default on the underlying obligation. So the fund is said to be *selling protection* on the underlying obligation to the bank. The bank in turn is referred to as a *buyer of protection*.

Thus, one should be careful in using the terms "buyer" and "seller" to emphasize what exactly is being bought and sold. The buyer of credit risk is the seller of protection, while the seller of credit risk is the buyer of protection. In this chapter, we mainly use the terms "buyer" and "seller" to refer to the buyer and seller of protection.

# Uses of Credit Derivatives

We provide here a summary of the main advantages of using credit derivatives, that is, of what can be achieved with credit derivatives that would be difficult or impossible without them. We elaborate further on these benefits in the chapter in the context of discussing specific products.

First, consider a potential buyer of protection (i.e., the seller of credit risk). For example, think of a bank that is managing its loan portfolio. Credit derivatives enable the bank to actively manage credit exposure in the portfolio even where cash market sales of the underlying instruments are impossible (say, because of illiquid loan markets) or undesirable (for relationship reasons—the bank may not want its client, the borrower, to know that it is shedding the client's loan from its portfolio). In particular, the bank can use credit derivatives to transfer the risks in specific loans to third parties; that is, it can *hedge* those loans by creating *synthetic short positions* using credit derivatives. Such hedging would be impossible without an active credit derivatives market. Similarly, too, the bank can take on new exposures by creating *synthetic long positions* in loans or other instruments using credit derivatives. In turn, this facilitates the active management of both external (regulatory) constraints on lending operations as well as internal ones (e.g., restrictions on lines of credit to individual borrowers). Superior portfolio management and balance sheet benefits result.

Second by enabling the decomposing and stripping of risks from securities, credit derivatives enable credit risk to be managed independently of other risks. For many buyers of protection, this is an attractive feature. For example, convertible arbitrageurs typically buy convertible bonds to "unlock" the cheap volatility in the bonds; they do not have an interest in the bond's credit risk, per se. By buying protection to maturity or first call of the bond, they can eliminate credit risk considerations and focus on the conversion optionality in the bond.

For the sellers of protection (i.e., the buyers of credit risk), the main advantage of credit derivatives is that they allow investors to access entire new asset classes (e.g., syndicated loans) which only a limited set of market participants could access earlier. Too, leverage is often built into the credit derivative, making it more attractive to take on the exposure via a credit derivative than the cash instrument. Further, credit derivatives offer another vehicle for expressing directional views: an investor who is skeptical about the prospects of Widget Corporation can buy protection on the company as an alternative to shorting its shares.

A particular advantage of credit derivatives, from both the buyer's and seller's standpoints, is that they enable the creation of synthetic instruments of any desired maturity. For example, a seller of protection can take on two-year credit exposure to a given entity (say, Widget Corporation) using a credit derivative even if there are no two-year credits issued by Widget Corporation. Similarly, a bank that holds a five-year loan (say) of Widget Corporation on its books and feels that the company's prospects do not look bright over the next two years but believes that the company should do well if it survives the next two years, can buy two-year protection on the five-year loan.

# A Taxonomy of Credit Derivatives

The range of credit derivative products is huge, so some form of classification helps. A simple one is to first divide the derivatives into two categories: ones that depend on just the credit risk of a single entity ("single-name credit derivatives") and those that depend on several entities ("multiname," "basket," or "portfolio" credit derivatives, often also called "correlation products"). Within each category, there is considerable variety.

### Single-Name Credit Derivatives

At one end of the single-name credit derivative category are *total return swaps*. As the moniker suggests, these are products that transfer *all* the risk in a product, market risk as well as credit risk, from one counterparty (the total return "payer") to another (the total return "receiver"). Consider, for example, a total return swap on an underlying bond. The bond may lose value because of an increase in riskless interest rates (market risk), a deterioration in the issuing corporation's creditworthiness ("spread-widening" risk, one aspect of credit risk), or even default on the bond. In all cases, the loss in value is shouldered by the total return receiver.

One level further specialized are "spread" products, such as *credit spread forwards* and *credit spread options*. Credit spread options are options on the credit spread above a reference risk-free rate: buying them involves making an up-front premium payment, and the options pay off if the spread is above (or below) a specified strike spread. Thus, they provide one-sided protection against a deterioration (including default) or improvement in the creditworthiness of the issuing entity. Credit spread forwards are cash-settled forward contracts whose payoff at maturity depends on the difference between the actually prevailing credit spread on the reference obligation and a specified spread. Credit spread options and forwards transfer both spread-changing risk (resulting from a change in creditworthiness of the issuing entity for the reference obligation) and default risk from one counterparty to the other; but unlike total return swaps, they do not transfer market risk.

Even more specialized are event-triggered products such as *credit default swaps*. A credit default swap (CDS) pays off only if a specified credit event occurs, and pays nothing otherwise. (For now, think of the credit event as default. The actual event referenced in credit default swap contracts is a little wider, as we explain later.) Thus, a CDS offers a payout in the event of default, but not if spreads widen.[1] CDSs have become by far the most important component of the credit derivatives market. Many other products—credit-linked notes, basket default swaps, synthetic CDOs, and credit indices such as CDX—are based on the CDS.

Total return swaps and credit default swaps are off-balance-sheet unfunded products: like forwards or swaps, there is no up-front payment to enter into these contracts. On-balance-sheet funded versions of the instruments can also be created by embedding them in other instruments. A particularly popular example is a *credit-linked note*, a note issued by one entity in which the coupon payments and/or principal repayment is tied to default on a specified instrument issued by another (usually unrelated) entity. A variant, a *credit-sensitive note* (a.k.a. "performance sensitive debt"), is one in which the issuer of the note references its *own* credit quality in the note, typically making the coupon size a function of its credit rating. Many other exotic single-name credit derivatives also exist.

### Multiname Credit Derivatives

The most popular multiname credit derivatives are *basket default swaps*, *collateralized debt obligations* or CDOs, and index products such as the CDX and iTraxx indices.

Basket default swaps are natural extensions of credit default swaps. Instead of a single name, we begin with a basket of $K$ names (typically, 5 to 10). A "first-to-default" basket pays off when at least one name in the basket experiences a credit event; a "second-to-default" basket pays off when at least two names experience credit events; and so on. Since the number of defaults in the basket is governed by not only the individual default probabilities but also the correlation of these events, such swaps are called "correlation products."

---

[1] To be sure, CDSs can also be used as a hedge against spread-widening. Such widening typically implies an increase in default likelihood, so the price of new protection will increase. This implies a marked-to-market gain for those who are already long protection. This gain may be realized by unwinding the contracts.

A collateralized debt obligation pools debt issued by various entities and tranches out the resulting cash flows. Tranching is the specification of how the cash flows are paid out, including, in particular, who takes the losses on account of default on the underlying debt. All CDOs have an "equity" tranche that takes the first set of losses up to some prespecified amount, say the first 5% of losses. One or more "mezzanine" tranches would take the next set of losses above the equity loss limit (say, the next 10% of losses), and the "senior" tranche takes losses only after the loss limits of the mezzanine tranches are reached. The more junior the tranche, the greater the likelihood of losses on account of default, so the higher the coupon received by the holders of that tranche. CDOs are, evidently, also correlation products. Traditionally, CDOs were created using bonds (or loans) issued by various entities, but *synthetic* CDOs, those in which the CDO cash flows were created using credit-default swaps rather than bonds, became popular in the early- to mid-2000s. The financial crisis of 2008–09 has had a severe effect on the CDO market, and it is to be seen whether, and in what form, the market returns.

Credit indices such as the CDX and iTraxx indices offer a reading of the credit health of the entire market in much the same way as equity indices offer a reading of the entire equity market. In North America, for example, the investment-grade index (CDX.NA.IG) is computed using the CDS prices of the leading 125 investment-grade names, chosen using specified rules. Similarly, there is a North American high-yield index, a European investment-grade index, etc. Credit indices offer investors the ability to hedge against economy-wide changes in credit risk.

## Outline of This Chapter

The first part of this chapter discusses single-name credit derivatives, beginning with total return swaps and credit-spread products. We then move to the centerpiece of this discussion, credit-default swaps (CDSs). Following this, we present a description of credit-linked notes (CLNs) and credit-sensitive notes (CSNs). Building on this foundation, the second part of the chapter discusses correlation products, especially basket default swaps and CDOs.

# 31.2  Total Return Swaps

Total Return Swaps (TRSs) were, in the early days of the credit derivatives market, among the most popular of credit derivatives. Also called a *Total Rate of Return Swap*, a TRS is a bilateral financial contract in which one counterparty (called the "total return payer") pays the total return on a specified asset (called the "reference obligation") to the other counterparty (the "total return receiver") in exchange for a specified cash flow (typically Libor plus a spread on the notional amount of the swap).

The maturity of the TRS need not be, and very often in practice is not, the same as that of the underlying reference obligation. Thus, for example, one can have a three-year total return swap on an underlying ten-year bond. In this case, the total returns experienced on the bond over the three-year horizon are transferred from the total return (TR) payer to the TR receiver.

The "total return" in a TRS refers to returns received in the form of cash flows from the underlying reference obligation (e.g., coupons or interest payments if the underlying is a bond or a loan) as well as any changes in the capital value of the reference obligation. The change in value of the reference obligation can be positive (if the obligation appreciates in value) or negative (if it depreciates). Thus, the total return can be positive or negative. If the total return is negative, then the TR receiver makes a payment to the TR payer.

For example, suppose a bond pays a coupon of $2.50 during a specified period but also loses $5 in value over that period (say, because of a deterioration in creditworthiness of the issuer of the obligation). Then the total return over the period is −$2.50. This negative return accrues to the TR receiver, who must now make a payment of $2.50 to the TR payer.

The change in value settlements may be at maturity of the swap or periodic. In the former case, only the cash flows from the underlying reference obligation are exchanged during the life of the swap. The change in value payments is exchanged once and for all at the swap's maturity. In the latter case, each exchange of cash flows involves not only the coupons or other cash flows received from the reference obligation but also the change in value of the reference obligation from the time of the previous payment. For specificity, we will assume the former structure for the swap throughout our discussion. Only minor and obvious modifications are required to cover periodic settlements of value changes.

What happens if there is a default on the reference obligation during the life of the swap? Simple: the swap terminates with a final exchange to reflect the loss in value of the obligation consequent to default. The loss in value may be measured, depending on the contract, from the par value of the reference obligation or from the initial value of the reference obligation at the swap's inception. (The two will not coincide if the obligation was not trading at par at the swap's inception.)

This final exchange itself is effected in one of two ways. If *physical settlement* is used, the TR payer delivers the defaulted obligation to the TR receiver in exchange for a cash payment of the reference obligation's par (or, depending on the contract specifications, its initial) value. If *cash settlement* is used, then the TR receiver makes a cash payment to the TR payer equal to the loss in value of the defaulted obligation, that is, equal to the par (or initial) value of the reference obligation minus the post-default market price of the obligation. The post-default market price is identified using a specified mechanism (for example, a dealer poll). Of course, from an economic standpoint, cash and physical settlement are equivalent, but cash settlement has the advantage that there is no need for the TR payer to source the defaulted obligation to deliver it, while physical settlement has the advantage that there is no need to identify a potentially contentious post-default market price. Figure 31.1 summarizes the TRS assuming physical settlement at maturity.

## TRSs as Synthetic Long/Short Positions

As this discussion makes clear, the TRS effectively creates a *synthetic long position* in the reference obligation for the TR receiver; that is, even though the TR receiver does not own the instrument, the cash returns he receives are the same as would have been received from actual ownership of the instrument. (Note, however, that any other benefits of actual ownership—voting or servicing rights, for example—are not conferred by the TRS.)

**FIGURE 31.1**

A Total Return Swap

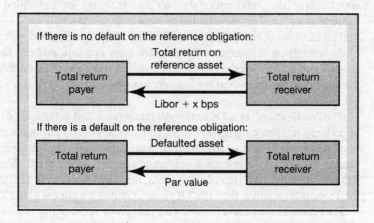

If there is no default on the reference obligation:

Total return payer → Total return on reference asset → Total return receiver

Total return payer ← Libor + x bps ← Total return receiver

If there is a default on the reference obligation:

Total return payer → Defaulted asset → Total return receiver

Total return payer ← Par value ← Total return receiver

Similarly, the TRS creates a *synthetic short position* in the reference obligation for the TR payer. This could be a "naked short," that is, the TR payer does not need to actually hold the underlying asset in order to enter into a TRS. But if the TR payer does hold the reference obligation too, the TR swap provides a hedge: it eliminates the risk in owning the obligation by transferring all returns to the TR receiver—but without transferring other benefits of ownership such as voting rights.

## TRS as a Form of Financing

In many ways, a TRS resembles a lease: in exchange for making regular payments, the TR receiver obtains the "use" of the underlying asset. Thus, the TRS is effectively a form of *financing*: the TR payer lends the use of the asset to the TR receiver for the swap duration. Assuming the TR payer holds the asset on its books, it is lending the use of its balance sheet to the TR receiver.

It follows that low funding-cost entities—that is, high-rated entities that can access assets cheaply on their balance sheets—fit naturally into the role of payers in TRS transactions, while lower-rated entities are more naturally TR receivers. (Intuitively, if I can access funds more cheaply than a leasing company, it does not pay for me to lease a car from them since the lease rate would have to reflect not only their cost of funds but also a mark-up to cover their other costs.) This gives rise to "funding-cost arbitrage," a term used to describe transactions in which entities with relatively high funding costs access assets synthetically using TRSs by borrowing the balance sheets of entities with lower funding costs. We describe a simple example below.

Obtaining cheap financing may not be the only reason for using TRSs. The TR receiver may simply not have access to the asset or find the asset difficult to access, while the TR payer has ready access. For example, a New York–based hedge fund looking to gain exposure to treasury bonds of an emerging market might find it easier to gain this exposure by entering into a total return swap with a global bank that can more readily access the underlying instruments. Moreover, TRSs provide leveraged exposure. The hedge fund may be required to post a collateral of (say) 20% of the face value of the bonds in exchange for which it gets full exposure, via the TRS, to changes in the bonds' value; the leverage in this case is 5:1.

## Funding-Cost "Arbitrage"

As mentioned above, funding-cost arbitrage is essentially a situation in which a high-funding cost entity uses the balance sheet of a lower-funding-cost entity to gain a desired exposure. The general idea is quite simple as the following example illustrates.

| **Example 31.1** | Consider two banks, Bank A, a relatively high-quality bank with a low funding cost, and Bank B, a lower quality bank with a higher funding cost. For specificity, suppose that Bank A's funding cost is Libor ($L$) flat while Bank B's funding cost is $L + 40$ basis points. Suppose too that the reference obligation in question is currently yielding $L + 70$ basis points. |
|---|---|

If Bank B were to buy the asset outright, this would result in a pick-up over funding costs of only 30 basis points, whereas if Bank A were to buy the asset, the pick-up is 70 basis points. Suppose Bank A bought the asset and entered into a TRS with Bank B in which B pays $L + x$ basis points in exchange for receiving the total returns on the asset.

The potential advantages to Bank B from this transaction are obvious. If $x < 40$ basis points, Bank B obtains the use of the asset off-balance-sheet at a cheaper cost than it could access it on-balance-sheet. For example, if $x = 30$ basis points, then Bank B effectively experiences a 10 basis point pick-up over what it could obtain by funding the asset on its balance sheet.

**FIGURE 31.2**
Funding Cost
Arbitrage Using a
TRS: Example

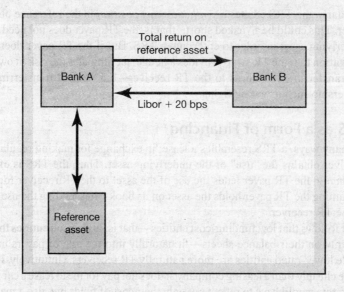

But why might Bank A want to enter into this transaction? Consider first the credit quality of the asset Bank A holds. Bank A is not exposed to the credit risk of the reference obligation since that risk has been transferred to Bank B. Nor is Bank A exposed to the credit risk of Bank B, since ownership of the asset resides with Bank A. Rather, what Bank A is exposed to is the risk of *joint* default of Bank B and the reference obligation. The lower the correlation between Bank B and the reference obligation, the higher is the quality of this synthetic asset. For example, if Bank B is rated A−, the reference obligation is rated BBB, and there is zero correlation between them, then the synthetic asset that Bank A holds has an implied rating of A+. Thus, the TRS enables Bank A to create a synthetic asset exposed to the risk of joint default of Bank B and the reference obligation, which may have a superior yield to similarly rated assets traded in the market.

Regulatory considerations too may push Bank A to go in for the synthetic asset rather than purchasing outright a cash asset with the same rating as the implied rating of the synthetic asset. Under Basel capital adequacy regulations, a bank in an OECD country buying a credit risky asset is required to hold a specified amount of capital as protection against default. But a bank that holds an asset and buys protection from another OECD bank is required to hold only 20% of that capital since the risk is now much smaller. So, in our example, if Bank A were to buy a cash asset outright, it would have to hold the full amount of capital, but if it buys the reference obligation and enters into a TRS, it is required to hold only 20% of this amount.[2]

Returning to our example, what values of $x$ might arise in the TRS? As we have seen, $x$ has to be at most 40 basis points, or Bank B will prefer to buy the asset outright to accessing it via the TRS. On the other hand, we must also have $x \geq 0$, or Bank A will not make up even its funding cost on the transaction. This creates a 40 basis point range within which $x$ could lie. (The figure of 40 basis points is just the difference in funding costs, i.e., the saving that arises from having A buy the asset rather than B.) A possible outcome, one that splits the gains from trade equally, is shown in Figure 31.2. In this outcome, Bank A gets a pick up of 20 basis points over its funding cost for taking on the risk of joint default, while Bank B obtains the use of the asset for $L + 20$ basis points, 20 basis points below its funding cost. ∎

---

[2] As noted earlier in the chapter, the regulatory treatment of credit derivatives may well undergo some change following the financial crisis that erupted in 2008. For the latest regulatory requirements, we refer the reader to the website of the Bank for International Settlements, http://www.bis.org.

### TRS: A Summary

To summarize, a TRS is an instrument that creates synthetic long and short positions (for the TRS receiver and payer, respectively) in an underlying reference obligation. From the standpoint of the receiver, the advantages of the TRS are that it may enable access to a desired asset class such as syndicated loans to which no access is otherwise available; it can be used to create new assets with maturities not available in the market; it may be used to obtain financing cheaper than on-balance-sheet purchase of an asset; and it provides levered exposure to the asset. For the TR payer, the main advantages are that the TRS creates a hedge for both price risk and default risk even while ownership is retained by the TR payer and that the TRS enables creating high-quality synthetic assets (with possibly low regulatory capital requirements) if there is sufficiently low correlation between the counterparty and the reference asset.

## 31.3   Credit Spread Options/Forwards

Credit spread products are derivatives on the credit spread. They may be written directly as options on the spread (with respect to Treasuries or Libor or asset swap spreads) or indirectly as options on bonds. A call option on the spread pays when spreads increase. A call option on a bond pays when bond prices increase, i.e., when the credit spreads decrease. Thus, a call option on spreads is akin to a put option on bonds and vice versa. (The analogy is not quite pristine. Bond options are not pure credit spread options. Bond prices may also change because of fluctuations in the riskless interest rate.) Credit spread forwards are instruments (usually cash settled) for which the payoff is a linear function of the final spread relative to an agreed-upon benchmark level.

The popularity of credit spread options has been declining over time. The British Bankers Association estimates that they accounted for around 5% of the credit derivatives market in 2000 but only around 1% in 2006. In part, this was because options on credit default swaps (credit default "swaptions") became increasingly popular over this period. Credit default swaps are the subject of the next section.

## 31.4   Credit Default Swaps

Credit default swaps (CDSs) are today by far the most important component of the credit derivatives market. Hugely important in their own right, they also form the building block for several portfolio credit derivatives such as synthetic CDOs and the CDX and iTraxx credit indices. Other products such as basket default swaps are natural generalizations of the CDS structure.

A CDS is a bilateral contract in which one party (the "protection buyer") makes a periodic payment to another party (the "protection seller") in exchange for a single contingent payment following a "credit event" on a specified underlying instrument (the "reference obligation"). The reference obligation may be any credit-risky obligation issued by an entity, for example, the obligation of a corporation, sovereign, or semi-government institution. As in a TRS, the maturity of the CDS need not, and in practice often does not, match that of the reference obligation. CDS maturities vary from 1 to 10 years. The most popular maturity in the market is 5 years, but over the years good liquidity has also developed at other maturities.

Figure 31.3 illustrates the CDS. The lower panel in the figure assumes physical settlement if a credit event were to occur. (Physical settlement was described in the discussion on total return swaps.) Alternative settlement procedures are explained later in this section.

**FIGURE 31.3**

A Credit Default Swap

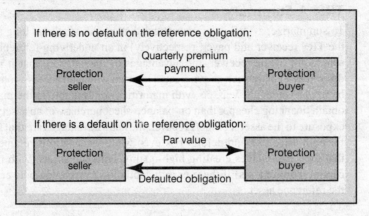

There are three key questions concerning a CDS: (a) What constitutes a "credit event"? (b) If a credit event occurs, what is the payment to be made by the protection seller to the protection buyer? (c) How is this payment to be effected? We turn to a description of these issues.

## The Credit Event

The contract definitions set by the International Swaps and Derivatives Association (ISDA) specify six possibilities that may constitute credit events in CDS contracts:

1.  **Failure to Pay**  This is subject to a materiality threshold (the amount due must be at least some specified minimum) and a grace period (usually three days).
2.  **Bankruptcy**  The corporation becomes insolvent or unable to meet its debts. Obviously, this is not relevant for sovereigns.
3.  **Repudiation/Moratorium**  The borrower declares a moratorium on servicing the debt or repudiates the debt.
4.  **Obligation acceleration**  The obligation becomes due on account of non-financial default.
5.  **Obligation default**  The obligation becomes capable of being due and immediately payable.
6.  **Restructuring**  This is a "soft" credit event that is explained in detail below.

Of these six events, the first two are self-explanatory and are uniformly used in CDS contracts. The third, fourth, and fifth, while admissible as credit events, are, in practice, never used in G-7 corporate contracts (although the third is used in emerging market contexts). Thus, effectively, for corporate CDS contracts, the credit event consists of bankruptcy, failure to pay, and restructuring.

What is "restructuring"? We discuss this in some detail below after discussing settlement alternatives. While restructuring is an important credit event, we note that going forward, it may become just a historical curiosity in the North American context: new North American CDS contracts traded following the "Big Bang" of April 2009 (see Appendix 31A) will trade without restructuring as a credit event. However, European CDS contracts are expected to include the Mod-Mod-R restructuring clause described below.

## Settlement Alternatives

Alternative settlement methodologies in CDS contracts are illustrated in Figure 31.4. There are two basic settlement methods: *cash settlement* and *physical settlement*.

**FIGURE 31.4**
Settlement
Alternatives in CDS
Contracts

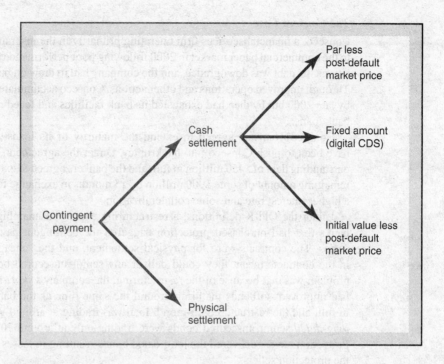

In a cash-settled CDS contract, the protection seller makes a cash payment to the protection buyer of an amount equal to the loss-given-default or, more precisely, the loss in value on account of the credit event. This loss is usually measured from par: that is, the cash settlement amount is defined as the par value of the obligation minus the post-default market price of the obligation. The initial value of the obligation (the value at inception of the CDS) is sometimes used instead of the par value. If the obligation was trading far from par at the inception of the CDS, then obviously these two alternatives have very different consequences. Some cash-settled CDS contracts (known as "digital CDS" contracts) specify simply a fixed sum to be paid if a credit event were to occur.

In physically-settled CDS contracts, the protection buyer delivers the defaulted obligation to the protection seller and receives the par value of the obligation in exchange. Economically, this is, of course, equivalent to cash settlement. The protection buyer in physically-settled CDS contracts has a "cheapest-to-deliver" option: the delivered obligation may be any obligation of the defaulting entity that ranks *pari passu* with the reference obligation. This option sometimes becomes valuable, especially following a restructuring, as in the Conseco case described below.

## Restructuring: Old-R, Mod-R, Mod-Mod-R, and No-R

The restructuring clause in CDS contracts introduced by ISDA in 1999 (and now called Old-R) triggers protection if one of the following happens:

- There is any reduction in interest or principal payable.
- There is a postponement of interest or principal repayments.
- There is a change in the priority of the reference obligation.
- There is a change in currency of payment.

A number of cases in the early 2000s pointed to the need to modify this clause. The most famous of these cases was that of Conseco.

### The Conseco Case

Conseco, a financial services firm operating primarily in the insurance market, lost access to the commercial paper market in 2000 following poor performance and some failed acquisitions. Its debt was downgraded, and the company had to draw on bank backstop facilities. Through improved operations and other actions, Conseco accumulated $450 million in cash by late 2000 but by then had exhausted its bank facilities and faced repayment of maturing bank loans.

Conseco's bankers agreed to extend the maturity of its loans; the alternative would have been to push Conseco into bankruptcy. Under the agreement, Conseco would repay outstanding debt of $450 million in full, and the bankers agreed to extend the maturity of the remaining amount of some $900 million by 15 months in exchange for which they obtained a higher interest rate and some collateralization.

Under the Old-R definitions, a restructuring event had unambiguously occurred, and banks that had purchased protection triggered the contingent payment on their default swaps. The contracts were for physical settlement, and the "cheapest-to-deliver" option in the contracts meant they could deliver any senior unsecured bonds of Conseco. The problem was that because of the restructuring, the company's *short-term* financial position had improved, so bonds maturing around the same time as the bank facilities were paid in full, and the restructured 15-month loan was trading at around 92% of face value, but *long-dated* senior unsecured bonds were trading only at around 70% of their face value. Protection buyers delivered the long-dated bonds resulting in losses of over $60 million to the protection sellers.

Spurred by the Conseco case among others, ISDA modified the restructuring clause in 2003. A new clause, the Mod-R clause, was introduced for the North American market. Under Mod-R, the maturity of deliverable obligations following a restructuring was limited to a maximum of 30 months; more specifically, to the maximum of the remaining maturity of the CDS contract or the lesser of (a) 30 months after the restructuring date and (b) latest final maturity date of any *restructured* loan or bond.

For various reasons, Mod-R was unsuitable for the European market, so a further modification, Mod-Mod-R, was introduced for European CDS contracts. Mod-Mod-R too placed limits on the maturity of the deliverable obligations following a restructuring, in this case to the maximum of the remaining maturity of the CDS contract and 60 months (for restructured bonds/loans) or 30 months (for other deliverable obligations).

Since 2003, users of CDS contracts have had four choices concerning restructuring: Old-R, Mod-R, Mod-Mod-R, or No-R, the last of which refers to a CDS contract that *excludes* restructuring as a credit event. Most North American CDS contracts on investment-grade names have traded Mod-R, while those on high-yield names have traded No-R. In Europe, the popular contract form has been Mod-Mod-R. As mentioned earlier and elaborated on in Appendix 31A, much of this may become just a historical footnote for North American contracts. Following the "Big Bang" of April 2009, new CDS contracts in North America will trade only No-R. It appears likely, however, at the time of writing that the new European contracts will continue to trade Mod-Mod-R rather than No-R.

## Some Uses of CDS Contracts

As is immediately apparent from the definitions, a credit-default swap is just a form of insurance against default (or, more accurately, against the credit event): the protection buyer gets nothing if there is no credit event and is compensated for the loss in value (i.e., is "made whole") if there is a credit event.

As insurance, a CDS is a potentially valuable tool for banks and other institutions looking to hedge loan or bond portfolios. By buying protection on specified assets in the portfolio, it

**FIGURE 31.5**
CDS Spreads for
Selected Financials:
2008

The upper panel shows the behavior of five-year CDS spreads on Morgan Stanley from late 2007 to early 2009. The lower panel does the same for Goldman Sachs. Note the sharp rise in CDS spreads in September 2008.

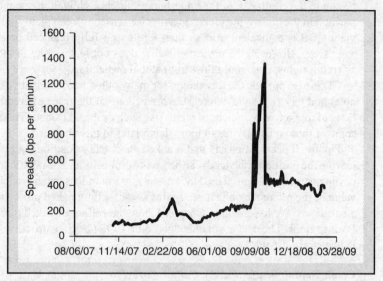

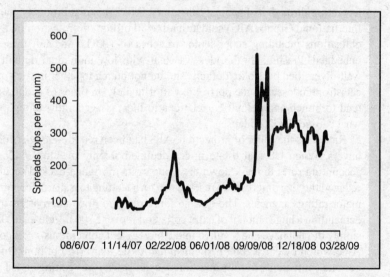

enables them to transfer the credit risk in those assets (essentially to taking a short position in the underlying credits) without transferring ownership. This enables active management of credit-risky portfolios even where trading in the underlying credits is difficult or impossible. Note, however, that unlike a TRS, *market risk* remains with the protection buyer; only credit risk in the underlying obligation is transferred.

To be sure, investors need not own the asset in order to buy protection. Indeed, CDSs have become a popular alternative vehicle for expressing negative credit views. (Figure 31.5 shows, for example, the way that CDS spreads on Morgan Stanley and Goldman Sachs reacted during the height of the financial crisis in September 2008 when market sentiment turned sharply negative on the entire financial sector.) An investor anticipating deterioration in an entity's financial condition can buy protection on that entity. If the deterioration occurs as anticipated, the price of protection will rise, leading to a marked-to-market gain on the contract held by the investor.

From the standpoint of the protection seller, the CDS enables obtaining unfunded exposure to the credit risk of the underlying reference obligation, essentially to taking a long position in the underlying credit. In a precise sense, as we explain shortly, selling protection via a CDS is equivalent in cash flow terms to a fully financed position in a bond or an asset swap. However, the protection seller does not receive any of the other benefits, such as voting rights, that would flow from actual ownership.

CDSs also provide the foundation for many other credit derivatives such as credit-linked notes and CDOs. As the market's favored gauge of the price of credit risk, CDSs form the basis of market-wide indices of credit risk such as the CDX and iTraxx indices. We explore some of these relationships in more depth later in this chapter.

Finally, it bears emphasis that a naked short CDS position (i.e., selling protection and leaving the position unhedged) can be a risky proposition. The maximum gain is the premium payments received from the CDS, but the maximum loss can be much larger, up to the par value of the reference obligation. In this sense, selling naked protection resembles writing a naked put. We have seen in Chapter 8 how the selling of naked puts on the Nikkei killed Barings Bank. The dangers of unhedged short CDS positions are correspondingly illustrated by the story of AIG.

### Credit Default Swaps and the Collapse of AIG

Operating through its financial subsidiary, AIG Financial Products, the US giant American International Group (AIG) sold around $450 billion of protection on a variety of reference obligations including super-senior tranches of CDOs, and left these almost completely unhedged. Presumably the idea was that with low individual default probabilities and a well-diversified portfolio, defaults should not bunch together in such quantities as to cause catastrophic losses in the portfolio. Unfortunately, in times of economic crisis, defaults do tend to bunch and default correlations to increase generally, though that is not precisely what caused AIG's collapse.

Rather, as the seller of protection, AIG had been required to post collateral to protection buyers. When US real estate prices declined steeply in 2008, AIG was required under accounting rules to mark down the value of its mortgage-backed securities portfolio. This reduced the size of its capital reserves, in turn leading to a sharp downgrading of AIG by the major ratings agencies. The downgrading resulted in counterparties to the CDS contracts demanding a huge amount of extra collateral—over $100 billion in all. This was money AIG simply did not have and resulted in the huge—and contentious—US government bailout of AIG, which by early 2009 had consumed more than $150 billion. One reason the bailout became contentious was the question of exactly who was getting bailed out; many, including members of the US Senate and writers in the financial press, argued that it was as much the CDS counterparties that were beneficiaries of the US injection of funds. The initial reluctance of AIG and even of regulators to reveal exactly who these counterparties were and how much each of them had received in extra collateral did not help matters.

It is true that it was the steep decline in the US real estate market and the consequent losses on mortgage-backed securities that provided the proximate cause of AIG's collapse. But the reason these factors constituted more than just a manageable financial setback for the insurance giant was the hundreds of billions of dollars worth of protection AIG had sold and left unhedged.

## Funding-Cost Arbitrage with a CDS

Funding-cost arbitrage with a CDS works in a similar way to that with total return. Here is an example.

| Example 31.2 | Consider the same simple setting used in the TRS setting. Bank A, a highly rated bank, has a funding cost of Libor ($L$) flat, while Bank B, a lower rated entity, has a funding cost of $L + 40$ basis points. Bank A has on its books an obligation currently yielding $L + 60$ basis points. Bank B wants exposure to the credit risk of that obligation. |
|---|---|

If Bank B were to buy the obligation outright, its pick-up over its funding cost would be only 20 basis points. An alternative arrangement that exploits Bank A's lower funding cost is for Bank B to enter into a credit-default swap with Bank A in which Bank A buys protection from Bank B at a premium of $x$ basis points. As long as $x \geq 20$, Bank B benefits: it obtains more than 20 basis points for taking on virtually the same credit exposure.

What about Bank A? Once it has entered into the credit default swap, Bank A's credit exposure is to the *joint default* of Bank B and the reference obligation. The lower the correlation between Bank B and the reference obligation, the higher the quality of this synthetic asset. For example, if Bank B is rated A, the reference obligation is rated BBB, and they are uncorrelated credit risks, the implied rating of a security exposed to joint default is AA−. Creation of such synthetic assets providing a greater yield than similarly-rated cash assets is one possible motivation for Bank A.[3]

As in the TRS, regulatory capital requirements could be another motivation. If Bank B is an OECD bank, the capital requirement is only 20% of the amount that would be required for holding a similarly-rated cash asset. And, lastly, balance sheet management may be another motivation. Both external constraints (freeing up capital for other purposes) and internal constraints (expanding lines of credit to the entity that issued the reference obligation) may be addressed using the CDS. ∎

## The "Fair Price" of a CDS

A CDS is a derivative contract on credit risk. Can it be priced by replication? The answer is a qualified "yes," as we explain.

Suppose that we have a five-year CDS on some reference obligation issued by Widget Corporation. Let the CDS premium be $y$ basis points per annum. Under idealized conditions, the fair price of this CDS (i.e., the value of $y$) can be determined by replication and arbitrage considerations. Assume first that there is a floating-rate note issued by Widget Corporation that

- is currently trading at par;
- has the same maturity as the CDS (in this case, five years); and
- has the same seniority as the reference obligation.

Let the coupon on the floating-rate note be Libor $(L) + x$ basis points. Next, assume too that you can fund the purchase of the note at Libor flat. Lastly, assume that the CDS and bond markets are perfectly liquid so one can take long and short positions with equal facility. We will show that under these conditions, we must have $y = x$, that is,

*The fair price of a CDS is equal to the spread on a par floater that (a) is issued by the same reference entity, (b) has maturity equal to the CDS, and (c) has the same seniority as the reference obligation.*

To see this, note the following two preliminary points. First, cross-default provisioning ensures that if Widget Corporation is in default on the reference obligation, it is also in default on the five-year floating-rate note (and vice versa), so the event of default is the same for the two instruments. Second, since the reference obligation and the note have the same seniority, they experience the same loss-given-default.

---

[3] Of course, some caution is in order here. Estimating default correlations is a tricky task. With high correlation, the credit quality of the synthetic asset will be little better than the weaker of the two assets.

For specificity, suppose that the par value of the note is 100. (By assumption, this is also its initial price). Consider a portfolio consisting of a long position in the five-year floating rate note funded by borrowing 100 at Libor. There are two possibilities:

- There is no default on the note to maturity. In this case, you receive $L + x$ on the note and pay $L$ in financing costs, so the portfolio results in a cash flow of $x$ basis points per annum for five years. At maturity, you receive the par value from the note and use this to repay the initial Libor borrowing, so there is no net cash flow on this account.

- There is a default before maturity. Let $R$ denote the recovery on the floating-rate note. Then you receive $R$ from the floating-rate note and pay 100 on the borrowing, for a net loss of $100 - R$.

This structure of cash flows is *identical* to that received from selling protection on the CDS. If you sell protection, there are two possibilities:

- There is no default over the five years. In this case, you receive $y$ basis points per annum for five years.

- There is a default within five years. Since the reference obligation and the par floater have the same seniority, they have the same recovery rate, so the loss on selling protection is also equal to $100 - R$.

It follows easily now that if $x \neq y$, there is an arbitrage:

- If $x > y$, buy the par floater, finance the purchase at Libor, and buy protection. This will result in a cash flow of $x - y$ basis points to maturity or until default. There are no cash-flow consequences of default on account of the purchased protection.

- If $x < y$, short the par floater, invest at Libor, and sell protection. This will bring in a cash flow of $y - x$ basis points per annum to maturity or default, and once again, there are no net cash-flow consequences of default.

In practice, there may be many factors causing a divergence from this idealized world: most importantly, the existence of a floater with the desired properties but also liquidity issues in the bond and CDS markets, financing costs, and so on. A common alternative that is used is the *asset swap spread*.

### The Asset Swap Spread

An asset swap is a package consisting of a bond with fixed coupons and an interest rate swap that converts the fixed coupons into Libor plus a spread $x$ (which could, in principle, be negative). Since this results in a synthetic floating-rate bond of the reference entity, the spread to Libor $x$ is then interpreted as the price of that entity's credit risk and is known as the "asset swap spread."

Two points about asset swaps are important. First, asset swaps are commonly par instruments. That is, the buyer of the asset swap pays par at inception for purchase of the package. If the bond is not trading at par, then the value of the swap at inception must offset this difference so that the asset swap costs par. For example, suppose the bond is trading at 105 against a par value of 100 when the swap is initiated. Then the swap has to be worth −5 at inception, which means that at inception, the asset swap seller has a credit exposure to the asset swap buyer. The reverse is true if the bond is trading at a discount, say at 90. In this case, the buyer of the asset swap package has bought a bond worth 90 and a swap worth 10, so the asset swap buyer has a credit exposure to the seller.

An alternative, but less popular, version of asset swaps is those that trade at the market price of the bond ("market-in, market-out" asset swaps). In this case, at inception, the asset swap buyer pays the market price of the bond, say $P$, for the package. However, in market asset swaps, there is also a final exchange of cash flows at maturity when the asset swap buyer pays par and receives the initial market price $P$ of the bond.

Second, the swap in an asset swap package does not terminate if the underlying bond defaults. So the buyer of the asset swap has the risk that upon default, the fixed coupon payments will have to continue being made on the swap even though no coupons are received from the bond. Equivalently, the buyer has the risk of having to close out the swap at the marked-to-market value.

These features mean that a financed par asset swap package is akin to a CDS if the bond is trading at par but not if the bond is far from par. As an example, suppose the bond is trading at 90 at inception, and immediately after inception the bond defaults. Suppose the post-default price of the bond is 40. Then, the buyer of the par asset swap has paid 100, recovers 40, and has a swap with a marked-to-market value of 10, for a total loss of 50. Similarly, if the bond is trading at 105 at inception of the swap and defaults immediately after inception, the asset swap buyer has paid 100 for the asset swap, recovers 40 on the bond, and has a swap with a marked-to-market value of $-5$, so has a total loss of 65. However, in either situation, the loss in a CDS would have been par minus post-default market price, which is 60. It is only where the bond was trading at (or near) par that the losses on the CDS and asset swap would resemble each other.

### The CDS-Asset Swap Basis

The *CDS-asset swap basis* (sometimes also referred to as the CDS-bond basis) is the difference between the CDS spread and the corresponding asset swap spread. In principle, the similarity between these instruments means that arbitrage forces should drive these spreads close together, but while the difference is often small, it is also often substantial. Here are some reasons.

- **Negative Credit Views** When credit-market views turn negative on a name, one can either short the bond or buy protection. The difficulty of shorting corporate bonds may cause the basis to diverge as protection buyers may be willing to pay more than the benchmark spread reflected in the asset swap.
- **Convertible Issuance** Convertible arbitrageurs' primary interest in convertible bonds is in the optionality component. It is not uncommon to hedge the credit risk in the convertible for at least an initial period of time. This is easiest to do via buying protection rather than shorting the bond, so again will generally cause the CDS-asset swap basis to diverge.
- **Synthetic CDO Issuance** Synthetic CDOs became particularly popular in the early 2000s. In a synthetic CDO, the issuer of the CDO sells protection on individual names to raise the cash required to meet coupon payments on the various tranches. This tends to drive CDS spreads down relative to asset swap spreads, i.e., to narrow the basis.
- **Debt Not Trading at Par** If debt is trading below par, the loss on debt will be less than the loss on a CDS which is measured from par. Consequently, the CDS spread will be wider to account for this. Conversely, if debt is trading above par, the loss on debt will be greater than the loss on a CDS, so the CDS spread will be tighter.

## Changes to CDS Contracts in 2009: The CDS "Big Bang"

The credit derivatives market has been in continuous evolution since its birth in the early 1990s, and its flagship product, the CDS, is no exception. The most significant alterations to the contract terms in North America came in April 2009, an event termed the "CDS Big Bang." The CDS Big Bang is described in Appendix 31A.

# 31.5 Credit-Linked Notes

Credit default swaps are unfunded off-balance-sheet instruments; there is no up-front payment to purchase a CDS. Credit-linked notes (CLNs) represent one method by which CDSs are converted into funded form. A CLN is essentially a credit-default swap embedded in a note. The purchaser of the note pays for the note up front. Coupons and principal repayment on the note are tied to performance of a reference obligation. If the reference obligation does not experience a credit event, coupons and principal are paid on the note as promised. If the reference obligation experiences a credit event, then the loss in the value of the reference obligation is taken out of the note, and the balance is returned to the investor. As compensation for taking on the risk of the reference obligation defaulting, the purchaser of the note receives a higher coupon than would otherwise be the case. Thus, the purchaser plays the role of a protection seller: if the reference obligation does not default, he receives the higher coupon, while if there is a default, he suffers the loss-given-default.

CLNs serve many purposes. Investors whose mandates do not allow them to use off-balance-sheet derivatives cannot sell protection via a CDS; however, they can achieve effectively the same end using a CLN. In principle too, CLNs may be bought and sold like other fixed-income instruments. From the standpoint of the protection buyer, buying protection obtained through a CLN has advantages to protection obtained via a CDS. Unlike a CDS, the protection seller in a CLN (i.e., the investor in the note) pays for the instrument up front; so neither the credit rating of the investor nor the correlation between the credit risks of the investor and the reference obligation is important.

The actual mechanics of a CLN are a bit more complex than the foregoing description of the product may suggest. At the heart of the CLN structure is a special-purpose vehicle or SPV. The SPV is the legal entity that acts as an intermediary between the buyers and sellers of protection. On the one hand, the SPV issues the CLN to investors (and so buys protection on the reference obligation from them). On the other, it sells protection via CDSs on the reference obligation to protection buyers; the maturity of the CDSs equals the maturity of the CLN. The collateral received from the sale of the notes is invested in AAA-rated securities.

Thus, the SPV receives cash from two sources: from selling protection and from its investment in AAA-rated collateral. It uses the cash raised to pay investors the promised coupon on the CLN. If there is a default on the reference obligation, the SPV liquidates the collateral and uses this to first satisfy the claims of the protection buyers. Any remaining amount is paid back to the investors in the note. If there is no default, the collateral is liquidated at maturity of the CLN, and the investors are repaid their principal.

An example will help clarify these mechanics. The example is a modified and disguised version of an actual transaction to the details of which one of the authors had access.

---

**Example 31.3**

Consider the following setting. There is a large manufacturer whose bonds are currently trading at the Treasury rate $T$ plus 90 basis points. The credit quality of the manufacturer is dropping and its suppliers, mostly small firms for whom the manufacturer's business constitutes a large part of cash flows, are balking at granting generous 120-day credit terms to it, proposing instead to reduce these terms to 60 days. Were this to happen, the manufacturer would face a drastic increase in its requirement for working capital, further worsening its credit condition.

A bank undertakes the following series of transactions. It first sets up an SPV. The SPV enters into credit default swap transactions with the suppliers of the manufacturer in which it sells protection to them with the bonds of the manufacturer as the reference obligation. (The protection may not be solely on the manufacturer's defaulting; the trigger could be even a significant deterioration in the creditworthiness of the manufacturer, for example, a decline in its credit rating below a threshold level or an increase in its bond spreads above a threshold level.) Suppose that the spread in the CDS contracts is 75 basis points per annum. Having purchased this protection, the suppliers agree to retain the 120-day credit terms they currently provide the manufacturer.

A natural question to ask at this point is why the suppliers would purchase the CDS and agree to extend favorable credit terms to the manufacturer. For many of the suppliers, by assumption, a large share of their business depends on the manufacturer. Now that they are insured against a deterioration in the manufacturer's creditworthiness, it is in their interest to continue the business relationship rather than to tighten the screws and take the chance that the manufacturer may go out of business.

The SPV then issues a CLN with principal amount equal to the notional on the CDSs it has sold. The coupon and principal repayment on the note are linked to the performance of the manufacturer's bonds, and the note carries a coupon of $T + 100$. Investors in these notes are taking on the risk of the manufacturer's credit standing deteriorating; for this risk, the note pays them $T + 100$ rather than the $T + 90$ they could get by a straight investment in the manufacturer's bonds.

Finally, the SPV invests the proceeds received from the note issuance in AAA-rated collateral yielding $T + 30$ basis points. The entire structure is summarized in Figure 31.6. There are now two possibilities:

1. **The Reference Bond Does Not Default** In this case, the suppliers pay their premia of 75 basis points, the SPV receives $T + 30$ basis points from the collateral, and the SPV pays out $T + 100$ to the investors in the note. Thus, the SPV makes a five basis points pick-up.

2. **The Reference Bond Defaults** In this case, the SPV liquidates the collateral, uses the proceeds to first repay the buyers of protection (i.e., the suppliers) and then returns any remaining amount to the investors. The SPV is terminated.

What is the net effect of the transaction? First, suppliers are able to continue their businesses as usual without worrying about the default of the manufacturer. Second, the manufacturer obtains the credit terms it needs to stay in business. Third, the investors in the note obtain 10 basis points more than they would have obtained for essentially the same risk. (Note the risks are not completely the same. Investing in the CLN also involves the risk that the collateral be managed properly. Mismanagement of the collateral will reduce the proceeds received by investors.) Lastly, the SPV registers a five-basis points pick-up until maturity (or default). ∎

**FIGURE 31.6**
Credit-Linked Note: Example

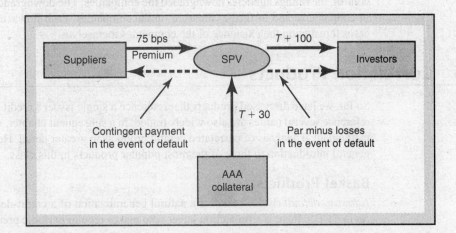

## A Variant: Credit-Sensitive Notes

A variant of the credit-linked note structure, called a *credit-sensitive note*, is one in which the cash flows from the note are linked to the credit rating of the issuer itself rather than to a third party's obligation. Credit-sensitive notes (CSNs) are also known as step-up bonds.

One of the earliest issues of CSNs was by Enron in 1989. Enron at that time had a barely investment-grade rating of Baa3 (Moody's) and BBB− (S&P). Enron issued $100 million in CSNs in which it promised the holder of the note a steep increase in coupons if it got downgraded even a notch (to Ba1/BB+) but only a gradual decrease in the coupon size if its rating improved. The coupon that Enron promised to pay was dependent on the *worse* of its Moody's and S&P ratings, and was given by the following:

| Rating | | Applicable Rate (%) |
|---|---|---|
| Moody's | S&P | |
| Aaa | AAA | 9.20 |
| Aa1–Aa3 | AA+−AA− | 9.30 |
| A1–A3 | A+−A− | 9.40 |
| Baa1–Baa3 | BBB+−BBB− | 9.50 |
| Ba1 | BB+ | 12.00 |
| Ba2 | BB | 12.50 |
| Ba3 | BB− | 13.00 |
| B1 or lower | B+ or lower | 14.00 |

In issuing this note, Enron was aiming to send a credible signal to the market that it expected its rating to improve, and most certainly did not expect it to decline. The credibility of the signal depended on the fact that it was *costly* to send the signal—the smallest downgrading would cost Enron 250 bps in coupon size. The security offering was especially expedient since it was issued at the time of the collapse of the high-yield debt markets when marginal investment-grade firms were hard pressed in their attempts to raise money from bond market investors.

Shortly after Enron's issue, there was a spate of CSN issues culminating in the late 1990s and early 2000s with large issues by telecom and airline companies including Deutsche Telekom, France Telecom, and British Airways. The bursting of the Internet bubble at that point and the recession that followed showed that CSNs were not without their downsides for the issuer. When business slowed in the recession for reasons beyond the companies' control, the ratings agencies downgraded the companies. The downgrade led to an increase in coupon size and to further pressure on the companies' cash flows, and so on, in some cases threatening the existence of the companies themselves.

## 31.6 Correlation Products

So far, we have discussed products that reference a single issuer's credit risk. Products that reference several names are also widely traded. In a subsequent chapter, we will take up the mathematical analysis of correlated default products in greater detail. Here we undertake a general introduction to three of the most popular products in this class.

### Basket Products

A *first-to-default* (FTD) basket is a natural generalization of a credit-default swap (CDS). As in a CDS, there is a protection buyer who makes regular periodic premium payments to a protection seller for protection against a credit event. The key difference is that instead of a single reference entity, there is a *basket* of reference entities. Protection is triggered at the first point where one of the credits in the basket experiences a credit event. Second-to-default (STD) baskets and, more generally, $n$th-to-default (nTD) baskets are defined similarly.

A typical basket structure has 5–10 names. For a specific example, consider a basket of 10 credits with a notional of $10 million on each credit. The protection buyer pays the seller a regular premium (typically quarterly). In an FTD basket, if any of the credits experiences a credit event, the protection seller pays $10 million in exchange for the protection buyer delivering $10 million in face value of the defaulted credit. The basket default swap then terminates. As with CDS contracts, physical delivery has been the settlement method of choice in this market, although this is changing.

### Why Basket Default Swaps?

Why FTD baskets? For the seller of protection, using an FTD basket provides the seller with leverage. As we discuss later on in the chapter on reduced-form models, the fair spread on a defaultable instrument is given approximately by $\lambda(1 - \phi)$ where $\lambda$ is the (risk-neutral) default likelihood and $\phi$ the anticipated recovery rate. By considering a basket rather than a single credit, the likelihood of a credit event, $\lambda$, increases. Assuming that all the credits in the basket have roughly similar recovery rates denoted by $\phi$, this increases the fair spread $\lambda(1 - \phi)$. As a consequence, the premium from selling FTD protection on a basket can be a multiple of the individual CDS spreads on the credits in the basket. However, the maximum loss the seller of protection can have is $1 - \phi$, which is the same whether protection is sold on one name or the basket. Thus, selling protection on an FTD basket is "like" selling CDS on each credit in the basket but with much lower potential losses.

From the buyer's standpoint, the FTD basket provides an equity cushion, an imperfect but inexpensive hedge against defaults on a portfolio. Consider an investor managing a portfolio of (say) 10 names. One way to protect the portfolio is to buy protection on each single name in the portfolio. A cheaper alternative is to buy FTD protection on the portfolio. The FTD protection is identical to the protection from a portfolio of CDSs if only one default occurs, but, of course, the FTD basket does not provide protection beyond the first default (which is why it costs less). There is a cost-benefit trade-off: if the investor does not think two or more defaults on the portfolio are a likely occurrence, then she may prefer the low-cost FTD route.

### Valuing Basket-Default Swaps

The FTD basket swap can be viewed as a basket of CDSs with a knock-out feature (the protection ceases to exist upon the occurrence of the first credit event). Upper and lower limits on the fair price of the basket are easily identified. First, the FTD basket premium clearly cannot exceed the sum of the premia on the individual CDSs; otherwise you could buy protection on each individual name and get more protection at less cost. Second, the FTD basket premium must be at least equal to the CDS premium for the weakest credit in the basket.

Unfortunately, beyond these broad limits, one cannot say much more about pricing without a formal model. The reason is that an FTD basket cannot be replicated with existing instruments (such as the individual CDSs), so replication-based arbitrage pricing is ruled out and only model-based pricing is possible.

What kind of inputs might a valuation model for a general $n$-th to default (nTD) basket need? Clearly, the value would depend on the number of credits $N$ in the portfolio, as well as the value of $n$. Clearly, too, it would depend on the qualities of the individual credits and their spreads, the anticipated recovery rates, the maturity of the basket, and so on. To a great extent, these are either observable variables or ones whose values can be inferred from other instruments (e.g., CDS spreads) using a model. The critical additional variable is *correlation*: how likely are credits to default together? This is not unfortunately, an observable variable.

Default correlation matters even for FTD baskets. Both systematic and idiosyncratic factors contribute to default, and default correlation is generally positive since most names have an exposure to overall macroeconomic conditions. In general, the effect of default correlation can be complex, but for FTD baskets, we can be more precise about the direction of impact. Intuitively, default correlation is the same as survival correlation. If names tend to default together, they also tend to survive together. So (again, intuitively), as correlation *increases*, the likelihood of zero defaults *increases*, which means the probability of one or more defaults must *decrease*. In turn, this means FTD premia must be a decreasing function of correlation.

## Collateralized Default Obligations (CDOs)

A natural extension of basket contracts is the securitization of default risk using an underlying basket or pool of debt obligations. This underlying pool is called the "collateral" or the "reference pool." Tranching and selling off baskets of default risk occur in the market for CDOs (collateralized default obligations).

CDOs are natural analogs to collateralized mortgage obligations (CMOs) in the securitization of mortgage risks. In a CDO securitization, tranches of debt are sold based on an underlying pool of debt. At the simplest level, there is a senior tranche, which has priority over cash flows. This is usually credit-enhanced by means of one or more "mezzanine" tranches, which provide the necessary subordination required to give the *A* tranche a high credit-quality rating. The residual tranche is called "equity" and is the backstop for first credit loss. By specifying the levels of credit loss for each tranche, the CDO can be tailored to meet specific investor demand. There may be various other credit enhancements in the CDO structure. Additional credit protection may be provided by early amortization clauses, which are imposed if the collateral defaults excessively or fails to generate cash at prespecified rates.

For a simple example of how a CDO tranching process works, consider a reference pool with 100 investment-grade names and a notional of $10 million each. The total notional of the CDO is then $1 billion. Suppose the cash flows from the pool are divided among three tranches: equity, mezzanine, and senior. The equity tranche takes all losses due to default on the pool up to a pre-specified maximum; let us suppose this in the example to be 5% of the notional amount (or $50 million). The mezzanine tranche takes all further losses from default again up to a pre-specified maximum; suppose this is 10% of the portfolio notional of $100 million. All remaining losses are absorbed by the senior tranche. Note that each tranche is specified by its *attachment point* (the point at which it begins to take losses) and its *width* (the percentage of losses it absorbs). In this example, the mezzanine tranche, for instance, has an attachment point of 5% and a width of 10%.

The one final point remaining is the distribution of cash flows from the collateral pool among the tranches. The equity tranche clearly has the greatest risk, so receives the highest coupon. The equity tranche is typically unrated. The mezzanine tranche has intermediate risk, so earns a lower coupon than equity; it usually carries a high speculative-grade/low investment-grade rating (e.g., BBB). The senior tranche is the least risky and carries the lowest coupon. To gauge the risk of the senior tranche in this example, note that the senior tranche is protected against the first $150 million of losses from default. If we assume an average recovery rate of 40% on defaulted names (a standard assumption in the industry), a single name's default costs $6 million. (Recall that the notional amount of each name is $10 million.) So for the $150 million cushion to be used up and for defaults to begin affecting the senior tranche, 25 names—or one-fourth of all the credits in the pool—have to default before the senior tranche is at risk.

How likely are 25 names to default? Obviously, this will depend on the credit quality of the individual names in the portfolio, the maturities, the anticipated recovery rates, and so on, but, as with basket default swaps, a critical driving variable is the hard-to-estimate and elusive default *correlation*. In times of economic crisis (the fourth quarter of 2008, for example), both individual default probabilities and default correlations across names tend to increase sharply, and a seemingly safe tranche can become very risky very quickly.

## The CDX and iTraxx Indices

The huge growth of the CDS market has resulted in the creation of indices based on CDS spreads. Credit indices now encompass all major corporate bond markets. There are two major families of indices: the CDX indices that cover North America (NA) and emerging markets (EM); and the iTraxx indices, which cover Europe and the rest of Asia. Each of these major indices also has a number of sub-indices based on sectors, geography, ratings, etc.

Credit indices are like equity indices in one sense. Just as equity indices are obtained by aggregating individual equity prices, credit indices are obtained by aggregating CDS spreads. However, there is one important difference. While equity is infinitely lived, CDSs are not. This means the index itself has a maturity. For example, if all the CDSs underlying the index have five-year maturities, we obtain a five-year index. Moreover, if we wish to maintain indices of given benchmark maturities (e.g., the popular five-year maturity), the precise underlying securities in the index have to be changed periodically. This is accomplished by "rolling" the index, a process we explain further below.

Since the number of indices and sub-indices available is huge, we confine attention here to describing just a few of these.

### North American Indices I: The CDX.NA.IG

This index is made up of 125 equally weighted North American (NA) investment-grade (IG) names. It is divided into five sector sub-indices: consumer, energy, financials, industrials and telecom, and media and technology. It also has a sub-index called HVOL consisting of the 30 highest volatility names in the index. The indices trade in a variety of maturities. The IG and HVOL indices trade in maturities of 1, 2, 3, 5, 7, and 10 years. The sectoral sub-indices trade in maturities of 5 and 10 years.

The credit ratings of the names in the index span the entire investment-grade spectrum but, reflecting the distribution of CDSs, are concentrated in the lower end of investment grade. Typically, over 50% are rated BBB or Baa, and another 30% are rated A. The index trades only No-R, i.e., the only credit events are bankruptcy and failure to pay.

### North American Indices II: The CDX.NA.HY

The North American high-yield (HY) index consists of 100 equally-weighted NA high-yield names. It has three sub-indices: a high-volatility index, a BB index consisting of all the BB-rated names in the index, and a B index, consisting of all the B-rated names in the index. A range of maturities is available. The main HY index trades in maturities of 3, 5, 7, and 10 years, while the sub-indices trade in 5-year maturities.

### European Indices I: iTraxx Europe

This is a benchmark index for the European investment-grade market. It consists of 125 equally-weighted CDSs on European investment-grade names. Two-thirds of the names come from the UK, France, and Germany. The main index trades in maturities of 3, 5, 7, and 10 years; there is also a high-volatility (HVOL) sub-index, as well as seven sectoral sub-indices.

### How the Indices Work

Each CDX or iTraxx index is like a CDS on a basket of names. The index is specified by a start date, an end date, a premium (or running payment), and a notional amount. The notional amount on the index is divided equally between the names in the index. For example, if an investor sells protection on $100 million of the CDX.NA.IG index, the notional on each name is $(100 million/125) = $0.80 million. This means selling $100 million of protection on the index is akin to selling $0.80 million of protection on each individual name but using a single contract.

### Index Rolls

Each index is "rolled" every six months. Rolling is the process by which new names are introduced and some old names dropped from the previous index. The process is governed by transparent rules and is based on dealer polls. Each roll increases the maturity of the "on-the-run" (the most current) indices by six months.

The composition of the old indices is not affected by the roll. They continue to trade as before. Since the new index composition is different from that of the old index, the new index may trade at a wider spread or a narrower spread than the previous one.

### Pricing Conventions

Each index comes with a fixed spread or "coupon." At inception, this spread will be roughly equal to the average spread of the names in the index. The spread represents the running premium payment received by sellers of protection on the index. Since the market price of protection on the basket of CDSs represented by the index will typically differ from this fixed spread, an up-front payment/receipt is required to compensate the seller and buyer. This up-front payment is equal to the (risky) present value of the difference between the market spread and the fixed spread.

For example, suppose that on February 1, 2009, an investor wishes to sell protection on $1 billion of the five-year CDX index maturing on December 20, 2013. Suppose that the fixed spread on the index is 100 basis points and that the current market spread is 163 basis points. Then, the investor will receive a running premium payment of approximately

$$0.25 \times 0.010 \times 1,000,000,000 = 2,500,000$$

In addition, the investor will receive an up-front payment equal to the risky present value of 63 bps on the notional principal amount of $1 billion.

### What If There Is a Default?

If a component of the index experiences a credit event (for simplicity, we call this a "default"), then the protection seller compensates the protection buyer via either physical or cash settlement. Restructuring is not a credit event in CDX contracts unlike in the pre-Big Bang US CDS contracts. The iTraxx European indices, however, do use Mod-Mod-R as a credit event. Following a credit event, the defaulting name is then removed from the index. The index continues to trade on the remaining names. The notional and all subsequent premium payments are reduced proportionately to reflect the altered portfolio.

For example, suppose a buyer has purchased €125 million of protection on the iTraxx Europe index (i.e., €1 million per name), and there is a credit event on one name. The protection seller then compensates the buyer for the loss-given-default on that name on a notional of €1 million via either physical or cash settlement. All subsequent premium computations are on a notional of €124 million. For example, if the running premium is 75 bps, then the new quarterly payments are approximately

$$0.25 \times 0.0075 \times 124,000,000 = 232,500$$

### Index Tranches and Correlations

In addition to the indices themselves, tranches on the indices with standard attachment points also trade. Figure 31.7 provides sample quotes from August 2005. The figure shows the standard attachment points for each tranche. On the North American investment grade index (NA.IG), for instance, there are five tranches available: 0–3% (the equity tranche),

**FIGURE 31.7**

Quotations for Various Indices

Source: Bear Stearns, Moody's. Indicative mid-market data derived from proprietary models

| Index tranche prices and implied correlation | | | | | |
|---|---|---|---|---|---|
| | est. ratings (Moody's) | 30 Aug 2005 level (bp*) | tranche correlation | 23 Aug 2005 level (bp*) | tranche correlation |
| **North America investment grade (five year)** | | | | | |
| Series | | DJ CDX NA IG 4 | | DJ CDX NA IG 4 | |
| Full index | Baa3 | 50.0 | | 49.0 | |
| 0–3% | Caa3 | 39.6% | 11 | 37.9% | 12 |
| 3–7% | Baa1 | 127.0 | 1 | 124.5 | 2 |
| 7–10% | Aaa | 36.0 | 12 | 35.8 | 12 |
| 10–15% | Aaa | 20.3 | 19 | 17.5 | 19 |
| 15–30% | Aaa | 9.8 | 33 | 8.4 | 33 |
| **North America high yield (five year)** | | | | | |
| Series | | DJ CDX NA HY 4 | | DJ CDX NA HY 4 | |
| Full index | B2 | 100.0 | | 100.5 | |
| 0–10% | C | 82.75% | 26 | 81.69% | 26 |
| 10–15% | Caa3 | 55.00% | 19 | 53.94% | 17 |
| 15–25% | Ba3 | 580.0 | 15 | 530.0 | 14 |
| 25–35% | A1 | 60.0 | 12 | 55.0 | 12 |
| **Europe investment grade (five year)** | | | | | |
| Series | | iTraxx 3 | | iTraxx 3 | |
| Full index | Baa2 | 36.0 | | 35.0 | |
| 0–3% | Caa2 | 24.0% | 16 | 22.8% | 17 |
| 3–6% | A3 | 82.5 | 4 | 77.5 | 4 |
| 6–9% | Aaa | 26.5 | 12 | 24.5 | 12 |
| 9–12% | Aaa | 14.5 | 18 | 13.5 | 18 |
| 12–22% | Aaa | 9.0 | 28 | 8.8 | 28 |
| **Japan investment grade (five year)** | | | | | |
| Series | | iTraxx CJ 3 | | iTraxx CJ 3 | |
| Full index | - | 22.8 | | 21.5 | |
| 0–3% | - | 13.0% | 26 | 12.4% | 26 |
| 3–6% | - | 90.0 | 9 | 80.0 | 9 |
| 6–9% | - | 28.0 | 18 | 25.5 | 18 |
| 9–12% | - | 20.0 | 29 | 20.0 | 29 |
| 12–22% | - | 14.3 | 40 | 13.0 | 40 |

3–7%, 7–10%, 10–15%, and 15–30%. For a given value of a tranche notional, the implied underlying portfolio notional can be computed using the width of the tranche. For example, if the equity tranche has a notional of $15 million, the implied underlying portfolio notional is $(15/0.03) million = $500 million. Similarly, if the notional on the 3–7% tranche is $40 million, the implied underlying portfolio notional is $(40/0.04) million = $1 billion.

As in a CDO, the attachment and detachment points of a tranche specify the loss taken by the tranche. The equity tranche in both the NA.IG and the European investment grade indices absorbs the first 3% of losses on the underlying portfolio. If, for instance, the underlying portfolio notional is €1 billion, then all losses on the portfolio up to €30 million are taken by the equity tranche of the Europe investment grade index. How many names must default for the equity tranche to be completely wiped out? This depends on the loss-given-default on a name. Since this index has 125 names in it, each name accounts for a notional of €8 million. Assuming a loss-given-default of 50%, default on each name would result in a loss of €4 million. So the equity tranche is wiped out only if there are at least eight defaults. Of course, a lower recovery rate means fewer defaults are needed to wipe out a tranche. If the loss-given-default is 75%, the equity tranche would be wiped out with only five defaults.

Investors may buy and sell protection on tranches. Sellers of protection receive a spread (a "coupon," as it is called) from the buyers of protection. This coupon is stated in basis points of the tranche notional. For example, Figure 31.7 shows that on August 30, 2005, a seller of protection on the 7–10% tranche of the NA.IG index would receive a coupon of 36 basis points per year from the buyer of protection, paid quarterly. For the equity tranches of the investment grade indices, the coupon is fixed at 500 basis points per annum, but the seller of protection also receives a portion of the notional amount up front. As Figure 31.7 shows, on August 30, 2005, these up-front payments were 39.6% on the NA.IG index and 24% on the Europe investment grade index. On the North American high-yield (NA.HY) index, the bottom two tranches trade with up-front payments (and no coupons). On August 30, 2005, these up-front payments received by the sellers of protection were 82.75% for the 0–10% tranche and 55% for the 10–15% tranche. The remaining tranches have specified coupons.

The other aspect of importance is tranche-implied default correlation. Since the default times of the issuers in the index are correlated, the number of defaults will depend on these default correlations. As correlations vary, the effects are similar to that of all default baskets: with increasing correlation, the equity tranche (analogous to a first-to-default basket) becomes less risky and the senior tranches (analogous to many-to-default baskets) become riskier. The tranche correlation number represents the average correlation of default across all issuers in the index that produces the exact spread (price) of the tranche seen in the quotations. The correlations are run through a market-standard model (known as a Gaussian copula), which we will investigate in Chapter 34.

Notice that each tranche has a different correlation! How might this be, given that all tranches are priced off the same underlying basket of issuers? It turns out that no single correlation in the model will produce a default loss distribution, which when translated into tranche spreads, matches the spreads of all tranches exactly. The fact that each tranche requires a different correlation to be priced correctly results in the phenomenon known as the "implied correlation smile," which is analogous to the notion of the implied volatility smile we encountered when pricing equity options. As in the case of equity options, the smile in implied correlations comes from the fact that the statistical structure of the market's standard Gaussian copula model does not capture the true joint default distribution of all issuers. However, as with implied volatility, implied correlation is used more as a quotation mechanism than as an indicator of true economic meaning.

Instead of tranche correlation, sometimes another form of correlation known as "base correlation" is quoted. In this case, the correlation for the equity tranche is the single average correlation that results in losses that match the spread level of the equity tranche. For the CDO equity, tranche correlation and base correlation coincide. But for the next mezzanine tranche, the base correlation is the level of correlation that matches the average price of both equity and mezzanine tranches, i.e., the correlation that corresponds to the average spreads of both the 0–3% and 3–7% tranches, or in other words, the 0–7% loss level. The base correlation for the 7–10% tranche will be the correlation that matches the average spreads of the 0–3%, 3–7%, and the 0–10% loss levels, i.e., the 0–10% loss bracket, and so on, for the remaining tranches.

## 31.7   Summary

Credit derivatives have transformed the derivatives landscape in dramatic fashion since the mid-1990s. By 2008, the credit derivatives market exceeded $50 trillion in notional outstanding worldwide, almost 10% of the world derivatives market's combined notional outstanding. The financial crisis of 2008–2009 took its toll on the market, particularly in its more exotic reaches into collateralized debt obligations (CDOs), but other portions of the market, notably the credit default swap (CDS) and index components, have also been affected.

A range of credit derivatives trade in the market today. Of these, the most important by far are CDSs. Useful in their own right, CDSs also constitute the building blocks for a range of other products including basket default swaps, credit-linked notes, synthetic CDOs, and credit indices such as those in the CDX and iTraxx families. The tremendous growth of credit derivatives in the years leading to 2008 was fueled at least in part by the wide-ranging applicability of these instruments, for example, in gauging the market's estimate of the credit health of a company or for taking short positions in credits. But the crisis of 2008 also revealed a dark side to this market. It appears likely at the time of writing (mid-2009) that the CDS and index markets will survive and even grow (perhaps in modified form as trading moves to centralized clearing houses), but it is less clear what the future holds for the more exotic correlation-driven parts of the market such as bespoke CDO tranches.

## 31.8 Exercises

1. If you are an equity asset manager and wish to diversify away from stocks, what credit derivative would you choose?

2. What are some of the advantages to a seller and a buyer in a credit spread option contract?

3. What is a credit-sensitive note (CSN)? How does it work? What is the advantage to the issuer? To the investor? What are the drawbacks to the investor?

4. What is an *n*-th to default contract? How does credit correlation impact this contract?

5. You expect that the market's expectation of recovery rates of a given issuer will be higher in a few weeks. There are two reference instruments for the same issuer: senior (S) and junior (J). Which of the following strategies would you prefer? Explain why.
   (a) Long S, long J.
   (b) Long S, short J.
   (c) Short S, long J.
   (d) Short S, short J.

6. In a CDO, suppose there are three tranches: A gets first claim to all cash flows from the collateral, B gets second claim, and there is a residual equity tranche E. Suppose the level of default risk in the economy declines but the correlations of default increase. What would be the likely impact of this on the values of the three tranches?

7. A credit default swap provides protection against the default of the reference issuer in the contract. Does it provide protection against the deterioration of the credit quality of the reference name before default occurs?

8. A bond fund wishes to speculate on the value of a five-year B-rated junk bond. It believes that, conditional on the bond surviving the next two years, it will rise in quality and be worth more. Suggest a risk management strategy for this trade.

9. In the previous question what should the fund manager do if instead he/she wanted to bear credit risk for the first two years but not for the remaining three?

10. EZFund can raise financing at six-month Libor plus 25 bps for five years. It finds that five-year Ampco bonds (BB rated) are trading at a yield to maturity of 10%. If total return swaps linked to the BB index are at 9.50% versus six-month Libor, what arbitrage trade may be available? What is the risk in this trade?

11. The credit default swap on a three-year bond is trading at a spread (premium) of 1%. If the credit spread on the bond is at 1.1%, suggest a trade to take advantage of this. Why do you think there might be a difference in spreads on the CDS and the bond?

12. You expect credit correlations to increase. If so, which of the following strategies is appropriate:

    (a) Long a first-to-default (FTD) contract and long a second-to-default (STD) contract.

    (b) Long FTD, short STD contracts.

    (c) Short FTD, long STD contracts.

    (d) Short FTD, short STD contracts.

13. Suppose you have a model for pricing convertible bonds that accounts for equity risk, interest-rate risk, and credit risk and is calibrated using observable stock prices, bonds, and credit default swaps. If the model price of the convertible bond exceeds that of the market and you believe the model is accurate, what broad strategy will you adopt to construct an arbitrage portfolio?

14. How might you convert a mortgage-backed securities (MBS) portfolio into a credit-risk-based CDO using CDS contracts? What should the CDS have as underlyings?

15. Can you suggest another credit contract that may be used to construct a synthetic CDO from a portfolio of MBS?

16. A CDO structure comes with a special clause for the A tranche whereby early amortization occurs if more than three issuers default within the first two years of the CDO. What happens to the value of the A tranche as we increase the number of issuers in the collateral?

17. Suppose we wish to price the spread on a two-year annual payment credit default swap. The constant interest rate is 10%. Suppose the conditional probability of default each year is also constant and is denoted $p$. Write down an expression that expresses the two-year fair value of the CDS spread ($s$) in terms of the other parameters of the model. Assume that all default payments are made at the end of the period, and all premium payments are made at the beginning of each period. Also assume that recovery is 40% of face value.

18. In the problem above, what is the fair spread $s$ if the premium payments are made at the end of each period only if the reference name has not defaulted? Is the premium higher or lower? Why?

19. If the correlation of default remains the same but the correlation of recovery between two issuers increases, what is the impact (ceteris paribus) on the price of a second-to-default contract?

20. In a synthetic CDO, does the issuer of the CDO tranches hold CDS contracts in long or short positions? Explain.

# The CDS Big Bang

Until 2008, the CDS market was an over-the-counter (OTC) market, and, as such, had several shortcomings to it. There was a high degree of counterparty risk in the system. The propensity for unconfirmed bilateral deals was high—it was estimated in 2005 that over half of all outstanding contracts were still pending confirmation. Since the system had no netting, hedging an existing position with a new contract resulted in multiple exposures, amplifying systemic risk. There was no auction protocol in place for finalizing the settlement of CDS contracts. Settlement could be based on a comparison of prices of the reference instrument before and after the credit event, and contracts sometimes failed to specify the dates for these valuations precisely. Finally, protection in CDS contracts usually became effective on the contract date. Since credit events sometimes are revealed only with a (possibly considerable) lag, buyers of protection might want the effective date of protection to pre-date the contract date. Spurred by these shortcomings, the Federal Reserve and 14 dealer banks began, in 2005, to develop the framework for an improved CDS marketplace. The resulting proposals, which resulted in the "Big Bang" of April 2009 in the CDS market, are described in this appendix.

## The New CDS Market

The exchange-traded CDS market has standardized contracts with a fixed-coupon convention. Conventional quotations of CDS spreads (where the spread quoted on each reference entity may be different) are called "par spreads." The par spread on a CDS is the spread that is charged on a periodic basis such that the expected present value of spread payments is equal to the expected present value of default payments. The new system will have a standardized spread (referred to as the "coupon") for all names of either 100 bps or 500 bps but with an up-front payment to reflect the fact that the fair spread may be different from this standardized spread.

For example, if the fair spread for a name is 160 bps, then 100 bps is too low a price to pay for protection, so the buyer of protection must compensate the seller of protection with an up-front payment. Conversely, if the fair spread is less than 100 bps, then the seller compensates the buyer with an up-front payment. The up-front payment now becomes the quotation for the contract.

The change to the quotation mechanism is significant. CDS quotations will be based on the ISDA CDS Standard Model. ISDA provides a standard tool for converting the conventional spread into a fixed-coupon plus up-front payment. Markit provides a calculator to convert the conventional spread into the new quotation, available at www.markit.com/cds.

The program code for the ISDA CDS standard model is now open source, and every trader may take this code and adapt it to its own use. Standardized inputs to be used with the code such as the daily yield curve and recovery assumptions for different debt seniority (senior 40%, subordinated 20%) are provided at www.cdsmodel.com.

Using these standardized contract terms, conversion from the conventional spread to the new fixed-coupon/up-front-payment model is done as follows.

1. The convention is that a constant hazard rate be assumed for default risk. (Hazard rate models are described in Chapter 33.) Premium payments are assumed to be free of default risk. Periodicity of the premium payments is quarterly. Discounting is undertaken using the yield curve published online.

2. Using the conventional spread quote $C$, the implied hazard rate $\lambda$ is computed by equating the expected present value of payments on the fee leg of the CDS to the expected present value of payments on the default leg.

3. Using $\lambda$ and assuming $C = 100$ or 500 bps as required, the difference between the expected present values of the default leg and of the fee leg is computed. This is the up-front payment.

## Example: Pricing New Contracts

Suppose a new five-year CDS contract, settling on March 23, 2009, with a maturity of March 23, 2014, has a conventional spread of 150 bps. The notional is 1 million dollars. The assumed recovery rate is 40%. By using the online CDS converter, the equivalent quotation for this contract is determined to be a fixed coupon of 100 bps and an up-front payment (from the protection buyer to the protection seller) of $20,144.45. If the conventional spread rises to 160 bps on the same day, then the equivalent 100 bps fixed coupon contract will have an up-front payment of $24,547.67, i.e., a mark-to-market gain to the buyer of the contract of $4,403.22.

## Example: Migrating Legacy Trades

Existing CDS contracts will need to be migrated to the new convention. Two features need to be preserved: (a) the notional on the contract should remain the same after the migration and (b) the periodic premium payment (usually quarterly) must stay the same. Suppose, as in the previous example, we had a $1 million notional CDS with a conventional spread of 150 bps. This could be converted into a portfolio of two possible contracts.

These two contracts are a 100 bps fixed-coupon contract with an up-front payment of $20,144.45, and a 500 bps fixed-coupon contract with an up-front payment of $-170,011.17$. Since in this case the fixed-coupon is higher than the conventional spread, the up-front payment is negative and results in a cash inflow to the protection buyer.

The original contract has a notional of $1 million and an annual premium of 150 bps, i.e., $15,000. We may use the two contracts above to obtain a replicating portfolio that gives the same notional and premium payments as follows. Let the dollar notional investment in the 100 bps contract be denoted $X$ and that in the 500 bps contract be denoted $Y$. We then require that the following two equations be solved so that we preserve notional and premium:

$$X + Y = 1,000,000$$

$$0.01\,X + 0.05\,Y = 15,000$$

Solving we get

$$X = 875,000, \qquad Y = 125,000$$

Hence, the original conventional spread contract is replaced with a 100 bps contract with a notional of $875,000 and a 500 bps contract of notional $125,000. There will also be an up-front one-time settlement amount to be paid computed as follows:

$$\$20,144.45\,X + \$(-170,011.17)\,Y = -\$3,625$$

implying that the buyer will receive a rebate of $3,625 at contract migration. This process of mass migration of legacy contracts at a predetermined date was dubbed the "CDS Big Bang."

# Chapter
# 32
# Structural Models of Default Risk

## 32.1 Introduction

Default risk and its measurement have always been a central concern of participants in financial markets. Early approaches to measuring credit risk took a statistical route, looking to distinguish between defaulters and non-defaulters using, for example, discriminant analysis. The most successful of these approaches was the Z-score model developed in the 1960s by Edward Altman. Altman's model assigns to each company a number (the so-called Z-score) based on five financial ratios:

$$Z = 1.2\,X_1 + 1.4\,X_2 + 3.3\,X_3 + 0.6\,X_4 + 0.999\,X_5$$

where

- $X_1$ = Working Capital/Total Assets
- $X_2$ = Retained Earnings/Total Assets
- $X_3$ = Earnings before Interest and Taxes/Total Assets
- $X_4$ = Market Value of Equity/Book Value of Debt
- $X_5$ = Sales/Total Assets

A high Z-score corresponds to a lower risk of default. The model classifies firms as "safe" if $Z > 3$, and as "distressed" if $Z < 1.80$, with Z-scores between 1.80 and 2.99 representing a zone of uncertainty. The Altman model predicts default two years ahead with good accuracy and continues to be used widely today.

In 1974, Robert Merton introduced a new option-theoretic approach to credit-risk modeling and measurement. Merton's model formalized and developed ideas that were implicit in Black and Scholes (1973). The class of models that has developed around the Merton (1974) approach is now called the class of "structural models."

The basis of the structural model approach is the observation that the value of the liabilities (debt and equity) of a firm at a point in time depends on the value of the firm's assets at that point as well as the outlook concerning that value. That is, debt and equity are *contingent claims* on the firm's assets. The value of the firm's assets acts as the central driving variable in structural models. In the typical structural model, the firm's debt and equity structure is taken as given, a process is posited for the evolution of the firm's asset value, conditions are specified that constitute "default," and debt and equity are priced off the posited process.

Since the firm's value process is unobserved, implementation of structural models is commonly effected in an indirect manner using the characteristics of the firm's equity. That is, given that equity is a contingent claim on the firm's assets whose value and other properties are observed, the implied value and other properties of the firm's assets may be backed out from this information. From this implied value, we may then calculate the desired output such as likelihood of the firm's default over any chosen horizon. One of the most successful commercial implementations of the structural model approach is that developed by KMV Corporation (now Moody's KMV) in the late 1980s. The KMV approach is described later in this chapter.

## Structural versus Reduced-Form Models

Structural models are distinguished from an alternative approach that was developed in the 1990s and that is now called the "reduced-form" approach. In a structural model, the likelihood of the firm's default over any horizon is derived from the model given the capital structure and the assumptions concerning the firm's value process and conditions determining default. Reduced-form models, the subject of the next chapter, take the default process as the model's "primitive": a process is directly posited for default likelihood that is then calibrated to the prices of securities issued by the firm or to the prices of derivatives based on those securities.

Reduced-form models thus have more of a financial engineering flavor than structural models. There are also differences in the implementation methodologies. As mentioned above (and as described in detail later in this chapter), structural model implementation is typically undertaken using equity market information. Reduced-form models, on the other hand, are commonly implemented using debt-market (usually bond-price) or credit-derivative (credit-default swap) data.

## Outline of This Chapter

This chapter discusses structural models. We first present the Merton model, the foundation of the structural model approach, in Section 32.2. Section 32.3 then discusses issues in the implementation of the model, in the course of which some extensions of the Merton model are also described. Section 32.4 describes the KMV implementation of the structural model approach. Theoretical extensions of the Merton model are the subject of Section 32.5. Finally, Section 32.6 presents an evaluation of the structural model approach to credit-risk measurement including a summary of its empirical performance.

# 32.2  The Merton (1974) Model

As with all structural models, the Merton model begins with a specification of the stochastic process for firm value (that is, the economic value of the total assets of the firm). Let $V_t$ denote the time-$t$ value of the firm. The model assumes that $V_t$ evolves according to a geometric Brownian motion:

$$dV_t = \mu V_t\, dt + \sigma V_t\, dW_t \tag{32.1}$$

where $\mu$ is the drift of firm value and $\sigma$ is its volatility.

The second input into a structural model is the capital structure of the firm. The Merton model assumes that the firm has equity and only a single issue of debt outstanding. Moreover, this debt is taken to be of zero-coupon form: the face value of the debt is denoted $D$ and the maturity date is $T$.

To complete the model, the conditions leading to default and costs in the event of default must be specified. The Merton model assumes that there are no covenants that could trigger default before $T$; default can occur only on date $T$. Moreover, absolute priority is assumed to hold at maturity of the debt: debt holders must be paid in full before equity holders receive anything. Finally, the model assumes away market frictions. In particular, there are no costs of liquidation or transfer of control in the event of default.

Under these assumptions, the Merton model derives its key insight: that risky debt issued by a firm is just an option on firm value and may be valued using option-theoretic techniques. We describe this next.

## Risky Debt as an Option

On date $T$, when the debt matures, there are two possibilities. If there is enough value in the firm to meet the amount due to debt holders (i.e., if $V_T \geq D$), debt holders are repaid the amount they are owed, and equity holders get the balance. However, if $V_T < D$, then debt holders receive whatever value there is in the firm, and equity holders get nothing. In notational terms, what debt holders receive is

$$\begin{cases} D, & \text{if } V_T \geq D \\ V_T, & \text{otherwise} \end{cases} \tag{32.2}$$

In shorthand notation, debt holders receive $\min\{V_T, D\}$. This may be rewritten as

$$D - \max\{D - V_T, 0\} \tag{32.3}$$

Expression (32.3) shows that the debt holders' claim is equivalent to a portfolio that is

- *Long* a default-risk-free bond paying $D$ at time $T$ (the first part of (32.3)).
- *Short* a put option on the firm's assets with strike $D$ and maturity $T$ (the second part of (32.3)).

That is, holding risky debt is equivalent to a situation in which debt is riskless (debt holders are going to get back $D$ for certain), but equity holders have the right to take back the payment of $D$ and give debt holders the firm in exchange, a right that will be exercised whenever $V_T < D$. It follows that the value of the firm's debt may be determined by identifying the values of the default-risk-free (henceforth, simply "risk-free" or "riskless") bond and the put. Denote these values by $B$ and $P$, respectively, and the value of the risky debt by $B^*$. We have

$$B^* = B - P \tag{32.4}$$

This decomposition also means that the *spread* on the risky debt—the difference between the promised yield on the risky debt and the risk-free rate—is completely determined by the value $P$ of the put. A higher value of $P$ increases the price difference between the risky and riskless bonds, increasing the spread. This makes it possible to identify how different factors affect credit spreads under the model's assumptions. For example:

- An increase in the volatility of the firm value process (the "underlying" for the put) increases the value of the put, so reduces the value of the risky debt and increases spreads.

- An increase in the risk-free rate decreases the value of the put (recall from Section 17.7 that put values vary inversely with the risk-free rate), so lowers spreads.

The principal observation made in this segment—that risky debt is equivalent to riskless debt minus a put on the firm—does not depend on the specific stochastic process driving firm value. But to give these observations *quantitative* expression, we must make use of the assumptions made in this regard. We turn to this next.

## Valuing Risky Debt

Let $t$ denote the current time. We have already assumed that the value process of the firm evolves according to a geometric Brownian motion. Suppose also that the risk-free rate of interest (expressed with continuous compounding) is a constant $r$.

Then, the value $B$ of riskless debt is just the face amount $D$ due at $T$ discounted to the present time $t$ at the risk-free rate $r$:

$$B = e^{-r(T-t)}D \qquad (32.5)$$

The value $P$ of the put can be identified using the Black-Scholes formula since all the conditions of the Black-Scholes model are met:

- The put is European in style with strike $D$ and maturity $T$.
- The price of the underlying (here, the firm value $V$) evolves according to a geometric Brownian motion with constant volatility $\sigma$.
- The risk-free rate of interest is a constant $r$.

Applying the Black-Scholes formula, the value of the put option is

$$P = e^{-r(T-t)}D\,N(-d_2) - V_t\,N(-d_1) \qquad (32.6)$$

where

$$d_1 = \frac{1}{\sigma\sqrt{T-t}}\left[\ln\left(\frac{V_t}{D}\right) + (r + \tfrac{1}{2}\sigma^2)(T-t)\right] \qquad (32.7)$$

$$d_2 = d_1 - \sigma\sqrt{T-t} \qquad (32.8)$$

and $N(\cdot)$ is the cumulative standard normal distribution.

Merton (1974) expresses the put price slightly differently. He defines

$$L = \frac{e^{-r(T-t)}D}{V_t} \qquad (32.9)$$

and writes

$$P = e^{-r(T-t)}D \cdot N(-d + \sigma\sqrt{T-t}) - V_t\,N(-d) \qquad (32.10)$$

where

$$d = \frac{1}{\sigma\sqrt{T-t}}\left[\ln\left(\frac{1}{L}\right) + \tfrac{1}{2}\sigma^2(T-t)\right] \qquad (32.11)$$

The term $L$ here is a measure of leverage: it is the ratio of the present value of debt to the total value of the firm. The reader is encouraged to compare the formulae (32.9)–(32.11) above to the original Black-Scholes formula (32.6)–(32.8) to confirm that the value of the put is exactly the same in the two cases.

Recall that $B^* = B - P$ is the value of the firm's debt. From (32.5) and (32.10), some simplification yields

$$B^* = e^{-r(T-t)}D\,N(d - \sigma\sqrt{T-t}) + V_t\,N(-d) \qquad (32.12)$$

Equivalently, (32.12) may be written as

$$B^* = e^{-r(T-t)}D\left[N(d - \sigma\sqrt{T-t}) + \frac{1}{L}N(-d)\right] \qquad (32.13)$$

**TABLE 32.1** The Merton Model: Inputs for Numerical Example

| Input Variable | Value |
|---|---|
| Current firm value ($V_t$) | 100 |
| Face value of zero-coupon debt ($D$) | 60 |
| Maturity ($T - t$) | 1 year |
| Volatility of firm value ($\sigma$) | 0.30 |
| Risk-free interest rate ($r$) | 0.10 |

Expression (32.13) provides a closed-form expression for the value of the debt issued by the firm in the Merton model. A numerical example illustrates.

**Example 32.1**

Suppose we are given the data in Table 32.1. Using these values, we first determine the price $B$ of riskless debt:

$$B = D \cdot \exp\{-r(T - t)\} = e^{-0.10 \times 1} = 54.29025$$

Next, using equation (32.13), we determine the price $B^*$ of risky debt. This works out to

$$B^* = 54.12146$$

This is lower than that of risky debt as is to be expected. The difference in the values of the two types of debt is precisely the value (32.10) of the put. ∎

### The Risk-Neutral Probability of Default

The Merton model can also be used to extract the *risk-neutral* probability of default, i.e., the risk-neutral probability of $V_T < D$. Indeed, this is simple. The risk-neutral probability of default is precisely the risk-neutral probability that the put $P$ finishes in-the-money. From Chapter 14, this probability is just

$$N(-d + \sigma\sqrt{T - t})$$

where $d$ is defined in (32.11). Expressed in full form, this probability is

$$N\left(\frac{1}{\sigma\sqrt{T - t}}\left[\ln\left(\frac{D}{V_t}\right) - \left(r - \frac{1}{2}\sigma^2\right)(T - t)\right]\right) \tag{32.14}$$

**Example 32.2**

Consider again the numbers given in Table 32.1. For the firm in this example, the risk-neutral probability of default is

$$\text{Prob}[V_T < 60] = N\left\{\frac{1}{0.3 \times \sqrt{1}}\left[\ln\left(\frac{60}{100}\right) - \left(0.10 - \frac{1}{2}(0.3^2)\right)(1)\right]\right\} = 0.029642$$

or about 2.96%. ∎

### And the Actual Default Probability?

Under the assumed process (32.1) for $V$, the actual ("real world") probability of default is the probability that $V_T < D$ given that $V_T$ has drift $\mu$ and volatility $\sigma$. In the risk-neutral world, the drift of the firm value process is the risk-free rate $r$. Since $\mu$ and $r$ may be different, the risk-neutral probability of default (32.14) may not be the same as the actual probability of default. Indeed, if $\mu > r$, the firm value in reality drifts upward faster than in the risk-neutral world, so the actual probability of default will be *lower* than the risk-neutral probability. Conversely, if $\mu < r$, the actual probability of default will exceed the risk-neutral probability of default.

A closed-form expression for the actual probability of default is not hard to obtain: it is simply the expression (32.14) with $r$ replaced with the true drift $\mu$:

$$N\left(\frac{1}{\sigma\sqrt{T-t}}\left[\ln\left(\frac{D}{V_t}\right)-\left(\mu-\frac{1}{2}\sigma^2\right)(T-t)\right]\right) \tag{32.15}$$

**Example 32.3**

Suppose that in addition to the information in Table 32.1, we are given the information that the actual drift of the firm is $\mu = 0.20$. Then, the real-world default probability is

$$N\left\{\frac{1}{0.3\times\sqrt{1}}\left[\ln\left(\frac{60}{100}\right)-\left(0.20-\frac{1}{2}(0.3^2)\right)(1)\right]\right\} = 0.013229$$

This is substantially lower than the risk-neutral default probability of 2.96%. ∎

From an economic point of view, we may interpret the higher risk-neutral default probability as comprising the actual probability of default plus a risk premium for the uncertainty around the timing and magnitude of default. (In the Merton model, there is no uncertainty considering the possible timing, but in more general models, and certainly in reality, there is.) The actual default probability will usually be less than the risk-neutral probability since we will typically have $\mu > r$.

From where do we estimate $\mu$? One possibility is to extract it using the equity return $r_E$ (determined from standard models such as the capital asset pricing model (CAPM) or other factor models for equity returns), and then de-levering it to determine firm value returns.

## Risk-Neutral Recovery Rates

The Merton framework admits a closed-form expression for the expected recovery rates under the risk-neutral measure, a useful feature of the model. At maturity $T$, if the value of the firm $V_T$ is less than the debt $D$ to be repaid, the firm is in default. The recovery amount will be some value less than $D$. If the recovered amount is denoted $a$, the *recovery rate* $\phi_T$ is defined to be the fraction $a/D$. The expected recovery rate as seen at time $t$ (contingent on default at $T$) is denoted $E_t[\phi_T]$. It is easy to derive this expected value under the risk-neutral measure, as we now show.

In the Merton model, there are no costs of liquidation or transfer of control and so the recovered amount $a$ in the event of default is just $V_T$. Thus, viewed from time $t$, the expected amount received by debt holders, contingent on default, is

$$E_t[V_T \mid V_T < D]$$

Letting $f(\cdot)$ denote the probability density function for $V_T$ (given the time-$t$ value $V_t$) and expanding this conditional expectation, we have

$$E_t[V_T|V_T < D] = \left(\int_0^D V_T f(V_T)\,dV_T\right)\Big/\left(\int_0^D f(V_T)\,dV_T\right)$$

The denominator is the risk-neutral probability that $V_T < D$. This is just the quantity given by (32.14): $N(-d + \sigma\sqrt{T-t})$. The numerator may be written as the difference of two terms:

$$\int_0^D V_T f(V_T)\,dV_T = \int_0^\infty V_T f(V_T)\,dV_T - \int_D^\infty V_T f(V_T)\,dV_T$$

The first term on the right-hand side is the time-$t$ expectation of $V_T$ under the risk-neutral measure, which is $e^{r(T-t)}V_t$. Expressed in the notation of this chapter, Section 15.4 (see expressions (15.37)–(15.44)) shows that

$$e^{-r(T-t)} \int_D^\infty V_T f(V_T) \, dV_T = V_t N(d)$$

so we obtain

$$\int_D^\infty V_T f(V_T) \, dV_T = e^{r(T-t)} V_t N(d)$$

Putting it all together, we obtain the following expression for the risk-neutral expected recovery rate in the Merton model:

$$\frac{1}{D} E_t[V_T | V_T < D] = e^{r(T-t)} \left( \frac{V_t}{D} \right) \left( \frac{N(-d)}{N(-d + \sigma\sqrt{T-t})} \right) \qquad \textbf{(32.16)}$$

## The Term Structure of Credit Spreads

The difference between the values of risky and riskless debt is commonly expressed in terms of a *credit spread*. The spread is the difference between the (promised) yield on the risky bond and the yield on riskless bonds.

Let $R$ denote the yield on the risky bond. By definition, $B^* = e^{-R(T-t)} D$, so

$$R = -\left( \frac{1}{T-t} \right) \ln \left( \frac{B^*}{D} \right)$$

The yield on the riskless bond is, of course, just the riskless rate $r$. Using (32.13), the spread $R - r$ is given by

$$R - r = -\left( \frac{1}{T-t} \right) \cdot \ln \left[ N \left( d - \sigma\sqrt{T-t} \right) + \frac{1}{L} \cdot N(-d) \right] \qquad \textbf{(32.17)}$$

The *term structure of credit spreads* refers to a plot of spreads against maturities By varying $T$ in (32.17), we obtain the term structure of credit spreads implied by the Merton model. From the definition of $d$, this term structure depends only on five variables: (i) the volatility of firm value $\sigma$, (ii) the risk-free rate $r$, (iii) the face value of debt $D$, (iv) the current value of the firm $V_t$, and, of course, (v) the maturity $T - t$.

---

**Example 32.4**

Consider again the inputs from Table 32.1. For the given maturity of one year, the value of the credit spread in this example is

$$R - r = -\ln \left( \frac{54.12146}{60} \right) - 0.10 = 0.003114$$

which is 31.14 basis points (or 0.3114%). ∎

More generally, using the other inputs from Table 32.1 but varying the maturity $T$, we may compute debt values and spreads for various maturities. The results for maturities ranging from 1 to 10 years are presented in Table 32.2. The term structure of credit spreads obtained from these input values is plotted in Figure 32.1.

Notice the humped shape of the plot. Spreads are low at short maturities, increase with maturity initially, and then decline at longer maturities. This shape is typical of what obtains in the Merton model when $V_t > D$. Intuitively, for very short maturities, default is an unlikely event, so spreads are low. As maturity lengthens, there is sufficient time for the bond to default as the firm value may drop below the value of debt, thereby resulting in higher spreads. For much longer maturities, the spread declines because, conditional on the bond not having defaulted for some time, the likelihood of the firm being far from default is high on average, thereby resulting in a lower probability of default.

**TABLE 32.2**

Merton Model Example: Term Structure of Credit Spreads

| Maturity (T) | Riskless Debt | Risky Debt | Spread (bps) |
|---|---|---|---|
| 1 | 54.2902 | 54.1215 | 31.1387 |
| 2 | 49.1238 | 48.5562 | 58.1090 |
| 3 | 44.4491 | 43.5873 | 65.2647 |
| 4 | 40.2192 | 39.1835 | 65.2249 |
| 5 | 36.3918 | 35.2708 | 62.5788 |
| 6 | 32.9287 | 31.7827 | 59.0387 |
| 7 | 29.7951 | 28.6639 | 55.2948 |
| 8 | 26.9597 | 25.8687 | 51.6363 |
| 9 | 24.3942 | 23.3590 | 48.1810 |
| 10 | 22.0728 | 21.1021 | 44.9705 |

**FIGURE 32.1**

Merton Model Example: Term Structure of Credit Spreads

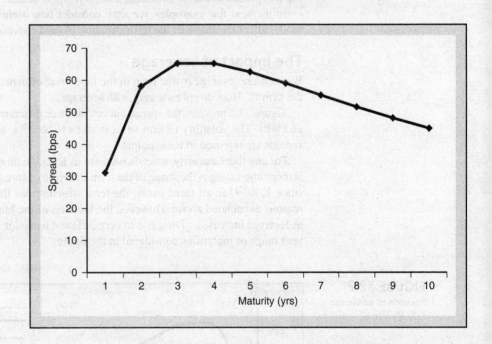

A simpler way of seeing the intuition is to think about two possible trajectories of firm value, one high and the other low. For short maturities, even if the firm took the low trajectory, there may not be sufficient time for it to reach default before the bond matures. At medium maturities, the low trajectory will be given enough play to allow sufficient time to reach default, and, hence, medium-term spreads tend to be higher than short-term ones. Finally, if the firm is still solvent after a long period of time, it is much more likely to have experienced a high trajectory, resulting in lower long-term spreads.

The same ideas may be put into an option-theoretic context. The extent of the credit spread is determined by the value of the European put option on $V_t$ with strike $D$ and maturity date $T$. Provided $V_t > D$, for very short maturities (small $T - t$) there is little likelihood of the put finishing in-the-money, so the value of the put is low, leading to low spreads. As maturity increases, the put value initially also increases since there is now a higher chance that the put will finish in-the-money. (For instance, suppose $V_t = 100$ and $D = 60$ as in Table 32.1. With a very short time to maturity—e.g., a day or a week—there is very little likelihood that the value of the firm will fall enough to push the put into the money, so the put will have little value. As maturity increases to, say, three months, there is a greater likelihood of this event, so a greater value for the put.) But at very long maturities, the put value again declines, since it is a European put. The maximum payoff from the put at maturity is $D$, which has a present value of $PV(D)$; so $PV(D)$ is an upper bound for the value of the put at any point. As $T \to \infty$, $PV(D) \to 0$, so the put value also goes to zero. This means spreads must decline towards zero at very long maturities.

One shortcoming of the Merton model that was mentioned above but bears stressing is the inability of the model to generate short-term spreads of the size observed in practice. Technically, the major reason for this is that the Merton model is based on Brownian motion, which evolves continuously. So if $V_t > D$, then it is unlikely over short horizons that the value will move below $D$ and default will result. If the process could include discontinuities (i.e., the value could suddenly "jump" down), then even over relatively short horizons, higher spreads would be generated since a jump to default is possible.

In the next few examples, we shall consider how some of the other parameters of the model affect the shape of the term structure of credit spreads.

## The Impact of Leverage

We measure leverage by the ratio of the face value of debt $D$ to the initial (time $t$) value of the firm $V_t$. How do spreads vary with leverage?

Figure 32.2 presents the spread curves for three different values of leverage: 50%, 65%, and 80%. The volatility of firm value is taken to be 25%, and the risk-free rate is 5%. The spreads are reported in basis points.

For any fixed maturity, spreads increase as leverage increases, which is expected. What is more interesting is the shape of the term structure of spreads in the three cases. In general, since $V_t > D$ in all three cases, the term structure has the classical hump shape for the reasons enunciated above. However, the location of the hump occurs at shorter maturities as leverage increases, giving rise to very different behavior in the curves over the 1 year–10 year range of maturities considered in the figure.

**FIGURE 32.2**

Spreads as Leverage $(D/V)$ Varies

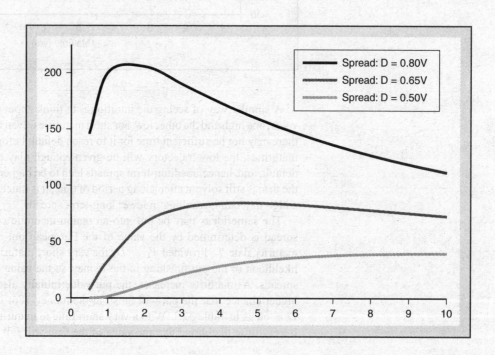

**FIGURE 32.3**

Spreads as *r* Varies

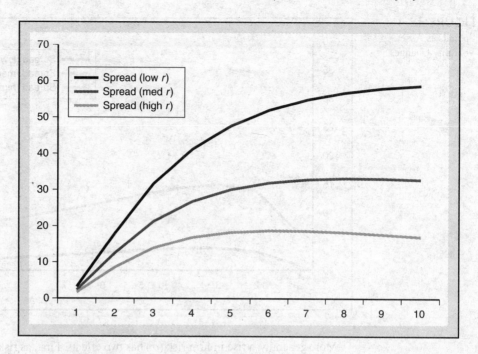

When $D/V = 80\%$, the term structure is effectively downward sloping over the 1 year–10 year range of maturities: the peak is reached very quickly. When $D/V = 65\%$, the peak is reached more gradually and the decline is not very visible in the figure. At $D/V = 50\%$, the term strucure of spreads is increasing over the entire horizon in the figure. Put differently, the Merton model implies an essentially downward-sloping term structure for highly levered or "risky" firms and an upward-sloping term structure for relatively safe firms.

## The Impact of Changes in the Risk-Free Rate

Next, we look at what happens to the term structure of spreads when the risk-free rate $r$ varies. The impact is captured in Figure 32.3. The figure considers three levels of the risk-free rate: 2%, 4%, and 6%. Volatility is fixed at 20%, and $D$ is taken to be 60% of the initial value of the firm. Spreads are shown in basis points

For fixed $T$, the plot shows an inverse relationship between risk-free interest rates and spreads: spreads decline as risk-free rates increase. The reason for this was noted earlier: the spread is determined by the value of a put option on the firm's assets, and put option values are negatively related to interest rates as explained in Section 17.7.

## The Impact of Changes in Volatility

Figure 32.4 captures the effect on spreads of changes in the firm's asset-value volatility $\sigma$. The figure considers three levels of volatility: 10.0%, 12.5%, and 15.0%. The risk-free rate is fixed at 5%, and the level of debt $D$ is taken to be 80% of the firm's initial value $V_t$. Spreads are shown in basis points.

For any fixed maturity, an increase in firm volatility increases spreads. Intuitively, additional risk means future firm values become more spread out. Debt holders, whose maximum payoffs are capped, cannot reap additional benefit from the higher firm values but stand to lose from the lower firm values. Thus, the higher volatility lowers debt value, in effect transferring value from debt holders to equity holders.

**FIGURE 32.4**

Spreads as Asset
Volatility Changes

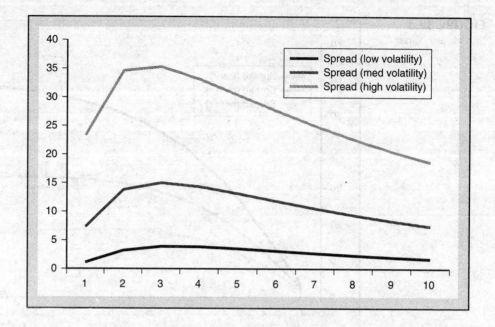

More generally, a rise in firm risk ($\sigma$) has two effects. First, as risk increases, the spread curve rises. This "level" effect is what we have described in the previous paragraph. Second, as risk increases, the hump of the spread curve is exacerbated. Because of higher risk levels, spreads initially tend to increase more rapidly with maturity, and then, conditional on survival, spreads decline just as dramatically. Thus, there is also a "shape" or "curvature" effect.

## 32.3    Issues in Implementation

The numerical examples of the previous section make the Merton model appear easy to implement in practice. However, a little thought shows two hurdles to be surmounted before the model can be applied to real-world firms:

1. Two key inputs, $V$ and $\sigma$, are unobservable.
2. The model assumes that the firm has a *single* issue of *zero-coupon* debt outstanding. Real-world debt structures will be more complex.

We discuss each of these problems below. The procedures we highlight here are those commonly used in practice to resolve these problems. Besides these, there are also some concerns with other aspects of the model, such as the assumption that the Absolute Priority Rule (APR) holds. We discuss these in a later section dealing with extensions of the Merton model.

### Problem 1: Unobservability of the $V_t$ Process

Although the firm value process $V_t$ and its volatility $\sigma$ are themselves unobservable in the marketplace, it is possible to use prices of traded securities issued by the firm to identify these quantities. Specifically, consider a publicly traded firm with observable equity prices $E$. In such a case, the *volatility* of equity prices $\sigma_E$ may also be estimated from the data. We explain how these two inputs $E$ and $\sigma_E$ may be used to obtain working estimates of current firm value $V$ and volatility $\sigma$.

The first step is to express equity value $E$ as an option on firm value $V$. On the maturity date $T$ of the debt, the amount $E_T$ received by equity holders is any remaining amount after paying back the debt holders what they are owed:

$$E_T = \begin{cases} V_T - D, & \text{if } V_T \geq D \\ 0, & \text{otherwise} \end{cases} \qquad (32.18)$$

In shorthand notation, this is $\max\{V_T - D, 0\}$. Thus, equity value is the value of a *long call option* on the firm's assets with strike $D$ and maturity $T$. Intuitively, equity holders have the right at time $T$ to take control of the remaining assets of the firm by paying the debt holders the amount $D$ they are owed, or they can walk away from the firm and receive nothing.

The time-$t$ value of equity $E_t$ is the time-$t$ value of this call, which in turn depends on the value and volatility of the underlying (i.e., on $V_t$ and $\sigma$), as well as on the observable variables $D$ (the strike), $T - t$ (the maturity), and $r$ (the risk-free rate). Letting $f$ denote the call-pricing function and suppressing dependence on the observable variables $(D, T - t, r)$, we write

$$E_t = f(V_t, \sigma) \qquad (32.19)$$

The pricing function $f$ depends on the specific assumptions made concerning the firm's asset value process. For example, under the geometric Brownian motion assumption made by the Merton model, $f$ is simply the Black-Scholes formula for the price of a call with underlying $V_t$, strike $D$, and maturity $T - t$:

$$f(V_t, \sigma) = V_t \cdot N(d) - e^{-r(T-t)} D \cdot N(d - \sigma\sqrt{T - t}) \qquad (32.20)$$

where $d$ was defined in (32.11) and $N(\cdot)$ is the cumulative standard normal distribution.

Now, since equity is an option on firm value, the *volatility* of equity, denoted $\sigma_E$, is also a function of $V_t$ and $\sigma$. Denote this function by $g$:

$$\sigma_E = g(V_t, \sigma) \qquad (32.21)$$

Again, once we have made specific assumptions about the firm value process, the form of $g$ may be identified. For example, in the Merton model, it can be shown using Ito's Lemma (Chapter 15) that

$$g(V_t, \sigma) = \sigma V_t \cdot \frac{f_V}{f} \qquad (32.22)$$

where $f$ is the call-pricing function (32.20) and $f_V = \partial f / \partial V$ is the delta of the call option at time $t$ (which under the Black-Scholes assumptions is just $N(d)$).

Expressions (32.19) and (32.21) give us two (nonlinear) equations for the two unknowns $V_t$ and $\sigma$ in terms of

- Equity value $E_t$.
- Equity volatility $\sigma_E$.
- Other observable variables $(D, T - t, r)$.

Since equity values are observable and equity volatilities may be computed from observable stock price histories or implied from option prices, we can use these two equations to solve for the two unknowns $V_t$ and $\sigma$.

**Example 32.5**

Suppose we observe the following current (time $t$) equity value and equity volatility in the market for some given firm:

$$E_t = 45.88, \qquad \sigma_E = 0.6445$$

Suppose too that a check of the company's balance sheet reveals that it has a single issue of debt outstanding with face value $D = 60$ maturing in one year. The one-year risk-free rate of interest is 10%.

Using equations (32.19) and (32.21), we plug in the input values above. This results in two equations with two unknowns, $\{V_t, \sigma\}$. The solution to these equations may be readily computed using numerical methods, even on a spreadsheet. Carrying out the computations reveals:

$$V_t = 100 \qquad \sigma = 0.30$$

This means the value of the firm's debt is

$$B_t^* = V_t - E_t = 100 - 45.88 = 54.12$$

The corresponding price of risk-free debt with the same face value and maturity, given the risk-free rate of 10%, is

$$B_t = e^{-r(T-t)} = 54.29$$

Thus, the spread on the firm's debt is

$$R - r = -\frac{1}{T-t} \ln\left[\frac{B_t^*}{B_t}\right] = 0.003114$$

or 31.14 bps.    ∎

## Problem 2: More Complex Capital Structures

The second problem with the Merton model is that it assumes too simplistic a capital structure. Capital structures in practice are far more complex than assumed by the model. There are usually many issues of debt outstanding, with varied coupons, maturities, and subordination structures. From an implementation standpoint, this presents us with two alternatives:

1. Extend the theoretical structure of the model to enable it to handle more complex debt structures.
2. Simplify reality to make it fit within the existing model.

Both alternatives have been examined in theory as well as in practice. We examine each in turn.

### Solution 1: Extending the Theoretical Model

The first solution appears intuitively attractive and the economically correct way to proceed. Robert Geske and others have developed extensions of the Merton model that allow for the simultaneous existence of multiple debt issues that can differ along many dimensions such as (a) the size of coupons, (b) maturity, and (c) seniority or subordination (see Geske (1977), Geske (1979), and Delianedis and Geske (1998)). In addition, these models can also incorporate issues such as safety covenants, sinking-fund provisions, amortization, etc.

Pricing risky debt in the extended model is conceptually not difficult but is technically more complex than in the Merton model. In particular, equity now becomes a *compound option* on firm value rather than a simple European option. Why is this the case? Because each payment presents the equity holders with an option: they can make the payment, in which case they retain control of the firm until the next payment, or they can default, in which case control passes to the debt holders and equity holders receive nothing. Effectively, each payment provides the right to proceed to the next payment, so is an option on the option represented by the next payment.

Here's a slightly more formal explanation. Imagine a situation in which a company owes debt payments $D_1, \ldots, D_n$ at times $t_1, \ldots, t_n$. The payments could be coupon and/or principal repayments and could come from one or several different debt issues. We derive the compound option nature of equity in steps.

***Equity Value between $t_{n-1}$ and $t_n$*** Suppose the first $n-1$ payments have been made, and consider any time $t$ between $t_{n-1}$ and $t_n$. At this point, there is only a single payment left, so we are effectively in the Merton setting. The value of equity at $t$ is therefore the time-$t$ value $C_t$ of a European call option on the firm's assets with strike $D_n$ and maturity $t_n$. (In particular, $C_{t_{n-1}}$ denotes the value of equity at $t_{n-1}$ just after the payment due at $t_{n-1}$ has been made.) The payoff of this option at maturity is

$$C_{t_n} = \max\left\{ V_{t_n} - D_n, 0 \right\} \qquad \textbf{(32.23)}$$

***Equity Value between $t_{n-2}$ and $t_{n-1}$*** Now, consider the equity holders' decision choice at $t_{n-1}$. At this point, equity holders can:

- Make the payment $D_{n-1}$, in which case the firm remains in equity holders' control. The value received by the equity holders is $C_{t_{n-1}}$.
- Default on the payment, in which case control of the firm's assets passes to the debt holders and equity holders receive nothing.

So equity holders' payoff at $t_{n-1}$ is

$$\max\left\{ C_{t_{n-1}} - D_{n-1}, 0 \right\} \qquad \textbf{(32.24)}$$

This is the payoff at maturity from a call option with strike $D_{n-1}$ and maturity $t_{n-1}$ whose underlying is the $t_n$-maturity call with maturity payoffs of (32.23). Thus, at any $t$ between $t_{n-2}$ and $t_{n-1}$, the value of equity is the value of this call-on-call compound option. Denote this value by $C_t^{[2]}$, with the superscript 2 indicating that the option is a call-on-call. In the Black-Scholes setting, the closed-form solution for this compound option involves a bivariate normal distribution (see Section 18.5).

***Equity Value between $t_{n-3}$ and $t_{n-2}$*** The same line of reasoning shows that at time $t_{n-2}$, equity holders can either

- pay $D_{n-2}$ and continue the firm, in which case they receive the time-$t_{n-2}$ value of the compound option that pays (32.24) at $t_{n-1}$; or
- default, in which case they receive zero.

Thus, their payoffs at time $t_{n-2}$ are

$$\max\left\{ C_{t_{n-2}}^{[2]} - D_{n-2}, 0 \right\} \qquad \textbf{(32.25)}$$

This is the payoff from a call option with strike $D_{n-2}$ and maturity $t_{n-2}$ whose underlying is the call-on-call with time-$t_{n-1}$ payoffs of (32.24). Thus, at any $t$ between $t_{n-3}$ and $t_{n-2}$ the value of equity is given by a compound option that is a call-on-call-on-call. In the Black-Scholes setting, the closed-form solution for this option involves a trivariate normal distribution.

And so on . . .

With each additional payment due, the "compound" nature of the call increases one additional level. The resulting solution for equity values does continue to have a closed-form representation but an increasingly complex one: if there are $n$ promised payments remaining, the closed-form expression involves an $n$–dimensional multivariate normal distribution.

The added complication is not without its potential upside. One example is the notion of forward default probabilities described in the model of Delianedis and Geske (1998). Delianedis and Geske undertake a minimalist expansion of the Merton model by collapsing a firm's capital structure into two debt "buckets" (rather than one as in the Merton model): a short-term debt bucket and a long-term debt bucket. This means equity is a compound option (a call-on-call). Because there are two maturities of debt, two probabilities of default exist in the model: a short-term probability (the likelihood of default occurring on the short-term debt) and a conditional long-term probability (or what Delianedis and Geske call the "forward" default probability). Useful information is obtained by comparing the short-term and long-term default probabilities. We may also calculate the total probability of default, i.e., of defaulting at either of the two maturity dates. The Delianedis-Geske model is described in more detail in Appendix 32A.

Nonetheless, the complexity of the solution for equity values creates problems in implementation. On the one hand, the full-blown model requires precise and complete information on the actual debt structure. On the other, the process of inverting equity values and volatility to identify the unobservable firm values and volatility gets significantly more complicated than in the Merton model. These are serious hurdles. The alternative to complicating the Merton model is to simplify reality so as to make it fit within the model's structure. We describe this next.

### Solution 2: Simplifying Reality

The Merton model assumes a single debt issue outstanding that is further required to be of zero-coupon form. Capital structures in practice are much more complex. To make them fit within the Merton model, we seek to replace the given debt structure with an equivalent zero-coupon structure. The challenge, of course, is in identifying what is "equivalent." There are many ways one could go here. One, for example, is to take a zero-coupon bond that has the same duration as the given debt structure. This is similar to the approach taken by Delianedis and Geske (1998) in their empirical analysis.

An alternative that is used in the popular Moody's KMV vendor model is to take the zero-coupon equivalent level $D$ to have a maturity of one year and a face value that is the sum of (i) the face value of all short-term (less than one year) liabilities in the given capital structure, and (ii) half the face value of all longer-term liabilities.[1] The Moody's KMV approach is based on the observation that, in practice, default tends to occur when the market value of the firm's assets drops below a critical point that typically lies below the book value of all liabilities but above the book value of short-term liabilities.

Of course, there is a certain arbitrariness in these approaches to simplifying the debt structure, but ultimately, the question is whether the models do well in practice, and the available evidence, both empirical as well as the popularity of the Moody's KMV and related approaches, suggests an affirmative answer.

---

[1] The actual rule is a little more complicated than this since Moody's KMV also allows for other securities in the capital structure than just equity and straight debt. We also note that Moody's KMV updates and revises the model on an ongoing basis.

## 32.4   A Practitioner Model

In the 1980s, Moody's KMV (then an independent firm called KMV Corporation) developed a particular implementation of a structural credit-risk measurement model. The Moody's KMV (henceforth, MKMV) framework is based on the classical Merton model but also differs from it in significant ways. This section provides a description of the MKMV approach. Since MKMV revises and updates the model on an ongoing basis, readers are encouraged to consult the company website (http://www.moodyskmv.com) for more information.

Broadly speaking, the MKMV approach uses a four-step procedure to track changes in credit risk for publicly traded firms. The first step is to collapse the firm's capital structure so as to make it fit within the Merton model's zero-coupon structure. This is accomplished as described above: that is, by setting the face value $D$ of the zero-coupon debt (called the "default point") to be equal to the sum of the face values of the short-term liabilities and a fraction of the face values of the longer-term liabilities.

The second step is to use the default point $D$ together with the firm's equity value and equity volatility to identify firm value $V$ and firm volatility $\sigma$. The procedure for accomplishing this has also been described above in equations (32.19)–(32.22).

At this point, we are still very much within the framework of the Merton model, but here is where the MKMV approach ploughs a different path. Having obtained the firm value and volatility, the third step is to define what is called the "distance to default." Intuitively, the distance to default is the number of standard deviation moves the firm value has to make before the firm is in default. Technically, this should use the lognormal distribution assumption on $V$; indeed, given the drift $\mu$ and volatility $\sigma$ of $V$, the distance to default is precisely the point at which $N(\cdot)$ is evaluated in (32.15). But MKMV define the distance to default $\delta$ in a simplified way as[2]

$$\delta = \frac{V_t - D}{\sigma V_t} \qquad (32.26)$$

The numerator is just the distance, measured in dollars, between the current value of the firm $V_t$ and the default point $D$. The denominator normalizes this distance by the "dollar standard deviation." The ratio $\delta$ represents the number of standard deviations the firm is from default. Normalizing the distance in this fashion makes it possible to compare how far two firms are from default even if they differ substantially in other ways. A higher distance to default implies a safer firm.

In the final step, the MKMV approach applies the estimated distance to default $\delta$ to a proprietary default database, and asks the question: of all firms in the database that had a distance to default close to $\delta$, how many actually defaulted within one year? This is the *expected default frequency*, or EDF. The EDF, the model's principal output, is the likelihood the given firm will default within one year. The EDF may, of course, be calculated for any horizon, not just one year. As of the time of writing, MKMV provides EDFs out to five years.

The following example illustrates the MKMV procedure.

| **Example 32.6** | Suppose we carry out the first two steps of the KMV procedure on a hypothetical firm and obtain the following results: |
|---|---|

1.  Estimated default point: $D = \$15$ billion.
2.  Estimated market value of the firm: $V_t = \$45$ billion.
3.  Estimated volatility of firm value: $\sigma = 20\%$.

---

[2] See Equation (2), p. 9, of Crosbie and Bohn (2003).

The next step is to estimate distance to default. In dollar terms, the firm is $30 billion from default (its value is $45 billion against a default point of $15 billion). One standard deviation of firm value is approximately $\sigma V_t = 0.20 \times 45$ billion, or $9 billion. Thus, in standard deviation terms, the firm is a distance

$$\frac{45 - 15}{0.20 \times 45} = \frac{30}{9} = 3.33$$

from default. That is, it would take a 3.33 standard deviation move in the firm value to put the firm into default.

For the final step, suppose that MKMV's database shows that historically, firms with a distance to default of 3.3 to 3.4 defaulted with a frequency of 1 in 300. (This is for illustrative purposes only; it is not based on MKMV's actual database.) Then, the EDF assigned to the firm is 1/300 = 0.33%.

Now, suppose a year from the time of our initial estimate, we examine the firm's credit risk again. Suppose that over this year, the firm's debt has decreased but that its equity value has also decreased (say, because its business prospects appear poorer). Has the firm's debt become riskier? If so, how much? The MKMV model (as, of course, with any structural model) enables a quantification of the answers. Specifically, suppose that based on the new data, we identify the following values for the new default point and for the firm value and volatility:

1. Default point $D = \$12$ billion.
2. Firm value: $V_t = \$40$ billion.
3. Firm volatility: $\sigma = 25\%$.

The lower firm value and higher volatility reflect the poorer business prospects of the firm, while the lower default point reflects the lower level of indebtedness. The new distance to default is

$$\frac{40 - 12}{0.25 \times 40} = \frac{28}{10} = 2.8$$

The lower distance to default indicates the firm's credit risk has worsened over the course of the year. Computing the EDF for the new distance to default enables us to put a number on just how much riskier the firm has become. Suppose, for example, that MKMV's empirical database yields an EDF of 1 in 210, or 0.48%. Then, this means that the likelihood of the firm's default over the next year is almost $1\frac{1}{2}$ times the level it was earlier. ∎

### Comments

In principle, given a firm's drift, volatility, and default point, we should be able to compute its theoretical default probability using the assumption that the firm value process is log-normally distributed. In practice, there are two problems with taking this route. First, the drift of firm value is difficult to estimate with any degree of accuracy. Second, investigations of this approach suggest that this results in an (often very large) underestimate of default probabilities compared to the data. MKMV's unusual mixed theoretical-empirical approach sidesteps both problems. It obviates the need to estimate the firm's drift, and by construction, it is broadly consistent with the default probabilities in the data.

One reason for underprediction of default in the Merton model is its assumption of normality in the returns distribution. Reality is considerably more fat-tailed (leptokurtic), meaning that extreme events (including default) are far more likely than under the assumed returns distribution. From a theoretical standpoint, one way to address this problem is to use a different returns distribution that is leptokurtic (e.g., **stable** Paretian); an alternative is to create fat tails by adding features to the model that induce this **effect** (jumps or stochastic volatility). While these theoretical extensions are not hard to carry **out**, they are certainly harder to implement in the context of measuring credit risk.

In this context, KMV's approach guarantees, by construction, a degree of empirical consistency with the data. Nonetheless, there are some potential shortcomings of the approach that should be noted. The Merton model, like all contingent claims modeling, is a forward-looking model. Its implementation uses the expectations of market participants as embedded in security (particularly equity) prices. However, in translating a specific firm's distance to default into a default probability for the firm, the procedure maps the distance to default into a historical database of defaults. The resulting default probability is thus no longer purely forward-looking and is no longer purely specific to the firm in question over the period of interest. In particular, the historical database of defaults may include defaults by firms of differing sizes, from a range of industries, and over periods of recession and expansion. These are all concerns from a conceptual standpoint. Nonetheless, the approach pioneered by MKMV has so far proved a popular one in practice.

## 32.5   Extensions of the Merton Model

As noted earlier, the Merton model involves a number of other simplifying and potentially restrictive assumptions. One of these—the simplicity of the assumed capital structure—has been discussed above. Other restrictive assumptions in the Merton setting include:

1. The assumption that default is possible only at maturity of the firm's debt. In particular, the model assumes that there are no covenants that could trigger default before the maturity date.
2. The assumption that the absolute priority rule holds in default with debt holders paid in full before equity holders receive anything. Available evidence in the US suggests that absolute priority is often violated in practice.
3. The assumption that no renegotiation of debt is allowed, contrary to casual empirical observation.
4. The assumption that liquidation/transfer of control is costless, i.e., that the deadweight costs of bankruptcy are nil.

Besides these are a host of other issues: the use of normality in the returns distribution rather than one allowing for tail fatness; the assumption of nonstochastic interest rates; the lack of a clearly defined cash-flow process from which the firm asset value process is defined, and the management of that cash-flow process between debt repayment, dividend payments, and cash reserves; the static nature of the capital structure of the firm, although evidence suggests that firms may have target leverage ratios; and so on.

Over the years, a number of attempts have been made in the finance literature to address these shortcomings. A brief discussion of some of these papers follows. We emphasize that this description is meant to be indicative rather than comprehensive.

An early extension of the Merton model was undertaken by Black and Cox (1976). They retain much of the Merton structure but assume that default can occur before maturity if the value of the firm falls sufficiently. Specifically, a default barrier $M_\tau$ is defined, and it is assumed that default occurs at the first time $\tau$ such that $\tau V_\tau \leq M_\tau$. Because there is the additional possibility of default before maturity, spreads in the Black-Cox model are usually wider than in the Merton model.

The Black and Cox (1976) model was extended by Longstaff and Schwartz (1995) who also allowed for stochastic interest rates. This injects an extra source of stochastic variation in the model, and also affects the firm value process through the correlation between changes in interest rates and firm value. Leland (1994) and Leland and Toft (1996) further extend this approach by endogenizing the default boundary: equity holders seeking to maximize the value of equity optimally choose the point of default. They also introduce tax benefits of debt into the model and derive closed-form solutions for the optimal capital structure.

Anderson and Sundaresan (1996) and Mella-Barral and Perraudin (1997) allow for costs of liquidation/transfer of control. They argue that the presence of such costs provides equity holders with incentives to indulge in "strategic" debt service, i.e., to renegotiate debt payments downwards since rejecting the proposed offer and liquidating the firm might make debt holders even worse off. The possibility of such opportunistic behavior by equity holders is, in equilibrium, factored into the pricing of debt; it lowers debt prices and raises spreads.

Anderson and Sundaresan (1996) model the underlying cash-flow process that generates firm value, but all periodic cash flows in their model must be paid out as debt service or dividends. Acharya, Huang, Subrahmanyam, and Sundaram (2006) extend this setting to allow for cash reserves and "optimal" (equity value-maximizing) dividend and debt-service policies. While cash reserves are intended to raise equity values, it is shown that such reserves may benefit debt holders as well, so spreads are lower than when reserves are disallowed. Moreover, because the option to service debt strategically affects the cash reserve policy, strategic debt service may not always act to raise spreads, and may even result in *lower* spreads in some situations.

Zhou (1997) addresses the issue of fat tails in returns. He models the firm value process as a jump-diffusion. As in Black and Cox (1976) and Longstaff and Schwartz (1995), Zhou assumes default can occur before maturity if firm value drops below some exogenously specified level (in his model, a constant $K$). Because firm value can jump down, the value at default time could be strictly less than $K$; this is not possible in Black-Cox or Longstaff-Schwartz. As a consequence, recovery rates in default in Zhou's paper are naturally stochastic. Zhou shows that jumps can have a significant effect on model outputs including spreads.

Collin-Dufresne and Goldstein (2001) incorporate another observed empirical regularity into their model: that firms appear to target leverage ratios. They develop a model with stochastic interest rates and mean-reverting leverage ratios and find that the model generates spreads that are generally more consistent with patterns in the data than earlier models.

Among vendor models of credit risk that have a structural basis is the CreditGrades model developed by RiskMetrics. The model's main objective is to eliminate the inability of pure Merton models to generate realistic short-term spreads. The model is similar in some respects to Black-Cox, but in the CreditGrades model, the default barrier is allowed to be stochastic, which creates a stochastic recovery rate in the model. This feature generates sufficiently large short-term spreads because of the additional source of random variation in the model.

## 32.6   Evaluation of the Structural Model Approach

From a conceptual standpoint, there is much to recommend the structural model approach. The model has a sound economic basis. It is a causal model: the key driving variables can be observed and analyzed. Recovery rates (risk-neutral) are also naturally defined in the model in a manner consistent with the probabilities of default. The implementation of the structural models makes use of current market price information, in particular, information from equity markets, which tends to be more liquid and informative than credit markets. It is a forward-looking model (although the use of historical data in approaches such as Moody's KMV qualifies this statement to a degree). Empirically, various versions of structural models have been found to have good predictive power for defaults and ratings transitions.

All this is to the good. But balancing this are some weaknesses. The model is computationally challenging for all but the simplest debt structures. In particular, for firms with debt of varying seniority, to value a particular tranche of corporate debt, one has to simultaneously value all issues senior to it. In fact, in practice, the model is rarely used to value specific tranches of debt; rather, it is used primarily as an indicator or predictor of distress.

Structural models are also primarily models of a single corporation, not general-purpose credit- or counterparty-risk models. They cannot be used to value sovereign debt from emerging markets, much less emerging market credit derivatives.[3] Even as models of corporate risk, structural models are difficult to apply to *private* companies because of the unavailability of traded equity prices.

Nor do structural models facilitate the valuation of most credit derivatives (although Das (1995) shows how some credit derivatives may be priced within this framework). Finally, the models make many stylized assumptions that are often violated in practice. Although the literature has developed generalizations to handle many of these issues, the practical applicability of many of these generalizations is limited.

## The Empirical Performance of Structural Models

Finally, there is the question of the empirical performance of these models. Here the evidence is mixed. Early investigations (e.g., Jones, Mason, and Rosenfeld, 1984) found that the Merton model tended to underpredict spreads, often by wide margins. Collin-Dufresne, Goldstein, and Martin (2001) examine the determinants of *changes* in credit spreads. They find that the key variables identified by structural models as determinants of spreads can explain only a small fraction of the changes in spreads even when supplemented by a range of financial and macroeconomic variables.

Eom et al. (2004) test five structural models—Merton, Geske, Longstaff-Schwartz, Leland-Toft, and Collins-Dufresne and Goldstein—on a common data set of bond prices from 1986 to 1997. They find that while the Merton model does substantially underpredict spreads, the others suffer from the problem of *over*predicting spreads on average, severely overstating the credit risk of riskier bonds even while they underestimate the risk of safer bonds.

Huang and Huang (2003) take a different approach to comparing models and also come up with different conclusions. They compare six models: Longstaff-Schwartz; a strategic debt-service model based on Anderson and Sundaresan (1996) and Mella-Barral and Perraudin (1997); an endogenous default barrier model based on Leland (1994) and Leland and Toft (1996); the mean-reverting leverage model of Collins-Dufresne and Goldstein (2001); and two new models that they introduce in the paper. Huang and Huang calibrate each model to data on historical default experience and find that all the models generate roughly the same credit spreads for these choices of parameters. However, these spreads are substantially smaller than observed spreads, particularly for short maturities and high-quality bonds.

Taken together, these studies suggest that the ability of structural models to explain the levels of spreads may be limited. On the other hand, one concept coming out of structural models—the notion of distance to default—has been shown to be useful in a variety of ways, as we discuss below.

---

[3] Some efforts have been made to extend structural models to sovereign debt, in particular to define the notions of asset and equity values for sovereigns. See, for example, Gray, Merton, and Bodie (2006) or Gapen, Gray, Lim, and Xiao (2005).

## Distance to Default and the CAP Curve

Samples of observed bankruptcies may be used to assess the predictive validity of default models. Since distance to default is a normalized metric, it may be used to rank order firms according to how likely they are to fail. A firm's propensity to default increases as its distance to default decreases. If the sequence of firm failures exactly matches the ordering of firms by distance to default, then the model is 100% accurate. Think of firms queued up in order of increasing distance to default. The firms at the front of the queue are the ones with the smallest distances to default. As we go down the queue, distance to default increases. If actual defaults occur more or less from the front of the queue, we can safely assume a high degree of predictive validity for the model. However, if firms fail randomly from anywhere in the queue, the model is not a good one.

A formal statistical metric for measuring the forecast validity of distance to default is the cumulative accuracy profile (CAP) of the model. A CAP curve is the plot of the cumulative percentage of defaulted firms (plotted on the y-axis) in each cumulative percentile of the population of all firms sorted by the default metric (plotted on the x-axis). For example, assume we have a population of 1000 firms, and of these, 25 default. We sort firms by distance to default and find that of the first 10 firms, we have 9 defaults. In the next 10, there are 8 defaults. Percentile three has 5 defaults and percentile four has 3 defaults. The first four percentiles account for all 25 defaults. The values on the CAP curve would appear as shown in Table 32.3.

The CAP curve is drawn by plotting the fourth column of Table 32.3 against the third column. It rises steeply initially and then tapers off, finally peaking out at 100% and remaining flat thereafter necessarily. The curve rises sharply in this example because the model has high predictive power. If the default model has no predictive ability, then the average outcome for the CAP curve will be seen as a 45-degree line. Therefore, the area between the CAP curve and the 45-degree line may be used as a metric of predictive ability. Denote this area as $A$. Likewise, denote the area between the CAP curve of a perfectly predictive model (the fifth column in Table 32.3) and the 45-degree line. Denote this area as $B$. The ratio $A/B$ is known as the "accuracy ratio" (AR) of the model. This quantifies the performance of the model. A schematic diagram of the relation between CAP curves and accuracy ratios is shown in Figure 32.5. The accuracy ratio for the example values in Table 32.3 is 99.72% (the reader is encouraged to rework this as an exercise).

There is substantial evidence showing that structural models do well in default prediction. Accuracy ratios vary from 65–90%, depending on the specifics of the model and the universe of firms. For example, Duffie, Saita, and Wang (2007) mix distance to default along with

**TABLE 32.3** A
Cumulative Accuracy
Profile (CAP)

| Percentage Range of All Firms | Percentage of Defaulted Firms | Cumulative Percentile of All Firms | Cumulative Percentage of Defaulted Firms | Cumulative Percentage of Perfect Model |
|---|---|---|---|---|
| 0 | 0 | 0 | 0 | 0 |
| 0–1 | 36 | 1 | 36 | 40 |
| 1–2 | 32 | 2 | 68 | 80 |
| 2–3 | 20 | 3 | 88 | 100 |
| 4–5 | 12 | 4 | 100 | 100 |
| 5–6 | 0 | 5 | 100 | 100 |
| ⋮ | ⋮ | ⋮ | ⋮ | |
| ⋮ | ⋮ | ⋮ | ⋮ | |
| 99–100 | 0 | 100 | 100 | 100 |

**FIGURE 32.5**
Cumulative Accuracy
Profile and Accuracy
Ratio: The CAP Curve

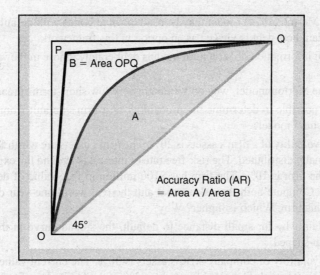

other covariates, macroeconomic and from the equity markets, and achieve accuracy ratios
of over 85%. These so-called hybrid models that use variables other than just firm-specific
ones look to improve on models based purely on distance to default.

## 32.7 Summary

This chapter demonstrates how derivatives models and observable market information may
be used to determine the default risk of a firm. The main idea underlying the approach in this
chapter germinated in the seminal work of Black and Scholes (1973) and Merton (1974).
These papers showed how equity option formulae could be used to treat debt in the firm as
containing an embedded option, which could then be valued using other traded observable
securities.

The main philosophy behind the structural model and its implementation is that equity
markets provide the best assessment of the default likelihood of a firm. This is reasonable
insofar as equity is often the most liquid security issued by a firm. But there are two
shortcomings to this. First, there is often no place in the implementation procedures for
information from other securities markets (like bond markets) or derivatives markets (like
options or credit-default swap markets). Second, it makes the model difficult to apply to those
corporate entities whose equity is not publicly traded, and, even more so, to non-corporate
entities such as emerging-market sovereigns.

On the other hand, there is no doubt that as far as public firms are concerned, the structural
model approach has yielded rich insights, most notably concerning default probabilities and
its drivers. As Leland (2006) notes, structural models also provide insights into corporate
finance decisions such as optimal leverage, maturity, and investment decisions. Perhaps the
biggest shortcoming of most structural models remains their inability to match empirical
short-term spreads especially from low-risk firms, although models incorporating jump risk
(e.g., Zhou, 1997) and/or recovery-rate uncertainty (e.g., the CreditGrades model) show that
significant improvement is possible in tractable frameworks.

## 32.8 Exercises

1. The Merton (1974) model may be used to value bonds with default risk in a company. Explain how debt is viewed as an option in this framework.

2. What information do structural models deliberately ignore in the valuation of debt in a firm?

3. In the Merton model, why do we obtain very low short-term spreads?

4. Is it possible to determine the probability of a firm's default from the Merton (1974) structural model?

5. The volatility of a firm's assets is 20%. The firm's assets are worth $200 million and are normally distributed. The risk-free rate of interest is 2% and the expected rate of return on the firm is 10%. The firm has $100 million in face value of debt maturing in one year. Compute both the risk-neutral and the real-world one-year default probabilities for this firm. Which is higher? Why?

6. Explain why for small distance to default, the spread curve in the Merton model is hump-shaped.

7. The volatility of company ABC's assets is 30%. The current value of its assets is $50 million. The risk-free rate of interest is 3%. If the face value of two-year maturity debt is $30 million, what is the value of the firm's equity? Use the Merton (1974) model. What is the value of debt?

8. If the risk-free rate of interest is 4%, firm value is 75 million, and equity is 50 million, what is the credit spread on the bonds of the firm if they are of zero-coupon form with face value 30 million and expire in one year? (Assume continuous compounding.)

9. If the value of the firm is $100 million, the value of equity in the firm is $40 million, the risk-free rate is 4%, and debt has a face value of $70 million with zero coupons and a maturity of three years, what is the firm's volatility of returns on its assets? What is the risk-neutral probability of the firm becoming insolvent in three years if we assume that the Merton (1974) model applies?

10. In the question above, what is the firm's distance to default based on the Moody's-KMV model?

11. Express the distance to default in terms of the risk-neutral probability of default.

12. Firm ABC has a current equity price of $50. The face value of zero-coupon debt per share with maturity one year is $50. If the one-year implied volatility of equity from the prices of options is seen to be 40% and the risk-free rate of interest is 3%, what is the value of the debt per share if there are no dividends on the stock? Assume the Merton (1974) model.

13. ABC Co has equity trading at a price of 50. The volatility of the equity is given to be 50%. If the face value of zero-coupon debt per share in the firm is 60 and the risk-free rate of interest is 10%, compute the term structure of credit spreads for 1–10 years using the Merton model, assuming the debt in each case is of maturity ranging from 1–10 years as well.

14. Assuming that you have good historical data, how would you convert the risk-neutral default probabilities from the Merton model into default probabilities under the real-world measure?

15. In the Geske-Delianedis model, there are two tranches of debt, short term and long term, hence allowing for short-term and long-term risk-neutral probabilities of default. If short-term debt has a maturity of one year, the probability of default is $p_1 = 2\%$, long-term debt has a maturity of two years, and the cumulative probability of default is $p_2 = 3\%$, what is the forward probability of default between one and two years?

16. If short-term debt has a maturity of one year, the probability of default is $p_1 = 2\%$, long-term debt has a maturity of five years, and the cumulative probability of default is $p_2 = 10\%$, what is the annualized forward probability of default between one and five years?

17. In order to stay within the Merton model framework, one way to accommodate firms with multiple debt issues in their capital structures is to collapse all debt into zero-coupon form at some representative maturity (e.g., one year). For example, one approach is to treat the debt face value at maturity of one year as being equal to the sum of all short-term debt plus one-half of long-term debt. The reason for taking only half of long-term debt is:

    (a) Long-term debt is less valuable than short-term debt because its present value is less.

    (b) Long-term debt has a maturity greater than one year.

    (c) It is possible to take steps in time to avoid bankruptcy in the long run.

    (d) Only the coupons on long-term debt are due at the end of one year.

18. Assume we modify the Merton (1974) model as follows. Whereas in the Merton model default can occur at maturity only if the firm's value $(V)$ is lower than the face value of debt $(F)$, we now assume that default also occurs whenever the firm hits a barrier level before maturity denoted $\phi F$ for $\phi < 1$. Here $\phi$ is the fixed recovery rate on default. There is a deadweight loss on default $\xi F$, $0 < \xi < 1$. Analyze whether credit spreads will be higher or lower than that in the Merton model.

19. In the Merton (1974) model with maturity 1 year, assume that $V = 100$. Let $r = 0$, and $F = 75$. Then if we vary the Moody's-KMV distance to default (DTD) to take values in the set $\{1, 2, 3\}$, compute the credit spread curve for 1–10 years (in annual steps) for each of the DTDs (i.e., three spread curves). Explain what you see in your answer.

20. Write down the cumulative risk-neutral probability of default in the Merton model.

# The Delianedis-Geske Model

This appendix describes the model of Delianedis and Geske (1998) (henceforth DG). There are two tranches of zero-coupon debt, face value $D_1$ with maturity $T_1$ and face value $D_2$ with maturity $T_2$, and $T_2 > T_1$. The values of debt are denoted $B_1$ and $B_2$, respectively, and we are interested in computing the prices of these two tranches of debt. Since there are two dates, equity holders have two points in time at which they choose to default if their residual claims in the firm are worthless. Thus, the DG model involves a compound option pricing approach.

At the first maturity date $T_1$, the firm is solvent if

$$V_{T_1} > D_1 + B_{2,T_1},$$

If it is solvent, then we assume it will refinance the first tranche of debt with equity. The same model may be implemented by assuming that refinancing is not permitted, but this would be less realistic as it would adversely impact the second tranche of debt. Thus, the condition above defines a critical cut-off value $V^*$ for firm value at $T_1$, which is analogous to the strike price of the first option in a compound option. Therefore,

$$V^* = D_1 + B_{2,T_1} \tag{32.27}$$

The strike price for the second option at date $T_2$ is just the face value of the second debt tranche, i.e., $D_2$.

The price of equity today is the value of the compound option with two exercise prices as above. Delianedis and Geske (1998) provide the following solution:

$$E_t = V_t N_2[d_1 + \sigma\sqrt{T_1 - t}, d_2 + \sigma\sqrt{T_2 - t}; \rho]$$
$$- D_2 e^{-r(T_2-t)} N_2[d_1, d_2; \rho] - D_1 e^{-r(T_1-t)} N(d_1) \tag{32.28}$$

$$\rho = \sqrt{\frac{T_1 - t}{T_2 - t}}, \tag{32.29}$$

$$d_1 = \frac{\ln\left(\frac{V_t}{V^*}\right) + (r + \frac{1}{2}\sigma^2)(T_1 - t)}{\sigma\sqrt{T_1 - t}} \tag{32.30}$$

$$d_2 = \frac{\ln\left(\frac{V_t}{D_2}\right) + (r + \frac{1}{2}\sigma^2)(T_2 - t)}{\sigma\sqrt{T_2 - t}} \tag{32.31}$$

Here, $N_2[.]$ is the cumulative bivariate standard normal distribution with correlation coefficient $\rho$.

DG provide three *risk-neutral* probabilities from their model as follows:

$$\text{Total default probability} = TRNPD = 1 - N_2[d_1, d_2; \rho] \tag{32.32}$$
$$\text{Short-term probability} = RNPD_1 = 1 - N(d_1) \tag{32.33}$$
$$\text{Long-term probability} = RNPD_2 = 1 - \frac{N_2[d_1, d_2; \rho]}{N(d_1)} \tag{32.34}$$

The total default probability is the probability of the firm defaulting at either $T_1$ or $T_2$. The short-term default probability is the probability of default at time $T_1$. The long-term probability is the probability of default at $T_2$ *conditional* on not having defaulted at the first maturity date $T_1$ and is the forward default probability.

The DG model has the appealing feature that it captures the short-run and long-run default characteristics of the firm. There are many firms that are of poor quality yet have, conditional on short-term survival, reasonable long-term prospects. A model of this type keys into these features more precisely since the long-run default probability would reflect the possibly increasing value of the firm conditional on survival. Likewise, the model also captures current adverse circumstances accurately through short-run probabilities of default. Hence, this parsimonious extension of the Merton model results in a rich framework within which to analyze each firm's credit risk. Rating agencies that rate firms "through the business cycle" may also prefer to use the long-term default probability instead of default probabilities from the Merton (1974) model. Delianedis and Geske empirically find that the model is able to forecast rating changes well.

---

**Example 32.7**

The DG model is easy to implement, and we illustrate this with a numerical example. The ideas are essentially the same as with the implementation of the Merton model. We use the equity price in the market and the equity volatility to back out the value of the firm and its volatility. To do so, we need two equations. One of the equations is the equity-pricing equation using the compound option formula presented in (32.28). The second equation is the volatility equation, which is the same as in the Merton (1974) model (the underlying firm value process is identical in both models) and is as follows:

$$\sigma_E = \frac{\partial E}{\partial V} \frac{V}{E} \sigma \approx N(d_1) \frac{V}{E} \sigma \qquad (32.35)$$

Once we have $V_t$ and $\sigma$, the rest of the model follows from the equations provided in the previous subsection.

Say we observe the following equity price and volatility in the market:

$$E_t = 54.73, \qquad \sigma_E = 0.5425$$

We are also given the following balance sheet values: the short-term debt per share in the firm is $D_1 = 30$, and the maturity of this zero-coupon debt, as is usual in these models, is taken as one year ($T_1 - t = 1$). The long-term debt is of maturity five years and is of face value $D_2 = 30$. Once again, this is zero-coupon debt. The risk-free interest rate is $r = 0.10$.

The only additional complexity of the DG model over the Merton model arises from the additional variable $V^*$ (the cut-off value), which also needs to be solved for in the problem. Hence, our solution program solves for $\{V_t, \sigma, V^*\}$ using equations (32.28), (32.35), and (32.27). For the parameter values above, we have the following solution:

$$V_t = 100$$
$$\sigma = 0.30$$
$$V^* = 49.57689$$

Using these values, we can check that we recover the equity price correctly. Next we compute the risk-neutral default probabilities of interest using the formulae in equation (32.33). These are:

$$TRNPD = 1 - N_2[d_1, d_2; \rho] = 0.0186$$

$$RNPD_1 = 1 - N(d_1) = 0.0058$$

$$RNPD_2 = 1 - \frac{N_2[d_1, d_2; \rho]}{N(d_1)} = 0.0129$$

The total probability of defaulting on either of the bond issues over five years is about 1.86%. The probability of default within the first year is much lower, only 0.58%. And we have the forward default probability for the interval between one and five years, which is about 1.29%.

We can use the model to undertake a sensitivity analysis. Suppose we want to know what the default probabilities are if the equity price were to drop to $50 from its current price of $54.73. Recomputing the model provides the following results:

$$V_t = 95.28$$
$$\sigma = 0.2876$$
$$V^* = 49.6721$$
$$TRNPD = 1 - N_2[d_1, d_2; \rho] = 0.0179$$
$$RNPD_1 = 1 - N(d_1) = 0.0067$$
$$RNPD_2 = 1 - \frac{N_2[d_1, d_2; \rho]}{N(d_1)} = 0.0113$$

There are several interesting outcomes from this analysis. Since the equity price has dropped, the firm value correspondingly falls. But firm volatility has also dropped because it reflects the lower call option value of equity. The fall in volatility has made the firm less likely to default since the total risk-neutral probability of default has declined from 1.86% to 1.79%. The drop in equity value has resulted in an immediate increase in the short-term default probability from 0.58% to 0.67% but with a corresponding decline in the long-term probability of default from 1.29% to 1.13%. This is because conditional on surviving the first debt maturity, the lower firm volatility has reduced the forward probability of default. But it has pushed up the short-term default probability because the lower equity value signifies a lower value of the firm. Thus, we can see how a change in a market-observed variable such as the equity price results in a change in the slope of the term structure of default probabilities. ∎

# 33

# Reduced-Form Models of Default Risk

## 33.1  Introduction

In structural models, default is based on the properties of the firm's assets and its capital structure. The likelihood of the default event is endogenously determined from these inputs. In this sense, structural models have an "economic" basis. In contrast, *reduced-form models* (a term coined by Duffie and Singleton 1999a) directly posit a stochastic process governing the time-to-default. This process is specified exogenously without necessarily referencing the underlying firm value or its capital structure. Thus, the reduced-form approach has a flavor of financial engineering to it.

The parameters of the posited default process in a reduced-form model are commonly calibrated to or estimated from observed debt prices, another contrast with structural models which are typically implemented using equity prices. A third point of distinction has to do with the default event itself. In the typical Brownian motion-driven structural model, default is not a "surprise" since the firm-value process is continuous. Firms gradually "diffuse" to default. In reduced-form models, default is always (by definition) a surprise event; the underlying entity experiences a jump-to-default in the manner described in the binomial example in Section 16.2.

Reduced-form models may appear less intellectually satisfying than structural models since they do not explicitly model the processes leading to default or the drivers of default. Nonetheless, they enjoy some important advantages over the structural approach. By allowing the modeler freedom in specifying the default process rather than requiring this to be pinned down by other variables, they offer greater flexibility in fitting the data. Since there is no underlying asset value process, the model can be applied to sovereigns and other entities that do not fit within the structural paradigm. Finally, since implementation is done from debt market prices, the requirement of a traded equity price—central to the common implementation of structural models—is also eliminated, making the models applicable to private firms also.

The key component of a reduced-form framework is the process that governs the likelihood of default over any given horizon. Through much of this chapter, we examine the most popular approach to modeling this process, one based on default "intensities." Section 33.2 opens with an introduction to intensity processes and intensity-based default modeling, while Section 33.3 adds some comments on recovery-rate specification and modeling. Section 33.4 then looks at what is perhaps the earliest member of the reduced-form class, the model of Litterman and Iben (1991). A key theoretical valuation result derived by

Duffie and Singleton (1999a) and its implications for reduced-form modeling is the subject of Section 33.5. Section 33.6 describes the class of "defaultable" Heath-Jarrow-Morton (HJM) models.

An alternative approach to reduced-form default modeling was proposed by Jarrow, Lando, and Turnbull (1997) (henceforth, JLT). The JLT approach is based on the use of ratings-transition matrices rather than default intensities. In such an approach, a firm's financial health—as measured by its credit rating—can not only deteriorate suddenly to default but also jump to other (better *or* worse) ratings. The JLT methodology for identifying *risk-neutral* ratings transition matrices from historical ones is discussed in Section 33.7.

As an application of this material, a final section then describes the pricing of credit-default swaps in reduced-form models.

# 33.2   Modeling Default I: Intensity Processes

Default in the reduced-form approach is most commonly handled through an "intensity" process $\lambda_t$. The intensity process determines (in a manner explained below) how likely default is over any given time interval. Loosely speaking, a higher intensity of default implies a greater likelihood of default over any given time horizon. A good place to begin the description of intensity-based modeling is with constant intensity processes, the simplest class of intensity processes.

## Constant Intensity Processes

A constant intensity process is one in which $\lambda_t = \lambda$ for all $t$ where $\lambda > 0$. The intensity $\lambda$ has the following interpretation: The likelihood that a firm will "survive" at least $t$ years (i.e., will *not* default over the horizon $[0, t]$) is given by

$$\psi(t) = e^{-\lambda t} \tag{33.1}$$

Note that for any $\lambda > 0$, this survival probability goes to zero as $t \to \infty$, so all firms eventually fail. Note also that for any given horizon $[0, t]$, a higher value of $\lambda$ implies a lower probability of survival over the horizon since $e^{-\lambda t}$ decreases as $\lambda$ increases.

The likelihood that default will happen in the interval $[0, t]$ is denoted $\varphi(t)$ and is just one minus the probability of survival over the interval:

$$\varphi(t) = 1 - e^{-\lambda t} \tag{33.2}$$

The higher is $\lambda$, the higher is the probability of default over any given horizon, and, of course, the probability of default goes to 1 as $t \to \infty$. Figure 33.1 plots the default probability curves for different values of $\lambda$.

## The Mathematical Context

Intensity processes are intimately linked to Poisson processes, which were introduced in Chapter 16 in describing jump-diffusion processes. Poisson processes are used to describe the random arrival rates of some event (e.g., the arrival of customers at a coffee shop or, as in Chapter 16, the incidence of jumps in the stock price). In the context of credit risk, default is equated with the *first* jump time of the Poisson process. Second and subsequent jumps are not relevant; implicitly, the assumption is one of jump-to-default.

In a *homogeneous Poisson process with intensity* $\lambda$, the number of arrivals between times $s$ and $t$ follows a Poisson distribution:

$$\text{Prob}(N_t - N_s = k) = \frac{e^{-\lambda(t-s)}[\lambda(t-s)]^k}{k!} \tag{33.3}$$

**FIGURE 33.1**

Default Probabilities
for Different Constant
Intensities $\lambda$

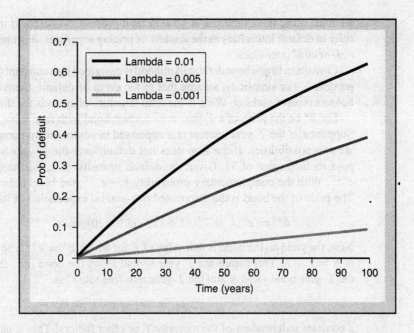

Let $T_1, \ldots T_n, \ldots$ denote the arrival times of the event being modeled. The *inter-arrival time* $T_{k+1} - T_k$ is the random time that elapses between the $k$-th arrival and the $(k + 1)$-th arrival. If $N$ is a homogeneous Poisson process with intensity $\lambda$, then the inter-arrival times are independent and are exponentially distributed:

$$\text{Prob}(T_{k+1} - T_k \le \tau) = 1 - e^{-\lambda\tau} \qquad \textbf{(33.4)}$$

Default is viewed as the *first jump time* of the counter $N$. The time of default is the distribution of the first arrival time $T_1$, which is exponential:

$$\text{Prob (Default before } t) = \text{Prob}(T_1 \le t) = 1 - e^{-\lambda t}$$

This is equivalent to saying that the probability of the firm surviving past $t$ is $e^{-\lambda t}$. Of course, these expressions for default and survival are just the expressions (33.1)–(33.2). The intensity $\lambda$ itself is just the conditional default arrival rate:

$$\lim_{h \downarrow 0} \frac{1}{h} \text{Prob} \left( T_1 \in (t, t + h] \parallel T_1 > t \right) = \lambda \qquad \textbf{(33.5)}$$

In words, expression (33.5) says that over very short time intervals $dt$, the likelihood of default between $t$ and $t + dt$ (given no default up to $t$) can be approximated by $\lambda \times dt$.

## Limitations of Constant Intensities

Constant intensity processes are easy to work with but are of limited value in describing most real-life situations. For example, the arrival rate of customers at a coffee shop is likely to be higher at certain times of the day and is perhaps also dependent on the season and the weather. In the context of credit risk, the default arrival rate $\lambda$ is similarly likely to depend on industry and economic conditions and other factors. Ignoring these considerations results in unrealistically restrictive implications for the spread curves.

This limitation is illustrated below, but an important point first. Recall that for pricing purposes, what matters is the *risk-neutral* likelihood of different states of the world. Default is just another state of the world, so to price defaultable securities using risk-neutral methods, we must make use of the risk-neutral default process. So here and in the sequel, when we refer to default intensities in the context of pricing securities, it is understood that these are *risk-neutral* intensities.

Consider a firm whose default likelihood is described by a constant (risk-neutral) intensity process $\lambda$. For simplicity, assume that in the event of default, there is zero recovery: debt holders receive nothing. What is the term structure of spreads for this firm?

Let $B^*$ be the price of a $T$-year zero-coupon bond with face value \$1 issued by the firm. Suppose $r$ is the $T$-year interest rate expressed in continuously-compounded terms. There are two possibilities. If the firm does not default over the $T$-year horizon, then the bond pays its face value of \$1. Given the default intensity of $\lambda$, this happens with probability $e^{-\lambda T}$. With the complementary probability $1 - e^{-\lambda T}$, the bond defaults and pays nothing. The price of the bond is the discounted risk-neutral expectation of its payoffs, so we have

$$B^* = e^{-rT} \left[ e^{-\lambda T} \cdot 1 + (1 - e^{-\lambda T}) \cdot 0 \right] = e^{-(r+\lambda)T} \qquad \textbf{(33.6)}$$

Now, the yield on the bond is that value of $R$ for which $B^* = e^{-RT}$, so from (33.6), the yield is $R = r + \lambda$. This means the $T$-year spread $s_T$ on the bond (i.e., the difference between the $T$-year bond yield $R$ and the $T$-year risk-free rate $r$) is

$$s_T = (r + \lambda) - r = \lambda$$

a constant independent of the maturity $T$ or other factors! This is patently unrealistic. For richer and more realistic spread curves, we must use richer specifications of the default process.

## Non-Constant Intensity Processes

The notion of a homogeneous Poisson process with a constant $\lambda$ is readily generalized to that of a non-homogeneous Poisson process with a time-varying intensity $\lambda_t$. Given $(\lambda_t)$, define

$$m_t = \int_0^t \lambda_\tau \, d\tau$$

In a *non-homogeneous Poisson process with intensity* $(\lambda_t)$, the number of arrivals between times $s$ and $t$ is determined probabilistically by

$$\mathrm{Prob}(N_t - N_s = k) = \frac{e^{-(m_t - m_s)}[m_t - m_s]^k}{k!} \qquad \textbf{(33.7)}$$

Of course, if $\lambda_t = \lambda$ for all $t$, then $m_t = \lambda t$, so (33.7) reduces to (33.3).

The distributions of default and survival times generalize accordingly: the survival and default probabilities are now given by

$$\psi(t) = \text{Prob of survival up to } t = \exp\left\{ -\int_0^t \lambda_\tau \, d\tau \right\} \qquad \textbf{(33.8)}$$

$$\varphi(t) = \text{Prob of default before } t = 1 - \exp\left\{ -\int_0^t \lambda_\tau \, d\tau \right\} \qquad \textbf{(33.9)}$$

where we have written $\exp\{x\}$ for the exponential function $e^x$.

## Spread Curves with Non-Constant Intensities

More interesting spread curves obviously result than with constant intensities. Consider a zero-coupon bond with maturity $T$ and face value \$1. Given the time-varying default intensity process $\lambda_t$, the price $B_T^*$ of this bond (continuing with the assumption of zero recovery in default) is

$$B_T^* = e^{-rT} [\psi(T) \cdot 1 + (1 - \psi(T)) \cdot 0] = e^{-rT} \psi(T)$$

Substituting for $\psi(T)$ from (33.8), the bond price is

$$B_T^* = \exp\{-rT\} \times \exp\left\{-\int_0^T \lambda_t \, dt\right\} = \exp\left\{-\left(rT + \int_0^T \lambda_t \, dt\right)\right\}$$

It follows that the $T$-year yield on the bond is

$$R = \frac{1}{T}\left(rT + \int_0^T \lambda_t \, dt\right) = r + \frac{1}{T}\int_0^T \lambda_t \, dt$$

Therefore, the $T$-year spread on the bond, denoted $s_T$, is

$$s_T = \frac{1}{T}\int_0^T \lambda_t \, dt$$

For example, if the intensities are affine in $t$ ($\lambda_t = a + bt$), the $T$-year spread is

$$s_T = \frac{1}{T}\int_0^T (a + bt) \, dt = a + \frac{1}{2} bT$$

Thus, now we can get both constant ($b = 0$) and upward-sloping ($b > 0$) or downward-sloping ($b < 0$) spread curves, although we are still limited to *linear* spread curves.[1] Similarly, if the intensities are quadratic in $t$ ($\lambda_t = a + bt + ct^2$), we obtain

$$s_T = a + \frac{1}{2} bT + \frac{1}{3} cT^2$$

so the spread curves are themselves now quadratic. Figure 33.2 plots the spread curves for quadratic intensities for three values of $c$ (taking $a = 0.005$ and $b = 0.001$). By choosing other forms of $\lambda_t$, we can generate a variety of spread curves.

The Litterman-Iben model described below uses a time-varying but deterministic intensity of the sort described here. In that model, $\lambda_t$ is calibrated to observed spreads in the market. The Litterman-Iben approach is commonly used on trading desks to estimate the term structure of default probabilities from credit-default swap spreads.

Nonetheless, from a conceptual standpoint, deterministic intensities are limiting. Such intensities imply that the only factor that affects the future likelihood of default is current time, i.e., survival to the current point. In particular, the intensity cannot depend on even the state of the economy or the industry, factors that one would intuitively judge to be important in evaluating credit risk. A richer class of intensities that admits such dependence is the class of *stochastic* intensities. We discuss these next.

## Stochastic Intensities

Stochastic intensities were introduced in a number of papers in the 1990s (e.g., Duffie and Singleton (1999a) or Lando (1998)). A popular approach uses *Cox processes* (also known as "doubly stochastic processes") to represent stochastic intensities. In a Cox process, the

---

[1] Downward-sloping curves arise if $b < 0$, but care has to be taken with $b < 0$ to ensure that the intensity $\lambda_t$ does not become negative. That is, the intensity can have the affine form $a + bt$ only over that horizon $[0, t]$ where $\lambda_t$ remains positive.

**FIGURE 33.2**
Spread Curves with
Quadratic Intensities

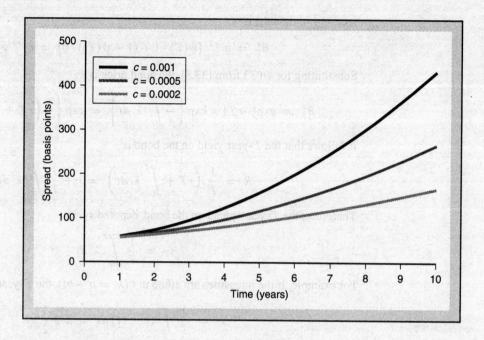

probability of default by time $T$ *conditional on a specific realization of* $\Lambda = (\lambda_t)$ is given by (33.9): that is,

$$\text{Prob}\{\text{Default before } T \parallel \Lambda\} = 1 - \exp\left\{\int_0^T \lambda_t \, dt\right\} \qquad \textbf{(33.10)}$$

But since $\lambda$ is itself stochastic, the unconditional probability of default over a $T$-year horizon is obtained by taking the expectation of (33.10) with respect to the distribution of $\Lambda$:

$$\text{Prob}\{\text{Default before } T\} = 1 - E\left[\exp\left\{\int_0^T \lambda_t \, dt\right\}\right] \qquad \textbf{(33.11)}$$

Stochastic intensities are, in general, more difficult to work with than deterministic ones, but they can be surprisingly tractable. Appendix A of Duffie and Singleton (2003) gives several examples of doubly stochastic intensities for which survival probabilities can be calculated explicitly in closed form. The principal theoretical valuation result in models with stochastic intensities is derived in Duffie and Singleton (1999a), who show that under certain conditions, an analytically attractive form obtains for the valuation equation. The Duffie-Singleton result is described in Section 33.5 below.

A key input into the Duffie-Singleton result is the convention for stating recovery rates in the event of default. Several different conventions have been proposed in the literature. A discussion of these conventions is essential before we examine specific reduced-form models.

# 33.3    Modeling Default II: Recovery Rate Conventions

There are two components to credit risk: the likelihood of default and the amount recovered in the event of default. The previous section focused on the first of these components. Here, we offer a few comments on the recovery rate.

**TABLE 33.1**

Recovery Rates on US Corporate Bonds, 1982–2004

(Numbers in the table are a percent of face value of defaulted debt.)

| Subordination Level | Average | Median | Min | Max | Standard Deviation |
|---|---|---|---|---|---|
| Senior secured | 57.4 | 55.3 | 35.7 | 83.6 | 14.3 |
| Senior unsecured | 44.9 | 45.2 | 23.1 | 62.8 | 11.2 |
| Senior subordinated | 39.1 | 43.5 | 20.3 | 67.9 | 11.4 |
| Subordinated | 32.0 | 33.4 | 12.3 | 46.2 | 10.5 |
| Junior subordinated | 28.9 | 23.7 | 7.8 | 62.0 | 18.9 |
| All levels | 42.2 | 43.1 | 25.7 | 61.7 | 8.7 |

A glance at the data shows that recovery rates exhibit considerable variability. Table 33.1 presents data on recovery rates on US corporate bonds by seniority for the period 1982–2004. The data is from Moody's and is based on Table 27 of Hamilton, Verma, Ou, and Cantor (2005). The table shows that mean recovery rates are indeed increasing with seniority, going from 28.9% for junior subordinated debt to almost twice that for senior secured. But what is remarkable is the variability within each seniority class: the difference between the minimum and maximum recovery rates within each class is at least 34% and ranges as high as 54%.

Reduced-form models state recovery rates in one of three ways in the modeling process. The first is what is called *Recovery of Par* or RP. (This is also called Recovery of Face Value or RFV.) In this case, recovery rates are stated as a percentage of the par value due at maturity of the bond. Recovery of par is the common convention in practice for stating recovery rates. The recovery rates in Table 33.1 are as a percentage of par.

While recovery of par is market convention, it turns out that for technical reasons, it is sometimes easier to define recovery in one of two other ways. Jarrow and Turnbull (1995) introduce a recovery notion that is now called *Recovery of Treasury* or RT. In this convention, the recovered amount in the event of default at some time $t$ is stated as a fraction of an otherwise identical default-risk-free (or "Treasury") bond. ("Otherwise identical" means identical in maturity, coupons, payment dates, etc. to the defaulted bond.) Intuitively, it is as if upon default, the defaulting bond is replaced with $\phi$ units of the Treasury bond, where $\phi$ is the recovery-rate fraction in this convention. For instance, if $\phi = 50\%$, then a zero-coupon bond with a face value of \$100 that defaults at any time in its existence pays \$50 *on its maturity date*. In contrast, if we were using the RP convention, a recovery rate of 50% means that the defaulting bond pays \$50 *at the time of default*.

Jarrow and Turnbull (1995) and Jarrow, Lando, and Turnbull (1997) develop reduced-form models based on the RT assumption. The role of the RT assumption in providing analytical tractability in specific settings may be seen in our descriptions below of the Litterman-Iben and Jarrow-Lando-Turnbull models (Sections 33.4 and 33.7, respectively).

Duffie and Singleton (1999a), who are responsible for the terminology for describing different recovery rate conventions, introduce a third way of capturing recovery rates, *Recovery of Market Value* or RMV. In RMV, the recovery rate upon default at time $t$ is stated as a fraction of the market value of the security at time $t-$, i.e., immediately prior to default. For example, if a security with a face value of \$1 trades at a price of 0.75 immediately prior to default, and its post-default value is 0.50, the recovery rate is $0.50/0.75 = 66.67\%$. Duffie and Singleton show that RMV has very significant analytical advantages in describing valuation expressions in general reduced-form models with stochastic intensities. Their result is described in Section 33.5.

# 33.4 The Litterman-Iben Model

Litterman and Iben (1991) were perhaps the first to introduce a model of credit risk in what we would today call a reduced-form framework. Their paper provides a simple but instructive way in which information concerning default probabilities and their evolution may be extracted from the prices of traded debt instruments.

Time is discrete in the Litterman-Iben world and is indexed by $t = 0, 1, 2, \ldots$. The model uses three inputs:

- The current term structure of (default-)risk-free interest rates.
- The current term structure of risky bond yields (from some given issuer). This is the set of current yields of defaultable zero-coupon bonds of various maturities $t$ issued by that entity.
- A model for the evolution of risk-free interest rates.

Using these inputs, the model may be used to derive two outputs. The first is the *forward default probabilities* for the risky bonds: at each $t$, given no default up to that point, what is the probability of default in period $t$? The second is *the stochastic evolution of credit spreads* (i.e., of the excess of risky bond yields over risk-free bond yields) implied by the model. The second point is discussed in the original paper only briefly and informally. We formalize the ideas and provide a more comprehensive discussion of the process.

Notice that we have not mentioned recovery rate assumptions. The Litterman-Iben paper takes losses in the event of default to be 100% (zero recovery). We present here a generalized version of their model in which positive recovery rates are admitted. Specifically, we will make the Recovery of Treasury (RT) assumption:

Upon default of the risky bond, the holder of the defaulted bond receives $\phi$ units of a risk-free bond with the same maturity.

We take the fraction $\phi$ $(0 \leq \phi \leq 1)$ to be a constant in this presentation, although it is not difficult to generalize this to allow $\phi$ to depend on time $t$. The case $\phi = 0$ is the setting of the Litterman-Iben paper.

The face value of all bonds is normalized to \$1. All yields are quoted with annual compounding. The $t$-year risk-free rate is denoted $r_t$ and the price of a $t$-year risk-free zero is denoted $B_t$. We have, by definition,

$$B_t = \frac{1}{(1+r_t)^t}$$

Similarly, $r_t^*$ and $B_t^*$ will denote, respectively, the risky $t$-year yield and the price of a risky $t$-year zero. Again, by definition:

$$B_t^* = \frac{1}{(1+r_t^*)^t}$$

The $t$-year spread is denoted $s_t$. Of course, $s_t$ is just $r_t^* - r_t$.

The model overlays this information on a risk-free interest-rate model. Any term-structure model that has been calibrated to current data may be used for this purpose. For specificity, we use the Black, Derman, and Toy (1990) model of short-rate evolution, which was described in Chapter 29. This is also the model used in the Litterman-Iben paper.

To aid in the presentation, we work through a specific numerical example to illustrate the working of the ideas. With the exception of the recovery rate, the example uses the same inputs as the one in the Litterman-Iben paper. The example uses periods that are spaced one

**TABLE 33.2** Prices of Risky and Risk-Free Bonds

| Year | Riskless Yields | Spread | Risky Yields | Riskless Bond Prices | Risky Bond Prices |
|------|-----------------|--------|--------------|----------------------|-------------------|
| 1 | 10.00 | 0.50 | 10.50 | 90.91 | 90.50 |
| 2 | 11.00 | 0.55 | 11.55 | 81.16 | 80.36 |
| 3 | 12.00 | 0.60 | 12.60 | 71.18 | 70.05 |
| 4 | 12.50 | 0.65 | 13.15 | 62.43 | 61.01 |
| 5 | 13.00 | 0.70 | 13.70 | 54.28 | 52.63 |

**TABLE 33.3** Evolution of the Risk-Free Rate

| Year 1 | Year 2 | Year 3 | Year 4 | Year 5 |
|--------|--------|--------|--------|--------|
|  |  |  |  | 25.53 |
|  |  |  | 21.79 |  |
|  |  | 19.42 |  | 19.48 |
|  | 14.32 |  | 16.06 |  |
| 10 |  | 13.77 |  | 14.86 |
|  | 9.79 |  | 11.83 |  |
|  |  | 9.76 |  | 11.34 |
|  |  |  | 8.72 |  |
|  |  |  |  | 8.65 |

year apart and has a horizon of five years. Table 33.2 contains the information on the prices and yields on risk-free and risky zero-coupon bonds of maturities 1, 2, 3, 4 and 5 years. For the interest-rate model, we use the five-year short-rate tree from the Black-Derman-Toy paper, which is described in Table 33.3 (see Chapter 29 for the derivation of the first three periods of this tree); the risk-neutral probabilities of up and down moves in this tree are each 0.50. Finally, we take the recovery rate $\phi$ to be 0.40.

## The Forward Probabilities of Default

Consider a one-year risky bond. At the end of one year, the bond pays its face value of \$1 if there is no default. If there is a default, the bondholder receives $\phi$ units of a one-year risk-free bond, which means the holder of the risky bond receives $\phi$ at the end of one year. So the payoff at maturity from a one-year risky zero-coupon bond is

$$\begin{cases} 1, & \text{if no default occurs} \\ \phi, & \text{if default occurs} \end{cases}$$

Let $p_1$ be the (risk-neutral) probability of default in one year. Then, the expected return on the risky bond is

$$\frac{(1 - p_1) \cdot 1 + p_1 \cdot \phi}{B_1^*}$$

Since $p_1$ is a risk-neutral probability, this expected return should be equal to the one-year risk-free rate. This gives us

$$\frac{(1 - p_1) \cdot 1 + p_1 \cdot \phi}{B_1^*} = \frac{1}{B_1}$$

Solving, we obtain

$$p_1 = \left( \frac{1}{1 - \phi} \right) \left( 1 - \frac{B_1^*}{B_1} \right) \tag{33.12}$$

Given the numbers in our example, this results in $p_1 = 0.007541$. That is, there is approximately a 0.75% risk-neutral probability of default occurring in the first year.

Now, we use $p_1$ to identify $p_2$, the conditional probability of default in year 2 given no default in year 1. Consider a two-year risky bond. If there is a default in the first year, the bondholder receives $\phi$ units of a two-year risk-free zero-coupon bond, so effectively receives $\phi$ at maturity (i.e., at the end of two years). If there is no default in the first year, then two further possibilities result. If there is default in the second year, then again the bondholder receives $\phi$ units of a zero-coupon bond maturing at the end of the two years, so receives $\phi$ at maturity. If there is no default in the second year either, the bondholder receives the promised face value of $1 at maturity.

Summing up, the payoffs at maturity from the risky two-year zero are:

| Event | Payoff | Probability |
| --- | --- | --- |
| Default in period 1 | $\phi$ | $p_1$ |
| Default in period 2 | $\phi$ | $(1 - p_1)\, p_2$ |
| No default | 1 | $(1 - p_1)(1 - p_2)$ |

Note the use of the RT assumption here. Regardless of when default occurs, the RT assumption implies that the payoff can be translated into a payoff of $\phi$ at maturity of the original bond. Of course, differences in the recovery rates in periods 1 and 2 can easily be accommodated by changing the payoffs in the first two lines to $\phi_1$ and $\phi_2$, respectively.

From these payoffs, the risky zero's payoff in two years is

$$\begin{cases} \phi, & \text{with probability } p_1 + (1 - p_1)\, p_2 \\ 1, & \text{with probability } (1 - p_1)(1 - p_2) \end{cases}$$

Therefore, by the usual risk-neutral pricing arguments, its initial price is

$$B_2^* = \frac{(1 - p_1)(1 - p_2) + [p_1 + (1 - p_1)\, p_2]\phi}{(1 + r_2)^2}$$

or, equivalently, using $B_2 = 1/(1 + r_2)^2$

$$B_2^* = \{(1 - p_1)(1 - p_2) + [p_1 + (1 - p_1)\, p_2]\phi\} \times B_2$$

Solving, we obtain

$$p_2 = \frac{1}{(1 - p_1)(1 - \phi)}\left[1 - p_1 + p_1\phi - \frac{B_2^*}{B_2}\right] \qquad (33.13)$$

We have already solved for $p_1$ (expression (33.12)), the values of $B_2$ and $B_2^*$ are known, and we have taken the recovery rate $\phi$ to be 0.40. Using this information in (33.13), we obtain $p_2 = 0.008920$.

Working similarly, we can solve for the remaining forward probabilities of default. The probabilities in our example are summarized in Table 33.4.

## The Evolution of Spreads

In identifying the forward probabilities of default, we made no use of the short-rate process. Now we use the forward probabilities of default together with the short-rate process to derive a stochastic process for the evolution of spreads.

At the end of year 1, there are two states that can occur: one where the riskless short rate is 14.32% and the other where it is 9.79%. Corresponding to these rates, there are two

**TABLE 33.4**

Forward Probabilities of Default in the Litterman-Iben Example

| Year | Forward Probability of Default |
|------|-------------------------------|
| 1 | 0.007541 |
| 2 | 0.008920 |
| 3 | 0.010275 |
| 4 | 0.011779 |
| 5 | 0.013210 |

possible prices for the price of a riskless one-year bond. In the state $u$, the bond will be worth

$$B_1(u) = \frac{1}{1.1432} = 0.8747$$

In the state $d$, the bond will be worth

$$B_1(d) = \frac{1}{1.0979} = 0.9108$$

Consider a one-year risky zero-coupon bond at this stage. Let $B_1^*(u)$ and $B_1^*(d)$ denote its prices in the states $u$ and $d$, respectively. As we have already seen, the one-year probability of default of the bond at this stage is 0.008920. Therefore, regardless of states $u$ or $d$, the expected payoffs on this bond are

$$(1 - 0.008920) \cdot 1 + (0.008920) \cdot \phi = 0.991080 + 0.008920\,\phi$$

Thus, the expected return on the bond in the state $u$ is

$$\frac{0.991080 + 0.008920\,\phi}{B_1^*(u)}$$

This expected return must, by definition of the risk-neutral probability, be equal to the one-year risk-free rate at this state, so

$$\frac{0.991080 + 0.008920\,\phi}{B_1^*(u)} = \frac{1}{B_1(u)} = 1.1432$$

Solving, we get $B_1^*(u) = 0.870056$, so the return on the risky one-year bond at the node $u$ is

$$\frac{1}{B_1^*(u)} - 1 = 1.1494 - 1 = 14.94\%$$

Thus, the one-year spread at the node $u$ is $0.1494 - 0.1432 = 0.0062$, or 62 basis points.

Exactly the same sequence of arguments shows that the expected return on a one-year risky bond at the node $d$ is

$$\frac{0.991080 + 0.008920\,\phi}{B_1^*(d)}$$

Equating this to the one-year risk-free rate of 9.79% at the node $d$, we obtain a risky one-year zero price at this node of $B_1^*(d) = 0.9060$, so the yield on a one-year risky zero at the node $d$ is 10.38%. This implies the one-year spread at this node is $0.1038 - 0.0979 = 0.0059$, or 59 basis points.

Combining all of this information, we have shown that the one-year spread, which is 50 basis points initially, moves either to 62 basis points (in the state $u$) or to 59 basis points (in the state $d$). Repeating the same arguments at the remaining nodes in the tree, we obtain the tree of one-year spreads (expressed in %) shown in Table 33.5.

**TABLE 33.5**
Evolution of One-Year Spreads in the Litterman-Iben Model

| Year 1 | Year 2 | Year 3 | Year 4 | Year 5 |
|--------|--------|--------|--------|--------|
|        |        |        |        | 0.987  |
|        |        |        | 0.858  |        |
|        |        | 0.736  |        | 0.940  |
|        | 0.613  |        | 0.817  |        |
| 0.500  |        | 0.701  |        | 0.903  |
|        | 0.589  |        | 0.787  |        |
|        |        | 0.676  |        | 0.876  |
|        |        |        | 0.766  |        |
|        |        |        |        | 0.854  |

In a similar fashion, by using riskless yields and risky bonds of longer maturities, we can also identify the evolution of risky yields of longer maturities. Having identified the processes for the evolution of the spreads, we can price derivatives on these instruments (for example, options on the one-year spread) in the usual way.

## Litterman-Iben and Intensity Processes

What intensity process underlies Litterman-Iben? That is, what is $\lambda_t$? The model does not explicitly introduce an intensity, but since information is available only at discrete time points, the most natural form to assume for $\lambda_t$ is a deterministic time-varying intensity that has a "step-function" form:

$$\lambda_t = \begin{cases} a_0, & \text{if } t \leq t_1 \\ a_0 + a_1, & \text{if } t \in [t_1, t_2) \\ a_0 + a_1 + a_2, & \text{if } t \in [t_2, t_3) \\ \vdots & \vdots \end{cases}$$

where $t_1$, $t_2$, etc., correspond to the maturities at which we observe the zero prices (in the Litterman-Iben model, this is years 1, 2, etc.). An intensity of this form introduces as many free parameters as there are maturities, so the spread curve can always be matched exactly. More precisely, it is the presence of as many free parameters as the number of pieces of information that allows the Litterman-Iben procedure to use the information in the entire yield curve in extracting default information. If we begin with a parametric specification of the intensity, whether deterministic or stochastic, that depends on only a finite number $m$ of parameters, we will be able to match only $m$ points on the spread curve exactly.

Thus, the Litterman-Iben model is mostly an exercise in curve fitting. As is apparent from the model description, the procedure can be used to extract default probabilities not just from bond prices but also from the term-structure of credit-default swap (CDS) spreads. As the spread curve changes from day to day, the model is recalibrated to the new data, and new values are identified for the parameters of the intensity process.

Intensity processes defined in this form have the virtue that they fit the data on any given day exactly (this is true by construction), but they lack any interesting properties. As deterministic functions of time alone, they cannot exhibit state-dependence; for instance, the Litterman-Iben forward-default probabilities depend on time but not on *which* node in the tree we are currently in. Nor does it allow for correlation between the interest-rate and default processes. To capture richer situations, we must turn to stochastic intensities.

# 33.5 The Duffie-Singleton Result

The paper by Duffie and Singleton (1999a) coined the term "reduced-form models" to describe approaches to credit-risk modeling that work directly with default (and recovery) processes rather than derive these from primitive assumptions concerning firm values. The paper discusses and relates several different reduced-form approaches, particularly with respect to recovery rate modeling. In this section, we describe the main result of the paper, the valuation formula that is derived for defaultable claims under the RMV convention for recovery rates.

The model is set in continuous time. Three exogenous processes, all specified under the model's risk-neutral measure $Q$, constitute the main inputs into the model:

1. The short-rate process $r_t$ describing the evolution of the default-risk-free short rate.
2. The intensity process for default, $\lambda_t$, which may be stochastic.
3. The recovery rate in the event of default, $\phi_t$.

The recovery rate in the model is stated in terms of the Recovery of Market Value or RMV convention. Recall that under this convention, if a security defaults at time $t$, the recovered value is $\phi_t V_{t-}$ where $V_{t-}$ denotes the value at which the security was trading at time $t-$, i.e., "just before" default occurred at $t$. The model is consistent with any term-structure model for the short-rate process $r_t$ and permits any desired correlation structure between interest rates, default intensities, and recovery rates.

The main result demonstrated by Duffie and Singleton is the following. Consider a defaultable claim that *promises* to pay $Z$ at time $T$. (The amount $Z$ could be state-dependent, as in the case of an option or other derivative, or it could be a constant amount as in the case of a bond.) Then, the time-$t$ arbitrage-free price of the claim is given by

$$V_t = E_t^Q \left[ \exp \left( - \int_t^T R_s \, ds \right) Z \right] \tag{33.14}$$

where

$$R_t = r_t + \lambda_t (1 - \phi_t) \tag{33.15}$$

As the superscript "$Q$" emphasizes, expectations in the valuation expression are taken under the risk-neutral measure $Q$.

In words, the Duffie-Singleton result says that defaultable claims can be valued *exactly* as default-risk-free claims, namely by taking expectations of their discounted *promised* payoffs under the risk-neutral measure. The key difference is that for a default-free claim, the discounting is done at the risk-free rate $r_t$ while for a defaultable claim, it is done at a risk-adjusted rate $R_t = r_t + \lambda_t (1 - \phi_t)$. If there is no likelihood of default ($\lambda_t \equiv 0$) or if there is no loss in the event of default ($\phi_t \equiv 1$), then there is no credit risk, and (33.14) reduces to the standard risk-neutral pricing expression for default-risk-free claims.

In Appendix 33A, we describe a simplified (and intuitive) derivation of the Duffie-Singleton result in a discrete-time setting. The role of the RMV convention in obtaining the valuation expression (33.14) is central. In contrast to the simplicity of the expression (33.14), valuation formulae obtained using, for example, the RP convention tend to be much more complex (see Lando 1998). One setting in which the precise recovery convention is irrelevant is that of zero recovery; some intuition for the Duffie-Singleton may be obtained by considering this case.

## The Special Case of Zero Recovery

Suppose there is no recovery in the event of default: $\phi_t = 0$. Conditional on specific paths for $r_t$ and $\lambda_t$ (and conditional on survival up to $t$), the time-$t$ probability of survival up to $T$ (see (33.8)) is

$$\psi(t, T) = \exp\left\{-\int_t^T \lambda_s \, ds\right\}$$

while the discount factor for the horizon is

$$B_{t,T} = \exp\left\{-\int_t^T r_s \, ds\right\}$$

Thus, conditional on these paths and given that there is zero recovery in the event of default, the time-$t$ value of the payoff $Z$ at time $T$ is the payoff $Z$ multiplied by the risk-neutral probability of survival, discounted back to time $t$:

$$B_{t,T} \times [\psi(t, T) \times Z] = \exp\left\{-\int_t^T (r_s + \lambda_s) \, ds\right\} \times Z$$

Taking expectations over the risk-neutral distributions of the possible paths of $(r_t, \lambda_t)$ gives us the unconditional time-$t$ value of the claim $Z$:

$$E_t^Q\left[\exp\left\{-\int_t^T (r_s + \lambda_s) \, ds\right\} Z\right] \tag{33.16}$$

This is just the special case of the Duffie-Singleton valuation expression (33.14) corresponding to $\phi_t = 0$. With zero recovery, the fractional loss rate in expected terms is just the default intensity $\lambda_t$. With non-zero recovery, the fractional loss rate is the likelihood of default $\lambda_t$ times the loss-given-default $(1 - \phi_t)$. Using this fractional loss rate in place of $\lambda_t$ in (33.16) results in the full valuation expression (33.14).

## Using the Valuation Expression

The key benefit of the Duffie-Singleton result is that standard term-structure models may be adapted to a credit-risk context by replacing the term-structure model's short rate $r_t$ with the risk-adjusted short rate $R_t$. (That is, we require of $R_t$ the properties we would have required of $r_t$.) This makes possible analytically tractable models for defaultable bond pricing. In particular, any term-structure model that yielded closed-form solutions for the prices of default-risk-free zero-coupon bonds can also be adapted to obtain closed-form solutions for the prices of defaultable bonds.

Alternatively, we may place conditions separately on the short rate $r_t$ and the "short spread" $s_t = \lambda_t(1 - \phi_t)$ in such a way as to ensure tractability of the overall model. [Note that the Duffie-Singleton result depends only on the short spread, not on its individual components $\lambda_t$ and $\phi_t$. The short spread is so called because it measures the spread between the risk-adjusted short rate $R_t$ and the risk-free short rate $r_t$.] One example of this approach is provided by the paper of Duffee (1999). Duffee models the short-rate $r_t$ as

$$r_t = \xi_0 + \xi_1 X_{1t} + \xi_2 X_{2t}$$

where $\xi_1, \xi_2 > 0$, and $X_1$ and $X_2$ are independent square root diffusion processes under the risk-neutral measure. He further specifies the short spread process as

$$s_t = \zeta_0 + \zeta_1 X_{1t} + \zeta_2 X_{2t} + \zeta_3 X_{3t}$$

where $X_3$ is a square root diffusion process that is independent (under the risk-neutral measure) of $X_1$ and $X_2$. Correlation between $r_t$ and $s_t$ is built in through their common dependence on the factors $X_1$ and $X_2$. The sign of this correlation depends on the signs of $\zeta_1$ and $\zeta_2$. That spreads depend on an additional factor means they are not perfectly instantaneously correlated with risk-free rates; this third factor may capture firm-specific or industry-specific risks. Since $r_t$ and $s_t$ are each affine processes in Duffee's specification, so also is $r_t + s_t$. Appealing to the standard results in the literature on affine term-structure models, we can obtain pricing expressions for defaultable bonds in this model.

The analytical tractability provided by the Duffie-Singleton result has made the doubly stochastic framework a popular modeling choice and the basis of a number of theoretical and empirical studies, both on individual issuer defaults and in the study of correlated defaults by multiple issuers. As some examples: Duffee (1999) examines the ability of the model to price non-callable corporate bonds and finds the average pricing error in the sample used is under 10 basis points. Driessen (2005) uses the model to decompose empirical bond returns into default, liquidity, and tax factors. He identifies the risk premium associated with the default event, and finds that significant risk premia exist with respect to common intensity factors. Longstaff, Mithal, and Neis (2006) study the liquidity component of corporate bond yield spreads. They compare corporate bond yield spreads to credit default swap (CDS) spreads, and under the assumption that the liquidity component of the latter is zero, identify the non-credit component of bond yield spreads. They find that this component has a strong relationship to both bond-specific illiquidity as well as bond-market liquidity factors. Duffie, Pedersen, and Singleton (2003) utilize a reduced-form framework to study the more complex problem of sovereign (in their case, Russian) default.

Despite its attractive theoretical properties, however, empirical work by Das, Duffie, Kapadia, and Saita (2007) suggests that the doubly stochastic model may be too restrictive in describing the data, notably in the context of multifirm defaults. In a multifirm context, one implication of the doubly stochastic process is that default events in some firms cannot affect the default intensities of other firms. A number of alternatives have been proposed in the literature that allow for feedback from events to intensities; see, for example, Giesecke and Goldberg (2005).

## 33.6 Defaultable HJM Models

An alternative reduced-form approach to modeling defaultable debt is to generalize the framework of Heath-Jarrow-Morton (HJM) to also incorporate default risk. Such extensions have been provided in Schönbucher (1998), Duffie and Singleton (1999a), and Das and Sundaram (2000). The presentations in Schönbucher and Duffie-Singleton are in continuous time, while Das and Sundaram develop their framework in discrete time.

The distinguishing feature of defaultable HJM models is that the primitive inputs in the model are "forward spreads" rather than default intensities and recovery rates. To the extent that spreads are observable and their volatilities can be calculated on the basis of historical data, this facilitates implementation of the model. Since spreads are a function of both default intensities and recovery rates, the implied default intensities in these models can be recovered from assumptions concerning the recovery process.

Recall that the principal result in the HJM model (Chapter 30) is that the drifts of the forward rates under the risk-neutral measures are functions of the volatilities of the forward rates. This result makes it possible to implement the HJM model on the basis of volatilities alone. Defaultable HJM models show that an analogous result also holds for defaultable bonds, namely that the risk-neutral drifts of the "forward spreads" on defaultable bonds are functions of the volatilities of these spreads and the risk-free forward rates. We describe the discrete-time derivation of this result from Das and Sundaram (2000) in this section.

## Description of the Model

The horizon of the model is $T^*$. Time periods are of length $h$ years. The initial (current) time is time 0, so the time points in the model are of the form $h, 2h, 3h, \ldots, nh = T^*$. For notational ease, we denote a typical time point by $t$ or $T$.

Denote by $B(t, T)$ the time-$t$ price of a default-risk-free zero-coupon bond of maturity $T \geq t$ and by $B^*(t, T)$ its risky counterpart. All zero-coupon bonds are taken to have a face value of \$1. Let $r(t, T)$ and $r^*(t, T)$ denote the corresponding spot yields expressed with continuous compounding:

$$B(t, T) = \exp\{-r(t, T) \cdot (T - t)\}, \qquad B^*(t, T) = \exp\{-r^*(t, T) \cdot (T - t)\}$$

Denote by $f(t, T)$ the time-$t$ forward rate for default-risk-free investment or borrowing over the period $(T, T + h)$. As shown in Chapter 26, the forward rates are defined from the spot rates as

$$f(t, T) = \frac{1}{h}\left[r(t, T + h) \cdot (T + h) - r(t, T) \cdot T\right]$$

When $t = T$, the forward rate $f(t, T)$ will be called the "short rate" and denoted by $r(t)$. Define the "risky" forward rates $f^*(t, T)$ analogously:

$$f^*(t, T) = \frac{1}{h}\left[r^*(t, T + h) \cdot (T + h) - r^*(t, T) \cdot T\right]$$

The *forward spread* $s(t, T)$ is defined by

$$s(t, T) = f^*(t, T) - f(t, T)$$

The forward spread plays a central role in this approach. Rather than model the default-risk-free and risky forward rates, we model the default-risk-free forward rates and forward spreads.

For future reference, note that the forward rates and bond prices are related via the following expressions:

$$B(t, T) = \exp\left\{-\sum_{k=t/h}^{T/h-1} f(t, kh) \cdot h\right\} \qquad \textbf{(33.17)}$$

$$B^*(t, T) = \exp\left\{-\sum_{k=t/h}^{T/h-1} f^*(t, kh) \cdot h\right\} \qquad \textbf{(33.18)}$$

One final definition is required. Let $M(t)$ be the time-$t$ value of a "money market account" that uses an initial investment of \$1 at time 0 and rolls the proceeds over at the rate $r(t)$:

$$M(t) = \exp\left\{\sum_{k=0}^{t/h-1} r(kh) \cdot h\right\} \qquad \textbf{(33.19)}$$

As in the HJM model, $M(t)$ is taken to be the numeraire security. Let $Q$ be a risk-neutral probability with respect to $M(t)$ as numeraire. All stochastic processes defined below are under the probability $Q$.

The first assumption in the model concerns the default-risk-free forward rates $f$. These forward rates are taken to evolve according to a standard one-factor discrete-time HJM setting:

$$f(t + h, T) - f(t, T) = \alpha(t, T)h + \sigma(t, T)X_1\sqrt{h} \qquad \textbf{(33.20)}$$

where $\alpha$ is the drift of the process and $\sigma$ its volatility; and $X_1$ is a random variable. Both $\alpha$ and $\sigma$ may depend on other information available at $t$, such as the time-$t$ forward rates.

The second assumption concerns the evolution of the forward spreads (and so of the risky forward rates). These spreads are taken to follow the process

$$s(t + h, T) - s(t, T) = \beta(t, T)h + \eta(t, T)X_2\sqrt{h} \qquad \textbf{(33.21)}$$

where $\beta(t, T)$ and $\eta(t, T)$ are the drift and volatility coefficients, respectively, and $X_2$ is a random variable. Both $\beta$ and $\eta$ may depend on other information available at $t$. No restrictions are required on the joint distribution of $X_1$ and $X_2$; thus, changes in risk-free and risky forward rates could be arbitrarily correlated.

## The Main Result

In the HJM model, it is shown that the drift $\alpha$ of the default-risk-free forward rates under the risk-neutral measure is a function of the volatilities $\sigma$. Extending this result, Das and Sundaram show that the drift $\beta$ of the spread process under the risk-neutral measure is a function of the volatilities $\sigma$ and $\eta$. Thus, all that is required to implement the model are the term-structures of volatilities $\sigma$ and $\eta$.

Here is a formal statement of these results. In the one-factor discrete-time HJM model introduced above, the drifts $\alpha$ are related to the volatilities $\sigma$ via the recursive relationship

$$\sum_{k=t/h+1}^{T/h-1} \alpha(t, kh) = \frac{1}{h^2} \ln\left( E^t\left[\exp\left\{ -\sum_{k=t/h+1}^{T/h-1} \sigma(t, kh)X_1 h^{3/2} \right\}\right]\right) \qquad \textbf{(33.22)}$$

Das and Sundaram show that a similar recursive relationship holds between $\alpha$ and $\beta$ on the one hand and the volatilities $\sigma$ and $\eta$ on the other:

$$\exp\left\{ \sum_{t/h+1}^{T/h-1} [\alpha(t, kh) + \beta(t, kh)]h^2 \right\}$$

$$= E^t\left[\exp\left\{ -h^{3/2}\sum_{t/h+1}^{T/h-1} [\sigma(t, kh)X_1 + \eta(t, kh)X_2] \right\}\right] \qquad \textbf{(33.23)}$$

Since we have solved for $\alpha$ in terms of $\sigma$ using (33.22), we may now use (33.23) to solve for $\beta$ in terms of $\sigma$ and $\eta$. Appendix 33B contains a proof of (33.22)–(33.23).

Das and Sundaram discuss and illustrate implementation of this model and the pricing of credit derivatives using an "endogenous default" approach similar to that used in the Das and Sundaram (2007) model which was described in Chapter 21. For a general continuous-time approach to defaultable HJM models, see Duffie and Singleton (1999a) or Bielecki and Rutkowski (2002).

# 33.7  Ratings-Based Modeling: The JLT Model

Jarrow, Lando, and Turnbull (1997) describe another reduced-form approach to modeling defaultable debt: one based on ratings, for example as provided by ratings agencies such as Moody's or Standard and Poor's (S&P). The fundamental input into such a model is a *ratings migration matrix* or a *ratings transition matrix*. Such matrices are available from ratings agencies themselves.

**TABLE 33.6** A
Ratings Transition
Matrix

| "From" Rating | "To" Rating | | | | | | |
|---|---|---|---|---|---|---|---|
| | 1 | 2 | 3 | 4 | 5 | 6 | Default (D) |
| 1 | 0.9081 | 0.0833 | 0.0068 | 0.0006 | 0.0012 | 0.0000 | 0.0000 |
| 2 | 0.0070 | 0.9065 | 0.0779 | 0.0064 | 0.0006 | 0.0014 | 0.0000 |
| 3 | 0.0009 | 0.0227 | 0.9105 | 0.0552 | 0.0074 | 0.0026 | 0.0006 |
| 4 | 0.0004 | 0.0035 | 0.0597 | 0.8695 | 0.0532 | 0.0119 | 0.0020 |
| 5 | 0.0020 | 0.0031 | 0.0084 | 0.0790 | 0.8070 | 0.0901 | 0.0123 |
| 6 | 0.0068 | 0.0079 | 0.0092 | 0.0111 | 0.0716 | 0.8414 | 0.0588 |
| D | 0 | 0 | 0 | 0 | 0 | 0 | 1 |

The ratings transition matrix takes as given a firm's current rating and provides, for each rating class in which the firm might conceivably be after a given period of time (typically, one year), the probability of being in that rating class. For example, the Moody's transition matrix describes the probabilities that a firm rated A by Moody's today will be rated Aa (or Aaa or Baa or Ba . . . ) in one year's time. [Moody's and S&P each employ eight basic ratings classes: Aaa, Aa, A, Baa, Ba, B, C, and Default (Moody's), and AAA, AA, A, BBB, BB, B, C, and Default (S&P).]

Table 33.6 provides a numerical illustration of a ratings transition matrix. There are six nondefault ratings classes in the matrix. The highest class is rating class 1 and the lowest is rating class 6. There is also a seventh class denoted $D$ (for "default"). The matrix depicts the probability of moving from one rating class to another over one year. Thus, for example, according to the table, the probability of a firm that is currently in rating class 2 still being in rating class 2 after one year is 90.65%. Such a firm would have improved its rating (i.e., moved to rating class 1) with probability 0.70%, while with probability 7.79%, its rating would have declined to class 3. Note that rating category $D$ is an "absorbing" class: the probability of transiting from $D$ to any other class is zero, and the probability of staying on in $D$ is 1. (This may not be literally true in practice because firms do restructure and emerge from default. However, the assumption that default is an absorbing state is commonly made; it helps ensure that there is a well-defined event of default in the model.)

The rating transition matrix in practice is estimated using a historical data sample that goes back suitably long. Actual rating transitions are used to determine the frequency of each cell in the matrix.

If we assume that the matrix does not change from period to period (a good first-order approximation), then we can use the single-period transition matrix to obtain multiperiod transition matrices. For example, to find the probability that a firm in rating class 2 in our example would continue to be in rating class 2 after *two* periods, we find all possible "paths" by which the firm could be in rating class 2 in two periods' time, identify the probabilities of these paths, and add them up. In the example, there are six such paths: the firm could be in any of six rating classes 1, . . . , 6 after one period and then from each of these classes, the firm could move to rating class 2 after the second period. So the probability that it will still be in rating class 2 after two periods is

$$(0, 0070)(0.0833) + (0.9065)(0.9065) + (0.0779)(0.0227)$$
$$+ (0.0064)(0.0035) + (0.0006)(0.0031) + (0.0014)(0.0079) = 0.8241$$

Mathematically, expressing these multiperiod transition probabilities is easier than these computations make it appear. If we denote the single-period transition matrix by $\Pi$, the two-period transition matrix is just $\Pi^2$ (i.e., $\Pi \times \Pi$), the three-period transition matrix is $\Pi^3$ (i.e., $\Pi \times \Pi \times \Pi$), and so on.

The ratings transition matrices provided by ratings agencies contain *historical* probabilities. For valuation purposes, what we need are *risk-neutral* probabilities of moving from one rating class to another. The JLT model addresses this issue and proposes one possible method for identifying the risk-neutral transition matrix. The proposed method is a recursive procedure that generates the risk-neutral transition matrix from the historical matrix under some assumptions concerning the "risk premium." We describe the JLT model in this section.

The JLT model begins with two assumptions:

1. There is no correlation (under the risk-neutral measure) between changes in interest rates and ratings migration probabilities.
2. Recovery rates, stated in terms of the Recovery of Treasury convention, are a constant $\phi$. Upon any default, the bondholder receives $\phi$ units of an otherwise identical treasury bond.

The model uses two main inputs: a model for the evolution of default-risk-free interest rates, and the historical rating transition matrix. To describe the model further, some notation is necessary.

## Notation

Time is discrete and is indexed by $t = 0, 1, 2, \ldots$. There are $K$ rating classes. Classes $1, \ldots, K-1$ are the nondefault classes, while class $K$ is default. The one-period historical (or "statistical") rating transition matrix is denoted $\Pi$. $\Pi_{ij}$ is the probability of moving from rating class $i$ to rating class $j$ in one period. We will use $\Pi_i$ to denote the vector $(\Pi_{i1}, \ldots, \Pi_{iK})$. The $t$-period statistical transition matrix is just $\Pi^t$.

The one-period risk-neutral transition matrix at time 0 is denoted $Q = (Q_{ij})$. $Q_{ij}$ is the risk-neutral probability that an entity that was in rating class $i$ at time 0 will be in rating class $j$ at time 1. The $t$-period risk-neutral transition matrix from time 0 is denoted $Q(0, t)$. Note that $Q(0, 1) = Q$.

The $t$-period risk-free interest rate is denoted $r(t)$, while the $t$-year spread on a zero-coupon bond currently in rating class $i$ is denoted $s_i(t)$. Interest rates are quoted in simple terms with a compounding frequency equal to the length of time between periods. Thus, for example, \$1 invested at the risk-free rate for

- one period grows to $(1 + r(1))$ by maturity
- two periods grows to $(1 + r(2))^2$ by maturity

and so on.

The time-0 price of a risk-free zero-coupon bond with maturity $t$ (and face value \$1) is denoted $B(t)$. The corresponding price for a bond in rating class $i$ is denoted $B_i(t)$. We have

$$B(t) = \frac{1}{(1 + r(t))^t} \qquad B_i(t) = \frac{1}{(1 + r(t) + s_i(t))^t}$$

We begin with the identification of the one-period risk-neutral transition matrix $Q$.

## Identifying $Q = Q(0, 1)$

Consider a one-period zero-coupon bond in rating class $i$. The current price of the bond is

$$B_i(1) = \frac{1}{1 + r(1) + s_i(1)} \qquad \textbf{(33.24)}$$

After one period, the bond is at maturity. At this point, it pays

- $1 if the bond is in rating classes $i \in \{1, \ldots, K-1\}$.
- $\phi$ if the bond is in rating class $K$.

By definition of the risk-neutral probabilities $Q_{ij}$, the current price of the bond is the discounted expectation under $Q$ of its payoffs in one period:

$$B_i(1) = \left(\frac{1}{1+r(1)}\right)[Q_{i1} + \cdots + Q_{i,K-1} + \phi Q_{iK}] \qquad \textbf{(33.25)}$$

Since (33.24) and (33.25) are equivalent, we have

$$\frac{1+r(1)}{1+r(1)+s_i(1)} = [Q_{i1} + \cdots + Q_{i,K-1} + \phi Q_{iK}] \qquad \textbf{(33.26)}$$

The problem is that we have just one equation but $K-1$ unknowns, $Q_{i1}, \ldots, Q_{i,K-1}$. (The $K$-th risk-neutral probability is just 1 minus the sum of the other $K-1$ probabilities.) There is no way to identify just a single solution.

JLT propose using an "adjustment factor" $\alpha_i$ whose effect is to reduce (33.26) to just one unknown and so uniquely identify the probabilities $Q_{ij}$. This factor, which is specific to each rating class, links the risk-neutral transition probabilities to the statistical probabilities. Specifically, the JLT proposal is to set

$$Q_{ij} = \begin{cases} \alpha_i \cdot \Pi_{ij}, & \text{if } j \neq i \\ 1 - \sum_{j \neq i} Q_{ij}, & \text{if } j = i \end{cases} \qquad \textbf{(33.27)}$$

In words, all "off-diagonal" risk-neutral probabilities $Q_{ij}$ are the same linear multiple $\alpha_i$ of their statistical counterparts, while the diagonal probability $Q_{ii}$ is determined by the requirement that the probabilities have to sum to one.

What should the value of $\alpha_i$ be? This is easy. Substitute the forms (33.27) for the $Q_{ij}$'s into (33.26). The right-hand side of (33.26) is then a function solely of $\alpha_i$ and the statistical probabilities $\Pi_{ij}$. Since the statistical probabilities are known, we have one equation in the one unknown $\alpha_i$. Solving this and using the solution in (33.27), we get the risk-neutral probabilities $(Q_{i1}, \ldots, Q_{iK})$.

## Identifying $Q(0, t)$ for $t > 1$

The next step is to extend the arguments to identify the $t$-year risk-neutral transition matrix $Q(0, t)$. Simplifying this procedure is the following observation. The probability, beginning from state $i$ in period 0, of reaching state $j$ in period $t$ is the sum over all $k$ of the probability of reaching state $k$ in period $t-1$ times the probability of transiting from state $k$ in period $t-1$ to state $j$ in period $t$. In matrix notation, $Q(0, t)$ is the product of

- the $t$-step risk-neutral transition matrix $Q(0, t-1)$, and
- the risk-neutral matrix of transition probabilities $Q(t-1, t)$ between $t-1$ and $t$.

Suppose $Q(0, t-1)$ is known. (This is certainly true for $t = 2$.) We show how to identify $Q(t-1, t)$ and, therefore, $Q(0, t)$. As earlier, suppose that $Q(t-1, t)$ is related to the one-step statistical transition probabilities $\Pi$ via "adjustment factors" $\alpha_i(t)$:

$$Q_{ij}(t-1, t) = \begin{cases} \alpha_i(t)\Pi_{ij}, & \text{if } j \neq i \\ 1 - \sum_{j \neq i} Q_{ij}(t-1, t), & \text{if } j = i \end{cases} \qquad \textbf{(33.28)}$$

Consider a $t$-year zero-coupon bond whose issuer is in rating class $i$ at time 0. The initial price of this bond is

$$B_i(t) = \frac{1}{(1 + r(t) + s_i(t))^t} \qquad (33.29)$$

This bond price must also equal the risk-neutral expectation of the discounted cash flows from the bond. If the bond does not default, it pays \$1 at $t$. If it defaults at any point, then, by the RT assumption, it pays \$$\phi$ at $t$. Thus, to value the bond using risk-neutral probabilities, we need identify only the risk-neutral probability of the bond surviving until date $t$.

This survival probability is just $1 - Q_{iK}(0, t)$. Now, $Q(0, t) = Q(0, t-1) \times Q(t-1, t)$. The first term, $Q(0, t-1)$, is known, by assumption. By (33.28), the second term, $Q(t-1, t)$, depends only on one unknown $\alpha_i(t)$. This means that the survival probability—and hence, the risk-neutral pricing expression for the bond—contains just one unknown $\alpha_i(t)$. Equating this expression to the bond price (33.29), we can solve for $\alpha_i(t)$.

Identifying all the $\alpha_i(t)$'s in this manner finally enables us to identify $Q(t-1, t)$, and so $Q(0, t)$, completing the recursion.

A simple example will help illustrate the JLT procedure.

**Example 33.1**

We work through a two-period example with each period representing one year. Assume there are four ratings classes: investment grade ($I$), mezzanine grade ($M$), junk grade ($J$), and default ($D$). The following inputs are used in the example:

1. The risk-free spot rates are 0.03 (for one period) and 0.04 (for two periods).
2. The statistical transition matrix $\Pi$ is given by:

$$\Pi = \begin{matrix} I \\ M \\ J \\ D \end{matrix} \begin{bmatrix} 0.85 & 0.05 & 0.05 & 0.05 \\ 0.10 & 0.70 & 0.10 & 0.10 \\ 0.05 & 0.10 & 0.70 & 0.15 \\ 0 & 0 & 0 & 1.00 \end{bmatrix}$$

3. The one- and two-period credit spreads by ratings levels are:

$$s_I = \begin{bmatrix} 0.005 \\ 0.010 \end{bmatrix}, \quad s_M = \begin{bmatrix} 0.010 \\ 0.020 \end{bmatrix}, \quad s_J = \begin{bmatrix} 0.020 \\ 0.030 \end{bmatrix}$$

4. The recovery rate (in the RT convention) is $\phi = 0.50$.

From this information, we can compute the initial values of risky zero-coupon bonds of maturities one period and two periods:

$$B_I(1) = \frac{1}{(1 + 0.03 + 0.005)} = 0.9662$$

$$B_I(2) = \frac{1}{(1 + 0.04 + 0.010)^2} = 0.9070$$

$$B_M(1) = \frac{1}{(1 + 0.03 + 0.010)} = 0.9615$$

$$B_M(2) = \frac{1}{(1 + 0.04 + 0.020)^2} = 0.8900$$

$$B_J(1) = \frac{1}{(1 + 0.03 + 0.020)} = 0.9524$$

$$B_J(2) = \frac{1}{(1 + 0.04 + 0.030)^2} = 0.8734$$

At maturity, the bond will be in one of four states $\{I, M, J, D\}$. If it is in any of the first three states, the principal is repaid in full. In the last state, the bondholder receives $\phi$. We denote these terminal cash flows by a vector $C$:

$$C = \begin{bmatrix} 1 \\ 1 \\ 1 \\ 0.50 \end{bmatrix}$$

We first identify $\alpha_I(1)$, the adjustment that must be made to the statistical transition probabilities to obtain the risk-neutral one-period transition probabilities for grade $I$. The one-step statistical transition probabilities for grade $I$ are given by

$$\Pi_I = [0.85 \quad 0.05 \quad 0.05 \quad 0.05]$$

As suggested by JLT, take the one-period *risk-neutral* transition probabilities for grade $I$ to have the form

$$Q_I(0, 1) = [1 - 0.15\alpha_I(1) \quad 0.05\alpha_I(1) \quad 0.05\alpha_I(1) \quad 0.05\alpha_I(1)]$$

The value of $\alpha_I(1)$ must be such that the expected value under the risk-neutral measure of discounted cash flows equals the initial price of the bond:

$$B_I(1) = \frac{1}{1 + 0.03} \times Q_I(0, 1) \times C$$

or

$$0.9662 = 0.9709[1 \cdot (1 - 0.10\alpha_I(1)) + 1 \cdot 0.05\alpha_I(1) + 1 \cdot 0.05\alpha_I(1) + \phi \cdot 0.05\alpha_I(1)]$$

This yields $\alpha_I(1) = 0.1932$.

Analogous procedures for grades $M$ and $J$ yield

$$\alpha_M(1) = 0.1923$$
$$\alpha_J(1) = 0.2540$$

This gives us the one-period risk-neutral transition probability matrix as

$$Q(0, 1) = \begin{matrix} I \\ J \\ M \\ D \end{matrix} \begin{bmatrix} 0.9710 & 0.0097 & 0.0097 & 0.0097 \\ 0.0192 & 0.9423 & 0.0192 & 0.0192 \\ 0.0127 & 0.0254 & 0.9238 & 0.0381 \\ 0 & 0 & 0 & 1.0000 \end{bmatrix}$$

We now move on to the two-period risk-neutral transition matrix. As outlined in the JLT procedure, this is accomplished by first identifying the *forward* transition matrix $Q(1, 2)$ that specifies the risk-neutral transition probabilities for the period $(1, 2)$. The statistical transition matrix for the period $(1, 2)$ remains $\Pi$. Using the usual JLT adjustment procedure on $\Pi$ (and denoting the second-period adjustment factors by $\alpha_I(2)$, etc.), we may write the matrix $Q(1, 2)$ as the matrix $\Pi$ adjusted by the factors $\alpha_i(2)$:

$$Q(1, 2) = \begin{bmatrix} 1 - 0.15\alpha_I(2) & 0.05\alpha_I(2) & 0.05\alpha_I(2) & 0.05\alpha_I(2) \\ 0.10\alpha_M(2) & 1 - 0.30\alpha_M(2) & 0.10\alpha_M(2) & 0.10\alpha_M(2) \\ 0.05\alpha_J(2) & 0.10\alpha_J(2) & 1 - 0.30\alpha_J(2) & 0.15\alpha_J(2) \\ 0 & 0 & 0 & 1 \end{bmatrix}$$

To identify the three unknown variables, we must set the initial values of two-period bonds from each category equal to the risk-neutral prices obtained using the matrices $Q(0, 1)$

and $Q(1, 2)$:

$$\begin{bmatrix} B_I(2) \\ B_M(2) \\ B_J(2) \\ B_D(2) \end{bmatrix} = \begin{bmatrix} 0.9070 \\ 0.8900 \\ 0.8734 \\ - \end{bmatrix} = Q(0, 1) \times Q(1, 2) \times C \times \frac{1}{(1 + 0.04)^2}$$

Note that while we have written these equations in matrix form to be concise, each adjustment factor $\alpha_i(2)$ can be solved for individually as we did in the first period. However, it is computationally easier to solve them all at once using matrix computations. The solutions are:

$$\alpha_I(2) = 0.5554$$
$$\alpha_M(2) = 0.5680$$
$$\alpha_J(2) = 0.5101$$

This means the matrix $Q(1, 2)$ resolves from $\Pi$ as

$$Q(1, 2) = \begin{bmatrix} 0.9167 & 0.0278 & 0.0278 & 0.0278 \\ 0.0568 & 0.8296 & 0.0568 & 0.0568 \\ 0.0255 & 0.0510 & 0.8470 & 0.0765 \\ 0 & 0 & 0 & 1.0000 \end{bmatrix}$$

Now, the risk-neutral transition matrix over two periods is just the product of the transitions from periods 0 to 1 and from 1 to 2:

$$Q(0, 2) = Q(0, 1) \times Q(1, 2)$$

Carrying out the multiplication, we obtain

$$Q(0, 2) = \begin{bmatrix} 0.8909 & 0.0355 & 0.0357 & 0.0379 \\ 0.0716 & 0.7833 & 0.0703 & 0.0748 \\ 0.0366 & 0.0685 & 0.7842 & 0.1106 \\ 0 & 0 & 0 & 1.0000 \end{bmatrix}$$

completing the example. ∎

## Comments on the JLT Approach

The JLT model offers a good starting point for thinking about the integration of Treasury markets with default information provided by rating agencies. It is also a model that can be used for the pricing and hedging of derivatives that depend explicitly on ratings.

The model makes some special assumptions. Some of these may be relaxed without losing analytical tractability. For example, Das and Tufano (1996) show that the JLT requirement that there be zero correlation (under the risk-neutral measure) between risk-free interest rates and changes in ratings may be generalized to allow for arbitrary correlation. Das and Tufano also show that the RT condition, which appears less natural than RP or even RMV, can be modified to allow for recoveries on defaulting bonds to occur immediately rather than at maturity.

JLT also propose a very specific method for moving from the statistical transition probabilities to the risk-neutral ones. Now, there are many different adjustments that could be applied to reduce (33.26) from a one-equation/$(K - 1)$-unknowns system to a one-equation/one-unknown system. As one example, Das and Tufano offer a computationally advantageous alternative that is a slight variant on the JLT procedure. However, the two procedures result in different risk-neutral transition matrices. There are no theoretical grounds for preferring one approach over the other—or a third approach to either of them—nor is empirical guidance available. The material below elaborates.

## A Comment on the JLT Adjustment Factors

In each step of the JLT model, the adjustment factors are applied to the statistical transition matrix $\Pi$ from which the forward transition matrices $Q(t, t+1)$ are successively recovered. Then, from knowledge of $Q(0, t)$, the $(t+1)$-period transition matrix $Q(0, t+1)$ is determined as $Q(0, t+1) = Q(0, t) \times Q(t, t+1)$.

Das and Tufano (1996) propose an alternative method in which the $t$-period risk-neutral transition matrix $Q(0, t)$ is recovered *directly* from the $t$-period statistical transition matrix $\Pi(0, t)$ in the same manner in which $Q(0, 1)$ is recovered from $\Pi$. That is, the adjustments are performed directly on the off-diagonal elements of $\Pi(0, t)$. This method is computationally advantageous compared to the JLT method since a formula is available for calculating the adjustment factors $\alpha_i(t)$.

Here is how the procedure works. First, we identify $\Pi(0, t)$. This is just $\Pi^t$, the $t$-th power of the matrix $\Pi$. Let $\Pi_{ij}(0, t)$ denote the $(i, j)$-th element of $\Pi(0, t)$. Define $Q_{ij}(0, t)$ similarly. Now let

$$Q_{ij}(0, t) = \begin{cases} \alpha_i(t)\Pi_{ij}(0, t), & \text{if } i \neq j \\ 1 - \sum_{j \neq i} Q_{ij}(0, t), & \text{if } j = i \end{cases}$$

The risk-neutral valuation of a bond that is initially in category $i$ and is maturing in $t$ periods can be identified using $Q(0, t)$ and the $t$-period risk-free rate. Equating this to the current price of the bond, we can identify the required $t$-year adjustment factor $\alpha_i(t)$. The following example illustrates.

---

**Example 33.2**

We continue with the two-period setting of Example 33.1. Under the Das-Tufano (DT) procedure, the first-period risk-neutral transition matrix is the same as under JLT since the procedures are identical for $t = 1$. Consider $Q(0, 2)$. To identify this matrix in the DT procedure, we first identify $\Pi(0, 2)$. This is just $\Pi^2$:

$$\Pi(0, 2) = \begin{bmatrix} 0.7300 & 0.0825 & 0.0825 & 0.1050 \\ 0.1600 & 0.5050 & 0.1450 & 0.1900 \\ 0.0875 & 0.1425 & 0.5025 & 0.2675 \\ 0 & 0 & 0 & 1.0000 \end{bmatrix}$$

Now apply the adjustment to $\Pi(0, 2)$ to obtain:

$$Q(0, 2) = \begin{bmatrix} 1 - 0.27\alpha_I & 0.0825\alpha_I & 0.0825\alpha_I & 0.1050\alpha_I \\ 0.1600\alpha_M & 1 - 0.4950\alpha_M & 0.1450\alpha_M & 0.1900\alpha_M \\ 0.0875\alpha_J & 0.1425\alpha_J & 1 - 0.4975\alpha_J & 0.2675\alpha_J \\ 0 & 0 & 0 & 1.0000 \end{bmatrix}$$

The risk-neutral pricing argument tells us that the initial prices of two-period bonds are just the discounted values of the expected payoffs under the risk-neutral probabilities, i.e.,

$$\begin{bmatrix} B_I(2) \\ B_M(2) \\ B_J(2) \\ B_D(2) \end{bmatrix} = \frac{1}{(1 + 0.04)^2} \times [Q(0, 2) \times C]$$

Here $C$ is the column vector of terminal payoffs $(1, 1, 1, \phi)$ that was defined earlier in the JLT example. These values must be equal to the given initial values of these bonds.

$$\begin{bmatrix} B_I(2) \\ B_M(2) \\ B_J(2) \\ B_D(2) \end{bmatrix} = \begin{bmatrix} 0.9070 \\ 0.8900 \\ 0.8734 \\ - \end{bmatrix}$$

Equating these, we can solve for the values of the adjustment factors $\alpha_i(2)$:

$$\alpha_I(2) = 0.3611$$
$$\alpha_M(2) = 0.3935$$
$$\alpha_J(2) = 0.4134$$

This results in the final transition matrix under the risk-neutral measure as follows:

$$Q(0, 2) = \begin{bmatrix} 0.9025 & 0.0298 & 0.0298 & 0.0379 \\ 0.0630 & 0.8052 & 0.0571 & 0.0748 \\ 0.0362 & 0.0589 & 0.7943 & 0.1106 \\ 0 & 0 & 0 & 1.0000 \end{bmatrix}$$

∎

The entries in this matrix (barring the last column) differ from the $Q(0, 2)$ matrix computed using the JLT procedure. This means ratings-dependent derivative prices may differ under the two procedures. Since each procedure is somewhat arbitrary, there are no real theoretical grounds for preferring one to the other.

From a computational standpoint, the DT procedure does have one important advantage. The adjustments $\alpha$ can be computed in closed-form in this procedure. Specifically, let $\mu_i(t)$ denote the probability of default from grade $i$ over $t$ periods. Then the risk-adjustment factor for grade $i$ in computing the $t$-period risk-neutral transition probability matrix is

$$\alpha_i(t) = \left[ 1 - \left( \frac{1 + r(t)}{1 + r(t) + s_i(t)} \right)^t \right] \left[ \frac{1}{(1 - \phi)\mu_i(t)} \right]$$

where $\mu_{it}$ is the total probability of default under the statistical measure for the entire period from time 0 to the maturity of the security.

# 33.8 An Application of Reduced-Form Models: Pricing CDS

Credit default swaps (CDSs) were introduced in Chapter 31 as the most important single-name credit derivative and as the building block of other credit derivatives such as credit-linked notes or synthetic collateralized debt obligations (CDOs). In this section, we illustrate the pricing of CDS contracts using a reduced-form model. As we show, the process is not complex. Once the forward probabilities of default are determined, the pricing scheme follows automatically.

A CDS is a contract in which one party makes a steady stream of premium payments in exchange for a single contingent payment that is made if a "credit event" occurs on the underlying reference instrument. For simplicity, we refer to the credit event as simply "default," although default is only one component of a credit event in CDS contracts (albeit the most important one). The contingent payment is specified in the contract and usually involves compensation in the amount of the loss in value (measured from par) on the reference instrument.

From a theoretical standpoint, the fair value of the periodic premium that is paid for this contract must be such that the present value of the premium payments made equals the present value of the payout received in the event of default. With a reduced-form model in hand that specifies the risk-neutral probabilities of defaults over different future time intervals, these present values are easily calculated and the CDS priced.

To illustrate the process, say that there are $T$ years in the horizon. Let $t$ index the time points at which payments are made. Let $h$ denote the time interval between payment periods (measured in years), and suppose there are $N$ payments due in all if no default occurs (i.e., assume that $Nh = T$).

Denote the risk-neutral forward probability of default for the $j$-th time interval $(t - h, t)$ by $\lambda_j$. This is the probability of default over the interval $(t - h, t)$ for $t = jh$. The corresponding recovery rate is denoted $\phi_j$. The pricing is carried out at time 0 and the expectations are taken at time 0. The short forward rates at any time point $t$ are denoted by $f(t, t) = f_t$.

We first compute the present value of the "premium leg." For this purpose, we compute the present value of \$1 premium payments made over all future periods or until a default event occurs. Call this $PV1$. Note that if the actual premium payment is \$$p$, then the present value of the premium leg is just $p \times PV1$. Assuming that premium payments are made at the start of each period, we have

$$PV1 = E_0 \left\{ 1 + \sum_{t=1}^{N-1} \left[ \prod_{j=0}^{t-1} (1 - \lambda_{j+1}) e^{-f_j h} \right] \right\} \tag{33.30}$$

To interpret this expression, note that the initial payment made at time 0 is \$1. (It is assumed that the reference asset is not in default at inception of the contract!) In each successive period, a premium payment is made only if there has not been a default so far. The likelihood of this is captured by the products of the survival probabilities $(1 - \lambda_j)$ from inception to the payment date. These expected payments are then discounted back to the present. Summing these over all the payment periods provides the required present value.

***Remark*** The payments under this model may be adjusted to be paid at the end of the period as well. CDS contracts often follow the convention that when payments are made at the end of the period, if default occurs within the period, then a pro rata premium payment is made for the time between the last premium paid and the time of default. Hence, it is important to adjust formulae such as those provided in this section appropriately for varying premium conventions.

This formula undergoes minor modification if the contract specifies that premium payments are to be made at the end of each time period in the model. Assuming for simplicity that full payment is made even if default occurs in that period, the applicable equation is

$$PV1 = E_0 \left\{ e^{-f_0 h} \left( 1 + \sum_{t=1}^{T-1} \prod_{j=1}^{t} (1 - \lambda_j) e^{-f_j h} \right) \right\} \tag{33.31}$$

Next, we calculate the present value of the "payment leg," i.e., of the contingent payment made in the event of default. For simplicity, we assume that these payments occur at the end of each time period. This present value, denoted $D$, is

$$D = E_0 \left\{ \sum_{t=1}^{T} \lambda_t (1 - \phi_t) \prod_{j=0}^{t-1} (1 - \lambda_j) e^{-f_j h} \right\} \tag{33.32}$$

The term $\prod_{j=0}^{t-1} (1 - \lambda_j) e^{-f_j h}$ represents the probability of not defaulting until the end of period $(t - 1)$, and the term $\lambda_t (1 - \phi_t)$ is the probable loss in period $t$ given as the product of the probability of default and the loss on default.

Since the value of the premium and payment legs should be equal, we find the following expression for the fair value of a CDS:

$$\text{CDS spread in bps} = \frac{D}{PV1} \times \frac{1}{h} \times 10,000 \qquad (33.33)$$

The division by $h$ and multiplication by 10,000 are done to express the CDS spread in basis point units per annum as is customary.

In the calculations in this section, we have assumed that default and contingent payments occur only at the premium payment time points. In fact, since default can occur at any time, including between payment points, a more sophisticated model would allow for this possibility also. The present value expressions become somewhat more complicated, but the principle behind identifying the fair value of the CDS remains the same.

## 33.9 Summary

The reduced-form class of models presented in this chapter complements the structural models of the previous chapter. Together these models comprise a large portion of the analytic techniques used in quantitative credit modeling. The reduced-form class of models uses debt-market information directly rather than equity market information as in structural models. They work through positing directly stochastic processes that determine the likelihood of default over any horizon. These processes most commonly take on the form of stochastic intensities (or what are called "doubly stochastic processes"), although there are also reduced-form models that operate via ratings transitions.

Reduced-form models generally tend to be analytically tractable, thanks to results in the theoretical literature that show that under some general conditions, reduced-form valuation of defaultable claims is essentially equivalent to risk-neutral valuation of the promised payoffs but with a credit-risk-adjusted discount factor. As a result, the models described in this chapter are relatively easy to use for the pricing of credit derivatives relative to structural models. They are also easy to calibrate because credit-linked securities may be used directly to extract default information. The flexibility in the choice of intensity process, recovery model, and term-structure model make this class of models very useful across a wide sprectrum of applications.

## 33.10 Exercises

1. If default intensity $\lambda = 3$, what is the probability of two or more defaults in a quarter of a year?

2. If $\lambda = 2$, what is the probability of survival for three years?

3. Suppose that the default intensity of a firm varies over time $t$ and is given by the following function:

$$\lambda_t = 0.5 - 0.01t$$

What is the probability of the firm defaulting in two years?

4. State a few important differences between reduced-form models and structural models of default risk.

5. Assume continuous compounding. Suppose the firm has a constant default intensity $\lambda = 2$. The risk-free rate of interest is $r = 0.02$. The recovery rate is $\phi = 0.5$, and all recovery of a defaulted security is assumed to occur at the original maturity of the

security. Price a two-year zero-coupon bond without default risk. Also price the same bond with default risk.

6. You are given that the intensity of default is $\lambda = 0.5$, and recovery rate is $\phi = 0.5$. The risk-free rate of interest is $r = 0.01$. In contrast to the previous question, the recovery amount is obtained at the time of default, *not* at the stated maturity of the security. Find the price of a one-year defaultable security that pays off \$1 at maturity.

7. The intensity of default is constant, $\lambda = 0.5$. What is the conditional probability of default at time $t$?

8. You are given that the cumulative probability of default for one year is 6% and for two years is 10%. The intensity is given by the following function of time

$$\lambda(t) = a + bt$$

   What are the values of $a, b$?

9. We examine the pricing of a semiannual pay, one-year credit default swap (CDS). The premium payments are made at the beginning of each semiannual period, and default payments are made at the end of each period. The default intensity is given by the following function

$$\lambda(t) = \begin{cases} 2a & \text{if } t \in (0, 0.5) \\ 2a + b & \text{if } t \in (0.5, 1.0) \end{cases}$$

   The CDS spreads for a half year and one year are

$$s(0.5) = 0.02, \quad s(1.0) = 0.04$$

   The risk-free rate is $r = 0.01$ and the recovery rate is $\phi = 0.6$. Recovery is a fraction of par. Solve for $a, b$ assuming the CDS contracts are fairly priced.

10. Given that $\lambda = 0.2$, the risk-free rate $r = 0$, and the recovery rate $\phi = 0.5$, price a CDS contract with maturity for two years, with semiannual premium payments made at the start of each period. Default payments are made at the end of each period.

11. Assume there are three debt ratings: $A$, $B$, and $D$, where $D$ stands for default. The one-period risk-neutral transition probability matrix for ratings is given as:

$$Q = \begin{bmatrix} 0.9 & 0.1 & 0 \\ 0.1 & 0.8 & 0.1 \\ 0 & 0 & 1 \end{bmatrix}$$

   What is the probability of default of an $A$-rated firm in one period, two periods, and ten periods?

12. Using the transition matrix from the previous question, what is the price of a five-year defaultable, $A$-rated zero-coupon bond if the risk-free rate is $r = 0$ and the recovery rate is $\phi = 0.7$?

13. The default intensity is given as $\lambda = 0.1$ per period. The recovery rate is $\phi = 0.5$. The risk-free rate of interest is $r = 0.10$ per period. Compute the price of a zero coupon bond with a maturity of two periods under the following assumptions:

   - No default risk (i.e., Treasury).
   - Default risk with recovery of par (RP).
   - Default risk with recovery of Treasury (RT).
   - Default risk with recovery of market value (RMV).

14. Consider a class of firms with hazard rate equal to 3. The default of one firm is unrelated to that of the others.

    (a) What is the average number of firms that will default in this class in one quarter of a year?

    (b) For the same firms, what is the average time to the first default?

    (c) What is the probability of two or more firms defaulting in the first year?

    (d) What is the probability of no firm in this class defaulting in two years?

15. The risk-free rate of interest is constant and is 10%. The credit spread for an issuer is also constant and is 2%. If the recovery rate is 50%, all componding and discounting is continuous, and default is assumed to occur at the end of the year,

    (a) What is the probability of default in one year?

    (b) What is the price of a one-year $1 zero-coupon bond issued by this firm?

16. The risk-free rate of interest is constant and is 10%. The credit spread for an issuer is also constant and is 3%. If the recovery rate is 40%, then given continuous compounding,

    (a) What is the probability of default over a two-year period?

    (b) What is the price of a two-year $1 zero-coupon bond issued by this firm? Assume all cash flows occur at maturity, whether or not the bond defaults in the interim period.

17. The one-year riskless interest rate and spread are 5% and 1%, respectively. At the end of the year, the next year's riskless rates are either 7% or 4% with equal risk-neutral probability. If the riskless rate is 7%, then the spread over the next year will be 0.5%, and if the riskless rate is 4% then the spread will be 2%.

    (a) Depict the rates and spreads on a binomial tree.

    (b) If the recovery rate is 40% (RMV), what is the price of a two-year bond with an annual coupon of 6%? Assume that compounding and discounting are continuous.

    (c) What is the probability of default over the first period?

    (d) What is the probability of default over the second period from each of the nodes on the tree at the end of the first period?

    (e) At what annual spread (in basis points) will a two-year CDS trade? Assume that payments on default are made at the end of each year and premiums are paid at the start of each year.

18. This question deals with a reduced-form model of risky debt. Suppose we can depict the risk-free interest rates on a tree (each period is one year) for which the current interest rate is 10%. Rates can change after one year and will become 12% or 9%. The recovery rate is constant at 40%.

    (a) Find the price of a risk-free Treasury bill that pays off 100 at the end of two years (it has no coupon).

    (b) There is a defaultable bond that we want to value using a reduced-form model. You are given the following default probability function at each node of the tree that depends on the risk-free interest rate:

$$\lambda = 1 - \exp(-a\,r)$$

    Here $r$ is the risk-free interest rate and $a$ is the hazard rate parameter. Suppose the credit spread on the bond is 20 basis points. Find the price of the defaultable zero-coupon bond, which also pays off 100 at the end of two years, and the value of the hazard function parameter "a." (You will need a spreadsheet and solver to work this out.)

19. This question refers to the model of Litterman and Iben presented in the chapter. The model takes as input the prices of riskless and risk-free bonds and generates forward probabilities of default. At the end of Section 33.4 is Table 33.4 presenting the forward default probabilities. This question relates to reverse engineering the spreads in the Litterman-Iben model.

Suppose all forward probabilities of default increased by 1% per annum. What should the new credit spreads in the model be to be consistent with the revised forward default probabilities?

20. This question requires you to implement the Das-Sundaram (DS) model presented in the chapter. The notation is the same as that used in the chapter. You are given the following table of forward rates and spreads along with their volatilities:

| Period $(T - h, T)$ | $T$ | $f(0, T)$ | $\sigma$ | $s(0, T)$ | $\eta$ |
|---|---|---|---|---|---|
| (0,0.5) | 0.50 | 0.10 | 0.020 | 0.020 | 0.002 |
| (0.5,1.0) | 1.00 | 0.11 | 0.018 | 0.030 | 0.003 |
| (1.0,1.5) | 1.50 | 0.12 | 0.016 | 0.040 | 0.004 |
| (1.5,2.0) | 2.00 | 0.13 | 0.014 | 0.050 | 0.005 |
| (2.0,2.5) | 2.50 | 0.14 | 0.012 | 0.060 | 0.006 |
| (2.5,3.0) | 3.00 | 0.15 | 0.010 | 0.065 | 0.007 |

The correlation between spreads and interest rates is −0.30.

(a) Build the tree in interest rates and spreads for five periods using all the data provided above.

(b) Generate another tree with just the probabilities of default at each node on the tree if the recovery rate is taken as two times the short rate at each node.

(c) Use the tree of forward rates and default probabilities to price a three-year semiannual premium credit default swap on the issuer. Express your answer for the premium in basis points credit spread.

# Duffie-Singleton in Discrete Time

We derive a version of the Duffie-Singleton valuation expression (33.14) here in a discrete-time setting.

## A One-Period Model

Begin with a simple one-period model. Consider a bond that pays $1 in one period if there is no default, and suppose the bond pays $\phi$ if there is a default. Let $t$ denote the length of the period, and let $1 - e^{-\lambda t}$ denote the risk-neutral default probability over the one period. Finally, let $s$ be the current spread on the bond and let $r$ denote the risk-free rate, both in continuously-compounded terms.

The current price of the bond is

$$V_0 = e^{-(r+s)t} \tag{33.34}$$

Its value computed using risk-neutral valuation is the discounted value of its expected payoff at maturity:

$$e^{-rt} [e^{-\lambda t} + \phi(1 - e^{-\lambda t})] \tag{33.35}$$

Equating these two values, we obtain

$$e^{-st} = e^{-\lambda t} + (1 - e^{-\lambda t})\phi$$

Using the approximation $e^x = 1 + x$, which is a very good approximation for small values of $x$, we see that for small values of $t$, the LHS is approximately $1 - st$ while the RHS is approximately $1 - \lambda t + \lambda t \phi$. This gives us

$$1 - st \approx 1 - \lambda t + \lambda t \phi$$

so canceling common terms results in

$$s \approx \lambda(1 - \phi) \tag{33.36}$$

Substituting this in (33.34), we obtain $V_0 \approx e^{-r+\lambda(1-\phi)}$, which is the Duffie-Singleton formula in this simple world.

Expression 33.36 provides a simple approximate relationship between the spread, the probability of default, and loss-given-default. Called the "credit triangle," this relationship is commonly used on trading desks to obtain quick estimates of default probabilities from observed spreads given assumptions concerning recovery rates.

## A Multiperiod Setting

Duffie and Singleton (1999a) provide a multiperiod discrete-time motivation of their result. Suppose the current time is $t$, periods are spaced $\Delta$ years apart, and maturity of the defaultable claim is at $T = t + n\Delta$. Let $\phi_\tau$ be the time-$\tau$ recovery rate in the event of default expressed in the RMV convention. In discrete time, this means that if default takes place at time $\tau + \Delta$, the recovered amount $\Phi$ is

$$\Phi_\tau = \phi_\tau E_\tau[V_{\tau+\Delta}] \tag{33.37}$$

where for any $s$, $V_s$ is the value of the claim at time $s$ contingent on it not having defaulted so far, and $E_s[\cdot]$ denotes expectation taken at time $s$ conditional on all the information available at that point.

Now, in general, risk-neutral pricing gives us the following recursive pricing relation:

$$V_t = \lambda_t \Delta e^{-r_t \Delta} \Phi_t + (1 - \lambda_t \Delta) e^{-r_t \Delta} E_t(V_{t+\Delta}) \qquad (33.38)$$

The first term on the RHS is the present value of the amount received on default, and the second term is the value if there is no default. Taking the expectations of these payoffs (under the risk-neutral probability of these events) and discounting it back gives us the present value of the instrument. This is equation (33.38).

Using (33.37) in (33.38), we obtain the simplification

$$V_t = e^{-r_t \Delta} [\lambda_t \Delta \phi_t + (1 - \lambda_t \Delta)] E_t(V_{t+\Delta}) \qquad (33.39)$$

Define $R$ by $e^{-R_t \Delta} = e^{-r_t \Delta} [\lambda_t \Delta \phi_t + (1 - \lambda_t \Delta)]$. Then,

$$V_t = e^{-R_t \Delta} E_t(V_{t+\Delta})$$

Carrying the recursion forward to maturity, we obtain

$$V_t = E_t \left[ e^{-\sum_{j=0}^{n-1} R_j \Delta} Z_{t+n\Delta} \right] \qquad (33.40)$$

Expression (33.40) is a discrete-time version of the Duffie-Singleton valuation result (33.14). It says that the present value of the defaultable claim may be identified by taking its promised payoffs at maturity ($Z_T = Z_{t+n\Delta}$) and discounting these payoffs back at a credit-risk-adjusted rate. Indeed, for small values of $\Delta$, $R_t \approx r_t + \lambda_t(1 - \phi_t)$, so the approximation becomes progressively closer to (33.14) as the time-period $\Delta$ shrinks.

## Appendix 33B

# Derivation of the Drift-Volatility Relationship

We derive here the recursive relationships (33.22) and (33.23) in the defaultable HJM model of Section 33.6. We first derive (33.22). To this end, denote by $\lambda(t)$ the probability of default by time $t + h$ given that default has not occurred up to $t$. Concerning the recovery rate, the model utilizes the Duffie-Singleton RMV convention. Let $\Phi^t$ denote the recovery amount in the event of default at $t$. The RMV condition then states that conditional on default occurring at time $t + h$, the time-$t$ expectation $E^t[\Phi^{t+h}]$ of the amount bondholders will receive is given by

$$E^t[\Phi^{t+h}] = \phi(t) E^t[B^*(t + h, T)] \qquad (33.41)$$

where $\phi(t)$ denotes the time-$t$ "recovery rate."

Let $Z(t, T)$ denote the price of the default-risk-free bond $B(t, T)$ discounted using $M(t)$:

$$Z(t, T) = \frac{B(t, T)}{M(t)} \qquad (33.42)$$

Since $Z$ is a martingale under $Q$, for any $t < T$ we must have $Z(t, T) = E^t[Z(t + h, T)]$, or, equivalently,

$$E^t \left[ \frac{Z(t + h, T)}{Z(t, T)} \right] = 1 \qquad (33.43)$$

Now, $Z(t+h, T)/Z(t, T) = (B(t+h, T)/B(t, T)) \cdot (M(t)/M(t+h))$. Using (33.17), some algebra shows that the first term is

$$\frac{B(t+h, T)}{B(t, T)} = \exp\left\{-\left(\sum_{k=t/h+1}^{T/h-1} [f(t+h, kh) - f(t, kh)] \cdot h\right) + f(t, t)h\right\}$$

**(33.44)**

The second term $M(t)/M(t+h)$ is just $\exp\{-f(t, t)h\}$. Combining these, we obtain

$$\frac{Z(t+h, T)}{Z(t, T)} = \exp\left\{-\sum_{k=t/h+1}^{T/h-1} [f(t+h, kh) - f(t, kh)] \cdot h\right\}$$

**(33.45)**

Using (33.45) in (33.43), the martingale condition becomes

$$E^t\left[\exp\left\{-\sum_{k=t/h+1}^{T/h-1} [f(t+h, kh) - f(t, kh)] \cdot h\right\}\right] = 1$$

**(33.46)**

Substituting for $(f(t+h, kh) - f(t, kh))$ from (33.20), this is the same as

$$E^t\left[\exp\left\{-\sum_{k=t/h+1}^{T/h-1} [\alpha(t, kh)h^2 + \sigma(t, kh)X_1 h^{3/2}]\right\}\right] = 1$$

**(33.47)**

Since $\alpha(t, \cdot)$ is known at $t$, it may be pulled out of the expectation. This gives us after some rearranging the recursive HJM expression relating the risk-neutral drifts $\alpha$ to the volatilities $\sigma$ at each $t$:

$$\sum_{k=t/h+1}^{T/h-1} \alpha(t, kh) = \frac{1}{h^2} \ln\left(E^t\left[\exp\left\{-\sum_{k=t/h+1}^{T/h-1} \sigma(t, kh)X_1 h^{3/2}\right\}\right]\right)$$

**(33.48)**

We now derive the analogous result (33.23) for the drifts $\beta(t, T)$. The following result relating the "short spread" to the default probabilities and recovery rates comes in handy:

$$s(t, t) = -\frac{1}{h} \ln[1 - \lambda(t) + \lambda(t)\phi(t)]$$

**(33.49)**

To see (33.49), consider a risky bond at $t$ that matures at $(t+h)$. By definition, its time-$t$ price is given by

$$B^*(t, t+h) = \exp\{-(f(t, t) + s(t, t)) \cdot h\}$$

**(33.50)**

Now, a one-period investment in this bond fetches a cash flow of \$1 at time $(t+h)$ if there is no default at $t+h$ and a cash flow of $\phi(t)$ if there is a default. The discounted expected cash flow under the risk-neutral probability must equal the current price of the bond, so

$$B^*(t, t+h) = \exp\{-f(t, t)h\}[1 - \lambda(t) + \lambda(t)\phi(t)]$$

**(33.51)**

Expression (33.49) is an immediate consequence of (33.50) and (33.51).

Now, pick any $t < T$ and consider a one-period investment in $B^*(t, T)$ at $t$. Viewed from time $t$, there are two possibilities regarding expected cash flows at $t+h$ from this investment:

- If the bond has not defaulted by $t+h$, there is an expected cash flow of $E^t[B^*(t+h, T)]$.
- If the bond has defaulted, the expected cash flow is $\phi(t)E^t[B^*(t+h, T)]$.

Since the probability of default by $t + h$ is $\lambda(t)$, the expected cash flow at $t + h$ is

$$(1 - \lambda(t)) \, E^t[B^*(t + h, T)] + \lambda(t)\phi(t) \, E^t[B^*(t + h, T)] \qquad \text{(33.52)}$$

which is the same as

$$[1 - \lambda(t) + \lambda(t)\phi(t)] \, E^t[B^*(t + h, T)]$$

By definition of $Q$, when discounted at the short rate $r(t)$, this expected cash flow must equal $B^*(t, T)$, so we have

$$E^t \left[ \frac{[1 - \lambda(t) + \lambda(t)\phi(t)] \, B^*(t + h, T)}{\exp\{r(t)h\}B^*(t, T)} \right] = 1 \qquad \text{(33.53)}$$

Now using (33.18) and the relation $s(t, t) = f^*(t, t) - f(t, t)$, some algebra reveals that

$$\frac{B^*(t + h, T)}{\exp\{r(t)h\}B^*(t, T)}$$

$$= \exp \left\{ - \left( \sum_{k=t/h+1}^{T/h-1} [f^*(t + h, kh) - f^*(t, kh)] \cdot h \right) + s(t, t)h \right\}$$

$$\text{(33.54)}$$

Further, by (33.49), we know that $[1 - \lambda(t) + \lambda(t)\phi(t)] = \exp\{-s(t, t)h\}$. Combining this with (33.53) and (33.54), we obtain

$$E^t \left[ \exp \left\{ - \sum_{k=t/h+1}^{T/h-1} [f^*(t + h, kh) - f^*(t, kh)] \cdot h \right\} \right] = 1 \qquad \text{(33.55)}$$

Using the definition $f^*(t, T) = f(t, T) + s(t, T)$, we can substitute for $(f^*(t+h, kh) - f^*(t, kh))$ from (33.20) and (33.21). Some rearranging now gives us the second recursive relation, this one defining $\alpha$ and $\beta$ in terms of $\sigma$ and $\eta$:

$$\exp \left\{ \sum_{t/h+1}^{T/h-1} [\alpha(t, kh) + \beta(t, kh)]h^2 \right\}$$

$$= E^t \left[ \exp \left\{ -h^{3/2} \sum_{t/h+1}^{T/h-1} [\sigma(t, kh)X_1 + \eta(t, kh)X_2] \right\} \right] \qquad \text{(33.56)}$$

Since we have solved for $\alpha$ in terms of $\sigma$ using (33.48), we may now use (33.56) to solve for $\beta$ in terms of $\sigma$ and $\eta$. This completes the derivation of the risk-neutral drifts in terms of the volatilities.

# 34

# Modeling Correlated Default

## 34.1 Introduction

In the preceding chapters, we discussed the modeling of credit risk for individual issuers, with Chapters 32 and 33 presenting, respectively, the structural and reduced-form approaches to estimating this risk. It is natural to ask how these models may be extended to the analysis of multiple credits so as to determine the joint risk of issuers in credit portfolios. We provide the answers in this chapter.

Modeling joint default risk has become essential in the pricing and risk management of products that are based on correlated default. These include collateralized debt obligations (CDOs), basket default swaps, credit index tranches, and others. In Chapter 31, we introduced these products; now, in this chapter, we will examine the technicalities of modeling these securitizations.

There are many ways to model correlated default, and we present several approaches in this chapter with an eye to their practical application. Over the course of the chapter, we work our way through several papers on the subject, including the non-parametric models in Chen and Sopranzetti (2003), hazard models of Lando (1994), the stopping time copula models of Li (2000), the fast recursion method of Andersen, Sidenius, and Basu (2003), implied copulas of Hull and White (2006b), the top-down correlated default models of Longstaff and Rajan (2006), and a tree model for correlated default (Hull and White, 2006a). We will also present a simple classification of correlated default products. By working through simple examples, we hope to provide a fundamental understanding of the ideas in different models as well as the differences between these models.

## 34.2 Examples of Correlated Default Products

Modeling correlated default is critical for several products in credit markets. One example is the CDO or collateralized default obligation. CDOs were described in Chapter 31. A CDO is a pool of underlying credits (the "collateral") whose cash flows are tranched out according to specified rules. The senior or "A" tranche has primary claim over cash flows; no other tranche can receive its promised cash flows until the claims of the senior tranche are fully met. Next comes the subordinated "B" tranche (mezzanine notes) whose cash-flow claims are junior only to the A tranche; there may be more than one subordinated tranche. Last comes the "equity" tranche, which has the juniormost claim on cash flows and takes the first set of losses on the portfolio. Correlations between securities in the CDO collateral determine the value of the tranches. For example, as default correlations increase, the senior tranche becomes more likely to experience losses and falls in value, while subordinated tranches may gain in value. Correlation is also key to valuing losses on credit indices such as the CDX and iTraxx which comprise many underlying names.

Another product that requires correlated default analysis is the basket default swap. In a basket default swap, a payoff is triggered when a specified number of credits in a given basket of credits experience a credit event. The general form is an $n$th-to-default (nTD) basket, a security which pays off when the $n$th default occurs in a given basket of $N$ securities. The most popular nTD baskets are first-to-default (FTD) and second-to-default (STD) baskets. In the next section we will see that nTD baskets are highly sensitive to credit correlations. Some, such as first-to-default baskets, increase in value as credit correlations decline. Others, such as second-to-default baskets, increase in value as credit correlations increase.

This chapter is intended to be a brief but comprehensive introduction to modeling default loss distributions for credit portfolios. The exposition that ensues is aimed at exposing the reader to mathematical details that are simple and germane to understanding the techniques applied in practice for valuing the products briefly mentioned in this section. Before proceeding to the technical details, we describe two very broad classes of correlated default models: bottom-up models and top-down models.

## Bottom-Up versus Top-Down Approaches

Bottom-up models begin by modeling the probabilities of default of individual names in the credit portfolio. The joint loss distribution is then based on specifying the correlations of default among all names in the portfolio. By simulating draws of individual default with the appropriate correlation between the names, the modeler generates a credit-loss distribution of the entire portfolio. The bottom-up model arrives at the portfolio loss distribution by aggregating the losses from individual names, hence, the moniker. Credit correlation in this class of models is obtained by positing correlations between the names in the portfolio, and then calibrating correlations to portfolio credit products such as CDOs and tranches of CDOs.

In contrast, the top-down approach does not the default of individual issuers in the credit portfolio, choosing instead to model the aggregate loss level directly. A stochastic process for loss arrivals that may be a function of other underlying latent variables is posited. The model is calibrated directly to prices of portfolio credit products such as CDO tranches. Credit correlation in this class of models is modeled only to the extent that it impacts the shape of the aggregate loss distribution of the credit portfolio, and this is manipulated in the model by setting the appropriate number and level of latent variables driving defaults in the portfolio. This is a more direct approach and is somewhat easier to implement, but since individual defaults are not tracked in the model, it makes hedging the risk of individual names more difficult and is limited to products that depend only on aggregate default levels.

Much of this chapter will focuses on the bottom-up approach although we discuss the top-down model as well. We begin with a simple exposition of correlated default mathematics. The simple concepts we introduce here are essential one wishing to understanding the more generalized forms of correlation that we eventually get to later in the chapter.

# 34.3   Simple Correlated Default Math

## Basic Variables and Relationships

Default modeling centers on the event of default. We denote this event by means of an indicator variable $D_i$, which indicates if firm $i$ has defaulted:

$$D_i = \begin{cases} 1 & \text{if firm } i \text{ defaults} \\ 0 & \text{if firm } i \text{ does not default} \end{cases} \tag{34.1}$$

Denote by $p_i$ is the probability of default for firm $i$. Since $D_i$ is an indicator variable, we have

$$E(D_i) = [1 \times p_i] + [0 \times (1 - p_i)] = Pr[D_i = 1] = p_i \tag{34.2}$$

$$\text{Var}(D_i) = p_i(1 - p_i) \tag{34.3}$$

This non-parametric approach was introduced in Chen and Sopranzetti (2003). The development of this section adopts their approach.

Extending this notation, we can also define the default correlation of two firms $i$ and $j$. This is

$$\rho_{ij} \equiv Corr(D_i, D_j) = \frac{E(D_i D_j) - E(D_i)E(D_j)}{\sqrt{Var(D_i)Var(D_j)}} \tag{34.4}$$

$$= \frac{E(D_i D_j) - p_i p_j}{\sqrt{p_i(1 - p_i)p_j(1 - p_j)}} \tag{34.5}$$

In order to simplify exposition, we write $Pr(D_i)$ for $Pr(D_i = 1)$. Then, the probability of joint default is

$$Pr(D_i \cap D_j) = E(D_i D_j) \tag{34.6}$$

$$= p_i p_j + \rho_{ij}\sqrt{p_i(1 - p_i)p_j(1 - p_j)} \tag{34.7}$$

which follows from equation (34.5). Therefore, the probability of joint default is linear in the correlation of joint default. But it is important to note that they are not the same.

Note that the correlation $\rho_{ij}$ cannot be arbitrarily specified. Since the probability of $i$ and $j$ *both* being in default cannot exceed the individual probabilities of default, we must have

$$p_i p_j + \rho_{ij}\sqrt{p_i p_j(1 - p_i)(1 - p_j)} \leq \min\{p_i, p_j\}$$

Equivalently, we may write

$$p_i = \min\{p_i, p_j\} \implies \rho_{ij} \leq \sqrt{\frac{p_i(1 - p_j)}{p_j(1 - p_i)}}$$

For example, if $p_i = 0.01$ and $p_j = 0.10$, then

$$\rho_{ij} \leq \sqrt{\frac{(0.01)(0.90)}{(0.10)(0.99)}} \approx 0.3015$$

**Example 34.1** Assume that $p_i = 0.01$ and $p_j = 0.10$. The following table provides a comparison of the probability of joint default and the correlation of default. Note that the maximum possible correlation in this case is roughly 0.3015.

| $\rho_{ij}$ | $Pr(D_i \cap D_j)$ |
|---|---|
| 0.000 | 0.00100 |
| 0.025 | 0.00175 |
| 0.050 | 0.00249 |
| 0.075 | 0.00324 |
| 0.100 | 0.00398 |
| 0.125 | 0.00473 |
| 0.150 | 0.00548 |
| 0.175 | 0.00622 |
| 0.200 | 0.00697 |
| 0.225 | 0.00772 |
| 0.250 | 0.00846 |
| 0.275 | 0.00921 |
| 0.300 | 0.00995 |

■

The probability of joint default may also be written in the following forms, exploiting the fact that $D_i$ is an indicator (0, 1) variable:

$$Pr[D_i \cap D_j] = Pr(D_i) + Pr(D_j) - Pr[D_i \cup D_j] \tag{34.8}$$

which is analogous to

$$E(D_i D_j) = E(D_i) + E(D_j) - Pr[D_i \cup D_j] = p_i + p_j - Pr[D_i \cup D_j] \tag{34.9}$$

These expressions are based on well-known set theoretic relationships. Using this, we may rewrite the correlation of default as follows:

$$\rho_{ij} = \frac{p_i + p_j - Pr[D_i \cup D_j] - p_i p_j}{\sqrt{p_i(1 - p_i)p_j(1 - p_j)}} \tag{34.10}$$

which extends equation (34.5). These various forms of the joint default relationship come in handy because the data may come in different forms, and one or the other expression for default correlation may be more applicable.

## Conditional Default

Conditional default probability is an alternative way of thinking of default correlations. For instance, we may be interested in the proliferation of default within an industry and the cascading effect of further defaults once initial defaults occur. We therefore care about the conditional probability of default of firm $j$ given firm $i$ has already defaulted. This conditional probability is written as $Pr[D_j|D_i]$. The probability of joint default may then be written as

$$Pr[D_i \cap D_j] = Pr[D_j|D_i] \, Pr(D_i)$$

$$= Pr[D_i|D_j] \, Pr(D_j)$$

which is just an implementation of Bayes' theorem.

**Example 34.2**

Let $p_i = 0.01$ and $p_j = 0.10$, and $Pr[D_j|D_i] = 0.8$ (if firm $i$ defaults, then $j$ defaults 80% of the time, signifying an increase in $p_j$ after conditioning). This implies that

$$Pr[D_i \cap D_j] = 0.8 \times Pr(D_i) = 0.8 \times 0.01 = 0.008$$

We consider two interesting questions:

1. What is the default correlation given the conditional probability of default? In this example, we compute the default correlation as follows:

$$\rho_{ij} = Corr[D_i \cap D_j] = \frac{Pr(D_i \cap D_j) - p_i p_j}{\sqrt{p_i(1 - p_i)p_j(1 - P_j)}}$$

$$= \frac{0.008 - (0.01)(0.10)}{\sqrt{(0.01)(0.99)(0.10)(0.90)}}$$

$$= 0.2345$$

2. What is the reverse conditional probability of default, i.e., $Pr[D_i|D_j]$? This may again be computed applying Bayes' theorem as follows:

$$Pr[D_i|D_j] = \frac{Pr[D_i \cap D_j]}{Pr(D_j)}$$

$$= \frac{0.008}{0.100} = 0.08 = 8\%$$

∎

How does correlation affect first-to-default contracts? Conditional default is useful in analyzing products such as first-to-default baskets. These are contracts that pay off when any one of a set of bonds in a chosen basket defaults. In the case of two issuers $i$ and $j$, this is clearly dependent on the following probability:

$$Pr[D_i \cup D_j] = Pr(D_i) + Pr(D_j) - Pr[D_i \cap D_j]$$

$$= p_i + p_j - Pr[D_j|D_i]\, p_i$$

We may analyze two cases:

1. When there is perfect positive conditional default, i.e., $Pr[D_j|D_i] = 1$, then

$$Pr[D_i \cup D_j] = p_i + p_j - 1.\ p_i = p_j$$

2. When there is zero conditional default, i.e., $Pr[D_j|D_i] = 0$, then

$$Pr[D_i \cup D_j] = p_i + p_j - 0.\ p_i = p_i + p_j$$

This gives the interesting result that the first-to-default basket contract will be more valuable when there is weak conditional default. This is intuitively convincing as well—when the correlation is low, there is little dependence between the credits, and hence, any one can default independently of the other. This makes the chance of any one firm defaulting more likely.

How does correlation affect second-to-default contracts? The pricing of contracts based on conditional default can be counterintuitive. For example, the reader may wish to consider whether the intuition of the first-to-default basket carries over to a second-to-default basket. The latter is a contract in which the payoff occurs only after two bonds in a basket have defaulted. Hence, the payoff depends on the probability of joint default. We have seen in equation (34.6) that this probability of two defaults increases in the correlation of default. Therefore, the value of this contract increases with default correlation, exactly opposite to what occurs in the case of first-to-default contracts.

What is the relationship of conditional default probability to default correlation? We may use conditional default expressions as a way to reexpress the correlation of joint default.

$$\rho_{ij} = \frac{Pr[D_i \cap D_j] - p_i p_j}{\sqrt{p_i(1-p_i)p_j(1-p_j)}}$$

$$= \frac{Pr[D_j|D_i]p_i - p_i p_j}{\sqrt{p_i(1-p_i)p_j(1-p_j)}}$$

$$= \frac{p_i(Pr[D_j|D_i] - p_j)}{\sqrt{p_i(1-p_i)p_j(1-p_j)}}$$

$$= \frac{\sqrt{p_i}(Pr[D_j|D_i] - p_j)}{\sqrt{(1-p_i)p_j(1-p_j)}} \equiv \frac{\sqrt{p_j}(Pr[D_i|D_j] - p_i)}{\sqrt{p_i(1-p_i)(1-p_j)}}$$

The last line follows from the symmetry of Bayes theorem. Rearranging, we also have another expression for conditional default:

$$Pr(D_j|D_i) = \frac{1}{p_i}\left[\rho_{ij}\sqrt{p_i(1-p_i)p_j(1-p_j)} + p_i p_j\right] \qquad \textbf{(34.11)}$$

which can be seen to be *linear* in default correlation.

# 34.4   Structural Models Based on Asset Values

Since correlated default products, such as CDOs, are based on baskets of hundreds of issuers, tranches written on such collateral with many constraints and conditions comprise some of the most complex derivatives in existence. Vast simplification of the assumptions underlying these products may sometimes result in closed-form solutions, but most cases require substantial numerical handling.

In this section, we will develop the basic intuition for the way in which we may simulate correlated default. The approach here is based on the structural model framework described in Chapter 32.

Assume that firm $i$ has asset value denoted by $A_i$ and that the volatility of these assets is $\sigma_i$. For now, assume that the asset return is normally distributed; we will relax this assumption eventually. The firm has zero-coupon debt in the amount of $F_i$. The distance to default for this firm is defined to be:

$$d_i = DTD_i = \frac{A_i - F_i}{\sigma_i A_i}$$

The distance to default $d_i$ specifies the number of standard deviations of its value the firm is away from default (implicit here is an assumed maturity for the debt of the firm, which may be taken as one year when not specified otherwise). Default is denoted as before by the indicator variable $D_i$ taking a value of 1.

The firm's probability of default may be stated in terms of the distance to default, i.e.,

$$\text{Prob of default} = p_i = N(-d_i) = 1 - N(d_i)$$

where $N(.)$ stands for the cumulative normal density function. Therefore, if we are given the probability of default, we may switch to the distance to default and vice versa, i.e.,

$$d_i = N^{-1}[1 - p_i]$$

For this initial discussion, we ignore the time horizon over which default risk is being assessed. However, both $p_i$ and $d_i$ are implicitly based on a time horizon chosen by the modeler or investor.

In order to simulate default for this issuer, we generate a number from the standard normal distribution, i.e., $x_i \sim N(0, 1)$, and then check whether it is less than the distance to default, in which case the default event $D_i = 1$ is deemed to be triggered. Thus, we have

$$D_i = \begin{cases} 1 \text{ if } x_i \leq -d_i \\ 0 \text{ if } x_i > -d_i \end{cases} \qquad \textbf{(34.12)}$$

In the model, default is precipitated when the random variable $x_i$ is drawn from far enough out in the left tail of the distribution so as to be less than the distance to default.

To illustrate how to use this approach to simulate correlated default, we specify another firm $j$, with distance to default $d_j$. We assume that the correlation of asset values is

$$Corr(A_i, A_j) = \rho_{ij}$$

If the two firm's assets are distributed as multivariate normal, then from the relationship of $d_i$ in terms of $A_i$, the correlation of default is induced by the correlation of both firms' assets. We generate joint default draws from the following distribution:

$$\begin{bmatrix} x_i \\ x_j \end{bmatrix} \sim MVN \left[ \begin{pmatrix} 0 \\ 0 \end{pmatrix}; \begin{pmatrix} 1 & \rho_{ij} \\ \rho_{ij} & 1 \end{pmatrix} \right]$$

Therefore, we draw $x_i$ and $x_j$ and then check each against its respective distance to default, $d_i, d_j$, determining separately whether default has occurred. In general, this two-firm example may be extended to many firms, and we draw a vector of values from the following system:

$$\mathbf{x} \sim MVN[\mathbf{0}; \mathbf{R}]$$

where the vector $\mathbf{x}$ is drawn from the mean zero sample with correlation matrix $\mathbf{R}$. Default is generated by comparing the following inequality element by element:

$$\mathbf{x} \leq -\mathbf{d}$$

where $\mathbf{d}$ is a vector of all firm distances to default. We will demonstrate the generation of correlated default with a simple example.

---

**Example 34.3**

Consider the case of 10 issuers, all of whom have distance to default equal to 2. The correlation of asset values is taken to be an average for all firms and is 0.20 in one simulation and 0.80 in another. Using the Octave program (below), we generate 100,000 iterations of the random vector $\mathbf{x}$, and in each iteration, we check for the number of firms that default. Keeping a count, we generate a histogram for both correlation levels. These are presented in Figure 34.1.

```
%Program to simulate defaults in asset values model
%Input Variables
n = 10;    %number of firms
d = 2;    %dtd
rho = 0.8;   %avg correlation across firms

%Set up correlation matrix
R = rho*ones(n,n);
for i=1:n;
    R(i,i) = 1;
end;
```

**FIGURE 34.1**
Histogram of Joint
Default Frequencies

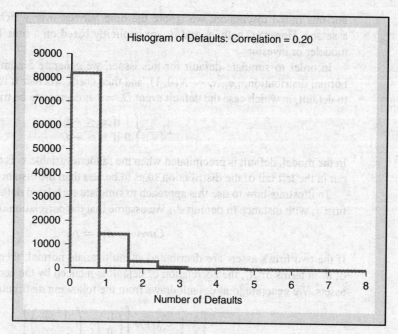

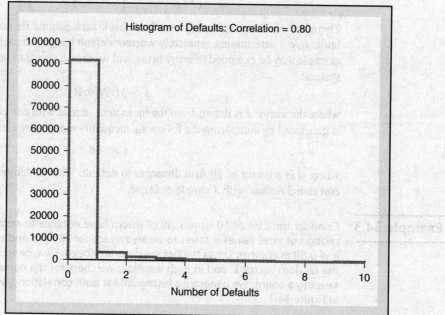

```
%Generate many correlated defaults
iter = 100000;
x = mvn_rnd(R,iter);
numdef = zeros(iter,1);
for i=1:iter;
    numdef(i) = length(find(x(i,:)<=-d));
end;
```

```
%Plot Histogram
grid;
title('Histogram of Defaults: Rho = 0.80');
hist(numdef);
```

The above `Octave` program uses a special-purpose function that we created for generating correlated random normal vectors, and the function is provided below (see the function `mvn_rnd`). The function uses Cholesky decomposition to generate random correlated vectors (more detail on this will be specifically provided in Chapter 36).

```
%Octave function to generate multivariate standard random normal variates
%You need to pass the correlation matrix only (all diagonal elements are 1)
function u = mvn_rnd(corr,n);
    m = length(corr);
    z = randn(m,n);
    L = chol(corr)';
    u = (L*z)';
```

An examination of the histograms in Figure 34.1 shows that most times, there are no defaults of any of the 10 firms. However, this is more prevalent when the asset values are more correlated. When $\rho = 0.8$, the probability of zero defaults is more than 90%, and when $\rho = 0.2$, the probability of zero defaults is lower, around 80%. The intuition for this comes from conditional default reasoning. When default correlations are high, conditional on the nondefault of one firm, the nondefault of the other firms is more likely as well. (We had undertaken this analysis earlier when considering first-to-default and $n$-th to-default contracts). Notice also that when the correlation is high, the probability of all firms defaulting is also higher. Thus, we see that a first-to-default contract will be worth more when correlations are low than when high.

On the other hand, consider a second-to-default contract. In this contract, the payoff is triggered only when two or more issuers default. From the histograms, we see that when $\rho = 0.2$, the probability of this happening is roughly of the order of 3%, but when $\rho = 0.8$, the probability is 4%. (We can get these values by subtracting the probability of 0 and 1 default from unity.) Hence, the second-to-default contract is more valuable when correlations are high, which reverses the effect noticed in the case of first-to-default contracts. ∎

## Reducing the Dimension of Large Systems

The simulation based on asset values is easy to implement as we have seen. But the speed at which the implementation works is misleadingly efficient for small problems such as basket contracts. When the same implementation needs to be undertaken for baskets of obligors numbering in the hundreds, the computation can become very time consuming, and handling a correlation matrix of a size such as $1,000 \times 1,000$ can quickly become infeasible. Specifically, drawing a vector of 1,000 random numbers is slow because Cholesky decomposition degrades in speed very quickly when the size of the correlation matrix increases. In such situations, reducing the dimensionality of the problem becomes an urgent necessity.

There are two ways in which we may address the high dimension issue. First, we can carry out what we will choose to call a "block" simulation. Second, we may adopt the method of projecting the system onto a parsimonious set of factors. In this subsection, we will analyze the former approach, leaving the second for the next subsection.

We assume that the firms in the basket or CDO collateral may be subdivided into $M$ "sectors." These sectors may be based on any chosen classification, for example, an industry breakdown. The number of firms within each sector $j$ is denoted $N_j$. We denote the correlation matrix of aggregate sector asset values as **R**. Therefore, **R** is of dimension

$M \times M$. We then draw a random vector $\mathbf{y} \in \mathbb{R}^M$ from this system, i.e.,

$$\mathbf{y} \sim MVN[\mathbf{0}; \mathbf{R}]$$

The values in this vector are for the average firm from each sector. Such a firm does not exist in reality, but the random vector $\mathbf{y}$ will be used to support the simulation for each individual firm as well. For now, this vector $\mathbf{y}$ is the default variable for each sector. Since the correlation matrix $\mathbf{R}$ is used, this approach ensures that a cross-sector default correlation is implemented. It also ensures that the dimensionality of the system is low, for it is restricted to the number of sectors that are stipulated, this being far fewer than the total number of firms.

The next step is to draw default variables for each individual firm. This is done sector by sector using the within-sector correlation matrix, which we denote $\mathbf{R}_j$ for each $j$. This correlation matrix is of dimension $N_j \times N_j$. Using this, we draw a random vector $\mathbf{x}'_j$ with the following distribution:

$$\mathbf{x}'_j \sim MVN[\mathbf{0}; \mathbf{R}_j]$$

This is done for each industry, i.e., for all $j$. Finally, the default variable is determined for each individual firm within an industry as follows:

$$\mathbf{x}_j = \mathbf{x}'_j + y_j \mathbf{1}, \quad \forall j$$

where $\mathbf{1}$ is a unit vector of dimension $N_j$. We then compare each element of this vector with the corresponding distance to default to determine which firms fail.

To recap, this reduction in dimension of the problem emanates from breaking the simulation of default for a large system into two steps. First, the default level for each sector in the system is simulated. This provides an average effect for each entire sector in the credit basket. Second, the default levels for each individual firm within a sector are generated using the intra-sector correlation matrix. Then, the sector average effect is added to the within-sector effect to get the final default variable for each firm. These may then be compared to the individual firm distances to default to determine which firms are in default.

The largest dimension of correlation matrix being handled here is limited to that of the biggest sector, or the number of sectors, i.e., $\max(\max(N_j), M)$. Unless the distribution of the number of firms within sectors is extremely skewed, this dimension is much smaller than that of the entire set of firms, which is $\sum_j N_j$. Hence, this provides a large computational benefit. Further, the breakdown into sectors effectively imposes a simple factor structure on the simulation model, such that each sector is treated as if it has its own loading on a factor, i.e., there are $M$ factors in the system. In the next subsection, we will discuss reducing the dimensionality of the model even further, such that the number of factors is strictly less than $M$.

## Factor Models

A common approach to capturing correlated default is based on a factor model. There are many variants of this class of models, naturally arising from a range of factor structures that may be chosen. Factor models also vary because of the form in which they are implemented.

Here, we will work with the distance to default $d_i$ of firm $i$. We denote the return on the firm's assets as $R_i$, which is the simple ratio of the asset value of the firm at the end of the period to that at the beginning minus 1; i.e., over period $(0, T)$, this is $\left(\frac{A_T}{A_0} - 1\right)$. We model $R_i$ as a function of firm-specific variables, which are fixed, and a factor set, which varies over time. This may be written generally as

$$R_i = f_i(\mathbf{X}; \ \boldsymbol{\beta}_i, \boldsymbol{\theta}_i)$$

The vector of factors is denoted $\mathbf{X}$, and the factor loadings for firm $i$ are denoted $\boldsymbol{\beta}_i$. The vector $\boldsymbol{\theta}_i$ comprises a set of firm-specific variables that remain fixed in time, such as the firm's target debt-to-equity ratio, and other policy variables. The factors may be chosen to be market or macroeconomic variables, such as equity and bond indexes, GDP growth, inflation, currency proxies, the level and slope of the term structure of interest rates, the VIX volatility index, etc. See Duffie, Saita, and Wang (2007) for a nice exposition of the power of well-chosen state variables to explain the cross section of defaults in the economy. Because all firms' returns will depend on the same factor set, this will induce correlation across defaults in the system. For example, a very simple factor model may be in linear form as follows:

$$R_i = \boldsymbol{\beta}_i' \, \mathbf{X} + \epsilon_i, \quad \forall i$$

where $\epsilon_i$ is the idiosyncratic (nonfactor) component of return. This model ignores firm-specific variables altogether and may be easily fitted using a time-series regression. Here, the variance of firm returns follows automatically from the regression, i.e.,

$$\sigma_i^2 = \boldsymbol{\beta}_i' \, \Sigma \, \boldsymbol{\beta}_i + \sigma_{\epsilon_i}^2$$

where $\Sigma$ is the factor covariance matrix, and $\sigma_{\epsilon_i}^2$ is the variance of $\epsilon_i$. Once the model is fitted for all firms, then simulation of correlated default involves the following steps:

1. Draw a sample of the factors using the multivariate factor distribution. For example, if this is multivariate normal, then we have

$$\mathbf{X} \sim MVN[\boldsymbol{\mu}; \Sigma]$$

where $\boldsymbol{\mu}$ is the mean of factor levels. The factor system may be translated into mean-zero terms and then $\boldsymbol{\mu} = \mathbf{0}$. We also draw the value of idiosyncratic return, as follows:

$$\epsilon_i \sim N\left(0, \sigma_{\epsilon_i}^2\right)$$

Thus, the generated return will be:

$$R_i = \boldsymbol{\beta}_i' \, \mathbf{X} + \epsilon_i$$

2. The factor vector is used to compute the values of returns for all the firms, which may then be used to determine whether default has occurred. This is done by comparing the normalized return

$$x_i = \frac{R_i}{\sigma_i}$$

with the distance to default $d_i$. Thus, default occurs if

$$x_i < -d_i, \quad \forall i$$

The last step here requires further explanation, and we show how to link it to the discussion on distance to default. Recall that the distance to default for firm $i$ is as follows:

$$d_i = \frac{1}{\sigma_i} \left[ \frac{A_i - F_i}{A_i} \right]$$

where $F_i$ is the face value of zero-coupon debt of firm $i$. Assuming that at the outset $A_i > F_i$, the value in square brackets above is the return by which the firm value needs to fall to trigger default. Therefore default occurs if

$$R_i < - \left[ \frac{A_i - F_i}{A_i} \right]$$

Dividing both sides by $\sigma_i$, we see that default is triggered when

$$x_i \equiv \frac{R_i}{\sigma_i} < -\frac{1}{\sigma_i}\left[\frac{A_i - F_i}{A_i}\right] \equiv -d_i \qquad (34.13)$$

This is equivalent to the condition we stipulated above. We can see that the framework of comparing a random default variable $x_i$ with distance to default $d_i$ is followed here as in prior sections. The difference lies in the way in which $x_i$ is generated for each firm.

In this factor model, the two main advantages are as follows. First, the computations required to generate the random variables are parsimonious because the dimension of the random vector is restricted to the number of factors, usually much smaller than the number of sectors, and substantially smaller than the number of firms. Second, the correlations among firm returns follow easily from the factor equation, which may be estimated using standard models.

In sum, the factor model uses a set of basis factors to generate returns for each firm. The post-return firm values are implicitly compared against debt value to determine whether default has occurred. This is done explicitly by comparing normalized returns with distance to default.

All the models looked at so far are based on a comparison of a default variable $x_i$ with distance to default $d_i$. The models differ in the degree of detail of the correlation structure used. Our first model was the most detailed and required the correlation matrix of individual firms. The second model reduced the dimension of the correlation matrix by grouping firms by sector. The third model based on a simplified factor structure was the most parsimonious.

# 34.5　Reduced-Form Models

In addition to structural models, which are based on asset value correlations, reduced-form models also enable the simulation of correlated default. Here joint default is driven by the correlation of default intensities, which were described in Chapter 33. We will use the results in that chapter as a basis for the framework presented here.

The basic unit of analysis is a default rate $\lambda_i$ for firm $i$. The rate or intensity is stochastic and changes over time. Given a time interval $(0, t)$, the intensity implies a survival probability

$$s_i(t) = \exp\left[-\int_0^t \lambda_i(u)\, du\right]$$

Note the similarity of this expression to the probability of zero events in a Poisson density function. The probability of default is 1 minus the probability of survival, i.e.,

$$p_i(t) = 1 - s_i(t)$$

Reduced-form models reside in the class of "doubly stochastic" models because there are two sources of uncertainty. First, the intensity is stochastic. Second, conditional on a given level of intensity, the default event is also probabilistic. In the default context, doubly stochastic processes are called Cox processes; see Lando (1994)—the main feature is that after we have conditioned on intensities, the actual default of firms is independent. In other words, all default correlation comes from the correlation of intensities. There are no further sources of correlation such as contagion effects. The presence of contagion would imply that even after fully accounting for the correlation between obligor intensities, additional correlation is experienced when defaults occur. To account for contagion, simulation models must draw random default times in a correlated manner, even after accounting for the correlation of default intensities.

One should note here that the doubly stochastic feature of these models also exists in the class of structural models. In the discussion preceding this section, we assumed that the distance to default $d_i$ was already determined and the event of default was drawn probabilistically. This is akin to drawing default in the reduced-form model *conditional* on a given intensity level.

Therefore, simulating default in a basket of issuers comprises first sampling intensities with the appropriate correlation, and thereafter, if the doubly stochastic assumption is violated, sampling default events with the correct additional dependence. The following example will make these ideas more explicit.

| | |
|---|---|
| **Example 34.4** | Suppose we have 10 issuers in a basket of credits. The constant default intensity for each issuer is $\lambda_i = 0.1$, $\forall i = 1 \ldots 10$. If the horizon for the analysis is one month (i.e., $t = 1/12$), then the one-month default probability is |

$$p_i = 1 - \exp(-\lambda_i t) = 0.0082987$$

Now we assume that default is conditionally independent, i.e., we sample 10 independent *uniform* random variables $x_i$ and check if $x_i \leq p_i$, $\forall i$. For example, we generated 10 random numbers from $x_i \sim U[0, 1]$ and obtained:

0.8807160    0.6384585    0.5407283    0.1113356    0.2733150
0.1002537    0.9708890    0.9470903    0.6617928    0.0022545

Only one of these values—the last one in the set of numbers above—is less than 0.0082987. Hence, one of the 10 firms defaults in this random draw.    ∎

In reduced-form models, the first level of correlation comes from drawing the set of $\lambda_i$s with the appropriate correlation (in the example above, we assume this was already done). If the doubly stochastic assumption holds, then there is no further correlation and, as above, independent random uniform numbers are drawn to check for default.

Of course, if the defaults are not conditionally independent, then the uniform random numbers would need to be drawn with the appropriate correlation. This may be done efficiently using the technique of "copula" functions and will be taken up later in this chapter.

Generating the set of intensities in a dependent manner requires a correlation matrix of intensities. Hence, the dimensionality of the simulation depends on the number of issuers. Since this may be a large number, the computational effort may grow rapidly. As before, the way in which high dimensionality may be addressed is by reducing the system to a much smaller one based on a factor set. By specifying intensities as modeled on a parsimonious set of factors, the computational complexity is curtailed successfully.

## 34.6    Multiperiod Correlated Default

So far, we assumed that the simulation of correlated default was undertaken for just one period. We may extend the model to many periods. To fix ideas, consider the modeling of a CDO with a collateral of many issuers and a maturity of 10 years. Suppose the discrete interval in our model is set to be annual. Then we need to run 10 annual simulations of correlated default to determine the total set of defaults over the full life of the CDO.

The probability of default (indicated by the default intensity in reduced-form models and by the distance to default in structural models) can no longer be assumed to be a constant over the entire period. Therefore, in a multiperiod setting, we need to use stochastic processes for the default intensities of each firm if we are working in a reduced-form model. If we work in a structural model, then we need to simulate the asset values of each firm over time.

A brief list of the steps in the procedure is as follows:

1. Generate the default intensity from a stochastic model for all firms (if the framework is reduced form) or generate the return on the firm's assets if the framework is structural. During this process, ensure that the correlations are factored in while simulating the new values.

2. Conditional on these values, determine which firms default within the first year. Unless conditional independence is imposed on the model, make sure that the default variables used to check for default are generated with appropriate correlations.

3. Using the values of default intensity or firm value (as the case may be) at the end of the first year, we proceed back to step 1 above and repeat the process for the next year. We continue to do this loop until all years have been accounted for. We make sure to record all defaults that occur in each year.

The outline of the multiperiod simulation is intentionally very general and admits many specific implementation forms. It applies to both structural and reduced-form models. This would be the approach used if one were pricing the tranches of a cash-flow CDO. Each period needs to be simulated so as to generate cash flows appropriately and check various covenants and conditions.

Synthetic CDOs are often easier to simulate. The method outlined above, although general, is inefficient if implemented literally. It is more efficient to simulate *default times* than default occurrences. This brings us to the concept of a *stopping time*. In brief, one may think of a stopping time as the time at which the event in question occurs. Therefore, the simulation of default may be thought of as the generation of *random* default times for each issuer.

The stopping time approach is not very different from that outlined earlier in which we simulated a default variable (which we denoted $x_i$) and compared it with the distance to default $d_i$ (in structural models) or with $p_i$ (in reduced-form models). In the stopping time framework, a variable $x_i$ is also generated but is compared with a time horizon. The method is best explained with an example.

---

**Example 34.5**

Assume again a set of 10 firms for which we have generated default intensities, which are constant and equal, i.e., $\lambda_i = 0.10$. We are interested in simulating defaults over the interval of time $(0, t)$. Conditional on these intensities, we need to generate stopping times $\tau_i$, $\forall i = 1 \ldots 10$. Since default arrival is Poisson, the time between Poisson arrivals is exponentially distributed. We exploit this distributional property in our simulation algorithm. Our procedure for generating stopping times is as follows.

1. Generate a default variable for each obligor: $x_i \sim U[0, 1]$, $\forall i$. This generates 10 uniform random numbers between 0 and 1.

2. Transform these uniform random numbers into default times using the exponential distribution, i.e., set

$$x_i = \exp(-\lambda_i \tau_i)$$

A transformation of the previous expression gives the stopping time $\tau_i$ as follows:

$$\tau_i = -\frac{1}{\lambda_i} \ln(x_i)$$

**3.** Compare the stopping time with horizon $t$, and establish default as follows:

$$D_i = \begin{cases} 1 \text{ if } \tau_i \leq t \\ 0 \text{ if } \tau_i > t \end{cases}$$

Therefore, if the stopping time occurs after the horizon, the interpretation is that default has not occurred. If the stopping time is less than the horizon, default is triggered.

As is now familiar, the stopping times may be generated independently conditional on the intensities. But this may be relaxed, and stopping times can be generated in a correlated manner too, by drawing the $x_i$s with appropriate correlation.

To complete the example, we present one sample draw for the 10 firms assumed above, taking default to be conditionally independent once the intensities are generated. The horizon is set to $t = 1$, i.e., one year. The Octave code is as follows:

```
octave:1> x = rand(10,1)
x =
   0.086135
   0.449259
   0.307056
   0.243939
   0.125794
   0.912623
   0.664363
   0.732090
   0.731622
   0.458583

octave:2> lambda = 0.1; tau = -log(x)/lambda
tau =
   24.51845
    8.00156
   11.80724
   14.10837
   20.73112
    0.91433
    4.08927
    3.11851
    3.12491
    7.79614

octave:3> t=1; def_firm_no = find(tau<t)
def_firm_no = 6
```

We first generated the default variables $x$ from a uniform distribution. These are then transformed into stopping times tau ($\tau$) using the stated intensities. Finally, the stopping times are compared to the horizon $t$ to find the firms that are in default. In our example, exactly one firm had a stopping time under 1 year, i.e., firm number 6 (its stopping time was 0.91433 years).

Now if the horizon was 10 years, i.e., $t = 10$, then more firms would be in default in the single sample draw depicted above, as can be seen from the results of the following Octave code.

```
octave:10> t=10; def_firm_nos = find(tau<t)'
def_firm_nos =
    2   6   7   8   9   10
```

Of the 10 firms, 6 defaulted in this random draw over a 10-year horizon.   ∎

Simulating stopping times is a highly parsimonious way of generating defaults especially when the time horizon is long, as is usually the case in products such as CDOs. Only one sample of default variables $x_i$ is required for the entire period of time. In the alternative approach in which default is generated (say) each year at a time, the simulation needs to be repeated once for each year, leading to a lot more computation. The stopping time approach is faster because it exploits the fact that each issuer can default only once and no more. For more details on simulating correlated default in a practical manner, see the paper by Duffie and Singleton (1999b).

## 34.7 Fast Computation of Credit Portfolio Loss Distributions without Simulation

From the preceding sections, we see that computing loss distributions is easy to do by means of simulation in either a structural or reduced-form framework. By drawing a vector of random variables from a specified joint distribution and checking these against the probability of default of each name in the portfolio, we are able to build up an entire loss distribution. However, like all simulation approaches, computation tends to be slow when the dimension of the problem becomes large, and in cases where the tails of the distribution matter, we need an extremely large number of simulation draws to ensure that the loss distribution is not an aberrant one. We will now examine an alternate analytic approach to computing the loss distributions of credit portfolios.

The work of Andersen, Sidenius, and Basu (2003) provides a fast semianalytic computation scheme to obtain the credit portfolio loss distribution. Once we have been given the set of default probabilities of all the issuers in the credit portfolio, a *recursion* scheme computes the loss distribution in run time that is linear with respect to the number of names in the portfolio. The approach works in three steps:

1. **Generate the Set of State-Dependent Probabilities of Default** Assume we have distance to defaults $d_k$ for $K$ issuers. Conditioning on state variable(s) $X$, generate a set of default probabilities for each name $k$ out of the total number of issuers $K$ drawn from a model in which the appropriate default correlation is maintained. For simplicity, assume a one-factor model of default such that a single factor drives all default correlation between the issuers in the portfolio. Let this common factor be normalized and denoted $X \sim N(0, 1)$. Assume that each issuer has a default variable

$$Y_k = \sqrt{\rho_k}\, X + \sqrt{1 - \rho_k}\, Z_k$$

where $\rho_k$ is the correlation coefficient relative to the common factor $X$. $Z_k \sim N(0, 1)$ is an idiosyncratic shock term that is different for each issuer. This means that $Y_k$ is also normally distributed with a mean of zero and a variance equal to 1. Normality is imposed here for illustrative purposes only, and any distribution may be applied in the equation above. Suppose we are given the distance to default of each issuer in the portfolio, denoted $d_k$. Then the probability of an issuer defaulting, denoted $p_k$, specified as follows is

$$p_k = \text{Prob}[Y_k < -d_k] = \text{Prob}[\sqrt{\rho_k}\, X - \sqrt{1 - \rho_k}\, Z_k < -d_k]$$

Since $Z_k$ is normally distributed, we can then denote $p_k$, *conditional on* $X$ as

$$p_k | X = N\left[\frac{-d_k - \sqrt{\rho_k}\, X}{\sqrt{1 - \rho_k}}\right]$$

2. **Generate the State-Dependent Loss Distribution $L(X)$** For a given level of the state variable $X$, we use the vector of probabilities $p_k|X$ to compute a loss distribution $L(X)$, which is described in detail below. The approach uses a recursion scheme.

3. **Generate the Aggregate Loss Distribution $L$** Repeating step 2 for the entire range of $X$ values gives a set of loss distributions, one for each value of $X$. Combining all of these loss distributions results in the total loss distribution of the credit portfolio, $L = \int_X L(X)\,\text{Prob}(X)\,dX$.

We now describe in detail the recursion approach of Andersen, Sidenius, and Basu (2003) to build up the loss distribution $L(X)$ analytically (step 2 above). Note that in the ensuing discussion, we are looking at the "inner" loop of the scheme in which we compute but one loss distribution $L(X)$ for a fixed value of $X$. The "outer" loop combines the various $L(X)$ distributions into the aggregate loss distribution $L$ (step 3). To keep the notation simple, we write $p_k|X$ as just $p_k$ and drop the conditioning (on $X$) notation, bearing in mind always that we are computing the loss distribution for a given value of the state variable $X$.

Our credit portfolio comprises the $K$ issuers: $k = 1, \ldots, K$. Let $w_k$ be the loss level of the $k$-th name. This is fixed, and hence, implies that conditional on the issuer defaulting, the dollar loss amount is prespecified and is constant. The set of loss levels (in round dollars) is denoted as

$$l = \{0, 1, \ldots, l_{max}\}$$

The probability of a total loss level of $l$ if the first $k$ firms is considered is denoted $P^k(l)$. Andersen, Sidenius, and Basu (2003) applied the following recursion:

$$P^{k+1}(l) = P^k(l)[1 - p_{k+1}] + P^k(l - w_{k+1})p_{k+1} \qquad \textbf{(34.14)}$$

Therefore, the probability of a loss level of $l$, after considering $(k + 1)$ firms, is equal to the sum of two terms: (a) the probability of a loss of $l$ after considering $k$ firms, and the $(k+1)$st firm does not default and (b) the probability of a loss of $l - w_{k+1}$ after considering $k$ firms, and the $(k + 1)$st firm does default. This simple recursion equation is the key to building up the entire loss distribution. This distribution $L(X)$ is, of course, a set of discrete loss levels and corresponding probabilities of these loss levels. We showcase the implementation with a numerical example.

**Example 34.6**

Let the number of names be $K = 4$, and the individual loss for each firm be specified as

$$w = \{w_1, w_2, w_3, w_4\} = \{2, 1, 7, 3\}$$

Hence, the maximum possible loss occurs when all firms default, and $l_{max} = 13$. We have 14 loss bins $l = 0, 1, \ldots, 13$. Since $K = 4$, we will have four iterations of equation (34.14) in total in the algorithm.

1. In the first iteration, only two possible outcomes exist: either that the first name does not fail or that it fails, so the loss will be 0 or 2:

$$P^1(0) = 1 - p_1$$
$$P^1(2) = p_1$$

There are no other possible loss levels if only the first issuer is considered. Hence, all other $P^1(l)$ values are zero, i.e., $P^1(l) = 0$, if $l \neq \{0, 2\}$.

2. For the second iteration, we need all combinations of losses from the first two names, i.e., we apply the recursion equation (34.14) for $k = 2$:

$$P^2(0) = P^1(0)[1 - p_2] = (1 - p_1)(1 - p_2)$$
$$P^2(1) = P^1(1)[1 - p_2] + P^1(1 - 1)p_2 = 0 + (1 - p_1)p_2$$
$$P^2(2) = P^1(2)[1 - p_3] + P^1(2 - 1)p_2 = p_1(1 - p_2) + 0$$
$$P^2(3) = P^1(3)[1 - p_2] + P^1(3 - 1)p_2 = 0 + p_1 p_2$$

Therefore, after accounting for the second firm (iteration 2), the maximum loss level is 3, given that firm 1 has a loss level of 2 and firm 2 has a loss level of 1. After $k = 2$, there are four possible loss levels, {0, 1, 2, 3}, and these have the four probabilities given above. The probabilities sum to 1. Note how, after iteration 2, we have a loss distribution that describes losses in a credit portfolio comprised of the first two issuers.

3. We proceed to iteration 3. Here the third firm may default as well, and so the maximum loss level is 10. We can write down a few of the probabilities for the possible loss levels as follows:

$$P^3(0) = P^2(0)[1 - p_3] = (1 - p_1)(1 - p_2)(1 - p_3)$$
$$P^3(1) = P^2(1)[1 - p_3] + P^2(1 - 7)p_3 = (1 - p_1)p_2(1 - p_3) + 0$$
$$P^3(2) = P^2(2)[1 - p_3] + P^2(2 - 7)p_3 = p_1(1 - p_2)(1 - p_3) + 0$$
$$P^3(3) = P^2(3)[1 - p_3] + P^2(3 - 7)p_3 = p_1 p_2(1 - p_3) + 0$$
$$P^3(7) = P^2(7)[1 - p_3] + P^2(7 - 7)p_3 = 0 + (1 - p_1)(1 - p_2)p_3$$
$$P^3(8) = P^2(8)[1 - p_3] + P^2(8 - 7)p_3 = 0 + (1 - p_1)p_2 p_3$$

Likewise, we can write down $P^3(4)$, $P^3(5)$, $P^3(6)$, $P^3(9)$, and $P^3(10)$. We may move on in this way to the fourth issuer as well, and compute the entire loss distribution. This is left as an exercise.

It turns out that this approach is exceedingly simple to program. Let the set of probabilities of default of the four firms be $p_1 = 0.10$, $p_2 = 0.05$, $p_3 = 0.03$, and $p_4 = 0.20$. The Octave program to implement this scheme is as follows:

```
%INPUTS
%PROGRAM: asb_recusrsion.m
w = [2,1,3,7];   %Loss weights
p = [0.1, 0.05, 0.03, 0.2]; %Loss probabilities

%BASIC SET UP
N = length(w);
maxloss = sum(w);
bucket = [0:maxloss];
LP = zeros(N,maxloss+1);  %probability grid over losses

%DO FIRST FIRM
LP(1,1) = 1-p(1);
LP(1,w(1)+1) = p(1);

%LOOP OVER REMAINING FIRMS
for i=2:N;
    for j=1:maxloss+1;
        LP(i,j) = LP(i-1,j)*(1-p(i));
```

```
            if bucket(j)-w(i) >= 0; LP(i,j) = LP(i,j) + LP(i-1,j-w(i))*p(i); end;
    end;
end;

%SHOW HISOTOGRAM OF LOSS DISTRIBUTION
lossprobs = LP(N,:);
fprintf('CHECK: Sum of final probs = %10.6f \n',sum(lossprobs));
[bucket'  LP']
```

The loss distribution computed from the program is as follows:

```
octave-2.9.17:4> asb_recursion
CHECK: Sum of final probs =   1.000000
ans =
```

| | | | | |
|---|---|---|---|---|
| 0.00000 | 0.90000 | 0.85500 | 0.82935 | 0.66348 |
| 1.00000 | 0.00000 | 0.04500 | 0.04365 | 0.03492 |
| 2.00000 | 0.10000 | 0.09500 | 0.09215 | 0.07372 |
| 3.00000 | 0.00000 | 0.00500 | 0.03050 | 0.02440 |
| 4.00000 | 0.00000 | 0.00000 | 0.00135 | 0.00108 |
| 5.00000 | 0.00000 | 0.00000 | 0.00285 | 0.00228 |
| 6.00000 | 0.00000 | 0.00000 | 0.00015 | 0.00012 |
| 7.00000 | 0.00000 | 0.00000 | 0.00000 | 0.16587 |
| 8.00000 | 0.00000 | 0.00000 | 0.00000 | 0.00873 |
| 9.00000 | 0.00000 | 0.00000 | 0.00000 | 0.01843 |
| 10.00000 | 0.00000 | 0.00000 | 0.00000 | 0.00610 |
| 11.00000 | 0.00000 | 0.00000 | 0.00000 | 0.00027 |
| 12.00000 | 0.00000 | 0.00000 | 0.00000 | 0.00057 |
| 13.00000 | 0.00000 | 0.00000 | 0.00000 | 0.00003 |

The left column in the tableau of shows the various possible loss levels (buckets), and each column thereafter shows the loss distribution after each iteration. Hence, the right-most column shows the final loss distribution probabilities.

Note that the results do not depend on the sequence in which the firms are processed in the iterations. The reader may enter the program into `Octave` and try shuffling the sequence of losses in variable w and respective probabilities p at the top of the program. The last column will be the same each time, though the intermediate columns will be different. ∎

# 34.8   Copula Functions

In this section, we will generalize the modeling approaches for correlated default to multivariate settings in which we may choose from various different joint distributions. The technique will use what are known as copula functions. These were introduced to the arena of correlated default by Li (2000). But before delving into the specifics of copulas, it is best to recap what we know so far:

1. Individual default probabilities ($p_k$,  $k = 1 \ldots K$) for issuers may be determined in either structural or reduced-form models.

2. Defaults of individual issuers are determined in a simulation setting by drawing numbers $Y_k$ *with appropriate correlation* from a multivariate probability distribution and then comparing these numbers to cutoff values $d_k$ that are based on the probabilities of default $p_k$ in order to ascertain which issuers default and which do not. In

general, $d_k = F_k^{-1}(p_k)$, where $F(\cdot)$ is a distribution function. Clearly, whether $p_k$ comes from a structural model or a reduced-form model *does not matter*. The application of copulas is therefore agnostic to the class of default model that generates the default probabilities.

3. The key to correlated default modeling lies in generating the values $Y_k$ with the right correlation. In this section, we will look at how this is done using copula functions. A copula function takes as input the various distribution functions $F_k(\cdot)$ and "couples" them into a joint distribution with the required shape. As we will see (a) copula functions are able to couple univariate distributions, all of which may be different, into a multivariate one and (b) copulas may also be chosen in a manner that specifies the shape of the joint distribution (specifically, how fat its tails are).

Copulas are functions that, as the name suggests, couple individual probability functions into joint probability functions. It is easy to intuit that there are many ways in which individual probability functions governed by a given correlation matrix can be coupled into a multivariate one—in other words, the joint distribution is not unique. It will depend very much on the coupling scheme, i.e., on the chosen copula.

We follow a two-step creation of the joint distribution.

1. First, the individual or marginal probability functions are chosen.

2. Second, these are coupled into the joint function using a copula. There are many copulas available, such as the Gaussian, Student's $t$, Gumbel, Frank, and Clayton. Each of these imposes different properties on the joint distribution.

A good reference (somewhat technical) on copulas is the book by Nelsen (1999).

The separation of the choice of marginal distribution from that of the joint distribution is a key practical benefit of using copula techniques. It offers great flexibility in creating the required correlation structure. This idea is best exemplified as follows. Consider two very different scenarios, $A$ and $B$. We have two random variables $x_1, x_2$, and they have a correlation equal to 40% in both scenarios. In scenario $A$, extreme values of the random variables tend to be more correlated than nonextreme ones. The opposite occurs in scenario $B$ where nonextreme values are more correlated. Even though, on average, both scenarios have the same correlation, the *pattern* of correlation is quite different. One can easily imagine the scenarios to be economic regimes, and it is easy to come up with examples of random variables that may be more like one scenario than the other. For instance, default correlations in the high-yield debt market are higher in poor economic conditions (extremal observations of firm value) than when times are normal. Such episodes result in "tail fatness" in the joint distribution.

To look at how the joint distributions with the same correlation can embody varying amounts of tail fatness, we look at plots that depict a scatter plot in the bivariate distribution. In Figure 34.2, we provide two graphs. The one on the left side shows the joint distribution of two standard normal variates with a correlation of 40%. The right-side plot is based on two variates drawn from a Students's $t$ distribution with the same correlation and degrees of freedom equal to 5. Since the correlation is positive, the scatter is heavy along the positive sloped diagonal for both plots. Even though the correlations are identical across the two plots, the shapes of the depicted bivariate distributions are quite different. The Student's $t$ distribution is more stretched (less circular, more ellipsoid) and has a much fatter tail, which may be seen from a comparison of the range of the axes in both plots. There are many more extreme outliers than in the case of the normal variates. With this informal discussion on why the shape of the joint distribution matters, we move on to an explicit consideration of copula functions.

**FIGURE 34.2**
Comparison of Plots
from Normal and
Student's *t* Bivariate
Distributions

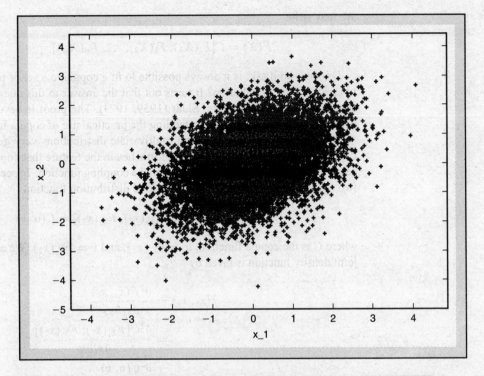

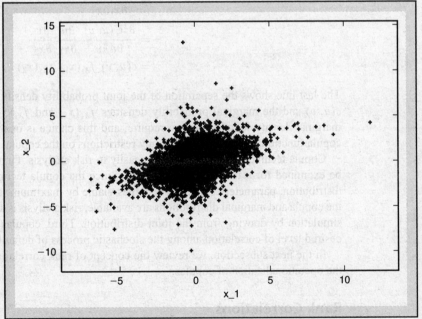

The formal definition of a copula begins by modeling an *m*-variate distribution. A random draw from this distribution comprises a vector $X \in R^m = \{X_1, X_2, \ldots, X_m\}$. Each of the *m* variates has a marginal distribution, which we denote $F_i(X_i), \quad i = 1 \ldots m$. The joint distribution is denoted $F(X)$. The copula associated with $F(X)$ is a function $C : [0, 1]^m \to [0, 1]$, which maps an *m*-dimensional space onto a line interval $[0, 1]$.

We may write

$$F(X) = C[F_1(X_1), F_2(X_2), \ldots, F_m(X_m)] \qquad \textbf{(34.15)}$$

One may well ask: is it always possible to fit a copula to a set of marginal distributions to create a joint distribution? It turns out that the answer to this question is yes. This was shown in well-known papers: Sklar (1959, 1973). The proof is beyond the scope of this book, and not essential to understanding the practical use of copula functions.

Copulas are useful in modeling multivariate distributions very generally with flexible dependence structures. The reason for this lies in the feature that copula density functions separate the univariate distributions from the coupling function. To see this, assume we have two random variables $X_1$ and $X_2$, with joint distribution function

$$F(x, y) = C[F_{X_1}(x_1), F_{X_2}(x_2)] = C(u, v)$$

where $C$ is the copula function, $u = F_{X_1}(x_1)$, and $v = F_{X_2}(x_2)$. We can easily see that the joint density function is given by

$$
\begin{aligned}
f(x_1, x_2) &= \frac{\partial^2 F(x_1, x_2)}{\partial x_1 \partial x_2} \\
&= \frac{\partial^2 C[F_{X_1}(x_1), F_{X_2}(x_2)]}{\partial x_1 \partial x_2} \\
&= \frac{\partial^2 C(u, v)}{\partial x_1 \partial x_2} \\
&= \frac{\partial^2 C(u, v)}{\partial u \partial v} \frac{\partial u}{\partial x_1} \frac{\partial v}{\partial x_2} \\
&= c(u, v) \, f_{X_1}(x_1) \, f_{X_2}(x_2)
\end{aligned}
$$

The last line shows the separation of the joint probability density into the copula density $c(u, v)$ and the marginal probability densities $f_{X_1}(x_1)$ and $f_{X_2}(x_2)$. We may choose any marginal density functions as we require, and this choice is unaffected by the choice of copula function, nor does it impose any restrictions on the copula.

Copula techniques lend themselves easily to risk analysis. First, different copulas may be examined for statistical fit to the data. Since the copula technique provides the joint distribution, parameter estimation becomes viable by maximum likelihood. Second, once the copula and marginal distributions are available, risk analysis is also feasible via scenario simulation by drawing from the joint distribution. Third, copulas enable injection of the desired level of correlation among the stochastic process of default of individual issuers.

In the next subsection, we review the concept of rank correlation, which is needed for the operationalization of copulas.

## Rank Correlations

If random variables track together, then the measure of linear correlation used earlier in this chapter would reflect this and would be positive. When a copula is applied to marginal distributions, it effects a scale transformation on the original distributions, and the linear correlations may change. This would not occur if rank correlations (i.e., the correlations of ranks, to put it very loosely) were used. Since rank correlation is invariant to scale transformations, the rank correlation in the joint distribution will be preserved irrespective of the copula that is used.

One measure of rank correlation is Kendall's $\tau$. If $(X_1, Y_1)$ and $(X_2, Y_2)$ are two independent draws from a joint distribution of $X$ and $Y$, then

$$\tau = Pr[(X_2 - X_1)(Y_2 - Y_1) > 0] - Pr[(X_2 - X_1)(Y_2 - Y_1) < 0] \quad \textbf{(34.16)}$$

If $(X_2 - X_1)(Y_2 - Y_1) > 0$, the pair of random draws is *concordant*, else it is *discordant*. If we define $c$ as the number of concordant pairs and $d$ as the number of discordant pairs, then we can also define the rank correlation as:

$$\tau = \frac{c - d}{c + d} = \frac{c - d}{\frac{n(n-1)}{2}}$$

$$= \frac{2}{n(n-1)} \sum_{i < j} \text{sign}[(X_i - X_j)(Y_i - Y_j)] \quad \textbf{(34.17)}$$

Rank correlation has the following properties:

- $\tau \in [-1, 1]$.
- If $X, Y$ are independent, then $\tau = 0$.
- $\tau$ is invariant under strictly monotonic transformations, that is, if $f(X), g(Y)$ are strictly increasing or decreasing functions. Then, $\tau[f(X), g(Y)] = \tau(X, Y)$.

In particular, with the normal distribution,

$$\tau[\Phi(X), \Phi(Y)] = \tau[X, Y] = \frac{2}{\pi} \arcsin(\rho(X, Y)) \quad \textbf{(34.18)}$$

which connects the rank correlation $\tau$ with the linear correlation coefficient $\rho$. The following program code is a fast and parsimonious function to compute Kendall's $\tau$ based on an implementation of equation (34.17) above.

```
function u = ktau(x,y);
  k=length(x);
  xminusx = triu(kron(x,ones(1,k)) - kron(x',ones(k,1)),1);
  yminusy = triu(kron(y,ones(1,k)) - kron(y',ones(k,1)),1);
  u=2*sum(sum(sign(xminusx.*yminusy)))/(k*(k-1));
```

To illustrate this, we generate two random columns of data from a bivariate normal distribution with correlation equal to 0.4 and compute the $\tau$ value. The code snippet is as follows:

```
octave:1> x = mvn_rnd([1 0.4; 0.4 1],1000);
octave:2> ktau(x(:,1),x(:,2))
ans = 0.29548
octave:3> corrcoef(x)
ans =
   1.00000   0.44774
   0.44774   1.00000
octave:4> ktau(x(:,1),exp(x(:,2)))
ans = 0.29548
octave:5> corrcoef([x(:,1),exp(x(:,2))])
ans =
   1.00000   0.33849
   0.33849   1.00000
```

Here, we first generate 1000 values each of two standard normal variates with correlation 0.4. Next we compute the rank correlation and obtain $\tau = 0.29548$. The linear correlation is

0.44774. We transform the second variable by exponentiating it and then rerun the rank correlation between the first (untransformed variable) and the second transformed one. Kendal's $\tau$ remains 0.29548 even for the transformed variables. But when we compute linear correlation $\rho$ for the transformed variables, we get 0.33849, which is not the same as 0.44774, showing that linear correlation is not preserved under monotone nonlinear transformations of the variables. Thus, we see that the exponential transform does not affect the rank correlation, but it does change linear correlation. Hence, Kendall's $\tau$ is unaffected by nonlinear transforms.

We also verify the relationship between linear correlation $\rho$ and Kendall's $\tau$ of equation (34.18), which is

$$\tau[x_1, x_2] = \frac{2}{\pi} \arcsin(\rho(x_1, x_2))$$

$$\Downarrow$$

$$0.29548 = \frac{2}{\pi} \arcsin(0.44774) = 0.29554$$

which is verified in the code below (the small difference being a matter of rounding):

```
octave:6> 2/pi*asin(.44774)
ans = 0.29554
```

Next we consider how to sample random variables from a normal copula.

## Sampling Random Variables with the Normal Copula

The Gaussian copula is a popular one for scenario generation because of its parsimony and ease of use. One approach to generate joint random variables $\{x_i\}$ using the Gaussian copula is as follows.

1. Compute the matrix of rank correlation coefficients prior to the simulation. This may be computed from the data or it may be derived from an economic model. Denote this matrix as $\{\tau\}_{ij}$.

2. Convert this matrix into the linear correlation matrix by computing values from the inverse of the transform equation used above, i.e.,

$$\rho_{ij} = \sin\left[\frac{\pi}{2}\tau_{ij}\right]$$

3. Generate multivariate random normal numbers with mean zero and correlation matrix $\{\rho\}_{ij}$, to get a random vector $(Z_1, Z_2, \ldots, Z_m)'$.

4. Let $u_i = \Phi(Z_i)$, $i = 1..m$. Here $\Phi(Z_i)$ is the cumulative normal distribution function over $Z_i$.

5. Finally, we get $x_i = F_i^{-1}(u_i)$, $i = 1 \ldots m$, where $F_i$ is the marginal distribution and may be different for each $i$.

A similar approach may be used to generate samples from a Student's $t$ distribution using copulas. Or for that matter, any other distribution. Each $x_i$ comes from its own distribution $F_i$. This procedure is best illustrated with an example.

**Example 34.7** Suppose we have two random variates $x_1, x_2$, which are from different distributions. We assume that $x_1$ comes from an exponential distribution with mean 0.1, and $x_2$ is standard chi-square with degrees of freedom equal to 3. We specify that the rank correlation between the two variables is 0.6. Our goal is to generate a scatter diagram of the two variables based on their marginal distributions coupled together by a Gaussian copula. We implement the following steps:

1. Convert the rank correlation into a linear correlation parameter, i.e.,

$$\rho_{12} = \sin\left[\frac{\pi}{2}\tau_{12}\right] = \sin\left(\frac{\pi}{2} \times 0.6\right) = 0.80902$$

2. We generate 1000 correlated pairs of random normal values using $\rho_{12}$, and the code is as follows:

```
octave:2> z = mvn_rnd([1 0.80902; 0.80902 1],1000);
```

3. Convert these $z$ values into [0, 1] variates using the normal CDF, i.e.,

```
octave:3> u1 = normal_cdf(z(:,1)); u2 = normal_cdf(z(:,2));
```

4. Generate the random values by parsing the $u_i$ through their respective marginal distributions. This is done by inverting the CDF for each marginal distribution.

```
octave:4> x1 = exponential_inv(u1,0.1); x2 = chisquare_inv(u2,3);
```

We can then also examine the correlation between the variables $x_1$ and $x_2$. This is equal to 0.78936, and is computed as follows:

```
octave:5> corrcoef([x1  x2])
ans =
  1.00000  0.78936
  0.78936  1.00000
octave:6> ktau(x1,x2)
ans = 0.59775
```

The rank correlation we started out with, i.e., $\tau = 0.6$, is preserved, as the final rank correlation is also almost the same, i.e., 0.59775. The linear correlation is also almost the same as its original value of 0.8, but this need not in fact always be the case. The scatter plot of the bivariate distribution is presented in Figure 34.3.   ∎

## Tail Dependence

The significant benefit of the copula method lies in the ability to tune "tail dependence" in the joint distribution. What does this mean? In nontechnical terms, tail dependence is the extent to which the correlation in the joint distribution comes from extremal observations rather than central observations. As we have seen in Figure 34.2, the Students's $t$ simulation generates a scatter plot with many more jointly extreme observations. Hence, its tail dependence would be higher than that of the normal distribution. Tail dependence is usually spoken of more specifically as left- or right-tail dependence, depending on which tail evidences higher correlation relative to the central part of the joint distribution.

Intuitively, tail dependence depends on the interaction of the various distributions coupled together by the copula. The choice of the copula may also permit the choice of tail dependence. For instance, when using a Students's $t$ copula, the lower the degrees of freedom, the higher is the tail dependence that is achieved. Many other copulas also have parameters that permit tuning of the extent of tail dependence. One special class is that of Archimedean copulas.

## Archimedean Copulas

The Archimedean copula structure is generally written as the function

$$C(F_1, \ldots, F_m) = \Omega^{-1}[\Omega(F_1) + \ldots + \Omega(F_m)]$$

**FIGURE 34.3**
Exponential and
Chi-Square with a
Normal Copula

The x-variable relates to an exponential distribution with parameter 0.1; the y-variable is based on a chi-square distribution with 3 degrees of freedom. The rank correlation between the variables is assumed to be 0.6.

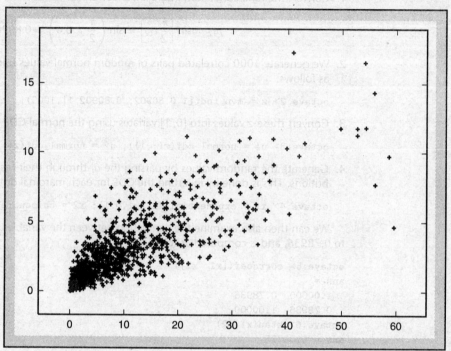

The function $\Omega(F)$ is known as the "generator" of the copula. Frees and Valdez (1998) summarize various examples of generators. For instance, the Gumbel copula has a generator $\Omega(F) = (-ln(F))^\alpha$.

**Example 34.8**

An example will illustrate some of the features of Archimedean copulae. Consider a Gumbel copula with random variables from two distribution functions $F_1$ and $F_2$. The copula is as follows:

$$C(F_1, F_2) = \Omega^{-1}[(-\ln F_1)^\alpha + (-\ln F_2)^\alpha]$$

where $\Omega(F_i) = (-\ln F_i)^\alpha = y$ is as above. Inverting this function, we get

$$\Omega^{-1}[y] = e^{-y^{1/\alpha}}$$

Substituting and rearranging, we get

$$C(F_1, F_2) = \exp\left\{-\left[\left(\ln\frac{1}{F_1}\right)^\alpha + \left(\ln\frac{1}{F_2}\right)^\alpha\right]^{\frac{1}{\alpha}}\right\}$$

To check that this does result in a joint distribution function on [0, 1] we verify the following:

$$\lim_{\substack{F_1 \to 0 \\ F_2 \to 0}} C(F_1, F_2) = 0, \qquad \lim_{\substack{F_1 \to 1 \\ F_2 \to 1}} C(F_1, F_2) = 1$$

In the Gumbel copula, tail dependence depends on the parameter $\alpha$. As $\alpha$ increases, the extent of tail dependence increases. In Figure 34.4, we see how the density function varies

**FIGURE 34.4**

Tail Dependence in the Gumbel Copula

This graph shows how the density function varies as the tail dependence parameter $\alpha$ is varied. We hold $F_1 = 0.5$ and then compute the density function as $F_2$ varies from 0 to 1. When $\alpha = 2$, as in the left-side plot, the graph is less leptokurtic than when $\alpha = 4$ as in the right-side plot.

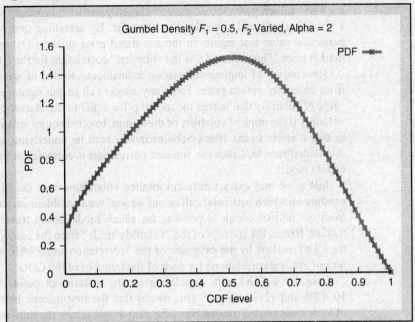

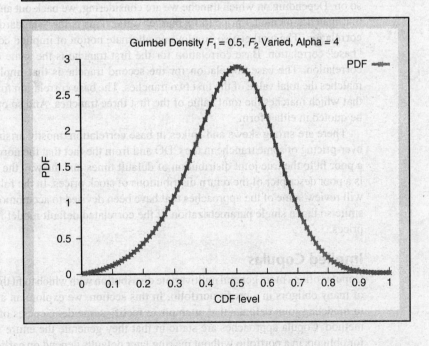

as the tail dependence parameter $\alpha$ is varied. We hold $F_1 = 0.5$ and then compute the density function as $F_2$ varies from 0 to 1. When $\alpha = 2$, as in the left-side plot, the graph is less leptokurtic than when $\alpha = 4$ as in the right-side plot.  ∎

## Implied Correlation from Copulas

In practice, the price of a CDO tranche may be used to "imply" the correlation of default times among the reference names in a CDO. This assumes that all obligors in the CDO have the same pairwise correlation coefficient $\rho$. If the default probabilities of the obligors are known, then given the single correlation parameter $\rho$, we simulate loss samples from a normal copula and price the CDO tranche. By searching over values of $\rho$, we find its particular value that results in the simulated price of the CDO tranche that matches its market price. This value of $\rho$ is the "implied" correlation for the CDO tranche.

The concept of implied correlation is analogous to that of implied volatility extracted from an equity option price. From any single call or put option on a stock, we find the value of volatility that makes the model price equal to the market price of the option. This volatility is the implied volatility of the option. Implied equity volatility is model dependent in that it refers to the Black-Scholes model with its underlying assumption of normally distributed returns. Likewise, implied correlation is extracted with reference to a normal copula model.

Just as we may extract different implied volatilities from the Black-Scholes model depending on which particular call or put we use, we also obtain varying implied correlations from the normal copula depending on which model-based tranche price is matched to market. Hence, the concept of the "volatility smile" from the equity markets is mirrored in the CDO markets by the existence of the "correlation smile." The correlation smile is the plot of implied correlations for each of the tranches of the CDO.

Consider a CDO with tranches given by attachment points 0–3%, 3–7%, 7–10%, 10–12% and 12% onward.[1] This means that the first tranche bears entirely the first 3% of losses, the second tranche bears the next 4% of losses, the third tranche the next 3%, and so on. Depending on which tranche we are considering, we back out an implied correlation that matches its model price to its market value. This is the "standard" notion of implied correlation. The market also employs an alternate notion of implied correlation, known as "base" correlation. Base correlation for the first tranche is the same as standard implied correlation. The base correlation for the second tranche is that implied correlation that matches the total value of the first two tranches. The base correlation for the third tranche is that which matches the total value of the first three tranches. And so on. Correlations may be quoted in either form.

There are strong skews and spikes in base correlation, mostly arising from the relative over-pricing of some tranche in the CDO and from the fact that the normal copula provides a poor fit to the true joint distribution of default times just the way the normal distribution is a poor descriptor of the return distributions of stock prices. In the following sections, we will review some of the approaches that have been devised to accommodate the correlation smile so that a single parametrization of the correlated default model fits all CDO tranche prices.

## Implied Copulas

Copulas offer a more general multivariate distribution with which to fit the joint default times of many obligors in a credit portfolio. In this section, we explore an alternative approach to modeling joint defaults that attempts to rectify some deficiencies of the normal copula method. Copula approaches are static in that they generate the entire set of default times for obligors in a portfolio without making later defaults depend on earlier ones. Hence, it is

---

[1] Attachment points circumscribe the loss ranges for each tranche. Hence, the 3–7% tranche bears all losses from 3% of the face value of the CDO to 7%.

not easy to impose path dependence in defaults in copula settings. Hull and White (2006c) argue that in particular, the Gaussian copula model implies a reduction in uncertainty about future hazard rates as the horizon increases, which does not accord well with empirical data. Using the $t$-copula may provide an antidote to this problem since the extra tail fatness in the distribution of hazard rates of default fits the data better.

Copula models calibrated to underlying issuer CDS quotes are not empirically able to exactly match prices of CDS on CDX indexes and their tranche prices simultaneously. This is reflected in the fact that the implied correlation between obligors in a CDO structure is different depending on which tranche we imply the correlation from. This is prima facie evidence that the shape of the joint distribution generated by the copula model is different from the empirical one implied by the prices of CDO tranches. In short, it is well-nigh impossible to exactly match the prices of all CDO tranches with one set of copula parameters. Hence, fitting a copula to a system of joint default is known to be an imperfect exercise. Nevertheless, market participants still use copulas, particularly the Gaussian copula, simply because it is tractable. They have also become comfortable with different "base" correlations calibrated to different tranches, resulting in the "correlation smile" in almost the same manner in which traders in options are intuitively comfortable with the volatility smile.

The "implied copula" technique, developed by Hull and White (2006b), is an attempt to rectify the imperfect fit of copula models. Hull and White christened their implied copula model as a "perfect" copula. While there is no rigorous definition of "perfectness" that we know of, certainly a system of joint default that exactly matches all tranche prices at a given point in time has a certain appeal. It is conceptually similar to the ideas developed in Rubinstein (1994) for fitting an option tree that exactly matches the prices of all options of a given maturity.

Consider a one-factor model driven by a single common variable $X$. Each obligor $j$ has a default indicator $Y_j$ related to the common factor through the following model:

$$Y_j = \rho_j X + \sqrt{1 - \rho_j^2} \, Z_j, \quad \forall j$$

where the coefficient $\rho_j$ provides the link that makes all obligors in the credit portfolio correlated via the common factor $X$. $Z_j$ is an idiosyncratic shock variable with distribution function $H_j$. $Y_j$ has a distribution function denoted $F_j$. We are interested in generating the distribution of default times $\tau_j$, denoted $G_j$, by mapping the distribution of $Y_j$ to that of $\tau_j$. The correlation that exists in $Y_j$ induces a correlation in the default times $\tau_j$ of all obligors in the credit portfolio. Hence, we consider the mapping defined by $\tau_j = G_j^{-1}[F_j(Y_j)]$. Such mappings exist in all copula models; see, for example, the implementation scheme outlined in Section 34.8.

Conditional on a fixed value of $X$, the probability of default may be defined by the likelihood of random variable $Y_j$ being less than a cut-off level $Y$ (based on the probability of default of the obligor), i.e.,

$$\text{Prob}[Y_j < Y | X] = H_j \left[ \frac{Y - \rho_j X}{\sqrt{1 - \rho_j^2}} \right]$$

Since this maps directly into default time, we may also write the probability of defaulting in time $\tau$ as

$$\text{Prob}[\tau_j < t | X] = G_j(t | X) = H_j \left[ \frac{F_j^{-1}[G(t)] - \rho_j X}{\sqrt{1 - \rho_j^2}} \right] \tag{34.19}$$

We can see that as $X$ increases, the probability of default decreases (which is clear from either one of the preceding equations). The key here is that the joint default of firms depends mainly on the time path of the driving factor $X$. Hence, by choosing a model with a rich enough structure for the evolution of $X$, we should be able to exactly fit the prices of all tranches in a CDO structure. This is analogous to "finding" the perfect copula.

Let us assume that we are interested in finding the system that best matches the prices of a five-year CDS on the CDX index and five tranche prices, that is, six prices in all. We proceed through the following steps.

1. Select distributions $H_j$ for all obligors. The normal distribution for $X$ would be a natural choice.

2. Select distributions $F_j$ and $G_j$ for all obligors. These will describe the mapping from $Y_j$ to default times $\tau_j$ and implicitly define the copula that is being used. (This is analogous to the choice of distributions $F$ and $\Phi$ in Section 34.8.) This is where the connection to copulas arises in this model.

3. Calibrate the values of $\rho_j$ such that the model prices of individual CDS on the obligors match market prices. The loss distribution of each issuer is based on default probabilities from equation (34.19) computed over all values of $X$.

4. Generate $n$ possible values of $X$, that is, $X_i$, $i = 1 \ldots n$ and denote the probabilities of each outcome as $p_i$, $\sum_i p_i = 1$. These should be chosen in a way to cover the range of values $Y_j$. Hull and White (2006b) suggest that $n \geq 50$. Each value of $X$ implies a default time distribution $G_j(\tau|X_i)$ for all obligors. This also implies an expected set of cash flows (a recovery rate needs to be assumed) for the CDO and its tranches, which may then be used to value these securities. By appropriately choosing the sets of $\{X_i, p_i\}$, match the prices of all securities.

Of course, this approach has many more degrees of freedom than needed. Fitting should be easily achieved. If $n = 50$, then there are 100 parameters (50 values of $X$ and 50 of $p$) with which to fit just six prices. There are an infinite number of ways in which to achieve this. Which one do we choose? Hull and White (2006b) suggest that the $X$ values be chosen in a manner that imposes equal spacing between the different values of $X$. If we assume that $X$ is normally distributed, then centering its values around zero should suggest a range of values spaced equally apart between $-3$ and $3$. For other distributions, the standard ranges suggest themselves just as easily. By imposing some smoothness properties on the probabilities $p$, a natural choice of the implied copula is feasible. Therefore, it is possible to narrow down the range of "implied" distributions that are employed. The overfitting that is undertaken here is a natural consequence of setting up a model that mimics an incomplete markets setting in which the number of states being used exceeds the number of securities being spanned. This is analogous to extracting the probability distribution induced by options in the approach pioneered by Breeden and Litzenberger (1978), which is, however, a complete markets approach.

Hull and White (2006c) report that the fitting scheme is extremely stable. We refer the reader to their paper in which they suggest an optimization approach to select the system of $\{X_i, p_i\}$ that is calibrated to market prices. The outcomes of this approach are said to be less sensitive to the interpolation procedures used and to minor variations in base correlations, both problems that occur frequently with regular copulas. Most important, the model prices in this approach, by dint of being exactly matched to market, are arbitrage free by fiat, a desirable property for any model. The implied copula approach may, however, lead to overfitting in sample with the result that out-of-sample values might be less accurate. This is, of course, an empirical matter.

# 34.9   Top-Down Modeling of Credit Portfolio Loss

We have seen how credit portfolio loss distributions may be built up from individual loss distributions in the so-called bottom-up approach in which probabilities of default are determined either in a structural or a reduced-form framework. Further, we have seen how the joint distribution of default may be specified as multivariate Gaussian or much more generally using copula functions.

In this section, we will consider the "top-down" class of portfolio credit models in which the object of interest is the aggregate portfolio credit loss distribution, not individual loss distributions. Here aggregate loss is modeled directly without recourse to individual probabilities of default.

## Longstaff and Rajan's Model

An empirically implemented example of the top-down class of models is by Longstaff and Rajan (2008). They show that a three-factor top-down model provides the best fit to CDX (CDO index) data. To keep the exposition simple, we will examine only a one-factor version of their model here. The extension to more factors is simple and will be described at the end of this section.

Let the underlying credit portfolio be normalized to a face value of \$1 and contain $M$ issuers, each with equal face value. For example, the CDX (North America) index is equally weighted among 125 issuers. We start at time 0 and let the cumulative portfolio loss at time $t$ on this \$1 portfolio be denoted as $L_t$. Naturally, $L_0 = 0$.

The instantaneous proportional loss on the current value of the portfolio is therefore given by $dL/(1 - L)$, and Longstaff and Rajan (2008) specify this as follows:

$$\frac{dL}{1 - L} = \gamma \, dN(\lambda)$$

where $N$ is a Poisson counter with intensity $\lambda$, i.e., losses arrive at rate $\lambda$ per unit time (usually annual). The variable $\gamma$ is the loss size. Hence, every time a loss event occurs, the portfolio's total loss increases by an amount $\gamma$. Integrating the equation above, we arrive at the expression for losses $L_t$:

$$\int_0^t \frac{dL}{1 - L} = \int_0^t \gamma \, dN$$

and solving given that $N_0 = 0$ gives

$$L_t = 1 - e^{-\gamma \, N_t(\lambda_t)}$$

Hence, the number of default events $N_t$ translates naturally into the loss level $L_t$. There are many possible stochastic specifications for this model. The arrival rate of default events $\lambda$ may be either constant or based on a stochastic process. We will explore both cases here. The loss severity $\gamma$ may be a constant or drawn from a distribution. Both $\lambda$ and $\gamma$ may be functions of underlying state variables and, thus, default and loss severity may be set up to have general correlation to each other.

Suppose that $\gamma$ and $\lambda$ are constant. Then the probability distribution of $L_t$ is determined entirely by the probability function $p_j \equiv \text{Prob}(N_t = j)$, where $j = \{0, 1, 2, 3, \ldots\}$. That is,

$$p_j = \frac{e^{-\lambda} \lambda^j}{j!}$$

The discrete loss distribution is very easy to compute.

What if $\gamma$ is constant but the rate of default $\lambda$ comes from a distribution or from a stochastic process in which its value changes over time (as in the case of the Longstaff and Rajan, 2008, model)? In this setting,

$$p_j = \int_{\lambda_t} \frac{e^{-\lambda_t} \lambda_t^j}{j!} f(\lambda_t) \, d\lambda_t$$

where $f(\lambda_t)$ is the probability density function of $\lambda_t$.

To illustrate, let the distribution for $\lambda_t$ come from a beta distribution with parameters $\{\alpha, \beta\}$ denoted as follows:

$$f(\lambda_t) = \frac{\Gamma(\alpha + \beta)}{\Gamma(\alpha)\Gamma(\beta)} (1 - \lambda_t)^{\beta-1} \lambda_t^{\alpha-1}$$

Then the probability function would be

$$p_j = \int_{\lambda_t} \frac{e^{-\lambda_t} \lambda_t^j}{j!} \frac{\Gamma(\alpha + \beta)}{\Gamma(\alpha)\Gamma(\beta)} (1 - \lambda_t)^{\beta-1} \lambda_t^{\alpha-1} \, d\lambda_t$$

Any function $g(L_t)$ of loss $L_t$, such as the price of a CDO tranche, is also a function of $N_t$, and is driven by probability function $p_j(\lambda_t)$. These pricing functions may be computed in closed-form in special cases, else numerical computation of the expectation $E[g(L_t)]$ is feasible. In our simple version here, the pricing model would have three parameters: $\{\alpha, \beta, \gamma\}$, and we could calibrate the parameters of the model by using three or more CDO tranche prices. Since the CDO tranches can be priced in the model using the loss probability distribution, a simple least squares fit of tranche prices to model prices may be undertaken to find the best values of the unknown parameters. Hence, the Longstaff and Rajan (2008) model is very easy to fit to the data.

The model may be generalized to $n$ factors by setting the specification to be

$$\frac{dL}{1-L} = \sum_{k=1}^{n} \gamma_k \, dN_k$$

with a solution given by

$$L_t = 1 - \exp\left[ -\sum_{k=1}^{n} \gamma_k N_{tk}(\lambda_k) \right]$$

Now the number of parameters increases for as many processes as are used to drive the loss process of the credit portfolio. The number of processes might be increased until the mean-squared pricing error is within tolerable bounds.

## Self-Exciting Default Models

Other authors have provided alternative implementations of top-down models. For an early example, see Giesecke and Goldberg (2005). A special enhancement of top-down models is that of Errais, Giesecke, and Goldberg (2006). In this model, the hazard rate of default $\lambda$ is specified as a function of the current loss level $L$ itself. The main point of this specification is that it captures the clustering of default identified in Das, Duffie, Kapadia, and Saita (2007). Since the default intensity $\lambda$ grows with accumulating defaults, it makes defaults cluster in just the same manner as seen in the data.

In a one-factor setting, the model of Longstaff and Rajan (2008) would be specified as follows:

$$\frac{dL}{1-L} = \gamma \, dN(\lambda(L))$$

where $\partial\lambda/\partial L > 0$; the only enhancement to the model of Longstaff and Rajan (2008) is that intensity is specified as $\lambda(L)$. And for strong clustering, the second derivative will be positive as well. A process such as this is known as a Hawkes process and is called "self-exciting" or "self-affecting." Specifically, think of intensity $(\lambda_t)$ following a simple stochastic process of the form

$$d\lambda = \alpha(\beta - \lambda)\, dt + \delta\, dL$$

That is, there is a jump in intensity every time there is a loss-triggering event ($dL > 0$). We require that $\delta > 0$ for the effect to be self-exciting. Hence, every time there is a loss, the intensity jumps and then slowly reverts to its mean level $\beta$ at rate $\alpha$. Therefore, the self-exciting loss process is a simple yet powerful extension to the class of top-down correlated default models. Errais et al. (2006) provide closed-form expressions for the loss distributions in this model. Loss distributions in this model have fatter tails than those of a Poisson distribution.

## Top-Down Models with Binomial Trees

Hull and White (2006a) show how we can implement the top-down modeling approach on a binomial tree. Despite being simple, the approach allows for dynamic modeling of portfolio losses, in contrast to modeling correlated default times using copulas, which is a static approach. We present a simple version of their model and then discuss how it may be extended to more complex settings.

The main idea in the Hull and White (2006a) model is that portfolio credit derivatives are priced off expected cash flows (for the entire portfolio or for specific tranches of the portfolio) at discrete points in time. By modeling these cash flows directly, the pricing of CDOs, tranches on CDOs, and other basket derivatives can be considerably simplified. The expected cash flows are functions of *each* issuer's cumulative survival function $S(t)$, which is the well-known expression:

$$S(t) = \exp\left[-\int_0^t \lambda(u)\, du\right]$$

where $\lambda(t)$ is the hazard rate of default. The probability of default up to time $t$ is the expectation $q = E[1 - S(t)]$. We also note that $S(0) = 1$ and $S(t) \geq 0$.

The model is based on a time line where defaults and cash flows occur at discrete points in time: $t_1, t_2, \ldots, t_m$. Let the time interval be constant, i.e., $t_i - t_{i-1} = h$. Noting that $\lambda(0) = 0$, at every point in time, we assume that the change in $\lambda$ is given by the following scheme:

$$\Delta\lambda = \mu\, h + J$$

where $\mu \geq 0$ is a drift term, and $J \geq 0$ is a jump in intensity that occurs with probability $p$. Therefore, with probability $p$, $\lambda$ jumps by $J$, but with probability $(1 - p)$, there is no jump. For now, we assume that $\mu$, $J$, and $p$ are all constant.

The movement in $\lambda$ over time may be represented on a binomial tree as follows. Starting at time $t = 0$, the value of $\lambda(0)$ is zero. In the next period, we have that accumulated $\lambda$ intensity will be either $\mu\, h + J$ with probability $p$ or $\mu\, h$ with probability $(1 - p)$. We will denote the accumulated intensity with the variable $I$. After two periods, $I(t_2)$ will be one of three values:

$$I(t_2) = \{2\mu\, h + 2J, \quad 2\mu\, h + J, \quad 2\mu\, h\}$$

**FIGURE 34.5**

Binomial Tree with the Values of $I$, the Cumulated Intensity Process for Each Issuer

Each up move occurs with probability $p$ and down moves with probability $(1 - p)$.

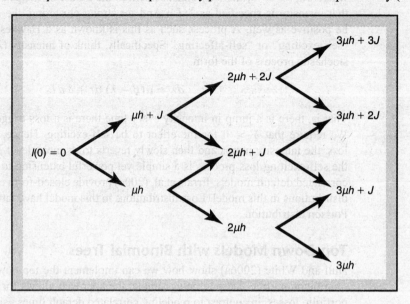

with probabilities

$$\{p^2, \quad p(1 - p), \quad (1 - p)^2\}$$

respectively. The survival function at each node on the tree will simply be $S(t) = \exp[-I(t)]$. The tree of values of $I$ is shown in Figure 34.5.

Since at each node of the tree we have the accumulated intensity $I$, we also have the survival function $S = e^{-I}$ and the cumulative probability of defaults $q = 1 - S$. Assuming that there are $N$ identical issuers in the credit portfolio, each with face value $1/N$, gives us a normalized credit portfolio value at the outset of \$1. Let the recovery rate on default be constant and denoted $\phi$. The probability that $n$ of these $N$ names has defaulted by the time we reach a given node on the tree is given by the binomial formula

$$P(n) = \frac{N!}{n!(N - n)!} \, q^n (1 - q)^{N-n}, \quad \forall n = 0, 1, \ldots, N \qquad \textbf{(34.20)}$$

Then it is easy to calculate the expected principal balance ($B$) of the credit portfolio at this node as

$$E(B) = \sum_{n=1}^{N} P(n)[1 - (n/N)(1 - \phi)]$$

Suppose that we have a derivative that pays rate $s$ on the principal balance over time; we may easily price this by working out $E(B)$ at each node of the tree, multiplying it by $s$, and then discounting the cash flows on the tree by backward recursion using the branching probabilities $p, 1 - p$ to weight the cash flows.

As another example, say we are interested in a tranched security with lower and upper attachment points $(x_l, x_u) \leq 1$. The expected principal balance at each node will be given by

$$E(B) = \sum_{n=1}^{N} P(n)T(n)$$

where

$$T(n) = \begin{cases} 1 & \text{if } (n/N)(1-\phi) \leq x_l \\ \frac{x_u-(n/N)(1-\phi)}{x_u-x_l} & \text{if } x_l < (n/N)(1-\phi) \leq x_u \\ 0 & \text{if } (n/N)(1-\phi) > x_u \end{cases}$$

And any function of these cash flows may be taken to construct a tranche derivative.

The same process may be run in reverse in order to calibrate securities in the model. We may choose a set of CDOs and CDO tranches and then choose the values of $\mu$, $J$ (maybe even $\phi$) such that model prices best match observed prices in the market. Note also that if more degrees of freedom are needed to fit market prices, it is easy to make $J$ dependent on both time and state on the tree. If we make $J$ higher for nodes on the upper levels of the tree relative to lower levels, then we are also accounting implicitly for contagion in the credit portfolio. Therefore, this model is quite flexible while remaining easy to calibrate.

As with all top-down models, modeling credit portfolio losses is parsimonious in the Hull and White (2006a) model. Their model is especially useful since its representation on the tree makes it simple to implement as well as easy to understand. It also offers easy generalization to state and time dependence of default rates. The downside, of course, is that given $n$ defaults out of $N$ issuers, there is no way to identify which names defaulted along any path. This is a crucial difference between all top-down models and their distant cousins, the bottom-up models. The other drawback of the model presented above is that we assumed all issuers to have identical trees for cumulated intensity processes. This made the calculation in equation (34.20) simple. This is denoted by Hull and White (2006a) as the "homogenous" case of their model. The case in which intensity trees are different for each issuer in the credit portfolio is called the "heterogenous" case. In this setting, the method for computing the loss distribution at each node of the aggregate tree and, hence, the principal balance, would proceed along the lines of the fast recursion scheme presented earlier in the model of Andersen et al. (2003).

## 34.10   Summary

We have seen that modeling default correlations is more complex than modeling return or price correlations. This is because default correlations are based on the comovement of indicator (i.e., discrete, binomial) variables, whereas correlations are usually based on variables over a continuous range of values. Nevertheless, we portrayed the probability calculations required in a simple manner so as to be able to implement basic models of correlated default with a view to pricing a range of basket default securities.

We explored how to simulate correlated defaults in baskets of issuers in both frameworks, structural models and reduced-form models. In fact, one can safely say that this analysis of correlated defaults shows that these two model classes are not as different from each other as one might imagine when looking at the models separately in Chapters 32 and 33. Simulating correlated default raises the challenge of managing high-dimensional random vector generation, and we examined how these large-scale systems could be circumscribed using projections onto smaller factor spaces.

But simulations are always time consuming, and in the fast-paced, competitive environs of Wall Street and trading arenas around the world, the search is on for quick algorithms to generate credit portfolio loss distributions. For simpler payoffs on security baskets, there are a few fast approaches that have been developed. Some use Fourier transforms with probability generating functions—see the papers by Burtschell et al. (2005), Gregory and Laurent (2003), Gregory and Laurent (2004)—or use a recursion approach (see the paper by Andersen et al., 2003). All these approaches begin with modeling individual firm default risk and build these up to the portfolio level using appropriate correlation structure. We called this the "bottom-up" approach.

More recently, the failure of the bottom-up approach to correctly calibrate to the prices of CDO tranches has increased disillusionment with this method. Turning everything on its head, the "top-down" approach in which the goal is to model directly the shape of the loss distribution rather than to model individual credits is gaining favor. Papers in this vein that represent the early work in the field are by Giesecke and Goldberg (2005), Longstaff and Rajan (2008), Schonbucher (2005), and Sidenius, Piterbarg, and Anderson (2005).

## 34.11 Exercises

1. What is the main difference between a cash flow CDO and a synthetic CDO?

2. What is the primary goal of the following tranche holders in a CDO: (a) the A-tranche, (b) the mezzanine tranche, and (c) the equity tranche?

3. In an $n$-th to default basket in which payment is triggered if there are $n$ defaults in a basket of $m$ bonds, does the value of the contract increase or decrease if (a) $n$ increases, (b) $m$ increases, or (c) the average correlation of bonds increases.

4. In an $n$-th to default basket, assume there are but two bonds. If the correlation of default between these two bonds increases, then what is the impact on (a) a first-to-default basket and (b) a second-to-default basket?

5. There are two firms, A and B, with the probability of A defaulting being 0.05. The conditional probability of B defaulting given A defaulted is 1. If the correlation of default of A and B is 0.30, then what is the probability of B defaulting?

   (a) 0.10

   (b) 0.28

   (c) 0.37

   (d) 0.50

6. For a maturity of $T = 1$ year, let the default probability of a firm be $p = 0.1$. Define an indicator variable $d = 1$ if default occurs and $d = 0$ if default does not occur.

   (a) What is $E(d)$?

   (b) What is $Var(d)$?

7. There are two firms with default probabilities $p_1 = 0.1$, $p_2 = 0.2$. The correlation of joint default $\rho(d_1, d_2) = 0.5$ where $d_1, d_2$ are indicator variables for default of each firm. What is the probability of both firms defaulting?

8. If $Pr[d_1 \cap d_2] = 0.08$ and $p_1 = 0.1$, $p_2 = 0.2$, what is $Pr(d_1|d_2)$ and $Pr(d_2|d_1)$?

9. Given two firms, if the probability of neither defaulting is 80% and the probability of each defaulting is $p_1 = 0.1$ and $p_2 = 0.2$, what is the probability of both defaulting?

10. If $Pr(d_1 \cap d_2) = 0.01$ and $p_1 = 0.1$, $p_2 = 0.2$, what is the probability of exactly one default?

11. In the previous question, what is the expected payoff of a first-to-default and a second-to-default contract, both of which pay $100 if the contract is triggered?

12. Given two firms, if the probability of default of firm 1 is $p_1 = 0.2$ and the conditional probability of firm 2 defaulting if firm 1 defaults is $Pr(d_2|d_1) = 0.9$, find the expected payoff (based on $100) of a first-to-default and a second-to-default contract if you assume that the probability of neither firm defaulting is half that of both firms defaulting.

13. Based on a structural model that assumes a normal distribution of firm value, the distance to default for firm 1 is $DTD_1 = 2$. Likewise, for firm 2, $DTD_2 = 1$. If the correlation of default between the two firms is 0.3, what is the probability of joint default?

14. Suppose default intensities are lognormally distributed for $n$ firms with identical intensities given by $\lambda = e^x$ where $x \sim N(\mu, \sigma^2)$. Explain the sequence of steps you would follow to generate $\lambda_1, \lambda_2, \ldots, \lambda_n$ from a Gaussian copula with common correlation $\rho$ among all firms.

15. If intensities $\lambda_i \sim \exp(\mu_i)$, $i = 1 \ldots 5$, where $\mu_i = 10$ is the parameter of an exponential distribution with mean $1/\mu_i$, then use a Gaussian copula to simulate defaults from 10,000 runs with a correlation of $\rho = 0.5$. Find the probability that the number of defaults in one year is more than or equal to 2.

16. If the intensity of default is 0.2, what is the expected time to default?

17. If the expected time to default is four years, what is the probability of default in less than two years?

18. Two firms have rank correlation of default given by Kendall's tau $= 0.6$. The probability of default of the first firm is $p_1 = 0.05$ and that of the second firm is $p_2 = 0.20$. Find the probability of joint default if default is triggered using correlated random variables as follows: generate $x_1, x_2$ from a bivariate standard normal distribution; default is triggered if $N(x) < p$. Repeat the exercise but draw from a Student's $t$ $(0,1)$ distribution with degrees of freedom equal to 5 and the same correlation. Default is triggered if $t(x) < p$. Compare your results from the two distributions.

19. In a system of three firms, we simulate default by drawing three $x_i \sim N(0, 1)$ random variables. We say that default occurs if $x_i < -2$. What is the probability of all three firms defaulting if their joint distribution is described by a Gumbel copula with tail dependence parameter $\alpha = 2$? Does the probability of all firms defaulting increase if $\alpha = 5$?

20. The following several questions relate to models for 20 issuers in a correlated default framework. You are required to develop a model for correlated default using the Octave programming language if required. You need to provide (a) a well-documented answer to all questions, (b) program code used, and (c) results from run-time execution of the program to demonstrate that the program works.

    Assume that you are forming a credit portfolio using 20 issuers, all of which have default intensity of $\lambda = 0.05$. This default intensity is constant. The recovery rate on each issuer's securities in the event of default is also given as 40% of the par value of the security. The correlation of default of all issuers is 0.3. For a five-year horizon, what is the expected loss on an equally weighted portfolio of $100 in value?

21. If you assume that the joint distribution of default times is multivariate normal, then what is the standard deviation of the loss distribution?

22. Show the steps in Octave that are needed to simulate the losses from this set of issuers using a Gaussian copula that combines a set of Gaussian marginal distributions and report the mean of the loss distribution for this portfolio.

23. Find the value of a first-to-default basket option with a maturity of one year. Assume that the payoff is $100.

24. What would happen to the price of this first-to-default security if there were no correlation of default between issuers?

25. Find the value of a second-to-default basket option with a maturity of one year. Keep the assumptions the same as in the previous question.

# Bibliography

Acerbi, Carlo, Nordio, Claudio, and Sirtori, Carlo (2001). "Expected Shortfall as a Tool for Financial Risk Management". http://www.gloriamundi.org/var/wps.html, Working Paper.

Acerbi, Carlo and Tasche, Dirk (2002). "Expected Shortfall: A Natural Coherent Alternative to Value at Risk". *Economic Notes*, 31(2):379.

Acharya, Viral, Huang, Jingzhi, Subrahmanyam, Marti, and Sundaram, Rangarajan (2006). "When Does Strategic Debt Service Matter?" *Economic Theory*, 29(2):363–378.

Ahn, Dong-Hyun, Figlewski, Steve, and Gao, Bin (1999). "Pricing Discrete Barrier Options with an Adaptive Mesh Model". *Journal of Derivatives*, Summer:33–43.

Amerio, Emanuele (2005). "Forward Prices and Futures Prices: A Note on Convexity Drift Adjustment". *Journal of Alternative Investments*, 8(2), Fall, 80–86.

Ames, William (1992). "Numerical Methods for Partial Differential Equations". *Academic Press*, 3rd edition, San Diego.

Amin, Kaushik and Ng, Victor (1992). "Equilibrium Option Valuation with Systematic Stochastic Volatility". *University of Michigan*, Working Paper.

Andersen, L. and Brotherton-Ratcliffe, R. (1997). "The Equity Option Volatility Smile: An Implicit Finite-Difference Approach". *Journal of Computational Finance*, 1:5–38.

Andersen, Leif, Sidenius, J., and Basu, S. (2003). "All Your Hedges in One Basket". *RISK*, November:67–72.

Anderson, Ronald and Sundaresan, Suresh (1996). "Design and Valuation of Debt Contracts". *The Review of Financial Studies*, 9:37–68.

Artzner, Philipe, Delbaen, Freddy, Eber, Jean-Marc, and Heath, David (1999). "Coherent Measures of Risk". *Mathematical Finance*, 9:203–228.

Back, Kerry (1996). "Yield Curve Models: A Mathematical Review". Option Embedded Bonds: Price Analysis, Credit Risk, and Investment Strategies, Ed: I. Nelken, Irwin, New York:3–36.

Backus, David, Foresi, Silverio, Li, Kai, and Wu, Liuren (1997). "Accounting for Biases in Black-Scholes". *New York University: Stern School of Business*, Working Paper.

Bardhan, Inderjit, Berger, Alex, Derman, Emanuel, Dosembet, Cemal, and Kani, Iraj (1994). "Valuing Convertible Bonds as Derivative". *Goldman Sachs Quantitative Strategies Research Notes*, November.

Barone-Adesi, Giovani, Engle, Robert, and Mancini, L (2004). "GARCH Options in Incomplete Markets". *University of Zurich*, NCCR-FinRisk Paper No. 155.

Bates, David (1996). "Jumps and Stochastic Volatility: Exchange Rate Processes Implicit in DM Options". *Review of Financial Studies*, 9(1):69–107.

Beaglehole, David and Tenney, Mark (1992). "Corrections and Additions to 'A Nonlinear Equilibrium Model of the Term Structure of Interest Rates' ". *Journal of Financial Economics*, 32:345–353.

Bielecki, Tomasz and Rutkowski, Marek (2002). "Credit Risk: Modeling, Valuation, and Hedging". *Springer*, New York.

Black, Fischer (1976). "The Pricing of Commodity Contracts". *Journal of Financial Economics*, 3:167–179.

Black, Fischer and Cox, John (1976). "Valuing Corporate Securities: Some Effects of Bond Indenture Provisions". *Journal of Finance*, 31(2):351–367.

Black, Fischer, Derman, Emanual, and Toy, William (1990). "A One Factor Model of Interest Rates and Its Application to Treasury Bond Options". *Financial Analysts Journal*, January–February:33–39.

Black, Fischer and Scholes, Myron (1973). "The Pricing of Options and Corporate Liabilities". *Journal of Political Economy*, 81(3):637–654.

Bollerslev, Tim (1986). "Generalized Autoregressive Conditional Heteroskedasticity". *Journal of Econometrics*, 31:307–327.

Bolster, P., Chance, Donald, and Rich, Donald (1996). "Executive Equity Swaps and Corporate Insider Holdings". *Financial Management*, 25 Summer:14–24.

Boudoukh, Jacob, Richardson, Matthew, and Whitelaw, Robert (1995). "Expect the Worst". *Risk*, 8(9):100–101.

Boyle, Phelim (1977). "Options: A Monte Carlo Approach". *Journal of Financial Economics*, 4:323–338.

Boyle, Phelim, Broadie, Mark, and Glasserman, Paul (1997). "Monte Carlo Methods for Security Pricing". *Journal of Economic Dynamics and Control*, 21:1267–1321.

Boyle, Phelim and Lau, S.H. (1994). "Bumping up Against the Barrier with the Binomial Method". *Journal of Derivatives*, 1(4):6–14.

Brace, Alan, Gatarek, Darius, and Musiela, Marek (1997). "The Market Model of Interest Rate Dynamics". *Mathematical Finance*, 7:127–155.

Breeden, Douglas and Litzenberger, Robert (1978). "Prices of State-Contingent Claims Implicit in Option Prices". *Journal of Business*, 51:621–651.

Brennan, Michael and Schwartz, Eduardo (1979). "A Continuous Time Approach to the Pricing of Bonds". *Journal of Banking and Finance*, 3(2):133–155.

Brennan, Michael J. and Schwartz, Eduardo S. (1985). "Evaluating Natural Resource Investment". *Journal of Business*, 58(2):135–157.

Brenner, Menachem and Dan Galai (1989). "New Financial Instruments to Hedge Changes in Volatility". *Financial Analysts Journal*, July–August 1989, 61–65.

Brenner, Menachem and Dan Galai (1993). "Hedging Volatility in Foreign Currencies". *Journal of Derivatives*, Fall 1993, 53–59.

Brigo, Damiano and Mercurio, Fabio (2001). "Interest Rate Models—Theory and Practice". *Springer-Verlag*, Berlin.

Broadie, Mark, Glasserman, Paul, and Kou, Steve (1997). "A Continuity Correction for Discrete Barrier Options". *Mathematical Finance*, 7(4):325–349.

Broadie, Mark and Sundaresan, Suresh (1992). "Quality and Timing Options in Treasury Future Markets, Theory and Evidence". *Columbia University*, Working Paper.

Burghardt, Galen (2003). "The Eurodollar Futures and Options Handbook". *McGraw-Hill*, New York.

Burghardt, Galen and Hoskins, William (1995a). "The Convexity Bias in Eurodollar Futures: Part I". *Derivatives Quarterly*, 1(3):47–55.

Burghardt, Galen and Hoskins, William (1995b). "The Convexity Bias in Eurodollar Futures: Part II". *Derivatives Quarterly*, 1(4):59–76.

Burtschell, X., Gregory, J., and Laurent, J-P. (2005). "A Comparative Analysis of CDO Pricing Models". *BNP-Paribas*, Working Paper.

Capozza, Dennis and Li, Y. (1994). "The Intensity and Timing of Investment: The Case of Land". *American Economic Review*, 84(4):889–904.

Carayannopolous, Peter and Kalimipalli, Madhu (2003). "Convertible Bonds and Pricing Biases". *Journal of Fixed Income*, 13(3):64–73.

Carr, Peter and Linetsky, Vadim (2006). "A Jump to Default Extended CEV Model: An Application of Bessel Processes". *New York University*, Working Paper.

Carr, Peter and Wu, Liuren (2003). "Finite Moment Log Stable Process and Option Pricing". *Journal of Finance*, 58(2):753–777.

Carr, Peter and Wu, Liuren (2009). "Variance Risk Premiums". *Review of Financial Studies*, 22(3): 1311–1341.

Casassus, Jaime and Collin-Dufresne, Pierre (2005). "Convenience Yields Implied from Interest Rates and Commodity Futures". *Journal of Finance*, 60(5): 2283–2331.

Chan, K.C., Karolyi, Andrew, Longstaff, Francis, and Sanders, Anthony (1992). "An Empirical Comparison of Alternative Models of the Short-Term Interest Rate". *Journal of Finance*, 47(3):1209–1227.

Chance, Don M. and Peterson, Pamela P. (2002). "Real Options and Investment Valuation". *Research Foundation of the AIMR*, Monograph.

Chance, Donald (2003). "Equity Swaps and Equity Investing". *Lousiana State University*, Working Paper.

Chance, Donald and Rich, Donald (1995). "The Pricing of Equity Swaps and Swaptions". *Journal of Derivatives*, 5(4):19–31.

Chang, Carolyn and Chang, Jack (1990). "Forward and Futures Prices: Evidence from the Foreign Exchange Markets". *Journal of Finance*, 45(4):1333–1336.

Chaput, Scott and Ederington, Louis (2003). "Option Spread and Combination Trading". *Journal of Derivatives*, 10(4):72–88.

Chincarini, Ludwig (2006). "The Amaranth Debacle: What Really Happened". *Georgetown University*, Working Paper.

Collin-Dufresne, Pierre and Goldstein, Robert (2001). "Do Credit Spreads Reject Stationary Leverage Ratios?" *Journal of Finance*, 56:1929–1958.

Collin-Dufresne, Pierre, Goldstein, Robert, and Martin, J. Spencer (2001). "The Determinants of Credit Spread Changes". *Journal of Finance*, 56:2177–2208.

Coopers and Lybrand (1992). "Equity Swaps: A Self-Study Guide to Mastering and Applying Equity Swaps". *Probus Publishing*, Chicago and London.

Cornell, Bradford and Reinganum, Marc (1981). " Forward versus Futures Prices: Evidence from the Foreign Exchange Markets". *Journal of Finance*, 36(5):1035–1046.

Coval, Joshua and Shumway, Tyler (2001). "Expected Option Returns". *Journal of Finance*, 56(3):983–1009.

Cox, John, Ingersoll, Jonathan, and Ross, Stephen (1981). "The Relation between Forward Prices and Futures Prices". *Journal of Financial Economics*, 9(4):321–346.

Cox, John, Ingersoll, Jonathan, and Ross, Stephen (1985). "A Theory of the Term Structure of Interest Rates". *Econometrica*, 53(2):385–408.

Cox, John and Ross, Stephen (1976). "The Valuation of Options for Alternative Stochastic Processes". *Journal of Financial Economics*, 3:145–166.

Cox, John, Ross, Stephen, and Rubinstien, Mark (1979). "Option Pricing: A Simplified Approach". *Journal of Financial Economics*, 7:229–265.

Crosbie, Peter and Bohn, Jeffrey (2003). "Modeling Default Risk". *Moodys KMV*, White Paper.

Culp, Christopher and Miller, Merton (1995a). "Corporate Hedging in Theory and Practice: Lessons from Metallgesellschaft". *Risk Books*, London.

Culp, Christopher and Miller, Merton (1995b). "Metallgesellschaft and the Economics of Synthetic Storage". *Journal of Applied Corporate Finance*, Winter:62–76.

Curran, Michael (1994). "Valuing Asian and Portfolio Options by Conditioning on the Geometric Mean Price". *Management Science*, 40(12):1705–1711.

Das, Sanjiv (1995). "Credit Risk Derivatives". *Journal of Derivatives*, 2(3):7–23.

Das, Sanjiv, Duffie, Darrell, Kapadia, Nikunj, and Saita, Leandro (2007). "Common Failings: How Corporate Defaults Cluster". *Journal of Finance*, 62:93–117.

Das, Sanjiv and Sundaram, Rangarajan (1999). "Of Smiles and Smirks: A Term Structure Perspective". *Journal of Financial and Quantitative Analysis*, 34(2):211–240.

Das, Sanjiv and Sundaram, Rangarajan (2000). "A Discrete-Time Approach to Arbitrage-Free Pricing of Credit Derivatives". *Management Science*, 46(1):46–62.

Das, Sanjiv and Sundaram, Rangarajan (2007). "An Integrated Model for Hybrid Securities". *Management Science*, 53:1439–1451.

Das, Sanjiv and Tufano, Peter (1996). "Pricing Credit Sensitive Debt When Interest Rates, Credit Ratings and Credit Spreads Are Stochastic". *Journal of Financial Engineering*, 5(2):161–198.

Davis, Mark and Lischka, Fabian (1999). "Convertible Bonds with Market Risk and Credit Risk". *Tokyo-Mitsubishi Intl, PLC*, Mimeo.

DeGeorge, Francois, Patel, Jayendu, and Zeckhauser, Richard (1999). "Earnings Management to Exceed Thresholds". *Journal of Business*, 72(1):1–33.

Delianedis, Gordon and Geske, Robert (1998). "Credit Risk and Risk Neutral Default Probabilities: Information about Rating Migrations and Defaults". *UCLA*, Working Paper.

Demeterfi, Kresimir, Derman, Emanuel, Kamal, Michael, and Zou, Joseph (1999). "More Than You Ever Wanted to Know about Volatility Swaps". *Goldman Sachs*, Working Paper.

Derman, Emanuel and Kani, Iraj (1994). "The Volatility Smile and Its Implied Tree". *Quantitative Strategies and Research Notes*, Goldman Sachs.

Dezhbaksh, Hashem (1994). "Foreign Exchange Forward and Futures Prices: Are They Equal?" *Journal of Financial and Quantitative Analysis*, 29(1):75–87.

Dixit, Avinash K. (1989). "Entry and Exit Decisions under Uncertainty" *Journal of Political Economy*, 97(3):620–638.

Dothan, Uri (1978). "On the Term Structure of Interest Rates". *Journal of Financial Economics*, 6:59–69.

Driessen, Joost (2005). "Is Default Event Risk Priced in Corporate Bonds?" *Review of Financial Studies*, 18(1):165–195.

Duan, Jin (1995). "The GARCH Option Pricing Model". *Mathematical Finance*, 5(1):13–32.

Duan, Jin-Chuan, Ritchken, Peter, and Sun, Z. (2005). "Jump-Starting GARCH: Pricing and Hedging Options with Jumps in Returns and Volatilities". *University of Toronto*, Working Paper.

Duffee, Gregory (1999). "Estimating the Price of Default Risk". *Review of Financial Studies*, 12:197–226.

Duffie, Darrell (1989). "Futures Markets". *Prentice-Hall*, Englewood-Cliffs, NJ.

Duffie, Darrell (1996). "Dynamic Asset Pricing Theory". *Princeton University Press*, 2nd edition, New Jersey.

Duffie, Darrell and Kan, Rui (1996). "A Yield Factor Model of Interest Rates". *Mathematical Finance*, 6(4):379–406.

Duffie, Darrell, Pan, Jun, and Singleton, Ken (2000). "Transform Analysis and Asset Pricing for Affine Jump Diffusions". *Econometrica*, 68:1343–1376.

Duffie, Darrell, Pedersen, Lasse, and Singleton, Kenneth (2003). "Modeling Sovereign Yield Spreads: A Case Study of Russian Debt". *Journal of Finance*, 58(1):119–159.

Duffie, Darrell, Saita, Leandro, and Wang, Ke (2007). "Multi-Period Corporate Default Prediction with Stochastic Covariates". *Journal of Financial Economics*, 83:635–665.

Duffie, Darrell and Singleton, Kenneth (1999a). "Modeling Term Structures of Defaultable Bonds". *Review of Financial Studies*, 12:687–720.

Duffie, Darrell and Singleton, Kenneth (1999b). "Simulating Correlated Default". *Stanford University*, Working Paper.

Duffie, Darrell and Singleton, Kenneth (2003). "Credit Risk: Pricing, Measurement, and Management". *Princeton University Press*, New Jersey.

Duffie, Darrell and Stanton, Richard (1992). "Pricing Continuously Resettled Contingent Claims". *Journal of Economic Dynamics and Control*, 16:561–574.

Dupire, Bruno (1994). "Pricing with a Smile". *Risk*, 7(1):18–20.

Engle, Robert (1982). "Autoregressive Conditional Heteroskedasticity with Estimates of the Variance of U.K. Inflation". *Econometrica*, 50:987–1008.

Engle, Robert (1990). "Stock Volatility and the Crash of 87: Discussion". *Review of Financial Studies*, 3:103–106.

Eom, Young Ho, Helwege, Jean, and Huang, Jing-Zhi (2004). "Structural Models of Corporate Bond Pricing: An Empirical Analysis". *Review of Financial Studies*, 17:499–544.

Errais, Eyman, Giesecke, Kay, and Goldberg, Lisa (2006). "Pricing Credit from the Top-Down with Affine Point Processes". *Stanford University*, Working Paper.

Fama, Eugene (1965). "The Behavior of Stock-Market Prices". *Journal of Business*, 38(1):34–105.

Figlewski, Stephen, Silber, William, and Subrahmanyam, Marti (1992). "Financial Options: From Theory to Practice". *Business One-Irwin*, Chicago.

Figlewski, Steven and Gao, Bin (1999). "The Adaptive Mesh Model: A New Approach to Efficient Option Pricing". *Journal of Financial Economics*, 53(3):313–351.

Flavell, Richard (2002). "Swaps and Other Derivatives". *Wiley*, New York.

Foresi, Silverio and Wu, Liuren (2005). "Crash-O-Phobia: A Domestic Fear or Worldwide Concern?". *Journal of Derivatives*, 13(2):8–21.

Frees, Edward and Valdez, Emiliano (1998). "Understanding Relationships Using Copulas". *North American Actuarial Journal*, 2:1–25.

French, Kenneth (1980). "Stock Returns and the Weekend Effect". *Journal of Financial Economics*, 8:55–69.

French, Kenneth (1983). "A Comparison of Futures and Forward Prices". *Journal of Financial Economics*, 12: 311–342.

Gapen, Michael, Gray, Dale, Lim, Cheng Hoon, and Xiao, Yingbin (2005). "Measuring and Analyzing Sovereign Risk with Contingent Claims". *International Monetary Fund*, Working Paper 05/155.

Geske, Robert (1977). "Valuation of Corporate Liabilities as Compound Options". *Journal of Financial and Quantitative Analysis*, 12(4):541–522.

Geske, Robert (1979). "Valuation of Compound Options". *Journal of Financial Economics*, 7:63–81.

Giesecke, Kay and Goldberg, Lisa (2005). "A Top-Down Approach to Multi-name Credit". *Stanford University*, Working Paper.

Glasserman, Paul (2003). "Monte Carlo Methods in Financial Engineering". *Springer-Verlag*. New York.

Glosten, Larry, Jagannathan, Ravi, and Runkle, David (1993). "Relationship between the Expected Value and the Volatility of the Nominal Excess Return on Stocks". *Journal of Finance*, 48:1779–1801.

Gray, Dale, Merton, Robert, and Bodie, Zvi (2006). "A New Framework for Analyzing and Managing Macrofinancial Risks of an Economy". *NBER*, Working Paper No. 12637.

Green, Richard (1984). "Investment Incentives, Debt and Warrants". *Journal of Financial Economics*, 13:115–136.

Gregory, J. and Laurent, J-P. (2003). "I Will Survive". *RISK*, June:103–107.

Gregory, J. and Laurent, J-P. (2004). "In the Core of Correlation". *RISK*, October:87–91.

Gupta, Anurag and Subrahmanyam, Marti (1999). "An Empirical Examination of the Convexity Bias in the Pricing of Interest Rate Swaps". *New York University*, Working Paper.

Hamilton, David, Verma, Praveen, Ou, Sharon, and Cantor, Richard (2005). "Default and Recovery Rates of Corporate Bond Issuers, 1920–2004". *Global Credit Research, Moody's Investor Services*, New York.

Harrison, Michael and Pliska, Stanley (1981). "Martingales and Stochastic Integrals in the Theory of Continuous Trading". *Stochastic Processes Applications*, 11:215–260.

Harrison, Michael J. and Kreps, David (1979). "Martingales and Arbitrage in Multiperiod Security Markets". *Journal of Economic Theory*, 20:381–408.

Heath, David, Jarrow, Robert, and Morton, Andrew (1990a). "Contingent Claims Valuation with a Random Evolution of Interest Rates". *Review of Futures Markets*, 9(1):54–82.

Heath, David, Jarrow, Robert A., and Morton, Andrew (1990). "Bond Pricing and the Term Structure of Interest Rates: A Discrete Time Approximation". *Journal of Financial and Quantitative Analysis*, 25(4):419–440.

Heath, David, Jarrow, Robert, Morton, Andrew, and Spindel, Mark (1992). "Easier Done Than Said". *Risk*, 5(9):77–80.

Heath, David, Jarrow, Robert A., and Morton, Andrew (1992b). "Bond Pricing and the Term Structure of Interest Rates: A New Methodology for Contingent Claims Valuation". *Econometrica*, 60(1):77–105.

Hemler, Michael (1990). "The Quality Delivery Option in Treasury Bond Futures Contracts". *Journal of Finance*, 45(5):1565–1586.

Heston, Steve (1993). "A Closed-Form Solution for Options with Stochastic Volatility with Applications to Bond and Currency Options". *The Review of Financial Studies*, 6(2):327–343.

Ho, Thomas and Lee, Sang-Bin (1986). "Term Structure Movements and Pricing Interest Contingent Claims". *Journal of Finance*, 41(5):1011–1029.

Hsia, C.-C. (1983). "On Binomial Option Pricing". *Journal of Financial Research*, 6:41–46.

Huang, Jing-Zhi and Huang, Ming (2003). "How Much of the Corporate-Treasury Yield Spread Is Due to Credit Risk?" *Penn State University*, Working Paper.

Hull, John and White, Alan (1987). "The Pricing of Options with Stochastic Volatilities". *Journal of Finance*, 42(2):281–300.

Hull, John and White, Alan (1990). "Pricing Interest-Rate Derivative Securities". *Review of Financial Studies*, 3(4):573–592.

Hull, John and White, Alan (2006a). "Dynamic Models of Portfolio Credit Risk: A Simplified Approach". *University of Toronto*, Working Paper.

Hull, John and White, Alan (2006b). "The Perfect Copula". *University of Toronto*, Working Paper.

Hull, John and White, Alan (2006c). "Valuing Credit Derivatives Using an Implied Copula Approach". *Journal of Derivatives*, 14(2):8–28.

Jackwerth, Jens and Rubinstein, Mark (1996). "Recovering Probability Distributions from Options Prices". *Journal of Finance*, 51(5):1611–1631.

James, Peter (2003). "Option Theory". *Wiley*, New York.

Jamshidian, Farshid (1997). "LIBOR and Swap Market Models and Measures". *Finance and Stochastics*, 1:293–330.

Jarrow, Robert, Lando, David, and Turnbull, Stuart (1997). "A Markov Model for the Term Structure of Credit Spreads". *Review of Financial Studies*, 10:481–523.

Jarrow, Robert and Oldfield, George (1981). "Forward Prices and Futures Prices". *Journal of Financial Economics*, 9(4):371–382.

Jarrow, Robert and Turnbull, Stuart (1995). "Pricing Options on Financial Securities Subject to Default Risk". *Journal of Finance*, 50:53–86.

Johnston, E. and McConnell, John (1989). "Requiem for a Market: An Analysis of the Rise and Fall of a Financial Futures Contract". *Review of Financial Studies*, 2(1):1–23.

Jones, Philip, Mason, Scott, and Rosenfeld, Eric (1984). "Contingent Claims Analysis of Corporate Capital Structures: An Empirical Investigation". *Journal of Finance*, 39:611–627.

Jong, Frank De, Driessen, Joost, and AntoonPelsser (2001). "Libor Market Models versus Swap Market Models for Pricing Interest Rate Derivatives: An Empirical Analysis". *University of Amsterdam*, Working Paper.

Jorion, Philippe (1988). "On Jump Processes in the Foreign Exchange and Stock Markets". *Review of Financial Studies*, 1:427–445.

Kester, Carl W. (1984). "Today's Options for Tomorrow's Growth". *Harvard Business Review*, 62 (March–April): 153–160.

Kreps, David (1982). "Multiperiod Securities and the Efficient Allocation of Risk: A Comment on the Black-Scholes Option Pricing Model". *The Economics of Uncertainty and Information* (J. McCall, Editor). *University of Chicago Press*.

Lando, David (1994). "Three Essays on Contingent Claims Pricing". *Cornell University*, Ph.D. Thesis.

Lando, David (1998). "On Cox Processes and Credit Risky Securities". *Review of Derivatives Research*, 2:99–120.

Leland, Hayne (1994). "Corporate Debt Value, Bond Covenants, and Optimal Capital Structure". *Journal of Finance*, 49:1213–1252.

Leland, Hayne (2006). "Structural Models in Corporate Finance, Lecture 1: Pros and Cons of Structural Models". *UC Berkeley*, Presentation Slides.

Leland, Hayne and Rubinstein, Mark (1988). "Comments on the Market Crash: Six Months After". *Journal of Economic Perspectives*, 2(3):45–50.

Leland, Hayne and Toft, Klaus (1996). "Optimal Capital Structure, Endogenous Bankruptcy, and the Term Structure of Credit Spreads". *Journal of Finance*, 51:987–1019.

Li, David (2000). "On Default Correlation: A Copula Approach". *Journal of Fixed Income*, 9:43–54.

Litterman, Robert and Iben, Thomas (1991). "Corporate Bond Valuation and the Term Structure of Credit Spreads". *Journal of Portfolio Management*, Spring:52–64.

Litterman, Robert and Scheinkman, Jse (1991). "Common Factors Affecting Bond Returns". *Journal of Fixed Income*, June:54–61.

Longstaff, Francis, Mithal, Sanjay, and Neis, Eric (2006). "Corporate Yield Spreads: Default Risk or Liquidity? New Evidence from the Credit-Default Swap Market". *Journal of Finance*, 60(5):2213–2253.

Longstaff, Francis and Rajan, Arvind (2008). "An Empirical Analysis of the Pricing of Collateralized Debt Obligations". *Journal of Finance*, 63:509–563.

Longstaff, Francis and Schwartz, Eduardo (1995). "A Simple Approach to Valuing Fixed and Floating Rate Debt". *Journal of Finance*, 50:789–819.

Longstaff, Francis and Schwartz, Eduardo (2001). "Valuing American Options by Simulation: A Simple Least-Squares Approach". *Review of Financial Studies*, 14:113–147.

Luenberger, David (1997). "Investment Science". *Oxford University Press*, New York.

Madan, Dilip, Carr, Peter, and Chang, Eric (1998). "The Variance Gamma Process and Option Pricing". *European Finance Review*, 2:79–105.

Majd, Saman and Pindyck, Robert (1987). "Time to Build, Option Value, and Investment Decisions". *Journal of Financial Economics*, 18:7–27.

Majd, Saman and Pindyck, Robert S. (1989). "The Learning Curve and Optimal Production under Uncertainty". *Rand Journal of Economics*, 20(3):331–343.

Margrabe, William (1978). "The Value of an Option to Exchange One Asset for Another". *Journal of Finance*, 33:177–186.

Markham, Jesse (1987). "History of Commodity Futures Trading and Its Regulation". *Praeger Publishers*, New York.

Marshall, John and Yuyuenyonwatana, Robert (2000). "Equity Swaps: Structures, Uses, and Pricing". *The Handbook of Equity Derivatives* (Jack Francis, William Toy, and Gregg Whittaker, Editors). *John Wiley*, New York.

McCulloch, Huston (1971). "Measuring the Term Structure of Interest Rates". *Journal of Business*, 44:19–31.

McCulloch, Huston (1975). "The Tax Adjusted Yield Curve". *Journal of Finance*, 30:811–830.

McCulloch, Huston (2003). "The Risk-Neutral Measure and Option Pricing under Log-Stable Uncertainty". *Ohio State University*, Working Paper.

McDonald, Robert and Siegel, Daniel (1986). "The Value of Waiting to Invest". *Quarterly Journal of Economics*, November:717–727.

McKenzie, Donald (2004). "The Big, Bad Wolf and the Rational Market: Portfolio Insurance, the 1987 Crash and the Performativity of Economics". *Economy and Society*, 33(3):303–334.

Mella-Barral, Pierre and Perraudin, William (1997). "Strategic Debt Service". *Journal of Finance*, 52(3):531–556.

Merton, Robert (1973). "Theory of Rational Option Pricing". *The Bell Journal of Economics and Management Science*, 4(1):141–183.

Merton, Robert (1974). "On the Pricing of Corporate Debt: The Risk Structure of Interest Rates". *Journal of Finance*, 29:449–470.

Merton, Robert C. (1976). "Option Pricing When Underlying Stock Returns Are Discontinuous". *Journal of Financial Economics*, 3:125–144.

Miltersen, Kristian, Sandmann, Klaus, and Sondermann, Dieter (1997). "Closed Form Solutions for Term Structure Derivatives with Log-normal Interest Rates". *Journal of Finance*, 52(1):409–430.

Moel, Alberto and Tufano, Peter (1997). "Bidding for Antamina: Incentives in a Real Option Framework". *Harvard Business School*, Case 297-054.

Muralidhar, Arun S. (1992). "Volatility, Flexibility and the Multinational Enterprise". *Massachusetts Institute of Technology*, Ph.D. Thesis.

Nelsen, Roger (1999). "An Introduction to Copulas". *Springer-Verlag*, New York.

Nelson, Charles and Siegel, Andrew (1987). "Parsimonious Modeling of Yield Curves". *Journal of Business*, 60(4):473–489.

Nelson, Dan and Ramaswamy, Krishna (1990). "Simple Binomial Processes as Diffusion Approximations in Financial Models". *Review of Financial Studies*, 3:393–430.

Nelson, Daniel B. (1990). "ARCH Models as Diffusion Approximations". *Journal of Econometrics*, 45:7–38.

Nelson, Daniel B. (1991). "Conditional Heteroskedasticity in Asset Returns: A New Approach". *Econometrica*, 59(2):347–370.

Neuberger, Anthony (1990). "Volatility Trading". *London Business School*, Working Paper.

Paddock, James L., Siegel, Daniel R., and Smith, James L. (1988). "Option Valuation of Claims on Real Assets: The Case of Offshore Petroleum Leases". *Quarterly Journal of Economics*, August:479–508.

Pearson, Neil (2002). "Risk Budgeting: Portfolio Problem Solving with Value-at-Risk". *John Wiley and Sons*, New York.

Pelsser, Antoon (2000). "Efficient Methods for Valuing Interest Rate Derivatives". *Springer-Verlag*, London.

Pindyck, Robert S. (1991). "Irreversibility, Uncertainty, and Investment". *Journal of Economic Literature*, 29:1110–1148.

Pindyck, Robert S. (1993). "Investments of Uncertain Cost". *Journal of Financial Economics*, 34:53–76.

Pozdnyakov, Vladamir and Steele, J. Michael (2001). "Convexity Bias in the Pricing of Eurodollar Swaps". *Methodology and Computing in Applied Probability*, 4:181–193.

Rebonato, Ricardo (2002a). "Modern Pricing of Interest Rate Derivatives". *Princeton University Press*, New Jersey.

Rebonato, Riccardo (2002b). "Modern Pricing of Interest-Rate Derivatives : The LIBOR Market Model and Beyond". *Princeton University Press*, New Jersey.

Reiner, Eric and Rubinstein, Mark (1991). "Breaking down the Barriers". *Risk*, September:28–35.

Richard, Scott (1978). "Arbitrage Model of the Term Structure of Interest Rates". *Journal of Financial Economics*, 6(1):33–57.

Richard, Scott and Sundaresan, Suresh (1981). "A Continuous-Time Equilibrium Model of Forward Prices and Futures Prices in a Multi-Good Economy". *Journal of Financial Economics*, 9(4):347–371.

Ritchken, Peter and Trevor, Robert (1999). "Pricing Options under Generalized GARCH and Stochastic Volatility Processes". *Journal of Finance*, 54(1):377–402.

Roll, Richard (1988). "The International Crash of October 1987". *Financial Analysts Journal*, 44(5):19–35.

Rubinstein, Mark (1991a). "Double Trouble". *Risk*, December/January:53–56.

Rubinstein, Mark (1991b). "Options for the Undecided". *Risk*, April:70–73.

Rubinstein, Mark (1991c). "Somewhere over the Rainbow". *Risk*, November:63–66.

Rubinstein, Mark (1994). "Implied Binomial Trees". *Journal of Finance*, 49(3):771–818.

Rubinstein, Mark (1995). "On the Accounting Valuation of Employee Stock Options". *Journal of Derivatives*, Fall:8-24.

Rubinstein, Mark (1998). "Comments on the 1987 Stock Market Crash: Eleven Years Later". http://www.in-the-money.com/pages/author.htm, Mimeo.

Samuelson, Paul (1972). "Mathematics of Speculative Price". *Mathematical Topics in Economic Theory and Computation*. SIAM (R.H. Day and S.M. Robinson, Editors).

Samuelson, Paul (1973). "Mathematics of Speculative Price". *SIAM Review*, 15:1–42.

Schöbl, R. and Zhu, J. (1999). "Stochastic Volatility with an Ornstein Uhlenbeck Process: An Extension". *European Finance Review*, 3:23–46.

Schönbucher, Philipp (1998). "Term Structure Modeling of Defaultable Bonds". *Review of Derivatives Research*, 2:161–192.

Schonbucher, Philipp (2005). "Portfolio Losses and the Term Structure of Loss Transition Rates: A New Methodology for the Pricing of Portfolio Credit Derivatives". *ETH-Zurich*, Working Paper.

Schroder, Mark (1988). "Adapting the Binomial Model to Value Options on Assets with Fixed Cash Payout". *Financial Analysts Journal*, November/December:54–62.

Shalen, Catherine (2002). "The Nitty-Gritty of CBOT DJIA Futures Index Arbitrage". http://www.cbot.com/cbot/docs/29685.pdf.

Sidenius, Jakob, Piterbarg, Vladimir, and Andersen, Leif (2005). "A New Framework for Dynamic Credit Loss Modeling". *Royal Bank of Scotland*, Working Paper.

Sklar, A. (1959). "Functions de repartition a n dimensions et leurs marges". *Publ. Inst. Statist. Univ. Paris*, 8:229–231.

Sklar, A. (1973). "Random Variables, Joint Distributions, and Copulas". *Kybernetica*, 9:449–460.

Smith, Donald (1994). "Aggressive Corporate Finance: A Close Look at the Procter & Gamble–Bankers Trust Leveraged Swap". *Journal of Derivatives*, 4(4):67–79.

Stein, Elias and Stein, Jeremy (1991). "Stock Price Distributions with Stochastic Volatility: An Analytical Approach". *Review of Financial Studies*, 4(4): 727–752.

Stulz, Rene (1982). "Options on the Maximum or Minimum of Two Assets". *Journal of Financial Economics*, 10:161–185.

Sundaram, Rangarajan (1997). "Equivalent Martingale Measures and Risk-Neutral Pricing: An Expository Note". *Journal of Derivatives*, Fall:85–98.

Svensson, Lars (1994). "Estimating and Interpreting Forward Interest Rates: Sweden 1992–1994". *International Monetary Fund*, Working Paper 94/114.

Tavella, Domingo and Randall, Curt (2000). "Pricing Financial Instruments: The Finite-Difference Method". *John Wiley*, New York.

Trigeorgis, Lenos (1993a). "Real Options and Interactions with Financial Flexibility". *Financial Management*, Autumn:202–224.

Trigeorgis, Lenos (1993b). "The Nature of Options Interactions and the Valuation of Investments with Multiple Real Options". *Journal of Financial and Quantitative Analysis*, 28(1):1–20.

Tsiveriotis, Kostas and Fernandes, Chris (1998). "Valuing Convertible Bonds with Credit Risk". *Journal of Fixed Income*, 8(3):95–102.

Turnbull, Stuart and Wakeman, Lee (1991). "A Quick Algorithm for Pricing European Average Options". *Journal of Financial and Quantitative Analysis*, 26:377–389.

U.S., Senate (2007). "Excessive Speculation in the Natural Gas Market". *Committee on Homeland Security and Governmental Affairs*, Senate Report.

Vasicek, Oldrich (1977). "An Equilibrium Characterization of the Term Structure". *Journal of Financial Economics*: 5:177–188.

Vorst, Ton (1992). "Prices and Hedge Ratios of Average Exchange Rate Options". *International Review of Financial Analysis*, 1:179–193.

Whaley, Robert (1993). "Derivatives on Market Volatility: Hedging Tools Long Overdue". *Journal of Derivatives*, 1:71–84.

Whaley, Robert (2008). "Understanding VIX". *Vanderbilt University*, Working Paper.

Wiggins, James (1987). "Option Values under Stochastic Volatility: Theory and Empirical Estimates". *Journal of Financial Economics*, 19:351–372.

Ye, George (2005). "Asian Options Can Be More Expensive Than Plain Vanilla Counterparts". *Journal of Derivatives*, 13(1):56–60.

Zhou, Chunsheng (1997). "A Jump-Diffusion Approach to Modeling Credit Risk and Valuing Defaultable Securities". *Federal Reserve Board, Washington, D.C.*, Working Paper.

# Name Index

Note: Page numbers in **boldface** type indicate material on website only. Page numbers followed by n indicate material in footnotes.

# Subject Index

Note: Page numbers in **boldface** type indicate material on the website only. Page numbers followed by n indicate material in footnotes.